Debian GNU/ Linux 2.1

ocs(p)

664
257
160
985
1008
261?
636
733
856
747

108 or 513 (SMTP = "Single..." or "Simple...")

Mario Camou and Aaron Von Cowenberghe

SAMS

Debian/GNU Linux 2.1 Unleashed

International Standard Book Number: 0-672-31700-1

Library of Congress Catalog Card Number: 99-62803

Printed in the United States of America

First Printing: December 1999

01 00 99 4 3 2 1

Trademarks

All terms mentioned in this book that are known to be trademarks or service marks have been appropriately capitalized. Sams Publishing cannot attest to the accuracy of this information. Use of a term in this book should not be regarded as affecting the validity of any trademark or service mark.

Warning and Disclaimer

Every effort has been made to make this book as complete and as accurate as possible, but no warranty or fitness is implied. The information provided is on an "as is" basis. The authors and the publisher shall have neither liability nor responsibility to any person or entity with respect to any loss or damages arising from the information contained in this book or from the use of the CD or programs accompanying it.

Acquisitions Editor
Don Roche

Development Editor
Jeff Durham

Managing Editor
Charlotte Clapp

Senior Editor
Karen A. Walsh

Copy Editors
Nancy Albright
Kris Simmons
Chuck Hutchison

Indexer
Johnna VanHoose Dinse

Proofreaders
Gene Redding
Mary Ellen Stephenson
Maryann Steinhart

Technical Editors
Rob Rati
Jose Neif
Edward Betts
Vincent Jenelle
Gerardo Horvilleur

Team Coordinator
Pamalee Nelson

Media Developer
Dan Scherf

Interior Design
Gary Adair

Cover Design
Aren Howell

Copy Writer
Eric Borgert

Production
Cheryl Lynch

Contents at a Glance

Contents

About the Authors

Mario Camou has been working with Linux for more than six years, since the days of the 0.99 kernels. He has worked with almost all Linux distributions, on hardware ranging from a 386 SX to Pentium IIIs, doing everything from software development to systems and network management. He was the director of technology at Umbral, one of the fastest-growing international Internet portals, until this past year when he moved to Spain to work as a Java developer for a major company. He currently lives in Madrid. In his free time, he likes to read science fiction and watch movies with his lovely wife, Angie.

John Goerzen has been a developer for the Debian GNU/Linux operating system project since 1996 and currently works with package integration and porting to the 64-bit Alpha platform. He currently works as a system administrator and developer for an Internet firm. As the founder of the Air Capital Linux Users Group of Wichita, Kansas, John has been active in getting people involved with Linux for some time.

Jeff Licquia has had an interesting and diverse career in the 10 years he has worked professionally in the information industry, from process control driver programming on Windows to network administration on one of the largest NT-based networks in the world. He first discovered Linux in 1991 (before it could boot multiuser) and became an avid proponent in 1993, successfully deploying it in varied environments for many purposes. Currently, he is network administrator for Springfield Clinic, a regional health clinic in his home town of Springfield, Illinois. Outside of the wired world, Mr. Licquia is active in his church and enjoys his time with his wife and two children.

Aaron Von Cowenberghe has worked with Debian for several years and is a member of the Debian dpkgv2 development team. Aaron is one of those fascinating young people in the Linux community—he will be a freshman at Cal Poly Tech this year. He has worked with advanced software development for six years and is a vocal advocate for Linux.

Gerardo Muñoz is a computer science graduate from Instituto Tecnológico y de Estudios Superiores de Monterrey (ITESM) in Mexico. He has been working in the Information Technology field as system administrator, software engineer, technical support consultant, and developer. He has experience on different UNIX flavors—such as AIX, Solaris, and Linux (of course)—and also in Windows environments. He's the MIS manager at Umbral Global (`www.umbral.com`), an Internet portal with headquarters in Mexico City and Miami. Gerardo Muñoz resides in Mexico City and can be reached at `gemunoz@usa.net`.

Steve Wells was first introduced to the Internet by fellow Linux developer Matt Messier in 1992, while attaining a business degree at Bryant College in Rhode Island. Steve then moved to Iowa, where he was introduced to the technical administrator for the local public libraries, Mike Dargan. Mike advised Steve in the creation of a consulting business, where he was introduced to Superhighway Consulting of Illinois, eventually gaining partial ownership of the company. Steve was instrumental in creating WebPromote.com and Starting-Point.com, each of which is worth several million today. He has since moved on to teach and present Internet-related studies, consult on a business and technical level for various companies, and work as the Chief Technical Officer of LiquidInternet.net. His most recent GNU project involves work with co-developer Brian Gannon at price-hunter.com, where he can be reached via email. He currently resides in Cedar Falls, Iowa with his wife, Hope.

Gerardo Horvilleur discovered, when he was 10 years old, that programming computers was fun. Now, 28 years later, computer programming is still providing him with lots of fun. Since 1983, he has played with a wide variety of UNIX distributions, which he has configured, installed, fine-tuned, and managed on systems ranging from a small single-user computer to a nationwide, distributed network with hundreds of nodes. Linux is now his favorite operating system and main software development platform.

Gerardo is the author of Montage, one of the first applications to be written entirely in Java. Montage was featured by Netscape in the 1997 Java World Tour. Montage Lite, a component version of Montage, is part of Sun Microsystems' JavaStudio.

Gerardo works as an independent Java consultant in Mexico City, where he lives with his wife, two sons, and one dog.

Dedication

To my parents, Carmen and Mario, who gave me life; to my wife, Angie, who gave my life meaning; and to my spiritual guide, Lou, who gave me the tools to live a better life.

—Mario Camou

Tell Us What You Think!

As the reader of this book, *you* are our most important critic and commentator. We value your opinion and want to know what we're doing right, what we could do better, what areas you'd like to see us publish in, and any other words of wisdom you're willing to pass our way.

You can fax, email, or write me directly to let me know what you did or didn't like about this book—as well as what we can do to make our books stronger.

Please note that I cannot help you with technical problems related to the topic of this book, and that due to the high volume of mail I receive, I might not be able to reply to every message.

When you write, please be sure to include this book's title and author as well as your name and phone or fax number. I will carefully review your comments and share them with the authors and editors who worked on the book.

Fax: (317) 581-4770

Email: `michael.stephens@macmillanusa.com`

Mail: Michael Stephens
Associate Publisher
Sams Publishing
201 West 103rd Street
Indianapolis, IN 46290 USA

Introduction

Linux is a UNIX-like operating system that has taken the world by storm. Born not in the engineering labs of some anonymous company but in the hearts and minds of thousands of hackers worldwide, Linux has rightfully gained a reputation for stability, performance, and robustness. This, coupled with the growing support that many software companies have announced over the last year, has ensured an extraordinary growth in the usage of Linux.

Debian GNU/Linux 2.1 Unleashed shows you most of the things you need to know to set up, operate, and manage Debian GNU/Linux. Although heavily oriented toward Debian, much of the information applies to all Linux distributions, which are based on the same core components. Because Linux is continually evolving, in many cases we provide pointers to online information that will often be more current than this book. Linux also includes a large amount of online documentation in the form of manual pages, info files, text files, and HTML files. *Debian GNU/Linux 2.1 Unleashed* covers the basic concepts you need to know (although usually the term "basics" covers things that aren't basic at all!) and provides pointers to places where you might research the topics more deeply. We believe that it is better (and more useful) to present the basic information and the techniques used to learn in this new environment, rather than present a step-by-step list of tasks to perform. This way, if something goes awry, you will have the necessary knowledge to troubleshoot things yourself.

Even though some Linux distributions (and most UNIX systems) offer graphical tools for systems administration (and Debian includes some "form-based" tools to help you install and configure some things such as networking), the underlying UNIX system is always configured using text files. It is best to learn how the system's files are organized and formatted, so you can fix things when the graphical tools go wrong, or to automate tasks beyond what is possible with the graphical tools. Because of this, one of the first things you will learn is how to use a text editor.

With this book, you also will explore setting up Web, FTP, news, mail, and other kinds of Internet servers; coexisting with Microsoft networks; setting up a firewall; programming with scripting languages; setting up centralized network administration; and many other subjects.

Who Should Read This Book

This book is oriented toward systems and network administrators who want to run or are already running Debian GNU/Linux, or who are familiar with another distribution of Linux and want to use Debian. Previous knowledge of basic UNIX or Linux commands and the UNIX/Linux philosophy can be very useful, although Part I gives an introduction to these topics. However, we do assume at least a passing knowledge of other operating systems, such as Microsoft Windows, OS/2, or MacOS. Knowledge of basic PC hardware, configurations, and terminology is also required.

What Software Will You Need?

The included CD-ROM contains most of the software mentioned in the book. Some packages may need to be downloaded from the Internet; in that case, the URL of the site is included in the text. This applies especially to software that may use strong encryption, because of international regulations.

How This Book Is Organized

We have tried to make each chapter in the book as self-contained as possible without unduly repeating information. If you're looking for information on some specific topic, you can jump in at the proper section. The book is organized in a logical progression, so later chapters do contain references to previous material.

This book is divided into the following parts:

- **Part I: The Basics** This part contains an introduction to the basic concepts you will need to use and manage Linux. It first introduces the Debian Linux system, including the open-source licenses. You will also learn about the different shells, which are the command-line programs you use to communicate with any UNIX system; the X Window System, which provides a graphical user interface to all UNIX systems; and how to use the most common UNIX command-line utilities. There is also a chapter on end-user applications for Linux, such as word processors, spreadsheets, presentation programs, and others.
- **Part II: Debian System Administration** In Part II, you will learn all about system administration, including how to install, upgrade, and remove software; how to customize the Linux kernel, which is the basic program that controls all the system; how to set up system logging and accounting; and how to recover your system in case it crashes. You will also learn about setting up and managing network servers—including Web, email, news, and FTP servers—and also servers that enable you to integrate to other network types, such as Microsoft Windows and Novell networks.
- **Part III: Security Issues** If you ever connect to the Internet (actually, if you ever turn on your computer!), you need to be aware of the possible dangers involved, as well as how to defend yourself and your system against them. In Part III, you deal with the things you have to know and do to make your computer safe.

- **Part IV: Development Environment** Part IV deals with software development. It covers development in languages ranging from C and C++ to scripting with `tcl/tk`, Python, and other scripting languages that can make managing your systems a lot easier and enjoyable.
- **Part V: Linux Applications** Part V of this book deals with programming large Linux applications, including how to take advantage of tools developed in the Linux community specifically for solving the problems involved in developing applications with large, distributed, and loosely coupled development teams.
- **Part VI: Appendixes** Appendix A covers installing Debian GNU/Linux using the included CD-ROM set. Appendix B contains an annotated listing of useful online references, organized by chapter. Appendix C contains the full listing of some open-source licenses that comply with the Debian Free Software Guidelines, and Appendix D includes other open-source licenses. Appendix E describes each of the options that the system asks when you configure the kernel.

Conventions Used in This Book

The following typographic conventions are used in this book:

- Code lines, commands, statements, variables, and any text you type or see onscreen appears in a mono typeface. Bold mono typeface is often used to represent the user's input.
- Placeholders in syntax descriptions appear in an italic mono typeface. Replace the placeholder with the actual filename, parameter, or whatever element it represents.
- Italics highlight technical terms when they're being defined.
- The ➥ icon is used before a line of code that is really a continuation of the preceding line. Sometimes a line of code is too long to fit as a single line on the page. If you see ➥ before a line of code, remember that it's part of the line immediately above it.
- This book also contains Notes, Tips, and Cautions to help you spot important or useful information more quickly. Some of these are helpful shortcuts to help you work more efficiently.

The Basics

PART I

IN THIS PART

CHAPTER 1

Introduction to Debian Linux

by Aaron Von Cowenberghe

In This Chapter

In 1991, a Swedish student attending the University of Helsinki announced his first release of a highly experimental operating system (OS). This operating system, which carried no name in its first incarnation, was created as a clone of a popular UNIX variant of the day, Minix, with a number of significant enhancements. During this project's fledgling stage, Linus Torvalds (our student attending U. of Helsinki) downplayed it as nonportable and monolithic. Linux, as his operating system came to be known, was not expected to evolve to the level of any commercial product—Torvalds was soundly convinced that this was just a small project that was likely to go nowhere.

There were a few problems the community initially perceived in Linux. First, it ran only on 386s when other UNIXes could run on numerous platforms; Torvalds hand-tuned each of its routines to be as efficient as it could be for this architecture, but this gain in speed hurt Linux's flexibility. Additionally, Torvalds abandoned recent trends in UNIX development, becoming somewhat of a heretic in operating system development. Needless to say, some were adamantly opposed to his standards; Linux's shortcomings threatened to doom it to eternal oblivion as just another traffic anomaly on the Internet.

As time progressed, however, additional devoted enthusiasts emerged to help Linux along. As a result, it overcame its organizational difficulties, and has dominated the UNIX market by a landslide. By not allowing himself to be influenced by the agendas of others, but instead following his own judgment, Torvalds inadvertently catalyzed one of the largest voluntary international collaborative efforts man has seen: the free software movement.

The greatest example of this movement is Linux itself. Linux began in 1991, and its sources have grown from absolutely nothing to a gigantic 60MB! From any corporation's standpoint, this is a major software project, one requiring a ridiculous amount of manpower and about ten years of time. Many companies have tackled similar operating system projects in the past, devoting tremendous amounts of resources to their products. However, the nature of the free software movement affords Linux more momentum than any individual corporation can hope to exceed.

Free Software

In 1984, Richard M. Stallman quit his job working in the Artificial Intelligence Lab at MIT, and started working on a new operating system to be called GNU. The idea was to provide source code for all the software used in the system, so that others could modify the code and redistribute it. This is what is known as *free software*.

More than one and a half decades later, GNU is still not complete. This is not a bad thing. The authors of GNU are not motivated by money. They have no release date to meet,

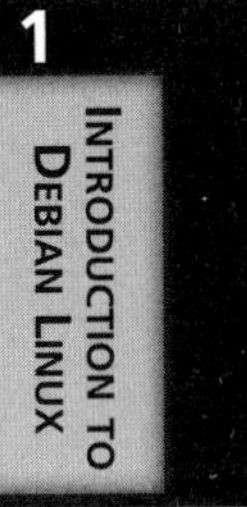

and they want to get their program right. However some people want to actually use computer systems, as opposed to spending the time writing them. The main thing that has been holding up the GNU is that the kernel, the software that interfaces between the computer hardware and the software applications, is unfinished.

Open-Source Software, GNU, and the Free Software Foundation

Most licenses that come with commercial software today are discouragingly restrictive. A typical software license disallows use of the software by more than one person or on more than one computer, or modification of the software in any way by reverse engineering or otherwise. In addition, just about every software vendor reserves the right to revoke each of their customers' licenses without reason or prior warning.

Stallman set out to change that when he began the GNU project. His vision was a complete, all-purpose OS that was entirely free. Not only could users redistribute the software, they could modify it in any way they saw fit and distribute their modifications.

This development model greatly encourages comprehensive development—when individuals can contribute enhancements to a project as their own personal needs dictate, those features that the contributors need most in everyday operation is implemented quickly. A product that a community produces collectively will most likely meet that community's needs; this is the paradigm of free software.

The community basically lost interest in the Hurd, and Linux came to the forefront as the OS that solves problems quickly. That is, instead of aiming for an ideal that would solve all future hypothetical problems, it became the only free OS known for gaining new features as quickly as they came into demand.

But where was Linux to get all its software? Achieving a platform with a fully functional development environment is not a project to be taken lightly; it is another daunting and time-consuming task. However, for any operating system to survive it must meet these needs.

The answer is simple. Torvalds and others simply expended the time necessary to port those necessary components from the endless list of GNU utilities to Linux. From the very beginning, the GNU project included development of free drop-in replacements for just about every useful utility that was shipped with the commercial UNIXes. Most of the time, these were expensive and proprietary (restrictively licensed or not standards-compliant). Stallman, however, headed the development of Emacs (an insanely powerful developer's editor), gcc (a free, portable C compiler), and almost countless other applications and utilities of necessity, as well as the Hurd.

The GNU project today continues to include development of the Hurd, which is still largely unfinished yet quickly progressing (`http://www.gnu.org/hurd`), but is mostly made up of various software projects aimed at development. Stallman's original goal is realized—that is, the availability of an operating system that is 100% free and comes with applications for every need at no cost.

Protecting the Community: Reservations in Free Software Licenses

To some readers who have encountered other free software, *open source* may seem to be just a new name for public domain. Public-domain software is licensed in such a way that there are absolutely no restrictions placed on its use or redistribution.

However, open-source software is quite different. There are several major problems with public-domain development. Notably, any large corporation can hijack a public-domain project—that is, improve greatly on the project, relicense it, and sell it as its own product. Needless to say, this defeats the purpose of free development. Who would be foolish enough to get involved in a project that could be so easily exploited?

Many individuals came up with their own solutions to this problem, but none were professional. This is the reason that the Free Software Foundation (FSF) was created. A friend of Stallman's who was a lawyer volunteered to write a license that would protect the integrity of free software. Later in the same year, the FSF published the GNU General Public License version 1.

This license explicitly grants all the freedoms previously mentioned, including modification, redistribution, and free use. It has one clause, however, that makes changing the license on a piece of software illegal without consent of each author. This type of licensing curbs the power of villainous corporations to capitalize on such movements as free software; it has come to be known as *copyleft*.

What Is Linux?

Today, Linux is widely known for being the fastest growing UNIX compatible operating system. It has come from a small, private project buried in the corners of the Internet to one of the highest-profile network operating systems of our time. However, Linux carries significantly more capability than a network server: it is capable of running as a graphics workstation, a desktop for office applications, or a router as powerful as any of the most advanced Cisco products. The possibilities are simply endless!

An *operating system*, simply put, is an environment that gives programs all the resources they need for proper operation. Although Linux generally comes bundled with multiple CDs full of powerful software, Linux itself is just a small program known as the operating system *kernel*. This is the part of the system that makes programs possible, but by itself, it's mostly useless.

Linux Distributions

With all the programs available for Linux scattered haphazardly across the Internet, it would be a daunting project to put together a Linux system with the needed environment. In reality, it's a project of gigantic proportions, because just about every application comes in source form with flaws to be overcome. There's no way any nontranscendent being (which is all of us, I hope!) can be expected to achieve this without an extreme amount of experience.

Software Management

Because everybody has heard so much about all the wonderful capabilities of Linux, it should be easy to use, right? Traditionally no, but this is what a *distribution* does. Red Hat, Debian, SuSE, and every other distribution play the basic role of providing powerful tools for installing and configuring applications and maintaining the system.

Every distribution does you the service of providing packaged software and a graphical user environment (GUI) to make software installation and system configuration simple. Each package holds software that would possibly have taken even the advanced user hours to configure manually, and the beginner perhaps would have been incapable of setting it up. A distribution makes setup simple; all that's required are a few keystrokes to install any available software.

Debian fills this role nicely, with a handful of tools suited to different situations. The main interactive package management tool for Debian, called `dselect`, has just as much functionality as any of the tools provided by Red Hat or any other distribution. It is Debian's other tools for package management, however, that give it its edge of superiority. `dpkg`, Debian's core package manager, contains more useful features than any in wide use today. (Most distributions today use `rpm`, Red Hat's package management system.)Debian's current software management system surpasses all because of a program that has recently come into existence. `apt`, a text front end for `dpkg`, lives up to its name. `apt` is capable of performing systemwide software upgrades without a hitch. Many times, when your software installation goes wrong with other methods, one invocation of `apt` is able to set everything right. `apt` makes zero downtime upgrades a reality. This is one boon Debian grants enterprises: Mission-critical servers cannot afford to be brought down for administration or upgrade, so Debian makes every effort to keep the distribution as dependable and flexible as possible.

Why Linux Is Better

For as long as any network administration guru can remember, UNIX has been the standard server platform for every need. Only recently has Windows NT overtaken the market as a popular solution; this can be attributed to Microsoft's gigantic marketing budget. When people hear one product's name more often than another, they are more likely to use it, whether or not it's a good product.

Windows NT, however, learned to speak the language of the Internet just a few years ago. It's not refined by any stretch of the imagination, but plagued with bugs and inconsistencies. Businesses need a solution that they can put online and expect to remain available 100% of the time, but Windows NT cannot meet this need. On the contrary, a Windows NT administrator's most common job is crash recovery; he wastes too much time doing busywork, such as booting servers that have gone down.

Linux has thrived among the dying embers of other UNIXes despite Microsoft's desperate attempts to monopolize this market, and this is no coincidence. Because of Linux's wealth of virtues, its userbase remains unmoved.

Flexibility

Linux is capable of filling any need. It handles every task equally well and has been tailored to be anything from a graphical desktop for offices to a powerful router or network server.

As well as Linux's flexibility, the wealth of applications it runs is astounding. My computer, for example, shows the current release of Debian offers 2,692 packages. Just about every major type of application is provided. Word processors, spreadsheets, money managers, and almost anything else you could name are available. Most of the time, you would pay hundreds of dollars to acquire such a variety of programs.

Beyond desktop applications, numerous information servers and networking packages are available. These can transform a modest Linux computer into a production quality Web server, email gateway, database, or any number of other information servers. There are also many packages available for making a regular desktop PC into a full-fledged router, firewall, or proxy. Systems custom-tailored for this purpose usually run thousands of dollars (see your local Cisco reseller for specifics), but because of Linux, the cost associated with such a solution is considerably lower.

Freedom

The biggest surprise in the corporate arena is the price of Linux and its associated software. Because of the licenses most of these programs are under, you can receive these two CDs full of software for almost nothing (all charges cover only the vendor's production costs and the price of the CDs). If you opt to retrieve everything over the Internet, the price is even lower—nothing. This software is entirely free. Not only does free mean zero cost, it also implies numerous other freedoms. No restrictive license is placed on the software, and no rights are reserved by the original author, allowing him to revoke all licenses without prior warning. Modification of the software is allowed, even encouraged, because doing so adds momentum to the free software movement and speeds the weakening of Microsoft's various virtual monopolies. You are granted the right to reverse-engineer the software if you so choose, although it's unnecessary because the full and uncensored sources are included for your perusal.

At the risk of stating the obvious, this is foreign to any product in the commercial arena, where everything with an exploitable market is tightly controlled. If you or your business needs a new feature in any of your software, tough luck. Even if this feature would take one afternoon's work to complete, most software licenses explicitly forbid modification even for private use, let alone for resale. This gives you only two choices: switch vendors (which wastes time, effort, and money) or beg your current vendor to add a feature to its software. Neither option is truly appealing.

You may ask who writes all this free software, and why. The answer is fairly straightforward. Linux and its applications draw all their manpower from people contributing on the Internet. Corporations, small business, contractors, consultants, and even hobbyists have contributed to this codebase, making Linux and its software more of a self-sustaining entity than an organized project. FSF's growth is directly related to the size of the Internet, giving it the potential to overtake the software industry.

Efficiency

As mentioned at the beginning of this chapter, Linux's first incarnation was highly optimized for its architecture. This optimization rendered Linux completely nonportable, but that situation has been rectified. Now, Linux is simultaneously released (and still highly optimized!) for a number of platforms, including the various generations of Intel CPUs, Compaq (formally DEC) ALPHAs, Motorola 6800, Power PCs, SPARCs, StrongARM, and a number of others.

Anybody who has been using computers in a business environment for a substantial amount of time has undoubtedly noticed the downward trend of speed in operating systems. Technology attains new heights, allowing operating system developers (such as Microsoft) to add new (often unneeded) features, bloating and slowing down systems.

Between operating system releases, most vendors will claim that the new version of their system is some percentage faster than all prior revisions, but this is almost never the case. For example, Microsoft claimed that Windows 98 would be considerably faster than Windows 95 because of its new, optimized filesystem, which it dubbed FAT32. However, I would not install Windows 98 on anything less than a Pentium 166 with 32MB of RAM; this setup is extremely painful for the user, yet Windows 95 will live comfortably on a 486 100 with 16MB of RAM.

History shows that although commercial operating systems cannot live up to their claims and have become notorious for being exponentially slower at each release, Linux does the exact opposite. In my experience, Linux is noticeably quicker on the same hardware at each major release. This is consistent with the nature of the free software community; when sources are open and changeable, individuals are more likely to improve the software. Because of this, Linux, as well as its applications, has a propensity toward quickly becoming more refined.

Reliability

Linux provides pre-emptive multitasking; it is designed so that a program running as a standard user cannot crash the system, and in most cases this is true. This results in a very reliable system; some computers running Linux have been doing so for over a year without restarting. However, Linux is still young and although a lot of the evidence points toward it being very reliable, much of this evidence is empirical. It is generally considered to be more reliable than other operating systems designed for personal computers, and on a similar level to other UNIX-like operation systems.

Standard Compliance

Microsoft's well-known legacy has been, for some time, the domination of all software markets. Where necessary, Microsoft has not hesitated to replace existing, developed specs with a poorly written fledgling of its own. It may come as a surprise to most readers that many of these specifications that Microsoft finds so threatening spent their infant days among UNIXes.

Academia, for as long as anybody can remember, has thrived with UNIX solutions. Because Linux, in particular, is so freely available and open, collaborative research products are simple. As a side effect, most Linux applications and servers are designed around the standards that have been proven to be most effective in the professional arena.

Standard compliance is one of the basic pillars of the open-source community; with it, multiple platform support is easily attained in many areas. As an example, take `egcs`, the most widely used C compiler on Linux. `egcs` is by far the most portable C compiler I have personally encountered (not only `egcs` itself, but code written to be compiled by `egcs`).

Other side effects of this community mentality include Linux's compatibility with other popular operating systems, such as Windows. There are enterprises that would have you believe it's impossible to get Windows and a UNIX machine to work together; however, this is simply not true. Linux offers a gamut of Windows compatibility daemons and can be made to perform such complicated tasks as emulating a full-fledged Windows NT server.

Why Choose Debian?

Debian is the second most widely used distribution on the Internet, weighing in just under Red Hat's market share. Debian is the largest non-commercial distribution in use. The Linux Counter (`http://counter.li.org/`) reports that 24% of Linux users use Red Hat and 21% use Debian. However, there's no way these statistics can be entirely accurate. Linux can be downloaded free and many people dual-boot their machines. Debian, because of its emphasis on technical superiority above ease of use, has gained a vast and often religiously devoted userbase.

> **Note**
>
> Debian, being a noncommercial endeavor, persistently evades accurate quantification. It has no commercial distribution channels, no controlled "official" royalty copies, no pointy-haired managers. As such, it's simply impossible to claim representative data. Instead, the community is given complete control of Debian's destiny, allowing it to grow to its maximum potential. Debian permeates every corner of the Internet—to see for yourself, check the `README.mirrors` file on any Debian mirror to see the great number of companies that have donated resources to Debian GNU.

There are side effects to this development model, notably the fact that Debian is fairly exclusive about whom its complexity favors. Anything with such a high learning curve (that is, difficulty level) suffers this way. However, Debian has long boasted of its domination as the most hands-off distribution for maintenance needs. Debian's package management system has the capability of performing complete, seamless, and in-place upgrades. System administrators are in complete control; no upgrade will corrupt configurations that were toiled on for hours. On the contrary, Debian strives to achieve zero downtime and comes closer to that goal than *any* other distribution, commercial or public.

Many of the developers who work on Debian are computing professionals who make use of it on a daily basis. This results in a high quality, highly integrated distribution.

Free Software

Debian is entirely devoted to the free software community. No software comes on the official Debian CD set that has adversely restrictive licensing. This is ensured with the Debian Free Software Guidelines (DFSG), which all software must conform to if it is to be allowed into the main distribution. The DFSG states plainly the core values of the open-source development model, as presented in the following sections.

Redistribution

You are granted free access to all applications that come with Debian. You can't be charged for any of it; shipping and reproduction costs don't apply here. You are also encouraged to disseminate or sell copies of the software as you choose, so long as all licensing remains intact.

Source Code and Derived Works

All software that an official Debian CD set comes with has source code available. In addition, users are encouraged to make changes and redistribute those changes as they see fit, assuming those changes are also under a free license.

No Discrimination Against Groups or Fields of Endeavor

No software that comes with Debian may have a license that changes depending on who is using it. Additionally, no license may limit use for any purpose whatsoever.

No Contamination of Other Software and Other Special Conditions

Some software packages come with licenses that outlaw the use of the software under certain conditions; Debian disallows anything that's blatantly illogical. For example, if one piece of software has a license that makes its use illegal if you have package *XXX* installed on your computer, it won't be allowed into Debian. In addition, no software is included in Debian whose license is specially written to be used only for Debian systems.

This means that there are no unusually confusing restrictions placed on any of Debian's software.

Size

In addition to Debian's freeness, consider its size. Debian is by far the largest Linux distribution in the world, containing over 2,600 packages and five complete ports.

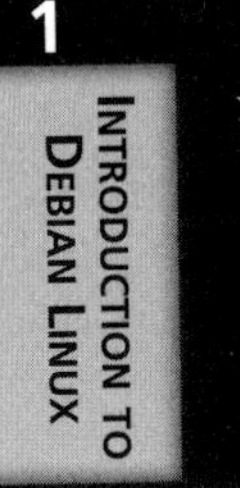

This makes Debian the largest free software project as far as disk space goes, having gobbled up a total of almost 3GB, counting only the latest versions of those ports to be released with Debian 2.2! The project as a whole takes a good 8.1GB!

Security

Debian, being open-source, is always being improved by the community. The instant a security advisory is released that affects Debian, somebody is working to fix the problem. Usually, major security flaws are fixed before they've been heard about by enough malicious hackers to be a threat.

Technical Superiority

Debian aims for zero downtime systems that can be completely upgraded in place without any reboots. Remember the days of Windows when the answer to every problem was a complete reinstall? Debian is very good at fixing problems automatically—when something too complicated to be recovered by this mechanism occurs, there's still nothing to be worried about. Problems are almost always very localized (depending on how essential a component fails) and fixable with a minimum of fuss.

This has been a basic pillar of the Linux community's philosophy for some time, and Debian as a rule sides with these opinions and works toward realizing them. For this reason, not only are zero downtime and in-place upgrade addressed, but efficiency, stability, and flexibility as well.

Who Makes Debian?

Debian is made on the spare time of over 500 hobbyists and professionals worldwide. I am a member of this development team, and receive no compensation but personal satisfaction for my efforts. Debian is a very flexible organization; very little control is exerted over the voluntary members.

It's a wonder to some that a mixed group of completely unpaid workers has been able to come up with such a solid product. To me, however, it's no surprise at all. When the community directs a product to its desires, that product generally meets the needs of the same community! If this were not true, the Debian organization wouldn't be effective.

Because of this philosophy, Debian is usually more professional, dependable, and efficient than its counterparts. On the other hand, it suffers in the area of user friendliness, because none of its contributors need that. Again, who would spend time writing something he or she didn't need?

Debian functions as a group of individuals, in a semidemocratic fashion. Participation in the political end of this work is entirely voluntary, as well as every other aspect of involvement. Because of this business layout, sometimes there are internal squabbles and/or inefficiency, which hinders progress. However, as a whole, Debian continues to serve the needs of the community as the most powerful and flexible Linux distribution on the planet.

Summary

Linux is the one software project that has discovered a powerful enough development model to make Microsoft leery. Although Microsoft has dominated the server market with Windows NT for some time, Linux is beginning to gain ground, having an estimated 8 million systems and servers worldwide. Red Hat took the initiative to perform some market research regarding this issue, and the results show the estimated growth of the Linux community for the last few years.

Obviously, this is an upward trend. This growth is directly related to the size of the Internet, so there is no way any individual software vendor can even hope to overtake this movement. Free software is simply untouchable by the corporate sector; the debut of entirely no-cost, technically superior platforms is complete. Now all that looms is the future and what new heights this self-sustaining community reaches in the years to come.

CHAPTER

Shells

by John Goerzen

IN THIS CHAPTER

When you work with the Linux command line, there is always a program called a *shell* that reads your commands, processes them, directs the flow of data in or out of programs, and allows scripting to automate tasks. There are a number of shells available for your use under Linux, each with its own particular characteristics. This chapter explores two of the most popular modern shells: `bash` and `tcsh`. You'll find that both shells offer you a great amount of power; they simply use a different approach for getting things done.

bash: The Bourne-Again Shell

When you first log in to a Debian machine and see a command prompt, you're already using `bash`; it's Debian's default shell.

History of bash

`bash` is an enhanced version of the Bourne shell, `sh`. What this means is that `bash` is designed to be able to run all scripts that ran under `sh`, which was a traditional UNIX shell for many years. This enables you to continue to run older scripts under `bash`.

`bash` also incorporates many features from the Korn shell, `ksh`, an earlier improvement upon `sh`. A few features found in the C shell (`csh`) have made their way into `bash` as well, but generally with a more Bourne-like syntax.

All of this means that `bash` can be used to run a wide variety of shell scripts, and should be a familiar environment for anyone used to using `sh` or `ksh` on another UNIX platform.

bash Syntax

When you start to use `bash`, you type basic commands. These commands can be something simple, such as

```
ls
```

This runs the program called `ls`, which displays a listing of files in your current directory. You can also specify additional options for commands, such as `ls`:

```
ls -l
```

`bash` passes along the `-l` to `ls`. This addition to the command is often called a *parameter* or an *argument* to `ls`. When you run the previous command, you get a longer listing with more detail of the same files because `bash` passed along the additional information to `ls`.

In general, you can separate the command from its options with a space, and you can also add other options, separating them from each other with a space as well. Many commands accept a wide range of arguments and may accept a list of files on which to operate as well.

Wildcards

You'll find that there will often be times when it is necessary to refer to a whole group of files. Rather than specifying each one individually, `bash` includes a mechanism called *wildcards* that enables you to specify files as a whole group. Wildcards work by enabling you to specify a pattern that is then compared to filenames to come up with the group of files on which to operate.

Here is a list of the most commonly used wildcards in `bash`:

Wildcard	*Matches*
`*`	Zero or more characters
`?`	Exactly one character
`[abcde]`	Exactly one character listed
`[a-e]`	Exactly one character in the given range
`[a-e,q-z]`	Exactly one character, taken from any of the given ranges
`{fox,goose}`	Exactly one entire word from the options given

Wildcard Examples

Let's consider a few examples. Your `/dev` directory has many hundreds of entries. This makes a great place to experiment with wildcards.

Try this:

```
cd /dev
ls
```

Notice that many filenames scroll by. If you're looking for just one bit of information, such as the names for your serial ports, you see too much information to be able to easily pick them out. So, try using wildcards:

```
ls ttyS*
```

Now you see only four entries—much better! Note that in this case, you could also have use `ttyS?` with the same result, because the `*` wildcard matches only one character in this situation.

Now, try this:

```
ls ttyS[0-2]
```

This time, `ls` displays only three files for you.

Let's use a more complicated pattern now:

```
ls [sh]d[a-c]?
```

This displays all files that start with either s or h, followed by d, then any character between a and c, and finally any one character.

The following pattern

```
ls {sd,hd}[a-c]?
```

matches exactly the same files as the previous one does. Note that the difference is that we're asking for files that begin with sd or hd, instead of just a single character.

A frequent use of wildcards is to select files by type. By convention, in UNIX, file type is indicated by the file extension. For instance, a filename that ends in .txt is a text file. You can use wildcards to your advantage to perform actions on files based on type, like so:

```
cp *.txt textfiles
```

This copies all the .txt files in your current directory to another directory named textfiles, assuming that the textfiles directory already exists.

As you can see, wildcards can be extremely powerful tools. They enable you to select dozens or even hundreds of files at once, with only a few keystrokes. Because bash interprets the wildcards, you can use wildcards on the command line of any program (for instance, ls or cp) that expects filenames.

Environment Variables

Every UNIX process has certain environment variables associated with it. bash is no exception. bash, in fact, enables you to set variables both for internal bash uses (such as are described later in this chapter)and for ones that should be passed along to other programs.

You can get a listing of your current environment variables by running the following:

```
printenv
```

Notice that the system has already assigned numerous variables for you. These include things such as PATH, HOME, and the like. Also note how bash displays the variables for you: the name, an equal sign, and then the value of the variable. This is also exactly how you set environment variables for yourself; try typing this at the prompt:

```
MYVAR=myvalue
```

This sets up MYVAR as an internal bash variable, and sets its value to myvalue. You can check the value of any variable in bash by using echo:

```
echo $MYVAR
```

The system displays myvalue for you. Now, run this:

```
export MYVAR
```

This marks `MYVAR` as a variable that will be passed on to programs that you start inside your current `bash` session. Note that `echo` can still display `MYVAR`, but now it also appears inside the `printenv` output, whereas it would not have appeared there had you not exported it first.

Sometimes, you may want to remove the definition of a variable (erase it); to do so, you use `unset`:

```
unset MYVAR
```


Special Syntax

Earlier, you learned how command lines contain a command and then some optional parameters, separated by spaces. This sounds quite nice, but you can run into some trouble. One common sticking point occurs if you are dealing with files whose names contain spaces. When you do that, you have to enclose the filename in single quotes (`'`) to prevent `bash` from thinking you are trying to give it two separate options instead of just one filename. Consider the following:

```
ls 'File With Spaces.txt'
```

If you leave off the single quotation marks, `ls` tries to display a listing of three files: `File`, `With`, and `Spaces.txt`. Adding single quotes in this fashion is called *quoting the filename*.

You can also use the backslash character (`\`) to deal with these situations. The backslash tells `bash` to not interpret the next character specially. Consider the following:

```
ls File\ With\ Spaces.txt
```

This achieves the same effect as quoting the filename did previously. You also can use backslashes to suppress the effect of the wildcard characters. For instance, you may be working with a file that has a question mark in its name. You can use the backslash to force `bash` to treat the question mark as a normal question mark instead of as a wildcard character:

```
ls Memo\?.txt
```

Now, instead of matching, for example, `Memo1.txt`, `Memo2.txt`, and `Memo?.txt`, it matches only `Memo?.txt`. The technique of using the backslash is called *escaping characters*.

So, now you may be wondering how to deal with a backslash in a filename. To do that, you simply double the backslash:

```
ls File\\.txt
```

This will match a file called `File\.txt`.

So far, you've learned the use of the single quote character and the backslash. In `bash`, however, you can also use the double quotation mark ("). This acts like the single quote character, but with one important exception: you can refer to variables inside a string with double quotes, but not inside one with single quotes; that is, the single quote represents the "stronger" quote of the two.

Quoting Example

Let's look at an example:

```
MYFILE=/dev/ttyS0
```

Here, we set `MYFILE` to hold the name of a specific file, `/dev/ttyS0`. Let's use this with `ls`:

```
ls $MYFILE
```

This displays an entry for `/dev/ttyS0`. Now, try that inside single quotes:

```
ls '$MYFILE'
```

`ls` complains that it can't find the file or directory named `"$MYFILE"`. This is because `ls` is literally looking for a file whose name begins with a dollar sign (`$`). Now try double quotes:

```
ls "$MYFILE"
```

This time, `ls` obliges and gives you the output you wanted: `/dev/ttyS0`. Look at the differences in wildcards:

```
ls '*'
ls "*"
ls *
```

The first two both generate errors; both the `'` and `"` escape characters cause `bash` to treat the asterisk (`*`) literally, and `ls` is actually looking for a file with a single asterisk as its name. The third option displays the listing of all files in the current directory, as you might expect, because the asterisk is not quoted there.

Redirection

So far, we've looked at a few basic things that can be done with the Linux command line. You can select groups of files and perform actions on them. But the power of `bash` goes far beyond this. Linux shells also give you the ability to "glue" different programs together. This is generally implemented by taking the output from one program and saving it to a file or feeding it directly to another program. *Redirection* enables you to tell programs where to send their output. Instead of displaying things on the screen, they are redirected to save their output to a file, to send it to a printer, or to send it across the Internet by piping to a program such as mail or telnet. With Linux, these different actions are completely transparent; every command-line Linux program automatically supports redirection, giving you tremendous power and flexibility.

Let's start with redirecting the output of a simple program, such as `ls`. The output redirection operator is the greater-than sign(>). Here's an example of its use:

```
cd
ls /dev/ttyS* > mylisting.txt
```

Notice that when you run `ls` this time, you don't get anything on your screen; the command prompt simply returns. `ls` did run, though; you simply instructed it to save the file listing into the file `mylisting.txt` instead of displaying the results to the screen. You can use a program called `cat` to view this file:

```
cat mylisting.txt
```

Now you see the output from `ls`! You could perhaps email this file to somebody, or maybe you'd just like to delete the file:

```
rm mylisting.txt
```

One thing to be careful of when using the > operator is that it will erase the file that you are writing the data to. For instance, if you already have a file named `mylisting.txt` and then use the previous `ls` command, the existing contents of `mylisting.txt` will be erased and replaced by the `ls` output. Usually, this is the desired behavior; however, sometimes you'd rather add on to the file instead of erase and start over. For that purpose, there is the >> operator, also known as the *append operator*. Here's an example of its use:

```
ls /dev/ttyS* > mylisting.txt
ls /dev/hda* >> mylisting.txt
```

Let's analyze what happens here. First, we save the listing of the `/dev/ttyS*` files to `mylisting.txt`, automatically erasing the file first if it already exists. Then, we add a listing of the `/dev/hda*` entries to the end of that file. You can now view both listings with the following:

```
cat mylisting.txt
```

Note that the two previous `ls` commands are actually equivalent to the following single `ls` command:

```
ls /dev/ttyS* /dev/hda* > mylisting.txt
```

As you can see, Linux gives you many different ways to approach a single problem. You can use whichever way works best for you.

Thus far, we've redirected only the standard output, or stdout, of a program. In Linux, each program has three predefined methods of reading or writing: standard input (stdin), standard output (stdout), and standard error (stderr). By default, stdin reads information from your keyboard, stdout displays information to your screen, and stderr also displays information to your screen. With the previous commands, you were redirecting stdout only.

Because `ls` doesn't read anything from the keyboard or print any errors in normal operation, you didn't notice anything odd. Let's try another command:

```
grep Linux /lib/* > /dev/null
```

You should see at least one error message on your screen, complaining that `/lib/modules` is a directory. For now, we'll not worry about why that message appeared or what `grep` does. Notice how stdout was redirected to `/dev/null`. `/dev/null` is a "bit bucket" device; that is, you can send data to it and it will just be thrown away. We could have used `mylisting.txt` again, but you would just have had to erase it later.

Note that even though you redirected stdout, the error message still appeared on your screen. This is because stderr was not redirected. You can redirect *all* of them with the `&>` operator:

```
grep Linux /lib/* &> /dev/null
```

Now, all the output from `grep` was sent to `/dev/null`, and nothing appears on your screen.

Although redirecting output can be quite useful, it can also be useful to redirect the input to a program. That is, some programs that might normally expect typed input can be sent input from a file instead. As an example, let's use the `tac` program. `tac` is a simple program that reads input from the keyboard and then displays it to you with all the lines reversed. You can try it at the command prompt; just type `tac` and press Enter. Now type a few lines of text and press Ctrl+D when you're done. `tac` then displays the text with the lines reversed.

Let's try a practical example of `tac`:

```
ls -l --sort=size /bin > mylisting.txt
tac < mylisting.txt
```

The first line instructs `ls` to generate a long listing of the files in `/bin`, sorted by size, and save the results into `mylisting.txt`. So far, so good—but this command puts the largest files first and the smallest files last. What if you want the smallest files first? Well, you could look up the `ls` option to do that (`-r`, in case you're wondering), or you can use `tac`.

The previous `tac` line reads its input from `mylisting.txt`, reverses the order of the lines, and displays it on your screen.

Another thing you can do is get a count of the files in `/bin`. Try this:

```
ls /bin > mylisting.txt
wc -l < mylisting.txt
```

`wc` will now tell you how many entries are in `/bin`. You're starting to see how powerful the "glue" of the Linux shell can be!

Piping

It gets even better yet. So far, we've examined redirecting the input and output of programs. But Linux takes it a step further: You can actually take the output of one program and send it to another as the input. This is called *piping*. The operator for piping is the ¦ symbol, which is a vertical or broken vertical line almost always found above the backslash key (\) on your keyboard.

Let's begin the discussion of piping by examining another way of doing the `ls` and `wc` commands shown previously:

```
ls /bin ¦ wc -l
```

You will get the exact same result displayed on your screen as you got earlier when you used the `mylisting.txt` file. The difference here, though, is that Linux starts both `ls` and `wc` for you simultaneously; that is, both programs are running at once. It then sets them up so that anything that `ls` sends to stdout (the file listing) goes to stdin of `wc`. That way, you avoid having to use an intermediate file. This can be great, especially if you're dealing with a large amount of data.

You can also use piping with the `tac` example:

```
ls -l --sort=size /bin ¦ tac
```

Again, you can avoid the temporary file here.

Piping Examples

Let's examine some more powerful things you can do with piping. One program that is commonly used on Linux is `grep`. `grep` reads input, compares it to a pattern supplied as an argument, and then displays only the lines that contain that pattern. As you may imagine, this program has almost no use when reading directly from the keyboard; but when you combine `grep` with piping or redirection, it becomes extremely powerful.

Let's say that we'd like a list of all the files in `/bin` that contain the letter *m* in their names—sorted by size, with the largest files listed last. We could use a wildcard of `/bin/*m*` to achieve this effect, but let's pretend for the moment that you don't want to use wildcards. Then, you might use a command such as this:

```
ls -l --`sort=size /bin ¦ grep m ¦ tac
```

Notice how you can use several commands at once here. For this command, Linux starts up *three* programs for you. The listing from `ls` is sent as input to `grep`. `grep` filters out all lines that don't contain the letter *m* and sends the result to `tac`, which reverses the order of the list. You could also use `wc -l` instead of `tac`, which gives you a count of the number of files in `/bin` whose names contain the letter *m*.

If you want to use only redirection to accomplish the same results, it takes some more effort. You have to do something like this:

```
ls -l --sort=size /bin > mylisting1.txt
grep m < mylisting1.txt > mylisting2.txt
tac < mylisting2.txt
rm mylisting1.txt mylisting2.txt
```

Piping makes this much easier!

Combining Programs

You can even take it a step further. Let's say you want to get the listing of *m*-containing files, as described previously, and mail the list to your system administrator. You can then do this:

```
ls -l --sort=size /bin | grep m | tac | \
  mail -s 'File Listing' friend@example.com
```

Here, you actually use four separate programs: `ls`, `grep`, `tac`, and `mail`. Notice that the command line is a very long one. You can type it all on one line if you want, but if you do that, omit the backslash. If you stick the backslash at the very end of one line and then press Enter, Linux waits for another line of input as part of the command line, sticks them all together, and then runs your request as if you typed it all on one large line.

Let's go over what this example does in more detail. First, `ls` generates the sorted long listing that we're familiar with. Then, `grep` reads that listing directly from `ls` and filters out any lines that don't contain the letter *m*. `tac` receives this list from `grep` and reverses it. `mail` then receives the reversed list from `tac` and sends it as the body of an email to `friend@example.com` with the subject line of `File Listing`.

You also can achieve the same result by using these commands:

```
cd /bin
ls -l -d -r --sort=size *m* | mail -s 'File Listing' \
  friend@example.com
```

Here, the `-d` and `-r` `ls` options and the `*m*` wildcard are used instead of a `grep` and a `tac` command. You are free to use whichever method you prefer; as before, Linux gives you many possible solutions to a problem.

Aliases

As we've gone through commands, you've seen how some of them can get a bit on the long side. To save you time, `bash` provides a facility called *aliases*. Aliases enable you to define shortcuts, or aliases, for commands. Let's consider, for example, that you might frequently want to issue the command `ls -l`. You could define an alias for it:

```
alias ll='ls -l'
```

After that, you can simply type `ll`. `bash` will see that it's an alias and will actually run `ls -l`. You can also put longer things into aliases; for instance:

```
alias lbin='ls -l --sort=size /bin | grep m | tac'
```

After this, whenever you run `lbin`, the longer command will actually be executed. You can also combine aliases with other things on the same command line:

```
lbin | mail -s 'File Listing' friend@example.com
```

Effectively, `bash` expands `lbin` and then tacks the mail command on after it, so the output from `tac` gets sent to mail just as before.

You can also get a list of all the aliases that are currently set by running the following:

```
alias
```

And finally, to delete an alias, you use `unalias`:

```
unalias ll
```

Job Control with bash

Linux provides you with many opportunities for multitasking. As you'll read later, one way to do this is by opening several programs in the graphical X interface. However, you can do some basic multitasking without ever having to start up something such as X—thanks to `bash`'s job-control features.

`bash` enables you to interrupt running processes, to set existing processes to run as a background task, and to switch between processes.

Suspending Programs

As an example, let's open up the `emacs` editor to work with a file:

```
emacs -nw
```

The editor appears onscreen. So far so good. You may go around editing files, or playing some of the games built into `emacs`. But let's say that you want to get back to the command prompt. To do so, you can press the suspend key combination, Ctrl+Z.

Now, your screen looks something like this:

```
erwin ~$ emacs -nw

[1]+  Stopped                 emacs -nw
erwin ~$
```

You're back to the prompt. `emacs` is still in memory, but its execution has been temporarily suspended. You can now run commands such as `ls`, or `mail`, or even another instance of `emacs`. When you're ready to return to `emacs`, you might type the following:

```
jobs
```

This shows you the `[1]+` line as previously. You can now return to `emacs` by typing the following:

```
fg %1
```

This tells `bash` to take job `1` from the listing and put it into the foreground again.

You can fire up lots of commands at once and switch between them by using this feature. Doing so is called *task-switching*.

You can also use multitasking features with `bash`. This is done by placing some processes into the background. If you are using solely `bash` features, you are generally restricted to using this capability for things that do not need to interact with the screen or keyboard—a prime candidate for things that use redirection. If you need to do multitasking with interactive programs, you need to use something like the virtual console support in Linux, the GNU screen program, or the X Windowing System.

Let's consider a small example. Type this:

```
emacs -nw
```

Next press Ctrl+Z (to suspend `emacs`). Then type the following:

```
cat < /dev/zero > /dev/null
```

This last command is basically reading a lot of nonsense and then discarding it; it's doing nothing useful, but it is using CPU time so it makes a good illustration of the process. Now go ahead and press Ctrl+Z to suspend `cat` as well. Then run the `jobs` command; you ought to see output such as this:

```
erwin ~$ jobs
[1]-  Stopped                emacs -nw
[2]+  Stopped                cat < /dev/zero >/dev/null
erwin ~$
```

Now, type the following:

```
bg %2
```

This puts job `2` into the background. If you run `jobs` again, you see the following:

```
erwin ~$ jobs
[1]+  Stopped                emacs -nw
[2]-  Running                cat < /dev/zero >/dev/null &
erwin ~$
```

You see that the `cat` job is now running in the background; the ampersand (`&`) at the end of it signifies this. In fact, a shortcut to starting a program and then suspending it and placing it into the background is to start it with an ampersand at the end:

```
cat < /dev/zero > /dev/null &
```

This starts cat and automatically places it into the background.

Now, you can use fg %1 to return to emacs and let your cat jobs go ahead and do their thing in the background. But, you may wonder how to stop the cat processes. Well, as usual, Linux gives you several ways. The first way is to restore it to the foreground and then press the interrupt key, Ctrl+C. Type the following:

```
fg %2
```

Then press Ctrl+C.

If you run jobs again, you'll notice that cat is no longer listed. Note that Ctrl+C enables you to terminate almost any program that you run in a Linux shell. Another thing you can do is run the following:

```
kill %2
```

which terminates the cat process without your having to use fg on it first.

Special bash Variables

Earlier, we looked at environment variables in the shell. Although there are many programs that can use variables that you export for them, bash itself can use variables that you set for it. In this section, you'll read about many of these differect variables and what they can do for you and for bash.

PATH and HOME

Arguably, the most important of these variables is PATH. The reason is that, to start almost any program, the shell has to know where to find it. This is the purpose of PATH. Take a look at what it's set to:

```
erwin ~$ echo $PATH
/usr/local/bin:/usr/bin:/bin:/usr/bin/X11:/usr/games
```

Recall from before that $PATH causes the shell to expand the PATH variable and that echo displays it. PATH tells bash where to look for a program when you try to run it. Try running this command at the prompt:

```
type ls
```

It responds by telling you that it's in /bin/ls. How does it know this? Well, that's where PATH comes in. bash searches each directory listed in PATH, in order, for ls. The first place it finds it, /usr/bin/, is the place that it uses. You can, in fact, run this:

```
ls -l /usr/bin/ls
```

and get information about ls itself.

If you install your own software, you might install it under a directory such as bin underneath your home directory. In that case, you might issue a command such as this:

```
PATH=$PATH:$HOME/bin
```

Let's examine how this works. First, bash replaces $PATH with the current contents of the PATH variable. Second, bash replaces $HOME with the contents of the HOME variable—your home directory. Note that the colon (:) and /bin are not replaced by anything; they are simply added to the appropriate place in the result. Finally, bash assigns the result to the PATH variable. You can now use the following:

```
echo $PATH
```

You'll see your home directory listed at the end of the PATH display. Now, you can put software in your bin directory, and bash will automatically find it when you type the program name on the command line.

PS1: Your Prompt

You can customize your prompt in bash; to do this, you need to modify the PS1 variable. First, let's consider an example:

```
PS1='\u@\h \w\$ '
```

As soon as you type this, you'll notice that your prompt changes to indicate your username, your hostname, and your current working directory, such as the following:

```
username@localhost ~/bin$
```

Note also that you need to put your prompt setting in quotes as previously, because it often contains special characters. Here is a complete list of the tokens bash offers for your use in PS1:

\a	Causes bash to beep each time a prompt is displayed
\d	Today's date
\e	Terminal escape character, 0x1B
\h	Your system's hostname
\H	Your system's fully qualified domain name
\n	Creates a new line at this location
\r	Carriage-return character
\s	The name of your shell
\t	24-hour time in HH:MM:SS format
\T	12-hour time in HH:MM:SS format (see also \@ for AM/PM)
\u	Your username
\v	The bash version

`\V`	The `bash` version and patch level
`\w`	Your current working directory
`\W`	The last component of your current working directory
`\!`	The number of this command in the history
`\@`	AM or PM, as appropriate for current time
`\#`	The command number of this command (since the start of the shell instead of the start of the history)
`\$`	A `$` character (unless you are logged on as `root`—in which case, it generates a `#` character)
`\\`	A backslash
`\[`	Begins terminal code string
`\]`	Ends terminal code string
`\nnn`	Inserts the character specified by the octal number `nnn`

MAILCHECK

`bash` can automatically check for new mail. You can set `MAILCHECK` to tell `bash` how frequently to do this. By default, `MAILCHECK` is set to `60`; that is, it checks for new mail every 60 seconds and lets you know whether you have new mail.

HISTSIZE and HISTFILESIZE

In the later section, "`bash` Command History," you'll learn about `bash`'s command history features. These two variables control how much history to store in memory and on disk, respectively. By default, both are set to `500`. The history file is written to disk whenever you exit `bash` so that your history is preserved between multiple shell sessions.

LANG

Debian GNU/Linux defaults to using English. However, many system functions are available in non-English versions as well. So, if you prefer to work in another language, you can set the `LANG` variable as appropriate. Generally, you set it to your country's ISO code. For instance, to set your system to interact with you in German where possible, you use the `de` code (short for Deutschland):

```
export LANG=de_DE
```

Now when you run a command such as the following:

```
man cat
```

you get the German version if available, and `bash` displays information for you in German where possible. Not all Linux programs have translations into all other languages, so setting this variable can best be thought of as communicating your preference for a certain language to the system.

bash Command History

As you run commands, `bash` keeps track of what you type. This enables you to easily recall previous commands to save typing. You can get a complete list of `bash`'s current command history by running the following:

```
history
```

However, this list is likely more than a screen long, so you will probably want to run it like this instead:

```
history | less
```

You will see a list of all the commands you have typed that `bash` remembers for you. There are three ways to select these:

- You can use the up arrow to select previous commands.
- You can select by number by typing:

  ```
  !100
  ```

  This selects command 100.
- You can select a command by matching the first parts of it:

  ```
  !export
  ```

  This selects the most recent command that started with

  ```
  "export"
  ```

You can also add things to the end of your command. For instance, if command 100 was `ls -l --sort=size`, you can run this:

```
!100 | tac
```

This results in the following:

```
ls -l --sort=size | tac
```

As a special shortcut, you may also use `!!` to match the most recent command that you issued. You can, of course, add things to the end of a command retrieved with `!!` as well.

You learned previously that you can use `\#` in your `PS1` so that your prompt displays the history number of the current command. If you find yourself using the history frequently, this can be a great time saver; you'll no longer need to find the history number, and giving a number takes generally less typing than matching the first part of a command.

Directory Stack

The command history can be a great way to save typing when you're working on tasks that involve similar commands. `bash` also offers a way to save time when working on tasks that involve many of the same directories. This mechanism is called the *directory stack*.

The directory stack enables you to store the directories in which you have been working, and to return to those locations without having to type the full pathname.

The first step to using the directory stack is to use the command pushd instead of cd. Let's start with a sample session such as this one:

```
cd
pushd /usr/doc
pushd /bin
pushd /usr/local
pushd /etc
pushd /boot
pushd /home
```

After the last command, bash displays:

```
/home /boot /etc /usr/local /bin /usr/doc ~
```

This is your directory stack. The first entry is your current directory, /home. The second is the one that you went to with your most recent pushd command; the third, the one you went to with your second most-recent pushd command; and so forth. You can also recall this list at any time by typing dirs at the prompt.

Now, you've done your work in /home and you'd like to return to /boot. To do that, you type popd. bash changes your directory to /boot and displays the directory stack for you again. The stack now reads

```
/boot /etc /usr/local /bin /usr/doc ~
```

Notice how /home has disappeared off the stack. If you type popd again, you change to /etc and /boot will disappear off the stack. You can continue issuing popd commands until you return to your home directory.

Also note that it is possible to use cd even after using pushd; directories entered with cd will simply not be put on the stack for later retrieval.

You've been introduced to a lot in this section—wildcards, redirection, piping, and special environment variables. As you go on to the next section on tcsh, you'll notice that some things remain the same between the two shells. Others, such as special variables, can be quite different.

tcsh: The Tenex C Shell

As mentioned before, another shell that you will find on many different UNIX platforms is csh, the C shell. Like sh, the Bourne shell, csh can be used both for interactive commands and for shell programming. csh is designed to have a syntax that resembles the programming language C; however, you'll find that it is similar to bash in many respects.

tcsh is an enhanced version of csh; interestingly, it adds to csh some of the same features that bash adds to sh, although of course tcsh has syntax that is like csh instead of like sh.

tcsh Syntax

Like bash, tcsh commands are split into the command name itself and its arguments, separated by spaces. You'll find that some of the bash wildcards apply to tcsh as well, but there are also some important differences to be aware of.

In tcsh circles, wildcards are referred to as *glob* patterns, and their use is called *globbing*. The difference between globbing and using wildcards is semantic only; they both refer to the same action.

Like bash, tcsh supports the wildcard characters *, ?, the [asdf] syntax, and the {word1,word2} syntax. These operators function the same in tcsh as they do in bash. Additionally, you'll find that escaping in tcsh works as it does in bash; the ', ", and \ operators function in the same fashion.

Working with Variables

However, in tcsh, shell and environment variables are dealt with differently than in bash. In tcsh, there are two commands that you use to find out information about variables: printenv and set. Try them now; you'll see printenv display a list of environment variables similar to the list in bash. set, however, displays a list of tcsh-specific settings, although some, such as path and home, correspond to certain environment variables. To set a variable in tcsh, you use the command setenv:

```
setenv MYVAR value
```

This sets the environment variable MYVAR to the value value. This command is the tcsh equivalent of the following bash command:

```
export MYVAR=value
```

As with bash, you can view the contents of MYVAR with echo:

```
echo $MYVAR
```

To remove MYVAR from the environment, you use unsetenv:

```
unsetenv MYVAR
```

To deal with internal tcsh variables, you use the set and unset commands. Generally, these variables control aspects of tcsh behavior or give you information about the system in which tcsh is running. In bash, these are all available using the same set of commands; tcsh draws a distinction between the two.

To set an internal variable in `tcsh`, use the following:

```
set myintvar=myvalue
```

You can still use `echo` to display internal variables in `tcsh`:

```
echo $myintvar
```

And to erase `myintvar`, you use `unset`:

```
unset myintvar
```

Note that when using `setenv`, you do *not* use the = sign; but when using `set`, the equal sign is mandatory. As a further distinction, note that the equal sign is always mandatory when setting variables in `bash`. `bash` actually enables you to use the `set` syntax of `tcsh`, but it is not mandatory and is not commonly used in `bash`.

Redirection in `tcsh` is almost identical to that in `bash`. The < operator redirects standard input, the > operator redirects standard output, the >> operator redirects standard output with append, and the ¦ sets up a pipe.

However, to redirect standard error, you use the `>&` syntax instead of `bash`'s `&>` syntax. For instance

```
grep Linux /lib/* >& /dev/null
```

You can also use the `>>&` syntax to append both standard output and standard error to the end of a file; this is an extension to the >> syntax that you find in both `bash` and `tcsh`.

Aliases

Like `bash`, `tcsh` has an alias facility. It functions almost identically to the one in `bash`. Let's set an `ll` alias:

```
alias ll 'ls -l'
```

Note the lack of an equal sign here. Now, `ll` will function as `ls -l` did. As with `bash`, you can add other things to the command line after the alias:

```
ll ¦ tac
```

You can view a list of all your currently defined aliases by running the following:

```
alias
```

And finally, to remove an alias, run this:

```
unalias ll
```

Job Control with tcsh

Like `bash`, `tcsh` provides you with the ability to do task-switching and multitasking from the shell. The mechanism for doing so in `tcsh` is almost identical to that of `bash`.

The largest difference, in fact, is simply that `tcsh` displays the `jobs` output for you less frequently, but you can still explicitly request it by simply typing `jobs` at the command line. As in `bash`, the background task facility in `tcsh` is most useful for programs that do not read from the keyboard or write to the screen—perhaps that are set up with redirection or pipes.

Special `tcsh` Variables

`tcsh` also has some special internal variables. These are accessed with the `set` and `unset` commands, and traditionally are stored in all-lowercase form. These will be illustrated in the following sections.

Of special note is the `path` variable. This variable is automatically set based on the `PATH` environment variable. Note that variable names are case-sensitive in `tcsh` as they are in `bash`. The recommended way to modify the path in `tcsh` is to modify the `PATH` environment variable directly; it uses a colon-separated list of directories just as `bash` does. Further, `tcsh` automatically updates its internal `path` variable every time you modify the `PATH` environment variable. In this way, programs that you run inside of `tcsh` can see the correct `PATH` as well.

The `autologout` Variable

`tcsh` has a feature in which it can automatically log you out: the `autologout` variable. This feature can be useful to increase security if you walk out of the room and leave your shell unattended, for instance. `tcsh` can also lock your terminal, meaning that you are not logged out but you have to enter your password to get back to work.

In its simplest form, `autologout` controls only the timeout before automatically logging you out. Unlike many other time variables in `tcsh`, `autologout` times are specified in minutes rather than in seconds. So, you might use this:

```
set autologout=60
```

This tells `tcsh` to automatically log you off after one hour of inactivity. If you also want to enable automatic locking, you might specify a value such as this:

```
set autologout=(60 30)
```

This automatically locks the shell after 30 minutes and automatically logs out after 60 minutes of inactivity.

Note that the `autologout` feature does not take effect if you are running some other program under the shell, you are running the shell under the X Windowing System, or if you have used a facility such as telnet to log in to the shell remotely.

The `history` Variable

The `history` variable is similar to the `HISTSIZE` variable in `bash` in that it controls how many lines are kept in your history. Its default value is 100. However, it can also be used to set the format used by the time; this is done with the second word shown in the code below. It uses the same tokens used by `prompt`, so there is no need to learn another set. When you assign more than one thing to an internal `tcsh` variable, you use syntax such as this:

```
set history=(100 '%h\t%t\t%R\n')
```

This tells `tcsh` to remember 100 commands. The second part tells it the format of the history file line. It starts by printing out the history number of the command. Then, the `\t` instructs it to display the tab character, which is used to insert some space between the command and the next part. Then, `%t` tells `tcsh` to display the time, followed by `\t` for another tab. Finally, the special token `%R` represents the command, and `\n` ends the line.

The `mail` Variable

Like `bash`, `tcsh` can periodically check your mailbox for new mail. It does this periodically—every 10 minutes by default. You can set both how frequently it checks for mail and the location of your mailbox.

You can set your mailbox location like so:

```
set mail=(/var/spool/mail/username)
```

You can also add a number, which indicates how frequently to check for new mail:

```
set mail=(60 /var/spool/mail/username)
```

This instructs `tcsh` to check your mailbox in `/var/spool/mail/username` for new mail every 60 seconds.

The `prompt` Variable

The `prompt` variable is the `tcsh` version of `PS1` in `bash`. As in `bash`, `tcsh`'s `prompt` variable is rich with replaceable tokens; you'll discover, in fact, that `tcsh` features a few more of them than `bash` does. Table 2.1 shows a complete list of the available tokens.

TABLE 2.1 A Complete List of Tokens

Token	*Meaning*
`!`	Same as `%h`
`%B`	Begins bold mode
`%b`	Ends bold mode
`%c`	The last part of the current working directory name

continues

TABLE 2.1 continued

Token	*Meaning*
%c2, %c3, and so forth	The last two, three (and so forth) components of the current working directory
%C	Like %c, but uses the long form of directory names
%d	The current day of the week
%D	The numeric day of the month for today
%h	The current command's history number
%l	The shell's current controlling terminal
%L	Erases everything from the end of the prompt to the next line
%m	The machine's hostname
%M	Your machine's fully qualified domain name
%n	Your Linux username
%p	12-hour time in "precise" format (meaning it includes seconds)
%P	24-hour time in "precise" format (meaning it includes seconds)
%S	Begins standout mode
%s	Ends standout mode
%t	The time in 12-hour format
%T	The time in 24-hour format
%U	Begins underline mode
%u	Ends underline mode
%w	The name of the current month
%W	The number of the current month
%y	The year in 2-digit format
%Y	The current year in 4-digit format
%%	The % character
%!	Like %h; the current command's history number
%@	Like %t; the time in 12-hour format
$#	Expands to > for normal usage and to # if you are running as root
%/	The full name of the current working directory
%~	The current working directory in short form
^C	The control character matching C; for example, ^G for Ctrl+G
\a	Causes tcsh to beep whenever a prompt is displayed
\e	Terminal escape code, 0x1B
\f	Terminal formfeed code

Token	Meaning
`\n`	Starts a new line at this position
`\r`	Carriage return code
`\t`	Tab
`\v`	Vertical tab
`\nnn`	The character specified by octal number `nnn`

Let's examine a sample usage:

```
set prompt='%U%m%u:%B%~%b%# '
```

This sets the prompt to Debian's default. Breaking it down, you see the first: underlining is turned on. Next, your machine's short hostname is displayed. Underlining is then turned off, and a colon is displayed. Now, bold is turned on, the short form of your current directory is displayed, and bold is turned back off. Finally, a closing character (either > or #) is displayed, followed by a space. That is, your prompt might look like this:

```
localhost:~/bin>
```

The `rmstar` Variable

The `rmstar` variable is a safeguard against accidental deletion of files. A common way to delete all files in the current directory is to use `rm *`. If you type `set rmstar`, `tcsh` prompts you before carrying out your actions:

```
set rmstar
```

Note that in this situation, it is not necessary to assign anything to the variable; you simply turn it on by using `set rmstar`.

Although this can be a great help, a word of caution is in order: beware that if you ever use a different shell, or ever work on a computer elsewhere, you will not have this protection; so it is best to assume that you do not have it but be glad when it's there for you.

The `savehist` Variable

`tcsh` can automatically save your history when you exit the shell, just as `bash` does. This variable controls whether your history is automatically saved, and if so, how much of it is saved and in what fashion.

First, you simply set the variable with the following:

```
set savehist
```

You automatically turn on history saving. You may also indicate how many lines to save; for instance

```
set savehist=50
```

This turns on automatic history saving and saves the most recent 50 lines from the command history. Note that you must set this to a value less than or equal to the size specified in the history variable.

Finally, you can also tell `tcsh` to merge your saved history with the existing one instead of replacing it; to do so, you use a command such as this:

```
set savehist=(50 merge)
```

This tells `tcsh` to save at most 50 lines into your history file. Furthermore, it merges your current history with whatever is already in the file, sorted by the time at which the commands were entered to the shell.

tcsh History and Directory Stack

`tcsh` provides both a command history facility and a directory stack feature. Both are similar to `bash`; the directory stack is almost identical to it in fact. Like `bash`, `tcsh`'s history enables you to save typing by recalling previously issued commands and combining them with new arguments. `tcsh`'s facility, though, has a few unique features to discuss.

First, you can get a history listing by using the history command:

```
history
```

As with `bash`, you can refer to commands by number, by first few characters, or by using the up arrow. Also, as with `bash`, you can add new arguments to commands recalled by the history facility:

```
ls -l
!! --sort=size
```

Recall from the discussion on `bash` that `!!` is a shortcut for your most recent command. Using this syntax, your second command will effectively become the following:

```
ls -l --sort=size
```

Summary

In this chapter, various aspects of using Linux's two most popular modern shells—`bash` and `tcsh`—were discussed. The mechanisms for selecting groups of files are very important to saving time and keystrokes. `bash` calls these wildcards, and `tcsh` calls them globs. Wildcards have a powerful syntax that can be used to form sophisticated patterns; or you can use them to form simple patterns, such as `*.txt`, which selects all text files.

Environment variables are variables that are accessed both from within a shell and from within any programs that you start from the shell. To set an environment variable, you use the `export` syntax in `bash` and `setenv` in `tcsh`. Shell variables are variables that are used only internally by the shell; they are not passed on to other programs. They are set by using the standard equal notation in `bash` and the `set` command in `tcsh`.

Redirection is a powerful way to glue together various programs that you can find on your GNU/Linux system. You can store the output from a program to a file using the > operator, read the input from a file using the < operator, append the output to a file with the >> operator, and pipe to another program with the ¦ operator. `bash` enables you to redirect standard error with `&>`; `tcsh` uses `>&` for the same purpose.

You can set up a pipeline containing many programs. In this way, it becomes easy to combine many small pieces to solve a larger problem. This type of data sharing is one of GNU/Linux's greatest strengths.

Aliases enable you to make shorter forms of frequently used commands. Both `bash` and `tcsh` support these, and the syntax is very similar on both shells. Both shells enable you to use an alias as part of a larger command line.

Job control enables you to perform task-switching and multitasking with your shell. The methods for doing this are almost identical between the two shells. Important commands and keystrokes include Ctrl+Z, which puts a process on hold and returns your command prompt; `bg`, which puts a process into the background; `fg`, which puts a process into the foreground; and `jobs`, which lists the processes you are running in a given shell. Additionally, adding `&` to the end of a command line automatically puts the process into the background.

Both `bash` and `tcsh` have a variety of shell and environment variables that can be used to customize how the shell works. Some of the highlighted ones include specifying the shell's search path and telling the shell how frequently it ought to check for new mail.

The command history facility enables you to recall recently used commands without having to retype them. You can recall commands by number, by the first part of the command, or by using the up-arrow key.

Finally, the directory stack helps you save keystrokes by keeping track of the directories that you have recently visited.

CHAPTER 3

The X Window System Environment

by Matt Hunter

More properly known as *X11* (for X version 11), or simply *X*, the X Window System environment provides a platform-independent, network-transportable graphical display standard. X is the primary graphical display system for most modern UNIX systems, and versions for most other operating systems exist. Although X is generally not a requirement for use with Linux, any system used in a workstation role would do well to make use of the capabilities X provides. Many useful programs are intended to run in an X environment. Systems used solely in a server role or with users who are never logged in from the console might want to forego using X to conserve memory and disk space.

X employs a client/server operating model. This model is quite different from the ones with which you may be familiar on other operating systems. Because of this difference, it's important to spend a little time understanding what is going on when you run programs in X. The X server component provides the display capabilities that X client applications use to display their interface. This can be somewhat counterintuitive, but if you keep in mind that the X server is providing display services to its clients, you should have few problems.

As a consequence of the client/server model, X clients do not actually do the work of displaying their interface on the screen. Instead, they communicate with an X server, which takes the client's display commands, converts them into something the graphics hardware can display if necessary, and then handles the actual display process. Input is handled in the same way; that is, it passes to the X server and is then passed from there to the client that is expecting it. This approach gives you platform independence and network transparency.

Platform independence, in the context of X, means that an X application running on any architecture can display itself on an X server of any *other* architecture, as well as its own. An i386-architecture X server can happily display X applications from a Sun Sparc workstation. Neither client nor server knows the difference. This example also illustrates the second major benefit of the X client/server model: network transparency.

All X applications are network-transparent. As long as a network connects two computers, an X application can run on one and display its interface on the other. The applications do not know the difference; in both cases, they are simply sending commands to the X server. The X server must be aware of the difference somewhat, for security reasons, but in practice, it does not care; as long as the remote application is allowed to connect and use that display, it works exactly as if it were local.

It is important to note that X itself is only a standard for displaying graphics data. It does not provide a user-interface per se but instead provides the capability for other programs to do so. Each program is responsible for its own interface (often using an interface toolkit, such as Motif or GTK), and a window manager is responsible for managing interactions between application windows and directing user input to the proper place.

This component-oriented approach allows for a great deal of flexibility but can also result in more complexity than otherwise necessary. Because the window manager controls the appearance and operation of application windows, it is responsible for a large part of how the system appears to the user, yet two window managers need not look or behave alike. As an example, some window managers mimic the appearance of other operating systems (most commonly Windows 95, but there are window managers providing the appearance of a Macintosh or Amiga).

Because of these features, you get an amazing capability: You can run an X program on a computer anywhere in the world, regardless of computer type, and have it display and interact with you locally as if it were running on your own machine and using your own preferences and settings.

X Server Requirements

To run an X server, you need to install the appropriate Debian packages on your Debian Linux system, purchase and install a commercial X server, or download, compile, and install the XFree86 programs manually. Because X is a large and complex system, using the Debian packages is the recommended course. You also need to know some details about your graphics card and monitor. Be sure you have that information handy before beginning the install process.

The entirety of the X standard and X extensions is far too great to cover here. Those interested can find more information from The X Consortium (`http://www.x.org/`), the XFree86 development team (`http://www.xfree86.org/`), and many other sites.

The remainder of this chapter covers the basic concepts, installation, setup, and configuration of the XFree86 implementation of X running on Debian Linux. There are several different commercial X implementations that work on Debian Linux, which you might want to investigate. These commercial distributions might be of particular use if you require drivers for a graphics card not yet available from XFree86. However, XFree86 is included and free and meets most needs. Support for modern hardware in XFree86 is advancing rapidly as manufacturers begin to develop and support Linux drivers for their cards.

Basic X Concepts

X is a very powerful GUI system. This power means that X takes a quite different way of looking at things than other GUI systems with which you might be familiar. In the following sections, you'll learn about some of the basics of X that will help you on your way to working with it.

A Client/Server Graphics System

Understanding the nature of X's client/server design is essential to doing interesting things with X, such as running programs remotely but interacting with them locally. Fortunately, the concepts are simple. An X server provides graphics display capabilities to clients. That means that the X server handles all communication with the graphics hardware of your computer. By contrast, the clients do nothing more than talk to the server, telling it what to draw on the screen. In normal use, the clients know nothing at all about the graphics hardware on which they are being displayed, only certain characteristics of the display itself (such as resolution, color depth, and so on).

X Resources

X provides a standard way for you to store configuration data for the X server. X applications can then use a standard protocol to request this information from the server. This configuration mechanism, called *X resources*, is usually used to store application defaults similar to the standard command-line arguments described later, in addition to whatever other defaults the application wants to define.

An X resource consists of an application name, a resource name, and a resource value. Different applications can have different values for the same resource.

X resources are managed by `xrdb`, which allows the user to load his resources into the X database from a file and otherwise manipulate the values.

On a Debian Linux system, X resources are stored in many different files. System-wide resources can be set in the `/etc/X11/Xresources` directory, stored in one file per application. Individual users on the system can override these resources or set their own by creating a `$HOME/.Xresources` file. The format of all these files is

```
application*parameter: value
```

As an example, you might include the following in a resource file:

```
Xterm*reverseVideo: true
```

This line will cause the `xterm` program to default to reverse video (white on black) mode by default.

Typically, users use `xrdb` to load, save, and modify their X resources in order to change how applications behave. To load your X resources from a file, simply issue the following command and they are passed to the currently active X server:

```
# xrdb .Xdefaults
```

To query the current X resources, use the following:

```
# xrdb -query
```

Window Managers

The window manager is one of the most important aspects of using X. The window manager is a special client application that exists only to manage the windows displayed to the user. The window manager determines which window receives user input, how the windows themselves can be controlled (moved, resized, closed, iconified, and so on) by the user, which window should display when two or more are superimposed, and so on. Most window managers provide graphical facilities to perform these tasks, so your window manager is responsible for a great deal of the appearance of your X display as well.

These tasks are complex enough, but many window managers go a few steps beyond them. It is common for a window manager to provide external utilities or modules for displaying status information, starting applications, or performing special tasks. Most window managers also provide virtual desktops, which appear to extend the display area available by creating multiple screens the user can switch between. There are many other interesting enhancements available for various window managers.

X Keyboard Basics

Although you might use your mouse to navigate with X, the keyboard is also important. The X keyboard model is divided into keycodes and keysyms. The *keysyms* (keyboard symbols) are the symbols displayed on the keyboard itself and are server-independent. The *keycodes* are server-dependent and represent the physical keys (or more appropriately, the signals generated by the keyboard when the key is pressed). X translates keycodes into keysyms using a keymap table, which contains a simple mapping.

More detailed information about keyboard operation under X appears in the X manual pages. In most cases, you do not need to worry about the details.

The `xmodmap` Program

`xmodmap` allows you to redefine your keyboard mapping to suit your own preferences. Most people do not need it because the default key mapping works fine. But remapping your keyboard is useful for the occasional, unusual case or when something other than the default is required. (Some people, for example, like to remap their keyboards to the Dvorak layout or to a different language with non-English characters, such as German.)

Some useful options for `xmodmap` are

```
# xmodmap -pk
# xmodmap -pke
```

Both of these options print the current keymap. The latter prints the keymap in a way that can be fed back to `xmodmap` later, which is useful if you have spent a long time getting your current keymap to work properly and you want to save it. The following command evaluates the expression passed on the command line immediately:

```
# xmodmap -e <expression>
```

It is useful for performing interactive testing of a new keyboard mapping before committing to using it in the future. Do test using this option.

A common use for xmodmap is correcting the infamous Backspace-Delete problem, which has plagued some other distributions of Linux. Although Debian Linux itself should not suffer from this problem, it might turn up when running applications remotely. In short, the problem is that the Backspace and Delete keys are mapped in reverse; typing Backspace results in delete, and typing Delete results in backspace. This can often result in a confusing mess because not all applications read Backspace and Delete through X directly, so some applications work, others don't, and still others work in odd ways. You can correct the problem with

```
# xmodmap -e "keycode 127 = Delete"
# xmodmap -e "keycode 22 = BackSpace"
```

You might need to change other settings that dictate how the Delete and Backspace keysyms are handled, but this code corrects the root problem by ensuring the keys are mapped correctly. See the man page for xmodmap for more information.

Displaying Applications Across the Network

As stated previously, X uses a client/server architecture. The X server manages the display and user input. Client applications communicate with the X server, describing what should be displayed and receiving user input. Barring bugs or design limitations, applications can communicate with any X server that allows them to do so. This communication often happens locally, running the application on the same computer as the display, but it is easy to display an X application running on a remote computer on a local display. Doing so requires two steps: telling the remote application where to send its display and telling the local X server to allow that application to do so.

Caution

A word to the wise: Running X over a network consumes a lot of bandwidth and can operate *very* slowly over a typical modem connection. You should avoid using X over slow networks if possible. If it cannot be avoided, look into the LBX extension (Low Bandwidth X), which might improve the situation. Another option is the dxpc protocol compression system; however, the lbxproxy is now included officially with XFree86, so you'll be able to find it on more systems.

The DISPLAY Environment Variable

To redirect the remote application to the local display, you need to set the DISPLAY environment variable on the remote computer before running the application. The value of this variable should be *hostname*:0.0. The 0.0 refers to the display number and screen number for computers running several keyboards or monitors at once. Some remote-access applications, such as SSH (Secure Shell), enable X forwarding automatically.

To set the variable yourself in a korn-type shell such as Debian's default of bash, do

```
set DISPLAY hostname:0.0; export DISPLAY
```

If you have changed your shell to a csh-type shell, do

```
> setenv DISPLAYhostname:0.0
```

Local applications work almost exactly the same way. The DISPLAY variable is set automatically for all children of that session when you start a local X server, which means you don't have to worry about this variable most of the time. The local applications don't have to know or care whether their display server is local or remote; they simply connect to the server specified in the DISPLAY variable or on the command line. The only difference you are likely to notice is speed.

xhost and xauth

xhost and xauth tell the X server to allow the client to display. Most X servers refuse a remote client if they are not specifically told to accept it. Otherwise, anyone could display anything to your local X server or even duplicate the display on their own! It pays to notice security issues when running X applications remotely.

You can use xhost to manipulate the access control lists of your local X display.

To add a host to the access control list (thus allowing users on that host to access your X display), type

```
# xhost +hostname
```

Caution

This command will allow *any* users on the new host to access your display. If you want to allow only specific users, you'll need to use xauth instead.

To remove the host when finished, type

```
# xhost -hostname
```

Note that the access control here is based on *hostname*. There are other methods. Using xhost with the host-based access control is convenient, and is not as bad as using X with no access control at all, but should not be considered a secure solution unless the network and the remote machines are thoroughly trustworthy.

Another authentication mechanism available for your use is xauth. xauth relies upon generating a random magic cookie when you start X. Any client that can present this cookie is allowed to connect; all others are rejected. Therefore, if you communicate the cookie to your user account on a remote machine and store it in a file to which only your account has read access, you can effectively allow connections from only your user on a remote machine.

You can use the rstart program (contained in a separate rstart package) to start programs remotely. This program will log on to the remote machine, pass the xauth information, and invoke the specified program. You simply use this syntax:

```
rstart hostname program [arguments]
```

As an example, you might use this:

```
rstart workstation2 xterm -rv
```

This will start xterm with reverse video mode, running on workstation2, but displaying on your own machine.

Because X can do so much over a network and across platforms, it can provide a lot of capabilities for the enterprising hacker looking for a way in if permissions are not set properly. Be careful with it.

Note

If you are considering running X applications remotely, you need to learn something about security first. The X protocol is widely known and does not include any form of encryption. Anyone with access to the network you are using to transport your X applications can see everything you see.

Several remote login protocols exist that alleviate this problem. The most common is SSH (Secure Shell), which handles the complex task of granting access to the local X display securely as well as encrypting the communication between you and the remote host. It also handily avoids the problem of transmitting passwords unencrypted over the network with Telnet, which is another surprisingly common security problem.

It should be noted that this security problem does not in the least apply to running local X applications, and in some situations, you might decide your local network is trustworthy or that you simply aren't doing anything that needs protecting. Still, you should behave securely unless there is reason not to.

Standard X Application Options

X applications typically accept a number of standard parameters, either as X resources or as command-line parameters. These parameters deal with the initial size and position of the application's window, the X server on which to display the window, the title of the initial window, and other X resources. Here is a list of the commonly used options.

- `-display`
- `-geometry`
- `-title`
- `-name`
- `-xrm`

You can use the `-display` option in place of the `DISPLAY` environment variable to redirect the application's display. It has the same basic format and function but is convenient when redirecting a single application somewhere other than the default:

```
# xterm -display hostname:0.0
```

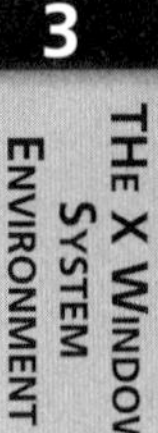

The `-geometry` option specifies the initial position and size of the application window. The exact format depends somewhat on the application itself. Text-based applications (`xterm`, many editors) usually interpret the width and height values as character values. Other applications generally use pixel values. Position settings are always in pixels:

```
# xosview -geometry 100x150+50+600
# xterm   -geometry 80x25+50+600
```

These commands cause `xosview` to open its window 50 pixels right and 600 pixels to the below (0,0), which is the top left of the display, and to make that window 100 pixels wide by 150 pixels tall. The `xterm` command opens a window 80 characters across by 25 characters down, but starting in the same place as the `xosview` window. You can also use negative position settings, in which case you start at the opposite edge and subtract the number of pixels. These options allow you to specify a default size and location of windows and are particularly useful if you want to script the initialization of applications as in a startup script.

The `-name` option specifies the resource group name of the application (with regard to X resources). Normally, this is set to the name of the application. It is useful for distinguishing different instances of the same application (perhaps multiple `xterm`s for different purposes, for which you have different preferences).

The `-title` option specifies the title that should appear in the application window. Normally, this is set to the name of the application.

The `-xrm` option dynamically sets a resource for the application (rather than add it to the general database with `xrdb`).

Now that you know how to run the various X clients and set configuration options for them, let's move on to the installation and configuration of the X system itself.

Installing and Configuring X

You can install and configure X in several different ways. The following section describes installing and configuring X through the mechanisms provided by the standard Debian Linux X packages. X installations can occupy anywhere from 40MB to 400MB of disk space, depending on the options you choose to install, although a typical X installation requires an amount toward the smaller end of that range.

You can apply most of the information in this chapter to any X installation, but the installation and configuration sections are limited to Debian Linux and XFree86. If you already have XFree86 installed and working on your computer, you should be able to use your prior configuration file without difficulty, assuming the X versions are similar and both support your video hardware.

Before beginning the installation and configuration process, gather the following information about your computer:

- What type of mouse you use (PS/2 or serial), along with the model name and manufacturer. If in doubt, you can take a guess that your mouse is either a PS/2 one or a Microsoft-compatible serial mouse.
- The model name, number, and manufacturer of the video card in your system. If possible, also acquire the chipset used in the card.
- The amount of video RAM your video card has. This is not your system RAM but is somewhere between 256KB (for really, really old cards) and 32MB (for the latest cutting-edge 3D card). Most modern cards have somewhere between 2MB and 8MB of memory.
- Your monitor's vertical and horizontal refresh rates. If you get the wrong values here, you can damage your monitor. These values can be found in the manual accompanying your monitor. The X configuration tool offers a rock bottom (standard VGA) option that you can use, but you'll be able to get a much better picture if you get the exact values for your monitor.

Note

You can check the version of X you are using with

```
# X -showconfig
XFree86 Version 3.3.2.3 / X Window System
(protocol Version 11, revision 0, vendor release 6300)
Release Date: July 15 1998
...
```

Note that not all of the output is shown.

The XFree86 Packages

Debian Linux provides a number of XFree86 packages designed for use with Debian Linux. Installing these packages is the easiest way to install X on Debian Linux. There are several packages that you'll need to install: those for the X server, those for the fonts, and those for other programs.

Selecting an X Server

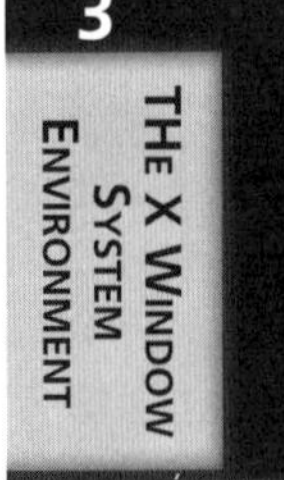

Here is a listing of the various X servers available:

```
xserver-s3_3.3.2.3a-11.deb
xserver-s3v_3.3.2.3a-11.deb
xserver-mono_3.3.2.3a-11.deb
xserver-mach32_3.3.2.3a-11.deb
xserver-mach64_3.3.2.3a-11.deb
xserver-8514_3.3.2.3a-11.deb
xserver-agx_3.3.2.3a-11.deb
xserver-i128_3.3.2.3a-11.deb
xserver-p9000_3.3.2.3a-11.deb
xserver-vga16_3.3.2.3a-11.deb
xserver-svga_3.3.2.3a-11.deb
xserver-mach8_3.3.2.3a-11.deb
xserver-w32_3.3.2.3a-11.deb
```

These packages contain the various X servers available. Each server package contains an X server designed to support a certain type of video card or chipset. In most cases, the name of the package includes the name of the card or chipset the package is intended for.

Generally, you only need one X server package installed. Which one depends on your video card and chipset. If you know what video card you have and can recognize it on the list of packages, then you only need to install that package. If you will be using the `XF86Setup` graphical configuration tool, you'll need to have at least the `xserver-vga16` package installed.

Laptops are especially tricky in this regard, so you should make an effort to discover your laptop's display chipset before installing, and read the Linux-Laptop HOWTO along with any available documents relating to your specific laptop. Many laptop video chipsets are supported, but most require some additional effort to configure and use to their full capabilities.

If you are unsure, install all of the packages; it won't hurt, and you can always remove them later.

During the configure stage of package installation, each X server package you choose to install asks whether it should be the default X server. If you know which X server you want to use, you may as well say yes. If you aren't sure, then you can set no default (saying no each time) or say yes to the VGA16 server, which works with most video cards.

Installing the Font Packages

The X environment requires fonts in order to display text. Those fonts come in separate packages to let you choose which font packages you want to install. The X packages recommend font packages from the Debian distribution to you. You can also add your own fonts, if you want. At a minimum, you should always install xfonts-base and xfonts-75dpi.

If you have the disk space to spare, you should install them all because some other applications depend on having those additional fonts available. Generally, you don't need to do anything extra to make those fonts available to X because the configuration is handled by the package system.

Fonts that are not packaged require a bit more work. X has two methods for accessing fonts: internally by the X server itself and externally through a font server. Debian's X is configured to use a font server by default, so you should add new fonts to the font server's configuration. The font server is normally started by `init` on system boot (see `/etc/init.d/xfs`).

The X font server's configuration file is located by default in `/etc/X11/xfs/config`. The initial contents of that file are reproduced in Listing 3.1.

LISTING 3.1 The X Font Server Configuration File

```
# /etc/X11/xfs/config
#
# X font server configuration file

# allow a maximum of 10 clients to connect to this
#font server
client-limit = 10
```

```
# when a font server reaches its limit, start up a new one
clone-self = on
# log errors using syslog
use-syslog = on
# paths to search for fonts
catalogue = /usr/X11R6/lib/X11/fonts/misc/,/usr/X11R6/lib/X11/fonts/Speedo/,
➥/usr/X11R6/lib/X11/fonts/Type1/,/usr/X11R6/lib/X11/fonts/75dpi/,
➥/usr/X11R6/lib/X11/fonts/100dpi/
# in decipoints
default-point-size = 120
# x1,y1,x2,y2,...
default-resolutions = 75,75,100,100
```

To add a new font package, simply add the location of the fonts to the list of paths following `catalogue`.

Type `[man xfs]` for more information.

Choosing Optional Packages

`xpm4g` contains the X pixmap library, a library for dealing with X pixel maps (a type of image file). Many applications, including commercial ones, depend on it and might not run without it. If you are running on an x86 platform, you should be sure to also install the `libc5` versions of the package for compatibility with older applications.

`xmanpages` and `xlib6g` contain manual pages and client libraries for X developers. They are useful if you are developing X applications.

`XF86Setup` contains one of the X configuration utilities. Installing this file is quite useful when first installing X, unless you have a prewritten config file from a previous installation. You can safely remove it afterwards, if you want.

`xdm` is a login manager for X. If you intend to keep X running all the time, it is useful.

IceWM, IceWM-GNOME, TWM, and FVWM2 are all window managers.

A number of packages have a `kde` or `gnome` prefix or suffix. KDE and GNOME are desktop managers, similar to window managers. The packages so marked are applications supporting KDE or GNOME along with the desktop managers themselves.

Using 3D Hardware Under X

Hardware-accelerated 3D graphics are getting a great deal of attention lately. Although X has the necessary capabilities to support hardware-accelerated 3D, `XFree86` has been somewhat lacking in this area. At present, few 3D accelerated video cards are supported, and even the supported cards can be difficult to properly set up. The release of the next version of XFree86 (4.0) should dramatically improve the situation.

At present, the `3dfx` chipset has the most 3D support. Cards with the Riva chipset and the Matrox cards also have some support. Describing how to set up a 3D card under XFree86 is a complex topic and beyond the scope of this section, but you can see the following Web sites for more information:

Mesa (`http://www.mesa3d.org/`)

XFree86 (`http://www.xfree86.org/`)

Linux 3D (`http://www.linux3d.org/`)

Running `XF86Setup`

`XF86Setup` is a program designed to help you configure X properly without needing to be an X expert. The following section describes the process of configuring X using `XF86Setup`; other programs perform a similar function (`xf86config`). Much of the advice applies regardless of which program you are using.

`XF86Setup` is an X application. If you can see `XF86Setup`, then your card is supported at a minimal level at least. Even if nothing else works, you should be able to limp along with X server settings similar to the ones `XF86Setup` is using until support is available for your card. If `XF86Setup` does not work, that is a good indication that your video card is not supported, at least not with this version of X; it could also mean you did not install the right X server or that you're missing some necessary components.

You might be able to get X working with time and effort even if `XF86Setup` fails, but the specifics depend entirely on your hardware and the current state of support for that hardware. You can take it as a learning experience, an opportunity to help with driver development, or as a hint to learn more about the Linux console. In any case, don't despair because support is likely already on the way.

Caution

In the process of configuring X, you are asked for several parameters related to your monitor's display capabilities. It is important to answer those questions correctly. Giving the wrong parameters might result in sending a video signal that exceeds your monitor's display capabilities and might damage your monitor. Most modern monitors detect when a signal is outside their capabilities and shut down, but older monitors or extremely cheap monitors might not do this. Be careful.

486: mouse protocol = MouseSystems device = dev/logibm

XF86Setup helps you configure your graphics hardware for basic use but does *not* provide a fully optimized configuration file for all chipsets. In some rare cases, the generated file might not even work properly. Refer briefly to the chipset- and X-server-specific information available in /usr/doc before running XF86Setup. Doing so will give you an idea of what to do if the generated configuration file fails or if you want to add settings for optimization.

The first thing XF86Setup does is attempt to start a minimal X server on your system, in order to display its interface. On most systems, this works fine, but on some, it fails (laptops typically have problems). If it fails, make sure you have your manual handy, and run xf86config instead; the latter utility works entirely in text mode and gives you the opportunity to specify everything. You can then manually make changes to the file xf86config creates as required to get a working system.

The XF86Setup interface consists of different sections for configuring different parts of X. The row of buttons across the top selects the section to configure, and the interface for that section is displayed in the area below. At the bottom are two buttons, Abort and Done, that abort the entire process and save a finished configuration for testing. If you get stuck, you can also look at the Help button for information about your current screen.

You have the opportunity to configure your mouse, keyboard, video card, monitor, and screen modes. Some of these steps might be unnecessary if you are satisfied with the defaults, but generally, you should try to configure X to exactly match the hardware you have.

If you have trouble, you should concentrate on first getting a basic X configuration that works, even if it does not use all the capabilities of your video hardware. You can run XF86Setup again later (or edit the configuration by hand, if you prefer) to try to get more out of the system. This is much easier with a working configuration to start from.

Configuring Your Mouse

You need to know both what kind of mouse you have and how it is connected to your computer. There are many different types of mice, a number of different ways to connect them to your computer, and some additional options that are useful but not necessary. The XF86Setup mouse configuration interface is shown in Figure 3.1. If your mouse already works, you got lucky and the default settings already present are probably acceptable. If not, you should see a text message describing how to configure your mouse within the GUI using only the keyboard. If you have trouble and your mouse is not yet active, you may press Alt+H (taking care to use the left Alt key) to bring up the help information for keyboard navigation.

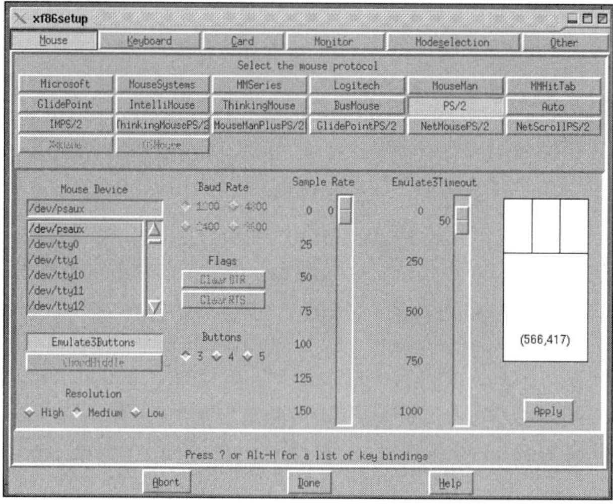

FIGURE 3.1
The XF86Setup *mouse configuration interface.*

Take a look at your mouse connector; if it is round, you probably have a PS/2 mouse. Try the PS/2 option first (click PS/2 from the row of buttons across the top, and select /dev/psaux from the list on the left). A trapezoid connector probably means a serial mouse, which can use any one of several protocols. If you know exactly what type of mouse you have, and it matches one of the types listed, choose that protocol from the top; otherwise, try the Microsoft protocol first and then the bus mouse protocol.

Determining the name of the device your mouse is connected to can be tricky. If you are using a PS/2 mouse, choose /dev/psaux from the list on the left. Otherwise, your mouse is probably connected to a serial port. The usual i386 serial ports are /dev/ttyS0, /dev/ttyS1, /dev/ttyS2, and /dev/ttyS3. The numbers at the end correspond to the number of the serial port. If your mouse is set up correctly with another operating system, you might be able to determine which serial port it is connected to there. Some manufacturers also label their serial ports. In the worst case, you can simply choose each in sequence and test.

The Baud Rate and Flags options are needed for some older mice. You should leave them set to the defaults when possible. If the defaults don't work or cause strange behavior, you can try changing these parameters.

The white mouse image at the far right displays your mouse coordinates and responds to clicking the three mouse buttons. You can use it to test your mouse configuration.

The Emulate3Buttons option allows you to emulate a third button on a two-button mouse by pressing both buttons simultaneously. You want to do this unless you have a three button mouse; X expects three-button mice for historical reasons, and many X applications make some use of the third button.

The Sample Rate and Emulate3TimeOut parameters are preferences; you can leave them at the default values or change them to your liking.

Configuring Your Keyboard

After setting up your mouse, you should proceed to set up your keyboard. You need to select a keymap from a list; normally, you want the basic 101-key layout (Generic 101-key PC from the Model list) with the appropriate layout for your language (normally U.S. English from the Layout list). The keyboard interface is pictured in Figure 3.2.

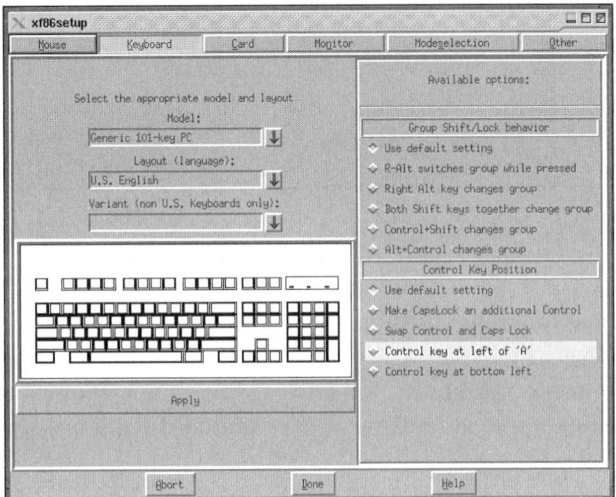

FIGURE 3.2
The `XF86Setup` *keyboard configuration interface.*

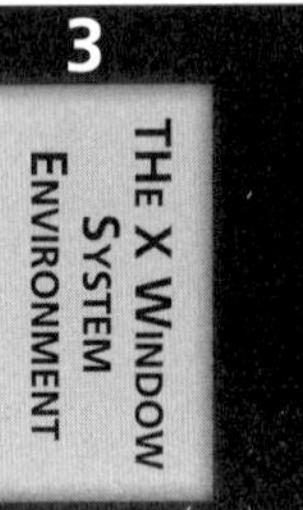

The two drop-down lists just above the keyboard are the important elements. Most users want the default settings for a generic 101-key PC keyboard using U.S. English. If you are using something else, select it here. The options on the right are keyboard preferences that you might find useful but are not necessary.

Configuring Your Video Card

The two parts to the video card configuration interface are pictured in Figures 3.3 and 3.4. The former is the card selection database, which you see first and from which you should select your video card if it is listed. If your card is listed, you do not even need to look at the other part of the interface. You should click the button to view the associated `README`, if any, and move on to configuring your monitor.

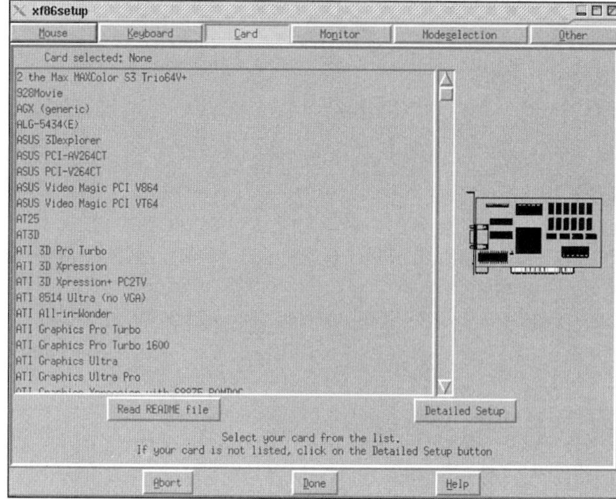

FIGURE 3.3
The `XF86Setup` *video card database.*

The second half of the interface is accessible from the Detailed Setup button, at the lower right. You should only use this section if you are having problems with your video card or if your video card was not listed in the card database. It allows you to configure the individual parameters for your video card manually. This should only be necessary when your card or chipset is not directly supported, if your card or chipset causes problems when X attempts to probe it, or if you are a perfectionist and want to tweak your system.

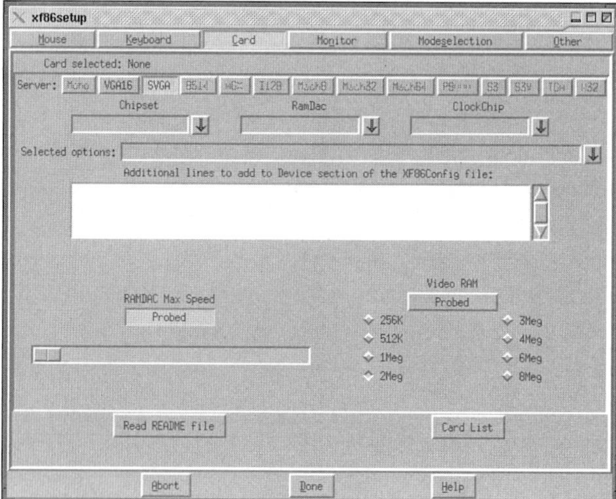

FIGURE 3.4
The `XF86Setup` *detailed video card configuration.*

The row of buttons across the top show the available X servers. The current server is pressed, the available ones are displayed normally, and the servers that have not been installed are shown hashed out.

Below the server selection buttons are three drop-down lists, which allow you to select the chipset, ramdac, and clockchip to use. Many of these values can and will be autodetected, but if they are not, you can try specifying them based on your hardware. You do not need to specify all of them even if you specify one.

The RAMDAC speed at the bottom should be left alone because RAMDAC speed can nearly always be probed. But if it is not and you know it, you can set it directly.

The Video RAM selection area can be probed, but probing is not as reliable as with the RAMDAC. If you know how much video RAM you have, you might want to set it specifically here to ensure X knows about it. If X has assumed you have less than you actually do, everything will work fine, but your available resolutions and color depths will be more limited. Beware of setting this too high; that can cause real crashes.

Note

X probing is a common cause of problems with cheap or old cards. When X is given minimal parameters to start with, it can try to determine the actual values of those parameters by probing the video card. Usually, this works fine. With some cards, however, it breaks—and so does X. Even with cards that can be probed, the actual probing might take some time, so specifying the exact parameters might reduce X startup time slightly.

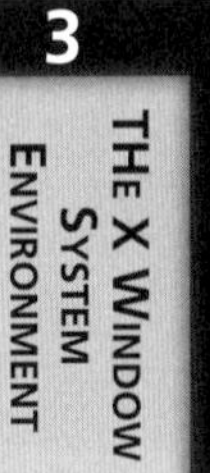

Configuring Your Monitor

The next step consists of defining your monitor's display capabilities. Make sure you have your monitor's manual handy so you can input the right settings. Using the wrong settings here might accidentally damage your monitor later, if you specify a mode your monitor cannot display properly. The interface is shown in Figure 3.5.

Most people can select a monitor with similar capabilities to theirs from the list. Be conservative. If you are using the resolutions available in another operating system as a guide, make sure you have actually tested the resolution you are choosing. The other operating system might not know any more about the monitor than Debian Linux does.

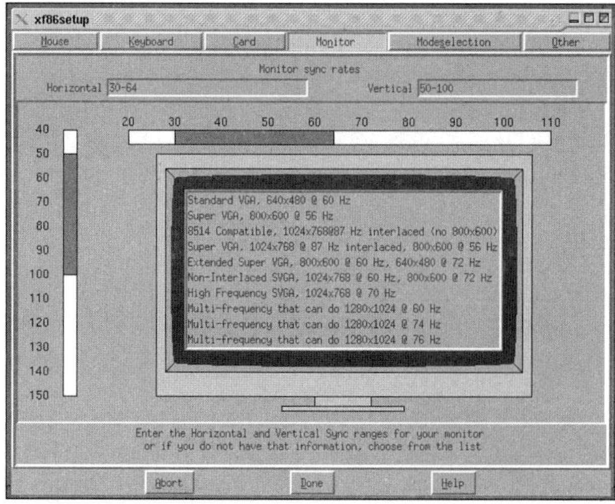

FIGURE 3.5
`XF86Setup`*'s monitor configuration screen.*

If you have no idea at all, the first entry (standard VGA) is almost always safe.

If you have your monitor's manual handy and want to be able to make the most use of the display, you can enter the range manually from the values in the manual. Be wary of typos.

If you are afraid of damaging your monitor after all these warnings, relax a little; most modern monitors shut off rather than allow themselves to be damaged. Those that do not generally complain loudly and obnoxiously about what you are doing, so you normally have ample time to panic and turn it off yourself. You just need to be careful.

Configuring the Default Display Mode

This section allows you to configure the display modes you want to have available to you. The list down the center shows the common display resolutions, and the row of buttons along the bottom show the common color depths. The resolution list lets you select multiple elements. Simply select the resolutions you want to have available to you. Then select the default color depth. On startup, X performs some calculations to enable only the modes your hardware and monitor can display, so you don't have to worry about those factors here.

You can change resolutions and color depths within an X session later.

You shouldn't need to change anything here, and if you do, you shouldn't need to read this paragraph to find out how.

Celebrating a Successful Configuration

Congratulations; You have configured X (we hope)! Click Done at the bottom, and the configuration is saved. `XF86Setup` then attempts to restart the X server with the new parameters you have defined. If it succeeds, you're done; copy the configuration file somewhere you won't lose it, just in case (it should be in `/etc/X11/XF86Config`) and enjoy the world of X.

If the test does not work, you need to try again. Generally, you should make sure all your information about your hardware was correct, and then read all the documentation concerning your hardware. This usually appears in `/usr/doc/xserver-servername`, depending on which server supports your card. If there is none, your video card might not be supported at all with this release of X. (In fact, the version of XFree86 shipped with this version of Debian Linux is already somewhat out of date; you should be able to use `dselect` to download an updated set of packages.)

After reading the documentation for your hardware, if any, go back in `XF86Setup` and use the detailed video setup to specify your hardware, along with any tips the documentation has. Then try again.

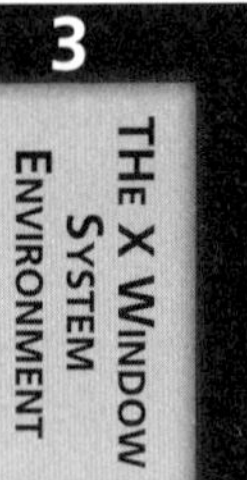

If X still fails, double-check all the parameters you entered, and read the XFree86 FAQ (`http://www.xfree86.org`) and the documents concerning the X server you are running (in `/usr/doc/x-`*`servername`*). You might also find it helpful to search for information on the Web or on Usenet; many people post their config files for general use after getting a particularly annoying card working. Appendix B also lists resources that may be useful.

Remember, however, that if you can use `XF86Setup` at all, the card you have is at least supported by `XF86_VGA16`; `XF86Setup` is itself an X application and is starting an X server to display its interface.

Supporting Different Resolutions and Bit Depths Under X

X can only display a single resolution and bit depth at a time, but it can store information concerning all available display modes and dynamically switch between them. By default, pressing Ctrl+Alt++ (keypad plus) switches to the next higher mode (higher resolution). Pressing Ctrl+Alt+– (keypad minus) performs a similar operation in reverse.

X can define two types of display resolution: real and virtual, but this is not done by default. Real is the resolution of the image displayed on your monitor. Virtual is commonly set to be the same as the real resolution but can be set larger, in which case the display acts as a window on the virtual display, using the mouse to scroll. This is sometimes useful when working with a limited-resolution display.

`XF86Setup` by default only defines screen modes for resolutions up to 1,024 by 768. If your graphics hardware can display better than that, you need to add the resolutions to your config file, which can be tricky. At the end of your `xf86config`, you should find the code in Listing 3.2.

LISTING 3.2 One of the Screen Sections from an `xf86config` File

```
#The Color SVGA server

Section "Screen"
    Driver      "svga"
    Device      "Generic VGA"
    #Device      "My Video Card"
    Monitor     "My Monitor"
    Subsection "Display"
        Depth       8
        #Modes       "640x480" "800x600" "1024x768"
        ViewPort    0 0
        Virtual     320 200
        #Virtual     1152 900
    EndSubsection
EndSection
```

You need to make changes to this section in order to support higher color depths or higher resolutions. There are actually several of these sections, each slightly different depending on the X server you chose to use. Make sure you make any changes to the appropriate section for your choice of X server, or they will not have any effect!

`Driver` Line

The `Driver` line indicates which X server is described by this configuration section. The `Device` and `Monitor` lines refer to other sections in the configuration file, specifying the capabilities of your video card and monitor.

`Display` Section

The `Display` subsection is the immediate concern. There can be any number of `Display` subsections (typically, one per color depth). Each one lists the color depth (`Depth`), a list of screen resolutions (`Modes`), and possibly some other settings.

The `Depth` Line

The `Depth` line indicates the color depth for the modes defined in this subsection (in bits). A depth of 8 provides 256 colors.

The `Modes` Line

The `Modes` line indicates which of the defined resolutions are available at this color depth. The resolutions are actually defined earlier in the configuration file (search for `Modeline`) and are only referenced here. Most common resolutions are already defined. You should simply list the ones you desire to use. Defining a new screen resolution from scratch is beyond the scope of this chapter.

The `Virtual` Line

The `Virtual` line indicates a virtual desktop resolution, which provides a way for lower-resolution displays to get more screen space. The physical display acts as a window on a larger display area and is scrolled with the mouse. Generally, this setting is more confusing than useful; you should probably comment out the line (by placing a `#` as the first character).

There may be other lines in this section; generally, you should leave them untouched.

In case you find switching resolutions is not working as expected, the following paragraphs describe some things to look for.

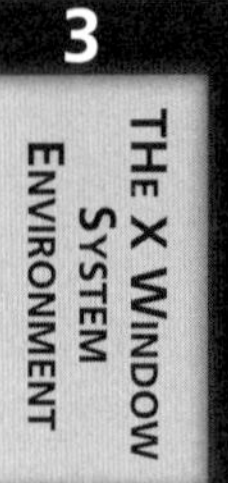

X will refuse to display a resolution if your monitor, as defined in the configuration, cannot display that resolution. If your monitor settings are correct, this shouldn't be a problem, but some modes are borderline and might not quite fit. You can see that this is happening by watching the X startup; it says `Removing mode XXXXxYYYY`. Sometimes, this can be corrected by tweaking the display mode a little. Sometimes, it means you entered incorrect settings for your monitor.

If your images seem grainy or less than colorful, you might be running at too low a color depth. A color depth of 8 bits is sufficient for most applications, but many graphical applications are happier with 16 bits or more. This can be particularly troublesome if you are running several applications that all require a large number of colors or even a single such application on a 256-color display.

If you are stuck with an 8-bit display, as many older computers are, then you can ask color-intensive applications to install their own color map. This allows each application to use all the colors available when it is active, instead of trying to share them with all the applications using the display. The price of this approach: The applications other than the one using its own colormap will have their colors altered. The result is ugly but usable.

If you can't seem to get X to display using the desired color depth, there are a number of possible causes. You can test it using the following from the terminal:

```
#startx -- -bpp color_depth_as_number_of_bits
#startx -- --bpp 16
```

The latter example will give you an X display with a color depth of 16 bits. If it fails entirely, you probably don't have any valid 16-bit modes defined or the video card does not support 16-bit color. (A valid mode for 8 bits will sometimes, but not necessarily, work for higher depths.)

Some applications, commonly Netscape, although it is by no means the only culprit, will not run with odd color depths. Normal color depths are 8, 16, 24, and 32. Commonly used odd color depths are 15 bits (slightly less memory than 16 bits), 2 bits (black and white), and 4–7 (grayscale).

You can find out details about your current X display by using `xdpyinfo`. You can tune some of the parameters of your current display, primarily useful for centering the display on your monitor, by using `xvidtune`. (You should be careful to only make small changes with this tool; trying to make large changes will not work and might cause damage to your monitor.)

Starting X

It should come as no surprise that there are several ways to start X. You can start it either from the command line or automatically at system boot time.

Manual Start with `startx`

`startx` is a script that starts an X session. It is typically invoked at the console to start an X session for the current user. It has several arguments.

Automatic Start with `xdm`

`xdm` is an X application that performs the same function as `login`, only with an X environment. It displays a graphical prompt for username and password, starts the user's specified environment upon a successful authentication, and retakes control of the display when the user logs out.

Under Debian Linux, an `xdm` startup script is provided in `/etc/init.d/xdm`. Running that script as root with a parameter of `start` starts the X environment at the `xdm` login prompt if a valid X configuration exists. The Debian environment attempts to start this script on system boot by default, but before it can do so, you must configure X for your graphics hardware and monitor.

Besides installing and setting up your X server, you also have many X window managers from which to choose. These can have a dramatic effect on the appearance and functionality of your X session; the same applications may appear quite different with different window managers.

Window Managers

X provides a graphical display and user input mechanism but does not provide an actual interface. The interface is left up to the window manager and individual applications. Without a window manager, an X display is not very useful.

Creating the Look and Feel

Your window manager is responsible for providing the look and feel of most generic window decorations—that is, the borders of each window and appropriate gadgets to close, minimize, maximize, move, and otherwise manipulate the different windows on the desktop. The contents of each window, within the borders, are handled entirely by the application.

Many window managers also provide facilities to perform other actions. Nearly all provide application menus, in order to start new applications; this is one of the most important functions of a window manager. Other common capabilities are docks (for organizing iconified windows) and status displays. Together with Debian's menu package, your menus can appear synchronized in every window manager you may try.

Handling User Interaction

A large part of a window manager's job involves determining which window the user's input should be sent to—that is, which window has the focus. With many windows on the screen, making this determination is not always an easy task, particularly when the user wants to move between several tasks rapidly, as is commonly the case for a multitasking operating system such as Linux.

The strategy a window manager uses for allocating the input focus is called a *focus model*. There are two common focus models, at least one of which most window managers implement, and individual window managers often implement their own hybrid focus models. The most common ones are

- `ClickToFocus` is the simplest model. Whichever window the user clicks becomes active (acquires the focus). Little or nothing else changes the focus.
- `FocusFollowsMouse` is an old standby for many UNIX users. Whichever window the mouse pointer is in has the focus. Although this focus model can be a little confusing for novice users, it is popular among people who do a great deal of multitasking (because it allows them to switch between windows easily).
- `SloppyFocus` is a common hybrid focus model. It works just like Focus Follows Mouse (FFM), except that windows are not deactivated when the mouse moves onto the background. The result is a little less strict than FFM.

Most window managers also provide a means of changing the focus through the keyboard, without using the mouse at all. It is generally useful to learn how your window manager provides for this because changing focus with the keyboard can save your hand a trip to the mouse and back.

Window management operations, such as moving, closing, resizing, and iconifying windows, are also within the purview of the window manager. Most window managers provide each window with borders, often containing buttons or gadgets. The borders are typically used to move and resize the window, and the gadgets handle closing, iconifying, or otherwise manipulating the window. Collectively, the borders and gadgets added to windows are known as *window decorations*. Although the appearance and placement of these decorations can vary widely, the functionality is usually similar.

Window managers are also partly responsible for placing new windows; that is, when a window is first opened by an application, the window manager determines where that window appears. There are several different policies in use, and certain applications attempt to provide hints as to where they want to be. By default, most attempt to place the new window in an area of empty space, if one is available and large enough. Some request that the user manually place some or all new windows. This is usually configurable.

Many window managers take every opportunity to present a menu to the user. Generally, at least one of the window decorations presents a menu of window management functions. Pressing each mouse button (due to the origins of X, this means three; if you have a two-button mouse, pressing both buttons together simulates the third button) while over the screen background generally provides a different menu for each button.

Many window managers provide a feature called *virtual desktops*. In brief, these are ways of increasing available display space by allowing the user to switch between different display areas, each of which can contain different applications.

Note

A word to the wise: When an X application crashes, you probably experience two things. First, you experience joy because everything else you were doing should still be working fine. Second, you experience dismay because you now have a huge window on your X display that won't go away even if you click the close button. Do not despair; for just this situation, X distinguishes between the close and destroy window operations, and your window manager provides access to both.

Selecting a Window Manager

If you want to get started immediately, Debian Linux provides a default window manager that should meet most common needs. If you are going to be working with X a great deal, however, you should probably take some time to choose the window manager that most suits you.

If you are using Debian Linux on a fast computer with a large amount of memory, the most important consideration in choosing a window manager is your personal taste. You should spend some time with each of the common window managers described here in order to get a feel for them. Examining the documentation briefly is also worthwhile because many of the window managers can be configured to behave in many different ways.

If your computer system is somewhat older, with less memory or a slower processor than a modern computer, you want to consider efficiency as much as personal taste. You probably do not want to use a desktop manager at all; those available are invariably expensive in terms of memory and processor time.

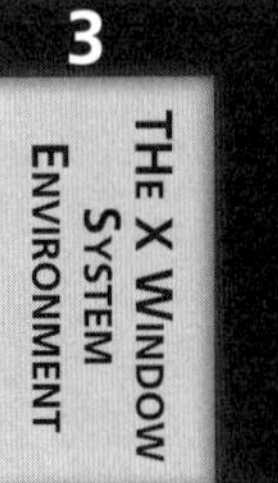

If you are not familiar with UNIX, you should ensure that the window manager you choose provides a simple user interface for configuration or comes with a suitable default configuration. (Most do come with suitable defaults.) Learning window managers after you are accustomed to one can take a surprising amount of time and effort.

There are a number of other window managers available. The window managers described in this section are

- IceWM
- FVWM
- WMaker
- KWM (the KDE window manager)

IceWM

IceWM is a modern window manager with a mixture of new and traditional features. It has a very nice look, it supports themes, and it has many useful and innovative features. Its configuration is not as complex as that for FVWM, but it's also not as flexible. Although IceWM has theme capability, much of the actual operation is dictated by the structure of the code rather than the user's configuration. If you don't mind editing text files but feel daunted by the power to configure everything, IceWM might be for you. There is also a GUI-based configuration utility, by an independent author, called IcePrefs.

More information concerning IceWM appears on the IceWM home page at `http://www.kiss.uni-lj.si/~k4fr0235/icewm/`.

The IcePrefs utility is located at `http://members.xoom.com/SaintChoj/icepref.html`.

IceWM-GNOME?

IceWM-GNOME is simply IceWM with the extensions for the GNOME desktop manager. If you intend to use GNOME, you should install it. Otherwise, you do not need to, although it won't hurt.

Using IceWM

The default IceWM configuration on Debian is straightforward, as shown in Figure 3.6. A taskbar occupies the bottom part of the screen, with a number of buttons and status displays active. There is a general menu button at the far left, along with a window list menu button next to it. The next two buttons are application launchers (for a terminal and the FTE text editor by the same author). The four buttons following switch between four virtual desktops. At the far right is a clock and to the left of that, a load meter. The space between the virtual desktop buttons and the loadmeter is filled by application bars representing each of the active X applications.

FIGURE 3.6
The default IceWM configuration on Debian Linux.

The default IceWM window decorations are shown in Figure 3.7 and consist of an icon representing the application (or a red X for unknown applications) and providing access to a menu of window operations, the title bar itself, and a trio of buttons that perform the minimize, maximize, and close operations in a single click.

FIGURE 3.7
The default IceWM window decorations.

Configuring IceWM

IceWM is configured through four files located in `$HOME/.icewm`, with defaults in `/etc/X11/icewm`. Unlike most window managers, the documentation is not covered in the man page, but instead in a series of HTML documents located in `/usr/doc/icewm`.

Changing the Focus Model

IceWM supports four standard focus models through a combination of several parameters. Three approximate the normal focus models offered by most window managers, and the fourth is an experimental model called `explicitFocus`. To change the focus model, you should search through the preferences file in the `$HOME/.icewm` directory for the focus model you want to use (from `ClickToRaise`, `ClickToFocus`, `PointerFocus`, and `ExplicitFocus`). Below each term are four lines; the currently active focus model has those lines active, and the other three have them commented out. Simply comment out the old model, and uncomment the new lines. You could conceivably also generate your own combination. There is a sample in Listing 3.3.

LISTING 3.3 The Focus Model Section from the IceWM Preferences File

```
#### ClickToRaise ###
ClickToFocus=1
RaiseOnFocus=1
FocusOnMap=1

#### ClickToFocus ###
#ClickToFocus=1
#RaiseOnFocus=0
#RaiseOnClickClient=0
#FocusOnMap=1

#### PointerFocus ###
#ClickToFocus=0
#RaiseOnFocus=0

#### ExplicitFocus ###
#ClickToFocus=1
#RaiseOnFocus=0
#RaiseOnClickClient=0
#FocusOnMap=0
#FocusOnMapTransient=1
```

Configuring the IceWM Taskbar

The taskbar has a number of configurable elements. Most of the simple ones can be configured by changing the settings in the `$HOME/.icewm/preferences` file. The examples that follow are only examples; examine the documentation for an exhaustive list of the preferences available.

To hide the taskbar completely, type

```
ShowTaskBar = 0
```

To move the taskbar to the top of the screen, type

```
TaskBarAtTop = 1
```

To hide the taskbar when not in use, type

```
TaskBarAutoHide = 1
```

The other configuration files work in basically the same way, except for the menu file, which is automatically generated based on available programs.

FVWM

FVWM is one of the most traditional UNIX window managers still in common use today. It is highly customizable in most respects. Several different versions exist, including some with the appearance of a Windows 95 interface, complete with a start menu. In addition, you can configure FVWM to require very little memory, so it is suitable for systems where memory is limited.

More information about FVWM appears on the FVWM home page at `http://www.fvwm.org/`.

Differences in the FVWM Family

Due in part to its age, FVWM has spawned several branches of development. Currently, these are FVWM (the original), FVWM95 (with modifications intended to aid use as a Windows 95 look-alike), and FVWM2 (a rewritten version that remains similar in function to the original FVWM). They are relatively similar in many ways but vary widely in others. In the section "Configuring FVWM" later in this chapter, we present configuration options for FVWM and FVWM2. FVWM95 options are similar in some areas and different in others; consult the documentation.

Using FVWM2

The following section details the default Debian Linux configuration. FVWM2 can be extensively modified in many areas such as mouse focus model and window decorations, and after such modification, it might not resemble the default configuration at all.

The default FVWM2 focus model is `FocusFollowsMouse`, which means your input is directed to the topmost window your mouse pointer is over. There is a small button on the left of each decorated window, containing a menu of common window functions. Three buttons on the top right of each window provide one-click access to minimize, maximize, and close. Windows can be moved by clicking and dragging on their title bars and resized by clicking and dragging the small external borders on any side or the corners. A virtual desktop area of nine screens (three by three) is used by default and is visible in the FVWMPager module at the lower-right area of the screen. The default configuration does not allow you to scroll across the screen borders.

Configuring FVWM

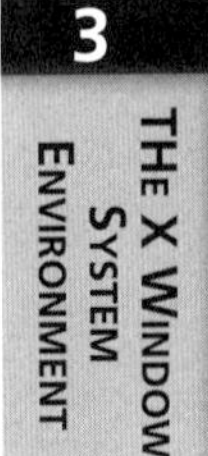

There are two useful things to have when configuring any member of the FVWM family: the documentation and a sample configuration file. FVWM is normally configured using manually edited text files in traditional UNIX fashion. Although the configuration is not difficult, it does require absorbing a lot of information at once. Trying to write an entire FVWM configuration by hand is a good way to feel overwhelmed.

To make things easier, FVWM provides a default configuration file that is used when the user does not have her own. The contents of this default file are pretty basic and offer an excellent starting place for experimentation. Accordingly, the first step to configuring FVWM is to locate the default configuration file (in `/etc/X11`, with the name depending on which variant of FVWM you want) and copy it to the appropriate location in your home directory.

Once you have this file available as a sample, you can open it in your favorite text editor (with the FVWM documentation available for reference) and begin making changes. You need to restart FVWM after making each set of changes and saving them; depending on your configuration, this choice might be available as a menu option or you might need to restart X. With a Debian FVWM2 installation, another option is to have the system administrator modify the system-wide files such that the menus will still work; the FVWM2 documentation documents this as do the system-wide FVWM2 configuration files.

FVWM provides three basic focus models. You can change them with FVWM simply by including the name of the desired focus model in the `.fvwmrc` file (although it is preferable to find the old focus model line and comment it out):

- `ClickToFocus`: Clicking a window gives it the focus.
- `FocusFollowsMouse`: Moving the mouse gives the focus to the window the mouse is over.
- `SloppyFocus`: This is like `FocusFollowsMouse`, but when the mouse leaves a window and enters the root window, the focus remains with the original window.

Changing focus in FVWM2 is only a little trickier. FVWM2 employs the concept of *styles*, which allow certain parameters to be applied to a set of applications. Changes are commonly made to the default style. Hence, the following changes the focus behavior for the entire window manager

```
Style "*" ClickToFocus
```

Menus

To do useful manipulation of windows in FVWM, two things are required. First, you must define a useful menu, and then you must create a way to invoke that menu. Invoking the menu is simple; you use the `Menu` command and bind it to a key or mouse event. There is more information on configuring key bindings in the next section. Note that most of the available mouse actions already have bound menus, so you can simply add entries to those. Here is a sample menu entry from FVWM; in FVWM2, Debian defines the menus itself, so you do not need to mess with them.

```
Mouse 1 R       A       Menu RootMenu Nop
```

Creating the menu is where most of the work is. A sample is shown in Listing 3.4.

LISTING 3.4 The Section of the Default `.fvwm2rc` That Defines the Root Menu

```
AddToMenu RootMenu      "Root Menu"      Title
+                       "XTerm"          Exec exec xterm
+                       "Rxvt"           Exec exec rxvt
+                       ""               Nop
+                       "Remote Logins"  Popup Remote-Logins
+                       ""               Nop
+                       "Utilities"      Popup Utilities
+                       ""               Nop
+                       "Fvwm Modules"             Popup Module-Popup
+                       "Fvwm Window Ops"          Popup Window-Ops
+                       "Fvwm Simple Config Ops"   Popup Misc-Ops
+                       ""               Nop
+                       "Refresh Screen"   Refresh
+                       "Recapture Screen" Recapture
+                       ""               Nop
+                       "Exit Fvwm"      Popup Quit-Verify
```

Key Bindings

Key bindings are used to cause some event to occur when a certain key or key combination is pressed. The section of code in Listing 3.5 is reproduced from the default `.fvwm2rc`.

LISTING 3.5 The Key Bindings Section from the Default `.fvwm2rc`

```
# Section: Key bindings
#
# This section binds some actions to keys. The bindings have been
# inspired by MWM, Windows, and nightmares. Everything that these
# key bindings do, can be done without them. Therefore they should not
# be too much of a burden on new users, but it definitely _can_ be
# confusing to press a key by accident and have it do something
# completely unexpected.
#

Key Tab         A       M       Next [CurrentPage !iconic] focus-and-raise
Key Tab         A       MS      Prev [CurrentPage !iconic] focus-and-raise
Key Tab         A       CM      Next [CurrentPage] deiconify-and-focus
Key Tab         A       CMS     Prev [CurrentPage] deiconify-and-focus
Key Left        A       M       Scroll -100 0
Key Up          A       M       Scroll +0 -100
Key Right       A       M       Scroll +100 +0
Key Down        A       M       Scroll +0 +100
Key F1          A       M       Popup Window-Ops
Key F2          A       M       Popup /Debian
Key F3          A       M       Lower
Key F4          A       M       WindowList
Key F5          A       M       CirculateUp
Key F6          A       M       CirculateDown
Key F7          A       M       Move
Key F8          A       M       Resize
Key F9          A       M       Iconify
Key F10         A       M       Maximize
```

The columns are the command (`Key`), a keysym specifier, two modifiers, and the internal FVWM command to perform. Some of the commands call functions that were defined earlier in the default configuration file, but others use the built-in commands. The syntax for FVWM and FVWM2 is the same, but the commands available might differ. You need to read the FVWM man pages to determine the available commands.

Virtual Desktops

FVWM provides virtual desktops. You can move within a display area larger by some integer multiple than your physical display.

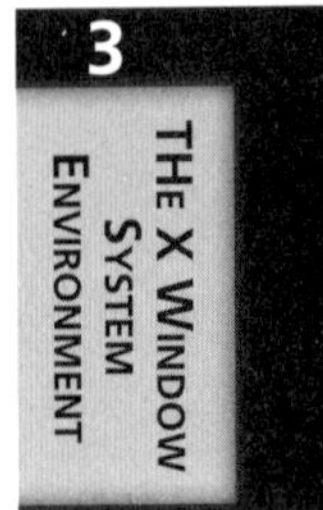

To use the large display area, add the command

```
DeskTopSize HorizontalxVertical
```

to your `.fvwm2rc` (where *Horizontal* and *Vertical* are integers). Note that when using this feature, applications start in the desktop area you are currently viewing. You can cause them to start in a different desktop area by switching to that area before starting the application (you can do this automatically by binding several commands to a single input sequence) or by specifying a geometry with coordinates outside the physical display.

The latter method looks like (for 640-by-480 display)

```
command -geometry 100x100+641+481
```

and will start the application at the first pixel of the virtual display area to the right and down from the current one.

Generally, the latter method is easier when starting applications from an initialization script. The former is more difficult to set up but ensures applications always start in the same area, regardless of which area is currently being viewed.

Moving to a Different Desktop

Moving within a large virtual desktop can be accomplished in one of several ways:

```
EdgeScroll horizontal_% vertical_%
```

This allows you to move the mouse off one side of the screen, causing the display to shift to the new area available in that direction.

You can bind control keys to move the mouse by a single unit of screen area (commonly done with the cursor keys) or to switch to different numbered screens. (The function keys are commonly used here.) See the section “Key Bindings,” earlier in this chapter, for more information.

The different ways virtual desktops are used can be confusing if you are not careful. To keep them straight, remember that the X server provides a virtual screen, which simulates a larger physical area and allows you to scroll with the mouse. To simplify things, this is commonly set to the same area as the physical display. You can then ignore the X virtual desktop entirely and concentrate on those provided by your window manager. FVWM provides a *physical area* desktop, which can be imagined as a rectangular window with many panes of glass. FVWM also provides virtual desktops, which can be imagined as a number of panes of glass without any surrounding window frame; the panes can be thought of as a stack, from which you can display any one you choose.

Modules

FVWM provides several modules that often come in handy. You should read through the FVWM man pages for information on them. However, the FVWMPager module bears mention here, for it will simplify your dealings with virtual desktops immensely. The module provides tiny windows showing the entirety of your virtual desktop; you can switch to a given desktop by clicking on its miniature image.

WMaker

WMaker (also called WindowMaker) is a window manager that attempts to mimic the look of NEXTSTEP. The NEXT-style interface has many fans (enough to have produced several different window managers imitating the interface) and is certainly due consideration.

Most of the WMaker configuration can be accessed through GUI utilities rather than text files, so it is a suitable window manager for novices. However, WMaker tends to be rather colorful, so it is poorly suited for display devices of less than 256 colors.

More information about WMaker appears on the WMaker home page:
`http://www.windowmaker.org/`.

The user's guide to WMaker is located at
`http://people.delphi.com/crc3419/WMUserGuide/index.htm`.

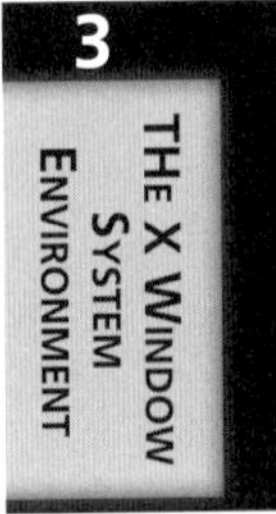

Using WMaker

The default WMaker configuration is shown in Figure 3.8.

FIGURE 3.8
The default WMaker configuration.

The images on the right are application launchers. You can change some aspects of their behavior by moving the mouse over the icon and holding down the right mouse button, which displays a menu of options. The icons are a drag-and-drop utility to set the background, an xterm launcher, and a configuration utility for WMaker itself. The icons to the lower left of the screen represent the applications with windows, whether currently displayed or iconified. You can restore an iconified window by double-clicking the icon.

The icon in the top left of the screen performs several functions. The number in the upper left of the icon itself indicates the desktop number currently displayed. Left-clicking the arrows in either corner increases or decreases the desktop number by one. Holding down the right mouse button over the icon provides an extensive menu of window operations.

The default window decorations (shown in Figure 3.9) are a square (representing a window) on the left side of the title bar and an X on the right side. The X closes the application when left-clicked. The square iconifies the application's window, so it appears in the row at the bottom of the screen.

xterm

FIGURE 3.9
The default WMaker window decorations.

Configuring WMaker

The default Debian configuration includes easy access to WindowMaker Preferences, which is a GUI-based configuration utility offering access to all the options you are likely to want to change. The common options modifiable by WindowMaker Preferences are discussed in this section. Because WindowMaker Preferences works by modifying and saving the configuration files, you need to restart WMaker in order to use the new settings.

The WindowMaker Preferences utility offers a horizontal row of icons across the top of the screen. Those icons determine the type of settings to be modified; left-clicking one presents the interface for configuring that icon's options in the window space below the icon bar.

Window Focus Preferences

This section (illustrated by Figure 3.10) deals with the focus model options. You can select from all of the common focus models with the Input Focus Mode chooser. New windows can automatically receive the focus if desired, and with click-to-focus models, the initial mouse click that sets the focus to that window can be consumed by the window manager or passed on to the application.

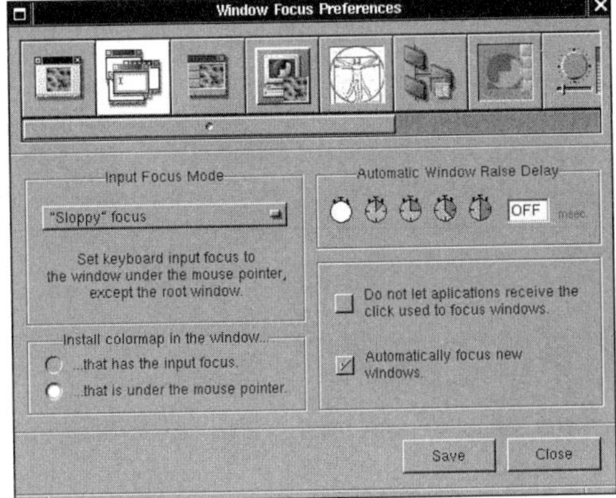

FIGURE 3.10
The WMaker Window Focus Preferences.

Workspace Navigation

Several different options relate to workspaces (referred to earlier in this chapter as *virtual desktops*; the terminology sometimes varies between window managers). Each option is presented with a button and explanatory text. If the option is disabled, a large red X covers the graphic of the button. The options are

- Drag Windows Between Workspaces: When active, windows can be dragged across the edge of the screen and into a new desktop or workspace.
- Switch to First Workspace: Workspaces can be viewed as a line or a loop.
- Create New Workspace When Switching Past the Last Workspace: This option dynamically creates a new workspace when dragging a window past the end of a line of workspaces.

The interface is shown in Figure 3.11.

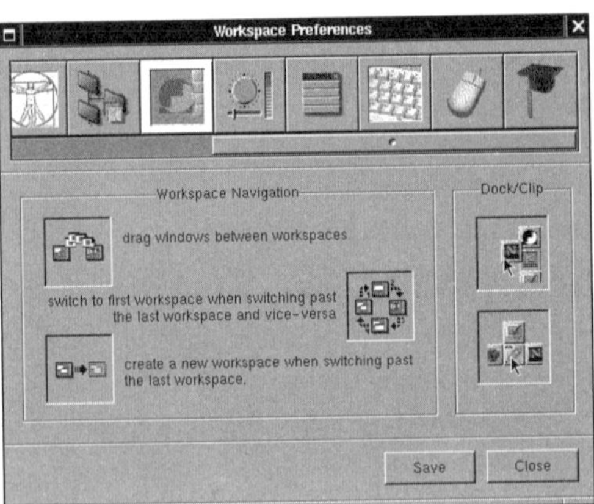

FIGURE 3.11
The WMaker Workspace Navigation Preferences.

KDE

KDE is a desktop manager that includes a relatively small window manager called KWM. There isn't much point in using the KDE window manager outside of the rest of the KDE environment. On the other hand, it is possible to use normal window managers with KDE (although they might not fit in as well visually). KDE as a desktop manager is described in the next section.

Desktop Managers

Window managers, as the name suggests, are intended to manage windows. This is a necessary function but leaves a great deal to be desired for functions such as file and session management. Desktop managers are an attempt to fill that gap. They occupy an unusual place in the X environment, somewhere between a window manager (most desktop managers include window manager functionality or can cooperate with window managers) and a normal application.

A desktop manager is not a requirement in the way that a window manager is. File management can be handled through applications (such as Midnight Commander) or simple shell commands. Session management can be handled through `xsm`, a dedicated session manager, or manually (by starting applications in the `.xsession` or `.xinitrc`), or simply ignored. Many people, particularly those who have spent a long time with UNIX, are comfortable with these mechanisms and prefer them. Most newcomers to UNIX, however, prefer to use a desktop manager. In particular, those whose previous computing experience is with other platforms (Windows 95/98, Macintosh, Amiga, or BeOS) will probably feel most comfortable with a desktop manager.

Application Integration

Desktop managers attempt to provide applications with a common set of available capabilities. These enable applications to store information and user preferences automatically, as well as to interact with each other. For example, a desktop manager might provide drag and drop capabilities, allowing you to drag files onto the desktop.

Common Look and Feel

The X display system allows each application to determine its own look and feel within its windows and allows the window manager to determine the look and feel of the window borders. In the past, this has resulted in applications with widely varying appearances and little common organization. Desktop managers take this concept a step forward, attempting to provide a common look and feel for all basic applications.

An application's look and feel consist of several things:

- How the application's GUI elements (menus, buttons, and so on) are drawn
- How the application's windows are drawn (A function of the window manager)
- How the application's menus, buttons and other interactive features are laid out on the screen
- How the application's features are named (on buttons and menus)
- How keyboard input is handled within the application

Providing a common look and feel means providing a standard for all of these elements, clearly a difficult task. The first two can be ensured by using a common toolkit (which handles the details of drawing buttons and menus for an application) along with a window manager that also uses that toolkit or is designed with a similar appearance. The rest are issues for each application and are generally addressed as matters of convention rather than requirement. These conventions are commonly specified in style guides.

This common look and feel cannot be enforced (due to X's design), so instead of enforcing a common look to all applications, desktop managers attempt to provide an application with their look and feel for every basic need. For example, both GNOME and KDE (the two desktop managers in common use on Linux) provide a simple WYSIWYG (what you see is what you get) text editor, calculator, and so on with their look and feel.

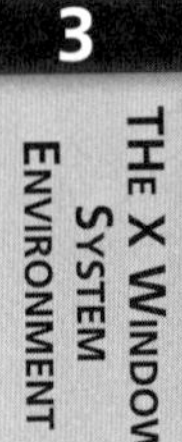

Desktop Functions

Because separate desktop managers are relatively recent developments, there is some overlap between desktop functions and the functions performed by most window managers. Desktop functions performed by desktop managers usually include file management, various (configurable) status displays, and application launchers.

File management is the area of greatest innovation for desktop managers. Typically, a desktop manager includes a graphical representation of the available file systems, complete with drag-and-drop functionality. This representation is generally considered more user friendly for the novice and is often convenient for the expert.

Session management is not strictly a function of the desktop manager, but some desktop managers provide it. A session manager attempts to preserve the applications you are running when logging out of one X session into the next. For example, if you have several shell terminals and a word processor open when you exit, the next time you log in, your session manager attempts to start those same shell terminals and word processor for you. The amount of success the session manager has depends on the applications you are using; some (such as shell windows) are simple enough to work well, but others (such as the word processor) require support for the session manager to properly restore their operation.

Traditionally, the functions of a session manager have been provided by starting all the desired applications in the X startup scripts (`.xinitrc` or `.xsession`). Once the applications have been started, manual manipulation serves to bring up any prior work that is required. Because most applications need special support in order to do more than that, and because mixing `.xinitrc` or `.xsession` launching with a session manager does not work well, session management has not gained a great deal of success.

Finally, both desktop managers presented here include suggested (but not required) sound managers as well. Sound on Linux is still in a somewhat uncertain state; the kernel provides basic access to sound hardware but does not mask the details of the hardware from the developer and does little processing of the sound itself. When running a single application, this does not cause problems because the application knows what to do. When running several sound-using applications, however, the Linux kernel allows the first application access to sound resources and denies that access to all subsequent applications, until the first releases the resources. This obviously causes problems with multiple sound-using applications, and both GNOME and KDE attempt to solve those problems by providing sound daemons.

A *sound daemon* is a program that requests control of the sound hardware from the kernel and then provides an interface for other programs to request sounds to be played. In this way, multiple programs can play short sounds with less chance of interfering with each other. Unfortunately, not all programs use the sound daemon interface, and those programs do not get access to the sound hardware at all. It is not an ideal solution, but it has advantages for a desktop situation, and the situation will improve as more programs adapt to using a sound daemon interface. However, if you are experiencing troubles with sound when running a desktop manager, and if sound works fine when you are not running the desktop manager, disabling the sound daemon could solve your problem.

KDE—The K Desktop Environment

KDE—the K Desktop Environment—is the first of two popular desktop managers available for Linux. The designers intend it to be similar but superior to the Windows 95/98/NT interface, which most users are familiar with. KDE was not intended to be a great leap forward in user-interface technology, but rather a decent interface done cleanly and well. It also provides basic session-management functionality, attempting to open supported applications you were running previously to the same state and position as when you left.

KDE is built around the Qt toolkit. Qt has been developed in a partially open-source manner by a commercial software company; the Linux version is free and open-source, but licenses for other platforms are more restrictive. This has been the cause of much uproar in the Linux community at times, resulting in modifications to the Qt license, and was at least one of the motives behind the development of GNOME (which is entirely open-source, licensed under the GPL). So far, the use of Qt has not caused problems beyond the controversy, however. If you intend to develop applications for KDE using Qt, you should read the license. If you merely want to use KDE, this will not present a problem.

More information concerning KDE appears on the KDE Web pages at `http://www.kde.org`.

Installing KDE

At the present time, KDE is not included with Debian due to licensing problems. You need to download KDE yourself by going to the KDE Web page and downloading the package files.

You need to download `kdebase-`*`version`*`.deb`, `kdelibs-`*`version`*`.deb`, and `kdesupport-`*`version`*`.deb`, where *`version`* is the same for all three and represents a version number. There is an internationalization package in the same directory as the former three packages, which you can also download if you expect to be using KDE with non-English languages.

Once downloaded, install each package by

```
# dpkg -i packagename
```

You can then run `dselect` and choose to configure installed packages.

The KDE Window Decorations

The KDE window decorations are produced by KWM, the KDE window manager. Normally, however, you don't have to worry about the window manager as a separate entity.

The title bar includes, from left to right, a menu of window operations, a tack, the application title display, a minimize button, a maximize button, and a close button. Windows can be moved by dragging the title bars or resized by dragging from any of the four borders or the resize area at the lower-right border.

The KDE Desktop

You can use KDE as your window manager by adding the command `startkde` to your `.xinitrc` and your `.xsession`. This section describes the default KDE desktop and tools, without attempting to cover other configurations.

The KDE environment will seem quite familiar to prior users of Microsoft's Windows 95/98/NT, both visually and functionally. An application bar occupies the top of the screen, with a rectangular bar representing each displayed window; clicking the bar activates the window. The bottom of the screen has a similar bar, with application launchers, status displays, and menus. The root window has an icon-based file manager.

By default, the file manager displays a trash can, a Templates directory, and an Autostart directory. All of the icons represent directories. The trash can provides a delayed delete function, programs dropped into Autostart are started when KDE is started, and Templates is a special directory the file manager uses when creating a new file.

Clicking any of the three (or in fact any directory displayed on the desktop or in a file-manager window) will display the contents of that directory. The files can be manipulated as you would expect, by selecting and dragging into a new location with the left mouse button or clicking the right mouse button for a menu of other options.

Most of your interaction with KDE happens with the file manager and the application bar, called `kpanel`. On this bar, menu buttons (buttons that display a menu when clicked) are indicated by a small black triangle, pointed upwards. Icons without that triangle are normal buttons. Right-clicking on most of the buttons provides options to move or remove the button and might provide additional options (commonly, Properties, which allows you to configure the behavior of the button). The specific function of each button is described in more detail later in this section.

Using KDE's Suite of Tools

KDE provides many tools, some original and some that have been modified from existing tools to conform to the KDE look and feel. There are far too many to detail them all individually. A brief selection of the more useful tools is described here; they are also covered in more detail within the KDE help system.

The KDE desktop panel appears in Figure 3.12.

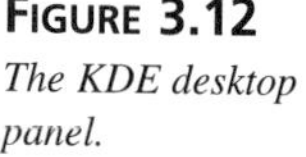

FIGURE 3.12
The KDE desktop panel.

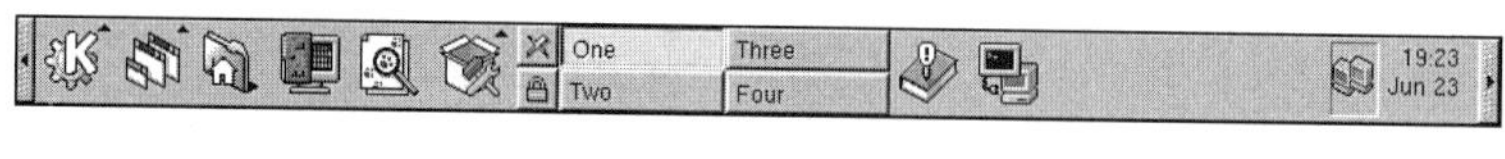

The left-right hide buttons, located on the far left and far right of the panel, allow the panel itself to be hidden. Clicking one causes the panel to shrink until only the clicked button is visible. Clicking again expands the panel to its prior position.

The K menu button provides for basic interaction with the KDE system. You can use this menu to log out of KDE (ending your X session in most cases), to start common applications that the system knows about, and so on.

The Three-Windows menu contains a list of all active windows on the all desktops; selecting a window activates it. It also contains an entry for each of the other three desktops configured by default. Selecting one of those three switches to the selected desktop.

The Home-Folder button is an application launcher that starts the KDE file manager in your home directory. The same function is available from the K menu as Home Directory.

The Control-Center button is another application launcher, configured to start the KDE control center. The control center is the KDE preferences application and allows you to configure most aspects of KDE and X.

The Footprints button is an application launcher that starts a simple graphical interface to the find system utility. Use it to find files easily even if you don't remember their names or if you want to find all files matching some criteria. (Hint: If you can remember part of the filename, try Locate first; it uses a database of files built nightly and can be much faster.)

The Toolbox menu provides a list of three common tools for quick access.

The Logout button is a one-click logout button.

The Lock button activates the screensaver's password lockout feature. The screen is blanked and requires you to enter your password to unblank.

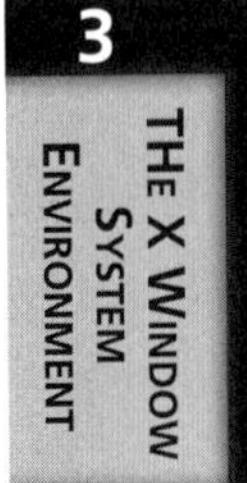

The four Workspace Selection buttons allow you to switch between workspaces (virtual desktops) in a single click. The currently pressed button indicates the current workspace.

The Lightbulb manual starts the KDE browser on the KDE help files.

The Terminal button starts a new terminal.

A right-click on the Display button produces a menu of several display-settings programs, from which you can change your background images, screensaver preferences, and so on.

The Clock is, well, a clock. It reminds you what time it is. Clicking it doesn't do anything.

The KDE Terminal is pictured in Figure 3.13.

KDE provides KVT, a terminal emulation program based on `rxvt` for displaying textual applications and shell windows. Most configuration options are available through the graphical interface. When started with no arguments, KVT opens a new terminal window with your default shell.

FIGURE 3.13
The KDE terminal.

The sophisticated KDE File Manager (see Figure 3.14) contains the functionality of a Web browser, FTP client, and archiving utility (for tar archives, a UNIX standard). It also provides network services for other applications. Output for most functionality is displayed using HTML as a Web browser would. File management is performed using a Web-browser model, with pages displaying directories and files generated automatically or overridden by manually created pages. (If a file named `index.html` or `.kde.html` is present in an open directory, it displays that file rather than the default directory display.)

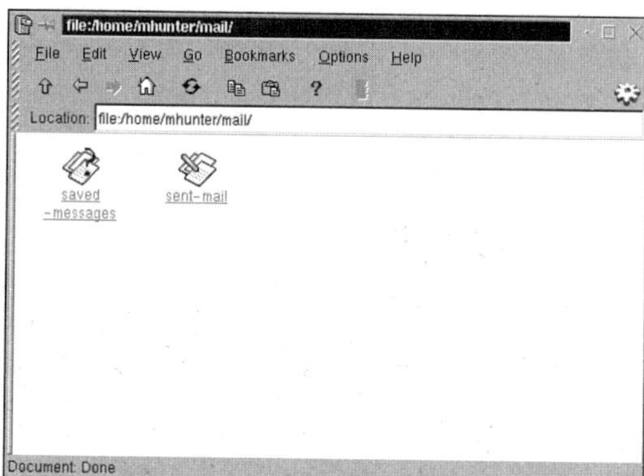

FIGURE 3.14
The KDE File Manager.

KFM also understands some KDE-only conventions, such as the # character in filenames, and `*.kdelink` files. The former can be used to refer to a file inside of a tar archive (as in `archive.tar#myfile`), and KFM will perform the operation on only that contained file, not the whole file. `*.kdelink` files allow things such as dragging an FTP directory onto your desktop. (It is saved as a text file containing a description of the protocol and location, and KFM knows how to use that information to access the file as if it were local.)

The different icons for the files in the window are determined based on the type of file and can be changed to your preferences.

GNOME: The GNU Network Object Model

GNOME is a desktop manager (see Figure 3.15) similar at first glance to KDE; the look and feel are sometimes different, but the functionality, niche, and intent seem similar. In fact, in many areas, GNOME has borrowed from the earlier work of KDE in terms of visual appearance and interaction. From a developer's perspective, however, GNOME offers much more. The difference is perhaps best summarized by the name: GNOME is a network object model, an attempt to take object-oriented technology and apply it to the desktop interface. It is an experimental system in that regard, although as a user you will only reap the benefits.

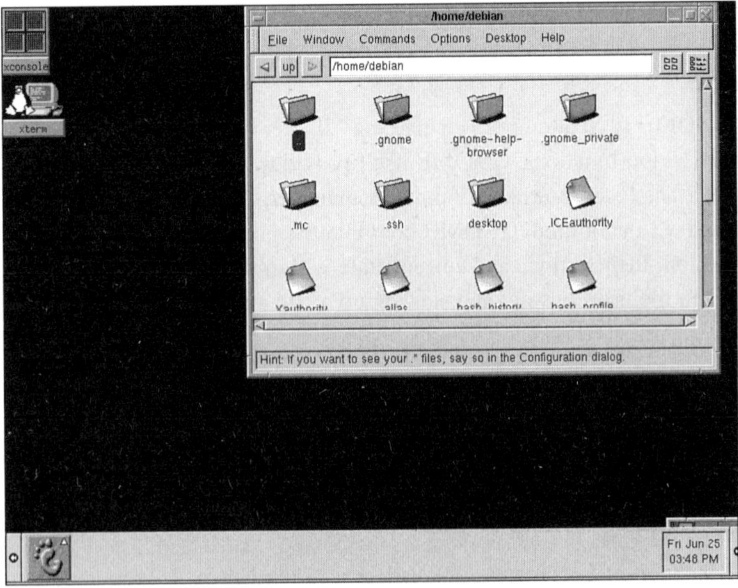

FIGURE 3.15
The GNOME display by default (FVWM as window manager).

GNOME either comes with or requires, depending on how you see it, a large number of shared libraries for various purposes. You should try to install GNOME either all at once or not at all and use the package management system whenever possible. Updating some portions of GNOME or the required libraries but not others can also lead to problems. The package management system in Debian helps you out with many of these situations. If you are not confident of your problem-solving ability, stick to major releases.

One of the more important required libraries is GTK, the Gimp ToolKit (so named because it originated with GIMP, a graphics editor). Most of GNOME itself was built using GTK. Other libraries include both sound and image utilities that were often in common use before GNOME.

Of the two desktop managers discussed in this chapter (GNOME and KDE), GNOME is the more open-source option. For some people, this is only minor trivia, but for others, it is a point of much debate and political contention.

GNOME—More Than a Desktop

Traditional desktops (whether implemented through X or otherwise) provide primarily user-interface elements. Applications are left to handle preferences, data, and the like through their own methods. The operating system interfaces available for these purposes are unfortunately rather poorly suited for operating a desktop (although they are just fine for many other types of applications). These interfaces are difficult to change for various reasons, not least because of the effort programmers have invested in learning to work around them!

GNOME is an attempt to change that. It attempts to provide an object-oriented interface to desktop functions. GNOME itself provides all the traditional components of a desktop interface (user-interface toolkit, file manager, application toolbars, and interface style guides). In addition, GNOME-compliant applications can use the GNOME functionality to store their settings and current state within the GNOME environment, shutting down when the user logs out and starting up again automatically when the user logs in again.

GNOME uses an object model (called Baboon) and persistent object store defined according to the CORBA standard. That allows GNOME applications to be written in any language with CORBA support, rather than be limited to the language GNOME itself was written in. Baboon itself provides many capabilities to the modern programmer that otherwise are not normally available; in essence, it makes writing complex desktop applications easier.

For more information on GNOME, check the GNOME Web page (`http://www.gnome.org`), including the GNOME FAQ, or the documentation included with your Debian CD (under `/usr/doc/gnome`, if you installed it). Development is rapid, and the version of GNOME included on the Debian CD is probably already out of date.

Installing GNOME

Installing GNOME with Debian packages is simple compared to most other methods but can still be pretty daunting. Use `dselect` to choose the GNOME packages you want. (At a minimum, you need `gnome-core`, `gnome-panel`, `gnome-session`, `gnome-gmc`, and `gnome-control-center`, along with all the packages they depend on.) GNOME requires a large number of libraries and support packages, so don't be surprised to see a large list of dependencies!

GNOME is located in the optional package section. If you search through `dselect` using `gnome` as a keyword, you encounter a number of additional utilities that are not part of the official GNOME distribution but do offer GNOME support. Some of these are probably worth installing if you have installed GNOME.

Using GNOME

There are several different ways to use GNOME. The most common is as a desktop manager, in which case GNOME provides all of its capabilities to the user. GNOME can function in this manner with or without session management, although the default is to use session management. If desired, however, you can use some of the GNOME utilities (particularly the GNOME panel and applets) without making use of GNOME as a desktop manager at all.

You still need a window manager to use GNOME properly. GNOME requests that the window managers used with it have certain extensions to help integrate them with GNOME. As of this writing, Enlightenment, IceWM, FVWM2, and several other window managers are adding the GNOME extensions. You can also use window managers without the GNOME extensions, but you might not be able to use the capabilities GNOME offers.

If you want to use GNOME with session management, start GNOME with `gnome-session`. GNOME looks in the environment variable `WINDOW_MANAGER` for the name of your window manager and starts it for you. When you log out of GNOME, GNOME attempts to store all of the applications you were using and restart them on your next login.

If you merely want to use the GNOME utilities, start the utilities you want to use in your `.xsession` or `.xinitrc` as you would normally. If the GNOME panel is one of these, you can start it as the last item in your `.xsession` or `.xinitrc` (as you would your window manager), in which case logging out of the GNOME panel would end your X session, or you can start it as you would any other program.

Startup methods are still somewhat in flux at the time of this writing; you should read the documentation carefully if you are not using the GNOME distribution included with this book or if you have updated the GNOME packages.

The GNOME Panel

The panel is the basic GNOME application, which looks like a solid gray bar across one (or more) of the borders of your screen. It provides display space for GNOME applets, including the common application launchers and system monitors as well as more interesting applications. By default, it also includes the GNOME menu button (designated by the GNOME logo, which resembles a footprint).

You can have any number of GNOME panels, and they are extremely flexible regarding screen placement. As bars, they can be placed on any of the four borders of the display or changed to occupy a corner of the screen. Panels can be hidden by sliding them off the screen (automatically or manually) or set up to occupy only the space required for applets to display. By default, unoccupied space in a panel is a light gray, but this can be changed to a color or a pixmap. To change a panel's attributes, look in GNOME, Panel, This Panel Properties.

Each panel provides space for a number of different applications that the user can add. These can be installed separately, but a number of small applets are provided with the GNOME packages. The applets of most interest are the GNOME menu button, the app launcher (a button that launches an application when clicked), and various system monitor applets.

The GNOME menu includes ready access to all of the included applets, by selecting GNOME, Panel, Add Applet. Positioning the mouse over an applet and holding down the right mouse button reveals a set of menu options. There are options to remove the applet or reposition the applet within the panel, and some applets provide ways of setting various parameters that way. Overall, it is a friendly interface compared to editing text files.

Managing Files with GNOME

GNOME produces an extensively modified version of Midnight Commander (a popular text-based file manager) as its file manager. The GNOME version, Gmc, has had an extensive GNOME interface added to it (see Figure 3.16). Using GMC, you can perform all the normal file management functions by the usual drag-and-drop, plus more advanced functions such as comparing two directories, treating compressed tar archives as directories, and providing network access. Overall, it is an impressive offering.

Sometimes, problems may crop up, regardless of what window manager or desktop manager you may be using. The next section aims to give you some useful tips for tracking down these problems.

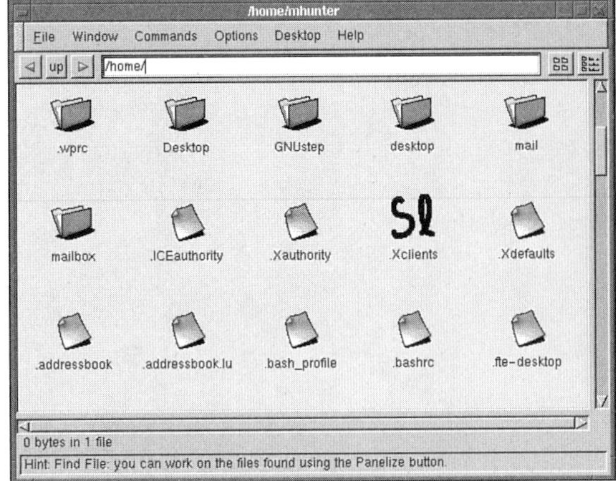

FIGURE 3.16
The GNOME file manager, GMC.

Troubleshooting X

You have a number of resources for troubleshooting X. Which to use depends on the problem. Good general resources include the XFree86 Web site, particularly the FAQ located there, Usenet newsgroups such as `comp.os.linux.x`, Usenet archival and searching services such as DejaNews, and Linux and X-related mailing lists.

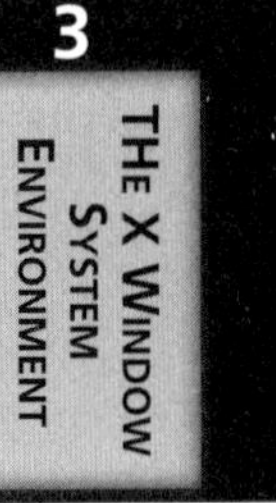

If you are having problems getting your video card to work, it's a good bet someone else has had problems, too. Check the manufacturer's site, along with the Usenet newsgroups, and search the Web; many people post their configuration files after a struggle with a particularly difficult card.

If you are having trouble getting X installed and configured, you may want to look at the following resources:

The XFree86 FAQ	`http://www.xfree86.org/FAQ/`
DejaNews	`http://www.dejanews.com/`

X generates a lot of text when it starts. (You see it scroll briefly before the X display opens.) Often, this text contains clues to problems you are having, so it's worth reading when trouble strikes.

Summary

This chapter covered the basic installation, configuration, and use of XFree86 on Debian Linux. It includes an overview of basic X concepts, along with descriptions and configuration information for some of the common window managers and desktop managers. After reading this chapter, novices should gain a better understanding of X, and experts should learn a few useful tidbits.

CHAPTER 4

User Applications

by Gerry Muñoz

In This Chapter

Users always look for tools that better fit their needs, so providing them with the most suitable tools to carry out their daily activities is a very important task of a computer system. Unlike other UNIX flavors, Linux has extended user-applications support that enables users to handle their daily computer-based activities in the simplest way.

Word processors, spreadsheets, CD players, Web browsers, mail readers, and graphics tools are some of the most useful tools that users require. This chapter shows some useful user applications supported by Linux.

Office Applications

The fact that most Linux users have a technical background doesn't mean that they don't do office work. Even the number of Linux's nontechnical users increases every day. They work at companies where Linux is not installed on their computers; therefore, it's very important for them to use applications that enable them to share documents and information with other people at their companies. This section presents an outline of some applications; it is not a user's guide for the applications mentioned here.

The Siag Office Suite

Siag Office is a free package office suite that features a word processor (Pathetic Writer), a spreadsheet (Siag scheme in a grid), and presentation graphics (Egon). Although Siag is the name of the spreadsheet, all the previous applications are considered part of the Siag Office Suite. The Siag packages are included on Debian's disc. Siag Office is a good option for most types of users, because it's easy and simple. The applications that form the Siag Office Suite have one important thing in common: all are open-source. Siag Office enables users to use expressions in different programming languages, such as C, SIOD, Guile, and Tcl.

Pathetic Writer, a Word Processor

Pathetic Writer is the word processor provided by Siag Office. Its user interface is simple and easy to understand (see Figure 4.1).

Even though Pathetic Writer is a good word processor, it seems as if it doesn't support many file formats. There are many proprietary file formats that are used by commercial applications that can't be used by other applications without the permission of their owners. The following are Pathetic Writer–supported file formats:

- Text
- Rich Text Format
- HTML (Hypertext Markup Language)
- PostScript

FIGURE 4.1
Pathetic Writer.

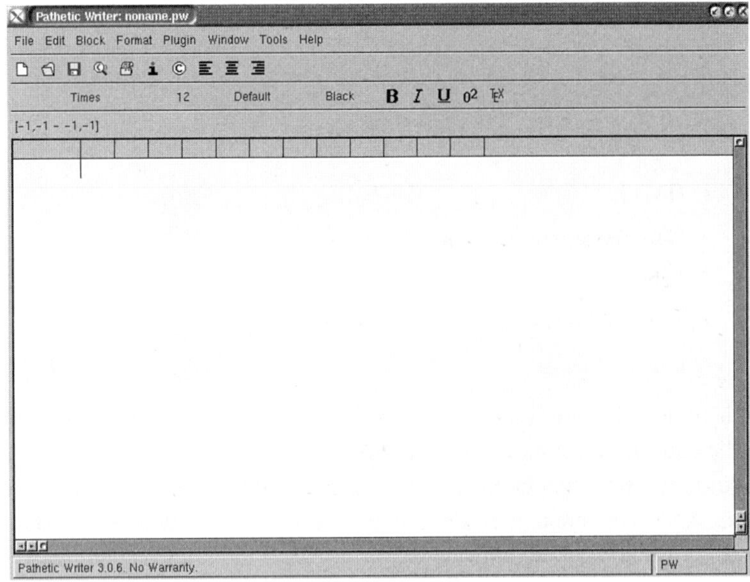

Siag (Scheme in a Grid), a Spreadsheet

Siag stands for *scheme in a grid* (see Figure 4.2). Siag is a full-featured spreadsheet that is available both on text and X formats. The look and functionality of Siag is similar to most spreadsheets; its user interface looks simple, but it is powerful.

FIGURE 4.2
Siag: scheme in a grid.

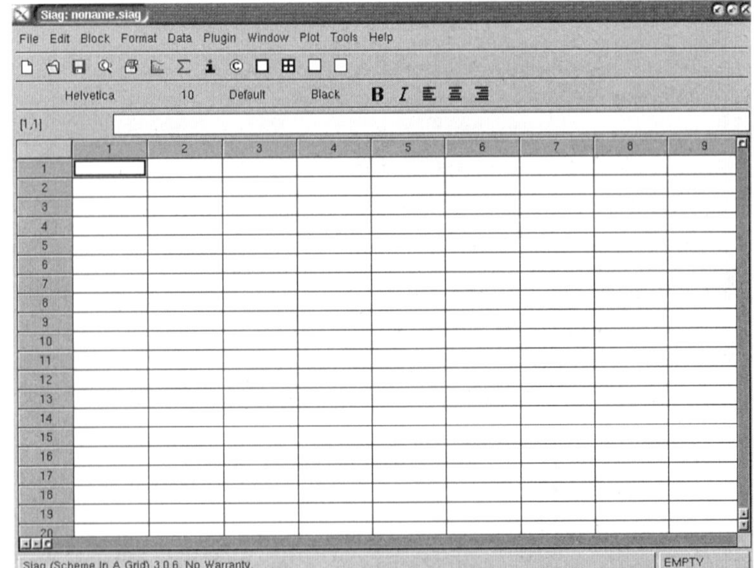

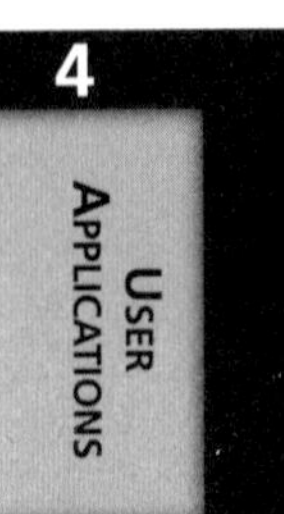

Siag, like Pathetic Writer, supports many different file formats:

- Text
- Lotus 1-2-3
- PostScript
- HMTL
- Comma-separated value
- Scheme code
- Troff table
- Latex table

The functionality of Siag is completely different from commercial spreadsheets, such as Microsoft Excel or Corel Quattro Pro. Formulas, data, and information are introduced in a different way than in other spreadsheets. Also the nomenclature of the cells is different. Siag uses numbers to indicate both rows and columns, whereas most commercial spreadsheets use numbers to indicate rows and letters to indicate columns.

Egon Animator, a Presentation Creating Tool

Unlike Pathetic Writer and Siag, Egon is very different from most commercial presentation and animation tools, such as MS PowerPoint (see Figure 4.3). Objects are added to the animation, and the user tells them what to do and when. The user interface is completely different than commercial applications.

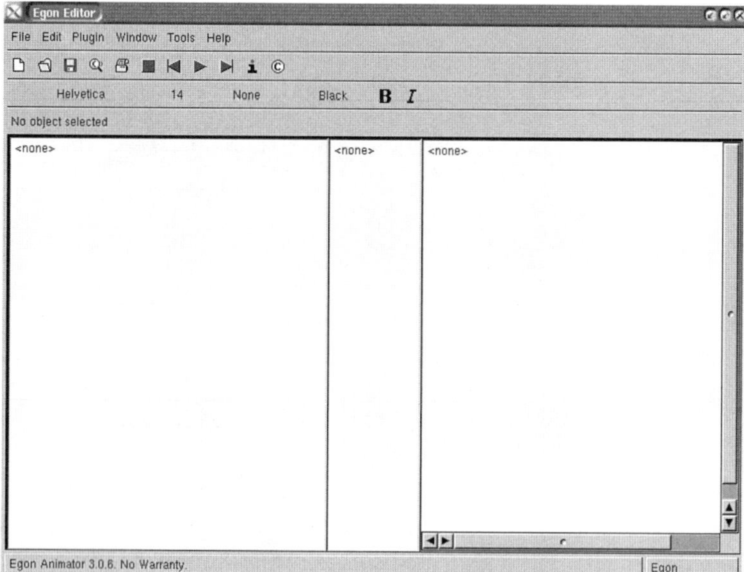

FIGURE 4.3
Egon Animator.

Egon supports the following file formats:

- C source
- Animated GIF
- PostScript
- Scheme code

Siag Office is a good option for technical users. It is powerful and has a nice user interface. Nevertheless, nontechnical users could get confused using Siag.

StarOffice

StarOffice is a non–open-source office suite manufactured by Star Division. The latest release, 5.1, uses an independent desktop environment that looks very similar to the MS Windows desktop. The StarOffice desktop (see Figure 4.4) includes a start button that has the same functionality as the Start button on MS Windows. I think the similarities between StarOffice and MS Windows might help get the attention of many users. StarOffice also can handle most of Microsoft's office file formats—another good reason for using Linux instead of MS Windows.

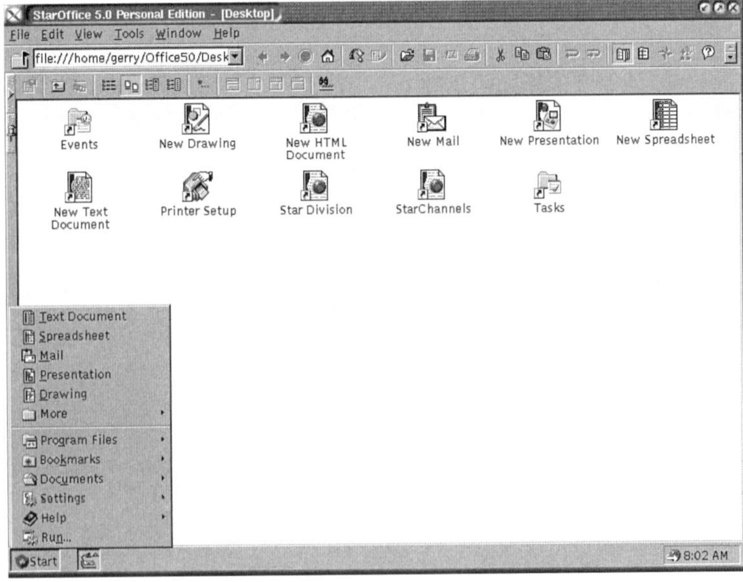

FIGURE 4.4
StarOffice desktop.

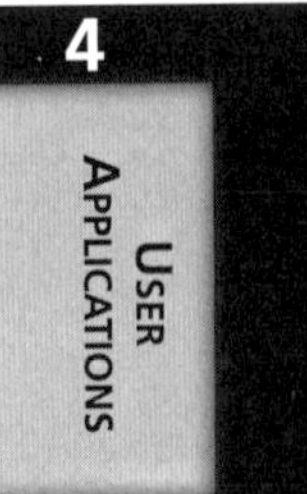

The software license is free for personal use. You should register first to obtain a product serial number and key. The installation process is quite simple: A setup script runs the installation program. The system prompts you to fill out and submit a registration form (see Figure 4.5) and then enter your product serial number and key.

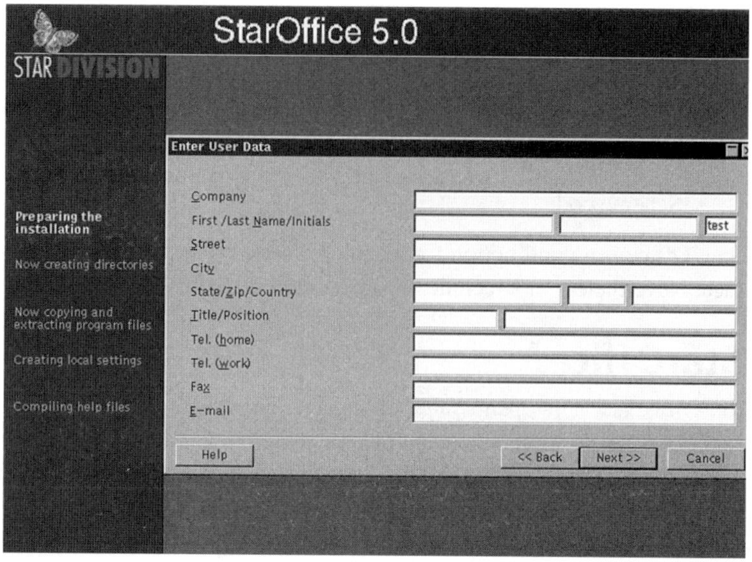

FIGURE 4.5
StarOffice registration form.

Running the setup script with the `/net` flag provides a network-install option of StarOffice. After the installation process is finished, each user should run the setup script to personalize StarOffice's preferences.

StarWriter (see Figure 4.6) is a full-featured word processor that looks like MS Word. I found StarWriter powerful and friendly. The menus and buttons are very well-organized and the way they're displayed also customizable, so you can organize it as you want. Maybe the most important reason to use StarWriter, regardless of its user interface, is that it has extended support to handle documents created by other applications. The following are supported formats:

- HTML
- StarWriter 3.0, 4.0, 5.0, and 5.1
- Simple Text
- Text Ansi
- Text Mac
- Text DOS
- Rich Text
- MS Word 6, 95, and 97
- Text WIN

StarCalc is StarOffice's spreadsheet application. The look and feel of StarCalc (see Figure 4.7) are very similar to those of Microsoft Excel—even the commands and functions are almost the same. StarCalc supports most common spreadsheet formats, including the following:

- StarCalc 3.0, 4.0, 5.0, and 5.1
- MS Excel 5.0, 95, and 97
- SYLK
- DIF
- dBASE
- Text

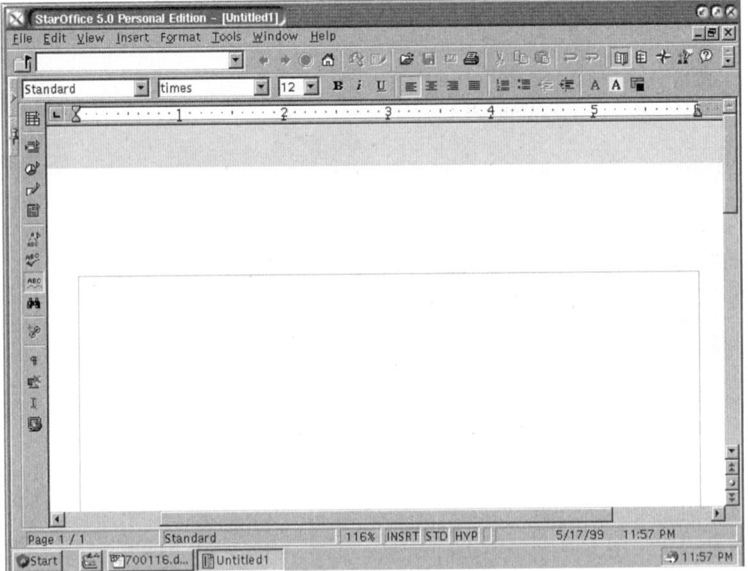

FIGURE 4.6
The StarWriter word processor.

StarCalc is a well-designed spreadsheet that enables users to work in a MS Windows-like environment running under Linux. It might make the change easier for those users who want to migrate from MS Windows to Linux.

StarImpress is the StarOffice's presentation tool. Even StarImpress's functionality is quite similar to MS PowerPoint, although its user interface (see Figure 4.8) looks a little different. StarImpress can open presentations from MS PowerPoint 97, but there is no support for other versions of PowerPoint. Presentations created with StarImpress can contain transition effects and background music.

In addition to the tools already covered, StarOffice features many applications that you'll find useful (see Table 4.1).

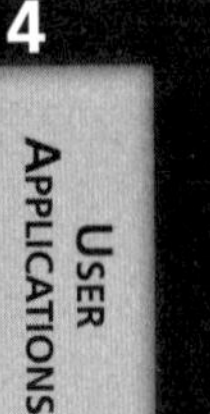

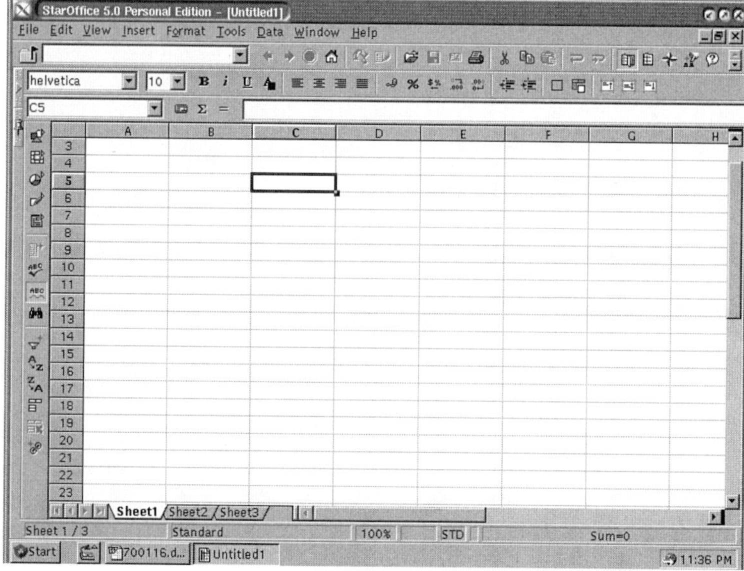

FIGURE 4.7
The StarCalc spreadsheet.

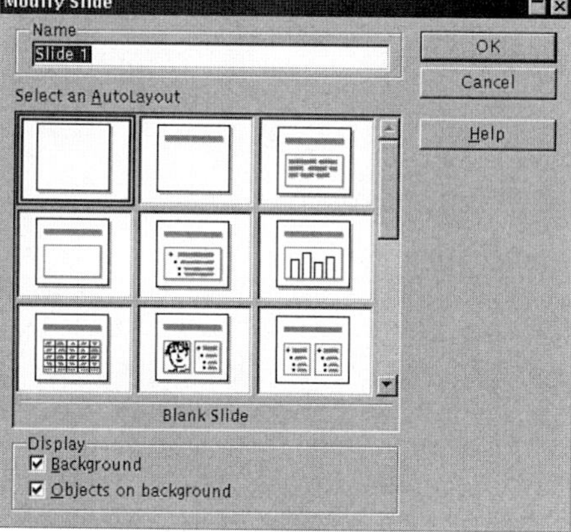

FIGURE 4.8
The StarImpress presentation tool.

TABLE 4.1 StarOffice's Miscellaneous Applications

Name	*Description*
StarSchedule	Appointment and task planning tool
StarDraw	Tool for assembling images
StarBase	Relational database tool
StarMail	Electronic mail user application
StarChart	Chart- and graph-building application

Unlike Siag Office Suite, StarOffice is an excellent option for users who want to use a Linux box, but need to share documents with others who use MS Windows. StarOffice is also a great tool for Web developers, because it has extended support for HTML conversion.

StarOffice is more complete than Siag Office Suite. Its user interface, functionality, and file-format support makes it easier to migrate from MS Windows to a Linux-based system.

WordPerfect

Corel WordPerfect is an office application that provides the same word processing capabilities for other platforms, including simple drawing and charting modules, spelling and grammar checking, auto correction, and so forth.

WordPerfect has been one of the most powerful and complete word processing tools for years. The version available for Linux is free for personal use; nevertheless, you must register your copy. The user interface (see Figure 4.9) is very well-organized and easy to use; there are menus and buttons that provide access to WordPerfect's facilities.

WordPerfect also features a small panel of easy-to-access menus for handling preferences, windows, and program options. The Preferences window (see Figure 4.10) has a graphical user interface that enables users to change preferences simply by clicking on the icons shown.

WordPerfect is a good option for those users who want to start working with Linux, but who are accustomed to working with Windows or Macintosh applications.

Gnome Office Suite

Gnome Workshop Project is a productivity suite for the GNOME Desktop (see Chapter 3, "The X Window System Environment," for more details on Gnome). There are a number of Gnome productivity applications under development, and the Gnome Workshop Project promises to be a very strong and complete office suite. Table 4.2 lists some Gnome productivity applications.

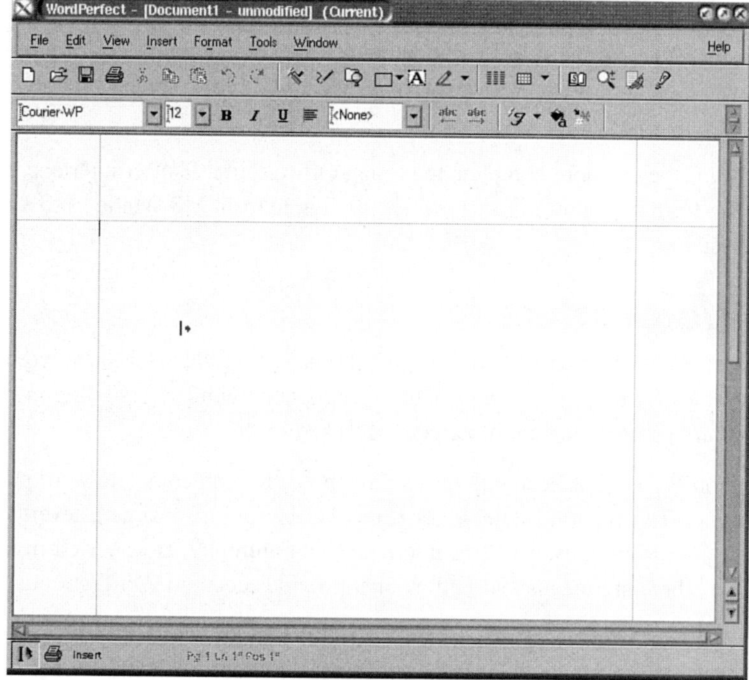

FIGURE 4.9
Corel WordPerfect 8.

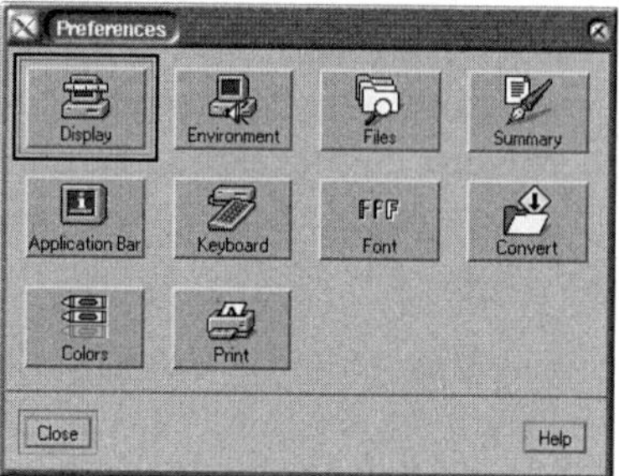

FIGURE 4.10
The Preferences window.

TABLE 4.2 Gnome Productivity Applications

Name	*Description*
Achtung	A presentation tool
Gnumeric	A spreadsheet
Gwp	A set of two word processors
Dia	A diagram editor
Guppi	A plot tool
Gnome-db	A database front-end

Name	Description
Gnome-pim	A scheduling tool
Genius	A scientific calculator

The Gnome Workshop Project is actually in development, so there are many changes coming. To learn more about the Gnome Workshop Project, check out `http://www.gnome.org/gw.html`.

MSWordView

These days, many documents are written on MS Word's format, because there is a computer running MS Windows almost everywhere. But what happens if you need to open an MS Word document on a UNIX machine?

MSWordView is an application that understands the MS Word format and converts it to HTML, so anyone with a Web browser is able to open it. MSWordview is not a word-processing tool; it's just a conversion tool. MSWordView is a good option for viewing MS Word documents, even though it works only with MS Word 8 (Office 97) documents.

The format conversion is fully functional; it's very similar to the conversion that MS Word makes when the option Save as HTML is enabled.

LyX

LyX is a very sophisticated and powerful word processor based on LaTeX, so users can do formatting that is also possible with LaTeX (see Chapter 7, "Typesetting," for more details on LaTeX). LyX is not a standard word processor; it's a smart writing tool that requires a minimum of user's concern about the look of the document.

LyX has many predefined styles that enable users to make any processing changes without being concerned about changing the style. For example, suppose you're writing a document and you're introducing text in the standard way. Suddenly, you change your mind and decide the text should be a comment. If you are using a conventional word processor, you need to follow many steps to make the change. On LyX, you just select the text with the mouse and click on the correct style—you don't even have to worry about tabulation or indent spaces.

The user interface (see Figure 4.11) is simple and features toolbars and menus, which is helpful for most types of users.

LyX has many other features, but it would take an entire chapter of this book to talk about its facilities.

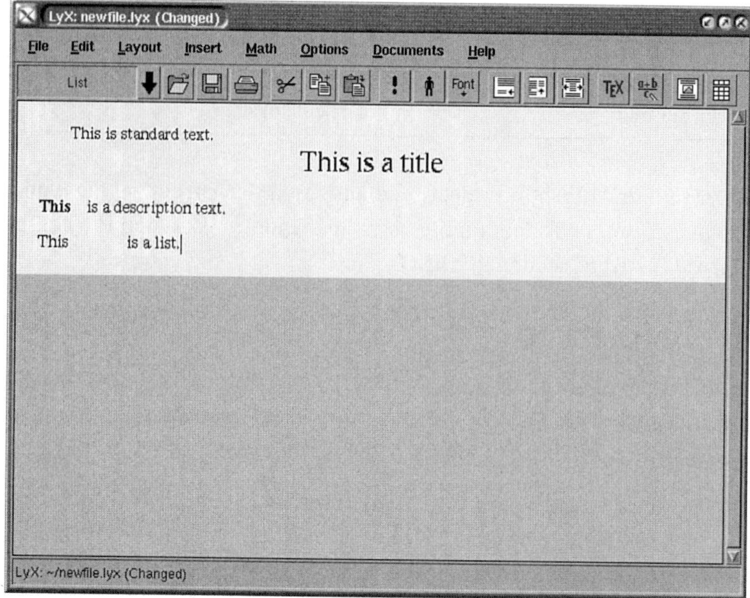

FIGURE 4.11
The LyX user interface.

There are several office applications currently running under Linux and certainly there will be many more. In the near future, these kinds of applications will be found in small offices, homes, and even in large organizations.

Network Applications

These days, there are networked computers almost everywhere. Even if your computer is not directly connected to a LAN, your computer becomes a networked computer when you get access to the Internet. One of the most acclaimed features of Linux is its enhanced network support. This section describes some useful network applications that run under Linux.

Setting Up a Dial-Up Internet Connection

Most users get access to the Internet by using the services of an Internet service provider (ISP). The most common way to establish a connection between the user's computer and the ISP's network is by using a PPP (Point-to-Point Protocol) connection. Figure 4.12 shows the process for accessing the Internet using a PPP connection.

Setting up a dial-up connection under Debian is a piece of cake, because it has a tool for configuring such connections. There are a few steps that must be followed, however.

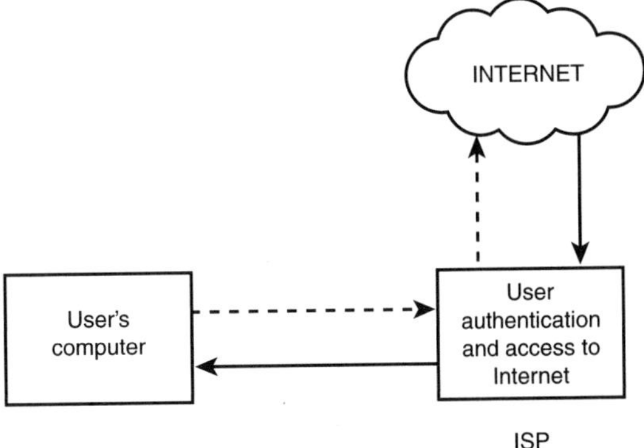

FIGURE 4.12
Access to the Internet using a PPP connection.

First, you must be sure that the kernel has the PPP support enabled (see Chapter 12, "Customizing the Bootup Procedure," for more details on configuring the kernel). If the kernel has PPP support as a module, you need to be sure that the PPP module is active.

Next, run the `pppconfig` program. This opens the Main Menu (see Figure 4.13). Select the Create a Connection option and press the Enter key.

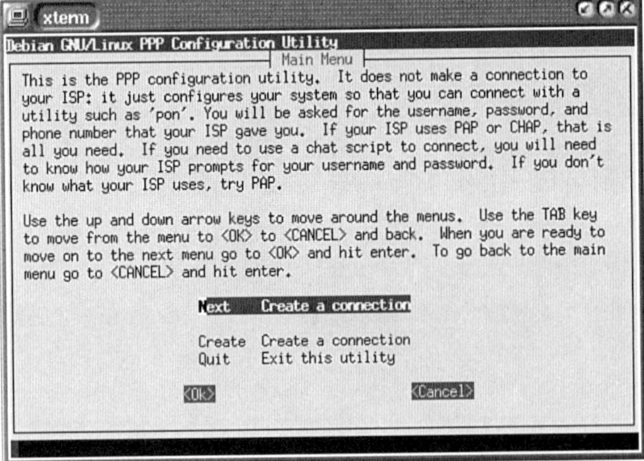

FIGURE 4.13
The PPPconfig main menu.

The next step is to complete the information that the program asks for. Providing the information required is very simple; each window has a description that you'll find useful. You also are asked for information about your modem and dial-up account settings. When you finish providing all the information required by the system, a review of that information (see Figure 4.14) is displayed. At this point, you can correct any mistake you have. If all the information is correct, select the Finished option to save the configuration and return to the main menu.

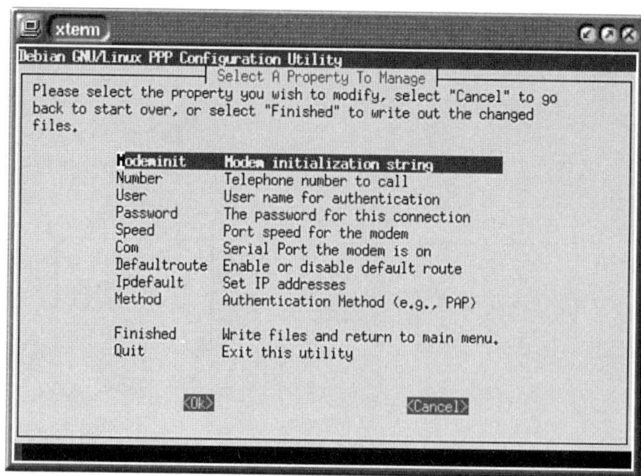

FIGURE 4.14
The PPP Configuration Utility.

The next step is to start the connection. To do this, run the `pon` command. When you finish using the dial-up connection, you execute the `poff` command.

And that's it! You are now ready to connect to your ISP and enter the marvelous world of the Internet.

Mail

Electronic mail (email) is an application that provides messaging services and message storage for users on either standalone or network computers. Each user has a unique directory for storing messages, called a *mailbox,* and a unique email address. The email address is formed by combining a user IF and a domain name, as in `gerry@my.domain`. Each user can read and handle the messages stored on his or her own mailbox.

RFC 821 describes the way that the Single Mail Transfer Protocol (SMTP) works (see Figure 4.15).

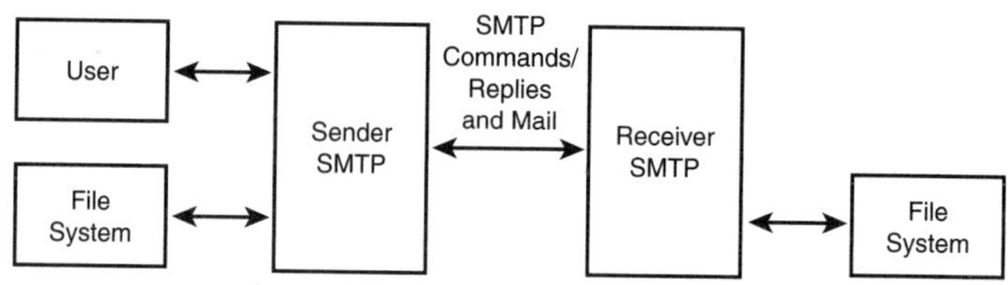

FIGURE 4.15
Model for SMTP use according to RFC 821.

The SMTP design is based on the following model of communication: As the result of a user mail request, the sender-SMTP establishes a two-way transmission channel to a receiver-SMTP. The receiver-SMTP may be either the ultimate destination or an intermediate. SMTP commands are generated by the sender-SMTP and sent to the receiver-SMTP. SMTP replies are sent from the receiver-SMTP to the sender-SMTP in response to the commands.

When the transmission channel is established, the SMTP-sender sends a `MAIL` command indicating the sender of the mail. If the SMTP-receiver can accept mail, it responds with an `OK` reply. The SMTP-sender then sends a `RCPT` command identifying a recipient of the mail. If the SMTP-receiver can accept mail for that recipient, it responds with an `OK` reply; if not, it responds with a reply rejecting that recipient (but not the whole mail transaction). The SMTP-sender and SMTP-receiver may negotiate several recipients. When the recipients have been negotiated, the SMTP-sender sends the mail data, terminating with a special sequence. If the SMTP-receiver successfully processes the mail data, it responds with an `OK` reply. The dialog is purposely lockstep, one-at-a-time.

Components of a Mail System

A mail system is formed by four components:

- Mail User Agent (MUA) Reads, writes, and replies to email
- Mail Transport Agent (MTA) Takes the mail package and transports it to the correct destination machine
- Mail Delivery Agent (MDA) Delivers mail packages to the mailboxes of users
- Mailbox A unique directory where the messages are stored

Following are the steps for mail delivery:

1. The user writes an email message using the MUA.
2. The MUA handles the message and takes it to the MTA.
3. The MTA carries the message to the destination machine.
4. The MDA receives the message and delivers it to the right mailbox.

Figure 4.16 shows the mail flow diagram.

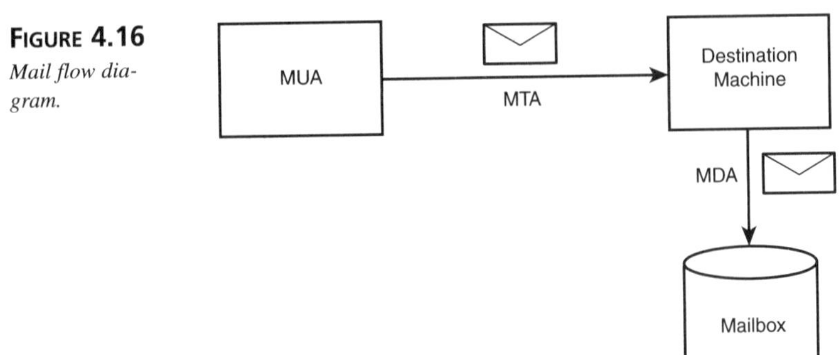

FIGURE 4.16
Mail flow diagram.

Mail Filtering

These days, it is very common to find messages that don't interest you in your email, or maybe you want to stop receiving messages from someone or from a discussion list to which you used to subscribe. To solve this problem, there are email filter facilities that can handle incoming messages in different ways, such as storing in a specific directory, deleting, forwarding, or performing other actions with the message.

There are different ways to establish a filtering policy. It can be done by looking at the Subject or From lines, or even the message headers. These filtering policies will be followed by any mail client. In this section, I use elm mailer tool for mail filtering. You must be sure that that `procmail` package is installed on your system (see Chapter 10, "Software Management," for more details on packages). Then, you need to create a file called `.procmailrc` under your home directory. The `.procmailrc` file must be created using a text editor. In this example, I use vi (see Chapter 6, "Advanced Text Editing," for more details on vi):

```
#cd
#vi .procmailrc
```

Enter a modified version of the following text on the `.procmailrc` file:

```
#Turn on and off the verbose mode.
VERBOSE=off

#Indicate your mail directory
MAILDIR=$HOME/Mail

#Directory for storing procmail log and rc files
PMDIR=$HOME/.procmail
LOGFILE=$PMDIR/log
#INCLUDERC contains the path of a file containing filter rules. You can have as
many INCLUDERC lines as you need.
INCLUDERC=$PMDIR/rc.debian
```

The next step is to create a new directory under your home directory called `.procmail` and a file in it called `rc.debian`:

```
#cd
#mkdir .procmail
#cd .procmail
#vi rc.debian
```

Enter the following code in the `rc.debian` file:

```
:0:
^Sender:.*debian
IN.debian
```

This code means that if the sender includes the word "`debian`", the message will be stored in the folder `$MAILDIR/IN.debian`.

Now you create a `.forward` file under your home directory:

```
#cd
#vi .forward
```

and insert the following code into the `.forward` file:

```
#Replace "gerry" with your own user ID
"¦IFS=' ' && exec /usr/bin/procmail -f- ¦¦ exit 75 #gerry"
```

And that's it! Now you're able to create any rc files that contain filter rules for your messages. Mail filtering is really helpful for avoiding junk mail or just for keeping your mail messages in order.

Setting Up a Local MTA

Debian's disc (like most UNIX discs) contains the Exim mailer, and it will install by default to run from `inetd.conf` (see Chapter 16, "TCP/IP Networking Essentials," for more details on `inetd`). Exim is a powerful MTA that was designed as an Internet mailer, so it provides extended facilities, such as junk mail detection and management of a large number of local domains.

To configure Exim is quite simple; just edit the `/etc/exim.conf` file. The `/etc/exim.conf` file is divided into several parts according to the purpose of the commands described in each section. The following are the sections of the configuration file:

- Main configuration section   In this section, you specify all the basic configuration settings that will apply for the MTA. You can set up local domains and define default domains for messages, domains to relay for, the received messages' headers, and so forth.
- Transports configuration section   Actual deliveries on Exim are made by *transports*. The only external transport currently implemented for Exim is an SMTP transport over a TCP/IP network (see Chapter 16 for more details on TCP/IP). In this section, you can set up the transport configuration for message delivery and determine how the system will handle the different internal transports defined here.
- Directors configuration section   Exim uses *directors* to handle addresses that include one of the local domains. This section is used to specify how local addresses are handled.
- Routers configuration section   Remote addresses are handled by routers on Exim. Remote addresses are those with a domain that doesn't match any of the local domains configured in the Main configuration section. In this section, you specify how remote addresses are handled.

Even though I'm talking about user applications in this section, it'll be useful to take a deeper look into the Transports configuration section. There are many configurable transports in this section, all of which relate to the way the system handles deliveries. Table 4.3 shows transports and their functions.

TABLE 4.3 Transports That Define How the System Handles Deliveries

Name	*Description*
`local_delivery`	Used for local delivery to user mailboxes. You can select the path of the user's mailbox.
`address_pipe`	Used for handling pipe addresses generated by alias or forward files.
`address_file`	When Exim founds a forward file or alias that points to a file, this transport handles the file address.
`address_directory`	When a forward file or alias points to a file that ends with "/", Exim understands that this is a directory instead of a file and uses this transport to deliver the message to a unique file in the directory.
`address_reply`	Used to handle autoreplies generated by a filtering option.

When you finish setting up Exim as an MTA, you're able to use any MDA to write and send email to both local and remote users.

Mail Readers

There are many applications that can work as an MUA that are called *mail readers*. Basically, the function of this kind of application is to enable users to read and write email messages.

Netscape Messenger

Netscape Communicator has a mail reader called Messenger that is a powerful tool for reading mail and news messages. Messenger enables users to read and write email easily, due to its menu- and button-based interface. Figure 4.17 shows Messenger's user interface for both mail and news.

The look of Messenger varies between versions; Figure 4.17 shows the look for Messenger included on Netscape Communicator 4.51. Messenger's main window is divided into four sections. The first section is located at the top of the window and contains the toolbar and menus. The second section is located on the left side and shows a list of the current folder, including the Mail and News folders. The third section is located below the toolbar and shows the messages contained in the selected folder. The fourth section is the big window located below the messages list and contains the body of the selected message.

Messenger is capable of working with both POP or IMAP protocols. Figure 4.18 shows Messenger's Preferences menu for Mail Servers.

FIGURE 4.17
Netscape Messenger.

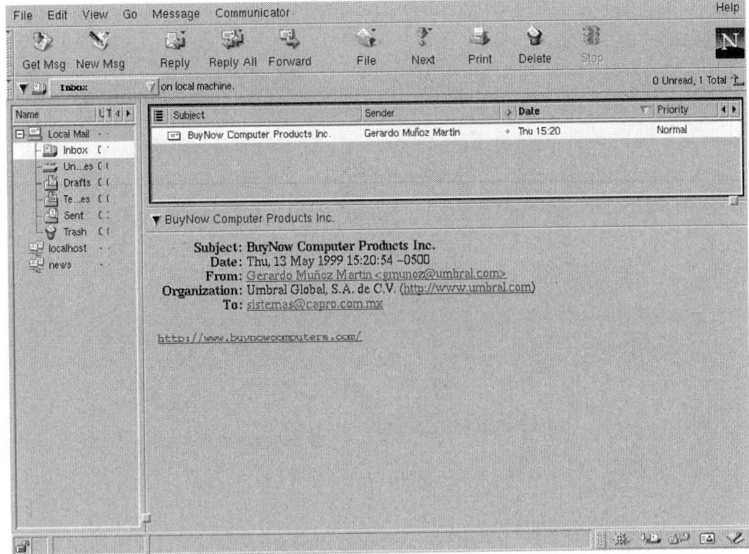

FIGURE 4.18
Netscape Communicator preferences.

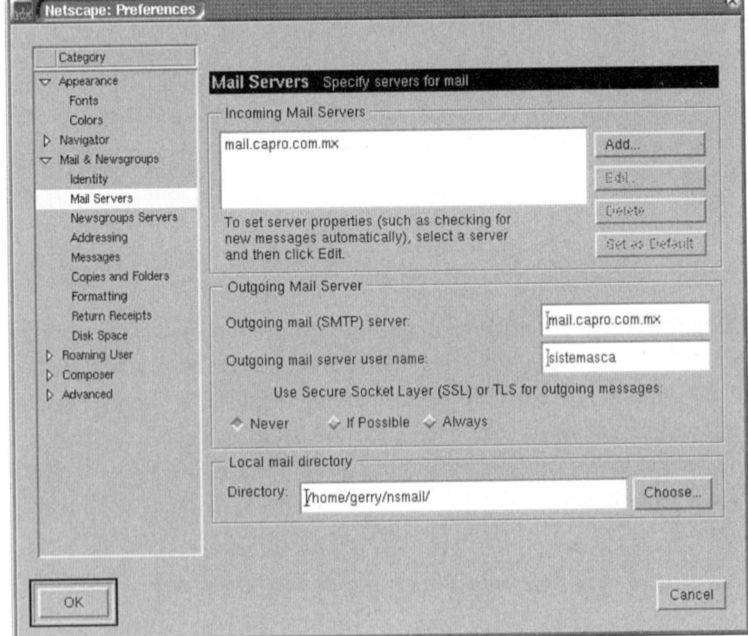

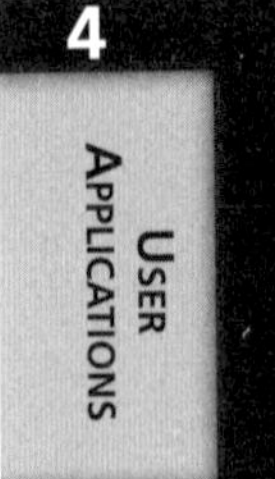

In the Mail Server section of the Preferences menu, you can set up a mail server that Messenger will use to send and receive mail messages. Messenger has extended features that make a user's life easy: mail filtering, image displaying, sending email in HTML format, and many others.

Balsa

Balsa, a package included on Debian's CD-ROM, is an X-based mail reader that enables users to read and write mail messages. Its user interface is quite simple and looks similar to Netscape Messenger, but it has few facilities. Figure 4.19 shows the Balsa user interface.

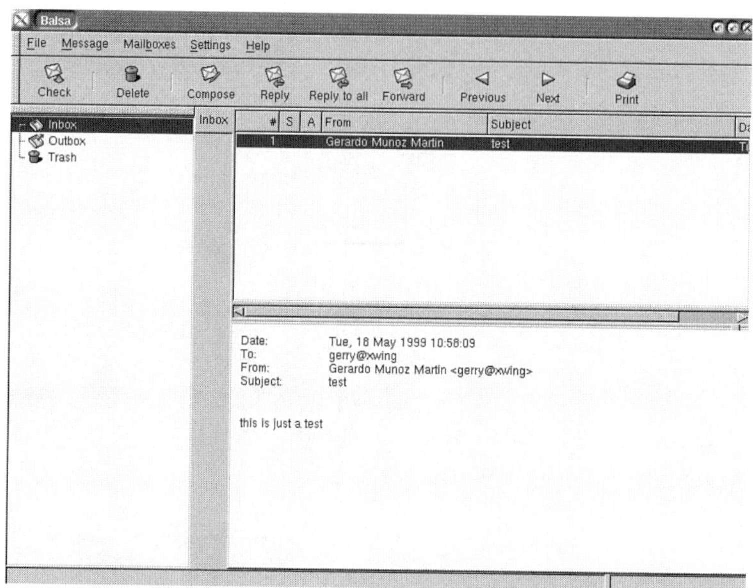

FIGURE 4.19
The Balsa mail reader.

Balsa is capable of retrieving mail messages from remote mail servers using IMAP. Balsa's user interface is divided into four sections. The first section is located at the top of the window and contains the toolbar and menus. The second section is located on the left side, below the toolbar, and shows the list of folders. The third section is located on the right side, below the toolbar, and shows the message list of the selected folder. The fourth section is located below the message list and contains the body of the selected message.

Mutt

Mutt is a text-based mail reader that can be used to read local mail. Mutt's user interface is good; even in its text mode, the commands are clearly shown and the area for message reading is separated from the command bar. It is available on Debian's CD-ROM. Figure 4.20 shows Mutt's user interface.

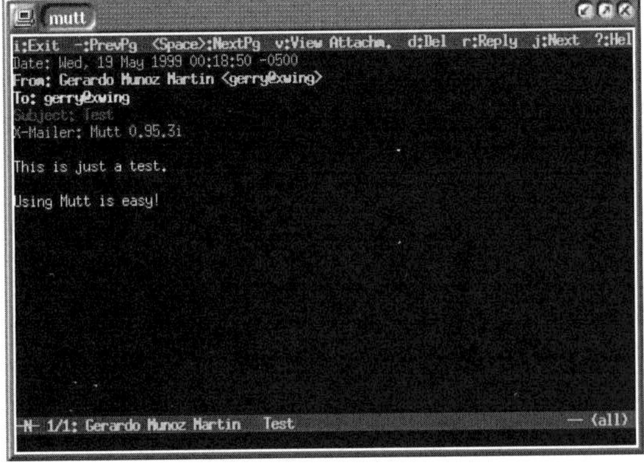

FIGURE 4.20
The Mutt text-based mail reader.

Mutt works based on vi commands (see Chapter 6 for more details on vi). When creating a new mail message, vi commands are used for editing the body of the new mail message. Mutt is a good option for users with Linux boxes without an X server running.

News

These days, newsgroups are very popular, but what's a newsgroup? A newsgroup is a discussion list about a particular subject, consisting of notes written to a central Internet site and redistributed through USENET, a worldwide network of news discussion groups. This section describes some news reader applications.

Netscape Messenger

Netscape Messenger is capable of reading messages to newsgroups using the Network News Transfer Protocol (NNTP). The Messenger user interface is the same for both Mail and News (refer to Figure 4.17). The Preferences menu has a section for setting up newsgroup servers. Figure 4.21 shows the Messenger's Preferences menu page for News.

Messenger can set up different newsgroups servers, a great deal for users who subscribe to various newsgroups.

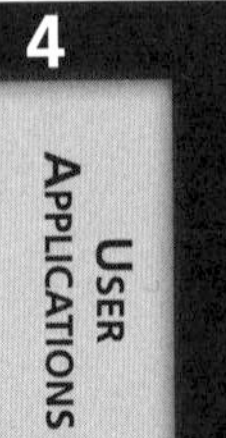

Knews

Knews is an X-based news reader that has an easy-to-understand user interface based on buttons without menus. Every action that Knews can perform is shown on a button, so nonexpert users will find it helpful. Figure 4.22 shows the Knews user interface.

Knews is very simple to use, but it doesn't support different news servers for reading messages. Knews has many limitations, but it is a good option for users who want an easy-to-use news reader. Knews is included on Debian's CD-ROM.

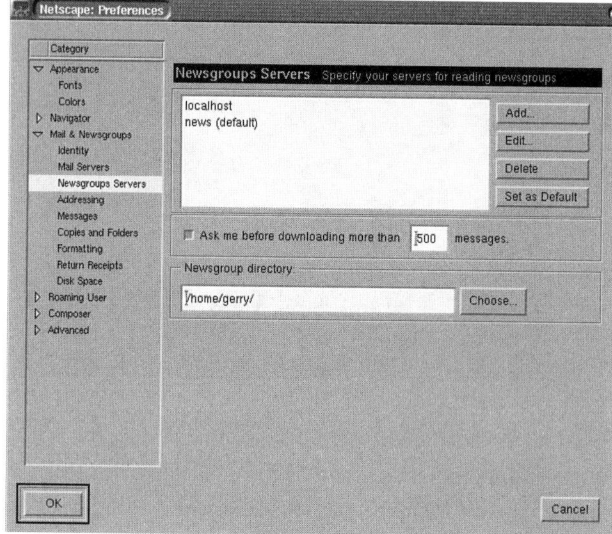

FIGURE 4.21
Netscape Communicator news preferences.

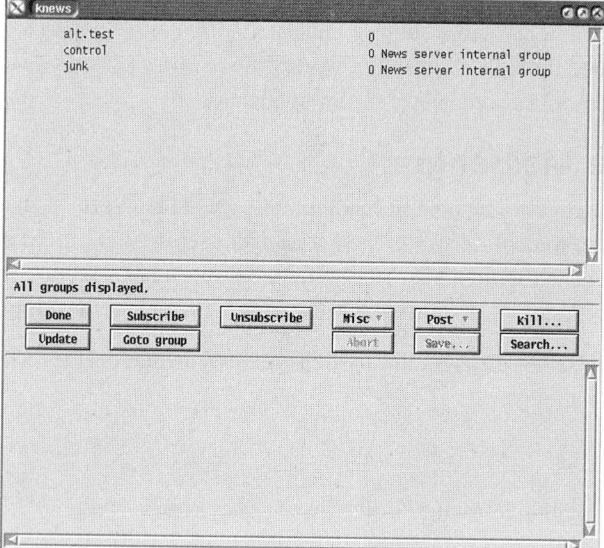

FIGURE 4.22
The Knews news reader.

Web Browsers

A Web browser is an application that provides a way to look at and interact with all the information available on the World Wide Web (WWW). Web browsers use the Hypertext Transfer Protocol (HTTP) to access a Web site. Documents on a Web site are written in

HTML, so the Web browser reads the HTML code from the Web site and interprets it to show the final document that users see on the Web browser main window.

Netscape Navigator

Netscape Navigator is the Web browser included in Netscape Communicator. Navigator is one of the most famous Web browsers used today, and it offers many facilities that make it a very complete application. Figure 4.23 shows the Navigator user interface.

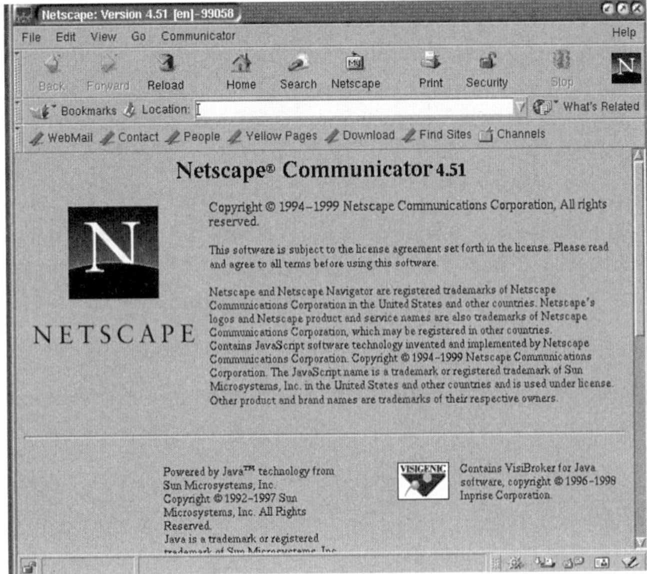

FIGURE 4.23
Netscape Navigator 4.51.

Navigator's user interface is divided into two main sections. The first section is located on top of the window and displays the toolbar and menus. The second section is located below the toolbar and displays the HTML document requested.

Navigator customization is really complete; it enables users to handle font colors and sizes, toolbars location, bookmarks, and so forth. Navigator is a very good option for everyone who wants to get in touch with the WWW.

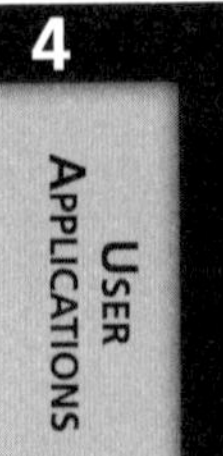

Lynx

Lynx is a text-based Web browser, which mean that you won't be able to see images, videos, or animations through a Web site. Lynx is very useful for those users who have a Linux box without X server running or have a slow connection to the Internet. The functionality of Lynx is pretty good; it can have fast access to Web sites because it doesn't have to load images.

Web browsing with Lynx sometimes becomes a little complicated. The mouse won't work while using Lynx. You must use the keyboard arrows to select a hyperlink, and you are forced to pass over all the hyperlinks until you get the desired one. Even the user interface is text-based; you'll find it useful because the commands are shown at the bottom of the window.

File Transfer

One of the great advantages of being connected to a network is the ability to share resources and files. File transfer is a common task today. People in different cities or even different countries can share information at any time—all they need is a computer with a modem or connection to a network. Following are some of the applications used for file transfer.

FTP

File Transfer Protocol (FTP) provides a simple way of file transferring across a network. UNIX includes it, and some other platforms, such as Macintosh and Windows, have their own versions. Using FTP is easy—let's try an example.

```
#ftp xwing
```

This command uses the `ftp` command to establish an FTP connection to the machine called `xwing`. After you're connected to the remote machine, the following message is displayed:

```
Connected to xwing.
220 xwing FTP server (Version 6.2/OpenBSD/Linux-0.10) ready.
Name (xwing:gerry): gerry
331 Password required for gerry.
Password:
230- Linux xwing 2.0.36 #11 Fri May 14 09:40:21 CDT 1999 i586 unknown
230-
230- Copyright  1993-1999 Software in the Public Interest, and others
230-
230- Most of the programs included with the Debian GNU/Linux system are
230- freely redistributable; the exact distribution terms for each program
230- are described in the individual files in /usr/doc/*/copyright
230-
230- Debian GNU/Linux comes with ABSOLUTELY NO WARRANTY, to the extent
230- permitted by applicable law.
230 User gerry logged in.
Remote system type is UNIX.
Using binary mode to transfer files.
ftp>
```

Now, I want to change to the `docs/` directory and list its contents:

```
ftp> cd docs
250 CWD command successful.
ftp> ls
```

```
200 PORT command successful.
150 Opening ASCII mode data connection for '/bin/ls'.
total 6
drwxrwsr-x   2 gerry    gerry        1024 May 18 17:11 mail
-rw-rw-r--   1 gerry    gerry        4779 May 19 19:08 mail1.html
226 Transfer complete.
ftp>
```

Next, I want to transfer the `mail1.html` file from remote host to local host:

```
ftp> get mail1.html
local: mail1.html remote: mail1.html
200 PORT command successful.
150 Opening BINARY mode data connection for 'mail1.html' (4779 bytes).
226 Transfer complete.
4779 bytes received in 0.0792 secs (59 Kbytes/sec)
ftp>
```

And that's it! I got a copy of the file on my local machine. Now I want to finish the FTP connection to return to my local host:

```
ftp> bye
221 Goodbye.
[gerry@gerry ~]$
```

FTP's command line accepts many UNIX commands, such as `cd`, `ls`, `mkdir`, and so on. You can obtain additional information about FTP by looking at FTP's online documentation (see Chapter 5, "Your Virtual Toolbelt," for more details on online documentation).

wget

`wget` is a utility that retrieves documents through the WWW using HTTP and FTP. This utility works similar to FTP, but `wget` is not interactive, which means it can work in the background even when the user is not logged in. `wget` is capable of analyzing remote server responses, so it can distinguish between correctly and incorrectly retrieved documents. It retries retrieving them as many times as necessary or until a limit of retries is reached.

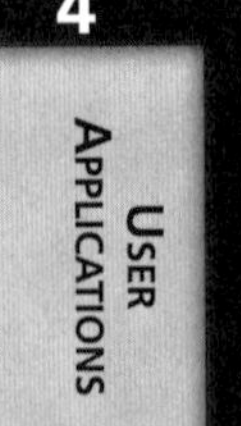

The recursion method used by `wget` makes it easier to copy the entire directory tree from a remote host without the supervision of a user. This means that you can simply execute `wget` and it does all the work for you. When calling the `wget` command, you should specify an URL to retrieve from, the following are valid URL formats:

```
http://host[:port]/path

ftp://host[:port]/path

http://user:password@host/path

ftp://user:password@host/path
```

Let's create an example using wget. Suppose that you want to retrieve all the files contained on a directory called test on the host called xwing. Because this directory is not a public directory that can be accessed using HTTP, we'll use ftp:

```
#wget ftp://user:password@xwing/test/*
```

If no user and password are specified, wget tries to gain access as an anonymous user. You can use a filename instead of the asterisk (*) to retrieve a single file. As a result of the previous command, the following response is displayed:

```
--09:09:51--  ftp://gerry:xxxxxxxx@xwing:21/test/*
           => '.listing'
Connecting to xwing:21... connected!
Logging in as gerry ... Logged in!
==> TYPE I ... done.  ==> CWD test ... done.
==> PORT ... done.    ==> LIST ... done.

    0K ->

09:09:52 (7.62 KB/s) - '.listing' saved [390]

Removed '.listing'.
--09:09:52--  ftp://gerry:xxxxxxxx@xwing:21/test/abstracts.txt
           => 'abstracts.txt'
==> CWD not required.
==> PORT ... done.    ==> RETR abstracts.txt ... done.
Length: 2,161

    0K -> ..                                                   [100%]

09:09:52 (21.32 KB/s) - 'abstracts.txt' saved [2161]

--09:09:52--  ftp://gerry:xxxxxxxx@xwing:21/test/index.txt
           => 'index.txt'
==> CWD not required.
==> PORT ... done.    ==> RETR index.txt ... done.
Length: 328

    0K ->                                                      [100%]

09:09:52 (23.93 KB/s) - 'mail1.html' saved [4779]

--09:09:52--  ftp://gerry:xxxxxxxx@xwing:21/test/resume.txt
           => 'resume.txt'
==> CWD not required.
==> PORT ... done.    ==> RETR resume.txt ... done.
Length: 2,054

    0K -> ..                                                   [100%]

09:09:53 (18.57 KB/s) - 'resume.txt' saved [2054]

#
```

Now you have a copy of all the files contained on the `test` directory on the host `xwing`. You can obtain additional information about `wget` by looking at `wget`'s online documentation (see Chapter 5 for more details on online documentation). `wget` will make your life easy when you're doing file transfer.

SCP

Secure CoPy (SCP) copies files between hosts on a network on a secure mode. It is based on Secure SHell (SSH) for authentication and data transfer, so it asks for passwords or pass phrases whenever it needs them. See Chapter 20, "Conceptual Overview of Security Issues," for more details on SCP.

Remote Access

Remote access offers the capability of logging on a network from a distant location. Generally, this implies a computer, a modem or network adapter, and some remote access software to connect to the network. Remote access refers to the remote computer actually becoming a full-fledged host on the network. Some applications used for remote access are described in the following sections.

telnet

The `telnet` command is used for communication with remote hosts in an interactive way. It works by opening a user session on a remote host and displaying the session on a window on the local host. After you're connected to the remote host, it seems as if you are working on the console of the remote host. Suppose that I want to gain remote access to the host called `xwing`. I call the `telnet` command to connect to the remote host:

```
#telnet xwing
```

The local host sends a request to the remote host and obtains a response:

```
Trying 10.0.2.2...
Connected to xwing.
Escape character is '^]'.
Debian GNU/Linux 2.1 xwing

xwing login: gerry
Password:
Linux xwing 2.0.36 #11 Fri May 14 09:40:21 CDT 1999 i586 unknown

Copyright  1993-1999 Software in the Public Interest, and others

Most of the programs included with the Debian GNU/Linux system are
freely redistributable; the exact distribution terms for each program
are described in the individual files in /usr/doc/*/copyright

Debian GNU/Linux comes with ABSOLUTELY NO WARRANTY, to the extent
permitted by applicable law.
Last login: Thu May 20 08:41:25 on tty1.
No mail.
$
```

Now I'm connected to the remote host, and I'm able to execute any command as if I were on my local host:

```
$ ls
DisplayGrab.ppm      docs                 nsmail
GNUstep              filter1.html         ntscmailandnews.tif
Mail                 filter2.html         rfc0821.txt
Office50             internew.gif         soffice
campus               mail                 wget.txt
cosim.gif            mail1.html           xkarma
debianUnleashed      mail2.html           xwp
$
```

`telnet` is a good option for those who need access to remote hosts and don't need to get all possible security—for example, users who access a remote host in the same subnet segment.

SSH

SSH provides access to remote hosts in a secure way. This means that all the information travels encrypted across the network. See Chapter 20 for more details on SSH.

Linux offers a wide range of network applications; this section only shows the applications that are used with the most common network services. You'll find that Linux almost always has the right tool to help you get the most out of of your network computer.

Multimedia Software

More frequently, computers feature multimedia devices, such as CD-ROMs, sound cards, or video cards. Because Linux has also extended support for those kinds of devices, there are many software applications that enable users to get the maximum from their computers' multimedia devices.

Graphics Editors

Graphics editors are tools that enable users to create or edit images. You might think that UNIX is not the best platform for graphics editing. Take a look at this section, and I'm sure you'll change your mind.

The GIMP, a Photoshop Clone with Some Twists of Its Own

The GIMP (GNU Image Manipulation Program) is a freely distributed program suitable for such tasks as photo retouching, image composition, and image authoring. The GIMP is famous among Linux users, because it is a very powerful tool. The user interface of The GIMP is like most image manipulation programs; it shows a toolbar and a window to display the image you're working with. Figure 4.24 shows The GIMP's user interface.

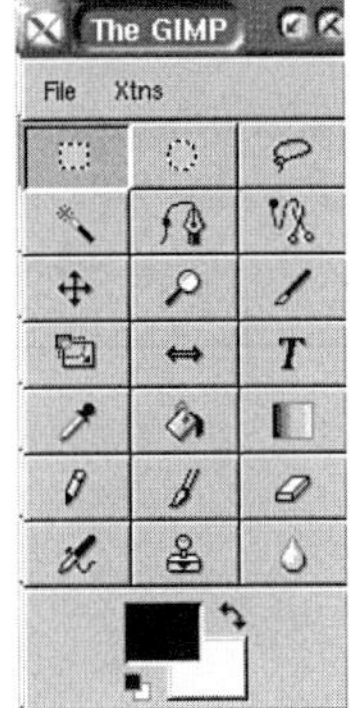

FIGURE 4.24
The GIMP.

The GIMP has many dialog windows that enable users to open or create image windows; modify preferences; and access tool options, brushes, the color palette, patterns, layers, and channels. It also has a gradient editor. When creating an image, you can choose the background type for the image; this is useful when creating images for the WWW.

The GIMP also features a mail tool that enables users to send images via email and access a Web browser. The GIMP supports the following file formats:

- BMP
- HRZ
- JPEG
- PCX
- PNM
- SUNRAS
- TIFF
- XWD
- MPEG
- PIX
- PNG
- PostScript
- Xpm

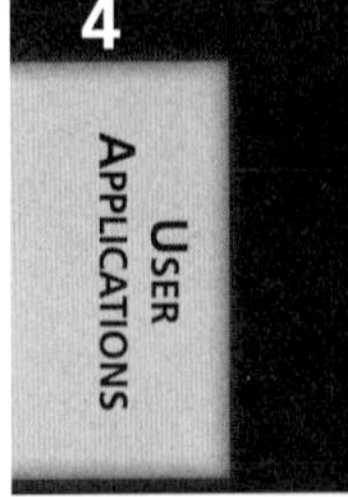

The GIMP is a powerful tool that wins acceptance from Linux users every day. There are many Web sites dedicated to The GIMP; the official one is `http://www.gimp.org`, where you can find the latest news and available plug-ins and resources.

Blender

Blender is a program for modeling, animation, rendering, and postproduction in a 3D format. One advantage to using Blender is that it enables you to save an entire project on a single file, making file management easier. The user interface of Blender looks complicated; there are a lot of buttons around the window. Figure 4.25 shows Blender's user interface.

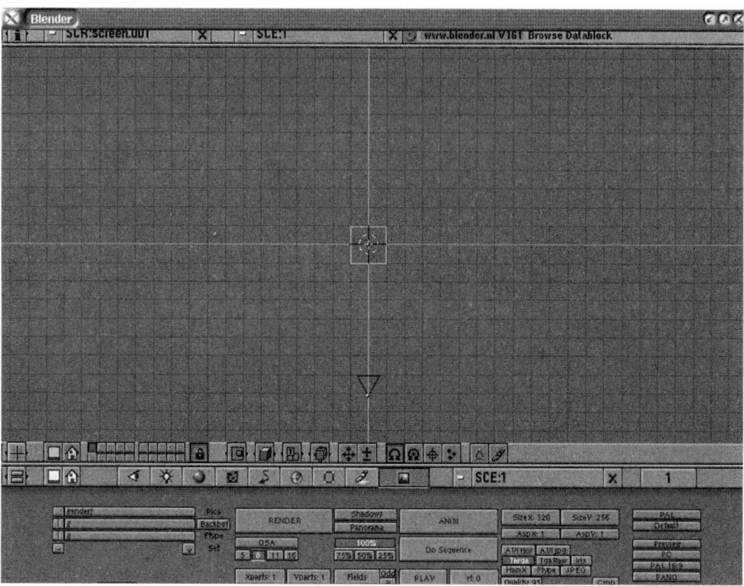

FIGURE 4.25
Blender.

Blender files can be used as libraries for other applications, and there are plug-ins for textures and postproduction. The following file formats are supported by Blender:

- TGA
- JPG
- Iris
- SGI Movie
- IFF
- AVI

Blender is a powerful tool, but understanding the way it works is not easy.

Graphics Viewers and Converters

When dealing with graphics, it's easy to get confused by the large number of image file formats. Different image file formats are used for graphics design than for photography, for example. There are applications that can open image files in different formats, and some of them can even make the conversion from the original format to a different one.

Electric Eyes

Electric Eyes is a graphics viewer application that enables users to handle several images and even convert them to a different image format. The user interface is quite simple; to make the menu appear, just right-click in the Electric Eyes window. Figure 4.26 shows the Electric Eyes main and edit windows.

FIGURE 4.26
Electric Eyes.

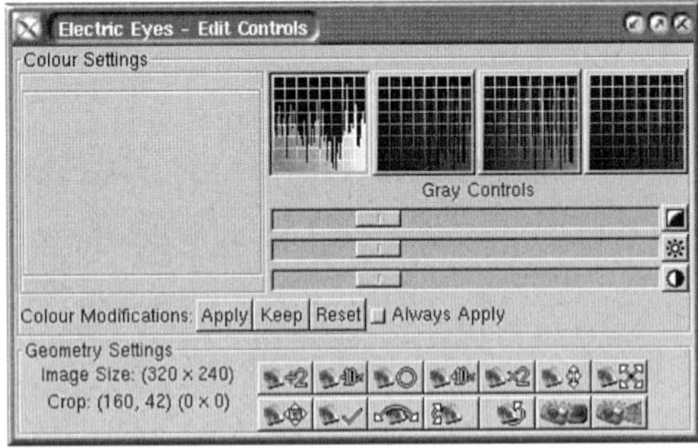

To make the edit menu appear, click the middle button of the mouse over the main window. The following formats are supported by Electric Eyes:

- PPM
- PGM
- JPEG
- PNG
- TIFF

Electric Eyes also includes a screenshots capture, the ability to put images as background on the desktop, and many other features that make it very useful.

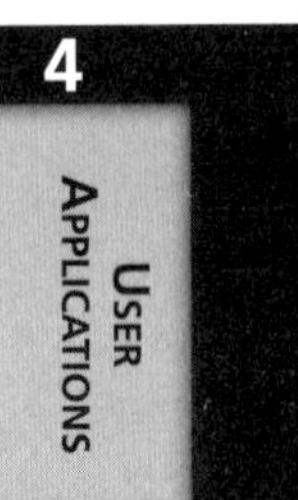

Xanim

Xanim is an X-based program for playing a wide variety of animation, video, and audio formats. Xanim runs mainly on UNIX systems, but there are also versions for other platforms. The following file formats are supported by Xanim:

- AVI
- Quicktime
- SGI
- RMF
- FLI

- IFF
- GIF87 and GIF89
- Dl
- JFIF
- MPEG
- WAV
- AU

Xanim also provides options that enable the user to modify colormaps and playback speed, and many other interesting facilities.

Audio Editing and Encoding Applications

When you acquired a sound card, you certainly expected to get the maximum out of its capabilities. Audio editing and encoding applications provide you with a wide range of tools for getting the most from your card.

Timidity

Timidity is a command-line MIDI file player, along the lines of Playmidi. Timidity is capable of enabling people with ordinary sound cards (of the prewavetable vintage) to enjoy reasonable-quality sound from their MIDI files. Timidity is really good at converting MIDI files to WAVE files.

Grip

Grip is a gtk-based CD player and front-end for CD rippers and MP3 encoders. It enables you to rip entire tracks or pinpoint a section of a track to rip. There is a Grip variant called GCD that is just a CD player; it's a good option for those who aren't interested in track ripping/encoding. Grip's user interface (see Figure 4.27) looks good and works even better.

BladeEnc

BladeEnc is a powerful X-based MP3 encoder that is capable of reading WAV and AIFF file formats. Any number of WAV or AIFF files can be specified on the command line, and you can even use wildcards to specify more than one file at a time.

Audio Players

Many users have a CD-ROM drive in their computer, but only a few of them use it for playing CDs. Actually, there are some applications that provide CD playback running under Linux.

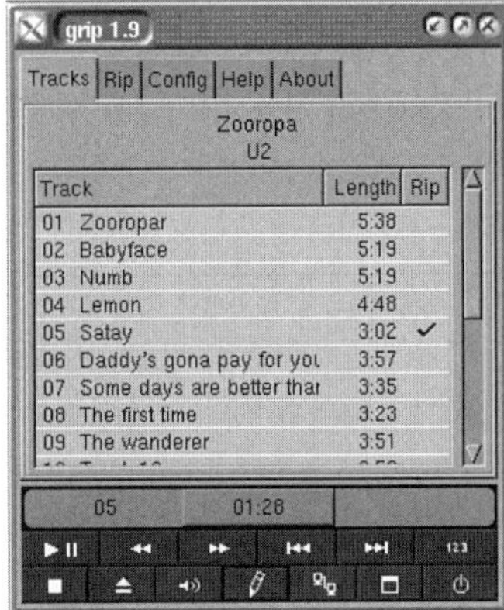

FIGURE 4.27
Grip.

Note

Music is also an intellectual work. International and local laws apply to protect composers against the illegal use of their works. Illegal use includes copy, editing, and public performance without the composer's authorization.

You can find many sites with music content on the Internet. You should be careful about accessing illegal sites—please visit only official musical sites.

FreeAmp

FreeAmp is an audio player that provides a number of the most common features users have come to expect in a clean, easy-to-use interface. It's capable of playing back MPEG 1, MPEG 2, and MPEG 2.5 encoded files; playing songs over the Internet using HTTP; recording a playlist; and so on. Figure 4.28 shows FreeAmp's user interface.

FIGURE 4.28
FreeAmp.

XplayCD

XplayCD is an X-based application for playing audio CDs. It has a database that stores the CD name and its track titles. You can change the play order of tracks, and it has a shuffle mode. The user interface (see Figure 4.29) is easy to understand.

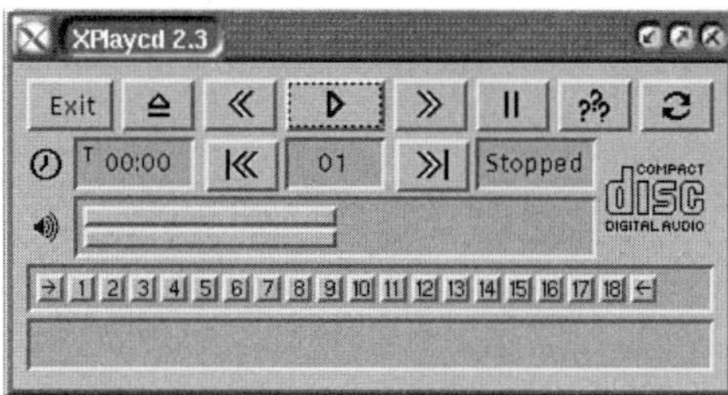

FIGURE 4.29
XplayCD.

Summary

User applications are one of the main reasons why users choose one operating system instead of others. The success that MS Windows has reached in the last few years is mainly due to its user applications and the capabilities they provide to the common user. As you noticed in this chapter, there is almost always a Linux application that will fit your needs. The user applications described in this chapter, along with several other applications, will ensure that users get interested in Linux.

Your Virtual Toolbelt

by Gerry Muñoz

In this Chapter

finished 000920

Many operating systems don't allow users to perform different tasks that would be useful for them, such as getting online information or help, examining files without using an application program, handling archives, and so forth. One of the greatest advantages in a UNIX system is the wide range of built-in commands to make the user's life easier by providing him with tools to perform such tasks. This chapter talks about some of these useful tools.

Online Documentation

Imagine you've just bought a new microwave oven. The first thing you do is unpack it and take a look at the control panel. It looks like the microwave oven that you used to use at your parents' place, so you just plug it in to the power and use it as you used your parent's oven.

Three months later you notice a green button labeled Popcorn that is located on the control panel. You don't know exactly how this button works, so you look for the oven's user manual, and you discover that the oven features a preprogrammed function to prepare microwave popcorn using the mysterious button.

Maybe it sounds a little stupid, but it's very common for users to skip reading the manual. I'm sure that if, when users pressed the button twice, the oven displayed a brief description of the functions of that button, many users would be capable of preparing popcorn from the moment they unpacked their oven. This idea is applied in UNIX. Online documentation provides you with the clear and brief information needed to get the most from your operating system.

man

You use the `man` command to get online help on UNIX systems. It's an interface to the online reference manuals—in other words, it is the system's manual pager. It works by calling `man` with an argument specifying the name of a program, utility, or function. The system looks for a page associated with the argument and displays it. There are different sections where the manual page can be found, and those sections can also be specified as an argument. Table 5.1 shows the section numbers and the pages they contain.

TABLE 5.1 Sections of the Manual Pages

Section	*Type of Pages Contained*
1	Executable commands or shell commands
2	System calls
3	Library calls
4	Special files
5	File formats and conventions

Section	Type of Pages Contained
6	Games
7	Macro packages and conventions
8	System administration commands
9	Kernel routines
n	New
l	Local
p	Public
o	Old

Manual pages are useful when using a command or application for the first time or for finding the argument needed to perform a specific action.

apropos

All the manual pages contain a short description of the purpose of the command apropos. apropos searches for keywords and displays the command name and its brief description. It's useful to use apropos to find out which command could be used for a specific task. For example, suppose you want to know which command or commands are used for encryption. It'll be helpful to use apropos and encryption as keywords:

```
#apropos encryption
```

As a result of the previous command, the following will be displayed:

```
crypt (3)              - password and data encryption
```

To know a brief description of what the mkdir command does, you type the following:

```
#apropos mkdir
```

Then the following information is displayed:

```
mkdir (1)              - make directories
mkdir (2)              - create a directory
```

The keyword argument may contain wildcards using the -w option or regular expressions using the -r option.

info

The hypertext-based tool info is a GNU program for reading documentation. You can navigate within the documentation using the keyboard. The syntax for using info is the following:

```
info [--option_name option_value] menu_item...
```

Table 5.2 shows the available options for `info`.

TABLE 5.2 Options for the `info` Command

Option	*Description*
`-f`	Filename. Specify a particular `info` file to visit.
`-n`	Node name. Specify a particular node to visit in the initial file that `info` loads.
`-o`	Direct output to a specified file instead of starting an interactive `info` session.
`-h`	Produce a relatively brief description of the available `info` options.

For example, while viewing a document with `info`, you can select any of the hyperlinks by locating the cursor on it and pressing the Enter key.

You can go to the next page by pressing the N key, or to the previous page by pressing the P key. Several actions can be performed using `info`, so navigation becomes really easy.

`info` is a good option for users who want to obtain information in a well-organized way. The menus and pages are correctly designed; this makes it easy to find anything within the documentation.

Online documentation is helpful to provide users with information about the available commands. It's also useful to guide users to use the command that best fits their needs.

Managing Files

Each operating system has its own way of managing files. Like any other UNIX system, Debian is command-line–based to handle files. Some users don't like it, but when you become familiar with using commands, you'll really appreciate the powerful features it provides.

Tools for File Management `ls`

The `ls` command lists or displays the contents of a directory. The command without any option shows files in alphabetical order from *a* to *z*, using the following priorities:

1. Numbers
2. A–Z
3. a–z

For example, if you type the command `ls` and no directory name is given, the list of the files on the actual directory is shown:

```
$ ls
campus       docs         internew.gif  wget.txt
cosim.gif    freeamp.gif  rfc0821.txt   xkarma
$
```

Options for Listinf Files

There are some options for use with the `ls` command. The first option is `-l`, which provides a long list referring to each file and shows the following information from left to right:

```
$ ls -l
total 157
lrwxrwxrwx   1 gerry    gerry          9 May 26 18:06 campus -> ../campus
-rw-r--r--   1 gerry    gerry      12617 May 26 17:57 cosim.gif
drwxrwsr-x   2 gerry    gerry       1024 May 26 18:05 docs
-rw-rw-r--   1 gerry    gerry      12283 May 26 17:57 freeamp.gif
-rw-r--r--   1 gerry    gerry       7787 May 26 17:57 internew.gif
-rw-rw-r--   1 gerry    gerry     120432 May 26 18:04 rfc0821.txt
-rw-rw-r--   1 gerry    gerry       1222 May 26 18:04 wget.txt
-rwxrwxr-x   1 gerry    gerry         32 May 26 18:06 xkarma
$
```

- The first column shows the modes. In a moment, you'll see just the first character of this section. The first character is an `l` if the file is a symbolic link, a `d` if this is a directory, and a hyphen (`-`) if it's an ordinary file.
- The second column shows the number of links. If the file is a directory, this shows the number of subdirectories within the directory. If the file is an ordinary file, this shows the number of links pointing to the file.
- The third column shows the owner. It is the user ID of the owner of the file.
- The fourth column shows the group ID of the file.
- The fifth column shows the file size, given in bytes.
- The sixth column shows the date and time of the last modification of the file.
- The seventh column shows the name of the file.

The `-a` (all) option is used to display all the files on the actual directory, including hidden files.

```
$ ls -a
.             .Xauthority   cosim.gif     internew.gif  xkarma
..            .emacs        docs          rfc0821.txt
.B.blend      campus        freeamp.gif   wget.txt
$
```

Option `-F` identifies which files are directories, executable files, or links. Table 5.3 shows characters displayed using option `-F` and their descriptions.

TABLE 5.3 Characters Displayed Using `ls -F` and Their Descriptions

Character	*Description*
/	Directory
*	Executable file
@	Symbolic link

Here is an example of the use of `ls -F`:

```
$ ls -F
campus@       docs/         internew.gif  wget.txt
cosim.gif     freeamp.gif   rfc0821.txt   xkarma*
$
```

The `-R` option lists files recursively; it means list files, directories, and subdirectories. Here's an example:

```
$ ls -R
campus        docs          internew.gif  wget.txt
cosim.gif     freeamp.gif   rfc0821.txt   xkarma

docs:
01new       03newrev    700104.doc  work
02sent      04revised   misc

docs/01new:
04fig01.bmp  04fig05.tif  04fig10.tif  04fig15.tif  04fig20.tif
➥04fig25.tif
04fig01.tif  04fig06.tif  04fig11.tif  04fig16.tif  04fig21.tif
➥04fig26.tif
04fig02.tif  04fig07.tif  04fig12.tif  04fig17.tif  04fig22.tif
➥04fig27.tif
04fig03.tif  04fig08.tif  04fig13.tif  04fig18.tif  04fig23.tif
➥04fig29.tif
04fig04.tif  04fig09.tif  04fig14.tif  04fig19.tif  04fig24.tif
➥images.tar

docs/02sent:

docs/03newrev:

docs/04revised:

docs/misc:
nbi.doc       nbi.rtf       redhat_b.doc  unlcheat.doc

docs/work:
$
```

As you can see, this command returns the list of all the files and directories contained in the actual directory. It also displays the name of all the subdirectories and the files contained in each one of them.

Wildcards can be used while using `ls`. Table 5.4 shows wildcard characters.

TABLE 5.4 Wildcards (Metacharacters)

Character	*Replaces*
*	Zero or more characters
[]	Any character inside
?	Any simple character

Let's look at some examples using wildcards. The following command displays a list containing all the files that begin with the letter c:

```
$ ls c*
campus     cosim.gif
$
```

The following command displays a list containing all the files with the extension `.txt`:

```
$ ls *.txt
rfc0821.txt  wget.txt
$
```

The following command displays the list of all the files that are called `04fig0`*`anysinglecharacter`*`.tif`:

```
$ ls 04fig0?.tif
04fig01.tif  04fig03.tif  04fig05.tif  04fig07.tif  04fig09.tif
04fig02.tif  04fig04.tif  04fig06.tif  04fig08.tif
$
```

The following command displays the list of all the files that are named `04fig01.tif`, `04fig02.tif`, or `04fig03.tif`.

```
$ ls 04fig0[1-3].tif
04fig01.tif  04fig02.tif  04fig03.tif
$
```

All the options mentioned can be used together. You can combine the options you want in the following way:

```
#ls -option1 -option2 -option3...
```

mv

The mv command has two functions; the first is to rename files or directories without altering their information or content, and the second is to move one or more files to a directory. The syntax of the mv command is

```
mv [option] file1 file2
mv [option] directory1 directory2
```

For example, to rename the file called sample.txt to sample2.txt, the following command should be executed:

```
#mv sample.txt sample2.txt
```

To move the file sample2.txt to the ./docs directory, preserving the filename, the following command must be typed:

```
#mv sample2.txt ./docs
```

The -i option means interactive mode. When using the interactive mode, if the second name already exists, a warning message for rewriting the file2 or directory2 will be displayed. For example, if you want to rename the file wget.txt to sample.txt without replacing this file if it already exists, you use the following command:

```
# mv -i wget.txt sample.txt
mv: replace 'sample.txt'? n
#
```

cp

The cp command is used to copy files and directories. The following is the syntax for using this command:

```
cp [options] sourcefile destinationfile
```

Table 5.5 shows the options allowed by the cp command:

TABLE 5.5 Options for the cp Command

Option	*Action*
-p	Preserve the last modification time and modes of the source file.
-r	Copy directories, including subdirectories and files contained in the source directory.
-i	Interactive mode. A message will be displayed warning to rewrite the file or directory, if it already exists.

Let's create some examples using cp. When listing my actual directory, the following is displayed:

```
# ls -l
total 159
lrwxrwxrwx   1 gerry    gerry          9 May 26 18:06 campus -> ../campus
-rw-r--r--   1 gerry    gerry      12617 May 26 17:57 cosim.gif
drwxrwsr-x   8 gerry    gerry       1024 May 29 11:06 docs
-rw-rw-r--   1 gerry    gerry      12283 May 26 17:57 freeamp.gif
-rw-r--r--   1 gerry    gerry       7787 May 26 17:57 internew.gif
-rw-rw-r--   1 gerry    gerry     120432 May 26 18:04 rfc0821.txt
drwxrwsr-x   2 gerry    gerry       1024 May 29 11:13 sample
drwxrwsr-x   2 gerry    gerry       1024 May 29 11:06 test
-rw-rw-r--   1 gerry    gerry       1222 May 29 00:08 wget.txt
-rwxrwxr-x   1 gerry    gerry         32 May 26 18:06 xkarma
#
```

If you want to copy the file called `rfc0821.txt` to a new file called `SMTP.txt`, use this:

```
#cp rfc0821.txt SMTP.txt
```

Now, let's list the actual directory again:

```
# ls -l
total 278
-rw-rw-r--   1 gerry    gerry     120432 May 29 11:19 SMTP.txt
lrwxrwxrwx   1 gerry    gerry          9 May 26 18:06 campus -> ../campus
-rw-r--r--   1 gerry    gerry      12617 May 26 17:57 cosim.gif
drwxrwsr-x   8 gerry    gerry       1024 May 29 11:06 docs
-rw-rw-r--   1 gerry    gerry      12283 May 26 17:57 freeamp.gif
-rw-r--r--   1 gerry    gerry       7787 May 26 17:57 internew.gif
-rw-rw-r--   1 gerry    gerry     120432 May 26 18:04 rfc0821.txt
drwxrwsr-x   2 gerry    gerry       1024 May 29 11:13 sample
drwxrwsr-x   2 gerry    gerry       1024 May 29 11:06 test
-rw-rw-r--   1 gerry    gerry       1222 May 29 00:08 wget.txt
-rwxrwxr-x   1 gerry    gerry         32 May 26 18:06 xkarma
#
```

As you can see, the new file `SMTP.txt` has the same size as the file `rfc0821.txt`, because both files are the same but with different names and modification dates. Now, let's make a copy of the same file but preserve the modification date. The new file is called `SMTP2.txt`:

```
#cp -p rfc0821.txt SMTP2.txt
```

When listing the directory, the following is shown:

```
# ls -l
total 397
-rw-rw-r--   1 gerry    gerry     120432 May 29 11:19 SMTP.txt
-rw-rw-r--   1 gerry    gerry     120432 May 26 18:04 SMTP2.txt
lrwxrwxrwx   1 gerry    gerry          9 May 26 18:06 campus -> ../campus
-rw-r--r--   1 gerry    gerry      12617 May 26 17:57 cosim.gif
drwxrwsr-x   8 gerry    gerry       1024 May 29 11:06 docs
-rw-rw-r--   1 gerry    gerry      12283 May 26 17:57 freeamp.gif
-rw-r--r--   1 gerry    gerry       7787 May 26 17:57 internew.gif
-rw-rw-r--   1 gerry    gerry     120432 May 26 18:04 rfc0821.txt
```

```
drwxrwsr-x   2 gerry    gerry       1024 May 29 11:13 sample
drwxrwsr-x   2 gerry    gerry       1024 May 29 11:06 test
-rw-rw-r--   1 gerry    gerry       1222 May 29 00:08 wget.txt
-rwxrwxr-x   1 gerry    gerry         32 May 26 18:06 xkarma
#
```

The files `rfc0821.txt` and `SMTP2.txt` are exactly the same but with different names.

It is possible to copy several files to a single destination directory. For example, to copy the files `cosim.gif`, `rfc0821.txt`, and `xkarma` to the directory `./test`, the following command should be executed:

```
#cp cosim.gif rfc0821.txt xkarma ./test
```

When listing the `./test` directory, the following is shown:

```
#ls ./test
cosim.gif    rfc0821.txt  xkarma
#
```

Suppose you want to copy the file `rfc0821.txt` to the directory `./test`, but you're not sure whether you did it already and you don't want to overwrite the file. The interactive mode is helpful at this moment:

```
# cp -i rfc0821.txt ./test/
cp: overwrite `./test/rfc0821.txt'? n
#
```

If you want to copy all the files and subdirectories contained in the directory `./test` to the directory `./sample`, you use the following command:

```
#cp .-r ./test/* ./sample
```

The directory `./sample` now contains the following files:

```
# ls -l ./sample
total 134
-rw-r--r--   1 gerry    gerry      12617 May 29 14:19 cosim.gif
-rw-rw-r--   1 gerry    gerry     120432 May 29 14:19 rfc0821.txt
-rwxrwxr-x   1 gerry    gerry         32 May 29 14:19 xkarma
#
```

Use the following to copy the entire directory `./test` into the directory `./sample`, preserving the directory tree:

```
#cp -r ./test ./sample
```

Listing the contents on the `./sample` directory, you notice that there is a copy of the `test` directory:

```
# ls -l ./sample/
total 1
drwxrwsr-x   2 gerry    gerry       1024 May 29 14:22 test
#
```

find

The function of the `find` command is to look for a specific file in a directory. This command is useful to find any file that has a location you're unsure of. The following is the syntax for this command:

```
find directory_name option file_name -print
```

Table 5.6 shows the options for the `find` command.

TABLE 5.6 Options for the `find` Command

Option	*Action*
`-name` *`filename`*	Search for a specified file.
`-type` *`filetype`*	Search for a specific type of file. Example: `l` for links, `d` for directories.
`-group` *`groupname`*	Search for files with the specified group name.
`-newer` *`filename`*	Search and display the file that has been modified after the specified file.
`-user` *`username`*	Search and display files owned by a specified user.
`-print`	Print on the display the result of the search.

Let's create some examples. The following command searches for the file named `rfc0821.txt`. The period (`.`) indicates that the search must be performed within the current directory and its subdirectories:

```
# find . -name rfc0821.txt -print
../rfc0821.txt
../test/rfc0821.txt
../sample/test/rfc0821.txt
#
```

The result obtained from executing the previous command indicates that there are three files named `rfc0821.txt` in the actual directory and its subdirectories. The following command searches for the files in the `/tmp` directory that are owned by user `gerry`:

```
# find /tmp -user gerry -print
/tmp/ssh-gerry
/tmp/ssh-gerry/agent-socket-223
/tmp/SMTP.txt
/tmp/SMTP2.txt
/tmp/rfc0821.txt
/tmp/wget.txt
#
```

The following command searches for all the directories contained under the actual directory:

```
# find . -type d -print
..
../docs
../docs/01new
../docs/02sent
../docs/03newrev
../docs/04revised
../docs/misc
../docs/work
../test
../sample
../sample/test
#
```

Users will find that Linux has powerful and easy-to-use tools for file management that will be helpful in their daily activities.

Examining Files

When you list the contents of a directory, you may find that there are a lot of files that you didn't know existed. When this happens, you'll be grateful for a UNIX system. UNIX provides many tools to examine files in different ways.

cat

The `cat` command concatenates and displays the information of the specified file or files. The following is the syntax for this command:

```
cat [options] file1 file2 ...
```

Table 5.7 shows options for the `cat` command.

TABLE 5.7 Options for the `cat` Command

Option	*Action*
`-b`	Enumerate file rows, omitting white lines.
`-ev`	Display a string character at the end of each row without omitting white lines and add the string character at the beginning of those rows. Also display the nonprintable characters.
`-n`	Enumerate all rows on file without omitting white lines.

Let's create some examples using `cat`. The following command displays the information contained in the file called `pcmcia.txt`:

```
#cat pcmcia.txt
The following vendors have assisted in the development of the Linux
PCMCIA driver package by contributing hardware and/or technical
documentation about their products.  It could be inferred that
```

```
since these vendors support Linux development and have provided
technical help, that their cards are likely to be better supported
under Linux.

        3Com/Megahertz  [ ethernet, modem, and multifunction cards ]
        Intel           [ linear flash memory cards ]
        Linksys         [ ethernet and multifunction cards ]
        Ositech         [ ethernet/modem combo cards ]
        Sandisk         [ ata/ide flash cards ]
#
```

Now, let's enumerate the rows on the same file, `pcmcia.txt`:

```
#cat -n pcmcia.txt
     1  The following vendors have assisted in the development of the
Linux PCMCIA driver package by contributing hardware and/or technical
documentation about their products.  It could be inferred that since
these vendors support Linux development and have provided technical
help, that their cards are likely to be better supported under Linux.
     2
     3          3Com/Megahertz  [ ethernet, modem, and multifunction
             ➥cards ]
     4          Intel           [ linear flash memory cards ]
     5          Linksys         [ ethernet and multifunction cards ]
     6          Ositech         [ ethernet/modem combo cards ]
     7          Sandisk         [ ata/ide flash cards ]
     8
```

As you can see, the entire first paragraph is contained in a single line. The following command enumerates the rows omitting white lines:

```
#cat -b pcmcia.txt
     1  The following vendors have assisted in the development of the
Linux PCMCIA driver package by contributing hardware and/or technical
documentation about their products.  It could be inferred that since
these vendors support Linux development and have provided technical
help, that their cards are likely to be better supported under Linux.

     2          3Com/Megahertz  [ ethernet, modem, and multifunction cards ]
     3          Intel           [ linear flash memory cards ]
     4          Linksys         [ ethernet and multifunction cards ]
     5          Ositech         [ ethernet/modem combo cards ]
     6          Sandisk         [ ata/ide flash cards ]

#
```

Let's put a string character at the end of each row. It's useful to mark rows:

```
# cat -ev pcmcia.txt
The following vendors have assisted in the development of the Linux ><
<>PCMCIA driver package by contributing hardware and/or technical ><
<>documentation about their products.  It could be inferred that since ><
<>these vendors support Linux development and have provided technical ><
<>help, that their cards are likely to be better supported under Linux.$
```

```
$
        3Com/Megahertz  [ ethernet, modem, and multifunction cards ]$
        Intel           [ linear flash memory cards ]$
        Linksys         [ ethernet and multifunction cards ]$
        Ositech         [ ethernet/modem combo cards ]$
        Sandisk         [ ata/ide flash cards ]$
#
```

Next, let's take a look into the contents of the file called `prepaid.txt`:

```
#cat prepaid.txt
This card expires six months from the date of its first use. Payphone ><
<>calls may be subject to additional fees. Service fee of 99 cents per ><
<>month and applicable taxes apply after first call.

#
```

The following command concatenates and displays the content of the files `pcmcia.txt` and `prepaid.txt`:

```
#cat pcmcia.txt prepaid.txt
The following vendors have assisted in the development of the Linux ><
<>PCMCIA driver package by contributing hardware and/or technical ><
<>documentation about their products.  It could be inferred that since ><
<>these vendors support Linux development and have provided technical ><
<>help, that their cards are likely to be better supported under Linux.

        3Com/Megahertz  [ ethernet, modem, and multifunction cards ]
        Intel           [ linear flash memory cards ]
        Linksys         [ ethernet and multifunction cards ]
        Ositech         [ ethernet/modem combo cards ]
        Sandisk         [ ata/ide flash cards ]

This card expires six months from the date of its first use. Payphone ><
<>calls may be subject to additional fees. Service fee of 99 cents per ><
<>month and applicable taxes apply after first call.

#
```

more/less Pagers

The `more` command displays the information of each specified file, paginating according to the size of the window and showing at the bottom of the window a status of the percentage of the file content reached while displayed. The following is the syntax for the `more` command:

```
more [-number_of_rows] [+row_number] file1 file2 ...
```

number_of_rows displays the information according to the specified block size.

row_number enables you to indicate a specific row to be the beginning of the display.

When several filenames are given as an argument, each file is displayed after the previous file display finishes. For example, the following command displays the contents of the file `pcmcia.txt`, followed by the contents of the file `prepaid.txt`:

```
# more pcmcia.txt prepaid.txt
::::::::::::::
pcmcia.txt
::::::::::::::
The following vendors have assisted in the development of the Linux
➥PCMCIA driver package by contributing hardware and/or technical documentation
about <
➥their products.  It could be inferred that since these vendors support Linux
➥development and have provided technical help, that their cards are likely to be
➥better supported under Linux.
        3Com/Megahertz  [ ethernet, modem, and multifunction cards ]
        Intel           [ linear flash memory cards ]
        Linksys         [ ethernet and multifunction cards ]
        Ositech         [ ethernet/modem combo cards ]
        Sandisk         [ ata/ide flash cards ]

::::::::::::::
prepaid.txt
::::::::::::::
This card expires six months from the date of its first use. Payphone
➥calls maybe subject to additional fees. Service fee of 99 cents per month and
➥applicable taxes apply after first call.

#
```

As you can see, both files' contents were displayed and the filename was displayed at the top of the character block.

The `less` command is a program similar to `more` but with some additional features. Several files can be opened at the same time, so it's possible to navigate from one file to the previous or next file. Some vi-like commands are allowed while using `less` (see Chapter 6, "Advanced Text Editing," for more details on vi). Table 5.8 shows some commands for using `less`.

TABLE 5.8 Commands for `less`

Command	*Action*
/	Search forward in the file for lines containing the pattern.
n	Repeat previous search forward.

continues

TABLE 5.8 continued

Command	*Action*
`N`	Repeat previous search backward.
`:e filename`	Examine a new file.
`:n`	Examine the next file.
`:p`	Examine the previous file.
`:x`	Examine the first file in command-line list.

head

The `head` command displays the first *n* rows of the specified files. This command is useful, for example, for checking the first lines of a log file to know the date it begins. The default number of rows is 10. The syntax for the `head` command is the following:

```
head [-number_of_rows] filename
```

The following command displays the first 10 rows of the file called `pcmcia.txt`:

```
#head pcmcia.txt
                Linux PCMCIA Supported Device List

                Last updated: 1998/08/20 23:01:39

The following cards are known to work in at least one actual system.
Other cards may also work -- if you can get a card to work that is n
on this list, please let me know.  This list is complete to the best
of my knowledge.

        -- David Hinds <dhinds@hyper.stanford.edu>
#
```

It's possible to specify the number of rows to be displayed at a time. The following command displays the first 5 rows of the file `pcmcia.txt`:

```
# head -5 pcmcia.txt
                Linux PCMCIA Supported Device List

                Last updated: 1998/08/20 23:01:39

The following cards are known to work in at least one actual system.
#
```

tail

The `tail` command displays the last rows of a file; by default, the number of rows displayed is 10. This command is useful, for example, for checking the last lines of a log file to know the last event recorded on the log. The syntax for `tail` is the following:

```
tail +row_number -number_of_rows filename
```

row_number is the number of the first row to be displayed.

number_of_rows is the number of rows to be displayed at a time.

Let's create some examples. First, we display the last 10 rows of the file `pcmcia.txt`:

```
bash-2.01$ tail pcmcia.txt
documentation about their products.  It could be inferred that since
these vendors support Linux development and have provided technical
help, that their cards are likely to be better supported under Linux.

        3Com/Megahertz  [ ethernet, modem, and multifunction cards ]
        Intel           [ linear flash memory cards ]
        Linksys         [ ethernet and multifunction cards ]
        Ositech         [ ethernet/modem combo cards ]
        Sandisk         [ ata/ide flash cards ]

#
```

Now, we display the file `pcmcia.txt` starting from line 335 to the end of file:

```
# tail +335 ../pcmcia.txt
        Panasonic KXL-D720, KXL-D745
        SMC 8016 EliteCard
        Telxon/Aironet wireless adapters
        Xircom CE II Ethernet/Modem
        Xircom CE-10BT Ethernet

The following vendors have assisted in the development of the Linux
PCMCIA driver package by contributing hardware and/or technical
documentation about their products.  It could be inferred that since
these vendors support Linux development and have provided technical
help, that their cards are likely to be better supported under Linux.

        3Com/Megahertz  [ ethernet, modem, and multifunction cards ]
        Intel           [ linear flash memory cards ]
        Linksys         [ ethernet and multifunction cards ]
        Ositech         [ ethernet/modem combo cards ]
        Sandisk         [ ata/ide flash cards ]

#
```

Finally, let's display the last 5 rows of the file `pcmcia.txt`:

```
# tail -5 ../pcmcia.txt
        Intel           [ linear flash memory cards ]
        Linksys         [ ethernet and multifunction cards ]
        Ositech         [ ethernet/modem combo cards ]
        Sandisk         [ ata/ide flash cards ]

#
```

file

The `file` command determines the type of the files by examining file content. There are different existing file types; the `file` command is able to identify the following types:

- Data
- Text in English
- Directory
- ASCII text
- Library
- Executable shell script

The following is the syntax for the `file` command:

```
file [options] name_file
```

`name_file` is a text file that contains the names of the files to be analyzed. There must be only one filename per line of the *`name_file`*. Table 5.9 shows options for using `file`.

TABLE 5.9 Options for the `file` Command

Option	*Action*
`-f`	Read the names of the files to be examined from *`name_file`* before the argument list.
`-z`	Look up in compressed files.
`-b`	Do not print the filename to output lines.

Let's create some examples. The following command verifies the file called `rfc0821.txt` and displays its type:

```
#file rfc0821.txt
rfc0821.txt: English text
#
```

Now, let's use the option `-f`. I've already created a *`name_file`* called `files_to_analyze` that contains the filenames `phantom.gif`, `pcmcia.txt`, `xkarma`, and `xwp`. You can create your own *`name_file`* using vi or any other text editor (see Chapter 6 for more details on vi). The following command checks the file type for the files contained in `files_to_analyze`:

```
#file -f files_to_analyze
phantom.gif: GIF image data, version 87a, 512 x 287,
pcmcia.txt:  English text
xkarma:      ASCII text
xwp:         symbolic link to /software/wp8/wpbin/xwp
#
```

Finally, the following command prints the file types of the files contained in `files_to_analyze`, omitting the filename:

```
# file -b -f files_to_analyze
GIF image data, version 87a, 512 x 287,
English text
ASCII text
symbolic link to /software/wp8/wpbin/xwp
#
```

diff

The `diff` command compares two files and indicates the differences between them. Table 5.10 shows the possible characters to be returned when executing `diff`.

TABLE 5.10 Characters Returned by `diff`

Character	*Meaning*
a	Add
c	Change
d	Delete
<	Rows belonging to the first file
>	Rows belonging to the second file
1,n	From row 1 to n
n	The n row
---	End of the first file and beginning of the second one

Let's check the differences between `file1` and `file2`, and what needs to be done to make both files the same:

```
# diff file1 file2
```

The following is the result of the previous command and its interpretation:

```
1,3c1,3
```

From row 1 to 3, the words change.

```
< bullet
< colony
< fly
```

From `file1` `bullet`, `colony`, and `fly`.

```
---
```

The end of `file1` and beginning of `file2`.

```
> plane
> colonel
> flying
```

From `file2` `plane`, `colonel`, and `flying`.

```
5a6
```

On the fifth row of `file1`, add the sixth row.

```
> vehicle
```

The word `vehicle` from `file2`, which is not included on `file1`.

cmp

`cmp` stands for *compare*. This command briefly indicates whether two files are different. The following is the syntax for `cmp`:

```
cmp filename1 filename2
```

Table 5.11 shows the options for `cmp`.

TABLE 5.11 Options for the `cmp` Command

Option	*Action*
`-s`	Silent. Display nothing even if the files are different, but it is possible to evaluate the return values: `0` = equal files, `1` = different files, and `2` = system error or missing arguments.
`-l`	Print the byte number (in decimal) and the differing bytes (in octal) for each difference between both files.

Let's create some examples:

```
# cmp  file1 file2
file1 file2 differ: char 1, line 1
#
```

The result of the previous command indicates that `file1` differs from `file2` in the first row. The system stops here and doesn't check whether there are other differences.

```
# cmp -s file1 file1
#
```

Because this command uses the `-s` option, after executing the command nothing else is displayed. The following is the result of the previous command:

```
# echo $?
0
#
```

The return value is `0`, which indicates both files are equal. Next, let's use the same command but with different files:

```
# cmp -s file1 file2
# echo $?
1
#
```

This time, the return value is `1`, which indicates that both files are different. Finally, let's use the `-l` option:

```
# cmp -l file1 file2
     1 142 160
     2 165 154
     3 154 141
     4 154 156
     6 164  12
     7  12 143
     8 143 157
     9 157 154
    10 154 157
    11 157 156
    12 156 145
    13 171 154
    18  12 151
    19 163 156
    20 164 147
    21 141  12
    22 162 163
    24  12 141
    25 163 162
    27 162  12
    28 157 163
    29 156 164
    30 147 162
    31  12 157
cmp: EOF on file1
#
```

The previous command shows all the differences between both files, indicating byte number in decimal and differing bytes in octal.

Linux provides several tools for file examination. Users will find these commands useful whenever they need to examine a file for a specific purpose.

Manipulating Data

Sometimes the information is not in the optimum format. For example, suppose you have a file containing the names, ages, and phone numbers of your employees, but you just care about the names and phone numbers. UNIX provides powerful tools to manipulate and modify data so the user is able to decide where, when, and how the information will be used. This section presents some of the most useful tools to manipulate data.

cut

The `cut` command is used to take out fields of a file. The following is the syntax for `cut`:

```
cut [options] filename
```

Table 5.12 shows the options for `cut`.

TABLE 5.12 Options for the `cut` Command

Option	*Action*
`-c`*RANGE*	Cut out the characters specified in *RANGE*.
`-d`*CHARACTER*	Specify that the filed delimiter is *CHARACTER*.
`-f`*RANGE*	Cut out the fields in *RANGE*.

RANGE could be in any of the following formats:

number`-` means cut out all from the character number specified to the end of the line.

number1`-`*number2* means cut out all from the first specified character number to the second one.

number1`,`*number2* means cut out the characters specified in *number1* and *number2*.

Now is a good time for you to have a little practice on using `cut`. The following command cuts the first character of every line of the file `players.txt`:

```
# cut -c1 players.txt
L
A
C
L
R
F
R
#
```

The following command cuts the characters `1` to `14` and `24` to `30` of every line in the file:

```
# cut -c1-14,24-30 players.txt
Luis Garcia:         Guadala
Alberto Garcia:     Mexi
Carlos Pavon:        Celaya
Luis Hernandez:      Mont
Ramon Ramirez:      Mexic
Felix Fernande:      Cela
Rafael Garcia:       Toluc
#
```

The following command cuts the second field of every line of the file:

```
# cut -d: -f2 players.txt
                Chivas
                America
                Celaya
                Tigres
                America
                Celaya
                Toluca
#
```

paste

The `paste` command prints lines consisting of sequentially corresponding lines of each given file, separated by tabs, terminated by a new line. The following is the syntax for `paste`:

```
paste [-s] [-d delimiter] file1 [file2 ... fileN]
```

Assume you've already created the files `dates.txt` and `events.txt`. The mentioned files contain the following information:

```
# cat dates.txt
1492
1910
1945
1969
# cat events.txt
Discovery of America.
Mexican revolution.
End of World War II.
Man walks on the moon.
```

The following command merges the contents of both files:

```
# paste dates.txt events.txt
1492    Discovery of America.
1910    Mexican revolution.
1945    End of World War II.
1969    Man walks on the moon.
#
```

It is possible to specify a delimiter character to be used instead of the tabs. The option `-d` is used to specify the delimiter character. The following command merges the files `dates.txt` and `events.txt`, using a colon (:) character to separate the contents of both files:

```
# paste -d: dates.txt events.txt
1492:Discovery of America.
1910:Mexican revolution.
1945:End of World War II.
1969:Man walks on the moon.
#
```

The option -s pastes the lines of one file at a time rather than one line from each file. Here's an example:

```
# paste -s events.txt
Discovery of America.  Mexican revolution.    End of World War II.    Man
walks on the moon.
#
```

sed

sed is a stream editor designed for noninteractive editing. It's a useful tool for using in shell scripts to modify files. sed by itself won't modify files; it's necessary to do that by other methods combined with sed—for example, a command shell. The following is the syntax for sed:

```
sed [commands] filename
```

sed uses vi-like commands (see Chapter 6 for more information on vi) and regular expressions (see Chapter 9, "Regular Expressions," for more information on regular expressions) to modify files. Let's look at an example. Assume that you've already created a file called test.txt containing the following information:

```
first
second
third
forth
fifth
```

The following command substitutes the word fourth for forth:

```
# sed 's/forth/fourth/g' test.txt
first
second
third
fourth
fifth
#
```

The character s used in the command indicates that a substitution will take effect, and the character g indicates that the substitution will be global (on the entire file).

grep

grep stands for *global regular expression and print*. This command is used to search for character strings contained within a specific file. If the search pattern is found, it's displayed with the line number of the file. The following is the syntax for grep:

```
grep [options] string filename
```

Table 5.13 shows options for grep.

TABLE 5.13 Options for the grep Command

Option	*Action*
`-c`	Display the number of rows in which the string appears in the file.
`-i`	Not case-sensitive.
`-n`	Display the row number at the beginning of the corresponding line of the file.
`-v`	Inverse search. Display all the lines of the file excluding those containing the string.

Before looking at some examples using `grep`, let's create a file called `SMTP.txt` containing the following text:

```
The objective of Simple Mail Transfer Protocol (SMTP) is to transfer mail
➥reliably and efficiently.
SMTP is independent of the particular transmission subsystem and requires
➥only a reliable ordered data stream channel.
An important feature of Smtp is its capability of relaying mail across
➥transport service environments.
```

First, search for the string `SMTP` on the specified file:

```
# grep SMTP SMTP.txt
   The objective of Simple Mail Transfer Protocol (SMTP) is to transfer
   SMTP is independent of the particular transmission subsystem and
#
```

Now, search the same string but ignore case:

```
# grep -i SMTP SMTP.txt
   The objective of Simple Mail Transfer Protocol (SMTP) is to transfer
   SMTP is independent of the particular transmission subsystem and
   An important feature of Smtp is its capability of relaying mail across
#
```

So far, we have displayed the lines of the file containing the string, but it's possible to display just the number of rows containing the string. The following command displays the number of rows that exactly match the string:

```
# grep -c SMTP SMTP.txt
2
#
```

The following command displays the number of rows that match the string, ignoring the case:

```
# grep -ic SMTP SMTP.txt
3
#
```

The following command enumerates and displays the rows containing the string ignoring the case:

```
# grep -in smtp SMTP.txt
1:   The objective of Simple Mail Transfer Protocol (SMTP) is to transfer
4:   SMTP is independent of the particular transmission subsystem and
7:   An important feature of Smtp is its capability of relaying mail across
#
```

The following command displays all the rows of the file, excluding those that contain the string:

```
# grep -v SMTP SMTP.txt
   mail reliably and efficiently.

   requires only a reliable ordered data stream channel.

   An important feature of Smtp is its capability of relaying mail across
   transport service environments.
#
```

It is also possible to search for sentences within a file. Here's an example:

```
# grep "Simple Mail" SMTP.txt
   The objective of Simple Mail Transfer Protocol (SMTP) is to transfer
#
```

As you could see, data manipulation is helpful to change the information's format to better fit users' needs. Linux provides several useful tools for manipulating data.

Handling Archives and Compression

Sometimes you'll find that there are too many files stored on a directory to be easily moved or copied to another directory, or too many to make backups of your information. Archiving and file compression are two different methods that are helpful to store, move, or copy many files. This section demonstrates that archiving and file compression can save storage space, time, and headaches.

tar

The `tar` command is a helpful utility to archive files, and it's standard on UNIX systems. The use of `tar` is quite simple but powerful. The following is the syntax for `tar`:

```
tar forced_options[options] archivename filename1 [filename2,...]
tar forced_options[options] archivename directory1 [directory2,...]
```

One of the forced options must be used when executing `tar`. Table 5.14 shows forced options for `tar`.

TABLE 5.14 Forced Options for the `tar` Command

Option	*Action*
`-A`	Append `tar` files to an archive.
`-c`	Create a new archive.
`-d`	Find differences between archives and file system.
`-delete`	Delete from the archive.
`-r`	Append files to the end of an archive.
`-t`	List the contents of an archive.
`-u`	Append files that are newer than the copy stored in archive.
`-x`	Extract files from an archive.

There are some additional options that can be used with `tar`. Table 5.15 shows options for `tar`.

TABLE 5.15 Options for the `tar` Command

Option	*Action*
`-b`	Block size given in N×512 bytes. The default block size is N = 20.
`-C DIR`	Change to directory `DIR`.
`-f`	Use archive file or device.
`-h`	Dump the real files that the symbolic links point to.
`-k`	Do not overwrite existing files.
`-N DATE`	Archive only files newer than `DATE`.
`-p`	Preserve the same permissions to the files.
`-P`	Preserve absolute paths.
`--remove-files`	Remove files after adding them to the archive.
`--same-owner`	Extract files preserving the ownership.
`-v`	Verbosely list files processed.
`-w`	Ask for confirmation for every action.
`--exclude FILE`	Exclude the file `FILE` from the archive.

Let's create some examples using `tar`. The following command creates an archive called `test.tar` of all the files contained on the directory `test`:

```
# tar -cf test.tar test
```

If the option `-v` (verbose) is added to the previous command, a list of the dumped files is shown during the creation of the archive:

```
# tar -cvf test.tar test
test/
test/cosim.gif
test/rfc0821.txt
test/xkarma
#
```

The following command lists the files contained on the archive `test.tar`:

```
# tar -tvf test.tar
drwxrwsr-x gerry/gerry       0 1999-05-29 11:06 test/
-rw-r--r-- gerry/gerry   12617 1999-05-29 11:06 test/cosim.gif
-rw-rw-r-- gerry/gerry  120432 1999-05-29 11:06 test/rfc0821.txt
-rwxrwxr-x gerry/gerry      32 1999-05-29 11:06 test/xkarma
#
```

Now, let's extract the files contained on the recently created archive into the directory `stuff`:

```
# tar -xC stuff -f test.tar
# cd stuff/
# ls -R
test

test:
cosim.gif    rfc0821.txt  xkarma
#
```

As you can see, the archive was extracted to the specified directory preserving the hierarchy; the new directory `test` created under the directory `stuff` contains the same files as the original directory.

gzip

`gzip` is a tool used for file compression for the purpose of ease of storage. The original file is substituted by another with the same name but containing the extension `.gz` and preserving the ownership, permissions, and creation and modification times of the original file. The following is the syntax for `gzip`:

`gzip` *`[options] file1 ... fileN`*

Table 5.16 shows options for `gzip`.

TABLE 5.16 Options for the `gzip` Command

Option	*Action*
`-l`	For compressed files, list the compressed and uncompressed size, compression ratio, and uncompressed name.
`-r`	Recursive compression. If the specified file is a directory, compress also all the files contained on the directory.

Option	*Action*
`-t`	Check the integrity of the compressed files.
`-v`	Display the name and percentage reduction.
`-number`	Perform different levels of compression. `-1` is the fastest method but with less compression, and `-9` is the slowest method but with larger compression. If it's not specified, the default value (`6`) is used.

Let's have some practice. The following command compresses the file called `SMTP.txt`:

```
# gzip SMTP.txt
#
```

Now, we use the option `-v` to get the compression percentage information:

```
# gzip -v SMTP.txt
SMTP.txt:                37.3% -- replaced with SMTP.txt.gz
#
```

It's possible to corroborate whether the information given by the option `-v` is correct. Let's use the option `-l` to do that:

```
# gzip -l SMTP.txt.gz
compressed  uncompr. ratio uncompressed_name
      242       343  37.3% SMTP.txt
#
```

As you can see, the information given by using the option `-v` matches the one provided by using the option `-l`.

The command `gunzip` is used to decompress files. Its use is quite similar to `gzip`, and even the options are the same. The following command is used to expand the file `SMTP.txt.gz` previously generated:

```
bash-2.01$ gunzip SMTP.txt.gz
#
```

It's possible to use the option `-v` to know the percentage of the file compression:

```
# gunzip -v SMTP.txt.gz
SMTP.txt.gz:             37.3% -- replaced with SMTP.txt
#
```

The z Commands

It's possible to handle archived or compressed files in the format they actually have. UNIX provides the tools to explore and manipulate information stored in archives and compressed files.

zcat

zcat uncompresses either a list of files on the command line or its standard input and writes the uncompressed data on standard output. It's useful to know the content of a compressed file without decompressing it. The following command shows the content of the compressed file SMTP.txt.gz:

```
# zcat SMTP.txt.gz
   The objective of Simple Mail Transfer Protocol (SMTP) is to transfer
➥mail reliably and efficiently.

   SMTP is independent of the particular transmission subsystem and
➥requires only a reliable ordered data stream channel.

   An important feature of Smtp is its capability of relaying mail
➥across transport service environments.
#
```

zgrep

zgrep works in the same way that grep does, but it's used for compressed files. It searches into compressed files for a regular expression. zgrep uses the same options as the grep command previously described in this chapter.

The following command searches the expression SMTP on the compressed file SMTP.txt.gz:

```
# zgrep SMTP SMTP.txt.gz
   The objective of Simple Mail Transfer Protocol (SMTP) is to transfer
   SMTP is independent of the particular transmission subsystem and
#
```

zcmp

zcmp is the version of cmp for compressed files. zcmp uses the same options as the cmp command, described earlier in this chapter.

The following command compares the compressed files SMTP.txt.gz and SMPT2.txt.gz:

```
bash-2.01$ zcmp SMTP.txt.gz SMTP2.txt.gz
- /tmp/gz01013aaa differ: char 1, line 1
#
```

File compression is useful for saving storage space. Archiving is helpful to group files and back up information.

Informational Commands

Under certain circumstances, it is very useful to count with utilities that can provide information about the system, such as who is logged on, for how long the system has been turned on, and so on. UNIX provides many different tools to get information about the system and its status.

Using /bin/true and /bin/false

When using shell scripts (see Chapter 8, "Conventional Means, Extraordinary Ends: Powerful Scripting Tools," for more information on shell scripts), it is very important to know the result of executing a command or performing an action. A simple way to obtain return codes from the system is to use the commands `true` and `false`.

`true` does nothing but return an exit code `0` that means "success," and it can be used when successful command execution is required within a shell script. `false` is the opposite; it returns an exit code `1` that means "failure." The use of `true` and `false` is treated in depth in Chapter 8.

uname

The `uname` command displays information about the computer and the operating system installed. Using `uname`, it's possible to know basic information about the system, such as operating system name and version, type of processor, and other important information. Table 5.17 shows the options for `uname`.

TABLE 5.17 Options for the `uname` Command

Option	*Action*
`-m`	Display the computer type.
`-n`	Display the network node name of the computer.
`-r`	Display the operating system release.
`-s`	Display the operating system name.
`-v`	Display the operating system version.
`-a`	Display all the information of the system.

Linux terminology differs from that of other UNIX flavors. Release in Linux's `uname` refers to what Linux users call version, and version reports build information.

If no option is given, `uname` uses the option `-s` by default:

```
# uname
Linux
#
```

The following command shows the version of the operating system:

```
# uname -v
#13 Tue Jun 8 22:12:25 CDT 1999
#
```

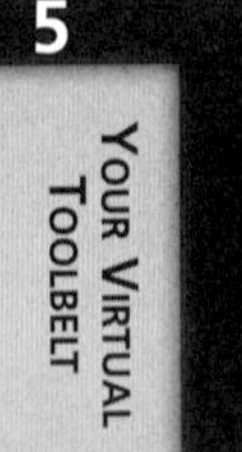

Using the option -a, all the available information about the system is displayed:

```
# uname -a
Linux xwing 2.0.36 #13 Tue Jun 8 22:12:25 CDT 1999 i586 unknown
#
```

The result given by the previous command is interpreted as follows:

`Linux` is the name of the operating system (option `-s`).

`xwing` is the network node name of the computer (option `-n`).

`2.0.36` is the operating system release (option `-r`).

`#13 Tue Jun 8 22:12:25 CDT 1999` indicates that the kernel has been compiled 13 times, and the last one occurred on Tuesday June 8, 1999, at 22:12:25 (option `-v`).

`i586 unknown` is the computer (processor) type (option `-m`).

hostname

The `hostname` command is used to either set or display the hostname of the computer. The computer's hostname is used by many network applications to distinguish the machine from others on the same network. Table 5.18 shows the options for `hostname`.

TABLE 5.18 Options for the `hostname` Command

Option	*Action*
-a	If existing, display the alias name or names of the computer.
-i	Display the IP address(es) of the host.

If no option is given when using `uname`, the actual hostname will be displayed:

```
# hostname
xwing
#
```

The following command displays the IP address of the host:

```
# hostname -i
10.0.2.2
#
```

It's possible to change the name of the host using the command `hostname`. The following command changes the hostname from `xwing` to `tiefighter`. You must be `root` to execute this command:

```
# hostname -v tiefighter
Setting hostname to 'tiefighter'
#
```

Let's verify that the hostname change is done:

```
bash-2.01$ hostname
tiefighter
#
```

id

The `id` command displays information about a specific user. If no username is given, the default user will be the one that is actually logged on the tty. The following is the syntax for `id`:

```
id [options] [user_name]
```

Table 5.19 shows the options for `id`.

TABLE 5.19 Options for the `id` Command

Option	*Action*
`-g`	Display only the group ID.
`-G`	Display only the supplementary groups.
`-n`	Display the username instead of the ID.
`-u`	Display only the user ID.

If no option is given, `id` displays the real user ID, real group ID, effective user ID if different from the real user ID, effective group ID if different from the real group ID, and supplemental group IDs. The following command displays the information of the user that is actually logged on the system:

```
# id
uid=1000(gerry) gid=1000(gerry) groups=1000(gerry), 0(root), 24(cdrom), ><
<>25(floppy), 27(sudo), 29(audio), 37(operator), 100(users)
#
```

The following command displays the user ID of the user `mario`:

```
# id -u mario
1002
#
```

logname

The `logname` command prints the calling user's name. `logname` is useful to find the user who is logged on a computer. Here's an example:

```
# logname
gerry
#
```

As you can see, the user logged on the system is `gerry`.

who and w

The `who` and `w` commands are used to find out who is logged on the system. Both commands display the users logged on, but the `w` command can also display what the users are doing.

Table 5.20 shows the options for `who`.

TABLE 5.20 Options for the `who` Command

Option	*Action*
`-m`	Display information about the user who is calling the command.
`-q`	Display the login names and total number of users.
`-i`	Display the time that users have been idle since they logged on.

Table 5.21 shows the options for `w`.

TABLE 5.21 Options for the `w` Command

Option	*Action*
`-s`	Don't display the login time, JCPU, or PCPU times.
`-h`	Display the information without the header.

The following command is used to display the users logged on the system:

```
# who
gerry    tty1     Jun 02 11:16
test     tty2     Jun 02 17:50
gerry    ttyp1    Jun 02 17:30 (:0.0)
#
```

The following command is also used to display the users logged on the system, but it also displays what they are doing:

```
# w
  5:53pm  up  6:40,  3 users,  load average: 0.02, 0.02, 0.02
USER     TTY      FROM              LOGIN@   IDLE   JCPU   PCPU  WHAT
gerry    tty1                      11:16am  6:36m  2:15   0.09s  xinit
test     tty2                       5:50pm 34.00s  0.25s  0.04s  man who
gerry    ttyp1    :0.0              5:30pm  1.00s  0.18s  0.07s  w
#
```

uptime

The uptime command is used to display the current time, how long the system has been running, how many users are currently logged on, and the system load averages for the past 1, 5, and 15 minutes. Here's an example:

```
# uptime
  6:08pm  up  6:55,  3 users,  load average: 0.34, 0.11, 0.02
#
```

The result given by the previous command is interpreted as follows:

The actual time is 6:08 pm.

The system has been up for 6 hours and 55 minutes.

There are 3 users currently logged on.

The load average for the last minute is 0.34, for the last 5 minutes is 0.11, and for the last 15 minutes is 0.02.

You'll find the informational commands helpful for discovering what's happening in the system and who is logged into the computer.

Disk Space

It is always useful to know the amount of available space on disks. Like other UNIX flavors, Linux provides useful tools for monitoring the disk space used and available in the system. This section describes some of the tools that will make your life easier.

df

The df command shows the amount of free space available on a disk and the total space (used or not) on the disk. The space is measured in block sizes of 1024 bytes (1KB). Here's an example:

```
# df
Filesystem         1024-blocks  Used Available Capacity Mounted on
/dev/hda2            1918862 1131395    688280      62%       /
#
```

du

The du command displays the amount of disk space used by each argument and for each subdirectory of directory arguments. The most common measure used is 1KB. Table 5.22 shows the options for du.

TABLE 5.22 Options for the du Command

Option	*Action*
`-a`	Display disk usage for all files, not just for directories.
`-k`	Display sizes in kilobytes.
`-b`	Display sizes in bytes.
`-s`	Display only a total for each argument.

The following command displays the disk usage for the directory called `test`:

```
# du test
135     test
#
```

The following command displays disk usage for the directory `test` and all the files that it contains:

```
# du -a test
14      test/cosim.gif
119     test/rfc0821.txt
1       test/xkarma
135     test
#
```

It is important to constantly monitor disk utilization to better prevent disk saturation.

Process Management

Because the way UNIX runs programs and executes applications is based on a process-based model (see Chapter 11, "Administration Essentials," for more information on the UNIX process model), it's very important to know how to handle processes. UNIX provides some tools to make the process management as easy as possible. This section introduces some process management tools that you'll find helpful.

ps

The `ps` command is used to report the status of the UNIX processes. Table 5.23 shows options for the `ps` command.

TABLE 5.23 Options for the ps Command

Option	*Action*
`l`	Show processes on long format.
`u`	Show processes ordered by username and start time.
`j`	Show processes in jobs format.

Option	Action
f	Show processes in "forest" family tree format.
a	Show all processes, including the processes of other users.
x	Show processes without controlling terminal.
h	Do not display header.
r	Show running processes only.

The following command shows the actual processes on the system:

```
# ps
  PID TTY STAT TIME COMMAND
  244   1 SW   0:00 (bash)
  253   1 SW   0:00 (xinit)
  261   1 S    0:03 /usr/X11R6/bin/icewm
  407   1 R    2:52 /software/Office50/bin/soffice.bin
  419   1 S    0:00 /software/Office50/bin/soffice.bin
  420   1 S    0:00 /software/Office50/bin/soffice.bin
  421   1 S    0:00 /software/Office50/bin/soffice.bin
  425   1 S    0:00 /software/Office50/bin/soffice.bin
  426   1 S    0:00 /software/Office50/bin/soffice.bin
  654  p0 S    0:00 (bash)
 1112  p1 S    0:00 bash
 1265  p0 Z    0:00 (sh <zombie>)
 1266  p0 S    0:00 /usr/bin/pager -s
 1364  p1 R    0:00 ps
#
```

Now, let's list only the currently running processes:

```
# ps r
  PID TTY STAT TIME COMMAND
 1111   1 R    0:01 /usr/bin/X11/xterm
  407   1 R    2:53 /software/Office50/bin/soffice.bin
 1368  p1 R    0:00 ps r
#
```

The following command shows the processes in the "forest" family tree format:

```
# ps f
 PID TTY STAT TIME COMMAND
 244   1 SW   0:00 (bash)
 253   1 SW   0:00  \_ (xinit)
 261   1 S    0:03      \_ /usr/X11R6/bin/icewm
 407   1 R    2:54          \_ /software/Office50/bin/soffice.bin
 419   1 S    0:00              \_ /software/Office50/bin/soffice.bin
 420   1 S    0:00                  \_ /software/Office50/bin/soffice.bin
 421   1 S    0:00                  \_ /software/Office50/bin/soffice.bin
 425   1 S    0:00                  \_ /software/Office50/bin/soffice.bin
 426   1 S    0:00                  \_ /software/Office50/bin/soffice.bin
 654  p0 S    0:00 (bash)
```

```
1112  p1 S    0:00 bash
1369  p1 R    0:00  \_ ps f
1265  p0 Z    0:00 (sh <zombie>)
1266  p0 S    0:00 /usr/bin/pager -s
#
```

The previous information is interpreted as follows: process 244 (`bash`) is the parent of process 253 (`xinit`); process 253 (`xinit`) is the parent of process 261 (`/usr/X11R6/bin/icewm`); and so on.

kill

The `kill` command finishes the process(es) indicated by sending them the `TERM` signal. The following is the syntax for `kill`:

```
kill [-signal_number] pid
kill [-signal_name] pid
```

Table 5.24 shows the most commonly used signal numbers and names.

TABLE 5.24 Signal Numbers and Names for the `kill` Command

Signal Number	*Signal Name*	*Action*
-1	-1	Superuser's broadcast to all processes or user broadcast to user's processes
2	INT	Interrupt
3	QUIT	Quit
6	ABRT	Abort
9	KILL	Forced kill
14	ALRM	Alarm clock
15	TERM	Software termination signal
	HUP	Restart process

Assume that the following processes are currently running:

```
# ps
  PID TTY STAT TIME COMMAND
  244   1 SW   0:00 (bash)
  253   1 SW   0:00 (xinit)
  261   1 S    0:04 /usr/X11R6/bin/icewm
  407   1 R    3:01 /software/Office50/bin/soffice.bin
  419   1 S    0:00 /software/Office50/bin/soffice.bin
  420   1 S    0:00 /software/Office50/bin/soffice.bin
  421   1 S    0:00 /software/Office50/bin/soffice.bin
  425   1 S    0:00 /software/Office50/bin/soffice.bin
  426   1 S    0:00 /software/Office50/bin/soffice.bin
```

```
  654  p0 S    0:00 bash
 1112  p1 S    0:00 bash
 1382  p0 S    0:00 telnet localhost
 1385  p1 R    0:00 ps
#
```

The following command kills the process that is performing a Telnet to `localhost` (pid 1382):

```
# kill -9 1382
#
```

top

The `top` command is used to display the currently running processes according to CPU utilization. The following is an example of `top`:

```
  9:43pm  up 10:31,  3 users,  load average: 0.16, 0.10, 0.10
55 processes: 53 sleeping, 2 running, 0 zombie, 0 stopped
CPU states:  1.8% user,  4.6% system,  0.0% nice, 93.5% idle
Mem:   14848K av,  14388K used,    460K free,   9964K shrd,    156K buff
Swap: 130748K av,  12460K used, 118288K free                  5984K cached

 PID   USER   PRI   NI  SIZE  RSSSHARE  STAT LIB  %CPU   %MEM    TIME     COMMAND
m
1407   gerry    3    0   732  732  564  R       0   6.5    4.9    0:00     top
   1   root     0    0   112   76   56  S       0   0.0    0.5    0:03     init
   2   root     0    0     0    0    0  SW      0   0.0    0.0    0:00     kflushd
   3   root   -12  -12     0    0    0  SW<     0   0.0    0.0    0:00     kswapd
   4   root     0    0     0    0    0  SW      0   0.0    0.0    0:00     nfsiod
   5   root     0    0     0    0    0  SW      0   0.0    0.0    0:00     nfsiod
   6   root     0    0     0    0    0  SW      0   0.0    0.0    0:00     nfsiod
   7   root     0    0     0    0    0  SW      0   0.0    0.0    0:00     nfsiod
 244   gerry    0    0   304    0    0  SW      0   0.0    0.0    0:00     bash
 245   test     0    0   308   48   48  S       0   0.0    0.3    0:00     bash
 187   root     0    0   424  184  108  S       0   0.0    1.2    0:00     omniNames
 112   root     0    0   248  196  140  S       0   0.0    1.3    0:00     syslogd
  16   root     0    0    52   28   16  S       0   0.0    0.1    0:00     update
 117   root     0    0   320  164  124  S       0   0.0    1.1    0:00     klogd
```

As you can see, the information about the processes is quite similar to the information obtained using `ps` (described earlier in this chapter), but `top` allows monitoring of different processes at the same time.

Communication with Other Users

Communication with other users across the network is helpful in certain situations, and there are different ways to do that. Using UNIX, it's possible to establish communication with other users when they're logged on the same computer or even if they are logged on a different node in the same network. This section presents some tools to establish communications with other users.

write

The `write` command is used to copy text lines from your terminal to be displayed on the other user's terminal; in other words, it's used to send messages to another user. The following is the syntax for `write`:

```
write username [terminal_name]
```

You should insert an Enter at the end of each line of the message. Here's an example:

```
# write meli
Hi! did you do the homework?
^d
#
```

The `^d` (Ctrl+D) command indicates the end of the message. The user `meli` will receive the message as follows:

```
Message from gerry@xwing on ttyp1 at 16:48 ...
Hi! did you do the homework?
EOF
```

The first line indicates that `gerry` has sent a message to `meli`, `gerry` is logged on `xwing` at terminal `ttyp1`, and the message was sent at `16:48`. The second line is the message body. The third line indicates the end of the message. Now, `meli` sends a response to `gerry`:

```
# write gerry ttyp1
Sure! what about you?
^d
#
```

In this case, `meli` decides to indicate the terminal name (`ttyp1`) to ensure that `gerry` will receive the message at his terminal. The message is displayed as follows:

```
Message from meli@xwing on ttyp1 at 16:51 ...
Sure! what about you?
EOF
```

wall

The `wall` command is used to send broadcast messages to all users currently connected to the system, whether they're logged local or remotely. Only superuser is able to send messages to all users, overriding the allow-messaging permissions of each user. The following is the syntax for `wall`:

```
wall [filename or text]
```

There are two different ways to send a broadcast. The first is just by calling `wall` and typing the text to be displayed, for example

```
# wall
Where is the tennis court?
```

```
^d
#
```

The message will be displayed on the terminals of all users that have allow-messaging enabled as follows:

```
Broadcast Message from gerry@xwing
        (/dev/ttyp1) at 17:14 ...

Where is the tennis court?
```

The second way to send broadcast messages is using a previously created file as argument:

```
# wall warning.txt
#
```

The message contained in the file will be displayed on the terminals of each user currently logged on the system. This is a helpful tool for scheduled tasks (see Chapter 11 for more information on scheduled tasks). The message will be displayed as follows:

```
Broadcast Message from root@xwing
        (/dev/ttyp1) at 17:19 ...

             This is a message from the system administrator.

The system will be turned off in 5 minutes,please save your documents and
logout now!
```

mesg

The `mesg` command allows or disallows other users to send messages to your terminal. Using `mesg`, it's possible to have messaging permissions to avoid being bothered by other users. The following command allows other users to send messages to you:

```
# mesg y
#
```

The following command is used to disallow other users to send messages to you:

```
# mesg n
#
```

When you've disallowed other users to send messages to you, nobody but `root` is allowed to send you messages. The following message is displayed if someone tries to send you a message:

```
# write meli ttyp0
write: meli has messages disabled on ttyp0
#
```

Communicating with other users is useful especially when performing administrative tasks that require you to notify the users of the system.

Managing the System

A UNIX system administrator frequently needs to perform administrative tasks to maintain the system integrity and stability. For example, UNIX systems have a special process to be turned off. System management differs from process management in that it is referred to the whole system instead of just processes. This section describes different tools for system management.

free

The `free` command is used to display the amount of free and used memory in the system. It is possible to show the memory information expressed in bytes:

```
# free -b
             total       used       free     shared    buffers     cached
Mem:      15204352   14778368     425984    9502720     163840    7118848
-/+ buffers/cache:    7495680    7708672
Swap:    133885952   11202560  122683392
#
```

or kilobytes (default):

```
# free -k
             total       used       free     shared    buffers     cached
Mem:         14848      14448        400       9100        160       6852
-/+ buffers/cache:       7436       7412
Swap:       130748      10892     119856
#
```

or even megabytes:

```
# free -m
             total       used       free     shared    buffers     cached
Mem:            14         13          0          8          0          6
-/+ buffers/cache:          7          7
Swap:          127         10        117
#
```

The option `-t` displays a line showing the totals:

```
# free -t
             total       used       free     shared    buffers     cached
Mem:         14848      14336        512       8852        208       6628
-/+ buffers/cache:       7500       7348
Swap:       130748      10828     119920
Total:      145596      25164     120432
#
```

The option `-s` activates continuous polling delay seconds apart. The following command makes a refresh every `2` seconds:

```
# free -s 2
             total       used       free     shared    buffers     cached
Mem:         14848      14440        408       8968        208       6768
-/+ buffers/cache:       7464       7384
Swap:       130748      10800     119948

             total       used       free     shared    buffers     cached
Mem:         14848      14396        452       8964        208       6736
-/+ buffers/cache:       7452       7396
Swap:       130748      10816     119932
```

Shutting Down, Stopping, and Rebooting the System

There are different ways to restart or turn off the system. This section explains how to shut down, stop, or reboot the system.

reboot and halt

The `reboot` command is used to restart the system. This command terminates all processes currently running and restarts the system. The following is the syntax for `reboot`:

```
reboot [-n] [-w] [-f] [-i]
```

The `halt` command is used to turn off the system. This command terminates all processes currently running and displays a message to turn off the system. The following is the syntax for `halt`:

```
halt [-n] [-w] [-f] [-i]
```

Table 5.25 shows options for `reboot` and `halt`.

TABLE 5.25 Options for the `reboot` and `halt` Commands

Option	*Action*
`-n`	Do not sync before `reboot` or `halt`.
`-w`	Write to the logs without `reboot` or `halt` the system.
`-f`	Forced.
`-i`	Shut down all network interfaces before `reboot` or `halt`.

The use of managing commands are recommended and commonly used by the system administrator.

Miscellaneous Commands

UNIX features miscellaneous commands to perform different actions on the system. This section introduces some useful commands provided by Linux for different purposes. That's why they're named miscellaneous.

date

The `date` command is used to display the actual date on the system:

```
# date
Sun Jun 13 21:51:39 CDT 1999
#
```

It is possible to display the time in the GMT format by using the option `-u`:

```
# date -u
Mon Jun 14 02:52:20 UTC 1999
#
```

This command also enables the user to change the system time and date. The following is the syntax to change the date and time:

```
date [MMDDhhmm[[CC]YY][.ss]]
```

For example, to set the date to June 20, 1999, and the time to 22:00, use the following command:

```
# date 062022001999
Sun Jun 20 22:00:00 CDT 1999
#
```

hwclock

The Hardware Clock is the clock on the BIOS of the computer. The `hwclock` command is a tool for accessing the Hardware Clock. You can display the current time, set the Hardware Clock to a specified time, set the Hardware Clock to the System Time, and set the System Time from the Hardware Clock.

For example, assume you've just changed the date and time of your system by using the `date` command described earlier in this chapter. It is possible to write the date and time to the Hardware Clock using the following command as superuser:

```
# hwclock ---systohc
#
```

Done! Your hardware clock has the date and time you previously defined.

cal

The `cal` command is a calendar tool that is able to display a simple calendar. The following is the syntax for `cal`:

```
cal [options] [[month] year]
```

The option `-j` displays the calendar using Julian dates.

The option `-y` displays the calendar for the actual year.

The month must be specified by number of the month (`01` for January, `02` for February, and so on), and the year should be specified in the 4-digit format (`1999`, `2000`, and so on).

If no options (neither month nor year) are given, `cal` displays the calendar for the actual month and year:

```
# cal
     June 1999
 S  M Tu  W Th  F  S
       1  2  3  4  5
 6  7  8  9 10 11 12
13 14 15 16 17 18 19
20 21 22 23 24 25 26
27 28 29 30

#
```

The following command displays the calendar for the actual year:

```
# cal -y
                               1999

       January               February               March
 S  M Tu  W Th  F  S    S  M Tu  W Th  F  S    S  M Tu  W Th  F  S
                1  2       1  2  3  4  5  6       1  2  3  4  5  6
 3  4  5  6  7  8  9    7  8  9 10 11 12 13    7  8  9 10 11 12 13
10 11 12 13 14 15 16   14 15 16 17 18 19 20   14 15 16 17 18 19 20
17 18 19 20 21 22 23   21 22 23 24 25 26 27   21 22 23 24 25 26 27
24 25 26 27 28 29 30   28                     28 29 30 31
31
        April                  May                   June
 S  M Tu  W Th  F  S    S  M Tu  W Th  F  S    S  M Tu  W Th  F  S
             1  2  3                      1          1  2  3  4  5
 4  5  6  7  8  9 10    2  3  4  5  6  7  8    6  7  8  9 10 11 12
11 12 13 14 15 16 17    9 10 11 12 13 14 15   13 14 15 16 17 18 19
18 19 20 21 22 23 24   16 17 18 19 20 21 22   20 21 22 23 24 25 26
25 26 27 28 29 30      23 24 25 26 27 28 29   27 28 29 30
                       30 31
```

```
         July                   August                 September
 S  M Tu  W Th  F  S    S  M Tu  W Th  F  S    S  M Tu  W Th  F  S
             1  2  3    1  2  3  4  5  6  7             1  2  3  4
 4  5  6  7  8  9 10    8  9 10 11 12 13 14    5  6  7  8  9 10 11
11 12 13 14 15 16 17   15 16 17 18 19 20 21   12 13 14 15 16 17 18
18 19 20 21 22 23 24   22 23 24 25 26 27 28   19 20 21 22 23 24 25
25 26 27 28 29 30 31   29 30 31               26 27 28 29 30

       October                November               December
 S  M Tu  W Th  F  S    S  M Tu  W Th  F  S    S  M Tu  W Th  F  S
                1  2       1  2  3  4  5  6             1  2  3  4
 3  4  5  6  7  8  9    7  8  9 10 11 12 13    5  6  7  8  9 10 11
10 11 12 13 14 15 16   14 15 16 17 18 19 20   12 13 14 15 16 17 18
17 18 19 20 21 22 23   21 22 23 24 25 26 27   19 20 21 22 23 24 25
24 25 26 27 28 29 30   28 29 30               26 27 28 29 30 31
31

#
```

Summary

Linux has different tools to make your life easier. This chapter divides the tools into different types according to their purpose.

- Online documentation tools include `man`, `apropos`, and `info`.
- Managing file tools include `ls`, `mv`, `cp`, and `find`.
- Examining file tools include `cat`, `more`, `less`, `head`, `tail`, `file`, `diff`, and `cmp`.
- Manipulating data tools include `cut`, `paste`, `sed`, `grep`, and the `z` commands.
- Tools for handling archives and compression include `tar`, `gzip`, and `gunzip`.
- Informational commands include `true`, `false`, `uname`, `hostname`, `id`, `logname`, `who`, `w`, and `uptime`.
- Disk space tools include `df` and `du`.
- Process management tools include `ps`, `kill`, and `top`.
- Communication with other users include `write`, `wall`, and `mesg`.
- System management tools include `Free`, `reboot`, and `halt`.
- Miscellaneous commands include `date`, `hwclock`, and `cal`.

CHAPTER

Advanced Text Editing

by Steve Wells

IN THIS CHAPTER

There are many UNIX-based text editors—emacs, Crisp, Breif, and xedit come to mind—but the longest running to date is *vi*. It all began in 1976 when Bill Joy combined the source code of two line editors (ed and ex) to create vi for an early BSD release. Shortly thereafter, AT&T integrated it into its UNIX system, and it became the standard UNIX editor outside of MIT until emacs was born in 1984. Though there is no hard POSIX standard for vi, several clones have developed with various levels of improvements over the original implementation. The elvis, nvi, and vim clones are distributed with Debian, and this chapter focuses on the one with the most features, vim.

vim originally stood for Vi IMitation when it was first introduced by its author, Brian Moolenar, as yet another version of vi. It was based on Stevie (STvi), which was created by Tim Thompson, G.R. (Fred) Walter, and Troy Andrews. Today, it comes as part of several Linux distributions, and is made up of a very advanced feature set. vim is now named for its vast improvements over vi. These improvements include multilevel undo, syntax highlighting, command-line editing, online help, and file completion, making "vim" now stand for Vi IMproved.

Distinguishing a Text Editor from a Word Processor

One thing should be clear before we continue, vim is not a word processor. It is a text editor. As such, it is useful for manipulating text, rather than formatting text for viewing as with Word Perfect or Microsoft Word. Programmers, scriptwriters, and administrators will find vim very useful, because a large part of those jobs entails manipulating text. A word processor is useful for formatting text in a way that is meant to be read by others, but vi documents are usually read by other programs rather than by end users.

As a text editor, vi is very efficient. It enables users to keep their hands on the keyboard to move around the document and does not require a mouse or any other input device. Be forewarned though: It is not easy for beginners to grasp, because there are many commands to learn. When you first sat down to learn to type, it was a tedious process, much slower than your two-finger, hunt-and-peck method. After some time, however, you realized that you could type far faster and much more accurately when you could make use of all your fingers in an organized manner. vi follows this same method; it enables the user to more effectively move, edit, and organize configuration files, scripts, and programs.

The rest of this chapter will discuss vi using the vim clone and the features that are available within it. Obviously, a complete in-depth look at the program will not be covered in this short section, but you will have enough understanding to effectively use vim for your editing needs. You will also be given the skills to find solutions that are not covered here by utilizing the help section of the program.

Understanding vi Components

I will make use of examples that build on each other as we progress from here. It is best to start with a clean directory if you want to follow along using your computer, to ensure that you are not randomly changing files, such as deleting your hosts file—or even worse, making some obscure change in a sendmail configuration.

Editing Your First File Using vim

To create a new, temporary directory and change your working directory to that new directory

```
#mkdir /tmp/learnvi
#cd /tmp/learnvi
```

Now we need a file to work with. Rather than starting off by creating a file, simply copy a file from elsewhere on your system. The message-of-the-day file is located in your `/etc` directory. It displays a message to each user of your Linux system whenever he or she successfully logs in to your machine. Let's start by copying that file into your new working directory (do not forget the final period (`.`):

```
#cp /etc/motd .
```

Then view its contents via

```
#cat motd
```

Next, it's time to start up vi. vi works like most other UNIX commands—it is run with arguments after it. In order to view or edit a file in vi, you use the following syntax: `vi` *`FILENAME`* where *`FILENAME`* is the file you want to edit. In this case, we want to look at the `motd` file located in the current directory. Therefore, the following command

```
# vi motd
```

starts vi and then opens the file `motd`. If `motd` did not exist in our current directory, vi would assume that we were creating a new file with the name `motd`.

If you start up vi with the message-of-the-day file, you may notice the tilde character (~) filling up the rest of the screen. This is an attempt to show you where the end of the file lies and is not part of your document; please ignore it. At the bottom of the screen, you will notice the filename (`motd`), the number of lines in this file, and the number of characters in the file. The blinking cursor is an underscore (_) under the first character in the file.

Thus far, vi has made a copy of the file from the disk into memory. At this stage, you can make changes without actually changing the file on the hard drive, which enables you to make mistakes without affecting the original file. Because this is a copy of the `/etc/motd` file, you are free to experiment any way you want without actually changing the real message-of-the-day file.

vi Commands for Different Inputs

vim has three different commands for different modes of input:

- Command mode, for entering your commands
- Insert mode, for inserting text
- Visual mode, for visually highlighting and selecting text

The Command mode is the default mode, but can be achieved by pressing the Esc key on your keyboard if you are in another mode. You will learn about the other modes later, but for now you should learn how to exit vi.

Many commands in vi start with a colon (`:`). When you type a `:`, it drops the cursor to the bottom of the screen on the left side and waits for you type a command. In this case, the command to quit vi is `:quit!`.

There is a shortcut that enables you to type `:q!` instead of typing out the whole word. This tells vi to drop everything and bring you back to the prompt. It does not write anything to the disk and therefore won't enable you to save your changes.

In most cases, you'll want to save your changes (otherwise, vi does little more than `cat`, more-or-less); the command is `:w` to write the file back to disk and then `:q` to quit. These commands can be combined into one convenient method, `:wq`, which writes the file from memory back to disk before exiting. There is a shortcut for this method that can be used; type `:x`. The only difference is that `:x` won't write anything back to disk unless you make a change to the document, which is usually what you want in any case.

Cursor Movement

The cursor movement keys may be difficult to grasp at first if you are used to the arrow keys, but you will be glad you learned to use them as you become more proficient. The arrow keys do work in vi, but you don't have to move your fingers far from the Home key to move around the document if you use the keyboard keys. If you type `h`, you move the cursor one character to the left. The `j` key moves the cursor down one, and the `k` key moves it up one. The `l` key moves the cursor one character to the right.

It may be surprising that you can make the cursor jump a number of lines by typing a number first. For instance, `5j` drops the cursor down 5 lines, and `10h` moves it 10 characters to the left. Sometimes when you move the cursor, it will drop off the screen; if you move too far to the left, for instance, the cursor will simply go as far as it is able. Most commands in vi have this optional prefix, whereby if you enter a digit before entering the command, vi performs the action that number of times.

There are several UNIX games that enable you to more readily use these keys—NetHack, ogue, moria, omega, worm, and snake to name a few. I'll leave installing them as an exercise for you, but you may want to search `http://www.freshmeat.net/` as a start.

Creating and Editing a File

Up to this point, you have learned how to open a file from the command line or within the vim editor. Once a file is open, you know how to use the cursor movement keys to maneuver within the file. You could save the file and finally exit back to the command line. Armed with this information, you could use vim as a method for reading long text files or for copying them to new locations using the Save command. Obviously, vim is much more useful than this, and this next section will help you create and edit files as well.

It's about time we actually change a file. From the command line, let's create a new file using the following command:

```
#vi myfile
```

Now you should see a series of tildes (~) going down the left side, and the word `myfile` in quotation marks and `[New File]` next to that at the bottom of the screen. Your cursor should be blinking in the upper-left corner of the screen. In order to add new text to a file, you need to change from Command mode to Insert mode. To do this, type the letter `i`. The bottom of the screen changes to display `-- INSERT --`, letting you know that you are in Insert mode. Type the following:

```
(2)  If what you're doing is not working, stop doing it.
```

If you make a mistake, use your Backspace key to erase it and go on. When you are finished, press the Esc key to go back to Command mode. You know that you are in Command mode because the `-- INSERT --` message at the bottom of the screen will disappear. Now type the following command:

```
:x
```

to write the file back to the disk and exit vi. At this point, you can type

```
#ls
```

to view the files in your directory, which should read:

```
motd    myfile
```

Now type

```
# cat myfile
```

to view the contents of the file you just created and verify that everything worked properly. It should read as follows:

```
If what you're doing is not working, stop doing it.
```

Adding a Line to the Existing File

Now we need to add a line to the existing file we just created. To edit the file, type the following:

```
#vi myfile
```

You'll see the screen just as you left it before. Notice though, that at the bottom of the screen, it no longer reads `[New File]`; rather, it tells you the number of lines and characters in the file:

```
"myfile" 1 lines, 56 characters
```

With your cursor in the upper-left portion of the screen, type `i` to enter the Insert mode again; then type

```
(1)     If what you're doing is working, keep doing it.
```

Remember to follow the sentence with the newline character by pressing the Enter key. When you are finished, you should have the following:

```
(1)     If what you're doing is working, keep doing it.
(2)     If what you're doing is not working, stop doing it.
```

Go back to Command mode from Insert mode by pressing the Esc key, and then exit again using the `:x` command. To view the contents of this edited file, type

```
# cat myfile
```

At this point, you know how to do the following:

- Start vi to create files (vi *NEW_FILENAME*)
- Edit existing (vi *EXISTING_FILENAME*) files
- Move around within vi (`h,j,k,l`)
- Understand the command (`Esc` and insert (`i`) modes

You could probably get by at this point by editing and creating any text file using vi, but it would still be very inefficient. All the other commands in vi help increase your efficiency in creating and editing text files.

Accessing Help and Undo

vim (vi) has a very detailed online help system. Beginners may feel overwhelmed by the number of features in a program such as this, because it's hard to imagine that so much can be done with a text editor. To access its online help system, you need to be in Command mode (press Esc); then type

```
:help
```

To go back to your document and exit the help system, type

```
:q
```

As you can see, this closes the help window and brings you back to the original cursor location. If you forget a command or want to know more about a particular subject, type `:help`, followed by the command you need help with. For instance, if you can't remember how to access the Insert mode, you can type

```
:help insert
```

and the first item in the list shows that you should type the letter `i` in lowercase in order to insert text. It gives more detail on the commands, as well as displaying the following:

```
I    Insert text before the cursor [count] times.
```

This means you could type `4i`, followed by `hello`, and it would output the word `hello` four times after you left the Insert mode. Because we need to cover the Undo command, now is a good time to use the `#i` command. Move your cursor to the first occurrence of the letter `d` in the second line and type

```
4i
```

This starts the Insert mode and you are able to type. Type the following word:

```
hello
```

Leave the Insert mode and return to the Command mode by pressing Esc.

Notice how the word `hello` was repeated four times before the cursor position. Obviously, this does not have a good effect on the document at this stage and does little to enhance the quality of our work. Probably the most alluring feature to vim's feature-rich set of commands is the Undo command. While in command mode, type

```
u
```

This removes the four `hello` parts and returns the file to its previous state. The `u` command undoes the previous command. If you were to change more than one item on a line and want them undone, you could type `u` multiple times, because it remembers each event that took place. But there is an easier method. The uppercase `U` command remembers all the events that took place on a line and undoes all of them at once.

If you mistakenly use Undo and want the ability to redo the command, press Ctrl+R, holding down the Ctrl key and the R key simultaneously). As you create and edit more of your text documents and programs, you will find that Undo and Help are some of your most useful features. The multiple levels of Undo quickly become an invaluable resource and it is worth mentioning that this is one of the many features available in vim as opposed to other vi clones. The extensive Help command is also a feature of vim and is necessarily universal among clones. You are urged to read through the Help commands in an effort to uncover other secrets within vim that will make your work easier.

Using Insert

You have already learned how to open the file and insert new text. The insert command is made up of many commands, though, that help speed up adding new items. Most notable is the `o` command. By typing `o`, you insert a new line after the current line that the cursor is positioned on.

Position your cursor at the beginning of the second line that reads

```
(2)   If what you're doing is not working, stop doing it.
```

Now type the letter `o`. The cursor moves down a line and the bottom of the screen changes to show that you are in Insert mode. At this point, you can start typing. Enter the following line:

```
          -- Loeb's Medicine
```

Press Esc to get out of the Insert mode and into the Command mode.

If you want to insert a line above where the cursor was located, the command is `Shift+O`. With your cursor located anywhere on the last line you typed (`--Loeb's Laws`), press Shift+O.

Notice that the line you were on moved down one line and you are in Insert mode ready to type at this point. Enter the following lines:

```
(3)   If you don't know what to do, take off
(4)   Above all, never let a surgeon get hold of your patient.
```

Remember to go back to the Command mode again (press Esc).

Adding Text to the Last Line

Next, we want to add some text to the last line, `--Loeb's Medicine`. It should read, `-- Loeb's Laws of Medicine`. Use the command `a` to insert text after the cursor, as opposed to the `i` command, which inserts text before the cursor. Move the cursor so it sits under the letter `s` in the word `Loeb's` and type

```
a
```

Then add the following text:

```
Laws of
```

so that the line reads

```
-- Loeb's Laws of Medicine
```

After pressing Esc to get back to Command mode, move the cursor to line 3, where we are going to append a word. The command `Shift+A` moves the cursor to the end of a line and changes the mode to Insert, enabling you to append text to the end. When you have moved your cursor to the line, type the following:

```
Shift+A
```

Now type this word:

```
anything.
```

At this point you know how to do the following:

- Insert text before (i) and after the cursor (a)
- Open a new line above (O) and below (o) the cursor
- Append text at the end of a line (A)

Additional Possibilities with Adding Text

There are other commands that help you add text. The command `Shift+R` enables you to overwrite text until the Esc key is pressed. You probably already noticed that the phrase `take off` in the third line of the code we have written doesn't fit well with the last word, `anything`, because it seems to imply that in states of confusion we should remove our clothes. If you believe it is doubtful that Loeb's Laws of Medicine would make such a statement, you would be correct. It does provide us with the opportunity to overwrite the phrase `take off` with the correct phrase `don't do`, giving you the following sentence:

```
(3)    If you don't know what to do, don't do anything.
```

With vim, you could go into Insert mode, use the Backspace key to remove the `take off`, and then insert the new text. But to achieve this most efficiently, overwrite the phrase `take off` with `don't do`. Move your cursor to the `g` in `give up` and type

```
Shift+-Rdon't do
```

The command `Shift+R` puts you in Insert mode the same as `i` or `A`, but it allows you to overwrite text instead of inserting or appending to the line.

The following should be the final results of your file:

```
(1) If what you're doing is working, keep doing it.
(2) If what you're doing is not working, stop doing it.
(3) If you don't know what to do, don't do anything.
(4) Above all, never let a surgeon get hold of your patient.

-- Loeb's Laws of Medicine
```

Finally, press Esc to go back to Command mode.

As you can see, there is remarkable flexibility in vi when inserting text, using only a few commands and without removing your hands from the keyboard. These powerful features allow you to

- Append (A)
- Insert (i)
- Add (a)

- Overwrite (Shift+R)
- Add new lines before the current line (O)
- Add new lines after the current line (o)

Although there are several ways to perform these actions, some certainly are better than others in certain situations. You are urged to make use of them all.

Delete

Many times when working on a project that needs certain environment variables to be set, I change my `~/.login` or `~/.profile` to include the new variables so I don't have to enter them manually when I log in. After the project has been completed and shipped onto the client, I no longer need those environment lines. vi has very efficient methods for deleting a line, a word, a character, or even a block of text.

The command `x` removes a character from a line. Be sure that you are in Command mode (press Esc) and position your cursor under the character you want to remove; then type `x` to see it in action. It removes the character and slides the rest of line over to fill the gap. If you want to remove several characters, enter the number of characters you want to remove and immediately type `x` to remove them.

Using the Delete Method

Move your cursor to the second line:

```
If what you're doing is not working, stop doing it.
```

Now position the cursor under the `d` in the second instance of the word; `doing`. Type `x` to remove the `d` and slide the rest of the line into its place. The line now reads as follows:

```
If what you're doing is not working, stop oing it.
```

To remove the rest of the word, enter the number of characters you want to remove. Enter the command `4x`, and it removes the rest of the word. At this point, you have a line with two spaces. The command `Shift+X` removes the character before in the same way that the earlier commands `Shift+O` and `Shift+o` inserted a line of text before and after the cursor position, respectively. Much of vi becomes intuitive the more you use it. Your line should now be

```
If what you're doing is not working, stop it.
```

If you hold down the x key, it removes a series of characters; but suppose you want to delete a word. The command `dw` enables you to do that. It actually deletes only from the cursor position to the end of word, but as long as your cursor is positioned under the first character, it removes the word. It has the added advantage of removing the space after the word as well, and the rest of the line slides in to fill the gap.

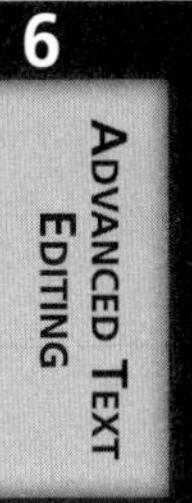

To see this in action, move your cursor under the word `it` in the second line and type `dw`. Notice that the period is not removed. If it had been a space, it would have been removed with the word, but the period is not considered part of the word and is therefore not removed.

Your sentence should now be

```
If what you're doing is not working, stop .
```

Remembering the Undo feature, you can restore the sentence by typing `Shift+U`, which restores all changes on a line. If you simply type `u`, it restores only the last change, although you could type it several times to restore all the changes in turn or prefix the command with a number to run it multiple times.

The command `dd` removes a line of text from within vi. It works based on the cursor location, so wherever the cursor is positioned, it removes that line. Let's remove the third line from our example to see how it works.

Position your cursor anywhere on the third line of text:

```
(3)    If you don't know what to do, don't do anything.
```

Now type `dd` to remove the line. Removing the line moves the rest of the document up by one line. This command works like most other commands in vi: If you place a number before it, it performs the action that number of times. To remove a block of four lines, prefix the command with the number `4`.

Move your cursor to the uppermost line of the file and type `4dd` to remove all four lines. Use the undo character (`u`) to restore them.

At this point, you can remove

- A character (x)
- Several characters (#x)
- A word (dw)
- Several words (#dw)
- A line (dd)
- A block of text (#dd)

For those of you familiar with regular expressions, the next command is intuitive for removing a line from the cursor position to the end of the line. The command `d$`' does just that. It removes everything from the cursor position to the end of line. You could use the number prefix with this command to remove everything from the cursor to the position at the end of the line, as well as the entire next two lines by using the command `3d$`. This works because the first instance of the command removes the rest of the line and the next command locates the cursor position at the beginning of the next line. Therefore the command removes the rest of the line.

Visual Mode

This is a good time to look at the Visual mode, which enables you to block text visually so you don't need to count the number of lines you want to block off. Please note that the Visual mode is only available in vim and may not work with other vi clones. To enter the Visual mode, type `v`. The bottom of the screen changes in the same manner as the Insert mode, only now, of course, it displays this:

```
-- VISUAL --
```

If you move your cursor down one line, you'll notice that the text becomes highlighted from the cursor position to the point where the cursor rests. As you move your cursor around, you select that block of text. If you want to delete a block of text visually, you highlight the block you want to delete and type `d` for delete.

Using the Visual Mode

Let's try an example. Be sure you are in Command mode (press Esc) and move the cursor to the top of the document at the beginning of the first line. Now type `v` to enter Visual mode. Observe that the bottom of the screen has changed to notify you that you are no longer in Command mode. Now move the cursor down to highlight lines 1 through 4 and type `d` for delete. As soon as you type `d`, you exit Visual mode and move back into Command mode. The following appears at the bottom of the screen:

```
4 fewer lines
```

This alerts you to what has been altered from within Visual mode. Also notice that the four lines have been removed from the document. To get them back, the trusty Undo (`u`) command comes to your rescue again. After typing `u`, the status at the bottom of the screen changes to the following:

```
4 more lines
```

As lines are inserted and removed, vi gives you updates on the process. You will see more of this in the section, "Further Capabilities for Cutting and Copying Text," later in this chapter. These updates are helpful when you are working with very large scripts, programs, or configuration files, ensuring you that the procedure was accurate.

For instance, let's say I have a large script and I need to remove a large subroutine from the document. After removing it using the visual method, rather than counting all the lines in the subroutine and scrolling through the text, I realize that I mistakenly removed the wrong routine. Without panicking, I simply type `u` for Undo. Yet the following appears in the status bar at the bottom of the screen:

```
3 more lines
```

I'm quite sure that the subroutine was much larger than the three lines I'm trying to put back; then I remember that I removed some comments further down in the document that

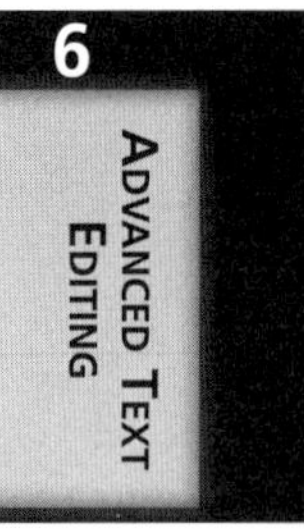

related to the missing subroutine. The Visual mode gives a status warning only when dealing with three or more lines, so you should expect it to give you a status report many lines long when you remove a block of text that you know to be long. In this case, I simply type u again until it reports that the large function is back in place.

Status and Jump

As any programmer knows, when a program gives you an error, it tries to return the line number that it suspects the error came from. When my Perl script fails, for instance, and returns this error

```
Can't locate object method "new" via package "CGI"
at nph-search.cgi line 29
BEGIN failed--compilation aborted at nph-search.cgi line 72
```

it means that there was an error at line 29 and that the BEGIN routine failed at line 72.

Using vi, it's very easy to jump around a document by lines. Remember that vi was originally based on ed, which is a line editor rather than a text editor such as vi.

Using Status and Jump

vi provides special commands for getting status information on a file or opening a file at a specific line number. To open the file nph-search.cgi and start editing at line 72 from the command prompt, I type the following:

```
#vi +72 nph-search.cgi
```

This tells vi to open the file nph-search.cgi and immediately move the cursor to the beginning of line 72. At this point, I see that I'm at the end of my BEGIN statement just as the error statement showed. I really want to be at line 29 where the object method is missing.

There are two ways to get there. One is to exit vi and type the following:

```
#vi +29 nph-search.cgi
```

The other way is to move the cursor to the top of the screen and type j 29 times. Neither is very appealing. I don't drive a standard very often, but when I get into a high gear I certainly don't like dropping back down and having to remember to use the clutch again. For the same reason, I don't want to drop out of vi and restart it just to get back to a specific line number.

To find the line number you are on within a file, the command Ctrl+g displays it in the status bar:

```
"nph-search.cgi" line 72 of 267 --27%-- col 1
```

This enables you to see the filename, the line number I'm currently on, and how many lines are within the document. The percent shows how far into the document I am located—in this case, 27%, which we can calculate by dividing the lines before (72) by the lines ahead (267). If we think of this document as a giant table with each cell holding one character, the `col` number is how many columns I am from the beginning of the line or how many characters into the line I am located.

The status line indicates only the position of the cursor at the time you press Ctrl+g. It does not update as you move around the document, although the status line remains static. To see the line at another point in the file, you press Ctrl+g again.

This enables you to traverse the file and find where you are at each point, so you don't have to count as you traverse the file looking for your line. But it's still not as effective as it could be.

The command `Shift+g` moves you immediately to the bottom of the document. This is useful if you need to append information to a file, but doesn't help much to jump to a specific line. The only reason it bounces you to the end of the file is that it defaults there unless you prefix it with a number.

Suppose we want to jump to line 29 from within our document and use the following command:

```
29Shift+g
```

This takes us immediately to the first character in line 29 that is not a space. If that line is blank, it stops at the beginning of the line. We can use the `Ctrl+g` command at this point to verify that we have moved to line 29. The following is the result for the `nph-search.cgi` file:

```
"nph-search.cgi" line 29 of 267 --10%-- col 12
```

The `col 12` is there not because we moved the cursor; rather, the first character in that line is located twelve spaces in from the beginning of the line. As you can see, debugging in vi is very effective. The error message from my script occurred because I commented out the part of the script that includes the CGI library. Using vi, it was easy to quickly locate and fix the error.

Search and Replace

Many times you open a configuration file or a script and need to search for that part of the file that contains some unique identifier so you can make changes around that area. An example might be a subroutine that needs updating or a long `/etc/hosts` file that needs an IP number updated. In a small file, it is not a problem to scroll through looking for the spot that needs updating, but in a large file it can be nearly impossible.

vi includes some powerful search routines to help in situations such as this—all using just the keyboard. Let's go back to the `nph-search.cgi` example. I have a routine that reads and holds prices of various books and the URLs where they were found. It returns an ordered list by price, and it's called `cheapest`.

If I want to make an update to that routine using vi, I open the file and call the search function. In the Command mode (press Esc), you use the slash character (/) to start a search. As soon as you type /, the cursor drops to the bottom of the screen and awaits input as to what you want to search. In the case of my book-price routine, I type sub cheapest to locate the beginning of the subroutine, and press Enter. It immediately takes me to the beginning of the subroutine.

Let's now go back to the previous example using the file that you created earlier. Your file should now look like this:

```
(1)    If what you're doing is working, keep doing it.
(2)    If what you're doing is not working, keep doing it.
(3)    If you don't know what to do, don't do anything.
(4)    Above all, never let a surgeon get hold of your patient.

-- Loeb's Laws of Medicine
```

Move the cursor to the beginning of the file in the uppermost line and type

```
/do
```

This moves the cursor to the first entry with the letter d followed by the letter o. To find the next place that the letter d is followed by the letter o, you could enter the command again—but there is a more effective shortcut.

The n command, when you are in Command mode, moves the cursor to the next match. Typing n, in this case, moves the cursor to the second occurrence of the word doing in the first sentence. Pressing it again drops the cursor down one line to the first instance of the word doing, and so forth, until you reach the last do in the third sentence. If you type n again, you will notice that the status bar has changed to the following:

```
search hit BOTTOM, continuing at TOP
```

In other words, as you progress through the document searching for the next instance, it loops around after it has found the last match. If you would like to search in the opposite direction, use the ? command rather than the / command to do your search.

Move your cursor to the beginning of line 2 of the document and type the following:

```
?do
```

It moves the cursor up to line 1 because it is searching in the opposite direction than before. If you continue to type n, / searches forward within the document and ? searches backward.

If you want to search in the opposite direction, you can also use Shift+n instead. If you type your search as ?do, and then Shift+n, it searches forward; if you use /do, it searches backward.

Now you know how to search for text within the document—forward (/) and backward (?)—as well as how to find the next match—in the same direction as the original search request (n) and in the opposite direction (Shift+n). Next, you need to know how to replace a series of characters with another set. Those who are familiar with regular expressions will again be glad to know that the search-and-replace methods in vi closely resemble regular expressions in other programs.

In order to search and replace instances of characters, the command requires the colon (:) to start. The syntax is `:s/`*SEARCH*`/`*REPLACE*`/` where *SEARCH* is the set of characters you are searching for and *REPLACE* is the set of characters you want to replace them with. You can change the next instance of the *SEARCH* set this way—but only one instance.

Place your cursor at the end of the first line in the document and type

```
:s/If/Since/
```

The command changes the next instance of the word `If` to `Since`. If you want to change *every* occurrence of the word `If` with the word `Since`, you add a percent symbol (`%`) to the previous command:

```
:%s/SEARCH/REPLACE/
```

Place your cursor at the end of the first line in the document again and type

```
:%s/If/Since/
```

Every occurrence of the word `If` throughout the document is now changed to `Since`.

We have looked at how to

- Change the search for a series of characters (/*SEARCH*).
- Search and replace the next iteration (:/*SEARCH*/*REPLACE*).
- Change the whole document with one command (:%s/*SEARCH*/*REPLACE*/).

Changing a Specific Part of the Document

What if you want to change only part of a document? vi provides the capability of searching and replacing characters located on a single line by appending the letter `g` to the end of the search command. This is very similar to the regular expressions syntax, which makes the search global and recursive by appending the letter `g`. The syntax is as follows:

```
:s/SEARCH/REPLACE/g
```

Place your cursor on line 2 of your file, which reads

```
Since what you're doing is not working, stop doing it.
```

If we want to replace the word `doing` with `experiencing` and want to be sure it is changed only on this line, the command is as follows:

```
:s/doing/experiencing/g
```

Observe that although the first line has the word `doing` in it, it was unaffected by the command. We have limited the effect to a single line.

If you would rather limit the effect to a block of lines, that is easily achieved. Prefix the search with the line numbers you want to change, and you can limit the search to a specific block. The syntax for block search-and-replace is

```
:#,#s/SEARCH/REPLACE/g
```

where the #s are the beginning and ending line numbers of your block.

Enter this command:

```
:1,3s/you/YOU/g
```

Every occurrence of the word `you` is now changed to uppercase, but it affects only those matches that occur on lines 1 through 3. Notice that although line 4 does contain the word `your` (a superset of `you`), it is unaffected by the command.

Locating Encapsulation Characters

If you are a programmer, you can't help but occasionally run into that hard-to-find [bracket], (parenthesis), or {bracket}. I have had times when I'm learning a new language when they are nearly impossible to find—and I wasn't even using lisp! vi to the rescue yet again. If you move your cursor to any bracket or parenthesis and type the percent character (`%`), it makes the cursor jump to its counterpart.

Place your cursor on any of the open parentheses within your document and type `%`. The cursor jumps to the closing parenthesis immediately following it. Type `%` again and the cursor jumps back to the original location. This is an invaluable resource to most scriptwriters, although scheme and lisp writers will see it as a blessing bestowed especially on them:

```
X Cut/Copy-n-Paste (move copy)
```

As programs and configurations evolve, inevitably they need to have components moved around or lines copied. The real hacker finds unique ways to use blocks of text more effectively and with less typing. Moving and copying text becomes a fundamental component of organizing text.

Further Capabilities for Cutting and Copying Text

vi provides various ways of cutting and copying text that appeal to very different methodologies. Moving simply consists of deleting text from the current document and copying it to some type of Clipboard (buffer), and then copying the text from the

Clipboard back to a new place within the document. Copying takes the same method, but you must move the text three times: once from the document to the Clipboard, again from the Clipboard back to the original document in the same location, and then again from the Clipboard to the document in a new location.

vi enables you to perform both moves and copies from both the visual and the Command modes. No matter which mode you use, it is always a three-step process. First, to move text you must delete it. When vi deletes characters, it actually moves those characters to a new buffer or memory location. The deleted information still exists in memory as long as you don't close the program. When you shut down vi, that memory is freed and cleaned up for other programs to use, but vi saves this information to a special file that you can retrieve from disk the next time you open a file. This enables you to effectively copy and paste between files.

Recall from the section "The Delete Method" that you can use `dd` to delete a line or `#dd` to delete a block, where `#` is the number of lines to remove. Another way to delete a block of text is to use the Visual mode to select the text and then type `dd`. After you remove the text, it is now in the buffer (Clipboard) and you can move your cursor to the place you want to insert the cut text. When positioned, type `p` to paste the text after the cursor or `Shift+p` to paste it before the cursor.

Switching Lines in a Document

First, let's switch lines 2 and 3 in our document. They currently read as follows:

```
Since what you're doing is not working, stop doing it.
Since you don't know what to do, don't do anything.
```

To switch the two lines, move your cursor to line 2 and type `dd` to cut the line. The line is removed and line 3 moves up to fill the gap. The advantage is that we do not need to move the cursor to insert the line again below line 3; type `p`, and line 2 is inserted after line 3. Type `2u` to undo the switch.

Next, we want to move a block, and in this case we'll move lines 1 and 2 after lines 3 and 4. The first step is to select the two lines we want to move, so first move your cursor to the first column of line 1 and type `v` to enter the Visual mode. Highlight the first two lines by moving your cursor to the end of line 2. When selected, the next step is to cut the lines with the `d` command. This puts you back into Command mode. Move your cursor past lines 3 and 4 so that it rests on the line below `(4)`. Finally, type `p` to insert the first two lines again and you're done. Type `2u` to undo the move.

Copying and Pasting a Line in a Document

To copy a line and paste it elsewhere in the document, perform the same commands as when moving, but paste it into the document twice. First, we'll copy line 1 and paste it under line 4. To begin, we must delete the line, so move the cursor to line 1 and type `dd`

to cut the line. At this stage, we have the line copied to the Clipboard. To paste the line back into the same place, do not move your cursor yet and press Shift+P. Move your cursor to line 4 and type `p` to paste the line from the Clipboard into the document. Type `u` to undo the final paste.

Anything that has been copied to the Clipboard can be pasted from the Clipboard multiple times. Just remember the technique requires that you cut the text and then paste (`p`) it in the locations that you want it to reside in. These commands work for all versions of cut, including `x`, `dw`, and `d$`, as well as prefixing numbers to those commands to get more characters included. The paste command supports the number prefix and will put several copies of the Clipboard into your document if used.

The command `yy` allows you to pull a line into the Clipboard (Buffer) as opposed to first cutting the line and then pasting it back to its original location. It works in the same way as removing a line and pasting it back without moving the cursor. Use this technique to copy and paste lines more efficiently.

The Shell Command

Let say, for example, you have spent your time connecting to an FTP site that is remarkably busy and slow (especially for 3:30 in the morning), but luckily you got in on only your tenth try and now you want to upload the new releases you finished before you call it a night. You can't remember what you called the files now (it took so long to connect). Which of the following should you do?

- Log out of FTP to check the filename and hope you can get back in before the sun rises.
- Open a new terminal or telnet session to log in and find the filename.
- Quickly shell out, find the file, and shell back in without leaving FTP.

The shell command has proved to be quite a timesaver in many situations, which explains why it is so prevalent in so many UNIX programs. vi is no exception, and it uses the same shell command as FTP, Lynx, and Pine—the `!`. The only difference is that you need to type `:` for this command because it can make use of arguments as well.

Let's say you want to look at the files within the current directory from within vi. Simply type `:!ls` to view them. You can perform virtually every shell command, even going so far as to start up another vi session and edit another file or telnet to a remote host to get more information before continuing. The real benefit of the shell command occurs when you are programming, scripting, or changing a configuration file. You can check the results without having to stop your current vi session by saving your work `:w` and then shelling out to compile, run, or check the results.

You can suspend your vi session for longer tasks using the command Ctrl+z, which drops you back to the prompt. In order to get back into vi, you may need to double-check with your shell, but most shells use the command `fg` to bring the process back to the foreground and allow you to continue editing.

Variables for Customizing vi

Looking back to our search-and-replace methods, it is obvious that the searches were case-sensitive. When we searched for the word `If`, for instance, we had to enter the word with a capital `I` or vi wouldn't have found any of them. In order to find matches that were case-insensitive, we could have used a variable to change the setting to ignore case.

vi has far too many variables that can be set to list them all here. I'm going to discuss only a couple to get you familiar with setting them. When you are ready to start editing them yourself, please use the command `:help options` to view them all.

Each variable within vi uses the `set` command, which is the same as the environment variables for your shell. In fact, only environment variables within vi that are used during that vi session can be set this way. The command to set any variable is `:set VAR[=VALUE]`. In many cases, the `=VALUE` component is optional if the variable is a Boolean that can be switched on or off as needed.

Therefore, if you want to set up your searches to ignore case, use the command `:set ic`. It sets the Boolean variable `ic`, which is a shortcut for "ignore case", to the on position. The default is off, so the first time you call it, the searches you do from there forward are considered to be case-insensitive.

Setting Tab Stops with Variables

Tab stops are set through variables as well. The default tab stop is eight columns, which means that each tab displays the text eight columns into the document. If you would like to test it, enter the Insert mode on a new line `o` and press Tab; then type some text. The next step is to set the tab stop and watch the text move. First, be sure you are in Command mode (press Esc), and then type `:set tabstop=20`. Be sure to watch the text you entered; it moves after you press Enter. Tab stops do nothing to the document itself, but do change the display in vi.

Using a Visual Bell

If you are on a terminal that has a bell (I'm sorry) or you are sick of hearing that annoying bell (I understand), vi gives you the option of turning it off and using a visual bell. You merely set the variable `visual bell`. To do this, type `:set visualbell` and you won't hear that annoying beep anymore; instead, the screen flashes—which could prove equally annoying, so you may want to switch it back.

These variables enable you to customize your version of vi. If you find many variables that you would like set each time you start vi, you may set these up in your `~/.vimrc` file, where the `~` is your home directory and the `.vimrc` file is your personal configuration file for vi. Remember that the version of vi that comes with the Debian distribution is vim; this helps you recognize why it's called .vimrc.

To be sure that every search you do is not case-sensitive, enter the following from the command line:

```
#echo 'set ic' >> ~/.vimrc
```

This adds the command `set ic` to your `~/.vimrc` file and assures that the `ic` variable is set each time you start vi.

Abbreviations

Abbreviations are useful when you need to type something many times, have a word that is difficult to spell, or both. They enable you to type a shorter word as a replacement for a longer word or set of words. vi then fills in the rest of the word whenever the abbreviation is typed.

The command for abbreviations is `:ab` *`ABBREVIATION REPLACEMENT`*. If, for instance, you are using a long URL or your email address in your document, you may want to create an abbreviation for it, as in the following examples:

```
:ab _homepage http://www.debian.org/

:ab _email me@myaddress.com
```

Within the document, any time that `_homepage` is typed, it is automatically replaced with the URL `http://www.debian.org/`; any time `_email` is typed, it is replaced with `wells@cedarnet.org`.

As a quick example, let's create the abbreviation `_name` and link it with your name in the document. To achieve this, enter the following:

```
:ab _name <YOUR NAME>
```

replacing *`YOUR NAME`* with your name. It should be noted at this point that the abbreviation can be any word you like. It does not necessarily need to start with an underscore (_), this was done to avoid conflicting with other words in the document and to note it as an abbreviation.

Move to the last line in the document and type `o` to insert a new line. Then type the following:

```
_name
```

It is replaced with your name and the abbreviation has taken place. Please note that if you had the word `_name` in the document before you created the abbreviation, it would remain unaffected.

Abbreviations are another great example of personalizing your vi program. These commands can be placed in your `~/.vimrc` file and used each time you start vi. They can be great time-savers and you are urged to use them. To place them in your personal configuration file (`~/.vimrc`), you add this line:

```
ab _name YOUR NAME
```

Now each time that you load vi, the abbreviation is set for you.

The `map` Command

vi is a programmers' program, so it is no wonder that vi is, itself, programmable. You can customize many parts of vi, including the keys you use. The `map` command enables you to map certain keystrokes to any key on the keyboard.

For instance, suppose you are doing a lot of cutting and pasting. You may want to map the F4 function key to the `dd` command, which, if you remember, removes a line from the document. You could then map the F3 function key to the `p` character, which pastes the deleted line back into the document.

Mapping Keystrokes

Start by mapping the F3 key to the letter `p` using the following command:

```
:map <F3> p
```

Next, map the F4 key to the `dd` command by entering the following:

```
:map <F4> dd
```

Now test the results by moving your cursor to line 1 of your test document. It should read

```
Since what you're doing is working, keep doing it.
```

Press the F4 function key to remove the line and move your cursor to the bottom of the document. Pressing the F3 key places the line back into the document in the new location. Enter `2u` to undo your move and return the document to its original entries.

Obviously, when you can use such simple commands, it is not appropriate to map a function key to them, but it makes a good start. Your key mappings can be made into very complex functions if you want. Just remember that function keys are denoted as `<F1>` through `<F12>`, that the Escape key is `<Esc>`, and that the Enter key is written as `<CR>` (carriage return). Also note that the Delete key is `<Del>`, and any control keys (keys in which you hold down the control key and type a character) are denoted as `<C-CHARACTER>`. For example, to enter the command Ctrl+H, you type `<C-H>`. Each of the commands that you want to have mapped needs to be entered exactly as you type it.

Your key mappings enable you to customize your version of vi, but like the abbreviations and variable settings, they quickly become a nuisance to enter each time. As you become more familiar with vi, you'll soon realize the value of the `~/.vimrc` file; it can save so much time when trying to customize your version. Key mappings are a large part of most vi users' `~/.vimrc` files because they have so many uses. If, for instance, your Backspace key sends a delete character over your terminal emulation, you can simply map the Delete key to a backspace in your `~/.vimrc` file by editing the file and entering the following:

```
map <Del> <C-H>
```

Now when the backspace is pressed, it doesn't matter that the command is recognized as a delete character, because the delete character (`<Del>`) is mapped to the backspace character (`Ctrl+H>`).

Please take the time to look over other customized versions of vim. Many of them are posted on the Web, and as your skills evolve you may do the same. Many of these users have well-commented versions of their personal `~/.vimrc` files posted at `http://www.vim.org/`, and you are urged to read through them to draw upon their techniques in customizing your own version.

Regular Expressions

vim's ability to implement regular expressions makes it the most versatile vi clone of all. I won't go into detail about every tag it offers, but you should know a few common ones anyway. When you are ready to dig into it even more, use the online help system by entering the command `:help regexp`.

Recall that vi was based on two other programming languages, ed and ex. ed, a line editor, was based on an earlier version called qed. The man who wrote qed, Ken Thompson, also wrote an article in the "Communications of the ACM" titled "Regular Expression Search Algorithm" in 1968. He then incorporated a regular-expression compiler into his program, qed. As you can see, regular expression support has been involved with vi from its beginnings.

Regular expressions enable extended searching, matching, and replacing of text. For instance, if you wanted to search for the word `Debian` or `Linux`, you could either first go through your document searching for `Debian` (`/Debian`) and then search for the word `Linux` (`/Linux`), or you could use one regular expression, `:/Debian\¦Linux`, to do both at once. The `\¦` characters mean "or" in this statement, so as the search takes place, it is looking for the letters `D-e-b-i-a-n` or the letters `L-i-n-u-x` in sequence.

A search with a dot (`.`) in it means to match any character, and an asterisk (`*`) means zero or more times. If you combine these commands, you can build searches that search for any line containing the letter `d`, followed by any number of characters and then the letters an, for instance. The command becomes /d.*an/, and it would match dan, divan, dean, and debian. In this case, it would also match bedpan, indian, drank, and freudian. In fact, it will match any line that contains the letter d and the letters an somewhere after it.

Understanding Word Boundaries

The command to specify a word boundary in vi is, \< for the beginning of the word and \> for the end. You also need to limit your search from matching everything to matching only alphabetic characters. To match only alphabetic characters, you need to use the command [a-z], because it will match only lowercase letters. If you want to match only words that start with the letter d and end with the letters an, you write the search this way:

```
/\<d[a-z]*an\>
```

Read this as a word boundary (\<), followed by the letter d, followed by any number of lowercase letters (assuring us that you won't match spaces, punctuation marks, and so forth), and ending with the letter a, followed by the letter n and an ending word boundary (\>). As you learn to use regular expressions, you will see how powerful they are.

Searching for Word Occurrences

In your test document, we will now search for every occurrence of a word that starts with the letter d and ends with the letters ng. Using regular expressions, we would use the command:

```
/\<d[a-z]*ng\>
```

This matches only the word doing in the document. Observe that line 3 would match if we used the command /\<d.*ng\>/ because the word don't precedes the word anything, which ends in ng. It also matches only the first occurrence of the word doing in the previous sentences, because .* matches as much as it can. In this case, it matches d—everything right through the second word doing on that line, up through the final ng.

If you have never used regular expressions, vi is good place to start. They are powerful enough to perform searches for any letter, followed by any character, followed by the same letter again in a single line using

```
/([a-z]).\1
```

This says that we will search for any lowercase character, but the parentheses say to save the result of that match. The period following the closing parenthesis matches any single character, and the \1 is a special character that holds the result of the parentheses.

Maybe you want to search for prices through a document. You could try something as simple as this:

```
/\$[0-9]*\.[0-9][0-9]
```

This command says that a dollar sign ($), followed by any number of digits, followed by a period, and ending with exactly two digits should be matched. There are some problems with this type of match; it won't match values such as `$1`, because it won't match the period and two digits after it. In most cases, you have some idea of the data you are looking for and can compensate without having to write a really long and comprehensive regular expression, although that is always a possibility.

Wrapping Up vi

vi enables its users to quickly edit files and efficiently build new ones. Its availability on UNIX machines is unmatched and has spread to many other platforms with good reason. It contains powerful features that have been proven effective over its 20-plus–year growth, and development continues today. vi may not provide all the bells and whistles as emacs, but it is excellent for quickly editing and creating text files.

emacs

In 1975, Richard Stallman wrote some additional features into the line editor, TECO. Most notably, he added the functionality to easily add macros to the editor—hence the name *emacs,* meaning Editing Macros. It was easy for others to add to the editor at this point and programmers everywhere started pouring in new enhancements. Soon, TECO was left behind and emacs was born.

Several versions of emacs have risen from this initial stage, including some commercial versions, such as Unipress and CCA. Some other notable emacs versions are MicroEmacs, MG, JOVE, Freemacs, and Epsilon; but the most prevalent is GNUEmacs.

GNUEmacs is distributed with the Debian Linux distribution, and version 20.3 is the most recent version as of this writing. The term GNU stands for GNUs Not UNIX and was a project started in 1984 to develop a UNIX-like operating system in which all the programs were free and included the source code so developers could expand on them.

GNUEmacs is still maintained by Richard Stallman, whom you should recognize as the founder of the Free Software Foundation. The Free Software Foundation has produced core parts of the Linux system, including the `gcc` and `g++` compilers, the `gdb` debugger, `flex`, and `bison`, which are alternatives to `lex` and `yacc`, as well as the `bash` shell. They even distribute the Debian version of Linux.

Richard Stallman himself is a very influential and outspoken advocate of free software. He received the Grace Hopper Award from the Association for Computing Machinery for his creation of the first emacs editor. Probably the most noteworthy contribution that Richard Stallman ever made was to give us the GNU General Public License, which set the standard by which free software is distributed today. The `Linux` kernel itself is distributed under this license, as well as popular scripting languages (Perl and Python),

GNOME software (GIMP), and literally thousands of other programs you can find all over the Internet.

Using Start/Stop

To start up your emacs editor you simply type the word `emacs` at the prompt. emacs behaves differently when started from X Windows as opposed to the Terminal mode and you should be aware of this. All the features that you receive from the terminal are available from the X Windows environment as well, except that more features are added when using the GUI.

This chapter cannot provide you with a comprehensive, in-depth feature list of emacs, because there are enough features to write a complete book on that topic alone. Rather, this chapter introduces you to the most widely used commands and helps you make your decision as to what text editor you want to use. If you are editing a small text file and want to use a simple editor, such as pico or ed, or if you want to simply echo a line to the end of a file (`echo myline >> filename`), please feel free. I am not advocating one text editor over another, because each job requires different needs and handles different purposes.

You will inevitably run into those who feel that vi is the editor of choice because it requires less memory, works under more diverse terminal conditions, and comes with every UNIX variant. Freedom of choice seems to invoke advocacy in one form or another. emacs does take more memory, but does not approach MS Word or Word Perfect in that respect. Most of us don't require our editors to handle substandard terminal settings. emacs has been ported to virtually every UNIX variant, as well as OS/2, Windows95/98/NT, MacOS, Atari, Amiga, NextStep, VMS, and DECwindows, so you can install it yourself if it doesn't come preinstalled. You should know what each tool is capable of before picking one as your own.

The next sections do not cover the X Windows commands and menu feature set; they are duplicates of the terminal-based feature set, simply providing alternative methods to achieve the same thing. Rather, you will look at those techniques that enable creating and editing documents from the base feature set, because it should prove useful to everyone.

Starting emacs

emacs can be started at the prompt by itself or take a filename as its argument. Let's start by creating a new directory and copying a text file into it. Enter the following commands at the prompt to first create a temporary directory, copy the message-of-the-day file to that new directory, and then change your current directory to the new directory:

```
#mkdir /tmp/learnemacs
#cp /etc/motd /tmp/learnemacs
#cd /tmp/learnemacs
```

At this point, your current directory should be /tmp/learnemacs, and you should have only one file in it, motd. Let's start emacs and edit the motd file in one step by entering

```
#emacs motd
```

The first thing you'll notice is that you are viewing the contents of the motd file. Across the top of the screen, you'll see the following menu items highlighted:

Buffers displays buffers you have access to.

Files manages files and windows.

Tools manages text and documents.

Edit includes Cut/Paste, Undo, Spelling, and so forth.

Search includes Search/Replace Options, Bookmarks, and so forth.

Mule includes Multilingual features.

Help includes Help commands.

These can be accessed by pressing F10 or Alt+'. Alt can always be switched with the Esc key, and vice versa. Alt and Esc are interchangeable in emacs, so use whatever you find easiest. Then use the PgUp and PgDn keys to maneuver through the top menus. When you find the command you are looking for, press the up or down arrow key until your option appears. Press Enter to select it or use the letter of the item that points to the command you want to select.

emacs has several command-line switches that can be given to it before you enter the filename you want to edit. One common switch is the plus sign (+), which needs a number as its argument. This number is the line number of the file you want to edit. If for instance, I want to edit my hello.c file and need to add some line after line 100, I use this command:

```
#emacs +100 hello.c
```

emacs opens and my cursor is resting on line 100 of the hello.c program. When you start your emacs program, it is possible to edit several files at once. To do this, append several filenames to the end of your command. For instance, if you want to edit the files hello.c, goodbye.c, and linux.c, you use this command:

```
#emacs hello.c goodbye.c linux.c
```

If you append the + syntax to the command, it applies only to the first file that you want to edit.

Shutting Down emacs

To shut down emacs, press Ctrl+x followed by Ctrl+c. This line appears at the bottom of the screen:

```
Save file /tmp/learnemacs/motd? (y, n, !, ., q, C-r or C-h)
```

It certainly gives you a lot of commands to try, but for now just remember that if you forget to save your file, when you try to exit it will give you the opportunity to save. If you want to save the file back to disk, type `y` for yes; otherwise, type `n` for no. It scrolls through each file that is opened and asks whether you want to save it. If for some reason you don't want to save a file, it gives you the opportunity to back out of the exit entirely by asking the following:

```
Modified buffers exist; exit anyway? (yes or no)
```

It is not advisable to start and stop emacs if you want to do something in the shell and then start it back up. More information is covered in the "SHELL Command" section, but in the meantime you should know how to suspend and restart emacs without having to shut it down completely and restart it.

Suspending emacs

The suspend command is the common UNIX suspend command `Ctrl+z`. The word `suspended` appears at the bottom of the screen, and you find yourself back in your shell. After you do what is needed in your shell, you can reenter emacs by typing `fg` at the prompt; it returns you to the same place you were when you left it.

Neither suspending nor shutting down emacs is the most effective way to perform outside tasks. emacs itself can surround the shell and provide the framework with which to perform your shell commands. We will cover more on this in the "SHELL Command" section. You will find that emacs tries to become an operating environment. You can start up at the beginning of the day and never exit it until your day is done.

Moving the Cursor Around a Document

There are numerous ways to move your cursor around a document in emacs. As you keep using emacs you will find that eventually it will become second nature to you and not seem so intimidating. The most basic keys enable you to move up and down and side to side, as do your cursor keys. You are urged not to use the cursor keys, though, when moving around a document, because it is far more efficient to use the control keys.

Let's start by opening your personal message-of-the day file, as we did in the previous section, and using the cursor keys to go through it. The Ctrl+f key moves the cursor forward, whereas the Ctrl+b key moves the cursor backward on a line. To move to the previous line or up, use the command Ctrl+u, and to move to the next line or down, the command is Ctrl+n. emacs commands are much more intuitive than vi in this sense.

By now, you may have noticed that the commands in emacs all seem to start with a Ctrl or Alt key. The reason for this is that you need some way to differentiate between commands and characters that you want in your document. emacs does this by using those keys that don't have any effect on the text in the document. There is also a rule of thumb that further sets the use of the Ctrl and Alt keys. The Alt key usually takes on words and sentence structure, whereby the Ctrl key is commonly used in dealing with characters and lines. This may sound confusing at first, but as we continue, you will find it becomes much clearer and helps in recalling which key to use for specific commands.

Jumping Forward in a Document

Let's study other ways to move around your document. To jump forward by a word instead of by a single character, use the command Alt+f. Remember that the Alt key usually specifies sentence structure rather than characters and lines. It stands to reason that if you move forward one character using the `Ctrl+f` command, which is a base of a line, the Alt+f command moves you one word, because it is a base of a sentence. To move one word back, you use Alt+b, because it correlates to Ctrl+b, which moves you one character backward.

In the same manner, moving to the end of a line uses the command `Ctrl+e`, so moving to the end of a sentence is Alt+e. A word of caution: A sentence needs to follow a very strict rule set. It needs to have punctuation followed by two spaces before it can be considered the end of a sentence. Moving to the beginning of a line, the command is `Ctrl+a`, and moving to the beginning of a sentence is Alt+a.

Using emacs Commands

Let's create a new file and try out some of these commands. For now exit emacs and then start it up again with no arguments:

```
#emacs testdoc
```

Most of the screen is now blank and in the lower-left corner, you will see the phrase `(New file)`, letting you know you aren't overwriting some other file.

Enter the following bit of text, being sure to use the Backspace key if you need to delete something to make it look right. Do not worry about pressing Return after each sentence, but make sure that there is a blank line between the first and second paragraphs:

```
A couple I know were discussing their wallpaper, which had just been
hung. Dov was annoyed at Debby's indifference to what he felt was a
poor job. "The problem is that I'm a perfectionist and you're not,"
he finally said to her.

"Exactly!" she replied. "That's why you married me and I married you!"
```

When you look at what you typed, it looks strange because those lines that scroll to the next line seem chopped off and a \ is at the end of them. emacs has ways of automatically reformatting a paragraph for you, but first move the cursor to the first character in the first paragraph and type `Alt+q` to format the paragraph automatically.

Now, with the paragraph properly formatted and your cursor in the upper-left position, press Alt+f twice. It should place your cursor in the space between `couple` and `I`. Type `Alt+b` twice to return to the beginning of the line. Now type `Alt+e` twice, and the cursor will move ahead two sentences to sit after the period after the word `job`. At this point, type `Ctrl+e` to move to the end of the line immediately following the quotation mark and press the Home key on your keyboard.

Using the Home Key

The Home key immediately moves to the beginning of a buffer. A *buffer* is an area that emacs has set aside for editing your file. In most cases, it's just as easy to say that the Home key moves you to the beginning of your file; but you first need to understand that emacs doesn't actually edit your file. It edits a copy of it. When you make changes in emacs, it makes a copy of your file in memory before you start making changes. Those changes do not take place on the disk until you tell them to by saving the file. This means that it is more technically correct to say that the Home key brings you to the beginning of the buffer rather than the file, though you may think of it that way.

A very observant individual will also notice that when you pressed the Home key, the words `Mark set` appeared at the bottom of the screen. Ignore it for now, but it will become a very useful feature as we continue.

Using the End Key

The End key performs the opposite operation of the Home key; it moves you to the end of the document and sets a mark. By pressing the End key within your current document, you'll see the cursor set one line below the last line. From the home position, type `Alt+}` (you need to hold down the Shift key to enter a `}`) to move to the first blank line between a paragraph. If you press it again, it takes you to the next paragraph and so on. It is a quick technique for jumping between paragraphs. To go back up by paragraphs, type `Alt+{`.

You are about to enter some more paragraphs, but rather than having to press `Alt+q` to reformat each paragraph, let's turn on emacs word wrap. In emacs, the word wrap command is called *auto-fill-mode* and can be accessed by entering `Alt+x` followed by `auto-fill-mode`. After you press Enter, the `/` will not appear at the end of each line and word wrap is on. This command is a Boolean command, meaning that you can toggle it off again by simply reentering it.

At this point, you need to enter some text, because we will be traversing through a document and learning how to scroll by screen. You may choose whatever you'd like as far as text goes, but I recommend that it be in paragraph form. You could retype a page of this chapter, for instance, or choose something from your favorite magazine. Whatever you choose, be sure that it is in Paragraph mode and enter several screens' worth.

Entering Text

Press Ctrl+v, which moves the cursor down by one screen. Press it again to move down two screens, and so forth. You can use Alt+v to move back up one screen at a time as well.

An alternative to the Home and End keys is the use of the Alt+< and Alt+> key combinations. They jump to the beginning and end of the buffer, respectively. These keys set a mark at the bottom of the screen just as the Home and End keys do. They perform the same function without your having to move your fingers from the main keyboard area.

You can also move forward and backward by page. If you use the command to move forward a page, you will find that it takes you immediately to the bottom of the buffer. This is because you haven't noted where the page breaks are located. When we uncover the mystery of modes, you will learn how to make page breaks in Text mode, and then the commands to jump by page will be much more useful. Until then, just remember that they are `Ctrl+x ]` to move forward one page and `Ctrl+x [` to move back.

If you're using emacs on your machine and someone sends you a message, it tends to break up the screen. The program is running perfectly behind the scenes, but the screen will seem out of place with the message in it. In most programs, the command `Ctrl+l` (that's a lowercase *l*) refreshes the screen, and emacs is no different in this respect. Apart from refreshing the screen, it centers the line your cursor is on in the middle of the screen. This makes it easy to find the cursor and is helpful when dealing with multiple windows as well.

Move your cursor to the bottom of the screen and type `Ctrl+l` to see it refresh and move the line the cursor is on to the middle of the screen.

In this section, "Using emacs Commands," we have covered many ways to move around your document in emacs:

`Ctrl+p`	Forward one character
`Ctrl+b`	Backward one character
`Ctrl+p`	Previous line
`Ctrl+n`	Next line
`Alt+f`	Forward one word
`Alt+b`	Backward one word
`Ctrl+a`	Beginning of line
`Ctrl+e`	End of line
`Alt+a`	Backward one sentence
`Alt+e`	Forward one sentence

continues

`PageUp`	Screen up
`PageDn`	Screen down
`Home`	Beginning of buffer
`End`	End of buffer
`Alt+}`	Forward one paragraph
`Alt+{`	Backward one paragraph
`Ctrl+v`	Scroll down
`Alt+v`	Scroll up
`Ctrl+x [`	Forward one page
`Ctrl+x ]`	Backward one page
`Alt+<`	Beginning of buffer
`Alt+>`	End of buffer
`Ctrl+l`	Refresh and center

One more line should be added to the list:

`Ctrl+u`	Number of times to perform action

Here's how it works. Take any command and run it multiple times by preceding it with `Ctrl+u`. If, for instance, you want to jump down 30 pages, you simply type `Ctrl+u` followed by the number `30`, and end the command with `Ctrl+x [`. emacs will run the `Ctrl+x [` command 30 times, and your cursor will jump down 30 pages.

Move your cursor to the home position (press Home) and enter the command `Ctrl+u 30<Enter>Ctrl+f` to move the cursor 30 characters forward in your document. If you left the wallpaper joke as the first few lines in the document, your cursor should be on the letter `g` in the word `discussing`, because it is 30 characters into the document. The `Ctrl+u #` command works for nearly every command in emacs.

We have covered a lot of ground concerning cursor movement in a short period of time. I recommend starting off with a sort of cheat-sheet when you begin using emacs; eventually, the commands will become intuitive.

HELP/UNDO Commands

emacs has an extensive online help program that enables you to look up commands, search for keywords, or just read through it at your leisure. It also provides a very comprehensive Undo feature. Both of these features will soon become invaluable as you begin to incorporate emacs into your daily routine.

Using the command `Ctrl+x u` triggers the Undo method. It remembers the last changes that took place in your document, but does not save things such as cursor movement.

Undo is a very common command for some of us, and, as such, you may use the shortcut key as well, `Ctrl+_`; However, if you have to use the Shift and the Control keys at once, you may wonder what kind of shortcut you are actually getting.

Accessing Online Help Routines with Intuitive

The very comprehensive online help routines can be accessed with the intuitive command `Ctrl+h`. If you need help with a specific key, the argument `k` must be appended to it: `Ctrl+h k`. At this point, you need to type the command that you need help on.

For instance, if I were looking for help on the Undo command, I would type the following, `Ctrl+h k Ctrl+x u`. It splits the screen into two sections, and you can read the section on that key. To return to the document and get back to one screen, use the command `Ctrl+x 1`.

A word of caution concerning the help documentation: When the documentation states a command such as `C-LETTER`, it is the same as `Ctrl+LETTER`. When it states `M-LETTER`, it stands for `Meta`, but it is the equivalent of `Alt+LETTER` or `Esc+LETTER`. In fact, all the documentation is set up this way, and you should be aware of this as you continue. I will continue to use the full `Ctrl` and `Alt` keys because they are easier to follow. To recap

- Ctrl+x u = Undo
- Ctrl+_ = Undo
- Ctrl+h = Help

After entering `Ctrl+h`, you can find help on a specific key by then entering `k`. At this stage, you can enter any key and get a quick help message concerning it. To get back to the main document, enter `Ctrl+x 1`.

The UNIX `apropos` command can be accessed from your prompt using the command `apropos` *`KEYWORD`*, where *`KEYWORD`* is the name of any word having to do with the command you are searching for. It is the equivalent of `man -k` *`<KEYWORD>`*. For instance, if you want to search for every command having to do with the word *GNU,* you use this command:

```
#apropos gnu
```

It would find such commands as the following:

```
bison (1)        - GNU Project parser generator (yacc replacement)
gdb (1)        - The GNU Debugger
make (1)        - GNU make utility to maintain groups of programs
```

As you can see, `apropos` searches for the keyword embedded within the description. emacs has the same command built in to its help system, and it can be accessed using the command `Ctrl+h` followed by the letter `a`. For example, if you want to know every command that had the word `file` as part of its description, enter the following from within emacs:

```
Ctrl+h a file
```

This lists more than 50 commands that are used with files. To scroll through those commands, press and hold the Ctrl and Alt keys at once. Then type `v` to move down. When you have finished, use the command `Ctrl+x` followed by the number `1`, and it will bring your main window back into view.

Regular expressions can be used with the `apropos` command in emacs. If you are familiar with regular expressions, you will know that the caret character (`^`) at the beginning of a regular expression stands for the beginning of the search string. In this case, if we were searching for any command that starts with the word `file`, we would use this command:

```
Ctrl+h a ^file
```

The results single out the command `file-cache-minibuffer-complete`. Because regular expressions can be made very complex, your searches within the emacs help section can be made equally elaborate.

As you can see, the emacs online help section is very comprehensive. It provides the capability of looking up commands, searching through the descriptions of those commands, and even using regular expressions when searching. An online tutorial is built into emacs as well and can be accessed using the command `Ctrl+h` followed by the letter `t`. It is very useful for beginners to get a feel for emacs and you are urged to use it if you are just starting out.

INSERT/DELETE Commands

As you know by now, when creating your document in emacs all you need to do is sit down and type. Any letters that are part of your document are automatically entered into the main body of the screen and instantly become part of your document. You can insert new information by simply moving your cursor to the position where you want to insert and just start typing. You can delete information by holding down the Backspace key, and it removes the characters before it.

Overwriting Document Parts

If, instead, you want to overwrite parts of your document, you can use a minor mode called, amazingly, Overwrite mode. Overwrite mode is a Boolean command that toggles like a light switch. It's either on or off and can be accessed the same way each time. To change to this minor mode, press Alt+x and type `overwrite-mode`. emacs is very good at finishing words for you in the same manner as some shells do when you press the Tab key. This creates a convenient shortcut: Press Alt+x, type `ov`, and press Tab to have emacs fill in the rest. This works with many commands, and you are urged to use the Tab key whenever possible to finish the word.

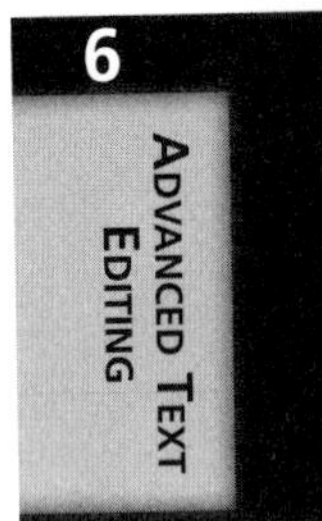

After you change to Overwrite mode, you will notice that the highlighted status bar at the bottom of the screen has changed slightly. After the word `Fundamental`, the letters `Ovwrt` have been inserted. This assures you that what you type will overwrite the text already in place. Start by typing something to see how Overwrite mode works and then toggle it back off by again pressing Alt+x, typing `ov`, and pressing Tab. You will notice that the `Ovwrt` mode disappears from the status bar.

Inserting a File

Another insert method is to insert a file. Enter `Ctrl+x` followed by the letter `i` to insert a file at the cursor position. At this point, the current directory can be seen at the bottom of the screen and you are required to enter a filename. Enter the message-of-the-day file, `/etc/motd`. Your current document now contains a copy of the message-of-the-day file embedded within your text.

As long as you are using auto-fill-mode (word wrap), you won't need to press Return at the end of each line. You should see the word `Fill` in your document's status bar at the bottom of the screen. You turned it on before you typed your text, so let's toggle it off now by typing `Alt+x` preceded by `auto-fill-mode`. You will notice the word `Fill` has now disappeared from the status bar.

Now move your cursor to end of one of the lines, using `Ctrl+e` (be sure it is not a blank line) and insert the message-of-the-day file again using the command `Ctrl+x` followed by the letter `i`. Enter the file `/etc/motd`. The file was appended to the line, but because word wrap was not on, it should have produced an exceptionally long line. The `\` character is now put into place to recognize that word wrap is not on. It's best when working with text to be sure that the word wrap is on.

To reformat the paragraph, enter `Alt+q` or press Enter at the beginning of the insert. At this point, we should toggle back the word wrap (`Alt+x auto-f <TAB>`) and continue on to more dangerous things, such as yanking things from the kill-ring.

The Kill-Ring

The kill-ring is like purgatory for your text. When you delete groups of text from the document, it doesn't actually enter oblivion yet. emacs has a special buffer saved for them called the *kill-ring*. It might be easier to relate it to the Clipboard if you are used to that term, but in emacs documentation you will see it called the kill-ring. The reason that it is called a ring is that you can cycle through it to get your data back because it saves the last 30 entries. You can change this number by entering `Alt+x` and then `set-variable`, and pressing Enter. The bottom line of the screen then displays `Set variable:`. You type `kill-ring-max` and again press Enter to continue. The bottom line changes again to `Set kill-ring-max to value:`. At this point, you can enter the number of deletions and copies you want saved in the kill-ring.

You already know how to remove text from your document using the Backspace and Delete keys, but if you didn't have access to them on your keyboard, you could use the command `Ctrl+d` to remove a character.

emacs provides many ways of deleting text and places them in your kill-ring, but you should be warned that when you remove a single character, it is not put in the ring. The only way to get back a single character that has been deleted with Backspace, Delete, or Ctrl+-d> is to use the undo command (`Ctrl+x u`).

Deleting a Word

If you want to delete a word, the command is `Alt+d`, which follows the pattern of having the Alt key deal with words and sentence structure and the Ctrl key remove the characters and lines. If you want to remove the previous word, use the command, `Alt+`<Delete> instead. If you want to remove an entire line, `Ctrl+k` will do the trick. In the same manner, the command `Alt+k` removes a sentence. Use the command `Ctrl+x` followed by the Backspace key to remove the previous sentence.

Each of these commands takes the cursor position into account when it removes characters. This means that if you delete a word and your cursor is not at the beginning of the word, it removes only the rest of the characters. The same goes for a sentence, a line, or any other delete command. Enter the following sentence:

```
You know you've been spending too much time on the computer when your
friend misdates a check, and you suggest adding a ++ to fix it.
```

Now move your cursor to the apostrophe in the word `you've` and delete the rest of word by typing, `Alt+d`. It moves only the last part of the word because the cursor wasn't at the beginning of it. Now move your cursor to the `,` after the word `check` and enter `Alt+k` to remove the rest of the sentence. Now move up a line and move the cursor to the space between `time` and `on`. Remove the rest of the line by pressing `Ctrl+k`. Each command takes the cursor position into account as it performs the command.

Your sentence should now read

```
You know you been spending too much time
friend misdates a check
```

The next command will make use of those changes. It's the yank command, but I must warn vi users that yank in emacs is very different than in vi. In emacs, it is the equivalent of paste (or put), whereas in vi it means to copy. emacs sees the yank command as yanking the text back from the kill-ring into your document. (I realize that these terms are rather violent but you get desensitized to it after a while.)

The Yank Command

To use the yank command, press Ctrl+y or Shift+Insert, and the first item in the kill-ring (the last thing you put there) will be placed back on the screen. Try it out by placing your cursor at the end of the word `time` in the previous sentence and press Ctrl+y; what you cut (yanked) will magically appear again, assuring you that you never really deleted it—it was just located in another buffer.

In fact you can access all the commands you just removed by pressing Alt+y. As you successively press Alt+y, each of your previous deletions shows up on the screen. Remember, though, that your last command must be yank Ctrl+y in order to use this trick or it won't work.

emacs carries with it a comprehensive suite of insert and delete options. It gives you the ability to use the following:

`Alt+x overwrite-mode`	Overwrite text
`Ctrl+k`	Insert file
`Ctrl+d`	Delete a character
`Alt+d`	Kill a word
`Alt+Delete`	Kill the previous word
`Ctrl+k`	Kill a line
`Alt+k`	Kill a sentence
`Ctrl+x Delete`	Kill previous sentence
`Ctrl+y`	Yank
`Shift+INSERT`	Yank
`Alt+y`	Scroll through the kill-ring

The Insert and Delete commands are very comprehensive, but soon you will see how they correlate with other commands that enhance your ability to use emacs to edit text. The yank command is a very powerful command when it comes to editing text and we will be discussing it much more in the section "Moving Text from the Kill-Ring."

STATUS/JUMP Commands

The status line at the bottom of the screen has some useful items you should be aware of. The two asterisks near the left side indicate that the file has been changed from what is on disk. If the file has not been changed or you have just saved it, the asterisks are replaced by dashes. Reading left-to-right, the next portion displays the filename of the current buffer you are working on. Use this keyword to jump back to this buffer when your main screen is editing some other file or buffer. The parentheses display both the major and minor modes. There are then two dashes followed by the letter `L`. In this case, `L` stands for the word, *line*, and the number following it correlates with what line number the cursor is on. Two dashes after that is a percent sign, which displays what percentage of the document is above the cursor.

When programming, many times the error messages deal with line numbers. In these cases, you may want to jump to a specific line to find the error. emacs enables you to do this through its use of the `goto-line` command. To access the command, enter `Alt+x` followed by the command `goto-line`, and press Enter. You are then prompted with `Goto line:` and expected to enter the line number that you want to jump to.

If you need to jump ahead a certain number of characters, that command is available as well. It is accessed the same way as the `goto-line` command, except the command is `goto-char`. To test it, enter `Alt+x` followed by `goto-char`, and press Enter. This changes the prompt to `Goto char:`, and you can enter the number of characters you want to jump ahead.

To recap, the following commands jump to certain lines or characters in your document:

```
Alt+x goto-line # - Jump to a Particular Line Number
Alt+x goto-char # - Jump Forward a Particular Number of Characters
```

The status bar and goto commands are an integral part of the emacs system. When looking through the help sections, you will see that the status bar is usually referred to as the *mode line* because it displays both the major and minor mode used in that buffer. You now know that it displays much more than that as well. The `goto` command, especially the `goto-line` command is very useful when editing scripts and programs—something emacs specializes in. There are ways to customize emacs for programmers and emacs itself can be programmed using LISP.

SEARCH/REPLACE Commands

emacs has more methods of searching for something than any line editor, text editor, or word processor that I have used. Its search modes include the following:

- Simple search—Every editor with search capabilities
- Incremental search—Search as each character is entered
- Word search—Limit search to full words or phrases
- Regular expression search—Includes RegEx engine
- Incremental regular expression search—A mix of the two

In most cases, you will use the incremental search method, and that is what is covered here. There are advantages to it over a simple search, although if you have a firm grounding in regular expressions, you may be more inclined to use the incremental regular expression search. To start your search, enter `Ctrl+s`. The bottom line displays `I-search:` and waits for your search request. As you start to enter the word or phrase you want to search for, you will see your cursor jump to the closest possible match for each letter you enter.

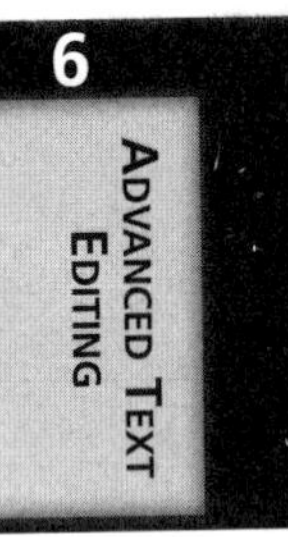

If for some reason the search fails to locate a match, you will immediately see `Failing I-search:`, followed by those characters you have entered thus far. At this point, it's best to either abandon the search or use your backspace (press Backspace) key to back out of the search until you can refine it to something that does match.

After you have a match, to find the next match you simply press Ctrl+s again. This works for each subsequent search and will traverse through the document until it finds the last match. If you press Ctrl+s at this point, the last line changes and displays `Wrapped I-search:`, followed by the search pattern. This means that the search could not find any more matches to the end of the document and therefore started again from the beginning of the document in order to find a match.

Canceling a Search

If at any time you want to cancel a search (or any other command for that matter), use the `Ctrl+g` command to back out. The last line displays the word `Quit`, informing you that you have successfully ended the command without executing it. This is useful not just for searches, but for virtually any of the commands you may use in emacs.

If you want to search in the opposite direction for your search pattern, use `Ctrl+r` instead of `Ctrl+s`. You will notice that the last line now displays `I-search backward:` instead of saying simply `I-search:`. Just enter your search request as you normally would, and the searches will move toward the top of the screen rather than the bottom.

A very quick and easy way to perform searches for specific words is to search for the word that the cursor is currently on. The easiest way to do this is with the command `Ctrl+s` followed by the command `Ctrl+w`. This inserts the word the cursor currently sits on into the search form, enabling you to quickly find the next instance of any particular word.

If, instead, you want to insert an entire line, you can move to the beginning of the line and enter `Ctrl+s` to start the search and then `Ctrl+y` to grab everything from the cursor position to the end of the line and put it in the search request. If you would rather have just part of the line, you should move your cursor into the line that you want and it will grab the rest.

A simple search does not jump through the document as you enter your search request. It is invoked using the same method as the incremental search using `Ctrl+s`, but before you start typing to start a simple search, press the Enter key. The last line now displays `Search:`, and the blinking cursor after it indicates that you should enter your search request here. Press Enter after entering your request, and it will drop you down to the first match for that search. To go to the next match, use `Ctrl+s`, as in the Incremental Search mode.

The simple search works in the same manner as the incremental search when looking for matches in reverse direction. Press Ctrl+r to start the search and then press Enter before entering your search query. Now the last line displays `Search backward`, followed by the blinking cursor, informing you that your simple search request will be performed in the reverse.

Replacing

Replacing is very much like searching; you must search for the characters you want to replace before replacing them. To initiate the replace command, enter `Alt+x` and enter the text `replace-string`. Press Enter to bring up the prompt `Replace string:`, which is where you enter your search request. This is the set of characters you want to replace. After entering them, press Enter to see the prompt now change to `Replace string [`*`YOUR SEARCH QUERY`*`] with:`, where `[`*`YOUR SEARCH QUERY`*`]` is the search request you entered.

At this stage, you enter what you want the text replaced with. To remove all occurrences of a word, you can enter nothing at this point and just press Enter, but in most cases you will want to exchange the text with something else. Enter the replace string and press Enter to immediately start a search-and-replace from the point the cursor is located throughout the rest of the document. It displays the number of occurrences it found and replaced at the bottom of the screen, enabling you to more-or-less verify that it performed as you intended it.

If you want to be sure that you replace all occurrences within a file, rather than just the point at which the cursor resides onward, be sure to move your cursor to the home position (Home or `Alt+<`) before starting your replace routine.

In many cases, you will not want to blindly search and replace throughout your document. Many times, you will want to look over the text that is to be replaced and confirm whether a switch should take place. emacs provides a powerful method for doing just that. It's called a Query-Replace, and it is invoked by entering `Alt+%`. You are now prompted with `Query replace` at the bottom of the screen and, as previously, you first enter the text you want to search for and press Enter. The prompt changes to `Query replace` *`YOUR SEARCH QUERY`* `with:`, where *`YOUR SEARCH QUERY`* is what you entered previously. Now enter the word or phrase you want to change it to and press Enter. Each time a successful match is found, the bottom line prompts you with `Query replacing` *`YOUR SEARCH QUERY`* `with` *`YOUR REPLACEMENT`*`:` where *`YOUR REPLACEMENT`* is what you last entered for a replacement to the search query. Now using either the spacebar or y and Backspace or n keys, you may choose whether to change each phrase.

To recap the search-and-replace keys, we explored the following:

- Ctrl+s — Start an incremental search.
- Ctrl+s <Enter> — Start a simple search; Also used to find the next match after the initial search.
- Ctrl+r — Start an incremental search in the reverse direction.
- Ctrl+s Ctrl+w — Immediately search for the word the cursor is on.
- Ctrl+s Ctrl+y — Immediately search for the line the cursor is on.
- Alt+x replace-string — Start a search and replace routine.
- (<HOME> or Alt+<) — Move cursor to top left-hand position useful for replacing within entire document.
- Alt+% — Query Replace—choose which replacements take place:

  SPACEBAR or 'y' to replace

  Backspace or 'no' toskip

  Cut/copy-and-paste to move/copy

Further Ideas on the Kill-Ring

By now, you already know about the kill-ring, which holds all the text you have killed. The kill-ring is used the same way as a Clipboard or a buffer. It doesn't hold only the text you kill, but the text you copy into it as well. In any case, the command `Ctrl+y` still holds true for pasting the information back from the kill-ring, and the command `Ctrl+y` followed by `Alt+y` scrolls through, replacing itself with the previous kill-ring entry. When it reaches the end of the list, it cycles back through—hence the term *ring*. If you want to get back characters that you have deleted, but you did not enter them within the kill-ring, you need to use the Undo (`Ctrl+x u`) command, because it remembers each process that took place.

The technique that emacs uses to select a block of text is to set an invisible mark within the document. The text from this mark to the cursor position marks out the block of text. In order to set a mark, you need to move the cursor into position and use either the Ctrl+@ or the Ctrl+Spacebar keys. This sets a beginning mark; your cursor position sets the ending mark by simply moving the cursor to the end of the text you want to block.

Recall that earlier when you pressed the Home and End keys, a message at the bottom of the screen appeared that displayed `Mark Set`. The Home and End keys automatically set an invisible mark at the start and end of your document. If you want to select the first paragraph, for instance, you can press the Home key, which takes you to the beginning of the document and sets a mark. Follow that with `Alt+}`, which moves the cursor forward by one paragraph. The first paragraph is selected.

Unfortunately, it is difficult to tell whether a block is selected, because there is no indication on the screen. The text is not highlighted, and there is no evidence that an area is blocked off. Luckily, there is something you can do. You can reverse the marked point and the point at which your cursor is located. This enables you to see the selected area, because the cursor is visible and you can see where the mark was set.

The command to do this is `Ctrl+x` followed by `Ctrl+x` again. It toggles the cursor and the mark, thereby enabling you to get some indication of the block size.

If you want to mark the entire buffer, you can use the command `Ctrl+x` followed by the letter `h`. It causes the cursor to jump to the beginning of the buffer and to set a mark at the end. The message `Mark set` appears at the bottom of the screen. You can prove that the whole buffer has been selected by pressing `Ctrl+x` followed by `Ctrl+x` again.

When you have blocked off some text, there are three things you can do with it. You may delete, move, or copy the text to a new location in the document. Here, you will see how the kill-ring becomes an integral part of the process.

Moving Text from the Kill-Ring

First, to delete the text, press `Ctrl+w`, which causes it to be removed from the current document and placed in the kill-ring. It is also placed in the undo buffer and can be recalled immediately from either by entering `Ctrl+x` followed by `u` for the undo feature or `Ctrl+y`, either of which places the selected text back into the file in the same location.

If you want to move the text at this point, you select the text using the command you just learned (`Ctrl+@`) to make a mark and then move the cursor to the end of the text you want to select. Now delete it using the command `Ctrl+w` and move your cursor to a new location where you would like it to be inserted. Remember that `Ctrl+y` is used to yank text back from the kill-ring, and you can place it back into the document at any new cursor location.

If you want to copy the text, first mark the area you want to copy and press Alt+w. It leaves the text on the screen but also copies the selected text to the kill-ring. This enables you to move your cursor to a new location and enter the yank command (`Ctrl+y`) to copy it from the kill-ring back into your document.

Remember to use the `Ctrl+x Ctrl+x` command to jump back and forth from the cursor location to the mark point in order to see the size of your selected text.

Let's recap the cut/copy and paste commands:

- Ctrl+y — Yank (paste) retrieves a line from the kill-ring
- Alt+y — Toggle through the kill-ring (30 entries max) (must be used immediately following a yank command)
- Ctrl+@ — Set a mark
- Ctrl+<SPACEBAR> — Set a mark

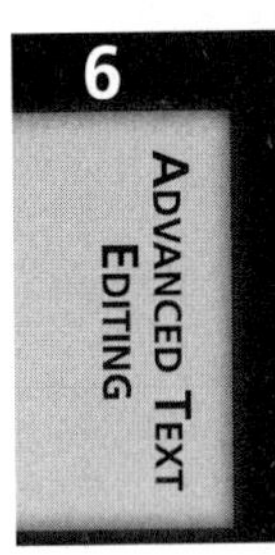

• Ctrl+x h	Select the entire buffer
• Ctrl+x Ctrl+x	Swap the mark with the cursor location
• Ctrl+w	Delete a block
• Alt+w	Copy a block
• Alt+<Insert>	Copy a block

SHELL Command

Many times, you just want to jump back to the shell and perform some simple task before continuing with your editing. It may be to catch a filename or look up a command. There are times when you may need to get your information from another machine. emacs makes performing this very simple with its shell features.

Looking Up a Single Command

If all you need to do is look up a single command, for instance, you can simply type `Alt+!` followed by the command you want to run. For instance, enter `Alt+!` from anywhere in the document, and you'll see the prompt at the bottom of the screen displaying `Shell command:`. From here, you can look up all the files in your current directory by entering the `ls` command. Upon pressing Enter, you will see another buffer (window) open up. The buffer is called *Shell Command Output*; the files in your directory are listed within this window.

To go back to the main window, type `Ctrl+x` followed by the number `1`.

emacs can be suspended by entering `Ctrl+z`. This drops you immediately to the shell, but you can re-enter emacs exactly where you left it by entering the UNIX foreground command `fg`. If the `fg` command is not supported by your shell, try entering `%emacs` to return.

Certain shell programs are built into emacs, such as `Alt+x` followed by `telnet`. After pressing Enter, the prompt changes to `Open connection to host:`; at this point, you enter the site you want to connect to. To test it, enter `localhost` and press Enter. You will notice that the screen has changed to your local login prompt, but it is still in emacs. All the emacs commands, such as cut-and-paste, search-and-replace, and so forth, work within this new buffer.

Because you have changed the buffer, in order to change it back you need the command `Ctrl+x` followed by the letter `b`. The prompt has now changed to `Switch to buffer:`; it defaults to the main buffer at this stage, so you can simply press Enter. If you didn't want the default buffer name, you can type the first few characters of one of the buffers and press Tab to finish it off. If you don't know the name of any of the buffers, press Tab without entering anything else to cause a new window to open with a list of each of the current buffers.

ABBREVIATIONS/SPELLING Commands

If you want to run a spell checker in emacs, `ispell` is a probable choice. To access it, enter the command `Alt+x`, follow it with `ispell-buffer`, and press Enter. The first word that is not recognized by the spell checker is now highlighted and the window has been split. In the upper window, the spell checker gives hints as to what to do. The spacebar takes you to the next word that is considered misspelled. Use the number of the suggestion at the top of the screen to change the word, or start typing the new word if the spell checker has not suggested it. If you are curious about other commands that deal with the `ispell` program, you can type `?` to view them. When the spell checker has finished, you are automatically taken back to your document.

Abbreviations are used to quickly change a word to another word or phrase. Many times, I see people type the word `seperate` when they really mean the word `separate`. Using emacs, it is possible to automatically change a common misspelled word to the correct version if you set it up that way.

Entering Abbreviation Mode

First, you enter the Abbreviation mode. To do this, enter the command `Alt+x` followed by `abbrev-mode`, and then press Enter. You will notice that the highlighted status bar at the bottom of the screen has changed to include the minor mode `Abbrev`, informing you that you are indeed in Abbreviation mode.

Now move your cursor to the word you want to change. Each time this word is entered, it is changed to the new word you are about to enter.

Abbreviations can be set up as either global or local abbreviations. To create a global abbreviation, use the command `Ctrl+x` followed by the letters `aig` (`add-inverse-global`). If, instead, you want to enter the command as a local command, use the command `Ctrl+x` followed by the letters `ail` (`add-inverse-local`). The prompt changes to either `Global expansion for "KEYWORD"` or `Local expansion for "KEYWORD"`, where *`KEYWORD`* is the word that the cursor was on when the command was invoked.

Now test it by entering the keyword, and as soon as you press the space bar, it changes to the new word or phrase.

To recap these commands:

Alt+x spell-buffer	Spell checker using the ispell program
Alt+x abbrev-mode	Change to minor mode, abbreviation
Ctrl+x iag	Add a global abbreviation
Ctrl+x ial	Add a local abbreviation

map Command

With emacs, you have the ability to change the commands your keys produce. The most efficient technique for this is to edit a personal customized file. This file needs to be located in your home directory and is called `.emacs`. To remap a key, you need to use the commands `global-unset` to unset a preset key or command set and `define-key` to tie a command with a key.

The Ctrl key is defined by the letter `\c`, and the Alt key is defined by the letter `\m`. This enables you to type a command such as `Ctrl+h` as `\c-h` or `Alt+h`as `\m-h`. The Esc key is defined as `\e`.

If you want to remove a command, such as the escape character (I don't recommend this unless it's someone else's file), you enter this line:

```
(global-unset-key "\e")
```

If you want to unset more than one key, simply place them between the double quotes. Here is yet another example:

```
(global-unset-key "\c-h\c-h")
```

This removes the `Ctrl+h`, followed by the `Ctrl+h` key again.

So far, you have learned how to remove keys, but the addition of keys is usually more important. To add a key, you need to bind it to a command.

For instance, if you want to find the search process to `Ctrl+x` followed by the letter `s`, you enter the following command:

```
(define-key global-map "\c-xs"'isearch-forward')
```

I should warn you that if you use this command, you overwrite the save command. It might not be a good idea. Nevertheless, it does show how to bind multiple keys to a command.

Summarizing emacs

emacs includes nearly every command you could imagine. It is extremely extendable through lisp programming and enables anyone to quickly add new commands. This is one of the reasons why emacs has become so popular.

There are also many more facets to emacs that we have not covered because they go into too much detail, such as the capability of reading and writing email and newsgroup postings or even viewing Web pages. It has special capabilities for handling various programming and scripting languages. emacs has several functions when dealing with X Windows and can be customized using your personal `.Xdefaults` file. There are also numerous techniques for managing version control systems using emacs.

emacs tries to be all things to all users and arrives quite close to succeeding in this respect. One of the icons that usually comes with emacs in X Windows environments is one of a sink that is overflowing with water. Emacs certainly has everything—including the kitchen sink.

Summary

Both vi and emacs make excellent text editors and there are serious advocacy wars as to which one is more effective. Users of vi like to point out how quickly they can make changes to a document, as the fingering was designed for efficiency rather than ease of learning. Users of emacs like to use the same argument, revealing that their system is easier to learn and therefore an individual can start producing documents more quickly with it. Ultimately, the decision lies in your hands as to which one you choose. Now you can approach that decision with a little knowledge rather than hype.

Typesetting

by Ossama Othman

In This Chapter

By now, you've been introduced to a multitude of useful Linux applications, including some word processing applications. In this chapter, tools for creating publication-quality documentation, such as the type produced by modern word processing packages, are described. The processes of document creation described in this chapter fall under the general category "Typesetting."

Typesetting Versus WYSIWYG Editors

Typesetting, in terms of the way it is described in this chapter, is achieved by using a simple text editor to enter the contents of the document you are creating. Such text editors need not have any particular formatting capabilities themselves. Rather, they are just a simple means for you to enter text into a document and store it. The final appearance of the text isn't shown when using such editors. You may wonder just how formatting, such as choosing a particular typeface or a specific document style, is achieved with simple editors.

Formatting is achieved by *marking up* the text to be set in a particular way by placing it between *tags* that denote where the desired formatting should begin and where it should end. HTML documents, for example, are formatted using tags. Markup tags are comprised of a particular sequence of characters that are easily recognizable by a user or even a computer. Both the actual document text and the markup tags are stored as plain, human-readable text.

To view the appearance of the formatted document, an external program must *render* the text. Formatting tags are interpreted by a viewer and converted into a preset graphical representation of the typeset text. In the case of a tag that denotes emphasized text, the text between the tags may be rendered using an italic font. Text that is marked up as a title may be rendered using a large boldface font. *WYSIWYG* (What-You-See-Is-What-You-Get) editors, on the other hand, render text on-the-fly and display the results of the rendering immediately on your screen.

Most users are accustomed to creating documents using WYSIWYG. Most word processors today are WYSIWYG editors. The terms *word processor* and *WYSIWYG editor* are used interchangeably in this chapter. WYSIWYG editors make it easy to create aesthetically pleasing documents with relative ease. However, the ease of creating such documents comes at a price. You may not realize it at first—in fact, you may even disagree—but a great deal of flexibility and power is lost by using WYSIWYG editors.

Flexibility

Most WYSIWYG editors contain proprietary code that is not usually readable in other editors. For this reason, you are usually confined to editing and viewing the document in the editor it was created for. Another aspect that restricts users of WYSIWYG editors is that the document is usually restricted to a certain type of output (that is, your screen or printer), although some do offer limited choices of conversions. For some users, these types of limitations don't present problems, but for more advanced users, a more powerful solution is needed.

Power

By focusing on appearance instead of content and structure, WYSIWYG editors lack the power of being able to use other tools to process the contents of your document. The typesetting tools described in this section can take advantage of tools designed for specific tasks. For example, one tool can be specifically designed to prepare a document for processing by another tool designed specifically for rendering a document. WYSIWYG editors attempt to accomplish such tasks without the aid of other tools. This limitation prevents a WYSIWYG editor from using a tool much better suited to accomplish a certain document processing task than itself.

Focusing on the content and structure of a document is also what allows improved automation when parsing a document.

Automation: Content-Oriented Markups

The canonical example used to demonstrate how content-oriented markup improves automation is the example of the content-oriented Web search. Search engines run through documents on the World Wide Web using some specified search criteria. Suppose you wanted to search for product XYZ. Normally, you'd specify a number of criteria in addition to `XYZ` to help narrow your search, but that search may still find occurrences of `XYZ` that are completely unrelated to product XYZ. The ability to search for a *product* called XYZ would improve the results of the search greatly. Appearance-oriented markup prevents such a search from occurring, but a *content-oriented* markup makes such a search entirely possible. In fact, this is one of the goals of XML, described later in this chapter.

In the next chapter we will discuss some of the features of markup-based document preparation tools such as DocBook and XML and their uses.

DocBook and XML

Now that you've been introduced to some of the reasons why using markup-based document preparation has many advantages over document preparation with a WYSIWYG editor, descriptions of some of the ways of doing markup-based document preparation follow.

This section describes typesetting using SGML-based methods. The next section describes typesetting using $\TeX$-based methods.

SGML

The typesetting methods described in this section are based on *Standard Generalized Markup Language* (SGML). It is a language that is used to *define* other markup languages. For example, HTML (the language used for creating World Wide Web pages) is defined using SGML.

Typesetting with SGML alone is not possible. Rather, an *instantiation* of SGML must be used to do typesetting. Typical instantiations of SGML include LinuxDoc, HTML, DocBook, and XML. Such instantiations are defined by using a *Document Template Definition* (DTD).

A DTD contains definitions of the *elements* used in the language being defined. An element is a part of the document structure defined by the DTD. Titles, chapters, sections, and paragraphs, for example, are elements that a DTD may define.

In addition to defining the elements used in the language defined by a DTD, a DTD also defines how the elements are related to each other. For example, it could define that a chapter is composed of title, section, and subsection elements. A chapter element could be part of a book or an article, both of which could be elements themselves. In other words, a DTD also defines the *structure* of a document. In parser terminology, a DTD defines a *grammar*.

SGML Tags

Tags are used to mark the beginning and end of a given DTD element in a document. SGML tags begin with a left angle bracket < and end with a right angle bracket >. Suppose a DTD defines a footnote element; a marked-up footnote would look like the following:

```
<footnote>
Typesetting with SGML is a snap!
</footnote>
```

In this example, the tag that marks the beginning of the footnote is `<footnote>`. The tag that marks the end of the footnote is `</footnote>`. Notice the forward slash `/` in the ending tag. All SGML tags that mark the end of a given region follow the convention of using `/` to denote that it is a closing tag. In general, each opening tag must have an accompanying closing tag.

Opening and Closing Tags

Opening and closing tags must be used at the same hierarchical level in your document. In other words, tags must be nested consistently. Here is an example of valid use of opening and closing tags, assuming that the tags shown in the example are defined in the DTD being used for the example:

```
<chapter>
    This is chapter text.
    <section>
        This is section text.
    </section>
</chapter>
```

In this example, the chapter tags surround chapter text and surround a section. The section tags surround section text. The actual document text does not have to be written using the spacing shown in the example. The additional spacing was simply used to illustrate that a hierarchy exists in the example. Nevertheless, the spacing does aid in making the structure of the document clearer for a user other than yourself. Now suppose the tags are placed at incorrect hierarchical levels:

```
<chapter>
    This is chapter text.
    <section>
        This is section text.
    </chapter>
</section>
```

In this example, the chapter is properly closed but the section isn't. This is a syntax error. An SGML tool will detect this error and usually let you know where the error occurs in your document.

Attributes

Tags can also contain *attributes*. A tag attribute provides additional information about the text enclosed by the tags. In HTML, an attribute can state the desired color of the text between tags. An attribute is found in the starting tag:

```
<employee job=engineer>John Doe</employee>
```

The attribute in this marked-up text is `job`. Such a tag could be defined in a DTD or in an XML document.

Each DTD defines its own set of tags. The HTML tags you may be familiar with are all defined in the HTML DTD, for example. You may not have realized that HTML is defined by a DTD. In fact, in order for your Web page to be certified as containing valid HTML, all the HTML in your Web page, including document structure, must conform to the HTML DTD and contain a line stating that your document uses the HTML DTD.

An SGML document that has properly balanced and nested tags is considered *tag valid*. Generally speaking, an SGML document that follows all the rules of a particular instantiation of SGML dictates but doesn't contain a line that states what DTD is being used is considered *well-formed*. A document is considered *type valid* if it conforms to its underlying

DTD. The line that specifies which DTD should be used for the document is described in the next discussion.

Viewing an SGML Document

What does an SGML document look like? You've already seen some examples of what some parts of an SGML document may look like. A detailed explanation of the different parts of an SGML document follows.

An SGML document consists of, at least, a main document file and a DTD. The main document file can also include the contents of other SGML text files. All SGML documents should begin with a line of the following form:

```
<!DOCTYPE  book PUBLIC ?-//Davenport//DTD DocBook V3.0//EN">
```

First, notice that the text shown is also a valid tag because it is placed between starting < and ending > tag characters. The following list describes each part of the line:

- `!DOCTYPE` informs the SGML tool being used that this tag identifies the document type of the document being processed.
- `book` is the document type. The document type name is also the name of the starting and ending tags that come immediately after the SGML declaration. All document content should be placed between these tags. In this case, an SGML document may look something like

  ```
  <!DOCTYPE  book PUBLIC ?-//Davenport//DTD DocBook V3.0//EN">
  <book>
    document text and elements...
  </book>
  ```

  Other DTDs define other document types. For example, the document type for simple Web pages is HTML, as defined by the HTML DTD, which is why valid HTML Web pages should be of this form:

  ```
  <!DOCTYPE HTML PUBLIC ?-//W3C//DTD HTML 4.0//EN"
       ?http://www.w3.org/TR/REC-html40/strict.dtd">
  <HTML>
     HTML head and body content...
  </HTML>
  ```

- `PUBLIC` and the text in quotes comprise the formal public ID (FPI). Different parts of the FPI are delimited by two forward slashes `//`.

  The first character in the FPI denotes the registration status with an approved registration service. A registration status of + indicates that the FPI is formally registered, whereas a registration status of - indicates that it is not. The second part of the FPI is the owner of the file. The third part of the FPI contains a keyword and a description that describes the content of the file. A DTD file will have the keyword `DTD` in the keyword description. Other keywords include `ELEMENT` and `TEXT`. See any source about SGML for a more detailed description of the FPI. The fourth part of the FPI indicates what language is being used for the file. In the previous examples, EN indicates that language used in the given file is English.

SGML elements can also be declared inside an SGML document. This is achieved by placing all SGML elements local to a document between square brackets in the `<!DOCTYPE />`:

```
<!DOCTYPE  MyDoc PUBLIC ?-//Foo Bar//DTD Foo's Document//EN" [
...some SGML declarationsv
]>
```

Declaring SGML elements in this way enables you to define your own SGML elements without creating or modifying an entire DTD. This can be useful, for example, when you want to define a macro for some SGML element.

If < and > denote the beginning and end of a tag, how can you use them literally in your document, such as in a mathematical equation? In situations where characters are reserved for use by SGML tags, a special sequence of characters beginning with an ampersand & and ending with a semicolon ; can be used to mark where the characters they represent should be substituted. This sequence of characters is an *SGML macro*. For example, in text where the < character would appear, you use the `<` macro. Some commonly used SGML macros are listed in the following table.

Character	*SGML Macro*
&	`&`
<	`<`
>	`>`
</	`&etago;`
$	`$`
#	`#`
%	`%`
~	`˜`

Many times, it is useful to place comments in an SGML document that are ignored by document processors. If you want to express some comments for a particular section of your document without having the contents of your comments appear in the final form of the document, SGML comments certainly are useful. Comments are useful for reminding yourself or telling others some important thoughts, or for explaining portions of your document to others who may view your "raw" SGML. SGML comment declarations begin with <! and end with >, respectively. SGML comments begin and end with the -- and -- delimiters, respectively. The following are valid SGML comments:

```
<!-- Foo -->
<!-- Foo -- -- Bar -->
```

As you can probably tell, SGML focuses on the structure and content of a document instead of its appearance. Notice that nothing was mentioned about the aesthetic appearance of SGML documents. Only the structure and content of SGML documents were discussed.

The following sections describe some specific SGML applications, DocBook and XML.

DocBook Tags

The DocBook DTD is fairly large and slightly intimidating at first. However, if you have a basic understanding of how SGML works, you will quickly find yourself making complicated documents with relative ease. DocBook provides four document hierarchies:

- Books
- Sets (a collection of books)
- Reference entries
- Articles

Only the DocBook book element is described in this book. See the *User's Guide for the DocBook DTD* for information about the remaining DocBook document hierarchies. In any case, when you understand how to use one of the hierarchies, it becomes fairly straightforward to use the others. The rest of this section describes some of the DocBook tags used in the book element. A simple book generally contains front matter, body matter, and back matter. As described earlier, an SGML document should begin with a line that declares the document type. A DocBook book document should begin with a line such as

```
<!DOCTYPE  Book PUBLIC ?-//Davenport//DTD DocBook V3.0//EN">
```

This line tells the SGML tool that you use to process your DocBook document that the document uses the book element found in the DocBook DTD. The entire document is wrapped inside `Book` tags:

```
<Book>
  ...Book content goes here...
</Book>
```

Keeping that in mind, meta-information—such as the date the book was written and the book title—can be written as follows:

```
<BookInfo>
  <Date>1999-06-01</DATE>
  <Title>A Simple Book</Title>
</BookInfo>
```

A preface can be written as follows:

```
<Preface>
  <Title>Preface</Title>
```

```
    <Para>
      This is the preface of my simple book.
    </Para>
  </Preface>
```

A table of contents and one or more list of tables can also be used in the book. The DocBook DTD does not require them, however. This completes the front matter. Let's move on to the body matter.

Suppose the body matter consists of one chapter (yes, a very small book) with a few subsections; the chapter is marked up using DocBook tags:

```
<Chapter>
  <Title>A Simple Chapter</Title>
  <Para>
    Here lies some introductory chapter text.
  </Para>
  <Sect1>
    <Title>A Simple Chapter Section</Title>
    <Para>
      This is some opening section text.
    </Para>
   <Sect2>
     <Title>A Simple Chapter Sub-Section</Title>
     <Para>
     Have you ever seen an angry penguin?
     </Para>
     <SimpleSect>
       <Title>Penguins: Do They Get Angry?</Title>
       <Para>
         If your home was so cold, wouldn't you be angry?
       </Para>
     </SimpleSect>
   </Sect2>
  </Sect1>
</Chapter>
```

DocBook supports five chapter section levels, `Sect1` through `Sect5`. `Sect1` is the highest chapter section. Chapters and sections must be nested properly. For example, a `Sect3` subection must be nested inside a `Sect2` subsection. A `SimpleSect` is an unnumbered subsection that can be placed at any level in a chapter. Additional chapters are added immediately after the one that precedes it. Forgoing the back matter, the complete `Book` document that was just described would look like this:

```
<!DOCTYPE  Book PUBLIC ?-//Davenport//DTD DocBook V3.0//EN">
<Book>
  <BookInfo>
    <Date>1999-06-01</DATE>
    <Title>A Simple Book</Title>
  </BookInfo>
  <Preface>
    <Title>Preface</Title>
```

```
      <Para>
        This is the preface of my simple book.
      </Para>
    </Preface>
    <Chapter>
      <Title>A Simple Chapter</Title>
      <Para>
        Here lies some introductory chapter text.
      </Para>
      <Sect1>
        <Title>A Simple Chapter Section</Title>
        <Para>
          This is some opening section text.
        </Para>
       <Sect2>
         <Title>A Simple Chapter Sub-Section</Title>
         <Para>
         Have you ever seen an angry penguin?
         </Para>
         <SimpleSect>
           <Title>Penguins: Do They Get Angry?</Title>
           <Para>
             If your home was so cold, wouldn't you be angry?
           </Para>
         </SimpleSect>
       </Sect2>
      </Sect1>
    </Chapter>
</Book>
```

There are many more elements in the DocBook DTD. The elements that were presented in this section should be enough for you to get started writing documents using the DocBook DTD.

DocBook lends itself well to writing computer documentation because its structure is parallel to the format of a book, although it is not limited to this use. In the next section, we will discuss XML, which makes it easier to define custom document types.

XML Tags

XML is the *eXtensible Markup Language*. It is a subset of SGML that enables an author to create a DTD with greater ease than creating one with pure SGML. It also enables an author to create custom markup tags without using a DTD! Why is this important? For the following reasons:

- Dependence on inflexible document types, such as HTML, is no longer a problem, because XML provides an author with the ability to define custom document types.
- SGML is very powerful, but it is also very complex. XML is based on a simple but very useful subset of SGML, thus greatly simplifying the task of creating a custom document type.

The capability of creating custom document types with relative ease is one of XML's major strengths. With XML, you can create custom tags that enable you to focus on the content of a document instead of the appearance.

Some HTML marked-up text could look something like the following:

```
<em>
Product XYZ
</em>
```

This may be useful if you care only about how a product is rendered in a Web browser, for example. What if you want to search the document for all the products listed in it? It would certainly be very difficult to isolate the products from other text marked up with the same tags. Defining XML tags that describe content instead of appearance makes it easy to search a document for products. In this case, a tag such as `<Product>` could be used:

```
<Product>
Product XYZ
</Product>
```


Writing an XML Document

How is an XML document written? The procedure for writing a *well-formed* XML document can be broken down into several basic steps:

1. Make an XML declaration.
2. Create a root element.
3. Write the document in XML.

Notice that this procedure is basically the same procedure that is followed when creating any type of SGML document.

Here is an example of an XML declaration:

```
<?xml version=?1.0" standalone="no? encoding="UTF-8"?>
```

The following are the XML declaration components:

- `<?xml` starts the XML declaration.
- `version` describes the version of XML being used. Currently, XML version 1.0 is the only version available.
- `standalone` specifies whether external markup declarations may exist.
- `encoding` specifies which character encoding to use. The default encoding is UTF-8, which is an 8-bit subset of the Unicode character set. UTF-8 is equivalent to ASCII.
- `?>` ends the XML declaration.

Well-formed XML documents generally begin with the following XML declaration:

```
<?xml version=?1.0" standalone="yes??>
```

The next step after creating the XML declaration is to create a root element. The root element encloses all other elements, just like any other SGML root element. A root element's name should be chosen to describe the contents of your document. A document that contains information about weather patterns could use a root element called WEATHER. In that case, the XML document would look something like

```
<?xml version=?1.0" standalone="yes??>
<WEATHER>
...WEATHER related XML content...
</WEATHER>
```

When a good root element is chosen, the content of the XML document can be written. A WEATHER document could look something like the following:

```
<?xml version=?1.0" standalone="yes??>
<WEATHER>

<PATTERN type=?storm">
<NAME>Monsoon</NAME>
</PATTERN>

<PATTERN type=?wind">
<NAME>Tornado</NAME>
</PATTERN>

</WEATHER>
```

Notice the use of attributes in the PATTERN elements. Attributes aren't necessary, but they can certainly be useful to further describe the text between the tags. As you can see, XML's flexibility enables you to create descriptive markups with ease. The previous document is a well-formed XML document; so how do you create a valid XML document?

As described in the section "SGML," earlier in this chapter, a valid SGML document must conform to the DTD specified in the line that contains a description of the DTD being used. XML is no exception. For a document to be considered valid XML, it also must contain a line that describes the DTD to use. This DTD is one that you as an author would typically write.

Writing a valid XML document typically involves the following steps:

1. Write a document type definition.
2. Make an XML declaration.
3. Include the document type declaration.
4. Write a valid XML.

Suppose you want to write a simple research paper DTD. Your DTD could look like this:

```
<!ELEMENT paper (title,abstract,chapter+,bibliography?)>
<!ATTLIST paper field (literature¦philosophy¦science) ?science">
<!ELEMENT abstract (paragraph+)>
<!ELEMENT chapter (title,paragraph+,section*)>
<!ELEMENT section (title,paragraph+)>
<!ELEMENT bibliography (title,paragraph+)>
<!ELEMENT paragraph (#PCDATA¦keyword)*>
<!ELEMENT title (#PCDATA¦keyword)*>
<!ELEMENT keyword (#PCDATA)>
```


This may seem confusing or complex, but it will become much clearer as it is broken down into smaller chunks in the next section.

XML Operators

Each element contains certain operators that modify the structure of the element (see Table 7.1).

TABLE 7.1 XML Operators and What They Mean

Operator	*Description*
,	Separates elements that must be used in the order they are listed.
¦	States that any of the elements in the list delimited with this operator can be used within the element containing the list.
+	States that *one* or more of the elements this operator is placed after must be used.
*	States that *zero* or more of the elements this operator is placed after must be used.
?	States that the element this operator is placed after is optional.

If you are familiar with regular expressions, you should have noticed that the last four operators listed in the table are used in regular expressions the same way.

The root element is the first line of the DTD, in this case `paper`. It is comprised of a title, an abstract, one or more chapters, and an optional bibliography. In this particular DTD, an *attribute* was defined for the root element `paper` that describes the field of research the paper document belongs to. The attribute defined in the DTD states that a paper could be a literature, philosophy, or science paper. If no attribute is specified in the document, the default will be `science`, as denoted by the last quoted string in the attribute. An abstract contains one or more paragraphs. A chapter contains a title, one or more paragraphs, and zero or more sections. Both the section and bibliography elements contain a title and one or more paragraphs. A paragraph contains either `#PCDATA`, which is just text, or a keyword—but not both. In either case, both can be left out of a paragraph, as denoted by the asterisk * on the end. The same applies for the `title` element. The `keyword` element simply contains text.

This simple DTD defines the entire structure of the `paper` document with only a few simple lines. This simplicity is part of what makes XML so powerful and flexible. Now that a DTD has been written, the rest of the XML paper document can be written.

First, an XML declaration is needed. In this case, a DTD to be used for the paper was defined, meaning that the document will not be a *standalone* document. Standalone in this context means one that doesn't call external declarations. The XML declaration would be something like this:

```
<?xml version=?1.0" standalone="no? encoding="UTF-8"?>
```

This XML declaration states that XML version 1.0 is being used in the document, external markup declarations must be used, and the character encoding used in the document is UTF-8. Because this paper document is supposed to be valid XML, external markup declarations must be used. Note that *external markup declarations* simply means that markup declarations exist outside the main document. Remember that the main document is found between the root elements. Anything outside the root elements is external to the document. This means that the DTD that was just defined can be placed in the same file as the document or in a separate file.

For this document, the DTD will be placed in the same file as the main document. This is done by placing the DTD in the SGML declaration section of the standard SGML document type declaration:

```
<?xml version=?1.0" standalone="no? encoding="UTF-8"?>

<!DOCTYPE paper [
<!ELEMENT paper (title,abstract,chapter+,bibliography?)>
<!ATTLIST paper field (literature¦philosophy¦science) ?science">
<!ELEMENT abstract (paragraph+)>
<!ELEMENT chapter (title,paragraph+,section*)>
<!ELEMENT section (title,paragraph+)>
<!ELEMENT bibliography (title,paragraph+)>
<!ELEMENT paragraph (#PCDATA¦keyword)*>
<!ELEMENT title (#PCDATA¦keyword)*>
<!ELEMENT keyword (#PCDATA)>
]>
```

The DTD could have been placed in a separate file, such as `paper.dtd`, and used in the document as follows:

```
<?xml version=?1.0" standalone="no? encoding="UTF-8"?>

<!DOCTYPE paper SYSTEM ?paper.dtd">
```

The complete paper document would look something like this:

```
<?xml version=?1.0" standalone="no? encoding="UTF-8"?>

<!DOCTYPE paper [
<!ELEMENT paper (title,abstract,chapter+,bibliography?)>
<!ATTLIST paper field (literature¦philosophy¦science) ?science">
<!ELEMENT abstract (paragraph+)>
<!ELEMENT chapter (title,paragraph+,section*)>
<!ELEMENT section (title,paragraph+)>
<!ELEMENT bibliography (title,paragraph+)>
<!ELEMENT paragraph (#PCDATA¦keyword)*>
<!ELEMENT title (#PCDATA¦keyword)*>
<!ELEMENT keyword (#PCDATA)>
]>

<paper field = ?philosophy">

<title>Zen and the Art of Linux</title>

<abstract>
<paragraph>Pretend some real abstract data would go here.</paragraph>
</abstract>

<chapter>
<title>Does this Chapter Really Exist?</title>
<paragraph>You read it in this chapter, so it exists!</paragraph>
</chapter>

</paper>
```

That's all there is to writing basic XML documents. There are some things you should be aware of when writing XML documents, as explained in the next section.

Other Factors in Creating XML Documents

XML is case sensitive, meaning the case in tags must match. A tag such as `<Bird>` must have a matching ending tag `</Bird>`. Tags such as `<Bird>` and `</BIRD>` are not correctly matched.

Another thing to be aware of is that XML treats whitespace (spaces, tabs, new lines, and so on) differently. Typically, most typesetting systems handle spacing for you. This includes suppression of excessive whitespace. XML interprets whitespace literally. Whatever whitespace you put in your XML document will be passed unchanged to a Web browser or other application that processes your XML document.

If you care about how your document is rendered—in a Web browser, for example—you accompany your XML document with a stylesheet. A stylesheet is generally written using CCS, XSL, or DSSSL. See the World Wide Web Consortium's Web page `http://www.w3.org/` for more information about stylesheets.

The next section describes how to process your SGML documents using two popular tools.

Tools for Interpretation

The final step of writing an SGML document is to interpret and render it to some form of output. Some typical forms of output include PostScript, DVI, and your display. Two popular sets of open-source tools in widespread use that perform such processing are sgmltools and Jade.

sgmltools

sgmltools is a set of tools that processes SGML documents. Some of the capabilities that sgmltools provide are SGML conversion error checks and SGML document rendering to several different forms of output, including plain text, groff, HTML, GNU info, LaTeX, LyX, DVI, PostScript, and RTF.

Each of the supported conversion formats has a corresponding replacement file that contains a mapping of linuxdoc SGML elements to the converted output format. For example, a linuxdoc chapter tag could be mapped to a LaTeX chapter tag. If a direct mapping of a particular tag to another format isn't available, an interpretation of what that tag would look like in the other format is performed.

sgmltools is primarily used for processing SGML documents that use the linuxdoc DTD. It does provide experimental support for some other DTDs, but they shouldn't be used unless you really know what you are doing.

To make sure that no error will occur when processing your SGML document into a rendered form, you can use the `sgmlcheck` script:

```
$ sgmlcheck doc.sgml
```

If there are no problems with your document, the only output you should see is `Processing...`. Assuming you are satisfied with the condition of your document, render your document using one or more of the commands in the following table.

Output Format	*Command Invocation Example*
Plain text	`sgml2txt doc.sgml`
groff man page	`sgml2txt --man doc.sgml`
HTML	`sgml2html --imagebuttons doc.sgml`
GNU info	`sgml2info doc.sgml`
LaTeX	`sgml2latex doc.sgml`
DVI	`sgml2latex --output=dvi doc.sgml`
PostScript	`sgml2latex --output=ps doc.sgml`
LyX	`sgml2lyx doc.sgml`
RTF	`sgml2rtf doc.sgml`

See the corresponding documentation for each of the tools shown in this table for complete descriptions of the available command-line options.

Jade

Jade, like sgmltools, formats SGML documents into some supported form of output, such as RFT, T_EX, XML, SGML, and fot, which are described in Table 7.2. Whereas sgmltools uses replacement files to determine how to map SGML tags into formatted output, Jade uses Document Style Semantics and Specification Language (DSSSL) to perform document formatting.

DSSSL provides a means for specifying how an SGML document should be processed. DSSSL instructions for document processing are placed in style sheetfiles, more appropriately called DSSSL specifications because more than one stylesheet can be found in a DSSSL specification. Both terms are used synonymously in this section.

One popular DSSSL transformation stylesheet specifies how to convert DocBook documents to HTML. A typical invocation of Jade that performs this conversion would look like

```
$ jade -d /usr/lib/sgml/stylesheets/dbtohtml.dsl -t sgml yourdoc.sgml
```

This converts `yourdoc.sgml`, which uses the DocBook DTD, into an HTML document. If you want to convert your DocBook document into a T_EX-formatted document, you issue the following command:

```
$ jade -d /usr/lib/sgml/stylesheets/docbook.dsl -t tex yourdoc.sgml
```

Both of these examples assume that the stylesheets specified by the `-d` command-line option exist. Your installation may place stylesheets elsewhere.

Jade uses the SP package as its DSSSL parsing engine, so it will accept all valid SP command-line options. Only Jade-specific command-line options are discussed in this section.

Jade supports several forms of output. All forms of output are described in the following basic command-line option table under the `-t` option description.

TABLE 7.2 Command-Line Options and What They Mean

Command-Line Option	*Description*
`-d` *`stylesheet`*	This specifies that the file *`stylesheet`* contains the DSSSL specification to be used.
`-t` *`output`*	*`output`* is the form of output Jade should generate. Valid values include
	`fot` XML representation of the flow object tree

continues

TABLE 7.2 continued

Command-Line Option	*Description*
	`rtf` Rich Text Format
	`tex` TEX
	`sgml` For SGML-to-SGML transformation (for example, DocBook-to-HTML)
	`xml` For SGML-to-XML transformations
`-o` *`output_file`*	Write output to *`output_file`* instead of the default. By default, if an output file is not specified, the extension of the input file will be stripped and replaced with an extension appropriate for the form of output.

Armed with simple but powerful tools such as sgmltools and Jade, you should be able to generate formatted documents with greater quality then most, if not all, WYSIWYG editors.

You have seen that there are powerful tools for creating very professional-looking documents. Now we will explore some typesetting tools such as TEX and LaTeX.

TEX and Friends

TEX is an extremely popular typesetting system in use by many scientific journals and publications. As with SGML, text is typeset using markup tags. When you know one markup language, learning another one, such as TEX, shouldn't be difficult. This section describes TEX and its many descendents.

TEX and Distributions

TEX is another document preparation system that uses markup tags to dictate the structure and appearance of a document. Because TEX is a markup language, many of the same benefits that SGML has over WYSIWYG editors also apply.

When writing a TEX document, you provide instructions about how you'd like the document to appear. This differs from the content- and structure-oriented nature of SGML. Nevertheless, TEX still provides very high-quality typeset documents. In fact, its typesetting capabilities are generally far superior to those of a WYSIWYG editor.

Documents can be written using the basic TEX program alone, but there are many TEX *macro* distributions that simplify and extend some of the capabilities of the basic TEX package. LaTeX is one such macro package. It provides predefined document classes—such as `book`, `journal`, and `report`—and also adds comprehensive sectioning and cross-referencing capabilities. AMS-TeX and AMS-LaTeX provide macros for documents that contain extensive mathematical content. BibTeX provides bibliography support. FoilTeX provides support for slide generation. There are many other TEX macropackages available. This section concentrates on LaTeX.

WYSIWYG editors enable you to interactively view what your document will look like in its final form, but it doesn't prevent the user from committing structural mistakes, such as incorrectly formatting a chapter heading or incorrectly numbering a section heading. LaTeX handles all these issues for you. You simply specify the document type a given document should use, and LaTeX handles proper font sizing, section numbering, and other such issues that a professional typesetter would handle. You are freed from worrying about any such problems.

TEX Special Characters

Before you continue, there are some things about TEX (and consequently, LaTeX) that you should know. As with SGML documents, TEX and LaTeX documents use some special characters in their markup tags:

```
$ & % # _ { } ~ ^ \
```

In order to use these characters in your document without having them interpreted as TEX special characters, you have to *escape* them with a backslash `\`. To use an ampersand in your document, for example, you enter `\&` instead of `&` alone. There is one exception, however. The backslash character `\` cannot be escaped by using `\\`, because that is the TEX line-break character. The TEX command `$\backslash$` should be used instead.

Comments can also be placed in TEX documents that are ignored by the TEX program. Comments begin with a percent sign `%`. If a comment extends beyond one line, the remaining comment lines should also begin with `%`. Anything after an unescaped `%` is considered a comment, which is why you must escape it if you want to use a percent sign literally in your document text. You can also use the `%` special character to split long lines where no line breaks or whitespace is allowed. The following:

```
This is an % bogus comment
     example of%
  splitting a sentence across several lines.
```

will produce

```
This is an example of splitting a sentence across several lines.
```

The next section describes LaTeX tags.

LaTeX Tags

LaTeX tags are generally referred to as *LaTeX commands*. They are case sensitive. LaTeX commands consist of a beginning backslash `\`, followed by a command name (letters only). A nonletter, such as a space or a number, terminates a LaTeX command of this form. If a command accepts a parameter, that parameter is placed between curly braces `{ }` following the command name. Additional options for that command, if any, are placed between square brackets `[ ]` after the command name and prior to the paramater. Options between square brackets are a comma-separated list. Typical LaTeX commands of this form look like the following:

- `\TeX{}`
- `\today`
- `\documentclass[a4paper,11pt]{article}`

The other LaTeX command form consists of a backslash followed by only one special character. An example of a LaTeX command of this form is the TEX line-break command `\\`.

TEX, meaning LaTeX as well, ignores extraneous whitespace. For example, two spaces between words will be compressed to one space. This being the case, how do you place a space after a LaTeX command (because the space after the command will terminate it)? Remember that LaTeX commands can accept parameters—even empty ones `{}`. To make sure a space is placed after a command that isn't terminated with a nonletter, simply use an empty parameter, as shown in the following example:

```
This is a \TeX{} sentence.  Now we end this sentence with the command \TeX.
\TeX{} it issimple.
```

Notice that the second sentence in the example doesn't use an empty parameter, because it ends with a nonletter (a period).

Writing a LaTeX document is similar to writing an SGML document. Every LaTeX document must begin with a command that specifies what kind of document your document will be. Document types must be chosen from the ones supported by LaTeX, such as `book`, `article`, and `report`. The document type or class is specified as follows:

```
\documentclass{document_type}
```

where *`document_type`* is one of the supported LaTeX document classes. After specifying the document class, additional commands can be specified that affect the style of the document. In addition, new commands can be specified via macro definitions. The section where these commands and macro definitions occur is called the *preamble*. Immediately following the preamble, if you have one, is the LaTeX command that marks the actual beginning of the document:

```
\begin{document}
```

A document is ended with a corresponding tag:

```
\end{document}
```

All document content should be placed between these two tags. Here is an example of a very simple LaTeX document:

```
\documentclass{article}
\begin{document}
This is a very small and simple LaTeX document.
\end{document}
```

The complete DocBook document example given in the section "DocBook," earlier in this chapter, could be written using LaTeX as follows:

```
\documentclass{book}
\date{1999-06-01}
\title{A Simple Book}
\begin{document}
\frontmatter
\chapter{Preface}
This is the preface of my simple book.
\mainmatter
\chapter{A Simple Chapter}
Here lies some introductory chapter text.
\section{A Simple Chapter Section}
This is some opening section text.
\subsection{A Simple Chapter Sub-Section}
Have you ever seen an angry penguin?
\subsubsection*{Penguins: Do They Get Angry?}
If your home was so cold, wouldn't you be angry?
\end{document}
```

Notice that most of the DocBook tags have analogous LaTeX book tags. Where the DocBook example uses the `<SimpleSect>` tag, this example uses the LaTeX `\subsubsection*` tag as its analog. The asterisk `*` after the `\subsubsection` indicates that that section should be unnumbered and should not be listed in the table of contents, if one exists.

Some other useful LaTeX commands are listed in Table 7.3.

TABLE 7.3

LaTeX Command	*Description*
`\footnote {`*`footnote text`*`}`	Text between the curly braces will automatically be placed in the appropriate location in the document, such as the bottom of the page the footnote is located on. In addition, the correct footnote number will automatically be placed in the document where the `\footnote{...}` is located.
`\emph{`*`text to be emphasized`*`}`	Text between the curly braces will be italicized.

continues

TABLE 7.3 continued

LaTeX Command	*Description*
`\begin{quote}`, `\end{quote}`	These commands are useful for quotes, phrases, and examples. Text placed between corresponding `\begin{quote}` and `\end{quote}` tags, for example, may be rendered as an indented paragraph.
`\begin{quotation}`, `\end{quotation}`	`quotation` is useful for quoting several long paragraphs, because it doesn't indent the beginning of each paragraph.
`\begin{verse}`, `\end{verse}`	`verse` is useful where line breaks are important, such as in poems. A `\\` is placed at the end of a line, and an empty line is placed between each verse.
`\begin{verbatim}`, `\end{verbatim}`	All text, including line breaks, between corresponding `\begin{verbatim}` and `\end{verbatim}` tags will be interpreted literally without any LaTeX command execution.

Tools for Interpretation

When you're ready to see what your rendered LaTeX document looks like, you have to run the LaTeX program on your document:

```
$ latex yourdoc.tex
```

This creates a DVI (DeVice Independent) file `yourdoc.dvi` that contains your formatted document. You can view your typeset document using the program `xdvi`:

```
$ xdvi yourdoc.dvi
```

Before your formatted text is displayed, you may notice some output with numbers between square brackets, such as `[23]`, displayed on your screen. This output always occurs when fonts have to be generated. Depending on how your system is configured, this may occur only once or may occur at another point in the future. It depends on whether your installation removes generated fonts to conserve disk space.

After the fonts are generated, `xdvi` displays your formatted document. You can use the Page Up and Page Down keys to scroll through your document. You can also click on any part of your displayed document to get a magnified view of the text in proximity to your mouse pointer. Left-clicking gives the smallest magnified view, middle-clicking gives you a slightly larger magnified view, and right-clicking gives you the largest magnified view. In all of these mouse clicks, the amount of magnification remains the same. Only the amount of text that is shown changes.

Printing the Document

If you want to print your formatted document, you typically need to convert the generated DVI file into PostScript. This is achieved by using the `dvips` program. To print your DVI file to a PostScript file, you use the following:

```
$ dvips yourdoc.dvi
```

This converts your document into PostScript and then sends it to your default printer. If you want to create a PostScript version of your DVI file without printing it, use the following:

```
$ dvips yourdoc.dvi -o
```

This creates a PostScript file called `yourdoc.ps`, which contains your formatted document. If you specify an argument to the `-o` option, the PostScript will be written to the file in that argument. The following writes your formatted document into a PostScript file called `foobar.ps`.

```
$ dvips yourdoc.dvi -o foobar.ps
```

groff

groff (GNU Troff) is the GNU implementation of the troff text-formatting system found on essentially all UNIX and UNIX-like operating systems, including Linux. It is a fairly old formatting system but it is still in wide use. Unlike SGML, groff concentrates more on the appearance of a document instead of its structure. This section describes the basics of using groff.

roff Dialects

The original formatting program upon which contemporary roff programs were based is called runoff (as in "run off a document"). UNIX versions of runoff were abbreviated to the name roff. A newer, more flexible implementation of roff was then created called nroff. Later, a new version of nroff was written called troff, based on the term "typesetter roff." The troff program also distributed nroff with it. Both are essentially the same program, except that nroff was designed more for line printers and ASCII terminals and ignored some troff commands such as font changes.

troff provides some fairly low-level typesetting commands. For that reason, several troff preprocessor packages were created. These preprocessors would transform certain parts of a document into troff. Some of the preprocessors groff supports include eqn, pic, and tbl.

The eqn preprocessor allows simpler typesetting of mathematical equations. The pic preprocessor provides drawing functions. Finally, the tbl preprocessor is used for formatting tables. In addition to preprocessors, groff also supports postprocessors.

groff produces device-independent output that may be fed to a postprocessor. A groff postprocessor converts the groff device-independent output into a format suitable for use by another device. groff currently supports postprocessors that produce ASCII, $\TeX$ DVI, PostScript, and X Windows output.

Because troff is somewhat difficult to use alone, troff macro packages were created. They encapsulate many of the same types of document entities that LaTeX does for $\TeX$. This encapsulation greatly simplifies the task of typesetting documents using troff. Two of these macro packages are `man` and `me`. The `man` macro package supports generation of man pages. The `me` macro package is used for formatting papers. There are several things you should know when using macro packages. The next section describes the basic markup syntax groff uses.

groff Markup Syntax

The groff analog to an SGML tag or a TEX command is a *request*. groff requests are placed on separate lines from the actual text. Here is an example:

```
Linux rules!
.ps 14
Linux rules!
```

The `.ps 14` request changes the point size of the letters on the next line to 14. The text in the example would be formatted as follows:

```
Linux rules!  Linux rules!
```

groff requests begin with a control character that is either a single quote (`'`) or a period (`.`). To start a line with a control character and not have it interpreted as a control character, precede the line with `\&`. This is a zero-width space, which will not affect your output. Multiple arguments to a request are separated with a space:

```
.uh Foo Bar
```

This invokes the `.uh` (unnumbered section head) macro with two arguments: `Foo` and `Bar`. To pass `Foo Bar` as one argument, enclose it in quotes or escape the space between the two words as follows:

```
.uh ?Foo Bar"
.uh Foo\ Bar
```

Comments in groff begin with the `\?` character sequence. Everything after this character sequence will be ignored by groff. If you begin a line with a comment, it is generally a good idea to precede the comment with a period:

```
.\? comment beginning of line
A line of text.\? end of line comment
```

The period at the beginning of the line causes the line to be interpreted as a request line, but because there is a comment immediately following the period, the line will be treated as an undefined request. The period at the beginning of a comment line isn't necessary, but it does prevent an extraneous newline character from occurring after the comment is ignored. Another thing to keep in mind regarding comments is that you shouldn't use tabs to line up your comments, because groff doesn't interpret tabs as whitespace.

As with T_EX, groff combines lines separated by a single line into a form suitable for output. For instance, the following text

```
The cow
jumped over
the moon.
```

will be formatted as follows when the document is processed for output:

```
The cow jumped over the moon.
```

Here is another example that demonstrates how groff markup can be used:

```
.B foo-config
.I OPTION
.B [
.I OPTION
.B ... ]
.B [
.I LIBRARY
.B ]
```

This particular example is for use with the groff `man` macro package. The formatted output of this example would look like this:

`foo-config` *`OPTION`* `[` *`OPTION`* `... ] [` *`LIBRARY`* `]`

Depending on the output device you specify to groff, the italicized text may be underlined instead. groff handles text and paragraph spacing for you.

Invocation of groff

A typical invocation of groff could be something like the following:

```
groff -man -Tascii foo-config.1
```

This invocation makes groff use the `man` macro package, because `foo-config.1` presumably uses macros from that package. The output is formatted as ASCII text and is sent to *standardout*, typically your screen. Suppose you wanted to print the `foo-config.1` man page with all formatting intact. One way to do this is to tell groff to format the output as PostScript and send it to the default printer as follows:

```
groff -man -Tps foo-config.1 ¦ lpr
```

This causes the PostScript generated by groff to be *piped* to the `lpr` program, which then prints the formatted PostScript output to a printer.

If you use another macro package, such as the me macro package, simply invoke groff in a way similar to the following:

```
groff -X –me yourdoc.me
```

This makes groff use the macros available in the me macro package, format yourdoc.me for the default output device, ps, and preview the output using the gxditview program.

Descriptions of some basic groff command lines are listed in Table 7.4.

TABLE 7.4 Basic groff Commands and What They Do

Command Line Option	*Description*
-h	Prints a help message.
-man, -me, -mm, -ms, and so on	Use specified macro package. Make sure the macro package you use matches the macros you use in your document.
-l	Sends the output to a printer.
-T*dev*	Prepares formatted output for the devices specified by *dev*. Supported devices are ps PostScript dvi $\TeX$ DVI format X75 Output for a 75dpi X11 previewer X100 Output for a 100dpi X11 previewer ascii Typewriter-like devices latin1 Typewriter-like devices using the ISO Latin-1 character set
-X	Preview with gxditview. The best output is achieved when this option is used with the -Tps option.

Summary

As with all things new, using any of the tools shown in this chapter takes time and practice, but after a short investment of time and effort, you will reap the rewards of a highly configurable, feature-rich set of document creation tools.

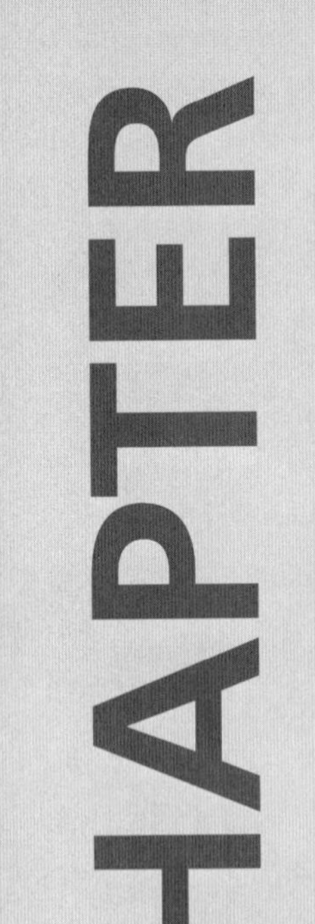

Conventional Means, Extraordinary Ends: Powerful Scripting Tools

by Mario Camou

In This Chapter

An important part of the UNIX philosophy is that "Small Is Beautiful," and large programs are made out of the joining of many small parts. Although pipes and input/output redirection are powerful constructs in their own right, by themselves they aren't flexible enough to enable the building of really powerful programs out of the "bricks" provided by UNIX. What's needed is some kind of "mortar" or "glue" that will allow you to build large programs out of smaller parts. This "glue" is provided by scripting languages.

Scripting languages are similar in concept to the batch or Job Control Language files provided by other environments, because they are designed to control the orderly execution of programs. However, they are much more powerful, because they include variables, looping, conditional execution, and more.

There are several scripting alternatives in UNIX. To begin with, all the UNIX shells (`bash`, `tcsh`, `ksh`, and others) can be used for scripting. There are also other specialized scripting languages, such as Perl, `tcl/tk`, Python, and Scheme. These last three are coverd in Chapters 26–28. In this chapter we focus on the two most common scripting languages: the `bash` shell and Perl. Although a full discussion of these languages (especially Perl) would take up a complete book, this section will get you up and running quickly and introduce some of the more salient features of these two scripting languages.

Scripting Basics

Programs written in scripting languages are known as *scripts*. A script is a file containing the commands that are executed when the script runs. It's similar to the source code of a program, except scripts are usually not compiled; the source code itself is executed. This means that there's no intermediate compilation step to generate the executable.

A script usually starts with a line such as the following:

```
#!/bin/bash
```

Although the `#` character usually introduces a comment, the special comment `#!`*`programname`* tells the shell that this is a script that should be run using *`programname`*. In the example, the script would be run using `/bin/bash`, the `bash` shell.

When you edit and save your script, you need to tell the system that it's an executable. That is done by setting the execute bits using the `chmod` command:

```
chmod a+x scriptname
```

After the execute bit is set, you can execute your script in the same way you execute any other program:

```
./programname
```

In scripts, variables usually don't need to be declared because the values stored in them are internally represented as strings (even if they are numbers), and their values are generally interpolated. This means that to use a variable name, you just place it in the middle of wherever you want it to go. For example, you can say `"The value of the variable is $variable"`, and the value of the variable will be included instead of its name, `$variable`.

Most UNIX scripting languages follow the quoting conventions of the UNIX shells (see Chapter 2, "Shells," for more information on the UNIX shells). That means that a string between double quotes (`"`) is interpolated, a string within single quotes (`'`) is taken as is, and a string within back quotes (`` ` ``) is executed as a program.

Scripting with the bash Shell

The Bourne shell and its derivative `bash` (Bourne-again shell) are probably the most popular scripting languages in the UNIX world, because one or the other (or both) are included in every UNIX system.

To write a shell script, you need to understand the concepts of Variable Substitution and Command Substitution. You also have to know which are the control flow statements and built-in functions understood by the shell. But, before that, let's see how to tell Linux that a file contains a shell script.

A `bash` script starts with this line:

```
#!/bin/bash
```

You can also use `/bin/sh` if your script doesn't use any of the `bash` extensions, such as functions, arrays, arithmetic, or tilde expansion. Although this section is centered on the extensions that `bash` provides to the standard Bourne shell, there is enough information here even for a person who has never programmed in the Bourne shell.

Tip

The program name in the first line of a script can also contain options or parameters to the script interpreter. For example, if you want a `bash` script to echo each line of code as it is executed, you can use the following:

```
#!/bin/bash -x
```

You can find more information on other parameters you can give `bash` in the `bash(1)` man page.

Displaying Information—The echo Command

One of the most common things you want to do when programming is display some output. In bash, this is done using the echo command. echo simply takes whatever is passed to it as a parameter and sends it to standard output. For example, the command

```
echo This is a test
```

outputs the text `This is a test` to standard output.

echo accepts two flags. The -n flag suppresses the linefeed at the end of the output. This is useful when building a line in steps, or when warning a user that a long process will take place:

```
echo -n "Wait a while..."
# Long process goes here
echo "Done"
```

In this case, `Wait a while...` and `Done` will be displayed in the same line.

The other flag is -e. It tells echo to interpret the backslash (\) character followed by some letter as a special character. Table 8.1 lists the escape codes.

TABLE 8.1 Shell Escape Codes

Escape Code	*Displays*
\a	Alert (bell)
\b	Backspace
\c	Suppress trailing newline
\e	Escape character
\f	Formfeed
\n	Newline
\r	Carriage return
\t	Horizontal tab
\v	Vertical tab
\\	Backslash
\nnn	The character whose ASCII code is nnn (octal)

Variables and Variable Substitution

bash variables work on the principle of *variable substitution*. This is a bit different from the way things work in nonscripting languages, such as C. When you want to use the name of a variable (such as when setting its value), you type its name by itself. If you want to substitute its value, you type its name, prepended by a dollar sign ($). For example:

```
#!/bin/bash
VAR=x
echo The value of VAR is $VAR
```

This script prints the following text:

```
The value of VAR is x
```

As you can see, the value of the variable has been substituted. No special operators or commands are needed to use the variable's value.

Exporting Variables

After a variable's value has been set, it is available only in the current shell. Any programs or scripts that are spawned by the current shell won't, by default, inherit the variable's value. To make the variable's value available to programs spawned by the current shell, the variables must be *exported* using the `export` command. For example, suppose you have the following script in the file `/usr/local/bin/testprog`:

```
#!/bin/bash
echo The value of VAR is $VAR
```

If you execute the following script:

```
#!/bin/bash
VAR=test
/usr/local/bin/testprog
export VAR
/usr/local/bin/testprog
```

you get the following output:

```
The value of VAR is
The value of VAR is test
```

As you can see, in the first call to `testprog`, the value of `VAR` isn't seen by the child program, because `VAR` hasn't been exported.

You can set a variable's value and export it in a single operation using the syntax `export` *`variable`*`=value`. You can also export several variables at the same time:

```
VAR1=value1
VAR2=value2
export VAR1 VAR2
```

Command-line Parameters

When you start a `bash` script, variables `$0` through `$9` are set to the values of the parameters passed from the command line. For example, take the following script:

```
#!/bin/bash
echo The values of the parameters are:
echo 1: $1
```

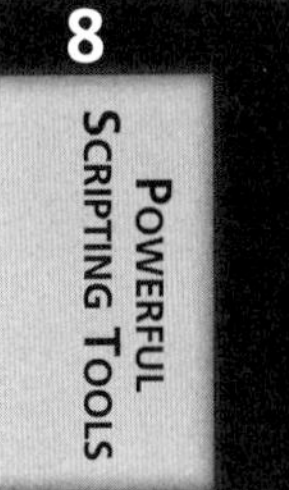

```
echo 2: $2
echo 3: $3
```

If you save it as `test.sh` and then run it as `test.sh this "is a" test`, you get the following output:

```
The values of the parameters are:
1: this
2: is a
3: test
```

Note that the double quotes used to group words into a single parameter are removed.

There are several special variables in `bash`. One of them, `$#`, is initialized to the number of parameters passed to the script. In the previous example, `$#` would have the value `3`.

Delimiting Variable Names with Braces

There are some cases where it's not clear where a variable's name ends. For example, suppose you want to display the value of the variable followed by an *s*. You might think the way to do it would be the following:

```
echo $VARs
```

However, in this case, the shell will be confused, thinking that you want to display the value of variable `VARs` instead of the value of the variable `VAR` followed by the letter *s*. Nothing will be displayed. This is because in `bash`, as in most other scripting languages, variables are declared implicitly the first time they are used. So `bash` looks for a variable called `VARs` and, not finding it, creates a new variable with an empty value.

The way around this is to use curly braces (`{}`) to delimit the name of the variable. In this way, the previous example should be written like this:

```
echo ${VAR}s
```

which does what you want—namely, display the value of the variable followed by the letter *s*.

Other Tricks with Braces

There are a few tricks that can be played using the curly brace notation. For example, the construction `${`*`variable`*`:-`*`value`*`}` substitutes *`value`* if *`variable`* is unset or `null` (that is, an empty string), or *`variable`*'s value if it is set. *`value`* can itself contain other expansions. For example, take the following:

```
echo ${var1:-${var2:-${var3}}}
```

The value of `var1` will be displayed if it is set. If `var1` is unset but `var2` is set, `var2`'s value will be displayed. Otherwise, `var3`'s value will be displayed.

Other special sequences are shown in Table 8.2.

TABLE 8.2 Special Constructions for Variable Substitution

Construction	*Meaning*
`${variable:-value}`	If `variable` is `null` or unset, substitute `value`. Otherwise, substitute `variable's` value.
`${variable:=value}`	Same as `${variable:-value}`, plus assigns `value` to `variable` if `variable` is `null` or unset.
`${variable:?value}`	If `variable` is `null` or unset, `value` is echoed to standard error and the execution of the script ends. If `variable` is set, its value is substituted.
`${variable:+value}`	The opposite of `${variable:-value}`. If `variable` is `null` or unset, substitute `null` (an empty string). Otherwise, substitute `value`.
`${#variable}`	Substitutes the number of characters in `variable's` value.

Special Variables

`bash` sets many variables when executing a script. Their names are usually special characters. The most commonly used `bash` special variables are listed in Table 8.3. Note that all these characters must be prefixed with the dollar sign ($) to get their value (for example, `$$` expands to the shell's process number).

TABLE 8.3 `bash` Special Variables

Variable	*Function*
*	Expands to all the script's parameters (`$1`, `$2`, and so on). If it is used within double quotes (`"`), it inserts the character provided by the `IFS` variable between the parameters (for example, if `IFS` contains the value `c`, `"$*"` expands to `"$1c$2c..."`.
@	Same as `*`, but if used within double quotes, each parameter expands as a single word (for example, "$@" expands to `"$1" "$2"`, and so on.
#	Expands to the number of parameters supplied in the script's command line.
?	Expands to the status (return code) of the most recently executed foreground command.
!	Expands to the status (return code) of the most recently executed background command.
$	Expands to the shell's process ID.
0	Expands to the script's full pathname.

Using Array Variables

bash provides one-dimensional arrays. Arrays are variables that can hold more than one value, indexed by an integer. The index is placed within square brackets. For example, the following code fragment:

```
ARR[0]=zero
ARR[1]=one
ARR[2]="element two"
ARR[8]=eight
ARR[9]=nine
```

assigns values to five elements of the ARR array variable. You may also assign several values in a single assignment in this way:

```
ARR=(zero one "element two" [8]=eight nine)
```

As you can see, elements are listed between parentheses, starting at index zero and separated by spaces. You can skip elements or assign to specific indexes by enclosing the index within square brackets and adding an equal sign and the desired value.

To get the value of an array index, you use a variation on the curly brace syntax, such as this: `${variable[index]}`.

You can also use the asterisk (`*`) or at-sign (`@`) as indexes. `${variable[*]}` substitutes all the elements of the array, as does `${variable[@]}`. As with `$*` and `$@` (refer to Table 8.2), the difference is when the expressions are used within double quotes ("). In this case, `"${variable[*]}"`is substituted by a single word consisting of all the elements of the array, separated by the first character of the value of the IFS variable. `"${variable[@]}"` is substituted by one word for each element.

More Substitutions and Expansions

Aside from variable substitution, bash performs a number of other substitutions before executing a command.

Command Substitution

You can substitute the output of a command using either backquotes (`) or the construct `$(command)`. For example, the following script:

```
#!/bin/bash
DATE=$(date)
echo The date is $DATE
USER=`whoami`
echo Your username is $USER
```

prints out something similar to

```
The date is Tue May 4 17:04:03 CDT 1999
Your username is mcamou
```

You can use a complete pipeline (see Chapter 2 for more information on pipelines) to massage the output into the format you need. For example, take the following script, `killall.sh`:

```
#!/bin/bash
PIDS=$(ps xea ¦ egrep "$*" ¦ egrep -v egrep ¦ sed -e "s/^  *//" ¦ cut -d\  -f 1)
echo Killing processes $PIDS
kill $PIDS
```

This script kills all processes matched by the regular expression given in its command line. The `PIDS` variable holds the process IDs of all the processes whose names contain the command-line arguments. For more information on regular expressions and the `egrep` and `sed` commands, see Chapter 9, "Regular Expressions." For more information on the `ps` and `cut` commands, see Chapter 5, "Your Virtual Toolbelt."

Arithmetic Expansion

`bash` has a full complement of arithmetic operators. To do arithmetic expansion, you use the construct `$[`*`expression`*`]`. The expression is evaluated and the result is substituted. The arithmetic operators shown in Table 8.4 are supported by `bash`, with the precedence listed in the table.

TABLE 8.4 Arithmetic Operators

Operator	*Meaning*
( )	Subexpressions in parentheses
+ -	Unary plus, –
-! ~	Logical and bitwise negation
* / %	Multiplication, division, remainder
+ -	Addition, subtraction
>> <<	Bitwise shifts, left and right
<= >= < >	Comparison
== !=	Equality
&	Bitwise AND
^	Bitwise XOR
¦	Bitwise OR
&&	Logical AND
¦¦	Logical OR
= *= /= %= += -=	Assignment
>>= <<= &= ¦=	

Any variable expansions in the expression are performed before performing the calculation. Constants that start with a 0 will be considered octal (base-8) values; constants that start with a 0x will be considered hexadecimal (base-16) values. For example,

```
i=1
i=$[$i+0xa+010]
```

In this case, the final value of i is 19. Note the dollar sign before the i inside the $[...] construct. That is needed to get the value of i.

Flow Control

Every computer language must have flow control statements that allow it to execute code based on different conditions or execute it multiple times. Scripting languages, and specifically bash, are no exception. bash has a full complement of flow control structures.

Exit Status

In bash, all flow control constructs are based on the *exit status* of commands. In UNIX, every command has an integer exit status. For bash, an exit status of zero is considered successful or "true." This is the opposite of traditional languages, such as C. A nonzero exit status means something failed or a false result. You can get a command's exit status in the special variables $? and $! for foreground and background commands, respectively. See Chapter 2 for more information on foreground and background commands.

Conditionals: if, test, and case

This is a typical conditional:

```
if /usr/local/bin/testprog1
then
  echo return from testprog1 is true
elif /usr/local/bin/testprog2; then
  echo return from testprog2 is true
else
  echo both returned false
fi
```

bash first executes /usr/local/bin/testprog1. If the return value from testprog1 is true (that is, zero), the script displays return from testprog1 is true. If testprog1 returns false (that is, nonzero), the script executes /usr/local/bin/testprog2; if its return value is true, the message return from testprog2 is true is displayed. Otherwise, the message both returned false is displayed.

As you can see, the if keyword introduces a conditional, then introduces the code that will be executed if the condition is true, else is used to introduce the code that will be executed if the condition is false, and elif is a shorthand for "else if." fi is used to end the conditional. This is usual in bash, where commands that apply to code blocks are usually closed by the same keyword used to open them, spelled backward.

The `if` keyword is commonly used with the `/usr/bin/test` program—so much so that the `[` character serves as a shorthand for `/usr/bin/test`. For example, the following code tests whether a file exists:

```
if [ -f /etc/passwd ]; then
  echo File exists
fi
```

`test` has many parameters that enable it to check whether strings are equal or different, the status and type offilenames, and much more. Table 8.5 shows the most commonly used options available to the `test` program. The full set of options can be found in the `test(1)` man page.

TABLE 8.5 Options for the `test` Program

Option	*Returns True If*
`-e` *`file`*	*`file`* exists.
`-d` *`file`*	*`file`* exists and is a directory.
`-f` *`file`*	*`file`* exists and is a regular file.
`-r` *`file`*	*`file`* exists and is readable.
`-w` *`file`*	*`file`* exists and is writable.
`-x` *`file`*	*`file`* exists and is executable.
`file1` `-nt` *`file2`*	*`file1`* is newer than *`file2`*, according to their modification dates.
`file1` `-ot` *`file2`*	*`file1`* is older than *`file2`*.
`-z` *`string`*	The length of *`string`* is zero.
`-n` *`string`*	The length of *`string`* is nonzero.
`string1` `=` *`string2`*	The strings are equal.
`string1` `!=` *`string2`*	The strings are not equal.
`! expr`	*`expr`* is false.
`expr1` `-a` *`expr2`*	Both expressions are true.
`expr1` `-o` *`expr2`*	Either expression is true.
`arg1` `OP` *`arg2`*	*`OP`* is one of `-eq`, `-ne`, `-lt`, `-le`, `-gt`, or `-ge`. These arithmetic binary operators return true if *`arg1`* is, respectively, equal-to, not-equal-to, less-than, less-than-or-equal-to, greater-than, or greater-than-or-equal-to *`arg2`*. *`arg1`* and *`arg2`* may be positive integers, negative integers, or the special expression `-l` *`string`*, which evaluates to the length of *`string`*.

Selection

As its name implies, selection is used to select code to execute depending on a value. This is a `bash` selection structure:

```
case "$1" in
  start¦"")
    echo Program is started
    ;;
  stop)
    echo Program is stopped
    ;;
  *)
    echo Invalid argument
esac
```

The `case` statement is introduced by the keyword `case` followed by the value to be tested. It is usually placed within double quotes so any spaces that appear will be included in the argument. This is followed by the keyword `in` and a series of options.

Each value to be tested is placed as a label by its own on a line, with a closing parenthesis (`)`) after it. The value to be tested may include the wildcards `?` to symbolize any character and `*` to symbolize any sequence of characters. You may match several values in the same line by separating them with the vertical bar (`¦`).

After the value, comes the code to execute if the tested value matches the label. After the code ends, there should be a line containing only whitespace and two semicolons (`;;`). This means that this option is over and execution should transfer to the line after the `esac`.

Loops: `for`, `while`, and `until`

There are two types of loops in `bash`. The `for` loop takes a list of words as a parameter and executes the loop once for each word. The `while` and `until` loops take a condition as a parameter. `while` executes the loop while the condition is true; `until` executes the loop while the condition is false. In both cases, the condition is evaluated before entering the loop.

If you want to break out of a loop in its middle, you can use the `break` statement. The `continue` statement jumps to the beginning of the loop and reevaluates the condition. Both take an optional integer parameter, which must be greater than or equal to 1; it specifies how many enclosing loops to skip. For example:

```
while [ $i < 10 ]
do
  while [$j < 20 ]
  do
    # do some processing
    if [ ! -f /tmp/file ]
    then
      break 2
    fi
    # Some more processing
  done
```

```
done
echo Finished
```

The `break 2` statement breaks out of the second enclosing loop, so the next line executed will be `echo Finished`.

Using the `for` Loop

This is an example of a `for` loop:

```
#!/bin/bash
index=1
for word in "$@"
do
  echo "Arg $index: $word"
  $index=$[$index+1]
done
```

After the `for` keyword comes the name of a variable that will hold, in turn, each of the values. After that, comes the keyword `in`, followed by the parameter list. In this case, the parameter list is the list of command-line arguments, so the loop will be executed once per command-line argument (if instead of `"$@"` we had said `"$*"`, the loop would be executed only once, passing the full argument list as a parameter).

The `do...done` syntax is used in both types of loops. It is the exception to the rule mentioned previously about finishing a block with the same keyword spelled backward. The code contained between `do` and `done` is executed once per loop.

In this case, if the previous code were a shell script called `./looptest.sh`, the output would be the following:

```
$ ./looptest.sh one two "three four" five
Arg 1: one
Arg 2: two
Arg 3: three four
Arg 4: five
```

Using the `while` Loop

This is an example of a `while` loop:

```
#!/bin/bash
num=${1?"You must supply a numeric parameter"}
total=1
while [ $num -gt 0 ]
do
  $total=$[$total*$num]
  $num=$[$num-1]
done
```

This script calculates the factorial of its parameter. After the `while` keyword comes a test, just as with the `if` statement shown previously. This test will be executed each time the loop runs. As long as the test returns a true return code, the loop will run.

As with the `for` loop (shown previously), the code to be executed in the loop is within a `do...done` pair.

Functions

A function serves the same purpose as a procedure or subroutine in other languages, that is, storing a piece of code for later execution. In `bash`, a function is introduced by the `function` keyword followed by the function's name and the code within curly braces:

```
function kill {
  local pids
  pids=$(ps xea ¦ egrep "$*" ¦ egrep -v egrep ¦ sed -e "s/^  *//" ¦ cut -d\  -f 1)
  kill $pids
}
```

This function kills any processes whose names match a regular expression provided as a parameter. It may be called just as any other command or program:

```
kill "netscape.*"
```

This kills any process whose name contains the characters `"netscape"`. Note that for this to work, the function must either be included in the same script where it is called from or be included in the script that executes the script it is called from and exported using the `export` command with the `-f` option.

The `local` keyword is similar to the `export` keyword in that it is followed by one or more variable names. However, it indicates that the following variables will be local to the function. This means that they won't be accessible outside the function, and that, if there's another variable with the same name, its value will not be modified by the function. In essence, it creates variables with the supplied names that are valid only within the function.

Any parameters provided to the function become command-line parameters while the function is executed. Their values are accessible via the special variables `$1`, `$2`, `$3`, and so on. The value of `$#` is also modified to reflect the number of parameters passed to the function.

A function behaves the same way as a variable regarding scripts that are executed from within the current shell—namely, the function will not be visible within the script unless it has been exported. To export a function, you use the same `export` command used to export variables, but with the `-f` option: `export -f` *`functionname`*.

More bash Built-In Commands

There are other commands that are built into `bash` and are useful when writing `bash` scripts.

exec—Replace the Current Shell with Another Program

The `exec` command stops executing the shell and executes another command in its place. It's useful when you're writing a shell program whose purpose is just to set up the environment for another program and then execute it. If you execute the program without the `exec` command, there will then be two processes taking up memory and slots in the process table: the shell that is running the script and the program itself. If you use the `exec` command, you wind up with just one process: the program you want to run.

You must be careful, however. If there is some cleanup task that must be executed after running the program, such as removing temporary files, you shouldn't use the `exec` command. This is because `exec` *replaces* the script with the executed program. For example,

```
#!/bin/bash
DEBUG=1
export DEBUG
exec /usr/local/bin/someprogram /tmp/logfile
mail -s "Log File" someuser < /tmp/logfile
rm /tmp/logfile
```

In this case, the intended result is that `someprogram` will generate a log file which will then be emailed to `someuser` and deleted. However, because of `exec`, the script will never get to the `mail` command. In this case, the program should be executed normally, without `exec`.

readGet Input

A script sometimes needs to get input, either from the user or from a pipeline it's embedded in (see Chapter 2 for more information on pipelines). The `read` command is used for this. For example:

```
#!/bin/bash
echo Enter something
read first second rest
echo First: $first
echo Second: $second
echo Rest: $rest
```

When you run this script, you'll see the message `Enter something`. Whatever you enter will be split into words, with the first word ending up in `$first`, the second one in `$second`, and the rest of the line in `$rest`. You can change the character used for separating words by setting the `IFS` variable. Suppose that you have a file containing numeric test scores for a class. Each line contains three test scores for one of the pupils, separated by commas. You want to generate a report with each pupil's scores and average, plus a class average for each test and a global class average. The script in Listing 8.1 does precisely that, sending the report to standard output, where it can be displayed, redirected to a file, or piped to another program (such as the print spooler `lpr`).

LISTING 8.1 The `classavg.sh` Script

```
#!/bin/bash
# Set variables
i=0
IFS=,
# Read each of the scores, save it and accumulate it
while read name[$i] test1[$i] test2[$i] test3[$i]
do
  avg[$i]=$[${test1[$i]}+${test2[$i]}+${test3[$i]}]
  sum1=$[$sum1+${test1[$i]}]
  sum2=$[$sum2+${test2[$i]}]
  sum3=$[$sum3+${test3[$i]}]
  i=$[$i+1]
done
# Print the report header
echo -e "Name\t\tTest 1\tTest 2\tTest 3\tAverage"
# Now print out the report
i2=0
while [ $i2 -lt $i ]
do
  # This assumes that each name is >8 characters long (one tab stop)
  echo -e "${name[$i]}\t${test1[$i]}\t${test2[$i]}\t${test3[$i]}\t${avg[$i]}"
done
# Get the class averages and print them out
$avg1=$[$sum1/$i]
$avg2=$[$sum2/$i]
$avg3=$[$sum3/$i]
$classavg=$[($sum1+$sum2+$sum3)/($i*3)]
echo -e "Average\t\t$avg1\t$avg2\t$avg3"
```

Listing 8.1 pulls together many of the things we've covered in this section. The `read` command will return a nonzero (that is, false) return code when it hits an end-of-file. As you can see, arrays can be read as well as standard variables.

Although `bash` is a very powerful scripting language, it does have shortcomings. For example, array indexes must be numeric. Most operations have to be made by starting other programs, which takes time, memory, and slots in the process table. The built-in arithmetic operations available are limited. No debugger is available where you can, for example, single-step through a script and inspect variable values as the script runs. `bash` programs are usually less than about 100 lines long, because `bash` provides few tools for larger programs.

Perl: Scripting on Steroids

Although other scripting languages exist, such as TCL, Python, and Scheme (which is discussed in Chapter 27), Perl is probably the most widely used scripting language in the UNIX environment. Perl programs also usually run much faster than other scripting languages, because Perl uses a precompiler. With a precompiler, when you start a program, the program is at that moment compiled into an intermediate code that is then executed much faster than an interpreted script. This results in speed close to that of a pure compiled language, such as C, with the advantages of scripting, such as immediate execution, without compiling.

Perl is the programming equivalent of a Swiss Army Knife—it contains all the tools you'll probably need. Tasks that used to require a combination of shell, awk, and sed scripts plus some C programming can now easily be handled with a single Perl script. Furthermore, you can find on the Internet (`http://www.cpan.org`) a wide variety of free Perl scripts and modules.

One of the things to consider when writing Perl programs is that, in the words of Larry Wall, Perl's creator, "There's always more than one way to do it." Perl is so flexible that there usually is no single "right" solution to a problem.

A Perl script usually starts with the following line:

```
#!/usr/bin/perl
```

so that Linux knows which program should be invoked to execute this script.

> **Note**
>
> In most Linux distributions, the Perl interpreter is located in `/usr/bin`. However, when downloading scripts from the Internet or using scripts developed for some other UNIX variant, you must keep in mind that Perl might reside somewhere else in the filesystem (such as `/usr/local/bin`). This is one of the first things to check if you have problems running a Perl script.

As with `bash` scripts, you can use flags to modify the operation of the Perl interpreter. For example,

```
#!/bin/perl -d
```

runs the script using the Perl debugger.

All commands in a Perl script must end with a semicolon (`;`). In most cases, you can place newlines in any place that a space may appear; this may increase readability of some scripts.

Variables

Perl has several variable types. The basic types are summarized in Table 8.6.

TABLE 8.6 Perl Variable Types

Type	*Symbol*	*Use*
Scalar	$	Stores a single integer or string value
Array/list	@	Stores a group of values indexed by an integer
Hash	%	Stores a group of values indexed by any scalar
Filehandle	(none)	Used to access open files

The *symbol* is used at the beginning of a variable's name to indicate its type; for example, `$FOO` is a *scalar* variable, `@FOO` is an *array* or *list* variable, `%FOO` is a *hash* variable, and `FOO` by itself is a filehandle. These four variables are completely distinct, so a program can use all of them for different purposes (although it's good programming style not to name different variables with the same name!).

It isn't necessary to indicate whether a scalar should be an integer or a string; Perl automatically detects which it should use depending on the context. Take, for example, the following code snippet:

```
$var1=10;
$var2="20";
$result1=$var1+$var2;
$result2=$var1.$var2;
```

Note that Perl differs from `bash`, because variables are always preceded by the type character, whether their values are being set or accessed. In this case, `$var1` has a numeric value, and `$var2` has a string value. However, `$result1` will end up containing the numeric value `30`, and `$result2` will have the string value `1020`. There are three *contexts* regarding string or numeric value, depending on what it's expecting at a particular moment. The `.` operator, for example, sets up a *string context*, and the `+` operator sets up a *numeric context*. In a numeric context, an empty or non-numeric string has the numeric value `0`.

There is an additional context, the *don't-care context*, which takes the value of a variable the way it is. All Boolean operations are examples of a don't-care context. In Boolean operations, numeric `0` means false and any other number means true; a `null` (empty) string or the string `"0"` means false, and any other string means true.

Variables in Perl are initially undefined. They are automatically defined upon their first use. The `undefined()` function can be used to check whether a variable is undefined; it returns a `true` or `false` Boolean value. There is also a special value, `null`, which means that a variable is defined but has no value. `null` and undefined values are treated as a `null` string in a string context, and as `0` in a numeric context.

Array and hash elements are accessed using `$array[index]` or `$hash{index}`. The dollar sign ($) indicates that the result of the operation will be a scalar, and the type of brackets used indicates the type of the variable (square brackets for arrays, curly braces for hashes). Array indexes in Perl always start at `0`.

Using Files and Filehandles

Perl excels at manipulating the contents of text files. As such, the operations of reading from and writing to a file are very easy.

First, you need to associate a *filehandle* to a physical file on the disk. This process is known as *opening* the file, and is done by the `open` function:

```
open (HOSTS, "</etc/hosts");
```

This statement opens the file `/etc/hosts` for reading and associates it with the filehandle `HOSTS`. Filehandles are usually all-uppercase to distinguish them from normal variables.

The less-than character (<) at the beginning of the filename specifies that the file should be opened for reading. A greater-than character (>) means the file should be opened for writing, and its contents should be deleted. >> means that the file should be opened for appending (writing at the end). A plus sign (+) before the < or the > opens the file for both reading and writing, without deleting its contents.

You can also start a process and write to its standard input or read from its standard output. This is done using the pipe character (¦). A ¦ at the beginning of the filename means the process should be started for writing, its standard input redirected to the handle. A ¦ at the end means the opposite, that its standard output should be redirected to the handle. For example,

```
open (SORTOUT, "¦sort > /tmp/sorted)";
open (FILELIST, "ls -R¦");
```

The <> operator is used to read from an open filehandle:

```
$line = <FILELIST>;
```

You can also use it to read from the standard input, by not including a filehandle:

```
$line = <>;
```

When you're finished with a filehandle, you should close it with the `close` function:

```
close (HOSTS);
```

Manipulating Lists

In some cases, the meaning of an array variable can change depending on the context. For example, the + operator forces a *scalar context*, which means that its arguments must be scalar. In this case, an operation such as `@var1+@var2` would force the arrays to be scalars. When used in a scalar context, arrays and hashes return the number of elements they contain, so `@var1+@var2` would return the sum of the number of elements in both arrays. The special prefix `$#array` returns the number of the last index of the array, which is usually one more than the number of elements (because array indexes usually start at `0`).

As seen, some operations detect the context in which they are running and appropriately return an array or a scalar. In other cases, an operator can alter the way it works depending on whether it's called within an array or a scalar context. One example is the <> operator used to read from an open filehandle:

```
open PASSWD "</etc/passwd>";
$line = <PASSWD>;
@file = <PASSWD>;
```

The second line reads the first line from `/etc/passwd`. The third line reads the whole contents of the file (except for the first line, which was read by the first line) into array `@file`.

Perl enables you to assign arrays in a single assignment operation. In Perl, arrays can be manipulated as lists. Lists are one of Perl's most flexible data structures. As such, there exist several ways of manipulating them. You can easily insert or delete elements, as well as truncate lists. Take the following fragment:

```
@a=(0..4);          # Same as @a=(0, 1, 2, 3, 4);
@b=(a,b,@a,c,d)     # Same as @b=(a, b, 0, 1, 2, 3 ,4, c, d);
@a=2;               # Same as @a=(2);
@a=();              # Same as $#a=-1, makes @a a null list
```

The *range operator* (`..`) returns a list containing all integers between its first and second arguments. As you can see, a Perl array can be assigned in a single operation. You can also split an array into a list of variables in a single assignment operation. This is useful when a function call returns an array:

```
open PASSWD "</etc/passwd>";
$line = <PASSWD>;
($user,$pass,$uid,$gid,$name,$home,$shell) = split (/:/,$line);
```

The `split` function is covered in the section "Built-In Functions," later in this chapter. For the moment, it is enough to say that it takes a string, splits it in pieces according to a delimiter, and returns an array. In this case, we split a line from the `/etc/passwd` file into its component fields and store each field into a variable. This makes the program more readable, because it is more understandable to work with `$user` than with, for example, `$passwd[0]`. For more information about the `/etc/passwd` file and its format, see Chapter 11, "Administration Essentials."

Operators

Perl has a full complement of arithmetic and string operators. It also contains advanced operators used for pattern matching. Many of Perl's operators have been borrowed from the C language. Also, some of Perl's operators have *left associativity*, and some have *right associativity*. This means that `5*3/2` is equivalent to `(5*3)/2` (left associativity), and `5**3**2` is equivalent to `5**(3**2)` (right associativity). Other operators, such as `..`, have no associativity, meaning that expressions such as `3..5..8` don't make sense. Table 8.7 lists most of Perl's operators and their associativity, in order of decreasing precedence.

TABLE 8.7 Perl Operators

<table>
<tr><th>Operator</th><th>Associativity</th><th>Meaning</th></tr>
<tr><td>List operators (leftward)</td><td>Left</td><td>See the section “Understanding List and Named Unary Operators,” later in this chapter</td></tr>
<tr><td><code>-></code></td><td>Left</td><td>Object reference</td></tr>
<tr><td><code>++ --</code></td><td>None</td><td>Autoincrement/autodecrement</td></tr>
<tr><td><code>**</code></td><td>Right</td><td>Exponentiation</td></tr>
<tr><td><code>!</code> ~ unary + and -</td><td>Right</td><td>Negation</td></tr>
<tr><td><code>=~ !~</code></td><td>Left</td><td>Pattern matching</td></tr>
<tr><td><code>* / % x</code></td><td>Left</td><td>Multiplication, division, modulo, string repetition</td></tr>
<tr><td><code>+ - .</code></td><td>Left</td><td>Addition, subtraction, string concatenation</td></tr>
<tr><td><code><< >></code></td><td>Left</td><td>Bitwise shift</td></tr>
<tr><td>Named unary and file test operators</td><td>None</td><td>See the sections “Understanding List and Named Unary Operators” and “File Test operators, later in this chapter</td></tr>
<tr><td><code>< > <= >= lt gt le ge</code></td><td>None</td><td>Comparison</td></tr>
<tr><td><code>== != <=> eq ne cmp</code></td><td>None</td><td>Equality</td></tr>
<tr><td><code>&</code></td><td>Left</td><td>Bitwise AND</td></tr>
<tr><td><code>| ^</code></td><td>Left</td><td>Bitwise OR and exclusive-OR</td></tr>
<tr><td><code>&&</code></td><td>Left</td><td>Logical AND</td></tr>
<tr><td><code>||</code></td><td>Left</td><td>Logical OR</td></tr>
<tr><td><code>..</code></td><td>None</td><td>Range</td></tr>
<tr><td><code>?:</code></td><td>Right</td><td>Conditional</td></tr>
<tr><td><code>= += -= *= etc.</code></td><td>Right</td><td>Assignment</td></tr>
<tr><td><code>, =></code></td><td>Left</td><td>Comma</td></tr>
<tr><td>List operators (rightward)</td><td>None</td><td>See the section “Understanding List and Named Unary Operators,” later in this chapter</td></tr>
<tr><td><code>not</code></td><td>Right</td><td>Logical negation</td></tr>
</table>

continues

TABLE 8.7 continued

Operator	*Associativity*	*Meaning*
`and`	Left	Logical AND
`or xor`	Left	Logical OR and exclusive-OR

Understanding List and Named Unary Operators

In Perl, many functions may also be called as *named operators*. Those that take a single argument are called *named unary operators,* and those that take multiple arguments are called *list operators*. A named unary operator functions just like any other unary operator: It takes whatever comes next to it as a parameter.

A list operator takes everything to its right and turns it into a parameter list. For example,

```
print $foo 2 3 4 5 $bar;
```

is equivalent to

```
print ($foo, 2, 3, 4, 5, $bar);
```

This is important to consider in some cases. For example,

```
exec '/usr/local/bin/program' 'parameter' * 20
```

is equivalent to

```
exec ('/usr/local/bin/program','parameter' * 20)
```

which is probably not what is desired. It is always better to add parentheses to show exactly what is wanted:

```
exec ('/usr/local/bin/program','parameter') * 20
```

Perl always assumes that an opening parenthesis following a list operator encloses the function's parameters (if it looks like a function call, it will be taken as such). For example,

```
print ($i+20) * 3;
```

will probably not do what is expected, because `($i+20)` will be taken as the parameter list to `print`, and the result from `print` will be multiplied by `3`. In this case, you can use either of the following:

```
print (($i+20) * 3);

print +($i+20)*3;
```

Tip

If you are not sure how Perl will interpret an expression and then add parentheses to make sure Perl does what you want, remember: It is better to have too many parentheses than too few! When in doubt, parenthesize.

A list operator can have two different precedences, depending on the side of the operator. To its left, it has a very high precedence, because it gobbles up everything to its right. However, to its right, it has a very *low* precedence, because everything to its right is evaluated before evaluating the operator. For example,

```
print (1, 2, sort 3, 4);
```

prints `1 2 4 3`, because the `sort` operator takes all the list elements to its right.

Numeric Operators

As you saw in Table 8.7, Perl supports the standard numeric operators `+`, `-`, `*`, `/`, `%`, and unary minus. It adds the exponentiation operator, `**`, to elevate its first argument to the power specified by its second.

The autoincrement and autodecrement operators work just like their C counterparts. They increment or decrement their parameter and return the value either before or after the operation. Their position with respect to the parameter specifies whether the returned value will be the value before or after the operation. For example,

```
$a = 2;
$b = ++$a;
$c = $a++;
```

In this case, `$b` will contain the value `3`, because placing the ++ operator *before* the variable (preincrement) does the increment first and then returns the value. `$c` will also contain the value `3`, because placing the ++ operator *after* the variable (postincrement) means get the value first, and then do the increment. In any case, `$a` will contain the value `4`, because it has been incremented twice.

Perl also has a full complement of bitwise operators, which operate on the bits of their arguments. The bit-shift operators << and >> shift their first argument the number of bits specified by their second argument.

Caution

The result of a bit shift depends on the computer's underlying architecture (is it a 32-bit or 64-bit processor?) and is not portable between processors. Beware!

There are also bitwise numeric operators, which apply a Boolean operation to each of the bits of its arguments: `&` for `AND`, `¦` for `OR`, and `^` for exclusive-`OR`. The bitwise negation operator, `~`, inverts all the bits in its single argument.

String Operators

As expected from a language whose primary strength is string manipulation, Perl has a couple of string operators. The `.` operator concatenates (puts together) its two parameters, so `01.23` will result in the string `"0123"`. The string repetition operator, `x`, repeats its first parameter the number of times specified by its second parameter, so `"ab"x3` results in `"ababab"`.

There are many other string manipulations possible in Perl, but they are done by pattern matching or by functions.

Comparison and Equality Operators

Perl supports the standard comparison operators, <, >, <=, and >=, as well as the equality operators == (equal-to) and `!=` (different-than). It also supports the comparison operator <=>. This operator returns `0`, `1`, or `-1`, depending on whether its first argument is equal to, greater than, or less than its second argument.

These operators set up a numeric context. There are equivalent operators for string comparisons:

Numeric Operator	*String Operator*
<	`lt`
<=	`le`
>	`gt`
>=	`ge`
==	`eq`
`!=`	`ne`
<=>	`cmp`

File Test Operators

Perl includes a full range of operators to test files. The most common are shown in Table 8.8. See the `perlfunc(1p)` man page for a complete list.

TABLE 8.8 File Test Operators

Operator	*Meaning*
`-r`	File is readable by effective uid.
`-w`	File is writable by effective uid.

Operator	Meaning
-x	File is executable by effective uid.
-o	File is owned by effective uid.
-e	File exists.
-z	File's length is zero.
-s	File's length is nonzero and returns file size in bytes.
-f	File is a plain file.
-d	File is a directory.
-l	File is a symbolic link.

Pattern Matching

Another of Perl's strong points is pattern matching. Perl provides operators for matching and substituting patterns, as well as the capability of marking portions of patterns and accessing them from other parts of the code.

Regular Expressions

Perl's patterns are based on regular expressions. Basically, a *regular expression* is a sequence of characters, some of which (called *metacharacters*) have special meanings. This section covers the most basic of them; regular expressions are covered in depth in Chapter 9.

Here's a list of the most common metacharacters used in Perl regular expressions:

Character	Meaning
\	Quote the next metacharacter (remove its special meaning)
^	Beginning of a line
$	End-of-line
.	Any character (except newline)
*	Zero or more repetitions of the previous subexpression
+	One or more repetitions
?	Zero or one repetition
[ ]	Character class
¦	Alternation
( )	Grouping

A *character class* matches any one of the characters contained within. For example, the regular expression `[0123456789]` matches any digit. You may specify character ranges, so that `[0-9]` is equivalent to `[0123456789]`, and `[A-Za-z]` matches any alphabetic character. You may also specify the negation of a character class using a caret as its first character, so `[^0-9A-Za-z]` matches any nonalphanumeric character.

Alternation matches what is before a character or what is after it. For example, `a|b` is equivalent to `[ab]`, and `ab|AB` matches either `ab` or `AB`, but not `aB`.

Parentheses are used to group subexpressions so they can be used later. This will be further explored in the section "Subexpressions," later in this chapter.

Pattern-Matching Operators

There are two pattern-matching operators in Perl. One is `m//`, which matches a regular expression. The other is `s///`, which substitutes a regular expression for another. Patterns are applied to variables using the `=~` and `!~` operators. If no variable is specified, `m//` and `s///` are applied to the default variable `$_` (see the section "Special variables," later in this chapter). The slash characters in `m//` and `s///` specify the delimiters. As such, `m//` takes only one pattern, and `s///` takes two. For example,

```
$var = "the quick brown fox jumped over the lazy dog";
$var =~ s/b.*n/red/;
```

results in `$var` containing `"The quick red fox jumped over the lazy dog"`. There are *modifiers* that may be applied to pattern matching. These are placed after the last delimiter. The modifiers supported by Perl are

Modifier	*Meaning*
`g`	Apply pattern repeatedly.
`i`	Match will be case-insensitive.
`m`	Match multiple lines.
`s`	Match single line.
`x`	Allow whitespace and comments within the pattern to make it more legible.

For example:

```
$var1 = "The quick brown fox jumped over the lazy dog";
$var2 = $var1;
$var3 = $var1;
$var1 =~ s/the/a/;
$var2 =~ s/the/a/i;
$var3 =~ s/the/a/ig;
```

In the end, `$var1` will contain `"The quick brown fox jumped over a lazy dog"`. The first pattern matches only the second occurrence of `"the"`, because, by default, pattern matches are case-sensitive. `$var2` will contain `"a quick brown fox jumped over the lazy dog"`. The second pattern matches the first occurrence of `"The"`, because it includes the case-insensitive modifier `i`. However, it stops after the first match. To match all occurrences, you have to include the global modifier g, as in the third pattern. In this case, $var3 will contain "a quick brown fox jumped over a lazy dog".

The m and s modifiers affect the way Perl does matches when a string contains multiple lines (that is, has embedded newlines). By default, ^ matches the beginning of the string, $ matches its end, and . matches any character except a newline. The m modifier makes ^ match the point after a newline (that is, the beginning of a line) and $ match the point before a newline (that is, the end of a line). s makes . match newlines as well as any other character. For example:

```
$var1="the quick brown fox\njumped over\nthe lazy dog";
$var2=$var1;
$var1=~s/^the/^a/g;
$var2=~s/^the/^a/gm;
```

Remember that \n represents a newline. In the end, $var1 will contain the text:

```
a quick brown fox
jumped over
the lazy dog
```

because the ^ character by default matches the beginning of the string, not the beginning of a line. $var2 will contain the text

```
a quick brown fox
jumped over
a lazy dog
```

because of the m modifier.

Subexpressions

One of the most common uses of pattern matching in Perl is extracting parts of strings using regular expressions. When you use parentheses in a regular expression, the subexpressions that match whatever is within the parentheses will be assigned to a set of special variables. The subexpression corresponding to the first opening parenthesis is assigned to $1, the one that matches the second opening parenthesis ends up in $2, and so on until $9. For example

```
$expression = "The quick brown fox jumped over the lazy dog";
$expression =~ /([^ ]+) fox .*([^ ]+) dog/;
$color = $1;
$active = $2;
```

As you can see, the m in the m// operator is optional. In this case, $color will hold the value "brown", and $attribute will hold the value "lazy". The expressions within the parentheses match any sequence of one or more nonspace characters. This means that any nonspace characters that come before the characters "<space>fox" will be matched to $1, and any nonspace characters that come before "<space>dog" will be matched to $2. The .* will match any length (*) sequence of any characters (.) needed to make the regular expression match. It is a "greedy" operator, meaning that if there are several possible matches (for example, if the phrase had contained more than one occurrence of "dog" after "fox"), it will always match the longest one.

Here's an example closer to the real world. As you will see in Chapter 16, "TCP/IP Networking Essentials," the /etc/hosts file is used to translate hostnames to network addresses, and vice versa. Here's an example of an /etc/hosts file:

```
10.0.1.50       chaos myhost
127.0.0.1       localhost
10.0.1.150      tumbolia   database   firewall
10.0.1.254      router
```

As you can see, each line has the basic structure *<address><whitespace><name><whitespace><aliases>*. Suppose you're processing this file and need to separate the parts of the line. Your code could look like the following (although there are other, probably more readable, ways of doing it! Remember: There's always more than one way):

```
open HOSTS "</etc/hosts";
while ( <HOSTS> ) {
  chop;
  /([0-9.]+)[ \t]+([a-z0-9]+)[ \t]+(([a-z0-9]+)*)/g
  $ip = $1;
  $name = $2;
  $aliases = $3;
  $firstalias = $4;
  # Now we can do some processing
}
```

Several things stand out in this example:

- What variable is matched? That is the strength of Perl's *default variable*, also known as $_. Many operations, such as reading from a file and pattern matching, use the default variable if no variable is specified. This makes more compact code.
- Perl has a while loop. The while loop and other control structures are examined in the section "Control Structures," later in this chapter.
- A read from a filehandle within a while loop without an assignment returns true if anything was read, and false on end-of-file. The read line is stored in $_.
- Lines read from a filehandle contain the newline at the end. The chop operator eliminates the last character from its argument. If no argument is provided, it deletes the last character from $_.
- Parentheses in subpatterns can nest. They are numbered in order of the opening parentheses.
- Parentheses can also be used to group stuff for other operators (consider the ([\t]+[a-z0-9]+)* subexpression).
- Regular expressions can be very complex and can be made to match practically anything.

You can also use the $<digit> variables in the right side of a substitution operation. Suppose you need to swap the hostname and the IP address, leaving the aliases alone. You could use the following expression to do it in a single line:

```
s/([0-9.]+)([ \t]+)([a-z0-9]+)([ \t]+([a-z0-9]+)*)/$3$2$1$4/g;
```

Note the parentheses used to capture the whitespace that separates the words, and note the order of the variables in the right side of the substitution operator. This sort of operation is used extensively when manipulating text files.

Special Variables

Perl has many special variables. Special variables are variables that already have a predefined meaning and whose value is automatically managed by Perl. The most common special variables are summarized in Table 8.9.

TABLE 8.9 Perl Special Variables

Name	*Use*
`$_`	"Default" variable. Many functions and statements use this variable if none is supplied.
`$<digit>`	Matched substrings from the corresponding opening parenthesis in the last pattern-matching operation.
`$[`	First index in an array. May contain a `0` or a `1`. The default is `0`, but you can set it to `1` to make Perl arrays start at `1`.
`$/`	The Input Record Separator, newline by default. This is the delimiter used to read lines.
`$?`	The return code from the last closed pipe, backtick (\` \`) command, or `system()` operator. It merges the actual return code with the signal number that the process died from, so `($? >> 8)` is the actual return code, and `($? & 255)` is the signal number.
`$@`	The Perl syntax error message from the last `eval()` command. If `null`, the `eval()` parsed and executed correctly. It may be set by a `die()` operator inside an `eval()`. die and eval will be covered in the section, "Built-In Functions," later in this chapter.
`$$`	Process number of the Perl interpreter running this script.
`$0`	Filename of the currently executing script.
`@ARGV`	Command-line parameters passed to the script.
`@INC`	Array of directories used to search files for use with the require, do, or use commands.
`@_`	Within a function or subroutine, contains the function's parameter list.

continues

TABLE 8.9 continued

Name	*Use*
`%ENV`	Hash whose keys are the shell or environment variables that are active in the shell that called Perl. The values are the values of the variables. Changing the hash changes the environment only for child processes.
`STDIN`	Filehandle for standard input, the default handle for `<>`.
`STDOUT`	Filehandle for standard output, the default handle for `print`.
`STDERR`	Filehandle for standard error.

Control Structures

Perl has a full array of statements to control program flow. In Perl, control statements apply to a *block*—that is, a sequence of statements delimited by curly braces (`{}`). This means that, unlike C, the braces are mandatory. However, Perl supports a *postfix* notation for control statements, which enables you to do away with the brackets in control statements that apply to a single line. For example, the following two fragments are equivalent:

```
if (! -f $file) {
  print "File not found";
}
```

```
print "File not found" if (! -f $file);
```

The one you use depends on personal style and readability; most people find the second style is usually a bit more readable.

Executing Block with Conditionals: `if` and `unless`

The `if` statement executes a block depending on a condition. For example,

```
if ( ! open (FILE1, $file1) {
  die ("Cannot open $file1");
} elsif (! open (FILE2, $file2) {
  die ("Cannot open $file2");
} else {
  print ("Both files successfully opened);
}
```

The `die` operator is covered in the section "Built-In Functions," later in this chapter.

The `elsif` clause works as a shorthand for `else if`; otherwise, because braces are mandatory, the previous fragment would have to be written as this:

```
if ( ! open (FILE1, $file1) {
  die ("Cannot open $file1");
} else {
```

```
  if (! open (FILE2, $file2) {
    die ("Cannot open $file2");
  } else {
    print ("Both files successfully opened);
  }
}
```

The `if` statement can also be used in postfix notation. The `unless` statement is the opposite of `if` and can be used only in postfix notation, executing the statement only if its condition is false. The postfix notation often makes for more concise and/or readable code. For example,

```
die ("Cannot open $file1") unless (open (FILE1, $file1);  # or if (!open...
die ("Cannot open $file2") unless (open (FILE2, $file2);
print ("Both files successfully opened);
```

Note that the `unless` statements have inverted the condition of the `if` previous statements.

Another way of doing conditionals is using the `¦` and `&` operators and their low-precedence equivalents `or` and `and`. The `¦` and `or` operators evaluate its left argument first. If it is true, the second argument is not evaluated (because the value of the Boolean expression is already known; the `OR` operation is true if any of its parameters are true). Conversely, `&` and `and` will not evaluate its second argument if the first argument is false:

```
open (FILE1, $file1) or die ("Cannot open $file1");
open (FILE2, $file2) or die ("Cannot open $file2");
print ("Both files successfully opened);
```

As you can see, there are many ways to do things in Perl, depending always on personal taste. At first sight this might seem complicated, but if you read it out loud you'll notice it sounds similar to the way one might say it in plain English.

Loops: `while`, `until`, `for`, and `foreach`

Perl has two kinds of loops. *Conditional loops* loop based on whether a condition is true or false, and *enumerated loops* loop on all the elements of a list, assigning each of them in turn to a variable.

Conditional Loops: `while`, `until`, and `for`

This is an example of a `while` loop. It is designed to read an email message from standard input and gather some information from the headers:

```
while (<>) {
  chop;
  last if /^$/;
  $subject = $2, next if (/^Subject: (.*)/);
  $from = $2, next if (/^From: (.*)/);
  $date = $2, next if (/^Date: (.*)/);
}
```

Several things stand out in this example. Some were already noted in the section "Subexpressions," earlier in this chapter, and are repeated here for completeness:

- The <> operator without an assignment and placed as a loop condition returns `true` if it read any lines, and `false` on end-of-file. The read line gets assigned to `$_`. If no filehandle is provided, it reads from standard input.
- The `last` statement is used to end a loop.
- The `next` statement is used to continue at the beginning of a loop.
- The comma operator (`,`) can be used to place several instructions in a single statement. It amounts to "do this, discard its results, and then do this and return the value." This can be used to make code more understandable.

In Perl, any prefix loop (that is, one that isn't in postfix notation) can be labeled, and the label can be referred to by `last` and `next`. For example,

```
FILE: while (<>) {
  chop;
  open (DATA, $_);
  while (<DATA>) {
    chop;
    next FILE if /^$/;
    # Process file data in $_
  }
}
```

In this case, a list of filenames is passed in standard input. Each of these files is opened and processed. However, if any file contains a blank line, it indicates the end of the data (anything below the blank lineis a comment).

Any prefix loop may also contain a `continue` clause, which will always be executed at the end of the loop before evaluating the condition. For example,

```
i = 1;
while (<>) {
  chop;
  next if /^$/;
  print "$i: $_";
} continue {
  $i++;
}
```

This example prints and numbers every nonblank line of the standard input. Blank lines are counted but not printed. The `continue` loop is executed even on those times where `next` makes the condition be reevaluated.

The previous loop may be expressed more succinctly as a `for` loop:

```
for (i = 1; <>; $i++) {
  chop;
  next if /^$/;
```

```
  print "$i: $_";
}
```

A `for` loop contains three statements, separated by semicolons (`;`): the *initializer*, the *condition,* and the *increment*. It is identical to the `for` loop in C.

`while` can be used in postfix notation. As with `if` and `unless`, `while` has its converse postfix operator, `until`. Thus, these two expressions are equivalent:

```
print while (<>);

print until (!<>);
```

Both these lines copy their standard input to standard output. The `print` operator prints its argument to a provided file descriptor. If no file descriptor is provided, it prints to standard output. If no argument is provided, it prints the default variable `$_`.

`while` and `until` always evaluate their conditions before executing the loop. To evaluate the condition after the loop (thus ensuring that the loop will always be executed at least once), you can place the loop within a `do` block:

```
do {
  $_ = <>;
  chop;
  $subject = $2, next if (/^Subject: (.*)/);
  $from = $2, next if (/^From: (.*)/);
  $date = $2, next if (/^Date: (.*)/);
} until (/^$/);    # or while (/.+/); or while (!/^$/);
```

Again, there is more than one way of expressing the same thing.

Enumerated Loops: `foreach`

There are many cases in which you want to execute a loop once for every element of a list. You could do the following:

```
for ($i = 0; $i < $#list; $i++) {
  $element = $list[i];
  # Process $element
}
```

However, that is what the `foreach` loop is for. Here's the equivalent loop using `foreach`:

```
foreach $element (@list) {
  # Process $element
}
```

If no variable is specified, `foreach` assigns the list values to `$_`. You may modify the list elements themselves by modifying the elements inside the `foreach` loop. For example, if you want to eliminate all commas in a file before processing it:

```
@lines = <>;
foreach (@lines) {
```

```
  s/,//g;
}
# Now process @lines
```

Remember that <>, when used in an array context, reads the entire file into the array.

`foreach` is often used with the range operator (`..`). The following two lines are equivalent:

```
for ($i = 0; $i < 10; $i++) {

foreach $i (0..9) {
```

Subroutines

All modern languages provide a way of specifying and executing subroutines. Perl is no exception. This is an example of a Perl subroutine:

```
# Returns the user ID  given a uid. Returns undefined if no users match.
sub getUser {
  my ($searchUid) = shift @_;
  local ($retUser) = undef;
  open PASSWD, "</etc/passwd" or die "Can't open /etc/passwd";
  while (<PASSWD>) {
    ($user,$pass,$uid,$gid,$name,$home,$shell) = split (/:/);
    $retUser = $user, last if ($uid == $searchUid);
  }
  $retUser;
}
```

This subroutine is called like this:

```
$userName = getUser (500);
```

This example shows several things:

- Perl subroutines start with the keyword `sub` followed by the subroutine name and the code within curly braces.
- Parameters are received in the `@_` array.
- The keywords `my` and `local` are used to introduced local variables. As a matter of fact, they can be used inside any block. Their parameter is a list of local variables.
- The value returned from the subroutine is the last value evaluated.
- Subroutines are called in the same way as built-in functions.

Built-In Functions

Besides using subroutines to build your own functions, you can also access the Perl built-in functions. Perl has an incredibly extensive array of built-in functions—so many that a complete listing of them would take up a whole book. This section covers only the most commonly used functions to manipulate strings, arrays, and hashes; to read and write from files; and to interface to the underlying operating and system. For a complete listing, see the `perlfunc(1p)` man page.

Perl functions can also be called as named operators. They fall into two categories: named unary operators and list operators. The difference is their precedence with respect to the comma operator. A comma will act as a statement separator when placed after a named unary operator (which takes a single argument), but will act simply as an argument separator when placed after a list operator. Basically, when used as operators, functions that take a single argument can also be called as named unary operators, and functions that can take multiple arguments are called as list operators (even when they are called with a single argument).

String Functions

Perl has a full complement of functions to manipulate strings. Some of the most common are shown in Table 8.10.

TABLE 8.10 String Functions

Name (arguments)	*Function*
`chop ([{LIST¦VARIABLE}])`	Removes the last character of its argument. Used mainly to remove linefeeds at the end of strings that have been read from a filehandle.
`index (STR,SUBSTR,[POSITION])`	Returns the position of the first occurrence of *SUBSTR* within *STR*. The first character is at the position specified by `$[` (`0` by default). If *POSITION* is specified, returns the index of the first occurrence after *POSITION*.
`length (EXPR)`	Returns the length in characters of its argument expressed as a string.
`split ([/PATTERN/[, EXPR[, LIMIT]]])`	Returns an array that results from splitting *EXPR* into tokens, with *PATTERN* as delimiter. The delimiter is not returned. If *EXPR* is omitted, uses `$.` If *PATTERN* is omitted, uses whitespace (`/[ \n\t]+/`). If *LIMIT* is specified, no more than *LIMIT* fields are split, with the last element of the returned array being the remainder of the string.
`substr (EXPR,OFFSET,[LENGTH])`	Returns a substring of *EXPR*, starting at *OFFSET*. The first character is at offset $[. If *LENGTH* is provided, returns only *LENGTH* characters; otherwise, returns all characters to the end of the string.

Array Functions

Perl has a series of very powerful functions for array manipulation. You can insert or remove elements from an array, search it, sort it, and manipulate it as a stack, queue, or dequeue. The most common array functions are listed in Table 8.11.

TABLE 8.11 Array Functions

Name (arguments)	*Function*
`grep (EXPR,LIST)`	Evaluates *EXPR* for each element of *LIST* (setting $ to each element in turn) and returns the array of elements for which *EXPR* returned true. For example, if `@lines` contains the lines read from a file, `grep (!/^$/,@lines)` returns an array of all nonempty lines.
`sort ([SUBROUTINE] LIST)`	Sorts *LIST*. If *SUBROUTINE* is not specified, sorts in ascending string comparison order. *SUBROUTINE* specifies the name of a subroutine that compares the variables `$a` and `$b` and returns a negative integer if `$a` comes before `$b`, `0` if they are equal, and a positive integer if `$a` comes after `$b`.
`splice (ARRAY,OFFSET[,LENGTH[,LIST]]`	Replaces *LENGTH* elements of *ARRAY* starting at *OFFSET* with *LIST*. *ARRAY* grows or shrinks as necessary. Default for *LENGTH* is from *OFFSET* to the end of the array. Default for *LIST* is a `null` list. Returns the elements removed from the array.
`push (ARRAY,LIST)`	Treats array as a stack, adding *LIST* to the end of *ARRAY*. Equivalent to `splice (ARRAY, 0 $#ARRAY+1, LIST)`. Returns a `null` value.
`pop (ARRAY)`	Treats *ARRAY* as a stack, popping the last element and returning it. Equivalent to `splice (ARRAY, -1, 1)`.
`unshift (ARRAY,LIST)`	Similar to `push`, adds *LIST* to the beginning of *ARRAY*. Equivalent to splice `(ARRAY, 0, 0, LIST)`. Returns a `null` value.
`shift (ARRAY)`	Similar to `pop`, shifts the first element of *ARRAY* off and returns it. Equivalent to `splice (ARRAY, 0, 1)`.

Hash Functions

Perl hashes are associative arrays in which elements are stored and retrieved by using a symbolic key (a string) instead of their position in the array (a number).

Perl has a few functions to manipulate hashes, shown in Table 8.12.

TABLE 8.12 Hash Functions

Name (Arguments)	*Function*
`each (HASH)`	Iterates over a hash returning a two-element (`key,value`) pair in each iteration. Returns `null` at the end of the hash. For example, the following prints the script's environment: `while (($key,$value) = each %ENV) {print "$key = $value";}`
`keys (HASH)`	Returns an array containing the *HASH*'s keys. The order is the same as the order of the `values` or `each` functions, and is seemingly random.
`values (HASH)`	Returns an array containing the *HASH*'s values, in the same order as the `keys` function.

Input/Output Functions

Perl has many functions to handle input and output to streams, whether they are files or pipes. The most common are shown in Table 8.13.

TABLE 8.13 Input/Output Functions

Name (Arguments)	*Function*
`close (FILEHANDLE)`	Closes *FILEHANDLE*, flushing all unsaved output to disk.
`eof (FILEHANDLE)`	Returns true if *FILEHANDLE* is positioned at end-of-file.
`print ([FILEHANDLE] LIST)`	Prints *LIST* to the *FILEHANDLE*. If *FILEHANDLE* is omitted, prints to *STDOUT*.
`open (FILEHANDLE,EXPR)`	Opens the file or pipe indicated by *EXPR* for input, output, or both. The direction is indicated by the first or last character of *EXPR*. For files, the beginning of *EXPR* indicates how to open the file: > opens the file for output and truncates it to zero bytes. < opens the file for input. >> opens the file for appending.

continues

TABLE 8.13 continued

Name (Arguments)	*Function*
	`+>` and `+<` open the file for reading and writing.
	In the case of pipes, a pipe character (¦) placed at the beginning opens the pipe for input. Placed at the end, it opens the pipe for output.
`truncate ({FILEHANDLE¦EXPR},LENGTH)`	Truncates the file pointed to by *FILEHANDLE* or named by *EXPR* to *LENGTH* bytes.

System Interface Functions

One of the most common uses for Perl is automating systems administration tasks, because it has many functions to interface with the underlying operating system and filesystem. Some of these are shown in Table 8.14.

TABLE 8.14 System Interface Functions

Name (Arguments)	*Function*
`chdir ([EXPR])`	Changes the script's current working directory to *EXPR* if possible. If *EXPR* is omitted, changes to the user's home directory.
`chmod (LIST)`	Changes the permissions of a list of files. The first element of the list must be a numeric mode as used in the `chmod` command (see Chapter 5). The rest of the list specifies the name of the files to change.
`exec (LIST)`	Replaces the currently executing Perl with another program. If *LIST* has only one scalar argument that has any shell metacharacters, `exec` executes the program by passing *LIST* to `/bin/sh -c` for further parsing. If there are no metacharacters, *LIST* is split into words. In that case, or if *LIST* is more than one argument or is a list with more than one value, executes the program named by *$LIST[0]* with the rest of the elements of *LIST* as arguments.
`exit ([EXPR])`	Terminates the script with a return code specified by the numeric value of *EXPR*. The default value for *EXPR* is `0`. In the case of subroutines, it is preferrable to use `die` instead of `exit`, because the error can be captured by `eval`.
`kill (LIST)`	Sends the signal specified by *$LIST[0]* to the process IDs specified by the rest of the elements of *LIST*. More information on signals and `kill` can be found in Chapter 5.

Miscellaneous Functions

As with all languages, Perl has some functions that don't fit into any other category. Some of these are shown in Table 8.15.

TABLE 8.15 Miscellaneous Functions

Name (Arguments)	*Function*
`defined (EXPR)`	Returns true if *EXPR* is a defined value, either a defined variable or a subroutine that returns a defined value.
`die ([LIST])`	Outside an `eval`, `die` prints *LIST* to `STDERR` and exits the program with the current value of `$!` (the system *errno*). If `$!` is `0`, the return code is `($? >> 8)` (the status of the last `` `command` ``. If that is also zero, the return code is `255`. The default value for *LIST* is the string `"Died"`. Inside of an `eval`, `die` transfers control to the instruction after the `eval` and places the value of *LIST* in `$@`. If *LIST* doesn't end in a newline, the current script filename, line number, and input line number are appended to it.
`eval (EXPR)`	Evaluates *EXPR* as a mini-Perl script and returns the last expression evaluated. If any error occurs that would abort the execution of *EXPR*, the error message is placed in `$@`, and `eval` returns the undefined value. This makes `eval` useful for guaranteeing that a program will not crash unexpectedly, by trapping any errors that may occur.
`gmtime (EXPR)`	Converts a time as returned by the `time` function to a 9-element array with the time in GMT (Greenwich Mean Time). The array contains, in order, the seconds, minutes, hour, day of the month, month, year, weekday, day number within the year, and a Boolean flag that says whether Daylight Savings Time is active. The month is in the range `0–11` and the weekday is in the range `0–6`, with `0` being Sunday.
`localtime (EXPR)`	Converts a time as returned by the `time` function to a 9-element array with the local time. The format of the array is as specified in the `gmtime` function.
`require (EXPR)`	Loads and executes the Perl code contained in the file specified by *EXPR*. The file is searched in the directories specified by the `@INC` variable. A file that is `required` twice is not included twice.
`time`	Returns the current time, specified as the number of non–leap seconds since January 1, 1970 GMT.

More Perl Features

Perl has many more things to offer than what has been covered in this chapter. Full coverage of Perl would take up an entire book. In fact, entire books have been written about

Perl. If you want to learn Perl, an excellent book is *Sams Teach Yourself Perl 5 in 21 Days*, by David Till, published by Sams Publishing. An excellent reference is *Perl 5 Quick Reference,* by Michael Fonghlu, published by Que Corporation.

In this section, you take a brief look at some of the advanced things Perl has to offer.

The Perl Documentation

Apart from the usual man pages, Perl includes a system called *plain old documentation,* or POD. This is a series of files with the extension `.pod`, which are usually found under the `/usr/lib/perl5/pod` and can be viewed using the `perldoc` documentation viewer. A good place to start is by using `perldoc perldoc`.

POD files can be converted to other formats, using `pod2html`, `pod2man`, `pod2latex`, or `pod2text`. Many Perl packages found in CPAN (see the section "CPAN: The Comprehensive Perl Archive Network," later in this chapter) include their documentation in POD format.

The Perl Debugger

Perl has an excellent debugger, invoked via `perl -d` *`filename`*. Although it is command-line–based, it is very easy to use. It enables you to do all the usual stuff a debugger can do, including single-stepping, setting breakpoints, showing stack traces, displaying and changing variable values, and so forth.

The Perl debugger differs from the debuggers for other languages because it isn't a separate program; instead, the `-d` flag instructs Perl to insert additional debugging information at the precompilation stage, and to enter the interactive debugger mode instead of directly executing the script.

The Perl debugger contains online help, accessed via the `h` command. You can get more information on using the Perl debugger in the `perldebug(1p)` man page.

Object Orientation

The latest version of Perl, Perl 5, introduced object-oriented programming (OOP) into the Perl world. OOP has many advantages over traditional (structured) programming, especially in large projects. These advantages include ease of reuse, increased modularity, and increased robustness.

The documentation for Perl's OOP features can be found in the `perlobj(1p)` and `perltoot(1p)` man pages.

Graphical User Interfaces

It is possible to program graphical user interfaces (GUIs) in Perl, using an extension called Perl/Tk. Tk (short for "Toolkit") is a graphics extension to several scripting languages that started its life as an extension to the TCL language and has been added to many scripting languages, including Perl. It enables you to create GUI programs that are as portable as the scripting language itself (in the case of Perl, completely portable!).

Perl/Tk is provided in Debian in a package called `perl-tk`. After the `perl-tk` package is installed, you will find extensive documentation provided in POD files; you can get started by running `perldoc Tk::overview`.

Portable Database Connectivity

One of the most common things a program needs to do these days is connect to a database. Whether it's a personal database stored in a text file, an enterprise-class database such as Oracle or Sybase, or an open-source database such as MySQL or PostgreSQL, Perl provides a standard interface to all of them.

Originally, there were special versions of Perl to access each database; thus, there was `oraperl` to access Oracle databases and `sybperl` to access Sybase databases. However, all that has changed. There exists now a standard *database interface* (DBI). DBI is an abstract layer that supports connecting to a relational database, sending queries, getting results, and disconnecting. To access each specific database, DBI relies on *database drivers* (DBDs). There are DBDs for most major and quite a few minor databases, with more being added all the time.

The Perl DBI and DBD modules can be found in CPAN.

CPAN: The Comprehensive Perl Archive Network

Over time, many Perl libraries, or *modules,* have been built. These modules have many diverse functions, from simplifying the writing of CGI scripts to interfacing to databases and much more. However, the problem of actually *finding* a module to do a particular task became more and more difficult.

Thus was born the Comprehensive Perl Archive Network (CPAN). CPAN is a collection of sites whose aim is to provide all the information you might need about Perl, including documentation, examples, distributions, and most Perl modules in existence. It can be easily accessed through the Web at `http://www.cpan.org/`. It includes an automatic "multiplexer," that will automatically send you to the mirror site nearest you.

When you have to do anything using Perl, it's a good idea to check out CPAN before starting to code. You'll probably find something that makes the job easier.

Summary

UNIX is a modular system, where large things are accomplished by small programs working together. A scripting language is designed to provide the "glue" with which to stick together such small programs.

Scripting languages differ from standard languages, because they are usually interpreted (or a separate compilation step is necessary), their variables don't need to be declared, and the variable's values are used by interpolation. Scripting languages usually follow the UNIX shells' quoting conventions.

Linux provides an extensive array of scripting tools. The two most widely used UNIX scripting languages are `bash` and Perl. `bash` is an extension of the Bourne shell, and Perl is a complete language designed to easily process text files and patterns.

Both `bash` and Perl provide variables and a full array of control structures. `bash` programs depend on calling external programs for most functions, and Perl is a self-contained language that can also call external programs where needed. `bash` is more suited to short programs (less than 100 lines in length), and Perl programs can grow to thousands of lines.

CHAPTER 9

Regular Expressions

by John Goerzen

In This Chapter

Often in Linux, you deal with text-based data, such as comma-separated information, system files such as `/etc/passwd`, or reports. You may need to have Linux parse or read this data automatically. Ordinarily, this might be difficult with all but the simplest of data forms. Fortunately, in Linux you have a versatile tool for working with data: regular expressions (regexps). Many Linux applications, including Perl, `emacs`, `sed`, `awk`, `grep`, `less`, and others can work with regular expressions. This kind of widespread usage means that you can use this single powerful tool for many different things.

Regular Expression Basics

Put simply, a *regular expression* is a pattern. More precisely, your regular expression contains instructions for the computer on how to match a pattern. This is accomplished by using plain text and special tokens.

Here's a sample regular expression:

```
bob
```

This matches any bit of text that contains the text *bob*. For instance, the sentence "Bob was here" wouldn't match, because the first *B* is capitalized; regular expressions are usually case sensitive. However, it would match the phrase "They were bobbing for apples." Unless you explicitly request it, the regular expression ignores word boundaries.

Often, you'll find that the syntax of various programs or languages require you to enclose your regular expressions in slashes; in those systems, you would write the same expression as

```
/bob/
```

The "bit of text" mentioned previously varies between programs, but usually it is understood to be a single line in a text file. Some systems may provide options to apply regular expressions to other arbitrary bits of text. These are often referred to as *strings*.

Regular expressions can also contain *tokens*. These tokens are used in place of other text. For instance, if you say

```
bo.+b
```

the `.` and `+` are both tokens; in this case, the two together mean "match one or more characters." So, the example will match `boxes from cardboard` and `bo2b` but not `bob`.

Recognizing Patterns in Data

As you've seen, regular expressions can be used to precisely match different things. Almost anything that isn't completely free-form text can be matched by a regular expression. For instance, on Linux systems, the `/etc/passwd` file is easy to pick apart with regular expressions. In many cases, regular expressions can also be used to pick out bits of data from a longer string. Perl, for instance, makes extensive use of this capability.

Here's a sample line from `/etc/passwd`:

```
news:x:9:9:news:/var/spool/news:/bin/sh
```

Notice how the different parts of this line are conveniently separated by colons; regular expressions make it easy to separate this line into its parts: the username, the UID, the home directory, and so on. This pattern is fairly obvious (each line has colon-separated data) and easy to deal with, both with regular expressions and other types of parsing tools.

But not all data that you must deal with is so easy to parse. Data often comes in variable-length fields, sometimes having optional components. This can make parsing a real chore unless regular expressions are around to help.

For instance, many programs use command lines with optional arguments; just looking at a few man pages will surely demonstrate this point. Normally, parsing these arguments with optional components is quite difficult. However, with regular expressions, the task becomes a lot easier.

Sometimes, the patterns may be even more obscure. What about parsing English text for the purposes of analyzing it? Free-form text is highly variable, yet there are still patterns that computers can recognize. For instance, you might notice that all sentences in English end with one of these characters: ., !, or ?. Knowing just this bit of information enables you to use regular expressions to separate your input text into its various sentences.

So, even though a pattern may not be as obvious as you may like for the purposes of processing it automatically, you can still take advantage of the power of regular expressions. Although regular expressions, like computers, are extremely precise and do only what you tell them to (recall the previous example of the regular expression that didn't match `bob`), they contain many constructs that introduce an element of structured flexibility.

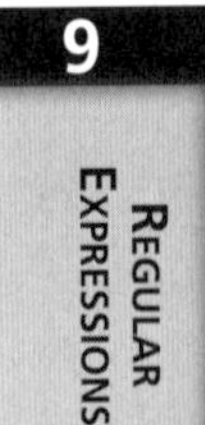

Uses of Regular Expressions

Now that you've seen how regexps can be used to parse most any type of input, it's time to move on to some simple examples of their use.

One of the simplest programs to use with regexps is `egrep`. On systems that use GNU `grep`, `egrep` is identical to the standard `grep`; however, on other non-Linux systems, the two are sometimes different. To avoid confusion, this chapter uses `egrep` in the examples.

`egrep` is simple; it reads a file of your choosing and prints the lines that match the pattern you specify. You can use a simple pattern such as this:

```
egrep root /etc/passwd
```

Here, `root` is actually a regular expression! It is used as the pattern that `egrep` is looking for in the `/etc/passwd` file. It looks just like a normal word, and it is. Regular expressions simply add additional tokens to normal words.

Note that the line would match not only the entry for the `root` user, but also an entry for a person named, for instance, `nonroot`. You need something more precise in order to get only the one account that you're interested in. So, let's try this:

```
egrep ^root /etc/passwd
```

The caret (`^`) means "match the start of the line." This gets rid of the problem with somebody named `nonroot`; the pattern matches only those lines that begin with `root`. But what if there is also somebody on the system named `root2`? The pattern would match that person. Let's restrict it a bit further:

```
egrep ^root: /etc/passwd
```

This line matches only the entry for the `root` user on the system. Regular expressions made the task remarkably simple, too!

Note that in this context, the colon is no special token for `egrep`; it's simply more text to match. Only the `^` has nonstandard implications.

Now that you know how to pick quick things out of text files, let's get a bit more complex. Suppose you want to select all people with a shell that ends in `sh` but is not `csh`.

First, let's review what a sample line from `/etc/passwd` looks like:

```
daemon:x:1:1:daemon:/usr/sbin:/bin/sh
```

Usage Example

Now, let's walk through some examples until we reach the desired effect.

First, you might try this:

```
egrep sh /etc/passwd
```

That's probably not terribly useful; at most places, it will probably list every account on the system! Furthermore, any username that contains the letters `sh` anywhere will be matched. Your first task, then, is to make sure that it matches only the end of the path to the users' default shell. Because the default shell occurs at the end of each line, you match the end of line by using the `$`. This works like the `^` used above, except it matches the end of a line instead of the start.

However, because the `$` is a special character to the shell, you enclose the search string in single quotes this time. These actually get stripped off before being passed to `egrep`; you could have used them for the previous commands as well:

```
egrep 'sh$' /etc/passwd
```

Thus far, you've eliminated the problem of matching the characters sh in someone's username. Next, you need to make sure that the shell isn't csh. Here's a first attempt at this:

```
egrep '[^c]sh$' /etc/passwd
```

This example introduces the brackets and a second use of the ^ character. The brackets are a character grouping operator; normally, they mean "match any one character between the brackets." However, when the ^ is the first character inside the brackets, the meaning changes to "match any one character *not* in brackets." So, the example means to match any line ending in sh, but not with csh. Although this regular expression isn't 100% perfect (people using tcsh would not be listed, for instance), it is close enough for your current purposes. You'll look at other operators for improving precision of regular expressions later.

Now that you've learned about the basics of regular expression uses, it's important to take a look at the differences between regular expressions and more traditional ways of parsing data. Properly adjusting your mindset to the idea of using regular expressions will allow you to better take advantage of them in your programs.

Ideas of Regular Expressions

Normally, you might use C functions such as strtok() to parse data. You often have to use these functions numerous times just to get basic information. Regular expressions serve as a substitute for both those and other facets of programming that are usually done with something else. Regular expressions can be used to find bits of text in something else (searching), to modify text based on replacement patterns, and for basic pattern matching. Languages such as Perl that are based on regular expressions don't need some of the syntax that you see elsewhere.

Another important fundamental idea about regular expressions is that they are character based; that is, you give patterns to match individual characters. Of course, these characters are part of a larger text string, but with a regular expression, you work on the character level.

For instance, C likes to copy whole strings or certain ranges (substrings). Functions such as strcpy() and the nature of C pointers help reinforce this philosophy. With regular expressions, on the other hand, it's almost as easy to pick three separate parts of a string and deal with them as it is to deal with the string as a whole.

You can build complex patterns that can pick apart things such as HTML or SGML documents. Or, you can use simple patterns that simply look for keywords in documents. This is possible because regular expressions enable you to tell the computer certain things about the characters you are expecting to find. For instance, you might tell it that you'll be expecting one or more instances of the letter *C* at a certain place. Or, perhaps you may or may not find the word `Linux` in the middle of a string; you can tell the computer that this word may occur—or it might not. You can tell the computer to match a range of characters by using character classes. Or, you can indicate a number of different multicharacter options for a match.

Matching a Set of Characters

You've learned the ways in which regular expressions can match sets of characters. You can give a simple word such as `root`, or you can use special tokens such as `^` or `[^c]`.

Although tokens may vary from program to program, Table 9.1 presents a list of ones that you can use in regular expressions. Don't worry about memorizing these; few people know all of them, and you can use this table as a convenient reference.

TABLE 9.1 Tokens Used in Regular Expressions

Token	*Matches*
`^`	Beginning of the line. Example: `^qwerty` matches any line beginning with the text `qwerty`.
`$`	End of the line. Example: `qwerty$` matches any line ending with the text `qwerty`.
`.`	Any character. Some languages define this as "any character except the newline character." Options may affect this interpretation. Example: `qwer.y` matches `qwerty`, `qweroy`, `qwer4y`, and many other pieces of text.
`\\`	A single backslash, `\`.
`[]`	Character range or list; `[a-zA-Z]` matches any lowercase or capital letter. Example: `[abqt]` matches the letters `a`, `b`, `q`, or `t`. If the `^` is the first character in the range, negation is indicated. Example: `[^abqt]` matches all characters except `a`, `b`, `q`, and `t`.
`¦`	Item separation; often, but not always, used with `()`. Example: `red¦blue` matches both `red` and `blue`.
`()`, sense 1	Enclosed items are returned or set as variables in your language. Example: `qwe(.)ty` returns the character matched after `qwe`, and generally sets `$1` or `\1` to that character.
`()`, sense 2	Indicates grouping. This usage also encompasses sense 1 of (). Example: `key:(qwerty¦dvorak)` matches either `key:qwerty` or `key:dvorak`.

Token	Matches
*	The preceding token 0 or more times. Example: qu* matches q, qu, and quu.
+	The preceding token 1 or more times. Example: qu+ matches qu and quu but not q.
?	The preceding token exactly 0 or 1 times. Example: qu? matches q and qu but not quu.
{x,}	The preceding token no less than x times. Example: qu{2,} matches quu and quuu but not qu.
{x,y}	The preceding token no less than *x* and no more than *y* times. Example: qu{2,3} matches only quu and quuu.
{x}	The preceding token exactly *x* times. Example: qu{2} matches only quu.
\d	A digit character; this is often the same as [0-9]. Example: a\d matches a1, a2, a3, and so on up to a9.
\D	A nondigit character.
\s	A space character; examples of these include spaces and tabs.
\S	A nonspace character.
\w	A "word" character; in English, this is the same as [a-zA-Z0-9]. Note that this matches just one character, not an entire word. In some languages, such as Perl, this also matches the underscore character.
\W	The opposite of \w; in English, this is the same as [^a-zA-Z0-9].
[:alnum:]	Similar to \w.
[:alpha:]	Alphabetical characters only.
[:cntrl:]	Control characters.
[:digit:]	Same as \d.
[:graph:]	Characters that are "visible" onscreen; for example, spaces do not fit this criterion.
[:lower:]	Lowercase letters.
[:print:]	Printable characters.
[:punct:]	Punctuation characters.
[:space:]	Same as \s.
[:upper:]	Uppercase characters.
[:xdigit:]	Hexadecimal digits.
\x or $x	Replaced with the matched text in the *x*th parenthetical group (see (), sense 1).

In addition, it's helpful to keep the following points in mind:

- Sometimes the special regular expression characters appear in the text you're dealing with; if you want the parser to take the character literally, simply preface it with a backslash: `\.`
- If you need to use the backslash itself in the pattern you are working with, use it twice: `\\`.
- There are often multiple methods of accomplishing something with regular expressions. As an example, the `.` character is the same as saying `{1,}`.
- The brackets are part of the special names in the table; for instance, to match one hexadecimal digit, you write `[[:xdigit:]]`.
- Not all programs that use regular expressions can use all these tokens.
- If you are providing a regular expression on a shell command line, keep in mind that it can be helpful to enclose it in single quotes if it contains any shell special characters.
- Some programs provide options that can influence how regular expressions are parsed; for example, you may be able to make them case-insensitive.
- In some languages, you need to enclose regular expressions between slashes.

As you can see from the sheer size of this table, regular expressions offer you a lot of flexibility.

Let's consider a command that uses these ideas:

```
egrep -v '^([^:]+).+:[^:]*\1:[^:]*$' /etc/passwd
```

This command displays a list of all users whose home directory does not contain their username at the end. If you're using a typical system, you'll get a list of a few system accounts that match these criteria. You'll examine the pattern in detail later; but first, there's a `-v` before the pattern. This causes `egrep` to reverse the sense of the match; instead of displaying all matching lines, it displays all that *don't* match. So, the pattern then matches everyone with his or her username as the last part of his or her home directory path, and `egrep` displays everything else.

Let's take a look at the parts individually. Recall that the single quotes around the pattern are for the shell's benefit and are not part of the pattern itself. Table 9.2 shows a breakdown of the pattern.

TABLE 9.2 Pattern Breakdown

Token	*Use*
^	Matches the start of the line; this, combined with the $ at the end, ensures that you deal only with the entire string.

Token	Use
`(...)`	Parentheses are used here to save the text matched inside the parentheses; this is used later by the `\1` token.
`[^:]`	Matches every character except a colon; in this way, you select all characters up to the colon.
`+`	Matches the previous item 1 or more times. In this case, it means that any non-colon character is matched 1 or more times. By using this, you guarantee that the entire username, but not the following colon, is selected.
`.+`	Recall that the period signifies "any character." Combined with the plus, it means "match one or more characters, ignoring what those characters are." In this case, it matches several colons and various fields; this data isn't important to us, so the `.+` effectively skips over it.
`:`	Matches a colon only.
`[^:]`	As before, matches any character except a colon.
`*`	The previous character should be matched 0 or more times. In this case, combined with the `[^:]` before it, it causes the pattern matcher to skip over any text at the start of the home directory path.
`\1`	Inserts the text that was saved by the parentheses earlier; in this case, that text is the username.
`:`	Matches another colon; this one separates the home directory from the shell.
`[^:]*`	Matches the user's default shell. Again, not something that you particularly care about.
`$`	Matches the end-of-line.

You can see how logical regular expressions are and how powerful they can be. This is only part of their power, however; you'll take a look at replacements using `sed` later in this chapter.

Logic

You may be wondering why certain things were done as they were in the previous example—for instance, the `[^:]+` at the start instead of `.+`. In this section, we'll examine why it is often necessary to restrict regular expressions so they do not match too much text through the use of devices such as quantifiers. These tokens also allow you to make your regular expression patterns match more text, in a specific and well-defined manner.

Quantifiers

Quantifiers such as `+` and `*` specify how many times the preceding item can be repeated in the matched pattern. You must use care when using quantifiers, however. If you do not use `\1` in this expression, you are forced to use `[^:]+` near the start of the regular expression instead of `.+`. In fact, even with the `\1` syntax, it's a good idea to do this.

Often, you can consider regular expression quantifiers to be greedy. That is, they match as much as they possibly can. In this case, the first `.+` matches several fields containing several colons. This is not the desired behavior, so you restrict it with `[^:]`.

Quantifiers can be combined with any normal character or token. For instance, `\s*` means to match 0 or more whitespace characters. Earlier, you saw the character class `[^:]` used with the quantifiers `+` and `*`. These are two examples of the different things you can do by combining quantifiers with other types of tokens. Of course, you can combine quantifiers with plain characters:

```
ba+ck
```

This matches `back`, `baack`, `baaack`, and so on.

Character Classes

Character classes are specified by brackets; you've already seen one. You can use either spelled-out options or entire ranges of characters in your classes. Table 9.3 presents some examples.

TABLE 9.3 Character Classes and Their Meanings

Class	*Meaning*
`[\s\d]`	Matches either whitespace or numeric digits.
`[^\s\d]`	Matches any character that is neither a whitespace character nor a digit character.
`[\S\D]`	This example is somewhat pointless; if any character satisfies either the condition that it is not whitespace or that it is not a digit, it matches. Because every character must match at least one of those, this matches every character; in this way, note that it is *not* the same as `[^\s\d]`.
`[a-cgj-mq-]`	Uses both ranges and separate characters. The first a-c means to match `a`, `b`, or `c`. The `g` means that the letter *g* is also a possible match. The sequence `j-m` specifies another sequence. The `q` means that the letter *q* is another possible match. Because the - is at the end of the sequence, it's treated as a separate character that can match instead of one that denotes a range.

Note that things such as `[:alpha:]` are *not* character classes, but rather special tokens.

Grouping and Alternation

Grouping is another facet of regular expressions. Grouping is similar in nature to character classes because it represents a number of alternatives; matching any one of them is considered a positive match.

Unlike character classes, however, grouping acts on larger patterns—for example:

```
(black|white)
```

This regular expression matches either `black` or `white`. Pretty simple!

You can also use standard regular expression tokens inside groups. Here's an example:

```
([j-z]|abc)
```

This matches either a single character in the range of `j` through `z` or the three characters `abc`.

Of course, you can also use more than two items in a group:

```
(red|white|gray|[q-z])
```

In some situations, it's also possible to use the alternation character (`|`) without enclosing it in parentheses. Here's an example:

```
red|white|P[1-8a-z]|foo
```

This reads the same as

```
(red|white|P[1-8a-z]|foo)
```

As you can see, using the `|` operator without the parentheses causes the entire regular expression to become part of the alternations. Sometimes this is what you want; other times, it's not. If in doubt, it's always safe to use the parentheses.

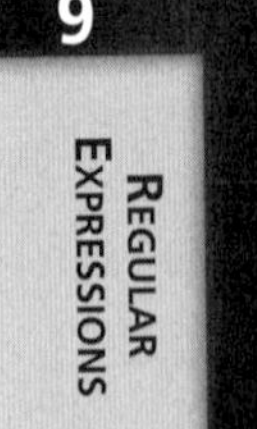

Anchors

Besides quantifiers, another useful way to limit the matches that occur is by using anchors. Whereas quantifiers limit how much text is matched, anchors limit where the text is matched.

You've already explored two anchors: `^` and `$`. Anchors don't actually match any text; rather, they match certain special places in text. Some languages, such as Perl, define special anchors that you can use; but these are highly variable between languages, so be careful when using special anchors from one language in another. For instance, one that matches a word boundary in Perl matches a backspace character in `awk`.

Tools That Use Regular Expressions

As I indicated at the beginning of this chapter, there are many programs and tools in Linux that take advantage of regular expressions. In this section, we'll explore these tools, cover some details on how to use them, and note language-specific differences in regular expression implementations where necessary.

egrep

You've seen a lot of what `egrep` can do, but it can be useful to see what other special functions this utility can provide. Table 9.4 presents some useful command-line options that relate to pattern matching.

TABLE 9.4 Command-Line Options Related to Pattern Matching

Option	*Meaning*
`-c`	Displays a count of the number of lines matching the given pattern instead of those lines themselves.
`-I`	Treats the supplied regular expression as case insensitive; normally, regular expressions are case sensitive.
`-v`	Negates the regular expression; that is, displays the lines (or counts with -c) that do not match the supplied pattern.
`-w`	Forces the supplied regular expression to match a whole word instead of an arbitrary portion of the line as usual.
`-x`	Forces the regular expression to match an entire line instead of part of it.

As you look at these options, you can see that several of them are what are called "syntactic sugar;" that is, they perform the same operations that could be done with regular expressions themselves. `-x` is one such option; you can use the `^` and `$` characters inside the pattern itself to achieve the same effect. `egrep` simply provides you with another way of doing it. As with many things in Linux, there's more than one way of doing something.

`egrep` also can search for a given pattern in a number of files; shell wildcards can be quite useful here. For instance, you may want to look for a line that contains `stream` at the beginning and `shell` toward the end. You might use this:

```
egrep 'stream.*shell' *
```

egrep searches through all the files in the current directory (selected by the *). When it locates a matching line, it displays the filename in which it occurred and then the line itself. Thus, you can search through quite a bit of data.

Multiple Files and Patterns

Not only can egrep use multiple files to search through, but it can also apply multiple patterns to its search. This is done through the use of a *pattern file*. This file holds a list of regular expressions to try, one per line. Any line of input that matches at least one is considered a match. Here's a sample pattern file:

```
root
daemon
mail
```

Those are simple regular expressions, but you can use full-blown ones as well.

You use -f to load a pattern file:

```
egrep -f patternfile < /etc/passwd
```

Running that command displays the following on the test system:

```
root:x:0:0:root:/root:/bin/bash
daemon:x:1:1:daemon:/usr/sbin:/bin/sh
mail:x:8:8:mail:/var/spool/mail:/bin/sh
alias:x:70:65534:qmail alias:/var/qmail/alias:/bin/sh
qmaild:x:71:65534:qmail daemon:/var/qmail:/bin/sh
qmails:x:72:70:qmail send:/var/qmail:/bin/sh
qmailr:x:73:70:qmail remote:/var/qmail:/bin/sh
qmailq:x:74:70:qmail queue:/var/qmail:/bin/sh
qmaill:x:75:65534:qmail log:/var/qmail:/bin/sh
qmailp:x:76:65534:qmail pw:/var/qmail:/bin/sh
```

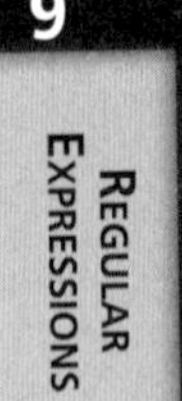

Another useful program is zegrep. zegrep is basically like egrep, except it can also automatically search inside g-zipped (.gz) files. This can be great for searching inside documentation that comes in /usr/doc, for instance.

One other benefit of this scheme is that you are free from shell interpretation of the patterns. That is, there's no need to quote or escape patterns to avoid the shell processing them; they're read directly by egrep.

You might use it like this:

```
zegrep 'stream.*shell' /usr/doc/bash/*
```

With this usage, you search through the files in /usr/doc/bash. zegrep automatically and transparently searches inside the compressed .gz files as well.

Note that with zegrep, if you use a pattern file, that file must still be uncompressed; zegrep can search through compressed files, not read compressed patterns.

sed

The name of sed describes its purpose: Stream EDitor. That is, sed reads input, can modify it, and produces output. sed is an entire language; this section discusses one of its most popular regexp-related features, fondly known as s///.

Here's a sample sed line:

```
sed s/root/haha/ < /etc/passwd
```

This tells sed to replace the first occurrence of the word root on each line with the word haha. In effect, the word root is the regular expression pattern to search for, and the word haha is the text that's used to replace it. You can also make sed act on every occurrence of root in every line by setting the "global" option:

```
sed s/root/haha/g < /etc/passwd
```

Notice the difference in the first line of the output. Where the first command changed only the username, the second command changed that as well as the home directory and full name (gecos) fields. Without the g, sed changes only the first instance of the search pattern on any given line.

One use of sed is to pick out certain patterns from text. Recall this earlier line:

```
egrep -v '^([^:]+).+:[^:]*\1:[^:]*$' /etc/passwd
```

Let's try a modified version with sed:

```
sed 's/:.*$//' < /etc/passwd
```

This displays all the usernames of all the accounts on your system. First, it starts matching at the first colon and continues to the end of the line, by virtue of the .* and $ characters. Then, that part is replaced by the null string because there's nothing between the final two slashes.

Multiple Patterns

It's also possible for sed to process multiple replacements at once. All you have to do is add a -e in front of each one on the command line. For instance, you can combine two previous sed statements:

```
sed -e s/root/haha/g -e s/:.*$// < /etc/passwd
```

This produces the same result as

```
sed s/root/haha/g < /etc/passwd | sed s/:.*$//
```

Using the -e method is the preferred way of handling multiple substitutions at once because

- It is faster. Executing additional copies of sed and setting up pipelines consumes CPU cycles.
- It makes cleaner, shorter, and more readable code.

If you're dealing with a very large number of requests, you can use what sed calls a script file. For instance, you might create a script file containing

```
s/root/haha/g
s/:.*$//
```

Then you can run sed with

```
sed -f scriptfile < /etc/passwd
```

This has several advantages:

- Because the shell is not involved with the patterns themselves, there's no need to quote them or otherwise deal with the shell.
- It's a lot easier to specify large numbers of commands with this method than to do so with many -e commands.
- You can save the file and reuse it later.

Perl

Regular expressions are an integral part of the Perl programming language. Perl enables you to use them for anything from simple parsing to counting how many times certain characters occur within a line.

Regexp Usage in Perl

Perl supports many operators and, by default, requires you to place regular expressions between slashes, as sed does. If you specify no explicit option, the m// (match) option is assumed. You can also specify the s/// operator, which works like the one in sed.

Perl regular expressions, by default, return true if they match and false if they don't. In list context, Perl regular expressions return a list of the text matched inside parenthetical expressions. They also set the $x (such as $1) variables to match the corresponding parenthetical expression. Thus, you have a number of options for getting information from regular expressions.

When you use a Perl regular expression, it works on $_ (the default argument) unless you specify otherwise. You can do so with the =~ operator.

Regular Expression Options

Perl also supports several options; these are used after the final slash of the regular expression. Table 9.5 presents the Perl options.

TABLE 9.5 Perl's Regular Expression Options and Their Meanings

Option	*Meaning*
`c`	Doesn't reposition search cursor when a match under option `g` is in progress.
`g`	Signifies a "global" match; that is, every instance of the pattern is matched instead of just the first one.
`i`	Acts case-insensitively.
`m`	Matches with multiple lines.
`o`	Runs the pattern through the compiler only once.
`s`	Matches as single line; things such as `.` now match the newline character.
`x`	Allows embedded comments in the regular expression.

Sample Usage

Let's consider some code samples. Assuming that you are reading in `/etc/passwd`, here is a code fragment:

```
while (<>) {
chomp;
($uname, $passwd, $uid, $gid, $gecos,
 $dir, $shell) =
/^([^:]*):([^:]*):([^:]*):([^:]*):([^:]*):([^:]*):(.*)/;
print "$uname, $shell\n";
}
```

Here's what this does:

- As you can see, the regular expression matches each of the seven fields in the `passwd` file. You use the `*` instead of `+` because some of these fields may be blank.
- The text in the parentheses is returned to Perl as an array.
- You assign the values of this returned array to various variables.
- The contents of a few of them are then printed.

You can do the same thing with this code:

```
while (<>) {
chomp;
/^([^:]*):([^:]*):([^:]*):([^:]*):([^:]*):([^:]*):(.*)/;
print "$1, $7\n";
}
```

This takes advantage of the `$x` syntax that Perl provides for you. Be careful, though, because later regular expressions can override the `$x` assignments made by previous ones, so it's often safer to use the list method.

Now let's say that you'd like to restrict it to displaying only people that have `root` as their username. The first attempt might be the following:

```
while (<>) {
chomp;
/^(root):([^:]*):([^:]*):([^:]*):([^:]*):([^:]*):(.*)/;
print "$1, $7\n";
}
```

However, this will print `root`'s line for each person. You probably want to do this:

```
while (<>) {
chomp;
if (/^(root):([^:]*):([^:]*):([^:]*):([^:]*):([^:]*):(.*)/) {
print "$1, $7\n";
}
}
```

Recall earlier that in scalar context (as encountered inside an `if` statement), a regular expression returns true if it finds a match and false otherwise. By testing the return value, you can see whether you need to print something. In this case, things are printed (and the `$x` variables are modified) only if the entire expression matches. Because `root` must be in the first field, the `if` statement skips the `print` statement for nonmatching lines.

Here's another twist:

```
while (defined($input = <>)) {
chomp $input;
if ($input =~ /^(root):([^:]+)/) {
print "$1, $2\n";
}
}
```

This example uses `$input` to hold the line read from `passwd`. You can see Perl's `=~` operator in action; `$input =~ /^(root):([^:]+)/` means to apply the regular expression to the contents of that particular variable. Another thing you might do is match without regard to case. As indicated earlier, the option for this is `i`. It is used like this:

```
while (defined($input = <>)) {
chomp $input;
if ($input =~ /^(root):([^:]+)/i) {
print "$1, $2\n";
}
}
```

Note the letter `i` after the pattern. This causes the regular expression to be case insensitive; that is, it will now match `root`, `RoOt`, and `ROOT`, among others.

Let's try working with the `s///` operator. Suppose that, for each line that matches, you'd like to use `s///` to print `r00t` instead of `root`. A first attempt might be

```
while (defined($input = <>)) {
chomp $input;
if ($input =~ /^(root):([^:]+)/i) {
$1 =~ s/root/r00t/i;
print "$1, $2\n";
```

```
}
}
```

You'll no doubt notice that this isn't particularly efficient or elegant code. However, it illustrates several important concepts. First, note that this code isn't actually going to work as you might think. In fact, Perl aborts with this error message:

```
Modification of a read-only value attempted
```

It's complaining about the `$1 =~ s/root/r00t/i;` line. The problem: the `$x` variables are treated as read-only in Perl. So, perhaps the next idea is to use a temporary variable:

```
while (defined($input = <>)) {
chomp $input;
if ($input =~ /^(root):([^:]+)/i) {
$myvar = $1;
$myvar =~ s/root/r00t/i;
print "$myvar, $2\n";
}
}
```

This is closer, but still not correct. Perl now complains

```
Use of uninitialized value
```

and then displays

```
r00t,
```

The second use of a regular expression (the `s///` operator) destroys the previous contents of both `$1` and `R2`. So, here's a correct, working version of the code:

```
while (defined($input = <>)) {
chomp $input;
if ($input =~ /^(root):([^:]+)/i) {
$myvar = $1;
$myvar2 = $2;
$myvar =~ s/root/r00t/i;
print "$myvar, $myvar2\n";
}
}
```

This works because the contents of both `$1` and `$2` are saved into `$myvar` and `$myvar2`. A more elegant solution to this problem would be

```
while (<>) {
chomp;
if (/^(root):([^:]+)/i) {
print "r00t, $2\n";
}
}
```

Recall how it was mentioned earlier that `m//` is equivalent to using the slashes by themselves. The previous code can be written as

```
while (<>) {
chomp;
if (m/^(root):([^:]+)/i) {
print "r00t, $2\n";
}
}
```

In addition to this, you can use other characters instead of the slashes. This is particularly useful if you want to match something with slashes in it—for example, directories. Normally, you have to escape slashes with backslashes, as illustrated in the following example:

```
while (<>) {
chomp;
if (m/:(\/home\/[^:]+):[^:]+$/i) {
print "$1\n";
}
}
```

This regular expression is a bit hard to follow. The following is an example of it rewritten to take advantage of the special Perl syntax:

```
while (<>) {
chomp;
if (m':(/home/[^:]+):[^:]+$'i) {
print "$1\n";
}
}
```

Now, the character `'` indicates the start and end of the regular expression pattern. This pattern starts by matching the colon character. Then it matches text that starts with `/home/` and continues matching until it reaches a colon. This text is saved into `$1` because it's inside parentheses. Then, another string is matched, with no colons, until the end of the input line. In this way, `$1` holds the home directory, but the entire expression matches only if the home directory path begins with `/home/`.

Perl regular expressions also have some extra escape sequences that are not in all languages that use regular expressions (see Table 9.6).

TABLE 9.6 Perl Regular Expression Escape Sequences

Symbol	*Meaning*
`\a`	ASCII bell (alarm)
`\cX`	The ASCII control character corresponding to X
`\e`	ASCII escape character
`\f`	ASCII formfeed character
`\n`	ASCII newline character

continues

TABLE 9.6 continued

Symbol	*Meaning*
`\r`	ASCII return character
`\t`	ASCII horizontal tab character
`\xyy`	The character represented by the two hexadecimal digits yy, for example, `\x2D`
`\yyy`	The character represented by the three octal digits yyy, for example, `\012`

Of course, these correspond to the standards for Perl strings in double quotes, and they are valid both places.

Variable Interpolation

Another feature of regular expressions in Perl is *variable interpolation*. With this feature you can use variables to determine part of the regular expression. One powerful use of this is to query the user for a search pattern and use the input in your program. There's no need to write your own matching routines; use Perl's existing ones. The interpolation works exactly as it does in double-quoted strings: Simply use `$VAR` to match:

```
while (<>) {
chomp;
$match = '(/home/[^:]+):[^:]+';
if (/:$match$/i) {
print "$1\n";
}
}
```

This has the same result as the previous example. `$match` in the regular expression is simply replaced with the contents of the variable, resulting in the same match pattern as used previously.

Perl also has some additional syntax that can be useful when used with regular expression matching, such as the previous example; this includes the `-n` switch, which adds an implicit loop:

```
#!/usr/bin/perl -n
chomp;
$match = '(/home/[^:]+):[^:]+';
if (/:$match$/i) {
print "$1\n";
}
```

You get the same results by using a `s///` pattern:

```
#!/usr/bin/perl -n
chomp;
if (s"^.+:(/home/[^:]+):[^:]+"$1") {
print "$_\n";
}
```

This example illustrates several important concepts. First, you learned earlier that you can use characters other than the slash with `m//` and `s///`. When you use these other characters, though, you get their standard Perl quoting syntax. For instance, if you use `m'foo'`, you get the quoting of the `'` in Perl. Variables will not be interpolated inside the string in that case. The previous example uses `m""`; this way, the `$1` can be interpolated.

Note that this pattern is a bit different than in the previous examples; we take care to match the entire line with the `^.+` at the start of the line. This is because the replacement pattern will delete everything in the line except the part in parentheses. If the start was not explicitly matched, it would not have been deleted by the replacement; the replacement applies only to the part of the line explicitly matched at the start.

Regular expressions in Perl are also useful in the context of a call to the `split` function. Recall that the earlier example used this to pick apart the fields in the `/etc/passwd` file:

```
while (<>) {
chomp;
($uname, $passwd, $uid, $gid, $gecos,
 $dir, $shell) =
/^([^:]*):([^:]*):([^:]*):([^:]*):([^:]*):([^:]*):(.*)/;
print "$uname, $shell\n";
}
```

With `split`, you can rewrite this as

```
while (<>) {
chomp;
($uname, $passwd, $uid, $gid, $gecos,
 $dir, $shell) = split(/:/);
print "$uname, $shell\n";
}
```

Notice how much easier this is. `split()` is great when you have data that is separated by a consistent character or pattern. Note that instead of `split(/:/)`, it would also have been possible to use an entire regular expression. The part of a string that matches the regular expression is never returned; it's simply taken to be a separator between more useful data. So, if you have a file whose fields are separated by either colons or semicolons, you might use this:

```
while (defined($input = <>)) {
chomp;
@arr = split(/[;:]/, $input);
}
```

Notice also how you can specify an explicit string to use for the split; in this case, `$input` is used. You can use entire complex regular expressions inside the context of a `split`, but you'll no doubt find that doing so is rarely necessary.

Other Regular Expression Variables

In addition to the $x variables that Perl provides, there are some others that are available. These are used more rarely, and their use can slow down the execution of your program, but they may be useful anyway. Like the $x variables, these are set automatically by Perl as it evaluates your regular expression: Below is a table showing the meaning of the regexp-related variables in Perl.

Variable	*Meaning*
`$&`	Holds the matched string
`$+`	Holds the string that the last character class matched
`` $` ``	Holds everything in the string prior to the matched area
`$'`	Holds everything in the string after the matched area

As you might see, these are another example of syntactic sugar; you can get the same information by using `()` and checking the $x variables or the returned list.

Regexp Applications

Now that you've looked at the regular expressions in Perl, let's put these concepts together. To do this, there are two examples. The first is a simple parsing job written in C without regular expressions, followed by the equivalent Perl code. You'll be able to see how much easier the Perl code with regular expressions is. The second example contains snippets from a program designed to parse simple PostScript files.

Let's look first at some C code. The task here is to write a simple shell-like parser. You can use redirection, but only with two commands (this makes the task easier). Here's part one of the C code:

```
cmdpart[0] = strtok(cmdline, "¦");
  cmdpart[1] = strtok((char *)NULL, "¦");
  parse_cmd(cmdpart[0]);
  if (cmdpart[1]) parse_cmd(cmdpart[1]);
```

Basically, the command is first split if there is a pipe symbol in it. Then, in `parse_cmd`, you have the following:

```
  tempstr = strtok(cmdpart, " ");
  while (tempstr && (counter < MAXARGS - 1)) {
    args[counter] = safestrdup(tempstr);
    args[counter + 1] = (char *)NULL;
    counter++;
    tempstr = strtok(NULL, " ");
  }
  if (tempstr) {                /* Broke out of loop because of num of args */
    fprintf(stderr, "WARNING: argument limit reached, command may be truncated.\
n");
  }
```

This example parses an individual command (or either side of the ¦ symbol) by splitting according to the space.

Here's a complete Perl program that does the same thing, and more:

```
#!/usr/bin/perl -w

$input = <STDIN>;
chomp $input;
@parts = split(/\s*\¦\s*/, $input);
foreach $part (@parts) {
@args = split(/\s/, $part);
print join(', ', @args), "\n";
}
```

Look at how much amazingly easier that is! The entire program is shorter than the snippet from C; there is no need to worry about pointers or memory allocation, and there is no need to worry about the destructive effects of `strtok()`. Note also the benefits you get from regular expressions (and some Perl language constructs):

- It's trivial to split the command into parts based on the ¦ symbol.
- You can deal with an arbitrary number of commands with pipes quite easily.
- The `split` itself can eliminate whitespace surrounding the pipe character.
- It's also trivial to pick apart the arguments in the individual commands.
- The parsing process is nondestructive. That is, `$input` is not modified. In C, `strtok()` modifies its input, rendering it useless for future use except as parsed. You don't need the input again in this particular case, but you may need it sometime. Note that if you use `s///` for parsing as in an earlier example, the process is destructive.

The pattern in the first `split`, `/\s*\¦\s*/`, is of interest. By surrounding the pipe character with `\s*` patterns, the split process automatically includes any whitespace surrounding the pipe character as a delimiter, and it will not result in either string. This means that the resulting strings in the array are "clean"; there are no leading or trailing spaces in them. Also note that because the pipe character ¦ is an alternation token, it is escaped with a backslash so that it takes on its literal meaning.

Let's now take a look at a second example of Perl code. This example comes from a program that parses some simple PostScript files that are known to come in a certain format. The first thing this program must do is ensure that the file doesn't contain any strange characters that shouldn't be found in PostScript files. In order to do this, there is a list of characters that are bad:

- Any character in the range NULL to Control+C
- Any character in the range Control+E to Control+H
- Control+K

- Any character in the range Control+M to Esc
- Any character in the range 0x7F to 0xFF

This is then processed fairly easily inside a while loop. The relevant code looks like this:

```
if(($rejchar) = $input =~ /([\x00-\cC\cE-\cH\cK\cM-\x1B\x7F-\xFF])/) {
        &badfile(ord($rejchar));
# Bad file!  Reject it!
      }
```

Notice how the character ranges translated quite directly to a regular expression character class. `ord(rejchar)` means to get the numeric value of the rejected character, for example, 7 for Control+G.

Next, the stream is rewound. The next thing to do is see whether the first line starts with `%!`. If it doesn't, it's not a PostScript file:

```
my $testline = <FILE>;
if ($testline =~ '^%!') {
print "File has " . CountPS() . " pages\n";
} else {
die "Not a PostScript file!";
}
```

So far, so good. The next thing to do is count the number of pages in the file; this is done in `CountPS`. Here's the code for that:

```
sub CountPS {
          my $counter = 0;       # Start out at zero pages.
     while (<FILE>) {
    $counter++ if (/^%%Page: /);
          }
return $counter;
}
```

Pretty simple! Loop through the file, looking through lines that start with `%%Page:` , and when one's found, increment a counter.

procmail

The mail sorting utility `procmail` uses regular expressions to determine what to do with incoming mail—separate it into folders, send it to programs, and so on. Like Perl, regular expressions are an integral part of `procmail`, and without them, `procmail` would be a far less useful tool.

`procmail` regular expressions are similar to most others, but there are a few important differences. First, `procmail` defaults to using regular expressions in a case-insensitive manner; most other software defaults to case-sensitivity. Second, `procmail` defaults to applying the regular expression to only the headers of a mail message, not to the entire body of the message.

procmail works with mail sorting rules; in order for a message to match the given rules, it must match one or more specified regular expression rules. procmail starts each line with a regexp pattern with * .

procmail Example

Here's a sample rule:

```
:0:
* ^Sender:.*mail-list@lists.example.com
maillist
```

This will match a message that contains mail-list@lists.example.com in its subject line. These messages will be saved into your maillist folder. You can also specify multiple regular expressions for a single message; if you do so, the message must match all of them in order to match the rule. Here's an example:

```
:0:
* ^From:.*joe@example.com
* ^Subject:.*regexps
joeregexps
```

In this case, if the message is both from joe@example.com and has a subject line of regexps, it will be placed into the joeregexps folder.

procmail starts by attempting to match your message to the first rule. If it fails, procmail then goes to the next rule. When it matches, procmail normally skips the rest of the rules and ends processing of the message.

Example of Negation

procmail also enables you to negate a regular expression by using the ! sign:

```
:0:
* ^From:.*joe@example.com
* !^Subject:.*regexps
joemail
```

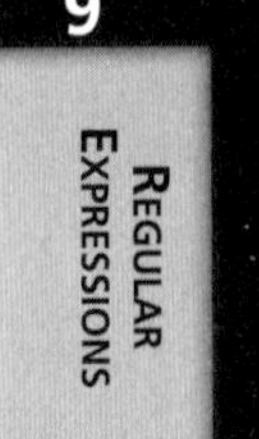

In this example, mail from joe@example.com but with a subject that does not contain regexps is placed into the joemail folder.

In these examples, you'll note that instead of simply saying From: joe@example.com, you use From:.*joe@example.com. You want to pick out the email address from anywhere inside the From: header line. In the message, the header might appear as From: Joe Smith <joe@example.com>, From: joe@example.com (Joe Smith), From: <joe@example.com>, or other variants. By using regular expressions such as these, it is possible to easily pick out the important part of the header: the email address.

Another thing to note is that procmail, by default, considers an "and" condition if you specify multiple conditions in a single rule. That is, all conditions must match in order for your mail to be directed as specified in the final line of the rule. There is no explicit "or" operation (one that causes the rule to be successful if at least one condition matches). However, you can achieve the same effect by using one of the following methods:

- The alternation syntax (`choice1¦choice2`) can be very helpful. For instance, you might say `* ^From:.*(joe@example.com¦jane@somewhereelse.com)`.
- If you want to match several different header lines, you can simply use a separate rule for each of them. For example, if you want to place a message in the `misc` folder if it comes from `jane@somewhereelse.com` or if it has a subject containing `green`, you can simply use two separate rules, each directing the messages into the same folder.

Let's provide an example of each. First, using alternation syntax:

```
:0:
* ^From:.*(joe@example.com¦jane@somewhereelse.com)
friendsmail
```

This is fairly straightforward—identical to `egrep`, in fact. The `procmail` documentation stresses that point: `procmail` regular expressions are interpreted as much like `egrep` as possible.

Now, if you want to use the second option to achieve a logical "or" effect:

```
:0:
* ^From:.*jane@somewhereelse.com
misc

:0:
* ^Subject:.*green
misc
```

If the message being processed has a `From:` line specifying `jane@somewhereelse.com`, the message is sent to the `misc` folder. If the `From:` line does not match, processing goes on to the second rule. At this point, if the `Subject:` line matches the text `green`, the message goes into the `misc` folder. If not, processing continues or the message ends up in your default incoming folder. So, you can see that a logical "or" is achieved. A message matches if the `From:` line contains `jane@somewhereelse.com` or the `Subject:` line contains `green`.

`procmail` defines a number of flags that affect regular expressions. These flags are placed on the first line of the rule immediately after the zero. The flags are as follows:

Flag	*Meaning*
`B`	Searches the message body instead of just the message header.
`D`	Distinguishes between upper- and lowercase. Unlike other regular expression systems, `procmail` defaults to matching in a case-insensitive fashion.
`H`	Searches the message header only. This is the default; there's no need to explicitly specify it.

There are also other procmail flags available; these are not directly related to regular expressions but are documented in the procmailrc(5) man page.

Nested Block Example

Here's a more complex example:

```
:0:
* ^X-Mailing-List: .*debian-\/[^ ]*@lists.debian.org
{
        LIST=`expr match $MATCH '\(.*\)\@' | sed s/-/./`

        :0:
        debian.$LIST
}
```

This is used to automatically split mail on the Debian mailing lists. This one rule catches mail for all the mailing lists hosted at lists.debian.org and puts mail into separate folders. Let's analyze how it works.

First, there is a standard matching rule; but there two new things:

- The \/ token is a special extension to the normal regular expression syntax. In this case, \/ means "save everything after me into the MATCH variable." It doesn't actually match anything specific; rather, it generates information that can be used later.
- The [^]* matches 0 or more nonspace characters in the middle of an email address. This particular part is the name of the specific list.

Then, you use a nested block inside of the existing one. procmail looks at the nested block only if the regular expression matched. In this way, you can use the result of the initial match in a command or a second match to follow.

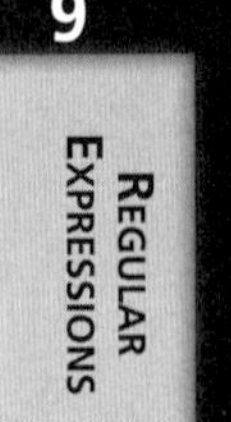

The text inside the backtick (`) characters is an actual shell command. procmail executes the specified command and uses its output in place of the backticks; this output then gets assigned to the LIST variable.

The command itself is interesting too. The expr part on the left is used to find only the list name part of the email address; the effect is the same as stripping the @ and the domain name that follows. Then, this result is piped to sed, which replaces any dash with a period in order to more closely match the desired folder naming scheme. Finally, procmail is instructed to use this LIST variable as part of the name of the destination folder itself, meaning that the folder name is determined in part from the email address.

It's also possible to replace the LIST line with a sed instead of an expr match; here's one way to do that:

```
:0:
* ^X-Mailing-List: .*debian-\/[^ ]*@lists.debian.org
{
```

```
        LIST=`echo $MATCH ¦ sed s/\@.*$// ¦ sed s/-/./`

        :0:
        debian.$LIST.procmail
}
```

You could also simplify that to a single sed call:

```
:0:
* ^X-Mailing-List: .*debian-\/[^ ]*@lists.debian.org
{
        LIST=`echo $MATCH ¦ sed -e s/\@.*$// -e s/-/./`

        :0:
        debian.$LIST.procmail
}
```

This usage takes advantage of sed's ability to process multiple replacement requests at one time.

Summary

You've seen many ways in which regular expressions can be used. They can do everything from analyzing PostScript files to sorting mail. As you use them in your program, you may find the following resources helpful:

- The perlre(1p) man page
- The perlop(1p) man page
- The gawk info pages
- The sed(1) man page
- The procmailrc(5) man page
- The procmailex(5) man page
- The procmail man page
- The egrep(1) man page

Debian System Administration

PART II

IN THIS PART

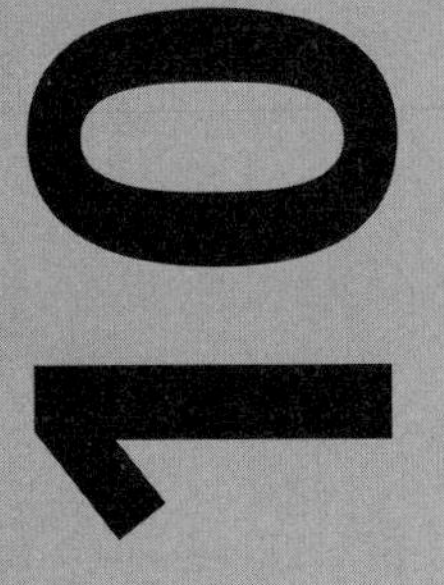

CHAPTER

Software Management

by Aaron Von Cowenberghe

In This Chapter

finished
000919

Debian's Package Management System

One of the most important aspects of any system is its software. The software you run on a system determines its purpose, whether it is a personal workstation or a production quality server.

In the world of commercial, proprietary software, every vendor supplies its own installation program. All development firms must forfeit an unacceptable amount of money if they want users to experience an installation consistent with common experience; in most cases, this comes from Microsoft's ridiculously priced development suites. Because user comfort is so highly valued, these near-monopoly software management packages are deemed essential; as a result, the end user pays more for his software. Other vendors, however, are known for growing their own systems for managing software installations. This makes software installation an inconsistent task for end users, causing a good deal of confusion for some in environments such as Windows.

Linux distributions, on the other hand, unify all software under a common application for managing software installation. Imagine if every piece of computer software in existence was kept in the same place, all of it installable instantly upon request. This is what Debian accomplishes: Every time you want to try a new application, you start the same package manager, where you're presented with a list of all the software available to you. No longer must you research various competitors, each of which touts itself as the best. Comparing similar programs is as simple as installing them all and trying them for yourself. In the world of commercial software, this is impossible.

Not only is package selection easy, but also software installation is greatly simplified with Debian. Every one of the thousands of available packages can be installed by simply typing a basic command. Imagine being able to specify a batch of powerful applications for installation (over the Internet or from media such as a CD) and sitting back and watching the install without having to switch CDs for every new program or being asked for registration codes. Debian accomplishes this and more. Have you ever complained about the difficulty of hunting down and retrieving important security updates? With Debian, this search is instantaneous.

Debian offers more than 2,600 packages, yet more are added to its master archive daily. Many of these applications rival (or surpass) their commercial counterparts in quality but are free and are organized for easy access. A handful of utilities come with Debian for the sole purpose of installing programs. This chapter discusses each of these in detail.

A Look Inside Debian's Package Formats

A *package*, in a few words, is an archive that contains something useful to a Debian user. Some contain programs, some documentation, some support libraries and development headers. These packages, however, perform more functions than act as a simple archive of data, like a `.zip` file you download off the Internet. Every bit of information needed to manage the software contained within is held in a consistent way inside every package. This includes scripts for setting up the software, records for uninstallation, and so on. This way, the installation, configuration, and uninstallation processes are consistent among every piece of software on your system.

In most cases in the Linux world, software comes as a compressed archive containing source code. *Source code* is the first representation of a program, the bowels of its inner workings. As such, it can't be used until it's "compiled" into a more useable form, such as an executable binary. Additionally, after building these programs from source, it's often necessary to build configuration files by hand. Often, the administrator doesn't care about these custom configurations; he only needs the software to work now, and forcing him to write his own configuration is a waste of his time. It's also impossible to remember every file that every program installs, and as a result, uninstallation is difficult in such a complicated environment as UNIX. For these reasons, compiling, installing, and setting up programs by hand in the traditional way consumes entirely too much time to be efficient in a professional setting.

A more complicated aspect of software management is the relationships various packages have with one another. These are commonly known as *dependencies*, where one piece of software depends on another to run correctly or perhaps interferes with another. A number of different kinds of relational needs exist, where one package requires your system to be configured a particular way before it will work correctly. When building system components by hand (from source), dependencies are your enemy; they can commonly require that you chase down new versions of several other pieces of software, some of which might have dependencies of their own. Building and installing several pieces of software to coax just one to work for you is painfully frustrating.

Debian provides all of its packages in an instantly useable form. The package management system takes care of installing your software, configuring it, and so on. These utilities are designed to minimize your effort as a system administrator and allow you to focus your energy on more important tasks. Debian's package management system provides all of the following for every package:

- A consistent interface for software installation
- Default configurations or easy-to-use configuration tools
- Protection for an administrator's customizations
- Dependency information
- Housekeeping records for uninstallation

First, all packages that require configuration files come preconfigured in such a way that they are useful to most people without customization. Often, the package maintainer (the person who donated the packages to Debian) goes one step further by creating a setup utility that eases advanced configuration. Some examples of such packages are `magic-filter` (printer drivers) and `exim` (an email server that's easily configurable as a satellite workstation), both of which contain software that is essential to most users' productivity but is too difficult to configure by hand, and for which a default configuration that works in most cases is impossible.

Unlike other package managers, `dpkg` (the one tool every other is based on) never overwrites an administrator's configurations if he has spent time modifying them by hand. Consider as an example ISPs that use Apache as their Web servers. A Web server generally requires a large investment of manpower to tune to any one situation. Now, suppose a new version of this Web server software has features most ISPs want to use. When a system administrator installs this new version, he is given the option to save his old configuration.

All distributions based on `rpm` (Red Hat's package manager), including SuSE, Red Hat, and other major players, simply overwrite these precious configurations that someone toiled over; not even a warning is emitted. Debian, on the other hand, notifies the administrator and asks for a choice on the course of action it should take (see Figure 10.1).

FIGURE 10.1
Admin choices.

```
[aaron@awac]
 ...~$ su
Password:
[root@awac]
 .../home/aaron# dpkg --pending --configure
Setting up libwine0.0.971116 (0.0.990523-1) ...

Setting up libwine-dev (0.0.990523-1) ...
Setting up wine (0.0.990523-1) ...

Configuration file `/etc/wine.conf'
 ==> File on system created by you or by a script.
 ==> File also in package provided by package maintainer.
   What would you like to do about it ?  Your options are:
    Y or I  : install the package maintainer's version
    N or O  : keep your currently-installed version
      Z     : background this process to examine the situation
 The default action is to keep your current version.
*** wine.conf (Y/I/N/O/Z) [default=N] ?
```

Dependency Information

Debian packages contain dependency information, just as most other package management systems of the day do. This is incredibly important, as there has to be a way to tell whether a particular package will work if it's installed. The way Debian handles this is by checking one package's dependencies against the software that's currently installed; `dpkg` in turn decides whether all prerequisites for this package's installation are met. If the package management system has no dependency handling, it will be too simple for an end user to break the system. Version mismatches and missing dependencies can throw a system into instant chaos, and most users don't have the knowledge to rectify such situations. Debian's dependency system assures your computer's stability.

Debian packages come in both source and binary formats, much like other open source software distributed by third parties. Debian's "source package" format contains the information needed to generate all binary packages associated with it, and a binary package is directly installable. *Binary packages*, as they are called, are the packages actual, useable software is stored in and installed from.

The Anatomy of Binary Packages

Binary packages for Debian are everywhere. The most common places to look for them is either a Debian FTP site (at `ftp://ftp.us.debian.org/debian`) or a CD you acquire as part of a book (like this one). Usually, these are named `package_version-release.deb`, where `package` is the package's name, `version` is the version of the program, and `release` is the revision on this Debian package. A new revision of a package is not necessarily a new version of the software; it usually just contains a few bug fixes.

Binary packages are simple, two-level archives. The `.deb` itself is an `ar` archive containing two gzipped tarballs (or tar archives), one containing information about the package and another containing the files that are to end up on the filesystem when the package installs. To illustrate this, find a `.deb` on the CD included with this book and move it to a new directory freshly created in your home space. Change to this new directory and type

```
ar x packagefile
```

where `packagefile` is the name of the file you moved here. Three new files will result from this command: `debian-binary`, which specifies the version of the C libraries this package's binaries are linked against, and `control.tar.gz` and `data.tar.gz`, which contain information describing this package to the package manager and the files that will end up in the filesystem after the package is installed, respectively.

The Anatomy of Source Packages

Source packages consist of several components. First, the original source tarball, which is identical to the entire upstream source tree (in most cases), is named `package-version.orig.tar.gz`. Changes that the package maintainer made to those sources for the purpose of creating packages (that is, building scripts and third-party patches) are contained in a file named `package-version_release.diff.gz`. Finally, information about the package that's needed before the source is extracted is kept in the file `package-version.dsc`.

After retrieving all three of these files for one source package, the archive can be extracted with the command `dpkg-source -x package-version.dsc`. If you don't have the package `dpkg-dev`, you can skip forward to the next section, which describes `dselect` (a user interface for package installation).

A new directory named *package-version* (both *package* and *version* are identical to those in the name of the source package) is created. This directory contains a standard source tree; the only thing Debian-specific resides in the debian/ directory underneath its top level. This directory, in turn, contains all scripts needed to build all useful software and data from the sources and create binary packages for them. This process is invoked by calling dpkg-buildpackage. (See dpkg-buildpackage(1) for more information.)

Source packages contain no dependency information; only the resulting binary packages do.

Now that you know what the various Debian packages are, let's move on to how you install and manage them.

dselect—A Text-Mode UI for Package Management

One of the most common complaints new, inexperienced Linux users have against Debian is the complexity and ugliness of its package management front end. (Figure 10.2 shows its introductory screen.) dselect, however, is one of the most powerful package managers around. It boasts an extensive help system, a condensed package listing and selection mechanism, and numerous installation methods. It is yet another of those things Debian has tailored to its audience of professionals; rather than waste effort on features that wouldn't be in demand (such as mouse input and other user-friendly features), the developers of dselect decided to focus on its power. As a result, dselect is more convenient for the experienced professional.

Those who know that applications centered around keystrokes are useable in a much more efficient manner than those with other methods for input will appreciate the way dselect works. It's easier to get simple or complicated tasks accomplished quickly with it than with any other package manager I have ever used in the past.

Running dselect

As with everything, it's always best to learn how to do things under Linux by actually doing them. Simply reading a large text file won't do you any good; as such, it's strongly recommended that you follow along and try things out as they are presented in this section.

Before running dselect, you must be root. After you have root permissions, run dselect by typing that command into your shell. Immediately, you are greeted with a screen identical to the one portrayed in Figure 10.2. You have a number of options; each of these serves a special purpose.

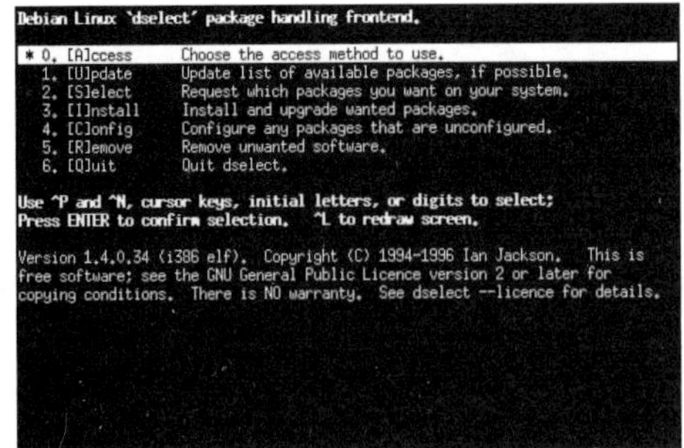

FIGURE 10.2
`dselect`*'s initial dialog.*

Acquiring Access to a Debian Mirror

Before you can install packages, you need a place to get them from; this place is called a *mirror*. The CDs included with this book, for example, contain a full Debian mirror. Mirrors can also be remote, accessed from your LAN or across the Internet.

The Organization of a Debian Mirror

Before you make your choice about how you're going to retrieve packages, a little introduction is in order. Debian, first of all, consists of many distributions, each of which has its own subdivisions. Debian and all of its software have been ported to several different architectures, several of which ship a stable distribution. Below this level, there is always a new distribution in progress for each architecture, which has more up-to-date software. This distribution in progress has come to be known as the "unstable" distribution, although common experience dictates that "unstable" is often more stable than what's labeled "stable." Last, when an unstable distribution is given additional attention for the purpose of stabilizing it for a new release of Debian, it is renamed "frozen." At any given time, you might have three distributions to choose from: stable, frozen, and unstable. You should not mix packages between the three until you become more experienced with Debian.

Below the distribution stability level is where the actual distributions live. Every piece of software that makes it into Debian is categorized according to its license and placed into one of the following distributions. The bulk of Debian's software goes in "main"; everything in this section complies entirely with the Debian Free Software Guidelines (DFSG, which was addressed in Chapter 1, "Introduction to Debian Linux"). Anything that is DFSG Free, but declares dependencies on any packages that aren't, goes in a distribution labeled "contrib." Finally, any software that doesn't comply with the DFSG is funneled into "non-free."

One special distribution lives apart from all others, "non-U.S." In this category, packages can be free or non-free, but U.S. export law bars them from being exported.

Because Debian organizes its mirrors in this way, you can take your pick of what type of system you need. If you want your computer to have no quirks and can handle having software without all of the latest features, pick the stable branch; it's been well tested and is known to contain only very minor bugs. If you need recent software and are willing to handle occasional, isolated flakiness in your software, pick unstable. If there happens to be a frozen branch, and you want to help test the new distribution before release, go ahead and choose that.

In turn, there is a great significance to which distributions you choose to peruse. If you want to advocate free software, or you don't have time to check licenses to be sure you're complying with the law when you use your system, use main. (The CD distributed with this book only contain main.) This assures you that everything on your system is DFSG compliant, hence useable for anything whatsoever. Anything in contrib is the same; however, packages in this section require packages from non-free, which might have restrictions. When you install a package from non-free, it's your responsibility to check `/usr/doc/`*`package`*`/copyright` for usage terms. By installing and using this software, you accept responsibility for the license's terms and suggest understanding.

Selecting an Access Method

Now that you've decided what stability branch and distributions to get your packages from, it's time to tell `dselect` where to access your chosen mirror. First, either enter A (`dselect` is case sensitive! that's uppercase) or use the arrow keys to highlight Access and press Enter. This shows you a list of access methods; you must select one (see Figure 10.3). Usually, people select multi-CD if they received an official Debian CD set, but if you want to get the most recent updates, it's perfectly acceptable to select the FTP method. However, for most cases besides CD installations, Apt is preferable. Apt is the most versatile access method, capable of handling parallel downloads and dependency-ordered installations. This utility is described in more detail in the section "Apt—An Intelligent Command-Line Package Manager" later in this chapter.

Beside each option is a short blurb describing its use. A more complete description of the selected access method is shown on the bottom half of the screen. It is recommended that you read each of these now unless you know what you're doing.

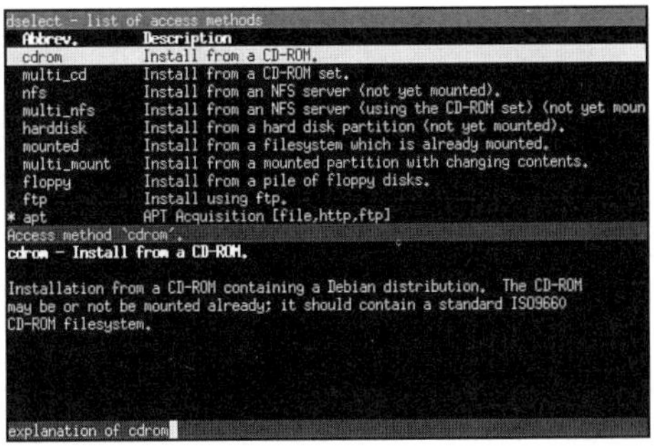

FIGURE 10.3
Selecting an access method.

```
dselect - list of access methods
  Abbrev.        Description
  cdrom          Install from a CD-ROM.
  multi_cd       Install from a CD-ROM set.
  nfs            Install from an NFS server (not yet mounted).
  multi_nfs      Install from an NFS server (using the CD-ROM set) (not yet moun
  harddisk       Install from a hard disk partition (not yet mounted).
  mounted        Install from a filesystem which is already mounted.
  multi_mount    Install from a mounted partition with changing contents.
  floppy         Install from a pile of floppy disks.
  ftp            Install using ftp.
* apt            APT Acquisition [file,http,ftp]
Access method `cdrom'.
cdrom - Install from a CD-ROM.

Installation from a CD-ROM containing a Debian distribution.  The CD-ROM
may be or not be mounted already; it should contain a standard ISO9660
CD-ROM filesystem.

explanation of cdrom
```

CD/Multi-CD

The CD installation method is obsolete and usually deprecated at this point in time, as it was replaced with good reason by the multi-CD method. Before Debian was too big to fit on one CD, the package management system wasn't designed to handle any more than that. Needless to say, in no time Debian outgrew this restriction and a replacement strategy was needed. For the CD set included with this book, you will most likely use the multi-CD installation method.

If you will be using the multi-CD method, select it now. You see yet another dialog asking what block device your CD drive is on. If you don't know, refer to Chapter 11, "Administration Essentials," for information on determining this. Before pressing Enter, be sure to put the last disc in your CD set into your CD drive, as this CD contains the package information for both CDs.

After a certain amount of drive activity, you are asked for the distribution top level. If you are using the CD set that came with this book, the answer is `/debian`, the default. Next, you are asked some questions about missing files; these issues are unimportant. When asked a question such as "Where is the non-free Packages.cd file?" just press Enter. After finishing these questions, `dselect` returns to its initial screen.

If you have followed these instructions and intend on using this installation method, you can skip the other install methods and proceed to "Updating the Package Availability Database" later in this chapter.

NFS/Multi-NFS

NFS is a file-sharing mechanism common in UNIX. This method is useful only if you are on a network and are hosting an NFS server locally. Usually, NFS installs are the best choice when the system being installed doesn't have a CD drive or a fast connection to the Internet. One machine with the media to hold all of the packages on the CD or a fast enough network connection to pull the latest packages from the Internet can serve the installation needs of a vast network.

Multi-NFS, on the other hand, is a special form of the NFS method that allows you to use package archives fragmented across multiple pieces of removable media (such as a CD set) across the network. This is really an uncommon case, so no more is said about it. See the `dselect` documentation for more information on using this access method.

After selecting NFS, you are asked for the name of your NFS server and the directory to request from that server. You cannot make this up; you must have an NFS server already running on the system you specify. For more information on setting up an NFS server, see Chapter 19, "Tools for Advanced Network Administration."

Hard Disk

The hard disk method is useful only when you have a Debian package archive on an unmounted hard drive partition. Upon selecting this method, you are asked for the block device name and filesystem type of the partition where it lives. After answering these questions, you are asked for the distribution top level.

Note

By selecting the hard disk method, you suggest that you've set up a Debian mirror on one of your hard-disk partitions. The work involved in setting up a mirror is beyond the scope of this chapter.

Mounted/Multi-Mount

The mounted method is similar to the hard drive access method. The only true difference is that when you use this method, the mirror is expected to be mounted manually before any installation takes place. Every other method handles mounting the filesystem for you. This method is most useful when you're using some kind of medium that's unsupported by any other access method (yet supported by the kernel) or a network filesystem that nobody's written an access method for.

FTP and Apt

FTP used to be one of the most common access methods. However, it's been greatly superceded by Apt, which is much more versatile than any previous method. As a rule, `dselect` access methods always install packages in sorted order, regardless of dependencies. As a result, errors are encountered while `dselect` attempts to install packages whose dependencies are entirely unresolved. When `dselect` encounters an unreasonable number of errors, it stops. This behavior forces the user to re-initiate installation several times before it's actually completed.

Apt, on the other hand, is a more versatile version of several installation methods. It implements mounted and FTP over again and adds a new method allowing access via HTTP (Web servers). Not only is Apt capable of handling all of these, but also it can address all of them during the same run.

The greatest reason Apt is superior is that it accounts for dependencies when installing or upgrading packages, making seamless upgrades and installations a reality. Never before has this level of simplicity been associated with mass software upgrades or installations. Electronic mirrors of the Debian package archives are listed at the URL `ftp://ftp.debian.org/pub/debian/README.mirrors`. You can use any one of the FTP sites for the FTP method, and all sites that include the HTTP mirrors are accessible via Apt.

Caution

Apt is one the most important new features of Debian 2.1, but it needs plenty of free space because it downloads all packages before installing them.

After selecting the FTP method, you are asked what site to connect to. Just pick a server that's close to you (geographically) from the aforementioned list. Afterwards, another prompt inquires whether to use passive mode; if you're not behind a firewall, proxy, or packet filter, the default should be fine. Next, `dselect` inquires about authentication information. In most cases, `anonymous` will suffice for your login name and your email address for your password. Next, you are asked where the Debian mirror lives on the server you specified; here, you should type in the directory listed for this mirror in `README.mirrors`, which you downloaded previously, I'm sure. If you want to go through an authenticated FTP proxy, say yes to the next question. However, this is unnecessary unless you know what you're doing, so the default is usually fine. If you have any doubt, refer to the sample answers `dselect` gives you before asking any questions.

The next question prompts you for a list of distributions to get. In the previous section, we described the layout of a Debian mirror, various stability branches, and the distributions available from each. The answer you give to this question tells the FTP method which distributions to retrieve. Each distribution should be of the form `dists/`*`stability-branch`*`/`*`distribution`*—so if you want to run the unstable branch and every distribution available from the U.S., your answer should look like `dists/unstable/main dists/unstable/contrib dists/unstable/non-free`. The non-U.S. distribution is hosted away from most Debian mirrors and as such must be accessed specially. See the upcoming section on Apt for more information on accessing non-U.S. servers.

Tip

The configuration of Apt is beyond the scope of this section. However, it is highly recommended over any other method for any purpose besides using network filesystems or removable media. For now, the default configuration should be fine; if you're using the CDs included with the book, simply use the multi-CD method. Otherwise, select Apt and press Enter at every prompt to get its default setup.

Updating the Package Availability Database

After you've chosen an access method, `dselect` needs to get a list of packages available from your mirror. This information goes into a database called the *package availability database*, which is located at `/var/lib/dpkg/available`. This database is `dselect`'s memory of every package available to it, where you can get them, and all kinds of other information about individual packages. To update this database, select the [U]pdate option from `dselect`'s main menu.

Updating your availability database isn't something you only do once. When a certain amount of time has gone by, new versions of packages (and sometimes brand new packages) may have been installed in the stability branch you're using. Running [U]pdate every time before you install any packages ensures that your system gets upgraded (if you want it to be) and that the newest software is installed.

If you're using any of the Multi access methods, be sure to put the last CD (or Zip disk or Jaz cartridge or whatever) in the drive before you update. If you don't, your package list will be incomplete.

Press U, or highlight Update and press Enter. Depending on which method you choose and how fast your network connection is (if your method uses the network), the amount of time this takes varies. If you're grabbing this information over a modem, go have a nice cup of coffee or take a ski trip or something. Realistically, if you're using a 56K modem, you should probably give this update around 10 minutes to complete.

Using the Package List Browser

After updating the package availability database, you can select new software for installation. `dselect`'s third option, the package list browser, is made for this purpose; choose the [S]elect option in `dselect`'s main menu to open it. This displays a dialog box from which you can manipulate your system's software installation in numerous ways.

The package list browser is probably the part of `dselect` that you will use the most. Because no other tool available with Debian 2.1 presents information about available packages in such an organized way as `dselect`, it's often used as nothing but a tool for research. Other programs, such as Apt, exist to make package management much easier either in conjunction with or independently of `dselect`. As you become more advanced, it's likely you'll find yourself using the simpler tools that don't carry a user interface; these are described later in this chapter.

The designers of `dselect` knew this step to be somewhat difficult; the browser is somewhat non-intuitive to those unfamiliar with it. Because of this, the first thing you see is the help screen. The first page displayed shows some basic commands, the most important commands for common use of `dselect`. As it's highly recommended you read at least this information, this screen is shown in Figure 10.4.

FIGURE 10.4
The package list browser dialog.

```
Help: Introduction to package list
Welcome to the main package listing.  Please read the help that is available !

You will be presented with a list of packages which are installed or available
for installation.  You can navigate around the list using the cursor keys,
mark packages for installation (using `+') or deinstallation (using `-').

Packages can be marked either singly or in groups; initially you will see that
the line `All packages' is selected.  `+', `-' and so on will affect all the
packages described by the highlighted line.  Use `o' to change the order of the
list (this also changes which kinds of group selections are possible).

(Mainly for new installations:) Standard packages will be requested by default.
Use capital `D' or `R' key to override this - see the keybindings help screen.

Some of your choices will cause conflicts or dependency problems; you will be
given a sub-list of the relevant packages, so that you can solve the problems.

When you are satisfied with your choices you should press Return to confirm
your changes and leave the package listing.  A final check on conflicts and
dependencies will be done - here too you may see a sublist.

Press Space to leave help and enter the list; press `?' at any time for help.
? = help menu    Space = exit help    . = next help    or a help page key
```

After you've browsed the online help a bit, press the spacebar to see the package list browser. You can open the help dialog again by pressing ? any time.

Tour of the Browser

The package list browser shows a categorized list of all software available for installation. Because Debian is such a huge distribution aimed at technically proficient people, the interface conventions used in presenting this list can sometimes overwhelm new users; because Debian is so huge, we try to represent these packages in as organized a way as possible.

The Status Database

The package browser deals with both the package availability database, which was presented previously, and the status database. The status database keeps track of your system's current profile—that is, what is installed, whether any packages' setup scripts didn't work, and so on. Your system profile represents software exactly as it's installed on your system. This database also holds a second system profile, called your *pending system profile*, which represents requested changes to software installation.

dselect's true job is to manipulate your pending system profile and then take appropriate action to get your software installation to reflect it. This information is kept in /var/lib/dpkg/status.

Package List Box

Figure 10.5 shows the package list browser. This dialog box, by being highly organized, manages to fit an immense amount of information into a very small space. To understand how to best use dselect, it's important to understand what all of this information means.

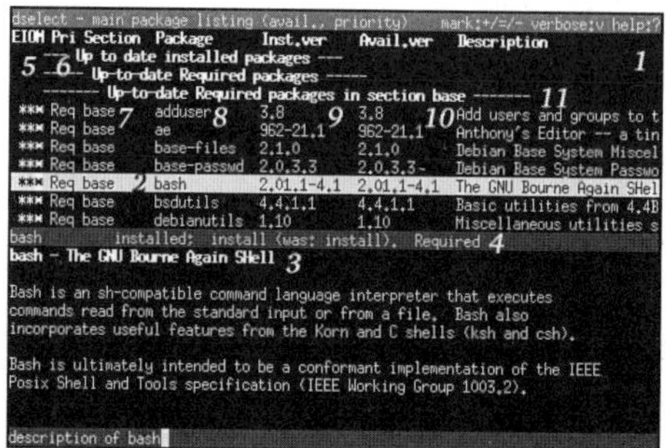

FIGURE 10.5
The package list browser.

The top half of the screen contains package records, one to each line. Each package has a name, a short description of the software contained within, some information about current installation status, version numbers, and the package's priority and category. The bottom half of the screen presents more in depth information about the currently selected package (or category of packages). The first line is brief and should give a layman's description of what the software does. The rest of this description is more in depth. If there is too much information to fit inside this segment of the screen, you can press u and d to scroll up and down. The dividing line between the two halves of the screen displays the package's name, some status info, and the package's importance.

As you can see, the package records are classified into specific categories. Operating on any category entry operates in turn on every package contained in it. For instance, if you read the initial help screen, you know that the + key marks a package for installation. If you scroll all the way up to the top until you see the highest level package category (All packages) and press the + key, you select all of Debian's 2,600+ packages for installation. This is definitely not recommended. (Press R to undo changes.)

Status Fields

The EIOM column in dselect is a readout of your system's software profile. Each one of these four letters (EIOM) in turn represents its own column:

- Error flag (E): If a package carries a mark in this column, its installation is seriously broken. Any time a package is labeled with an R in this column, it requires reinstallation.
- Installed State (I): This column represents the current state of your packages, namely your current system profile. If this column shows an underscore, this package has not been installed. A star here (*) shows this package to be completely installed, and a dash (-) means that configuration files remain from a previous installation of this package. A U signifies the package is unpacked but still requires configuration. C suggests that an error occurred during configuration of this package, and I only appears when the package could not be completely unpacked.
- Old mark (O): This column shows your pending system profile as it was before `dselect` was started. This is helpful in that you can refer to your previous settings even after you change the system's configuration; as you make changes, your previous selections are always left intact so you can refer back to them or revert as necessary.
- Mark (M): This column shows the pending profile in addition to any changes you have made during this run of the package browser. Every time you begin the browser, the O and M columns are identical, but as you mark new packages for installation or removal, those changes accumulate here. Upon exiting the browser, this field is saved into the pending system profile; entering the browser again shows that your changes have been moved to the Old mark field. The interface was written this way so that if you make a mistake, you can easily undo any changes.

Priority and Section

As you can see, choosing which software is important enough to install can be a difficult task! If packages were sorted only by alphabetical order, it would be almost impossible for a new user to decide what to mark for installation and what to leave alone, unless he spent hours reading every description. That's why packages are ordered by the functions they perform and their importance to the average user. The browser uses the Pri and Section columns to display this information. Software in Debian is divided among these sections:

- `admin/`—System and network administration tools.
- `base/`—Software necessary for the proper working of even the most minimal system.
- `comm/`—Software for use with serial communication devices.
- `devel/`—C/C++/Java development tools.
- `doc/`—Loads of exhaustive documentation.
- `editors/`—All kinds of text editors. Some for extreme simplicity and seemingly thousands for power.

- `games/`—The title says it all.
- `graphics/`—Multimedia editors and viewers. Movies, ray-tracing, graphics…you name it, it's there.
- `hamradio/`—Programs HAM operators might find interesting.
- `interpreters/`—Scripting languages and other more tailored interpreters. Languages such as Scheme, Python, Perl, and Tcl.
- `libs/`—C and C++ libraries for all purposes.
- `mail/`—Mail readers, servers, filters, and more.
- `math/`—Mathematical tools: scientific calculators, equation typesetting, and equation plotting.
- `misc/`—All kinds of stuff that just won't fit into any other category.
- `net/`—Network applications, servers, and tools.
- `news/`—News readers, servers, and more.
- `oldlibs/`—Compatibility libraries for maintaining compatibility with old systems.
- `otherosfs/`—Tools for interoperation with other operating systems.
- `shells/`—Shells. Umm, that thing you type commands into to make your computer do stuff.
- `sound/`—Editors for various sound formats, sound players, encoders, and so on.
- `tex/`—The popular and powerful typesetting system.
- `text/`—Other typesetting systems, various documentation formats, and their associated viewers.
- `utils/`—Software implementing highly useful commands that perform specific tasks.
- `web/`—Anything to do with the World Wide Web.
- `x11/`—Graphical applications for the X windowing system, along with development libraries.

Next is the priority setting on packages. These descend, in order, from Required through Important, Standard, Optional, and Extra. Debian has specific rules for figuring out which packages go into which category, but the rules aren't important to know; our prioritization scheme usually reflects the needs of the average user.

One last set of criteria for categorizing packages hasn't been discussed yet: how up-to-date they are. Any packages under a category that's updated has a new version available for download and installation. For example, "Updated Required packages in section base" is a category containing packages that are Required and come from the section base which have new versions available.

Because Debian knows when new versions of its software are available, it's relatively easy to do full, seamless system upgrades. We show you how to do this in the upcoming section on Apt.

Keystrokes

Every keystroke in the package list browser concerns one of three purposes: navigating, searching, or marking packages. The most important key to remember, however, is ? because this brings you to the help menu, which outlines all of these keystrokes in one screen.

Changing a Package's Status

All keys used to change a package's status modify the M field in `dselect` (which stands for Mark or the pending profile). These allow you to request new states of installation for any package:

- + (plus sign, install) tells `dselect` to mark this package for installation. If this flag is set on a package, `dselect` does not hesitate to upgrade it whenever a new version becomes available.
- - (dash, delete) marks a package for deletion but does not delete configuration files (which are often labored over for hours and as a result are usually worth saving).
- _ (underscore, purge) marks a package and its associated configuration files for deletion.
- = (equal sign, hold) stands for hold. A package with this status stays exactly as is. For example, a package that's installed but on hold is not upgraded when a new version becomes available.
- : (colon) takes a package off hold status.

The Dependency Resolution Screen

Often, asking for one package to be installed or removed disrupts another package's working environment. Some programs depend on the availability of others for proper operation, and as such, relationships between packages evolve. As a result, sometimes you can't install one package without installing another as well. Sometimes when removing one package, you break another; in this case, you're forced to remove the broken package as well. This is where dependencies come in.

When you come across a dependency conflict, the dependency resolution screen appears. This is depicted in Figure 10.6. For example, suppose I decide I need to install the console graphics viewer, `zgv`. Because it uses a display library called `svgalib`, which is in its own package, it can't work until I install that as well. Selecting `zgv` for installation yields the dialog in Figure 10.6. Notice that `dselect` modifies selections as necessary to resolve all problems; it does this every time the dependency resolution screen appears. To exit this dialog, press Enter or Q.

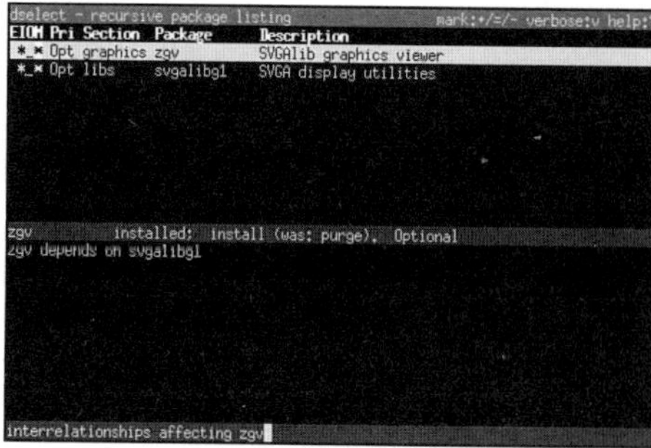

FIGURE 10.6
Dependency resolution screen.

Relationships between packages are fairly self-explanatory. A package can Depend upon, Suggest, Recommend (which is a less important suggestion), or Conflict with another package. Some relationships are more exotic; for example, some packages provide a replacement for or entirely replace another (the latter also suggesting the two cannot be installed simultaneously). In any case, the names for these relationships are fairly intuitive, and `dselect` usually makes a satisfactory choice.

Mass Operations

You can invoke any one of the previous keystrokes on a single package or on an entire category. Highlighting any package category and pressing one of these keys affects every package contained therein.

Other mass operation keystrokes exist. If you want to revert every change you made in the current dialog, press R; this also works in the dependency screen. In addition, pressing U sets all packages to the state suggested by `dselect`.

Searching and Reordering Data

The / (slash) key allows you to search the entire database of available packages for a particular keyword or phrase. You are presented a prompt, at which you can type a simple string, the next occurrence of which appears quickly. Pressing \ (backslash) finds the next occurrence of the previously specified search string.

Pressing O and V reorganizes the way information is presented in the package browser. Pressing O changes the way packages are divided into categories, and pressing V changes the way package records are displayed. Experiment with both to find your personal preference.

Exiting the Browser and Other List Dialogs

There are two ways you can leave any dialog in the browser: Either check dependencies and fix any problems first or just leave without regard to checking package relationships.

The former is always recommended, as this can save you considerable grief later. Pressing Enter at any dialog box from within the package browser will exit and display a list of unmet dependencies. Pressing Q exits a dialog without consideration of dependencies. You can use either of these keys within the dependency resolution screen as well as the browser. As a last resort, pressing Esc or X exits the browser, discarding any changes that were made.

Final Steps in Adjusting Your Software Installation

Now, we get to the step that follows the excruciating agony we've described: We actually install some software. However, we're going to discard all of this knowledge and move on to greener pastures with better and simpler software management tools. So why did we teach you `dselect`? Well, because it's important. No matter how good you are with Perl and searching big chunks of textual data (such as the status and availability databases), you will be forced to use `dselect` every now and again, even if the occurrence is rare.

Installing and Upgrading `dselect`

When you select [I]nstall from `dselect`'s main menu, it automatically looks over the packages you've marked for installation and those needing to be upgraded, and it fetches them by whatever method you specified in [A]ccess. It then unpacks them all and sets them up one at a time; some packages ask for input, but most don't. Because each package might ask questions differently, there's no way to cover this topic in its entirety; we'd end up with a 2,000-page book. Just wing it. If you don't understand what you're being asked and you don't remember what the package was for, chances are you won't use it often, and guessing probably won't hurt you.

One quirk of `dselect` is that all of its methods (besides Apt) are fairly stupid. They install packages in an order that exacerbates dependency problems. As a result, you often come across a situation where you have to run the Configure step two or three times after installing before problems are resolved. In bad cases, manual intervention with `dpkg` is required. However, once again, Apt is the solution to all.

Configuring Unconfigured Software in `dselect`

If the last message `dselect` gives you when installing is that `dpkg` failed on a number of packages, running the configure step will often solve the problem. This step re-attempts configuration of any packages that failed this step previously during the installation phase.

Any packages that appear with a C in the I (Installed state) column of status information in the package browser needs reconfiguration. If rerunning this step several times does not fix your problem, get to a root shell and run the command `dpkg --abort-after=500 --configure --pending` several times. This should get you through the configuration stage. For more information on invoking `dpkg` directly when `dselect` fails, see the coming section on `dpkg`.

Removing Packages

Any packages marked to be removed or purged are handled appropriately when you select [R]emove from `dselect`'s main menu.

Now that you've learned all of the ins and outs of `dselect`, it's time to move our attention to another helpful tool, Apt.

Apt—An Intelligent Command-Line Package Manager

Apt was written by Jason Gunthorpe to create a package manager that was easier and more functional than `dselect`. At this time, Apt is no more than a command-line tool, yet there are plans to replace `dselect` altogether with a more friendly GUI based on Apt. These plans, however, are stalled for the time being.

Because Apt does not have a mechanism for browsing and selecting packages (everything is done via the command-line interface), it is often used in conjunction with `dselect` as an access method. We explain how to accomplish this in the sections to come. After you become accustomed to Debian's package management system and no longer need an organized readout of your options to know what you need installed, Apt's command-line interface will most likely become the most powerful tool in your arsenal. Personally, I use it over `dselect` 95 percent of the time; this follows the reality that cryptic batch-oriented tools are much more efficient than interactive applications for those who have the necessary experience.

Advantages of Apt

Apt's main feature is its dependency handling. When you request that a package be installed on your system, Apt automatically installs the specified package along with any others that are needed to satisfy its dependencies. In addition, Apt installs packages in the order that dependencies dictate, avoiding the trouble `dselect` has in this area that forces the administrator to rerun the configuration and installation step several times to achieve a working system in many cases.

Basically, when one package depends on another, it requires that package to be configured before itself. Using the `zgv` example presented before, when `zgv` is installed, it requires that `svgalib` (the SVGA display library for console graphics) not only be installed, but properly configured as well. If you try to configure `zgv` before `svgalib`, `zgv` isn't truly configured correctly because not everything it depends upon is ready for use. Instead, `zgv`'s configuration scripts are never executed; `dpkg` (described in an upcoming section) complains that not all of `zgv`'s dependencies are met.

It follows, then, that any package manager installing a huge chunk of packages should be able to order them as their dependencies dictate to avoid installation errors. In the past, `dselect` methods have not been this smart. Instead, `dselect` iterates over the packages in some order it favors, installing and configuring packages without regard to dependencies. As a result, a huge number of errors sometimes accumulates, and when this happens, `dselect` bails halfway through installation. This is obviously not satisfactory because it forces the system administrator to rerun the configuration and installation steps multiple times before everything works correctly.

Not so with Apt. It has the redeeming feature that it understands the order in which packages should be installed. Only one run of Apt is ever required to install or upgrade any number of packages. I, personally, have used Apt to keep my entire system up-to-date (on two systems, notably) for three entire releases of Debian; that's way more than what's possible with any other operating system or any other Linux distribution.

Configuring Apt

Before you can use Apt, you need to configure it by giving it a list of mirrors to attempt to access. Apt is capable of accessing any volume that's on the Web or an FTP site or mounted somewhere on the local system. It keeps all of these package "sources" in `/etc/apt/sources.list`; the following code shows an example of this configuration file:

```
deb http://http.us.debian.org/debian stable main contrib non-free
#deb file:/cdrom stable main
deb http://pandora.debian.org/debian-non-US stable non-US
```

Each line in Apt's `sources.list` file names one location to retrieve packages from. These are in the format `deb` *`URI stability_branch distribution ...`*, where *`URI`* is the Universal Resource Indicator where packages can be obtained, *`stability_branch`* is the distribution to be retrieved, and *`distribution`* is one or more of main, contrib, non-free, and non-U.S. Note that you can comment out entries by placing a pound sign in front of them.

The second source in the preceding code is what you use for a CD drive or other medium that you can mount onto your filesystem. However, this is usually not satisfactory any more because Apt is incapable of handling sets of multiple CDs. The first is an example of a line to put in `sources.list` if you want to retrieve your packages from the Internet.

The URI used in each entry is the path to the distribution's top level. In most cases, the default configuration Apt is shipped with is satisfactory; however, it's always recommended that you use mirrors that are near you. `http.us.debian.org` is an alias for a cluster of about 15 machines and will work for most people in the U.S.

Apt performs parallel downloads whenever possible in an attempt to maximize bandwidth. However, one problem is introduced by this behavior: Because Debian mirrors all updates from the master server at different times, two mirrors often have different versions of the same packages available. How then does Apt decide which package to get when it has more than one version to choose from? As it turns out, Apt gives the first source the highest priority. When there is a version mismatch, it always gets the version available on the source that's listed first. Always place the source you expect to be the most up-to-date first, whenever you have two sources that will contain at least some of the same packages.

Using Apt

Apt's command-line interface is fairly straightforward. To see a short description of its options, type `apt-get -h`. As the output of this command shows, Apt can perform a number of tasks. These are the respective commands listed by `apt-get -h`. When invoking `apt-get`, you must specify a command, along with any additional information required by that command. These commands are `update`, `install`, `upgrade`, `dist-upgrade`, `dselect-upgrade`, and `clean`. They are described in the following list:

- `update`—The `update` command retrieves all package databases from every source, modifying your local information to reflect what is available from each. It's important to run this command before attempting to invoke any one of the installation or upgrade commands.
- `install`—The `install` command retrieves and installs all packages specified on the command line, along with any other packages necessary to meet their dependencies. The format of this command is `apt-get install` *`package_list`*. If you want to install the GNOME panel but don't feel like searching every piece of software it requires for proper operation, the simple command `apt-get install gnome-panel` installs every necessary package. Listing 10.1 shows the output for this simple command.

LISTING 10.1 A Sample Run of `apt-get`

```
.../home/aaron/docs/dglu# apt-get install gnome-panel
Updating package status cache...done
Checking system integrity...ok
The following extra packages will be installed:
libgtkxmhtml0 gnome-core libgtop1 libpanel-applet0
The following NEW packages will be installed:
gnome-panel libgtkxmhtml0 gnome-core libgtop1 libpanel-applet0
0 packages upgraded, 5 newly installed, 0 to remove and 0 not upgraded.
```

- `upgrade`—Invoking the upgrade `command` attempts to install the most recently available version of every software package already on your system. This particular command tries to do everything without changing the installation status of any package, whether dependencies call for it or not. This command is usually not used.
- `dist-upgrade`—The `dist-upgrade` command is much like `upgrade` but it is distinctive in that it changes the installation status of additional packages if dependencies call for it. This is the preferable command for complete system upgrades.
- `dselect-upgrade`—As mentioned previously, you can use Apt in conjunction with `dselect`. This command reads `dselect`'s status databases and attempts to upgrade your system to the profile you have specified in the package list browser. In this mode, Apt installs packages in the order that dependencies dictate (to avoid dangling misconfigurations) but does not change the installation status of any package.

To cause `dselect` to use Apt as its access method, all you have to do is configure Apt's sources and select it under `dselect`'s access method dialog. You are asked whether you want to change your list of sources. You can either take care of this before starting `dselect` (with your favorite editor) or from within this dialog box.

dpkg—The Core of Debian

Underneath every packaging front end is `dpkg`, the core package manager for Debian. Apt and `dselect` are incapable of the actual installation of packages; instead, they both simply retrieve packages, putting them on the local filesystem, and invoke `dpkg`.

dpkg Is Debian

All Linux distributions are basically the same. They all ship generally similar software, most of it under similar licenses. Most have the same capabilities for use in a production server environment. Every distribution gets its software from the same place: sources acquired on the Internet. Many contribute time back to the community in the form of additional software; Red Hat is known widely for its work on GNOME, and Debian is regarded as the defender of free software (SPI being the holder of the Open Source trademark; see Chapter 1) and is known for donating resources to such projects as Berlin and GNOME.

When it comes down to the fundamentals, however, all distributions are almost identical: they are all Linux, and they ship the same software. What sets one distribution apart from another? The answer to this question is fairly complex but always involves the only piece of software that's exclusive to most distributions: the package manager.

Of course, other issues are involved as well, including licensing policies, the number of people involved with developing the distribution, how well it's put together, the target audience, and so on. However, the package management system is always the foundation piece of software in a distribution. As it turns out, the information included in Debian's packaging format greatly dictates the look and feel of the system, and this packaging format is controlled by `dpkg`.

`dpkg` is a simple command-line tool that understands how to perform a small set of operations on individual packages. It has no graphical interface; that's what `dselect` is for. It is incapable of accessing packages that live anywhere but on your system in a file. As such, `dpkg` is a basic tool that the average user rarely uses.

Basic Operations (on Package Installation) with dpkg

`dpkg`'s command line is simple: It takes zero or more options and exactly one action flag. An *action* flag, of course, is one that performs some function, and *option* flags change the way these are carried out. All actions are fairly straightforward.

Action Flags

`dpkg` requires one of the following action flags to tell dpkg exactly what to do.

-i | - -install *package_files*

Both `-i` and `--install` perform the same action. Each package file listed on the command line (with *`package_files`*) is unpacked and installed (see the next two actions). If `--recursive` is specified as well, `dpkg` searches recursively under the directory specified (*`package_files`* is replaced with the directory you want scanned) for any packages and installs them in the order they are found. Many methods in `dselect` use this flag. You can also specify recursive installation with `-iGROEB` rather than `--install --recursive`.

To install a package in the file `foo.deb`, execute this command as root:

```
dpkg -i foo.deb
```

If you've got a directory that lives at `~/debian`, for example, populated with any number of other directories containing Debian packages that you want installed, execute this command as root:

```
dpkg --install --recursive ~/debian
```

Note

dselect and Apt both work by invoking dpkg. Both of them take responsibility for making sure packages are in a place where dpkg can access them. The CD and multi-CD methods of dselect use a special form of --install --recursive, specifically -iGROEB. This is almost the same, but with a few options added; these options are covered in more depth later. Specifically what -iGROEB does is tell dpkg to install all packages found anywhere under this directory (recursively), decline to downgrade anything, and only install those packages that have been selected for installation with dselect.

--unpack *package_files*

The --unpack *package_files* action flag performs a simple operation, namely unpacking the contents of a list of package files onto the filesystem. To preserve any previous setup you've done, any old files overwritten are backed up, and no configuration is performed by dpkg. This leaves packages in an "installed but not configured" state, which must be corrected by invoking --configure on them.

To unpack foo.deb onto your filesystem without performing any configuration, execute the following as root:

```
dpkg --unpack foo.deb
```

--configure *packages*

It becomes necessary to use dpkg directly when dselect confuses the installation process; often, one invocation with a --configure flag can right everything. Of course, --configure takes a package that's in an "installed but not configured" state and runs some number of scripts to set it up for use.

If -a or --pending is specified as well, dpkg will attempt to configure all packages that haven't been yet. Once again, dpkg isn't aware of the order it should handle packages, so errors are likely when dealing with a large number of packages. dpkg also has a failsafe in that when it encounters more than 50 errors, it exits. Often, when you're dealing with 100 or more packages needing to be configured, you have to invoke dpkg with these options a few times to get everything right. This happens for the same reasons that selecting configure in the dselect main menu doesn't always finish because dselect itself uses dpkg --pending --configure!

In this light, then, why would anyone invoke dpkg directly because it's already an option in dselect? The answer is simple. We can make dpkg oblivious to the errors, allowing us to get through this process much more quickly. Specifying --abort-after=500 tells dpkg to only abort if it encounters 500 errors.

To configure package `foo`, the command is

```
dpkg --configure foo
```

If you just installed a whole slew of packages from `dselect`, and you're stuck in an infinite loop trying to get everything configured, run

```
dpkg --pending --configure --abort-after=some_huge_number
```

Yes, if you have to bail from `dselect` and use more low-level programs, it's designed badly. A few different projects are under way to rectify this situation.

`--remove` *packages* and `--purge` *packages*

These options delete installed packages. If `--remove` or `-r` is specified, `dpkg` deletes the contents of listed packages but leaves their configuration files intact. If you spent any time hand-tuning any package's configuration, it's a good idea to save that work for a later time in case you decide to install this package again. In these situations, you should use `--remove`. The `--purge` option, on the other hand, deletes everything, including configuration files.

If `--pending` is specified as well, any packages that are slated for removal are removed (saving configuration), and any marked to be purged are entirely deleted. These selections are made through `dselect`, and this is the command `dselect`'s Remove option invokes.

To remove package `foo` but leave its configuration files intact, execute

```
dpkg --remove foo
```

or execute

```
dpkg -r foo
```

To entirely erase any traces of package `foo` from your system, run

```
dpkg --purge foo
```

To delete all packages you've marked for removal, invoke

```
dpkg --pending --remove
```

Informational Action Flags

Invoking `dpkg` isn't always for the purpose of modifying installation. Often, you can use `dpkg` to glean information about packages that either are installed or are available for installation. These action flags used for informational purposes can be useful for report generation with scripts or just to find out what's installed on your system.

--print-avail *package*

The `--print-avail` *package* switch lists all information your package subsystem knows about one specific package. This is, specifically, all control information; to know more about what it means, see Chapter 31.

Listing 10.2 shows some example output.

LISTING 10.2 One Entry in the Availability Database

```
[aaron@awac]
...~/docs/dglu$ dpkg --print-avail bash
Package: bash
Essential: yes
Priority: required
Section: base
Installed-Size: 783
Maintainer: Guy Maor <maor@debian.org>
Architecture: i386
Version: 2.01.1-4.1
Pre-Depends: libc6 (>= 2.0.7u), libncurses4, libreadlineg2 (>= 2.1-8)
Filename: dists/stable/main/binary-i386/base/bash_2.01.1-4.1.deb
Size: 450930
MD5sum: 2968895b420d43ea57e20f6c148c6931
Description: The GNU Bourne Again SHell
 Bash is an sh-compatible command language interpreter that executes
 commands read from the standard input or from a file.  Bash also
 incorporates useful features from the Korn and C shells (ksh and csh).
 .
 Bash is ultimately intended to be a conformant implementation of the
 IEEE Posix Shell and Tools specification (IEEE Working Group 1003.2).
```

To find out what version of package `foo` you have installed on your system, simply type

```
dpkg --print-avail foo ¦ grep Version
```

--list ¦ -l *pattern*

`--list ¦ -l` *pattern* lists all available and installed packages that match *pattern*. The pattern you pass to `dpkg` can have any wildcard characters supported by a POSIX-compliant shell. As such, it's important to quote the pattern so your shell's interpolation rules don't come into effect. Otherwise, you'll pass the list of files matching that pattern to `dpkg`, and this is definitely not desired behavior.

The output from this action lists package status and the package's name, installed version, and short description.

For example, suppose I want to see a list of GGI targets and know that their names all begin with `libggi-target-`. To show all available and installed GGI targets, type

```
dpkg -l '*ggi*'
```

The output should look something like this:

```
ii  libggi-target-a 990413-3       General Graphics Interface ASCII Art display
ii  libggi-target-e 990413-3       General Graphics Interface colour emulation
```

...with a lot more following.

-s ¦ --status *package_list*

The `-s ¦ --status` *package_list* action flag shows status information for all specified packages. This looks almost identical to the output of the `--print-avail` action, but it includes a status line and a section on configuration files. You can perhaps use this command to either check whether a package is installed correctly or find out where its configuration files live.

If I want to see where bash keeps its configuration files, I can type

```
dpkg --status 'bash'
```

-C ¦ --audit

When given a `-C ¦ --audit` flag, `dpkg` does nothing but check for any problems with package installations. If everything is fine, `dpkg` exits without any output. If there are packages with problems, however, more information is provided.

-L ¦ --listfiles *package_list*

The `-L ¦ --listfiles` *package_list* action lists all files that were installed by the specified packages. You can only invoke this on packages that have been installed.

To see all files on your filesystem that are owned by package `foo`, execute the command

```
dpkg -L foo
```

-S ¦ --search *file_pattern*

The `-S ¦ --search` *file_pattern* action takes a file (or pattern) and searches its databases to find out which package (or packages) it belongs to. Once again, if a pattern is specified, it should be enclosed in quotes; otherwise, your shell will tamper with its representation before `dpkg` processes it. This option is generally useful when you want to find out where a particular file came from.

For example, if you want to see which file the `true` command comes from, try this:

```
dpkg -S `which true`
```

That command's output is

```
shellutils: /bin/true
```

If you want to find out where every file in a particular directory came from, such as `/bin`, try this:

```
dpkg -S '/bin/*'
```

The output from this is fairly long, so it's omitted.

Altering dpkg's Behavior

`dpkg` has many universal options it can apply to every single action flag. Each of these modifies `dpkg`'s behavior in small, sometimes almost unnoticeable ways. As a great many options exist, we only present the most useful here; if you have additional needs, see the man page `dpkg`:

- `--abort-after=`*`num`* tells `dpkg` to abort after *`num`* errors.
- `--force-`*`thing`* forces `dpkg` to perform an action even though it would not normally. These options are usually useful only to experts, and if you're not experienced, you can severely damage your system by using these recklessly. However, using them might be necessary from time to time. To get a more complete list and description, run `dpkg --force-help`; this will list all of the `force` options and their effects.
- `--root=`*`dir`* makes `dpkg` install packages to and keep administration information in *`dir`*. This is generally useful when you're trying to build a `chroot` environment from a different distribution or managing the installation of a different machine over the network.
- `--largemem` and `--smallmem` tell `dpkg` to use as much (faster) or as little (slower) memory as it can. This is useful if you need `dpkg` to either go faster or if you don't have much memory.
- `-G` and `--refuse-downgrade` mean `dpkg` will not downgrade any packages, even if older versions of some packages are specified for installation on the command line.
- `-R` and `--recursive` handle all package files found under the directory specified, but search recursively. This is generally useful when you're dealing with a filesystem that has packages arranged in the standard way, separate categories stored under separate directories. This option can only be specified with the `--install` or `--unpack` options.
- `-O` and `--selected-only` only process those packages that are marked for installation in `dpkg`'s database, even if more packages are specified on the command line. This is generally useful when you've got a big number of packages in the same

place that you want to install, but they're mixed in with many you don't want to install. In this case, simply specify all of them with the `-O` flag; as a result, only those you need installed end up that way.

- `-E` and `--skip-same-version` skip the version of any installed package that matches that of one specified for installation on the command linc. This way, you don't waste time unpacking and setting up packages that are already installed.
- `-B` and `--auto-deconfigure` deconfigure any packages that require a package that is removed for any reason. This way, any packages that have unresolved dependencies are easily recognizable and act normally when their dependencies are fulfilled once again.
- `--ignore-depends` perform whatever actions are specified, even if dependencies dictate otherwise. Using this can result in a system with unworkable software; as such, it's recommended this is a seldom used member of your arsenal.

A dpkg Example

Consider a situation where you want to install all packages that you selected in `dselect` from your Debian CD, but you don't feel like waiting for a bazillion packages to install that are either old or haven't been upgraded. In addition, you don't want any status information in `dpkg`'s status database to be misleading. To perform this action, mount your CD, execute

```
dpkg -iGROEB path_to_CD-ROM_filesystem
```

and then sit back and wait. This can take some time. Not surprisingly, this is the command `dselect` uses to install packages with many of its access methods.

Advanced dpkg Issues

There is much to learn about what's under the hood of Debian's package management system. However, much of this information is only useful to a specific group of people, and as such, is only briefly presented here.

The Available and Status Databases

`dpkg` stores all of its data in two databases: the package and status databases. These are plain ASCII files, stored in `/var/lib/dpkg/{available¦status}`. The available database lists all packages `dpkg` knows that you have access to and every piece of information it needs to retrieve and install them. The status database lists packages and pieces of information about their status: current status and what the user has requested it be changed to.

One advantage dpkg has over rival package managers is that it keeps every one of its databases in ASCII. This means that if anything goes seriously wrong with the system that dpkg can't fix, you can use your favorite text editor to rectify the situation. Because RPM (which is the package manager of choice for many distributions) keeps everything in binary databases, when something serious goes wrong the only option is complete re-install. However, an ASCII database has one downside: It slows the package manager down a bit.

Summary

In this chapter, you learned all about dselect and Debian's package management system and how to use various package retrieval methods. You also learned about Apt as a more advanced alternative to dselect. Finally, you learned that both dselect and Apt rely on dpkg to work their magic and how to use dkpg directly for special purposes.

Debian, like all other distributions, has many tools for package management. Specifically, it has both a command-line tool and a second program that provides an easier user interface to the package management system. Both of these store all of their internal data in ASCII format, giving the system administrator that much more control over his system.

The biggest advantage Debian's package management system has over any other is Apt. With this tool, massive system upgrades and everyday software installations are so easy that you don't even need to think twice before performing them. This is contrary to many other distributions, where the only application that has this much capability is the graphical package manager—but none compare to Apt as far as dependability and ease of use.

11

Administration Essentials

by Gerry Muñoz

In This Chapter

System administration is not easy work; it is one of the most complex, fulfilling, and misunderstood professions within the computing area. System administration must ensure that the system works correctly and as efficiently as possible, so users can accomplish their daily activities easily and effectively. There are several different tasks that must be done so the system works properly; some of them should be done daily to ensure the system's integrity and effectiveness.

In this chapter, you'll learn about the basics of system administration and existing tools running under Debian that make system administration simple and more effective.

User Management

Users are the main reason computer systems exist. There are many different user-related tasks on a computer system, such as creating or removing a user. There are also different concepts that every administrator should know in order to manage users. In this section, you explore user management and concepts.

User Management Concepts

Because UNIX is a multiuser system, it is very important to differentiate between users; that's the main reason for creating an account for each user on the system. An account is a collection of information that basically specifies who the user is and what the user is allowed to do. The following are the components of a UNIX user account:

- Login `name.account`—Every user is assigned a unique login or username.
- User ID (UID)—A unique number given to every user on the system. It is used by the system to track user-related information.
- Group ID (GID) of the user's default group—GID is similar to the UID, only the GID is used for groups.
- Password—The account's password is the key that enables someone to use the account. A password is required for each user to get access to the system. The encrypted password is stored in the system.
- Full name—The user's real name, full name, and/or additional information.
- Home directory—Each user is placed in an initial directory when he or she logs in.
- Login shell—The shell that is started for the user at login time (see Chapter 2, "Shells," for more information on shells).

The /etc/passwd File

The file used for account configuration is the `/etc/passwd` file. This is a text file that contains valid usernames and their associated information. Each line of this file is divided into seven fields (see Table 11.1) separated by colons. The format is as follows:

```
name:encrypted password:UID:GID:comment field:home directory:login shell
```

Table 11.1 shows the fields contained on each line of `/etc/passwd`.

TABLE 11.1 Fields Contained on /etc/passwd

Field Name	*Description*
Login name	User's login name.
Encrypted password	Encrypted version of user's password. When using the `/etc/shadow`, no encrypted password will be shown.
UID	The user ID described earlier.
GID	The group ID described earlier.
Comment field	Usually contains full name and additional user-related information.
Home directory	The home directory described earlier.
Login shell	The login shell described earlier.

The following is an example of the `/etc/passwd` file:

```
# cat /etc/passwd
root:x:0:0:root:/root:/bin/bash
daemon:x:1:1:daemon:/usr/sbin:/bin/sh
bin:x:2:2:bin:/bin:/bin/sh
sys:x:3:3:sys:/dev:/bin/sh
sync:x:4:100:sync:/bin:/bin/sync
games:x:5:100:games:/usr/games:/bin/sh
man:x:6:100:man:/var/catman:/bin/sh
lp:x:7:7:lp:/var/spool/lpd:/bin/sh
mail:x:8:8:mail:/var/spool/mail:/bin/sh
nobody:x:65534:65534:nobody:/home:/bin/sh
gerry:x:1000:1000:Gerardo Munoz Martin:/home/gerry:/bin/bash
test:x:1001:1001:Testing account:/home/test:/bin/bash
```

The x character next to the login name indicates that the system is using the shadow passwords method (defined later in this chapter). It is possible to modify the information contained in the `/etc/passwd` file by using vi or any text editor (see Chapter 6, "Advanced Text Editing," for more information on vi).

> **Caution**
>
> To keep the system integrity, please do not modify this file unless you're really sure about what you are doing!

The /etc/group File

A *group* is a logical collection of users who share some characteristics. The /etc/group/ file maintains a list of the current groups on the system and the users that belong to each group. Each user is member of at least one group. A user can be a member of many groups; any additional groups the user is a member of are specified by entries in the /etc/group file. The format for /etc/group is the following:

```
Group name:encrypted password:GID:group members list
```

The following is an example of the /etc/group file:

```
# cat /etc/group
root:x:0:gerry
daemon:x:1:
bin:x:2:
sys:x:3:
adm:x:4:
tty:x:5:
disk:x:6:
lp:x:7:lp
mail:x:8:
users:x:100:gerry
nogroup:x:65534:
gerry:x:1000:
test:x:1001:
```

It's not necessary to have an entry in the /etc/group file for the default group; however, if the user belongs to any other groups, those groups must be added to the /etc/group file. This is done by using vi or any text editor (see Chapter 6 for more information on vi).

The /etc/shadow File

Many Linux systems have shadow passwords. With shadow passwords, the system doesn't store the encrypted passwords in the /etc/passwd file. Instead, they are kept in another file that only the root user can read, the /etc/shadow file. When installing Debian, the system prompts you to use shadow passwords. It's your choice, but I highly recommend using them to increase security. If you're not logged as root and try to read the /etc/shadow file, the following error is displayed:

```
# cat /etc/shadow
cat: /etc/shadow: Permission denied
#
```

The /etc/shadow consists of one line per user containing the following information:

```
login name:encrypted password:password last changed:days to may change:
➥days to must change:days before  expire:account expiration:days disabled:
➥reserved field
```

Following is a breakdown of the code:

- `password last changed` refers to the number of days since January 1, 1970, that password was last changed.
- `days to may change` refers to the number of days before password may be changed.
- `days to must change` refers to the number of days after which password must be changed.
- `days before expire` refers to the number of days before password is to expire that user is warned.
- `account expiration` refers to the number of days after password expires that account is disabled.
- `days disabled` refers to the number of days since January 1, 1970, that account is disabled.

Let's look at an example of the `/etc/shadow` file:

```
# sudo cat /etc/shadow
root:bsGobOJ3sjQmM:10717:0:99999:7:::
daemon:*:10717:0:99999:7:::
bin:*:10717:0:99999:7:::
sys:*:10717:0:99999:7:::
sync:*:10717:0:99999:7:::
games:*:10717:0:99999:7:::
man:*:10717:0:99999:7:::
lp:*:10717:0:99999:7:::
mail:*:10717:0:99999:7:::
nobody:*:10717:0:99999:7:::
gerry:0CSs535j9w/72:10717:0:99999:7:::
test:0eN8VyJvPufH.:10719:0:99999:7:::
```

The * character next to the login name indicates that the account has no password.

The `/etc/skel` Directory

It is a good practice to create a standard set of startup files to be copied to a new user's home directory. Creating a skeleton directory is an easy way to do that. The files contained in the `/etc/skel` directory are copied to the home directory when a new user is created. These startup files can be modified by users whenever they need to.

The following is a common set of startup files contained in the `/etc/skel` directory:

```
xwing:/etc/skel# ls -la
total 9
drwxr-xr-x   2 root     root        1024 May  6 12:13 .
drwxr-xr-x  66 root     root        4096 Jun 30 12:36 ..
-rw-r--r--   1 root     root         266 Jan 17 08:28 .alias
-rw-r--r--   1 root     root          68 Oct 19  1998 .bash_profile
-rw-r--r--   1 root     root          55 Oct 19  1998 .bashrc
-rw-r--r--   1 root     root         375 Jan 17 08:28 .cshrc
xwing:/etc/skel#
```

The system administrator can add, remove, and modify files from the `/etc/skel` directory to provide a standard environment for all users. It is highly recommended that no one but sysadmin modify the `/etc/skel` directory content to preserve, at most, the desired default environment for new users.

Programs for User Management

There are two basic tasks for user management: user creation and user deletion. Debian provides programs to easily create and remove users.

useradd—Creating a New User

There are six steps to follow to create a new user account:

1. Add the user to the `/etc/passwd` file.
2. Set an initial password for the new user.
3. Add the new user to the appropriate group(s).
4. Create the home directory for the new user.
5. Create the new user's mail file.
6. Create any startup files required for the user.

As you can see, to create a new user by hand, even when it's not complicated, is quite laborious. Fortunately, Debian has the `useradd` program that automatically creates a new user account. Assume that you want to create a new account for the user `meli`, whose real name is Carmen Delgado and who belongs to the group `users`. The home directory for the new user must be `/home/meli`. Use the following to create the new account for `meli` using the `useradd` program:

```
# useradd -g users -m -c "Carmen Delgado" meli
#
```

Let's ensure that the new user has been added to the `/etc/passwd` file:

```
# tail -5 /etc/passwd
nobody:x:65534:65534:nobody:/home:/bin/sh
gerry:x:1000:1000:Gerardo Munoz Martin,,+52(5)555-5121,,gemunoz@usa.net:
➥/home/gerry:/bin/bashtest:x:1001:1001: Testing account:/home/test:/bin/bash
mario:x:1002:1002::/home/mario:
meli:x:1003:100:Carmen Delgado:/home/meli:
#
```

As you can see, the line for the new user has been added at the end of the `/etc/passwd` file. The program by itself will not set up a password for the new user, so it's necessary to set up the new user's password yourself. Let's check the `/etc/shadow` to verify that no password has been set up:

```
# tail -5 /etc/shadow
nobody:*:10717:0:99999:7:::
gerry:0CSs535j9w/72:10717:0:99999:7:::
test:0eN8VyJvPufH.:10719:0:99999:7:::
mario:wFUayWmhFHAYw:10744:0:99999:7:::
meli:!:10774:0:99999:7:::
#
```

The `!` character next to the login name indicates that no password has been set. Usually a password is assigned when creating a user account, nevertheless sometimes it's omitted. Use the `passwd` command to set up the new user's password:

```
# passwd meli
Changing password for meli
Enter the new password (minimum of 5, maximum of 8 characters)
Please use a combination of upper and lower case letters and numbers.
New password:
Re-enter new password:
Password changed.
#
```

Now let's check the `/etc/shadow` file again:

```
# tail -5 /etc/shadow
nobody:*:10717:0:99999:7:::
gerry:0CSs535j9w/72:10717:0:99999:7:::
test:0eN8VyJvPufH.:10719:0:99999:7:::
mario:wFUayWmhFHAYw:10744:0:99999:7:::
meli:0aGoucfPI43mw:10774:0:99999:7:::
#
```

Note that the encrypted password now appears next to the login name.

Note

When not using shadow passwords, the encrypted password must appear next to the login name in the `etc/passwd` file.

The next step is to verify that the new user has been added to the proper group:

```
# grep users /etc/group
users:x:100:
#
```

The group ID for the group users in the `/etc/group` file matches the group ID for user `meli` in the `/etc/passwd` file. The option `-m` used when creating the account indicates that you should create a home directory for the new user if it doesn't exist under the `/home` (default) directory:

```
# cd /home
# ls -l
total 5
drwxr-sr-x  25 gerry    gerry        2048 May 03 13:04 gerry
drwxr-xr-x   5 mario    mario        1024 Jun  4 04:24 mario
drwxr-sr-x   2 meli     users        1024 Jun  23 19:59 meli
drwxr-sr-x   5 test     test         1024 May 18 16:50 test
#
```

The default files have also been copied to the new user's home directory:

```
# cd /home/meli
# ls -la
total 6
drwxr-sr-x   2 meli     meli         1024 Jun  23 19:59 .
drwxrwsr-x   6 root     staff        1024 Jun  23 19:59 ..
-rw-r--r--   1 meli     meli          266 Jun  23 19:59 .alias
-rw-r--r--   1 meli     meli           68 Jun  23 19:59 .bash_profile
-rw-r--r--   1 meli     meli           55 Jun  23 19:59 .bashrc
-rw-r--r--   1 meli     meli          375 Jun  12 19:59 .cshrc
#
```

And that's it! The new account is ready to be used. There are several options for the `useradd` program. Use the online documentation for `useradd` to learn about them (see Chapter 5, "Your Virtual Toolbelt," for more information on online documentation).

userdel—Removing a User

To remove a user from the system, the following steps must be executed:

1. Remove the user from the `/etc/passwd` file.
2. Remove the user from the `/etc/group` file.
3. Delete home directory.

Debian has a program to easily remove users from the system: `userdel`. Even when removing a user is not a big deal, `userdel` makes it simplier. Assume that you want to remove the user `meli` from the system. Type the following command:

```
# userdel -r meli
#
```

And that's it! The user `meli` no longer exists on the system. The option `-r` indicates the program to remove the user's home directory; if you do not want to delete the user's home directory, you should omit this option.

User management is not really a difficult task. Using the appropriate tools makes it easy to handle users on your system.

Programs and Processes

Processes are instances of a program. While a program is running it is called a process. Although there is just one copy of the program held on the filesystem, any number of processes can be invoked to run this program. This section is intended to describe what programs and processes are and how they work.

The UNIX Process Model

As said before, a UNIX process is an instance of an executing program that has separate existence from all the other processes on the system. Assume that three users use the vi editor. Each one has an individual process. There are three types of processes:

Process Type	*Description*
Interactive	Runs using a terminal
Batch	Runs separate from any terminal and probably at a different time
Daemon	A system process that runs all the time

Processes have a set of attributes; the following are some of them:

A unique process ID (pid), that distinguishes it from other processes

A parent process

The pid of its parent process

The user ID and group ID of the user who started the process.

A state that indicates whether the process is running, sleeping, runnable, zombie, or stopped.

The name of the terminal to which the process is attached. Usually, just interactive processes have a terminal attached.

UNIX enables you to send short messages, called signals, to processes. Depending on the signal, processes could either catch and interpret the signal or exit. Signals are also delivered when the process does something wrong or as a response when certain keys are pressed, such as Ctrl+C or Ctrl+Z. The way a process handles a signal depends on which signal it is.

Daemons

Daemons are processes that run in the background and perform a specified operation at predefined times or in response to certain events. A daemon is always active while the system is on or until it's instructed to stop.

Daemons are usually started at boot time or by the superuser. Many of the system programs run as daemons. A classical example of a daemon is the printing daemon, which is always waiting for print jobs to be processed.

The Login Process

The login program is in charge of authenticating the user and setting up an initial environment for the user by setting permissions for the serial line and starting the shell. Figure 11.1 shows the login process.

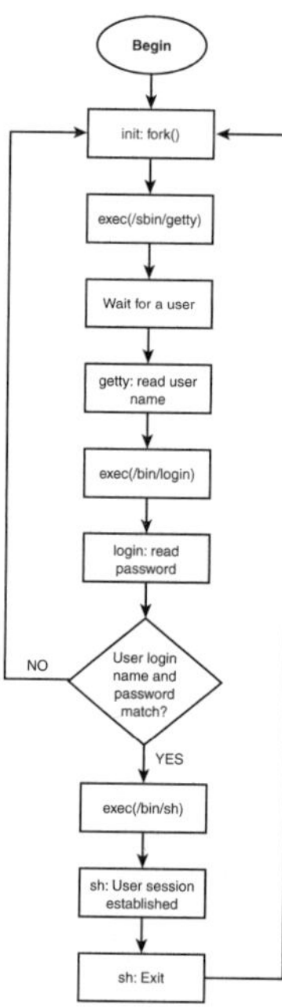

FIGURE 11.1
The login process.

`init` makes sure there is a `getty` program for the terminal or console connection. `getty` listens at the terminal and waits for the user to notify it that he or she is ready to log in. When it notices a user, `getty` outputs a welcome message, prompts for the username, and then runs the `login` program:

```
Debian GNU/Linux 2.1 xwing tty2

xwing login:
```

`login` gets the username as a parameter and prompts the user for the password. If both username and password match, `login` starts the shell configured for the user. Now the user session is established, and the shell executes the commands and programs indicated by the user:

```
Debian GNU/Linux 2.1 xwing
```

```
xwing login: gerry
Password:
Linux xwing 2.0.36 #15 Sat Jun 26 14:01:59 CDT 1999 i586 unknown

Copyright © 1993-1999 Software in the Public Interest, and others

Most of the programs included with the Debian GNU/Linux system are
freely redistributable; the exact distribution terms for each program
are described in the individual files in /usr/doc/*/copyright

Debian GNU/Linux comes with ABSOLUTELY NO WARRANTY, to the extent
permitted by applicable law.
Last login: Sat Jul  26 18:23:12 on tty3.
No mail.
#
```

If username and password don't match, `login` just exits and terminates the process. `init` notices that the process is terminated and starts a new `getty` for the terminal.

```
Debian GNU/Linux 2.1 xwing

xwing login: gerry
Password:
Login incorrect

xwing login:
```

The /etc/nologin File—Denying Login Access to the System

It's possible to deny access to common users. If the file `/etc/nologin` exists, logins are disabled and only superuser has access to the system. To create the file `/etc/nologin`, you can use the following `touch` command:

```
# touch /etc/nologin
```

Once the `/etc/nologin` file is created, the following message will be shown when someone different to superuser tries to log in to the system:

```
Debian GNU/Linux 2.1 xwing

xwing login: gerry
Password:
Connection closed by foreign host.
#
```

The file `/etc/nologin` can be created only by the superuser. When a user other than `root` tries to log in to the system, the system rejects the login:

```
Debian GNU/Linux 2.1 xwing

xwing login: gerry
Password:
Debian GNU/Linux 2.1 xwing

xwing login:
```

It is possible to add a message to the file `/etc/nologin` so the users of the system can read it. To add a message to the file `/etc/nologin`, superuser needs to edit the file using vi or any text editor. When the file `/etc/nologin` has the desired message, it's displayed any time a user tries to log in to the system:

```
Debian GNU/Linux 2.1 xwing

xwing login: gerry
Password:
Sorry, no access to this host is allowed at the moment.
Please try again later.

Debian GNU/Linux 2.1 xwing

xwing login:
```

The login process is quite simple. Denying access to common users could be helpful while making changes or fixing the system.

Printing

In today's world, printers are a common device attached to a computer system. This is the main reason that any serious operating systems has printer support. Its multiuser and multitasking nature and its extended support for printers make Debian a powerful tool for printing purposes. This section is intended to show the capabilities of Debian for handling printers and printing jobs.

The `lprng` Printing Model

Unlike other UNIX flavors, Debian has the `lprng` printing model, which is an enhanced, extended, and portable implementation of the common `lpr` print spooler functionality used by most UNIX flavors. `lprng` provides the same interface as `lpr`, while providing such additional features as the following:

- Lightweight `lpr`, `lpc`, and `lprm` programs
- Dynamic redirection of print queues
- Automatic job holding
- Highly verbose diagnostics
- Multiple printers serving a single queue

- Client programs that do not need to run SUID `root`
- Greatly enhanced security checks
- An improved permission and authorization mechanism

`lprng` is the native printing model for Debian, but it is not exclusive to it; `lprng` could be implemented in other UNIX flavors.

The /etc/printcap File—Setting Up Printing Queues

The file `/etc/printcap` is the printer configuration file. `/etc/printcap` is a colon-delimited text file where each printer has one entry. Here is an example `printcap` entry:

```
# /etc/printcap: printer capability database. See printcap(5).
# You can use the filter entries df, tf, cf, gf etc. for
# your own filters. See /etc/filter.ps, /etc/filter.pcl and
# the printcap(5) manual page for further details.

lp:\
        :sd=/var/spool/lpd/lp:\
        :mx#0:\
        :sh:\
        :if=/var/spool/lpd/lp/filter:\
        :af=/var/spool/lpd/lp/acct:\
        :lp=/dev/null:
```

An entry in `printcap` must fit on one line. Notice in the example that the `\` character is used to ignore the special meaning of the newline character at the end of lines. This effectively means that the entry is only one line.

The first field in each entry of the `/etc/printcap` file specifies the printer's name. A printer can actually have multiple names. Multiple names are separated using the `¦` character.

A printer called `lp` is the standard default printer. When a user prints a file without specifying the destination printer, the print job is sent to the printer called `lp`. You should always have one printer with the name `lp`.

See online documentation for `printcap` for a description of the `/etc/printcap` file layout (see Chapter 5 for more information on online documentation).

Managing Print Queues

There are different commands for managing print queues. This section explains those commands.

`lpc` is used by the system administrator to control the operation of the line printer system. For each printer configured in the `/etc/printcap` file, `lpc` may be used to

- Disable or enable a printer.
- Disable or enable a printer's spooling queue.
- Rearrange the order of jobs in a spooling queue.
- Find the status of printers and their associated spooling queues and printer dameons.

`lpd` is the line printer daemon and is normally invoked at boot time. It makes a single pass through the `/etc/printcap` file to find out about the existing printers, and prints any files left after a crash. It then listens to receive requests to print files in the queue, transfer files to the spooling area, display the queue, or remove jobs from the queue. In each case, it forks (create) a child to handle the request so the parent can continue to listen for more requests.

`lpq` examines the spooling area used by `lpd` for printing files on the printer, and reports the status of the specified jobs or all jobs associated with a user. Executing `lpq` without any given arguments shows the jobs currently in the queue. Table 11.2 shows `lpq` options.

TABLE 11.2 Options for `lpq`

Option	*Action*
`-P`	Specifies a particular printer to process the printing job
`-l`	Prints information about each of the files comprising the job entry

`lprm` removes a job, or jobs, from a printer's spool queue. Because the spooling directory is protected from users, using lprm is normally the only method by which a user may remove a job. The owner of a job is determined by the user's login name and the hostname on the machine where the lpr command was invoked. Table 11.3 shows the options for lprm.

TABLE 11.3 Options for `lprm`

Option	*Action*
`-P`*`printer`*	Specifies the queue associated with a specific printer
`-`	Removes all jobs that a user owns
`user`	Removes any jobs queued belonging to the specified user
`job #`	A user may de-queue an individual job by specifying its job number

The printing process is certainly a little more complicated in UNIX than in other operating systems such as Windows, but is also powerful.

Scheduling Tasks

It is always helpful to count on tools to schedule tasks. System administration often requires periodically running processes or executing programs to maintain the system in good shape—for example, system backups. This section is intended to show tools for scheduling tasks.

The at Tool

at executes commands at a specified time. It accepts times in the form HH:MM to run a job at a specific time of day. at also accepts "midnight," "noon," or "teatime" (4 p.m.) as valid time formats, and it's also possible to have a time-of-day suffixed with AM or PM for running in the morning or the evening. You can also say what day the job will be run, by giving a date in the form monthname day with an optional year, or giving a date of the form MM/DD/YY. The following is the syntax for at:

```
at [-f file] [options] TIME
```

Table 11.4 shows the options for at.

TABLE 11.4 Options for at

Option	*Action*
-V	Prints the version number to standard error
-m	Sends mail to the user when the job has been completed, even if there was no output
-l	Lists the jobs pending to be executed
-d jobnumber	Removes a job from the queue
-v	Shows the time the job will be executed

If the scheduled command produces an output, it's sent to the user by mail. Let's look at some examples using at. The following command executes the shell script xkarma at 2:00 p.m.:

```
# at -f /home/gerry/xkarma 2:00PM
warning: commands will be executed using /bin/sh
job 7 at 1999-06-30 14:00
#
```

The following command lists the contents of the /home/gerry directory at 1:35 p.m.:

```
# at 1:35PM
warning: commands will be executed using /bin/sh
at> ls /home/gerry
at> <EOT>
job 8 at 1999-06-30 13:35
#
```

If the -f option is not used, the system prompts you to type the commands to be scheduled. You should type the commands you want to run and then press Ctrl+d to finish the command. The message <EOT> and the date, time, and number of the scheduled job is displayed. The following is the result of executing the previously scheduled job:

```
Date:          Wed, 30 Jun 1999 13:35:03
To:         gerry@xwing
From:       Gerardo Munoz Martin <gerry@xwing>
Subject:    Output from your job   8

700105.doc
DisplayGrab.ppm
GNUstep
Mail
Office50
boot.img
campus
cosim.gif
debianUnleashed
docs
examining_files.txt
files_to_analyze
filter1.html
filter2.html
freeamp.gif
internew.gif
mail
mail1.html
mail2.html
managing_files.txt
miami
nsmail
ntscmailandnews.tif
pcmcia.txt
phantom.gif
rfc0821.txt
soffice
test
wget.txt
xkarma
xwp
```

Let's check again for pending jobs:

```
bash-2.01$ at -l
7       1999-06-30 14:00 a gerry
#
```

The following command removes the job 7 from the queue:

```
# at -d 7
```

The following command looks for the file meli.txt at 7:30 a.m. on November 18, 1999:

```
# at 7:30AM 11/18/99
warning: commands will be executed using /bin/sh
at> find . -name meli.txt -print
at> <EOT>
job 13 at 1999-11-18 07:30
#
```

The cron Tool

cron is a system daemon that executes other programs at the times specified in the appropriate configuration files. The daemon is normally started at boot time. The configuration files that control the operation of cron are called crontab files. These files contain information about the time, date, and command to execute. The crontab files can be modified using only the crontab command.

crontab files are text files, with each line consisting of six fields separated by spaces. The first five fields specify when to carry out the command, and the sixth field specifies the command. Table 11.5 shows the fields used on crontab files.

TABLE 11.5 crontab Fields

Field	*Purpose*
Minute	Minute of the hour
Hour	Hour of the day
Day	Day of the month
Month	Month of the year
Weekday	Day of the week
Command	The actual command to execute

The command crontab -l shows the contents of the crontab file:

```
# crontab -l
# DO NOT EDIT THIS FILE - edit the master and reinstall.
# (/tmp/crontab.17283 installed on Fri Mar 12 11:13:55 1999)
# (Cron version -- $Id: crontab.c,v 2.13 1994/01/17 03:20:37 vixie Exp $)
00 11 * * 1 /usr/local/sbin/totape
00 12 15 * * /usr/local/sbin/logtransfer
30 01 * * * /bin/rm /tmp/*
#
```

The first line without the hash mark (#) tells the system to run the shell script /usr/local/sbin/totape the first day of the week (Monday) of all months, regardless of the date, at 11 o'clock.

The second line indicates to run the shell script /usr/local/sbin/logtransfer on the 15th of every month at 12 o'clock.

The last line is used to daily remove the contents of the /tmp directory at 1:30 a.m..

Even though the crontab files are text files, they should not be modified using an editor. The option -e is used to edit the crontab files. This option creates an instance of the vi editor to edit the crontab file. Here's an example:

```
# crontab -e
# DO NOT EDIT THIS FILE - edit the master and reinstall.
# (/tmp/crontab.17283 installed on Fri Mar 12 11:13:55 1999)
# (Cron version -- $Id: crontab.c,v 2.13 1994/01/17 03:20:37 vixie Exp $)
00 11 * * 1 /usr/local/sbin/totape
00 12 15 * * /usr/local/sbin/logtransfer
30 01 * * * /bin/rm /tmp/*
~
~
~
~
~
~
~
~
~
~
~
~
~
~
~
~
~
"/tmp/crontab.3733" 6 lines, 295 characters
```

After the vi editor is opened, you can add or remove lines to your crontab file (see Chapter 6 for more information on vi). Each user of the system has his or her own crontab file, so there could be as many crontab files as users on your system.

The anacron Tool

anacron can be used to execute commands periodically, with a frequency specified in days. Unlike cron, it doesn't assume that the machine is running 24 hours a day. anacron reads the file /etc/anacrontab to get the list of the jobs that it controls. Each job entry specifies a period of time and a shell command to be executed. When the computer is turned on, anacron checks the entries in /etc/anacrontab for commands to be executed because of its time period of execution has been reached. Table 11.6 shows the options for anacron.

TABLE 11.6 Options for anacron

Option	*Action*
`-f`	Forces execution of the jobs, ignoring the time stamps
`-u`	Updates only the time stamps of the jobs to the current date, but doesn't run anything
`-s`	No new job will be started until the current job is finished
`-n`	Runs jobs now, ignoring the delay specifications in the `/etc/anacrontab` file

Disks and Filesystems

The primary job of any operating system is to store information. Like most operating systems, Unix makes use of a structured upside-down, tree-like hierarchy of files and directories. This section explores disks and filesystems.

Disk and Filesystem Concepts

For a better understanding of how UNIX handles disks and filesystems, there are some concepts to grasp. The system administrator has to manipulate files throughout the entire directory hierarchy. To do this efficiently, you need a good working knowledge of the directory structure.

The information ends up as binary information stored on the surface of a disk drive. The smallest accessible unit of measure on a disk is a block. A disk controller is an electronic device that tells the disk drive what to do, which block to read from where, and when. A single disk controller typically controls a number of separate disk drives. Every physical device has a different command language that it understands, including disk controllers. A device file is basically an entry point into a device driver and is usually located under the `/dev` directory. Device files are used by many parts of the operating system to send or retrieve information from a device.

Under UNIX, the part of the operating system responsible for structuring and understanding the information that is stored on disk is called the filesystem. UNIX can handle several filesystems at the same time.

Block Devices

On Debian, devices are typically classified into block-structured devices. The block devices are typically designated by names similar to `hd0` (MFM/IDE hard disk or CD-ROM devices) or `fd0` (floppy disk devices). Block device files are used for devices whose driver handles I/O in large blocks and where the kernel handles I/O buffering. Physical devices, such as disks, are defined as block device files—for example, `/dev/fd0`.

The `/dev` directory contains the special device files for all the devices. The device files are created during installation, and later with the `/dev/MAKEDEV` script. The `/dev/MAKEDEV.local` is a script written by the system administrator that creates local-only device files or links.

Filesystem Types

As said before, UNIX can manage many differentfilesystems at the same time. This is possible because the code associated with each filesystem translates how the information is structured on the disk into a standard UNIX programming interface. This standard programming interface is used by the majority of UNIX commands to access the services provided by the filesystem kernel code.

There are different filesystem types, which have different characteristics. Debian uses the `ext2` (second extended filesystem. The following are the most common filesystem types:

- MS-DOS—The standard MS-DOS filesystem. It supports a limit of only 8-character filenames with 3-letter extensions.
- `ext2`—The standard Linux filesystem. It supports up to 255-character filenames.
- `S5` (System 5 filesystem)—It supports up to 14-character filenames.
- `minix`—A local filesystem supporting filenames of 14 or 30 characters.
- `xiafs`—A local filesystem with longer filenames, larger `inodes`, and lots of other features.
- `hpfs`—A local filesystem for HPFS partitions.
- `iso9660`—A local filesystem used for CD-ROM drives.
- `nfs`—A filesystem for mounting partitions from remote systems.
- `swap`—A disk partition to be used for swapping.

`ext2` defines the filesystem topology by describing each file in the system with an `inode` data structure. An `inode` describes which blocks the data within a file occupies, as well as the access rights of the file, the file's modification times, and the type of the file. Every file in the `ext2` filesystem is described by a single `inode`, and each `inode` has a single unique number identifying it. The `inodes` for the filesystem are all kept together in `inode` tables.

Partitioning a Disk

Hard disks can be divided into other more logical disks called partitions. When using IDE disks, the boot partition must be completely within the first 1024 cylinders. This is because the disk is used via the BIOS during boot process, and BIOS can't handle more than 1024 cylinders. It is sometimes possible to use a boot partition that is only partly within the first 1024 cylinders. This works as long as all the files that are read with the BIOS are within the first 1024 cylinders. Because this is difficult to arrange, it is a very bad idea to do it;

you never know when a kernel update or disk defragmentation will result in an unbootable system. Therefore, make sure your boot partition is completely within the first 1024 cylinders. Some newer versions of the BIOS and IDE disks can handle disks with more than 1024 cylinders. If you have such a system, you can forget about the problem; if you aren't quite sure, put your boot partition within the first 1024 cylinders.

There are many programs for creating and removing partitions. Most operating systems have their own, and it can be a good idea to use each operating system's own, just in case it does something unusual that the others can't. Many of the programs, including Debian's, are called `fdisk` or variations thereof.

`fdisk` is a helpful tool for disk partitioning; it supports the following disk partition types:

```
Command (m for help): l

 0  Empty            9  AIX bootable    75  PC/IX          b7  BSDI
➥fs
 1  DOS 12-bit FAT   a  OS/2 Boot Manag 80  Old MINIX      b8  BSDI
➥swap
 2  XENIX root       b  Win95 FAT32     81  Linux/MINIX    c7  Syrinx
 3  XENIX usr       40  Venix 80286     82  Linux swap     db  CP/M
 4  DOS 16-bit <32M 51  Novell?         83  Linux native   e1  DOS
➥access
 5  Extended        52  Microport       93  Amoeba         e3  DOS
➥R/O
 6  DOS 16-bit >=32 63  GNU HURD        94  Amoeba BBT     f2  DOS
➥secondary
 7  OS/2 HPFS       64  Novell Netware  a5  BSD/386        ff  BBT
 8  AIX             65  Novell Netware

Command (m for help):
```

Caution

Disk partitioning is a very risky task. You could lose all the information stored in your hard disk if something goes wrong while disk partitioning. Do not modify the partition table unless you're sure what you're doing.

Creating Filesystems

The command used to create new filesystems is `mkfs`. There is actually a separate program for each filesystem type. `mkfs` is just a front-end that runs the appropriate program depending on the desired filesystem type. The type is selected with the `-t fstype` option. Table 11.7 shows the most important options for `mkfs`.

TABLE 11.7 Options for `mkfs`

Option	*Action*
`-t` *`fstype`*	Selects the type of the filesystem
`-c`	Searches for bad blocks and initializes the bad block list accordingly
-l *`filename`*	Reads the initial bad block list from the file *`filename`*

To create a new filesystem of the type `ext2fs`, you should use either of the following commands:

```
mkfs -t ext2fs
```

```
mke2fs
```

The following is the syntax for creating a new filesystem using `mkfs`:

```
mkfs [-t fstype] filesys [blocks]
```

`blocks` refers to the number of blocks to be used for the filesystem.

Checking Filesystem Integrity

Filesystem integrity means that there are no errors on the filesystem. Sometimes you need to check the filesystem integrity to look for possible disk errors—for example, when the computer has been powered off improperly. To check the filesystem integrity, you use the `fsck` tool. `fsck` checks and optionally repairs a Linux filesystem. Table 11.8 shows the options for `fsck`.

TABLE 11.8 Options for `fsck`

Option	*Action*
`-A`	Checks all the filesystems on the `/etc/fstab` file in one run
`-R`	When checking all filesystems with the `-A` flag, skips the `root` filesystem (in case it's already mounted read/write)
`-N`	Doesn't execute, just shows what would be done
`-P`	When the `-A` flag is set, checks the `root` filesystem in parallel with the other filesystems
`-s`	Serializes `fsck` operations
`-t` *`fstype`*	Specifies the type of filesystem to be checked
-a	Automatically repairs the filesystem without any questions
`-r`	Interactively repairs the filesystem (asks for confirmations)

To check the integrity of filesystems of the `ex2fs` type, you can also use the `e2fsck` command.

Whenever you need to create a filesystem, it's very important that you have in mind what type of filesystem you need. It's also important to frequently perform checks of your filesystems to ensure that they're in good shape.

The Buffer Cache

Accessing memory is much faster than reading from a disk. It is common to read the same part of a disk several times during relatively short periods of time. For example, consider how often the command `ls` might be run on a system with many users. By reading the information from disk only once and then keeping it in memory until no longer needed, you can speed up all but the first read. This is called disk buffering, and the memory used for the purpose is called the buffer cache.

Because memory is a limited resource, the buffer cache usually cannot be big enough. When the cache fills up, the data that has been unused for the longest time is discarded, and the memory thus freed is used for the new data.

Disk buffering also works for writes. Data that is written is often soon read again, so putting data that is written in the cache is a good idea. By only putting the data into the cache, not writing it to disk at once, the program that writes runs quicker. The writes can then be done in the background, without slowing down the other programs.

Mounting and Unmounting Filesystems

Before anyone can use a filesystem, it has to be mounted. The operating system then does various things to make sure that everything works. Because all files in UNIX are in a single directory tree, the mount operation makes it look like the contents of the new filesystem are the contents of an existing subdirectory in some already mounted filesystem. A mount point must be an empty directory and is the place in which a new partition joins the rest of the directory hierarchy. When a filesystem no longer needs to be mounted, it can be unmounted.

Mounting Filesystems Manually

To manually mount filesystems, you use the `mount` command. This `mount` command passes the kernel three pieces of information: the name of the filesystem, the physical block device that contains the filesystem, and where in the existing filesystem topology the new filesystem is to be mounted. The following is the syntax for `mount`:

```
mount [-fnrsvw] [-t vfstype] [-o options] device dir
```

Table 11.9 shows the options for `mount`.

TABLE 11.9 Options for `mount`

Flag	*Action*	
`-f`	Causes everything to be done except for the actual system call.	
`-n`	Mounts without writing in `/etc/mtab`.	
`-s`	Ignores mount options not supported by a filesystem type.	
`-r`	Mounts the filesystem read-only.	
`-w`	Mounts the filesystem read/write.	
`-t` *`vfstype`*	The argument following the `-t` is used to indicate the filesystem type.	
`-o`	Options are specified with a `-o` flag followed by a comma-separated string of options. The following are valid options:	
	`async`	All I/O to the filesystem should be done asynchronously.
	`qtime`	Updates `inode` access time for each access.
	`quto`	Can be mounted with the `-a` option.
	defaults	Uses default options: `rw`, `suid`, `dev`, `exec`, `auto`, `nouser`, and `async`.
	`dev`	Interprets character or block special devices on the filesystem.
	`exec`	Permits execution of binaries.
	`noatime`	Does not update `inode` access times on this filesystem.
	`noauto`	Can be mounted only explicitly.
	`nodev`	Does not interpret character or block special devices on the filesystem.
	`noexec`	Does not allow execution of any binaries on the mounted filesystem.
	`nosuid`	Does not allow set-user-identifier or set-group-identifier bits to take effect.
	`nouser`	Forbids an ordinary user to mount the filesystem.
	`remount`	Attempts to remount an already-mounted filesystem.
	`ro`	Mounts the filesystem read-only.
	`rw`	Mounts the filesystem read/write.
	`suid`	Allows set-user-identifier or set-group-identifier bits to take effect.
	`sync`	All I/O to the filesystem should be done synchronously.
	`user`	Allows an ordinary user to mount the filesystem.

Let's look at an example. The following command mounts the CD-ROM using the `/cdrom` directory as the mount point:

```
# mount /dev/cdrom /cdrom
mount: block device /dev/cdrom is write-protected, mounting read-only.
#
```

Mounting Filesystems on Boot

On many systems, there are other filesystems that should also be mounted automatically at boot time. These are specified in the /etc/fstab file. fstab is only read by programs, and not written; it is the duty of the system administrator to properly create and maintain this file. Each filesystem is described on a separate line; fields on each line are separated by tabs or spaces.

The /etc/fstab is formed by six fields, the first three of which you would typically need to modify. The first field describes the block special device or remote filesystem to be mounted. The second field describes the mount point for the filesystem. For swap partitions, this field should be specified as none. The third field describes the type of the filesystem. The fourth field gives the options that are to be used when mounting this filesystem; in most cases, defaults is used to indicate that no special options are necessary. The fifth field is optional and is used by the dump backup system to determine which filesystems are to be backed up. The final field specifies the order for mounting filesystems at boot, with filesystems having a lower number being mounted before those with a higher number. The following is an example of the /etc/fstab file:

```
/dev/hda1           /                   ext2    defaults        1 1
/dev/hda5           /export             ext2    defaults        1 2
/dev/hda6           /tmp                ext2    defaults        1 2
/dev/hda7           swap                swap    defaults        0 0
/dev/hdc1           /export/bak         ext2    defaults        1 2
/dev/fd0            /mnt/floppy         ext2    noauto          0 0
none                /proc               proc    defaults        0 0
```

Unmounting Filesystems

When a filesystem no longer needs to be mounted, it can be unmounted with umount. umount takes one argument: either the device file or the mount point. The umount command detaches the filesystem(s) specified from the file hierarchy. A filesystem cannot be unmounted while it's busy—for example, when a file in the filesystem is opened. The following command unmounts the CD-ROM device mounted on the /cdrom directory:

```
# umount /cdrom
```

Swap Space

When the physical memory in the system runs out and a process needs to bring a page into memory, the operating system must decide what to do. It must equally distribute the physical pages in the system between the processes running in the system; therefore, it may need to remove one or more pages from the system to make room for the new page to be brought into memory. How virtual pages are selected for removal from physical memory affects the efficiency of the system. Debian uses a page aging technique to fairly choose pages that might be removed from the system. This scheme involves every page in the system having an age that changes as the page is accessed. The more a page is accessed, the younger it is; the less it is accessed, the older it becomes. Old pages are good candidates for swapping.

UNIX Memory Management

UNIX supports virtual memory, which means using a disk as an extension of RAM so that the effective size of usable memory grows in the same proportion. The kernel writes the contents of a currently unused block of memory to the hard disk so that the memory can be used for another purpose. When the original contents are needed again, they are read back into memory. Of course, reading and writing the hard disk is slower than using real memory, so the programs don't run as fast. The part of the hard disk that is used as virtual memory is called the swap space.

UNIX can use either a normal file in the filesystem or a separate partition for swap space. A swap partition is faster, but it is easier to change the size of a swap file. When you know how much swap space you need, you should go for a swap partition. But if you are uncertain, you can use a swap file first, use the system for a while so that you can get a feel for how much swap you need, and then make a swap partition when you're confident about its size.

You should also know that UNIX allows you to use several swap partitions and/or swap files at the same time. This means that if you only occasionally need an unusual amount of swap space, you can set up an extra swap file at such times, instead of keeping the whole amount allocated all the time.

Creating a Swap Partition

To create a swap partition, you use the `mkswap` command. The following is the syntax for `mkswap`:

```
mkswap [-c] [-vN] [-f] device [size]
```

The device argument in this particular case is a disk partition. The Linux kernel does not look at partition IDs, but many installation scripts assume that partitions of type 82 (`LINUX_SWAP`) are meant to be swap partitions. Table 11.10 shows options for `mkswap`.

TABLE 11.10 Options for `mkswap`

Option	*Action*
`-c`	If the device is a block device, it is checked for bad blocks before the swap area is created
`-f`	Forces the creation of the swap area
`-v0`	Creates an old-style swap area (default)
`-v1`	Creates a new-style swap area

Creating a Swap File

Swap files are files that allow you to increment the swap area without defining a bigger swap partition. They can be created or removed as needed. A swap file is an ordinary file; it is in no way special to the kernel, and it must reside on a local disk. The only thing that matters to the kernel is that it has no holes, and that it is prepared for use with mkswap. A swap file without holes could be created using the following command:

```
# dd if=/dev/zero of=/extra-swap bs=1024 count=1024
1024+0 records in
1024+0 records out
#
```

Swap files can also be created using the mkswap command.

Activating and Deactivating Swap Areas

An initialized swap space is taken into use with swapon. This command tells the kernel that the swap space is ready to be used. The path to the swap space is given as the argument, so to start swapping on a temporary swap file, the following command must be used:

```
# swapon /extra-swap
#
```

Swap spaces can be used automatically by listing them in the /etc/fstab file described earlier in this chapter:

```
/dev/hda7 none swap sw 0 0
/swapfile none swap sw 0 0
```

The startup scripts run the command swapon -a, which starts swapping on all the swap spaces listed in /etc/fstab. Therefore, the swapon command is usually used only when extra swap is needed.

The command swapoff is used to disable swapping on specific devices and/or files. To stop swapping on a temporary swap file, the following command must be used:

```
# swapoff /extra-swap
#
```

To stop swapping from all files and partitions, the command swapoff -a should be used.

Summary

System administration comprises all the things you have to do to keep a computer system in usable shape. It includes things such as backing up files and restoring them if necessary, installing new programs, creating accounts for users and deleting them when no longer needed, making certain that the filesystem is not corrupted, and so on.

Debian provides several system administration tools that are wonderful help for system administrators and make their work easier. It's very important to maintain a computer system in the best shape possible to get the most of the system.

CHAPTER

Customizing the Bootup Procedure

by Aaron Van Cowerberghe

In This Chapter

In the world of Linux, there are several aspects of the system that have a part in system startup, some that determine a computer's most foundational behavior. A handful of these come into play long before the system is usable, during the bootup process. The operating system kernel, for example, is the piece of software that allows all your other software to run. It provides drivers for all the most common hardware and has perhaps the most impact on your system's performance. Because Linux is open source and highly configurable to any individual's needs, customizing it is one of the most common routes taken to optimizing system performance.

Linux Is the Kernel

There is a commonly held misconception about Linux that is attributable mostly to confusion. Some, when they hear the word *Linux,* think of their favorite distribution, with all its software. Basically, Linux is taken to mean the entire system. This is definitely wrong. Linux is the kernel, the very foundation of a powerful operating system, usually taking up only about 500KB of RAM; it allows the great environment that has developed around it to exist. This is somewhat of a paradox to explain to new users, but professionals will probably understand.

So, when you hear somebody refer to "Linux 6.2" in reference to the latest version of a specific Linux distribution, smirk and hold your peace, knowing you are superior. In reality, Linux is Linux, regardless of which distribution you're using.

The Linux Kernel

There is another popular misconception that kernel tuning is no place for the average user. In reality, this is both true and false: Like other features in Linux, the configuration possibilities are endless and deep, but you don't necessarily need to understand arcane PCI chipset mantras or the gory details of virtual memory to tailor a better Linux for your computer. Armed with nothing more than your computer manuals, you should be able to zero in on those features you need and leave the very technical tuning for some day down the road. If you do know all these technical details, Linux will not stand in your way, but if all you know is how to run a shell command, this section will show you how you can build a better Linux for your computer.

The core of a UNIX system is the *kernel,* the innermost layer of the operating system. The kernel provides a uniform interface to the local hardware. When your computer starts, the boot loader hands control to the kernel. The kernel then identifies your hardware, initiates the boot scripts, and launches your network and terminal daemons. After the boot, the kernel becomes the gateway to the local hardware, supplying applications with a standard interface to basic services, such as task switching, signaling, device I/O, and memory management.

Although the default kernel installed by your Debian CD-ROM stands a very good chance of running on your hardware, one kernel cannot be all things to all people. At some point, you will want to harness the real power of UNIX, the power of choice. In Linux, kernel tweaking can be as simple as adding a few command parameters to modify the kernel at boot time, picking and choosing from the ever-growing list of modules and kernel options, which are as in-depth as tuning memory and filesystem behavior or as deep as directly modifying or creating driver C code. The Linux kernel can be adapted for small memory machines, optimized as a router or firewall, or extended to support new hardware, alien filesystems, and a wide array of network protocols.

The sections that follow describe what makes the Linux kernel so special, even among UNIX-like systems, and includes tips and tutorials on configuring your Linux computer. These sections cover

- An overview of the Linux kernel architecture
- Obtaining and patching Linux kernel sources
- Compiling a kernel for multiple machines
- Kernel troubleshooting

After reading this section in tandem with Appendix E, "Kernel Configuration Options," you will be well-equipped to create a custom kernel for your particular machine. The size of this section may be a little daunting, but this only illustrates the flexibility of the Linux kernel; many readers will need only those few sections on installing their sound or special device. On the other hand, for those difficult problems of kernel optimization, advanced networking, or tailoring the kernel for embedded and other special situations, this section should equip you with a full overview of what is possible.

Caution

The worst that can happen while reconfiguring your kernel is boot failure. It happens to the best of us and usually happens because of incompatible settings or forgetting to run `lilo` after changing a kernel; there are few things as frightening as the dreaded `lilo` boot prompt.

Before you reboot a new kernel, you should take a few precautions to ensure a backup boot method. If your hardware has a floppy drive, keep your Red Hat install/rescue disks handy, and production machines should always keep a boot floppy with their current stable kernel; your `lilo` configuration should also include at least one backup kernel image.

continues

There is a penchant for reinstalling from scratch, a habit unfortunately instilled by another popular operating system. In Linux this is a rarity; with a Linux system, your darkest hour still probably does not require reinstalling Linux.

When the worst happens, use the rescue disks to boot your system, manually `fsck` and `mount` the hard drive, restore order, rerun `lilo`, and breathe easier. You can also find a number of rescue disks and tools in the Metalab archive at `ftp://metalab.unc.edu/pub/Linux`.

Linux Kernel Architecture

Linux is UNIX-like. Linux is not a version of UNIX, but a new OS highly reminiscent of UNIX, and that heritage has freed Linux from legacy code. Linux is designed to be UNIX-compatible but has been developed from scratch.

Kernel Version Numbers

Linux kernel version numbers identify the base design, the revision, and also whether you are running an experimental or a production release. The version in use by any Linux system can be queried with `uname -a`:

```
# uname -a
Linux nowhere.com 2.2.5 #2 Thu Apr 15 18:34:07 EDT 1999 i586 unknown
```

This line identifies my kernel as version 2.2.5 and gives the date when the kernel was compiled. A version number contains three parts:

- The major number
- The minor number
- The current revision

The first of these is easy: It is either 1 or 2 and, although there are enough of the old edition to be impressive, there are not many 1.*x* kernels around. For most practical purposes, though, the major number of the Linux kernel is 2. The last number has some special significance as well, especially with the experimental kernels; but for the moment, the important portion of the kernel version number is the middle digit, the minor number.

Odd minor numbers denote experimental kernels (kernels 2.1 and 2.3 for example), and even minor numbers would carry a stamp of respectability and be considered production editions. Today, although many Linux distributions carry a 2.0 kernel as the default, it is the newer 2.2 kernel that is generating most of the public and commercial interest in Linux; upgrading from 2.0 to 2.2 is very likely why you are reading this chapter.

Caution

During the rapid development of the odd-minor kernels, it is important not to simply jump in and expect to join the other kernel surfers; although the development group endeavors to release only stable code, very often a core change can create havoc for other users. These troubles are often traced to needing specific libraries, module, or compiler tools, and sometimes the development can inadvertently strand whole communities of developers. When surveying the patches, the best practice is to first check the Linux Kernel Changes Web site, and then to watch the Linux kernel development mailing list for trouble reports. Only then should you dive in to a development kernel revision that has been stable for at least a few days.

The official Web site for the kernel development team is `http://www.tux.org`.

Kernel Modules

For most purposes, building a Linux kernel means selecting those devices and services that you need and omitting those that don't apply to your situation. Starting with Linux 2.0, a new design feature was introduced into the kernel to provide a middle ground: Components can be dynamically loaded and unloaded from the kernel at runtime.

Kernel modules are services that are included in the kernel as needed and removed from memory when done. This can include support for filesystems or network protocols that are needed only for certain applications, or for dynamically adding support for a network interface such as PPP without carrying around this code while offline. Modules become very convenient for adding many services under tight memory constraints, such as in laptops or embedded systems, and it is largely because of modules that your Debian distribution was able to boot and install on your hardware; a quick look at `/lib/modules` shows many extraneous components that the install had ready on the chance you might need them.

Modules have one other important use: In certain situations, the configuration of the hardware may not be known at boot time, and loading the drivers as modules enables querying (or setting) the hardware configuration before loading the code. One example is with plug-and-play sound cards, where the boot process must initialize all needed interrupts before the module can be invoked.

Do you really need to recompile? There are numerous ways of modifying the configuration and default behavior of Linux. Only one of these is to set values in the kernel configuration and recompile from sources.

With all versions of Linux, many parameters, such as sound card ports, hard disk geometries, and IRQ assignments can be set using boot command-line options. Many characteristics of the running kernel, even delicate issues such as virtual memory and filesystem behaviors, can be queried and set through the `/proc` filesystem (if `/proc` is enabled in your kernel).

For example, if all you need to do is to set the proper address for an old SoundBlaster CD-ROM, you can add the line

```
append=?sbpcd=0x230,SoundBlaster
```

to your `/etc/lilo.conf` and rerun `lilo`; for testing purposes, most options can also be added manually after the `lilo` prompt when your system boots.

```
lilo: linux sbpcd=0x230,SoundBlaster
```

More information on `lilo` can be found later in this chapter.

In the sections on kernel options, many allow overriding default settings through boot command-line options. Others accept new settings by echoing some value to a `/proc` file.

Before you delve into a complete recompile, you can save a lot of time and bother by investigating these alternate tuning methods. However, in almost all cases, compiling and using a custom kernel will both optimize your system for speed and save some amount of memory.

Troubleshooting Modules

Modules are services of the kernel that are dynamically inserted and removed from the system as required. With the current kernels, almost all devices and services can be configured to load as modules.

Loading a module is done by the `/sbin/insmod` program with the obvious `/sbin/rmmod` to remove the module. Other utilities in this suite include `/sbin/depmod` to compute module dependencies and `/sbin/modprobe` to query a module for those modules upon which it depends.

One of three problems can occur when upgrading to a newer kernel:

- Module version numbers will mismatch.
- Module utilities will be incompatible.
- Module dependencies may conflict.

The first issue occurs when the kernel has been compiled with the option to check module version numbers, and those numbers do not exactly match (that is, including the build number). When this happens, the modules are rejected and, if your system depends on some critical module to function, your system may not come up. This is not an issue with the 2.2 kernel, because this test is no longer part of the configuration.

The second situation is more likely to happen, although the kernel modules have not changed in a long time (months!). If your module utilities meet the requirements spelled out in `linux/Documentation/Changes`, you will have no problem, but if you do happen to boot a kernel with old module utilities, you may hang.

The third problem can hit anyone and is one of those things that, when you know what has happened, you realize is just common sense. For example, suppose you compile Windows VFAT filesystem support as a module, but then your boot scripts try to use some file from your Windows partition prior to the module loading; or more likely, you configure your network support as a module, forgetting that the `httpd` will hang the boot scripts while trying to resolve the hostname.

The net advice is to use modules where they are appropriate. There will be some overhead in loading and unloading and some overhead in coding the driver as a module; if the code is needed frequently or continuously, or if it is critical to the boot process, perhaps it should not be compiled as a module.

Coping with New Kernels and Modules

Building and running the kernel depends on many different software components; these are all listed in `linux/Changes` and, before you attempt to run your new kernel, you must ensure your system is running at least the version numbers listed in the `Changes` file.

Similarly, the drivers provided with the Linux kernel may not be the latest, and if you have problems with a particular device or with very state-of-the-art hardware, such as new video or sound cards, you may want to search out an update before building your kernel.

Kernel changes may also require changes to your boot scripts, to `/etc/lilo.conf`, or to other configuration options elsewhere on your machine—for example, in the `/etc/conf.modules` file. The `linux/Documentation` collection contains many short `README` files for many different parts of the kernel, and each driver subdirectory may also contain additional information on installing or configuring difficult devices. Most kernel modules accept parameters either through the boot command line; through the `append` line of `/etc/lilo.conf`; or, for dynamically loaded modules, on the `/sbin/insmod` command line or in `/etc/conf.modules`.

If you give options both in `lilo.conf` and at the boot prompt, the option strings are concatenated, with the boot prompt options coming last. This enables you to override your installed options at the command line to preempt unwanted settings and is also why many modules include options to restore their default behavior.

KernelNotes is a good starting place for all your kernel needs, for build and module tool updates, and for new packages and device drivers. The Web site is at `http://kernelnotes.org`.

kernelnotes

Obtaining the Kernel Sources

Your Debian distribution should contain the sources for some version of the 2.2 or at least the last revision of the 2.0 series kernel. For most people, this will be as good as any for creating a new kernel more in tune with their computer hardware. Because new editions of Debian and other Linux distributions will include the new 2.2 series kernel, this chapter concentrates on the configuration and installation of the newer production release. The 2.2 kernel includes many options for devices and protocols that were unknown in 2.0, but the process of obtaining, configuring, building, and installing the kernel is identical regardless of your version.

Your Debian installation gives options to include the kernel headers and also to include the kernel sources. You must install the kernel headers if you plan to compile any software (that is, build your own binaries from source code) but, to build the kernel, you must also install the `kernel-sources .deb` or obtain kernel sources from some other location. The name of these packages in your software management system is `kernel-source-`*`version`* and `kernel-headers-`*`version`*, where *`version`* follows the conventions described previously.

The kernel sources can be found at `dists/stable/main/binary-i386/devel` on the CD-ROM shipped with this book.

Those looking to upgrade to the newer 2.2 kernel can obtain the sources from many sites, and it is good Netiquette to seek out a mirror site as close to you as possible. Although famous sites such as `ftp://ftp.cdrom.com` and `ftp://ftp.kernel.org` have the files you need, you should first check with `http://www.kernel.org` to find an appropriate mirror site. If you did install from the `kernel-source .deb` on your Debian CD-ROM, you will find the source directory at `/usr/src/kernel-source-`*`version`*; if you need to download your tarball from an official mirror, you will find the file in the `/pub/linux/kernel/v2.2` directory on that FTP site.

A kernel mirror FTP site will list two types of files: the whole-enchilada source tarballs and compressed patch files. Initially, if you are making the jump between minor version branches (that is, from 2.2 to 2.3) or if you want to start fresh, you need the complete sources, which are in a file with a name such as `linux-2.2.10.tar.gz`. These also come compressed with `bzip2`, which compresses files considerably farther; these carry exactly the same names but have a final extension of `.bz2` instead of `.gz`. Although this is a major chunk to download over a modem connection, when you have a relatively recent source tree, you can later update your sources by downloading only the much smaller patch files; the system I use now has been patched to 2.2.7 from 2.1.103!

Before you open any tar file, the first thing you should do is list the contents to see whether it is complete and get an overview of the directory structure it will install. Use either

```
# tar -tzf linux-2.2.10.tar.bz2
```

or

```
# tar -tyf linux-2.2.10.tar.bz2
```

This shows a long list of files, including directories for device drivers, modules, and architecture-dependent code for all the current Linux ports. The salient detail right now is that the `tar` is based in a directory called simply `linux/`.

Symbolic Links to the Kernel Sources

You should always manually create a directory for your kernel sources and symlink (`ln -s`) this directory to the generic `/usr/src/linux` location. For example, if you obtained `linux-2.2.10.tar.gz`, you should manually create `/usr/src/linux-2.2.10` and alias that to `/usr/src/linux`:

```
cd /usr/src
mkdir linux-2.2.10
ln -s linux-2.2.10 linux
```

This has two benefits. First, if your kernel `include` directory `/usr/include/linux` is also symlinked to `/usr/src/linux/include`, your `include` files will always belong to your current kernel. Second, you can keep several versions of the kernel, each in its own `/usr/src/linux-`*X.X.X* directory, and when you update your sources using the `patch` utility, the patch will then be applied to the appropriate kernel sources—this enables you to experiment with one version and later to quickly return to another version.

After you have created the new `/usr/src/linux-2.2.10` directory and symlinked this to `/usr/src/linux`, unpack the tarball from your `/usr/src` directory:

```
cd /usr/src
tar xzf /home/garym/incoming/linux-2.2.10.tar.gz
```

If all goes well, and you have enough disk space, you will find the Linux sources in `/usr/src/linux`. In that directory, you will find a `README` file with some basic information on bug reporting and other tidbits, but a more important directory to browse is `linux/Documentation`. This contains many detailed guides for every aspect of the Linux kernel and is essential reading if you are hoping to configure Linux for some new or rare hardware.

Note

Throughout this book, path names will be given as relative to your source directory. Unless a path begins with a slash (/), it will begin with a prefix of `/usr/src`.

A Script to Check Version Numbers

Version numbers of software pertinent to the kernel should always be checked against the `Documentation/Changes` file, but checking each package can be tedious, especially if, like me, you can't remember the syntax for all these commands. If you want to be sure your development environment fits the bill for building a new kernel, I've written a script that will check versions for you. This can be found at `tools/kernel-dep.sh` on the last CD-ROM shipped with this book. I originally wrote this as a poor man's version of the `versions` command available on Silicon Graphics IRIX machines.

So, if you want to be absolutely sure, run this script and check all the versions against what appears in `Documentation/Changes` of your kernel source. If you're feeling lucky, go ahead and try building the sources without checking dependencies. If you don't feel like dealing with it, just retrieve the kernel sources and everything they depend on to build by typing

```
apt-get install kernel-source-2.1
```

Patching the Source Tree

Even if your Linux distribution includes the 2.2 kernel, you may need to upgrade your system to the more recent version of this kernel to take advantage of performance, security, or device support improvements. Updates to the Linux kernel are always available on the standard mirror sites as patch files named for the version that will result from the patch—for example, the upgrade from 2.2.4 to 2.2.5 will be called `patch-2.2.5.gz`. Patch files are simply context `diffs`, that is, the output of the `diff` command (see `man diff`) listing the differences between the prior version and the new version. A patch is applied by running the output generated by `diff` through the GNU `patch` utility. `patch` is given the lines of context around the change and told to delete, add, or replace lines in the source files.

Caution

Patch files upgrade your sources by only one revision number; if you need to upgrade from 2.2.1 to 2.2.6, you need to obtain all the patches for the intermediate releases and apply them in order.

Patch files are created by comparing the sources of *totally clean* `linux` source trees. Before you apply any patches, it is very important to back up your `.config` file and clean your kernel source tree to the most pristine state using `make mrproper`:

```
cd /usr/src/linux
cp .config /usr/src/config-old
make mrproper
```

This ensures there are no residual generated files that could frustrate the patch or interfere with your subsequent kernel build; saving your old `config` (which would be removed by `mrproper`) enables you to bootstrap your next kernel `config` with the `oldconfig` option.

Patch files are typically very much smaller than the source tarball (at most a few hundred kilobytes)

Verifying a `patch` Update

After using the `patch` program to patch your sources, you should search your kernel tree for any "reject" files—these files will be the unapplied `diffs` and are most often the result of some innocuous difference in whitespace or tab stops between the sources owned by the creator of the `diff` and your own sources.

If you find any `*.rej` files, you must manually correct the associated source file before you compile your kernel. To understand how to accomplish this, first you must have significant programming experience; second, read `diff(8)` and learn the format of `diff` output. After you've done this, compare *`file`*`.rej` (where *`file`* is the name of the file before its `.rej` suffix) to the original file *`file`*. With this pair of files, you can often guess what the patch was supposed to do and correct the situation.

Kernel Configuration Shortcuts

After you have patched your sources, you can bootstrap your configuration by copying your backup `config` file to `.config` and running

```
cp /usr/src/config-old .config
make oldconfig
```

This sets all the options that were present in your previous installation, preserving all those fiddly options that are so easy to forget (such as the IRQ of your sound card!), but it stops and prompts for any new options that have been added by the new sources. After the `oldconfig` has run, the kernel can be configured and compiled.

New Features in Kernel 2.2

Linux 2.2 adds a number of new facilities to the suite of kernel options, including read-only support for the NT filesystem and experimental support for the distributed CODA filesystem. Many performance optimizations have also been added, including support for

MTRR registers, finer grain locking on SMP systems, user buffer checks, and directory entry caching. Also new with the 2.2 kernel is the ability for kernel programmers to mark sections of their code as being for initialization only; kernel memory is not swappable and, with this new facility, after the kernel has initialized, the marked code is jettisoned and the memory is freed. This makes the new kernel actually leave a smaller footprint in memory than the 2.0 kernel.

The 2.2 kernel will work on a system installed for a 2.0 kernel but will require upgrading some of the dependent utilities, such as the modules package and Net tools. Older systems also need to run the `MAKEDEV` script to ensure that obsolete devices are replaced by the current set. For developers of third-party kernel modules, the kernel interface has changed between 2.0 and 2.2; programmers wanting to port their code can find more information at

`http://www.atnf.csiro.au/~rgooch/linux/docs/porting-to-2.2.html`

Known Bugs in the Linux 2.2 Kernel

In any software project of 1.7 million lines of code that is intended to run on such a wide array of platforms and combinations, there will be bugs. If you encounter problems, your first stop should be to check Richard Gooch's Kernel Newsflash page for reports and patches on the latest kernel release:

`http://www.atnf.csiro.au/~rgooch/linux/docs/kernel-newsflash.html`

Your second stop should be the Linux Kernel FAQ and the Linux Kernel mailing list archives:

`http://www.tux.org/lkml/`

Configuring the Linux Kernel

Warning

If you are experimenting with kernel options, remember to set the `lilo delay` parameter to give you some grace time to select an alternate kernel. If your production system has a delay of zero seconds, you will not have the opportunity to preempt loading the default kernel, and if that kernel is faulty, your only option is to boot from a floppy disk. Again, further information on `lilo` is presented later in this chapter.

The Linux Makefile provides four methods of setting your configuration options:

- A command-line terminal program, `make config`
- An `ncurses`-based console program, `make menuconfig`
- A tk/tcl–based X11 GUI program, `make xconfig`
- A semiautomatic update program, `make oldconfig`

I remember sitting in a Linux User Group meeting one evening and complaining about having wanted to set some kernel option one way but letting it slip by or setting it wrong and having to abort the program and start again. Everyone gave me a rather strange look; I had been using the command-line interface for so long that I hadn't even considered there might have been other methods introduced in the intervening years.

Why have a command-line interface? Suppose you had an autonomous robot submarine, or perhaps a space probe, that was in the midst of maneuvers and needed a fast kernel `reconfig`. Simple dumb terminal interfaces can go places other interfaces cannot dream of going. Keep this in mind if you plan to read your email or news from some GUI-only package!

That said, outside of using the `oldconfig` option for generating an updated configuration from a previous `.config` file, I don't think I have used the command-line interface since that day. Without doubt, the X11/tk interface is the most elegant and appealing, although it does require that tk and X11 are both working—X11 is sometimes not practical to use, for example, when doing remote administration over a slow Telnet connection.

This leaves the Linux console `ncurses` configuration as the main workhorse of Linux configuration, with the X11 interface as the vehicle of choice when possible. Both the X11 and the `ncurses` configuration tools offer the same options in the same order and have roughly the same capability of navigating backward and forward through the configuration options.

The Configuration Process

To start the configuration, simply change to the `/usr/src/linux` directory and enter one of the first three configuration commands; if you choose either of the `ncurses` or X11 methods, you see a brief flurry of compiler activity while the user-interface programs compile, and then you are greeted by an overview screen with all the categories of kernel options.

root-Owned Source Directories and xconfig

Debian has always been very security conscious. Often, user ease is sacrificed for true system security—a trend that can cause quite some confusion for beginners.

Usually, `/usr/src/` will be owned by `root`. As a side effect, in order to unpack the `linux` archive, you must be `root`; this causes `/usr/src/linux` to also be owned by `root`. Finally, because `/usr/src/linux` and all the files under it are owned by `root`, only `root` can run any `build` scripts there. Unfortunately, Debian's default X configuration does not allow any application to display to the screen unless it is being run by the user that owns the current X session. This means that you can't become `root` and run `xconfig` in an X session you started as a regular user.

This renders `xconfig` useless when the `linux` source archive lives in `/usr/src`, unless you grant your user write access to all directories underneath. This is a fairly trivial task that can be accomplished with a short script. However, the preferred method of compiling the kernel that you'll be shown will often need to place files in the directory *above* your `linux` source directory. For anyone with any level of experience with compiling kernels, this may be surprising. Debian's reasons for doing things this way will be demonstrated later.

Because of these circumstances, you either have to do everything as `root` from `/usr/src` (in which case, you won't be able to run `xconfig` unless you started your X session as `root`), manipulate the permissions of `/usr/src` until your regular user account has write access to it and every subdirectory of `/usr/src/linux`, or perform this entire procedure from your home directory. Remember: No matter where your `linux` source tree is, it's highly important that you link `/usr/src/linux` to point to it.

Configuration Options

This is it. Hit the lights. This is the moment you have all been waiting for! In all the configuration methods, most kernel options can be set to be included, included as a module, or left out of the compile. On the `xconfig` and `menuconfig` screens, there are also options to include or exclude certain sections of the configuration, where disabling these sections grays out any dependent options (the dumb-terminal `config` option silently skips these sections).

Rather than hold your hand during this process, I am certain you can figure out 90 percent of what you need to know without my help. This guide does not attempt to describe every one of the 407 options in the Linux kernel but instead focuses on options that are required for a working system. If the entire process was outlined, some of these sections would be more interesting to new Linux users, and others would be of interest only to seasoned network or systems administrators and might become bogged in acronyms. As such, I will not outline any options in detail here; see Appendix E for an in-depth account of options of interest for specific applications.

The important feature on all the kernel configuration screens, whether you use the dumb-terminal, `ncurses`, or X11 method, is the `HELP` option. Almost all kernel features are well documented in the configuration screen and, whether you are looking at beginner options for installing network support or expert options for setting filesystem caching, most carry this reassuring advice: `If you are in doubt, say Y (or N)`. When you've got a question that neither this guide nor Appendix E can answer, read the help for whatever option you're considering.

Again, as stressed earlier, there's no harm in trying new things without really knowing whether they will work. Where uncertain, just give it a shot—you can't break anything.

Preparing for a Kernel Configuration

Before you can answer many of the questions about your new kernel configuration, you may need to know about the inside of your computer. Kernel configuration asks about your network card, your PCI chipset, your IDE and SCSI controllers, and a host of other highly personal questions.

For your first time, through, where you are in doubt you can use the defaults or the recommended option in the associated `HELP` page. For a zealous fit, keep your computer manuals nearby or run through your first configuration with the panels taken off your computer and a flashlight in hand.

Above all, take heart—it is not absolutely essential that you match your computer chipset perfectly on your first kernel configuration; the defaults have served you well so far. Wherever you're uncertain, read the help text and make your best guess.

Required Options

There are a few components that your kernel absolutely needs to start correctly. Some of these, in very specific cases, can be built as modules. As described previously, anything that is needed for bootup, before there is any possibility of loading modules, needs to be integrated directly into the kernel. For example, the filesystem driver for your `root` filesystem is usually `ext2`; you *need* this driver integrated, or your kernel will panic halfway through startup, complaining it can't mount the `root` filesystem. Other important aspects include the console driver (which allows output to your screen) and binary format drivers (which allow the kernel to execute commands). Those options absolutely required for a booting system, in most cases, are presented in the following sections.

Processor Family, Under "Processor Type and Features"

This optimizes the kernel for your particular CPU. A wrong setting won't harm anything; the resulting kernel just won't be as fast as it could.

Access to the Device Your `root` Filesystem Is Stored On

Because all modules are stored under the `root` partition (usually), the kernel doesn't have access to them until it's mounted. As such, any drivers needed to gain access to the `root` partition must be integrated directly with the kernel. If your `root` filesystem is on an IDE drive, you need `generic IDE/MFM/RLL disk/cdrom/tape/floppy support` under Block Devices enabled. If, on the other hand, it's SCSI, enable SCSI support and include drivers for the type of SCSI card your system has directly into your kernel.

Binary Format Drivers

Debian provides all binaries in ELF format. If your kernel doesn't support this type of binary, it will be unable to run `init`. In effect, it will be rendered useless. So say `Y` to Kernel support for ELF binaries under General Setup.

Filesystem Drivers

Your kernel is responsible for mounting the `root` filesystem and executing `init`. If it doesn't have drivers for the type of filesystem you use on your `root` partition, Linux can't boot. Debian, by default, uses the Second Extended Filesystem. So, enable Second Extended Filesystem Support under `Filesystems`.

Working Around Buggy Hardware

Often, serious bugs creep into hardware design. Sometimes, these bugs are so severe and widespread that instead of recalling every single piece of hardware affected, the manufacturer introduces software workarounds to various operating systems. However, often they do not and just ignore the problem. Once again, Linux's open source development process makes it shine, as developers around the world converge on common problems such as these. If a kernel you build doesn't work for mysterious reasons, check every component of your system's hardware against each bug workaround option in the kernel configuration. You may just find something that makes your system work.

However, most hardware isn't this buggy. As such, the defaults usually work just fine.

Hardware Options

Everything else is fair game for either including or omitting. From here, browse the help screens of individual options, enabling what looks useful as you go along. If you enable an option you have no use for, the worst agony you have inflicted upon yourself is a slightly slower system, and forgetting to enable an option will probably do nothing but cause a device on your system to not work. If you need everything laid out plainly, just jump straight to Appendix E, where every kernel option is described in detail.

Just remember, you can't break anything. As long as you follow precautionary measures for installing these untested kernel images, there's no way inexperience can harm you here. Safely installing new kernel images is outlined in the sections to come.

Saving Your Configuration

After the kernel is configured, the save-and-exit option creates the `.config` file and, if the kernel has been configured for sound, it generates `linux/include/linux/autoconf.h`; the kernel is now primed and ready for building.

Building and Installing the Kernel

After you've selected a set of options you think will work for you, it's time to build your newly configured kernel and attempt to install it.

The configuration program will have created one very precious file: `/usr/src/linux/.config`, which contains a long list of `#define` statements for all your selected options. To create a duplicate kernel, all that is required is this one file; when you have a configuration that works for your system, you may want to keep a copy someplace safe.

You can now use this configuration program to build the new kernel, create your modules, and install the works. It's also now time to give your wrists a break and return to the command line to put it all together.

Scheduling a Kernel Rebuild Using `at`

If you are reasonably certain a kernel build will not fail, you may want to schedule the build using the `at` command; this not only enables you to shift the added system load to offpeak hours, but the output of the build will be logged and sent to you as email.

Before building the new kernel, you need to regenerate all the dependency files to account for any changes in include or module file dependencies introduced by your new options; this is needed whenever the kernel configuration is changed. The Linux Makefile provides the commands to rebuild these files and another to ensure there are no stray generated files, and you can run both together with

```
# make dep clean
```

Building the Kernel Image

The next step is building the actual kernel image. There are several ways Linux is able to represent itself, but the differences are usually quite minuscule. The different types of kernel image usually differ only in their compression mechanism or in the steps automatically taken to install. Probably the most basic types are `zImage`, which is an image compressed with `gzip`, and `bzImage`, which uses `bzip2`. To generate these, execute either one of the following commands:

```
# make zImage
# make bzImage
```

Tip

You can also create the new kernel and have it automatically installed (that is, the build process installs the image and `lilo` for you):

```
# make zlilo
```

Next, to build and install any loadable modules you configured into this kernel build, run this:

```
# make modules modules_install
```

Note

The `modules_install` target *must* be run as `root`, because it installs files in `/lib`.

Both of the `zImage` and `bzImage` targets generate a file (`zImage` and `bzImage`, respectively) and place it in `arch/`*`architecture`*`/boot`. For example, if you're running an Intel-based PC and invoked the `bzImage` target, this file will end up as `arch/i386/boot/bzImage`. This kernel image should be moved somewhere onto the `root` filesystem and configured into `lilo`. For instructions on adding an image to `lilo`, see the following sections.

Debian Shortcuts to Kernel Compiling

Now that you're brainwashed into using the most rudimentary method of compiling and installing a kernel, it's time to introduce a much more elegant and simplified method. Debian provides a tool specifically for compiling and installing kernels. This convenient method can be invoked as simply as this:

```
make-kpkg kernel_image
```

This one command implements the following:

1. Perform the dependency file generation.
2. Clean the sources.
3. Create a compressed kernel image.
4. Create a Debian package for you.

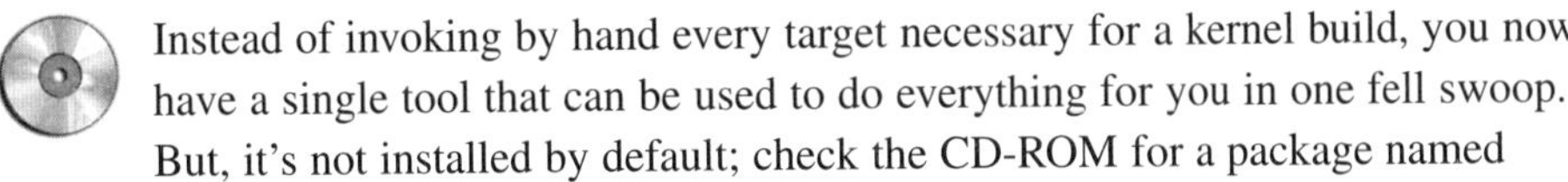

Instead of invoking by hand every target necessary for a kernel build, you now have a single tool that can be used to do everything for you in one fell swoop. But, it's not installed by default; check the CD-ROM for a package named `kernel-package`. This can be easily installed via

```
# apt-get install kernel-package
```

or through `dselect`.

fakeroot and make-kpkg

Be sure to run `make-kpkg` as `root`. If you followed the previous suggestion to place the `linux` source tree in your home directory, however, you have another option: `fakeroot`. The files generated by the build process need to be `root`-owned, but you don't necessarily need `root` permissions to build a piece of software stored under your home directory.

`fakeroot` eliminates this dilemma. It emulates a `root` environment, so that all permissions on generated files are as if `root` created them. Now you can invoke `xconfig` as yourself (not `root`) from this source tree in your home directory and build the kernel without any trouble! The command line you use for `make-kpkg` under `fakeroot` is as follows:

```
fakeroot make-kpkg kernel_image
```

The `.deb` produced by `make-kpkg` contains all information that Debian needs to install your new kernel image and its modules. Type `dpkg -i` *`package`* (*`package`* being replaced by the name of the file `make-kpkg` produced), and watch while Debian takes care of all the administrative tasks for you. However, Debian's `liloconfig`, which is executed after a kernel image is installed, isn't very robust (and can actually cause some major suffering for sysadmins), so I recommend that you bypass it entirely and configure `lilo` yourself. This process is described in the section "`lilo`," later in this chapter.

Scheduling a Kernel Build

When an administrative command has a long output—for example, patching or compiling a new kernel—a convenient way to keep a record is to run the command as an at job; output is automatically emailed to the task owner.

Manually Installing a New Kernel

A freshly generated kernel is always found in /usr/src/linux/arch/i386/boot/. Before it can be used, however, it must be installed using the lilo boot loader or some other Linux loader.

As one example, to emulate the Debian /boot path scheme, you need to copy the new zImage to /boot/vmlinuz-X.X.X (this is where the .deb created by make-kpkg puts things) and modify /etc/lilo.conf to include the new version. Always be sure to make backups of any kernel images and module directories that will be overwritten—this will happen only if you've recompiled and installed a kernel version that you already had installed.

Alternatively, to accommodate stubborn plug-and-play devices, you may need to copy this new kernel to your Windows 95 partition for use by the Linux loadlin.exe boot loader.

Note

The format of the /etc/lilo.conf configuration file is described in the sections to come about lilo.

One frequent requirement is to create boot floppies, a kernel copied directly to the floppy disk and set to mount the root filesystem from the hard drive.

Although it is far more mnemonic to create a boot floppy using this command:

```
# make zdisk
```

it is equivalent to using the dd command to copy the file directly to the disk device (that is, to the raw sectors of the disk):

```
]# dd if=arch/i386/zImage of=/dev/fd0
```

Compiling for a Remote Machine

When creating a kernel for some other machine (for example, a laptop), you can create the compressed kernel file and all modules into an alternate directory tree by adding the alternate values for the install path variable to the `make` command line:

```
INSTALL_PATH=/psitta \
INSTALL_MOD_PATH=/psitta ROOT_DEV=/dev/hda1 \
make bzlilo modules_install
```

This command moves the generated kernel, map, and module files to `/psitta/vmlinuz /psitta/System.map` and `/psitta/lib/modules`, where you can conveniently `tar` the whole directory for shipment to the remote machine:

```
cd /psitta && \
tar cf - vmlinuz System.map lib/modules/2.2.7 ¦ \
tar xCf / -
```

The `make` command also runs `lilo`, but because the `/etc/lilo.conf` file does not reference these new `/psitta` files, there is no side effect.

The only potential side effect of this process is a possible change to files in `/usr/include/linux`, which may affect programs subsequently compiled on the build host. Some care must be take to ensure the alternate kernel build does not leave unwanted changes in this directory on the build machine. Also, if the remote machine will be used to build software, after compiling the new kernel, the `/usr/include/linux` directory should also be copied or installed onto the remote machine.

Troubleshooting the New Kernel

`/proc` is your friend. With the 2.0 through 2.3 series of kernels, the pseudofiles in the `/proc` directory hold a wealth of diagnostic information and a simple means to set runtime parameters. Between these major revisions of Linux, `/proc` has some subtle differences. For the most part, however, the most commonly used files have remained the same.

The most frequently useful `/proc` diagnostic files are difficult to point out; you may have a use for information that nobody else would. As Linus iterates often, users are the least predictable part of any operating system, because you never know what they are going to want to do. Instead, take a look at the contents of the `/proc` directory; the filenames there are fairly self-explanatory:

- `cpuinfo` lists processor type, number of ports, and other essential information about the computer hardware:

  ```
  $cat /proc/cpuinfo
  processor       : 0
  ```

```
vendor_id       : AuthenticAMD
cpu family      : 5
model           : 8
model name      : AMD-K6(tm) 3D processor
stepping        : 12
cpu MHz         : 350.804507
fdiv_bug        : no
hlt_bug         : no
sep_bug         : no
f00f_bug        : no
fpu             : yes
fpu_exception   : yes
cpuid level     : 1
wp              : yes
flags           : fpu vme de pse tsc msr mce cx8 sep pge mmx 3dnow
bogomips        : 699.60
```

- `interrupts` maps IRQ lines to devices:

```
$ cat /proc/interrupts
           CPU0
  0:   30200579          XT-PIC  timer
  1:     251230          XT-PIC  keyboard
  2:          0          XT-PIC  cascade
  4:     996021          XT-PIC  serial
  5:          1          XT-PIC  soundblaster
  7:          2          XT-PIC  parport1
  8:          1          XT-PIC  rtc
 11:       3984          XT-PIC  MSS audio codec
 12:     973494          XT-PIC  eth0
 13:          1          XT-PIC  fpu
 14:    4253923          XT-PIC  ide0
 15:    4713361          XT-PIC  ide1
NMI:          0
```

- `sound` reports the current sound system configuration and the installed services:

```
$ cat /proc/sound
OSS/Free:3.8s2++-971130
Load type: Driver compiled into kernel
Kernel: Linux maya.dyndns.org 2.2.5 #2 Thu Apr 15 18:34:07 EDT 1999 i586
Config options: 0

Installed drivers:
Type 10: MS Sound System
Type 27: Compaq Deskpro XL
Type 1: OPL-2/OPL-3 FM
Type 26: MPU-401 (UART)
Type 2: Sound Blaster
Type 29: Sound Blaster PnP
Type 7: SB MPU-401
Type 36: SoftOSS Virtual Wave Table

Card config:
SoftOSS Virtual Wave Table
```

```
Compaq Deskpro XL at 0x530 irq 11 drq 0,0
Sound Blaster at 0x220 irq 5 drq 1,5
(SB MPU-401 at 0x330 irq 5 drq 0)
OPL-2/OPL-3 FM at 0x388 drq 0
Audio devices:
0: MSS audio codec (SoundPro CMI 8330)
1: Sound Blaster 16 (4.13) (DUPLEX)

Synth devices:
0: SoftOSS
1: Yamaha OPL3

Midi devices:

Timers:
0: System clock
1: SoftOSS

Mixers:
0: MSS audio codec (SoundPro CMI 8330)
1: Sound Blaster
```


- `parport` contains directories for each parallel port and reports on the devices attached to each port:

```
$ cat /proc/parport/0/hardware
base:   0x378
irq:    none
dma:    none
modes:  SPP,ECP,ECPEPP,ECPPS2
```

Recovering from Faulty Kernel Installations

It happens. You execute an orderly shutdown and reboot, the monitor flashes (or your connection goes dead), and you wait for the boot, only to be greeted with a partial `lilo` prompt or worse.

Typically, a faulty kernel installation will exhibit one of the following behaviors:

- The machine will cycle through repeated rebooting.
- You will see some substring of the `lilo` prompt—for example, `LIL-` followed by a halt.
- Linux will begin to load but halt at some point during the kernel messages.
- Linux will load but end in a kernel panic message.
- Linux will load, run, let you log in, and then die when it is least convenient.

If you are prepared, your prognosis for a full recovery is very good. If you can get up to the `lilo` prompt, the most convenient recovery is to load your backup kernel by specifying its label to the boot loader:

```
lilo: backup
```

Note

During a normal boot, there is a short delay after the `lilo` appears. Pressing the Alt key during that delay will change the message to the `lilo` prompt and allow you to enter alternate boot labels or parameters. For more information, see the sections on using `lilo`.

This boots from your previous kernel and allows you in to fix the problem and try your luck again. If you cannot get to the `lilo` prompt, your only alternative is to use your boot disk or to use a rescue disk. The boot disk makes life much easier, because the running system will be identical to your normal system; when you use a rescue disk, you must manually mount your system partitions, and this puts all your files (and any symlinks) off kilter, complicating running `LILO` or the RPM package manager.

Where alternate kernels and boot disks are not practical—for instance, on thin clients with limited diskspace—if you can reach the `lilo` prompt, you can try to start your system in single-user mode to prevent the probing and loading of many modules, such as your network card (a frequent culprit). The default configuration for single-user (run level 1) mode is specified by the files in `/etc/rc1.d`, and it is a good idea to double-check the symlinks in that directory after each system upgrade to ensure the choices are intelligent for the purpose. Single-user mode puts you directly into a system shell; when the problem has been corrected, you can either reboot the system or exit the shell to return to multiuser mode.

Note

Configuring run levels for `init` is an aspect of the bootup procedure that needs more than just a few lines like this; for more information, see the coming sections on `init`.

Repeated Rebooting

Nine times out of ten, repeated rebooting is caused by making changes to the kernel file and forgetting to run `lilo` to register the new image with the boot loader. `lilo` needs the raw sector location of the kernel; even copying a kernel image moves it to a new sector and leaves the previous pointer stored by `lilo` dangling into an abyss.

This problem can be corrected by booting from the boot floppy and running the `lilo` command, or by using a rescue disk, mounting the boot partition under `/mnt`, and running `lilo` with the options to use a relative path:

```
lilo -r /mnt
```

Partial `lilo` Prompt

A partial `lilo` prompt is the most terrifying of all kernel boot errors because it is often difficult to diagnose and fix. Each letter of `LILO` signifies a stage in the boot process and can be used to isolate the trouble:

- `L-` or `LIL` usually signifies a media error.
- `LI` or `LIL?` signifies that `/boot/boot.b` is missing, moved, or corrupt. The solution is the same: rerun `lilo`.

Kernel Halts While Loading

Device probing is a dangerous business and the most frequent cause of kernel halts while loading. For example, if you are configuring for a gateway/firewall machine with two network interfaces, the second probe may cause the kernel to halt. Other causes of kernel halts can be IRQ conflicts, memory conflicts, or mismatched devices (that is, selecting a similar but not quite identical driver).

Probing, memory, and IRQ conflicts can be avoided for most kernel modules and devices by supplying the correct configuration parameters in the `/etc/lilo.conf` `append` line. The exact parameters to use depend on your device, but advice is often found in the `README` files either in `linux/Documentation` or in the subdirectories of the driver source code.

Resolving IRQs and Memory Ports

If you have hardware that is particularly troublesome for IRQ and memory settings, and if you have a Windows partition, you can find the values used by Windows in the `ControlPanel:System:Devices` listings and then use these settings on the `lilo` command line or in the `/etc/conf.modules` file. It is unfortunate, but many manufacturers still believe their best business model includes restricting use of their hardware to only Microsoft users; as a result, techniques and interfaces for probing and configuring these devices are not available to Linux programmers. The good news is that more manufacturers have seen the light and happily provide any information you need to incorporate their products under Linux.

Kernel Oops and Bug Reporting

It is certainly true that a Linux machine is general highly stable and resilient to application failures, but when you start experimenting with odd kernel combinations or experimental editions, hardware, and configurations, stuff happens. In the parlance of the kernel developers, an *oops* is a kernel panic message, which seems to occur spontaneously, often mercilessly, and for no apparent reason. The message reported is similar to the kernel panic that can occur during the boot, but it may not be visible if you are running X-Windows. The cause of both the boot halting and a spontaneous oops is the same: The kernel has reached an impasse.

When an oops occurs during a user session, the kernel panic message may be displayed on one of the Linux Alt consoles and can be seen by pressing Ctrl+Alt+1 or by checking the system log file in `/var/log/messages`. If you can see the panic report, the activity just prior to this in the log may give some clues to the cause of the panic.

Linux is maintained and developed by volunteers, so the first advice for reporting problems and bugs is to be polite. Chances are, someone will take personal interest in this bug and you will have a fix or a workaround in record time, but you are also far less likely to get a timely response if you take your frustrations out on the developers. Unlike other proprietary systems, when dealing with the Linux community, you are not dealing with underpaid droogs, you are dealing with the masters themselves, people who take personal ownership and pride in their work. Show some respect and they will more than repay your kindness.

Your first line of support should always be to check to see whether this bug is known. If you have access to a Web browser, look into the kernel-developer's archive at `http://www.tux.org/lkml/`. If you have IRC access, you can ask directly on one of the `#linux` or `#linuxOS` channels on efnet or the undernet.

If you think you have found a new bug in the kernel, the kernel development community is more than interested—providing you can supply enough information to lead to a fix. If you can isolate the module where the oops occurred, you can locate the author of that module either in the `linux/Documentation/MAINTAINERS` file or in the source code of the module itself. You can also post your report to the `linux-kernel` mailing list.

When reporting a suspected bug, you should specify which kernel you are using and outline your hardware setup (such as RAM and CPU) and the situation where the problem occurred. If there is a kernel panic message, copy the message *exactly as displayed on your screen*.

Building and installing a kernel is probably one of the most important tasks you will do on your system. There's a lot of information in this section to learn. Do not let that discourage you from this aspect of Linux. Learning about the kernel and your hardware is important, and fun too.

Now that you know about the kernel, it's time to move on to how and when the kernel loads.

`lilo`

Before the kernel is even loaded into memory, another program is run that's known as a *boot loader*. Boot loaders have exactly one purpose: to load and boot an OS kernel. All operating systems have a boot loader; Linux's is just more powerful and less user friendly. Together, these two aspects can make `lilo` (the Linux Loader) a difficult thing to master for beginners.

First, a little introduction to the boot loading process. When your system first begins, it knows relatively little about itself: what hardware is installed, what software, and so on. Even after your system BIOS has discovered all your drives, it knows nothing about the software contained in them. The convention that's developed over the years to handle this dilemma is as follows: Your BIOS loads the first segment of your first drive into memory and executes that directly, as if it were a program. This very first piece of your first hard drive is known as your system's Master Boot Record, or MBR.

The program that's contained in this segment of your hard drive is known as the boot loader; in Linux's case, this is where `lilo` lives. After the OS has been properly loaded, the boot loader ceases to exist. `lilo`, as opposed to many less-flexible boot loaders, allows runtime selection from a list of kernel images and secondary boot loaders. A *secondary boot loader* is one that `lilo` passes control onto to load a different OS, such as the Windows boot loader.

The following sections describe `lilo` in detail, including

- Using `lilo`
- Installing `lilo`
- Configuring `lilo`
- Running `lilo`

Using `lilo`

After you install your Debian system, the first thing you will notice on bootup is a somewhat odd greeting from `lilo`. The four letters `lilo` will appear on your screen, and your system will seem to hang for five seconds or so; this is `lilo` waiting for input. After its timeout expires, it moves on to load the default operating system. By default with Debian 2.1, this will be an image of Linux 2.0.36.

When `lilo` is waiting for input, you're being given a chance to load an operating system or kernel image other than the default. If you press Shift, you're presented with yet another prompt, from which you can type the name of the kernel or OS you want to boot. To get a list of your available options, press Tab. For example, on my machine, I've got three old kernel images that I never spent the two minutes to delete. At the `lilo` prompt, this is what I might see:

```
lilo boot: <hit tab>
2.1.131 2.0.36 2.2.0 2.2.10
```

After you're at the `lilo boot:` prompt, typing the name of the kernel you want to load causes `lilo` to boot that one instead of the default. Also, any kernel parameters that you want to pass can be appended here. For example, if I wanted to run Linux 2.0.36 for this boot and force it to recognize my second ethernet card, I could type something like `2.0.36 ether=5,0x300,eth0 ether=7,0x320,eth1`. Kernel image names and default parameters are set in the `lilo` configuration, so you most likely won't have to do anything like this except for testing purposes.

Tip

Whenever you install a new kernel image, it's a good idea to keep the old one installed and make either the `delay` or `timeout` option (each does something a bit different; one will apply) nonzero. These options set how long `lilo` waits before moving on to load the default kernel. If your default kernel is broken and you have `lilo` set up so it won't wait for input, you're stuck.

When you have a second kernel image and `lilo` waits for input, on the other hand, fixing your broken kernel is as easy as booting your backup kernel and fixing whatever is wrong with your default.

Configuring `lilo`

Everything `lilo` knows about the kernel images you have installed will be in `/etc/lilo.conf`. This file defines a number of kernel images and foreign operating systems to give the user the option of loading. `lilo` can also take a number of behavioral directives from this file.

There are two main aspects to configuring `lilo`: defining a kernel image and global options.

Defining a Kernel Image

The format for a kernel image entry in `/etc/lilo.conf` is as follows:

```
image = /boot/vmlinuz-2.2.10
label = 2.2.10
other scoped options
```

This specifies a kernel image to `lilo` named `2.2.10`, which is actually stored at `/boot/vmlinuz-2.2.10`. Specifying `2.2.10` at the `lilo` prompt boots this image.

The `lilo` configuration file is *scoped*—that is, options either apply to the whole file or a very specific segment of it. In the previous example, any options inserted under the `label` tag (denoted `other scoped options` in the listing) apply to this one kernel image and no other.

For example, if I had a 2.0.34 kernel installed on my system that was meant to use an entirely different `root` filesystem than the rest of those that were available, and I wanted to force it to recognize my 128MB of RAM, I might append some kernel parameters to its invocation:

```
image = /boot/vmlinuz-2.0.34
label = 2.0.34
append="mem=128M"
root=/dev/hdc3
```

In a kernel image entry such as this, the kernel parameter `mem=128M` is passed, and whenever this kernel is booted it mounts `/dev/hdc3` as its `root` filesystem.

Options

However, `lilo.conf` also has *global options*—those that apply to every kernel image. Global options can be overridden within image definitions. See Listing 12.1 for details.

LISTING 12.1 An Example of `/etc/lilo.conf`

```
root = /dev/hda1
boot = /dev/hda
delay = 40
default = 2.2.10
read-only

image = /boot/vmlinuz-2.2.10
label = 2.2.10

other = /dev/hda3
label = windows

image = /boot/vmlinuz-2.0.34
label = 2.0.34
append = "mem=128M"
[CX]root = /dev/hdc3
```

In this example, `lilo.conf`, two images are specified: `2.2.10` and `2.0.34`. The first image listed is always the default, but we can explicitly specify the preferred image with the `default` global option. The `read-only` option is applied to every image, as is the `root` device (see the following section for details on specific options). However, the `2.0.34` image overrides the global `root` device setting with `/dev/hdc3`. You'll also see something new in this listing: a foreign operating system. The third option entry in this `lilo.conf` suggests that the user should be able to boot the operating system on `/dev/hda3` by specifying the keyword `windows` at the `lilo` prompt.

Commonly Used `lilo` flags

A number of options *must* be specified before `lilo` will work. First, `lilo` needs to know where to install itself. Second, it needs to know where at least one kernel image or foreign operating system is. Each kernel image, in turn, must have a `root` device associated with it (unless it's already set—but that's a more advanced issue). These options are as follows in `lilo.conf`:

- `boot = /dev/hda` (installs the master boot record on `/dev/hda`)
- `root = /dev/hda2` (sets the `root` filesystem; can be scoped or global)
- `image = /boot/vmlinuz` (already covered, specifies a kernel image)
- `other = /dev/hda3` (tells `lilo` that you want to be able to boot the OS on `/dev/hda3`, be it Windows or any other)

Each kernel image or `other` operating system must specify a label (covered in more depth earlier), which makes `lilo` associate a name with this image. In turn, typing a label into the `lilo` prompt loads the associated kernel or alien operating system.

As pointed out earlier, it's always a good idea to have a delay before `lilo` boots the default kernel. This is set with the `delay =` option, which takes a number in tenths of a second. Specifying `delay = 50`, for example, causes `lilo` to wait 5 seconds before it loads the default kernel.

The `boot` option tells `lilo` where to install itself. Generally, this will be the Master Boot Record (the Master Boot Record of `/dev/hda5` is stored at the beginning of `/dev/hda`, as an example) of the first drive on your system. If you're using a more advanced boot manager, such as System Commander, however, you should install `lilo` to the superblock of your `root` partition and let your other boot manager control the Master Boot Record.

`lilo` and Drive Access via the BIOS

`lilo` can load only images (and other OSs) that exist on the first 1024 cylinders of your hard drive. If your drive has more cylinders than this, turn on LBA in your BIOS. If the drive still has more than 1024 cylinders, you have to make sure that your entire `root` partition lives beneath this limit.

If it's already too late, don't despair: if you have any partition (of any filesystem type) contained beneath the first 1024 cylinders, you can use this to hold your kernel images. If you don't have even this option, you can always boot from a floppy.

rdev and Kernel root Devices

Every kernel image keeps its default `root` device stored internally. If you do not specify a `root` device for any given image to `lilo`, the default is used. However, depending on this aspect of kernel images is generally deprecated, because default behavior may change without warning in the future.

To see a Linux kernel's default `root` device, execute

```
$ rdev vmlinuz
```

Of course, you replace *`vmlinuz`* with the filename where your kernel image is stored. The image specified, however, can also be a block device; in this case, it's assumed that the superblock of the specified device contains a kernel image, and this is operated upon. This command will show you the block device that the specified `linux` image will mount as `root` by default. Adding a block device after the kernel image will set your image's default `root` device to whatever you specify. For example

```
rdev /dev/fd0 /dev/hda2
```

forces the kernel stored at the superblock of the floppy in `/dev/fd0` (made with `zlilo` or `dd` perhaps?) to mount `/dev/hda2` as its `root` filesystem.

Other utilities exist for setting specific parameters directly in the kernel. For more information, see `rdev(8)`. This manual page describes how to set the following within the kernel:

- root device
- Swap device
- RAM size (useful for systems that use insanely huge amounts of memory that aren't autoprobed)
- Video mode (useful if Linux insists on initializing your video card to an unworkable state)
- Flags used when mounting the root filesystem

You *can* omit the `root` device (and these other bits of information) from `lilo.conf` and just depend on the default set in your kernel image. However, when you collect more than two kernel images, this can become a confusing practice. Don't shoot yourself in the foot; keep important information together in one place.

A myriad of other options exists for `lilo`, but covering them all here would be wasted space. Almost nobody will ever make use of more than what I've outlined here. Most of the `lilo` configuration is to specify the disk geometry of hard disks. With modern BIOS technology, this is not needed. If `lilo` can't install or doesn't work for some reason, see

`/usr/doc/lilo/Manual.txt.gz`, `lilo.conf(5)`, and `lilo(8)` for a more thorough listing of directives.

Running `lilo`

To make your changes to `/etc/lilo.conf` take effect, you must execute `lilo` as `root`. In turn, it will dump a list of kernels that were successfully set up. Here is what that output would look like for the `lilo.conf` in Listing 12.1:

```
# lilo
Added 2.2.10 *
Added windows
Added 2.0.34
```

> **Note**
>
> `lilo` must be run as `root`, because it needs direct access to important block devices.

If any serious-sounding errors occur at this point, *do not reboot.* Make sure you have a working Linux boot floppy; if you don't, make one by using `dd` to copy a kernel image to a floppy, as follows:

```
dd if=vmlinuz of=/dev/fd0 bs=512
```

`lilo` is a powerful boot loader. Like many other aspects of Linux, `lilo` is completely customizable. Additionally, `lilo` can be configured to boot operating systems other than Linux.

Now that you know about `lilo`, it's time to move on to the actual Linux startup process.

`init` and Software Startup

Programs available under Linux are generally extremely small and task-oriented. (For example, `cat` displays things on the screen, `wc` does a word count, and `grep` searches for words.) This means, specifically, that tools are highly specialized to eliminate needless waste. However, this mentality inherently exchanges ease-of-use for power and speed. For example, under Debian, one program exists to construct the filesystem and one to prepare the swap space. One utility exists to open and dump the contents of a file, and one to search for specific data within.

Because programs under Linux are so highly specialized, simple tasks often involve stringing together long lists of commands. Starting up the system is no different in any of this; software for configuring the system at boot is highly specialized as well. For a good example, consider all the steps involved in starting a shell. First, one program is responsible for acquiring a virtual console and attaching to it. In turn, this program executes another that prints a login prompt and waits for input. When a username and password are received, yet another program is started to interpret commands, which is known as your shell.

Just about every part of system startup is this complicated, and for good reason. If any of these simpler programs were consolidated, the end result would be a bloated system with less flexibility. Because of this state of affairs, we need a capable piece of software to perform these rudimentary, repetitive tasks for us at each boot. This program is called `init`.

Run Levels

`init` has configurable software profiles, known as *run levels*. A run level can be thought of as a particular state of the system's software—what programs are running at any given time. You have a number of run levels that are configurable to your needs; each run level delimits an entirely different set of programs that should be running.

For example, suppose that on occasion you need to share files with your Windows system from your Linux system. The file sharing daemon, Samba, takes more memory than you might like if you rarely actually need this file server to be available. So, specify to `init` that Samba should be running in, for example, run level 2, but not any other. Perhaps you also want people to be able to use your computer as an FTP server, but only on occasion; you could configure FTP in a similar way as Samba for this purpose.

Often, starting these two daemons the way you need them to be involves quite a long command line or some scripting. Instead of specifying the whole command line each time you want either to be started, you could write one script for `init` that takes care of it. From here on out, `init` knows how to start and stop each one of these daemons.

Now suppose again that your computer often was used as an experimental server for a networked build daemon (a solution for sharing CPU cycles with other systems for compiling software). Something like this would take a great deal of CPU power and memory, so you want as little as possible running when your computer is being put to this use. You would then set up another run level (for example, 4) that shuts off everything, including X, and starts this piece of software.

The default run level is 3, in which anything that Debian considers important enough is started by default. Now, suppose your system needs to become a networked build server (as described earlier) for a few hours. Instead of shutting everything off and starting this experimental daemon by hand, you can now simply type

```
init 4
```

because you already configured run level 4 for use when you need a build server.

This is a powerful tool. Now your Linux computer can have every bit of capability you need it to, without having everything running 100 percent of the time (which would do nothing but slow the system down). By hand-tailoring run levels to specific purposes, you can easily jump back and forth between uses of your system.

Special Run Levels

Debian's `init` comes preconfigured for some very specific (and unchangeable) behavior in a few run levels. These all correspond to important tasks. Where possible, Debian conforms to established conventions. As such, these will be consistent with other distributions, for the most part.

Run Level 0

Run level 0 has a very simple task: shut down all programs and halt the computer. If you've got APM (Advanced Power Management) support compiled into your computer and you've got reasonably recent hardware, the system's power will automatically shut off.

Shutting Your Computer Down

Yes, you can just type `init 0` into a `root` shell and watch your system shut down. However, this command has a few aliases. The `shutdown` command halts the system, but can be scheduled; so, if you want your system to halt in exactly three hours, you can enter this command:

```
shutdown -h 3:00
```

or just this

```
halt
```

which is equivalent to this

```
shutdown -h now
```

Run Level 1

Run level 1 is reserved for single-user mode. In this run level, absolutely nothing is running except a single `root` shell. No filesystems are mounted except the `root` filesystem, which happens to be mounted read-only. This run level is generally useful for recovery purposes.

Run Level 3

Run level 3 is configurable and doesn't have any reserved use, but it's the run level Debian uses as default. This is the run level that's started when you boot your Debian system.

Run Level 6

Run level 6 is very similar to run level 0, but instead of halting the system, run level 6 reboots it. This can also be invoked with the `shutdown` command, either this

```
shutdown -r time
```

or this

```
reboot
```

which is equivalent to the following

```
shutdown -r now
```

Run Levels 2, 4, and 5

Debian has no specific policy on the configuration of run levels 2, 4, and 5. They are mostly open for your customization.

`init`'s Configuration File, `/etc/inittab`

Apart from all the scripts that `init` uses, it has one solitary configuration file that controls its most basic behavior. `inittab` specifies the first script that should be run *before* `init` goes into any run level, and what run level will be started after this script is complete. It then specifies what commands should be run to start the respective run levels.

The major function `inittab` has is to describe what programs should be started for bootup and normal operation and under what run levels. Every run level can be defined entirely from `/etc/inittab`, but Debian has a much more robust scheme called `sysvinit`, which is recognized as one of `init`'s most powerful applications.

The way Debian has organized `inittab` moves the definition of run levels, for the most part, out of `inittab` and into a hierarchy of scripts. The only programs that are started directly from `inittab` are `gettys`, which are used to start login prompts on virtual terminal devices. This is done only because they require special handling that would be much harder to accomplish outside of `inittab`.

LISTING 12.2 An Example of `/etc/inittab`

```
# /etc/inittab: init(8) configuration.
# $Id: inittab,v 1.8 1998/05/10 10:37:50 miquels Exp $

# The default run level.
id:2:initdefault:

# Boot-time system configuration/initialization script.
# This is run first except when booting in emergency (-b) mode.
```

2 = default

continues

LISTING 12.2 continued

```
si::sysinit:/etc/init.d/rcS

# What to do in single-user mode.
~~:S:wait:/sbin/sulogin

# /etc/init.d executes the S and K scripts upon change
# of run level.
#
# Run level 0 is halt.
# Run level 1 is single-user.
# Run levels 2-5 are multi-user.
# Run level 6 is reboot.

l0:0:wait:/etc/init.d/rc 0
l1:1:wait:/etc/init.d/rc 1
l2:2:wait:/etc/init.d/rc 2
l3:3:wait:/etc/init.d/rc 3
l4:4:wait:/etc/init.d/rc 4
l5:5:wait:/etc/init.d/rc 5
l6:6:wait:/etc/init.d/rc 6
# Normally not reached, but fallthrough in case of emergency.
z6:6:respawn:/sbin/sulogin

# What to do when CTRL-ALT-DEL is pressed.
ca:12345:ctrlaltdel:/sbin/shutdown -t1 -a -r now

# Action on special keypress (ALT-UpArrow).
kb::kbrequest:/bin/echo "Keyboard Request—edit /etc/inittab to let this work."

# What to do when the power fails/returns.
pf::powerwait:/etc/init.d/powerfail start
pn::powerfailnow:/etc/init.d/powerfail now
po::powerokwait:/etc/init.d/powerfail stop

# /sbin/getty invocations for the runlevels.
#
# The "id" field MUST be the same as the last
# characters of the device (after "tty").
#
# Format:
#  <id>:<runlevels>:<action>:<process>
1:2345:respawn:/sbin/getty 38400 tty1
2:23:respawn:/sbin/getty 38400 tty2
3:23:respawn:/sbin/getty 38400 tty3
4:23:respawn:/sbin/getty 38400 tty4
5:23:respawn:/sbin/getty 38400 tty5
6:23:respawn:/sbin/getty 38400 tty6

# Example how to put a getty on a serial line (for a terminal)
#
#T0:23:respawn:/sbin/getty -L ttyS0 9600 vt100
```

```
#T1:23:respawn:/sbin/getty -L ttyS1 9600 vt100

# Example how to put a getty on a modem line.
#
#T3:23:respawn:/sbin/mgetty -x0 -s 57600 ttyS3
```

The Format of /etc/inittab

Take a good look at Listing 12.2. Your system's inittab will look (at least somewhat) like this. This file has one basic type of directive, which specifies a command line, some action to be taken with it, and under what run levels it should be active. The format of these lines is basically as follows:

```
id:runlevels:action:command
```

where id is some arbitrary name (this doesn't really matter), runlevels is a string of numbers (standing for run levels), action describes when the command should be executed, and command specifies the actual command line to execute.

For example, take one of the lines that starts a getty:

```
1:2345:respawn:/sbin/getty 38400 tty1
```

Basically, this tells init that it should run the command /sbin/getty 38400 tty1 (see getty(8) for more details on exactly what this does) after boot in run levels 2–5. The action flag used here is respawn, which causes the command to be rerun whenever it exits (in this case, when a user types exit at a shell).

As you can see in Listing 12.2, there are six gettys active in run levels 2 and 3, but only one in 4 and 5. Suppose you want to have three shells available on virtual consoles during run level 4. You add the number 4 to the run levels field in the lines with ID 2 and 3. That is, you replace these two lines:

```
2:23:respawn:/sbin/getty 38400 tty2
3:23:respawn:/sbin/getty 38400 tty3
```

with these:

```
2:234:respawn:/sbin/getty 38400 tty2
3:234:respawn:/sbin/getty 38400 tty3
```

You can enact changes to inittab only by either rebooting or executing the following command:

```
telinit q
```

telinit

which instructs init to reload its configuration. For more information on telinit, read telinit(8).

12 CUSTOMIZING THE BOOTUP PROCEDURE

Action Flags

Many of the other lines in `/etc/inittab` look somewhat more complicated. Before we can go into more detail, we need to outline exactly what the other action flags mean. The action flags are as follows:

- `respawn` Start the command and monitor its execution. When the process exits, execute the command again. (Obvious use: login prompts on virtual terminal devices.)
- `wait` The process will be started when any of the specified run levels are entered, and `init` will pause until its execution finishes. This is used in Debian's setup for run level–specific software startup.
- `once` The process will be started once when any of the specified run levels are entered. I used to use this to dump `/var/spool/messages` to a virtual console (all users were trusted).
- `boot` The command will be run during system boot. Run levels are ignored in this type of directive.
- `bootwait` This command will be run during system boot, and `init` will wait for it to exit before moving on.
- `off` Disables a command in all run levels (that is, eliminates a directive without deleting it).
- `initdefault` This type of entry specifies what run level should be entered at system boot. The `runlevels` field is ignored.
- `powerwait` This type of directive gives a command to be executed in case of a power shortage. `init` pauses until this process is complete.
- `powerfail` This is similar to `powerwait`, but `init` doesn't wait for the process' completion.
- `powerokwait` This is executed when the power is brought back up. `init` pauses until the process completes.
- `powerfailnow` This is executed when a laptop's battery or an external UPS' battery is running low.
- `ctrlaltdel` This specifies what command to run when `init` catches `ctrl+alt+del`.
- `kbdrequest` This maps a special action onto a specific keypress. In Debian's case, this is `alt+UpArrow`.

Now you can see what happens with some of those more exotic lines. Debian's `init` setup defaults to rebooting on Ctrl+Alt+Del, shutting down when there is any kind of trouble with the power and starting some `gettys` in all multiuser run levels (multiuser is run levels 2–5).

However, it may be complicated how Debian manages to start all of its software with such a minimal `inittab`. Anyway, doesn't the format of this file seem somewhat of a cutoff to creating complicated profiles of software configurations?

My personal answer is yes. Managing every aspect of run levels from `inittab` is definitely possible, but not something anybody would want to do. The task would simply be huge. This is why we have the following lines in `/etc/inittab`:

```
l0:0:wait:/etc/init.d/rc 0
l1:1:wait:/etc/init.d/rc 1
l2:2:wait:/etc/init.d/rc 2
l3:3:wait:/etc/init.d/rc 3
l4:4:wait:/etc/init.d/rc 4
l5:5:wait:/etc/init.d/rc 5
l6:6:wait:/etc/init.d/rc 6
```

These are the lines that actually determine how your system acts in the various run levels. It might not seem obvious *how* they accomplish this, but let's take a look at their meanings. First, each is given a symbolic ID `lX`, where `l` stands for `level` and `X` is some number; hence `l6` stands for level 6. Second, each one is active in exactly one run level, which corresponds to the number in its symbolic ID. At the execution of each, `init` pauses until its process dies. Finally, each calls a script `/etc/init.d/rc X`, where `X` is the number of the current run level.

The short answer to the obvious question (so what?) is that this script (`/etc/init.d/rc`) is a gateway into a different, more elegant type of run level management. By invoking `init` with a number argument (standing for the run level), you in effect invoke `/etc/init.d/rc` with the same argument, giving it control of starting up all the software configured to run in that run level.

The `rc` Symlink Tree

Basic to Debian's `init` setup is the directory `/etc/init.d`. This directory contains scripts that start and stop important pieces of software. For simplicity, it was decreed that each one of these scripts should be able to handle the exact same set of arguments—exactly one, which is any of `start` or `stop`. Maintainers of individual packages can opt to add extra functionality to these scripts for user convenience, but `init` will not make use of them.

So, for example, you could call the following:

```
# /etc/init.d/apache start
```

to start Apache, and this

```
# /etc/init.d/apache stop
```

to shut it down.

First, this is extremely useful as a user tool, because it gives you the ability to start and shut down complicated programs that come with Debian, without being forced to read extensive documentation beforehand. So, before trying to figure out how to start a program, check in `/etc/init.d` to see whether there's already a script to do it for you.

Next, these are the mechanism by which you tune a run level to your needs, and by which `/etc/init.d/rc` is able to bring the system to the state you requested in a run level. In every one of the directories, `/etc/rcx.d` (of which there is one for every multiuser run level) is a group of symlinks pointing back to scripts in `/etc/init.d`. When entering a run level, `rc` iterates over the scripts in the run level's directory in logical order. First, every file prefixed with a `K` is executed with the parameter `stop` (in numerical and alphabetical order); then, each script prefixed with an `S` is executed with the parameter `start` (in the same order).

Customizing a Run Level

Now that you know how run levels work, it's time to construct one for yourself. Customizing a run level allows you to fine-tune the startup process, giving you more control over what starts and what does not and when.

As a test bed for this experiment, you use run level 5 and the directory `rc` associates with it, `/etc/rc5.d`. First, take a good look at the contents of that directory. Find out what each symlink in there does; view the file and decide what package it came from. Remember that in this run level, everything prefixed with a `K` will be turned off when this run level starts, and everything with an `S` will be started.

The established naming conventions in Debian have become such that a normal `rc` symlink will have a name of the form `^(S¦K)\d{2}.*` (remember your regular expressions?). The 2-digit number in that name doesn't really signify anything, but it gives you a way to order executions where necessary. For example, a link named `S02abcd` would be executed before `S19efgh`.

Take a good look at the contents of `/etc/rc5.d`. Find any `S` scripts that start programs you have no use for—they are most likely wasting your memory. To resolve this situation, remove them. Next, look for any scripts in `/etc/init.d/` that you *want* to run but that aren't included. For these, execute something similar to the following:

```
ln -s /etc/init.d/samba /etc/rc5.d/S20samba
```

as an example, if you wanted to start Samba (the Windows file server) in run level 5.

Additional Reading

Some other resources you might want to consider for further reading are

`http://www.vaxxine.com/pegasoft/portal/kernel_index.html`

```
http://www.tux.org/
http://www.linuxhq.com/
lilo(8)
lilo.conf(5)
/usr/doc/lilo/Manual.txt.gz
inittab(5)
init(8)
telinit(8)
/usr/doc/sysvinit/README.runlevels.gz
/usr/doc/sysvinit/examples/*
```


Summary

Linux is the kernel, and the kernel is Linux. Linus Torvalds writes that he never expected Linux would become the size of emacs, only he is quick to point out that "at least Linux has the excuse that it needs to be." The development of this beast over the past eight years has been meteoric and has probably left some broken hearts along the way, but the result of this experiment in community cooperation now stands as a major contender in the operating systems marketplace. Linux 2.2 has proven to be a worthy successor to 2.0 and the rollercoaster ride of 2.1 has been put to bed. In its place has risen a new, grander rollercoaster: Linux 2.3.

As with the Linux and X11 installation, configuring an optimal kernel does require planning, preparation, and some knowledge of the target machine to ensure an exact fit. It is not unreasonable to expect some day that the Linux kernel will be self-configuring (IRIX has done this for years). But for the forseeable future, although it is nowhere as frightening as it was even a year ago, kernel configuration still demands a certain attention and a small measure of sysadmin savvy.

If you have made it this far, you now know what the Linux kernel is and how it works. You know how to obtain, install, and patch kernel sources. You know how to interpret and select from kernel version numbers and how to prepare for, select, and execute a new kernel configuration. You know how to recognize and recover from kernel configuration problems. You know how to install kernels with `lilo`, Linux's boot loader, and how to configure `lilo` for flexibility, especially multiple kernels and operating systems.

Additionally, you know how to customize the startup of your system's software after the kernel boots by way of `init`. You also know how to configure a system run level, how to change run level-specific daemons such as `getty`, and how to change what runs on which virtual terminal.

Mostly, I hope you have learned how hand-tuning your system's configuration is not a rite of passage or a task to be feared. Kernel building is only a matter of some common sense, care, and attention and is yet another of the reasons you chose to run Linux in the first place. Modifying your `lilo` configuration is a matter of a few simple keywords in a configuration file. Finally, customizing `init` and its system run levels takes a little knowledge of scripting, but it's not an advanced task by any stretch of the imagination.

CHAPTER

System Logs and Accounting

by Mario Camou

In This Chapter

Log files are an important part of any system. They enable you to monitor how the system is working, and to detect whether anything anomalous is going on. They also enable you to glean statistics, such as your system's busiest time or the number of accesses per user. It is important to know how the Linux logging system works and how to configure it for your site.

Make a habit of looking at the contents of your log files periodically. This will give you a feeling for the number and kind of messages that appear when the system is functioning correctly; then when something goes wrong, you'll easily detect log entries that are symptomatic of an anomalous behavior. How often should you check your log files? On a heavily loaded server, you might want to check them once or even twice a day. On your personal workstation, once a week is probably more than enough.

Accounting is the process by which the system keeps track of the utilization of a particular resource. For example, *process accounting* keeps a record of how much CPU time and memory has been used by a particular process, and *network accounting* keeps track of bandwidth use. It is very useful, especially in production settings, where it is important to know who has used what resources (such as in chargeback environments) or to keep track of runaway processes so system performance isn't impacted.

In this chapter we will first examine how the two log daemons, `syslogd` and `klogd`, handle all logging activities in a Linux system and how to manage the log files they create. Then we will take a look at a wide variety of commands to monitor disk usage, network activity, process load, and user logins.

The System Logs

/var/log

Linux can log practically everything that happens in the system. Log files are usually found in the `/var/log` directory and are usually readable only by `root`, although you can configure the system and many programs to store their logs somewhere else and, in many cases, even send them to some other host on your network.

The Linux logging facility is based on two daemons: `syslogd` and `klogd`, which are contained in the `sysklogd` package. `syslogd`, the *sys*tem *log* daemon, is the workhorse of the logging system, receiving messages from different processes and dispatching them according to a configuration file. `klogd`, the *k*ernel *log* daemon, takes care of grabbing the messages generated by the kernel and forwarding them to `syslogd`.

The `syslog` Daemon

Most logging in a UNIX system is done by means of `syslogd`. This daemon is usually started on boot in every UNIX host, listening for logging requests from programs and other hosts and sending them to different destinations according to their source and severity. Some programs have the option of using their own log files or using `syslogd`. In those, it is usually a better option to use `syslogd`, because it assures a uniform interface to configure logging. Also, every message logged by `syslogd` is guaranteed to contain at least a time stamp, the name of the host that originated it, and usually the program name (although this last one depends on the logging program).

Let's take a look at how the `syslogd` daemon receives logging messages from other programs and how you can customize its behavior for each kind of message by modifying the `/etc/syslog.conf` file.

`syslogd` is extremely versatile. It can be configured to centralize logging for an entire network to a single host (or not), and to handle log messages in a variety of ways. For example, it can send some messages to the console, others to a file, still others to the terminals of particular users when they are logged on, and some to all of these destinations. This configuration is performed by editing the `/etc/syslog.conf` file, which is covered in its own section later in this chapter.

Using `syslogd`

`syslogd` is started automatically at system startup by the `/etc/init.d/sysklogd` script. It is linked to the `/etc/rc?.d` directories as `S10sysklogd`, so it starts very early in the boot process. For more information on the boot process and the `/etc/init.d` and `/etc/rc?.d` directories, see Chapter 12, "Customizing the Bootup Procedure." `syslogd` can take several options, which are listed in Table 13.1. If you want to use any of these options, you should edit `/etc/init.d/sysklogd` and add them to the line where `syslogd` is executed.

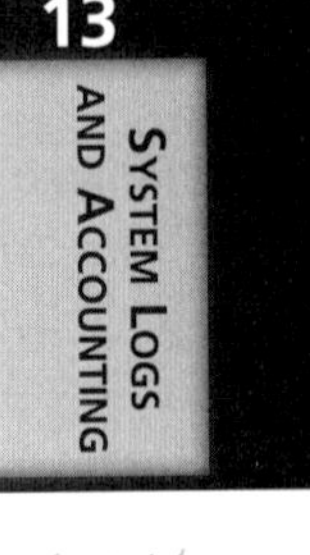

TABLE 13.1 `syslogd` Options

Option	*Meaning*
`-d`	Turns on debug mode. This is used only when debugging the `syslogd` program itself.
`-f config-file`	Uses a different configuration file than `/etc/syslog.conf`.
`-h`	By default, syslogd does not forward any messages it receives from other hosts. This switch specifies that `syslogd` should forward any messages it receives, according to the forwarding hosts defined in the configuration file.
`-l hostlist`	Any hosts specified in *`hostlist`* (separated by colons :) will be logged using just their simple hostname, and not their fully qualified domain names.
`-m interval`	Specifies the interval in seconds between mark messages. Mark messages are sent periodically by `syslogd` to the `mark` facility. The default is 20 seconds.
`-n`	Usually, `syslogd` sends itself to the background when started (like many other daemons). This option specifies that `syslogd` should stay in the foreground. This is very important in some cases, such as when starting `syslogd`

continues

TABLE 13.1 continued

Option	*Meaning*
	directly from `/etc/inittab`. For more information on `/etc/inittab`, see Chapter 12).
`-p socket`	Normally, `syslogd` listens to the `/dev/log` UNIX domain socket for log messages from local processes. This option changes the UNIX domain socket used.
`-r`	By default, `syslogd` doesn't listen to the network for logging messages. With this flag, `syslogd` listens on the socket listed as syslog in /etc/services, usually UDP port 514 (for more information about network protocols, see Chapter 16, "TCP/IP Networking Essentials").
`-s domainlist`	Any domains included in *`domainlist`* (separated by semicolons ;) is stripped off the hostnames before logging. The first match is used, so if a message comes from server.east.company.com and you specify `-s company.com:east.company.com`, the first match is taken and the host is logged as server.east. In this case, you should invert the domain names and use `-s east.company.com:company.com`.
`-v`	Prints the `syslogd` version and exits immediately.

`syslogd` responds to several signals, which can be used to communicate with a running `syslogd`. The process ID of the currently running `syslogd` is found in the `/var/run/syslogd.pid` file. If you need to send a signal to a running `syslogd`, you can do a `kill -`*`SIGNAL`* `` `cat /var/run/syslogd.pid` ``. Table 13.2 lists the signals that can be sent to `syslogd`.

TABLE 13.2 syslogd Signals

Signal	*Action*
`SIGHUP`	Reinitializes `syslogd`. `syslogd` closes all open files, reopens them, rereads its configuration file, and restarts the `syslog` system.
`SIGTERM`,	`syslogd` dies.
`SIGINT and SIGQUIT`	`syslogd` dies unless debugging is enabled.
`SIGUSR1`	Switches debugging on/off, but only if `syslogd` was started with the `-d` option.

The `/etc/syslog.conf` File

`syslogd` is configured through the `/etc/syslog.conf` file. Each line in `/etc/syslog.conf` has two parts: the *selector* and the *action*, separated by whitespace.

The selector indicates which messages to apply the action to, and the action specifies what to do to those messages. Anything from a hash (#) to the end of the line is a comment.

Selectors

Messages are selected by two parameters. The first of these is the *facility*. It indicates the program or service from which the message comes, although because facility names are limited, some programs have to use facility names that don't reflect their true names. The following facility names are available:

```
auth          user
auth-priv     uucp
cron          local0
daemon        local1
kern          local2
lpr           local3
mail          local4
mark          local5
news          local6
security      local7
syslog
```

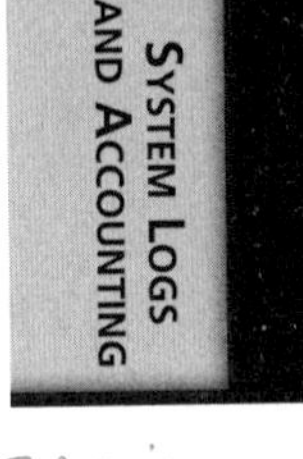

Some of these have special meanings. The `security` facility is an obsolete alias for `auth`, and `mark` is an internal facility that sends messages to `syslog` every 20 minutes. `local0` through `local7` are left open for any functionality defined locally.

The second parameter used to select messages is the *priority*. This is an indication of the severity of the message. In increasing order, the priorities are

```
debug         error
info          crit
notice        alert
warning       emerg
warn          panic
err
```

`error`, `warn`, and `panic` are obsolete aliases for `err`, `warning`, and `emerg`, respectively, and should not be used.

A selector has the form `facility.priority`. This form matches all messages of the selected priority and all higher ones; so, for example, `mail.info` matches all mail messages except debug. If you want to match a specific priority only, you can use an equal sign (=). Hence, mail.=info will match only mail messages of the info priority.

There are other special characters. An asterisk (*) means "everything," so mail.* matches all mail messages (and is equivalent to mail.debug), and *.crit matches all messages with priority crit and above.

An exclamation point (!) negates a condition, so mail.!info is equivalent to mail.=debug, and mail.info is equivalent to mail.!=debug.

You can combine several facilities in a single selector with a comma; for example, mail,news.crit matches all messages with crit-or-higher priority for the mail and news services. You can also combine several selectors with a semicolon. In this case, the special priority none can be used to specify no messages from a given service. For example, *.crit;mail.none matches all messages at crit level or above except those from the mail facility.

Actions

The action field specifies what to do with messages matched by a particular selector. The first character of the action specifies the action type.

An action that begins with a slash (/) specifies a filename to which messages will be appended (for example, /var/log/messages). If the file is a tty, special tty handling is used. If you want to send messages to the console, use /dev/console.

A dash followed by a slash (-/) also specifies a filename, but specifies that the file will not be flushed to disk after every write. This makes syslog more efficient, but carries the risk of losing messages if the system crashes. It should not be used for any critical logs—for example, -/var/log/ppp.log.

An at sign (@) specifies the name of a host to which log messages should be sent—for example, @logger.company.com.

A pipe sign (¦) specifies the name of a named pipe (fifo) to which messages will be written—for example, ¦/dev/xconsole. The pipe must have been created with the mkfifo command before starting syslogd.

Any alphanumeric character specifies the beginning of a list of users separated by commas. The message will be written to the terminals of those users if they are logged on—for example, mario,root,admin.

An asterisk (*) specifies that the message will be written to the terminals of all logged-on users.

Listing 13.1 shows the default /etc/syslog.conf file provided with Debian.

LISTING 13.1 The /etc/syslog.conf File

```
#  /etc/syslog.conf      Configuration file for syslogd.
#
#                        For more information, see syslog.conf(5)
#                        manpage.

#
# First some standard logfiles.  Log by facility.
#

auth,authpriv.*                 /var/log/auth.log
*.*;auth,authpriv.none          -/var/log/syslog
#cron.*                         /var/log/cron.log
daemon.*                        -/var/log/daemon.log
kern.*                          -/var/log/kern.log
lpr.*                           -/var/log/lpr.log
mail.*                          /var/log/mail.log
user.*                          -/var/log/user.log
uucp.*                          -/var/log/uucp.log

#
# Logging for the mail system. Split it up so that
# it is easy to write scripts to parse these files.
#
mail.info                       -/var/log/mail.info
mail.warn                       -/var/log/mail.warn
mail.err                        /var/log/mail.err

# Logging for INN news system
#
news.crit                       /var/log/news/news.crit
news.err                        /var/log/news/news.err
news.notice                     -/var/log/news/news.notice

#
# Some `catch-all' logfiles.
#
*.=debug;\
        auth,authpriv.none;\
        news.none;mail.none     -/var/log/debug
*.=info;*.=notice;*.=warn;\
        auth,authpriv.none;\
        cron,daemon.none;\
        mail,news.none          -/var/log/messages

#
# Emergencies are sent to everybody logged in.
#
*.emerg                         *

#
```

continues

13 SYSTEM LOGS AND ACCOUNTING

LISTING 13.1 continued

```
# I like to have messages displayed on the console, but only on a
# virtual console I usually leave idle.
#
#daemon,mail.*;\
#        news.=crit;news.=err;news.=notice;\
#        *.=debug;*.=info;\
#        *.=notice;*.=warn       /dev/tty8

# The named pipe /dev/xconsole is for the `xconsole' utility.  To use it,
# you must invoke `xconsole' with the `-file' option:
#
#    $ xconsole -file /dev/xconsole [...]
#
# NOTE: adjust the list below, or you'll go crazy if you have a
#       reasonably busy site..
#
daemon.*;mail.*;\
        news.crit;news.err;news.notice;\
        *.=debug;*.=info;\
        *.=notice;*.=warn       |/dev/xconsole

local2.*                -/var/log/ppp.log
```

If you want to have a single logging host on your network, you could change the `syslog.conf` file in every other host to something like the following:

```
# Send all logs to logger
*.*    @logger
```

If you do this, you have to edit the `/etc/init.d/sysklogd` on host file on host `logger`, add the `-r` switch to the line where `syslogd` is started, and run `/etc/init.d/sysklogd restart` (or reboot `logger`). Otherwise, the `syslogd` on `logger` won't listen to network messages.

The `klogd` Daemon

In Linux, kernel messages traditionally go to the console. However, in many cases this is not desirable. For example, an unattended server running in a remote location might send information regarding a system crash to the console, where nobody would read it. Even if an operator is available, the message might scroll off the screen, or might be erased if the server reboots.

The `klogd` daemon was created to solve this problem. `klogd` was designed to intercept all kernel messages and forward them to `syslogd`, which can perform more complex operations on those (and even display them in the system console, if that is what is desired).

If the `/proc` filesystem is mounted, the kernel makes its messages available on the `/proc/kmsg` virtual file. `klogd` reads messages from this file if it exists. If `/proc` isn't mounted, `klogd` reads messages using system calls. For more information on the `/proc` filesystem, see Chapter 15, "Advanced System Administration."

`klogd` logs messages with facility `kern`. The priority is given by the kernel itself and converted by `klogd` to the appropriate `syslogd` priority. The kernel priorities are listed in the `/usr/include/linux/kernel.h` file. Here is the relevant portion of this file, including the meanings of each message level:

```
#define KERN_EMERG      "<0>"   /* system is unusable               */
#define KERN_ALERT      "<1>"   /* action must be taken immediately */
#define KERN_CRIT       "<2>"   /* critical conditions              */
#define KERN_ERR        "<3>"   /* error conditions                 */
#define KERN_WARNING    "<4>"   /* warning conditions               */
#define KERN_NOTICE     "<5>"   /* normal but significant condition */
#define KERN_INFO       "<6>"   /* informational                    */
#define KERN_DEBUG      "<7>"   /* debug-level messages             */
```

Normally, you will want to log all messages about conditions that might have some impact on your systems behavior, namely those with priority `notice` or higher, and perhaps even `info`. Turning on all logging on your site for a few days to different files gives you a feeling of what messages are useful (of course, you shouldn't get any messages above `notice` priority!). To do this, you can add the following lines to `/etc/syslog.conf`:

```
kern.=debug     /var/log/kernel.debug
kern.=info      /var/log/kernel.info
kern.=notice    /var/log/kernel.notice
kern.=warning   /var/log/kernel.warning
kern.=err       /var/log/kernel.err
kern.=crit      /var/log/kernel.crit
kern.=emerg     /var/log/kernel.emerg
```

Log Administration and Maintenance

If left unchecked, the system logs grow until they fill the disk partition assigned to them. That is why it is a good idea to assign a separate disk partition to `/var` in any production server. If you don't do that, and the logs get too large, they fill the `root` partition and make the server practically unusable. For more information on partitioning disks, see Chapter 11, "Administration Essentials."

To prevent log files from growing out of control, Debian includes the `savelog` utility. The function of `savelog` is to manage log rotation. That is, it handles the task of periodically moving log files out of the way and keeping track of a configurable number of historical log files. Each time `savelog` runs, it renames the current *`logfile`* to *`logfile.0`*. If there is a *`logfile.0`*, it renames it to *`logfile.1`*, and so on. When the number of historical logs reaches a configurable number, the oldest file is deleted, so you can control how much history to keep for each log file. `savelog` can also optionally compress the historical log files so they take up less disk space. `logfile.0` is never compressed, because the program might still be writing to it while the rotation is taking place.

`savelog` is usually run periodically by `anacron` (for more information on `anacron`, see Chapter 11). It is run once for each rotated log file, so each logging application usually has its own script in `/etc/cron.daily` or `/etc/cron.weekly`. You may want to edit these files if you want to do something before or after rotating logs (such as generating statistics). `savelog` accepts as parameters the names of the files to rotate. It also accepts several switches, which are detailed in Table 13.3.

TABLE 13.3 `savelog` Switches

Switch	*Action*
`-m mode`	The mode of the historic files is changed to `mode` (in octal).
`-u user`	The owner of the historic files is changed to `user`.
`-g group`	The group of the historic files is changed to `group`.
`-c cycle`	cycle historic files are kept, with suffixes `.0` to `.(cycle-1)`.
`-t`	Creates an empty log file after rotating (the default is not to create it).
`-l`	Does not compress historic files (the default is to compress them).
`-p`	Preserves the mode, owner, and group of the log file.

There is one possible problem with `savelog`. The process that writes to the log file must close and reopen it after doing the rotation, or it will continue to write to `logfile.0`. If this is the case when `savelog` is run the next time, `logfile.0` will be renamed to `logfile.1`, which will then be compressed. If that happens, data will probably be lost. To make sure this doesn't happen, be sure to make the program close and reopen its log files just after running `savelog`. Many system daemons do that when sent the `SIGHUP` signal; others must be stopped and restarted. Check the daemon's documentation to see whether this is necessary, and how to do it.

`Syslogd` and `klogd` let us manage how logging messages, generated by processes and the Linux kernel, are written to log files. These log files are useful when we need to find out if a certain event took place.

Keeping logs is important, but is not enough. You also need to have some mechanisms to allow you to monitor the use of important resources such as CPU time, RAM space and disk usage. The next section describes some of these mechanisms.

Accounting

As mentioned before, accounting is the process of summarizing the resource usage of a user or process. There are several kinds of accounting, which can be used for different things. For example, you might want to count the time you are online if your ISP charges by the hour, or you might need to generate disk-space usage reports for department chargeback within your company. Although a large number of tools can be used for accounting, this section focuses on what is included in the stock Debian distribution, using additional packages only when necessary to cover an obvious lack of functionality.

Disk Accounting

Accounting for disk space is best handled by using quotas. However, quota information is very coarse-grained, being limited to the amount of disk space that a user occupies in each filesystem. If you need finer-grained information (such as which file is taking up disk space or which files are owned by a particular user), you can use two standard UNIX commands: `du` and `find`. Both are covered in Chapter 5, "Your Virtual Toolbelt;" in this section, we'll see a specific application of them.

Using du to Find Disk Hogs

`du`, combined with the `sort` command, is useful to "drill down" into a filesystem to find the exact file that is taking up all that disk space. Listing 13.2 shows a sample session where the `/var` filesystem is getting full, and you want to find out which file is taking up all that space.

LISTING 13.2 Using du to Find Disk Hogs

```
[root@atman ~]# df -k /var
Filesystem          1024-blocks  Used Available Capacity Mounted on
/dev/hda6              147983  147983         0     100%    /var
[root@atman log]# cd /var
[root@atman /var]# du -sk * .??* | sort -n
du: .??*: No such file or directory
1     local
1     nis
1     preserve
1     yp
2     lock
12     lost+found
15     named
20     run
4508     lib
12759     tmp
68620     log
75148     spool
[root@atman /var]# du -sk {log,spool}/{*,.??*} | sort -n
du: log/.??*: No such file or directory
du: spool/.??*: No such file or directory
0    log/spooler
0    log/xferlog
```

continues

LISTING 13.2 continued

```
1     log/lastlog.1.gz
[...output cut for brevity...]
244     log/maillog.2.gz
248     log/maillog.3.gz
621     log/maillog.8.gz
1174     log/auth
2304     log/maillog
2621     log/kernel
13245     spool/mqueue
57632     log/squid
61896     spool/smap
[root@atman /var]# du -sk {spool/mqueue,log/squid,spool/smap}/{*,.??*} \
                            | sort -n
du: spool/mqueue/.??*: No such file or directory
du: log/squid/.??*: No such file or directory
du: spool/smap/.??*: No such file or directory
0     spool/mqueue/dfEAA24999
0     spool/mqueue/qfEAA24999
0     spool/mqueue/xfEAA24999
0     spool/smap/xma000698
[...output cut for brevity...]
797     log/squid/access.log
799     log/squid/store.log.52.gz
813     log/squid/access.log.33.gz
815     log/squid/store.log
864     log/squid/store.log.33.gz
1054     spool/smap/xma014145
1475     spool/smap/xma002102
1531     spool/smap/xma010683
2118     spool/smap/xma029895
4154     spool/smap/xma010511
5117     spool/smap/xma011449
5117     spool/smap/xma014086
5117     spool/smap/xma016147
5117     spool/smap/xmaa09314
5117     spool/smap/xmaa14439
6840     spool/mqueue/dfWAB03562
17373     spool/smap/xma008414
[root@atman /var]#
```

As you can see, you can do a `du -sk * .??*`, which lists all the files and subdirectories of the current directory with their accumulated sizes in KB. If you pipe the output through `sort -n`, you get a list sorted by disk usage (the `-n` flag specifies a numeric sort). That way, the disk hogs will be at the end of the list (or you could use `sort -nr` to get the hogs at the beginning).

After you have identified the largest directories, you can use shell wildcards to drill further down, until you find which files or directories are taking the most space. In this case, it is some files in the the `smap` and mail queues (`smap` is a mail-forwarding program used in some firewalls) and the `squid` log files. The solution here is to check whether that many log files are needed, and perhaps modify the parameters to `savelog` so fewer historical copies are kept.

One thing to note here is that you can't forget hidden files (those starting with a dot). Although in this case there were none, in some cases (such as users' home directories), hidden files and directories can be the resource hogs. Thus, it is always a good idea to include `.??*` in the search (the `??` ensures that only files with at least two characters after the dot will be searched, thus skipping `.` and `..`, the current and parent directories).

Another flag that is useful with `du` is `-x`, which limits the search to the current filesystem. In Listing 13.2, this flag would have been necessary if, for example, `/var/log` was in a different partition (and thus you wouldn't want to search it).

It can also be useful to do a `du -k | sort -nr` every day and send the output to a file. Then if you do a `diff` to compare today's file with yesterday's, you automatically get a summary where you can see at a glance the changes in disk usage. You can do this by running the following script once a day:

```
#!/bin/bash
if [ -f ~/.today ]
then
        mv ~/.today ~/.yesterday
fi
du -k / | sort -nr > ~/.today
if [ -f ~/.yesterday ]
then
        diff ~/.yesterday ~/.today
fi
```

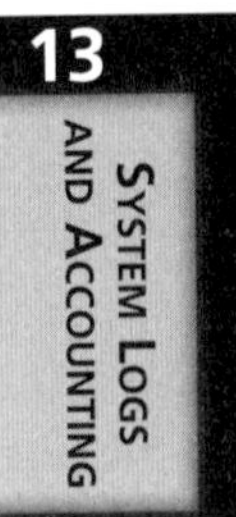

Using `find` to Locate Users' Files

In some cases, it is necessary to find all the files owned by a user. This might be the case, for example, when an employee leaves the company and all his files need to be archived and removed, or assigned to another employee. Or, the user might be over quota, and you might want to find any large files owned by him.

The `find` command is invaluable in these cases. Several of its options, which can be extremely useful when doing disk accounting, are shown in Table 13.4. `find` is covered in depth in Chapter 5 .

TABLE 13.4 `find` Switches That Are Useful for Disk Accounting

Switch	*Action*
`-xdev`	Stays in the same filesystem.

continues

TABLE 13.4 continued

Switch	*Action*
`-atime days`	File has been accessed *days* days ago. *days* can be prefixed with a plus, minus or equal sign (+, - or =) to specify that the access time is higher, lower, or exactly equal to the given parameter.
`-mtime days`	File has been modified *days* days ago. *days* can be prefixed the same way as `-atime`.
`-user uname`	File is owned by user *uname*.
`-uid uid`	File is owned by user ID *uid*.
`-group gname`	File's group is *gname*.
`-gid gid`	File's group ID is *gid*.
`-nouser`	File is owned by an unknown user (its user ID doesn't appear in `/etc/passwd`).
`-nogroup`	File's group is unknown (it doesn't appear in `/etc/group`).
`-size size`	File's size is *size*. *size* is expressed as a number followed by the units, where `c` means bytes (characters), `b` means disk blocks, `k` means kilobytes. *size* can also be prefixed as the *days* parameter to `-atime`.

For example, to find all files in all filesystems owned by user `mario`, you use the following command:

```
# find / -user mario -print
```

If you want to do a full listing of each file (such as `ls -l`), you could use this:

```
# find / -user mario -ls
```

Use the following to find all files larger than 1MB owned by user `mario` in the `/export/home` filesystem that haven't been accessed in the last 30 days, and to list the file's size in bytes, its name, and the time of its last access:

```
# find /export/home -xdev -user mario -size +1024K -atime +30 \
                    -printf '%s %p %a'
```

Finally, to delete all files owned by unknown users (for example, after removing several users from `/etc/passwd`), use this:

```
# find / -nouser -exec rm -f \{\} \;
```

Of course, this last option should be used very carefully, because when the files are deleted, they cannot be recovered. A better option would be to first generate a file list and use a tool such as `tar` or `cpio` (covered in Chapter 5) to back up the files before removing them:

```
# find / -nouser -print | cpio -oavH crc | gzip -9 > /archive/nouser.cpio.gz
```

As you can see, `find` is an extremely flexible tool that can help you manage your disks.

Network Accounting

Network administrators usually have to answer questions such as, "Who's using up our Internet bandwidth?" or "How saturated is our WAN connection?". Network accounting can give you the facts you need to answer those difficult questions.

A couple caveats apply here:

- You need to have a single measurement point. It can be the router that connects you to the WAN (a corporate WAN or the Internet), or it can be your firewall. However, it must be a Linux system. If you want to measure the traffic going through a third-party router or some other device, you need to use some other tool, such as the Multi-Router Traffic Grapher (MRTG), which you can find at `http://ee-staff.ethz.ch/~oetiker/webtools/mrtg/pub/`.
- If you are using a proxy server such as Squid (covered in Chapter 17, "Information Servers," and Chapter 22, "Firewalls and Proxies") and you want to monitor network usage for each computer on your network, you need to integrate the information found here with information from the proxy's log files.

In Linux, network accounting is configured using either `ipfwadm` (if you're running a 2.0 kernel, such as the one that comes with the standard Debian 2.1 distribution) or `ipchains` (if you're running a 2.2 kernel). See Chapter 12 for more information on kernel version 2.2, and Chapter 22, for more information on firewalls, `ipfwadm` and `ipchains`.

The Linux kernel keeps internal byte and packet counters for each firewalling rule (for `ipfwadm`) or chain (for `ipchains`). The basis of Linux network accounting is to create a rule or chain for each of the links you want to monitor. You then write a small program that polls the firewall counters periodically (say, every 5 seconds) and saves the information to a file. Finally, a second program takes that information and exploits it whichever way you want, whether it is summarizing, graphing, or storing it in a database.

In the following sections, we explore one way of gathering and processing this data. Remember: It is not the only way. In our examples, we will use the network shown in Figure 13.1. We will keep track of WAN bandwidth usage and total bytes transferred per each client node, plus grand totals. We will assume, for simplicity's sake, that either no IP masquerading is taking place, or the masquerading is done by some host or router (not the firewall).

The important data here are the IP addresses of the client nodes (10.0.1.1 and 10.0.1.2), the interface through which the firewall is connected to the LAN (eth0), and the interface through which it is connected to the WAN (eth1). Note that these could be any kind of interface: PPP, Token Ring, X.25, or something else. Using this information, we can see that we need to monitor the following (taken from the perspective of the firewall):

- Bytes coming from eth1 and going to 10.0.1.1
- Bytes going out on eth1 coming from 10.0.1.1
- Bytes coming from eth1 and going to 10.0.1.2
- Bytes going out on eth1 coming from 10.0.1.2
- Bytes coming into eth1
- Bytes going out on eth1

FIGURE 13.1
Sample network for accounting examples.

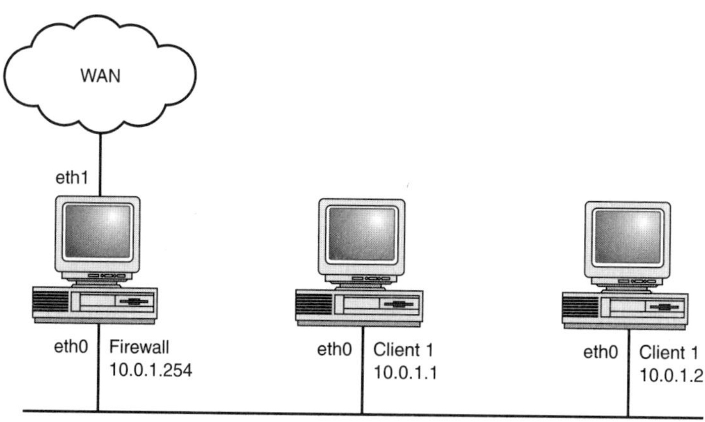

After we have this data, we can easily calculate both the total amounts (by simple addition) and the bandwidth usage (by dividing by the polling interval). To simplify this example, we simply generate a file, `/var/log/bandwidth.log`, that contains a time stamp in the first column, followed by the current value of the six byte counters. This data can then be fed to another program that runs less often (for example, every 5 minutes), which calculates the bandwidth and the totals and sends them to a graphing program, such as `gnuplot`.

Gathering Accounting Data with `ipfwadm`

The firewalling/accounting code in the 2.0 kernels works solely by *rules*. Each firewall rule is applied to each packet in sequence, until it is either accepted, rejected, or denied.

The 2.0 kernels have four kinds of rules: input, forwarding, output, and accounting. Input, forwarding, and output rules are covered in Chapter 22, which also covers general firewall configuration. In this section, we cover just the accounting rules and the subset of `ipfwadm` options needed for accounting.

In the first place, you need to enable IP accounting in the kernel. When configuring your kernel, go into `Network options` and activate option `IP: accounting`, recompile the kernel, and reboot. For details on configuring and compiling the kernel, see Chapter 12.

When you run a kernel with IP accounting enabled, you need to add the accounting rules. We will add a rule for each of the six data points we want to track, by typing the following commands at the shell prompt:

```
# ipfwadm -f -A
# ipfwadm -a -A in -D 10.0.1.1/32 -W eth1
# ipfwadm -a -A out -S 10.0.1.1/32 -W eth1
# ipfwadm -a -A in -D 10.0.1.2/32 -W eth1
# ipfwadm -a -A out -S 10.0.1.2/32 -W eth1
# ipfwadm -a -A in -W eth1
# ipfwadm -a -A out -W eth1
```

First of all, we flush (`-f`) the accounting rules. This is very important, because `ipfwadm` rules are always added to preexisting rules. If we don't flush any preexisting rules, weend up duplicating the rules, which gives confusing results.

Next, we add the rules one-by-one with the `-a` option. We specify that this is an accounting rule (`-A`), the direction we want to monitor (`in` or `out`), the source address and number of bits in its network part (`-S a.b.c.d/n`), and the interface we want to attach this rule to (`-W eth1`).

Finally, we zero the counters with the `-z` option so we get a clean start. Note that this will zero the counters for all accounting rules. The Linux kernel doesn't allow you to zero only a particular counter:

```
ipfwadm -z -A
```

To see the data from the counters, we can either use the `-l` option to `ipfwadm` coupled with `-e`, or we can read it directly from the `/proc/net/ip_acct` pseudofile. For more information on the files in `/proc`, see Chapter 15. We will use the second option, because it is much less expensive to open a file than to execute a program. Here's an example of a line from `/proc/net/ip_acct`:

```
00000000/00000000->00000000/00000000 ppp0 00000000 2000 0 0 30
➥1639        0 0 0 0 0 0 0 0 0 0 0 AFF X00
```

As you can see, the fields are separated by sequences of spaces. The field that interests us is the eighth (which contains the value `1639` in our example). The lines in the `ip_acct` file will be in the same order that the `ipfwadm` commands, so we don't have to do too much massaging.

We need a program that will poll the counters and save the information to `/var/log/bandwidth.log`. Because we want to poll relatively frequently (for example, every 5 seconds), we need to write a program that will run in an endless loop gathering the data, instead of a one-shot program called by `cron`, because `cron` can launch programs only in even minutes. Listing 13.3 shows a Perl program that first sets up the firewall rules and then polls the /proc/net/ip_acct file. For more information on Perl, see Chapter 8, "Conventional Means, Extraordinary Ends: Powerful Scripting Tools."

LISTING 13.3 Gathering Accounting Data from ipfwadm

```
#!/usr/bin/perl

# IP's to monitor
@LAN_IPS=('10.0.1.1','10.0.1.2');
# WAN interface name
$WAN_IF='eth1';
# Logfile name
$LOGFILE='/var/log/bandwidth.log';
# Path to the ipfwadm program
$IPFWADM="/sbin/ipfwadm";
# Polling interval in seconds
$INTERVAL=5;
# Name of the /proc file to read
$PROCFILE="/proc/net/ip_acct";

# Set up the firewall accounting rules
# First, flush the rules
system ("$IPFWADM -f -A");

# Set up incoming and outgoing rules for each IP
foreach (@LAN_IPS) {
  system ("$IPFWADM -a -A in  -D $_ -W $WAN_IF");
  system ("$IPFWADM -a -A out -S $_ -W $WAN_IF");
}

# Set up summarizing rules
system ("$IPFWADM -a -A in  -W $WAN_IF");
system ("$IPFWADM -a -A out -W $WAN_IF");

# Zero all firewall counters
system ("$IPFWADM -z -A");

# Clear logfile
open LOG, ">$LOGFILE";
close LOG;

# Now we go into an endless loop
while (1) {
  # Wait for data to accumulate
  sleep ($INTERVAL);
  # Read the data from the /proc file
  open PROC, "<$PROCFILE";
  @data = <PROC>;
  close PROC;
  # Write the data to the logfile
  open LOG,">>$LOGFILE";
```

```
  # First write the time stamp
  print LOG time();
  foreach (@data) {
    # Write each of the data points. The number of bytes is the
    # eighth field.
    @line=split (/ +/,$_);
    print LOG " ".$line[7];
  }
  print LOG "\n";
  # Close the logfile so it will be flushed
  close LOG;
}
```

We first set up several constants. This makes maintenance much easier (for example, if we need to add a new host or log to another file). We set up the accounting rules with `ipfwadm` and then go into an endless loop, polling every `$INTERVAL` seconds. Note that we close and reopen the `/proc` file each time, so we get new data on every loop. We also close and reopen the log file each time. On one side, this is a bit expensive; however, it ensures that the log file will always have the latest data and that no data will be left lying around in the filesystem buffers.

Gathering Accounting Data with `ipchains`

The concept behind accounting with `ipchains` is similar to `ipfwadm`: Add some firewall rules that accumulate the desired data, and then read them back periodically and store them in a log file. However, `ipchains` is much more flexible than `ipfwadm`. That, coupled with the fact that kernel 2.2 doesn't have a separate accounting functionality, changes some of the details.

First of all, a bit of background. The way `ipchains` works is, you create chains of rules. Each of the rules in each chain is applied to any packets that travel through it. If a packet matches any of the rules in the chain, it is accepted, rejected, or denied, depending on the chain policy.

There are three predefined chains: `input`, `output`, and `forward`. These are applied, respectively, to packets coming into the host, going out of the host, or being forwarded. The `forward` chain is applied after the `input` chain and before the `output` chain. There are also user-defined chains. To use these, you first define them and then add conditions to the predefined chains to jump to the user-defined chain. This is the basis of accounting in `ipchains`.

All packets that pass through each chain are counted, depending on the chain they came from. Thus, if we define a chain called `acct` and add it to both the `input` and `output` chains, the kernel counts each independently.

First, you need to enable IP firewalling in the kernel. When configuring the kernel, go into `Networking options`, enable the `Network firewalls` and `IP: firewalling` options, recompile your kernel, and reboot. When you run a kernel with IP firewalling enabled, you can add the ipchains rules for accounting. In the case of our example, you need to execute the following commands:

```
# ipchains -F input
# ipchains -F output
# ipchains -F acct
# ipchains -X acct
# ipchains -N acct
# ipchains -A input -d 10.0.1.1/32 -i eth1 -j acct
# ipchains -A output -s 10.0.1.1/32 -i eth1 -j acct
# ipchains -A input -d 10.0.1.2/32 -i eth1 -j acct
# ipchains -A output -s 10.0.1.2/32 -i eth1 -j acct
# ipchains -A input -i eth1 -j acct
# ipchains -A output -i eth1 -j acct
# ipchains -Z acct
```

We first flush the input and output chains. This is necessary because, since they reference the acct chain, we won't be able to flush or delete it. If you run this from your firewall, you have to individually delete (with the -D option) each rule that references the acct chain, because a flush deletes your firewall rules, too. After this is done, we need to flush and delete the acct chain to ensure that no data is left from previous runs.

After that, we create each of the needed rules, specifying the chain to add them to (output or input), the corresponding source or destination address (-s or -d), the desired interface (-i), and that we want to jump to the acct chain (-j). The acct chain itself will have no rules, because its single purpose is to count the number of bytes that come in or go out, and that is done automatically by the kernel.

Finally, we zero the counters of the acct chain (-Z), so we get a completely clean start. In ipchains, the -Z option can zero the counters for a single chain, so no other counters will be affected.

To read the data, we can either use the -L and -v options to ipchains, or read directly from the /proc/net/ip_fwchains pseudofile (for more information on the /proc filesystem, see Chapter 15). Reading directly from /proc is more efficient than starting a new program each time. Besides, the output of ipchains is meant to be readable by humans, which means it's more difficult to parse than the contents of the ip_fwchains file, so that is what we will do.

This is a sample from /proc/net/ip_fwchains:

```
   input 00000000/00000000->0A000101/FFFFFFFF eth1 0 0 0 0
➥1725          0          1704500          0-65535 0-65535
➥ AFF X00 00000000 0 0       acct
   input 00000000/00000000->0A000102/FFFFFFFF eth1 0 0 0 0
➥2843          0          4382420          0-65535 0-65535
➥AFF X00 00000000 0 0       acct
   input 00000000/00000000->00000000/00000000 eth1 0 0 0 0
➥38506          0          23048401          0-65535 0-65535
```

```
➥AFF X00 00000000 0 0      acct
   output 0A000101/FFFFFFFF->00000000/00000000 eth1 0 0 0 0
➥520         0          83000          0-65535  0-65535
➥AFF X00 00000000 0 0      acct
   output 0A000102/FFFFFFFF->00000000/00000000 eth1 0 0 0 0
➥310         0          62800          0-65535 0-65535
➥AFF X00 00000000 0 0      acct
   output 00000000/00000000->00000000/00000000 eth1 0 0 0 0
➥2340         0          2843020          0-65535 0-65535
➥AFF X00 00000000 0 0      acct
```

Each record has several space-delimited fields. We need several of them. The first field specifies whether this is an input or an output chain. As you can see, `ipchains` reorders the rules by chain, so we have to do some massaging before outputting the data. However, within each chain the records are in the same order as they were created.

The tenth field is the number of bytes, which is the actual data we want, and the last (eighteenth) field specifies the chain. In our case, we want only the data from the `acct` chain, so we have to select it.

Listing 13.4 shows a Perl program that takes the data from `ip_fwchains` and outputs it to our `/var/log/bandwidth.log` file.

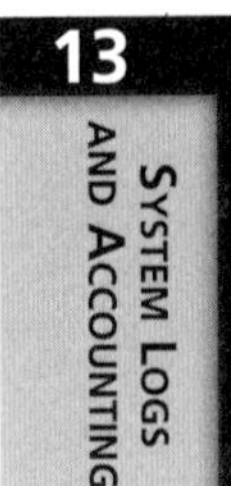

LISTING 13.4 Gathering Accounting Data from `ipchains`

```
#!/usr/bin/perl

# IP's to monitor
@LAN_IPS=('10.0.1.1','10.0.1.2');
# WAN interface name
$WAN_IF='eth1';
# Logfile name
$LOGFILE='/var/log/bandwidth.log';
# Path to the ipchains program
$IPCHAINS="/sbin/ipchains";
# Polling interval in seconds
$INTERVAL=5;
# Name of the /proc file to read
$PROCFILE="/proc/net/ip_fwchains";
# Name of our accounting chain
$CHAIN="acct";
# Field number of the input/output chain label
$IO_FIELD=0;
# Field number of byte count
$BYTES_FIELD=9;
# Field number of our chain
$CHAIN_FIELD=17;
# Tags for the IO field
$IO_INPUT="input";
$IO_OUTPUT="output";
```

continues

LISTING 13.4 continued

```
# Set up our accounting chain
# First, flush the chains
# WARNING: Don't flush the input and output chains if you're firewalling!
system ("$IPCHAINS -F input");
system ("$IPCHAINS -F output");
system ("$IPCHAINS -F $CHAIN");

# Now delete and re-create our accounting chain
system ("$IPCHAINS -X $CHAIN");
system ("$IPCHAINS -N $CHAIN");

# Set up incoming and outgoing rules for each IP
foreach (@LAN_IPS) {
  system ("$IPCHAINS -A input  -d $_ -i $WAN_IF -j $CHAIN");
  system ("$IPCHAINS -A output -s $_ -i $WAN_IF -j $CHAIN");
}

# Set up summarizing rules
system ("$IPCHAINS -A input  -i $WAN_IF -j $CHAIN");
system ("$IPCHAINS -A output -i $WAN_IF -j $CHAIN");

# Zero all firewall counters
system ("$IPCHAINS -Z $CHAIN");

# Clear logfile
open LOG, ">$LOGFILE";
close LOG;

# Now we go into an endless loop
while (1) {
  # Wait for data to accumulate
  sleep ($INTERVAL);

  # Read the data from the /proc file
  open PROC, "<$PROCFILE";
  @data = <PROC>;
  close PROC;

  # Create arrays for the data
  @input = ();
  @output = ();

  # Write the data to the logfile
  foreach (@data) {
    chop;
    s/^ +//;
    @line = split (/ +/,$_);
    # Check whether it belongs to our chain
    if ($line[$CHAIN_FIELD] eq $CHAIN) {
      # Add the bytes value to the appropriate array
```

```
      push (@input,  $line[$BYTES_FIELD])
                      if ($line[$IO_FIELD] eq $IO_INPUT);
      push (@output, $line[$BYTES_FIELD])
                      if ($line[$IO_FIELD] eq $IO_OUTPUT);
    }
  }

  # Now output the line to the logfile
  open LOG, ">>$LOGFILE";
  print LOG time();
  for ($i = 0; $i < @input; $i++) {
    print LOG " $input[$i] $output[$i]";
  }
  print LOG "\n";
  close LOG;
}
```

As you can see, we're doing the same thing we did with `ipfwadm`. The only difference is that we're filtering the data based on the chain name (because all chains appear in the same file), and we're using a pair of arrays to rearrange the data before writing it to the log file.

`ipchains` gives us more flexibility than `ipfwadm`. We could easily extend this program to log traffic with different characteristics, just by adding more of the `$IO_XXX` variables. With `ipfwadm`, we would have to add rules specifying each kind of packet we need to log; with `ipchains`, we just add the `-j` option command to jump to our `acct` chain wherever we want to do accounting.

Process Accounting and Performance Analysis

In process accounting, our focus is on the amount of system resources (memory and CPU) that a process takes up. Process accounting is useful when doing chargebacks, when analyzing server performance, or when doing capacity planning. Linux includes several tools for process accounting. This section covers `ps`, `top`, `vmstat`, and part of the GNU Accounting Utilities.

Using `ps` for Process Accounting

Linux includes several tools that help with process accounting. The first tool is the `ps` command, which lists processes running in the system, and can give several statistics on them. `ps` gives you a snapshot of the processes in the system at a particular moment.

The most useful options to `ps` for process acounting purposes are shown in Table 13.5, and Table 13.6 shows the meanings of the most significant `ps` data fields.

TABLE 13.5 ps Options That Are Useful for Process Accounting

Option	*Meaning*
m	Memory info. The important fields are SIZE, RSS, and SHRD.
u	User output. The important fields are %CPU, %MEM, SIZE, RSS, and TIME.
x	Shows processes with no controlling terminal (that is, daemons).
a	Shows processes that belong to other users.

TABLE 13.6 Important ps Fields

Field	*Meaning*
USER	Name of the user who owns the process.
PID	Process ID.
COMMAND	Command that the process is running.
SIZE	Total process virtual size in KB, including code + data + stack.
RSS	Resident set size in KB. This is the amount of RAM the process is currently using (including shared memory).
SHARE	Shared memory size in KB. This is the amount of RAM the process is sharing with other processes.
%CPU	Percentage of CPU time that this process is currently using.
%MEM	Percentage of system RAM that this process is using.
TIME	Total CPU time that this process has consumed, in minutes:seconds.

Using `top` to Monitor Processes in Real Time

The `top` command is an interactive, real-time version of `ps`. It shows the same basic statistics as the `ps` command, updating its display every 5 seconds. It enables you to sort the output by `%MEM`, `%CPU` or `TIME`, and enables you to show only the processes for a certain user or only nonidle processes. It also enables you to kill tasks.

`top` is useful in the day-to-day monitoring of a host, to spot runaway processes or processes that are taking up too much RAM. The columns it shows are the same as the `ps` command.

Using `vmstat` to Monitor Virtual Memory Statistics

`vmstat` is probably the most important workhorse for UNIX process accounting and performance management. While it runs, it periodically samples the system state and displays one line of output, which contains the average value of the system's vital statistics during that interval. `vmstat` is usually called with a single command-line argument that specifies the number of seconds between samples. Useful values usually range between 3 and 30 seconds, depending on the granularity you're looking for.

You can also specify a second numeric argument, which specifies the number of samples to take. This is useful for quick snapshots of the system status. Another useful option is `-n`. Usually, `vmstat` will redisplay the headers every 20 lines of output. If you're redirecting the output to a log file for later processing, you can include the `-n` option so the headers will be printed just at the beginning.

One important thing to note about `vmstat` is that you should always ignore the first line of output, which represents the average since the system was booted (and is usually meaningless). Useful values start at the second line of output.

When using `vmstat` for long-term logging, remember that it generates a 72-character line per sample. For example, a `vmstat` log with 5-second intervals generates more than 1MB of output daily.

Although vmstat stands for Virtual Memory Statistics, it is useful for monitoring the disk and CPU activity of your host. You should get into the habit of periodically running `vmstat` to get familiar with the numbers it displays when your host is under different load conditions. `vmstat` can also be used to detect if a performance problem is due to a disk or CPU bottleneck.

The fields in `vmstat`'s output are detailed in Table 13.7.

TABLE 13.7 `vmstat` Fields

Field(s)	*Meaning*
`procs: r`	Number of processes waiting to run. Usually, `r` shouldn't be more than the number of CPUs in the system. If `r` has a constantly high value, the system would benefit from more CPUs (especially if running kernel 2.2).
`procs: w`	Number of processes that are sleeping, waiting for something. They are usually waiting for an I/O request to complete.
`procs: b`	Number of otherwise runnable processes that are swapped out.
`mem: swpd`	Amount of swap space currently used (in KB).
`mem: free`	Amount of currently free RAM (in KB).
`mem: buff, cache`	Amount of memory used, respectively, for disk buffers and as disk cache, in KB. This memory is managed dynamically by the Linux kernel, so most of it can eventually be turned into free memory if the system is memory-starved.
`swap: si, so`	KB per second swapped in and out, respectively. If these numbers are consistently high, the host needs more RAM.

continues

TABLE 13.7 continued

Field(s)	*Meaning*
`io: bi, bo`	Blocks per second, respectively, received from and sent to a block device.
`system: in`	Interrupts per second received, including the clock.
`system: cs`	Context switches executed per second. A context switch happens when the processor is switched from one process to another.
`cpu: sy, us, id`	Percentage of CPU time spent, respectively, in the system, in user processes, and idle. If the idle percentage is consistently above 70%, the host's CPU is overloaded.

The GNU Accounting Utilities

The GNU accounting utilities are designed to provide a systems administrator with information on system usage: connections, programs executed, and utilization of system resources. They can be found in the `acct` package.

There are several utilities that can be used both for process and user accounting. In this section, we concentrate on the first. The utilities used for user accounting are discussed in the following section.

The GNU accounting utilities store their data in the `/var/account/pacct` file. Accounting is started with the `accton` command, which is called from the `/etc/init.d/acct` file. There are two commands to exploit that data for process accounting: `lastcomm` and `sa`.

Using `lastcomm` to List the Programs That Have Been Executed

`lastcomm` lists information about all the programs that have been executed (and finished their execution) since the beginning of the `/var/account/pacct` file. By default, this file is rotated daily by the `/etc/cron.daily/acct` file. If you want to accumulate data for more days, you can use the `-f` flag to read older files (after decompressing them) or modify the `/etc/cron.daily/acct` script. For example, if you want to rotate the file on a weekly basis, you should move the script to the `/etc/cron.weekly` directory and probably change the `-c` parameter to `savelog` so it saves less than seven historical files.

`lastcomm` lists the following fields:

- Executed command.
- Flags—`S` means the command was executed by the superuser. `F` means that the program did a `fork` (split into two processes) and didn't do an `exec` after it (which

would split the accounting into two processes). `D` means that the program terminated abnormally, generating a `core` file. `X` means that the program was stopped by a `SIGTERM` (usually generated by Ctrl+C).

- The user who executed the command.
- The `tty` that the command was executed from.
- The CPU time used by the process.
- The time the command's execution ended.

This information is most useful when doing chargeback for system resources consumed, because it can pinpoint who executed which commands, and how much CPU time each command occupied. You can add parameters to `lastcomm` that will work as search keys, displaying only the records that contain any of the parameters in any field. For example, `lastcomm tty1` displays only those programs started from the console, and `lastcomm tty1 mario` displays only programs for which one of their fields matches `tty1` or `mario`. If you want to match specific fields, you can use the `--user`, `--command`, or `--tty` files, so you could use `lastcomm -tty tty1 --user mario`.

Using sa to Summarize the Accounting Data

The `sa` command is used to summarize the information found in `/var/account/pacct`. Additionally, it can store the summarized information in the `/var/account/savacct` and `/var/acount/usracct` files.

`sa` can display the fields listed in Table 13.8.

TABLE 13.8 sa Fields

Field	*Meaning*
`cp`	Total CPU time, sum of system and user times
`re`	Total real execution time in seconds
`re/cp`	Ratio between real-time and CPU time
`u`	User CPU time in seconds
`s`	System CPU time in seconds

The field names aren't listed at the head of each column. Instead, they are appended to each value, so you might see a `25.7cpu`, meaning 25.7 CPU seconds.

`sa` takes several switches. The most useful ones for user and process accounting are listed in Table 13.9.

TABLE 13.9 sa Switches

Switch	*Meaning*
`-a`	By default, `sa` groups all commands with unprintable characters in their names and those that have been executed only once into a single entry labeled `***other`. The `-a` switch makes `sa` display all commands.
`-c`	`sa` prints percentages of the total time for each of the user, system, and real-time values.
`-l`	Separates the user and system time. Normally, they are added together and printed as CPU time.
`-m`	Prints the number of processes and CPU minutes for each user.
`-s`	Summarizes `/var/account/pacct` into the `savacct` and `usracct` files. Must be run as root.
`-t`	Prints the ratio of real time versus the total CPU time for each process. If the value is too small (CPU time is zero), it prints `**ignore**` in the corresponding field.
`-u`	Prints only the user ID and command name for each entry in the `pacct` file. If `-u` is specified, all other options are ignored.

User Accounting

Just as process accounting is concerned with the amount of system resources that processes consume, the purpose of *user accounting* is tracking the amount of system resources that each user consumes. As such, it is closely related to process accounting, and several of the programs used for process accounting can also provide user accounting data (that is, `lastcomm` and `sa`). However, there are a few utilities whose single purpose is tracking users, specifically users that log on directly to the server (as opposed to just using it as a file or database server, for example). These commands are `last` and `ac`.

These commands print out the data stored in the `/var/log/wtmp` file. This file is maintained by the `login` and `init` processes and can grow very large in a busy system. The `/etc/cron.monthly/acct` script rotates this file after summarizing its contents to `/var/log/wtmp.report`. However, if `/var/log/wtmp` doesn't exist, no logging will occur.

Using `last` to View Login and Logout Details

`last` prints the records in the `wtmp` file. Each record contains the following data:

- Username
- `tty` on which the login occurred

- Host from which the login came, or `console` if it was a local login
- Login time stamp, followed by a dash and the logout time stamp, or the text `still logged in` if the user hasn't logged out
- Total time spent logged in, within parentheses and specified as `hours:minutes`

The special user `reboot` marks the times when the system booted. However, it is impossible to know the time the system went down.

`last` can take the `-x` option, which also lists all run-level changes. This is useful to pinpoint orderly shutdowns (as opposed to system crashes), because they are stored as changes to run-level 0 (for shutdowns) or 6 (for reboots).

Using `ac` to View a Summary of Connect Time

Without parameters, `ac` just lists the total connect time in hours for all users of the system. `ac` takes a couple of switches. `ac -d` prints daily totals instead of a single grand total, and `ac -p` prints a total for each user. `ac -pd` summarizes by day and by user.

You can also specify a list of usernames to print, and the totals reflect the times for those users only. For example, `ac mario root` prints the total number of hours the users `mario` and `root` have spent logged on, and `ac -p mario root` also lists the totals for each user.

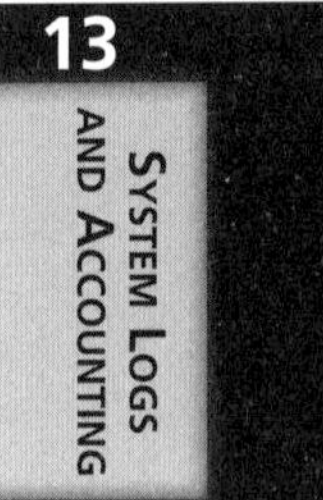

As you can see, many tools allow you to monitor the behavior of your Linux system. In fact, there are so many that, as the next section explains, it is sometimes useful to use a tool that automatically keeps track of everything.

Automated Monitoring Tools

Log files are no good if they aren't periodically monitored. However, the system logs usually grow so fast that it's impossible to monitor them constantly and thus detect possible problems before they occur. Besides, many problems (for instance, full disks) are better detected before they occur (for example, when the filesystem is 95% full).

To help with this, you may write programs that monitor the logs and vital statistics automatically and take some action when a condition occurs. For example, if the `/tmp` filesystem is full, the script might delete some temporary files you know aren't needed. If the system runs out of memory, you might automatically add a swap file. Or, if a database server goes down, you might send an email or page the system administrator.

There are several systems to automate the gathering of data from log files. An excellent tool in this category is `PIKT`, the Problem Informant/Killer Tool, which can be downloaded from `http://pikt.uchicago.edu/pikt/`. PIKT is a complete scripting language and explaining how to use it would require at least a complete chapter. However, for a small network or a single system this may be overkill. In that case, a sysadmin is probably better off writing his or her own scripts.

Suppose for example, that you want an email sent to you when the root filesystem on a server is full. Listing 13.5 shows a Perl script that can do just that.

LISTING 13.5 Monitoring Filesystem Capacity

```
#!/usr/bin/perl

# Command to monitor
$CMD="/bin/df / ¦";
# Line number to monitor (first line is 0)
$LINE_NO=1;
# Field separator regular expression
$FIELD_SEP="[ %]+";
# Field number to monitor (first is 0)
$FIELD=4;
# Threshold value (email if greater)
$THRESHOLD=75;
# Interval between samples (in seconds)
$INTERVAL=300;
# Person to email
$ADMIN="sysadmin\@company.com";

while (1) {
  # Get the command's output
  open DF, "$CMD";
  @lines = <DF>;
  close DF;

  # Split the interesting line
  @fields = split ($FIELD_SEP, $lines[$LINE_NO]);

  # Check the value
  if ($fields[$FIELD] > $THRESHOLD) {
    open MAIL, "¦ mail -s 'WARNING: Threshold passed!' $ADMIN";
    print MAIL "A threshold has been passed in the monitoring system\n";
    print MAIL "Line $LINE_NO, field $FIELD has value $fields[$FIELD],
➥which is higher than $THRESHOLD \n\n";
    print MAIL "This is the output of the '$CMD' command:\n\n";
    print MAIL @lines;
    close MAIL;
  }

  # Wait for next polling time
  sleep ($INTERVAL);
}
```

The program runs in a loop, executing the df / command every 5 minutes and checking its output. Configuring the program with variables at the beginning makes it very easy to reuse this program to check the output of other programs (for example, a ping to another server or a free command to check swap space). It easily could be applied to check a file (for example, /var/log/meminfo, where it also could get the information on available swap space).

Monitoring a continuously growing log file is even easier. The trick here is to open the file for reading, use the `seek` function to reach the end of the file, and then continuously read from it. Listing 13.6 shows a program that executes the `sendpage` command (a fictitious command that should send a message to a pager) whenever `root` logs in to the server. This might be used to monitor the security on a site.

LISTING 13.6 Monitoring Log Files

```
#!/usr/bin/perl

# Command to monitor
$FILE="tail -f/var/log/auth.log ¦";
# Regular expression to check
$REGEXP="login\\[.*\\]: ROOT LOGIN";
# Script to execute (syslog line appended to command)
$CMD="/usr/local/bin/sendpage 5835544 ";

# Open the file to monitor
open LOGFILE, "$FILE";

while (<LOGFILE>) {
  chop;
  tr/'`//d;
  system ($CMD.$_) if /$REGEXP/;
}
```

Again, this script can be easily adapted for your own needs.

Summary

System logging and accounting are two important system administration tasks. The main UNIX logging interface is done by means of the `syslog` daemon, which receives messages from programs and from other computers in the network and dispatches them to different log files, depending on the configuration of the `/etc/syslog.conf` file. The `klog` daemon takes care of grabbing kernel messages and passing them on to `syslogd`.

Log files have to be periodically rotated, or they grow boundlessly and fill up the disk. In Debian, rotating is done with the `savelog` program, which is executed periodically by the `anacron` program. `savelog` takes care of rotating the log files, compressing historical files, and removing old files.

Accounting is the process by which data is gathered about the usage of the system. Different kinds of accounting gather different data. The most important types of accounting are disk, network, process, and user accounting. Although standard day-to-day utilities can be used for some accounting purposes, there also are special tools for each of these.

Automated monitoring is one of the most important system administration tasks. Although specialized monitoring programs exist, a lot can be done using Perl scripts. These scripts can execute a program and take automatic action based on its output, or analyze a log file and act upon the messages that are sent to it.

CHAPTER

Disaster Recovery

by Jeff Licquia

In This Chapter

When you have Debian GNU/Linux installed, configured, tweaked, and customized to your heart's content, it's hard to imagine it ever having problems. Certainly the system's stability and security features make it much less prone to errors, crashes, and data loss, and one can be lulled into a false sense of security about it being "bulletproof."

Unfortunately, nothing could be further from the truth. All operating systems must run on hardware, and hardware is prone to firmware bugs, poor manufacture, age, abuse, and incompatibility problems. You can make a mistake and delete the wrong file or overwrite something important. A hacker might find a way into your system while you're surfing the Web or reading your mail (more about hackers and security in Chapter 20, "Conceptual Overview of Security Issues") and might do some things to your system that you don't like. And however unlikely it may seem, a bug might creep into Debian and cause a problem, or you might decide to try something new and different (such as the new 2.2 Linux kernel) that might cause a problem.

However it happens, if you work with computers for an extended period, it's inevitable that you will someday find yourself having a problem that needs to be fixed. When that day comes, you will be much better off if you have prepared ahead of time. This chapter will show you how to prepare and what to do when problems arise.

There are three things you can do to protect yourself against disaster, which we will cover in this chapter:

- Back up your system.
- Keep a recovery disk handy.
- Document how your system is set up.

Backup as the First Line of Defense

It seems that every sysadmin, network guru, and Linux wizard has one sage piece of advice whenever asked about good computing practice: back up your data! It may sound tired and trite from all the repetition, but it is no less true: The best thing you can do for yourself to keep your system safe is to back it up regularly.

Cost and convenience are the two reasons most often used to justify not backing up. In the past, these were valid concerns. Tape drives and tapes tended to be expensive, and floppies became impractical as a backup medium years ago. Typical PC software also did not have any mechanism for unattended backups, meaning that the user had to take time to start the backup job manually whenever it needed to be done. But today, most of these issues have answers. Tape drives have dropped in price even as they have grown in capacity. New media types have helped to speed up backups while providing other convenient features. And with Debian's inherent multitasking abilities and job scheduling system, backups can take place on a regular schedule automatically or semiautomatically, with little or no manual intervention required.

Deciding What to Back Up

The most important decision to make when planning your backup strategy is deciding what to back up. It would seem that this is probably the easiest decision to make; just point your backup program at the `root` directory and go from there. However, there are several good reasons why this is a bad plan:

- Some directories are not meant to be backed up. The `/proc` filesystem on Linux systems is made up of information about the running system held by the kernel, such as the processes running on the system, the current contents of core memory, and the state of the hardware, as well as some kernel configuration options. Because the information is dynamic and provided by the kernel, it does not need to be backed up, and some of those files can chew up quite a bit of valuable space (`/proc/kcore`, as just one example, is approximately the same size as the amount of physical RAM installed on your computer). Additionally, restoring some of these files from a tape backup can crash your system hard; the aforementioned `/proc/kcore` is one example of this.
- Temporary directories (such as `/tmp`) generally contain dynamic information that isn't needed over the long term.
- Other directories, although not necessarily bad to back up, are a waste of tape space. For example, if you ran a backup while you had a CD-ROM mounted, you could lose as much as 650MB of space backing up the CD in the drive.
- The data stored in some directories is highly standardized and doesn't change between installations of the same version of Debian GNU/Linux. This makes it easy to recover their contents through other means, such as reinstallation. If the capacity of your backup medium is a concern, they could therefore be dropped from the backup safely. The `/dev` and `/usr/doc` hierarchies are examples of this.
- Some data may be stored locally for the sake of convenience—for example, local mirrors of Internet archive sites. Losing this data might be inconvenient, but nothing would be lost; using the Internet archive mirror example, the mirroring script could be rerun to re-create the archive after some downloading time.
- Some directories on your system may be mounted over a network and may be backed up on another system. Keeping a second backup could be considered wasteful. (On the other hand, a second backup might be a good thing, because it provides a redundant backup source for critical data. Only you can decide that.)
- Your backup media may not be big enough to store everything on the system, and you may not be able to afford to upgrade; backing up only important data might not be best, but it would be better than no backup at all.

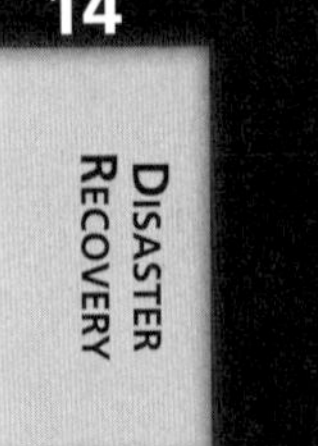

There are advantages to backing up everything (besides dangerous directories such as `/proc`). If you back up everything, you can restore the system from a rescue disk without having to reinstall, and the restore process is likely to be faster. But the information on a typical Debian system can be several hundred megabytes; if you are running tight on media space, you might consider leaving off some of the programs and other information installed with Debian.

"Important" information usually consists of configuration files for important programs or personal data. Ultimately, only you can decide for yourself what is important enough to back up and what is not. However, here is a guide to some directories that are more likely to contain important data:

- `/etc` All local configuration is stored here, along with certain important systemwide information, such as the user and group databases and the global mail alias database.
- `/home` All user data, with a few exceptions, is stored here, along with most user-specific configuration data.
- `/var` The exceptions mentioned previously for `/home` are usually stored here, as well as other systemwide data. Some important data stored here would include all users' mail inboxes, the installed package databases, the data files for some database servers, and the default document location for Web servers.

Choosing Media

After choosing what to back up, you should choose the medium to back up on. In some cases, your choice is determined for you; you may not be able to afford anything more than floppies, or your company may mandate that all servers be backed up using some standard backup media.

If you have a choice, your first consideration should be whether the technology you use is compatible with Linux. In general, any standards-based system will likely work (such as SCSI or IDE), and any technology that is proprietary has less of a chance. Keep the Hardware Compatibility HOWTO close as you evaluate solutions.

Another important consideration is the media type to use. There are several tried-and-true popular types, as well as a few new ones.

Tape

Tape drives, in some form, are the oldest and most widely used backup solution. They are capable of extremely high data density and are easy to use in today's typical configurations. Most likely, if you have a backup solution mandated to you or bundled with a product, it will consist of some kind of tape-based solution.

Tape is considered a *streaming* device; you *stream* data to the tape device, which writes it to the tape immediately. If you cannot stream data to the tape as fast as the tape can write it, the tape drive stops and waits for you to catch up; this has a dramatic effect on performance. It is difficult to read data in the middle of the tape; typically, this involves scanning a catalog for the right position or simply reading the tape from the beginning until the right data is found. Today's tape systems support a rudimentary filesystem; each file (or *session,* as it's sometimes called) appears sequentially on the tape, separated by *file markers,* with each file representing one backup session with many system files.

As with most devices on Linux, tape drives are represented by device files, usually stored in `/dev`. The name of the device file indicates what kind of hardware it uses; for example, `/dev/st0` is the first tape drive on your primary SCSI chain, and `/dev/ftape0` is the first *floppy tape* drive. This device is rather simple: To read the tape, read from the requested device file; to write to the tape, write to the device file.

Each tape drive has two devices associated with it. One of these is a *rewinding* device; when you're done with the tape, it automatically rewinds the tape to the beginning. The other is a *nonrewinding* device, which leaves the tape where it is after the device is closed. Nonrewinding devices are typically named with an `n` prepended; thus, the non-rewinding device for the first IDE tape drive will usually be named `/dev/nht0`.

This two-device approach is handy for doing multiple backups. If you make all backups but the last write to the nonrewinding device and the last backup write to the rewinding device, you end up with all your backups sequentially written to the tape and the tape rewound automatically for you.

Besides the normal actions of reading from and writing to the tapes, Linux supports controlling the tape drive directly. From the command line, the `mt` command performs this action. You invoke `mt` with a command such as this:

```
$ mt -f device command
```

The argument to `-f` should be the device file that controls the device. For most options, you should use the nonrewinding device; it certainly wouldn't make sense to rewind the tape after telling it to move ahead one file.

The following are some commonly used `mt` commands. To move the tape forward (`fsf`) or backward (`bsf`) `x` files:

```
mt fsf [x]
mt bsf [x]
```

To rewind the tape

```
mt rewind
```

To retension the tape

```
mt retension
```

Retensioning involves rewinding the tape, spooling the tape out to the end, and then rewinding it again. This ensures that the tape has even tension throughout its length; uneven tension can result in the tape unspooling at different rates, which can cause read errors.

To erase the entire tape

```
mt erase
```

To print the drive's current status

```
mt status
```

Types of Tape Media

"Tape" is not just one medium, but several. There have been many varied kinds of tapes, from the venerable tape spools to ultramodern cartridge tapes. The current field of tape drives supported by Linux essentially boils down to two distinct types, with a few variations in each type, as well as several new standards.

The old standby in tape technology is the QIC standard, for *quarter-inch tape*. This was originally created as a PC tape standard, with small cartridges that could hold 40MB. The QIC standard has been extended many times to accommodate larger disk sizes and has even changed physical format: The newer Travan tapes have a larger plastic cartridge that can hold more tape (and consequently more data). One popular manufacturer of QIC-based tape drives is Iomega with its Ditto series of tape drives; although they are nonstandard, they are supported. The highest-end QIC-style tape drives today can hold about 20GB.

Somewhat newer than QIC is the DAT standard. This was originally envisioned as a digital replacement for the cassette in the music world but was quickly adapted for digital backup purposes because of its higher reliability and greater capacity (at the time) than QIC. Drives are available that will hold as much as 96GB.

New tape technologies, not based on QIC or DAT, include DLT and AIT tapes (as well as several others). Some of these drives are able to hold hundreds of gigabytes.

Floppy Tape Drives

In the days before IDE could handle peripherals other than disks, the most popular way to attach a tape drive to a PC was through the floppy controller. Although floppy tapes allowed PCs to back themselves up locally, they were usually slow and unreliable, because the floppy controller was never intended to handle tape drives. Floppy tape has become more rare in recent years, but many older drives still support this standard.

Linux supports QIC-style floppy tape drives with the `ftape` kernel driver. However, the `ftape` driver supplied with the 2.0.*x* kernel (the standard kernel for Debian GNU/Linux 2.1) is extremely out of date and does not support many later tape drives. To overcome this problem, Debian supplies a current version of `ftape` as a separate set of packages, including both the driver itself and some utilities.

The driver itself is supplied in one of several `ftape-module-xxx` packages, where *xxx* is the kernel version the driver is compiled against. Unfortunately, the latest stable kernel (2.0.36) is not supplied; if you have this kernel, you need to compile your own kernel module from the source in `ftape-source` (see Chapter 12, " Customizing the Bootup Procedure" for more information on doing this). You also need the `ftape-util` package, which provides several utilities for managing the tape drive. When the new `ftape` module is installed and working, the tape devices for `ftape` (`/dev/qft*` and `/dev/nqft*`) should work with the standard tape tools.

One distinction with QIC floppy tape drives: Unlike other tape technologies, they require that you format the tapes before using them. This can be done with the `ftformat` utility supplied with `ftape-util`. Also, floppy tapes (precisely because of the formatting) are more sensitive to tape tension and stretching; you should definitely retension before writing to the tape, and retensioning before reads is recommended as well. Finally, remember not to use the floppy drive (this would include having it mounted) at the same time as the tape drive; the floppy controller cannot handle this.

Floppy-Disk Backup

Floppy-disk backup, although inefficient, is still useful for backing up small amounts of data. Its main advantage is that almost all computers today come with a floppy disk, making it nearly universally available. Linux accesses these disks using the device files `/dev/fd*`; most people use the device file `/dev/fd0` to enable autodetecting of the floppy drive type on the first available floppy (or drive A: in DOS parlance).

GNU `tar` supports multivolume backups (or *spanning*); it can prompt you when the device is full, allowing you to switch media. This was originally done for tapes, but it works for floppy disks as well. Use the `-M` option to enable this. (See the section "`tar`," later in this chapter, for more information.)

Besides allowing you to do traditional backups, floppies enable you to create filesystems on the disks and mount them, or to read them with tools such as the `mtools` suite. This enables you to do easy backups. If you don't need disk spanning or compression, doing a backup can be as easy as this:

```
mount /dev/fd0 /mnt/floppyrm -rf /mnt/floppy/*
cp -a ./myfiles/* /mnt/floppy
umount /mnt/floppy
```

Be warned, however: The format used by `tar` and other traditional backup utilities is not compatible with the kernel filesystem drivers. If you use a backup utility to make a backup, you should use the same utility to restore that backup. If you mount or use `mtools`, you should mount or use `mtools` to restore. (Mounting and `mtools` are compatible with each other if the disks used are formatted with the FAT filesystem, the filesystem used by DOS and Microsoft Windows.)

Hard Disk

With the dropping prices of hard disks, using a permanently mounted hard disk or partition as a backup medium is becoming more popular. Hard-disk backups have many advantages: speed, convenience, and low downtime in the event of a failure. They also have disadvantages: They are difficult to remove for offsite storage and, if they are kept in the computer, they can be compromised by the same catastrophe that compromised the running system.

Like floppies, hard disks can be used for "live" backups, where files are copied directly to a native filesystem on the disk instead of being written to directly. This is more effective with hard disks because of their large size; additionally, a live backup can be quickly mounted in place of defective data, which eliminates the need to go through a restore process. One problem with live media backups is their lack of compression, which can allow twice as much data to be backed up. To overcome this, some systems are set to write backup files to the disk, complete with compression.

If you are considering using a hard disk as a live backup medium, you should also consider using a RAID system of some kind. The section "Uninterruptible Power Supply (UPS)," later in this chapter, discusses RAID in more detail .

Other Backup Media

Although these are some of the most popular backup media, other, less traditional media have been used for backup purposes with success.

Removable hard-disk systems can be used in the same way as floppies for doing backups, with the advantage of higher storage capacity and greater speed. Debian GNU/Linux supports most of the popular types of removable media, including Iomega Zip and Jaz drives and LS-120. Any removable media format should be recognized if it uses the IDE or SCSI standards; others are supported that use a parallel port.

Another popular option is to create archive files and burn them onto a CD-ROM with a CD-R/RW writer. The disadvantage to this method is that you must have enough free hard disk space to store the backup files locally before they can be written; because the writing process is not tolerant of errors or delays, it's not recommended to stream directly to CD-ROM. However, CD-ROMs have the advantage of much greater reliability and higher shelf life.

Finally, there are also several options for backing up systems over the network, either to a backup medium such as tape or to an archive directory on the server's hard disk. In large environments, this makes backup strategies easier to manage, as well as saving money that would be spent on local tape drives, media, and so on.

The simplest form of network backup is to use file sharing systems such as NFS or Windows Networking to export the data and have a client run the backup. This method is simple and effective and can be used on smaller networks. For larger networks, client/server backup systems have been developed that allow finer control over the backup process, as well as lower bandwidth requirements.

Standard Backup Tools

Building on its heritage from UNIX, Debian GNU/Linux provides many tried-and-true backup tools from that environment. Besides the standard tools `tar`, `cpio`, and `dump`, Debian provides an enhanced `cpio` tool, called `afio`.

tar

`tar` is the standard archiving tool for UNIX. It is available for almost every UNIX and non-UNIX platform and has been selected as the *de facto* standard for creating UNIX file archives for distribution on the Internet. Essentially, `tar` reads files from the local filesystem and writes them into an archive file (this "file" may actually be a device such as a tape drive instead of a real file).

A typical `tar` looks something like this:

Clearer? - JAL -

```
tar [cdtx][other options][f archivefile] [directory]
```

The first letter argument for the `tar` command specifies which action to perform. The actions are

- `c` Create an archive. This creates a brand new archive in `archivefile`. If `archivefile` exists, it will be overwritten.
- `d` Diff an archive. Check the contents of the directory against the archive and print the differences.
- `t` List the contents of the archive.
- `x` Extract the archive into the specified directory.

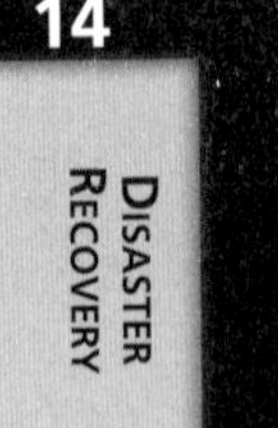

The `f archivefile` argument is optional, but only in theory. The default archive is `/dev/rmt0`, which doesn't exist in Debian. You must specify an archive filename.

Some other options that are useful include

- `z` Compress the archive on-the-fly before writing it, or uncompress the archive before reading it. Uses `gzip` to compress. *Note:* This can be dangerous; a single bit error in the middle of the archive can render the entire archive unreadable from that point forward.

l Stay in the same filesystem; don't cross into filesystems mounted under the given directory.

M Multivolume. If the current volume runs out, ask for another instead of quitting.

p Preserve file permissions when extracting files, including ownership.

v Display verbose information about the current process, including filenames.

W Verify the archive after writing it.

Note that Debian uses GNU tar, and therefore you can use more descriptive options if you want. For example, the following two tar command lines are equivalent:

```
tar cvzf /dev/nht0 /

tar --create --verbose --gzip --file /dev/nht0 /
```

For a complete list of options (and their long equivalents), consult the man page and GNU Info documentation for tar. (At the command line, you can do this by executing man tar and info tar, respectively.)

The following are a few sample command lines for doing some things with tar (both terse and descriptive).

To create a compressed archive in mysource.tar.gz in the parent directory of everything under the current directory

```
tar czf ../mysource.tar.gz .
tar --create --gzip --filename ../mysource.tar.gz .
```

To back up the entire root filesystem only, preserving all file permission information, to the first SCSI tape drive, rewinding the tape after the backup is finished

```
tar clf /dev/st0 /
tar --create --one-file-system --filename /dev/st0 /
```

To restore the backup you just created, including verbose information about filenames

```
cd /; tar xvf /dev/st0 .
tar --extract --verbose --directory / --filename /dev/st0 .
```

cpio/afio

The cpio command is similar to tar; it works on archive files (which, again, can be devices), copying files in and out of these files. Unlike tar, however, cpio reads the list of files to write to the archive from standard input. This makes it slightly harder to use but allows you very fine-grained control of exactly what files to back up. For example, if you were working on a program, tar cf archive. would back up all files, including object code and executable files, but cat MANIFEST ¦ cpio -o archive would back up only the files listed in the MANIFEST file (which could, conceivably, leave out the object and executable files). cpio can also be used as a fast copy command, reading the list of files to copy from standard input and copying them into the directory given.

Tip

Any of the standard utilities can be used to generate the file list for `cpio`; you don't have to use a manually generated static file. A good utility for this task is `find`, which looks through directories generating file listings according to the specifications you give it. For example, you can generate a file list of all true files (not directories, pipes, symlinks, or sockets) owned by user `me` under `/var` with this command:

```
find /var -type f -user me -print
```

This can be combined with other utilities as well; for example, here is one way to get a list of all C source files under a directory:

```
find /dir -type f -print | egrep '\.[chCH]$'
```

These can then be piped to `cpio` as a list of files to back up.

`afio` is an enhancement to `cpio` intended especially for backups. Its method of compression is to compress each file before storing it, instead of compressing the whole archive as one unit. Thus, if there is an error in restoring the compressed archive, you lose only one file. With `tar` and `cpio`, a single read error can cause the rest of the backup from that point to be unreadable. It is also more robust in dealing with read errors when restoring.

`cpio` (like `afio`) is invoked with a command line similar to the following:

```
cpio -(oip) [other options] < file-list [> archive-file]
    [directory]
```

The first option determines the mode `cpio` runs in: `-o` indicates copy-out mode (copying files out to an archive), `-i` indicates copy-in mode (copying files in from an archive), and `-p` indicates copy-pass mode (copying files from one directory to another, skipping the archive step).

The rest of the options are highly dependent on this mode. Without going through an exhaustive list of alternatives, the following are some common combinations.

To back up the files listed on standard input to the floppy tape drive and print each filename as it's processed

```
cpio -ov /dev/qft0
```

To restore the backup taken in the last command, preserve hard links and modification times, and report each file as it is restored

```
cpio -ilmv -I /dev/qft0
```

To copy the files listed in `files` to `/mnt/backup`, preserving hard links and modification times

```
cpio -plmv /mnt/backup < files
```

dump/restore

The `dump` and `restore` commands work differently. Although `tar` and `cpio` read each filesystem normally to perform their backups, `dump` works directly with the filesystem, bypassing the kernel. Thus, backups and restores can be performed on mounted or unmounted filesystems. `dump` takes either a raw filesystem or a directory argument and backs up that filesystem or all files under the given directory. Because it works directly with the filesystem, it can back up only filesystems it understands; currently, the `dump` provided with Debian works only with `ext2` filesystems.

`dump` can perform incremental or differential backups using a *dump level* system. Dumps are run at a dump level; files are backed up if they have been modified since the last dump at a dump level that is the same or lower. Under this scheme, a dump at level 0 is guaranteed to pull a full backup, and a level 1 dump pulls all files backed up since the last level 1 or 0 backup. Thus, any files backed up at level 2 will be backed up again with a level 1 backup. To manage this, `dump` keeps a record in the file `/var/lib/dumpdates` of when each dump was done and at what level.

Tip

Because `dump` works directly with the raw filesystem instead of through the kernel, it is possible to configure the system so a user can back up files he or she doesn't have access to. On Debian, this can be done by adding the user to the `disk` group; the user will then have the ability to dump the filesystem directly. Be careful with this, however! The user is granted full read/write access to the entire disk; this gives the user the ability to overwrite parts of the filesystem and even format it. If the user is clumsy, incompetent, or malicious, or if the user's account is cracked by an outsider, this could have disastrous results.

`dump` additionally can consult `/etc/fstab` to determine what filesystems to dump. The fifth field of `/etc/fstab` (the file used to determine what filesystems to mount at boot-time) contains a number; a nonzero number tells `dump` that this filesystem is intended to be backed up with `dump`. This enables `dump` to print information about what filesystems need to be dumped and when the last dump was taken.

If invoked interactively (in other words, not from an automatic process), `dump` writes output to its terminal concerning its current status. If there is a problem, it prints a diagnostic message and waits for an operator to come and answer its questions. It can also be told to alert all users in the `operator` group through a mechanism similar to `wall` if this happens.

Here is a typical command line for dump:

```
dump -0 -un -f /dev/nht0 /dev/hda1
```

This command executes a full dump of the /dev/hda1 filesystem, updates /var/lib/dumpdates with the dump information when it's finished, and notifies the operator group members if there is a problem. By using a different number in the first argument, dump can be made to do a dump at any level.

The restore process with dump is fairly complicated. In order to do a full restore of a backup made with dump, a blank filesystem must first be re-created, followed by restores of the latest dumps of thc relevant dump levels. The first restore is always the most recent level 0 dump. After this, the next dump to be restored is the dump with the lowest dump level; if multiple dumps have been done at that level, the latest is used. Then all remaining dumps that happened before this dump are discarded, and the dump with the next lowest dump level is then restored. This process continues until all dumps are accounted for.

An example is in order. Suppose I have taken dumps with these dump levels, in chronological order:

```
0 3 2 4 5 5 7 6 8 9
```

The first dump to restore is the level 0 dump. The next one is the level 2 dump (not the level 3 dump, because 2 is less than 3). The level 3 dump is discarded, and the next dump is the level 4 dump. Next comes the second level 5 dump (because it is later in time than the first level 5 dump, which is again discarded), and then the level 6 dump (7 is discarded also). Finally, the level 8 and 9 dumps are restored, and the restore is complete.

The restore program works in several modes, depending on whether you want to do a partial or full restore or just view the backup contents:

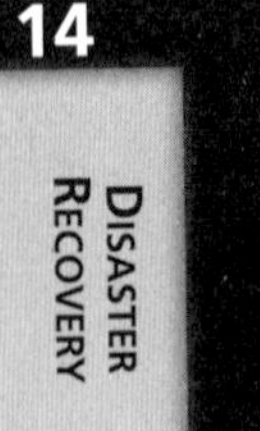

- -C (compare mode) This compares the files in the archive with the files on the disk.
- -r (restore mode) This restores the dump to the specified filesystem.
- -R (restore mode, multivolume) This flag is used to restore from the middle of a multivolume backup.
- -t (list mode) This lists the files in the archive.
- -x (extract mode) Named files and directories are extracted from the archive.
- -i (interactive mode) In this mode, restore acts as a shell, allowing you to browse the archive as if it were a filesystem, adding to and removing from the list of files to restore from the archive as you go. When all the necessary files are added to the extraction list, the extract command starts the actual restore.

An example command line for `restore` might be

```
$ restore -rvy -f /dev/nht0
```

This command restores the files archived in `/dev/nht0` to their original locations, prints verbose information about the restore, and always assumes the answer "yes" to any question you would otherwise ask. (Because any questions would have to do with errors, and the questions always ask whether the restore should continue, in most cases the right answer is "yes.")

rmt

When an archive file is requested as an argument for `tar`, `cpio`, `dump`, or `restore`, you can specify a file in the following format instead:

```
[user@]host:/path/to/file
```

This syntax uses the `rsh` system to invoke a program called `rmt` on the host system as the specified user (or as your current local username if not given). When connected, the local backup program gives `rmt` commands over the network connection to control the archive file on the remote server.

This allows a simple form of network backup between trusted hosts. One system acts as the *backup server*, and the others write their archives to a device on the backup server.

This method of doing network backups requires that `rsh` be set up and working between the systems. `rsh` can be rather complex to set up and is so full of security weaknesses that its use is not recommended. The `ssh` system provides a drop-in replacement for `rsh` that is much more secure.

Tip

Debian GNU/Linux ships with other, higher-level backup alternatives, with nicer user interfaces, more features, and easier restore options. Some of them simply provide nice interfaces for the lower-level tools; others are completely standalone and use their own system. Because they are a bit more obscure than the standard tools, however, it may be a bit more difficult to get good information or documentation on them; this is especially important if you run into problems with them in a disaster recovery situation.

If you decide to use one of these systems, you should read the documentation carefully and conduct some tests on your own. Make sure you understand the restore procedure well; it could be (and likely is) different from the procedure described here.

These are some of the systems shipped with Debian:

- `afbackup`
- `Amanda`
- `floppybackup`
- `KBackup`
- `taper`
- `tob`

Backup Schedules

After deciding what to back up, the media, and the tools, you have one step left: deciding the schedule.

For many situations, a simple schedule is best. If your backups don't take very much time, and if you can schedule them during a time where they are not likely to interfere with other activities on the system, something as simple as "back everything up every night" will do nicely. If things don't change much (and you don't mind losing up to a week of work), you could even go to a weekly full backup, although it's not a good idea to back up less frequently than that.

In today's world, however, with multigigabyte hard drives and all manner of things to fill them, such a simplistic backup system may not work well. With enough data, a full backup to tape can take many hours; on a large network with shared media, there may not be enough time to back everything up. Additionally, a full backup could require more than one media volume, making it inconvenient to perform often. A good schedule can alleviate many of these problems by minimizing the amount of data that has to be backed up per session, while still providing the ability to restore the system quickly should that be necessary.

Understanding Backup Types

Part of the process of scheduling involves deciding what to back up as well as when. To this end, there are several common backup types that can be combined in different ways to make up a schedule. Each backup type archives a slightly different set of data.

Full backups are the simplest: Back up everything. All backup strategies must include regular full backups to be effective.

Incremental backups store only files that have changed since the last backup. Restoring a system that uses incremental backups involves restoring the last full backup, followed by all incremental backups that follow it. This method is simple, but if the same files change every time, it can be wasteful because multiple copies of the same data with minor corrections must be restored during recovery.

Differential backups are similar to incremental backups; they work by backing up only files changed since a previous backup. Unlike incremental backups, however, differential backups can use any previous backup as the "last" backup, up to and including the last full backup. This system is the most complex, because it has to keep track of all previous backup times, and it must compare each file's last-modified time to the list so it can know whether to back up the file this time. The advantage is that differential backup tapes cover all the modifications stored in previous backups, making those backups available. Additionally, because several previous backed-up changes are covered in differential backups, restores are quicker and require fewer tapes.

Differential and incremental backups can be done with any of the standard backup tools. Under `dump`, it's possible to do incremental backups by using the number of days since the last full backup as the dump level; for differential backups, use the same dump level (such as 1) for all backups except the full backup.

The `tar` command accepts a date for the `-N` parameter and will back up only files newer than that date. This makes it simple to implement differential or incremental backups; simply store the date of the previous backup (for incremental) or the previous full backup (for differential) and pass that value to the `-N` parameter.

For `cpio` and `afio`, the process is more complex. Older files must be weeded out during the generation of the file list. One way to do this is to touch a file before every backup (or every full backup for differential backups) and use the `find` utility with the `-newer` option to generate the file lists. Here is a script that will do an incremental backup of the `/var` filesystem:

```
#!/bin/sh


# Backup script for incrementally backing up /var

# with cpio to the /dev/tape device.  (/dev/tape

# should be a symlink to the real backup device.)
# First, create a new file to mark the cutoff
# for the next backup.  For the sake of the admin,
# let's store the date in text form as well.
date > /etc/lastbackup.temp
# Now do the backup, using the previously saved
```

```
# date.
find /var -newer /etc/lastbackup -print ¦ \
  cpio -ov /dev/tape
# Assuming all went well, replace the lastbackup file.
if [ $? -eq 0 ]; then
  rm /etc/lastbackup
  mv /etc/lastbackup.temp /etc/lastbackup
else
  mail -s 'Backup Failure!' root < /dev/null
fi
```

The Grandfather-Father-Son System

One very popular backup schedule is known as the *Grandfather-Father-Son* schedule, or GFS. This method is especially useful for backup systems that maintain online catalogs of backed-up files, because it minimizes the size of those catalogs without compromising data integrity. It is also simple to use and understand, allows for relatively quick restores, and provides a method for keeping a year's worth of backups on a minimal set of tapes if desired. The GFS rotation is used in many environments (not just Linux) and is directly supported by some vendors as the preferred backup schedule.

GFS starts with a weekly schedule of incremental backups, with at least one full backup per week. The last full backup of the week is called the *father backup*; the other backups (full or incremental) are called *son backups*. The son backups are reused on a rotation basis every week, and the father backups are reused on a monthly rotation. The last full backup of the month is called the *grandfather backup*. This last backup is not reused; rather, it is labeled and placed in long-term storage.

Restoring the last backup involves restoring the last full backup taken (either the father or a full son backup), followed by all the incremental backups following that full backup.

It is possible as well to restore from historical backups. Any day up to the previous father backup can be restored. Additionally, the fathers can be restored to provide the last backup of each week, up to one month previously. Finally, the grandfathers provide historical information beyond one month, up to the limit that grandfather backups have been kept.

A variation on GFS uses differential backups instead of incremental backups, using the (grand)father as the reference. This shortens the restore process, because only two backups would have to be restored for any day, and allows the restoration of days preceding the father backup. Under a normal rotation, all the days up to one week previous can be restored; by adding tapes to the son rotation, it is possible to keep daily information up to the last grandfather backup.

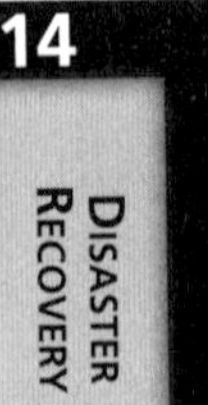

Other Backup Schedules

Although the GFS system has advantages, it is not "the correct system" by any means. By simply dropping the grandfather tapes in GFS, it is possible to simplify the system while still allowing historical restores going back as far as a month. Others use the very simple method of doing weekly full backups and incremental or differential daily backups, reusing each tape on a weekly basis.

The `dump` man page mentions a slightly different schedule, based on differential backups, that has the advantage of minimizing the number of tapes required while storing almost as much information as the GFS method. It works as follows:

1. Start with a backup at dump level 0.
2. Take daily backups after that, using this order of dump levels: 3, 2, 5, 4, 7, 6, 9, 8, 9. (The pattern is a Tower of Hanoi sequence.) If you need more, use 9 for all further dumps.
3. At regular intervals (weekly is recommended), take a backup at dump level 1. After taking this backup, start the sequence in step 2 again. This level 1 backup can be recycled, but only with the other level 1 backups.

This pattern can continue indefinitely, cycling in fresh media regularly to replace the daily and weekly tapes. At certain intervals, another level 0 backup can be taken in place of the level 1 backup to start the process over.

This system enables some historical restores to take place (each day up to one week previously, each week up to the oldest level 1 backup in the rotation, and the original level 0) and, with weekly rotations, ensures that no more than five restores will be necessary to fully restore the system.

Scheduling Your Backups

The best way to ensure that your backups happen when your schedule demands is to set up your system to start your backups automatically. This can be done even if your computer is not on all the time.

The `cron` and `anacron` packages are responsible for running scheduled jobs automatically. `cron` runs programs at certain times according to a schedule, and `anacron` ensures that jobs scheduled for `cron` get run eventually even if the computer is off when they are scheduled to run. These packages are discussed more thoroughly in Chapter 15, "Advanced System Administration."

The default configurations of `cron` and `anacron` includes several jobs that look in the `/etc/cron.daily`, `/etc/cron.weekly`, and `/etc/cron.monthly` directories for scripts and runs them. By placing backup scripts in these directories, you can schedule those jobs to run on a daily, weekly, or monthly basis without learning how to control `cron` and `anacron` more tightly.

By default, the jobs in these directories are scheduled to run between 6 a.m. and 7 a.m., the weekly jobs run only on Saturday, and the monthly job runs on the first day of the month. Make sure your backup scripts know what days not to run so they don't collide with each other or overwrite each other's data.

Other Backup Tips

Remember that no backup medium is perfect. Over time, they will wear out, and they may be defective even when new. Always be sure to verify backups and replace the backup media regularly. You don't want to find out that your backup failed when your system has crashed.

Whatever plan you create for your backup system, stick to it! A simple plan applied consistently will do much more good than a sophisticated plan that is never used. If you find that you are skipping or dropping parts of your original plan, rework it to be less of a burden on you.

Every so often, attempt to restore the last backup to another system. Random tests of the recovery process will tell you whether your plan is sound, may also uncover problems such as media or hardware failures, and will give you practice for the day when panic strikes.

After backups are set up, the next step is to collect the necessary tools and information. The most important tool to have in a pinch is a set of recovery disks.

Recovery Disks

When something goes wrong with your Debian system, the most important tool to have handy is a recovery disk. Many of the problems that can strike a Debian system will keep it from booting properly; others will render the system unusable when it has booted. In these situations, a recovery disk will get your system back to at least a minimal Linux system so you can work on finding the problem and fixing it.

When assembling your disaster recovery toolchest, you should put three recovery disk sets in it: the custom boot floppy you created at installation time, the Debian rescue disk, and a floppy-based Linux system.

The Custom Boot Floppy

During installation and whenever you install a new kernel, the system will give you the option of creating a custom boot floppy. If you didn't create the boot floppy then, you can create one at any time by inserting a formatted, blank floppy and running (as `root`)

```
dd if=/vmlinuz of=/dev/fd0

rdev /dev/fd0 [root filesystem device]

rdev -R /dev/fd0 1
```

This boot floppy allows you to boot your installed Linux system in the event of a problem with the boot system. If LILO gets confused, if the boot sector becomes corrupt, or if the kernel image is lost or corrupted, this floppy will bring your system up to a fully operational state. It does not help in situations where the problem isn't in the boot loader or kernel, because it relies on the system already installed on the hard disk.

The Debian Rescue Disk

The Debian rescue disk is the boot disk used to install the system. It is also helpful as a general boot disk for rescue purposes, especially if you don't have or can't find your custom boot disk.

The rescue disk is also helpful when you have kernel or hardware problems. Because it doesn't come with general hardware support, and because it's a known good kernel, it can sometimes boot in situations where a weird kernel interaction or hardware problem would prevent the custom boot floppy from booting.

Floppy-Based Systems

If your problem doesn't involve a boot loader or kernel problem, if hard-disk failure or some other problem renders your original system unreachable, or if the boot floppies mentioned previously fail, your "tool of last resort" should be a floppy-based system.

Floppy systems are complete Linux installations designed to boot entirely off one or more floppy disks. They are typically small but still powerful. Most provide all the standard GNU/Linux tools, and some even provide more powerful utilities, such as file managers. Some of these systems are provided as direct floppy images; others allow you to build your own custom system, with just the utilities you need.

Debian GNU/Linux ships with tools to create custom floppy systems in the package `yard`. `yard` consists of a set of Perl scripts that create a disk image, copy the user-specified files from your running system to the image, test the image for errors, and write the image to disk. The disk image ends up being compressed, giving you more space for utilities. You can also create a two-disk boot series if you prefer, with the kernel on one disk and the `root` filesystem on the other.

Tip

Having a problem fitting all the utilities you need on that small floppy? Never fear: Linux may be able to give you a bigger floppy drive for free!

With most regular floppy drives, Linux can format a standard 1.44MB floppy to hold more data, up to 1.74MB. The format is such that it is actually bootable on most computers and can be read by some other operating systems, such as MS-DOS. (If you're willing to give up booting and DOS support, it is possible to store up to 1.98MB on a single floppy; see the documentation on `fdutils` for details.)

To format a 1722KB floppy, use the `superformat` utility, with the following command line:

```
superformat --superverify /dev/fd0 hd sect=21 cyl=82
```

This command line formats the disk in the first floppy drive in high-density mode with 21 sectors and 82 cylinders, doing a write verify after formatting. The extra verification step is important to make sure that the floppy is able to handle the larger format; after you are sure that this works, you can remove that option.

Be careful; there are reports that this can damage your floppy drive. Listen for weird noises coming from the drive when writing or reading the disk at certain times, and don't use these large floppies if you hear them.

fdutils

Building a `yard` boot system is a matter of configuring what needs to be on the boot disk and then writing the disk. The configuration is controlled by two files, `/etc/yard/Config.pl` and `/etc/yard/Bootdisk_Contents`. `Config.pl` contains the configuration proper; it is a Perl script with definitions and settings used in the main script. The file itself is well documented, but here are some of the settings you'll likely have to change:

`$floppy`

`$floppy_capacity`

This should be set to the location and capacity of the floppy; the defaults (`/dev/fd0` and `1440`, respectively) will work for most modern systems, because they assume that the first (or only) floppy drive is a 3 1/2-inch high-density drive. If you use one of the high-capacity formats (as described in the previous Tip), you need to change both the capacity and the device; for example, if you use the 82-cylinder settings, you should set the device to `/dev/fd0H1722` and `1722`.

The following should be set to the type of system you want to build. For a single-floppy system, use `single`; for a two-floppy boot/root combo, use `double`:

`$disk_set`

This is a list of directories:

`@additional_dirs`

If a file is listed in `Bootdisk_Contents` without absolute path information, the regular system path will be searched for the file. Directories in this list will be searched first. The list should be written in standard Perl syntax, for example:

```
@additional_dirs = ("/etc/rc.d", "/lib", "/usr/lib");
```

`Bootdisk_Contents` is a list of files to include on the recovery disk. The default files are a good place to start. Make sure the device files for your backup media are included; in particular, tape devices will not be included unless symlinked in `/dev` to a file with `tape` in the filename, and other "odd" devices (Zip/Jaz drives, proprietary CD-ROM drives, SuperDisk drives, and so on) may not be included.

Certain files are set up to load from `/etc/yard/Replacements` instead of from their original location. This enables you to provide slightly changed files for the boot disk that are still based on the originals. This is most often used for statically linked versions of certain utilities, or where you want to provide different configuration files from the ones on your system.

After all the settings are checked properly, run `make_root_fs`. This builds the `root` filesystem for the floppy system, leaving it mounted at the location configured in `Config.pl` (by default, `/mnt/floppy`). If there are errors or warnings, you may have to change some of the settings in `Config.pl` or `Bootdisk_Contents` and run it again.

After this, run `check_root_fs`. This checks for common errors and omissions.

Finally, if you are satisfied with the system as defined, run `write_rescue_disk`. This compresses the `root` filesystem and writes everything to the boot disk(s), checking that everything will fit beforehand. If you were configured for a single-floppy system and not everything will fit on the disk, you will be asked if you want to write a two-disk system.

Be sure to test the system extensively. Boot it up on your system (or on another system if you can't spare the main one) and make sure you can get in. Test the programs you installed to make sure they work. You don't want to find out that you forgot a program when you're in a recovery situation.

Documenting the System

If you ever need to recover a system, you will be thankful for any documentation you have available. Do yourself a favor and write that documentation now, while everything's working fine. Make sure you print a copy (what good will an electronic copy do if the hard disk it's stored on has crashed?), and store it with the other recovery tools.

The following are some important things to document about the system:

- The type of system (Pentium, Pentium II, Alpha, and so on)

- Its general hardware configuration (how many CPUs, how much memory, peripherals such as modems or SCSI cards and their settings, and so on)
- Its disk configuration (IDE or SCSI, model number, size, drive settings such as cylinders and tracks, SCSI ID or IDE master/slave settings, status in a RAID array, and so on)
- Its backup system settings (media type, hardware info, and so on), backup schedule, and backup media storage locations
- System settings (name, authentication settings, and so on)
- Network settings (NIC hardware information, TCP/IP network settings, services run, firewall/NAT settings, and so on)
- Important software installed

Documenting this information doesn't have to be difficult or time consuming, because the system can do much of the work for you. This script, for example, prints information about your CPU, PCI bus, memory, filesystem, SCSI devices, hardware configuration, serial ports, network card, and shadow file configuration for you:

```
#! /bin/bash
# Script for printing information about your system that
# could be handy for disaster recovery.  The output can
# be piped to 'lpr' for printing.
uname -a; echo
echo "CPU INFORMATION"; echo
cat /proc/cpuinfo
echo
echo "PCI CONFIGURATION"; echo
cat /proc/pci
echo
echo "MEMORY CONFIGURATION"; echo
free
echo
echo "FILESYSTEM INFORMATION"; echo
df
echo
if [ -f /proc/scsi/scsi ]; then
  echo "SCSI INFORMATION"; echo
  cat /proc/scsi/scsi
  echo
fi
echo "SYSTEM HARDWARE INFORMATION"; echo
echo "IO Ports:"; cat /proc/ioports; echo
echo "Interrupts:"; cat /proc/interrupts; echo
echo "DMA channels:"; cat /proc/dma; echo
echo "SERIAL INFORMATION"; echo
setserial -vg /dev/ttyS? /dev/ttyS?? 2>/dev/null | grep -v 'unknown'
echo
```

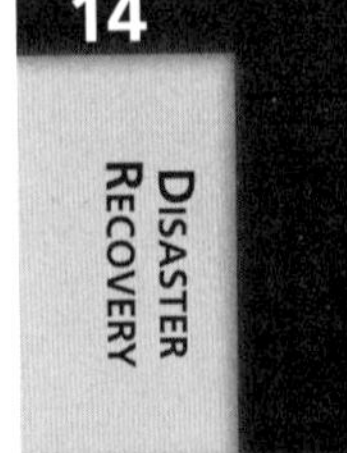

```
echo "NETWORK INFORMATION"; echo
/sbin/ifconfig
/sbin/route -n
if [ -f /etc/shadow ]; then
  echo "/etc/shadow detected."
else
  echo "No shadow password database detected."
fi
```

Tip

The command `dpkg --get-selections` prints out the list of installed Debian packages. If you save that output to a file with a command such as `dpkg --get-selections > packages.lst`, you can use that file to install the same software on a new or restored system. To install these selections, run

```
dpkg --set-selections <filename>

  apt-get update

  apt-get upgrade
```

Avoiding Problems

Preventing disaster is as important as preparing for it; it's obviously better to prevent problems than to recover from problems. It's possible to avoid serious outages even with random and uncontrollable calamities, such as hard drive failures or power blackouts.

Don't Use the `root` User

User error is a major cause of outages. An easy way to help prevent these outages—or limit their damage—is to avoid using `root` as your principal user.

The security system of Debian GNU/Linux can provide effective protection against many mistakes, such as accidental file deletion or overwriting. But because the sysadmin has to have the ability to work on any part of the system, the `root` user has no such restrictions.

Tip

If you're running a 2.2 kernel, there's another option available to you for avoiding system failures: RAID. RAID (Redundant Array of Inexpensive Disks) is a technology that enables you to combine a number of physical disks into one or more logical volumes, some of which include fail-safe benefits.

> Some RAID support is in the 2.0 series of kernels, but the fail-safe features are new to 2.2. These include RAID 1, or disk mirroring, where data is written simultaneously to two separate disks; RAID 4, which combines multiple disks into one volume with an additional *parity disk*, which contains information for recalculating the contents of a failed disk; and RAID 5, *parity striping*, which stores parity information on the other drives (similarly to RAID 4) but *stripes* that information across all the drives.
>
> Fail-safe RAID support is not a standard feature in the current version of Debian GNU/Linux; therefore, it will not be discussed here. For more information, please consult the Software RAID mini-HOWTO, from any Linux Documentation Project mirror or from its home site at
>
> `http://linas.org/linux/Software-RAID/Software-RAID.html`

You should always use a personal user ID to do everything on your system, only switching to `root` on rare occasions to perform specific tasks before switching back. The `su` and `sudo` utilities (as well as others) allow this quick switching without logging off and back on.

Uninterruptible Power Supply (UPS)

Problems with power can result in more problems with any computer, and Debian GNU/Linux is no exception. Because of the way Debian stores files and writes to the disk, it is important that your system be shut down properly every time; when it isn't, disk corruption can result. Additionally, power spikes and fluctuations can damage other parts of your hardware.

The best insurance against power problems is a device called an uninterruptible power supply (UPS). These range in size from beefy power strips to refrigerator-size cases. All of them plug in between your computer and the wall outlet, and all have large batteries in them, allowing your computer to keep running for a short time after the power goes out. Additionally, all maintain some form of power conditioning, filtering out power spikes and surges before they have a chance to damage your hardware.

Most UPSs also have another handy feature: the capability of talking to your PC and warning it when there's a power problem. Usually, this occurs through a serial cable connected to the power supply on one end and to a serial port on your PC on the other. Most models can warn the system of power outages and low battery conditions and also alert the system when power is restored; some more advanced models analyze the power system constantly and can provide more advanced information about the quality of the power line.

This feature works with Linux on most UPS models. At a minimum, Linux can handle the basic trouble signals from a UPS; with some models, finer-grained control is possible. To get this working, however, it's important to understand how Linux handles UPS power events.

How UPS Management Works on Debian GNU/Linux

Debian GNU/Linux manages UPS events through the `init` process, the master process on the system. A separate process watches the serial port the UPS is connected to, waiting for an event or some data to come in. When a critical event comes in, the process uses a signal—`SIGPWR`—to alert the `init` process of a change in status on the UPS and writes the current status to `/etc/powerstatus`. `init` checks that status and then runs a script—the `powerwait` script when power is first lost, the `powerfailnow` script when the battery starts to run low, and the `powerokwait` script if the power comes back on.

These scripts are usually set to work about the same way on all systems. In a `powerwait` situation, a shutdown is initiated within a set number of minutes; this prevents a total shutdown in the event of a momentary lapse of power, while preventing a total battery drain during an extended outage. The `powerfailnow` script usually starts the shutdown process immediately. The `powerokwait` script usually cancels impending shutdowns (although not shutdowns in progress, which are very difficult to abort properly).

Thus, the system is able to handle the basic procedures for handling a power outage, while leaving the actual task of communicating with the UPS to a separate program. This modular approach allows enhanced features to be supported without requiring customized versions of essential system software (such as `init`).

Software for a UPS

Debian GNU/Linux ships with several packages for talking to the UPS. These include

- `genpower` This is a good general-purpose UPS monitor. It contains sample configurations for several UPS models and handles the basic functions well.
- `upsd` Another basic UPS monitor, with a twist: It can work over a network, with a master `upsd` alerting client `upsd` monitors over the network. This should work well—assuming that the network equipment (hubs, routers, and so on) is also protected by a UPS.
- `apcd` This package is specific to APC's popular line of UPSs. It can talk to "smart" APC UPSs and can keep a log of extra power information.

Each of these packages works in the same way. A daemon process is started, which watches a serial port for interesting information from the UPS. When an important event is detected, the software writes the current status to `/etc/powerstatus` and signals `init`; it then continues to watch for more events, and do more updates as needed. Mostly, these packages need little more information than the model of UPS you're using and the serial port to work; for information on configuring this, check the documentation for the particular package you've chosen.

Sooner or later, despite all the planning and effort you put into the system, you will one day find yourself in a disaster situation. It is important to be prepared for that day, and to have in mind what you will do to recover from the problem.

Practice is a good way of testing your knowledge. If you can, build a duplicate of your current system from backups and then attempt some of these procedures on it. This way, you won't be caught unaware when disaster strikes.

There are three steps that must be taken in a disaster situation. First, assess the situation and find out what the problem seems to be. Second, fix it if possible. If there is permanent damage to your system, recovery steps may be needed; you may need to restore from backup or reinstall certain packages.

Assessing the Disaster

The first thing to do when your system is having problems is not to panic. Calmly assess the situation and look for solutions to the problem.

If some services on the system do not seem to be available, do some digging to find out what the problem is. Use the `ps` command to list the processes on the system. Is your errant process among them? If not, you may be able to get the process running again with a simple restart. Check the service's log files and the system log files in `/var/log` first, to see that there isn't some serious problem, and then restart the service with its script in `/etc/init.d`. If it starts up fine, you're okay.

Sometimes, you'll have some messages on your console or in your log files telling what went wrong. Do any of them have to do with your main filesystems? If so, that's a good indication that you will probably want to reboot and check them. Other filesystems (such as floppies or CD-ROM drives) are probably not as much of a problem; you should unmount them. You can unmount them and try remounting them if they are important.

If the system just crashed, look at the crash message to see what might have gone wrong, for future diagnostics or a bug report. Then try to reboot. The system will check all its filesystems at boot-time; in most circumstances, the filesystem will check out OK, and the boot will continue. If it doesn't, the system will print out a message about the failure and put you at a `root` prompt to give you a chance to fix the problem.

Other times, you will reboot for an unrelated reason, and the system will not boot properly. This indicates a problem with the boot process; perhaps a new kernel was not correctly installed, or some new software is interfering. Use one of the alternate boot methods to bypass the normal boot process to disable the offending program or fix it.

Booting the System

The first task to be done when the system is having problems is to boot properly. You may need a special recovery environment to work in, giving you all the tools you need for examining the problem while others are prevented from using the system, or the boot process itself may be having problems. Either way, you must get the system started before you can fix the problem.

Using a Special Boot Option

The Linux kernel recognizes several diagnostic boot options. For LILO or SYSLINUX boot systems (this would include the Debian rescue floppy, as well as the normal boot process), you can give these options at the boot command line, which will usually give you the `boot:` prompt. If you use LILO and do not see that, you may have to press the Shift, Control, or Alt key after `LILO` prints on the screen.

LILO supports the concept of named boot configurations; each boot image (including the default) has a name. If you do not want to boot normally, you need to give LILO the name of the boot image to use. If you press Tab, it gives you a list of boot images to try. You can then give boot options on the command line after the image, with each option separated by a space.

The `single` boot command causes Debian to come up in single-user mode; in the middle of the boot process, it asks for the `root` password and then gives you a normal `root` shell. At this point, only a minimum of processes will be running, and no one is able to log in or otherwise connect to the system. From here, you should be able to proceed with troubleshooting. You have the option of logging out of that shell to continue the boot process if you want; unless the fix was very simple, however, this is not recommended.

The `init=/bin/sh` boot command causes the system to bypass `init` completely, running a `root` shell in its place. At this point, nothing else is working on the system, and the only filesystem mounted is the `root` filesystem in read-only mode. This provides a good environment for checking the filesystem for errors, as described later in this chapter.

Booting with the Rescue or Custom Floppy

The Debian rescue floppy (which you used to install the system) or the custom boot floppy can be used to boot the system. For the rescue floppy, the rescue image is called `rescue`; the first boot argument should be the device name for your normal `root` filesystem. For example, if your normal `root` filesystem is `/dev/hda1`, type `rescue /dev/hda1`. The custom boot floppy knows about your `root` filesystem and should work. Either way, your old system should come up normally.

The custom boot floppy does not support boot options, because of the way the boot kernel is written to the disk. If you need special boot options and you cannot boot normally, you should use the Debian rescue disk.

Using a Floppy-Based System

If none of these boot methods works, you need your custom floppy-based system. This gives you a complete system independent of the filesystems on your disks. From here, you should be able to perform diagnostic tasks that might otherwise be impossible if certain portions of your system are messed up.

If the system does not boot from a floppy, you are likely looking at a serious hardware failure, perhaps on the motherboard or CPU. Although very serious, this is outside the scope of this book. Most likely, you will have to replace the system and restore it from backups. Check your system's warranty information, or take it to the place you bought it.

chroot

Sometimes, you may be working on your system and you may need to run a program that works from the `root` directory. If you are running from a floppy-based system, the program will work on the `root` of the floppy system, which is most likely not what you want. Some of these programs can be told to work on a different filesystem; for those that can't, they can be made to work with a utility called `chroot`.

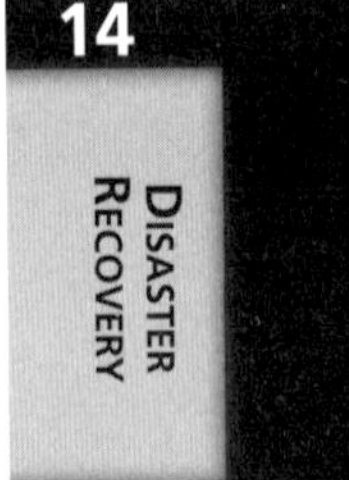

`chroot` is a utility that sets the `root` directory to point to some arbitrary directory before running a process; this process will be unable to use other directories not under the new `root`. It can run any program as the `chroot` process; it runs the user's default shell if no program is given.

When recovering a system from a floppy-based system, you can use `chroot` to set a process to use the `root` of the old system as its `root`. Then, programs that use hard-coded absolute paths will work, as will absolute symlinks.

Fixing Disk Problems

Disk corruption is one of the most common problems to deal with. Even if a crash was caused by some other problem, the crash will inevitably leave some damage to the filesystem in its wake.

The normal boot-time checks will catch most problems without any intervention. Sometimes, however, there will be a problem that cannot be safely fixed automatically. When this happens, the system will stop the boot process, provide an error message, and allow you to log in in single-user mode, after which the system will reboot.

Using `e2fsck`

If this happens, the next step is to log in and run `e2fsck` on the damaged filesystem. This command works much like the `chkdsk` program on DOS and Windows NT or the ScanDisk utility in Windows: It examines the data on the hard drive for errors, misplaced data, and other problems.

The standard notation for the `e2fsck` command is

```
e2fsck [options] filesystem-device
```

This should never be done on filesystems that are mounted read/write; you should either unmount the filesystem, or (in the case of the `root` filesystem, which cannot be unmounted) you should mount it read-only.

Some important options include the following:

- `-b` superblock   The superblock is the master block of the filesystem; it contains information necessary for reading the rest of the disk. Because of its importance, multiple copies of the superblock are stored on the disk. If the first superblock becomes unreadable, you can tell `e2fsck` to use one of the copies. These are usually stored at regular intervals in the filesystem; for example, one is usually stored at block 8193, another at block 16,385, and so on. You can get a list of superblocks in your filesystem with the `findsuper` command.
- `-y`, `-n`   These tell `e2fsck` to answer "yes" or "no," respectively, to any questions that would be asked.

Generally, you should run `e2fsck` in interactive mode so you understand what may be happening to your system.

Using `lost+found`

Every `ext2` filesystem has a `lost+found` directory. This special directory is intended for `e2fsck` to put file fragments without any associations to specific files.

You should always check the `lost+found` directory as soon as you can after running a manual `e2fsck`. Some of the files found there may be important files to the system. The files will have very strange names, but you should be able to tell what they are by their contents.

Restoring from Backup

In many cases, there is nothing you can do to salvage a filesystem. Serious crashes on busy systems are known to do this, as are disk failures. Rather than fight with `e2fsck`, it is often best to simply start over with the last backup.

There are several steps to restoring a filesystem from backup:

1. First, fix any problems that caused the corruption in the first place, if you can. A failed hard disk is not going to be any better at holding your data restore than it is at holding your current data.
2. If the `root` filesystem is involved, you have to boot a floppy-based system before restoring. Otherwise, it may be possible to boot from the hard disk. Make sure that the entire normal boot process is bypassed, using a boot command such as `init=/bin/sh`. (See Chapter 15 for details.)
3. Do any partitioning or reformatting of the hard disk that is necessary. The `fdisk` command provides a partitioning utility with a menu interface, and `mke2fs` formats and initializes each partition with the `ext2` filesystem. The command for `mke2fs` is as follows:

   ```
   mke2fs [-c] <filesystem-device>
   ```

   The `-c` causes `mke2fs` to check for bad blocks before writing information to the device.
4. Mount the newly formatted partition read/write to a directory.
5. At this point, you can run your `restore` utility to restore the backup. Be sure to restore to the right place! To recap, the basic commands for restoring a system with the major backup systems are

   ```
   tar:
     cd <directory-to-restore>; tar xvpf <backup-file>
   cpio/afio:
     cd <directory-to-restore>
     cpio -ilmv -I <backup-file>
   dump/restore:
     cd <directory-to-restore>; restore rf <backup-file>
   ```

   Be sure to match the other flags that are needed (for example, compression options).
6. If you used an incremental or differential backup system, restore the incremental backups.
7. Repeat this process for any other filesystems you may need to restore.
8. If you had to restore any filesystem involved with booting, ensure that LILO's boot options are reset. This can be done by mounting any boot-related directories the way they will be mounted in the regular system and then running

   ```
   lilo -r <root-directory>
   ```

Tips on Solving Problems

Tracking down and solving problems with computers is much like detective work; you have to find clues that point to the right solution to the problem. Fortunately, the computer itself (at least in the case of Debian GNU/Linux) does its best to collect those clues for you. Here are some tips for finding these clues and solving those problems:

- Did you just add or remove hardware to your system? If you did, try to restore things to the way they were. If the problem goes away, there may be some hardware interaction or driver problem that is causing the problem.
- Did you just install or remove some software? Again, try reversing what you just did to see if the new or removed software was the cause of the problem.
- Check your log files. Many of these are stored under `/var/log`. They often contain interesting information about what happens immediately before, during, and after the problem.
- Look at which software is running after the problem occurs (if your system didn't crash). Is anything missing? For example, you might suddenly lose the ability to work with the network at weird times. If you run a local name server and the name server isn't running at the times when the network appears to be missing, that could point to a problem with the name server.
- If the problem happens at regular intervals (such as every Sunday at 1 p.m. or every morning), check which jobs are set to run with `cron`. An errant job could be causing the problem.

Summary

Disasters are never fun; like death and taxes, however, they seem to be inevitable. It's important, therefore, to plan for them ahead of time, so their impact is as minimal as possible. By following a regular backup schedule, assembling necessary tools ahead of time, and moving carefully when a problem does arise most siturations can be handled quickly, letting you go on to the more important business of learning and using your Debian system.

CHAPTER

Advanced System Administration

by Jeff Licquia

IN THIS CHAPTER

red 01 02 18

It is arguable that the nature of the information technology industry makes it a never-ending classroom for those working in it; no one denies the need for constant learning and striving in order to stay competitive in the job market. It is fitting that UNIX-like systems, such as Debian GNU/Linux, have flourished in this market for so long; the incredible flexibility such systems offer makes learning them such a process. Even after years of experience, it's always possible to learn something new, to see something that has gone unseen for a long time.

This is the precise reason why a chapter on "advanced system administration" is such a misnomer. It implies that the "secrets of the universe" lie within its pages, and that, having reached this point, one has achieved the heights. Nothing could be further from the truth.

This chapter's goal is much different from that. Rather than present the ultimate secrets of administering a Debian machine, this chapter seeks to simply point the way to future discovery. By discussing some of the advanced tools and some tricks of the trade, it is hoped that the reader will use this as a stepping stone into exploring more of the possibilities that are available.

Rather than focus strongly on one issue, this chapter is structured as a series of tips and insights, loosely grouped together under the umbrella of "advanced system administration." It is not necessary to read the entire chapter through; each section is intended to stand on its own. You can therefore skip ahead to the section that interests you, explore it as long as you like, and then skip back and pick up something preceding it.

The tips given here were chosen either because of their usefulness (such as job scheduling, automounting, or quotas) or because they provide insight into how the system works (the boot process comes to mind here). None of these are strictly required for keeping up a regular Debian system; however, they provide many new options for those interested in learning them.

Understanding (and Hacking) the Boot Process

To many, the boot process is a bit of a mystery, `rooted` in the deepest magic of the system's internal workings. The complexity involved in getting all that stuff working seems insurmountable. In fact, the Debian boot process is remarkably simple, given all of the tasks it must complete. Furthermore, it is much easier to customize than the boot process of almost any other operating system, from seamlessly adding on a few procedures to rearranging the most fundamental steps to your liking.

Working with Boot Loaders and the Kernel

At the beginning, when the power first turns on, the computer's internal systems take over. After doing what they do—a process that should be familiar to anyone who's ever waited for the memory counter to finish ticking—the system looks for a valid and ready boot device and loads the first sector off that device. This sector is called the "boot sector"; its main function is to load the main operating system kernel.

The boot sector under Debian GNU/Linux is different for each architecture. For Intel and Motorola 68000 versions, it's called LILO; for SPARC, it's SILO; and for Alpha, it's called MILO. Although each boot loader has functions and attributes specific to its hardware, the general purpose is the same: to load the Linux kernel into memory and start it, optionally passing boot parameters to the kernel for controlling how it boots. Because most readers will be familiar with the Intel platform, this section discusses the procedures with LILO; the general principles, however, are applicable on any platform.

When an Intel-based computer hands control to it, LILO immediately reaches into the hard disk and loads the kernel into memory. LILO has only a bare understanding of the ext2 filesystem, so it must have the absolute location of the kernel file embedded into it; this is why you must run LILO every time you switch kernels. Linux kernels are usually compressed, so LILO must uncompress the kernel in memory. After the kernel is uncompressed, LILO passes control to it, transferring the boot parameters it hasn't used itself.

The Tecra Bug

This two-step process has caused a problem on Intel machines that isn't there on other platforms. Intel systems, because of their need to retain compatibility with DOS, initially start in real mode, which comes complete with one of DOS's major limitations: Only 640KB of memory is available for use at boot time. For LILO to uncompress larger kernels in memory, therefore, LILO must set up the rest of memory as old DOS-style extended memory, load the kernel up there, and execute it. The kernel then takes responsibility for switching the processor into protected mode, which is more like the regular mode other platforms start with. This is the source of the so-called "tecra bug" in many notebook computers and a few regular machines.

Configuring the Kernel

The kernel's first jobs involve configuring itself and finding out what kind of hardware it's running on. After parsing the boot parameters and extracting important kernel-level information from them, the kernel examines the major parts of the system, such as the CPUs, the amount of RAM, what buses are available (PCI, ISA, and so on), what console type is available, and so on. It then consults all of the drivers compiled into it, asking each of them to probe or search for the hardware they support; when applicable, boot options tell these drivers exactly where the hardware is. Finally, the kernel looks at its internal configuration or the kernel parameters for the `root` device; this device is then mounted as the `root` filesystem. Most of the time, the `root` filesystem is configured to be mounted read-only.

All this time, the kernel is writing information to the console about what it has found. These messages are later written to the system log and are vital to solving hardware and boot problems.

Once all the hardware is configured and ready, the kernel starts the first process. By default, the first program to be run is `/sbin/init`; the `init` boot parameter causes Linux to load whatever program is specified. For example, a common way to get to a shell when nothing else works is to specify `init=/bin/sh` as a boot parameter; the kernel then starts a shell as the first process.

The boot parameters that figure so prominently in this first stage of the process can be expressed in two places:

- The `append=` parameter in LILO's configuration file
- The `boot:` prompt LILO briefly prints before continuing

Most boot parameters parsed at this stage provide configuration settings for installed hardware, such as console video settings, memory size, hard disk identity and size, the location of expansion cards, and the like. For a more complete list of the possible parameters, consult the Boot Prompt HOWTO (part of the Linux Documentation Project).

Working with `init`

The master process, `/sbin/init`, is very important. As the first process, it is responsible, directly or indirectly, for creating every other process on the system. It watches for certain types of events, during and after booting, and reacts to them. It is ultimately responsible for both starting the system (after the kernel has done its part) and shutting down the system when needed (by stopping all processes and saving all cached data before telling the kernel to stop).

The standard init that ships with Debian GNU/Linux is organized around a general principle called a *runlevel*. A runlevel is simply a numbered property that describes the state init is in at a particular time. `init`'s configuration file, `/etc/inittab`, associates certain actions with certain runlevels; when `init` is started, it simply performs the actions specified in its configuration file according to the runlevel it is in.

init's Configuration File

The `/etc/inittab` file is structured as a series of entries, one per line. Each entry has the following fields, separated by colons: a one- or two-letter descriptor, the runlevels this entry applies to, a description of the type of entry it is, and a process to start for that entry. These are some of the more interesting entry types:

- `initdefault` — This entry defines the default runlevel, which `init` starts in unless overridden.
- `sysinit` — This entry tells `init` to run this process first as a system initialization program. The runlevel is ignored.
- `ctrlaltdel` — Execute this process whenever the Ctrl+Alt+Del key sequence is pressed and one of the specified runlevels is active.
- `kbrequest` — Execute this process whenever the special keystroke is pressed. This keystroke is defined by the keyboard setup macros as the key with the `KeyboardSignal` action associated with it. By default, this key is Alt+UpArrow.
- `wait` — Run the process once when one of the specified runlevels starts, and wait for it to complete before continuing.
- `respawn` — Run the process in the background when the specified runlevels start. If the process exits, run it again, continuously.

Starting init

When `init` starts, it first runs the program specified in the `sysinit` entry in `/etc/inittab`. It then switches to the default runlevel, either the one given as a boot parameter or the one specified as the default in `inittab`, and goes through the entire `inittab` file, line by line, performing the required actions as necessary. Once all actions have been performed, `init` goes into the background, waiting for an event it needs to handle (such as a respawned process exiting or a request to change runlevels).

The `inittab` file is generally left alone; most customization is generally left to later stages. The main exceptions are the `respawn` entries. These are useful for handling console login sessions and dial-up applications such as voice mail or fax. A typical respawn entry looks like this:

```
T3:23:respawn:/sbin/mgetty -x0 -s 57600 ttyS3
```

This entry manages a modem on the serial port `/dev/ttyS3` when in runlevels 2 and 3.

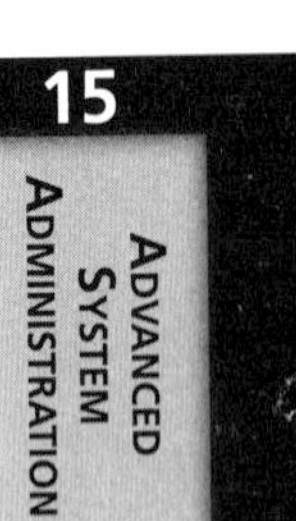

Understanding Startup Scripts

In the Debian GNU/Linux system, `init` launches two scripts: `/etc/init.d/rcS` and `/etc/init.d/rc`. Both of these scripts launch other scripts to do the actual setup of the system. The startup system they use is copied from System V UNIX and provides the run-level system with much of its power and flexibility.

All of the scripts used to start the system are stored in `/etc/init.d`. Each task has its own script. Each of the scripts takes a single argument indicating the action to take. The allowed values are

`start`	Start, initialize, enable, or otherwise run whatever this script does.
`stop`	Shut down, back out, quit, or otherwise stop whatever this script does.
`restart`	Cause this process, whatever it does, to re-initialize itself. This can fail if it would otherwise cause a loss of service.
`force-reload`	Force the process to re-initialize, no matter what loss of service might come.

When a parameter doesn't make sense, some of the scripts ignore it; for example, the script that checks the filesystems does not actually enable or start anything, so there is no need to stop or restart anything.

In addition, a series of directories under `/etc` start with `rc`. These directories contain symlinks to the scripts in `/etc/init.d`. Each directory is named after a runlevel, and ends in `.d`, so the directory for runlevel 2 is named `/etc/rc2.d`. Two extra rc directories also exist; both of them are associated with system boot initialization. `/etc/rcS.d` is organized similarly to the other `/etc/rc*` directories, and `/etc/rc.boot` contains its own scripts instead of symlinks. The `rc.boot` directory is depreciated and should not be used.

The symlinks in each of these directories use a naming convention that indicates when they are run and in what order. The first character in the name is a letter, either `S` or `K`. Following this is a number, and following that is the name of the script linked to. As an example, one of the symlinks installed under Debian is `S91apache`; as the name indicates, it is symlinked to the script `apache` in `/etc/init.d`.

When init runs one of its scripts to indicate a change in its state (either at bootup or when changing runlevels), the `init` script first looks in the directory of the new runlevel and runs all of the `K` scripts, in ascending numeric order by the number in the filename, passing the `stop` argument to each script. `init` then looks in the same directory and runs all of the `S` scripts, again in ascending numeric order by the number in the filename, passing the `start` argument to each of these as they run. At bootup, the `init` script additionally runs all of the `S` scripts in `/etc/rcS.d` (and any legacy scripts in `/etc/rc.boot`) before switching to the default runlevel and running the `S` scripts associated with it. (The `K` scripts are skipped because nothing is running yet.) The main script (`/etc/init.d/rc`) is optimized to not re-run an `S` script if there is an `S` script for it in the previous runlevel and there is no `K` script in the current one.

In the standard Debian inittab, init is configured to run all of these scripts before starting any of the respawn entries. When init is handed control at boot time, it first executes the system initialization scripts one by one until each is finished. It then switches into the default runlevel, runs all of the S scripts associated with the runlevel, and finally runs all of the respawn entries. At that point, the boot process is done; getty is running on the virtual consoles, and xdm (started from an init script) is providing a graphical login as well.

Special Runlevels

Within this runlevel system, the processes of shutting down and rebooting is implemented as two special runlevels. These are configured as runlevel 0 (for shutdown) and 6 (for reboot). Each of these run-level directories contain mostly K scripts for shutting down services gracefully, unconfiguring some devices, and so on. The S scripts do the final cleanup of the system—killing all remaining stray processes, unmounting filesystems, and the like. The last "startup" script actually halts or reboots the machine.

The single-user mode runlevel (1) is similar. It mostly runs K scripts to shut down the system. Its lone S script switches init into the S runlevel, which really isn't a runlevel at all; in this mode, init simply runs sulogin on the console and switches back to the default runlevel once that process exits.

Finally, the state that init is in before selecting a runlevel at boot has been given a pseudo runlevel: N. Many of Debian's run-level management tools recognize N. Its symlink directory is /etc/rcS.d.

Altering the Boot Process

This system gives the sysadmin powerful and flexible tools for altering and customizing the machine. It is possible to add your own scripts to run at boot without disturbing any of the files installed by the system. If multiple configurations are needed, they can each be assigned to a runlevel and selected at boot or switched at runtime. Services can be disabled and enabled without completely removing the software that runs them.

As an example, you might want to set up a system that normally boots to text mode, but can be switched in an instant to use xdm to allow graphical logins. This can be done by setting the xdm startup script to run only in a certain runlevel (not the default), and switching to that runlevel whenever you want graphical logins enabled.

New scripts should support the standard init script options. You can do the necessary symlinks yourself, or you can use the update-rc.d tool. update-rc.d has this syntax:

```
update-rc.d [-nf] script_name command priority runlevels
```

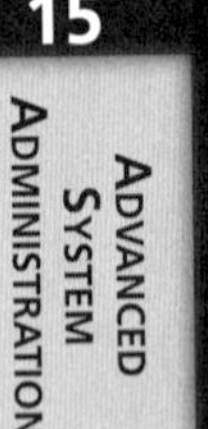

Each of these options works as follows:

- `-n` — Dry run. Don't actually do anything; just print out what would be done.
- `-f` — Force the configuration even if other symlinks are present. The default is to abort with an error if some other symlinks are present, so that a previously selected configuration is not overriden.
- *`script_name`* — The name of the script.
- *`command`* — The action to take. `remove` removes all symlinks to that script in the boot directories. `defaults` installs the default set of symlinks: `K` links in 0, 1, and 6 and S scripts in 2 through 5. `start` installs S symlinks in the given runlevels. `stop` installs `K` symlinks in the given runlevels.
- *`priority`* — The number used in the symlink name to order the script. It can be omitted, in which case the default value of `20` is used. Two numbers can also be given; these are interpreted as the `S` number and the `K` number, in that order. This option should be blank for `remove`.
- *`runlevels`* — The runlevels to install the symlinks to. Not used with `defaults` or `remove`.

`init` scripts are considered to be configuration files (conffiles) on Debian; this means that you can alter the scripts themselves if you need. This is not recommended, however; most of the time, you can customize that package through other means. Future versions of Debian might change this rule, and `init` scripts might lose their status as conffiles if that happens. If possible, see if you can achieve the same effect some other way, or disable the provided script and use a completely separate script to store your changes.

Scheduling Jobs with `cron`

Although easy administration of a system is always good, it is also always better that a system administer itself without intervention so admins aren't stuck with manually pruning log files, backing up the system, checking system integrity, managing quotas, and so on. For that to happen, there has to be a method for tasks to be automatically started when they're needed.

Debian GNU/Linux provides an enhanced form of the UNIX `cron` system for job scheduling. It allows packages and administrators to add arbitrary jobs at specified times, and it also can run jobs daily, weekly, or monthly, letting the system or an administrator choose the best exact time for running these jobs. And for machines that aren't left running all the time, Debian also provides a package to ensure that important jobs get run even if the machine is unavailable at their regularly scheduled time, and it also provides the ability to do quick one-time scheduling.

Format of crontab Files

/etc/crontab

Jobs are scheduled with cron using a special format called a crontab entry. Each crontab entry is on a line by itself, with all fields separated by spaces. The last field can contain spaces, but the fields before it cannot, since this would confuse cron's parser.

The fields are, in order:

```
min hour dom mon wk user job_command_line
```

The fields are generally self-explanatory. *min* is the minutes past the hour, *hour* is the hour in 24-hour format, *dom* is the day of the month, *month* is the month number where January is 1, *wk* is the weekday number with Sunday as 0 or 7, *user* is a valid username, and *job_command_line* is the command to execute at the specified time. For the months or the days of the week, you can use the first three letters of the name instead of the number.

The fields that specify the time can specify multiple values within the field. For simple multiple values, separate the values with a comma (without a space). For a range, the dash is used; for example, you can specify every hour between 3 PM and 6 PM with 15-18, and all the workdays can be expressed with Mon-Fri. It's also possible to use step values with a range by adding a slash and the step; for example, to run a job every two hours between 8 AM and 5 PM, you can use 8-17/2 in the hour field. Finally, the * character indicates every possible value for that field.

crontab files consist of one or more of these entries. Additionally, you can specify environment variables at the top of the file, and they are set before executing the jobs in the file. The LOGNAME entry cannot be set here, however, for security reasons. As with most Debian configuration files, comments can be prefixed with a # in the file and are ignored.

If anything happens that should be reported to someone (for example, if a program prints output to stdout or stderr or if the command fails), the status is sent via email to the user specified in the MAILTO variable (or to the owner of the crontab file if MAILTO is not set).

Adding Jobs with /etc/cron.d

Rather than have to append system jobs to run to the standard crontab file, Debian's cron supports using /etc/cron.d as a repository for individual crontab files. cron reads each file in /etc/cron.d and treats all of the entries there as if they had been entered in the master crontab file.

This is the preferred way to add jobs to cron that must run at certain times; for example, if a job needs to be run every 15 minutes, or must run after something else. This way is cleaner than editing /etc/crontab, easier to reverse, and allows the package management system to manage /etc/crontab properly.

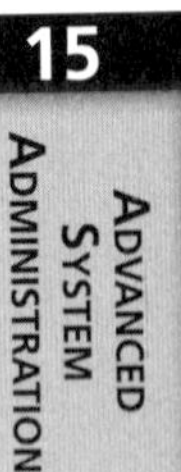

Adding Jobs with /etc/cron.time

Three other directories, /etc/cron.daily, /etc/cron.weekly, and /etc/cron.monthly, contain scripts or programs. At the specified intervals, all of the programs in the associated directory are executed. The exact time is configured in /etc/crontab and can be changed if the times aren't convenient, although their frequency should be preserved.

For most jobs, jobs that must run regularly and aren't sensitive to the exact time they run, this is the best way to schedule a job. Besides the cleanliness and ease-of-management issues, backup systems ensure that these jobs run as closely as possible to the standard intervals if the system is not available for some reason. See the section "Handling Machines That Don't Run Constantly," later in this chapter, for more details.

Using cron as a Regular User

cron can also be made available to non-root local users. Each user (including root) can have his or her own crontab file. Jobs specified in these cron files are run as the user.

The crontab command allows each user to manipulate his or her own crontab file. You can give one of the following options:

file Install the named file as the user's crontab file.

-l List the user's crontab file on stdout.

-e Edit the user's crontab file with the default editor (set in VISUAL or EDITOR).

-r Remove the user's crontab.

In addition, root can specify -u user, which allows root to manipulate a different user's crontab. User crontabs are stored in /var/spool/cron/crontabs; the permissions on that directory, however, restrict regular users from accessing that directory, so regular users must use the crontab command to change their crontab.

By default, all users are allowed to use cron. The files /etc/cron.allow and /etc/cron.deny allow you to restrict this permission; each file consists of a list of users, one per line. If /etc/cron.allow exists, users must be listed in that file in order to use cron. If /etc/cron.deny exists, users must not be listed in that file in order to use cron.

Handling Machines That Don't Run Constantly

The cron system was designed to work with computers that were always turned on, such as servers. Although it works well in this situation, it works less well when the computer is not running for certain periods of time; for example, if it is turned off or if it is a dual-boot machine and is running the other operating system.

To cover this situation, Debian provides the anacron package. This add-on to cron runs at boot and once per day (as a cron job). It stores information about what jobs have run when in a file and consults its own job entry file (/etc/anacrontab) to decide how often they should be run. After using this information to calculate what jobs are due to run, it runs these jobs, exiting after the last job is complete.

The default configuration for anacron is to run the /etc/cron.daily, /etc/cron.weekly, and /etc/cron.monthly jobs at their specified intervals. Thus, jobs in these directories are automatically picked up by anacron without any intervention. It is strongly recommended that you do not change this, although you can change the exact times anacron is run if necessary.

Quick Job Scheduling with at

Not all jobs need to be run repeatedly. Sometimes, it's handy to just run a job once, and you don't want to do it right away; for example, you might connect to the Internet, start a long download, and schedule a job to disconnect when the download has been given a reasonable amount of time to complete. For these tasks, the at schedule is preferable.

At jobs are entirely user-based; there is no "system level." A user wanting to run a job simply runs at, which takes the commands for the job on standard input. The job is entered into a queue and given a number, and the at scheduler (atd) runs those commands at the time indicated. at jobs can be listed (atq) and deleted by number (atrm) as well.

The at command is invoked as follows:

```
at [-c job [job...]] [-q queue] [-f file] [-m] time
```

The options perform the following tasks:

-c *jobs*	Lists the contents of the jobs with the given job numbers. You cannot use this option with any other option.
-q *queue*	Puts the job on the named queue. Queues are designated by single letters, either uppercase or lowercase. The default queue for at is a. Higher letters indicate higher niceness (or lower priority).
-f *file*	Reads the job commands from the file instead of stdin.
-m	Sends email when the job is complete, whether it's needed or not. The output of the job or any errors are always mailed to the job owner anyway.

The time you want the job to run is specified using a fairly flexible time format. Times are specified by *hh*:*mm*; you can use 24-hour format or AM and PM. Dates can be referred to by month name, day, and optional year or in short form with *mm*/*dd*/*yyyy*. Short-hand names exist: `today`, `tomorrow`, `now`, `midnight`, `noon`, and `teatime` (or 4 PM). You can specify dates and times together by giving a time followed by a date. You can also add times to time or date units; you must give the measurement with the time offset.

A few examples:

Now	Right now
1pm	At the next 1:00 PM
teatime tomorrow	Tomorrow at 4 PM
+ 1 hour	One hour from now (now is assumed)
midnight + 2 days	Two days from now, at midnight
15:30 Sep 15	September 15, 3:30 PM

`at` recognizes the files `/etc/at.allow` and `/etc/at.deny`, which work similarly to `/etc/cron.allow` and `/etc/cron.deny`.

Avoiding System Overload with `batch`

The `at` system also includes a handy utility called `batch`. `batch` has a similar command line to `at`, except that the time is optional; if the time is omitted, it defaults to `now`. `batch` submits jobs to the `at` queue in the same way as `at` (using a default queue of `b`).

The difference with `batch` is that jobs are only run when the system's load average is below a certain threshold. For long, CPU-intensive jobs on busy servers, this feature can help ensure that a job is run while not bogging down more important tasks or getting bogged down itself.

Switching User Identities

One precaution that's often repeated—but not often enough—is the old maxim, "Don't run as `root`." The `root` user wields awesome power over the system, with few safety nets in place. Thus, `root` access should be limited to only the few that can be trusted, and even they should avoid `root` access unless they need it.

All of this is fine and good when talking about maintaining a system in the abstract; it's another matter when working on a system. It's a pain to interrupt what you're doing, log off and back on as `root`, fix a problem, log off and back on as yourself, and try to pick up where you left off. Virtual consoles help, but not so well in a GUI environment; why should you need to start a completely separate desktop just to run a GUI admin tool for a minute?

Beyond that, there's the problem of delegating jobs. Full-fledged `root` access should be limited to only the people who need it; on the other hand, it is often handy to be able to give a single user the right to back up or restore files on the system, or reset a hung `getty` on a modem, or add and remove users. None of these tasks need the ability to reboot the computer, destroy the filesystem, or delete the log files.

Several utilities exist to address these problems. All of these programs act on the principle of switching users, where you take on the identity of another user for a short time without having to log off. This section covers two utilities that serve these purposes: `su` and `sudo`.

Using su

The `su` command allows you to run a shell as a different user. This shell can be interactive, or you can pass commands on the command line for it to execute before exiting, much like the shells themselves do. If a user is not given, the command assumes `root`.

If the user is not `root` to start with, `su` asks for the user's password before allowing the user to switch. By default, the minimum number of changes to allow you to take the identity of the user are made; thus, many of the settings (including even options such as `$HOME`) remain the same. If you specify a dash or pass the `-l` option to it, `su` runs a login shell, which attempts to mimic the environment of the new user identity as much as possible.

If `-c` *`command`* is not provided (to run a command as the user), the default action is to simply run an interactive shell as the user. This allows the user to execute an arbitrary number of commands as that user. When the shell exits, the old user identity is recovered.

Using sudo

Although `su` is handy for quick switching of users to get things done, it is only useful for those who already have privilege. `sudo`, on the other hand, allows the system administrator to delegate certain privileges to certain users while denying those users other privileges. It does so by restricting what programs users are able to run and what users they are able to run them as.

Setting Up sudo

`sudo` operates entirely from a single configuration file, `/etc/sudoers`. This file associates users with the commands they can (or cannot) run on the hosts they can run them on.

The file consists of entries, one entry per line (although as the lines get quite long, you can use the backslash to escape a newline and let an entry cover multiple lines). Standard user specifications list a single user, group, or NIS netgroup, followed by whitespace, followed by a series of access groups separated by colons.

An access group specifies a host and one or more commands that can run on that host, optionally as a user or users. The host comes first; this can be written as a DNS hostname, NIS hostname, IP address, or IP network number and netmask (to include an entire group of machines). The host identifier is followed by an equal sign. After the equal sign should come each command, separated by commas, which can be specified by absolute pathname or absolute path to a directory (which includes all programs under that directory). You can provide an argument for the command. If you need to restrict the user list for the command, the list of users (which can also include groups or netgroups) should precede the commands, enclosed in parentheses and separated by commas.

Setting Up Aliases

As a convenience, you can set up aliases for things that are conceptually similar—such as all of the printing commands or all the part-time sysadmins. The four types of aliases are host aliases, user aliases, command aliases, and runas aliases. Host aliases are useful in networked environments; they allow one shared configuration file to be used on a network. User aliases specify groups of users; members of an alias can be users, groups, or NIS netgroups. Runas aliases are similar to user aliases, except that they specify "target" users, or users that sudo is allowed to switch to. Command aliases specify commands (with optional arguments) in the same format as allowed in the user specification. Each of these is specified in the file with a keyword (`Host_Alias`, `User_Alias`, `Runas_Alias`, and `Cmnd_Alias`), followed by whitespace, followed by an equality statement like `ALIAS = item, item...`.

Simple, eh? The best way to learn this (and the exceptions and special cases that also exist) is to jump in and see a few examples. To make things simple, we assume a single-host environment; setting up host aliases and using them is similar to setting up other aliases.

First, let's set up a few aliases:

```
User_Alias ADMINS = jeff, mike, %wheel
```

This line sets up a user alias called `ADMINS` and puts the users `jeff` and `mike` in it, along with all members of the group `wheel`. (Netgroups are included by prepending a plus sign to the group.) Here's another alias:

```
Runas_Alias MAIL = mail, %mail
```

This runas alias is called `MAIL`, including the `mail` user and all the members of group `mail`. Next, we set up a command alias:

```
Cmnd_Alias MAILPRGS = /usr/sbin/sendmail, /bin/mailx, \
                      /usr/bin/fetchmail
```

This line sets up a command alias called MAILPRGS, which includes those programs for handling mail.

Now, let's get to some user specifications for giving some users privileges:

```
ADMINS          ALL=(MAIL) NOPASSWD:MAILPRGS, /sbin/shutdown
```

This line gives the members of the ADMINS alias (which we defined earlier) rights to run any of the commands in the command alias MAILPRGS, but only as a user in the run as alias MAIL, as well as the right to run /sbin/shutdown as any user. The ALL= specifies the hosts this applies to; ALL is a special alias that matches any item of the type that's expected (hosts in this case). Normally, sudo requires the user to type his or her own password before running the command; the NOPASSWD: option before the command disables that step.

The next line gives the user george the right to run tar or the adduser program as any user:

```
george          ALL=/usr/bin/tar, /usr/sbin/adduser
```

This allows george to do backups and add users, but nothing more (except what he could do normally as a user).

The next line gives the user vicki the ability to run any program as the user news except for the mail programs defined in the command alias MAILPRGS:

```
vicki           ALL=(news)ALL,!MAILPRGS
```

The ! can serve to negate certain classes of programs. Note: Although vicki cannot run the mail programs directly, if she can run a shell, she can then run any of the mail programs from the shell. Usually, if ALL with negations is used for commands, the shells are usually restricted as well—although any program that allows the user to execute arbitrary commands can be used in the same way to circumvent this protection.

Using sudo Privileges

Once sudo is set up, using it is easy:

```
sudo [command-option] [other-options] command
```

Only one command option is allowed (although it is not required). The valid command options are

-V	Prints the version and exits.
-l	Lists the allowed and forbidden commands for the user on this host.
-h	Prints a help message.

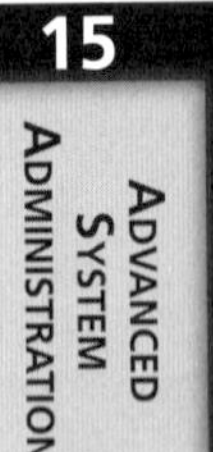

`-v`	Validates the user timestamp. Once you give your password once, `sudo` will allow access for a short time afterwards without asking for it again. To track the access, it uses a timestamp file that is updated whenever a command is run. By giving the `-v` option, you can keep the timestamp up to date without actually running a command.
`-k`	Removes the timestamp file. The next `sudo` command will require the password.
`-b`	Runs the command in the background.
`-p` *`prompt`*	Uses the given prompt to prompt for the password. A `%u` is replaced with the current username, and `%h` is replaced with the hostname.
`-u` *`user`*	Switches to the given user instead of `root` to run the command. Users can be specified by name or by numeric user ID. (Precede the user ID with a `#`.)

Quotas and Accounting

Quotas and accounting first became available in the days of UNIX timesharing, when people actually paid for CPU time and disk space. Although timesharing is no longer popular, the need for limiting a user's disk space consumption has continued in the age of file, Web, and mail servers. Additionally, quotas provide an important failsafe for applications: If they are in place, a runaway user process is prevented from consuming all available disk space.

Process accounting support has also found its place as well. Security-conscious sites can use the accounting logs to detect break-ins. On multiuser systems with performance problems, accounting provides statistics that can be used to tune the server's performance.

Using Quotas

Quota support is provided for any `ext2` partitions. It can be added on or removed at any time because it requires no special filesystem changes to implement. You can set quotas for users and for groups; if both are set up, the more restrictive set always applies, so a user can run out of quota space on a volume if she is a member of a group that has run out, even if she has remaining user quota space.

Turning on quotas in Debian is a four-step process: building a quota-aware kernel, installing the quota utilities, configuring the quota settings, and turning on quotas. The first step is easy; Debian builds its default kernels with quota support built in, so it should be taken care of if the system uses a standard kernel. If not, the custom kernel should be built with "quota support" turned on. Additionally, the second step—installing the `quota` package—is just as easy under Debian.

Setting the Initial Quota Configuration

To configure the quota settings, first edit the `/etc/fstab` file and add the `usrquota` or `grpquota` flags to the options field of all the filesystems for which you want to enable quotas. These options act as flags to the quota utilities and are ignored by the filesystem drivers; therefore, remounting the filesystems is not required.

After enabling quotas on the desired filesystems, the initial quota files can be created and quota support turned on by running:

```
/etc/init.d/quota start
```

This command builds the quota files for each mounted device, turns on quotas, and starts a quota server for any NFS-exported filesystems, if needed. By default, no quota limits are placed on any users or groups. When this process finishes, each filesystem with quota support turned on has up to two new files in its `root`: `quota.user` for user quota information and `quota.group` for group quota information. This command normally runs at boot; it adds a few seconds to your startup time to check quotas and turn them on.

Changing Quota Settings with `edquota`

After creating the initial files, you can edit the default quotas with the `edquota` command:

```
edquota user-or-group name ...
```

`edquota` reads the current quota settings (as well as the current disk usage) for each user or group passed to it and builds a small ASCII report on quota settings and usage. The default editor (specified with the `EDITOR` or `VISUAL` environment variables; by default, it is set to vi) is then run on the report. You edit the settings in the file, save, and exit the editor; `edquota` then reads the file, looking for changes to the quota settings in the report, and updates the quota records accordingly. The *`user-or-group`* indicator tells `edquota` whether the names on the command line are users or groups; it is either `-u` (for users) or `-g` (for groups).

A sample quota report looks something like this:

```
Quotas for user jeff:
/dev/hda2: blocks in use: 133287, limits (soft = 0, hard = 0)
        inodes in use: 5474, limits (soft = 0, hard = 0)
```

This user has no quotas set. It is possible to limit the number of block the user can use (each block is 1,024 bytes) and the number of inodes (an inode is the concrete representation of an object, such as a regular file, directory, symlink, device file, and so on, on a filesystem). The soft limits indicate the level at which the system will start warning the user about exceeding quota limits, and the hard limits indicate the level at which the kernel will start refusing to allow the user to allocate any more blocks.

When a user exceeds the soft limits, the system gives the user a grace period to reduce the space he is using below quota; after this grace period expires, the soft limit is treated as a hard limit, and the user is refused any more space until his used space is reduced to be below quota. The grace period timeout can be different for each filesystem and can be changed with `edquota -t`.

The quota suite also comes with reporting utilities. The `quota` command will report on a user's or group's quota limits and is invoked as follows:

```
quota [-g] [-qv] [name [name...]]
```

By default, quota reports on the current user's quotas. The `-g` flag tells quota to report on groups; by default, it reports on all groups that the user is a member of. The `-q` flag only reports on filesystems where the user is over quota, and the `-v` command prints a report for users who are not currently using the filesystem. The command also reports a non-zero status if the user is over quota; you can use this to test for quota status in scripts.

The other reporting utility is the `repquota` command. Using this command gives a more comprehensive report on quota limits and usage. You can pass it the filesystem to check or `-a` to check all filesystems with the quota flags in `/etc/fstab`. `-v` reports on users not using a filesystem, and `-g` causes `repquota` to report on group usage instead of user usage.

Using Process Accounting

Process accounting provides you with a log of every command run on the system, when it ran, how much time it took, and how long it ran. As mentioned before, these reports can be useful to detect security problems or "system hogs." The reports can either be summaries or detailed. You can view all of the programs that have been run recently or get information generally about system usage.

Installing process accounting is easy. You need a kernel capable of accounting; the standard kernels have it compiled in, and you can turn it on with a custom kernel by saying `Y` to BSD Process Accounting. You also need the `acct` package installed.

With those tasks completed, the system logs process accounting information to `/var/account/pacct`. The file is treated as a log file; it is rotated and compressed on a regular basis, and older files eventually are deleted.

You can read process accounting information with the `sa` and `lastcomm` commands. `lastcomm` prints out the last commands executed, sorted in time order, most recent first. You can give `lastcomm` a series of field values to search for; for example, `lastcomm tty0 fred` lists all commands run on a session connected to `tty0` or all commands run by the user `fred`. To require that all fields be present (in other words, do an AND search instead of an OR search), use the `--strict-match` flag.

sa is an advanced reporting tool that can sort by many fields, summarize, and build summary log files from the raw process logs. For more information about sa, check the man page or accounting info node.

Automounting

Many users of Debian GNU/Linux who migrate from the DOS world have a difficult time adjusting to the Debian concept of filesystems. In particular, the requirement that every file system be explicitly mounted before working with it is seen as a pain to many people. Most people are used to inserting removable media (such as floppy disks, CD-ROMs, or Zip disks) and immediately accessing it, without having to log in as `root` and type a long command line.

This is the precise purpose for the automounter. This software registers itself with the kernel to manage a specific directory and waits until the kernel signals that the directory is being accessed. It then wakes up, mounts the directory, and waits again. After the directory is no longer being accessed and after a timeout, the automounter automatically unmounts the directory, allowing ejection of the media.

Getting Started

Automounting support is as easy as it gets. It requires a kernel option, which is built in to the standard Debian kernels; for a custom kernel, select the Kernel automounter support option, either as a module or built-in. Additionally, the `autofs` package is required; you need to either reboot or manually start the automounter with `/etc/init.d/autofs start` after installation.

The default configuration uses the `/amnt` directory for automounting and includes support for standard floppy drives (at `/anmt/floppy`) and an IDE CD-ROM drive on `/dev/hdc` (`/amnt/cd`). You might need to edit the `/etc/auto.amnt` file and change the CD device (it's also advisable to comment out or remove the `boot` entry unless you really have an unmounted `ext2` filesystem on `/dev/hda1`) and run `/etc/init.d/autofs restart` to reload the configuration.

At this point, you should be able to stick a CD in your CD-ROM and type `ls /amnt/cd` and see the `root` directory of the CD. Additionally, you should be able to put in an `ext2`-formatted floppy in the floppy drive and run `ls /amnt/floppy`. (The automatic filesystem detector doesn't always work well with floppies formatted for Windows; if you work mostly with these, you want to change the `-fstype=auto` part of the floppy line to `-fstype=vfat`.)

Configuring the Automounter

The default configuration, with a few tweaks, works well with standard hardware and should suffice to provide "instant mount." But it has even more capabilities:

- Working with other removable media, such as Zip drives
- Automounting network shares

The Debian automounter uses a master configuration file, `/etc/auto.master`, to point to the master directories for automounted devices. You can use multiple directories; the `autofs` init script will start an automounter for each directory listed in `auto.master`. The file consists of entries, one entry per line, with two fields separated by whitespace: the master directory and the configuration file for the master directory. The default `auto.master` specifies `/etc/auto.amnt` as the configuration file for `/amnt`.

The directory configuration files also consist of entries, one per line, with three fields separated by whitespace. The fields are the mount subdirectory (which is created under the master directory when the device is mounted), the mount options separated by commas, and the device to mount. The mount options are identical to the options passed to the `mount` command. An additional option is supported: `-fstype=`*`type`*, which allows the filesystem type for the device to be configured. The device is specified in the format *`host`*`:`*`path`*; local devices can leave the host field blank (but must keep the colon).

Places to Learn More

These topics barely scratch the surface of the capabilities of Debian GNU/Linux. Tips to make your life easier when managing a Debian machine are available in many places, with more appearing every day.

Here are some places to look for more ideas:

- *The Linux Journal* (see `www.ssc.com` for subscription information) is an excellent magazine for gleaning helpful hints and tips. It is the oldest of the Linux-specific print magazines, and it still tends to be more technically oriented than the others.
- Online Linux-centered or Linux-friendly sites, such as the Linux Gazette (`http://www.linuxgazette.org`), often report on new software and new capabilities of Linux as they arrive.
- Of special mention is Freshmeat (`http://freshmeat.net`). This site acts as a central announcement site for new software for Linux, as well as an archive for old announcements and a general Linux software database. It is searchable and often has documentation, project home pages, and other information about software. Besides being a good place to see what new things are happening with Linux, it's helpful for chasing down "that software I saw that frobs foobars…what was its name?"

- The Debian Home Page (`http://www.debian.org`) has searchable package lists for checking whether a particular option is available for Debian, as well as searchable list archives chock full of good ideas.
- The Linux HOWTOs, available from the Linux Documentation Project (`http://metalab.unc.edu/LDP`, also available as the `doc-linux-*` packages in Debian) often contain helpful hints and tips. Browse the titles of both the HOWTOs and mini-HOWTOs; you might be surprised at all the things you can do with Linux!

Summary

As mentioned before, these tips are by no means the exhaustive list of the possibilities available in Debian GNU/Linux. Hopefully, they will serve as pointers into new areas to discover, as well as provide helpful advice for doing what needs to be done. By exploring and reading up on new things, it's hoped that you will be able to add greatly to the list of tips here.

CHAPTER

TCP/IP Networking Essentials

by Mario Camou

In This Chapter

TCP/IP (Transmission Control Protocol/Internet Protocol) is the most widespread networking protocol in use today, forming the base of many networks, including the Internet. Like all UNIX systems, Linux has extensive built-in support for TCP/IP. This chapter discusses the essentials needed to understand and configure network services under Linux.

The first half of the chapter explains basic TCP/IP concepts such as network addresses, netmasks, routing, and socket ports; the second half shows you what commands and files are used to configure TCP/IP services under Linux.

TCP/IP Basics

Before diving into the configuration of the TCP/IP network stack, let's get some basic stuff out of the way. If you're already familiar with how TCP/IP works and would like to go straight to the nitty-gritty stuff of how to configure your Linux system, you can skip this part and jump straight to the section titled "Configuring the Network."

This is just a quick overview of TCP/IP. To learn more about it, check the Internet Engineering Task Force's Web site at `http://www.ietf.org`. The IETF is the body charged with standardizing TCP/IP, and it publishes all the standards in the form of documents called Requests For Comments (RFC).

IP Addresses

Every computer in a TCP/IP network must have a unique *IP address*, which identifies it to other computers on the network. An IP address is composed of four bytes (or *octets* in networking parlance), written in the form *A.B.C.D*.

It is important not to assign just any IP address to a computer on a network. If the network is directly connected to the Internet, the IP addresses of all its computers must be assigned by the Internet Assigned Numbers Authority (IANA). If the network isn't connected to the Internet, or is connected to the Internet via a firewall, addresses should be selected from the private network addresses discussed in the next section. The network administrator is the person responsible for assigning IP addresses within an organization. You should contact him before assigning an IP address to any device.

Dividing the Network

As its name implies, IP was designed from the ground up for *internetworking*. This means that it was designed for interconnecting networks. Thus, an IP address is divided in two parts: a *network part* and a *host part*. The network part identifies all the hosts in a particular network and distinguishes one network from another one; the host part identifies a particular host in that same network.

Note

A computer network is built out of nodes and communication links between the nodes. A node can either be a computer or special networking equipment. A node that is a computer is called a host.

To manage an IP network, you use netmasks to split an address into a network part and a host part. This is the mechanism that allows you to configure your network as a set of interconnected subnetworks, and to determine how data packets are routed between subnetworks or between your network and the rest of the Internet. But, before you start assigning addresses to your hosts and networks, be aware that certain address ranges are assigned by default to particular network classes, and other address ranges are reserved for special uses.

Netmasks and Network Classes

An IP address is a 32-bit number (four bytes of 8 bits each). Some of the first bits are used to identify a network, and the remaining bits identify a particular host on that network.

How many bits of the address are used to identify the network and how many bits are used to identify the host is defined by the network mask, or *netmask*. The netmask is a four-byte number in which the bits of the network part are set to one and the bits of the host part are set to zero. For example, if a network has a netmask of 255.255.255.0 (11111111 11111111 11111111 00000000 in binary), all hosts in that network must have the same 3 first bytes in their IP addresses and must be distinguished only by the last byte. This means that there can, theoretically, be at most 256 hosts in that same network—although, as we shall see, the limit is a bit lower (see Figure 16.1).

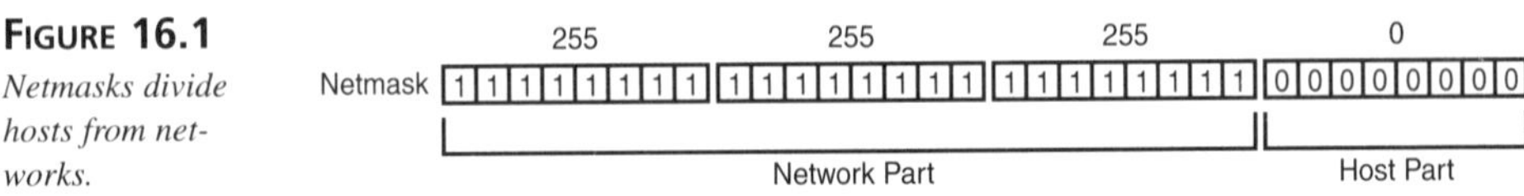

FIGURE 16.1
Netmasks divide hosts from networks.

Each network has a *network address* and a *broadcast address*. The network address is used to identify the network itself, and has all zero bits in the host part. The broadcast address is a special address that sends data to all the devices in the network, and has all ones in the host part. This means that the actual maximum number of hosts in a network is two less than the theoretical maximum, so a class C network can actually have a maximum of 254 hosts.

When you request IP addresses from IANA you are assigned a range of IP addresses. How many addresses are contained in the range depends on the network class you requested.

Networks are divided into *classes*. A class A network has an 8-bit network part and a 24-bit host part, so it contains a range of 16,777,216 IP addresses; only a few large government organizations use class A networks. A class B network has 16 bits each in the network and host parts, so it contains 65,536 IP addresses; class B networks are typically assigned to Fortune 500 companies, large universities, and Internet service providers. A class C network has a 24-bit network part and an 8-bit host part, which represents a range of 256 IP addresses; class C networks are typically assigned to medium and small companies or organizations. Class D networks are considered "multicast" addresses used for special purposes (such as broadcasting TV over the Internet). RFC-796 has assigned ranges of IP addresses for each of the network classes, depending on the first byte of the address (see Table 16.1). Most networking software automatically selects the right netmask based on the IP address; however, this can be overridden when configuring the network.

TABLE 16.1 Network Classes According to RFC-796

First Byte of Address	*Default Network Class*
1–127	A
128–191	B
192–223	C
224–239	D
240–254	Reserved

Subnetting

The division of a large network into smaller ones is called *subnetting*. It is usually done when an organization requests a large address block and needs to divide it between several different sites. For example, a large company may request a class C network address and then divide it between two different offices. Or, it may decide to use addresses in the 10.x.x.x private class A network for its internal hosts, and assign different class C networks to each of its offices.

To split a network into subnets, divide the host part into a subnet address and a (smaller) host address. If you take a C class network, which has an 8-bit part for the host address, you might decide to split the host part into a 3-bit subnetwork address and leave 5 bits for the host address.

When subnetting, it's important to note that the subnetworks that have addresses with all zeros and all ones are invalid. So, in the previous example where we divided the 8-bit host address into a 3-bit subnet address and 5-bit host address, we will only be able to have six subnetworks instead of the eight we might have expected because '000' and '111' are invalid subnetwork addresses. All zeroes and all ones is also invalid for a host address (these values are used for the network and broadcast addresses), so instead of having 32 hosts in each subnet, we can have at most 30. Our class C network, which before subnetting could have up to 254 hosts, now can only handle up to 180 hosts (6 subnets of 30 hosts each). Then, you might wonder, why would anyone want to subnet a network? The answer is that typically you don't want to, you have to. When you have to split your network over two or more physical locations, you must assign a subnet address to each location. Table 16.2 summarizes the different subnets that may be built inside a class C network.

TABLE 16.2 Subnets Inside a Class C Network

Netmask	*Usable Subnets*	*Hosts per Subnet*	*Total Hosts*
255.255.255.0	1	254	254
255.255.255.128	0	127	0
255.255.255.192	2	62	124
255.255.255.224	6	30	180
255.255.255.240	14	14	196
255.255.255.248	30	6	180
255.255.255.252	62	2	124
255.255.255.254	127	0	0

Reserved Network Numbers

There is also a standard, defined in RFC-1918, for private networks. These are networks that will never be connected to the Internet or that will be connected via an *address-translating* (also known as *masquerading*) firewall (see Chapter 22, "Firewalls and Proxies," for more details on firewalls and masquerading). It is important to use these addresses when first setting up a network even if the network is initially not to be connected to the Internet, because it is assured that no hosts on the Internet will have these same addresses. The private-network addressing standard is shown in Table 16.3.

TABLE 16.3 Private Network Addresses According to RFC-1618

Address Range	*Network Class*
10.0.0.0–10.255.255.255	A (1 class-A network)
172.16.0.0–172.31.255.255	B (16 class-B networks)
192.168.0.0–192.168.255.255	C (24 class-C networks)

There is another reserved class A network, with addresses in the range 127.0.0.0–127.255.255.255. This is known as the *loopback* network. It is a "virtual" network that points to the same host where the packet originates. The usual loopback address in any system is 127.0.0.1. So, if you want a program to connect to the same system it's running on, you can open a connection to 127.0.0.1. This is useful, for example, when running networking software in a system that isn't connected to a network.

Routing

Networks are connected by means of *routers*. A router is a device that has connections to two or more networks and takes care of moving packets between them. When a host sends out a packet whose destination lies in the same network, it sends it directly to the destination host. However, if the packet's destination lies in a different network, it sends the packet to a router so that the router will send it to the correct network. This is why it's so important to set a host's netmask correctly, because it's the parameter that tells the host whether to send the packet directly to the destination host or to the router (see Figure 16.2). A wrong netmask is one of the main reasons that cause a computer to fail to communicate with other computers on the network.

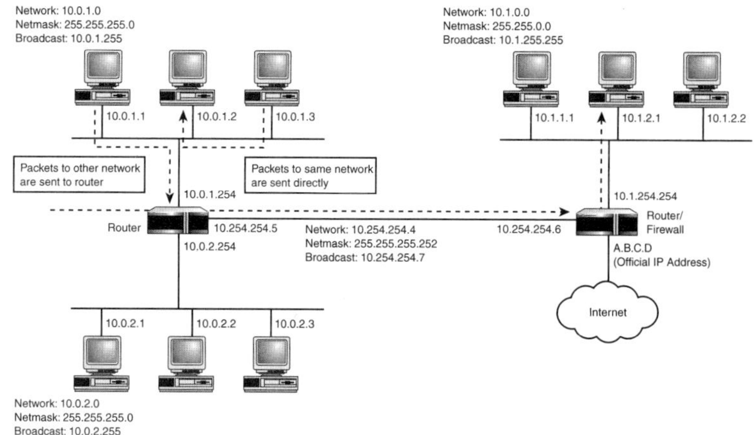

FIGURE 16.2
Routers connect networks.

A network usually has a *default router,* which connects it to other networks. In such a setup, all traffic whose destination is outside the local network gets sent to the default router. There may also be several routers in a network—for example, one to the Internet and another one to other internal networks. In this case, it may be necessary to use a *static route* to tell the host to send packets destined for specific subnets to a specific router, or to use *dynamic routing* by means of a routing daemon (such as `igrpd` or `routed`). These daemons are discussed in the "Network Daemons" section, later in this chapter.

The TCP/IP Protocol Suite

TCP/IP is actually not just one protocol, but a protocol suite. At the low level, it's composed of the following protocols:

- IP (Internet Protocol)
- TCP (Transmission Control Protocol)
- UDP (User Datagram Protocol)

The IP protocol is the lowest layer of TCP/IP. Every protocol at a higher level must eventually be translated into IP packets. An IP packet is self-contained in the sense that it contains within itself the addresses of its source and destination. It is in the IP layer where all the routing decisions take place; upper layers, such as TCP or UDP, don't know anything about netmasks or subnets.

On top of IP you have either TCP or UDP, depending on the type of service you require.

The TCP protocol is a *connection-based* or *stream-oriented* protocol on top of IP. This means that an application that communicates with another using TCP sends and receives data as a stream of bytes, and the TCP/IP stack takes care of splitting the data into packets and putting the packets back together in the receiving end. It also ensures that the packets arrive in order and requests retransmission of missing and corrupt packets. TCP is like having a phone conversation where you start by dialing a number. Then, if the number you dialed is not busy, somebody answers and you ask for the person you want to speak to. If that person is available you talk to her, and she hears the words you say *in the same order* you said them. Then the conversation ends when either of you hangs the phone.

On the other hand, the UDP protocol is a *datagram-based* or *packet-oriented* protocol. This means that the programmer must assemble the packets, and must ensure that the packets arrive in order and that there are no missing packets. However, UDP is much more efficient than TCP, and some applications (notably those where packet loss may not be significant, such as clock synchronization) benefit from its lower overhead. UDP is like sending postcards to someone; you don't know if they will receive them in the same order you sent them, and there is always the possibility that one of them might get lost in the mail and never arrive to its destination. Actually, to better understand the difference between TCP and UDP, imagine a world where sending a postcard is much faster than dialing a phone and asking for someone.

Application-specific protocols work on top of TCP and UDP. The following are some of these:

- SMTP (Simple Mail Transfer Protocol)
- HTTP (Hypertext Transfer Protocol)
- FTP (File Transfer Protocol)

SMTP

- SNMP (Simple Network Management Protocol)
- NFS (network file system)

There are many others. Each of these has different characteristics, depending on its intended use. Figure 16.3 shows the layers of the TCP/IP suite and the corresponding layers in the OSI reference model.

FIGURE 16.3
TCP/IP is a protocol suite composed of several layers.

Layer	Protocols
Application	Telnet, FTP, HTTP, etc...
Transport	TCP, UDP, etc...
Network	IP and others
Link	Network interface and device driver

Ports

A single computer may host several services. To separate these services, something more is needed than just the IP address of the host. *Ports* are analogous to the jacks in an old-fashioned manual switchboard. A single computer with a single IP address may host many different services, as long as each of them uses a different port number (see Figure 16.4). Each protocol has its own set of port numbers, so different services may use the same port number under TCP and under UDP.

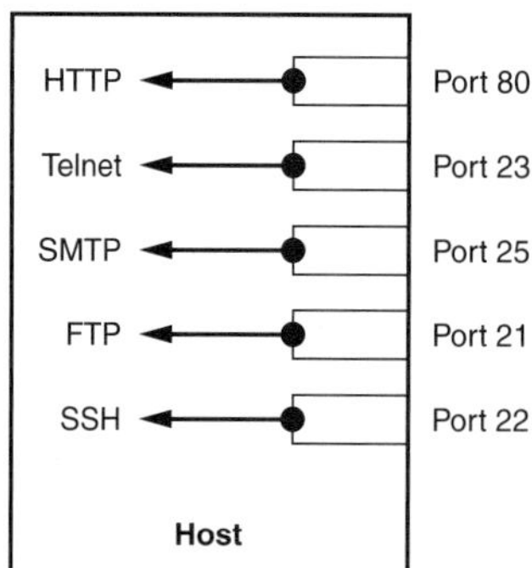

FIGURE 16.4
A single computer may host different services in different ports.

A server can listen on any port. However, if this decision were entirely arbitrary, things would be very complicated, because there would be no easy way of finding out what port a given service was listening on. That is why there are a number of *well-known ports*, assigned in RFC-1700. Some of these well-known ports are listed in Table 16.4.

TABLE 16.4 Some Well-Known Port Numbers

Port/Protocol	*Name*	*Use*
7/tcp	echo	Echoes everything it receives
13/tcp	`daytime`	Sends back the current date and time
23/tcp	`telnet`	Remote terminal emulation
25/tcp	`smtp`	Email transfer
53/udp	`domain`	Domain name system
80/tcp	`www`	World Wide Web traffic
110/tcp	`pop3`	Post Office Protocol, version 3
443/tcp	`https`	Secure Web traffic

Sockets

In network parlance, a *socket* is a network connection between two processes, which may be running on the same or different computers. Technically, an open socket is the quad (source host, source port, destination host, destination port). A closed socket has only the source port and source host.

Note that a socket has ports on both sides of the connection. When a client tries to connect to a server, it first asks the system for a free port (one that isn't being used by any other program). It then asks the system to connect to a destination host and port using that source port. That is why there can be several programs connected between the same two hosts (for example, a browser can have two or more windows open to the same host). The system keeps track of both the source and the destination port, and has different sockets for each connection.

Hopefully, you now have a basic understanding of IP addresses, netmasks, subnets, routing, ports, sockets, TCP, and UPD. The next section explains which files and commands are used to configure TCP/IP services under Linux.

Configuring the Network

In Debian, basic network configuration is done at installation time, when configuring the base system. As with other UNIX systems, all configuration data is stored in text files in the `/etc` directory.

An important thing to consider is that Linux, like other UNIX systems and unlike Microsoft operating systems, can be reconfigured on-the-fly—that is, most parameters can be changed while the system is operating, without rebooting. This makes it easy to experiment or correct configuration problems. On the other hand, many of the changes you made will disappear when you reboot the system because you only changed the in-memory configuration and didn't modify the files Linux uses at boot time to configure those services. If you want the changes to become permanent, make sure you also update the configuration files that Linux will use the next time it boots. After changing any configuration files it might be a good idea to reboot the system to make sure that the correct configuration is used when the system reboots.

This section deals with configuring the network statically, by editing the files stored in `/etc`. More advanced configuration options, such as using the Dynamic Host Configuration Protocol (DHCP) and the Network Information System (NIS), are covered in Chapter 19, "Tools for Advanced Network Administration."

Configuration Files

The most important network configuration files in a Linux system are the following:

- `/etc/hostname`
- `/etc/hosts`
- `/etc/services`
- `/etc/host.conf`
- `/etc/nsswitch.conf`
- `/etc/resolv.conf`
- `/etc/init.d/network`

We will explore each of them in turn in the following sections. All these files can be modified while a system is running. Modifications to them (except for `/etc/init.d/network`) will take place immediately, without having to start or stop any daemons. Note that most of these files accept comments beginning with a hash (#) symbol. Each of these files has an entry in Section 5 of the UNIX manual, so you can access them with the `man` command.

`/etc/hostname`—Name of the Host

The `/etc/hostname` file contains just one line with the name of the host. It is used when booting to set the hostname. Here's an example of the `/etc/hostname` file:

```
mycomputer
```

`/etc/hosts`—Map Between IP Addresses and Hostnames

The `/etc/hosts` file contains the mapping between IP addresses and human-readable hostnames. IP addresses were designed to make it easy for computers to route IP packets over a network, but it's hard for people to remember them. That's why the `/etc/hosts` file was created. Here's an example of the `/etc/hosts` file:

```
127.0.0.1     localhost
192.168.1.1    mycomputer
192.168.1.2    server
192.168.1.3    router
192.168.3.45    othercomputer    otheralias
209.81.8.242    www.debian.org
```

In this case, `othercomputer` also has an `alias`. It can be referred to also as `otheralias`.

In practice, `/etc/hosts` usually contains only the host's name and `localhost`. Other hostnames are usually resolved using the Internet domain name system (DNS). The client portion of DNS is configured in the `/etc/resolv.conf` file.

`/etc/services`—Map Between Port Numbers and Service Names

The `/etc/services` file contains the mapping between port numbers and service names. This is used by several system programs. This is the beginning of the default `/etc/services` file installed by Debian:

```
tcpmux       1/tcp               # TCP port service multiplexer
echo         7/tcp
echo         7/udp
discard      9/tcp     sink null
discard      9/udp     sink null
systat       11/tcp    users
```

Note that `/etc/services` also allows aliases, which are placed after the port number. In this case, `sink` and `null` are aliases for the `discard` service.

`/etc/host.conf` and `/etc/nsswitch.conf`—Configure the Name Resolver

The `/etc/host.conf` and `/etc/nsswitch.conf` files configure the UNIX name resolver library—that is, they specify where the system will find its name information. `/etc/host.conf` is the file used by version 5 of the `libc` library, and `/etc/nsswitch.conf` is used by version 6 (also known as `glibc` (see Chapter 24, "C/C++ Development Environment," for a discussion of `libc5` versus `glibc`). The important thing here is that some programs use one and some use the other, so it's best to have both files configured correctly.

`/etc/host.conf`

The `/etc/host.conf` file specifies the order in which the different name systems (`/etc/hosts` file, DNS, NIS) are searched when resolving hostnames. Each line of the `/etc/host.conf` file should consist of one directive followed by a parameter. The directives and their respective parameters are listed in Table 16.5.

TABLE 16.5 `/etc/host.conf` Format

Directive	*Function*
`order`	Indicates the order in which services will be queried. Its parameter may be any combination of lookup methods separated by commas. The lookup methods supported are `bind`, `hosts`, and `nis`, meaning, respectively, DNS, `/etc/hosts`, and NIS.
`trim`	Indicates a domain that will be trimmed of the hostname when doing an IP address-to-hostname translation via DNS. `trim` may be included several times for several domains. `trim` doesn't affect `/etc/hosts` or NIS lookups. You should take care that hosts are listed appropriately (with or without full domain names) in the `/etc/hosts` file and in the NIS tables.
`multi`	Controls whether a query to the name system will always return only one result, or whether it may return several results. Its parameter may be either `on`, meaning that several results may be returned when appropriate, or `off`, meaning that just one result will be returned. Default value is `off`.
`nospoof`	Controls a security feature to prevent hostname spoofing. If `nospoof` is `on`, after every name-to-IP lookup, a reverse IP-to-name lookup will be made. If the names don't match, the operation will fail. Valid parameters are `on` or `off`. Default value is `off`.
`alert`	If the `nospoof` directive is on, `alert` controls whether spoofing attempts will be logged through the `syslog` facility (see Chapter 13, "System Logs and Accounting," for a discussion of `syslog`). Default value is `off`.
`reorder`	If set to `on`, all lookups will be reordered so that hosts on the same subnet will be returned first. Default value is `off`.

This is the default `/etc/host.conf` file included with Debian:

```
order hosts,bind
multi on
```

which means that lookups will be done first to the `/etc/hosts` file and then to DNS. If several hosts match, all will be returned. This configuration is appropriate for most installations. This file is appropriate for most installations; however, installations using NIS or where the `nospoof` behavior is desired have to modify it.

/etc/nsswitch.conf

The `/etc/nsswitch.conf` file was originally created by Sun Microsystems to manage the order in which several configuration files are looked for in the system. As such, it includes more functionality than the `/etc/host.conf` file.

Each line of `/etc/nsswitch.conf` is either a comment (which starts with a hash (#) sign) or a keyword followed by a colon and a list of methods, in the order in which they will be tried. Each keyword is the name to one of the `/etc` files that can be controlled by `/etc/nsswitch.conf`. The keywords that can be included are the following:

Keyword	*Function*
`aliases`	Mail aliases
`passwd`	System users
`group`	User groups
`shadow`	Shadow passwords
`hosts`	Hostnames and IP addresses
`networks`	Network names and numbers
`protocols`	Network protocols
`services`	Port numbers and service names
`ethers`	Ethernet numbers
`rpc`	RPC names and numbers
`netgroup`	Networkwide groups

The keywords that may be included are the following:

Keyword	*Meaning*
`files`	Valid for all keywords except `netgroup`. Look up record in the corresponding `/etc` file.
`db`	Valid for all keywords except `netgroup`. Look up record in the corresponding database in the `/var/db` directory. This is useful for extremely long files, such as `passwd` files with more than 500 entries.To create these files from the standard `/etc` files, `cd` into `/var/db` and run the `make` command.
`compat`	Compatibility mode, valid for `passwd`, `group`, and `shadow` files. In this mode, lookups are made first to the corresponding `/etc` file. If you want to do NIS lookup of the corresponding NIS database, you need to include a line where the first field (username or group name) is a plus (+) character, followed by an appropriate number of colons (`:`) (6 for `/etc/passwd`, 3 for `/etc/group`, 8 for `/etc/shadow`). For example, in `/etc/password`, the following line would have to be included at the end: `+:*::::::`
`dns`	Valid only for the `hosts` entry. Lookups are made to the DNS as configured in `/etc/resolv.conf`

continues

Keyword	Meaning
`nis`	Valid for all files. Lookups are made to the NIS server if NIS is active.
`[STATUS=action]`	Controls the actions of the name service. *STATUS* is one of `SUCCESS` (operation was successful), `NOTFOUND` (record was not found), `UNAVAIL` (selected service was unavailable), or `TRYAGAIN` (service temporarily unavailable, try again). *action* is one of `return` (stop lookup and return current status) or `continue` (continue with next item in this line). For example, a line such as: `hosts: dns nis [NOTFOUND=return] files` results in looking up the host first in DNS and then in NIS. Only if neither of these were available would the `/etc/hosts` file be used.

This is the default `/etc/nsswitch.conf` included with Debian:

```
passwd:         compat
group:          compat
shadow:         compat

hosts:          files dns
networks:       files

protocols:      db files
services:       db files
ethers:         db files
rpc:            db files

netgroup:       db files
```

With this configuration, all names except network names will be looked up first in `/var/db` (for efficiency). If not found there, they will be looked up in the corresponding `/etc` files. Users, groups, and shadow passwords will also be looked up in NIS if an appropriate entry exists in the corresponding file,

/etc/resolv.conf—Configure the DNS Client

The `/etc/resolv.conf` file configures the DNS client. It contains the host's domain name search order and the addresses of the DNS servers. Each line should contain a keyword and one or more parameters separated by spaces. The following keywords are valid:

Keyword	Meaning
`nameserver`	Its single parameter indicates the IP address of the DNS server. There may be several nameserver lines, each with a single IP address. Nameservers will be queried in the order they appear in

Keyword	*Meaning*
	the file. Nameservers after the first one will be queried only if the first nameserver doesn't respond.
`domain`	Its single parameter indicates the host's domain name. This is used by several programs, such as the email system, and is also used when doing a DNS query for a host with no domain name (that is, with no periods). If there's no domain name, the hostname will be used, removing everything before the first dot.
`search`	Its multiple parameters indicate the domain name search order. If a query is made for a host with no domain name, the host will be looked up consecutively in each of the domains indicated by the `search` keyword. Note that `domain` and `search` are mutually exclusive; if both appear, the last one that appears will be used.
`sortlist`	Allows sorting the returned domain names in a specific order. Its parameters are specified in network/netmask pairs, allowing for arbitrary sorting orders.

There is no generic default `/etc/resolv.conf` file provided with Debian. Its contents are built dynamically depending on options given at installation time. This is an example of the `/etc/resolv.conf` file:

```
search my.domain.com other.domain.com
nameserver 10.1.1.1
nameserver 10.10.10.1
sortlist 10.1.1.0/255.255.255.0 10.0.0.0/255.0.0.0
```

This file indicates that unqualified hosts will be searched first as `host.my.domain.com` and then as `host.other.domain.com`. The nameserver at IP address `10.1.1.1` will be contacted first. If that server doesn't answer after a timeout, the server at `10.10.10.1` will be contacted. If several hosts are returned, the hosts in the class C network `10.1.1.0` will be returned first, followed by any other hosts in the class A network `10.0.0.0`, followed by any other hosts.

`/etc/init.d/network`—Host Address, Netmask, and Default Router

Unlike many other UNIX flavors and Linux distributions, Debian currently doesn't configure the network automatically from the `/etc/hostname` and `/etc/hosts` files. To change a host's default IP address, the `/etc/init.d/network` script must be edited directly to reflect the correct network configuration (see Chapter 8, "Conventional Means, Extraordinary Ends: Powerful Scripting Tools," for more information about scripts, and Chapter 12, "Customizing the Bootup Procedure") for more information about the scripts in `/etc/init.d`). This file contains variables specifying the IP address, netmask, network, broadcast address, and default router. This is an example of the relevant section of the file:

```
IPADDR=10.1.1.10
NETMASK=255.255.255.0
NETWORK=10.0.1.0
BROADCAST=10.1.1.255
GATEWAY=10.1.1.1
```

The variable names are self-documenting. The `GATEWAY` variable specifies the default router.

Configuration Programs

A configuration program is simply a program that you use to configure something. Linux is creating more and more of these, such as linuxconf. The files detailed in the previous section serve to configure general network parameters. Although most of them can be modified dynamically just by editing the proper file, there's one omission to this: configuring the host's IP address and routing table.

`ifconfig`—Configure the Host's Network Interfaces

The `/sbin/ifconfig` program is used to configure a host's network interfaces. This includes basic configuration, such as IP address, netmask, and broadcast address, as well as advanced options, such as setting the remote address for a point-to-point link (such as a PPP link).

Under Linux, all network interfaces have names composed of the driver name followed by a number. These are some of the network driver names supported by Linux:

Driver Name	*Device Type*
`eth`	Ethernet
`tr`	Token ring
`ppp`	Point-to-Point Protocol
`slip`	Serial line IP
`plip`	Parallel line IP

Interfaces are numbered starting from 0 in the order the kernel finds them, or, if the network drivers are loaded as modules, in the `/etc/conf.modules` file (see Chapter 12 for more information on kernel modules). By default, the Linux kernel will find only one network. If you have several network cards, you need to add a line such as the following to the `/etc/lilo.conf` file and then run the `lilo` command:

```
append="ether=IRQ,I/O,eth1 ether=IRQ,I/O,eth2"
```

(See Chapter 12 for more information on `LILO` and the boot process). This tells the kernel to add two more Ethernet devices, `eth1` and `eth2`, whose cards are at the IRQ and I/O address specified. If you want the kernel to autoprobe the I/O addresses and IRQs of the cards, you can use `0` for IRQ and I/O. The following sections get into more details regarding interfaces.

Basic Interface Configuration

This is the basic form of the `ifconfig` command:

```
ifconfig interface IP-address [netmask netmask] [broadcast broadcast-address]
```

This form of the `ifconfig` command can be used only by `root`. The netmask and broadcast parameters are optional. If they are omitted, `ifconfig` gets their values from the default class for the IP address (see the earlier section, "Netmasks and Network Classes," for more details). They should be included if subnetting is being used.

> **Caution**
>
> The command will do exactly as it's told; it won't check whether the broadcast address corresponds to the IP address and netmask supplied, so be careful!

This command loads the proper network driver and configures the interface.

It's not enough just to configure the interface. You need to tell the kernel how to get to the hosts on the network connected to that interface using the `route add` command.

Enabling and Disabling an Interface

An interface can also be brought down (deactivated) temporarily and brought back up without having to reconfigure it. This is useful for temporarily disabling a server's network connection (such as when reconfiguring a critical service). This is done with the following commands:

```
ifconfig interface down
ifconfig interface up
```

These forms of the `ifconfig` command can be used only by `root`.

Checking Interface Status

If you want to know the status of a network interface, just issue the command `ifconfig` *`interface`*. If you want to know the status of all active interfaces, use the command `ifconfig -a`. These versions of the `ifconfig` command can be used by any user. They show all the configuration information for an interface, including its IP address, subnet mask, broadcast address, and physical (hardware) address (the hardware address is set by the network card's manufacturer). They also display the interface status, such as whether it is up or down and whether it's a loopback interface, and other statistics and information, such as the Maximum Transfer Unit (MTU, the size of the largest packet that can be sent through that interface), the network card's I/O address and IRQ number, and the number of packets received, packets sent, and collisions.

You can also check the status of an interface with the `ifconfig -a` command. This prints out all the interfaces that are currently active with their parameters. Here's an example of the output of `ifconfig -a`:

```
$ /sbin/ifconfig -a
lo        Link encap:Local Loopback
          inet addr:127.0.0.1  Bcast:127.255.255.255  Mask:255.0.0.0
          UP BROADCAST LOOPBACK RUNNING  MTU:3584  Metric:1
          RX packets:1600 errors:0 dropped:0 overruns:0 frame:0
          TX packets:1600 errors:0 dropped:0 overruns:0 carrier:0
          Collisions:0

eth0      Link encap:Ethernet  HWaddr 00:20:87:3E:F0:61
          inet addr:10.0.1.10  Bcast:10.0.1.255  Mask:255.255.255.0
          UP BROADCAST RUNNING MULTICAST  MTU:1500  Metric:1
          RX packets:90506 errors:0 dropped:0 overruns:0 frame:0
          TX packets:92691 errors:0 dropped:0 overruns:0 carrier:1
          Collisions:667
          Interrupt:3 Base address:0x310
```

Network Aliasing—One Interface, Several Addresses

It is sometimes useful for a single network interface to have multiple IP addresses. For example, a server may be running several services, but you may want clients to access different IP addresses for each service to make reconfiguration easier in the future (if, for example, you need to split some services off to another server).

Linux, as most other UNIX flavors, provides a feature called *network aliasing*, which does just that. To be able to use network aliasing, you must have reconfigured and recompiled your kernel, and enabled the Network Aliasing and IP: Aliasing Support options in the Networking Options configuration section. The options can be either compiled into the kernel or compiled as modules (see Chapter 12 for more information on reconfiguring and recompiling the kernel and on kernel modules).

When you are running a kernel with aliasing enabled, creating an alias is as easy as issuing a standard `ifconfig` command. You merely append a colon and an alias number to the interface name:

```
ifconfig eth0:0 10.1.1.1 netmask 255.255.255.0 broadcast 10.1.1.255
```

This creates an alias `eth0:0` for Ethernet interface `eth0`, with the provided parameters.

To automate the creation of an alias each time the host boots, you can add the command to create it to `/etc/init.d/network`.

Other `ifconfig` Options

There are other options to `ifconfig` for some special circumstances:

- `ifconfig` *`interface local-address`* `pointopoint` *`remote-address`* enables a point-to-point interface (one that connects only to a single other host, not to a network). The interface must also be enabled in the remote host, switching the *`local-address`* and *`remote-address`* parameters.
- `ifconfig` *`interface local-address`* `tunnel` *`remote-address`* creates an IPv4 tunnel between two IPv6 networks. IPv4 is the current TCP/IP standard on the Internet. IPv6 is the next-generation IP standard. If there are two IPv6 networks that need to be connected via the Internet, a tunnel must be made that uses the IPv4 protocol.

`route`—Manipulating the Routing Table

The `/sbin/route` command is used to manipulate the kernel's routing table. This table is used by the kernel to see what needs to be done to each packet that leaves the host—whether to send it directly to the destination host or to a gateway, and on which network interface to send it.

The general form of the route command is

```
route [options] [command [parameters]]
```

Viewing the Routing Table

The simplest form of the command (with no options or command) simply outputs the routing table. This form of the command can be used by any user:

```
$ /sbin/route
Kernel IP routing table
Destination  Gateway          Genmask        Flags  Metric  Ref  Use  Iface
localnet     *                255.255.255.0  U      0       0     16  eth0
127.0.0.0    *                255.0.0.0      U      0       0      2  lo
default      router.company.  0.0.0.0        UG     0       0     71  eth0
```

The output has eight columns. They are described in the following numbered list:

1. The first column (`Destination`) indicates the route destination. If a corresponding entry exists in either `/etc/hosts` or `/etc/networks`, the name will be substituted. The special name `default` indicates the default gateway.
2. The second column (`Gateway`) indicates the gateway through which packets to this destination will be sent. An asterisk (`*`) means that packets will be sent directly to the destination host.
3. The third column (`Genmask`) indicates the netmask that applies to this route. The netmask will be applied to the value in the `Destination` column.

4. The fourth column (Flags) can have several values. The most common flags are
   - U Route is Up. Means this route is enabled.
   - H Target is a Host. Means this is a static route to a specific host (see the section "Host-Based Static Routes," later in this chapter.
   - G Use a Gateway. Means that packets will not be sent directly to destination host; instead the Gateway will be used.
5. The fifth column (Metric) indicates the distance to the target. This is used by some routing daemons to dynamically calculate the best route to get to a target host.
6. The sixth column (Ref) isn't used in the Linux kernel. In other UNIX systems, it indicates the number of references to this route.
7. The seventh column (Use) is the number of times the kernel has performed a lookup for the route.
8. The eighth column (Iface) shows the name of the interface through which packets directed to this route will be sent.

There will always be at least one active route, the localhost route, which is set up in the /etc/init.d/network script. There should also be at least one route per network interface, pointing to the network the interface is connected to.

The -n option modifies the display slightly. It doesn't do host or network name lookups, displaying instead numerical addresses:

```
$ /sbin/route -n
Kernel IP routing table
Destination     Gateway         Genmask         Flags Metric Ref    Use Iface
10.0.1.0        0.0.0.0         255.255.255.0   U     0      0       16 eth0
127.0.0.0       0.0.0.0         255.0.0.0       U     0      0        2 lo
0.0.0.0         10.0.1.254      0.0.0.0         UG    0      0       71 eth0
```

In this case, the default destination and the * gateway are replaced by the address 0.0.0.0. This output format is often more useful than the standard output format, because there is no ambiguity as to where things are going.

Tip

If you issue a route command and it seems to hang, press Ctrl+C to interrupt it and issue route -n. Name lookups, especially if DNS is configured and the host is currently not connected to the network, can take a long time.

Manipulating the Routing Table

The route command is also used to add and remove routes from the routing table. This is done by the following commands:

```
route add¦del [-net¦-host] target [gw gateway] [netmask netmask] [[dev]
interface]
```

The `add` or `del` commands indicate, respectively, whether you want to add or delete a route.

The optional `-net` or `-host` options indicate whether you want to operate on a net or a host route (see the next section, "Host-Based Static Routes," for more information on net or host routes). It is usually best to provide it, to eliminate any ambiguity (for example, the address `10.0.1.0` can be either the network address of a class C network or the address of a host in a class A or B network).

The *`target`* parameter is the host or network name of the destination of the target's IP address, or the keyword `default` for setting the default route.

The optional *`gateway`* parameter indicates which gateway to use for this route. If omitted, the `route` command assumes that the host or network is connected directly to this host. It's important to add a route to the local network after configuring an interface with `ifconfig`. The reasoning behind this is as follows: If there is no routing information, the network cannot work. If you have an internal network, you want to add the address to the route table so you can talk to other machine inside your private network.

```
# /sbin/ifconfig eth0 10.1.1.1 netmask 255.255.255.0 broadcast 10.0.1.255
# /sbin/route add -net 10.1.1.0
```

The optional *`netmask`* parameter sets, as its name implies, the netmask for the route, which will be applied to the *`target`* address. If omitted, the netmask will be taken either from the default netmask for the IP address (see the previous section, "Netmasks and Network Classes," for more information on the default netmask), or (in the case of routes to local networks) from the interface's netmask.

The optional *`dev`* parameter sets the interface on which the packets to this destination will be sent. If omitted, the `route` command checks the current routing table to find which interface has a route to the *`gateway`*. If no *`gateway`* is provided, it checks which interface can be used to get directly to the *`target`*.

Host-Based Static Routes

Most of the time the `route` command is used to manipulate network routes (those that point to a remote network), but sometimes it is necessary to add routes to specific hosts. This can be necessary, for example, if a host is connected through a point-to-point link—for example, through a modem or serial cable (see Figure 16.5).

In this example, host `10.1.1.1` won't know how to get to host `10.2.1.1` without the following `route` command:

```
# /sbin/route add -host 10.2.1.1 gw 10.1.1.2
```

FIGURE 16.5
Host-based static routes are needed when a host is connected via a point-to-point link.

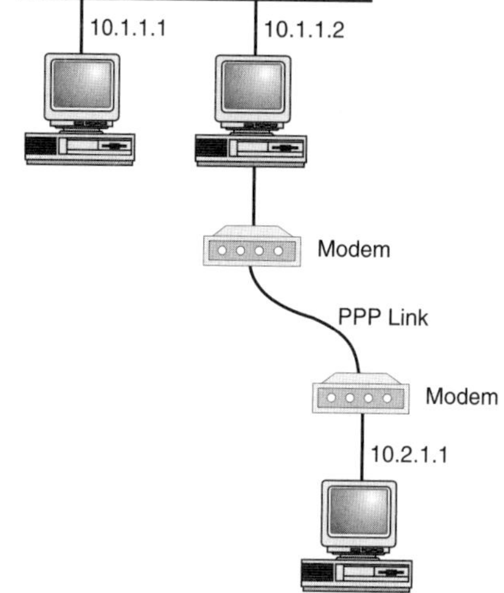

There are other uses for host-based static routes, which are covered in Chapter 14, "Disaster Recovery."

netstat—Checking Network Status

The `/bin/netstat` command displays the status of all TCP/IP network services. Status in this case is more than just up or down. netstat can give you a detailed description of ports, packets, and many other areas of a network that you might be interested in. It has several options, depending on the information you want to display.

`netstat` by itself lists all connected sockets. The `-a` (all) option lists all open or listening sockets, not just those that have connections. The information listed for each socket includes the following:

- The protocol (`tcp` or `udp`).
- Number of bytes currently in the send and receive queues (bytes that the local process hasn't read or that the remote process hasn't acknowledged).
- Addresses of the local and remote hosts. The remote host address is displayed as `*.*` for sockets that are in `LISTEN` state.
- Socket state. This can be one of `ESTABLISHED`, `SYN_SENT`, `SYN_RECV`, `FIN_WAIT1`, `FIN_WAIT2`, `TIME_WAIT`, `CLOSED`, `CLOSE_WAIT`, `LAST_ACK`, `LISTEN`, `CLOSING`, or `UNKNOWN`. In general, the SYN_ states indicate that a connection is in the process of being opened, the `WAIT` states indicate the socket is in the process of being closed, `ESTABLISHED` means the socket is connected, `LISTEN` means that a daemon is listening and waiting for clients to connect, and `CLOSED` means the socket is unused.

The -e (extended) option lists, in addition to this information, the user that is currently using the socket.

netstat -r (routes) lists the routing table. It lists the same information as the route command with no parameters.

netstat -i (interfaces) lists the network interfaces and statistics on each interface. It displays the same statistics as the ifconfig argument, but in table form for easy parsing.

As with the route command, you can also add the -n option to view numeric IP addresses instead of hostnames.

Network Daemons

As you saw in Chapter 11, "Administration Essentials," a *daemon* is a program that sits around waiting for another program to ask it to do something. Network daemons, in particular, are similar to the jacks in an operator's switchboard. They create one or more sockets and sit around listening to it, waiting for another process to connect. In Linux, as with most variants of UNIX, network services can be provided in one of two ways: as standalone daemons or as inetd-based servers.

Standalone TCP/IP Daemons

Originally, all UNIX network servers were standalone daemons. With standalone daemons, the function varies with the daemon. When you wanted to start a server, you ran a program that created the socket and listened to it. Many UNIX server programs currently run in this manner. Examples are squid, the Web cache/proxy server; Samba, the SMB file/print server; Apache, the Web server, and many others (see Chapters 17, "Information Servers," and 18, "Interacting with Microsoft Networks Using Samba").

Even though they have many different functions, most network daemons usually share a few characteristics:

- Their names end with a d (for *daemon*).
- They respond to the HUP signal (sent by the kill -HUP command) by rereading their configuration files.
- They are usually started at boot time by scripts in the /etc/init.d directory. These scripts minimally accept the start and stop parameters to start and end the daemons. Most of them accept the restart parameter to tell the daemon to reread its configuration files.
- When they receive a request, they create another copy of themselves to service it. Thus, there may be several copies of each daemon running simultaneously at any given time.

inetd, the "Internet Super-Server"

In the standalone daemon model, each service you run on a server has a corresponding daemon. This poses several problems:

- If you have many services on a server, you need to have many daemons running, even if they are idly waiting for something to happen. Although inactive daemons will probably be swapped out to disk, they still take up valuable resources, such as virtual memory and process table entries.
- There is no centralized way of modifying the daemons to provide services, such as encryption or access control. Each daemon program must be modified to provide these services.
- If a daemon dies because of user or programmer error, the service will be suspended until it is restarted. The restart procedure can be automated, but the program that restarts the daemon can also die.
- Programming a network daemon isn't easy, especially because most daemons must be multithreaded to be able to manage several requests at once.

Eventually, someone came up with a solution. How about a single daemon that could be configured to listen to any number of sockets and transfer control to different programs when it was needed? This daemon would also take care of multithreading and of managing the sockets. Thus was born `inetd`, the so-called "Internet Super-server".

`inetd` is a daemon that is started when the host boots. It reads a configuration file, `/etc/inetd.conf`, that tells it what sockets to listen to and what program to start when a connection is received in each of them. It handles the creation of the socket: listening until a connection is made; creating a new process to handle that connection; and passing to that process, as standard input and standard output, connections to the socket.

There is, however, one disadvantage to starting servers via `inetd`. The startup time for the server is longer. This is because, with a standalone daemon, the server process is always up and running. However, `inetd` has to load the server process each time it runs. Some servers, notably the Apache Web server (discussed in Chapter 17) can be started either as standalone daemons or via `inetd`. For sites that have a low load or where the Web server is accessed only sporadically, starting the server through `inetd` is an excellent choice. However, in high-traffic sites, the best option is using a standalone daemon.

inetd Configuration

As stated before, `inetd` is configured by means of the `/etc/inetd.conf` file. Each line of this file has the following format:

```
service socket-type protocol wait/nowait[.max] user[.group] server-program
program-arguments
```

The following sections go over these components in more detail:

- *`service`* is the name of the service, taken from the `/etc/services` file. From this, `inetd` gets the port number. It must be the "official" service name (that is, no aliases are allowed).
- *`socket-type`* is usually `stream` or `dgram`, depending on whether stream-oriented or datagram-oriented (connection-based or connectionless; see the previous section, "The TCP/IP Protocol Suite," for more details) service is desired.
- *`protocol`* is a valid protocol taken from `/etc/protocols`. It is usually `tcp` or `udp`.
- The *`wait/nowait[.max]`* entry applies only to datagram services. All other services should have `nowait` in this entry. There are two types of datagram servers. One of them, the multithreaded server, receives the connection and then connects to its peer, freeing the socket so `inetd` can continue receiving messages on it. The other kind, the single-threaded server, starts only one thread that receives all packets sequentially and eventually times out. For multithreaded servers, you should use `nowait`; for single-threaded servers, use `wait`. The optional *`max`* field, separated from *`wait/nowait`* by a period, specifies the maximum number of processes that may be created (in the case of a `nowait` server) in 60 seconds.
- *`user[.group]`* specifies the username and, optionally, the group name that the server should use.
- *`server-program`* is the full pathname of the program executable. Some services (notably `echo`, `chargen`, `discard`, `daytime`, and `time`) can be handled directly by `inetd`. In that case, the `server-program` should be the keyword `internal`.
- *`program-arguments`* is the list of arguments to the server program, if any. In most cases, it should include, as first argument, the program name (without the path).

Take, for example, the following line from `/etc/inetd.conf`:

```
telnet stream tcp nowait root /usr/sbin/in.telnetd telnetd
```

This line means that `inetd` should listen on port 23/tcp, the port assigned to the `telnet` service in `/etc/services`. It is a connection-oriented service. When a connection is made to that port, it should run the `/usr/sbin/in.telnetd` program with the single parameter `telnetd`.

Aside from ease of programming and a lower memory and process-table use on the host, the biggest advantage of using `inetd` is security. Because all connections can go through one centralized point (the `inetd` program), and because there is now a standardized way in which daemons are started, programs that enhance security may be built using the building-blocks approach: Don't modify the whole program; just build a small block that plugs into the program and gives it additional security. One such program that is included with Debian is `tcpd`, part of the *tcpwrappers* package, which is discussed in depth in Chapter 21, "Principles of Security." Briefly, `tcpd` is a program that is run from `inetd` instead of the standard server, and provides host-based access control to any `inetd`-based server by means of rules coded into the `/etc/hosts.allow` and `/etc/hosts.deny` files.

In the last section, we spent a lot of time dealing with network daemons. In the following section, we'll branch out a bit and get into network connections via a PPP dial-up server.

Setting Up a PPP Dial-Up Server

The Point-to-Point Protocol (PPP) is the most widely used way of connecting to the Internet. It is usually used to connect two hosts or networks by means of a modem. In Chapter 4, "User Applications," we explored setting up a basic PPP connection to an ISP. This section covers the other side of the equation: how to make your Linux host accept calls from other hosts and connect them to the Internet.

First, you must configure your Linux box so it will accept calls coming from a modem. That configuration is dealt with in Chapter 11. When a user can log on to your host through a modem using a terminal emulator, it is time to set up the PPP server. This allows other hosts to dial into your host to connect to the Internet (see Figure 16.6).

There are two ways of allowing users to use a PPP connection. The first involves allowing them to log in with a standard shell. This is useful if you want to allow your users both kinds of access: shell and PPP. If a user wants a PPP connection, he or she logs on and then executes a program that starts the PPP process.

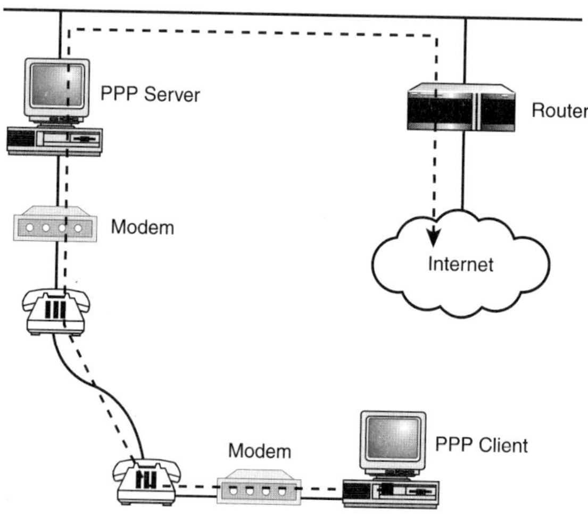

FIGURE 16.6
A PPP server allows other computers to connect to the Internet through it.

The second option is having the user connect directly to the PPP process. If you don't want users to have shell access through the modem (which is useful for security purposes), you will want to do this.

Basic Configuration

There are some configuration steps that need to be done, regardless of which way you choose for your users to connect. First of all, you need to compile your kernel with the following options set (either as modules or as built-in drivers):

PPP (from "Network device support")

IP: forwarding (from "Networking options")

You must have installed the `ppp` and one of the `getty` packages. If you don't want your users to have shell access, it's best to install one of the `mgetty` packages instead of the standard `getty` (see Chapter 10, "Software Management," for more information on installing packages and Chapter 11 for more information on `getty` and its cousins).

The `ppp` daemon is called, appropriately enough, `pppd`. It is configured by editing the `/etc/ppp/options` file. Note that `/etc/ppp/options` should contain options that apply to all PPP connections, incoming and outgoing. Here's a useful `/etc/ppp/options` file that should work for any connection:

```
asyncmap 0
netmask 255.255.255.0
proxyarp
lock
crtscts
modem
```

`asyncmap` sets which control characters should be escaped. Some modems have problems with some characters (notably Ctrl+S and Ctrl+Q), so those characters should be escaped. The parameter to `asyncmap` is a 31-bit number where each bit represents one of the 31 control characters (from ASCII 0 to ASCII 31)

`netmask` sets the netmask for the PPP interface.

`proxyarp` tells the host to answer any ARP (Address Resolution Protocol) queries on behalf of the remote system. An ARP query is sent by a host on a local network, effectively asking all other hosts which one can handle a particular IP address. A *proxy ARP* means that this host will tell all hosts on its LAN that it "owns" the remote host's IP address, thereby allowing other hosts on the LAN to see the remote host.

`lock` tells `pppd` to create a lockfile so no other process will try to use the same serial port.

`crtscts` tells `pppd` to use hardware handshaking through the serial port. All modern modems and modem cables support hardware handshaking.

`modem` tells `pppd` to use all other modem control signals, such as *Carrier Detect*, in its operation.

When the default `/etc/ppp/options` file has been set up, you should set up a file called `/etc/ppp/options.ttyXX` for each serial port you want to have a PPP server on. This is so the server program knows what ports to listen on and what the options are for that port. The most important configuration options in this file are the local and remote IP address. This is done so you have *dynamic IP addressing*, where IP addresses are not assigned to a particular remote host, but to a particular modem. The `/etc/ppp/options.ttyXX` file should minimally contain a line of the following form:

```
localaddress:remoteaddress
```

where *localaddress* is the address of the local side of the PPP interface, and *remote-address* is the address you want to assign the remote host. You must assign different local and remote addresses to each remote host. In this case, a netmask of `255.255.255.252` is useful, because it contains only two hosts per subnet. If different netmasks are desired for each connection type (incoming and outgoing), you can set the netmask using the `netmask` option in each of the `options.ttyXX` files instead of the general `options` file.

When the general setup is finished, it is time to decide which kind of setup you want: shell access or PPP-only access.

Setting Up PPP Access via the Shell

If you want your users to log in with a shell and from there start the PPP program, you must follow these steps:

1. Starting a PPP link involves several operations, including configuring a kernel device. This requires `root` privileges. Because the user will be starting `pppd` from his or her own account, the `/usr/sbin/pppd` executable has to be `setuid-root`, using the following command:

   ```
   chmod u+s /usr/sbin/pppd
   ```

2. To make it easier for users to start PPP, there should be either a global alias (set in the `/etc/bashrc` and `/etc/csh.cshrc` files) or a shell script in one of the directories accessible by all users through their `PATH` (that is, `/usr/local/bin`). For more information on aliases, see Chapter 2, "Shells." For more information on shell scripts, see Chapter 8. The alias or script should point or contain the following command:

   ```
   exec /usr/sbin/pppd -detach
   ```

   The `exec` command tells the shell to replace itself with the `pppd` program, thus saving memory. The `-detach` option tells `pppd` to remain in the foreground. This will ensure that no processes remain when `pppd` exits.

When your users log in with their standard shell accounts, all they need to do is execute the `ppp` command to start the PPP connection. This can be automated through a *chat script*, which depends on which platform they're running (Microsoft Windows, Apple Macintosh, some UNIX variant, or something else). For information on building PPP chat scripts in Linux, see the PPP section in Chapter 4.

Setting Up Direct PPP Access Without Shell Access

If you want the PPP program to start automatically when a user connects, you have to resort to using a type of authentication called *PAP* (Password Authentication Protocol) or *CHAP* (Challenge Handshake Authentication Protocol). Both are supported indiscriminately; however, some PPP clients (notably old Windows 3.1 TCP/IP stacks and others) don't support PAP or CHAP. For this kind of client to work, you have to work some magic with the `/etc/passwd` file.

To add automatic PAP/CHAP authentication, you need to make sure you're running one of the `mgetty` variants, not just standard `getty` or `agetty`. This means, first, making sure the `mgetty` package is installed (with `dpkg`, see Chapter 10) and then making sure your `/etc/inittab` entries for the modem ports point to `mgetty` (see Chapters 11 and 12). After this is done, PAP/CHAP authentication should automatically work. If it doesn't, edit the file `/etc/mgetty/login.config`. It should have a line such as the following:

```
/Autoppp/ -      A_Ppp   /Usr/Sbin/Pppd Auth -Chap +Pap Login Debug
```

If the line isn't there, or if it's commented, add it or uncomment it. If the line is there and PAP/CHAP still doesn't work, you might need some extra PPP options. Check the `pppd(8) man` page for more information. (See Chapter 5, "Your Virtual Toolbelt," for more information on `man` pages).

If some or all of your users' PPP programs don't support PAP or CHAP, you need to do a trick. Create the `ppp` script outlined in the previous section (it will have to be a script, not an alias), and set your users' login shell to, for example, `/usr/local/bin/ppp` in `/etc/passwd`. This makes `getty` start the PPP daemon instead of the standard shell.

Caution

This method isn't as secure as it should be. A knowledgeable user could use Ctrl+C to stop the script's execution, and in some cases would end up in a shell. Because of that, the best way would be to write a C program that used the `exec()` call to start the PPP daemon. However, that is beyond the scope of this book.

Summary

The TCP/IP protocol suite forms the basis of the Internet. It is organized in layers, with the lowest layer being the IP protocol, the next layer being formed by the TCP and the UDP protocol, and the application protocols on top. TCP/IP provides both for stream-oriented (TCP) and datagram-oriented communications (UDP).

TCP/IP was designed from the ground up with internetworking in mind. An IP address has a host part and a network part. The decision of which bits are in which part is made based on the netmask. Depending on the number of bits in the network part, a address can be a class A, class B, or class C network.

Routing is the process by which packets travel from one network to another. Most networks have a single default router that connects them to another, upstream network.

In Linux, the network is configured using two basic commands:

- `ifconfig`, which manages the network interfaces
- `route`, which manages the kernel routing tables

There are also several files in the `/etc` directory that serve to configure different networking parameters. The most important of these files are the following:

- `/etc/hostname` Sets up the host's machine name
- `/etc/hosts` Maps between IP addresses and names
- `/etc/services` Maps between port numbers and service names
- `/etc/host.conf` Configures the name resolver for `libc5`
- `/etc/nsswitch.conf` Configures the name resolver for `libc6`
- `/etc/resolv.conf` Configures the domain name service (DNS) client
- `/etc/init.d/network` Configures the network interfaces

There are two ways of running network daemons in Linux, via a standalone daemon or via `inetd`. `inetd` has the advantage of a centralized configuration file, authentication and encryption add-ins, and easier programming. `inetd` is configured through the `/etc/inetd.conf` file.

Finally, setting up a PPP server in Linux is easy.

CHAPTER

Information Servers

by John Goerzen

In This Chapter

red 010329

As you learned in Chapter 16, "TCP/IP Networking Essentials," networking is a large and powerful component in the Linux environment. Debian GNU/Linux comes with a wide assortment of server programs that can be used on your system. They manage everything from machine names to Usenet news. In this chapter, we discuss the installation, configuration, use, and maintenance of these servers.

In the pages of this chapter, you'll be introduced to `inetd`, the Internet super-server that handles many smaller services of the system. We'll then cover programs that provide services such as electronic mail, file transfer, telnet capabilities, secure login, Web services, name service, and Usenet.

inetd and TCP Wrappers

`inetd` is used to start small servers that handle a myriad of tasks. `inetd`'s job is to listen for connection requests from clients. When a request arrives for an `inetd`-handled service, `inetd` starts up the appropriate server process and sends the connection to it. In this way, it is possible to have a large number of server programs accepting connections without requiring each to use up a process on the system. So, `inetd` saves you process table entries and RAM. In this section, you'll learn how `inetd` works and how to configure it. After that, TCP wrappers will be discussed. They work alongside `inetd` to help you augment security and control access policies.

inetd Concepts

In addition to saving RAM, `inetd` provides other benefits:

- You get a single, unified file to edit for enabling or disabling a variety of servers.
- `inetd` itself provides an internal implementation for a number of simple services such as daytime.
- With `inetd`, you can use TCP wrappers provided by `/usr/sbin/tcpd`. By doing so, you get fine-tuned control over which machines (and in some cases, even which users on them) can access each service, as well as advanced logging capabilities.
- `inetd` can start servers as any UID or GID on the system. So, you can add an entry to the `/etc/inetd.conf` file to run a specific server as a nonroot user. A typical use is to run servers as the user `nobody` to improve security.
- `inetd` has built-in overload detection. That is, if a specific server is getting hit extremely frequently (perhaps due to a network malfunction or attack), `inetd` can automatically disable it and reenable it later.

On the technical side, `inetd` listens for a connection at each specified port number. When it receives a connection, it first checks to make sure nothing is wrong. Then it forks, sets its UID and GID if necessary, and executes the specified program to handle the request.

Configuring inetd

inetd.conf

The core of the inetd configuration lies in /etc/inetd.conf. Like many configuration files in Linux, this file contains entries for different items, one per line. Each line in inetd.conf contains six fields:

- The first field specifies the service name. This name is defined in /etc/services; it is always best to use the official name of a service whenever possible.
- The second item specifies the socket type. Generally, it is dgram for UDP protocols and stream for TCP protocols.
- The third item specifies the protocol type. This type is generally either udp or tcp. You can find a list of all valid protocols in /etc/protocols if you need to deal with other protocols.
- The fourth field should be set to nowait for stream services. For datagram services, it can be set to wait if the server handles all packets on the socket (presumably eventually timing out) or nowait if a new server should be started for each request.

  You can also specify a number for inetd to use to detect whether a given server is being started too fast. This number specifies the maximum number of servers to start in a given 60-second window and defaults to 40. You need to separate this number from the wait or nowait by a period.

  For example, nowait.60 means to allow up to one connection per second.
- The fifth field specifies the user account under which the server should be started. You can also optionally specify a group; again, you separate the two with a period. Common examples are nobody (to give the minimum set of permissions), root (to give access to everything), or others such as nobody.tty to give access to the nobody user and tty group.
- The sixth and remaining items specify the program to start and its arguments. For services handled by inetd itself, this field should be set to internal. Otherwise, you should specify the full path to the server daemon and, in some cases, the program's arguments. If you want to use TCP wrappers (which is a very good idea), you should use /usr/sbin/tcpd and then the real name of your program.

Also, note that inetd can handle protocols other than plain TCP or UDP; examples include the portmapper. However, these services are rarely used from inetd, and their usage is thus somewhat esoteric, so you are advised to look up the appropriate information in inetd.conf(5) if necessary.

When your Debian system gets installed, each protocol that you use installs entries into /etc/inetd.conf already. Therefore, with services that come with Debian itself, you don't need to add an entry from scratch. However, you often might want to tweak things. For instance, if you have a heavily used server, you might want to increase the maximum number of invocations per minute or even switch the server to standalone mode so that it doesn't use `inetd.conf` at all. You also might want to disable services (by inserting a `#` character at the start of the line) or add entries for your own services that may not ship with the operating system.

In some systems, when you make a significant change to the networking configuration as can be done in `inetd.conf`, you have to reboot the system. In Debian, rebooting is not necessary. After you have made the desired modifications to `/etc/inetd.conf`, you simply need to restart the daemon:

```
/etc/init.d/netbase reload
```

This line tells `inetd` to reread its configuration files without disrupting any service. In this manner, you can make changes to a running system.

TCP Wrappers

TCP wrappers work hand-in-hand with `inetd` (and today, a small handful of other applications) to improve system security. They work by restricting the people and systems that may use your servers. TCP wrappers allow you to set rules based on connecting IP address or hostname, local service name, and remote username if `ident` is in use.

As a general rule, you should not use TCP wrappers as your sole method of security for a given service. The reason for this is that hostname lookups, `ident` checks, and in some cases, even IP addresses can be forged or faked. Rather, you should think of using them as an additional useful preemptive strike against any potential security problem.

This behavior is regulated by two files: `/etc/hosts.deny` and `/etc/hosts.allow`. Not surprisingly, you specify those entities not allowed to use a given service in `hosts.deny` and those that are explicitly granted access in `hosts.allow`. If a conflict occurs, `hosts.allow` takes precedence. This capability is often exploited to use a generic rule in `hosts.deny` to reject all requests for a given server and then add a line in `hosts.allow` to grant access to a few specific machines.

Both files are laid out in the same format:

- One or more services to apply a given rule to. If you specify multiple services, separate them with commas.
- A colon, to separate the services from the rest of the rule.
- A list of hostnames or special tokens for which access is to be denied or granted.
- An optional shell command to run (preceded by a colon); however, this use is rather esoteric and generally not recommended for security and performance reasons. The `hosts_access(5)` and `hosts_options(5)` man pages contain more details on this usage.

Note that the service name used in the hosts.deny and hosts.allow files can be different from that used in /etc/inetd.conf. In the hosts.deny and hosts.allow files, the service name refers to the name of the daemon; for instance, in.rlogind instead of the name of the /etc/services service (such as login). Additionally, if a given invocation of a server matches neither in hosts.allow nor in hosts.deny, the default is to allow access. However, as we'll see soon, that default can be changed.

Finally, as with many configuration filesystems, lines starting with # denote comments, and lines ending with \ mean that the next line is a continuation of the current one and that they should be treated as one long line.

Let's analyze a few examples. After going through them, we'll summarize a few more special features of these files.

For the first example, let's say that you would like to prevent everyone with a machine in the example.com domain from telnetting in to your server. However, you have two friends in that domain you would like to allow in.

You can do so in two ways. Let's look at one way.

The First Approach

In your /etc/hosts.deny file, you can list the following:

```
in.telnetd: *.example.com
```

Then, in /etc/hosts.allow, you can add this line:

```
in.telnetd: friend1.example.com, friend2.example.com
```

Because hosts.allow has precedence over hosts.deny, the machines belonging to your two friends are allowed to connect to the Telnet server, but no other machines in example.com have that permission.

Note also that in.telnetd is used instead of just telnet. You can find the appropriate value for these files by looking in /etc/inetd.conf; the value you want occurs after /usr/sbin/tcpd on the relevant line. Strip away the path, and you have the daemon name for use in hosts.allow and hosts.deny.

The Second Approach

A second way of approaching this particular problem requires no modifications to hosts.allow. Instead, you list the following in hosts.deny:

```
in.telnetd: *.example.com EXCEPT friend1.example.com, \
friend2.example.com
```

In both `hosts.allow` and `hosts.deny`, you can specify exceptions to a given rule by giving the `EXCEPT` keyword, followed by a list of exceptions. Here, this feature is exploited to exempt `friend1.example.com` and `friend2.example.com` from the restriction on connecting to the Telnet server.

Also, note the use of the backslash at the end of the first line; it tells the parser to treat the two lines as one long line.

If the remote machines that connect to your servers have `ident` installed, you can also specify a username for connections. At this point, note that `ident` is not foolproof and, again, should not be used as the sole security mechanism. However, restricting access based on `ident` or logging `ident` information can be a valuable security precaution.

> **Warning**
>
> If your `ident` daemon is using TCP wrappers, you must never try to perform an `ident` lookup on `ident` requests coming in to your own `ident` daemon. Doing so can get you into nasty `ident` loops and can severely hurt several network services.

You can use `ident` lookups by specifying an `ident` username and an `@` sign before the machine name. Consider this example:

```
in.telnetd: ALL@*.example.com EXCEPT user1@friend1.example.com, \
user2@friend2.example.com
```

First, note the new use of the `ALL` keyword. If it is used on the left side of the `@`, it matches any result from `ident`. This keyword makes no difference for authentication purposes because any user is presumed to match unless a specific one is given. However, it causes the TCP wrappers to perform an `ident` lookup and log the results. This way, you can track down entries in your logs later.

`user1@friend.example.com` and `user2@friend.example.com` both indicate usernames and machines that are allowed to connect. This example further narrows down the people who can connect compared to the previous example; now, only one specific user on each machine is allowed to connect.

As a final example, you can change the default from allowing all connects to disallowing all connects by placing the following in `/etc/hosts.deny`:

```
ALL: ALL
```

If you want to log `ident` information, you can use this line:

```
ALL: ALL@ALL
```

Table 17.1 provides a list of the special keywords supported in `/etc/hosts.deny` and `/etc/hosts.allow`.

TABLE 17.1 Special Keywords

Keyword	*Valid Locations*	*Meaning*
`ALL`	Everywhere	Matches everything.
`EXCEPT`	Daemon name, client list	Specifies that the items following are to be taken as exceptions to a rule.
`KNOWN`	`ident` username	Matches any username for which the remote `ident` returns a valid username.
`KNOWN`	Client list	Matches any machine for which both the hostname and the address can be determined and are valid. This keyword should be used with caution because temporary network outages can cause false negative results.
`LOCAL`	Client list	Matches any hostname that doesn't contain a dot character. This keyword might not work with some DNS configurations.
`PARANOID`	Client list	Matches any machine whose hostname doesn't match its address. This result is determined by performing a reverse lookup in the IP address of the connection machine and then a forward lookup on that result. When used in `hosts.deny`, this keyword can be a good defense against some types of attacks. A common usage is `ALL: PARANOID`.
`UNKNOWN`	`ident` username, client list	Opposite of `KNOWN`.

Email

Now that you've seen one way that servers can be invoked on your machine, we'll turn to another service. Email is typically not run out of `inetd`; instead, it uses standalone servers and clients.

Long one of the most popular parts of the Internet, email is one of the most powerful—and complex—systems that you will encounter. Email involves several pieces of software in order to work:

- A Mail User Agent (MUA) is used by people to read and compose email. Examples of MUA software include GNUS, Elm, Mutt, Pine, and Netscape.
- A Mail Transport Agent (MTA), also known as a mail server, is used to handle sending and receiving mail. Examples of MTA software include sendmail, postfix, and exim.
- A transport is necessary to get the mail from place to place. These days, this transport is most commonly SMTP over the Internet, but it could also be UUCP using modems or a variety of other options.
- Other optional pieces include mail filters such as procmail, delivery agents such as deliver (they are sometimes built into the MTA), mailing list hosts, autoresponders, forwarding programs, anti-spam software, and more.

Debian includes dozens of mail readers (MUAs) and a number of mail servers as well. The setup and use of mail readers is generally fairly straightforward and generally doesn't even require any configuration at all. However, configuring a mail server can be quite a bit more complex. In the pages to come, you'll learn about installing and configuring the sendmail server, the Internet's most popular. You'll also learn how to set up mailing lists in Linux using the Listar mailing list server.

Sendmail

Sendmail is one of the most popular mail servers on the Internet. It has the distinction of being generally regarded as more configurable than any other mail server. In a basic configuration, you probably don't need to worry about any of them. However, if you have more specialized needs, you'll most likely end up editing at least one of the files in the following table. Table 17.2 provides an overview of some of the files that are found in a Sendmail installation.

TABLE 17.2 Sendmail Configuration Files

File	*Purpose*
`/etc/mail/sendmail.mc`	This Sendmail configuration file is either generated by the Debian configuration script or prepared manually. It is the master configuration file; most options can be tweaked here. Its syntax is defined in `/usr/doc/sendmail/cf.README.gz`.

File	Purpose
`/etc/mail/sendmail.cf`	This is the file that Sendmail uses internally. It is built by `/usr/sbin/sendmailconfig` from the data in `sendmail.mc`. You shouldn't modify this file directly; make all your changes in `sendmail.mc`.
`/etc/mail/sendmail.ct`	This file contains a list of trusted users, one per line. These users are trusted to provide nondefault message headers.
`/etc/mail/sendmail.cw`	This file contains a list of hostnames, one per line, for which this host can accept and process mail as if it were addressed directly to your mail server.
`/etc/mailertable`	This file denotes special delivery rules on a per-host basis; for instance, if mail to certain machines should be delivered using UUCP, that rule would be defined here. A DBM version of this file is generally available also.
`/etc/aliases`	In this file, you can specify that mail to a certain account on your server should be dealt with specially. It can be forwarded to a different recipient, to a whole group of recipients, piped into a shell command, or all the above.
`/etc/virtusertable`	This file specifies virtual users. It is frequently used when hosting mail for multiple separate domains on a single server. It allows you to specify that the mail for a certain person (regardless of whether the account exists) should be delivered to a different email address. This file is separate from `/etc/aliases` in that you specify complete email addresses here, with domains, and the destination must be a single email address. After you edit this file, run the `newaliases` program to rebuild the alias database.
`/etc/uudomain`	This file, generally in DBM format, establishes the correspondence between UUCP node names and Internet domain names. It is of use only if your site uses both UUCP and Internet domain names.

Having this overview of Sendmail in mind, let's take a look at the basic configuration process.

Using `sendmailconfig`

Debian provides a convenient Sendmail configuration program: `/usr/sbin/sendmailconfig`. This program can set up your `sendmail.mc` file based on your answers to a few questions. This setup will probably be adequate for many sites, but if you want

to customize your Sendmail configuration in more detail, probably what you want to do is start with the generated `sendmail.mc` file and go from there.

Let's step through the `sendmailconfig` prompts. Here is a list of the questions that you may be asked as well as some information about the questions.

- Configure Sendmail with the existing `/etc/mail/sendmail.mc`?

  If you already have set up a Sendmail configuration, you can answer Yes here, and `sendmailconfig` will simply rebuild the `.cf` file using your existing settings. However, if you answer No, you can re-create the file from scratch.

- Mail name?

  This question defines the visible domain name that appears on mail originating from your mail server. This information is useful, for example, if your mail server is named `somehost.example.com` but you want the mail to appear to have just `example.com` as the domain. You can select such an option here. This information corresponds to the masquerade options in the `mc` file.

- Smart host?

  If the machine you are setting up is part of a larger network that has a dedicated mail server, you should enter the name of this mail server here. When you do so, all mail that goes out from your own machine will be relayed through the server.

  If you are setting up a mail server separate from such a central one (or the central one itself), leave this response blank.

- Disable address canonification?

  Almost always, you should answer No here. Notable exceptions are when you are running Sendmail in environments in which live DNS may not be available or if the server is a mail relay. If you are running your own mail server but do not have name service yet, you may want to look at the section on DNS later in this chapter so you can configure your name service before setting up email.

- Enable the SMTP mailer?

  SMTP is the protocol used to send email across the Internet. If you don't enable this protocol, you render Sendmail essentially useless. Even if you don't plan to use SMTP, some other mailers (such as UUCP) require that SMTP be enabled anyway.

- Masquerade envelopes?

  Your answer to this question is a judgment call. If you want, you can have your mail name appear in the envelopes of SMTP transmissions as well as the message body. You can just accept the default here; the practical impact of doing so is negligible.

- All masquerade?

  Generally, you will say No here unless you know you have a reason for it. If enabled, this option causes all recipient headers including the local hostname to be rewritten with the mail name. Normally, only the From headers are rewritten in such a way. However, enabling All Masquerade can cause unpleasant conflicts with other configurations, so leaving it turned off is generally best unless you know you have a need for it.

- Always add domain?

  When you're sending mail from one user on the local machine to another, you don't need to specify the entire email address; the username portion alone will suffice. However, using just this portion can sometimes lead to confusion. So, Sendmail offers to automatically add the domain name to emails addressed in such a way. Enabling this option is generally a good idea.

  An exception is if your machine hosts mail for multiple separate namespaces (virtual domains, probably using `virtusertable`). In that case, this feature can put the wrong domain on email, and you should not use it.

- Accept mail for (mailname)?

  You ought to turn on this option unless there is some special reason that you are running a mail server that doesn't accept mail.

- Alternate names?

  If your machine has any names other than its normal hostname and mailname, you probably ought to list them here. This information corresponds to the contents of `/etc/mail/sendmail.cw`.

- Trusted users?

  You have an opportunity to define trusted users. They get saved into `/etc/mail/sendmail.ct`.

- Enable redirect option?

  Generally, you should leave this option disabled. If you are running a service such as an ISP in which accounts are created and removed on a regular basis, you might want to take advantage of this feature. It can return an error message with a new address of the intended recipient.

- Enable UUCP addressing?

  If you use UUCP, turn on this option. Most people do not use UUCP, so leave it off unless you know you have a specific need for it.

- Enable sticky host option?

  This option is almost never needed. It sets up a strange situation in which an email address without a domain name can be delivered differently than one with the normal local domain name. This delivery can result in some unpleasant side effects, so its use is generally discouraged.

- Enable DNS?

  Unless your server is not connected to the Internet, this option must be enabled.

- Assume best MX is local?

  With this option, your Sendmail automatically accepts mail for any machine for which the "best" MX is itself. It acts as if those machines were listed in `sendmail.cw`. However, this option can be a security risk and can generate a lot of DNS traffic, so its use is generally discouraged.

- Enable `mailertable` feature?

  Say Yes here if you would like to take advantage of the `/etc/mailertable` file, as described in Table 17.2. If you don't need that file, you can answer No.

- Use the Sendmail Restricted Shell (`smrsh`)?

  You can send data directly from Sendmail to other programs in various ways. You can set up a pipeline in `/etc/aliases` or `~/.forward`, a mailer definition can include it, and so on. `smrsh` restricts just which programs can be run. It can improve security in some cases, but it can also make things a lot more difficult. Nothing is inherently wrong with the normal capability to execute programs, but you may prefer to limit the capability to do so just for safety's sake. In general, answer No here unless you know you have a special need for this feature.

- Mailer name?

  This address is used for messages that Sendmail itself generates—usually messages informing a sender that his or her message bounced for some reason. The default of `MAILER-DAEMON` is good; use it unless you have some specific other needs.

- Enable me too option?

  Normally, the sender of a message doesn't receive a copy of his or her own message if it is sent to a list that contains his or her name. This option will change that behavior. The normal answer here is No unless you know you have special needs.

- Message timeouts? [4h/5d]

  This option defines how long Sendmail will continue trying to deliver mail. When outgoing email is sent, it is usually transmitted over the Internet to the remote server right away. However, sometimes something might prevent this process from happening. Perhaps a network problem occurred, or maybe the remote server had a hardware failure and is down, or any number of other things may have gone wrong.

The first value here defines how long Sendmail will continue trying to deliver the message before sending a warning back to the original sender. In this case, it will try for four hours. The second value defines how long Sendmail will continue with its delivery attempts before giving up and bouncing the mail back to the original sender. In this case, that value is five days.

In general, you should not decrease these values at all. If you modify them in any way, you will probably want to increase them.

- Reload the running Sendmail now with the new configuration?

  Answer Yes. If you don't, the Sendmail that's already running will still have the old configuration, which is probably bad.

At this point, your sendmail has been configured. The .mc file has been created and your mail server has been started.

The `.mc` File

Recall that the `/etc/mail/sendmail.mc` is the main configuration file for Sendmail. This file is created by `sendmailconfig` and is the one that you should edit if you need to tweak Sendmail behavior. Although `sendmailconfig` asks a number of questions and can set up `sendmail.mc` for a variety of situations, you still might need to edit `sendmail.mc` to customize Sendmail even more for your local situation.

The `sendmail.mc` file is processed by the GNU m4 macro language. As such, the syntax is slightly different from that of other configuration files with which you might be familiar. First, it is important to note that # is not a comment character, even though it may appear like it is. Rather, comments are denoted by `dnl`, which means "delete to new line." Anything on a line after `dnl` is ignored by the parser.

dnl

You'll no doubt notice that some items are enclosed inside single quotes; for instance:

```
define(`confTO_QUEUEWARN', 5d)dnl
```

It's important to note that you use the backquote (`) to start the string and the normal single quote (') to end it. In many cases, quoting the string like this is optional, but it never hurts to do so if you have any doubt.

Finally, note that you ought to put any local customizations in `sendmail.mc` at the end of the file, below the line:

```
## Custom configurations below (will be preserved)
```

This line is a flag to `sendmailconfig` to never touch those lines.

You can find the guide to `sendmail.mc` in `/usr/doc/sendmail/cf.README.gz`. This file is a comprehensive guide to all the options in the file, and you should consult it first when you have a configuration question.

Annotated Sample sendmail.mc

Let's look at a sample `sendmail.mc` file. It is presented here with comments interjected after the lines.

```
VERSIONID(`@(#)sendmail.mc      8.7 (Linux) 3/5/96')
OSTYPE(debian)
```

The preceding two lines are inserted automatically by the Debian configurator; they should not be modified.

```
FEATURE(nocanonify)
```

As mentioned previously, this line disables canonification of email addresses.

```
FEATURE(masquerade_envelope)
```

Again, the preceding line corresponds directly to a question asked by the installer program.

```
dnl FEATURE(always_add_domain)
```

This line is commented out (the leading `dnl` does that), so it is ignored. If it were not commented out, it would turn on the `always_add_domain` feature.

```
FEATURE(use_cw_file)
FEATURE(use_ct_file)
```

These two lines enable the `/etc/mail/sendmail.cw` and `/etc/mail/sendmail.ct` files, respectively.

```
FEATURE(redirect)
```

The `redirect` feature (again, asked by `sendmailconfig`) is enabled by this line.

```
dnl FEATURE(nodns)
```

The preceding is another commented-out line. If it were not commented out, it would disable DNS lookups.

```
FEATURE(local_procmail)
```

This line specifies that `procmail` is to be used to deliver mail locally. If it is used, all mail delivered to accounts on the mail server is automatically sent through `procmail`, so explicitly adding `procmail` to a `.forward` file is not necessary.

```
FEATURE(uucpdomain)
FEATURE(mailertable)
```

These two lines add in support for email over UUCP (with traditional Internet domain names) and the `mailertable` file, respectively.

```
MAILER(local)
```

The preceding line enables support for delivering mail locally.

```
MAILER(smtp)
```

And this line enables the SMTP support—pretty much a must these days.

```
MASQUERADE_AS(example.com)
```

Here, we make sure that all outbound mail appears to come from `example.com`.

```
define(`confTO_QUEUEWARN', 5d)
define(`confTO_QUEUERETURN', 10d)
```

These two lines substantially increase the limits before sending warnings or bounce messages.

```
## Custom configurations below (will be preserved)
```

This line signals `sendmailconfig` that it should never modify anything below this line in the `sendmail.mc` file. Even if you run `sendmailconfig` again and answer the questions differently, the remainder of the file will still remain untouched.

```
FEATURE(limited_masquerade)
MASQUERADE_DOMAIN_FILE(`/etc/mail/sendmail.cM')
```

These two lines provide a special-case handling of masquerading; in this case, only some hosts (those listed in the `sendmail.cM` file) will be enabled for masquerading instead of all hosts.

```
FEATURE(rbl)
```

This line enables support for Paul Vixie's MAPS RBL (Realtime Black List), which is a powerful tool to help thwart spammers.

```
FEATURE(virtusertable)
```

The `virtusertable` file is enabled by this line.

```
define(`confMAX_MESSAGE_SIZE',9145728)
```

The preceding line defines the general maximum message size, in bytes. If someone attempts to send a message larger than that to this server, it will be rejected (with any luck before transmission of the message itself even begins). This setting is already more than many people use; some use 1 megabyte or less.

```
define(`UUCP_MAILER_MAX',6145728)
```

This line defines a special, upper limit for UUCP.

```
MAILER(uucp)
```

This line enables the general UUCP mailer.

```
MAILER(procmail)
```

And this line enables the `Procmail` mailer; it works together with the `local_procmail` feature.

```
FEATURE(relay_entire_domain)
```

Sendmail has some strong anti-relay rules, which are excellent for preventing spam. However, this particular mail server acts as a mail relay for all machines in its domain (the other machines presumably have a "smart host" setting pointing to this server), so relaying is turned on—but only for hosts in this particular domain.

```
RELAY_DOMAIN(otherexampledomain.com)
```

Relaying is also allowed for hosts in `otherexampledomain.com`. Perhaps this mail server is used by two separate domains.

Using Database Files

If you decide to work with some of the additional Sendmail configuration files, such as the `mailertable` file, you'll notice that they are stored in database form. This measure is taken to improve the performance of the Sendmail daemon. With the database files, you edit a normal, plain-text file. Next, run `makemap` to generate the database version that is used internally by Sendmail.

For instance, for the `mailertable` file, you use the following:

```
makemap hash /etc/mailertable.db < /etc/mailertable
```

The same procedure applies to several other files such as `virtusertable`. Some people with several of these files create a shell script or Makefile to generate all necessary database files with a single command.

The `/etc/aliases` file is stored in a database, but it is generated in a different way. When you update `/etc/aliases`, after saving the changes, simply run the following:

```
newaliases
```

The system regenerates the aliases database as appropriate when you run that command.

Listar

One common use of electronic mail is for mailing lists. Mailing lists are used to facilitate group discussions on the Internet. The basic idea of a mailing list is this: Anybody who wants to have a message readable by the group needs to send it to a list submission address. A mailing list server then takes the message and sends it to everyone in its list of addresses. These lists can have as few as five people or reach into the tens of thousands. Many different projects use mailing lists; they range from everything from discussing home gardening to coordinating a release of Debian GNU/Linux.

Listar is a mailing list server program. Its job is to properly handle incoming messages, making sure that they get distributed to everyone subscribed to the mailing list. Listar also provides automated mechanisms that people can use to subscribe and unsubscribe to a list. This means that no human intervention is required (unless you tell Listar that you prefer it) to handle these routine tasks, and people get subscribed or unsubscribed faster.

Additionally, Listar has capabilities to make archives of messages, to help thwart spam, to handle moderated lists (ones in which a moderator must approve posts before they get sent to the entire list), to make list digests, and many more.

Listar made its debut in Debian in the potato (Debian 2.2 development) distribution. As you read this book, potato may not yet be released; in the interim, you can fetch `.deb` packages for Listar and its optional Web front-end from `ftp.debian.org` or `ftp.listar.org`. The `ftp.debian.org` site has Listar for all the Debian platforms in a potato version. The Listar site has current versions for i386 and alpha only. Additionally, until the next release of Debian, you may find i386 2.1 debs of Listar on the Web at `http://master.debian.org/~jgoerzen/slink/`.

Understanding Listar from the Users' Perspective

When a person on the Internet wants to participate in a mailing list hosted at your site, the first thing that user generally needs to do is subscribe to the list. This is done by writing to the user `listar` at your domain, using a specially formatted message. The message might be something as simple as this:

```
From: user@somewhere.gov
To: listar@example.com
Subject: whatever

subscribe funlist
```

Listar sees this message and the `subscribe` request. To verify that the `user@somewhere.gov` person really requested to be subscribed to the `funlist` mailing list, Listar replies with a *cookie*. `user@somewhere.gov` simply sends this cookie back to Listar, and then that person is a member of the list. At this point, `user@somewhere.gov` will see all the list traffic.

To post a message to the list, the user simply sends it to `funlist@example.com`. When this is done, Listar gets hold of it and sends it out to everyone subscribed to the list.

So, from the end user's perspective, Listar is fairly simple to deal with. Of course, `listar@example.com` has many more commands than simply `subscribe` and `unsubscribe`; it has dozens of options and settings that can be used by more advanced readers.

Understanding Listar from the Administrator's Perspective

Let's analyze the transaction from the preceding section from the perspective of the sys tem administrator of a machine running Listar.

First, the mail server (perhaps Sendmail) receives the email from `user@somewhere.gov`. Sendmail notices that the message is sent to Listar. `/etc/aliases` defines a special entry for Listar, specifying that mail sent to that address gets piped to the Listar mail-handling program. So, Sendmail invokes Listar and hands the message off to it. Listar parses the message, notices the `subscribe` request, and sends off a message to `user@somewhere.gov` containing a randomly generated cookie.

`user@somewhere.gov` then replies, sending back the cookie. Sendmail again looks in `/etc/aliases` and again delivers the message to the Listar mail-handling program. Again, Listar parses the message. This time, however, Listar detects the cookie. After ensuring that the cookie is valid, Listar adds `user@somewhere.gov` to the subscriber list for `funlist`; this list is stored in `/var/lib/listar/lists/funlist/users`. Listar then sends a confirmation message back to `user@somewhere.gov`.

When a message is received at `funlist@example.com` to be sent out to everyone subscribed, Listar again gets ahold of it. However, this time, Listar reads `/var/lib/listar/lists/funlist/users` for a list of everyone who should receive the message. After adding a few headers, Listar tells Sendmail to send the message to all the recipients.

As you can see, Sendmail's capability of piping data to programs in `/etc/aliases` is exploited by Listar to its advantage. This means that Listar integrates nicely with the mail server and that the configuration of Listar is fairly simple.

Installing Listar

When you install the Listar `.deb`, it automatically creates a user named `listar` on your system. All the configuration files and data files used by Listar should be owned by that user. Therefore, it's a good idea to use `su` (from `root`) to switch to that user before modifying any configuration files. You can also use `chsh listar` to set it to use your favorite shell, if desired.

After becoming the `listar` user, the first thing you need to do is edit configuration files in `/etc/listar`. It serves as a master configuration file. Some things are defined in here that cannot be changed elsewhere. Other things are simply treated as defaults; per-list configuration options can override them. For details on all the settings, you can take a look at the Listar configuration file quick-reference card on the Web at `http://www.listar.org/variables.html`. Of particular interest for first-time configuration is to change every occurrence of `yourdomain.com` to your real domain name.

The second thing you need to do is add the master Listar entries to `/etc/aliases`. You need to do so as `root`. The items to add are already available; you can add them with these commands:

```
cat /usr/doc/listar/examples/aliases >> /etc/aliases
newaliases
```


Now Listar is ready to answer queries. However, before it can do anything useful, you need to create a list.

Creating a List

To create a list, you need to run the following:

```
/usr/lib/listar/scripts/newlist.pl
```

First, it asks for a list name. This is a list name only; not an entire email address. So, if you specify `mylist`, the posting address will eventually become something like `mylist@example.com`. However, for this prompt, simply type **`mylist`**.

Next, it needs the email address of the list administrator. Probably, you will want to type in your normal email address here. This one must include the domain name.

Finally, it displays some lines that need to be added to `/etc/aliases`. Cutting and pasting in X or with gpm is handy here. Simply add these lines to `/etc/aliases` and rerun `newaliases`. Your list is now set up!

If you want to modify the configuration of the list, you can do so by editing `/var/lib/listar/lists/mylist`. To subscribe, just send **`subscribe mylist`** to `listar@example.com` (using your specific domain name, of course).

Administering Listar Daily

As the list administrator, you might need to deal with several situations. We'll discuss them here.

First, it's important to understand how Listar interacts with you and with the other list members. For security purposes, whenever you send Listar a command asking it to perform some action, it requires a cookie using the mechanism we described earlier. All the special list administrator commands work this way.

First of all, you'll notice that Listar keeps you up-to-date regarding the list. You get a small notice in your email box whenever someone subscribes to or unsubscribes from a mailing list for which you are acting as the administrator. No action is required; Listar has already handled the request automatically. Listar is simply keeping you informed regarding what it's done.

Approving Posts

Another point to note is that sometimes you might need to approve a post to the list. This is the case for all messages if you are running the list as a moderated one. Otherwise, this happens only if Listar detects an unusual post to a list. Perhaps the post looks like it might contain spam, or maybe someone mistakenly sent a `subscribe` request to the list posting address instead of to the Listar address. Listar is smart enough to detect some of these situations before sending the message to all the subscribers; this capability goes a long way toward keeping people on the list happy.

When Listar detects one of these situations, it sends the message to you. What you do then depends on the message. If Listar was right in rejecting the message, you can do nothing; just delete the message from your mailbox. However, if you decide that you would rather post the message to the list anyway, you need to forward it back to a special address. Listar includes these instructions at the top of the email it sends to you. For our example list, the address would be `mylist-repost@example.com`. Note that it's important to forward the message, not use a reply key. Also, if your mail client typically does anything to forwarded messages, such as indentation or something like that, make sure that the client does not modify this message at all.

When Listar receives the message at the `-repost` address, it is delivered to the list as usual.

Dealing with Bounces

Another type of message that you might receive is a mail bounce message. Unfortunately, for larger lists, receiving these messages is somewhat of a frequent occurrence. People who are subscribed to your list may close the accounts with which they're subscribed, or their mail servers may go down, or any number of other problems could occur that would cause mail going to them to bounce. For high-volume lists, which sometimes have thousands of subscribers and hundreds of posts per day, you can accumulate many bounces in a short period of time.

By default, Listar sends you a copy of every bounce mail message that results from the actions on a particular list. If you don't want it to do that, you can remove the `CCERRORS` flag from your account by writing to Listar and issuing the following command:

```
unset CCERRORS
```

Unlike many other mailing list servers such as Majordomo, which require the administrator to manually remove names of people whose email does not go through, Listar can, and by default does, automatically process these bounce messages. Its algorithm automatically removes names of people whose mail continually bounces, thus saving you a lot of work. You can tweak options such as `bounce-max-transient`, `bounce-max-fatal`, `bounce-timeout-days`, and `bounce-never-unsub` in either `/etc/listar/listar.cfg` or the `per-list` configuration files to make the algorithm work in different ways.

Therefore, these messages are generally sent to you for your information only because Listar can process them automatically.

Listar also periodically sends you a *watch report*, detailing the names of all the people for whom mail has bounced, how many times mail has bounced, and what Listar has done about it. This report is probably more valuable than the individual bounce messages themselves because it provides you with a summary of all the actions. This watch report, too, is for your information only; no additional action is required.

Manipulating Listar by Email

As we've already seen, Listar provides an email processor at `listar@example.com` to handle administrative list requests. It's probably a good idea to write to that address now and include the following in the body of your message:

```
help
commands
flags
```

Listar then sends back email instructions, containing a command summary and information on manipulating Listar by email.

Subscribing, Unsubscribing, and Setting Flags

One of the jobs you can do as administrator is subscribe, unsubscribe, or set flags for other people. Sometimes people may have trouble performing these tasks for themselves and ask you to do it for them.

For this purpose, Listar has an `admin2` wrapper. The following is a sample session:

```
admin2 mylist
subscribe foo@example.com
setfor foo@example.com digest2
```

These commands do the following:

First, the `admin2 mylist` command tells Listar that you are using administrator mode for the list `mylist`. Listar checks to make sure that you are a valid administrator for the list (and verifies this with a cookie as described next). The next line tells Listar to subscribe foo@example.com to mylist. Notice that you don't need to specify the list name here; Listar already knows that these commands apply to mylist because it was specified in the admin2 line. Finally, the last line specifies that the digest2 flag should be set for foo@example.com.

These commands aren't actually carried out immediately. Rather, Listar sends you back a message with a cookie. You need to forward this message back to Listar. It contains the verification cookie as well as the commands to execute. After Listar receives this second message, it carries out your commands. After doing that, it sends you a confirmation message indicating that foo@example.com has been subscribed and the flag digest2 has been set as per your request.

Because of this feature, the list administrator does not need to have an account on the list server. Many people exploit this capability by hosting lists on their Linux servers but allowing people with email access elsewhere to handle the day-to-day administrative details of the list.

Listargate

Listar also has another interesting feature: a Web-based front-end to the Listar program. This program, called Listargate, allows people to subscribe and unsubscribe from lists using a convenient Web page. It also allows them to see the subscription status and flag settings for lists, to see what lists are available on your Listar server, and to subscribe to or get information about those lists.

To use Listargate, you must first have a working Web server installed. Later in this chapter, we discuss the installation and configuration of Apache in the "Web Servers" section; it makes a great server for use with Listargate.

Then you must install the listar-cgi package. Debian's listar-cgi package includes both the Listargate CGI script itself and a module for Listar to add in the Listargate functionality to the Listar program. Simply install the listar-cgi package, and both are installed for you.

Now you need to edit your /etc/listar/listar.cfg file. In particular, you need to insert the following line:

```
lsg-cgi-url = /cgi-bin/listargate.cgi
```

Now save the file. Your Listargate installation is now ready for use. You can access it with /cgi-bin/listargate.cgi at your Web server; for instance, http://www.example.com/cgi-bin/listargate.cgi takes you to the Listargate interface if your Web server is named www.example.com.

From here on, you can access Listar in the same way as any other list reader would. At this time, Listargate doesn't handle administrator requests, so they still need to be done via the conventional email interface.

One point to note about Listargate: Like Listar itself, Listargate operates in a completely passwordless fashion. It therefore eliminates the need to store passwords on the server and also removes the vulnerabilities associated with transmitting passwords in cleartext through email. However, to verify that people using Listargate are really who they claim to be, Listargate still sends out email cookies. The people simply need to forward this message back to Listar as per the included instructions, and it is processed.

Therefore, Listar saves people from having to concoct their own emails with commands for Listar. It also gives them a convenient interface to view their current subscription status. Although this information is available on request from the Listar server, it can be more convenient to receive the information from a Web page.

Warning

Listargate is fairly early in its development cycle, so it may have some bugs or may take some time until it has all the features planned.

Mailing List Security

Security is an important concern with mailing lists as with many other aspects of Internet servers. Traditionally, mailing lists had a lot of security problems. Listar has a new design that does a great deal to address these traditional concerns. The primary line of defense against security problems is the cookie. Traditionally, no authentication mechanism existed at all. However, forging a From: line on email is easy enough that people were routinely sending forged messages to mailing list servers. The result is that people who didn't want to be subscribed to lists would be subscribed, and sometimes those who were subscribed would be unsubscribed.

The cookie mechanism prevents this problem by ensuring that all requests are from the person they claim to be from. By sending a cookie out to the From: address, Listar can guarantee that the person there is really the one who requested the change. This step alone goes a long way to defeating security problems.

Some other mailing list packages that allow remote administration use passwords. However, this mechanism poses several problems. First, as we discuss in the section about `ssh`, sending unencrypted passwords across the Internet is a very bad idea; it is too easy for crackers to intercept the passwords. By using cookies for those requests too, Listar can guarantee that the request is coming from somebody who really is an administrator for the list.

Another security hole that Listar addresses by default is that of alias expansion. It's sometimes possible for people to get a list of the email addresses of everyone subscribed to a given mailing list by issuing special commands to the lists' SMTP server. However, because Listar delivers the mail to Sendmail itself, this avenue of attack is not possible.

However, you still need to watch out for a few things. The biggest one is guarding your subscriber list. Letting people request the list of the email addresses of all list subscribers is generally a bad idea. This method is frequently a favorite for spammers to use to build their databases of people to send unsolicited email to. A good way to prevent this problem is to disable Listar's `who` commands. You can do so by using the following line in the `/etc/listar/listar.cfg` file or the `per-list` config files:

```
who-status = admin
```

This line prevents spammers from being able to fetch your subscriber list—a big win. Another thing to watch out for is archives. If you have enabled keeping archives (they're disabled by default) and place them under a location where the `get` command can reach them, it's a good idea to restrict those commands such that only list members can use them.

You can accomplish that feat by using this configuration file line:

```
file-archive-status = list
```

By taking these precautions, you achieve a good level of security, while avoiding inconveniencing yourself or your list subscribers.

If you have occasional trouble with people sending spam to the list posting address itself, several solutions are possible. One is to add patterns to the `/etc/listar/banned` file. Another is to make the list moderated. Making a list moderated means that you (or the list administrator or designated moderator) must approve every post before it gets sent out to the list subscribers. This means that spam can be stopped before it gets distributed to the subscribers. However, it also means that turnaround time is longer because all posts have to be manually approved before going through. Moreover, it creates more work on your part because you now have to process every list message before it gets sent out on the list. Whether these consequences are acceptable is a matter of individual needs. However, if you decide to use a moderated list, you do so by using this line in a configuration file:

```
moderated = yes
```

Another possible defense against spam is a compromise between the two. It's possible to allow Listar to automatically pass through all messages sent to the list from people who are also subscribed to it but to have all other messages sent to the administrator or moderator for approval. To enable this behavior, you can set the following:

```
closed-post = yes
```

Note that Listar looks for an exact match on the email address. Some people post from addresses different than they receive mail from, so their messages may still be sent to the moderator for approval.

As you have seen in this section, Internet mail service is a large and complex system to install and configure. However, along with this complexity, you get a tremendously powerful communication tool. With add-ons such as Listar, you can extend traditional email services to work in new and even more powerful ways. Now, we'll move on to covering a program designed to transfer files instead of messages: FTP.

FTP

FTP, an acronym for *File Transfer Protocol*, is used for the transmission of files from one computer to another over a network (usually the Internet). Normally, a person uses an FTP client to connect to the server and log in to FTP with the normal username and password. For this, all that you need is the standard FTP server in the `netstd` package. In this section, you'll learn about anonymous FTP, the FTP servers available in Debian, and how to install and configure FTP service for your own server.

netstd

Anonymous FTP

Another use of FTP is to make certain files available for download by anyone on the Internet. Because this mode doesn't require a preexisting account on the FTP server, it's called *anonymous FTP*. In general, from the client side, a person logs in to an anonymous FTP server with the username `anonymous` and a password of a normal email address.

From the server side, special security precautions must be taken. Generally, allowing anonymous visitors to access all areas on the system is not desirable; rather, the preference is to give them access only to the files specifically for anonymous FTP downloading. Additionally, because the FTP server uses some external programs (such as `ls`) to prepare information to send to FTP clients, it's generally desirable to limit access to external programs to just a small set of harmless ones.

These requirements are met by placing anonymous FTP in a `chroot()` environment. This means that, while an anonymous FTP user is logged in, the FTP server process has used chroot to set the root directory for the process to something other than the normal root directory. This means that the anonymous FTP users are effectively running in a *chroot box*; it's not possible to access other files.

However, because of this use, you need to place some system binaries and libraries in the chroot environment such that the FTP server process can still properly generate file listings and the like for people who access FTP anonymously.

Debian GNU/Linux provides a package called wu-ftpd-academ that contains a modern, fully featured FTP server. Even better, the install script for this package can automatically configure anonymous FTP services, saving you from having to set up the chroot environment yourself.

At install time, the installation script asks you whether to install anonymous FTP services. If you choose to do so, it defaults to setting up /home/ftp for this purpose. You are asked whether to set up an upload area; generally, you should say no unless you know you have a specific need for it.

Now you can create files in /home/ftp/pub for people to download. /home/ftp/welcome.msg contains a message that people see when they log in to FTP anonymously.

wu-ftpd-academ Configuration Files

The configuration files for the wu-ftpd-academ server reside in the /etc/wu-ftpd-academ directory. Of the files there, the most important one is ftpaccess.

ftpaccess defines which people have access to your server, what things they can do, and how many are allowed to connect simultaneously. The ftpaccess file is described in the ftpaccess(5) man page. The key to this file is classes. By default, Debian installs these lines:

```
#class  local   real,guest,anonymous *.my.domain 192.168.0.0
#class  remote  real,guest,anonymous *
class   all     real,guest,anonymous *
```

Notice how the first two lines are commented out, so they have no function by default. The class line is defined like this:

- The class keyword at the start.
- The name of the class that you are defining. It is something that you pick.
- The type or types of connections that this class should match. If you use more than one, separate them with commas. The valid options here are as follows:
    - real matches somebody logging in to a real account on your system.

- `guest` matches guest accounts (less frequently used).
- `anonymous` matches people logging in anonymously.

- Finally, the address or addresses that matches this class. Note that these addresses use wildcards similar to those in the TCP wrappers configuration files.

Then you can use a `limit` keyword:

```
limit   all     10  Any   /etc/wu-ftpd-academ/msg.toomany
```

This line says that there should be a limit, effective at any time, applicable to people in the `all` class, of a maximum of 10 simultaneous connections. If people try to connect and they don't have permission to do so, they see the message contained in `/etc/wu-ftpd-academ/msg.toomany`.

Perhaps you would like to deny access to people from a certain domain. You might do this:

```
class denied real,guest,anonymous *.example.com
limit denied 0 Any /etc/wu-ftpd-academ/msg.denied
```

Here, you set a maximum user count of zero for the `denied` class, effectively preventing people there from connecting. Note that this functionality may appear to overlap that of TCP wrappers. In some ways, it does; both can prevent people from connecting on a per-host basis. However, the `ftpaccess` file allows you to specify a message given to people who try to connect, which is a feature not present in TCP wrappers. On the other hand, TCP wrappers allow `ident` checks, which `ftpaccess` does not support. Finally, `ftpaccess` allows you to specify a simultaneous connection limit, a feature also unsupported by TCP wrappers. So, you might want to use both to your advantage.

FTP Security Concerns

Earlier, we touched on some security concerns related to anonymous FTP. The following are some more hints of issues to be aware of regarding FTP services:

- Placing a connection limit on all classes is a good idea. Otherwise, your network link can become saturated, possibly degrading more important services.
- Having an upload ("Incoming") directory for anonymous FTP is generally a bad idea. First, it can allow attackers to cause trouble by filling up your disk. Also, unless you are extremely careful with permissions, it can be possible for others to download files uploaded by the public. This is bad; crackers often exploit this directory to exchange data (often illegally) using high-bandwidth servers.
- The `passwd-check` line in `ftpaccess` can be beneficial. If you set it to `passwd-check rfc822 enforce`, it requires a valid-looking email address as a password for anonymous FTP users.

- Logging can be great to find out what files people are downloading and what sort of performance people are getting. Also, if a security issue ever develops, logs are extremely valuable when you're tracking down the cause and the perpetrator.
- `path-filter` (set up by default) restricts anonymous users to use only certain valid filenames. It also can be beneficial in preventing certain types of abuse, and you are advised to stick with the default.
- Passwords are transmitted in plain text over the network, so people should not be logging in to real accounts from anywhere on the Internet.

Telnet

Although FTP allows you to access files remotely, Telnet allows you to log in to a remote machine as if you were sitting at its console. Telnet clients connect to the server. The server opens a pseudo terminal (`pty`), runs the login program, and then the programs run on the server but display on and read input from the client machine.

Telnet servers are fairly straightforward; the standard networking packages in Debian automatically install `in.telnetd` for you.

You can use TCP wrappers with Telnet, but beyond that, there is nothing to be configured.

ssh

As noted previously, problems can occur when passwords are sent over the Internet. For example, eavesdroppers can "sniff" the network and catch passwords. This means that other computers on the network can spy on the traffic to and from your own workstation. They also can catch any other part of the session, and in some cases, even insert characters as if one end or the other had typed them. Finally, in some cases, people can pretend to be a certain server; not knowing that they're not communicating with the real server, people can supply passwords that can then be used for security breaches. These types of attacks aren't solely a problem in Linux or even in TCP/IP; every operating system that communicates across the Internet has the same types of vulnerabilities.

To address these concerns, a number of programs for Linux use encryption to achieve increased security. One such program is `ssh`. You can download `ssh` from `non-us.debian.org`; due to United States' export laws, all encryption software in Debian is stored on servers outside the U.S.; however, it is legal to import and use those programs inside the U.S.

`ssh` is a program that uses both encryption to increase security and compression to increase performance. `ssh` can be used in a fashion analogous to Telnet, and its included copy utility, scp, can be used in place of FTP for some situations. All data that goes between the local and remote computer when using ssh is encrypted, defeating all the vulnerabilities just mentioned.

Using ssh

To begin using ssh, you first need to make sure that ssh is installed on both the local and the remote machine. Then, to log on to a remote machine using ssh, you can use the following:

```
ssh remotemachine.example.com
```

You then are asked for your password and are logged on. ssh assumes that your username is the same on the local and remote machines; if this is not the case, you can explicitly specify the username to use on the remote as follows:

```
ssh -l user2 remotemachine.example.com
```

In this example, you log in to the user2 account on the host remotemachine.example.com.

After you're logged in, you can use the programs on the remote just as you can with Telnet.

scp

scp is a program that uses the ssh protocol to copy files from one machine to another. As with ssh, the data going across the network is always encrypted, which increases security.

The basic syntax of scp is as follows:

```
scp filename remotemachine:remotedir
```

or

```
scp remotemachine:remotefile localname
```

The first command copies a file from the local machine to the remote; the second, a file from the remote machine to the local one. Note that you must always include the colon and the remote directory, even if you are placing the file in your home directory on the remote. If you do not, scp simply acts like cp and copies files on the local machine. However, as a shortcut, you can simply use . as the remote directory if you are referring to your home directory.

Consider this example:

```
scp /bin/bash remote2.example.com:.
```

This example copies the `/bin/bash` file from the local machine to the home directory on `remote2.example.com`.

You can also specify your username on a remote server like this:

```
scp /bin/bash user3@remote2.example.com:.
```

This example copies `/bin/bash` to the `user3` account on the remote machine. Also, with `scp`, as with `cp`, you can specify a different filename for the remote like this:

```
scp /bin/bash user3@remote2.example.com:mybash
```

In this case, the file is saved as `mybash` in the home directory on the remote machine.

Tunneling with ssh

`ssh` allows you to send data other than files and normal Telnet-like communication over its secure channel. One thing that it can do is encrypt X data; that is, if you run X programs remotely, the data stream used to display the interface can be encrypted. When you `ssh` to a remote machine, `ssh` can set up X forwarding. In this way, if you run X clients on the remote to connect to the local server, the communication for those too will be encrypted. This capability gives your X session the same kind of security benefits that you enjoy for normal terminal use.

`ssh` automatically configures X forwarding whenever both ends of the connection support it. On the remote machine, it even sets the `DISPLAY` variable as appropriate, so you can start X programs right away, without having to do any additional configuration.

`ssh` also allows arbitrary TCP connections to be forwarded with encryption. This is done with the `-L` and `-R` options to `ssh`.

With the `-L` option, `ssh` listens at a specified port on the local side for connections. Then it forwards all communication on that port over its encrypted channel to a specified machine and port on the remote end. With `-R`, the process is reversed; `ssh` listens to a certain remote port and forwards the data to the local machine.

For instance, you can use the following:

```
ssh -L 5555:remote:5555 remote
```

This example logs you on to the remote machines and forwards any connections to the local port 5555 to the remote port 5555, using encryption along the way.

Configuring ssh

`ssh` stores its configuration in several files in `/etc/ssh`. The primary one of interest for the server is `sshd_config`. This configuration file is documented in the `sshd(8)` man page. Most of the items in `sshd_config` are defaults that are appropriate for almost all sites, so not a lot of tweaking is necessary.

On the client side, a configuration file can be located in `~/.ssh` or the site-wide `/etc/ssh/ssh_config` file. They are documented in the `ssh(1)` man page.

Web Servers

One of the most popular uses of a Linux machine today is as a Web server. The power, speed, and stability of Linux and its strong networking support make this a natural choice for many organizations. Debian GNU/Linux includes a wide variety of Web servers from which to choose, spanning the spectrum from the large and powerful to the small and fast.

The most popular Web server is, by far, Apache. This is for good reason: It is powerful, stable, and extremely versatile. Debian includes Apache as part of the distribution. Also included are a number of Apache modules that add additional features to the server.

Apache

When you install the Debian Apache package, you get a fully functional server that's ready to use. By default, the root of your server (`http://yourmachine.example.com/`) looks for documents in `/var/www` and tilde expansion is performed as for `http://yourmachine.example.com/~username/`, which serves documents out of `username`'s `public_html` directory. So, you can place your Web documents online in `/var/www` or your personal `public_html` directory, and your server is ready to go!

You can do a lot more with Apache, though. You can set up redirection, aliases, CGI areas, virtual hosts, and more.

Configuring Apache

Apache configuration files have several unique capabilities. Some options can be specified on a "global" basis; that is, they apply to all parts of the server. You can also specify options that apply only to documents underneath a particular directory or to documents served from a specific virtual host.

Some options are valid several different places (alias, for instance); others, only at one specific location. Usually, this is common sense; it doesn't make sense to load modules that apply to the whole server in a section of the configuration that applies to a single directory.

The main Apache configuration consists of three files in `/etc/apache`:

- `httpd.conf` is the main configuration file for the server. This file specifies which modules are used, what the server name is, and some basic performance-tuning options, for example.
- `access.conf` defines the access restrictions on your Web pages. Most frequently, this file contains a number of Directory sections.
- `srm.conf` defines where to find documents on the server and how to present them. This file is frequently the location for virtual host definitions and a variety of other items related to presenting documents.

Technically, it's possible to concatenate these files and have all the information in a single file, but the Apache authors decided to have the default layout be split; otherwise, the single file becomes huge, and navigating it can be difficult. In other words, the separation of options into different files is not enforced by Apache; it's something that's simply recommended.

As you'll notice by examining the configuration file, Apache sections are defined like this:

```
<Section>
  Option 1
  Option 2
</Section>
```

Everything between the opening and closing parts of the section is taken to be part of that specific section.

After you make a modification to the configuration file, you need to inform the server of this change. To do that, run the following:

```
/etc/init.d/apache reload
```

Let's take a look at some aspects of Apache configuration. Although the configuration system is so versatile that every option can't be covered here, we'll examine some of the more popular and complex configuration tasks.

Virtual Hosts

Virtual hosts are used to provide multiple separate namespaces (generally under separate domain names) on a single server. This capability is frequently used by ISPs and Web-hosting companies to be able to host pages for multiple customers on a single machine.

The two different methods for doing virtual hosting are name-based and IP-based. With IP-based virtual hosting, the kernel IP alias feature is used to make the system respond to multiple IPs (instead of just one, as is conventional). Apache then treats each specified IP as a separate virtual host. It's important to note that virtual hosts apply only to the second and additional hosts served by a given machine; the first (primary) namespace is never a virtual host.

The second method is name-based virtual hosting. Here, only a single IP address is used, and the server relies on a feature in the HTTP/1.1 protocol to figure out from which virtual host the browser is requesting documents. This means that HTTP/1.0 browsers aren't compatible with this method, but because HTTP/1.0 browsers are virtually nonexistent these days, that isn't really a large problem.

Because name-based virtual hosting is the easier one to set up since it doesn't require more advanced modification to the networking system, we'll discuss that system here.

Generally, you configure virtual hosting in the `srm.conf` file. First, you use a directive such as this:

```
NameVirtualHost 10.11.12.13
```

This directive tells Apache that all the name-based virtual hosts will be served from IP address 10.11.12.13. You can set this address to the same address as your normal server name if desired.

Then you set up a `VirtualHost` section for each virtual host that you want to serve, as in this sample:

```
<VirtualHost 10.11.12.13>
ServerName software.example.com
DocumentRoot /var/www/software
</VirtualHost>
```

That's all you need to use to configure your virtual host!Notice that the IP address in the `VirtualHost` section must correspond with the IP address specified in `NameVirtualHost` above. `ServerName` is the name that the server is to take; in this example, you could access `http://software.example.com/` and get this particular virtual host. Finally, `DocumentRoot` specifies the location of the documents to serve for this virtual host.

Note

If you are running your own DNS services, you need to add a `CNAME` for each virtual host that points to your Web server.

In the `VirtualHost` area, you can also use aliases and redirect statements just as you can for the entire installation; we discuss them next.

Aliases and Redirects

Aliases and redirects provide a powerful way to manage documents in your server. Aliases allow you to specify that documents under a certain path reside at a special location on your server. Consider this example:

```
Alias /doc/ /usr/doc/
Alias /icons/ /usr/share/apache/icons/
```

These two are commonly used on Debian-based Apache systems. In this example, if someone accessed `http://machine.example.com/icons/`, the documents served would be from `/usr/share/apache/icons/` instead of from `/var/www/icons/`. So, you can place things at different places in your filesystem and yet have them all appear as one coherent structure to browsers.

Redirects are most useful when something has moved. A redirect returns a code to the browser effectively saying, "The document isn't here. Look over there." The browser then reissues a request, this time for the location pointed to by the redirect. In this way, you can move documents on your server but still allow old links to be functional. Plus, because the browser becomes aware of the move, when readers of your site bookmark your pages, they get the new URL as well. Additionally, you can redirect people to an area not part of your own server because the new item returned to the client is a complete URL. This capability can be useful if your server changes names. In general, it is understood that redirects are a better solution technically than the `META REFRESH` trick used in HTML documents.

Let's look at a sample redirect:

```
Redirect /doc/ http://www.example.com/bigfiles/doc/
```

In this case, when someone requests files under `/doc` from your server (regardless of whether your server is named `www.example.com`), the reader's browser is directed to look for the file under `http://www.example.com/bigfiles/doc` instead.

Redirects can also use sophisticated regular expressions if you have the `rewrite` module loaded (see `httpd.conf` for details on the modules).

The following is a real-life example from a Web server. This snippet is from a site that provides archives of mailing lists. Only the server name is changed for the examples.

```
Alias /mailinglists/archives /var/lib/lists-archives/archives/
<Directory /var/lib/lists-archives/archives>
RewriteEngine On
RewriteOptions inherit
RewriteRule ^/(.+)-(9[0-9])([01][0-9])/(.*)$ /mailinglists/archives/$1-19$2$3/$4
[R=permanent] </Directory>
```

First, the server is told to look for documents requested by `http://www.example.com/mailinglists/archives` in the `/var/lib/lists-archives/archives/` path in the filesystem. This area holds archives generated from mailing lists, presumably placed in that path by some automated list archiving software.

Now, the `Directory` section describes the fancy redirect that takes place. The problem in this case is that the URL includes the year for mailing lists (archives are typically split by date), but it is in two-digit form—a classic Y2K problem. Everything needs to be changed to four-digit years, but doing so would ordinarily break all the preexisting links into the archives, which is clearly a bad thing. So, Apache's `rewrite` module comes to the rescue by allowing the URL to be rewritten, the result being sent back to the browser as a redirect.

The `RewriteRule` line is the one that's of interest. It contains three components: a regular expression, the text to change it to, and the type of redirect to use.

The regular expression part matches a part of the URL that occurs underneath `/mailinglists/archives/` in the URL. The expression then proceeds to match the listname (`.+`), a two-digit year in the nineties (`9[0-9]`) and a month number (`[01][0-9]`). They are assigned to the `$1`, `$2`, and `$3` variables as is typical for regular expressions. Then the new URL is concocted: It starts with `/mailinglists/archives/` and then includes the listname as before. However, this time it inserts `19` and then the year and month from the original URL. This works because it is known that all the existing list archives are in the twentieth century. Finally, the server is told that it should give the browser a code indicating that the requested document has moved permanently.

If the requested document's URL doesn't match the regular expression (as would occur if the reader used a URL that already had a four-digit year), the `rewrite` rule is ignored for that request.

This section has walked you through setting up a Web server for your system. If you are setting up your own network, you'll also need to provide name service so that other computers can easily reach you. In the next section, you can learn about setting this up.

DNS and Bind

DNS is one of the fundamental building blocks of the Internet. Every machine name that you see on the Internet relies on DNS to be looked up because, fundamentally, TCP/IP (the protocol used for communication on the Internet) relies on numeric IP addresses instead of hostnames for communication.

It didn't take long to realize that humans found large numbers were a suboptimal method of remembering hostnames. We find it much easier to simply use `www.companyname.com` for a company instead of using 10.201.59.197 or some other large number.

The purpose of DNS, the domain name system, is to resolve these textual names into the IP addresses used for communication by TCP/IP. Today, more advanced DNS features are also used to facilitate backup email servers and Web server farms, for example. For a Web server farm, you can use DNS to let you use several machines to serve the same pages, and allow clients to randomly select one for connections.

Bind is a software suite that provides a nameserver for use on your network. It will most likely be of use to you only if you have a dedicated Internet feed and are hosting your own name service or if you have a private in-house network for which you would like to provide name service.

Understanding the DNS Process

Let's consider everything that happens regarding DNS when a Web browser performs a typical lookup.

Let's say that someone types `http://www.uk.debian.org/` into a Web browser. The first thing that the Web browser has to do before it can connect to the Web server is look up its IP address (this is done with the `gethostbyname()` call). It is this call that uses the DNS.

When the resolver code gets invoked by `gethostbyname()`, it first builds a list of the nameservers to ask. This list is defined in `/etc/resolv.conf`. Generally, these nameservers are ones defined by an ISP. When the resolver finds a working nameserver, it sends the query to that nameserver.

This nameserver is most likely acting as a forwarding and caching server. So, this server first looks in its cache of recent lookups to see whether it already knows the IP address of `www.uk.debian.org`. If so, it gives the result to the client, and the process ends here. However, most likely it needs to look up the result itself.

The nameserver then queries one of the root nameservers to find out where `debian.org`'s nameserver resides. When it has this information, it proceeds to ask `debian.org` about the name.

It finds out from `debian.org`'s nameserver that a separate server is authoritative for the `uk.debian.org` subdomain. So, the query then proceeds to that server. There, it finally gets an IP address. The ISP's forwarding nameserver then passes this address back to the original client and stores it in a cache for future reference.

The Configuration Files

The current series of Bind, version 8, has a master configuration file and then a number of zone files.

The master configuration file resides in `/etc/named.conf`. This file records which domains you are hosting and what the corresponding zone files are.

You have zone files for each domain that your nameserver provides information for. In fact, you may often have two per domain: One is the forward file, and the other the reverse (with PTR records).

Zone File Concepts

DNS entries are defined in a file called a *zone file*. A zone file begins with an SOA (Start Of Authority) record, which lists a few things about the domain: how long it should be cached, what its serial number is, and so on. After that, a number of different types of records are listed:

- A records are "normal" records. They indicate the IP address of a particular hostname. You can achieve some fascinating effects by having multiple A records for the same hostname but with different IP addresses.
- CNAME records define aliases. They effectively tell machines looking for the IP address of one hostname to go look up the IP address of another instead. They are frequently used with `www` or `ftp` prefixes, for example, to direct the resolver to the appropriate hostname instead.
- HINFO records exist but are not used frequently these days. They are used to provide information about a given host, such as operating system, hardware platform, and so on.
- MX records are used for mail. A given machine can have both A and MX records, or MX records alone. MX records are used to tell mail clients where mail sent for a certain machine can go. But there's an added capability here: MX records can be duplicated, each one for a single host with a different priority. In this way, backup mail servers can be specified. If the mail server can't reach the first MX entry, it continues with the others until it finds one that accepts the mail. If you have both MX and A record for a single machine, you can use this to have mail delivered to a different server but other connects to the machine itself.
- NS records define the nameservers for the domain. They are useful because they allow Bind to notify the secondary nameservers to redownload the zone whenever it is updated, thus dramatically reducing the time it takes for changes to propagate to the secondary servers. These records are also used to delegate authority for subdomains to other servers.

- PTR records are used for reverse lookups—that is, looking up a name given an IP address. In general, every A record has a corresponding PTR record. However, unlike the other records, PTR records are generally listed in a zone file separate from the A records.

All these records are used as part of the domain name system. Without MX records, for instance, mail service wouldn't be able to be as resistant to failure as it is. The capability to have numerous A records for a single hostname allows server clusters—a number of different servers that are capable of providing the same information. This is useful for servers that serve a high volume of mostly static information.

Using Zone Files

Let's consider an example of a zone file. Listing 17.1 shows a sample; below, you'll find commentary about it.

LISTING 17.1 Zone File Example for `example.com`

```
@ IN  SOA alpha.example.com. root.example.com. (
                                1971122001  ;serial (yyyymmddrr)
                                7200        ;refresh (2 hours)
                                3600        ;retry (1 hour)
                                3600000     ;expire (1000 hours)
                                28800       ;minimum (8 hours)
                                )
  IN  A     10.11.12.13
  IN     NS     alpha.example.com.
  IN  NS    backupserver.othernet.com.
  IN  MX 10 alpha.example.com.
  IN  MX 20 beta.example.com.
  IN  MX 50 omega.example.com.

alpha         IN    A        10.11.12.13
IN     MX 10    alpha
IN     MX 20    beta
IN     MX 30    omega.example.com.

beta             IN    A        10.11.12.14
IN     MX 10    alpha
IN     MX 20    beta
IN     MX 30    omega

gamma         IN     CNAME    alpha.example.com.

omega         IN    A        10.11.12.15
IN     MX 10    omega
IN     MX 20    alpha
```

```
IN    MX 30    beta
IN    MX 40    foo.somewhereelse.com.

pi              IN    CNAME    www.calc3141592653.com.

www              IN    CNAME    omega
ftp              IN    CNAME    omega
```

We begin this zone file, as all zone files, with an SOA record. The `@` sign at the start signifies that this SOA record is for the domain this file describes; that domain is listed in `/etc/named.conf`. Then the `IN` denotes that this is an Internet record, and `SOA` specifies Start Of Authority. Next is the machine name from which this information is presumed to originate. Typically, it ought to be the machine that acts as your primary nameserver. Then you have the email address of the server administrator, with the `@` sign converted to a dot. It is important that you remember to make that change.

In the parentheses are five important numbers. The first number is the serial number. Every time you update the file, you must increment it. Also, you must *never* decrease that number, or else software can get extremely confused. Many people adopt a method of using `YYYYMMDDRR`, where `RR` is a two-digit revision number; this method is handy if you make more than one change per day. You can also just start at one and increase the value every time you make a change.

The remaining numbers are all time intervals, specified in seconds. The value for `refresh` defines how frequently the SOA information is to be reloaded. The `retry` value specifies how frequently nameservers should attempt to reach an authoritative server for the domain if an authoritative answer cannot be obtained for a given lookup.

`expire` defines how long secondary nameservers are allowed to keep the information without attempting to update themselves. It is best to keep this value large; that way, if a lengthy network downtime occurs for some reason (caused by a natural disaster, for instance), your DNS is not interrupted if you have an offsite secondary.

The `minimum` value is the default time-to-live (TTL) duration for the entries in the zone file.

Now, after the SOA record itself, we define a few things about `example.com` itself. First, we define an IP address—10.11.12.13. That way, if people try to look up an IP address of `example.com`, they get a value.

Next, the nameservers that are authoritative for `example.com` are specified. This also allows Bind to notify the secondary nameserver of updates whenever necessary so that the secondary can remain as up-to-date as possible.

The `IN NS` lines illustrate an important point about the zone files: Whenever you specify an entire domain name, you absolutely *must* use a terminating period after it. If you do not use this period, Bind automatically tacks on the current domain (`example.com` in this example). For instance, had the period been omitted in the first `NS` line, Bind would have calculated a value of `alpha.example.com.example.com`—definitely not what is desired.

After the nameserver specifications, we move on to define the mail exchangers for addresses ending in `@example.com`. In this case, three mail servers can receive mail for `example.com`. The one with the lowest number is considered the primary server; if a remote is unable to reach it, the remote server tries the second-lowest priority, and so on, until it either can deliver the message or gives up.

Here, `alpha` is used to receive mail. If `alpha` is unreachable for some reason, the machine named `beta` will receive the mail instead. If both are unreachable, `omega` will be used for mail.

After all this, we move on to four lines defining information about the machine named `alpha.example.com`. The first line contains an A record, specifying the IP address of `alpha`. Next, we define three mail servers that can accept mail addressed to `@alpha.example.com`. Just to illustrate the point that you can use either simple hostnames or complete names with a trailing period, we use just `alpha` and `beta` (the `.example.com` is appended automatically) and then `omega.example.com`.

Then we have four lines for the machine named `beta.example.com`. Again, it gets an IP address and has three mail servers specified.

Next, the name `gamma` is defined. This name doesn't correspond to a machine on its own; rather, it is treated as an alias for `alpha.example.com`. Anybody asking for the IP address of `gamma.example.com` will be given the IP address of `alpha.example.com`.

Then we have a machine named `omega`. This one has five lines. The first defines its IP address as usual. Next, its mail servers are defined. Unlike the previous definitions of `example.com`, `alpha.example.com`, and `beta.example.com`, this one says that `omega.example.com` is the primary mail server for mail sent to `@omega.example.com`, and that `alpha` and `beta` are backups. Finally, it says that if all the servers are unreachable, the server `foo.somewhereelse.com` should be used; presumably, it is an offsite backup server.

Next is a definition for `pi`. Like before, it is an alias for a different machine, but in this case, the alias points to a different domain: `www.calc3141592653.com`. Thus, `pi.example.com` and `www.calc3141592653.com` both connect you to the same place.

Finally, we have two more `CNAME`s: one for the Web server and the other for the FTP server. Although they are not strictly necessary (you could use `http:// omega.example.com/` just as you could use `http://www.example.com/`), many people prefer to use two names because it is somewhat of a standard. Plus, if the Web server is ever moved to a different machine, you don't need to update links; you can just update the zone file.

This zone file is to be loaded from a `named.conf` clause like this:

```
zone "example.com" {
type master;
file "db.example";
}
```

This example assumes, of course, that you have placed the zone file in Listing 17.1 into `/var/named/db.example`.

Now that you have set up a normal zone file for looking up your hostnames, it's time to set up a reverse zone file. This is used for other computer to determine a hostname from a given IP address.

Reverse-Lookup Zone File

Listing 17.2 shows a sample reverse-lookup zone file for our `example.com` domain.

LISTING 2.2 Sample Reverse-Lookup Zone File

```
@ IN  SOA alpha.example.com. root.example.com. (
                                1971122001  ;serial (yyyymmddrr)
                                7200        ;refresh (2 hours)
                                3600        ;retry (1 hour)
                                3600000     ;expire (1000 hours)
                                28800       ;minimum (8 hours)
                                )
13             IN    PTR    alpha.example.com.
14             IN    PTR    beta.example.com.
15             IN    PTR    omega.example.com.
```

Note several important points here:

- The first three parts of the IP address (10.11.12) are inferred from the `named.conf` file; more on this below.
- You need to specify the full domain name here—but don't forget the trailing period.
- In general, only machines with A records have a corresponding reverse-lookup entry.

In `named.conf`, you have a section like this:

```
zone "12.11.10.in-addr.arpa" {
type master;
file "db.example.rev";
}
```

Notice how this section takes the first three parts of the IP address (we're assuming a class C netblock here; you may use less if applicable) and reverses them. Then we add `in-addr.arpa` to the end.

Now that you have your name service running, let's move on to another feature of Linux: collaborative discussions with Usenet servers.

Usenet

Usenet is a system of carrying on public discussions online. Usenet is organized into thousands of newsgroups, each devoted to a specific topic. In this section, we are going to explore the issues surrounding running a news server.

When an article is posted to Usenet, it propagates through the network to each participating Usenet server. When a server receives an article, it adds that article to a local spool and keeps it around for some amount of time (often a week or so). Then an expiration process runs and cleans out older articles.

People who read news typically use a newsreader client that uses Network News Transport Protocol (NNTP) to communicate with their local news server. NNTP provides a way for the client to figure out how many articles are in a group and which ones are unread, and to pull down a summary of the articles without having to download and read each one.

Finally, newsreaders can post new articles using NNTP as well. Servers use a slightly different flavor of NNTP to communicate between each other and exchange news articles.

Usenet articles also can be carried by different protocols; UUCP was once a popular way to do so, and still has a presence. Various other tricks are possible as well, including piping articles to arbitrary programs or files, which allows an almost unlimited flexibility in transport.

Usenet newsgroups are organized in a hierarchy; for instance, the top-level `comp` is for computer-related items. Underneath that is `os` for operating system groups. Next is `linux` for items related to Linux, and finally, `announce` for announcements. Thus, you get `comp.os.linux.announce`.

The first point to note is that Usenet is a large and distributed network. There are the "big seven" semi-official areas. Outside those areas are hundreds of separate hierarchies. Some are widely distributed; others, distributed across only a few computers. Therefore, there is no single definition of exactly what the Usenet newsgroups are. In fact, it's possible for different servers to have differences in the thousands for the count of newsgroups carried—and both could be Usenet servers.

If your server is going to have a "full" feed, be prepared for it to use a significant amount of bandwidth and disk space. Such a feed easily uses many gigabytes. One trick that people often do to cut down on this space is to exclude some of the "binaries" newsgroups, which account for a significant chunk of bandwidth and disk space required.

Installing INN

The next step is to install INN, the InterNetNews server used for Usenet. This generally means installing the `inn` and `inewsinn` package. If you will be feeding anyone with the NNTP protocol (as is probably the case for most people), you'll also want to install `innfeed`.

INN's installation script asks you a few questions. They are as follows:

- Return mail name, which defines what domain will be used in From: lines in Usenet posts.
- Organization, which sets up the Organization: line in Usenet posts. Using something other than the default here is probably wise.
- Path hostname, the hostname of the news server itself.
- News server, which is generally (but not always) the same as the path hostname.
- The local manager of the news system, which should be your email address.

At this point, Debian's installer sets up some very basic newsgroups. But you have an active system. Next, let's take a tour of the configuration files in `/etc/news`.

Configuration File Overview

INN uses many configuration files, each for a specific purpose. Transport of Usenet articles can be a complex task, and like email, there are many things to configure. Here are the files that you can find in /etc/news and the purpose of each.

- `actsync.cfg` and `actsync.ign` configure the `actsync` program. `actsync` is generally used only by people carrying full Usenet feeds, and is used to keep the local active file (list of known newsgroups) in sync with that of a primary newsfeed provider.
- `boot` is a shell script used to start the server.
- `control.ctl` defines what happens to various control messages. Control messages appear in the special "control" newsgroup and request the server to do something: create or remove a group and so on.
- `expire.ctl` defines how long articles remain before they are expired out of the news spool.

- `hosts.nntp` defines the hosts that are taken to be as peers, presumably ones from which newsfeeds arrive.
- `hosts.nntp.nolimit` are those hosts that are exempt from the limits of incoming NNTP connections and connects per minute.
- `inn.conf` defines some basic configuration information; it is generally information that the configure script asked you for.
- The `innshellvars` files define file locations, names, and so on.
- `innwatch.ctl` defines what `innwatch` should do when the state of the news system reaches a certain point.
- The `moderators` file describes the proper posting address for moderated newsgroups. Moderated newsgroups don't allow posting directly to the group; rather, posts must first be sent via email to a moderator for approval. This file describes which email address to use for which groups.
- The `newsfeeds` file is one of the most important. It defines where articles are sent. Generally, unless you are running a completely isolated news server, you have entries in here ensuring that your users' posts propagate to the Usenet.
- `nnrp.access` defines which hosts (and users) can access the server with a newsreader, optionally defining passwords for them.
- `nntpsend.ctl` is used to configure the `nntpsend(8)` batch-file processor.
- `organization` simply holds your value for the Organization: header.
- `overview.fmt` describes the format of the overview database files, which are used by news clients requesting summaries of the articles in a group.
- `passwd.nntp` is used for defining passwords of remote NNTP servers.
- `send-uucp.cf` is used for the `send-uucp` script. It defines what sort of compression to use, a maximum precompression size, and the times to process the batches.
- `server` simply contains the local name of your news server, which the configure script asked you for.
- `whoami` contains the pathname; again, the configure script asked you for this information.

Additionally, the following are some relevant status files in `/var/lib/news`:

- `active` records all the newsgroups present on the system, whether each one is moderated, and the range of articles present for each group.
- `newsgroups` holds a description of many (but not necessarily all) groups. Some clients use this file to present the reader with more descriptive newsgroup names.

The newsfeeds File

The files listed in the preceding section are, for the most part, self-explanatory when you look at them. An exception here is the `newsfeeds` file. Recall that this file is used to describe where articles are sent.

This file has long entries, theoretically one per line, but the use of the backslash as a continuation operator is common. Each of the fields is separated by a colon in a fashion similar to files such as `printcap`.

The basic syntax is given as follows:

```
site[/exclude,exclude...]\
          :pattern,pattern...[/distrib,distrib...]\
          :flag,flag...\
          :param
```

Let's look at the meaning of each of these components. For some of these items, particularly the different types of feeds, you might want to consult the `newsfeeds(5)` man page for more details on the particular feed that you choose to use.

- `site` is the primary name of the remote machine.
- The `exclude` value or values name other aliases for the remote. This is so that we don't end up sending articles back to the remote that it sent here—even if they had a slightly different name on them.
- The `patterns` define which groups the remote is to receive.
- `distrib` describes essentially the same thing but relies on the Distribution header.
- The `flag` values set a number of options—what type of feed it is, size limits, and so on. You'll find more details on the flags in Table 17.3.
- `param` describes additional information for some of the flags.

TABLE 17.3 Available Flags

Flag	*Meaning*
`<x`	An article is selected for transmission only if its size is less than `x` bytes.
`>x`	An article is selected for transmission only if its size is greater than `x` bytes. For both `<x` and `>x` flags, the default is to have no limit.
`Ax`	This flag specifies certain criteria that must be met before the article will be allowed to be sent; the valid values for `x` are as follows: * `d`, which indicates that the article will not be sent unless it contains a Distribution: header. * `p`, which indicates that, except for the explicit exclusions, the Path: header is not checked for the remote name.

continues

TABLE 17.3 continued

Flag	Meaning
`Bx/y`	This flag applies only to three types of feeds: exploder, file, or channel. Normally, the server writes data synchronously; that is, it's written as soon as it arrives. This option, however, tells the server to buffer the data for a while. Buffering can provide a performance win for heavily loaded sites. Both `x` and `y` are numbers here. `x` defines the point at which the server should empty the buffer to disk, and `y` defines the point at which the server ought to begin buffering again. Thus, `x` is a "maximum" value, and `y` is a "minimum" value.
`Fx`	Here, `x` specifies a filename for sites fed in that way. Unless `x` is an absolute filename (beginning with a slash), it is assumed to refer to a file under `/var/spool/news/out.going`.
`Gx`	This flag allows articles to be sent to the specific site only if they are posted to no more than `x` newsgroups.
`Hx`	This flag allows articles to be sent to the specific site only if they have no more than `x` entries in the `Path` line. The default for `x` is `1`, meaning essentially that only those articles that are created locally will be sent to the feed. If you are not running a leaf site, you will no doubt want to increase this value.
`Ix`	For file feeds, this flag specifies the size of INN's buffer. The default is 16KB.
`Nx`	This flag allows articles to be sent to the site only if they meet the criteria of `x`. The possible values of `x` are as follows: * `m`, which means that only moderated messages will be sent. * `u`, which means that only unmoderated messages will be sent.
`Sx`	This flag specifies that data should be spooled to disk if the amount queued for the site exceeds `x` bytes. This flag is generally useful only for channel and exploder feeds. If the `F` flag is also specified, it denotes the location of the spool file.
`Tx`	This flag specifies the feed type for the site. The possible values for `x` are as follows: * `c`, for a channel feed. This type of feed is similar in concept to a program feed but differs in the semantics of communication between the news server and the destination program. * `f`, for a file feed. A line is written to the file specified in the `param` field for each article to be sent to the path. If `param` does not specify an absolute path, it is taken to be relative to `/var/spool/news/out.going`. Further, if `param` is missing altogether, it defaults to simply the name of the site. * `l`, to just log an entry. This is essentially the same as a file feed sending information to `/dev/null`.

Flag	Meaning
	* m, for a funnel feed. Funnels allow you to combine the data to be sent out to multiple sites into a single stream, probably for use with innfeed. For this, the param field specifies the name of a newsfeeds entry that is to be the target of this funnel. That particular entry, then, is a "pseudo-entry"; that is, it receives articles from the funnel and describes what to do with them, but it doesn't do anything else. * p, for a program feed. In this case, for each article received, INN forks and execs the program specified in param (which incidentally has some special capabilities; see the newsfeeds man page). It then pipes the article to the specified program. * x, for an exploder feed. This type of feed is similar to the channel feed, but INN can also pass specially formatted command-line arguments to them.
Wx	The W flag specifies which items are to be included for the feed. It is used only by file, channel, exploder, or program feeds. You can use one or more options for x for all the feeds except program; for program, only the asterisk option has any effect. The valid values for x are as follows: * b, the size of the article (in bytes). * f, the path to the article; an absolute path, starting with /var/spool/news. * g, the newsgroup in which the article can be found. If the article is cross-posted, this flag specifies the first newsgroup in which the article appears for this site. * m, the Message-ID: header contents for the article. * n, similar to f, but provides a relative path only (the /var/spool/news is implied). * p, the posting time of the article. This time is given in traditional UNIX form: seconds since epoch. * s, the site from which this machine received the article, according to the Path: line. * t, the time the article was received by this server—again, in seconds since epoch. * *, the names of the newsfeeds entries for a funnel feed, or the names of all sites to which the article is sent. * D, the contents of the Distribution: article header. If the article has no Distribution: header, this flag results in a ?. * H, all headers of the article.

continues

TABLE 17.3 continued

Flag	*Meaning*
	* N, the contents of the Newsgroups: header for the article. * O, the overview data for this article. * R, the replication information for the article.

The /etc/news/newsfeeds file comes with an assortment of examples. You can probably find a few in there that are relevant to your particular situation.

> **Note**
>
> Many of the options in newsfeeds—such as the pattern and distrib fields—can use wildcards such as the asterisk. Not only that, but the effect can be negated by appending ! (an exclamation mark) at the start of a particular pattern. If this occurs for a pattern entry, for instance, it means to not send the specified groups instead of to explicitly send them.

> **Note**
>
> newsfeeds contains a special entry for a site named ME. This entry refers to your local server. It must be the first entry in the file. The pattern given in ME, if any, becomes the default pattern list for all other sites in newsfeeds. If the distrib entries exist, then it restricts which Distribution: headers are allowed in incoming articles.

Setting Up a Newsfeed

To set up a bidirectional newsfeed—one in which articles are both sent to and received from the remote—you need to perform the following steps:

- Make sure that the remote is configured to send articles to and receive articles from your server.
- Add the appropriate groups to your local configuration. You do so either by using ctlinnd, as described in the next section, or by using actsync.
- Add the appropriate entry or entries to your newsfeeds file.

- Add an entry to `innfeed.conf` if appropriate. See the `innfeed.conf` man page for more details.
- Tell the server to reload everything by using `ctlinnd`.

Your feed is now ready.

ctlinnd

`ctlinnd` is a program used to issue commands to a running INN server. The `ctlinnd(8)` man page lists quite a few options available to you with `ctlinnd`. We'll highlight the most important ones here.

Note

One note beforehand: Several options ask for a "reason" argument. This argument is used for several purposes. In the simplest form, it logs the reason into a log file. For some options, though, the reason is saved for future use. For instance, if you issue a `pause` command, a later `go` command will want you to specify the same reason that you specified with the previous `pause`. The exact string used for the reason is arbitrary; you can select it yourself.

Table 17.4 presents some of the most useful `ctlinnd` commands.

TABLE 17.4 `ctlinnd` Commands and Their Meanings

Command	*Meaning*
`ctlinnd allow reason`	Specifies that NNTP connections are again allowed, after a previous `reject` command.
`ctlinnd changegroup group rest`	Modifies the active file entry for the specified group such that the fourth field in the active file becomes the value specified by `rest`. This command is typically used to change whether a group is moderated or unmoderated. For more details, see the `active(5)` man page.
`ctlinnd checkfile`	Tells the server to check the syntax of the `newsfeeds` file. If any problem occurs, a message is displayed, and the details of the error are logged in `/var/log/news`.

continues

TABLE 17.4 continued

Command	*Meaning*
`ctlinnd go reason`	Tells the server to resume processing after a previous command that took the server down from normal full operation status. The reason given here must match that given to the previous command.
`ctlinnd help`	Displays a summary of the commands available for `ctlinnd`.
`ctlinnd newgroup group rest creator`	Creates a new newsgroup on the local server and adds the corresponding entry to the active file. The `rest` parameter is `options`; it defaults to `y` if not specified. The `creator` parameter is typically the name of the person creating the group; however, it too can be omitted and defaults to being empty. For more information on these last two items, see the `active(5)` man page.
`ctlinnd pause reason`	Changes the status of the server such that no further incoming articles are accepted. This command does not prevent reading or close existing connections. To re-enable full operations, use `ctlinnd go`.
`ctlinnd reject reason`	Tells the server to reject NNTP connections. Those attempting to connect are given `reason` as an explanation for being rejected.
`ctlinnd reload file reason`	Tells the server to reread configuration files. For `file`, you can specify `all` to load all the configuration files or one of `history`, `hosts.nntp`, `active`, `newsfeeds`, or `overview.fmt`.
`ctlinnd rmgroup group`	Removes the active file record of the specified group. The articles in the spool directory `/var/spool/news` are not removed; however, they are deleted by the usual expiry process.
`ctlinnd shutdown reason`	Stops the server daemon. `ctlinnd` cannot restart the server after issuing this command; however, you can use `/etc/init.d/inn` start to restart it yourself. It is recommended that you use `ctlinnd throttle` prior to using `ctlinnd shutdown`.
`ctlinnd throttle reason`	Closes all existing NNTP connections and rejects new connection attempts.

Summary

Information servers are one of the most powerful and important features of Linux. They are used by many people and organizations to provide a variety of information and services on the Internet. When setting up your own network, the first thing you'll need is name service, which you can set up with Bind. You'll most likely also want email, which you can configure with sendmail. After that, you can add services that you want, such as Web and FTP servers. All can be hosted from your Linux machine, and together can make a robust information server.

CHAPTER

Interacting with Microsoft Networks Using Samba

by Mario Camou

In This Chapter

This chapter gives you the information you need to install, configure, and use the Samba suite of Server Message Block (SMB or Samba) With Samba, you can share a Linux filesystem with Windows 95, 98, or NT. You can share a Windows 95, 98, or NT FAT filesystem with Linux. You can also share printers connected to either Linux or a system with Windows 95, 98, or NT.

Samba is the protocol used by Microsoft's operating systems to share files and printer services. It doesn't matter to whom or from whom. It's just the protocol they use. Microsoft and Intel developed the SMB protocol system in 1987, and later, Andrew Tridgell ported the system to various UNIX systems and Linux.

Note

Microsoft is currently proposing another file sharing standard, Common Internet File System (CIFS). The standard has been submitted to the Internet Engineering Task Force, but CIFS is not yet widely adopted and does not currently exist for Linux.

The Samba suite of SMB protocol utilities consists of several components. The `smbd` daemon provides the file and print services to SMB clients, such as Windows for Workgroups, Windows NT, or LAN Manager, or other Linux and UNIX clients. The configuration file for this daemon is described in `smb.conf`. The `nmbd` daemon provides NetBIOS nameserving and browsing support. You can also run `nmbd` interactively to query other name service daemons.

The SMB client program (`smbclient`) implements a simple FTP-like client on a Linux or UNIX box. The SMB mounting program (`smbmount`) enables mounting of server directories on a Linux or UNIX box. The `testparm` utility enables you to test your `smb.conf` configuration file. The `smbstatus` utility tells you who is currently using the `smbd` server.

This is useful for accessing SMB shares on other compatible servers, such as Windows machines, and can also be used to enable a UNIX box to print to a printer attached to any SMB server, such as a PC running Windows 98.

The `testparm` utility enables you to test your `smb.conf` configuration file. The `smbstatus` utility enables you to tell who is currently using the `smbd` server. In the Debian 2.1 distribution, these files can be found in the following directories:

```
smbd and nmbd: /usr/sbin
smbclient, smbmount, testparm, smbstatus: /usr/bin
smb.conf: /etc
```

Installing Samba

First of all, you need to install Samba. You can install Samba during the Debian installation from CD-ROM or later using `dpkg` or `apt-get`. There are two packages to install: `samba` and `samba-doc`. See Chapter 10, "Software Management," for more information on using `dpkg` and `apt-get`.

When you configure the Samba installation, `dpkg` asks you the following question:

```
Run Samba as daemons or from inetd?
Press 'D' to run as daemons or 'I' to run from inetd: [I]
```

There are two ways of running Samba. You can run it as a daemon, started on boot from a file in `/etc/rc?.d`, or you can have `inetd` start it. Running as a daemon is best when the startup time when running from `inetd` can be an issue. This is referring to the time it will take for the Samba service to start when running from `inetd`. If Samba will be used only sporadically, it is best to run from `inetd`. Running as a daemon allows the superuser to reconfigure, shut down, or restart the service much easier than in inetd.

If you select to run from `inetd`, the Samba configuration adds the Samba service to `/etc/inetd.conf` and restarts the `inetd` daemon. If you select to run as a daemon, it creates soft links in `/etc/rc*.d` to start Samba in all run levels. See Chapter 16, "TCP/IP Networking Essentials," for more information on `inetd`, and Chapter 12, "Customizing the Bootup Procedure," for more information on run levels and the `/etc/rc*.d` directories.

Getting a Simple Samba Setup Running

Samba can be very complex, so it's important to get the simplest possible implementation of Samba running before making major configuration changes.

The main configuration file, `smb.conf`, is located in `/etc`. Listing 18.1 provides the default listing shipped with Debian 2.1. It is used by the Samba server software (`smbd`) to determine directories and printers, and to determine security options for those directories and printers.

LISTING 18.1 The Example `smb.conf` Samba Configuration File

```
;
; /etc/smb.conf
;
; Sample configuration file for the Samba suite for Debian GNU/Linux
;
```

continues

Listing 18.1 continued

```
; Please see the manual page for smb.conf for detailed description of
;     every parameter.
;

[global]
   printing = bsd
   printcap name = /etc/printcap
   load printers = yes
   guest account = nobody
   invalid users = root

; "security = user" is always a good idea. This will require a UNIX account
;     in this server for every user accessing the server.
   security = user

; Change this for the workgroup your Samba server will be a part of.
   workgroup = WORKGROUP

   server string = %h server (Samba %v)

; These socket options really speed up Samba under Linux, according to my
;     own tests.
   socket options = IPTOS_LOWDELAY TCP_NODELAY SO_SNDBUF=4096 SO_RCVBUF=4096

; Passwords are encrypted by default. This way, the latest Windows 95 and NT
;     clients can connect to the Samba server with no problems.
   encrypt passwords = yes

; It's always a good idea to use a WINS server. If you want this server
;     to be the WINS server for your network, change the following parameter
;     to "yes." Otherwise, leave it as "no" and specify your WINS server
;     below (note: only one Samba server can be the WINS server).
;     Read BROWSING.txt for more details.
   wins support = no

; If this server is not the WINS server, specify who is and uncomment
;     next line.
;   wins server = 172.16.0.10

; Please read BROWSING.txt and set the next four parameters according
;     to your network setup. There is no valid default, so they are commented
;     out.
;   os level = 0
;   domain master = no
;   local master = no
;   preferred master = no

; What naming service and in what order should we use to resolve hostnames
;     to IP addresses?
   name resolve order = lmhosts host wins bcast

; This will prevent nmbd from searching for NetBIOS names through DNS.
```

```
   dns proxy = no

; Name mangling options

   preserve case = yes
   short preserve case = yes

; This Boolean parameter controls whether Samba attempts to sync. the UNIX
;     password with the SMB password when the encrypted SMB password in the
;     /etc/smbpasswd file is changed.
   unix password sync = false

; For UNIX password sync. to work on a Debian GNU/Linux system, the following
;     parameters must be set (thanks to Culus for pointing this out):
   passwd program = /usr/bin/passwd %u
   passwd chat = *New\spassword:* %n\n *Re-enter\snew\spassword:* %n\n
*Password\schanged.* .

; The following parameter is useful only if you have the linpopup package
;     installed. The samba maintainer and the linpopup maintainer are
;     working to ease installation and configuration of linpopup and samba.
;   message command = /bin/sh -c '/usr/bin/linpopup "%f" "%m" %s; rm %s' &

; The default maximum log file size is 5MBs. That's too big, so this
;     next parameter sets it to 1MB. Currently, Samba rotates log
;   files (/var/log/{smb,nmb} in Debian) when these files reach 1000KB.
;     A better solution would be to have Samba rotate the log file upon
;     reception of a signal, but for now, we have to live with this.
   max log size = 1000

[homes]
   comment = Home Directories
   browseable = no

; By default, the home directories are exported read-only. Change next
;     parameter to "no" if you want to be able to write to them.
   read only = yes

; File creation mask is set to 0700 for security reasons. If you want to
;     create files with group=rw permissions, set next parameter to 0775.
   create mask = 0700

; Directory creation mask is set to 0700 for security reasons. If you want to
;     create dirs. with group=rw permissions, set next parameter to 0775.
   directory mask = 0700

[printers]
   comment = All Printers
   browseable = no
   path = /tmp
   printable = yes
   public = no
```

continues

LISTING 18.1 continued

```
   writable = no
   create mode = 0700

; A sample share for sharing your CD-ROM with others.
;[cdrom]
;   comment = Samba server's CD-ROM
;   writable = no
;   locking = no
;   path = /cdrom
;   public = yes
;
; The next two parameters show how to automount a CD-ROM when the
;     cdrom share is accessed. For this to work, /etc/fstab must contain
;     an entry like this:
;
;        /dev/scd0   /cdrom  iso9660 defaults,noauto,ro,user   0 0
;
; The CD-ROM gets unmounted automatically after the connection
;
; If you don't want to use automounting/unmounting, make sure the CD
;     is mounted on /cdrom.
;
;   preexec = /bin/mount /cdrom
;   postexec = /bin/umount /cdrom
```

> **Note**
>
> The ; character at the beginning of an `smb.conf` line indicates the line is a comment that is to be ignored when processed by the Samba server. The # character does the same thing. Customarily, the ; character is used to "comment out" option lines, and the # is used at the beginning of lines that are truly comments.

The `smb.conf` file layout consists of a series of named sections. Each section starts with its name in brackets, such as `[global]`. Within each section, the parameters are specified by key/value pairs, such as `printcap name = /etc/printcap`.

`smb.conf` consists of three special sections and one or more custom sections. The special sections are `[global]`, `[homes]`, and `[printers]`. Before describing them in detail, let's look at getting a minimal running Samba.

First, whatever username is used on the test client, make sure it exists on the Linux box. Add the user and password with the `adduser` and `passwd` commands.

Warning

Be sure to back up the original /etc/smb.conf file before making your first modification.

Note

Samba works only on functioning networks. To prevent frustration, always make sure the client and server can ping each other's IP address before attempting any Samba configuration or testing. Also, attempt to ping the server's hostname from the client to determine what to expect from smbclient or smbmount commands using the hostname instead of the IP address.

Testing with a Linux Client

The default /etc/smb.conf should be sufficient to run a simple Samba test with a Linux client. Run the following command:

```
smbclient '//192.168.100.1/homes' -U myuid
```

Note that this example uses 192.168.100.1 as the IP address of the Samba server. Substitute the IP address of your Samba server. Any name resolving to that same IP address can be used in its place. The preceding example uses myuid for the user name; please substitute the client's username. homes represents the [homes] section of smb.conf.

You will be asked for a password. Type the user's password. If the server password is different from the client password, use the server password. If all is well, you will then be greeted by the following prompt:

```
smb: \>
```

Type ls and press Enter. If all is well, you get a directory listing that includes the file .bash_profile. You have proved you have a simple Samba running.

If you get an error message resembling this:

```
error connecting to 192.168.100.1:139 (Connection refused)
```

it probably indicates that the smb daemon is not running on the server. If you selected to run Samba as a daemon, run the daemon with this command on the Samba server:

```
/etc/init.d/smb restart
```

Testing with a Windows Client

Samba is what makes a Linux computer show up in a Windows Network Neighborhood. What shows up in Network Neighborhood is the workgroup name attached to `workgroup=` in the `[global]` section of the Samba server's `/etc/smb.conf`. Samba works best with workgroup names that are all caps, 8 characters or under, and definitely not containing spaces. This is a limitation of Windows.

Next, in the `[global]` section, temporarily uncomment (which means to remove the comment character before the line, thereby activating the option) `password level` and `username level`. Make `password level` equal to the longest likely password on this system, and `username level` the longest likely username (`uid`). These specify how many characters are case-insensitive, which is very important with case-insensitive SMB clients such as Windows.

> **Note**
>
> The changes to username level and password level are typically not required. The preceding suggestion is simply to temporarily eliminate any possible case sensitivity problems. When the system is working perfectly, you'll want to re-comment the password level and user level.
>
> Whenever there's a troubleshooting question involving case sensitivity for users and passwords, you can once again uncomment them, and recomment them upon resolution.

Encrypted Versus Plain-Text Passwords

Now you have to decide whether to use clear-text passwords or encrypted passwords, and how to implement that decision. Early Windows SMB clients defaulted to clear-text passwords. Beginning with Windows 95 OEM Service Release 2, Windows defaulted to encrypted passwords. All Windows 98 clients default to encrypted. Likewise, the default behavior changed from clear-text to encrypted in Windows NT 4.0 Service Pack 3. All clients on the network must use the same scheme, so if any of your clients cannot use encrypted passwords (for example, if you have Windows for Workgroups clients) you must use clear-text passwords.

In the Debian GNU/Linux 2.1 shipping default `smb.conf`, encrypted passwords are enabled, so for Windows versions prior to 95-OSR2 or Windows NT versions prior to 4.0 Service Pack 3, either each plain-text client must be changed to encrypted passwords, or the server's `smb.conf` must be changed to disable encrypted passwords, and any encrypted-password clients must be changed to use clear-text passwords.

Note

The documentation packaged with Debian 2.1 contains detailed discussions of plain versus encrypted passwords, and their ramifications. See

```
/usr/doc/samba-doc/Win95.txt
/usr/doc/samba-doc/WinNT.txt.gz
/usr/doc/samba-doc/ENCRYPTION.txt.gz
```

Windows NT users: NT SMB clients present some additional challenges. Be sure to read these three documents carefully if you are having problems with Windows NT SMB clients.

Note that documentation files that end with `.gz` are compressed with the `gzip` program. To view these documents, you can use a command like the following:

```
zcat /usr/doc/samba-doc/ENCRYPTION.txt.gz | less
```

Disabling and Enabling Passwords

To disable encrypted passwords in the server, edit the `smb.conf` file. In the `[global]` section, comment lines `encrypt passwords = yes` and `smb passwd file = /etc/smbpasswd`.

To enable encrypted passwords in the client, start `regedit` and navigate to `[HKEY_LOCAL_MACHINE\System\CurrentControlSet\Services\VxD\VNETSUP]`. If it contains an object called `EnablePlainTextPassword`, set that object's value to `0`. If it does not contain that object, create that object as a `DWORD`, and give it a value of `0`. Exit `regedit`, and reboot the Windows machine.

Warning

This technique requires editing the Windows Registry, which involves significant risk, including risk of data loss and OS inoperability. If possible, it's preferable to handle this issue on the server, as explained previously. If you don't know what `regedit` is, you should definitely handle it on the server!

The Results of Your Work: Network Neighborhood

Ideally, after you've completed configuration and rebooted, the server's workgroup (defined in `[global]`, `workgroup=`) should simply appear inside the Entire Network folder of Network Neighborhood. Double-clicking the workgroup should produce an icon for the server, which, if double-clicked, should produce an icon for the user directory described in the `[homes]` section. Files in that directory should appear when that directory's icon is double-clicked. Note that files beginning with a period (such as `.bash_profile`) are considered hidden by Windows and can be viewed only if the folder's Windows Explorer view properties are set to see all files.

> **Note**
>
> Encrypted password support doesn't use the `/etc/passwd` file to store users' passwords. This is because the algorithm Windows uses to encrypt passwords is different from the algorithm used by UNIX. Because of this, a separate `/etc/smbpasswd` file is needed.
>
> When you add a user to Samba with encrypted passwords, you need to add the user to the `/etc/smbpasswd` file. This is done using the `/usr/bin/smbpasswd` utility. To add the client username `myuid` to the `/etc/smbpasswd` file, use the following command:
>
> ```
> smbpasswd -a myuid
> ```
>
> You should then type the password. If the password is not the same as it is on the client, the user will be prompted for the password the first time he or she accesses the Samba server.

Troubleshooting the Windows Connection

The preceding paragraph describes the ideal outcome. Often, there are difficulties even if you've set up everything exactly right. First, it can take Windows over a minute (sometimes several minutes) to "find out" that the server's Samba configuration has been changed and restarted. There are often password difficulties resulting from Windows being case-insensitive and Linux being case-sensitive. There may be problems with name resolution. And of course, there could be a basic network problem.

None of this presents a major obstacle. Take a few minutes' break to make sure Windows has "gotten the word." You may want to reboot Windows a second time. Then, make sure you have a network by confirming that the client and server can ping each others' IP addresses.

Next, it's often helpful to use `Start Button:Find:Computer` to try to find the server's IP address. Note that the ability to find the server is not absolutely essential to complete Samba use (*find* is not equivalent to *ping*). Remember to refresh the various Network Neighborhood screens often (the `F5` key does this). If problems continue, temporarily set `username level` and `password level` to `128` (overkill) and make sure they're uncommented. Make sure your client and server agree on the use of encrypted or clear-text passwords, as described earlier in this chapter. Then, if you're running Samba as a daemon, restart Samba on the server with the following:

```
/etc/rc.d/smb restart
```

If problems continue, it's time to view the documentation in the `/usr/doc/samba-doc/` tree. It's important to have a simple Samba (simple in this case meaning not much functionality) working before attempting serious configuration. When a working Samba has been established, it's a good idea to back up `/etc/smb.conf` (but be sure not to overwrite the backup of the original that came with Debian GNU/Linux 2.1).

Now that we've gone over a simple Samba setup, we'll move along to configuring this setup we've created.

Configuring Samba: The /etc/smb.conf file

Samba has hundreds of configuration options. This chapter discusses those options most likely to be useful. In the following sections, the examples are presented first and then analyzed.

Tip

Andrew Tridgell has written an excellent diagnostic procedure, called `DIAGNOSIS.txt`, for Samba. On the Debian 2.1 distribution, it's available at

`/usr/doc/samba-doc/DIAGNOSIS.txt.gz`

which is the location of the doc on the Linux box.

It's excellent for troubleshooting tough Samba problems.

The [global] Section

The `global` section controls parameters for the entire SMB server. This section also provides default values for the other sections.

```
workgroup = WORKGROUP
```

`workgroup=` specifies the Windows workgroup, which must be the same in all servers and clients. Try to keep it all uppercase, 8 characters or less, and no with spaces.

```
server string = %h server (Samba %v)
```

`server string=` specifies a human-readable string used to identify the server in the user interface of the client. `server string=` goes in the `[global]` section. Note the similarity to the `comment=` option, which identifies individual shares in the client's user interface. `%h` will be substituted by the server's hostname, and `%v` will be substituted by the Samba version number.

```
printcap name = /etc/printcap
load printers = yes
```

The preceding enables printing without fuss, and is uncommented by default. It enables printing to all the printers defined in `/etc/printcap`.

```
guest account = nobody
```

This line defines a `guest account` for clients logged in as users not known to the Samba server. These users have the privileges of the UNIX user mentioned in this line.

```
encrypt passwords = yes
```

Passwords are encrypted by default for Windows 95 OSR2 and beyond, but are clear-text for earlier versions. To enable Windows-encrypted passwords to work with Samba, these two lines must be uncommented and SMB-encrypted passwords added on the server with the `smbpasswd -a` command. For instance:

```
smbpasswd -a valerie
```

```
The preceding command adds SMB user valerie (who should already have a Linux
user ID) to the SMB-encrypted password file, and enables you to give valerie a
password.unix password sync = false
passwd program = /usr/bin/passwd %u
passwd chat = *New\spassword:* %n\n *Re-enter\snew\spassword:* %n\n
*Password\schanged.* .
```

If you set the `unix password sync` option to `true`, the UNIX `/etc/passwd` file is synchronized with the `/etc/smbpasswd` so that whenever a user's password is modified in `smbpasswd`, it ismodified in `passwd`. The `passwd program` and `passwd chat` options are necessary so Samba knows how to change the Linux password.

```
log file = /var/log/samba-log.%m
max log size = 50
```

The `log file` entry specifies the location of the log file for each client who accesses Samba services. The `%m` parameter tells the Samba server to create a separate logfile for each client. The `max log size` entry sets a maximum file size for the logs created.

The [homes] Section

The `[homes]` section enables network clients to connect to a user's home directory on your server without having an explicit entry in the `smb.conf` file. When a service request is made, the Samba server searches the `smb.conf` file for the specific section corresponding to the service request. If the service is not found, Samba checks whether there is a `[homes]` section. If the `[homes]` section exists, the password file is searched to find the home directory for the user making the request. When this directory is found, the system shares it with the network:

```
comment = Home Directories
```

The `comment` entry is a human-readable share identification string to be displayed by the client user interface to the clients to let them know what shares are available. Note that `comment=` is similar to `server string=`, but the latter is valid only in the `[global]` section.

```
browseable = no
```

The `browseable=no` entry instructs the SMB client not to list the share in a browser (such as Windows Explorer). However, by its nature, `[homes]` makes the user share it represents visible in the client browser.

```
read only = yes
```

The `read only` parameter controls whether a user can create and change files in his or her home directory when shared across the network.

```
preserve case = yes
short preserve case = yes
```

The `preserve case` and `short preserve case` parameters instruct the server to preserve the case of any new files written to the server. This is important because Windows filenames are not typically case-sensitive, but Linux filenames are case-sensitive.

```
create mask = 0700
directory mask = 0700
```

The `create mask` and `directory mask` entries specify the `umask` for user-created files and directories, respectively. The permissions set by the user are `AND`ed with the respective mask when the file is created, so a mask of `0700` means that files and directories will be created with read/write/execute permissions for the user, and none for the group and other. If you want your users to create files that can be read by users in the same group, you should set the mask to `0750`.

Warning

Linux and Windows use a different linefeed sequence in text files. When editing a file through Samba, the text file protocol is determined by the OS of the client. This means that if the same file is edited by clients of both operating systems, corruption can result.

The `[printers]` Section

There are two ways Samba can make printers available. One is to create a specific share section with a `print ok=yes` line, a specific `printcap` printer specified by a `printer name=` line, and possibly a list of valid users. The other way is to let the `[printers]` section do most of the work and list all `printcap`-defined printers to the client. The following two lines are sufficient to allow use of all printcap-defined printers on SMB clients, although they're certainly not ideal in terms of security:

```
[printers]
path = /tmp
```

Note

This section mentions /etc/printcap, printcap, and printcap printers several times. /etc/printcap is a file defining all the Linux system's printers. A printcap printer is a printer defined by name in /etc/printcap. For more information on printing and /etc/printcap, see Chapter 11, "Administration Essentials."

The simplest case of a dedicated print share is

```
[vals_lp]
print ok = yes
printer name = lp_mine
path = /home/everyone
```

In the dedicated print share, the print ok=yes (or the printable=yes synonym) is necessary, and it's necessary to name the printer with the printer name= line. The intent of the [printers] section is accessibility to all users with valid IDs. The intent of a special printer is typically to restrict access to a user or group, implying that it would be a good idea to add a valid users= line to the dedicated printer share. Beyond that, the [printers] section and dedicated print shares function pretty much the same.

The [printers] section defines how printing services are controlled if no specific entries are found in the smb.conf file. As with the [homes] section, if no specific entry is found for a printing service, Samba uses the [printers] section (if it's present) to enable a user to connect to any printer defined in /etc/printcap:

```
[printers]
   comment = All Printers
   path = /tmp
   browseable = no
   printable = yes
#; Set public = yes to allow user 'guest account' to print
   public = no
   writable = no
   create mode = 0700
```

The comment, browseable, and create mode entries mean the same as those discussed earlier in the [homes] section. Note that browseable= no applies to the [printers] section, not to the printcap printers, which are listed in the SMB client's front-end as a consequence of the [printers] section. If browseable= were yes, a share called printers would be listed on the client. That's clearly not what's needed.

The path entry indicates the location of the spool file directory to be used when servicing a print request via SMB. Print files are stored there prior to transfer to the printcap-defined printer's spool directory.

The printable value, if yes, indicates this printer resource can be used to print, so of course it must be set to yes in any printer share, including [printers]. The public entry controls whether the guest account can print to this particular printer. The writable=no entry assures that the only thing written to the spool directory are spool files handled by printing functions.

Samba Printer Troubleshooting Tips

These troubleshooting tips work not only for the [printers] section, but also for any dedicated printer shares. Dedicated printer shares all have print ok=yes, and they have a printer name= option as well.

Samba printer shares (including [printers]) usually work the first time. When they don't, it's important to remember a printer share won't work without a working Samba [global] section and a working printcap printer, and Samba won't work without a working network.

Therefore, before troubleshooting any printer share including [printers], make sure the client and server machines can ping each other's IP address. If not, troubleshoot the network.

Next, make sure you can see the [global]-defined workgroup in the client listing (Network Neighborhood or smbclient -L *Ipaddress*). If not, troubleshoot Samba as a whole before working on the printer. Use testparm (discussed later this chapter) to verify that smb.conf is internally consistent.

Next, make sure the printcap printer works properly. The printcap name can be deduced from the share's printer name= option, or if there's no printer name= in the share, from the client request. Do the following:

```
lpr -P printcap_printer_name /etc/lilo.conf
```

This should print /etc/lilo.conf to the physical printer defined as *printcap_printer_name* in /etc/printcap. /etc/lilo.conf is an ideal test file because it's short and it exists on most Linux machines. If your machine does not have it, use any short .conf file in the /etc directory. When the machines can ping each other, the client can see the workgroup defined in the [global] section, and you can print to the printcap printer, then you're ready to troubleshoot the Samba printer share.

Many Samba printer problems occur because the default printer command doesn't work. This is especially true if the `printcap` printer is a network printer instead of a local printer. First, try putting the following line in the printer share:

```
print command = lpr -P %p %s; rm %s
```

The command prints to printer `%p` (the printer name passed from the client) the file `%s` (the spool file passed from the client). This is the same command done in the `printcap` printer test described previously, so it should work.

If it still doesn't work, verify that the `path=` entry points to a directory to which the user has read and write access. Make sure any `printer name=` entry points to a working printer defined in `/etc/printcap`. Make sure the entry has a `printable=yes` or `print ok= yes` entry. Otherwise, it's not a Samba printer share. If the printer share has a `valid users=` entry, make sure the user in question is one of those users.

If it still isn't working, it's time to install your own test point. Temporarily create directory `/tmp/test mode 777` (all can read, write, and execute), comment out any `print command=` line in `smb.conf`, and add the following line:

```
print command = cp %s /tmp/test/%p.tst;rm %s
```

This copies the file to be printed to a file in `/tmp/test` with the same filename as the `printcap` printer with the extension `.tst`. This gives several pieces of information. First, the filename tells you what printer it's trying to print to. You can check `/etc/printcap` for the existence of that printer. You can print that file and see whether it comes out properly.

If the file does not exist, you know something's wrong on the client side of the `print` command. Be sure to check the queue on the client to see whether it's getting stuck. Sometimes a single failure on the server can jam the client queue. Also, be sure all users can read, write, and execute directory `/tmp/test`, or the `print` will bomb on permissions. When the problem is resolved, for security reasons be sure to remove the `/tmp/test` test directory you created.

Beyond these tips, remember that troubleshooting is simply a matter of keeping a cool head and narrowing the scope of the problem.

The following section will get into the concepts of sharing files and printer services.

Sharing Files and Print Services

After configuring your defaults for the Samba server, you can create specific shared directories limited to just certain groups of people or available to everyone. For example, let's say you want to make a directory available to only one user. To do so, you create a new section and fill in the needed information. Typically, you need to specify the user, directory path, and configuration information to the SMB server, as shown here:

```
[jacksdir]
comment = Jack's remote source code directory
path = /usr/local/src
valid users = tackett
browseable = yes
public = no
writable = yes
create mode = 0700
```

This sample section creates a shared directory called `jacksdir`. It's best to keep share names to eight characters or less to avoid warnings in the `testparm` utility, and to avoid problems on older SMB clients incapable of using longer share names. The path to the directory on the local server is `/usr/local/src`. Because the `browseable` entry is set to `yes`, `jacksdir` will show up in the client's network browse list (such as Windows Explorer). However, because the `public` entry is set to `no` and the `valid users` entry lists only `tackett`, only the user `tackett` can access this directory using Samba. You can grant access to more users and to groups by specifying them (using an at sign (`@`) prepended to the front of the group name) in the `valid users` entry. Here's the `valid users=` line after giving group `devel` access:

```
valid users = tackett, @devel
```

A printer share is created by placing a `print ok=yes` (or synonym) and a `printer name=` in the share. For instance:

```
[vals_lp]
print ok = yes
printer name = lp_mine
path = /home/everyone
valid users = valerie, @devel
browseable = yes
```

Here we have a printer that is listed as `vals_lp` on the client because of the `browseable=yes`. It prints out of `printcap` printer `lp_mine`. Its spool directory is `/home/everyone`, and valid users are `valerie` and the `devel` group.

The primary differences between a printer share such as this and the `[printers]` section is that the `[printers]` section displays all `printcap` printers without being browseable, whereas a printer share such as the preceding displays only the printer whose value appears in the `printer name=` option, and then only if a `browseable=yes` option appears. The `[printers]` section does not have or require a `printer name=` option, because its purpose is to display all printers to the client and allow the client access to all printers.

All the Samba printer troubleshooting tips previously listed in the `[printers]` section of this chapter apply to printer shares.

Now that we've moved through creating the various Samba components, it's now time to optimize them.

Optimizing Samba Performance

Samba usually performs excellently, so performance usually isn't an issue. If performance becomes an issue, there are several options to evaluate.

Note

The author tested all the following Samba configuration performance enhancement techniques, and was unable to attain any significant performance gains on an underloaded Samba Server with a Celeron 333, 64MB of RAM, a 7200rpm 14.4GB disk, and 100Mb wiring, using a test of copying an 11MB file back and forth. The conclusion is that gains depend on many factors, including but not limited to, system load. These techniques will not help if the bottleneck is the wire, which appears to be the case on the author's setup.

Samba's default for option `wide links=` is `yes`. Setting it to `no` gains some security benefits. However, significant performance costs have been reported in certain environments. If you have `wide links=` set to `no` in heavy usage environments, you may want to experiment with changing it to `yes`.

If `wide links=` is set to `yes`, further optimization may be gained by setting `getwd cache=` to `yes` in the `[global]` section (the default is `no`).

Some other possible enhancement techniques include faster network hardware and wiring, a better server hard disk, more server memory, or a server CPU upgrade.

The bottom line is that performance is bottleneck-limited, so to improve performance, it's essential to locate the bottleneck. After that's done, a performance-enhancement plan can be made. Until the bottleneck is located, speculation makes little sense.

One of the best bottleneck analysis techniques is to deliberately slow a suspected bottleneck. If system throughput slows by a similar proportion, you've found a bottleneck. If system throughput slows only slightly, continue looking.

Testing Your Configuration

After creating the configuration file, you should test it for correctness. Start by making sure the client and server can ping each others' IP addresses. Without a functioning network, Samba will not work.

Next, use the testparm program. testparm is a simple test program to check the /etc/smb.conf configuration file for internal correctness. If this program reports no problems, you can use the configuration file with confidence that smbd will successfully load the configuration file.

Caution

Using testparm is not a guarantee that the services specified in the configuration file will be available or will operate as expected. This kind of testing guarantees only that Samba is able to read and understand the configuration file.

testparm has the following command line:

```
testparm [configfile [hostname hostip]]
```

configfile indicates the location of the smb.conf file if it is not in the default location (/etc/smb.conf). The *hostname hostIP* optional parameter instructs testparm to see whether the host has access to the services provided in the smb.conf file. If you specify *hostname*,you must specify the IP number of that host as well, or the results will be unpredictable.

The following illustrates sample output from running testparm. If there are any errors, the program reports them, along with a specific error message:

```
[root@ns /etc]# testparm smb.conf ntackett 209.42.203.236
Load smb config files from smb.conf
Processing section "[homes]"
Processing section "[printers]"
Loaded services file OK.
Allow connection from ntackett (209.42.203.236) to homes
Allow connection from ntackett (209.42.203.236) to printers
Allow connection from ntackett (209.42.203.236) to lp
Allow connection from ntackett (209.42.203.236) to IPC$
```

Testing Your Printers with testprns

If you have configured your server to print to a printer on a Samba mount, you can test this configuration using the testprns command. testprns has the following command line:

```
testprns printername [printcapname]
```

printername is the name of the printer share, and *printcapname* is the name specified in the /etc/printcap file. Because the testprns command is simple, it is recommended that you specify the *printcapname*. The following is sample output:

```
[root@ns /etc]# testprns lp
Looking for printer lp in printcap file /etc/printcap
Printer name lp is valid.
```

Testing with `smbstatus`

The `smbstatus` program reports on current Samba connections. `smbstatus` has the following command line:

```
smbstatus [-d] [-p] [-s configfile]
```

`configfile` is by default `/etc/smb.conf`. `-d` provides verbose output, and `-p` provides a list of current SMB processes. The `-p` option is useful if you are writing shell scripts using `smbstatus`. The following is sample output:

```
[root@vishnu ~]# smbstatus

Samba version 1.9.18p10
Service      uid      gid      pid     machine
-----------------------
masters      liliana  management 20763   liliana  (10.0.1.101) Fri Jun 11
17:37:34

No locked files

Share mode memory usage (bytes):
   102232(99%) free + 112(0%) used + 56(0%) overhead = 102400(100%) total
```

Once you've checked everything out, the next thing to do is run the Samba Server.

Running the Samba Server

The Samba server consists of two daemons, `smbd` and `nmbd`. The `smbd` daemon provides the file- and print-sharing services. The `nmbd` daemon provides NetBIOS name server support.

You can run the Samba server either from the `init` scripts or from `inetd` as a system service. As mentioned before, when you install the Samba package, the configuration script asks you whether you want to run it as a daemon or from `inetd`. If you select running as a daemon—that is, from the `init` scripts each time you boot—you can use the command

```
/etc/rc.d/init.d/smb start¦stop
```

to start or stop the SMB server. Using the `init` scripts provides better response to SMB requests than continuously spawning the programs from `inetd`.

Accessing Shares

Samba shares can be accessed either by Windows or Linux platforms, although Linux doesn't need Samba to share items, but Windows does. Windows access is via Network Neighborhood and Windows Explorer. Linux access is via the `smbclient` and `smbmount` commands.

Using `smbclient` on a Linux Client

The `smbclient` program enables Linux users to access SMB shares on other, typically Windows, machines. If you want to access files on other Linux boxes, you can use a variety of methods, including FTP, NFS, and the SSH command `scp`.

`smbclient` provides an FTP-like interface that enables you to transfer files with a network share on another computer running an SMB server. Unfortunately, unlike NFS, `smbclient` does not allow you to mount another share as a local directory. `smbmount`, discussed later in this chapter, provides the capability of mounting `smb` shares.

`smbclient` provides command-line options to query a server for the shared directories available or to exchange files. For more information on all the command-line options, consult the man page for `smbclient`. Use the following command:

```
smbclient -L -I 10.1.1.25
```

to list all available shares on the machine `10.1.1.25`. If asked for a password, simply press the Enter key, because the command contains no user ID. Any name resolving to the IP address can be substituted for the IP address. The `-L` parameter requests the list. The `-I` parameter instructs `smbclient` to treat the following machine name as a DNS-specified entry, rather than as a NetBIOS entry.

To transfer a file, you must first connect to the Samba server using the following command:

```
smbclient //192.168.100.1/homes -U tackett
```

The parameter `//192.168.100.1/homes` specifies the remote service on the other machine. This is typically either a filesystem directory or a printer. Any name resolving to the IP address can be substituted for the IP address. The `-U` option enables you to specify the username you want to connect with. Note there are many additional `smbclient` command configurations—see the `smbclient` man page for full details. The `smbclient` utility prompts you for a password if this account requires one and then places you at the prompt:

```
smb: \
```

where \ indicates the current working directory.

From this command line, you can issue the commands shown in Table 18.1 to transfer and work with files.

TABLE 18.1 `smbclient` Commands

Command	*Description*
`?` or `help` `[`*`command`*`]`	Provides a help message on command or in general if no command is specified.
`! [`*`shell command`*`]`	Executes the specified shell command or drops the user to a shell prompt.
`cd [`*`directory`*`]`	Changes to the specified directory on the server machine (not the local machine). If no directory is specified, `smbclient` reports the current working directory.
`lcd [`*`directory`*`]`	Changes to the specified directory on the local machine. If no directory is specified, `smbclient` reports the current working directory on the local machine.
`del` *`files`*	The specified files on the server are deleted if the user has permission to do so. Files can include wildcard characters.
`dir` or `ls [`*`files`*`]`	Lists the indicated files or all files in current directory.
`exit` or `quit`	Exits from the `smbclient` program.
`get` *`remotefile`* `[`*`local name`*`]`	Retrieves the specified *`remotefile`* and saves the file on the local server. If *`local name`* is specified, the copied file will be saved with this filename rather than the filename on the remote server.
`mget` *`files`*	Copies all the indicated files, including those matching any wildcards, to the local machine.
`md` or `mkdir [`*`directory`*`]`	Creates the specified directory on the remote machine.
`rd` or `rmdir [`*`directory`*`]`	Removes the specified directory on the remote machine.
`put localfile [`*`remotename`*`]`	Copies the specified file from the local machine to the server.
`mput` *`files`*	Copies all the specified files from the local machine to the server.
`print` *`file`*	Prints the specified file on the remote machine. The share indicated on the command line must be a printer share.
`queue`	Displays all the print jobs queued on the remote server. The share indicated on the command line must be a printer share.

Mounting Shares on a Linux Client

To make life even easier, the `smbmount` command enables you to mount a Samba share to a local directory. To experiment with this, create a `/mnt/test` directory on your local workstation. Now run the following command as user `root`, or quoted in the tail of an `su -c` command:

```
smbmount '//WORKGROUP/homes' '/mnt/test' -I 192.168.100.1 -U myuid
```

Assume this command is given on the local workstation, and that workstation already contains a `/mnt/test` directory. Further assume a Samba server at `192.168.100.1`, accessible to the workstation via the network, whose `workgroup` in the `[global]` section of `/etc/smb.conf` is `WORKGROUP`. Note that any name resolving to the IP address can be substituted for the IP address. Running the preceding command on the local machine mounts to local directory `/mnt/test` the share defined in the server in the `[homes]` section, logged in as user `myuid`.

To unmount it, simply run this command as user `root`, or quoted in the tail of an `su -c` command:

```
smbumount /mnt/test
```

This capability is not limited to the user's home directory. It can be used on any share in `smb.conf` on the Samba server.

Mounting Shares on a Windows Client

A properly configured Samba share is accessible via Windows' Network Neighborhood, via this path: `Network_Neighborhood\Entire_Network\Workgroup\Machine_name\path`.

If there are problems, the usual suspects are: Windows doesn't yet know about it (find the computer, refresh the screen, wait a couple minutes, or reboot the Windows client), user and password case (username level and password level in `[global]`),or clear-text versus encrypted passwords (`encrypt passwords = yes` and `smb passwd file = /etc/smbpasswd` in the `[global]` section).

Next we'll go one step deeper into the discussion of optimization through discussing some traditional configuration options.

Common `smb.conf` Configuration Options

There are hundreds of Samba options. For complete documentation, view the `smb.conf` man page with this command:

```
man smb.conf
```

An understanding of a few options suffices for most tasks. A discussion of those options and conventions follows. Note that many options are followed by *(G)* or *(S)*, meaning they are intended for the `[global]` section or a share section, respectively.

Special Conventions

Many options expecting users as the value can also take groups. In these cases, the value is the group name preceded by an at sign (@). For instance, group acct can be represented as @acct.

There are several substitution characters that can be used in smb.conf. They are all explained on the smb.conf man page. Two, %u and %H, are especially useful. %u will be substituted with the username, and %H will be substituted with the home directory of the user. For instance, here's a share giving a document directory below /home/everyone to every user, as long as the sysadmin has created a directory with the user's username below /home/everyone:

```
[everyone]
comment = Accessible to everyone
path = /home/everyone/%u
browseable = yes
public = no
writeable = yes
create mode = 700
```

Note that the preceding is not the best way to accomplish this task. It's merely a demonstration of the %u substitution.

read only=, writeable=, writable=, and write ok= (S)

writeable=, writable=, and write ok= are synonyms, meaning they completely substitute for each other. read only= is an inverted synonym for writeable=, writable=, and write ok=, meaning that a read only=yes substitutes for a writeable=no, and so forth, and a read only=no substitutes for a writeable=yes, and so forth. Only one of these four options need be used to specify whether a share is writeable. If this option is specified in the [global] section, it serves as a default for all shares (this is true of all options that can be put in share definitions). Note that these options can be overridden by the write list= option.

```
read only=no
writeable=yes
writable=yes
write ok=yes
```

All four of these mean the same thing and are interchangeable. The default is read only=yes.

valid users= (S)

In any share, the lack of the valid users= option, or a blank value following the equal sign, makes the share accessible to everyone (probably not what you want). To limit access, place a comma-delimited list of valid users after the equal sign:

```
valid users = myuid, tackett, @acct
```

This option gives access to users myuid and tackett, and group acct. This option is overridden by the invalid users= option.

invalid users= (S)

This is a list of users who cannot access this share. This list overrides any users in the valid users= option for the share.

```
[ateam]
valid users = myuid,tackett,art
invalid users = myuid,tackett
```

The preceding smb.conf snippet allows only art to access [ateam].

read list= (S)

The value is a list of users to be given read-only access. This overrides any read only=, writeable=, and so forth, statements, restricting the listed users to read-only access. If any user on the read list= list is also on the write list= option for the share, read list= is overridden and that user can write in the directory.

Does read list= override valid users=? That's an interesting question. When a user not appearing in an existing valid users= list for the share appears in the read list= list, that user is prompted for a password, but no matter whose password is input, it kicks the user out. This behavior is exactly mirrored by Samba's smbclient program and Windows' Network Neighborhood. So no, it does not override valid users= or invalid users=. For instance:

```
[spec_dir]
path = /home/everyone/spec
valid users = valerie,tackett
writeable = yes
read list = valerie,tackett,myuid
write list = tackett
```

In this example, directory /home/everyone/spec can be read by valerie and tackett, but not myuid (no valid users= entry for myuid). User valerie cannot write the directory because her entry in read list= overrides the writeable= option. However, tackett can write it because his write list= entry overrides his read list= entry.

write list= (S)

Any share can have a list of users who can write to that share, no matter what the `writeable=` or `read list=` options say. Here's an example giving write access to `[billsdir]` for `bill`, `tackett`, and `myuid`, in spite of the fact that the directory is optioned to be read only:

```
[billsdir]
valid users = bill, tackett, myuid
read only = yes
write list = bill, tackett, myuid
```

path= (S)

`path=` is the directory accessed through the share. In the case of a print share, it's the spool directory (spool here before submitting to the `printcap` printer, which may also have its own spool). Note that if the `[global]` section contains a `root=`, `root dir=`, or `root directory=`, the `path=` will be relative to the directory specified as the root.

create mask= and create mode= (S)

`create mask=` and `create mode=` are synonyms. They specify the maximum permissions for a newly created file. The DOS permissions (read-only, hidden, and so forth) further restrict it. The default is `744`, meaning `user` gets all rights, but `group` and `other` get only read. If the owner later marks the file read-only from DOS, the file's actual mode on the Linux box is changed to `544` to reflect the loss of write permissions.

browseable= (S)

The `browseable=` entry instructs the SMB client whether to list the share in an SMB client's browser (such as Windows Explorer). It does *not* grant access to users not in the `valid users=` list, nor does `browseable=no` deny access to users in the `valid users=` list.

If set to `yes`, the existence of the share can be seen even by those without rights to the share. If set to `no`, it cannot be seen even by those in the `valid users=` list. However, in clients that allow a user to access a share not listed (`smbclient`, for instance), `browseable= no` does not prevent a valid user from accessing the share, as long as the user enters the proper command with the proper share name. As an example, take the following:

```
[valsdir]
comment = Valerie's special directory
path = /home/everyone/valsdir
browseable = no
valid users = valerie
```

Execute the following command:

```
smbclient -L 192.168.100.1 -U valerie
```

This yields the following:

```
Sharename       Type      Comment
---------       ----      -------
everyone        Disk      Accessible to everyone
IPC$            IPC       IPC Service (Jacks Samba Server)
jacksdir        Disk      Jack's remote source code directory
lp              Printer
myuidx          Disk      Myuid's remote source code directory
spec_dir        Disk
valerie         Disk      Home Directories
```

Notice that share `valsdir` is not listed. That's because it's not browseable. However, on SMB clients allowing a user to access an unlisted share by name, access is not affected. For instance, in `smbclient`, user `valerie` can issue the following command:

```
smbclient  //192.168.100.1/valsdir -U valerie
```

This brings up an `smbclient` prompt allowing user `valerie` to read and write to `/home/everyone/valsdir`.

In summary, `browseable=` governs the visibility, not the accessibility, of the resource. However, some SMB clients, such as Windows Network Neighborhood and Windows Explorer, make access of unlisted shares extremely difficult.

The default for `browseable=` is `yes`, so in tight security situations where listing on the client is not desired, you must insert a `browseable=no` line to make it invisible to the client browser.

`printable=` (S)

`printable=` allows printing from the share, so it should be used on any share that's a printer, and not used on other shares. In the `[printers]` section `printable=` defaults to `yes`. Everywhere else, it defaults to `no`.

`hosts allow=`, `hosts deny=`, `allow hosts=`, and `deny hosts=` (S)

`hosts allow=` governs which hosts or subnets can access a share. If this option is used in the `[global]` section, it becomes the default for all shares. If this option is used, it denies entry to all hosts and/or subnets not specifically allowed. To allow a single host, use the following:

```
hosts allow = 192.168.100.201
```

To allow an entire subnet, use its address and subnet mask:

```
Hosts allow = 192.168.100./255.255.255.0
```

`hosts allow=` overrides any `hosts deny=` options, which simply deny access to a host or subnet. `allow hosts=` is a synonym to `hosts allow=`, and `deny hosts=` is a synonym to `hosts deny=`.

`public=` (S) and `guest ok=` (S)

`public=` and `guest ok=` are synonyms. The purpose of this option is to allow those without a login on the server to access a share. This is a security compromise that sometimes makes sense on a printer. Usually with network printers, you want any user on the network to be able to print to it without giving them an account on the server. Care must be used to avoid the possibility of allowing a hostile exploit. For that reason the default is `no`.

`comment=` (S) and `server string=` (G)

`comment=` and `server string=` are related in that they both provide human-readable strings to identify Samba resources in the user interface of an SMB client. `comment=` describes a share, and `server string=` goes in the `[global]` section and describes the entire Samba server.

`domain logons=` (G)

`domain logons=` defaults to `no`; but if it is set to `yes`, it allows the Samba server to serve as a domain server for a Windows 95/98 workgroup. This is different from a Windows NT domain.

`encrypt passwords=` (G)

The `encrypt passwords=` option is vital to serving Windows clients, and is discussed extensively earlier in this chapter. The default is `encrypt passwords=no`.

`hosts equiv=` (G)

The dangerous option `hosts equiv=` points to a file containing hosts and users allowed to log in without a password. Obviously, it is an extreme security risk. The default is `none`, and the best policy is to leave this option absent from `smb.conf`.

`interfaces=` (G)

The `interfaces=` option becomes necessary when the server serves multiple subnets. Here's an example:

```
interfaces = 192.168.2.10/24 192.168.3.10/24
```

The /24s are subnet masks. 24 represents 24 bits of ones, or 255.255.255.0. Thus, this example serves subnets 192.168.2 and 192.168.3. Normal subnet notations with four dot-delimited numbers can also be used after the slash.

load printers= (G)

load printers= defaults to yes. A yes value loads all printers in /etc/printcap for Samba browsing.

null passwords= (G)

null passwords= defaults to no, meaning no user with a zero-length password on the server can log into Samba. Setting this to yes is an obvious security risk.

password level= (G) and username level= (G)

password level= and username level= determine the level of case insensitivity of username and password comparisons. The default is 0, meaning the client-provided password or username is first compared case-sensitively to the copy on the server. If that fails, the client username or password is converted to lowercase and compared to the copy on the server.

In troubleshooting Samba connection problems from Windows clients, it's often handy to set these high (such as 24), to see whether that fixes the problem. Although this represents a minor security problem and also slows initial connection, it often solves the problem. After problems have been fixed, an attempt should be made to re-comment these two options to beef up security.

Connection problems from Windows clients also are often solved with the encrypt passwords= option.

security= (G)

The default for security= is security=user, which enforces security by user and password. This is generally the best choice, with excellent security and predictability.

security=server and security=domain are used primarily when password authentication is actually done by another machine. security=domain is used to join Samba to an NT domain. security=share offers less security and less predictable operation, but it is sometimes a logical choice in less security-intense situations, such as those in which most of the client usernames don't exist on the server or in which most usage is with printers not requiring passwords.

This topic is important and is discussed further in documents /usr/doc/samba-doc/security_level.txt.gz and /usr/doc/samba-doc/DOMAIN.txt.gz.

workgroup= (G)

`workgroup=` indicates the workgroup in which the server appears. It also controls the domain name used with the `security=domain` setting. The default is `WORKGROUP`.

config file= (G)

`config file=` is a method of specifying a Samba configuration file other than `/etc/smb.conf`. When Samba encounters this option, it reloads all parameters from the specified file.

Samba Documentation Sources

With Debian GNU/Linux 2.1 installed, you have access to voluminous Samba documentation. Every program has its own man page, available with the Linux command:

```
#man programname
```

where *programname* is `smbtar`, `smbmount`, and so forth.

There is also text-based hyperlink help available with the info program:

```
#info programname
```

where *programname* is `smbtar`, `smbmount`, and so forth.

If you install the `samba-doc` package, you can find text-format Samba documentation in directory `/usr/doc/samba-doc`. An excellent SMB how-to is located at `/usr/doc/HOWTO/SMB-HOWTO.html` on your Debian machine.

Samba Applications Documentation Sources

Samba is a suite of programs (listed in Table 18.2) designed to give all necessary client and server access to SMB on your Linux-based computer. Each program has a man page and an info page.

TABLE 18.2 Programs Comprising the Samba Suite

Program	*Description*
`smbd`	The daemon that provides the file and print services to SMB clients, such as Windows for Workgroups, Windows NT, or LanManager. (The configuration file for this daemon is described in `/etc/smb.conf`.)
`nmbd`	The daemon that provides NetBIOS nameserving and browsing support.
`smbclient`	This program implements an FTP-like client that is useful for accessing SMB shares on other compatible servers.
`testparm`	This utility enables you to test the `/etc/smb.conf` configuration file.

Program	Description
`smbstatus`	This utility enables you to tell who is currently using the `smbd` server.
`smbpasswd`	This utility changes a user's SMB password in the `/etc/smbpasswd` file.
`smbrun`	This is an interface program between `smbd` and external programs.
`smbtar`	This is a shell script for backing up SMB shares directly to a UNIX-based tape drive.
`smbmount`	This utility enables you to mount an SMB filesystem.
`smbmnt`	This is called by smbmount to do the work. Generally not called directly.
`smbumount`	This utility enables you to unmount an SMB filesystem.

Configuration Option Documentation

Samba has hundreds of configuration options. For complete information, search for these three strings on the `smb.conf` man page: `"COMPLETE LIST OF GLOBAL PARAMETERS"`, `"COMPLETE LIST OF SERVICE PARAMETERS"`, and `"EXPLANATION OF EACH PARAMETER"`. All the same information is accessible in the `smb.conf` info page.

Other Documentation

The `smb.conf` file supports a number of variable substitutions. The `%H` and `%u` substitutions were discussed earlier in this chapter. For a complete list and description of these substitutions, search the `smb.conf` man page for the phrase `"VARIABLE SUBSTITUTIONS"`.

The `smb.conf` file has several options related to *name mangling*. Name mangling is a method of interfacing between the old DOS 8.3 filename convention, and modern file-naming conventions. It also relates to case sensitivity, default case, and the like. To see a complete treatise on the subject, search for the string `"NAME MANGLING"` in the `smb.conf` man page.

Summary

Samba enables a Linux computer to act as a secure, sophisticated file and print server. At this point, you should have a properly configured Samba server up and running, and have learned the commands and options to make that Samba server practical. You have learned several tips on troubleshooting your Samba setup.

Several advanced options are available for Samba and the various programs that make up the Samba suite. For more information about Samba, read the Samba how-to at `/usr/doc/HOWTO/SMB-HOWTO.html`. Finally, you can find a large amount of information on Samba by surfing to `http://www.samba.org`, choosing the mirror site closest to you, and following the `documentation` link.

CHAPTER

Tools for Advanced Network Administration

by Mario Camou

In This Chapter

Managing a network can be a daunting task. A network composed of UNIX systems is a bit easier to manage, because of the fact that you can actually log on to any UNIX host and execute tasks exactly the same way as if you were sitting at its console. However, there are several tools that can help you manage your network. As a matter of fact, if you play your cards right, you can get very, very close to the ultimate panacea—a network that needs absolutely no management of end-user nodes, where everything is managed at the server.

This chapter introduces a few of these tools:

- The Network File System (NFS), which allows you to mount a remote host's disks as if they were local
- The Network Information System (NIS), which centralizes the administration of many system files, such as `/etc/passwd`, `/etc/group`, and `/etc/hosts`
- Some additional tools to help you troubleshoot your network

NFS—The Network File System

The first application for computer networks was file sharing. Early PC networking technologies, such as Novell and Lantastic, were created just for the purpose of eliminating the "sneakernet" approach to file sharing. Even today, the primary use of many companies' internal networks is making available a server's disk space to many computers on the network. There are other file-sharing technologies in current use, the most widespread of which is Microsoft Windows' server message block (SMB) protocol. If you want to share disks with Microsoft Windows networks, see Chapter 18, "Interacting with Microsoft Networks Using Samba."

The centralization of disk storage is one of the first steps in reducing network administration headaches. By centralizing storage, you can make sure that important data is backed up. If all files are stored on the server and a user's PC breaks down, you can safely reformat its disk and reinstall or even replace the PC outright without losing any data.

What Is NFS?

NFS stands for *network file system*. It is a means by which a host may share its disk space with other hosts. Although NFS was created for UNIX and is the native way of sharing files between UNIX systems, there are commercial NFS clients and servers available for most other operating systems.

NFS has several advantages over other file-sharing systems. First, it runs over the UDP protocol (although recent versions can also run over TCP). The big advantage of this is that, because UDP is a connectionless protocol, filesystems mounted through NFS can survive network failures. Another advantage is that it will continue trying as an automatic feature. For example, suppose you're copying a file from a remote server to a local disk and a router between you and the remote server goes down for five minutes. With other file-sharing or file-transfer technologies, such as FTP or SMB, the copy would have to be aborted and restarted when the link came back up. NFS was designed to work reliably over unreliable networks, so it will continue retrying until the network comes back up.

Another advantage of NFS is security. A server can export a filesystem to only a select group of hosts. It can also export the filesystem read-only or map the remote user ID to another user ID. This is useful to disallow `root` access from client hosts to the server's filesystem.

NFS is an open protocol, specified in RFC-1094. This means that anyone is free to create his or her own implementation and can be sure that it will interoperate with any other existing implementation. As a matter of fact, implementations of NFS exist for practically every operating system in existence.

Remote Procedure Calls and the External Data Representation

NFS is what is known as an RPC (Remote Procedure Call) service. RPC is a service defined in RFC-1057, by which a client program running on one host can call code (known as a *remote procedure*) that is running on a server host in the same way that it calls code on a local host. It can pass any data structure as a parameter to the procedure and receive any structure as a return value. All the information the server code needs is encoded in the procedure's parameters, and the information the server passes back to the client is encoded in the procedure's return value. Thus, RPC services are completely *stateless*, which gives them more reliability.

Because an RPC server's interaction with its client is limited to procedure calls, it is usually not a good idea to start them via `inetd`; the server process' startup time in many cases is much longer than the time it takes to process the procedure call. Because of this, RPC servers are usually started as daemons.

RPC services don't use preassigned ports. Instead of this, they use *service numbers*. A daemon called the *portmapper* runs on the server and takes care of converting service numbers to port numbers. When an RPC server daemon starts, it opens a server port and registers its service and port numbers with the portmapper. When a client makes its first RPC call to a service on a particular server, it contacts the server's portmapper and looks up the particular service it needs. The portmapper returns the port number, and the client can then call the server process directly.

There is a problem that arises when trying to make remote procedure calls between hosts with different architectures. Because RPC is designed to transfer structured data, things such as byte ordering and structure padding (which differ between host architectures) affect the way data is stored in memory and can potentially affect the way it is sent over the network. Because of this, a standard called XDR (external data representation, defined in RFC-1014) was created. All data transferred over the network is first converted into XDR format by the sending host, and then converted back into internal format by the receiving host.

The NFS Daemons

The NFS system has three daemons that must run on the server:

- `/usr/sbin/portmap` is the portmapper daemon, which translates between the service numbers and port numbers.
- `/usr/sbin/rpc.mountd` is the daemon that speaks the *mount protocol*, which is actually separate from the NFS protocol. It takes care of serving mount requests, converting between a client's request and the server's filesystem.
- `/usr/sbin/rpc.nfsd` is the daemon that takes care of actually serving the data and acting upon client requests after the filesystem is mounted.

The subjects in this bulleted list will be further explained in the following sections.

`portmap`, the Portmapper Daemon

As mentioned previously, the portmapper takes care of registering RPC services and converting from RPC service numbers to port numbers. The `portmap` daemon is part of the `netbase` package, which is installed by default, and it is started in the `/etc/init.d/netbase` and `/etc/init.d/mountnfs.sh` scripts.

When an RPC server daemon starts up, it listens on any free port and then connects to the portmapper and registers its program and port numbers with it. When a client program needs to call an RPC server, it opens a connection to the server host's portmapper and gives it the program number. The portmapper replies with the port number that the server process is listening on. The client program can then either talk directly to the server process or ask the portmapper to mediate the conversation.

The usual form of controlling access to programs started by `inetd` is with the `tcpwrappers` package (see Chapter 21, "Principles of Security"). This isn't the case with the portmapper, because it is always started as a daemon. However, the Linux `portmap` daemon has been modified to use the `tcpwrappers` configuration files, `/etc/hosts.allow` and `/etc/hosts.deny`. You should use the program name `portmap` to allow or deny access.

Querying the Portmapper with `rpcinfo`

The `rpcinfo` program, also part of the `netbase` package, can be used to query the portmapper. Its most common usage is with the `-p` option, which lists all the registered programs. Listing 19.1 shows the output of `rpcinfo` on a host that is running the NFS daemons.

LISTING 19.1 Output from the `rpcinfo` Program

```
mario@chaos:~ 514 $ rpcinfo -p
   program vers proto   port
    100000    2   tcp    111  portmapper
    100000    2   udp    111  portmapper
    100003    2   udp   2049  nfs
    100003    2   tcp   2049  nfs
    100005    1   udp   1012  mountd
    100005    2   udp   1012  mountd
    100005    1   tcp   1015  mountd
    100005    2   tcp   1015  mountd
```

The program names are taken by `rpcinfo` from the `/etc/rpc` file. This file is used by all client programs to convert from program names to program numbers. As you can see, the `portmapper` service itself is an RPC server. However, it always runs on well-known port number 111 on both TCP and UDP.

You can also see that there are two `nfsd` processes running. Although there is a single `mountd` running, it can serve both version 1 and 2 requests on both TCP and UDP, so it is registered four times.

Listing 19.2 shows an `rpcinfo` query on a server that is also providing NIS services. For more information on NIS, see the section "NIS—The Network Information System," later in this chapter.

LISTING 19.2 Output from the `rpcinfo` Program

```
[mario@tumbolia mario]$ rpcinfo -p vishnu
   program vers proto   port
    100000    2   tcp    111  portmapper
    100000    2   udp    111  portmapper
    100004    2   udp    807  ypserv
    100004    1   udp    807  ypserv
    100004    2   tcp    810  ypserv
    100004    1   tcp    810  ypserv
    100009    1   udp    816  yppasswdd
    100007    2   udp    830  ypbind
    100007    2   tcp    832  ypbind
    100005    1   udp    635  mountd
    100005    2   udp    635  mountd
    100005    1   tcp    635  mountd
    100005    2   tcp    635  mountd
```

continues

LISTING 19.2 continued

```
    100003    2   udp    2049   nfs
    100003    2   tcp    2049   nfs
    300516    2   tcp       3
    300019    1   tcp     923   amd
    300019    1   udp     924   amd
```

As you can see, `rpcinfo` can also be used to query remote servers. The `rpcinfo` program has many more options; see the `rpcinfo(8)` man page for more information.

`rpc.mountd`, The Mount Protocol Daemon

After an NFS client has queried the portmapper for the `mountd` program, it contacts `rpc.mountd` with its mount request. `rpc.mountd` is part of the `nfs-server` package and is started from the `/etc/init.d/nfs-server` script. `rpc.mountd` takes care of several tasks:

- Verifying that the client is allowed to connect by using the `/etc/hosts.allow` and `/etc/hosts.deny` files
- Verifying that the requested filesystem is exported in the `/etc/exports` file (see the section "The `/etc/exports` File," later in this chapter)
- Verifying that the client is allowed access to the filesystem, and checking with which options (such as read-only or with a user mapping)
- Creating a file handle for the requested filesystem and returning it to the client
- Adding the client to the `/etc/rmtab` file
- When the client unmounts the filesystem, removing it from `/etc/rmtab`

Note that the contents of `/etc/rmtab` aren't completely reliable, because clients may crash without notifying `rpc.mountd`.

As with the portmapper, access to `rpc.mountd` can be controlled in the `/etc/hosts.allow` and `/etc/hosts.deny` files. It uses program name `rpc.mountd`.

`rpc.mountd` can take several options; most of them are used for debugging and are documented in the `rpc.mountd(8)` man page. An exception is the `-r` option, which can be used to allow `rpc.mountd` to export filesystems mounted from other servers via SMB (with the `smbmount` program—see Chapter 18), IPX (using the `mars_nwe` utilities), Appleshare (with the Appletalk utilities), or NFS. In this way, a Linux host running Samba can be used to export SMB shares to other UNIX hosts on the network. However, care must be taken when using this option, because the whole SMB filesystem will be mounted using a particular user's ID and will be exported as if owned by that user.

`rpc.nfsd`, the NFS Server Daemon

`rpc.nfsd` takes care of most of the work. After a client has mounted a filesystem, it queries the portmapper for the `nfs` program. It then contacts `rpc.nfsd` with any requests, such as opening and closing files, checking their status and type, and reading and writing data. `rpc.nfsd` is contained in the `nfs-server` package, together with `rpc.mountd`, and it is also started by the `/etc/init.d/nfs-server` script.

`rpc.nfsd` has several options, most of which are usually used for debugging. They are documented in the `rpc.nfsd(8)` man page. A useful option is `-r`, which has the same function as in `rpc.mountd` (see previous section)—that is, allowing for reexporting remote SMB, Novell, Appleshare, or NFS filesystems.

The /etc/exports File

The `/etc/exports` file controls which filesystems are exported, to which hosts, and with which options. The /etc/exports file would be used when you wanted to share a filesystem to another *nix type box. It's like a Samba share for windows, only much more secure. Each line of the file contains a path, followed by whitespace and the options that apply to it within parentheses. The options may be preceded by a hostname or wildcard, and several hostname-options sequences can be specified. Table 19.1 shows the options that may be applied to each filesystem.

TABLE 19.1 `/etc/exports` Security Options

Option	*Meaning*
`insecure`	By default, `rpc.nfsd` and `rpc.mountd` deny requests that come from nonprivileged ports (those above 1024). The `insecure` option allows these requests. Some older NFS clients require this option to work.
`secure`	The opposite of `insecure`, disallowing requests from nonprivileged ports.
`ro`	By default, filesystems are exported with read and write permissions. The `ro` option exports the filesystem read-only.
`rw`	The opposite of `ro`, exporting the filesystem read/write.
`no_access`	Disallows access to the filesystem. Useful when the filesystem is a subdirectory of a filesystem that has been exported, or to allow access to a filesystem to all hosts except a few.
`link_relative`	Converts all absolute softlinks into relative softlinks. For example, if `/usr/local/bin/program` is a softlink pointing to `/usr/local/packages/mypackage/bin/program`, clients will see it as pointing to `../packages/mypackage/bin/program`. This is useful when the links point within the exported filesystem. However, if they point to places outside the exported filesystem, strange things happen.
`link_absolute`	The opposite of `link_relative` and the default. Leaves all symbolic links as they are.

continues

TABLE 19.1 continued

Option	*Meaning*
`root_squash`	Requests coming from the UID/GID 0 on the client (that is, the `root` user) are mapped to the anonymous user. This is the default and the recommended option (for security).
`no_root_squash`	The opposite of `root_squash`, `no_root_squash` allows requests from `root` to be treated as they are. Useful mainly for diskless clients.
`squash_uids` and `squash_gids`	Maps certain UIDs and GIDs to the anonymous user. For example, `squash_uids=0-15,20,30-200` map UIDs 0 through 15, 20, and 30 through 200 to the anonymous user.
`all_squash`	Maps all UIDs and GIDs to the anonymous user. Useful for exporting FTP directories and news spools.
`map_identity`	Leaves all UIDs and GIDs unchanged. This is the default behavior.
`map_daemon`	Maps all UIDs and GIDs to the corresponding UID/GID based on the username or group names on the client. This requires that the client run the `rpc.ugidd` daemon. This queries `rpc.ugidd` on the client to get the username that corresponds to the given UID, and then look up the username in `/etc/passwd`. The `squash` options take precedence on the `map` options.

`map_static`	Maps UIDs and GIDs depending on the file given as an argument. For example, you might store the following file as `/etc/nfs/user.mapping` and use the `map_static=/etc/nfs/user.mapping` directive:
	`# Mapping for client foobar:`
	`#     remote     local`
	`uid  0-99       -       # squash these`
	`uid  100-500    1000    # map 100-500 to 1000-1500`
	`gid  0-49       -       # squash these`
	`gid  50-100     700     # map 50-100 to 700-750`

`map_nis`	Similar to `map_daemon`, but instead of contacting the client host, it contacts the client host's NIS server to get the user ID. The client's NIS domain must be specified as a parameter, as in `map_nis=company.com`.
`anonuid` and `Anongid`	Sets the anonymous user's UID and GID.

Note that some options reproduce the default behavior of `rpc.nfsd` and `rpc.mountd`. These are usually used to change the behavior for a subdirectory of an exported filesystem. For example, `/usr/local` may have been exported read-only, but you may want to export `/usr/local/common` read/write. In this case, you could use the following lines in `/etc/exports`:

```
/usr/local          (ro)
/usr/local/common   (rw)
```

You can also use it when you want to apply the default only to a few hosts. For example, you may want to export /usr/local read-only to all the network and read/write only to trustedhost and superhost. In this case, you could use the following line in /etc/exports to accomplish these goals.

```
/usr/local          (ro) trustedhost(rw) superhost(rw)
```

Listing 19.3 shows a sample /etc/exports file.

LISTING 19.3 Sample /etc/exports File

```
# sample /etc/exports file
/                master(rw) trusty(rw,no_root_squash)
/projects        proj*.local.domain(rw)
/usr             *.local.domain(ro) @trusted(rw)
/home/joe        pc001(rw,all_squash,anonuid=150,anongid=100)
/pub             (ro,insecure,all_squash)
/pub/private     (noaccess)
```

- The root filesystem is exported read/write, only to hosts master and trusty. master has the root_squash option enabled, and trusty will be allowed root access to the filesystem.
- /projects is exported read/write, only to those hosts whose hostname matches the wildcard proj*.local.domain.
- /usr is exported read-only to hosts whose domain matches local.domain (as looked up via inverse DNS) andread/write to hosts belonging to netgroup trusted. Netgroups are discussed later, in the section "NIS—The Network Information System."
- /home/joe is exported read/write, only to host pc001 (presumably Joe's PC). All requests are treated as if they came fromuid 150 and gid 100 (presumably Joe's UID and GId). This is useful especially for networks where you have PC clients, to ensure that a user's files can be read only from that user's PC.
- /pub is exported read-only to any host. All requests are mapped to the UID and GID belonging to the nobody account.
- /pub/private is marked as not exported, even though its parent directory, /pub, is exported.

Mounting and Unmounting Filesystems via NFS

To access an NFS filesystem, you must *mount* it on the client. The way Linux uses filesystem is by mounting them. The server may offer an NFS filesystem, but for the client to use it, it must mount it. All filesystems are mounted in Linux. Mounting a filesystem "splices" it onto your local filesystem at the specified point, making it accessible as a particular subdirectory. After the filesystem is mounted, you access files on it as if they were local.

There are two ways of mounting filesystems: via the `mount` program and via the `/etc/fstab` file. These have been covered in depth in Chapter 11, "Administration Essentials." This section covers the particulars of using them with NFS. A third way of dynamically mounting NFS filesystems is covered later in this chapter, in the section titled "NIS—The Network Information System."

Instead of specifying a device name on the `mount` command line or the `/etc/fstab` line, you must specify the hostname of the NFS server, followed by a colon and the server's directory name. For example, take the following command:

```
mount server:/export/share /usr/share
```

This splices the server's `/export/share` directory at the `/usr/share` directory on the local file, so if, for example, you access the `/usr/share/data/data1.dat` file, you actu-allyaccess `/export/share/data/data1.dat` on the server. It has the same effect as speci-fying the following line in `/etc/fstab`:

```
server:/export/share    /usr/share
```

There are several mounting options that apply specifically to NFS filesystems. They are covered in the `mount(8)` man page. Table 19.2 shows the most useful of them.

TABLE 19.2 Common Options for NFS Mounts

Option	*Meaning*
`rsize=`*nnnn*	Changes the read-buffer size to *nnnn* bytes. Setting this to `8192` makes your NFS connection much faster than the default 1024 bytes, although some NFS servers might not support it.
`wsize=`*nnnn*	Changes the write-buffer size to *nnnn* bytes. Same comments as with `rsize`.
`hard`	If the NFS server crashes, the process accessing it hangs until it is back online, at which point it continues executing as if nothing happened. You can't kill or interrupt the process unless you also specify the `intr` option.
`soft`	Allows the kernel to timeout if the NFS server doesn't respond within a set time (set with the `timeo=`*nnn* option). Useful if the connection to the NFS server isn't reliable; however, it usually causes too much trouble.
`intr`	Allows an NFS process that is accessing a filesystem mounted with the `hard` option to be interrupted or killed while it is waiting for the NFS server to respond.
`timeo=`*nnn*	Sets the timeout in seconds for `soft`-mounted filesystems.

Option	Meaning
`bg`	Mounts the filesystem in the background. The `mount` command returns immediately even if the filesystem hasn't been mounted yet. Useful in the `/etc/fstab` file, so that boot can continue while the mount is taking place.
`fg`	The opposite of `bg`. Mounts the filesystem in the foreground.

From here we'll move to a discussion of the Network Information System.

NIS—The Network Information System

One of the biggest headaches when managing UNIX networks is keeping the system files in all the hosts synchronized. For example, each time you add a new user, you must add him or her to `/etc/passwd`, `/etc/shadow`, `/etc/group`, and possibly to `/etc/netgroup` and `/etc/aliases`, and then propagate them to all the hosts on the network. Each time you add a host, you have to distribute the `/etc/hosts` file. There are other `/etc` files that might need to be distributed now and then: `/etc/ethers`, `/etc/rpc`, `/etc/services`, and so on.

The Network Information System (NIS) was created just for this. It was formerly known as Yellow Pages or YP, but ran into copyright infringement problems in the United Kingdom, where the Yellow Pages trademark had already been registered by the telephone directory company. However, the names of the programs and directories that comprise NIS still reflect this heritage, because they all start with the letters `yp`.

NIS is an RPC service (see the previous section "Remote Procedure Calls and the External Data Representation") whose function is precisely to distribute configuration file information throughout a network. A host is configured as an NIS server for an *NIS domain* (not to be confused with the DNS domains used in the Internet). Client hosts join the domain and get their configuration information from this host, instead of from local files.

An NIS domain is a group of hosts controlled by a particular NIS server. Several domains may share the same physical network, or one domain may span several physical networks (although there are some caveats to this—see the section "Configuring an NIS Client," later in this chapter). An NIS domain name is simply a sequence of characters that serve to specify which domain a server or client belongs to. Many organizations use their Internet DNS domain name as their NIS domain, although it isn't required.

Files Distributed by NIS

The files usually distributed by NIS are

/etc/aliases

/etc/passwd

/etc/group

/etc/shadow

/etc/hosts

/etc/networks

/etc/protocols

/etc/services

/etc/ethers

/etc/rpc

/etc/netgroup

Most of these have been covered elsewhere in this book. You can also add any configuration files for any applications you write. However, you have to edit /var/yp/Makefile on the NIS server.

Of note is the /etc/netgroup file, which is useful for access control in some subsystems (such as NFS, covered earlier). /etc/netgroup allows you to define groups of (host,user) pairs that belong to a particular network group. You can then configure access-control rules that will allow or deny access to a particular resource, based on whether the user accessing it and the host he's accessing it from belong to a particular netgroup. Here is a sample /etc/netgroup entry:

```
admin   (,superguy,) (adminhost,bill,) (bossman,bosshost,development)
```

The admin netgroup will match the following:

- The user superguy coming from any host. This entry will be valid in any domain.
- The user bill, but only if the request comes from the host adminhost. This entry will also be valid in any domain.
- The user bossman, only if the request comes from the host bosshost. This entry will be valid only if the host that receives the request is in the development domain.

Netgroups are especially useful when coupled with NFS, because they enable you to easily control access via user/group pairs without having to add complex lines to /etc/exports.

Installing NIS

The nis package contains both the NIS client and server programs. Because NIS is an RPC-based service (see the earlier section "Remote Procedure Calls and the External Data Representation"), you also need to install the netbase and netstd packages, which contain the portmapper and other support programs. After installing the NIS package, during package configuration, it will ask you for the host's NIS domain name.

There are two kinds of NIS servers: master servers and slave servers. With a *master server,* the master configuration files are kept; it is the authority for a particular domain. A *slave server* copies its configuration files from a master server. Its function is to serve as a backup for the master server when the master is down or when it is overloaded. You first need to install a master server. After that, you install NIS clients and perhaps convert some of those clients into slave servers. These two server types are covered in the next two sections.

Configuring a Master NIS Server

To configure a master NIS server, you must do the following after installing and configuring the nis package:

1. Verify that the /etc files in the server contain all the records for the whole network. For example, /etc/hosts must contain all the hosts in your network, and /etc/passwd must contain all users. In particular, the records in /etc/hosts must have the fully qualified domain name of each host as primary name and the hostname itself as an alias:

   ```
   10.0.1.250      myhost.company.com      myhost
   ```

2. Check the /etc/defaultdomain file. This file must contain your NIS domain name. It is checked only at boot, so if you change or create it, you either need to reboot or run the /bin/domainname program, passing your domain name as a parameter:

   ```
   # /bin/domainname mycompany.com
   ```

3. Edit /etc/init.d/nis. Set the NISSERVER variable to the value master:

   ```
   NISSERVER=master
   ```

4. Edit /etc/ypserv.securenets. This file contains information about which subnets will be able to access your NIS server. Although things will work with the default configuration (which allows access from any host), it is best to limit access to your server for security reasons. The file contains lines of the form

   ```
   netmask     IP_address
   ```

   So, if you want to allow access only from Class C subnet 10.0.1.0, you should remove or comment the 0.0.0.0 line and add the following line:

   ```
   255.255.255.0     10.0.1.0
   ```

5. Now you need to create the master server database. To do this, run `/usr/lib/yp/ypinit -m`. This creates a directory for your domain name under the `/var/yp` directory. This directory contains the *NIS maps*—that is, the master files used by the NIS server.

   `ypinit -m` asks you what NIS servers serve your domain. At the very least, this list should contain the fully qualified domain name of your master server. If you currently have any slave servers, you should enter their names, one per line. If you will be adding slave servers later, *don't* include their names at this time; later, you will return and rerun `ypinit -m`.

6. Stop and restart the NIS server. It is best to stop it just in case it is already running:

```
# /etc/init.d/nis stop
# /etc/init.d/nis start
```

That's it! If everything went well, you now have an NIS master server running. To check whether your NIS server is running, use the `ypwhich` command, which lists the NIS server that the host is currently bound to. In this case, because the NIS server is the same host, it should return `localhost`:

```
# ypwhich
localhost
```

After configuring your master NIS server, you need to configure at least one client to check your work. When they are configured as clients, the NIS information is filtered down through them. Also, slave NIS servers are first configured as clients.

Configuring an NIS Client

On the client box, you also need to install the `netbase`, `netstd`, and `nis` packages. After they are installed, if the NIS server is in the same physical subnet as the client, configuring the client is as easy as setting your domain name in `/etc/domainname`, running the `domainname` to set it without rebooting (see step 2 in the last section), and stopping and restarting the `/etc/init.d/nis` script (see step 6 in the last section). If everything goes fine, running `ypwhich` should return the fully qualified domain name of your NIS server:

```
# ypwhich
server.company.com
```

By default, NIS uses network broadcasts to find the server. Because broadcasts are limited to the physical subnet the client is in, if the NIS server is in a different subnet, you need to edit the `/etc/yp.conf` file. Uncomment the last line (the one containing the `ypserver` entry) and change the server name to your server's hostname or IP address. Because NIS services won't be running when this file is read, you need to add the hostname to the `/etc/hosts` file on the client or make sure that you have DNS and use fully qualified domain names. If you have several NIS servers on your network (a master and one or several slaves), you can list them in separate `ypserver` lines:

```
ypserver nisserver1
ypserver nisserver2.company.com
ypserver 10.0.1.250
```

This, of course, assumes that `nisserver1` exists in `/etc/hosts`, and that `nisserver2.company.com` exists in DNS or in `/etc/hosts`.

Again, after you edit `/etc/yp.conf`, you need to stop and restart `/etc/init.d/nis` and test using `ypwhich`.

When NIS is running, you have to edit the `/etc/nsswitch.conf`, `/etc/host.conf`, `/etc/passwd`, and `/etc/group` in the client host to use NIS for lookups. See Chapter 16, "TCP/IP Networking Essentials," for details on these files.

Configuring a Slave NIS Server

When a host is running as an NIS client, you can reconfigure it to be a slave NIS server. As stated above, slave servers are useful for load-balancing and redundancy. They are also useful in cases where you have multiple physical subnets. The easiest way of setting up NIS, in that case, is to have at least one slave server in each subnet, using `/etc/yp.conf` to point to the master server. Then, clients can use the default broadcast method to find their NIS server.

Setting up a slave NIS server is very similar to setting up a master server. After setting up the host as an NIS client, you need to do the following (note that steps 1, 2, and 4 are identical to the process of setting up a master server outlined previously):

1. Verify that the `/etc` files in the server contain all the records for the whole network. For example, `/etc/hosts` must contain all the hosts in your network, and `/etc/passwd` must contain all users. In particular, the records in `/etc/hosts` must have the fully qualified domain name of each host as primary name and the hostname itself as an alias:

   ```
   10.0.1.250      myhost.company.com      myhost
   ```

2. Check the `/etc/defaultdomain` file. This file must contain your NIS domain name. It is checked only at boot, so if you change or create it, you either need to reboot or run the `/bin/domainname` program, passing your domain name as a parameter:

   ```
   # /bin/domainname mycompany.com
   ```

3. Edit `/etc/init.d/nis`. Set the `NISSERVER` variable to the value `slave` (this step differs from step 3 in setting up a master NIS server):

   ```
   NISSERVER=slave
   ```

4. Edit `/etc/ypserv.securenets`. This file contains information about which subnets will be able to access your NIS server. Although things will work with the default

configuration (which allows access from any host), it is best to limit access to your server for security reasons. The file contains lines of the form

```
netmask     IP_address
```

So, if you want to allow access only from Class C subnet 10.0.1.0, you should remove or comment the `0.0.0.0` line and add the following line:

```
255.255.255.0     10.0.1.0
```

5. Instead of running `ypinit -m`, you run the following command:

   ```
   ypinit -s name_of_master_server
   ```

   This has a similar effect—creating and populating a directory under `/var/yp`—but with the additional characteristic that it will be a mirror of the directory on the master server.

6. Stop and restart NIS on the slave server:

   ```
   # /etc/init.d/nis stop
   # /etc/init.d/nis start
   ```

7. *On the master server,* edit `/var/yp/Makefile`. Find the `NOPUSH` variable and set it to `false`:

   ```
   NOPUSH=false
   ```

8. *On the master server,* rebuild the NIS maps by running `/usr/lib/yp/ypinit -m` and telling it about your NIS slave servers. This ensures that the master will keep the slave servers informed of any updates to the NIS maps.

9. *On the slave server,* it's a good idea (although not indispensable) to edit `root`'s `crontab` using `crontab -e` and add the following lines:

   ```
   20 *    * * *     /usr/lib/yp/ypxfr_1perhour
   40 6    * * *     /usr/lib/yp/ypxfr_1perday
   55 6,18 * * *     /usr/lib/yp/ypxfr_2perday
   ```

   This periodically runs commands that query the master server for any updates. This is recommended so that the slave will always be up-to-date, even if it misses an update because it was down when the master sent it.

How It All Works—NIS Under the Hood

The steps outlined in the previous sections will get you up and running. However, it is sometimes useful to know what is actually going on behind the scenes. If you're not interested in this, you can skip this part and jump to the "Using NIS" section following.

`ypbind` and `ypserv`

NIS is composed of two basic daemons, `ypbind` and `ypserv`, other daemons such as `rpc.yppasswdd` and `rpc.ypxfrd`, and programssuch as `yppasswd`, `ypwhich` and `ypcat`. These programs interact in the following way (see Figure 19.1).

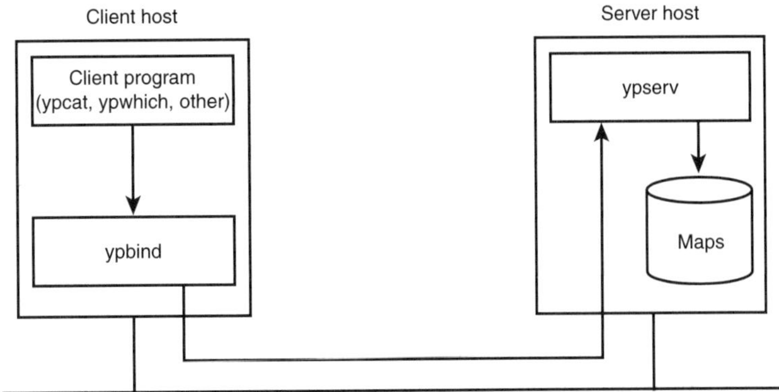

FIGURE 19.1
NIS is composed of several programs.

`ypserv` is the NIS server daemon. When it starts up, it registers with the portmapper (being an RPC service), gets its domain name from the system (it must have been previously set with the `domainname` program), and waits for calls from clients.

`ypbind` is the daemon that runs on the client host. When a program (for example, `/bin/login`) needs information from NIS, it contacts `ypbind` and gives it a map name and a key (for example, it might be looking for key `mario` in map `passwd`). `ypbind` makes an RPC call to`ypserv` and forwards the client's request. `ypserv` looks up the record in its maps, and either returns the found record(s) or returns an error stating the record doesn't exist. `ypbind` then forwards this information to the calling program.

Because maps have a single key, and lookups can usually be made by one or more fields (for example, the `hosts` map can be queried by hostname and by IP address), a single source file can be converted into several maps. For example, `/etc/hosts` is converted into `hosts.byname` and `hosts.byaddr`. The full name of a map is *`mapname`*`.by`*`keyname`*; however, there are several aliases that can be used for the most common queries. These can be queried using `ypcat` (other uses for `ypcat` and `ypmatch` are presented later):

```
# ypcat -x
Use "ethers"    for map "ethers.byname"
Use "aliases"   for map "mail.aliases"
Use "services"  for map "services.byname"
Use "protocols" for map "protocols.bynumber"
Use "hosts"     for map "hosts.byaddr"
Use "networks"  for map "networks.byaddr"
Use "group"    for map "group.byname"
Use "passwd"    for map "passwd.byname"
```

For more information on NIS, check the `/usr/doc/nis/nis.debian.howto.gz` and the following `man` pages:

`ypchsh(1)`	`ypmatch(1)`	`yppasswd(1)`	`ypwhich(1)`
`ypcat(1)`	`ypchfn(1)`	`yp.conf(5)`	`ypserv.conf(5)`

netgroup(5)	nicknames(5)	ypbind(8)	ypxfrd(8)
mknetid(8)	rpc.ypxfrd(8)	yppoll(8)	ypinit(8)
revnetgroup(8)	yppush(8)	ypxfr(8)	makedbm(8)
pwupdate(8)	yppasswdd(8)	domainname(8)	nisdomainname(8)
rpc.yppasswdd(8)	ypdomainname(8)	ypserv(8)	ypset(8)

Using NIS

When NIS is set up, it should be almost transparent to all users. In this situation, transparent means that users can't tell the difference. They can log in to a machine on the network with the same username and password. The only thing they should remember is that they should use `yppasswd`, `ypchsh`, and `ypchfn` instead of `passwd`, `chsh`, and `chfn`, respectively, to manipulate their `/etc/passwd` entries. Aside from that, NIS is usually completely unobtrusive.

There are two utilities that are very useful when running NIS: `ypcat`, which dumps all the lines of a map, and `ypmatch`, which finds a particular record. They are used as follows:

```
ypcat [-k] mapname
ypmatch [-k] key [key ...] mapname
```

By default, both commands list only the data associated with the map key (for example, the user ID in the `passwd` map). The `-k` option also displays the key itself. For more information, see the `ypcat(1)` and `ypmatch(1)` man pages.

Managing NIS

The main thing to remember when managing a network through NIS is that files aren't converted into maps automatically. So, each time that you edit an NIS-managed configuration file in `/etc`, you need to recreate the NIS maps from the source files.

To do this, change to the `/var/yp` directory and run `make`. There is a `Makefile` in `/var/yp` that checks which files have changed, recreates the maps, and pushes them to any slave servers. If you want to add your own files to be managed by NIS, you should edit this `Makefile` and add your files. The details of this, and of writing your program to take advantage of this, are beyond the scope of this book.

Aside from that, NIS simply works. When it has been set up, you usually don't need to tweak anything; just remember to run `make` in `/var/yp` each time you modify a file. It is usually best to write "wrapper" scripts to do it for you so you don't forget. For example, Listing 19.4 shows the `/usr/local/sbin/newuser` script, which I use to add users on an NIS network.

LISTING 19.4 `/usr/local/sbin/newuser` Script to Automate User Management

```
#!/bin/sh
# Validate the number of parameters
if [ $# -ne 3 ]; then
  echo Usage: newuser username groupname "'Real Name'"
  exit
fi

# Get the parameters into human-readable variables
login=$1
group=$2
comment=$3
home=/export/home/$login


# Add the user and ask the operator for the user's password
/usr/sbin/adduser -g $group -G everyone -d /home/$login  M  c "$comment" $1
mkdir $home
/usr/bin/passwd $login

# Initialize the user's home directory
cp -R /etc/skel/* /etc/skel/.??* $home
chown -R $login.$group $home

# Add the user to the aliases file
echo `echo $comment ¦ sed -e 's/ /./g'` $login >> /etc/aliases
newaliases

# Remake the NIS maps
cd /var/yp
make
```

As you can see, `/usr/local/bin/newuser` first calls the `/usr/sbin/adduser` script to actually add the user to `/etc/passwd`. It then creates the user's home directory, copies some skeleton files to it, changes its ownership so the user can work in it, and adds the user to `/etc/aliases`. Finally, it changes to `/var/yp` and remakes the modified maps. Scripts such as this can make systems administration *much* easier and fun.

One thing to note here is that the user's home directory in `/etc/passwd` and the directory that was actually created are different (`/home/`*`user`* versus `/export/home/`*`user`*). This is because we're using the automounter to mount the user's home directory. The automounter is another piece of the sysadmin puzzle, which will be covered in the next section.

The Automounter

Suppose you add a disk to your server—in `/export/public`, for example. You want all clients to mount it as `/resources/user`. Or, suppose the server's home directory partition, `/export/home`, fills up, and you add a new `/export/home1` partition for new accounts. You might even move some of the accounts from /export/home to /export/home1 to save space. So, after you reboot and reconfigure the server, your next task is modifying /etc/fstab in all your client workstations so they mount the new partitions, and then running mount -a. If you have a medium-to-large network, that can take a while. Of course, by using tools such as ssh you could automate it, but you will still have a while when some hosts on the network have the old configuration and some have the new one. And what happens if for some reason one of the client hosts is turned off?

Both of these scenarios are quite common nowadays. Wouldn't it be nice to be able to distribute /etc/fstab by NIS? The automounter to the rescue.

The function of the automounter is to mount filesystems on demand, when they are needed, and unmount them after they have been inactive for some time. On one hand, this reduces resource usage on both client and server, because mounted filesystems consume memory and bandwidth. On the other hand, the fact that the automounter can read its configuration from NIS makes it a perfect tool for network administration.

The automounter is configured to look at a certain subdirectory on your filesystem (the *automount point*). When any program tries to open a file within that subdirectory, it checks its configuration for the particular filename. If it finds it, its configuration file tells it where that mount point actually is (it can be a local device or a remote filesystem), and it automatically mounts the filesystem on the specified directory.

As a quick note, the automounter is a different package that works with NIS.

The automounter can also be used to dynamically mount local filesystems, such as CD-ROMs and floppies. Debian comes preconfigured with an automount point called /amnt, where CDs and floppies are automounted. If you have a softlink called /dev/cdrom pointing to your CD-ROM device (for example, /dev/hdc), inserting a CD and changing to /amnt/cd automatically mounts the CD-ROM.

Preparing to Use the Automounter

To use the automounter, you have to configure your kernel (see Chapter 12, "Customizing the Bootup Procedure"). First, make sure you have enabled Prompt for development and/or incomplete code/drivers in the Code maturity level options screen. Then, go into the Filesystems screen and select Kernel automounter support (experimental). You can compile it as a module if you prefer. Note that, although it is marked as experimental code, the Linux automounter is quite stable. After you have enabled the automounter, save your configuration, recompile the kernel, and reboot.

Automounter support is no longer experimental as of the 2.2.x kernels. Compiling it as a module isn't a good idea if on a network. The main reason to make it a module is to make the kernel smaller by default and the ability to add and remove that functionality whenever root wants.

When you run a kernel with the automounter enabled, you need to install the `autofs` package, which is included in the Debian CDs. This package contains the user-level programs and shared libraries needed for the automounter to work.

Automounter Configuration

The automounter is configured through files in `/etc` and corresponding NIS maps. The master automounter configuration file is `/etc/auto.master` and the `auto.master` NIS map. If a particular map exists both in `/etc` and in NIS, the contents of both are concatenated. In the remainder of this section, all maps are referred to by their NIS map name, but keep in mind that any of these can also be stored statically in `/etc`.

As mentioned, the master automounter map is `auto.master`. Each line in this map contains a directory name and the name of the map that specifies what subdirectories to mount under the directory. Listing 19.5 shows the `auto.master` map that comes by default with Debian.

LISTING 19.5 Default `/etc/auto.master` File

```
# Sample auto.master file
# Format of this file:
# mountpoint map options
# For details of the format look at autofs(8).
/amnt    /etc/auto.amnt
```

Listing 19.5 specifies that the subdirectories under `/amnt` should be handled by the automounter according to the rules in file `/etc/auto.amnt`. Listing 19.6 shows the default `auto.amnt` file supplied with Debian.

LISTING 19.6 Default `/etc/auto.amnt` File

```
# $Id: auto.misc,v 1.2 1997/10/06 21:52:04 hpa Exp $
# This is an automounter map and it has the following format
# key [ -mount-options-separated-by-comma ] location
# Details may be found in the autofs(5) man page

# Examples
#kernel  -ro                          ftp.kernel.org:/pub/linux
#debian  -ro
sunsite.org.uk:/public/Mirrors/ftp.debian.org/pub/debian

boot     -fstype=ext2                 :/dev/hda1
cd       -fstype=iso9660,ro           :/dev/hdc
floppy   -fstype=auto,nosuid,nodev :/dev/fd0
```

With the maps in Listings 19.5 and 19.6 in place, a user can do a `cd /amnt/cd`. At that moment, `/dev/hdc` will be automatically mounted (assuming it is a CD-ROM drive and that it contains a disc). After a user `cd`s out of `/amnt/cd`, and assuming no other processes are using files on the CD (or have a directory in the CD set as their current directory), the automounter waits (by default it waits 60 seconds) and unmounts the CD. The same thing happens with `/amnt/floppy` and the floppy drive.

As you can see in Listing 19.6, each line in an automounter map contains the name of the directory that will be mounted. This is known as the *key*. It is followed by the options to use when mounting the filesystem and the device to mount. If the device starts with a colon (`:`), it is taken to be a local device; otherwise, the device name should be of the form `server:filesystem`, like NFS mounts in `/etc/fstab`.

Note

Unlike other automounters (such as the one included in Sun's Solaris), the Linux automounter currently supports only *direct* maps. This means that the automounter will completely take over the managed directory (`/amnt` in the default `auto.master` file), and none of the files and directories that exist under it will be accessible. Other automounters also support *indirect* maps, where you can mix local and automounted subdirectories within the same parent directory.

Using the automounter for local devices can be useful, especially when you want a user to be able to mount devices with a minimum of fuss. No more manually mounting and unmounting CDs each time you need them! However, the real power of the automounter comes when you use it with NIS, NFS, and wildcard maps.

Listing 19.7 shows an `auto.master` map that is being currently used at a company with a Linux network. The map is stored in the server and is automatically pushed by NIS to all workstations. Listings 19.8 and 19.9 show the two maps mentioned in `auto.master`.

LISTING 19.7 A Real-Life `auto.master` Map

```
# $Id: auto.master,v 1.2 1997/10/06 21:52:03 hpa Exp $
# Sample auto.master file
# Format of this file:
# mountpoint map options
# For details of the format look at autofs(8).
#
/home       auto.home
/usr/sw     auto.software
/amnt       auto.amnt
```

LISTING 19.8 The `auto.software` Map

```
dl        -defaults,soft,intr        disksvr:/export/dl
drivers   -defaults,soft,intr        disksvr:/export/drivers
```

```
masters  -defaults,soft,intr       disksvr:/export/masters
src      -defaults,soft,intr       develsvr:/export/src
dist     -defaults,soft,intr,suid  disksvr:/export/dist
bin      -defaults,soft,intr       binsvr:/export/dist/linux/bin
config   -defaults,soft,intr       binsvr:/export/dist/linux/config
common   -defaults,soft,intr       disksvr:/export/common
mysql    -defaults,soft,intr       develsvr:/export/mysql-3.22.21
win      -fstype=smbfs             //winnt/public
web      -defaults,soft,intr       develsvr:/export/devel/web
```

LISTING 19.9 The auto.home Map

```
# This is an automounter map and it has the following format
# key [ -mount-options-separated-by-comma ] location
# Details may be found in the autofs(5) man page
#
-defaults,soft,intr  homesvr:/export/home/&
```

There are two automounter mountpoints: /usr/sw and /home. /usr/sw contains software that is used throughout the company, and common areas for things such as shared files and project files. The directories are mounted from four different servers, but clients just see the /usr/sw directory hierarchy. Of note is the win mountpoint. It is mounted from a Windows server via Samba (see Chapter 18), because the -fstype option specifies an smbfs filesystem.

The default NIS server configuration knows about the auto.master and auto.home maps; however, it knows nothing about auto.software. Because of this, to use custom maps, you have to edit /var/yp/Makefile. You have to add the name of your map at the end of the line that starts with all:, then go to the entry for an existing map (for example, auto.home), copy it, and substitute your map's name instead of the existing map.

/home is interesting, because with a single line it controls all the home directories. The key is specified as a wildcard that matches any directory. The mounted device includes an ampersand (&) at the point where the matched text should be inserted. In this case, if a user tries to cd into /home/mario, the filesystem homesvr:/export/home/mario is mounted on /home/mario.

A limitation of a wildcard is that it is an all-or-nothing proposition. Either you use a wildcard as your only line in the map, or you have to specify each directory by hand. However, you can substitute the wildcard several times. For example, suppose that each user's workstation is named after the owner's user ID and contains his home directory. You could use the following line:

```
*    -defaults,soft,intr  &:/export/home/&
```

However, if you want to cluster users' home directories in a few servers, you either have to list each user in auto.home or use an executable map.

An executable map is a program or script that takes a key as an argument and returns an automounter line, or no output if the key doesn't exist. It is specified in the `auto.master` map as a filename; the fact that it must be executable by `root` sets it apart. Listing 19.10 shows a sample bash script that maps users whose names start with letters from *a* through *m* to one server, and all other users to another server. This could, of course, be as complex as needed—for example, looking up another NIS map or querying a database.

LISTING 19.10 `/usr/local/sbin/usermap`, **an Executable Automounter Map**

```
#!/bin/bash
case "$1" in
  [a-m]*)
    echo "$1  -defaults,soft,intr  svr01:/export/home/$1"
    ;;
  default)
    echo "$1  -defaults,soft,intr  svr02:/export/home/$1"
    ;;
esac
```

To use this map, your `auto.master` file contains the following line:

```
/home    /usr/local/sbin/usermap
```

As you can see, the automounter, combined with NIS and NFS, can eliminate many of the headaches of managing a large Linux or UNIX network. For instance, if you add or remove a server, or if you need to move things between servers, you just need to modify the map on the NIS master server and push the maps out (via a simple `make`), and all clients will be automatically updated.

TCP/IP Troubleshooting Tools

After a TCP/IP network is configured, problems rarely appear. Rarely, however, does not mean never. Networking equipment does fail, lines do go down, and cables do get disconnected. Also, problems can arise during the initial configuration of a networked host.

In Linux, there are three basic network troubleshooting tools. Two of them (`ping` and `traceroute`) are concerned with the ability of a host to reach another, and the third one (`tcpdump`) is useful for analyzing the flow of traffic in a network. The following sections take a look at some of these tools.

`ping`

The most basic network troubleshooting tool is the `ping` program. Named after the pinging sound made by submarine sonars, `ping` sends packets to another host and waits for that host to reply to them. Ping is mainly used to see if the machines on a network can talk to each other. If they can ping each other, they should be able to send just about any other data to other machines on the network. `ping` uses ICMP (Internet Control Message Protocol), a protocol that runs over IP and is designed for control messages used for things such as routing and reachability information.

The most common way of using `ping` is to pass it a hostname or address:

```
% ping server.company.com
PING server.company.com (10.0.1.10): 56 data bytes
64 bytes from 10.0.1.10: icmp_seq=0 ttl=245 time=83.239 ms
64 bytes from 10.0.1.10: icmp_seq=1 ttl=245 time=80.808 ms
64 bytes from 10.0.1.10: icmp_seq=2 ttl=245 time=82.994 ms
64 bytes from 10.0.1.10: icmp_seq=3 ttl=245 time=81.635 ms
^C
--- server.company.com ping statistics ---
4 packets transmitted, 4 packets received, 0% packet loss
round-trip min/avg/max = 80.808/82.169/83.239 ms
```

In this case, `ping` pings the target host once a second, until you press Ctrl+C. At that moment, it prints the statistics for the run. In the statistics, aside from the number of packets transmitted and received, you can see the minimum, average, and maximum round-trip times, which helps youfind out how congested the path to the destination host is at the moment.

`ping` has many options. The most common ones are the following:

Option	*Function*
`-c` *`count`*	Sends only *`count`* packets instead of pinging forever.
`-n`	`ping` displays numeric addresses instead of hostnames. Useful when you can't get to the DNS server, or when DNS queries take too long.
`-r`	Records route. Sends an option in every packet, which instructs all hosts between the source and the target to store their IP address in the packet. This way, you can see which hosts a packet is going through. However, the packet size is limited to nine hosts. Besides, some systems disregard this option. Because of this, it is better to use `traceroute` (see next section).
`-q`	Quiet output. Outputs just the final statistics.
`-v`	Verbose. Displays all packets received, not just `ping` responses.

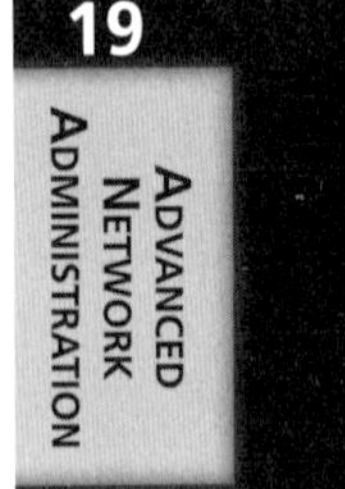

When troubleshooting network problems, you should first ping the IP address of the source host itself. This verifies that the network interface is set up correctly. After that, you should try pinging your default gateway, your default gateway's gateway, and so on, until you reach the destination host. Then you can easily isolate where a problem lies. However, after you've verified that you can get to the default gateway, it is better to use the `traceroute` program (described in the next section) to automate the process.

Note

All TCP/IP packets have a field called the Time-To-Live, or TTL. This field is decremented once by each router on the network. The moment it reaches zero, the packet is discarded. While `ping` uses a default TTL of 255 (the maximum value), many programs, such as `telnet` and `ftp`, use a smaller TTL (usually 30 or 60). That means that you might be able to `ping` a host, but not `telnet` or `ftp` into it. You may use the `-t` *`ttl`* option to `ping` to set the TTL of the packets it outputs.

traceroute

The `traceroute` program is the workhorse of TCP/IP troubleshooting. It sends UDP packets with progressively larger TTLs and detects the ICMP responses sent by gateways when they drop the packets. In the end, this maps out the route a packet takes when going from the source host to the target host.

This is how it works: `traceroute` starts by sending out a packet with a TTL of 1. The packet gets to a gateway, which can be the target host or not. If it is the target host, the gateway sends a response packet. If it isn't the target host, the gateway decrements the TTL. Because the TTL is now zero, the gateway drops the packet and sends back a packet indicating this. Whatever happens, `traceroute` detects the reply packet. If it has reached the target host, its job is finished. If not (that is, it received notification that the packet was dropped), it increments the TTL by one (its new value is 2) and sends another packet. This time, the first gateway decrements the TTL (to 1) and passes it through to the next gateway. This gateway does the same thing: checks whether it's the destination host and decrements the TTL. This goes on until either you reach the target host or you reach the maximum TTL value (`30` by default, but it can be changed with the `-m` *`max_ttl`* option).

`traceroute` sends three packets with each TTL,and reports the round-trip time taken by each packet. This is useful for detecting network bottlenecks.

`traceroute` is usually used the same way as `ping`—by giving it a destination address. Listing 19.11 shows an example of the output from `traceroute`:

LISTING 19.11 Sample Output from `traceroute`

```
mario@chaos:~ 511 $ /usr/sbin/traceroute www.umbral.com
traceroute to xmaya.umbral.com (207.87.18.30), 30 hops max, 40 byte packets
 1  master.spin.com.mx (200.13.80.123)  120.75 ms  126.727 ms  109.533 ms
 2  octopus.spin.com.mx (200.13.81.32)  110.042 ms  104.654 ms  99.599 ms
 3  200.33.218.161 (200.33.218.161)  119.539 ms  105.697 ms  109.603 ms
 4  rr1.mexmdf.avantel.net.mx (200.33.209.1)  131.556 ms  112.767 ms  109.6 ms
 5  bordercore1-hssi0-0.Dallas.cw.net (166.48.77.249)  159.54 ms  155.378 ms
169.598 ms
```

```
 6  core9.Dallas.cw.net (204.70.9.89)  159.483 ms  156.364 ms  159.628 ms
 7  dfw2-core2-s1-0-0.atlas.digex.net (165.117.59.13)  169.505 ms  156.024 ms
149.628 ms
 8  lax1-core1-s8-0-0.atlas.digex.net (165.117.50.25)  199.497 ms  194.006 ms
189.621 ms
 9  sjc4-core2-s5-0-0.atlas.digex.net (165.117.53.74)  199.489 ms sjc4-core2-s5-
1-0.atlas.digex.net (165.117.56.110)  191.025 ms sjc4-core2-s5-0-
0.atlas.digex.net (165.117.53.74)  210.25 ms
10  sjc4-core6-pos1-1.atlas.digex.net (165.117.59.69)  201.031 ms  196.195 ms
199.584 ms
11  sjc4-wscore2-p1-0.wsmg.digex.net (199.125.178.37)  360.468 ms  366.267 ms
199.481 ms
12  sjc4-wscore4-fa1-0.wsmg.digex.net (199.125.178.20)  582.272 ms  207.536 ms
198.275 ms
13  xmaya.umbral.com (207.87.18.30)  209.457 ms  3076.14 ms *
```

`traceroute` can give you quite a bit of information if you know how to look for it. For example, in Listing 19.11, we can see a few things:

- `www.umbral.com` is actually an alias for `xmaya.umbral.com`. `traceroute` always does a reverse DNS lookup and reports the official hostname of the host it's tracing.
- `xmaya.umbral.com` is connected to the Internet through a service provider whose domain is `digex.net` (probably an ISP called Digex) (lines 7–12; it is the domain of the last gateway).
- We are connected to the Internet through an ISP called `spin`, which is in Mexico (lines 1–2; it is the first gateway; the domain ends with `.mx`).
- The `digex` hosts that appear on line 9 are actually several hosts with the same IP address. This is done for redundancy.
- There seems to be some kind of hangup or bottleneck between hosts 10, 11, and 12. Notice how the response time, after slowly growing steadily until line 9, suddenly jumps from about 200 milliseconds to more than 300, and then to more than 500. This might be a temporary bottleneck (caused simply by the traffic load at the moment) or it may be a continuous problem, caused perhaps by a physical media problem or not enough capacity in the link.

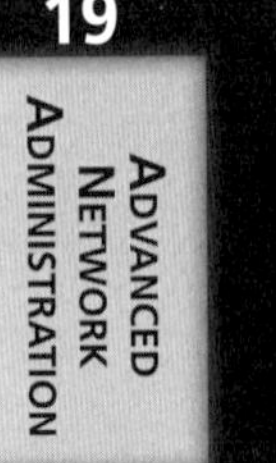

As you can see, `traceroute` can be an invaluable tool. There is much more information that can be gleaned from `traceroute` output; it is best to read the `traceroute(8) man` page for a complete discussion.

tcpdump

`tcpdump` is another invaluable tool for debugging some types of network problems. It basically works as a *packet sniffer*. This means that it listens to the network, looks at any packets that come by (whether destined for the host it is running on or not), and operates on it. It can store all or just some interesting parts of the traffic it sees, or perform a rudimentary analysis of the information it contains.

`tcpdump` works by setting the network card into what is known as *promiscuous mode*. Normally, a network card only "sees" packets that are meant for it. However, in promiscuous mode, it "sees" all packets that pass through the network and passes them to the operating system above. The OS then passes the packets to `tcpdump`, which can then filter them and display or store them. Because it modifies the configuration of the network card, `tcpdump` must be run by `root`.

Caution

`tcpdump` is a potential security hole. It falls into the category of programs known as *sniffers*, which listen to the network and have the capability of listening to all packets in the network and storing them. If users use programs such as `telnet`, which send passwords in the clear, a cracker might use a sniffer to "sniff out" the passwords. Because of this, `tcpdump` should never be installed `setuid-root`.

To detect whether a network interface is in promiscuous mode (and thus might have a sniffer running on it), use the `ifconfig` command to display the interface's configuration. The `PROMISC` flag will appear if the interface is in promiscuous mode:

```
# /sbin/ifconfig eth0
eth0      Link encap:Ethernet  HWaddr 00:60:97:3E:F0:61
          inet addr:10.0.1.50  Bcast:10.0.1.255  Mask:255.255.255.0
          UP BROADCAST RUNNING PROMISC MULTICAST  MTU:1500  Metric:1
          RX packets:0 errors:0 dropped:0 overruns:0 frame:0
          TX packets:5 errors:0 dropped:0 overruns:0 carrier:5
          Collisions:0
          Interrupt:3 Base address:0x310
```

If you run `tcpdump` without any arguments, you get a listing of all the packets that pass through the network:

```
# /usr/sbin/tcpdump
tcpdump: listening on eth0
22:46:12.730048 renato.1445323871 > vishnu.nfs: 100 readlink [|nfs]
22:46:12.734224 tumbolia.1012 > vishnu.808: udp 92
22:46:12.746763 tumbolia.22 > atman.1023: P 142299991:142300035(44) ack
3799214339 win 32120 (DF) [tos 0x10]
22:46:12.763684 atman.1023 > tumbolia.22: . ack 44 win 32120 (DF) [tos 0x10]
22:46:12.778100 vishnu.808 > tumbolia.1015: udp 56
22:46:12.780084 gerardo.1448370113 > vishnu.nfs: 124 lookup [|nfs]
22:46:12.780153 tumbolia.22 > atman.1023: P 44:596(552) ack 1 win 32120 (DF)
[tos 0x10]
```

The dump stops when you press Ctrl+C.

As you can see, tcpdump by default converts IP addresses to hostnames and port numbers to service names. It also attempts to interpret some packets (such as those where the line ends with lookup [¦nfs], which are NFS lookups). In some cases, the number of bytes that tcpdump looks at (68) might not be enough to fully decode the packet. If so, you may use the -s option to increase the number (see the -s option in Table 19.4, later in this chapter).

Many times (especially in medium-to-large networks), you don't want to see all the packets. Sometimes you want to see all the packets going between two specific hosts, or even those that use a specific service. tcpdump takes as a parameter an optional filter expression that selects only certain packets.

tcpdump's filter expressions consist of one or more primitives joined by the keywords and, or, and not. Each primitive consists of a qualifier followed by an ID. A qualifier consists of one or more keywords, the most common of which are shown in Table 19.4. The ID specifies the value the corresponding field must have to match the filter.

TABLE 19.3 Most Common tcpdump Qualifiers

Qualifier	*Matches*
src host	The IP address of the host where the packet comes from
dst host	The IP address of the host to which the packet is going
host	The IP address of the source or the destination host
src port	The port the packet is coming from
dst port	The port the packet is going to
port	The source or the destination port
tcp, udp or icmp	The specified packet's protocol

Tip

One common mistake is to run tcpdump through a remote connection, such as when connected through telnet or ssh, with a filter that will include all the telnet or ssh packets (for example, including just host thishost, where thishost is the host where tcpdump is running). In that case, you end up with an incredible amount of output, because the first packet that comes through generates output, which is transmitted through the network and captured by tcpdump, which generates more output, which is also transmitted through the network, and so on ad infinitum.

To prevent that, be more specific in your filter expressions. For example, you might include the primitive not port 22 to filter out ssh packets.

tcpdump also takes several switches, the most common of which are shown in Table 19.4.

TABLE 19.4 Most Common tcpdump Switches

Qualifier	*Matches*
-c *count*	Exit after receiving *count* packets.
-i *interface*	Listen on *interface*. By default, tcpdump listens on the first interface found after the loopback interface. You can see the order the interfaces are searched by using the ifconfig -a command.
-n	Don't convert numeric addresses and port numbers to host and service names (print numeric output).
-N	Print only the hostname, not its fully-qualified domain name.
-r *file*	Read packets from *file*, which must have been created with the -w option.
-s *snaplen*	Grab *snaplen* bytes from each packet. The default is 68, which is enough for IP, ICMP, TCP, and UDP packets. However, for certain protocols (such as DNS and NFS), a *snaplen* of *68* truncates some protocol information. This is marked by [¦*protocol*], where *protocol* indicates the protocol part where truncation occurred.
-v	Verbose mode. Print some more information about each packet.
-vv	Very verbose mode. Print lots more information about each packet.
-w *file*	Capture the packets into *file*.
-x	Print each packet in hex. Prints either the whole packet or *snaplen* bytes, whichever is less.

Summary

In this chapter, we explored how to reduce your systems administration headaches by using NFS and NIS. NFS gives you centralized storage, and NIS is an easy way of managing many of the system configuration files that live in /etc. Coupled with the automounter, which enables you to dynamically mount filesystems when they are required and to control this by means of an NIS map, NIS makes it possible to manage most of a network's functions from a single server.

We also looked at the three most important tools for network troubleshooting: ping, traceroute, and tcpdump. ping and traceroute concern themselves with TCP/IP connectivity between hosts, and tcpdump enables you to "peek under the hood" of the network protocols and find out what is going on in the network.

Security Issues

Part III

In This Part

CHAPTER 20

Conceptual Overview of Security Issues

by Mario Camou

IN THIS CHAPTER

finished
00 09 18

It has long been said that information is power. This is more true in today's information-based economy, where even most monetary transactions consist solely of information (consider, for example, e-commerce). For many purposes, an individual's very existence is based on the data on him or her available in some database (consider the IRS or the social security system).

Many companies spend huge amounts of money on physical security measures, such as security guards and access points. They then connect their internal networks to a public network (such as the Internet) without any protection. The purpose of this chapter is first to raise awareness of the perils of the information highway, to acquaint you with some basic security concepts, as well as the most common types of attacks used by crackers. The information security landscape is extremely large, so the information presented here should be regarded as a starting point. If you want to learn more (and you should!), an excellent reference is *Maximum Internet Security: A Hacker's Guide*, ISBN 1-57521-268-4, also published by Sams, and available online in the MCP Personal Bookshelf at `http://www.pbs.mcp.com`.

Security Concepts

It has been said that the only way to have a completely secure computer is to never, ever, plug it in or turn it on. If you do need to turn it on (which is probably the case unless you want it to be a very expensive paperweight), remove the floppy drive, CD-ROM, network connection, and any way of getting data into or out of it (including the keyboard and monitor). Even in that case, you have to worry about someone wandering by with a magnet.

As you can see, it's impossible to have a completely secure computer and get some work done with it! Information security deals not with making a computer *completely* invulnerable, but with making it so hard to get into it that it would take too much time and effort to break into it. Because technology is constantly advancing, this means that information security is an extremely fluid field.

The Security Policy: Your Master Plan

Before going into the nitty-gritty details of configuring firewalls or deciding on an encryption scheme, it is necessary to consider the following questions: What are you protecting, and who are you protecting it against? That is the basis of an organization's security policy.

The *security policy* is the master document containing the security guidelines for the organization. These guidelines contain both physical security measures (such as that employees must wear a badge at all times) and information security measures (such as that all passwords must be at least six characters long and must be changed monthly). It may be a long document that spans several binders, or it might be just one or two pages long (of course, somewhere between is best). The important thing is that you must know what you are protecting, who you are protecting it against, and what measures you are taking to protect it.

Some organizations might have extremely valuable classified information stored in their networks. Others might not even blink if someone steals or deletes the information on their computers. Because of this, it is impossible to make a general security policy that applies to all situations.

A security policy might also affect legal liability in some cases. For example, if someone breaks into a company's systems and publishes the customers' data without their express consent, some countries might find the company legally liable, unless the company's security policy demonstrates that appropriate measures were taken to prevent that from happening.

An important part of any security policy is the list of actions to take in case of a breach. How do you detect a break-in? What do you do about it? Do you disconnect your servers from the network? Do you leave them connected and try to trap the attacker? Who do you contact? What do you do to recover from an attack? All these questions should be answered in your security policy.

The Many Faces of Information Security

Information security deals with several things:

- Authentication
- Authorization
- Encryption
- Detection
- Recovery

Authentication

Authentication is the means by which a system knows who is accessing it. Examples of authentication methods are passwords and smart cards. There are three general categories of authentication methods, depending on the information they gather (see Figure 20.1).

The first and most common authentication category, known as *password authentication,* is based on *something you know*. An example of this category is the password used to log on to a computer or computer network.

The second category, *token-based*, is based on *something you have*. An example is the access badges used to enter many buildings or offices.

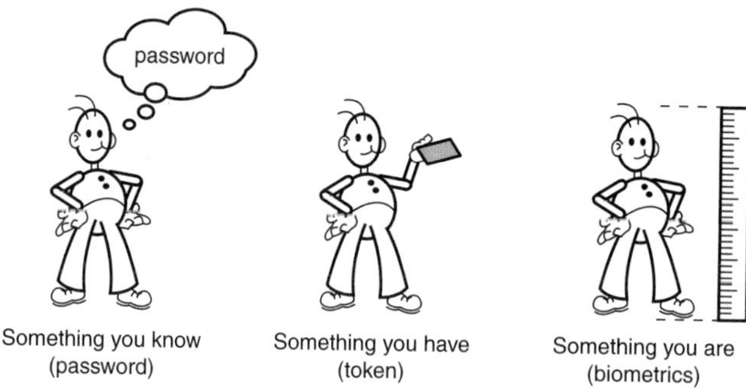

FIGURE 20.1
There are three types of authentication schemes.

The third category is known as *biometrics*. It is based on *something you are*. Examples of this are fingerprint or voice print scanners.

The best authentication systems combine two or all three of the previous categories. For example, banks combine password-based and token-based authentication in their ATM cards, where you need both the card itself (something you have) and its PIN (something you know) to access the ATM.

Linux uses the password authentication for everything needed by default. The other forms users will probably never see on their Linux boxes.

Authorization

After a system has verified who its user is (the term "user" is used loosely here; the "user" might be another system), it must somehow find out what that user is allowed to do. This is known as *authorization*. For example, an ATM must check a database to see which accounts a user has access to, and a building's access-control software must verify that a user is allowed to access a secured area. There are three broad types of authorization schemes, based on what they verify (see Figure 20.2).

FIGURE 20.2
There are three types of authorization schemes.

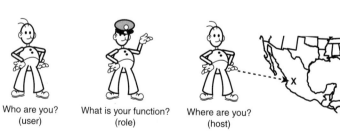

The first is *user-based* authorization, where a specific user is allowed access to specific services (the ATM is an example of user-based authorization). User-based authorization is based on *who* the user is.

The second type of authorization is *role-based* authorization. For example, a human resources system might let all managers see the salary of all the employees in their respective department. In this case, the authorization is given based on the role the person plays within the organization. Role-based authorization is based on *what* the user is or does.

A third type of authorization scheme, *host-based* authorization, is a subset of user-based authorization used in computer networks. In this case, the decision of whether to allow or disallow access is based on which host the request is coming from. The assumption here is that the particular host requesting service can be accessed only by authorized users. Host-based authorization is based on *where* the user is.

Encryption

Encryption is the means by which information is scrambled so that only the receiving party may read it. Most local-area network architectures are based on *shared media*. This means that data sent from one host to another can be seen by all the hosts on the LAN. If the data leaves the LAN bound for a host on a different network, it may be seen by all intervening hosts. Unencrypted data is like a postcard, whose contents may be seen by all.

Data is encrypted by means of a *key,* which is a sequence of bits used to encrypt and decrypt data. There are two categories of encryption schemes. *Shared-key* encryption is based on a single key. The same key is used to encrypt and to decrypt the message. The other category is *public-key* encryption, in which there are two complementary keys. You need one in order to decrypt data from the other. The data encrypted by the first key can only be decrypted by the second, and vice versa.

Public-key encryption was developed to deal with the problem of key distribution. Imagine that a group of 10 people want to communicate individually and securely with one another, with none of the other people in the group being able to read their messages. Each person would generate nine different keys, one for each of the other people in the group. A key is used to pass any kind of data in an encrypted setting. They then would have to give each of the other nine persons their respective keys. If the people aren't close to each other, how do they get the key to another person in a secure manner? See Figure 20.3.

With public-key encryption, each person wanting to communicate generates only a key pair. One of the keys is known as the *public* key, and is widely shared, perhaps even posted on a bulletin-board system or a Web site. The other key, known as the *private* key, is kept secret. That way, if John wants to send a private message to Anne, he looks up her public key and encrypts the message with it. Because the keys are complementary, the public key cannot be used to decrypt the message. The only person who can decrypt the message is Anne, using her secret key.

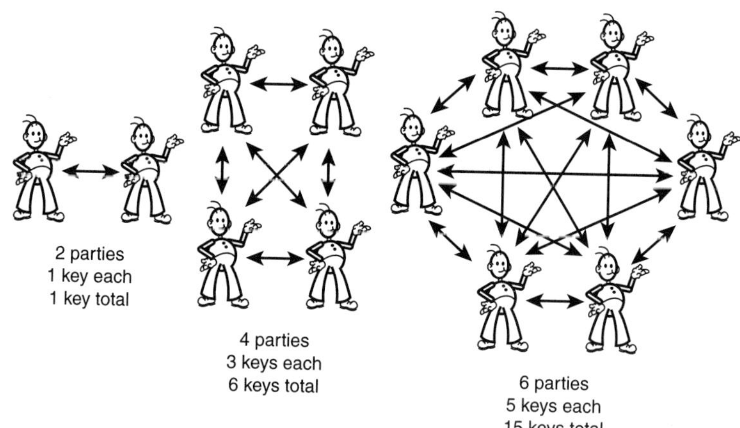

FIGURE 20.3
The key distribution problem.

The problem with public-key encryption algorithms is that they are usually very compute-intensive. Because of this, most public-key encryption schemes use an underlying shared-key encryption algorithm. They generate a random shared *session key* used to encrypt the message itself. They then encrypt the session key using a public-key algorithm and attach the session key to the encrypted message. See Figure 20.4.

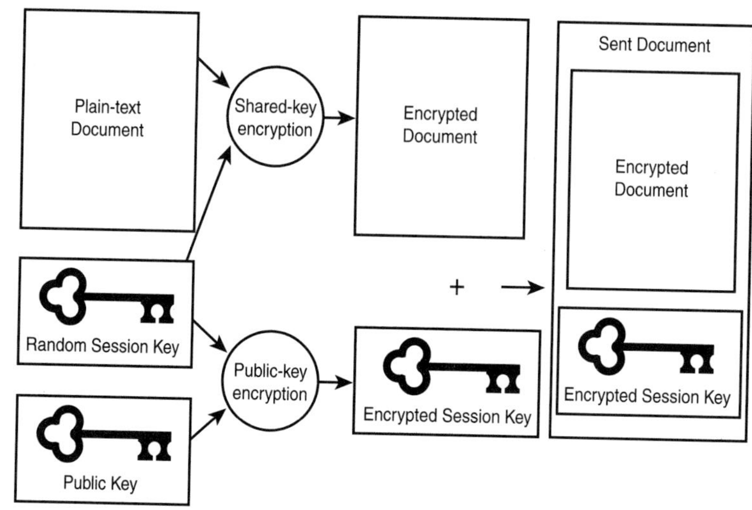

FIGURE 20.4
Public-key encryption schemes use underlying shared keys.

Detection

You might have a sophisticated authentication and authorization system in place. You might have included all three authentication methods and have a bulletproof authorization system where there is no possibility that a user will be able to do things he or she isn't authorized to do. Your hardware may also be perfect, so crashes never happen. In that case, you don't need a detection system. You also probably need a healthy dose of reality.

The reality of things is that systems are never perfect. As a frustrated programmer once said, "there is always one more bug." That means that you need a way of detecting when things go wrong with your security system—such as detecting when an intruder comes into your systems or is trying to get in, detecting when a server goes down, or verifying when someone has tampered with your systems.

Recovery

Another responsibility of information security is *recovery*. Recovery means restoring the data and the use of the system after an incident, regardless of the incident type. It might be a user (or even yourself!) accidentally typing `rm -rf .` when the current directory wasn't the one the user wanted to remove. It might be a disk crash. It might be an intruder playing "amateur sysadmin" with your servers. Or it might be the building falling on top of your data center because of an earthquake.

In any case, it is a responsibility of information security to be prepared for such eventualities. A recovery plan is essential. It doesn't matter whether the plan is stored in 20 binders or if it's written on a paper napkin; it is one of the critical pieces of documentation that any organization must have.

Common Misconceptions About Information Security

There are a lot of supposed "truths" about information security that are simply false. They are sometimes even propagated by the media and by vendors, and by misinformed users. We will try to debunk the most common of these.

Hackers Versus Crackers

One of the most common errors when talking about attacks and security incidents is mistaking the term *hacker* with the term *cracker*. Many people use them interchangeably, but they are completely opposite.

The term *hacker* is applied to people with a deep technical knowledge, who like to "hack away" at problems until they are solved. Hackers are the people ultimately responsible for the advance of computer science, because one of their passions is to think up new ways to use technology in ways it wasn't meant to be used.

A *cracker*, on the other hand, is a person who breaks into (or "cracks") other people's systems. Some of them are also hackers in their own right, using their deep systems knowledge to crack other systems. However, a great number of crackers fall into a category known as *script kiddies*. These are people who take the cracking knowledge provided by another cracker and apply it directly, recipe-like (see the section "Exploits and Script Kiddies," later in this chapter).

Gaining Security Through Non-Detection

In many organizations, the security policy can best be characterized as "If they don't know about your network, they won't come," a strategy widely known as *security by obscurity*. For example, suppose that there is a Web page that contains information that should be seen by only some people. Instead of setting up passwords for each of them (which might be an administrative burden), they simply don't publish the page's URL except to the select group. Their reasoning is, "If nobody knows where your network is, nobody will access it."

This works fine, until one person of the select group leaves the organization or gets reassigned to some other duty where he or she doesn't require access any more. Because the person knows the Web page's URL, the URL must be changed and then redistributed. Or perhaps someone outside the select group gets the page's URL and distributes it throughout the organization. In any case, keeping it secret becomes harder and harder.

Security by obscurity might have its place—if the hassle of keeping data secure is larger than the value of the data. But keep in mind that there are many ways that people can find out about things kept secret.

Security Through Non-Importance

Closely related with security by obscurity is the idea that an organization is so unimportant (or so new) that crackers won't find it interesting. This idea comes from the misconception that crackers are interested in cracking only important organizations, such as the Department of Defense, NASA, or large corporations.

The problem here is that they disregard one of the cracker's highest motivators: the fact itself of having cracked a system. Like airmen in war recording downed enemy planes, many crackers accumulate cracked systems as if they were "brownie points," taking pride in the number of systems cracked regardless of their importance. For them, the thrill of cracking is more important than what is being cracked.

These crackers use software such as port scanners to scan complete networks by IP address. They don't care whom the IP addresses belong to; they simply scan them to find crackable servers.

Our Systems Are Safe and We're Secure Forever

One of the constants of information systems is that software has bugs. Another one is that technology constantly advances.

These two constants make it a given that a security policy that is strong enough today will be hopelessly insecure sometime in the future. It is extremely important for any person responsible for information security to keep up with advances in cracker technology, as well as to keep up-to-date with bug reports and software versions. There are several email lists that can help you; the most useful are listed in Appendix B, "Online References."

Crackers Are "Somewhere Out There"

Many people believe that crackers are somewhere on the public networks, and as long as they have a firewall, nothing can happen to them. They don't realize that most attacks come from the inside. Disgruntled employees, saboteurs, and infiltrators exist in many organizations. In many cases, employees leave their computer screens open, displaying confidential information or allowing access to it to the first person that comes along. Many companies also don't have strict controls on where visitors may or may not go.

In many cases, it is necessary to build internal firewalls between different departments, and perhaps add measures such as biometrics to strengthen security.

Electronic Defenses Are Enough

Just as with firewalls, many people assume that if the network is secure from electronic intrusions, their information is secure. That is like building the most secure jail, and then forgetting to lock the doors. There are several attacks known as "meatspace attacks" (as opposed to "cyberspace attacks") because they work in the real world.

Social Engineering

Social engineering is probably the oldest form of gaining access to any kind of restricted area. It is based on the fact that the weakest link in any chain is the human link. Social engineering is actually a generic name for several different kinds of attacks, all of which have in common that they work through human beings.

For example, a cracker might call a legitimate user of a computer system, pretending to be a technical support employee. This false employee then asks the user to give the cracker his or her user ID and password, claiming that there are database problems and the cracker needs to run some tests. The user, trusting that this is a legitimate call, confidently gives the cracker his or her user ID and password, thereby letting the cracker into the system.

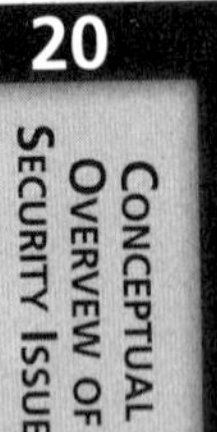

The only way of defending your systems against social engineers is to have clearly defined policies and educate the users, operators, and administrators of the system.

Trashing

We have an ingrained belief that when we throw something into the garbage can, it's gone. We are taught that you should never take things out of the garbage. The problem is that, when dealing with information, your trash can return to haunt you.

Many companies hire a special kind of cracker, known as a *trasher,* whose job is to sift through their competitors' garbage, looking for interesting information. Many people, for example, write their passwords on pieces of paper and then throw them into the trash can without thinking twice about it. Others discard printed reports or floppy disks. These are the trasher's treasures.

Users must be educated that practically all paper must be shredded. Floppy disks must be bulk-erased before being thrown away. Passwords must never be written down.

Other Types of Physical Attacks

There are many other kinds of attacks that take place in the real world. Computers can be stolen complete with their data, or their hard disks can be removed. Backup tapes and hard disks can be erased with a suitably placed magnet. Notebook computers have been stolen in airports and hotels. Executives sometimes use their notebook computers in airplanes and waiting rooms, without checking whether someone is looking over their shoulder.

Users, operators, and administrators have to be educated in the fact that information is property, and that it can be more valuable than any physical object it is stored in.

Perimeter-Based Versus Host-Based Security

There are two basic kinds of security measures that have to be included in any information security plan: perimeter security and host security. It is necessary to consider both. See Figure 20.5.

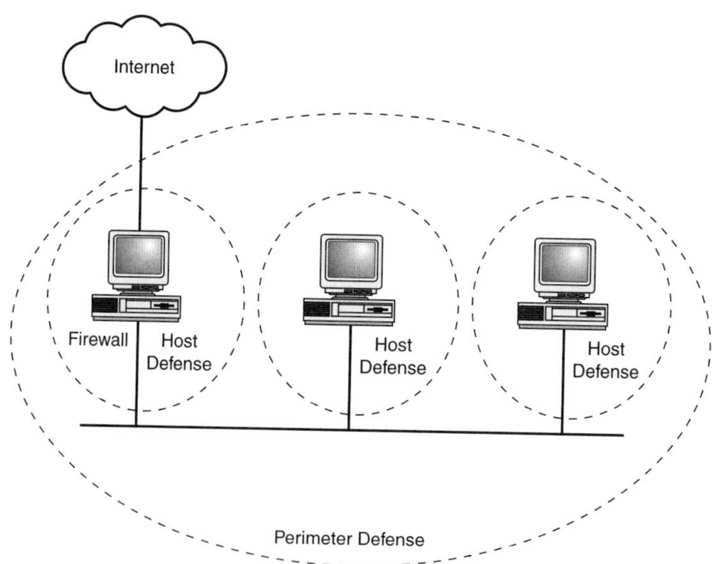

FIGURE 20.5
Perimeter-based versus host-based security.

Perimeter security takes care of protecting against people coming into the network. As its name implies, it protects the perimeter of the network against intruders. Perimeter security is usually enforced through firewalls (including internal firewalls between portions of the organization's internal network). Firewalls are covered in Chapter 22, "Firewalls and Proxies."

Host security concerns itself with protecting the host itself. It is on one hand the last bastion of defense against a cracker that might have penetrated the perimeter defense. On the other hand, it also protects against attacks from inside the organization. There are several tools to enforce host security, which are covered in Chapter 21, "Principles of Security."

Security Versus Ease-of-Use

Security is often at odds with ease-of-use and the free flow of information within an organization. For example, a company's security policy might require that a user log in once to access his or her files on the network servers, have another password to read his or her email, and perhaps a different password to access the internal systems.

It is important to consider this when drafting the organization's security policy. How important is the information? Is it really necessary to make a user log in three times to get at a particular item? On the other hand, how much can we trust the user? None of these questions have easy answers, and their answers are different for each organization. But be sure that you'll always have people who would like things to be easier.

The Principle of Least Access

A rule of thumb that helps when establishing a security policy is called the *principle of least access*. It basically means that a person should have the least access he or she needs to do the job. Many people would say that is simple common sense, but it's amazing how many organizations don't consider this when designing their security policies. Many systems are left open to all employees, when only a single department (or a single person) really needs access to them.

When defining access profiles, it is usually better to define roles, provide access on a role-per-role basis, and then assign roles to people. A person may have several roles. For example, in a human resources system, the same person may have access to some parts of the system as an employee, to other parts as a manager, and to still other parts as the manager of a particular office. If you assign access to the role instead of to the person, it makes it a lot easier to change things as a person moves through the organization.

Now that we've discussed security basics, we'll move on to the more complex subject of online attacks.

Types of Online Attacks

In this section, we explore some of the most common types of online attacks. We also look at some ways of preventing them. In all these cases, the first thing you have to do is to keep abreast of new developments and keep your systems up-to-date. Apply the latest vendor patches to allyour systems. As security manager, you should at least follow all CERT advisories and probably subscribe to the SANS Institute's Security Digest list (for information on these and other security-related resources, see Appendix B).

Denial-of-Service

In a *denial-of-service* (or DOS) attack, the cracker's objective is to make your legitimate users unable to access the system. For example, a cracker may send thousands of pieces of email to your server, thus filling up your disk. Or a cracker may open hundreds of simultaneous connections to your server and hold them open, making it impossible for the server to serve your users.

Because of their varied nature, it's practically impossible to prevent all kinds of DOS attacks. Some of them take advantage of flaws in the TCP/IP protocol itself. New DOS attacks and vendor patches to prevent them are published in the CERT advisories as they are found.

Sniffing

One of the first things a cracker does after getting access to a network (either legally through being a legal user, or illegally through cracking one of your servers), is installing a sniffer program. A *sniffer* is a program that listens to all packets that travel through the network, searching for user IDs and passwords. If you use `telnet` or `rlogin` to remotely manage one of your servers, the cracker will sniff out the `root` password—and then all bets are off. Even if you use encrypted communications, your users may not. When a cracker steals a normal user account on a host, it is usually easy work to get `root` access (see the section "Exploits and Script Kiddies," later in this chapter).

When you consider that the packets that travel over the Internet pass through many hosts and networks, you understand that you should never log in to a remote server through a clear channel. The only way of preventing a sniffer attack is by using tools that encrypt your communications, such as the secure shell (SSH), which was introduced in Chapters 4, "User Applications," and 17, "Information Servers," and is covered in depth in Chapter 23, "Encryption."

Password Cracking

Many users use easily guessed words as passwords. They often use their name, birthday, social security number, or the name of a favorite pet or movie. All these are subject to brute-force password-cracking attacks. To carry out one of these attacks, the cracker first gets a copy of the system's password file (this is easy if, for example, an anonymous FTP server isn't set up correctly, or if the cracker has access to another account on the same server). After the cracker gains possession of the password file, he or she feeds it to a program that tries hundreds of passwords per second. Because the algorithm that encrypts the password is publicly known, the program can try well-known words, encrypt them, and see whether they match what is found in the password file. Crackers can gain access to hundreds of accounts in one sweep.

There are several things you should do to prevent this kind of attack. The first is to use a utility that validates your users' passwords against a dictionary, or to use one of the cracker tools available on the Internet to try and crack your password file yourself. Users should also be forced to change their passwords periodically. Another important thing is to enable shadow-password support. In Debian, this is done during the installation (see Appendix A, "Installing Debian Linux." In standard UNIX installations (without shadow passwords), the encrypted password is kept in the `/etc/passwd` file, which many applications need to access simply to convert from user IDs to usernames. When you enable shadow passwords, the encrypted passwords are stored in `/etc/shadow`, a file that only `root` may read.

One common mistake is made when configuring an anonymous FTP server. Most FTP servers do a `chroot` call when an anonymous user logs in (thereby changing their "root" directory to a subdirectory in the filesystem, thus not allowing the user access to any files outside this new "root"). The problem is that, after the server makes the `chroot` call, it doesn't have access to the rest of the filesystem, so any files that are needed by the FTP server have to be copied to the protected filesystem. Many systems administrators simply copy the `/etc/passwd` file directly into the `chroot` directory, making it available to anyone who accesses the FTP server. You should create a fake `/etc/passwd` file for your FTP server, with all passwords removed (and perhaps even most user IDs).

Spoofing

In a *spoofing* attack, the attacker fabricates packets with fake source addresses, fooling the target host into believing that they come from another, trusted host. You must never use `rlogin` together with `.rhosts` or `/etc/hosts.equiv` to allow logging onto a host without a password; a cracker may fabricate fake `rlogin` packets that pretend to come from your trusted host and wreak havoc in your host. You must never trust the IP addresses of connections received through the Internet.

A spoofing attack is usually blind, unless the attacking host is in the same subnet as the target host or in a subnet between the target host and the trusted host, and the attacker is using a sniffer. This is because reply packets will be sent to the trusted host's IP address instead of the attacker's IP address. An attacker may combine *source-routing* with a spoofing attack. With source-routing, a packet includes in its header the list of hosts that a packet must go through to return to the source host. When one such packet reaches an unprotected host, the host will send its replies through the path that the packet specifies, instead of its default path, allowing the hacker to see the effect of his or her attack. To prevent against this, the Linux kernel has a configuration option in the "Networking options" section which, when activated, makes it drop all source-routed packets. You should always enable it.

Another use for spoofing is used by crackers to hide their tracks. For example, a cracker may use a tool such as `nmap` (see Chapter 21) to scan your network for vulnerabilities he or she can exploit. However, the cracker sends his or her scanning packets together with a bunch of spoofed packets that apparently come from all over the Internet. In this case, it is usually impossible to detect which are the real attack packets and which are just decoys, because the decoy packets seem to be just as real as the real packets.

The Man-in-the-Middle Attack

A *man-in-the-middle* attack occurs when an attacker intercepts communications going both ways and alters them. Thus, the client thinks it's talking to the server, and the server thinks it's talking to the client; however, both are actually talking to the attacker (see Figure 20.6).

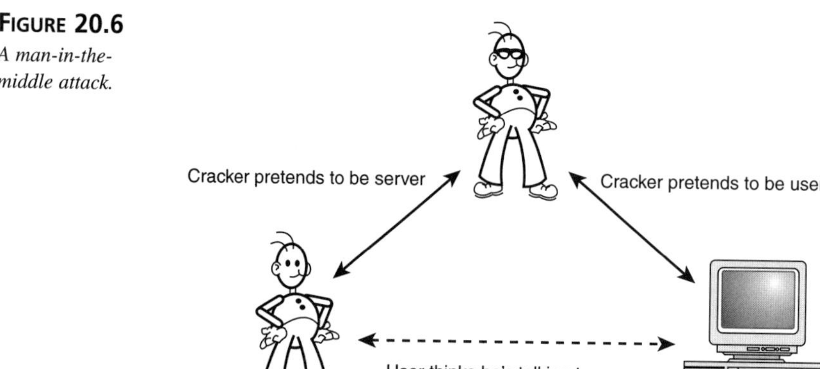
Cracker pretends to be server
Cracker pretends to be user
User thinks he's talking to server

FIGURE 20.6
A man-in-the-middle attack.

One target of man-in-the-middle attacks are Web commerce servers. The cracker intercepts the packets that travel between the client and the server. The cracker might then, for example, use the client's credit card numbers to commit fraud or use a *replay attack* so that the server thinks the client made several transactions. Imagine this happening when a customer is using a financial institution's Web site to make electronic payments!

End-to-end encryption with private/public key pairs can be used to help prevent this. Because data encrypted with the public key can be decrypted only with the private key, and vice versa, a private/public key pair can be used to "sign" information. Each party computes a checksum of the data and encrypts it with its private key, so the other party can decrypt it with the corresponding public key and see whether the checksum matches.

Note

Encryption is not enough to prevent a replay attack. The encrypted message must also contain a timestamp and a sequence number (which must also be encrypted) to detect replayed messages. Remember that a cracker doesn't need to understand the contents of a message in order to be able to send it again.

Hostile Code: Trojan Horses, Viruses, and Worms

A *Trojan horse* is a program that purports to do something, and when run, does something else. For example, a cracker might compromise an FTP site and replace a program he or she finds there (let's say it's a utility to detect intruders) with another that, apart from compressing files, grabs the host's `/etc/passwd` file and emails it to the cracker. Also, if it is run as `root`, it will install a back door that allows the cracker to enter the host at will (this scenario has actually happened). So, a trusting sysadmin downloads the utility, thinking it's a new version, and runs it to test it, giving the cracker complete access to his or her host.

A *virus,* by contrast, is a program that attaches itself to other programs and is executed when they are executed. It may be harmless, with its only function being to replicate itself, or it may be programmed to do harm when a condition is met (such as formatting a hard drive when the system clock reaches a particular date).

The last type of possibly harmful code is a worm. A *worm* works by replicating itself from one host to another through the network, without attaching itself to another program. It may, for example, exploit vulnerabilities in mail software (such as running as `root`) to replicate itself to other hosts, or read a user's email address book and send itself to every address it finds in it.

There are several things that you can do to defend yourself against all these kinds of hostile code.

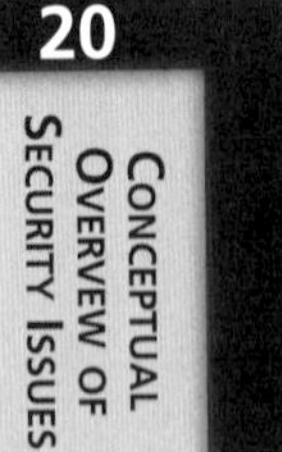

1. N*ever* run anything as `root` unless you absolutely have to. That way, if the program does any harm, it will be restricted to those pieces of the host that a normal user can access.
2. Never run untrusted code or code whose origin you aren't absolutely sure of on any production host. You may build a special "sacrificial lamb" host to do testing.

3. Whenever you download a program from the Internet, always check that its MD5 or PGP signature corresponds to that provided from the author. If possible, don't download the signatures from the same host you downloaded the program from, or download the program and the signature from two or more hosts and compare them. You can never be too careful!

Exploits and Script Kiddies

Many crackers disseminate their knowledge in the form of prepackaged programs called *exploits*. These programs take advantage of exploit-specific vulnerabilities. For example, suppose a bug has been detected in a particular version of an IMAP server that executes some code as `root` when a particular sequence of invalid commands is given to it. A cracker may write a program that does precisely that and publish it in sites such as `http://www.hackers.com` or `http://www.rootshell.org`. Other crackers may download the exploit and use it without even knowing how it works or what vulnerability it exploits. As mentioned before, these pseudocrackers are sometimes known as *script kiddies*, because they don't know what is actually going on and they limit themselves to running premade scripts.

The only way of defending against exploits is to keep abreast of the latest security bugs published in security lists such as Bugtraq, the CERT Advisories, or the SANS institute's newsletters (see Appendix B). You may also monitor sites such as `http://www.rootshell.org` for exploits that may affect your installed software.

From online attacks, we'll move into discussing monitoring and intrusion detection.

Monitoring and Intrusion Detection

So, you protect your site. You monitor all security advisories and sites. You have what you think is a airtight firewall. Your users have been educated. Now you can rest, right?

Well, you can rest if you're keen on losing your information and/or your job as security administrator. The fact is, security is a race between crackers and security administrators. All software has bugs, and all plans have weak spots. So, you should always plan for the worst and think what you will do when (not if) a cracker enters your vital systems. As the saying goes, "Hope for the best, plan for the worst."

What Is Anomalous Behavior?

When the doctor takes your temperature, he or she wants to check whether you have a fever. But, how does the doctor know whether you do have a fever? By comparing your temperature with the standard body temperature. However, the "normal" temperature can vary up to 2 degrees Celsius or more between individuals. So it is best for the doctor to know what *your* normal temperature is before checking for a fever.

The same thing happens in information security. You should monitor your systems for anomalous behavior. But, what exactly is anomalous behavior? It really depends on your environment. For example, a particular user logging in in the middle of the night might be anomalous in one organization and completely normal in another. A nonexistent log file might be normal—or might not. And so on. The only way of knowing what is normal and what is not is to monitor your systems *before* something abnormal happens. You should set up your automated monitoring systems and alarms before a cracker comes in, or you might never detect the intrusion.

What to Monitor

What should you monitor? Again, it depends on your particular environment. However, here are a few guidelines:

- You should monitor all logfiles in your system. After all, that's what they are for! This includes everything in `/var/log`, every file mentioned in `/etc/syslog.conf` (see Chapter 13, "System Logs and Accounting"), and any other log files generated by your server programs (such as database, Web, or email servers).
- On your firewall, you should enable logging of all packets that don't pass the accept rules (see Chapter 22). Then you might detect an intrusion attempt before it actually happens.
- You should periodically run the `tripwire` program to check the integrity of your system files. tripwire
- You should also turn on process and user accounting, and monitor the accounting files (see Chapter 13).
- Anything else you can think of! It might include periodically running a program against a server to see who is logged on to a particular service, or executing some utility and checking its output. Be creative!

You must remember, for security, the purpose of monitoring is to detect when anomalous use happens. Anything you think of that helps that end is valid.

Automated Monitoring

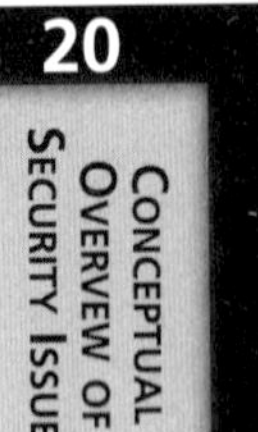

Monitoring your system by hand can be boring and error-prone. Sifting through line after line of very similar data, with perhaps one line in ten thousand being interesting can quickly turn into drudgery. Sometimes it can feel like looking for a needle in a haystack the size of the Empire State Building.

So, what can you do to ease the job? If you were looking for the proverbial needle, you might grab hold of an extremely powerful magnet to pull the needle out. In log file analysis, your magnet is a tool that can run through a log file and find patterns. Listing 20.1 shows a sample Perl script that analyzes the `/var/log/messages` file and detects some errors that might occur in it. It assumes that there's a program called `/usr/local/bin/call_pager`, which takes a pager number and a message and sends the message to an alphanumeric pager.

LISTING 20.1 A Simple Log File Analyzer Using Perl

```
#!/usr/bin/perl
$LOGFILE="/var/log/messages";
$ADMIN_PAGER="5544332";
$ADMIN_EMAIL="sysadmin";
$FILE_CMD="tail -f";
$PAGER_CMD="/usr/local/bin/call_pager";
$MAIL_CMD="/bin/mail -s 'logwatcher report' $ADMIN_EMAIL";

open LOG, "$FILE_CMD $LOGFILE |";
while (<LOG>) {
   if (/INVALID|REPEATED|INCOMPLETE/) {email ($_)};
   if (/PANIC|HALT|syslogd.*: restart/) {system ($PAGER_CMD, $ADMIN_PAGER, $_)};
}

sub email {
    open MAIL, "| $MAIL_CMD";
    print MAIL join (" ", @_);
    close MAIL
}
```

As you can see, the script can be easily extended depending on your needs. It takes advantage of regular expressions (covered in Chapter 9, "Regular Expressions") to match patterns that may occur in the log file. Other tools that may help in log file analysis are covered in Chapter 15, "Advanced System Administration." You will also find more tools to monitor your systems in Chapter 21.

Summary

This chapter laid the groundwork for the rest of the security chapters. We have covered a lot of ground in a small number of pages, to give you a quick snapshot of basic security.

The first thing you must do before starting to secure and monitor your site is create a security policy and make sure your users know and understand it. The security policy must state what is allowed and what is not, who is allowed to do what and who is not, as well as guidelines for things such as passwords. The security policy will be your master plan for implementing security in your site.

There are several aspects to information security: authentication, authorization, encryption, detection, and recovery. You must take each of these into account when drafting your security policy. It is important to note which methods are acceptable for each of thcsc arcas.

Security measures can be divided in two complementary categories depending on their scope: Host-based measures protect a particular host, and perimeter-based measures protect a group of hosts, which can be a particular LAN or a whole intranet. Many sites concern themselves with creating airtight firewalls (which secure the perimeter) and don't complement them with host-based schemes, such as encrypted communications channels and password-changing policies. These sites are extremely insecure, because when a cracker gains access to a single host within the network, the rest of the hosts are accessible to him or her.

There are many kinds of attacks that can be carried on upon information systems. They can be divided into electronic and meatspace attacks. Many sites take extensive measures to protect against electronic attacks and then leave their doors wide open to meatspace attacks.

The first step in detecting an attack is monitoring your hosts. It is extremely important to start monitoring before any attacks occur, so you can see what is normal and what is not. There are many tools to aid you in monitoring and protecting your site; these are covered in the next chapter.

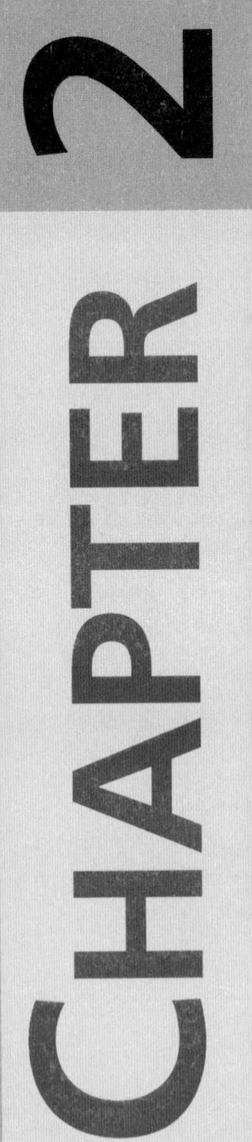

Principles of Security

by Mario Camou

In This Chapter

One of the problems with using a power network-oriented operating system such as Linux, or indeed any UNIX-like system, is security. The capability for you, a legitimate user or administrator, to perform nearly any task you want from a remote computer means that, potentially, so can someone else pretending to be you. Before the advent of the Internet, security was not such a big deal; you could generally only be attacked by someone with access to the physical machine or the local network that machine was on or, at worst, a dial-in line configured to accept connections. The growth of the Internet has made it much easier to reach many computer systems without needing any prior contact with that system or the organization that operates it.

Basically, before the Internet, an attacker first had to gain physical or dial-up access to the computer or network he wanted to attack. Running a secure installation, if you trusted all your legitimate users, was as simple as locking the door to your office at night and not configuring your computers to answer the phone for you. For computers on the Internet, however, the task is much harder.

Somehow, the computer must reliably separate legitimate users from attackers and allow the legitimate users access to the services they are supposed to have access to while denying those same services to the attackers. The computer also needs to deal with attacks aimed not at gaining access to a service, but at merely denying others access to the service (by consuming resources).

There is no denying that providing system security can be a difficult task. No security measures can protect you from all attacks, short of simply not owning or using a computer at all (which is rather counterproductive). However, you can make life very, very hard for most attackers—hard enough that the vast majority won't be successful and any who could perhaps succeed would need to spend quite a bit of effort doing so.

The idea behind securing a computer is to define a level of security that does not greatly hinder what you want to do with the computer, while requiring attackers to spend more time and effort trying to get past the security measures.

Most people using a Linux system for their home computing needs do not need to be overly concerned about security, although they should still follow the practices outlined in this chapter. If you are running a Linux system that is accessible over the Internet, particularly as a publicly accessible server, security should be one of your foremost concerns.

Common Security Concerns

Most security problems arise through ignorance or carelessness. Many of the Linux distributions in general use make the problem worse by defining defaults for their distributions that are less secure than they should be. This section covers the most common mistakes made by novice Linux users that can result in security holes.

The common goal of attacks on your system is gaining root (also know as superuser) access in order to execute code of some kind. Typically, this code installs some kind of easier backdoor for the attacker to use later.

Viruses, Trojan Horses, and Internet Worms

Linux is not vulnerable to viruses in the conventional sense because they generally require access to the system in order to spread effectively. Linux systems protect direct system access heavily, making life very hard for any virus that wants to spread that way. It is possible to do so, but the system security must be compromised first, and that is difficult enough to do for a live human looking for vulnerabilities.

Internet Worms

Internet worms are an interesting variant of the basic virus. These programs typically know about security flaws in one or two common programs (historically, the first such worm primarily used a hole in `sendmail` but knew several others) and know how to exploit that hole in order to replicate themselves on the remote system. Once the first system is cracked, the worm installs itself and looks for more systems to infect through virus-style propagation.

Trojan Horses

Trojans are another potential problem. A Trojan horse is similar to a virus in that, when run, it attempts to do something to your system, usually something annoying or destructive. However, Trojan horses generally cannot reproduce or spread effectively; they are dependent on the user running the program itself. Despite their inability to effectively spread outside of human control, they are extremely dangerous because their effect is usually to damage the system as much as possible.

Luckily, for any of these programs to do serious damage, they need access to the system—and that requires access to the superuser account, which normally requires breaking security. As long as you are careful what you do when you are `root` and maintain decent security, these malicious programs can't do any damage to your system.

Unfortunately, Trojan horses can still damage your own personal files, which (on a single-user system) is really all the important things anyway. You can protect yourself against this by being careful what you download. You might also want to create a special account just for testing downloaded software. The account should have access to nothing of any value.

It should be noted that the overall number of viruses, Trojan horses, and similar hostile programs targeted at Linux is tiny compared to the number of such programs targeted at unprotected operating systems (mostly versions of DOS and Windows or the Apple

Macintosh). This is partly due to popularity and partly due to the additional protection Linux offers.

The same sort of people who write viruses for unprotected operating systems tend to instead concentrate on finding and exploiting security holes in protected operating systems, such as Linux. This activity requires a higher degree of human knowledge and control, thus preventing the kind of widespread distribution that programs capable of self-replication receive.

This requirement has created a kind of attacker normally known as a "script kiddie." These attackers use prewritten scripts to exploit known security holes and then more prewritten scripts to install a range of additional backdoors on cracked systems. (The second half of the name comes from the typical age of such an attacker, usually in her early teens.) These attackers are generally not dangerous if you keep your system up-to-date but are often annoying far out of proportion to the danger they represent.

Running Unnecessary Services

Most Linux distributions install a large number of network services by default. They do this in order to ease the burden on the new sysadmin trying to install a server for his small workgroup, or his family, or whatever. In those environments, installing all these services is convenient and doesn't do any real harm. However, in an Internet environment, keeping all the network services is a dangerous practice; attackers can exploit a security hole in any of those services in order to gain access to the system.

The solution is simple: Find the services you are running and disable those you don't need. Any services you do need should be access-controlled so that only authorized users even know they are there, when that is possible. There are a couple different places to look for services. The first is your `/etc/inetd.conf` file, which is a configuration file for the `inetd` daemon.

The `inetd` daemon listens on the network sockets defined in its configuration file, and when a connection attempt is made, it starts the appropriate server program to handle the connection. This arrangement is most appropriate for small, not-often used daemons because it uses fewer resources than running the daemons all the time. Listing 21.1 offers a sample of the `inetd.conf`.

LISTING 21.1 Part of the `/etc/inetd.conf` File

```
# service_name sock_type proto flags user server_path args
#
#:INTERNAL: Internal services
#echo          stream  tcp     nowait  root    internal
#echo          dgram   udp     wait    root    internal
#chargen       stream  tcp     nowait  root    internal
#chargen       dgram   udp     wait    root    internal
```

```
discard         stream  tcp    nowait  root    internal
discard         dgram   udp    wait    root    internal
daytime         stream  tcp    nowait  root    internal
daytime         dgram   udp    wait    root    internal
time            stream  tcp    nowait  root    internal
time            dgram   udp    wait    root    internal

#:STANDARD: These are standard services.
ftp             stream  tcp    nowait  root    /usr/sbin/tcpd
➥ /usr/sbin/in.ftpd
telnet          stream  tcp    nowait  root    /usr/sbin/tcpd
➥ /usr/sbin/in.telnetd
```

The # character at the left indicates that a line is a comment; you should go through this file and comment out any lines for daemons you do not use. Don't delete the lines unless you know what you are doing because you might want to add the service later, especially if you run into problems after removing it.

Make sure you restart or signal `inetd` so that it can reread the configuration information.

Overuse of the Root Account

You should already know about the root account from previous chapters. It is the superuser account that performs system management functions and can override pretty much any of the security restrictions imposed on normal users. For obvious reasons, some things need to be done as the root. Just as obviously, the normal goal of an attacker is to compromise the root account and gain that unrestricted access to the system.

Once root access is gained, an attacker can do a great deal to cover his tracks, if he wants, or can basically destroy the system. Normally, this isn't a problem because the root account is just as well protected as other accounts (and in some ways, better, especially because an attentive administrator will carefully watch activity on the root account), but a determined attacker can still compromise it.

However, certain attacks can be a great deal easier if the root account is in active use for normal activities other than system administration. The attacks are easier partially because there is more active use of the account (and thus, there are more chances to compromise a password going over the network or similar things). They are also easier because there is the chance to trick the root user into running a compromised application and because the increased activity makes any suspicious activity stand out.

This isn't a narrowly defined security problem; those same risks occur with normal use of the superuser account. The idea is to minimize that use and restrict it to system administration tasks, to make spotting a compromised superuser account possible, and to reduce the chances of opening a vulnerability by mistake.

The "solution" is simple; don't use the superuser account for anything other than necessary system administration. Create and use normal user accounts, with normal access rights, for all normal computing tasks. In many cases, you can reduce the risks still further by careful use of file permissions (which can ensure that fewer tasks must be done as the root user) and use of other programs (such as `sudo`), which allow a single task to be performed as the superuser, but with some additional restrictions.

Note

Limited-root tools, such as `sudo`, provide temporary superuser powers from an ordinary account. They are used for two purposes: First, they can give an ordinary user access to some of the root functions, such as shutting down the system in a secure and limited way; second, they can be used by an administrator to avoid granting himself full root access for common tasks.

Sending Passwords in the Clear

Sending passwords securely is a common challenge when working with networks of any description. Most basic network protocols such as Telnet and FTP are not very concerned with security and will allow authentication by the use of passwords transmitted without any encryption. This becomes a problem when someone is in a position to listen to the packets being sent between the two computers. By doing that, they can determine the password that is exchanged and thus compromise that user's account.

The chances of this happening vary widely depending on the environment your computer is operating in. If you are running a home network, for example, you probably trust everyone else on the network, and everyone already has physical access to the computer anyway; security isn't really a concern. Larger networks, such as those in businesses or educational institutions, often present a more serious threat because you probably do not know or trust everyone on that network.

Using the Internet is a mixed bag. It is harder to "listen" to someone on the Internet because you must have access to a machine that is consistently "between" the two communicating computers with regard to the packets they are exchanging. This can be substantially difficult to arrange, but even so, sending packets over the Internet should not be considered secure.

You should assume that any service you do not know specifically uses encryption in fact does not.

Poorly Chosen Passwords

It is important to pay attention to security considerations when choosing passwords. Although it is difficult to guess a random user's password, a poorly chosen password can make it much easier. If you know the user whose password you are trying to find out, you can try a number of common passwords based on your knowledge of that user as an individual because the user is likely to try to choose something she can easily remember.

Examples of commonly used, poorly chosen passwords are

- Names of friends or family members
- Your own name or variations on your initials
- Important dates (birthdays and anniversaries)
- Words or phrases with some personal meaning
- Words that are in a dictionary

An ideal password is entirely random; the user takes the extra trouble to memorize it and destroys any location where it is written down.

Debian has a package named `pwgen` that can generate a password for you. You can use a command such as `pwgen -s 9` to generate a secure password for your use. Note that you should never write down a password in a location where others might potentially find it.

Password Cracking Programs

If an attacker can gain access to your system, even as a normal user, he might be able to get his hands on your `/etc/passwd` file. If you are using shadow passwords, this isn't a problem. If not, the attacker can in effect have access to your own passwords, but in a roundabout way. The passwords in that file are traditionally stored with a kind of weak, one-way encryption. The algorithm is generally standardized, and any application can read the encrypted password from the file, read the password supplied by the user, and run the user-supplied password through that same algorithm. If the result matches, access is granted, without the password being stored in plain text anywhere.

This system works well in practice, as long as you trust all the local users whom have access to that file. If an attacker has it, he can perform a brute-force attack on the password of any user in that file. This is similar to simply trying each possible password in sequence until you find one that works. It is time-consuming, but because the encryption is weak, a single person with a personal computer can eventually find the passwords. If she attempts this work over a network, it takes a great deal of time and effort and it leaves a trail in your logs. If she has your password file, it still takes time, but there is no indication of the attack in your log files; the first indication of the attack you have is the attacker logging in with the correct password.

Because the attacker has the correct password, this login does not show up as an unauthorized access. The only way to determine whether your system has been compromised in this way is to pinpoint a time when a user supposedly logged in when the actual user in question did not. This is obviously a nightmare for any number of users. Luckily, most attacks like this concentrate on the root account, which is commonly accessible to only a single person, or, at worst, a small group. By carefully watching your log files for activity from the root user that did not come from you, you can detect a root break-in.

Social Engineering

Social engineering refers to gaining entry into a system by the simple expedient of convincing someone to let you in. This can happen through subterfuge, persuasion (monetary or otherwise), blackmail, or similar extreme methods. It is one of the common methods employed by attackers trying to get into a specific system but does not work as well on random systems.

Social engineering is mostly a concern with large organizations that obviously have something valuable to protect. However, a number of cases have involved a prominent, nationwide ISP where users were asked for their passwords in email or instant message by someone claiming to be an administrator of the ISP. You should be aware of the possibility for this kind of attack, even if you never expect to face it. In a large organization where serious attacks are believed a possibility, it is worthwhile to take steps to guard against them.

Although not strictly considered social engineering, other similar techniques can allow attackers to gain access to specific systems they target. In the past, attackers have gained access through such prosaic means as digging through the trash cans of a targeted system. When talking about security, paranoia pays off.

As an individual user, you should simply be aware of the possibility that anyone asking for your password is not necessarily who he claims to be. Most ISPs and online services never actually need to know your password because they own and administer the systems anyway. Thus, it is unlikely that they would ask for it. If you initiate the contact, they might want to verify your identity, but you should first be sure about to whom you are talking.

"Open Relay" Mail Systems

Sometimes, an attacker doesn't even have to gain access to your system to cause trouble. If your email system is configured as an open relay, anyone can send an email to your system and have that forwarded to another destination. This feature is a great thing to have in a mailserver for your authorized users, but it becomes a security problem when you allow anyone to do the same. And it becomes a serious headache when a spammer finds your open relay and decides to send his latest batch of spam through it.

Until recently, many email systems (most notably `sendmail`, one of the most popular mail systems) were installed with the open-relay configuration as their default setting. This has changed somewhat, but it's still worth checking in any system you administer.

If you are running a system with a dial-up connection only, you don't have to worry too much about this; the transient nature of your connections and the dynamic IP status means that spammers will have a tough time finding your system to use. If you are running a system with a high-bandwidth Internet connection, the relay settings of your mail system should be one of the first things you check. There are several automated and semi-automated mechanisms for detecting open-relay systems on the Internet, and, once detected, such systems are almost inevitably being used by spammers. Once that happens, many, many mail servers automatically deny any further access from that mail server, even for legitimate mail.

Technically, an open relay is a mail server to which anyone can connect and use to send mail to any other system. A properly configured mail system allows anyone to connect and send mail to any local user but requires some kind of authorization before allowing someone to send mail to a remote system using the mail server as a relay. The exact nature of the authorization depends on the system in question.

Securing Email

Because SMTP (Simple Mail Transport Protocol) does not include an authentication mechanism for legitimate users, there is no standard solution for allowing access only to specific users. A number of solutions exist for different situations; the three most common follow:

- Do not allow access to SMTP from the network.
- Allow relaying from specific IP addresses; forbid by default.
- Allow relaying only after performing some authentication.

The first solution is most suited for standalone systems that should not be receiving mail directly anyway. The second is best for networks where all potential addresses for which relaying should be permitted are known. The last is best for situations where users might be using any number of different IP addresses to connect to the mail servers.

The Debian CD-ROM included with this book has several potential mail systems. Whichever one you install and use, you should make sure it is configured to deny mail relaying to anyone who is not an authorized user of your system. The exact procedure obviously depends on which mail system you are using.

Now that we've discussed some of the security risks you might face when setting up servers to use on the Internet, let's examine some things you can do to prevent problems.

Common Sense Precautions

The following section describes common precautions you can take to make your system more secure. None of them are particularly surprising or complicated techniques. Nor do they require a lot of effort to implement. Think of them as a simple checklist that will help keep you from leaving yourself wide open, but also, remember that they are not sufficient to protect you from a determined attacker. Many of these techniques are specifically intended to counter the security problems mentioned in the prior section.

Choosing Passwords Carefully

Making an effort to choose a difficult-to-guess password can pay off. Obviously, you shouldn't use anything closely related to you and publicly known (such as names of your family or friends, birthdays, and so on). Your password should be long enough to make it difficult to guess at random—at least eight characters long. By default, only the first 8 characters are significant; the remaining ones will be ignored. Ideally, it should include more than one character that is not a letter (numbers, punctuation, dollar signs; anything that you can type but isn't in the alphabet). And it should not be a word found in the dictionary because the number of possible English words is small compared to the number of possible random combinations of letters.

A number of tools can help point out poorly chosen passwords, and others can help you select good ones. Generally, the best choice of password is a random one that is then checked against a dictionary to eliminate real words from use. If you are supporting a number of users with passwords, you can be sure that some of them *will* choose poor passwords; you might want to simply assign random passwords and not allow the users to change them (and then change them yourself on a regular basis). This does tend to annoy the users, however, so you should carefully weigh the kind of security threat you are dealing with.

Using shadow passwords can get around some of the security problems related to the `/etc/passwd` file. This operates by moving the passwords out of the `/etc/passwd` file and into the file `/etc/shadow`, which is only readable by the root user. Thus, applications needing to read the `passwd` file can, but the passwords themselves are protected.

Security tools available for choosing secure passwords include

- John the Ripper (`http://www.false.com/security/john/`)
- Crack (`http://www.users.dircon.co.uk/~crypto/`)

Watching Your Logs

Most attacks leave a trail in your system's log files. Most daemons should leave the time, date, and username of any connections being attempted in their own or the system log

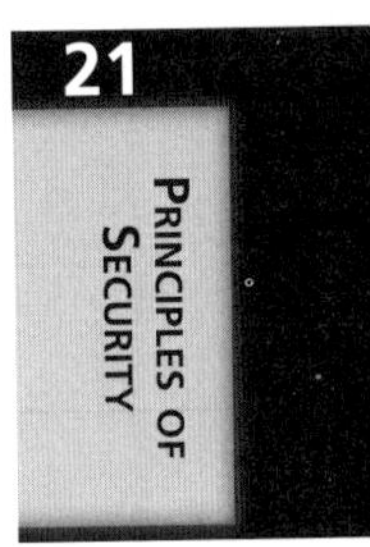

files, particularly for failed connection attempts. If you are the only user on your system, this trail can be particularly useful because you know any connection attempts you did not yourself make are from an attacker.

On Linux, logging is usually handled by the `syslog` facility (for normal system logging) and a kernel logging daemon (`sysklogd`). Both daemons simply accept messages from any program wanting to log information, often with additional details (such as the daemon generating the message, the priority of the log message, and so on). Some servers handle their own logging, however.

You should read your log files regularly; you don't need to go through them in depth, but just glance through and see whether anything unusual jumps out at you. Become familiar with what the log files usually look like so you can spot unusual situations easily. These could be repeated login failures, connections from a strange machine, or a variety of other possibilities.

If you are securing multiple machines, it can be helpful to use `syslog` to redirect log messages from all the machines to a single, central machine. This setup makes it easier to check for anomalies, but, more importantly, it ensures that if an attack succeeds, the attacker will need to break into two machines to cover his tracks.

You should pay close attention to the following log files:

- `/var/log/messages`
- `/var/log/auth.log`

These log files are the ones most likely to contain information about attempted attacks. The first is a catch-all category, covering general information that doesn't fit elsewhere. The latter contains authentication attempts, both successful and failed. You should also look at the other files in the `/var/log` directory because some of them will also be of interest, depending on the daemons you are running.

If the existing logs aren't generating enough information for you, you should look into `auditd` (available from `ftp://ftp.hert.org/pub/linux/auditd`). This program will allow you to record many of the actions that pass through the kernel, such as opening files or network connections. You can generate a lot of information using this tool.

Portscanning

Portscanning is a common method of probing a system, sometimes used as a preliminary to an attack, but also commonly used by network-savvy users with no ill intent. Using one or more ports, connections are attempted on the system to be scanned, and the response to the connection request is recorded. Portscanning a single port on a system, or even multiple ports on the same system, can be considered similar to knocking on a stranger's door to see whether they are home—perhaps a little intrusive, but not really offensive. However, if you run multiple machines and they are all being portscanned, or if your machine has had all of its ports checked (rather than just the common ones, such as HTTP and FTP), it is a pretty good indication of less than pleasant intent.

It is important to note that portscanning is not actually an attack. It can be used to find vulnerable points for later use in an attack, but, by itself, the technique is not a big deal. Nearly all systems on the Internet with a static IP are regularly portscanned by the curious, and mostly nothing comes of it.

Being Careful Who Gets Access

Attacks are generally much easier from the inside, that is, with access to the system you are attacking as a legitimate user. Remember also that whenever you give access to someone, you are also giving it to anyone he chooses to share it with (which is more common than you might think), and that the first level of security on your system is only as good as the security of your users. If your users commit any of the mistakes described earlier, they compromise their accounts on your system, and that can make the precautions you take against remote attackers meaningless.

Filesystem Security

Users typically should have write access to their home directories and the `/tmp` directory, but nothing else. Ideally, the `/home` directory (containing all the user's home directories) and the `/tmp` directory should both be on separate partitions, preventing a user from filling up important partitions (like `/`) by continually dumping data into those directories they can write to. This way, they can annoy other users, but the system shouldn't be bothered.

Useful Utilities for Security

You can use the `chown`, `chgrp`, `chattr`, and `chmod` utilities to manipulate file access rights. Each file has a number of different attributes and is owned by a user and a group. The first two utilities are used to change the user and group owner of a file:

```
# chown username filename
# chgrp groupname filename
```

You cannot change the user or group of a file to a user or group that you are not a part of, unless you are root.

The `chmod` utility modifies the access rights to a specific file for the (u)ser, (g)roup, and (o)ther (anyone). The possible rights are (r)ead, (w)rite, and e(x)ecute. Reading and writing are obvious; execute permissions have different meanings depending on context. For directories, "execute" means you can read the contents of a directory. For files, "execute" means you can run the file as a program. You are able to access files that are owned by you or by a group that you are a member of or that allow the access you need to

everyone. You will, of course, need the right permissions in order to change permissions with `chmod`:

```
# chmod ug+rwx filename
```

This command adds read, write, and execute permissions to *filename* for the user and group associated with the file.

The following command prevents anyone who is not the user or group owner of the file from reading, writing, or executing the file:

```
# chmod o-rwx filename
```

The `chattr` command allows you to change some of the attributes associated with the file. These are sometimes filesystem dependent. Useful attributes for the `ext2` filesystem (the standard Linux filesystem) include `setuid`, `setgid`, `immutable`, and `append-only`.

The `setuid` and `setgid` are intended for applications; when an application with those attributes is executed, the user and group IDs are changed to those of the file's owners. This is most often used with root, to give root permissions to a normal user when a specific task requires it; however, this move is not very secure without an additional layer such as `sudo`. `setuid-root` applications are one of the most common security holes.

The immutable bit indicates that a file should not be changeable at all, even by the owners. The owner must first remove the immutable bit, make the changes, and then reset the bit. Although this can be a pain when making legitimate changes, it makes life harder on attackers trying to break into the system; they might not have the access to remove the immutable bit before making changes.

The `append-only` flag is useful for log files. Any changes other than appending to the file will fail. This prevents attackers from covering their tracks in the logs without, again, getting full root access and removing the attribute first. Remember to remove the bit yourself if you have anything that needs to access the files, such as a log-maintenance utility.

You should also look at the section on disk quotas.

Don't Execute Untrusted Binaries as Root

Because the point of getting root access is to be able to perform tasks without the security restrictions of a regular user, but the root user itself is usually watched closely, a common type of attack seeks to "trick" the legitimate sysadmin into running an application that has been modified to suit the purposes of the attacker. Often, those purposes including inserting a known security hole into the system for later use.

Unless you are a programmer with a lot of free time on your hands, the best you can do to prevent this is to keep an eye on the applications you have installed and use as root (normally, this is done with TripWire or similar tools, which are discussed later) and also limit the PATH environment variable for the root user to the absolute minimum necessary.

The usual procedure for an attack of this type is to create an application, usually by modifying a common application already on the system, to perform the task you want. The attacker then inserts this binary into the system in a place where he hopes it will take precedence over the existing binary (or perhaps even replace the original binary entirely). Eventually, someone will run the program as root, at which point the system is compromised.

To guard against this, your best bet is to ensure that your root user has a very limited PATH. The especially paranoid insist that the root user should have no PATH at all (that is, that the root user must enter the full path manually for each command, as in `/bin/rm`). Most are content with keeping the basic system directories (`/bin`, `/sbin`, and `/usr/sbin`) in the PATH and leaving out anything localized.

One of the other things to be aware of is the behavior of the system when using `su` to another user account. Doing this does not give up root access rights! This often has the effect of appending the user's path to the root path as the user's initialization scripts are processed. All such a user has to do is create a binary directory with some corrupted binaries and then lure the system administrator to `su` to them under some pretense and run the affected command.

Securing from Remote Access

Securing a system from remote attackers is easy compared to the alternatives, but it can still be troublesome if you want to actually do anything with your machine. Mainly, you need to worry about the daemons you are running and, of course, manage not to do anything to make yourself vulnerable in other ways.

Network Daemons

When attackers do not have legitimate access to log in to a machine, or physical access to the machine, they need to convince something already running on the targeted machine to do what they want. In most cases, this is a network daemon, whose job is to listen for connections from the network and provide some service to anyone who connects. Some of the services require authentication, but others don't; typically, if the daemon functions properly, it is reasonably secure.

Sometimes, however, the daemon does not function properly. These situations are bugs, usually fixed as soon as they are found, but finding them is not easy. In fact, one of the arguments for open-source software is that the greater number of eyes examining the code, the more likely it is that bugs are spotted before they are found by an attacker and exploited. Obviously, an attacker who finds an exploit in a particular daemon has no incentive to report it!

In cases where a bug allows a remote user access, the remote user is typically able to perform any task that the daemon itself could; the most common attack simply opens a shell over the network link. If your daemon was running as the root user, which many do, that's all she wrote; your system is compromised. The good news is that many daemons do not need to run as the root user, and even for those that do, updates are usually released promptly when security holes are found.

The first thing to do, regarding network daemon security, is to regularly track the available updates and security fixes. The package manager on Debian Linux will let you do this for Debian packages easily. Any daemons that you installed without using the Debian package system need to be tracked and updated manually. The easiest way for an attacker to compromise your system is to find an old daemon you haven't updated and use a well-publicized attack on that daemon.

To guard against this, keep the daemons you need updated, and don't run daemons you don't need. You should sort through your startup scripts and figure out what each of the daemons does and whether you need them; if you don't, remove the daemon.

> **Note**
>
> Some daemons are secure in and of themselves but use access control based entirely on the IP address and hostname of the machine making the connection. This itself is not secure because that machine may itself have been compromised first, or the attacker might be able to pretend to be from an IP address or hostname that he is not really from.
>
> Services such as `rexec` and `rsh` use host-based authentication and thus are not trustworthy. Better alternatives are available.

tcp_wrappers

Once you have eliminated unnecessary daemons from your startup scripts and from `inetd`, you might want to further restrict access to the daemons you do use. One of the usual means of accomplishing this is the use of `tcp_wrappers`, a software package that provides simple access control for `inetd`-based services. Debian comes with `tcp_wrappers` installed and configured by default. For more information, refer to Chapter 17, "Information Servers."

When `inetd` receives a connection request, it finds the proper line in its configuration file and starts the program it was told to start, with the arguments it was told to use. On a system using `tcp_wrappers`, this is `/usr/sbin/tcpd`, with the actual daemon as the first argument following. The `/usr/sbin/tcpd` command checks the access rules for the connection, based on its own configuration files, and either accepts the connection and starts the daemon or closes the connection immediately.

The relevant configuration files are `/etc/hosts.allow` and `/etc/hosts.deny`. They are read each time a new connection is received, starting with `hosts.allow` for any specific allow rules and then `hosts.deny` for any specific deny rules. The default is to allow access, and entries in `/etc/hosts.allow` override entries in `/etc/hosts.deny`.

If you are extremely concerned about security, you should add the rule `ALL: 0.0.0.0/0.0.0.0` to your `/etc/hosts.deny` and then go through `/etc/hosts.allow`, adding each service you need with rules as specific as possible. For example, if only people on your local network should connect to your POP3 daemon, you would add the following rule to `/etc/hosts.allow`:

```
pop3: 192.168.1.0
```

This allows users from the `192.168.1.0` network to connect to the POP3 daemon, even if a global rule in `/etc/hosts.deny` denies access.

It should be noted that this security issue has nothing to do with the access control used by daemons not run from `inetd`! If a daemon is started from a script, and not by `inetd`, the controls in `hosts.allow` and `hosts.deny` are not effective unless the daemon reads those rules itself.

Terminals and the Root Account

Because of the vital nature of the root account, the root user is typically only allowed to log in from one of the local virtual terminals. Any attempt to log in from a terminal where root is not permitted to log in results in access being denied, even if the user has the correct password. This behavior is normally controlled from the `/etc/securetty` file, which contains a list of terminals considered secure enough for root logins.

Another way to prevent security problems is to address issues within your own organization. When combined with the steps outlined above, this can go a long way to a common-sense approach to securing your systems.

Securing from a Local Network

The most significant threat on a local network is someone using the network itself as part of the attack—listening to all traffic on the network, trying to identify the traffic that contains a user's password or other important information, and then using that for whatever presumably nefarious purpose. For general network security notes, see "Securing from Remote Access" earlier in this chapter.

You can defeat this attack by avoiding sending your passwords over the network or using encryption if you must do so. For more information on security, refer to Chapter 20, "Conceptual Overview of Security Issues."

A number of other security problems arise on untrusted local networks. Some of the common ones are described in the following sections.

Network File System

The NFS authentication method is particularly weak; it simply checks the user ID number against those on your own system. If your attacker knows the user ID of the user he wants to attack, NFS will allow him to read that user's files as if he were that user, if configured to do so. This is a problem because the NFS security mechanism is based on host security, not user security; if a given host is allowed to use NFS, then all users on that host can do the same, and it also assumes that the user IDs are the same across the systems. Both of those assumptions are wrong for an untrusted local network.

Clearly, NFS is not suitable for use in environments where the local network is not trusted. It can be useful in some situations; a cluster of workstations using disk space from a central server with their own local network, centrally administered, will get a lot of benefit from NFS. But using NFS where you don't trust the local network is asking for trouble.

Lack of Encryption

NFS has two major problems in that situation. First, it transmits the data entirely in the clear; no attempt at encryption is made. Assuming someone is willing to do the work to decode the NFS packet format, she can get access to any of the data you have sent via NFS.

Weak Authentication

NFS's second problem is with weak authentication. Because NFS uses host-based authentication, if you allow a host to mount a drive from your system, you can basically conclude that anyone on that host can read any file on that drive. If you don't want the file to be read, don't keep it on the NFS-exported partition. This makes NFS singularly unsuitable for such interesting tasks as sharing users' home directories (unless you can map users to host in a one-to-one fashion reliably), but it works fine for sharing things that are world-readable anyway. The contents of your `/usr` directory, for example, could be exported and save you disk space on each of the client machines because they would not need a `/usr` directory tree of their own.

Spoofing

Finally, there is a third potential security hole in NFS. Some attackers are able to modify the packets they send out in order to disguise their origin and make the attack harder to trace back to them (called *host spoofing*). Unfortunately, this can also have the effect of allowing the attacker to pretend to be a host you allow NFS shares to and gain access this way.

Besides securing your network from local attackers, you also need to secure your computer from users on it. In the next section, you'll get some pointers on doing just that.

Securing from Local Users

Maintaining a secure system when your local users are not trusted can be difficult. An authorized user of your system will have a lot more access than a random attacker off the Internet; he will know more about your system, have access to your system's resources, and might even be able to use those resources to help him in the attack itself. After all, if you don't trust him, why provide him access as a user at all?

Of course, the most common answer involves some form of monetary compensation for the service. In that case, you should ask yourself what the user is really paying for; does she want access to a UNIX-style shell on the Internet or just a place to store her email and put up Web pages? For the latter, she doesn't need to be a local user at all; simply arrange for your network daemons to use a database of user information other than your system's `/etc/passwd` file. Such a setup will neatly sidestep the whole problem.

Unfortunately in many cases, allowing the user to log in to the system via a shell is a requirement. The good news is that, even as an authorized user, an attacker must be skilled and determined to cause trouble in order to do any serious damage. The file permissions used with UNIX filesystems will, if configured properly, prevent any normal (non-root) user from doing serious harm. The user typically does not have access to server-type applications or similar important files.

As with most other types of attacks, the normal focus is the attempt to gain access to the superuser account. Once the attacker gains root access, he is unaffected by the system security restrictions and can do, basically, whatever he wants. If the attacker is less concerned about doing something useful and more concerned with simply doing as much damage as possible, he might also opt for a denial-of-service attack from inside the system. This is harder to defend against but usually means you will be able to spot the culprit easily and disable his account.

Login Spoofing

Login spoofing is a rather sneaky tactic intended to get passwords from unsuspecting users. The attacker obtains a program that has the exact appearance of the login prompt for the system she is attacking. This program is designed to mimic the login prompt perfectly, luring users to type their usernames and passwords as they would normally to log in. The program records the username and password somewhere and then either denies access with an error message or perhaps even logs on the user normally.

All this attack requires is a valid user account. Even a guest account with very few access rights will do, as long as the user can install and run his fake login program. Because Linux typically uses text-based logins, this is not a particularly difficult program to write. Worse, this attack is essentially invisible if the fake login program attempts to log the user in normally or simply reports a failure message and then exits to the system's login program. An attacker using this technique doesn't leave a trail of failed access attempts.

Luckily, you can usually determine which user was running the faked login program once you know that such a program has been in use. Telltale symptoms of this problem can include a long-running process on the console with a particular user's name, and users complaining of failed logins. Also fortunately, the user accounts compromised by this method are typically random and thus are usually just *users*, not administrators. If this sort of attack is a likely risk, administrators should be especially careful about where and how they log in as the superuser.

The canonical response to this attack is the use of a System Attention Key, which is a key sequence (typically Ctrl+Alt+Del) that is always intercepted by the operating system. After you press that key sequence, the OS guarantees that you are given a valid login prompt and does not allow applications to override it. To get around this, an attacker must break the system security anyway, and, if he can do that, he hardly needs to collect passwords from random users.

Another class of security problems is the one that doesn't seek to directly subvert your security mechanisms, but instead to cause your servers to crash or become otherwise unusable. This is discussed in the next section.

Securing from Denial-of-Service Attacks

A denial-of-service attack is not like most attacks on your system. The attacker in such an attack does not particularly care about gaining control of your system or having his attack go unnoticed. The goal of a denial-of-service attack is to deny your system the ability and resources to provide services to legitimate users, instead of tricking the system into thinking the attacker is a legitimate user. Because the goals of a denial-of-service attack are more modest, the task is somewhat easier to accomplish and in many cases much harder to defend against.

Attacks from Local Users

Denial-of-service attacks from local users generally consist of using various holes in the system to consume resources. It is possible to defend against them somewhat, but as authorized users, they have the right to use some of your system's resources; the tricky part is determining how much and what to do when they cross that line. It should be noted that "local users" in this section refers to people with valid accounts on the Linux system, regardless of their physical location. Physical security is discussed later in this chapter.

The obvious resources for an attacker to consume are CPU time, memory, and disk space. The latter is easy enough to deal with; Linux allows you to define per-user quotas, limiting how much space each user can use at a time. CPU time is much harder to deal with because the user theoretically has the right to consume some amount of CPU, and it's hard to fix a limit on how much is too much. Memory is easily restricted.

Preventing denial-of-service attacks from local users requires a combination of tactics, which are illustrated in the following sections.

User Limits

User limits are controls implemented by the shell a user uses, restricting what processes the shell spawns are able to do. The capabilities vary according to which shell is in use, so read the man pages for the shells available to your system when configuring this. The command is usually a shell-internal one named `limit` or `ulimit`.

Disk Quotas

Disk quotas limit the amount of space on the filesystem a user can consume. They are generally not necessary for single-user systems or systems where all the users are trusted, although in the latter case, disk quotas might make things a lot easier to administer. The idea behind disk quotas is simple: The kernel keeps track of how much space the user's files are taking up and prevents them from exceeding a specified limit.

Your kernel must be compiled for filesystem quotas, and you need quota-manipulation utilities installed.

Attacks from Remote Systems

Denial-of-service attacks from remote systems are similar in principle to attacks from local users, but much harder to deal with. The resources that the attacker attempts to consume are different; without direct access to memory, disk, or CPU resources, the attacker concentrates on consuming the resources he has access to (primarily incoming bandwidth, in most cases) and indirectly attempting to consume more vital resources. Although a denial-of-service attack from a remote system won't usually crash your computer, the difference is academic from the point of view of the network. A successful attack prevents your system from providing useful services to the network and thus is just as bad as actually being down, aside from the need to repair things later.

Certain types of denial-of-service attacks operate at the network level rather than the individual daemon level. Read the networking section of the Linux kernel documentation for information on how to respond to these attacks. Unfortunately, there isn't all that much you can do; by nature, network-based denial-of-service attacks just send you enough data so that very little real data gets through. The ability to do this usually depends more on the bandwidth available to your system and to the attackers than on the configuration of your software.

Mailbombs

One of the most common denial-of-service attacks from a remote system is the mailbomb, which is popular due to its ability to target a specific person and the ease with which it can be carried out. The concept is simple: Send as much data as is electronically possible via the mail system. This serves primarily to annoy the intended recipient by filling her mailbox with worthless data, possibly overflowing it (and thus preventing new mail from arriving), and making her spend a long time downloading the worthless email.

Secondary effects from this can cause problems at the system level. Depending on the amount of data involved, the mailbomb might fill up the mail queues on the targeted system, preventing anyone from sending or receiving mail until they are cleared out. Depending on the bandwidth available to the attacker, the network link might also be saturated as a side effect.

Typically, mail transport agents such as sendmail have settings that allow you to filter incoming and outgoing email based on size. The exact mechanisms depend on your mail transport program.

Dial-up users don't need to worry too much about this because there is little they can do anyway; any mailbombs sent to them are presumably received at the ISP's mail server, where they have little control over the measures taken. Check your mail retrieval program for options to limit the size of mail automatically downloaded, and you should be fine.

For additional reassurance, check the amount of free space available on your incoming mail partition (this is usually `/var/spool/mail`, with the partition usually being `/var` or just `/`). Unless you've been extremely conservative with space in your partitioning, you should have at least 10MB or 20MB of free space. Now, calculate how long that will take to download over a modem. Modern single-user systems can usually laugh hysterically at mailbomb attempts, aside from the effect on bandwidth (which is easy enough to deal with).

Users with faster connections to the Internet who run a mail server intended to receive mail directly might want to set up their mail transports with size or frequency-of-sending limits. From a practical perspective, however, mailbombs should not be first on your list of things to lose sleep over.

Securing from Physical Access

If an attacker has physical access to the machine you are trying to protect, it is extremely hard to prevent him from doing anything he wants. Nothing you do can stop someone with unlimited physical access to the machine from making use of the hardware for his own purposes. If you are exceptionally paranoid, you might be able to keep him from gaining access to your own data, but enforcing limited data access is nearly impossible; it's an all-or-nothing proposition.

Most of the time, the only people with real, physical access to a machine are authorized to use it; they are, in fact, the administrators. If this is true for you, there's nothing much to worry about. Simply lock the door to the server room when no one is there. If you need to make machines physically available for general users, however, things get a bit tricky.

If you can limit the physical access, you've made an important step. A number of security devices attempt to prevent users from either stealing machines outright or just opening them up. Install one on each machine, preferably one that activates an alarm if a breach is attempted.

Securing Bootup

Once you have denied your users physical control of the machine, your next step should be to prevent them booting anything other than your operating system of choice. The simplest way to manage this is to physically remove all the externally accessible drives. If you don't want to do this, your BIOS might provide features to help you: Set the BIOS to boot only from the hard drive, and then password-protect the BIOS itself. The user will need to guess the password to make the system boot from an external disk in that case.

After your BIOS figures out where to boot from, you need to arrange the boot process so that the user cannot make any changes. If you are booting from LILO, the only secure way to configure the system is to boot instantly, without offering the user a choice in the matter (set `delay=0` in `/etc/lilo.conf`). Otherwise, she will be able to pass options to the kernel when it boots, and all is lost. If your users need to select an OS to boot (such as for a dual-boot system), you need to use something other than LILO to be secure. Even if you can find a secure bootloader, you need to secure any operating system that can be loaded. (If one of those operating systems is Windows 95/98, don't bother; nothing you can do to that operating system will make it secure. If it's Windows NT, you at least have a chance.)

Once the OS boots, the problem reverts to a relatively normal situation.

Encrypted Filesystems

If you absolutely need to prevent certain data from falling into the wrong hands, put it on an encrypted partition that requires a password to mount, and ensure the partition is not mounted by default on system boot. Disable any swap space (because swap space contains the contents of RAM, and a determined attacker can read whatever fragments of data gets swapped out). Then, secure the computer from any network access and as much physical access as you can.

If you do this, the attacker will need to guess your password or steal your encryption key to access your protected data. Without the password and the key, all he can do is destroy it or, if extremely determined, try to brute-force the encryption.

It is possible to create a key that will take longer than the current age of the universe to break with current technology, even with massive computing power available; if that isn't secure enough for you, nothing is. Brute-forcing just the password, if you already have the key, might be easier, but it is still not trivial. If possible, you should deny the intruder access to the key as well as the password.

Specialized Security Tools

A number of tools are designed to aid the system administrator in building and maintaining a secure system. The following sections briefly describe several of the common tools along with pointers to further information.

SSH

SSH provides for a secure network by encrypting communications between hosts. By itself, it functions similarly to Telnet or `rsh`, allowing remote access to the host running the SSH daemon. Communications with that host are encrypted and optionally compressed, preventing passwords and other data from going over the network insecurely. It also provides for cryptographic authentication methods rather than strictly password-based methods, making it more convenient in many cases and more secure for those who feel a password is not enough.

SSH is available as a Debian package in the non-US section at `nonus.debian.org`. It is not quite free; there are restrictions on commercial use. Read the license if you work in a commercial environment.

PAM (Pluggable Authentication Modules)

PAM introduces a level of abstraction between programs requiring authentication and the actual methods of authentication. Most Linux distributions support it; Debian has it available but does not use it by default. If you expect to have a large number of users, you should probably install and use this. Otherwise, it is not necessary.

sudo

The `sudo` utility allows you to provide access to certain functions as a different user than the user currently logged in. If you have users who need access to occasional superuser-level functionality, but you don't want to give them full control over the system, `sudo` will help you. It is available as a Debian package.

super

The `super` utility is similar to `sudo` but provides more fine-grained access control functionality. It is available as a Debian package.

TripWire

TripWire is an intrusion-detection tool. It operates by performing a regular checksum of the important configuration files on your system and then regularly comparing those checksums to the current state. If there is a difference, it means the file has been changed since the last checksum, which could indicate a successful attack.

A number of similar tools exist for more limited situations. In fact, you can perform a similar function using two simple scripts:

```
# md5sum /bin/* /sbin/* /usr/bin/* /usr/sbin/* /usr/X11R6/bin/* /etc/*
➥>"/root/'date +"%Y%m%d"
```

This first command creates a checksum (using the `md5sum` program) for all the files commonly used by the superuser. The checksums are stored according to the date in the root user's home directory.

```
# md5sum /bin/* /sbin/* /usr/bin/* /usr/sbin/* /usr/X11R6/bin/* /etc/*
➥2>/dev/null | diff $1 - | awk '$1=="<" {print $3}".md5" 2>/dev/null
```

This second command creates checksums for the same files as before, but it compares each checksum to the stored checksum you specify as an argument. Any differences between the stored checksums and the newly generated checksums is printed. This provides a powerful intrusion detection tool, especially if you store the generated checksums offline where an attacker cannot update them to suit his newly installed binaries.

Saint/Satan

Satan is a provocatively named tool designed to probe a network for security problems. Its notoriety comes from the unpleasant fact that although it was designed for administrators trying to secure their networks, it can be used just as effectively by crackers trying to find a way in.

Saint is a tool for network security analysis based on Satan and is available from `http://www.wwdsi.com/saint/`.

Recovering from a Compromised System

Recovering from a system after it has been cracked can take a lot of work, depending on how heavily you had customized the system and how long it had been penetrated before the compromise was discovered. The rule of thumb is to treat a compromised system as entirely untrustworthy; every binary program on the system should be replaced and every configuration file rewritten from backups known to be safe or recreated by hand.

This process is made easier by modern Linux distributions; with a single CD and a few hours, you can restore your entire basic system to the starting state. From that point, you still must redo all the configuration, but you might have backups of the configuration data, and you certainly should have backups of whatever personal data and application data you were using.

The exact steps to recovery are, in order:

1. Isolate the compromised system (that is, take it off the network).
2. Determine the method of intrusion (by examining logs).
3. Reinstall the entire system (to eliminate compromised binaries).
4. Restore configuration from backups made before the attack.

   Alternatively, redo all configuration from scratch.
5. Eliminate the security hole used to gain entry.
6. Restore data from backups made before the attack.
7. Selectively restore important data from backups made after the attack, if necessary.
8. Bring the system back up on the network.

When reinstalling the system after a successful attack, it is strongly recommended that you format all the system partitions, to make absolutely sure that any compromised applications or data are destroyed. This is one case where using a multiple-partition scheme for certain portions of your filesystem layout can be useful; you might be able to leave some of the partitions unchanged while reinstalling the system, saving you the trouble of restoring them from backup. You should do this only with partitions that should not hold any application programs (typically, `/home` and perhaps `/etc` are candidates), and only if you are certain the attacker did not leave compromised binaries there to facilitate breaking in again later.

The one thing to be very, very careful about: As soon as you know the system has been compromised, take it off the network *immediately*. The attacker might be using it to attack other machines on the local network or might be *packet sniffing* (listening to all the packets passing through or near that machine) to find passwords to other machines. Of course, if the attacker can find an appropriate password in the network traffic, you won't have an easy time spotting a compromised system.

If you are going to take legal action, or something of that sort, your best bet is to preserve the compromised system as it is after the attack for a detailed examination. You can restore the configuration and data to a different system and use that to replace the compromised system until you are finished examining it.

Other Security Resources

A number of important security resources are available from the Internet. Many of them are Linux oriented, and others are more general.

One of the best introductions to security on Linux is the *Linux Administrator's Security Guide*, which covers the topic of security in far more depth than there is space to do here. The other Linux Guides from the Linux Documentation Project also have information on security considerations relevant to their subject matter. All of the guides are available from the Linux Documentation Project at `http://www.linuxdoc.org/`.

Once you understand the basics, you should keep an occasional eye on the various security-related Web sites and mailing lists available. These will alert you to any new security holes and often provide solutions for the same. New exploits for Linux and other systems are usually posted on RootShell (`http://www.rootshell.com`) among others.

Summary

This chapter discussed the common steps everyone should take to secure their Linux systems from attackers. Although such precautions should not be necessary, the world is not perfect and indeed is filled by malicious script kiddies. We discussed steps for defending against remote attackers, local users, and untrusted networks. However, for in-depth coverage of security topics, you should purchase a book devoted solely to security.

CHAPTER 22

Firewalls and Proxies

by Matthew Hunter

In This Chapter

With the growing importance of networks in general and the Internet in particular, security has become a particularly vital concern for anyone operating an Internet-connected server or network. Firewalls can serve as a barrier between the untrusted Internet and your relatively trusted internal network, allowing only authorized traffic to pass and potentially logging attempts at bypassing the firewall. Although having a firewall is not a panacea for network security, it is an important component of maintaining a secure network with access to and from the Internet.

A firewall is designed to sit between the internal network and the Internet in such a way that it can talk to both sides. Traffic to and from and the Internet must be routed through the firewall. This provides the firewall the chance to examine the traffic and to deny any traffic that appears to pose a security threat. Depending on the policy used, firewalls can let packets pass through them freely (though such a configuration is typically not called a firewall), deny packets based on a number of criteria, or deny all packets (which is very secure, but not very useful).

The use of proxy servers coupled with a firewall can provide even more security. Rather than passing packets through directly or denying them completely, proxy servers allow a machine on the internal network to access the Internet through the firewall itself; from the Internet, the internal network is not visible at all, but internal machines can use the proxy servers to access the Internet freely. All traffic goes from the internal machine to the proxy server on the firewall and is then sent to the Internet as if it originated from the firewall machine. Traffic in the other direction passes through the same steps. Thus, the firewall becomes the only computer visible from the Internet, and the only one accessible to attack; all other traffic is stopped at the firewall.

The use of proxies with a well-configured firewall provides protection for attacks on your internal network originating from systems on the Internet. Although internal systems will require some minor additional configuration to access Internet resources through the proxy servers, the extra cost is minimal compared to the security benefits. It is very difficult to maintain a large number of network workstations securely (particularly with operating systems not designed for that task!); proper use of a firewall and proxy servers can reduce the threat considerably.

In this chapter, a *proxy-only firewall* refers to a firewall that allows connections to and from the local network only through the proxy servers and does not forward packets directly. A *filtering firewall* passes some packets directly and denies others, based on various criteria. A *masquerading firewall* behaves like a filtering firewall, but also uses the IP masquerading feature of the Linux kernel, making proxy servers unnecessary for many functions. It should be noted that proxy servers can be run on any machine; filtering or masquerading firewalls can still offer proxy services if desired.

The most basic firewall arrangement is a machine with two network interfaces that is *not* configured to forward packets between those interfaces. Users are expected to log on to the firewall machine itself to access the Internet, or to use proxy servers on the firewall machine to perform the same essential task automatically. Such a firewall will completely deny normal traffic and allow contact only through the proxy servers.

This chapter is intended primarily for the network administrator configuring a Linux system to serve as a firewall or proxy between a local network and the Internet. The topics covered will include the configuration of both the firewall server and the network clients, configuration of the kernel and user tools, and security tips. If you are configuring a Linux machine as a client or server behind a firewall operating on a different machine, ask your network administrator for the proper settings.

Finally, before beginning to configure a firewall as described in this chapter, make sure that your two network interfaces are properly configured and working individually. You should be able to reach both networks normally from the firewall machine.

IP Masquerading

The Linux kernel offers a feature called *IP masquerading*, which operates in a manner similar to a firewall. However, packets passing through the firewall are transparently translated. Packets from the internal network are rewritten to appear as if they come from the firewall system, but without the use or need for proxy servers. In fact, the client machines are generally not aware of the difference at all. This capability is commonly used to provide Internet access for an entire internal network without obtaining an IP address for each computer on the internal network. IP masquerading is not perfectly transparent to the clients, but suffices for most situations and provides some of the benefits of a normal firewall.

Firewalls and the Linux Kernel

Because networking code is a part of the Linux kernel, you need to be familiar with making changes to your kernel in order to ensure that the firewalling capabilities you require are available to you. Please refer to Chapter 12, "Customizing the Bootup Procedure," for more information on customizing your kernel.

The Debian Linux version included with this book uses the v2.0 kernel. Most of the options discussed below are available with recent releases of this kernel. The v2.2 kernel (which is the next stable kernel version) has even more advanced capabilities. Unfortunately, the interface to those capabilities has changed significantly between the two versions. This chapter focuses primarily on detailing the v2.0 kernel.

You need to ensure that your firewall system has more than one network device available (commonly two ethernet cards, or one ethernet card and a modem). The two network interfaces are necessary to pass data from your internal network and your external connection. If you are using anything other than a proxy-only firewall, you also need to compile your kernel with specific options enabled. Proxy-only firewalls operate through the configuration of the proxies and do not need special kernel options.

The options relevant to firewalls will be found in the Networking Options section of the kernel configuration and are detailed in the following list. Options that are in the networking section of the kernel configuration, but which are not related to firewalls or routing, are not detailed. Options available only in the v2.2 kernel are so marked. You should read the kernel help for each option if you have doubts. Some options (most notably IP Forwarding) require that the user enable that option after booting, in addition to enabling the option in the kernel:

- Network Firewalls If you are reading this chapter, you should check this option. It is the basic enabler for firewall functionality.
- TCP/IP networking You should almost certainly select this option. If you don't, you won't have TCP/IP networking at all.
- IP Forwarding/Gatewaying This option refers to the capability of forwarding packets from one network to another, typically from a local network to the Internet or between two local networks. This option is useful only with at least two network interfaces (a dial-up modem connection can count as a second interface).

  If you are running a proxy-only firewall, you *do not* need this option. If you are running a masquerading firewall, you *do* need this option.
- IP syn cookies Although not directly related to firewalling functionality, this option should be turned on for firewall systems because it protects against a certain type of denial-of-service attack.
- IP Firewalling This option selects firewalling capability for the IP protocol. Unless your network does not use IP at all, you will want this option selected.
- Firewall Packet Logging This option logs information about incoming IP packets. The information is useful for diagnosing problems and detecting certain types of attacks.
- IP masquerading This option enables the IP masquerading capability described earlier. If you need it, enable it. If you don't, but might in the future, it is safe to compile with the option enabled; packets will not be masqueraded unless configured to do so at runtime (with `ipfwadm` or `ipchains`).
- IP: ICMP Masquerading If you selected IP masquerading, you almost certainly want this as well. This facility also masquerades the ICMP protocol (so that `ping` will work, among other things).

- IP always defragment   This option indicates that packets being forwarded should be defragmented. It is required for IP masquerading and is probably a good idea generally.
- IP accounting   This option allows packets to be tracked and statistics generated. You will need to activate the `/proc` filesystem in order to access the statistics and configure what information you want tracked with `ipfwadm` or `ipchains`.
- IP optimize as router not host   If this Linux system will be acting as a router more than sending and receiving packets as an individual host, select this option to get the benefit of different optimizations for that situation. Note that for a proxy-only firewall, most traffic is actually handled as a normal host, not as a router. This should not change the actual functionality at all, only the optimizations.
- IP tunneling   This is a bit tricky, but is of use for things such as Virtual Private Networks and similar tricks. If you need IP tunneling, your firewall is a logical place to use it. Most people won't need it, and if you do, you should spend time going through the documentation for this feature carefully.

Now that you have configured the kernel for firewall support, you need to move on to customization of the firewall installation for your needs.

Configuring a Linux Firewall

This section deals with configuring the firewalling capabilities in the Linux kernel's TCP/IP stack. You need to read this carefully if you are planning a filtering or masquerading firewall. Administrators using proxy-only firewalls do not need to make use of this section, except to configure their system to deny forwarding of all packets.

Configuring a Filtering Firewall

Typically you use the `ipfwadm` command (or `ipchains` for a v2.2 kernel) in a script to configure your firewall and forwarding policies. You will probably want to run this script automatically at boot-time, so it should be placed in the `/etc/init.d` directory. A good place to add these commands is the `/etc/init.d/network` script. The contents of the script will depend on exactly what you want to do. If you are using a filtering firewall, you may also want to use the script as a place to turn on IP forwarding in the kernel.

Enabling Packet Forwarding for Services

To enable a service, you need to know a few pieces of information about it:

- Which computers are authorized to use the service?
- Which computers are authorized to provide the service?
- Which "direction" do you want to allow traffic to flow?
- What port(s) does the service use?

/etc/services

The port information for most standard services can be found in the `/etc/services` file. You should ensure that you have this information for the services you want before beginning to configure the firewall.

`ipfwadm` (v2.0)

The script shown in the following listing is a good starting place for a v2.0 kernel. It denies access to everything. This is the most secure arrangement and is a good place to start because you know that only the traffic that you explicitly permit later will be allowed through. If you are running a proxy-only firewall, you can stop here. If you are running a filtering or masquerading firewall, you should look at the following section to learn how to enable the desired services. The man page for `ipfwadm` provides detailed usage information; this chapter is intended as a tutorial, not a detailed list of options.

The rules for `ipfwadm` fit into five categories: input, output, forwarding, accounting, and masquerading. The masquerading options are more limited than the other four. The categories are represented by the following options, which should occur first on the command line:

- `-A` Accounting
- `-I` Input
- `-O` Output
- `-F` Forwarding
- `-M` Masquerading

The `-A` option has an optional direction component, which can be `in`, `out`, or `both`. The default is `both`.

Following the category specification, you enter the command. The common command options are `-i [`*`policy`*`]` (insert the defined policy rule), `-a [`*`policy`*`]` (append the defined policy rule), `-d [`*`policy`*`]` (delete the defined policy rule), `-p [`*`policy`*`]` (sets the default rule when no specific match is found; must be one of `accept`, `deny`, `reject`, or `masquerade`), `-l (list all policy rules)`, and `-f (flush all rules)`. The following code denies forwarding for all packets (that is, nothing gets through the firewall). You should comment out the line starting with `echo` if you are using a proxy-only firewall.

```
#
# Configure IP forwarding
#
# Activate IP forwarding in the kernel
echo "1" > /proc/sys/net/ipv4/ip_forward
# By default DENY all services
ipfwadm -F -p deny
# Flush all commands
```

```
ipfwadm -F -f
ipfwadm -I -f
ipfwadm -O -f
```

Creating Firewall Rules

After configuring the firewall to deny packets by default, you can begin to enable the services you need. As you'll see below, you can enable services generally or only to and from a specific machine. You can also enable some services and deny others by allowing or denying access to their standard ports. You should know, however, that it is entirely possible for most services to use nonstandard ports if both sides of the communication know the nonstandard port ahead of time.

In order to configure the firewall to accept packets, you need to make use of the `-S` and `-D` options (which specify the source and destination addresses and port numbers, respectively). Addresses can be specified as a hostname, IP address, network address, or `0.0.0.0/0` (which means any address). The dotted quad is the IP address or network address, and the number after the slash specifies the netmask. The netmask can be specified in long form, as a dotted quad (`255.255.255.0` for class C addresses) or as a number indicating the number of 1s at the left side of the netmask in a binary representation (thus, 24 for a class C, equivalent to the long form shown previously). The netmask is not required for single IP addresses in most situations, but should always be applied to network addresses.

Port numbers can be specified as a single number or as a range of numbers (`1024:65536` being all ports between `1024` and `65535`, for example). The `-P` option specifies the protocol and can be one of `tcp`, `udp`, `icmp`, or `all`. The `-b` specifies bidirectional mode, allowing this rule to match packets in both directions:

```
ipfwadm -F -a accept -b -P tcp -S [source] 25 -D [destination] 1024:65535
```

This example enables SMTP connections (email) through the firewall to SMTP servers outside the firewall. SMTP typically uses port `25`. The port number range `1024:65535` is needed because of the way the TCP/IP protocol works; there are a finite number of ports available, and each connection uses one. Only the superuser has access to ports below `1024`, but ports above that range are allocated for user connections. Whenever you specify firewall rules, remember to specify access to the service port itself on either the source or destination component, and allow any ports between `1024` and `65535` to be used on the other side of the connection. Otherwise, your communication will work in only one direction.

The `-P` option specifies the `tcp` protocol only, because SMTP (along with most, but not all, services) uses the `tcp` protocol only. The `-a` accept option indicates that the rule should be appended to any existing rules.

Warning

You should not use this exact command, but instead replace the source address with your own network address (or with the IP addresses of each specific machine you want to allow). The `192.168.1.0` network is for internal purposes only and should not ever be directly connected to the Internet. If you are using a masquerading firewall, which is the *only* time you should be using a non-routable network address in a firewall forwarding rule, you should make certain the firewall is indeed going to masquerade the packets!

Assuming you want to allow access to any external email server from any machine on your internal network, and that your internal network is using the `192.168.1.*` address block, the actual command would be

```
ipfwadm -F -a accept -b -P tcp -S 192.168.1.0/24 25 -D 0.0.0.0/01024:65535
```

Similarly, to forward incoming email connections (from the Internet) to an internal email server, making the same assumptions as before, and also assuming that your internal email server is the first machine on the local network (that is, `192.168.1.1`), use the following:

```
ipfwadm -F -a accept -b -P tcp -S 0.0.0.0/0 1024:65535 -D192.168.1.1 25
```

This allows incoming connections to the mail server at `192.168.1.1`, on port `25`, from any computer. You'll need this if you want to receive email directly using SMTP, which is common if you are running your own Internet mail server. If you want to download mail from an external Web server, you need different settings to permit that (the appropriate protocols are usually POP3 or IMAP).

If you are running a Web server inside your firewall, you need to allow HTTP access through the firewall. HTTP typically uses port `80`:

```
ipfwadm -F -a accept -b -P tcp -S 0.0.0.0/0 1024:65535 -D192.168.1.1 80
```

You probably want to allow those on your internal network to browse the Web as well:

```
ipfwadm -F -a accept -b -P tcp -S 192.168.1.0/24 80 -D 0.0.0.0/0 1024:65535
```

To allow DNS lookups on an external DNS server, use the following:

```
ipfwadm -F -a accept -b -P udp -S 0.0.0.0/0 53 -D 196.1.2.0/24
```

Remember that these commands are configuring the kernel firewalling system and are not being saved to disk. You should enter the commands you use (after testing) into a script that will be run at boot-time, or they will be lost should your system need to reboot. Putting the commands in a script also makes changing the configuration later much easier. Don't forget to double-check your interface addresses.

Misconfiguring a Firewall

The result of misconfiguring your firewall depends on exactly what mistake you make. If you are careful and test everything before actually hooking a live network into the firewall, nothing much will happen; your rule will not quite work as intended, but the world will not come crashing down around you. However, there are certain mistakes you should make a serious effort to avoid, as they will potentially cause problems all over the Internet.

- Do not forward invalid IP addresses directly!
- Do not forward IP addresses that are not yours!
- If you have only one IP address from your access provider, do not forward anything at all! You must operate a proxy-only firewall or masquerade all packets in that situation.

Until the advent of Linux, most consumer-level operating systems did not have any routing capabilities at all. Most still do not. As such, there were not many mistakes users could make that would cause problems for anyone other than themselves. Linux offers you a great deal of power; as a consequence, you can make more serious mistakes. By using Linux, and particularly by using the IP routing and forwarding features discussed in this chapter, you are accepting the responsibility for using them competently and not making life harder on others.

All the examples in this section make use of the nonroutable IP address block `[192.168.1.*]`. You should change this to your own valid IP address block if you have one. If you do not have a valid IP address for each machine on your network, you should be using a masquerading firewall or a proxy-only firewall instead of direct forwarding.

Using one of the IP address blocks reserved for internal networks that are not connected to the Internet is recommended whenever possible, because these addresses can be detected and stopped by properly configured Internet routers; and even if a misconfigured router does route them, these addresses should not be in use by anyone else.

If you cannot use any of the reserved blocks, you should be particularly careful. If you route packets to the Internet from an IP address that you do not own and that someone else is using, you will annoy the person who owns those IP addresses. They will, in turn, annoy your connectivity provider, and your connectivity provider will make it his business to annoy you until you stop.

If you do make a mistake, correct it *immediately* if possible, and if not, disconnect until you can. If you are just configuring a firewall for a small home network over a dial-up line, don't worry too much; you won't be able to cause serious problems in a short time. If you have more bandwidth and a lot of users, you should make sure you get it right the first time.

Configuring a Masquerading Firewall

A masquerading firewall is one that modifies the addresses in packets as they pass through the firewall. This causes all packets to appear, on the outside, to come from the firewall host. Configuring a masquerading firewall is very similar to configuring a filtering firewall. The basic idea is the same; packets are received by the firewall system on one network interface and sent out to the other if the destination requires it. The only difference for a masquerading firewall is the extra step (masquerading) that takes place between receiving a packet and sending it.

There is, however, a difference in purpose between the two kinds of firewalls. A packet-filtering firewall is a security tool, designed to restrict network access to provide protection to an internal network from a presumably untrusted external network.

A masquerading firewall is generally intended as a way of providing access for a number of machines on an internal network without allocating an IP address for each machine individually. It is most often used in small networks where Internet access is important but resources for connectivity are not abundant, such as small computer businesses or a family with several computers and a technically inclined member. You cannot use a masquerading firewall to protect an externally accessible server; however, if you want to run externally accessible servers, they cannot be located behind the firewall. Obviously, this makes the security provided by masquerading somewhat moot.

The fact that internal services cannot be reached from outside your network makes configuration simpler if you are not especially concerned about security because each desired service does not have to be explicitly permitted. The masquerading process offers some measure of protection to the internal network even with a loose configuration. Because you cannot run an externally accessible server behind the masquerading firewall, you do not need to worry as much about people trying to get through your firewall to attack the server.

The next command sets the default policy to be masquerading. If you have IP forwarding turned on, your kernel compiled and installed properly, and so on, this will be all you need to have a masquerading firewall working. You should still use the brief script illustrated in the following listing to set the default policy and activate forwarding in the kernel. The network IP in the command should be the IP address and netmask of your local network (the one being masqueraded), in the same format used earlier:

```
ipfwadm -F -a masquerade -S [network IP] -D 0.0.0.0/0
```

Running an Internet-Accessible Server with Masquerading Connectivity

If you want to run an Internet-accessible server and provide masquerading connectivity for a network behind that server, you can do so by using the firewall machine as the server machine. However, this arrangement has serious security flaws, because your server will be completely accessible to the Internet; the firewall server itself receives no benefit from the firewalling it provides to the internal network.

You can be just as secure with a masquerading firewall as with any other kind, however, aside from the limitation on running servers. In fact, a masquerading firewall is more secure than a packet-filtering firewall by nature, because the masquerading process hides the IP addresses of the other machines on the network just as a proxy-only firewall does. If you want to do this, you should configure your masquerading default policy to be `deny`, and then configure masquerading for specific services following the same process as outlined under Configuring a Filtering Firewall. You need only to add the masquerading option (`-m`) to the same series of commands as for the forwarding option (`-F`).

You should not make masquerading your default policy because people who can manipulate their packet routing will be able to use that to get inside your network, and your firewall will masquerade their packets as well, thus hiding the source.

Note that the process by which IP masquerading operates is not foolproof. It works fine in most situations, but there are some operations that may cause it to break. This is unavoidable, because masquerading is by necessity working with very little information compared to a proxy server (which has cooperation from the applications). In general, any operation where the masqueraded machine is required to accept a connection initiated from the outside will fail. Because of this, you cannot, for instance, run a Web server or mail server on the internal side of a masquerading firewall.

The Masquerading HOWTO offers an in-depth explanation of the setup process.

Configuring IP Accounting

When your firewall has been properly configured to pass through the packets you want and deny those you don't, you may want to configure IP accounting. Although this accounting won't provide a lot of usage information, it can let you know when an attacker is probing your system or the systems you are firewalling for security holes.

First, flush the accounting rules:

```
ipfwadm -A -f
```

Then, set up an accounting rule that should match every packet your firewall sees, in either direction. This setup will vary depending on what you want to keep track of, so you should probably arrange your own configuration here:

```
ipfwadm -A both -i -S 0.0.0.0/0 -D 0.0.0.0/0
```

Of course, both commands should be added to the firewall configuration script so they are configured at boot-time.

`ipchains` (v2.2)

There is a shell script that is designed to ease the transition between the `ipfwadm` and `ipchains` interface. The script takes `ipfwadm`-style arguments and translates them into `ipchains`-style commands. This may be of use when making a transition between the two, especially with a pre-existing configuration. In addition, there is an IPCHAINS HOWTO dealing specifically with the `ipchains` utility.

Now that you have learned about configuring a firewall, let's shift gears and look at the configuration process for a proxy server, which uses a different method to provide you with security.

Configuring Proxy Servers

A proxy server is a daemon that listens for connections on one network and translates them into a request on another. The proxy daemon itself handles all the forwarding requirements; no packet forwarding is done by the TCP/IP implementation in the operating system for proxy server operation.

There are two kinds of proxy servers: generic proxies and application proxies. Application proxies are geared toward a specific application or protocol, and generic proxies can be used by any application that supports the proxy protocol. Both kinds typically require some degree of application support in order to be invisible to the user.

There are several open-source proxy servers, as well as commercial firewall toolkits.

Generic Proxy Servers

Generic proxy servers use a common protocol to allow any application with knowledge of the protocol to make use of the proxy server. This simplifies administration considerably, because the administrator needs to ensure only that all installed clients know about the generic proxy server and are configured to use it. No configuration of the firewall needs to be done in order to use a new client or protocol.

The disadvantage associated with using a generic proxy server is a loss of security and control. Users on the local network can use any application or client that understands the proxy protocol, and accesses cannot be logged in detail (short of logging every packet!).

Application proxies can overcome some of these disadvantages, at the cost of more configuration effort.

SOCKS

The SOCKS protocol is an implementation of the generic proxy idea that allows a supporting application to connect to the SOCKS server and request the server to make a connection to another machine. The SOCKS protocol deals only with requesting the connections through the firewall and passing the data transparantly through the SOCKS server, not with the meaning of the data being passed through the connection.

The Debian Linux version included with this book offers a SOCKS server implementing version 4 of the protocol and a client library:

- `libsocks4`
- `socks4-server`
- `socks4-clients`

You should install the first two packages because the SOCKS server uses the library. The client package is optional; your firewall system will not need it. The systems behind the firewall, however, will.

The SOCKS server is configured primarily through the file `/etc/sockd.conf`. Detailed configuration information can be found in the SOCKS man pages. However, most systems will require only the default configuration file, shown in Listing 22.1, with the appropriate network addresses filled in. The `.my.domain` entries should be replaced by the obvious.

LISTING 22.1 The `/etc/sockd.conf` File, by Default

```
deny    ALL  0.0.0.0              .my.domain  0.0.0.0
permit  .my.domain  0.0.0.0     ALL  0.0.0.0
```

Some systems require an additional file, `/etc/sockd.route`, to specify which network interface should be used to connect to a given host. Systems that need this are typically multihomed systems with IP forwarding disabled; this describes a typical proxy-only firewall. The default configuration file is shown in Listing 22.2.

The format of the route file is quite simple. All you need are the two addresses of the network interfaces and the addresses of the networks those interfaces are connected to. The interface address at the left specifies which interface should be used when a destination address matches those on the right. The destination address is simply an IP address for a single host or a network, followed by the netmask. In the sample file, the first noncomment line defines routing for external hosts to the local network. The second line defines routing from the local network through an external interface at `192.168.2.1`.

The `0.0.0.0` address with the same netmask will match any address and can thus be used to define the default route. The order of the lines in this file do matter; they are processed from top to bottom and processing halts at the first match. Listing 22.2 specifies the network interface to use for communicating with a given host on a multihomed system.

LISTING 22.2 An Example of an `/etc/sockd.route` File

```
# routes for sockd
#
# IP of interface        destination       netmask for destination
# eg: 10.0.0.254         10.0.0.28         255.255.255.255
  192.168.1.1            192.168.1.0       255.255.255.0
  192.168.2.1            0.0.0.0           0.0.0.0
```

If you aren't sure whether you need a route file or not, you can have the SOCKS daemon tell you:

```
# /usr/sbin/sockd -ver
 SOCKS server version 4.3
        SOCKS protocol version: 4A
        SOCKSified: No
        Stand-alone: No (must run under inetd)
        Supports RBIND: Yes
        Runs on Multi-homed server: Yes
        Needs route file: Yes
```

Configuring SOCKS

The purpose of a SOCKS proxy server is simple: to bypass a firewall conveniently. If you are setting up a firewall for security purposes, this should set off large alarm bells. If your SOCKS server is not configured properly, it can allow an attacker to bypass your firewall just as easily as an authorized user. In order to maintain security, pay attention to your SOCKS configuration.

Application proxy servers are less dangerous because they operate only for a specific protocol or application, thus limiting the damage that can be done, and because they will often examine the contents of the request before passing it on (ensuring that garbled requests are blocked).

Application Proxy Servers

Application proxies use a proxy protocol specific to each application or network protocol. Thus, you would have a proxy for the HTTP protocol, another for the FTP protocol, another for telnet, and so on. This obviously requires quite a bit of additional configuration, compared to a generic proxy, but allows for other potential advantages. Application proxies understand the protocols used by their clients and can perform detailed logging and access control if desired. In some cases, they can also offer additional advantages such as local content caching for improved performance.

HTTP proxies are an excellent example for describing the potential benefits of an application proxy. Basic operation is simple; the Web browser connects to the proxy server and requests a page. The proxy server connects to the remote Web server, downloads the page, and passes it on to the browser. The additional capabilities provided by this exchange are obvious: access control, detailed logging, user-independent caching and/or prefetching, and so on. The exact capabilities available will differ depending on the protocol and the proxy server chosen.

Proxies exist for various other protocols and provide benefits depending on the nature of the protocol. If you are running a proxy-only firewall, you should make sure you have a proxy for every protocol your users will need.

SQUID

SQUID is an application proxy for the HTTP, HTTPS, and FTP protocols. It provides all the capabilities mentioned previously. It is often used even where direct packet access to the Internet is available because browsers can speed up access times tremendously by reading a Web page over the local network from the SQUID cache instead of downloading it over the (often much slower) Internet link.

The following packages contain the SQUID proxy server and associated utilities:

- `squid`
- `squid-cgi`
- `squidclient`

The main proxy server is the `squid` package alone. The `squid-cgi` package is a configuration utility for SQUID that operates through a Web server's CGI interface; you connect to the Web server with a Web browser and change the configuration using forms. The `squidclient` package is a small command-line client that can fetch documents using the HTTP protocol through a SQUID proxy. You will need the `squid` package, but the other two are optional.

The main configuration file is `/etc/squid.conf`, which contains a great deal of information and commented-out configuration. You should be able to get a working configuration simply by uncommenting some of the lines from the examples. A full explanation of all the options would be too long to include here.

To start with, however, you should uncomment the `http_port` line and configure access control. A configuration that is not particularly secure would be

```
http_port 3128
http_access allow all
```

Test the configuration by configuring Netscape to use the SQUID proxy (see the client configuration section; SQUID is an HTTP proxy).

More information on SQUID can be found from the SQUID home page at

```
http://squid.nlanr.net/
```

It is worth noting that SQUID can do many interesting things; it is used as an HTTPD accelerator for static Web serving, can operate in a hierarchical network of caches, and is generally a very versatile tool.

Apache

The Apache Web server can also be configured to act as a proxy server. Information on doing so can be found in the Apache documentation. Generally it is easier and better to install a specialized proxy, but Apache is certainly adequate in most situations. More information on Apache can be found on the Apache Web pages at

```
http://www.apache.org/
```

Taking care of your server, whether it is a firewall or proxy, is only half of your task. You must also configure your internal machines to operate properly with your firewall or proxy.

Configuring the Local Network

The local network configuration will depend on the configuration of the firewall system:

- For a packet-filtering firewall, each local client should be configured with the firewall system as the TCP/IP gateway and *must* use valid IP addresses.
- For IP masquerading, each local client should be configured with the Linux firewall as its gateway (just as with packet-filtering firewalls), and should use IP addresses from one of the nonroutable network segments.
- For a firewall configured to deny all direct traffic, combined with appropriate proxy servers, each client should be configured to use the proxy servers individually. The configuration requirements will depend on the applications you want to configure and the details of the proxy they should use.

Configuring Application Proxy Clients

The details of configuring application-specific proxy clients depends on the client. The Netscape v4.61 proxy configuration dialog is displayed in Figure 22.1 and shows the various application proxies that Netscape can use. Other clients will differ, but the essential information required should remain the same.

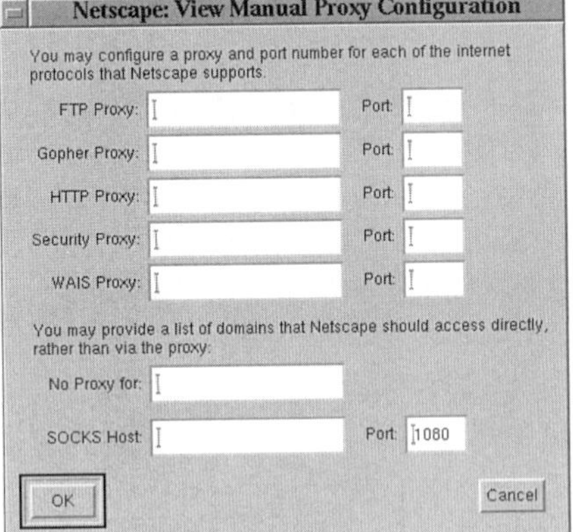

FIGURE 22.1
The Netscape proxy configuration dialog box.

Configuring SOCKS clients

The `socks-clients` package comes with several of the basic Internet utilities that have been modified to have SOCKS support. Those utilities are named by prefixing an `r` to the name of the standard utility (for example, `rfinger`, `rftp`, and so on). These utilities use the SOCKS library installed on the system and read their configuration from `/etc/socks.conf` (shown in Listing 22.3, which is for clients that use the provided SOCKS client library).

LISTING 22.3 The SOCKS Client Configuration File

```
# socks configuration
#direct                 127.0.0.1       255.255.255.255
#direct                 10.7.10.255     255.255.255.0
#sockd                  0.0.0.0         0.0.0.0
direct                  0.0.0.0         0.0.0.0
```

The format of this file is similar to the format of the `/etc/sockd.route` file. You have a routing method on the left and two dotted quads representing an IP and netmask of the destination. Take the first match from the right and use the specified route.

Note

If you have several computers in an internal network using TCP/IP, they each need an IP address. If you want to connect all the computers in the network to the Internet directly, you need to acquire an IP address from an official source (often an ISP providing connectivity). If you do not intend the network to be directly connected to the Internet, you should use one of the IP address ranges set aside for internal, nonconnected networks. The most common range is the class C network `192.168.1.*`, which has 256 addresses available.

If you are using IP masquerading or a firewall that allows access only through its proxy servers, the internal network should not be considered to have direct access. If your firewall does not use IP masquerading and allows packets through without using a proxy server, your network is considered Internet-connected and requires officially assigned IP addresses.

The Netscape proxy configuration dialog in Figure 22.1 also includes SOCKS configuration at the bottom.

Another situation that could arise is an instance where the machines behind a firewall are not simply workstations but actually servers. If you need to make the servers accessible from the Internet, you need to properly configure the firewall to allow access.

Running Servers Behind a Firewall

One of the common reasons for having a firewall is protecting an Internet server from attackers. This often provides an extra measure of protection to the server, but falls short of the full protection a firewall can offer (because the server, at least, must be visible to the outside world). You cannot run a server between a proxy-only or masquerading firewall without making a special exception to the firewall rules for that server. The exact nature of those exceptions will depend on what the server is expected to be doing. In general, the server must be able to freely send and receive packets (without a proxy) from any machine that is allowed to use its services.

A common means of allowing this is to use a single, Internet-connected computer for all Internet-accessible services, and have that same computer configured as a firewall for the local network. *This is not the most secure arrangement.* The Internet server, in this case, is connected to the Internet fully and is running a number of services that may have vulnerabilities; it is not protected by the firewall it provides to the local network. If an attacker can compromise that machine, he controls your Internet server and can bypass your firewall.

A more secure arrangement is to have a single machine as a dedicated firewall, running only the proxy servers needed to provide local clients access and the firewall itself. This minimizes the vulnerability of the firewall to attacks from outside. In addition, the firewall itself does not need to be accessible to anyone other than the network administrators; compromising the firewall machine through "social engineering" (that is, talking someone into giving up a valid password) is much harder. With the firewall difficult to compromise, it can protect any number of Internet servers on the local network from malicious traffic while remaining secure itself.

Even if the attacker manages to compromise the firewall, he or she must still compromise machines on the local network in order to do significant damage. This allows you the chance to detect the intrusion and correct the problem.

Another approach uses a proxy server on the firewall to arbitrate requests from the outside as well as from the inside. That works, but has significant disadvantages in practice.

If you have a security need or situation that we have not specifically addressed in this chapter, there are a number of resources that you might find useful; next, there are several suggestions for finding this information.

Online Documentation

There are many resources for Linux administrators who want to get a handle on security. In addition to the many books available on the subject, Linux administrators will want to consult the Linux System Administrator's Guide and the Linux Network Administrator's Guide (both part of the Linux Documentation Project). Much useful information about firewalls is available in the Firewall HOWTO; information about IP chains (the v2.2 kernel interface to firewalling and routing functionality) is available from the IP-Chains HOWTO. The Network Overview HOWTO provides pointers to additional network resources and a general overview of Linux networking.

Resources specifically geared toward security include the Security HOWTO and the Linux Administrator's Security Guide.

Most of these resources are available through the Linux Documentation Project at

`http://metalab.unc.edu/LDP/`

The Linux Administrator's Security Guide is available from

`https://www.seifried.org/lasg/`

Note

This chapter does not seek to provide anything approaching a full guide to network security; rather, it focuses specifically on the installation and configuration of firewalls and proxies. If you intend to run widely accessible servers, you are encouraged to purchase books specifically devoted to security. Short of that, there are three security principles that everyone should follow:

- Run only the services you need. With each additional service you run, you open up new possibilities for exploitation of security weaknesses or bugs.
- Read your log files regularly. Spotting suspicious behavior can be a first step to detecting both successful and failed attempts to breach security.
- Keep current with security-related updates. These can often include bug fixes for newly discovered security flaws in some services.

Remember that Linux makes an effort to be secure, but no security measures are perfect.

Summary

Firewalls can be an important security tool for Internet-connected networks. They protect the internal network from attackers by preventing unauthorized network traffic from crossing the firewall. A firewall can operate in three modes: filtering, proxy-only, or masquerading. A filtering firewall examines each packet and permits only authorized packets to pass, but does not hide the IP address of the machines on the internal network. A masquerading firewall performs a translation on each packet crossing the firewall, making the packet appear to originate from the firewall itself, and a similar translation in the other direction occurs. This has the effect of hiding the IP addresses of the internal network from the Internet, and of allowing multiple hosts to share a single IP address and network connection transparently. Finally, a proxy-only firewall uses several programs (called Proxies) to perform a similar translation for applications that support it.

CHAPTER 23

Encryption

by Mario Camou

IN THIS CHAPTER

A network is an insecure place. Most current local area networks (LANs) use *shared-media* technology. This means that when a host wants to send a message to another host, it puts it in the wire, where all hosts see it. Hosts usually ignore messages not destined to them. However, a host may be set to *promiscuous mode*, where it listens to all packets in the network, whether destined for it or not.

When we take wide area networks (WANs) into account, it becomes even harder to have security. A packet that travels through a WAN is closer to a postcard than a letter. Its contents can be seen by anyone on any host through which it passes. When a packet or message arrives at its destination, it may be intercepted by the systems administrator or by a cracker.

To continue with the mail system analogy, in the physical world, if we want a communication to be private, we put it in an envelope before sending it (the basic difference between a postcard and a letter). In the digital world, the equivalent of an envelope is encryption.

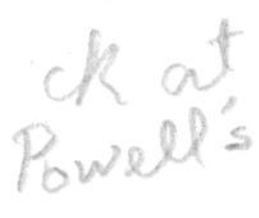

This chapter is an introduction to encryption technology in general and to some programs for encrypted communication. An excellent in-depth reference for encryption and security is *Internet Security Professional Reference,* Second Edition, published by New Riders Publishing, ISBN 156205760X.

What Is Encryption?

To *encrypt* a message means to scramble its contents in such a way that only the recipient of the message may unscramble it. For example, a simple encryption method might be to substitute for each letter a letter that is five places further along in the alphabet. So *A* turns into *F, B* into *G,* and so on. The end of the alphabet might wrap around, so that *X* turns into *C* and *Z* turns into *E*. Thus, if you wanted to send the following message:

```
THE QUICK BROWN FOX JUMPS OVER THE LAZY DOG
```

You would actually send this:

```
YMJ VZNHP GWTBS KTC OZRUJI TAJW YMJ QFED ITL
```

Modern encryption methods are, of course, much more complex. Central to most encryption algorithms is the concept of a key. A *key* is a sequence of bytes (or characters) that is used to encrypt or decrypt the message.

Using another simple example, suppose that your encryption algorithm (known as the *cipher*) involves respectively adding each character of the key to each character of the message, again wrapping around characters after *Z*. *A* is considered to have value 1 and spaces have value 0. So, assuming the key is `ABRACADABRA`, the encryption process might work like this:

```
  THE QUICK BROWN FOX JUMPED OVER THE LAZY DOG
+ ABRACADABRAABRACADABRAABRACADABRAABRACADABRA
  ------------------------------------------
  UJWATVMDMRCSQOOCGSYBBVNRWECPZFTRUIGRMDACAFGH
```

The message recipient needs to know two things: the cipher used and the encryption key. Usually, ciphers are widely known, and the security of the message depends solely on the key and the strength of the cipher. This, however, is much better than keeping the cipher secret, since it ensures that the cipher will be reviewed by a large body of people to ensure that it is secure. A secret cipher might have hidden holes in it that render it useless.

Shared-Key Versus Public-Key Encryption

There are two broad categories of ciphers: shared-key ciphers and public-key ciphers.

Originally, cryptography relied on *shared-key* ciphers. In these, the key used to encrypt a message is the same as the one used to decrypt it. Because of this, they are also known as *symmetric ciphers*. If a person wanted to communicate securely with two others, he or she had to have two different keys, one for each of the other parties. Otherwise, any party might forge messages or read the messages destined for any of the others. Also, there is the problem of distributing the keys without anyone else finding out. If the parties are in geographically distant locations, they must trust some means of transfer, whether it be a courier, a telephone system, or some other means. Anyone intercepting the key will be able to read, modify, or forge messages with it.

To solve the key management problems inherent in shared-key ciphers, Whitfield Diffie and Martin Hellman introduced the concept of *public-key* cryptography in 1976. In public-key cryptography, each person has two keys: a public key and a private key. These are related in such a way that messages encrypted with one can be decrypted only with the other, and vice versa. The public key is, as its name implies, widely publicized, and the private key is kept secret by each party. When a person wants to send a message to another, he or she encrypts it with the other person's public key. This ensures that the only way to decrypt the message will be using the recipient's private key.

Because public-key encryption is usually very compute-intensive, it is usually used in the following order (see Figure 23.1):

1. A random shared key is generated.
2. The message is encrypted with this shared key.
3. The shared key is encrypted using the recipient's public key.
4. The encrypted message and key are sent together.
5. The recipient decrypts the shared key using his or her private key and then uses it to decrypt the message.

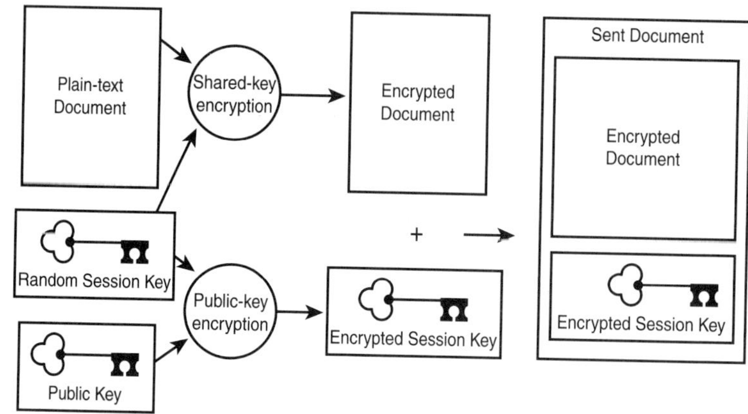

FIGURE 23.1
Public-key encryption usually relies on shared-key encryption.

Next we'll discuss some uses for encryption.

Uses for Encryption

Encryption is widely used—and not just to keep communications private. Most uses of encryption fall into three categories, or combinations of them:

- Privacy
- Authentication
- Nonrepudiation

These are covered in the following sections.

Privacy

Encryption is most commonly associated with privacy—that is, with keeping communications private. In this case, the message itself is encrypted before being sent.

Authentication

Suppose you send a message to another party. How can that party verify that the message sender is actually you, and that the message hasn't been modified in transit? In the physical world, the first question is managed by a signature. The second, question, verifying that the message has not been modified, is handled by the difficulty of modifying a physical document without trace, and might also be managed by special ink and/or watermarks.

In the digital world, both problems are handled by *digital signatures*. To create a digital signature, you first create what is known as a *digest* of the message. The digest is the result of applying one or several complex functions to the message. It is much shorter than the message, but it has the characteristic that a small change in the contents of the message is reflected in a large change in the digest.

After you have created the digest, you encrypt it and send it together with the message. The message recipient then calculates a digest of the received message, decrypts the digest that came with the message, and compares both digests. If they are equal, the recipient can be sure that the message came from you (because your key was used to decrypt the digest) and that it wasn't modified in transit (because both digests are equal).

Note that when public-key encryption is used for generating a signature, the roles of the public and private keys are reversed. The digest is encrypted with the sender's private key and decrypted with his or her public key, thus verifying that it actually came from the sender (see Figure 23.2).

FIGURE 23.2
Digital signatures are used to verify a message's origin and integrity.

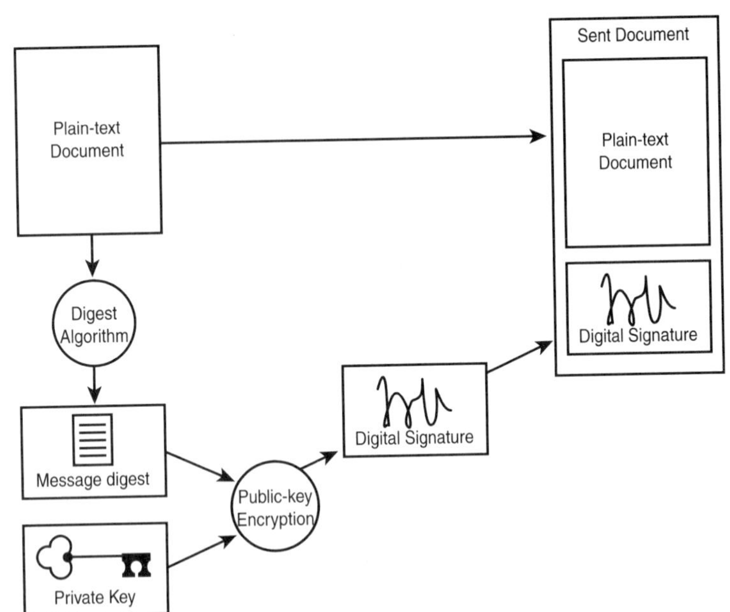

Nonrepudiation

In the physical world, when you make an agreement with another person, you usually write a contract that is signed by both parties. This is done in case one of the parties suddenly decides to change the terms of the contract, or wants to wriggle out of his or her obligations. This is known as *nonrepudiation*—that is, the document states something so that none of the parties may deny what it says.

In the digital world, digital signatures can also be used for the same thing. For example, if the terms to some transaction are agreed to by email, both parties may digitally sign the document so that there is proof that both agreed to such terms.

Legal Issues and Export Controls

Cryptography is a delicate issue in many countries. Because it can be used to hide information from others (including the government), many governments regard it as a dangerous thing. Because rules and regulations change all the time, the stuff covered in this section might change by the time you read this. Also, this section is by no means exhaustive; it covers simply the most important current issues: U.S. export controls and the Wassenaar Agreement.

Next we'll be getting into discussing tools for encrypted communication.

Tools for Encrypted Communication

There are many encryption tools for Linux, ranging from libraries to enable encryption to complete applications that use encryption. However, in this section we concentrate only on two applications that enable encrypted communication:

- SSH, the secure shell, which replaces programs such as `telnet`, `rlogin`, and `rcp` with equivalents that use an encrypted channel.
- PGP, Pretty Good Privacy, which enables you to encrypt and sign files, using public-key technology, for emailing.

There are many other applications that use encryptions, from Web browsers and email readers to filesystem modules that transparently encrypt the data stored on the disk. A full discussion of all of them would take an entire book. An excellent resource for more information on cryptography and cryptographic software is "SSH—Cryptography A-Z," at `http://www.ssh.fi/tech/crypto/`. Its links section is especially interesting.

Because of the export restrictions mentioned previously, the stock Debian distribution does not contain any cryptographic software. To install these packages using `apt`, you have to edit `/etc/apt/sources.list` and add the following line:

```
deb http://non-us.debian.org stable non-US
```

Note

As always when adding lines to `/etc/apt/sources.list`, be sure to use the mirror nearest you (especially if you are outside the U.S.). The list of Debian mirrors can be found at `http://www.debian.org/misc/README.mirrors`. For more information on using `apt` to manage software, see Chapter 10, "Software Management."

The `non-us.debian.org` server is currently located in Germany, and because it contains only open source software, it is not affected by the Wassenaar Arrangement. Adding this line enables you to install the export-controlled packages on your host with `apt-get`. Remember that you must not reexport any of the packages downloaded from it or any of its mirrors.

SSH, the Secure Shell

The problem with most Internet programs is that the Internet was initially created in academia, where the open environment encourages trust and experimentation. It wasn't created with businesses in mind, where the data stored in a server can be worth millions of dollars to a competitor. And even with a firewall in place, it has been reported that over 70% of system compromises originate within the firewall, either by disgruntled employees, by amateur crackers who want to see how systems work, or by competitors' spies.

So, what is a sysadmin to do? Use only the console? What about remote sites that you can access only via the Internet?

Enter the secure shell, also known as SSH. SSH is a suite of programs that allow you to log on to remote servers and transfer files in a secure manner. It is meant to be a replacement for `rlogin`, `rsh`, `telnet`, and `rcp`, which are insecure because they transfer data in the clear and depend on IP addresses and DNS queries (which can be spoofed) for authentication. SSH manages this using public-key encryption technology.

SSH uses public-key encryption, so each host and user has a private key and a public key. The public key is stored on the server, and the private key is kept on the client. Data encrypted with one key can be decrypted only with the other, and vice versa. This means that SSH can be used both for secure communications and for strong authentication, where you need to be sure that the host on the other side of the connection is actually what it pretends to be.

In Debian GNU/Linux, the `ssh` package contains both the SSH server daemon and the SSH clients. When you install it, it generates your host's public and private keys and starts the `sshd` daemon.

`ssh` uses two main configuration files: `/etc/ssh/sshd_config` to configure the server daemon and `/etc/ssh/ssh_config` to configure the client programs. The default files included in the `ssh` package work fine for most purposes. Their contents are covered in the section "SSH Configuration Files," later in this chapter

There are several `ssh` client programs. The most useful are `ssh` and `scp`. `ssh` allows you to log on to a remote host, execute remote programs, and redirect ports from the local host to the remote host and vice versa. `scp` is a replacement for the `rcp` program that allows you to copy files securely from one host to another. These client programs are further discussed in the following sections.

The ssh Command

The `ssh` command is used to log on to a remote server and execute a command. It has the following syntax:

```
ssh [options] host [options] [command]
```

`ssh` also handles X connection forwarding. Whenever you log on to a remote host using `ssh` from a host that is running X windows, `sshd` creates a dummy X server and sets the `DISPLAY` variable to point to it. All X traffic going to this dummy server is actually forwarded to the X server on your local host. X authentication is automatically taken care of via `xauth`. That way, the X traffic is also encrypted and secure. You don't have to do anything to make this happen, just log on to the remote server from an X session.

There are many options to the `ssh` command that can be included either before or after the hostname. The most common options to `ssh` are listed in Table 23.1.

TABLE 23.1 Most-Common `ssh` Options

Option	*Meaning*
`-f`	Sends process to background after authentication. Useful when you need to enter a password.
`-l` *`user`*	Logs in as *`user`* to the remote server.
`-o` *`'option'`*	Sets option in the same format as the configuration file. Useful for some options that don't have command-line switch equivalents.
`-v`	Verbose mode. Useful for debugging connections.
`-C`	Compresses. All data in the connection will be compressed. Useful especially over modem lines. The compression algorithm used is the same one used by `gzip`.
`-L` *`port:host:hostport`*	Forwards TCP port *`port`* to *`hostport`* on remote host *`host`*. This opens a local server socket on *`port`* and a socket on the remote host that connects to port *`hostport`* on *`host`*. All connections to *`port`* on the local host are forwarded to port *`hostport`* on *`host`*.
`-R` *`port:host:hostport`*	The reverse of `-L`. Forwards TCP port *`port`* on the remote host to port *`hostport`* on *`host`*.

Port Forwarding

The `-R` and `-L` options deserve special mention. They are useful especially in cases where you need to make a secure "tunnel" through an insecure network (such as the Internet). Consider the case where you have a Web server—for example, in California—and a database server in some other place—for example, in Florida. You want the Web server to access the database, but for security purposes you want the communication to be encrypted. Suppose the database listens by default to port 3306. You might run the following shell script on the Web server:

```
#!/bin/sh
while /bin/true
do
  ssh dbserver -L 3306:localhost:3306 sleep 87600
done
```

The `while` loop is needed because the `ssh` command (and thus the port forwarding) will run only as long as the command given on the `ssh` command line. In this case, the `sleep 87600` command simply waits for 87600 seconds (24 hours) before exiting. This command forwards port 3306 of the Web server (where you're running the command) to port 3306 on the `localhost` of the database server.

If you want to run this script on the database server, you use the `-R` option and invert the two port numbers. Because they are the same, the command is identical except for the option name.

Authentication

The previous scheme poses a problem. The `ssh` commandasks for the password of the remote user. There are two ways to automate the login process:

- Using `.rhosts` authentication
- Using private/public key-authentication

To use `.rhosts` authentication, you create an `.rhosts` file in the home directory of the remote user, as if you were using the `rsh` command. The difference here is that the remote host will be authenticated by its public key, instead of just by its IP address (which can be spoofed). Assuming the command was run by the `admin` user and that the Web server host is called `webserver`, the `.rhosts` file should contain the following line:

```
webserver  admin
```

If you don't like the idea of using an `.rhosts` file, or are sitting behind a firewall, you have to use private/public keys, using the following steps:

1. Log on to the local server.
2. Run the `/usr/bin/ssh-keygen` program to generate the private and the public keys. These are saved under the user's home directory as `.ssh/identity` and `.ssh/identity.pub`, respectively. `ssh-keygen` asks you for a passphrase, which will be used to encrypt the keys and will have to be keyed in every time you want to log on remotely. Because the purpose of this is precisely to be able not to use a password, leave the passphrase blank.

3. Copy the `.ssh/identity.pub` file to the `/tmp` directory of the remote server:

   ```
   scp $HOME/.ssh/identity.pub remoteserver:/tmp.
   ```
4. Log on to the remote server:

   ```
   ssh remoteserver.
   ```
5. Append the `/tmp/identity.pub` file to the `.ssh/authorized_keys` file under the remote user's home directory:

   ```
   cat /tmp/identity.pub >> .ssh/authorized_keys.
   ```
6. Log off the remote server and log back on using `ssh`. This time `ssh` shouldn't ask you for a password.

Caution

You should never use this procedure with the `root` user. This is because you don't want to give a cracker access to other accounts as root. Nor do you want something that a cracker could use to find out the root password. If you want to use strong authentication when logging in as `root`, be sure to use a passphrase! The passphrase should be 10–30 characters long,and should preferably not be an English phrase. If you forget the passphrase, you have to regenerate the keys.

For this kind of batch process, it is usually best to have a special user whose only function is to perform these processes. That way, if a host is compromised, the attacker will get access only to an unprivileged account.

SSH Configuration Files

As stated before, SSH uses two configuration files: `sshd_config` for the server daemon and `ssh_config` for the client programs. These files contain option/value pairs. Note that option names aren't case-sensitive.

Configuring the Server Daemon in `sshd_config`

`sshd`, the SSH daemon, reads its configuration from `/etc/ssh/sshd_config`. Each line of this file consists of a key-value pair separated by whitespace. Blank lines or lines starting with a hash sign (#) are comments. Many options can be placed in this file, all of which are documented in the `sshd(8)` man page. The most common are shown in Table 23.2.

TABLE 23.2 `sshd_config` Options

Option	*Function*
`AllowUsers/DenyUsers`	Followed by any number of usernames or `user@host` patterns separated by spaces, with `?` and `*` as wildcards. Hostnames can

Option	Function
	either be DNS fully qualified domain names or IP addresses. These options respectively allow the given users to log in or prevent the given users from logging in. If `AllowUsers` is specified, only the given users will be able to log in. If `DenyUsers` is specified, login will be allowed to all users except those specified. Note that all other authentication steps must be completed; this is just an additional restriction.
`AllowGroups/DenyGroups`	Followed by any number of group names separated by spaces, with `?` and `*` as wildcards. These options will respectively allow or deny the users whose primary group name is given to log on. If `AllowGroups` is specified, only users belonging to the given groups will be allowed to log on. If `DenyGroups` is specified, login will be allowed to all users except those whose primary group names are given.
`AllowHosts/DenyHosts`	Followed by any number of fully qualified hostnames or IP addresses, with `?` and `*` as wildcards. These options will respectively allow or deny login from the given hosts. If `AllowHosts` is specified, login will be allowed only from the given hosts. If `DenyHosts` is given, login will be allowed from all hosts except those specified.
`AllowTCPForwarding`	This option can have values `yes` or `no`, with the default being `yes`. If set to `no`, TCP forwarding will be disabled. See the previous section "Port Forwarding" for more details on TCP forwarding.
`IdleTimeout` *`time`*	Sets the idle timeout to `time`. The time unit is specified by a letter after the value (for example, `30s`), with `s` or nothing specifying seconds, `m` specifying minutes, `h` for hours, `d` for days, and `w` for weeks. If all connections through this session have been idle for *`time`*, the child is killed with a `SIGHUP` and the connection is closed.
`ListenAddress`	For hosts with more than one network interface, specifies the IP address to which `sshd` will listen.
`PermitEmptyPasswords`	This option can have values `yes` or `no`, with the default being `yes`. If set to `no`, the server will not allow login to accounts with empty passwords.
`PermitRootLogin`	This option can have values `yes` or `no`, with the default being `yes`. If set to `no`, `root` will not be able to log on through SSH. To gain `root` access, you must log on as another user and use `su` to gain `root` privileges.

continues

TABLE 23.2 continued

Option	*Function*
`X11Forwarding`	This option can have values `yes` or `no`, with the default being `yes`. If set to `no`, the forwarding of X-windows connections will be disabled, so graphical applications won't display on the client host.

Configuring the Client Programs with `ssh_config` and `.ssh/config` Files

The SSH client programs read their configuration from the `/etc/ssh/ssh_config` and the `$HOME/.ssh/config` files. The `/etc/ssh/config` file contains general options that apply to all users, and `$HOME/.ssh/config` contains options for each user. There are many options that can be placed in these files, which are documented in the `ssh(1)` man page. The most common are shown in Table 23.3.

TABLE 23.3 `ssh_config` Options

Option	*Function*
`Host` *`hostname`*	Introduces a new section. The *`hostname`* is matched against the hostname given on the command line. The options that follow apply to this host until the next `Host` directive. The `?` and `*` characters may be used as wildcards. You may use `Host *` to set defaults that apply to all hosts.
`HostName` *`hostname`*	The connection is made to *`hostname`*. This is useful to create "aliases" for particular connections (such as with different usernames or for port forwarding).
`BatchMode {yes¦no}`	When set to `yes`, `ssh` never asks for a password. It fails if it can't log in without a password.
`Compression {yes¦no}`	When set to `yes`, `ssh` compresses all data transferred to this host. The compression algorithm is the same one used by `gzip`. Equivalent to the `-C` command-line option.
`CompressionLevel {1-9}`	Specifies how much to compress the data. A `CompressionLevel` of `1` provides the least and fastest compression, and a level of `9` provides the most and slowest compression. The default value is `6` and is appropriate for most applications.
`User` *`username`*	Log in as *`username`*. Equivalent to the `-l` command-line option.

Option	Function
`LocalForward` *`port host:hostport`*	Forward local *`port`* to remote *`hostport`* on *`host`*. Equivalent to the `-L` command-line option.
`RemoteForward` *`port host:hostport`*	Forward remote *`port`* to local *`hostport`* on *`host`*. Equivalent to the `-R` command-line option.

From Secure Shell we move on to PGP, which is discussed in the next section.

PGP, Pretty Good Privacy

One of the first widespread applications for encryption was encrypting and signing files. The Pretty Good Privacy system (PGP) was originally written precisely with that in mind. It is a command-line system for encryption and signing based on public-key cryptography, designed for encrypting and signing files, which can then be attached to email messages or simply stored on the disk.

An important question in any cryptosystem is, how do you know you can trust a particular key? Other systems, such as SSL, rely on centralized Certification Authorities (CAs). The public keys of the CAs are preloaded in browsers and other programs that use SSL. To accept another person's public key, it must be signed by a CA that is known to the program. This signature in effect says that the CA is validating that the person is who he or she says that person is and that the signature belongs to that person.

In PGP, there is no such thing as a CA. Instead of that, PGP was originally based on the concept of *introducers*. That is, if Bob has Alice's key and knows for sure that the key is Alice's, and Steve has Bob's key and trusts him to introduce people, then Bob can sign Alice's key and give it to Steve. Steve knows that it is Alice's key because Bob says so. These introductions are incremental, so if later Angie also signs Alice's key, PGP keeps track of the fact that it has now been signed by two people. In that way, PGP can assign levels of trust to the keys it stores.

The first versions of PGP were written for DOS, before the World Wide Web existed. Because of that, it was impossible to have a centralized key repository that was easy to use. With the advent of the Web, it became easy to create public-key repositories. PGP5 introduces the concept of a keyserver. Keyservers use the Horowitz Key Protocol (HKP), designed by Marc Horowitz at MIT. The HKP allows you to connect to a central keyserver and from it get any public keys that you might not have in your public key ring.

For more in-depth information on PGP, see the `pgp-intro(7)` man page after installing the PGP packages (see the later section "Installing PGP").

Key Storage

PGP stores keys in *key rings*. A key ring is a file that stores one or more keys, together with the identity of the owner and whatever other keys were used to certify it. PGP manages two key rings: the secret key ring and the public key ring. The secret key ring stores your private key or keys, and the public key ring stores your public keys plus any other public keys you have received. These key rings are protected by a passphrase, which is similar in concept to a password but can be a whole phrase containing any number of characters.

You have to be extremely careful with your key rings. Because the secret key ring contains your private key, anyone who gets it can sign messages in your name and decrypt any encrypted messages written to you. It may be thought that the public key ring, because it contains only public keys, might not be as sensitive as the secret key ring. However, suppose someone tampers with your public key ring. If that person modifies the signatures on your key ring, you might end up sending messages to another party that the tamperer can read. The tamperer might even decrypt the message and reencrypt it to send it to the other person, so you would never think anything is amiss. On the other hand, the tamperer might also send you messages with his or her own signature, and make you believe that they come from someone you trust.

Because of this, you should never store your key rings in a computer that you don't personally control (such as a server at your workplace or your ISP's computer). Many people store their key rings in write-protected floppies that they insert whenever they want to sign or decrypt a message. Although this is a pain, it is probably the most secure way of storing your key rings, especially if you use two or more computers (for example, at work and at home).

Installing PGP

PGP contains encryption algorithms, so it cannot be exported from the United States. Because of that, to install PGP using `apt` you must first modify your `/etc/apt/sources.list` file, as mentioned previously in the section "Tools for Encrypted Communication." When you do that, you need to install the PGP package itself.

If you are outside the United States, you should install the `pgp5i` package. Inside the U.S., you need to download the PGP binary package from MIT. You should do the following:

1. Use your Web browser to go to `http://web.mit.edu/network/pgp.html`.
2. In the section titled How to obtain PGP from MIT, click on the link that says "To obtain the current version of PGP from MIT via the World-Wide Web, click here".

3. Read the licenses and, if you agree, select Yes in all the pull-down menus in the form. Click on the Submit button.
4. Click on the link titled PGP Freeware 5.0R1 for Linux (i386). The browser should ask you where to store the downloaded file. Select an appropriate directory to download the PGP binary distribution.
5. After downloading the file, go to a shell and `cd` to the directory where you downloaded it.
6. Extract the PGP distribution:

```
$ tar xvzf PGP-Linux-Binary.tar.gz
```

7. `cd` to the `PGP50` directory and run the `pgpinst` program. After reading the license, enter `Y` to indicate that you agree to it. To be compatible with the `pgp5i` package, you should place the binaries in `/usr/bin` and the man pages in `/usr/man`. However, many people prefer to store them in `/usr/local/bin` and `/usr/local/man` and modify their `PATH` and `MANPATH` variables accordingly.

Warning

PGP uses several encryption algorithms that are patented in the U.S. Because the algorithms aren't patented outside the U.S., the international version of PGP can use the algorithm with no problems. However, in the U.S., the only way you can use the RSA algorithm is by using the RSAREF library. The U.S. version is linked against RSAREF.

Note also that the PGP license allows you to use it with no cost only for non-commercial purposes. If you want to use PGP for commercial purposes, you to purchase a copy of PGP. PGP is now owned by Network Associates, Inc. The Web site is at `http://www.nai.com/`.

Using PGP

PGP 5.0 is composed of two basic programs:

`pgp`, which performs the actual encryption, decryption, signing, and verifying functions

`pgpk`, which is used to manage the key rings

There are also three programs that are actually symlinks to the `pgp` binary:

`pgpe`, used to encrypt and sign messages

`pgps`, used to sign messages

`pgpv`, used to decrypt and verify messages

Note

There are packages to integrate PGP into other email programs and editors. For example, `pinepgp` integrates PGP into Pine, and `auto-pgp` integrates into emacs. However, this chapter covers only the command-line programs for encryption, decryption, signing, and verifying.

Configuring PGP with the `pgp.cfg` File

PGP reads its configuration from the `${HOME}/.pgp/pgp.cfg` file. If the file doesn't exist, all the PGP programs warn you about it.

`pgp.cfg contains key=value pairs. All the options in the file can be overridden in the command line by prefixing them with two dashes (--). For example, you can usepgpe --MyName="John Smith <jsmith@altaddr.com>"`

to change the value of the `MyName` option.

The options that can be included in `pgp.cfg` are documented in the `pgp.cfg(5)` man page. Table 23.4 shows the most important ones.

TABLE 23.4 `pgp.cfg` Options

Option	*Meaning*
`Armor`	Activates ASCII armoring. Normally, PGP files and signatures are binary files. However, if `Armor` is specified, the file is converted to ASCII so it can be included directly in an email message. The default is off.
`AutoServerFetch`	If the key ring specified is not found, keys will be fetched from the keyserver. This option has some intelligence to prevent typos, so if the key ring obviously specifies a file (for example, if it starts with `/` or `./`) it will not attempt to contact the keyserver. Default is on.
`EncryptToSelf`	When encrypting files, encrypt with your own key, apart from encrypting it with the recipient's public key, by adding your own address to the recipient list. If you don't use this option, you won't be able to read any messages you send encrypted. Default is off.
`HTTPKeyServerHost`	Specifies your default keyserver host. The default is `pgpkeys.mit.edu`. It is recommended to change it to `wwwkeys.pgp.net`.
`HTTPKeyServerPort`	Specifies the port on which to contact the keyserver. The default is `11371`.

Option	Meaning
MyName	Specifies the key ID to use for signing and EncryptToSelf operations. There is no default; however, if MyName isn't specified, most operations use the first key on your secret key ring.

Generating Your Key Pair

To use PGP, you must first generate your personal key pair using `pgpk -g`:

```
$ pgpk -g
Cannot open configuration file /home/mario/.pgp/pgp.cfg
Choose the type of your public key:
  1)  DSS/Diffie-Hellman - New algorithm for 5.0 (default)
  2)  RSA
Choose 1 or 2: 1
```

First of all, pgpk asks you which key-generation algorithm to use. It is recommended that you generate one key with each algorithm. The DSS/Diffie-Hellman algorithm works only with PGP 5.0, so if you want your messages to be read or verified by people with older versions, you should generate an RSA key.

Next, the system asks you what key length to use. If you selected DSS/Diffie-Hellman, you have the following options:

```
Pick your public/private keypair key size:
(Sizes are Diffie-Hellman/DSS; Read the user's guide for more information)
 1)   768/768  bits- Commercial grade, probably not currently breakable
 2)  1024/1024 bits- High commercial grade, secure for many years
 3)  2048/1024 bits- "Military" grade, secure for forseeable future(default)
 4)  3072/1024 bits- Archival grade, slow, highest security
Choose 1, 2, 3 or 4, or enter desired number of Diffie-Hellman bits
(768 - 4096): 3
```

If you selected an RSA key, you have the following options:

```
Pick your public/private keypair key size:
  1)   768 bits- Commercial grade, probably not currently breakable
  2)  1024 bits- High commercial grade, secure for many years
  3)  2048 bits- "Military" grade, secure for the forseeable future
Choose 1, 2 or 3, or enter desired number of bits
(768 - 2048): 3
```

The key size affects two things: speed and security. The longer the key, the more secure it is, but the longer it will take when it is used to encrypt, decrypt, sign, or verify. However, in modern hardware this isn't a problem. Because the technology to break encryption is constantly advancing, you should use a key length of at least 2048 bits to be assured that your key won't be broken in the foreseeable future.

Next, pgpk asks you for the user ID that will be included with your public key:

```
You need a user ID for your public key.  The desired form for this
user ID is your FULL name, followed by your E-mail address enclosed in
<angle brackets>, if you have an E-mail address.  For example:
  Joe Smith <user@domain.com>
If you violate this standard, you will lose much of the benefits of
PGP 5.0's keyserver and email integration.

Enter a user ID for your public key: Joe Smith <jsmith@company.com>
```

To be able to use the keyservers, your email address must be in the stated form—namely, FirstName Lastname <email@domain.com>.

PGP keys can have expiration dates. After they expire, they are automatically revoked. pgpk asks you for how many days your key is valid. It is usually safe to make it valid forever:

```
Enter the validity period of your key in days from 0 - 999
0 is forever (and the default): 0
```

pgpk now asks you to enter your passphrase, which will not show up on the screen. Be sure to use a passphrase that you can easily remember, but that another party won't be able to guess. Use a mixture of upper- and lowercase letters, numbers, and punctuation. pgpk asks you for your passphrase twice, so it can be sure that you entered it correctly:

```
You need a pass phrase to protect your private key(s).
Your pass phrase can be any sentence or phrase and may have many
words, spaces, punctuation, or any other printable characters.
Enter pass phrase:
Enter again, for confirmation:
Enter pass phrase:
```

pgpk now generates random bits to generate your key pair. In Linux, this process is very fast. In other platforms (such as DOS or Windows), which don't have a built-in random number generator, it is necessary to type random text or move the mouse to make the numbers more random (the numbers are based on the intervals between keypresses). However, the random number generator in the Linux kernel is good enough for most purposes, so this isn't necessary:

```
Collecting randomness for key...

We need to generate 608 random bits.  This is done by reading
/dev/random.  Depending on your system, you may be able
to speed this process by typing on your keyboard and/or moving your mouse.
 608. 596. 584. 572. 560. 548. 536. 524. 512. 500. 488. 476. 464. 452. 440. 428.
416. 404. 392. 380. 368. 356. 344. 332. 320. 308. 296. 284. 272. 260. 248. 236.
224. 212. 200. 188. 176. 164. 152. 140. 128. 116. 104.  92.  80.  68.  56.  44.
32.  20.   8.   0 *# -Enough, thank you.
..******** .........................******* .

Keypair created successfully.
```

Finally, pgpk allows you to publish your key to a keyserver:

```
If you wish to send this new key to a server, enter the URL of the server,
below.  If not, enter nothing.
http://wwwkeys.pgp.net:11371
Looking up host wwwkeys.pgp.net
Establishing connection
```

It is usually best to use `http://wwwkeys.pgp.net:11371`. This URL randomly sends you to one of the keyservers on the Internet; because they replicate each other periodically, you don't need to submit your key to any other server.

Managing Keys with pgpk

PGP key rings are managed using pgpk. With pgpk, you can generate key pairs and add keys to your key rings (both public and private). See Table 23.5.

TABLE 23.5 pgpk Options

Option	*Meaning*
`-g`	Generates your own public/private key pair (see previous section).

`-a keyfile [keyfile ...]`	Adds a key file's contents to your public or private key ring. *keyfile* may also be an URL; supported protocols are hkp, http, and finger. If *keyfile* does not exist, pgpk attempts to download it from your default keyserver. pgpk automatically detects whether *keyfile* contains a public or a private key. For example:
	`pgpk -a keyfile #`
	`➥Local keyfile`
	`pgpk -a hkp://wwwkeys.pgp.net/user@domain.com #`
	`➥Get key from keyserver`
	`pgpk -a finger://host.company.com/user #`
	`➥Get key from "finger" output`
	`pgpk -a http://www.host.com/~user #`
	`➥Get key from user's webpage`
	`pgpk -a user@domain.com #`
	`➥Get key from default keyserver`

`-r userid`	Removes a key from your public key ring, and from your private key ring if it exists there.
`-ru userid`	Removes a user ID from your public key ring, and from your private key ring if it exists there.
`-rs userid`	Removes a signature from your public key ring.
`-e your_userid`	Edits your user ID or passphrase.
`-e her_userid`	Edits the confidence you have in a person as an introducer.
`-x userid -o keyfile`	Extracts a copy of a key from your public key ring into *keyfile*.

continues

TABLE 23.5 continued

Option	*Meaning*
`-xa` *userid* `-o` *keyfile*	Extracts a copy of a key from your public key ring into *keyfile*, in ASCII form.
`.-l[l] [`*userid*`]`	Lists the contents of your key rings. If *userid* is specified, it lists only the keys for *userid*; otherwise, it lists all keys. `-ll` lists more information on each key.
`-c [`*userid*`]`	Checks the signatures on your public key ring. If *userid* is specified, checks only the signature for *userid*.
`-s` *her_userid* `[-u` *your_userid*`]`	Signs someone else's public key on your public key ring. Used when you want to be an introducer for that person.
`-d` *her_userid*	Disables or reenables a public key on your public key ring.
`--revoke` *your_userid*	Permanently revokes your own key on your public and private key rings. Used when your secret key ring has been compromised. This option should be used very carefully, because it is permanent. After using this option, you have to re-create your key pair and redistribute your public key.
`--revokes` *her_userid*	Revokes a signature you made on someone else's key on your public key ring.

Signing a Message and Verifying Signatures

You sign a message using `pgps`. If you want to sign and encrypt it, you should use `pgpe`, which is covered in the next section, "Encrypting or Decrypting a Message." To sign a message, you must first save it into a file and then execute the following:

```
pgps filename.txt
```

This command asks you for your passphrase and generates an output file that contains both the data from `filename.txt` and the digital signature. If you specified ASCII armoring, the output file will be `filename.txt.asc`; otherwise, the file will be `filename.txt.pgp`.

Sometimes you may want to store just the signature in a file. This may be used, for example, to create a signature log to check tampering on a file. To do that, use the `-b` option:

```
pgps -b filename.txt
```

In this case, `pgps` generates a file called `filename.txt.sig` for a binary signature, or `filename.txt.asc` for an ASCII-armored signature.

To verify a signature, you use the pgpv program:

```
pgpv hosts.pgp            # For an embedded signature
pgpv hosts.pgp hosts.sig  # For a detached signature
```

pgps and pgpv take several options, which are documented in their respective man pages.

Encrypting or Decrypting a Message

You encrypt messages using pgpe. To encrypt a message with a particular recipient's public key, you use the following:

```
pgpe -r user@domain.com file.txt
```

This encrypts `file.txt` with `user@domain.com`'s public key and stores the encrypted message in `file.txt.asc` (if armoring is enabled) or `file.txt.pgp` (if armoring is disabled).

You can use several -r options to encrypt a message so several recipients can read it:

```
pgpe -r user1@host1.com -r user2@domain.com file.txt
```

The -s option signs and encrypts simultaneously:

```
pgpe -s -r user@host.com file.txt
```

To decrypt a message, you use pgpv, the same program used to verify signatures:

```
pgpv file.txt.pgp
```

Note that for encryption you cannot use detached signatures. pgpe and pgpv take several more options, documented in their respective man pages.

Summary

Encryption is a critical tool in today's open Internet, where you can never be sure exactly who is on the other side of a connection. Encryption is used for privacy, authentication, and nonrepudiation.

Cryptography is a delicate topic in many countries. Because of that, several countries (led by the United States) have policies that prevent the export of strong cryptography. However, this situation is currently in flux.

There are several useful tools for cryptography in Linux. These include SSH, the secure shell, for connecting to a remote host through an encrypted channel; and PGP, Pretty Good Privacy for encrypting files and email messages.

Development Environment

PART IV

IN THIS PART

CHAPTER 24

C/C++ Development Environment

by John Goerzen

In This Chapter

Programming in GNU/Linux often is centered around C (or C++). The Linux kernel itself is written in C, and so are many common system programs and utilities.

C has a rich history with UNIX, dating back to the early 1970s. C has proven to be a language well suited for systems programming, and its popularity continues today.

Debian GNU/Linux features a rich C/C++ development environment centered around the compilers and related tools from the Free Software Foundation. These tools, such as `gcc`, are extremely versatile, modern development tools. `gcc`, for instance, generates code on all Debian-supported platforms. It can also act as a cross-compiler, allowing you to compile code on one architecture that executes on a different one.

In this chapter, you'll learn all about Debian's rich C/C++ environment. The topics covered include compilers, libraries, debuggers, and build utilities.

The C/C++ Environment

The C/C++ environment consists of numerous components. We can separate these into the C/C++ development tools and the C/C++ runtime support components.

Here is a list of the development tools. Through the rest of the chapter, you'll be encountering these as you work with your programs.

- `gcc`, the GNU C Compiler. This is often regarded as the core of the C/C++ development environment. When you invoke `gcc` to compile your C programs, it can actually end up calling other programs such as `ld` and `cpp` in order to do preprocessing and linking. In addition to basic compilation, `gcc` handles syntax checking, optimizations, and the insertion of special debugging symbols.
- `g++` is the C++ compiler. Its function is quite similar to that of `gcc` and, in fact, typically operates as a front end for `gcc`.
- `cpp` is the C preprocessor. Its job is to manage `#include`, `#define`, `#ifdef`, and similar preprocessor directives. Generally, this is invoked as part of `gcc`. However, it is possible to use it separately—even for non-C uses.
- `ld` is the GNU linker. It takes all the modules, libraries, and necessary startup code and generates the resulting executable for your program.
- `gas` is the GNU Assembler. Its duty is to deal with assembler source code. One rarely encounters assembler source code outside of extremely low-level situations such as parts of the Linux kernel itself. However, `gcc` can emit assembly code, and `gas` converts this to object file (`.o`) form. Like `cpp`, `gas` is rarely invoked directly.
- `make` is the GNU project building utility. `make` is generally used for all but the tiniest of projects. `make`'s job is to manage the build process for your software. Given rules specified in a makefile, `make` can automatically determine what to compile and what commands to run in order to generate the executable or bring it

up-to-date. By giving it rules, you can allow `make` to determine that only some things may need recompilation—a great feature if, for instance, you have a project with 100 C source files and make a small modification to only one of them. Instead of recompiling everything, `make` can recompile just the modified part, relink the executable, and be done. This can represent a significant time savings.

- `gdb` is the GNU debugger. You can use `gdb` to diagnose runtime problems with your software. It allows you to interactively step through your source code line-by-line to see how it executes. It can also use breakpoints, which allow your code to execute at normal speed until a certain condition is reached, at which point you can take over and step through the code line-by-line. `gdb` can also display information from a core file of a program that crashed, it can debug programs on remote machines, and it can attach itself to already-running processes—a capability great for debugging daemons, for instance.
- `gprof` is the GNU profiler. `gprof` provides you with a tool to analyze the performance of your code in order to identify potential bottlenecks or candidates for manual optimizations.

In addition, another important piece of the puzzle is a programmer's editor. Many people doing development under Debian prefer to use one of XEmacs, GNU Emacs, or a vi derivative such as vim. A program such as XEmacs can serve as a standard editor, but you can optionally use it as an integrated development environment (IDE) as well. When it is used like this, you can integrate the editor, compiler, `make` utility, debugger, and related programs into a single front end.

The runtime tools include

- The runtime linker, which is responsible for loading the dynamic libraries required by your software at runtime. This process usually happens completely behind the scenes but, as we shall see later, it is possible to influence it.
- The C library, which is generally used as a dynamic library. This library provides many of the commonly used functions in C; without it, C programming is quite different from what you might be used to.
- The kernel, which provides certain essential services such as I/O for your software.

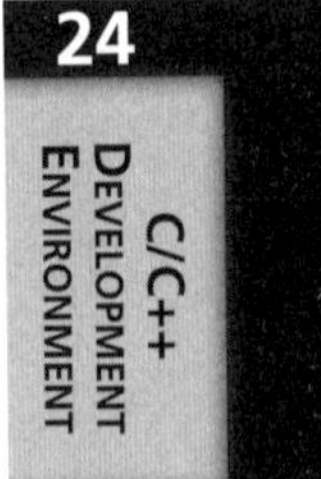

C's Role in Debian

As mentioned earlier, C has been with the Linux/UNIX heritage for years. Most of the programs in Debian are written in C or C++, and all of the major systems in the OS are as well. Therefore, if you plan to be working with programming on the systems level, it is good to have knowledge of the C and C++ systems in Debian.

Additionally, many of the non-C languages supported in Debian, such as Perl, Tcl, Python, shell scripting languages, Lisp, Scheme, and others, are all implemented with

C-based compilers or interpreters. There are a few notable exceptions, such as gnat (Ada), which is implemented in Ada itself.

Core functionality of the system is provided by the GNU C library, which has functions for such things as usage logging, terminal manipulations, and the like. Finally, C-based loadable modules are used as components in programs such as Apache and Listar.

C++ is typically used for graphical programs, particularly applications that run under X11. As C is still a strong influence on C++, this makes a natural step for C programmers and goes a long way toward maintaining the ties with the system at a low level.

Even if you don't program in C yourself, it can be useful to understand the mechanisms surrounding C programs in Linux. You no doubt will encounter a situation in which you would like to compile a C program for yourself or you need to know about the nature of dynamically loaded libraries in Linux.

Libraries in Linux

Libraries are one of the most powerful, and yet most complex, aspects of programming in the Debian GNU/Linux environment. In this section, you'll be introduced to both types of libraries: static libraries and shared libraries.

Library Basics: Static Libraries

As you are probably aware, many mid- to large-size C projects are split up into modules. This has a number of benefits: easier isolation of data, better abilities for collaboration on a project, quicker recompilation times if `make` is in use, and so on. Sometimes, there may be some functions—inside a module—that are useful inside a number of other programs. Examples of these include terminal interface libraries such as ncurses or graphic interface systems such as GTK.

To make these systems easier to use, from both a programmer's and a user's perspective, the functions and modules comprising them are grouped together into libraries.

Technically, these static libraries (`.a` files) are little more than collections of object (`.o`) files. These object files, in turn, contain functions and their associated data variables. In essence, a library is a collection of C or C++ code, grouped together in a convenient package.

To use a static library, it is linked into the final executable at link stage. That is, the contents of the compiled code that makes up the library actually become a part of the final executable. In this way, all the code necessary to run a particular program always accompanies it.

Static libraries were the de facto standard for libraries for some time. However, they have some drawbacks. They all stem from the fact that a static library is completely embedded inside each executable that uses it. Some of the drawbacks follow:

- Memory usage is higher than necessary. For commonly used libraries, each executable that uses it needs a separate copy of the code in memory. This is wasteful and can reduce performance of the system.

  On a related note, disk space is wasted by having a complete copy of the library in every executable that uses it.
- Library upgrades are difficult. When a library is upgraded, all programs on the system that use it must be recompiled—or at a minimum, relinked. If there is a serious bug or security hole in a library that is used by many programs, upgrades to fix this can be time-consuming and difficult.
- Another problem related to library versions is that different programs on the same system could end up using multiple versions of a single library. For instance, if one program was compiled against version 10 of a library but another program is compiled after version 11 is installed, the first program still uses the version 10 code (because it's embedded in the executable), but the second will use the new version 11 code. This can create nasty conflicts when libraries expect that only one version is present on a machine at any given time. This assumption is not altogether unheard of, especially with some of the more complex libraries in use today.
- There is no runtime control over which library code gets used by a given executable. For instance, with the shared library mechanism discussed later, it's possible to override the system's defaults for libraries used in a program and substitute one's own code. There is no such possibility for static libraries because all the library code is embedded in the executable. The only option is recompilation, which itself is not very attractive or practical for situations in which a single program might need to use multiple different libraries, depending on user settings.
- It is not possible to load additional code at runtime. Programs such as Apache and Listar make extensive use of Linux's dynamic library loading system to add code to the running program—but only that code specified by the administrator in a runtime configuration file. With a static library system, all possible modules must be declared beforehand and compiled directly into the executable. Adding other options requires a complete recompilation of the program. Alternatively, with systems such as Apache, you can add capabilities without requiring a recompilation—or even a server restart in some cases.

Shared Libraries

Shared libraries address the problems with static libraries discussed in the previous section. The primary idea of shared libraries is to move the link process for the library from compile time to runtime. Note that standard modules for an executable are still linked at compile time; it's only libraries that are shared by multiple different programs that benefit from a shared library system.

When a program that uses shared libraries is invoked, the dynamic linker (`ld.so`) takes care of ensuring that all required libraries are in memory. After doing this, control is passed to the program's `main()` function. Due to files such as `ld.so.cache`, this dynamic linking process is extremely fast and generally has no noticeable performance hit.

In Debian, shared libraries are the default way to go. `gcc` and related tools support shared libraries by default; in fact, your programs may have been using them all along without your realizing it!

Virtually every C program in Debian uses shared libraries as well; that solution simply fits a modern operating system such as Debian better than static libraries. In keeping with this idea, `gcc` won't use static libraries when you compile your programs unless there are no shared libraries available or it is explicitly told to use static libraries.

Shared libraries can pose a few potential problem spots as well. However, these are far less pronounced than those for static libraries in most cases.

One particular issue is for system recovery utilities that might run at a time at which the shared library files are not available. For this reason, some systems compile a few vital system recovery tools with static libraries instead of shared libraries. Debian goes a step further with the excellent rescue disk, which provides its own shared libraries, removing this particular issue.

Another is that of library upgrades. It is possible that newer libraries can change the interface used by programs. However, even there, the dynamic linking system has the answer. It is possible to have multiple versions of a single library (or even a backward-compatibility layer for a newer library) on the same system. The dynamic linker automatically chooses the appropriate version for any particular executable. In this way, you still keep a minimum of data in memory and make upgrades far easier. For those library upgrades with which the C interface doesn't change (as is the case with a majority of situations), a library upgrade is simply a drop-in issue. You simply install a new library, and whenever a program is invoked, it automatically takes advantage of the new library. Compare this to static libraries, in which all programs using the library must be recompiled in order to take advantage of the newer library.

`ld.so.conf` and the `LD_LIBRARY_PATH` Environment Variable

To properly load libraries at runtime, the runtime loader (`ld.so`) needs a search path. This tells it where to look for libraries. This path is defined in `/etc/ld.so.conf`. The `ldconfig` program reads this file, analyzes the installed libraries, and creates `/etc/ld.so.cache`, which is an optimized version to speed loading.

When an executable that uses shared libraries is invoked, it contains a built-in list of the libraries (and their versions) required for the program to run. The runtime loader then looks in the search path and loads any necessary libraries.

Barring a few security restrictions, users can override (or rather, prepend) the path by setting the `LD_LIBRARY_PATH` environment variable. This can define paths that should be checked for libraries prior to checking those specified in `ld.so.conf`. `ld.so` also understands some other environment variables; details on these appear in the `ld.so(8)` man page.

You can see which libraries your executable requires and where the system is finding them by using the `ldd` command:

```
ldd /bin/bash
```

This displays something like this:

```
libreadline.so.2 => /lib/libreadline.so.2 (0x40004000)
libncurses.so.4 => /lib/libncurses.so.4 (0x4002f000)
libdl.so.2 => /lib/libdl.so.2 (0x40071000)
libc.so.6 => /lib/libc.so.6 (0x40074000)
/lib/ld-linux.so.2 => /lib/ld-linux.so.2 (0x2aaaa000)
```

Thus, you can see exactly which libraries the `/bin/bash` program requires and the locations at which the system found them.

Shared Versus Static Libraries

In general, you should use shared libraries whenever possible. We've already highlighted many of the advantages.

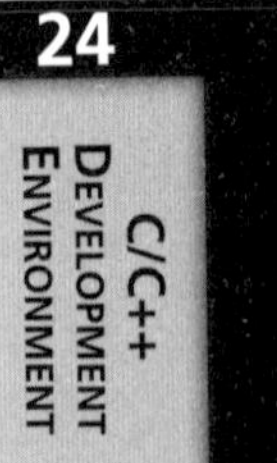

One other potential situation that could arise is a performance issue. On some architectures (most notably i386), it is possible that, due to requiring an additional CPU register, there could be a performance hit if your software uses library calls extensively. However, this is generally negligible, and the performance hit of having so many copies of the library in memory that the system must resort to swapping would certainly have a much larger impact. In fact, the only package in Debian that consciously chooses a static library over a shared one for performance reasons is `perl`; even so, it still uses numerous shared libraries, as `ldd` can show.

The only other real advantage for static libraries is in a situation in which shared libraries might not exist—for instance, system recovery tools.

The result is that you ought to always use shared libraries unless you know there is a specific reason not to.

C Library Revisions: FSF `libc5` and GNU `libc` 2.0 and 2.1

The C library plays a vital role in the operation of the system. Many of the functions that people consider to be part of C are actually implemented as C library calls. These functions might include such things as string-manipulation calls, which might count the number of characters in a string. The functions could be handling input and output from a program; the functions `printf()` and `puts()` are examples of functions implemented in the C library.

On Linux and other UNIX-like systems, there are a number of functions defined as part of the POSIX standard. Many of these are implemented in the C library as well. Examples include `getpwnam()`, which returns the `passwd` information for a given username. Typically, this might search `/etc/passwd`, but depending on other options such as shadow passwords, Pluggable Authentication Modules (PAM), or a network situation, it might get the information from a different location—perhaps a database or even a network.

Because of the C library, the calling program doesn't need to know where the information resides. The function in the C library is simply updated (or, better yet, looks in a configuration file somewhere) to get the information from the appropriate location and return it to the calling program. Thus, you can see that the C library plays a vital role in the system. Virtually every executable on the system uses the C library. Without it, even the tasks that might appear simple, such as logging in, become impossible.

In the recent history (since the switch to ELF) of the evolution of the GNU/Linux environment, we have seen the use of three major versions of the C library in the Linux distributions. The first has been known as version 5 of the C library, or `libc5` for short. `libc5` originated from the GNU project, but its code represents a fork in the development, and so `libc5` was maintained separately from the other platforms that were a part of the GNU `libc` project.

When version 2 of the GNU C library was released, it came with excellent support of the Linux environment. Therefore, since that time, there has been a switch to this library; Debian 2.0 (`hamm`) was the first Debian version to use it. This library is known both as `glibc2` and `libc6`—the former referring to its proper name within the GNU project and the latter referring to its place in the line of C libraries used on GNU/Linux systems. Both terms are interchangeable; they refer to the same thing.

Because of the vast number of changes that happened between `libc5` and `glibc2`, the two are not entirely compatible with each other; programs need to be recompiled to take advantage of `glibc2`. Due to the capabilities of the dynamic linker, those programs that have not yet been recompiled are still able to function in a `glibc2` environment; they automatically get a version of `libc5` that has additional `glibc2` compatibility modifications present.

Recently, the Free Software Foundation released `glibc2.1`, an enhancement to the `glibc2` series. Debian 2.2 (`potato`) is the first version of Debian to use `glibc2.1`. Because `glibc2.1` did not require large-scale changes in the library that could have broken compatibility with the existing library, it is generally not necessary to recompile existing programs to run under `glibc2.1`.

For a full summary of the changes from one version of the C library to the next, take a look at the `NEWS.gz` or `changelog.gz` files that appear in `/usr/doc/libc6` or `/usr/doc/libc6.1`.

Compiling and Debugging C and C++

Now that we have discussed how pieces of the C environment in Debian GNU/Linux fit together, let's move on to the usage of those particular items.

The first, and most obviously important, component of any C development environment is the C compiler. Debian GNU/Linux ships with the GNU C compiler, known as `gcc`. `gcc` is a modern optimizing C compiler with a whole range of options that you can use. The tools related to `gcc` include the GNU Assembler (`gas`), the GNU linker (`ld`), and the C preprocessor (`cpp`). There is also a C++ compiler to be found as part of the GNU suite in Debian; its name is `g++`.

In addition to all of these tools that are directly used to generate your C programs, you should be aware of some other related tools. GNU `make` is a program that understands makefiles and uses them to automate the build process for medium- to large-size projects. The GNU debugger, `gdb`, is used to isolate mistakes in the code and to perform post-mortem analyses of crash records such as core dumps. You can use the GNU profiler, `gprof`, to isolate performance bottlenecks in your programs in order to improve their execution speed. Let's look at them each in greater detail.

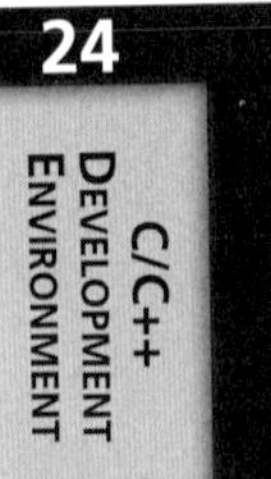

gcc, The C Compiler

`gcc` is the program invoked to start compiling a program. If you have just a single program to compile, the basic usage is this:

```
gcc -o programname programname.c
```

This compiles and links `programname.c` and places the resulting executable in a file named `programname`. The `-o` option tells `gcc` that the name of the executable follows.

You can also compile to just -o form (no link) by using

```
gcc -c test.c
```

This compiles the code in `test.c` and places the result in `test.o` but does not link or generate an executable.

You can later use a command like this to generate the executable:

```
gcc -o test test1.o test2.o test3.o
```

This takes the code from the three object files and generates the executable named `test`. It's also possible to specify different types of files:

```
gcc -o test test1.c test2.c test3.c
```

In this case, it compiles and links the three modules all in one step. Alternatively, you can use

```
gcc -o test test1.c test2.c test3.o
```

This assumes `test3.o` has already been compiled to `.o` form.

You can inform `gcc` to use additional libraries:

```
gcc -o test test.c -lncurses -lm
```

This links in the `ncurses` (`-lncurses`) and `math` (`-lm`) libraries for the generated executable. On your system, you can find these libraries in `/usr/lib` named `libncurses.so` and `libm.so`.

`gcc` also contains a number of useful options that can control exactly how it behaves while compiling your code.

`-O` controls optimization; we discuss that more later in this chapter. `-W` controls warnings. A typical use of `-W` is to use `-Wall` to turn on all warnings. This can help you spot bugs in your code before it even gets to runtime—and can often be extremely valuable in spotting potential typos that, while still valid C syntax, could pose a serious problem later.

Table 24.1 shows a more detailed list of the most useful `gcc` options.

TABLE 24.1 Commonly Used `gcc` Options

Option	*Meaning*
`-ansi`	Treats source as pure ANSI standard, without GNU/Linux extensions.
`-c`	Instructs `gcc` to disable the link step; that is, compile the source code and generate the resultant object file (`.o`).
`-D`*`macro`*	Defines the specified macro such that it can be tested with `#ifdef` in the source code.

Option	Meaning
`-Dmacro=value`	Defines the specified macro with the given value so it can be used as such in the source code for the program.
`-E`	Pipes the output from the preprocessor to standard output; does not compile.
`-ffast-math`	Enables faster math processing by allowing the generated code to violate some specifications to achieve faster performance.
`-g3`	Produces detailed debugging information for a debugger such as `gdb`. This option should not be used in conjunction with an `-O` option.
`-Idirectory`	Adds the specified directory to the beginning of the search path for include files.
`-Ldirectory`	Adds the specified directory to the beginning of the search path for libraries used in the linking stage.
`-llibrary`	Instructs the linker to include the specified library when generating the final executable.
`-O`	Turns on basic optimizations. Should not be used with the `-g` option.
`-O2`	Turns on more sophisticated optimizations. Should not be used with the `-g` option.
`-O3`	Turns on most optimizations, including those that save time at the expense of using more space. Should not be used with the `-g` option.
`-o filename`	Compiles and places the resulting file (executable, object file, assembler code, and so on) in the file named *`filename`*.
`-pedantic`	Is extremely strict about requiring standards adherence in the source code.
`-pg`	Generates the code necessary for profiling the program with `gprof`.
`-S`	Asks the compiler to generate assembler output from your source code.
`-v`	Displays verbose output.
`-Wall`	Enables all warnings.
`-Werror`	Aborts compilation when a warning is generated; that is, treats warnings as errors.
`-w`	Disables all warnings.

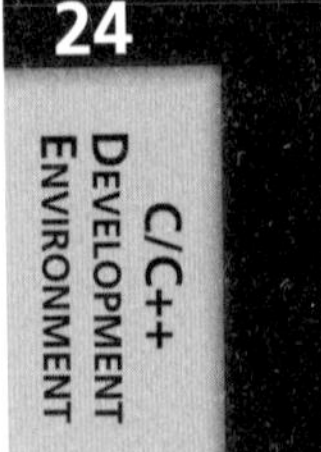

g++, The C++ Compiler

`g++` is used to compile C++ programs. Its syntax is essentially identical to that of `gcc`; in fact, in many cases, `g++` is a link to `gcc` itself. All of the options and remarks above relating to `gcc` also apply to `g++`. For `g++` to recognize your C++ sources as such, you need to use a special extension for them. This is typically an extension of `.C`; however, you can use others such as .cc and .cpp as well. Note that because header files are processed as part of the file in which they are included, extensions do not make a difference to the compiler at those locations.

Optimizing Compilers

One particularly fascinating feature of modern-day compilers is the optimizations that they can perform. Compilers today are capable of identifying code that might not be written in the fastest possible manner and rewriting it such that it performs faster—all without changing the logic of your source code. This is a remarkable and widely used feature of compilers. gcc is no exception; with the -O switch, you can enable gcc's optimization support.

For even more optimizations, you can use -O2. This turns on an even more aggressive optimizer inside gcc, which generates yet faster code.

It is important to note that although optimizations are exactly right 99 percent of the time, there can be circumstances in which you might want to disable them. These circumstances can arise when dealing with assembler code that talks directly to C code or when dealing with places in memory that can be modified by something outside the current process—another thread, perhaps. The latter can be effectively dealt with by using the volatile keyword; this tells gcc to disable certain optimizations relating to a particular keyword. volatile is a standard by now, so this code remains portable.

As an example of the benefit that your code can receive from optimization, consider the following sample C program:

```
#include <stdio.h>

int main(void) {
  int counter;
  int x;

  for (counter = 0;
       counter >= 0 && counter < 10000000 * 20 -
(100 / 2) + (200 * 100);
       counter++) {
    x = 10 + 901 - (185 * 192 / 15) - 998;
  }
}
```

Note several things about this code:

- There is an unnecessary test (counter >= 0); it is known that the counter will always be greater than or equal to zero because of the initialization.
- The upper boundary is set to a value calculated each time through the loop.
- The variable x is never used. Further, its value is calculated each time through the loop, rather than before or after it.

To analyze the code's performance, first it needs to be compiled:

```
gcc -o perftest perftest.c
```

Now, you can run it inside the `time` program, which reports the execution time:

```
time ./perftest
```

On a PII/366 laptop, `time` reports the following:

```
real    0m9.979s
user    0m9.960s
sys     0m0.000s
```

The keys here are the real and user times. The real value indicates how long it took to execute the program, as if you had timed it with an extremely accurate stopwatch. The user value indicates how much time your CPU actually spent doing calculations in user space (which is where the loop for this program takes place). These values might differ if your system is heavily loaded; in this case, the real time may be significantly higher if your program's execution was slowed due to other processes on the system. Additionally, the real time would include time the program spends waiting for user input or network traffic. Therefore, you might generally consider the user time to be a more accurate estimation of the actual amount of processor time your program required. As you can see, it takes nearly 10 seconds in both places.

Now, compile it with basic optimizations:

```
gcc -O -o perftest perftest.c
```

And re-run the benchmark:

```
time ./perftest
```

This time, the results are

```
real    0m2.861s
user    0m2.860s
sys     0m0.000s
```

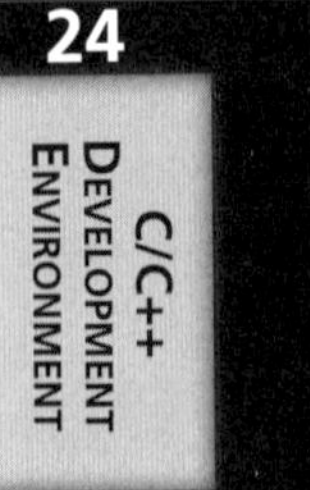

Wow! Already a significant difference—from 10 seconds down to only 3. Let's crank up optimizations even more:

```
gcc -O2 -o perftest perftest.c
```

And examine the results:

```
real    0m2.828s
user    0m2.800s
sys     0m0.000s
```

So you see, there are small improvements here, but noticeable nonetheless.

Finally, try it with `-O3`:

```
gcc -O3 -o perftest perftest.c
```

Now, the results:

```
real    0m2.332s
user    0m2.310s
sys     0m0.000s
```

There's another improvement in run time, but again, not as significant.

It's important to note that this is an extremely simplistic view of the optimizer; this code is specifically designed for the optimizer to be able to improve it. In most cases, the optimizer will most definitely not be able to make the code execute five times faster. Furthermore, the difference between `-O`, `-O2`, and `-O3` can be more significant than it was here. However, the point is important: The optimizer can make a significant difference on the performance of your code.

It's important to note that the optimizer is not a substitute for real analysis. As you might have noticed, that `for` loop really has no effect on the behavior of the program. You can write a program that effectively does the same thing by using this code:

```
int main(void) {
}
```

Even with no optimization at all, here is the time result:

```
real    0m0.003s
user    0m0.000s
sys     0m0.000s
```

That's a performance improvement of more than three thousand times compared to the the original version of the code. Again, this is a contrived example, but the principle holds for everything from the simplest code (such as this) to the most complex code.

`ld`, The Linker

`ld` is called to link together all of your object files with the necessary libraries and produce a final executable. Most of the time, `ld` is called automatically from `gcc` and you have no need to talk to it directly. However, you can use some options with `gcc` that can eventually get passed on to `ld`.

Key among these is `-l`, which tells `ld` to link in a library. Additionally, `-L` can specify an additional path in which to search for a library:

```
gcc -Wall -O2 -o test test.c -L/home/foo/mylibs -lmylib
```

This compiles the program `test.c` with optimization level 2, all warnings, and the `mylib` library. `ld` looks for this library in `/home/foo/mylibs`; presumably, `mylib` isn't to be found in the standard system library locations.

gdb, The GNU Debugger

gdb is an extremely powerful resource for tracking down problems. gdb allows you to track down logic bugs by tracing through your program line-by-line as it executes, examining the contents of variables as you go. You can also set breakpoints such that the program executes normally until it reaches a specified location. You can also specify conditional breakpoints that allow the program to execute normally until a certain condition is true, perhaps when your loop counter reaches a certain value.

Let's say you have a situation such as this:

```
$ ./test
Hi!
Segmentation fault
```

This doesn't provide a lot of help on figuring out just where in a program the problem occurred. Note, however, that unlike some other operating systems, Linux was smart enough to detect the problem and terminate the program rather than allow the system to crash; that itself can be a big help for the debugging process!

Let's examine the source code for the program that crashed:

```
#include <stdio.h>
#include <string.h>

void crashme(char *bar);

int main(void) {
  char *foo = "Welcome!";
  printf("Hi!\n");
  crashme(foo);
  printf("Hi: %s\n", foo);
}

void crashme(char *bar) {
  bar = 0;
  strcat(bar, "Hello.");
}
```

Here, life has been kind to you, and you find that the function that causes the problem is named crashme—but the problem is not so obvious in most cases. Most programs have hundreds, or even thousands, of calls to functions such as strcat() that deal with pointers. Knowing exactly where a crash occurred can be impossible or extremely difficult without a debugger.

Before you can fire up gdb to find out where the program is crashing, you need to compile the program with debugging symbols. Many people use -g3 to do this such that the maximum possible information is present:

```
gcc -g3 -o test test.c
```

Now, invoke gdb:

```
gdb test
```

gdb displays its welcome:

```
GNU gdb 4.18
Copyright 1998 Free Software Foundation, Inc.
GDB is free software, covered by the GNU General Public License, and you are
welcome to change it and/or distribute copies of it under certain conditions.
Type "show copying" to see the conditions.
There is absolutely no warranty for GDB.  Type "show warranty" for details.
This GDB was configured as "i686-pc-linux-gnu"...
```

and then its prompt

```
(gdb)
```

This means that gdb is ready to accept your input. We're going to be stepping through the code line-by-line, so the first thing we need to do is tell gdb to hand control over for manual tracing when main() is invoked:

```
(gdb) break main
```

gdb responds with something like this:

```
Breakpoint 1 at 0x8048426: file test.c, line 7.
```

Note that when you see memory addresses (the large hexadecimal numbers in gdb most frequently fall into this category), they will almost certainly be different on your machine than on the one used to prepare the examples for this book. Do not be alarmed; that is normal.

Now that gdb has been told to hand over control when main() is reached, it's time to start the execution of the program:

```
(gdb) run
```

gdb starts the program, displaying

```
Starting program: /home/username/test
```

Of course, the path to your program might differ from this path. Almost immediately, gdb informs you that it has hit a breakpoint:

```
Breakpoint 1, main () at test.c:7
```

Now, we are ready to trace through the code line-by-line. gdb displays the line number and the code on the line that will be executed next:

```
7           char *foo = "Welcome!";
```

In this case, line 7, containing an assignment to a pointer to a character, is about to be executed.

Now, type

```
(gdb) step
```

gdb executes the code on line 7 of the program and then displays the code for line 8 and pauses for your next command:

```
8         printf("Hi!\n");
(gdb)
```

Let's see whether it really set the foo pointer as it was told to:

```
(gdb) print foo
$1 = 0x80484e4 "Welcome!"
```

As you can see, foo does indeed point to a string containing the word "Welcome!" and, furthermore, the memory address that it points to is 0x80484e4.

You can also say

```
display foo
```

If you do that, not only does gdb print the value of foo at the present moment, but it also does so before each prompt in the future. This can be useful if you want to keep an eye on how your variables change over time. However, foo doesn't change here, so we're not going to do that; it would just be extra information on the screen without a real use.

Let's step past the next line. Note that you can just use s as a shortcut for step:

```
(gdb) s
Hi!
9         crashme(foo);
```

Recall that line 8, which this s command executed, is a printf() call that displays "Hi!". You can see the output of printf() right here in your gdb window. Let's proceed into the crashme() function.

One additional shortcut in gdb: Pressing Enter automatically re-issues the previous command given. If you press Enter here, it runs step again:

```
(gdb)
crashme (bar=0x80484e4 "Welcome!") at test.c:14
14        bar = 0;
```

Here, we have entered another function: crashme(). gdb informs you of this. It also displays all of the arguments passed in and their values, so you can get an idea of how things stand as the function begins. Finally, it lets you know that it's about ready to execute line 14. Let's set a display on bar:

```
(gdb) display bar
1: bar = 0x80484e4 "Welcome!"
```

Now, step on to the next line:

```
(gdb) s
15          strcat(bar, "Hello.");
1: bar = 0x0
```

Here's something suspicious! `bar` no longer points to a string but rather points to the address `0`, which is not valid.

Anyway, let's continue with the program and see what happens:

```
(gdb) s
Program received signal SIGSEGV, Segmentation fault.
0x40076040 in strcat () from /lib/libc.so.6
```

Good news! The program has crashed!

Ironic though that may sound, it's true: The culprit has been isolated. The program is crashing during the call to `strcat()`. From the display of `bar`, the reason is known: It is trying to add something to an invalid memory address.

Modifying Variables with gdb

That's one way of isolating the problem. Let's go back and try a different tactic: checking to see what would happen if the program executed past the `strcat()` statement.

First, let's exit `gdb`:

```
(gdb) q
The program is running.  Exit anyway? (y or n) y
```

Restart `gdb` with

```
gdb test
```

This time, however, set a breakpoint at line 14:

```
(gdb) break test.c:14
Breakpoint 1 at 0x8048463: file test.c, line 14.
```

Now, let's start the program running:

```
(gdb) run
Starting program: /home/username/test
Hi!

Breakpoint 1, crashme (bar=0x80484e4 "Welcome!") at test.c:14
14    bar = 0;
```

Notice how this time, the program goes right ahead and starts, calls `printf()`, and continues executing until it gets to line 14. Note the hex value of `bar`'s memory address; it will be important later.

Now, it's ready for a command at line 14. Go ahead and step:

```
(gdb) s
15    strcat(bar, "Hello.");
```

Let's verify that bar is indeed 0:

```
(gdb) print bar
$1 = 0x0
```

Recall from before that if gdb were told to step into line 15 at this point, the program would crash because bar is 0.

Let's formulate a hypothesis. It turns out that this hypothesis is partially wrong, but it helps to illustrate how you can use gdb to develop "what if" situations without needing to recompile or even restart your application.

Perhaps we hypothesize that the original author meant to say `bar[0] = 0` instead of `bar = 0`. This would have the effect of changing bar to a zero-length string, and the `strcat()` should then act as a `strcpy()`. Let's test this idea. First, restore bar to the value it had when the function was entered by using this:

```
(gdb) set variable bar = 0x80484e4
```

Of course, use the value for bar that you wrote down earlier instead of this particular one. You can now verify that bar has changed:

```
(gdb) print bar
$2 = 0x80484e4 "Welcome!"
```

Excellent! Notice that it now points to the string containing "Welcome!" again.

Recall that this variable comes from foo in `main()`, and foo has only enough space to hold "Welcome!". `strcat()` will still cause the program to crash; there isn't enough room for "Hello." afterward. Let's now use the command that perhaps was intended:

```
(gdb) set variable bar[0] = 0
```

This resets the string to be zero-length. What is bar set to now? Take a look:

```
(gdb) print bar
$3 = 0x80484e4 ""
```

Good! The memory address is correct and the string is empty. Now, step into the `strcat()` call:

```
(gdb) s

Program received signal SIGSEGV, Segmentation fault.
0x40076054 in strcat () from /lib/libc.so.6
```

As you can see, the program still crashes, despite the fact that foo now points to a valid location and strcat won't exceed the size of the allocated memory. As it turns out, the reason for this is that strcat() is attempting to overwrite read-only memory. Note how easy gdb made it to diagnose this; had we not tried to set the variable within gdb, it would have been necessary to recompile and restart the program to test the hypothesis, only to find that the crash still existed.

Let's modify the code so that it works:

```
#include <stdio.h>
#include <string.h>

void crashme(char *bar);

int main(void) {
  char *foo = strdup("Welcome!");
  printf("Hi!\n");
  crashme(foo);
  printf("Hi: %s\n", foo);
}

void crashme(char *bar) {
  bar[0] = 0;
  strcat(bar, "Hello.");
}
```

Notice that we now use strdup() to obtain an area of memory that we can write to. Furthermore, in crashme, the bar line is changed to that which worked better in gdb. After compiling and running the program again, we see

```
Hi!
Hi: Hello.
```

Success! No more crashing from this program.

Debugging with Core Files

As you may have noticed, Linux can create core files when there is a program that crashes. This action, called a core dump, saves the contents of the program's memory space into a file. Later, you can use this file by loading it into a debugger that can understand it. Given this file, gdb can pinpoint the location of a crash, the calls that lead up to it, the contents of memory at the time of the crash, and even the cause of the crash. Because gdb doesn't have to be running when core files are created, you can do all of this even if gdb wasn't running when the program crashed. Moreover, you can perform these analyses even if the program was running on a different computer when the program crashed.

Let's take some sample code. This is similar to the earlier code that crashed but has a few more details:

```
#include <stdio.h>
#include <string.h>

void dostuff(char *baz);
void crashme(char *bar);

int main(void) {
  char *foo = strdup("Welcome!");
  printf("Hi!\n");
  dostuff(foo);
  printf("Hi: %s\n", foo);
}

void dostuff(char *baz) {
  char quux[80];
  sprintf(quux, "%s; %s", baz, baz);
  crashme(quux);
}

void crashme(char *bar) {
  bar = 0;
  strcat(bar, "Hello.");
}
```

Compile with the same command line:

```
gcc -g3 -o test test.c
```

Now, we're ready to run. First, note that sometimes core dumps are not enabled. Enable them by running

```
ulimit -c unlimited
```

Now, start the program:

```
./test
```

It displays

```
Hi!
Segmentation fault (core dumped)
```

Let's look at the core file:

```
$ ls -l core
-rw-------   1 username username    61440 Jun 17 16:21 cor
```

This is the file created by the system. It's time to fire up gdb to analyze the core file. When we do that, the first parameter is the name of the executable, and the second is the name of the core file:

```
gdb test core
```

This time, the gdb startup messages are a bit different. It displays this:

```
GNU gdb 4.18
Copyright 1998 Free Software Foundation, Inc.
GDB is free software, covered by the GNU General Public License, and you are
welcome to change it and/or distribute copies of it under certain conditions.
Type "show copying" to see the conditions.
There is absolutely no warranty for GDB.  Type "show warranty" for details.
This GDB was configured as "i686-pc-linux-gnu"...
Core was generated by './test'.
Program terminated with signal 11, Segmentation fault.
Reading symbols from /lib/libc.so.6...done.
Reading symbols from /lib/ld-linux.so.2...done.
#0  0x40076040 in strcat () from /lib/libc.so.6
(gdb)
```

Notice, first, that it displays the name of the program that generated the core file—good. Next, it displays the reason that the program terminated: a segmentation fault. Then, it loads debugging information (if any) from the libraries used by the program. Finally, it displays the location of the crash—the `strcat()` function inside of the C library. Although that is useful for our particular situation, it often isn't; a given program might contain hundreds or thousands of calls to `strcat()`. Let's get some more information by requesting a stack backtrace. You can do this with either the `info stack` or the `bt` command:

```
(gdb) bt
#0  0x40076040 in strcat () from /lib/libc.so.6
#1  0x8048528 in crashme (bar=0x0) at test.c:22
#2  0x8048508 in dostuff (baz=0x8049858 "Welcome!") at test.c:17
#3  0x80484be in main () at test.c:10
```

Now, there's some more useful information! You can see exactly what functions had been called at the time of the crash. Reading from the bottom up, you can see that execution began in `main` and proceeded until it reached line 10, at which point control was transferred to a function. This function was `dostuff()`, which ran until line 17, at which point control was transferred to `crashme()`. That function, in turn, executed until line 22, when it called the `strcat()` function that crashed.

Already, we know exactly where the program crashed (the `strcat()` call in line 22 of `test.c`). The `bt` command gave a few clues as to the reason (`bar` is `0` at the time of the crash, for instance). But let's get some more information. It's possible to examine the variables in any of these areas by using the `frame` command.

You might not have even noticed it, but when `gdb` first loaded the core file, it displayed this line:

```
#0  0x40076040 in strcat () from /lib/libc.so.6
```

That indicates that the current frame is `#0`. The default frame is always the one in which the most recent code was executed, which in turn is always `#0`.

Let's go all the way back to main() and investigate the status of the variables there:

```
(gdb) frame 3
#3  0x80484be in main () at test.c:10
10          dostuff(foo);
```

Okay, now we're back in main. gdb even indicates exactly the last function called in main() prior to the crash. Let's investigate the foo variable in main:

```
(gdb) print foo
$1 = 0x8049858 "Welcome!"
```

Well, foo seems to be intact. Let's switch to frame 2:

```
(gdb) frame 2
#2  0x8048508 in dostuff (baz=0x8049858 "Welcome!") at test.c:17
17          crashme(quux);
```

We can now see that the foo variable arrived safely; it's named baz inside of dostuff(). Notice that the last command dostuff() called before the crash was crashme(). It is wise to make sure that the item passed to crashme(), quux, is in good order:

```
(gdb) print quux
$2 = "Welcome!; Welcome!\000\002@(\002@"
```

This is normal output. Don't worry about the fact that there might be extra junk after the text part of the string; the string really ends at the first \000. gdb is simply displaying the entire region of memory allocated for its use.

Because everything seems in order in frame 2, it's time to skip over to frame 1:

```
(gdb) frame 1
#1  0x8048528 in crashme (bar=0x0) at test.c:22
22          strcat(bar, "Hello.");
```

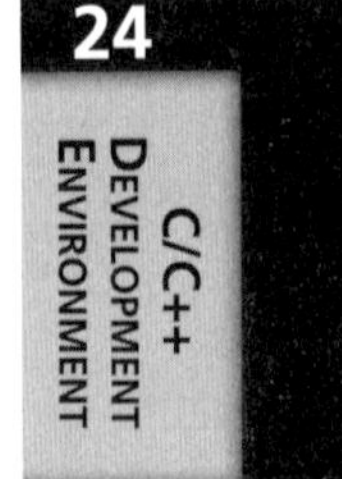

Now, we see that bar has been set to 0 and that the strcat() call is trying to concatenate something to that memory address—a definite problem.

It's possible to work backward from a crash and find out exactly how it happened. If there's no core dump available, you can work forward to find the problem as we described earlier. The bt and frame commands still work even if you've been simply stepping through the program; you don't have to be using a core dump to use them.

Debugging Already-Running Processes

One of the most powerful capabilities of gdb is its ability to attach to processes that have been started already, without gdb. This provides several advantages:

- Some processes, particularly those that use fork() or server daemons, cannot be easily started inside of gdb.
- Using this mechanism, it's possible to have the program run in one window and the debugger in another, effectively separating the output from the program from the

output from gdb. This can make the interface to debugging significantly cleaner, especially for programs that generate voluminous output.

- It's possible to attach only at a point where this is desired.

Let's step through an example of this type of attachment. First, here is the sample code that will be used for these examples:

```
#include <stdio.h>
#include <string.h>

void dostuff(char *baz);
void crashme(char *bar);

int main(void) {
  char *foo = strdup("Welcome!");
  printf("Hi!\n");
  dostuff(foo);
  printf("Hi: %s\n", foo);
}

void dostuff(char *baz) {
  char quux[80];
  sprintf(quux, "%s; %s", baz, baz);
  crashme(quux);
}

void crashme(char *bar) {
  printf("Enter greeting: ");
  fgets(bar, 20, stdin);
  printf("I didn't like that one.  Try again: ");
  bar = 0;
  fgets(bar, 20, stdin);
}
```

Notice that this is a modified version of the earlier code that caused a segmentation violation. Now, compile the code as usual with

```
gcc -g3 -o test test.c
```

At this point, maybe you want to go ahead and run the program to see what it does:

```
./test
Hi!
Enter greeting: Hello
I didn't like that one.  Try again: Hi
Segmentation fault
```

Now, start the program again. This time, after it asks for the first greeting, don't type it in. Rather, open another xterm or virtual console. You'll use this other terminal for gdb.

The first thing to do is find out the process of the test program. This ps command might help:

```
ps x ¦ grep test
```

You get a result that looks something like this:

```
1100 pts/3    S      0:00 ./test
```

Note the very first number on the line; it's the process ID of the test program, which you will need to pass to gdb. Now, it's time to start gdb. Tell it to use the test program and attach to the already-running process:

```
gdb test 1100
```

Of course, substitute your own result from ps instead of 1100.

This time, gdb displays the following while starting:

```
/home/username/foo/1100: No such file or directory.
Attaching to program: /home/username/foo/test, process 1100
Reading symbols from /lib/libc.so.6...done.
Reading symbols from /lib/ld-linux.so.2...done.
0x400bd784 in read () from /lib/libc.so.6
```

The first line is saying that gdb didn't find a core file named 1100; no big surprise there. It attaches to the process 1100 as specified. It loads the appropriate library symbols and then tells you where the current execution point is: deep inside the C library, in the read() system call, waiting for input.

Now, it is probably useful to figure out where this is relative to the rest of the code. Doing so will show you the functions that have been called so you can understand the execution up until the current point:

```
 (gdb) info stack
#0  0x400bd784 in read () from /lib/libc.so.6
#1  0x4010774c in __DTOR_END__ () from /lib/libc.so.6
#2  0x4006e791 in _IO_new_file_underflow () from /lib/libc.so.6
#3  0x4006f9d5 in _IO_default_uflow () from /lib/libc.so.6
#4  0x4006f8d0 in __uflow () from /lib/libc.so.6
#5  0x4006b885 in _IO_getline_info () from /lib/libc.so.6
#6  0x4006b82d in _IO_getline () from /lib/libc.so.6
#7  0x4006afe2 in fgets () from /lib/libc.so.6
#8  0x8048551 in crashme (bar=0xbffffc58 "Welcome!; Welcome!") at test.c:22
#9  0x8048528 in dostuff (baz=0x8049908 "Welcome!") at test.c:17
#10 0x80484de in main () at test.c:10
```

gdb is displaying a lot of information here that no doubt looks completely strange. It's showing you the stack frames inside the C library itself; this is inside the fgets() function that was called. This is probably something to be ignored because it is not your code; the key is in frame number 8, which shows where the execution is in the written code. Let's set a breakpoint so that the C library function can finish and then break back into the debugger when there's something else to do in the test code:

```
(gdb) break test.c:23
Breakpoint 1 at 0x8048554: file test.c, line 23.
```

Tell gdb to continue executing the program until it reaches the breakpoint:

```
(gdb) continue
Continuing.
```

At this point, gdb will just sit there, apparently doing nothing. Switch over to the other terminal and enter some short greeting. As soon as that is done, gdb indicates that the breakpoint has been hit and displays information and then the prompt:

```
Breakpoint 1, crashme (bar=0xbffffc58 "hi\n") at test.c:23
23          printf("I didn't like that one.  Try again: ");
```

Note how the interaction with the program takes place in one window and the interaction with gdb in another. Now, step through the printf():

```
(gdb) s
24          bar = 0;
```

You might be surprised to note that the prompt didn't actually appear in the program window yet. The reason is that output is buffered internally until a newline (\n) or an attempt to read from the terminal is encountered. This is done by the C library for performance reasons.

Go ahead and press s again:

```
(gdb) s
25          fgets(bar, 20, stdin);
```

Check on the contents of bar and stdin, just for good measure:

```
(gdb) print bar
$1 = 0x0

(gdb) print stdin
$2 = 1074814560
```

Looks good. The stdin is a pointer to a file handle, and as such, there is no surprise that it could be large. Now, go let gdb run the fgets() call:

```
(gdb) s
```

Note that the program executing in the other terminal displays the pending prompt because there is now a request for terminal input. Then, it waits for input. While it's doing all of this, gdb is paused, waiting for fgets() to return. Type some simple greeting to the test program and press Enter.

gdb comes back to life and mentions

```
Program received signal SIGSEGV, Segmentation fault.
0x4006b8d3 in _IO_getline_info () from /lib/libc.so.6
```

It's now obvious that the segmentation fault is occurring at the call to `fgets()`, and it's occurring because `bar` is `0`. The rest of this analysis is academic, but let's proceed anyway in order to demonstrate a few more items:

```
(gdb) bt
#0  0x4006b8d3 in _IO_getline_info () from /lib/libc.so.6
#1  0x4006b82d in _IO_getline () from /lib/libc.so.6
#2  0x4006afe2 in fgets () from /lib/libc.so.6
#3  0x8048579 in crashme (bar=0x0) at test.c:25
#4  0x8048528 in dostuff (baz=0x8049908 "Welcome!") at test.c:17
#5  0x80484de in main () at test.c:10
```

The stack backtrace reports results largely as expected; the last line executed in the test code prior to the crash was line 25 of `test.c`, and the crash occurred while inside the C library's `fgets()` implementation. At this point, it is possible to switch frames and analyze their contents as was done with the analysis of the core file; however, the procedure would be the same here as there, so we go ahead and exit the program:

```
(gdb) q
The program is running.  Quit anyway (and detach it)? (y or n) y
Detaching from program: /home/username/foo/test, process 1100
```

The debugger asks for confirmation that the program should be exited and then informs you that it has detached from the process being debugged.

Now, look at the window that was running the test code. It finally displays

```
Segmentation fault
```

The reason it didn't display the message earlier is that `gdb` had control and was not allowing execution to proceed until the exit. Note that it would also have been possible to issue the `continue` command to `gdb` instead of exiting; had that been done, it would have replied

```
(gdb) continue
Continuing.

Program terminated with signal SIGSEGV, Segmentation fault.
The program no longer exists.
```

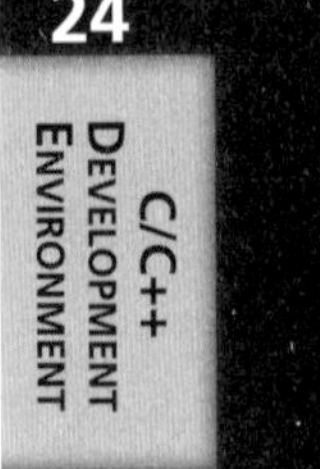

And the terminal window for the test then indicates that it encountered a segmentation fault. Note that because the program has actually terminated and the process has gone away, it's no longer possible to get a stack backtrace or examine the contents of variables.

Now that you've learned how to use `gdb` to debug programs, core dumps, and already-running programs, there are only a few more things to learn about `gdb`. Next, you are introduced to some commands for `gdb` that you may find useful.

Useful gdb Commands

Table 24.2 illustrates some useful gdb commands and their purposes. They are varied in purpose; some are used for starting execution, others for stopping, and still others for starting to debug an already-executing program.

TABLE 24.2 Some Useful gdb Commands

Command	*Purpose*
attach	Attaches to a separate process as if it had been specified on the command line.
break *location*	Sets a breakpoint at the specified location. *location* can be a function name, a line number, an offset from the current location (for example, +5 means to set it at five lines forward), or an address proceeded by an asterisk. If you want to set a breakpoint in a line of source different from the current one, you can specify the filename, a colon, and then the line number or function name.
bt	A synonym for info stack.
continue	Continues execution of the program being debugged without interruption until a breakpoint is reached, a signal is received, or the program terminates.
display *expression*	Like print, except the value of the specified expression is displayed each time gdb interrupts the program's execution.
frame *number*	Sets the active stack frame to that specified by the numeric argument. For a list of available frames, issue an info stack command.
help	Displays generic gdb help information.
help *command*	Displays a summary of the syntax for the given command.
info frame [*number*]	Displays information about the current or specified frame number.
info stack	Displays a stack backtrace, including frame numbers for later use with the frame command.
list [*location*]	Displays 10 lines of source, starting at the current position. You can also specify the location of source to display, using the same syntax as with the break command.
next	Executes the next line of code in the program being debugged. Unlike the step command, next does not go into the function if the source code calls one. Rather, it executes the function and waits until it returns before proceeding with another gdb prompt.
print *expression*	Displays the value of the given expression. Typically used to examine the contents of variables.

Command	Purpose
`run [arg...]`	Starts the execution of the loaded program. If arguments are specified to this `run` command, they are passed to the program as command-line arguments.
`set variable var = val`	Sets the value of the variable `var` to be that specified by *`val`*.
`step`	Steps the program. That is, it executes one line of the source and gives another `gdb` prompt when it is ready for the next instruction. The `step` command traces inside of functions whenever possible.
`watch expression`	Sets a watch point for your program. When you set one of these, execution of the program stops whenever the value of the specified expression changes.

More details appear in the info documentation for `gdb`. Also, `gdb` online help provides convenient listings of available commands and command summaries.

System Libraries and Headers

We've discussed how libraries work and the difference between static and shared libraries. Your Debian system comes with a wide range of libraries available for your use. These include everything from the standard C and C++ libraries to things that do such tasks as render 3D graphics, display photographs, monitor SNMP devices, and talk to SQL databases.

You are probably familiar with some of these libraries. For instance, the C library is automatically linked in to your executables by `gcc`. The C++ compiler automatically links in a C++ library as well. Other libraries you might frequently encounter are discussed in the following sections.

The X11 Library

The X11 library is linked in with `-lX11`. This library is a low-level one for using the X11 protocol for graphical applications.

The `xpm` Library

The `xpm` library is used for displaying X pixmaps (graphics), typically by programs that use one of the lower-level X libraries.

The Mesa Library

Mesa, linked with `-lMesaGL`, is meant to be a free clone of the OpenGL graphics system. Mesa is used to render 3D graphics and animation. Currently, quite a handful of programs use Mesa. You can see one example if you have the `xlockmore-gl` package installed:

```
xlock -mode pipes -nolock
```

This starts the 3D pipes mode of `xlockmore-gl`, which is a (simplistic) demonstration of one thing that you can do with Mesa.

The GTK Toolkit

GTK and its relatives GDK and GLib are used to write programs using the GTK widget set for the X windowing system. This is a modern, full-featured system used by applications such as the GIMP and many GNOME-based applications.

The `imlib` Library

`imlib` is an image manipulation library that is positioned as a replacement for `xpm`. Originally designed for use with the Enlightenment window manager, it is now used by quite a few other programs as well.

The ESD Library

The ESD library (linked with `-lesd`) is used to interface with the Enlightened sound daemon, a program that coordinates access to the sound card between all the programs on the system that generate sound. The purpose of ESD is to allow multiple programs to play simultaneously by mixing the sound; this library is used to communicate with ESD.

The Gnome Environment

The `gnome` and related libraries are used for writing programs that run in the Gnome environment.

The JPEG and TIFF libraries

The `jpeg` and `tiff` libraries are designed to allow programs to read and write from JPEG and TIFF images. They, too, are used by many programs, particularly image manipulation software.

For handling GIF files, Debian provides two libraries: `ungif` and `gif`. The `ungif` library is present in the main Debian distribution but can only read GIF files—not write them. This is due to patent problems with the GIF file format. The `gif` library in the non-free section, on the other hand, can both read from and write to GIF files.

The `ncurses` Library

The `ncurses` library is linked with `-lncurses`. `ncurses` is a library designed to handle full-screen I/O for applications running in a terminal. This library includes functions for doing such things as changing colors, drawing full-screen interfaces such as you might find in a program like mutt (although mutt actually uses a different library for the same task), positioning the cursor, changing modes for input (whether or not characters typed are echoed back, for instance), and more. ncurses programs generally automatically use the terminal information in the terminfo database. The ncurses library present in Debian is fully compatible with older programs or programs written on other platforms that expect to use the older curses library.

The paper Library

The paper library is used by programs that need to know what size of paper is in use locally. Previously, it was often necessary to set this for every application. Now, it is possible to define this in a single configuration file. Programs that use libpaper can then read their data from that one file.

The liblockfile Library

liblockfile (linked with -llockfile) is used to securely and correctly handle file-locking issues in C programs. In some situations, it is necessary to do proper locking over methods that do not traditionally support that, such as NFS. liblockfile provides a unified interface for programs that need to do this (especially programs such as mail clients) such that the locking can be honored between programs and that each individual program does the locking in a proper fashion.

The Z Compression Library

zlib (linked with -lz) is a library implementing the compression algorithm used by programs such as gzip. With this library, your program can have compression built in. This is used by some programs to use compression for data storage. Others use it to achieve better network performance by transparently compressing the data passing from one computer to another such that it requires less bandwidth for communication.

The math Library

The math library (linked with -lm) provides access to a number of mathematical functions, such as trigonometric and some advanced floating-point functions. In general, if you use the math.h header file, you probably need the math library as well.

In addition to libraries, your programs almost certainly need several header files. These header files define prototypes, contain typedefs, and define macros and other necessary details for your programs.

In many cases, when you look at documentation for C functions in the man pages, they inform you of the necessary headers. Table 24.3 is a list of some of the more common ones and why you might need to include them in your program.

To use these header files in your C programs, you generally put the name inside of angle brackets:

```
#include <string.h>
```

This includes the `string.h` header file. Sometimes, you need to include a header file from a subdirectory of the main include file search path:

```
#include <sys/stat.h>
```

The most frequently used header files are described in Table 24.3.

TABLE 24.3 Common Header Files

File	*Purpose*
`string.h`	Provides string-related operations such as copying, concatenating, searching, counting, and so on.
`math.h`	Deals with math functions, most of which go along with the `math` library. These include trigonometric and floating-point functions, among others.
`stdio.h`	Includes prototypes and macros necessary for dealing with the C standard input/output system. This file gets included in almost every program for this reason; it includes definitions for things such as `printf()`.
`stdlib.h`	Includes definitions for doing such things as converting strings to numbers and numbers to strings, some functions to generate random numbers, and other simpler math functions.
`unistd.h`	Defines a number of items relating to providing standard UNIX services, especially as defined by POSIX.
`time.h`	Provides definitions of items relating to date manipulation.
`stdarg.h`	Provides the macros necessary to implement the standard C variable-argument list support, which allows functions to receive a variable number of arguments.

System Library and Header Locations

For libraries, there are two issues at work: the dynamic loader's search path and the compiler's search path.

The former is defined in the `/etc/ld.so.conf` file, which lists paths, one per line, in which the dynamic loader ought to look in order to load libraries. Then, after the `ldconfig` utility is run, an optimized version of this is stored in `/etc/ld.so.cache`.

The search path for the linker largely mirrors this, although you can add additional directories by using the `-L` option to `gcc` or `ld`.

The general breakdown of the locations of library files is shown in Table 24.4.

TABLE 24.4 System Library Locations

Location	*Contents*
`/lib`	Basic, vital system libraries such as the C library and the dynamic loader.
`/usr/lib`	More general libraries, such as graphics libraries. Also, some application-specific libraries appear here.
`/usr/X11R6/lib`	Libraries for the X windowing system.
`/usr/lib/libc5-compat`	This directory, as well as `/lib/libc5-compat`, holds libraries that are used to provide an execution environment for those programs that arc linked against an old version of the C library.

For include files, there are several areas to check. These are generally all underneath `/usr/include`. Running a `find` command there can often determine the exact location of any given include file. Alternatively, you can look in the man page for your particular include file and the relative path for your function.

Table 24.5 shows a breakdown of the general locations for include files.

TABLE 24.5 System Header File Locations

Location	*Contents*
`/usr/include`	Basic top-level location for generic include files.
`/usr/include/sys`	Include files for "system" tasks, which tend to be more low-level interfaces to the system.
`/usr/include/arpa`	Contains header files for dealing with Internet protocols.
`/usr/include/net`	Header files for dealing with networking in general appear here.
`/usr/include/netinet`	More header files for Internet communications appear at this location.
`/usr/include/rpc`	Holds files for the Remote Procedure Call interface.
`/usr/include/linux`	Includes low-level header files from the Linux kernel source.
`/usr/include/asm`	Includes more low-level headers from the Linux source.

Summary

In this chapter, you learned about writing C and C++ programs on your Debian GNU/Linux system. The C/C++ development environment on Debian is full-featured and quite powerful. You can use the `gcc` program to compile your C programs and `g++` to compile your C++ programs.

Debian supports two types of libraries: static and shared. Static libraries are linked into the executable at build time but are difficult to maintain and upgrade. Shared libraries are linked into the in-memory image at runtime and offer more flexibility but at the cost of a more complex runtime-loading procedure and the possibility of performance loss.

The `gdb` debugger is used to tracc through your programs to find bugs with your code. It can also be used to analyze core dumps to determine the cause of a crash and to attach to already-running processes.

Debian includes a number of powerful libraries available for use in your program, some of which are listed in this chapter. These libraries cover everything from compression to processing JPEG files.

CHAPTER 25

Java Programming

by Gerardo Horvilleur

What Is Java?

Java is an object-oriented language. If you are already familiar with object-oriented programming, you know what a powerful tool it can be. If you don't have any experience in programming with objects, don't worry: It is simpler that you might have been led to believe.

Being object oriented is just one of the features that has made Java so popular. It also features portable object code, powerful dynamic linking, automatic garbage collection, built-in multithreading, and easy network programming.

But the most important feature is that it meets the two essential requirements for any programming language: It is fun and useful.

What Makes Java Special?

To really understand what makes Java special, we have to compare the way it compiles, links, and executes programs to the traditional compiling and linking model used in most C++ compilers.

The Traditional Compile and Link Model

When you write software in C++, you use a compiler to translate one or more source files into object code. For each source file, the compiler generates a file containing a translation of your C++ statements, definitions, and declarations into optimized machine language for a specific processor implementation. These object code files are then linked together, with maybe additional object code files coming from one or more libraries, to generate an executable file.

The Java Linking Model

When you write software in Java, you also use a compiler to translate one or more source files into object code. For each source file, the compiler generates one or more *class* files. Each class file has a `.class` extension and contains a translation of your Java statements and declarations into bytecodes for an abstract machine called the Java Virtual Machine (JVM).

Once you have compiled your program, you are ready to execute it. You don't need to link anything. You don't need to build an executable. If you want—maybe because it is easier for you to handle a single large file than a lot of small files spread out through many directories—you can group the contents of all your class files in a single *jar* file (with a `.jar` extension), but it doesn't make any difference for the JVM. Even when all the class files are placed inside a single jar file, there is no linking involved. A jar file is just an archive. Actually, it is a zip file.

When you run your program, the JVM dynamically loads and links the code for each class on an as-needed basis. If you run your program but you don't exercise the functionality implemented by a particular set of classes, those classes might never be loaded into memory. Some other classes might be loaded early into memory because they are part of the initialization code, but later, the JVM realizes that they aren't needed anymore so it unlinks them and frees the memory they used.

Although C and C++ were designed for static linking, all linking in Java is dynamic by default. One way to look at it is that Java always delays all linking decisions to the last minute (or maybe it's the last nanosecond?) in order to gain flexibility.

Java Bytecodes

Linking isn't the only area where Java delays the decision-making until the last moment. Whereas C and C++ compilers generate code for a specific processor architecture—even for a specific implementation of that architecture if we are using a good optimizing compiler—the Java compiler generates portable bytecodes that can be executed on any platform that has a JVM implementation.

Once again, a decision is delayed as long as possible in order to gain flexibility; now, it is the decision about the specific machine instructions that need to be executed when running a Java program. This late decision-making can be implemented in many ways.

Probably the easiest implementation, and the one used in all early versions of the JVM, is to write a bytecode interpreter. Interpreting bytecodes is easy: The interpreter runs in a loop, which fetches the next bytecode to be executed, examines it, and calls the appropriate routine. It is simple and easy to port to different architectures. Although it won't run as fast as a direct execution of machine code, it is fast enough for most applications.

For better performance, a JVM might implement a JIT (Just In Time) compiler that at runtime translates the bytecodes to optimized machine code for the processor it is running on. The JVM and its bytecodes are based on a stack architecture, which makes it relatively easy to extract the flow graph—all the possible execution paths—of a routine. This information allows a JIT to perform better code optimization. Later, we see that the flow graph is also used in the JVM verifier to ensure that the code being loaded over a network is a secure Java program.

Because a JIT generates code at runtime, it doesn't have the time to optimize it as thoroughly as a traditional compiler. Nonetheless, with a good JIT implementation, you can typically get about 70 percent of the performance you would obtain by using a traditional compiler. There might be some cases where a JIT will outperform a traditional compiler. For instance, when you use a traditional compiler, you must decide at compile time if you want to optimize the code for a 486 or a Pentium, but a JIT might know what processor it is running on and make the appropriate optimizations at runtime.

Note

For even more performance, Sun has introduced a technology known as HotSpot. HotSpot starts by executing all the code in an interpreted mode and measures the time taken by each routine in order to find out which routines are the bottlenecks (or hot spots) in your application. Once it decides that a routine must be translated into machine code, it uses all the information available to it to generate highly optimized machine code for the processor it is running on.

Because HotSpot doesn't try to compile everything—initialization routines that are executed only once don't need to be optimized—it has more time to run powerful optimization algorithms. Because it has more information—a traditional compiler might only guess where the bottlenecks are, but HotSpot knows where they are—it is able to generate better code for the specific combination of code and data at that particular point in time. As a matter of fact, HotSpot might decide that the environment has changed—new code dynamically loaded into the application or different distributions in the data being processed—and discard the machine code generated previously to substitute it with code optimized specifically for the new situation.

Unfortunately, at the time of this writing, the JIT compiler implementations available for Linux are not as good as the ones you can have for other operating systems such as Windows or Solaris. But it seems that, with the recent rise in the popularity of Linux, this inconvenience will soon vanish.

Java Security

Java security is implemented through three mechanisms: memory management, the bytecode verifier, and security managers, which are covered below.

Memory Management

One of the main reasons for the existence of Java is to have a language that allows programmers to create systems whose behavior can be safely modified at runtime by loading new code dynamically.

In C or C++, loading new code at runtime is a risky business. What happens if the code you just loaded has a bug and overwrites some arbitrary memory area? Maybe the code was written by a cracker that wants to break your program or extract confidential information.

To avoid these problems, Java was designed to make it impossible for any code to access memory areas that it is not supposed to handle. This is why in Java there is no pointer arithmetic, memory is garbage collected, array indexes are always checked, new memory is always initialized to zero, and local variables cannot be used if they haven't been initialized beforehand.

Many programmers love Java because they feel these features are like a safety net designed to catch their programming errors. Others hate Java because they feel they are being treated as small children that need to be protected from their mistakes; they claim that these are "beginner's" features that just impair performance and there should be a switch to turn them off. In a way, both are wrong. These features are there to support safe dynamic code; it is not a matter of whether you like them. All their side effects, either fortunate or unfortunate, as the case may be, are beside the point.

The Bytecode Verifier

Safety might be first, and performance might be second, but it is still an important second. One of the safety features we mentioned previously, making it impossible to use a local variable before it has been initialized, might be too expensive in terms of performance if it is implemented at runtime. For this reason, Java checks for this kind of error at compile time. If your code has any execution path where it is possible to access a local variable before it is initialized, the compiler rejects it with an error message and doesn't generate any code.

What happens if some cracker doesn't use the compiler at all and generates the bytecodes directly using some kind of assembler program for the JVM? To handle this problem, the JVM has a bytecode verifier that can examine the code at load time and check whether it complies with the local variables initialization rule.

How can the verifier do this just by looking at compiled code? It extracts the flow graph for the code it is verifying. (Remember, we said that one of the benefits of Java bytecodes was that they made it relatively easy to extract the flow graph for any piece of code.) Once you have the flow graph, the verifier can check whether there is any possibility that the content of a local variable might be used before it is initialized.

Although verifying bytecodes at load time is not unreasonably expensive in terms of performance, it might have an impact on the startup time of a large system. For this reason, most implementations of the JVM let you configure, through runtime switches, whether all code is to be verified. If you know that the code on your host is all valid, you can simply verify the code that comes from the network.

Security Managers

Okay, so Java is secure in preventing unauthorized access to memory areas. But what about the files in your hard disk? What prevents foreign code downloaded from a network from erasing the contents of your hard disk? Or reading confidential information and sending it to another host over the Internet?

This is where a security manager comes in. You can set up the environment so that any Java code downloaded from the network is denied access to the filesystem. You can also prevent the downloaded code from accessing the network or limit it so that it can only open a connection to the host it came from.

A security manager is a Java object that manages access to resources, so you can program your own security managers to implement the security policies you want to enforce. You can have multiple security managers so that, depending on where the code comes from, you can give it different permissions to access the system resources. You might configure your program so that your application code can have full access to the local filesystem and the network, code loaded from a user directory cannot write or erase files but can read them or open any network connection, code downloaded from another host in your intranet can only open network connections, and code downloaded from the Internet can only open connections to hosts outside of your corporate firewall.

Now that you have learned some of the basic principles of the Java language, it's time to get started with Java on your own system. To do this, you need to first download and install the system.

Getting and Installing Java

There are many Java implementations available for Linux. Probably the best starting point is to download Sun's standard Java Development Kit (JDK). Once you become familiar with the JDK, you might want to take a look at the other implementations. The Sun JDK is gratis, but it is not Free Software. Other projects, such as kaffe and gjc, are under way to produce versions of Java tools and libraries that comply with the DFSG (Debian Free Software Guidelines). In the sections that follow, you'll be able to select which version of the JDK to obtain and find out how to download it.

JDK Versions

There are three versions of the JDK: JDK 1.0, JDK 1.1, and JDK 1.2.

JDK 1.0 is the original Java implementation; it is now obsolete and, unless you are interested in software archeology, you probably don't need to waste your time on it.

JDK 1.1 is the most widely used version of Java. It comes with an extensive library that covers everything from GUI programming to managing compressed files. It is both solid and stable. All the examples in this chapter were tested using JDK 1.1.

JDK 1.2 is the latest incarnation of Java. Its main advantages over JDK 1.1 are a more optimized implementation of the JVM with support for the HotSpot performance engine and an even more extensive library. Sun now refers to the JDK 1.2 as the Java 2 platform and, in the not too distant future, it will probably replace JDK 1.1 as the most widely used Java implementation.

At the time of this writing, the better option is probably JDK 1.1: It has been well tested and debugged, it is extremely stable, and many of the new JDK 1.2 libraries such as Swing are available for it.

This explanation might have left you with the impression that there are many incompatible versions of Java, but that is not the case. Most of the changes between JDK 1.0, JDK 1.1, and JDK 1.2 are only improvements in the implementation of the JVM and additions to the standard libraries. Practically all code written for JDK 1.0 will still run with JDK 1.2. You don't even need to recompile it.

Unpacking and Configuring

The Linux port of the JDK is available for download at `http://www.blackdown.org`. Once you have downloaded it, the installation is simple. First, you must extract the contents of the archive file. A good place to install the JDK is in your `/usr/local` directory. Assuming you have downloaded an archive named `jdk_1.1.7-v1a-glibc-x86.tar.gz` into `/usr/tmp`, here is a sequence of commands that you can use to install it:

```
# cd /usr/local
# tar xvfz /usr/tmp/jdk_1.1.7-v1a-glibc-x86.tar.gz
```

Now, you must add the JDK's `bin` directory to your executable search path. If you're using bash, you can add this line to your `.bash_profile`:

```
export PATH=$PATH:/usr/local/jdk117_v1a/bin
```

(You need to change `jdk117_v1a` to the name of the directory that was created in `/usr/local` when you extracted the contents of the archive.)

Once you have unpacked the archive file and updated your executable search path, you can test whether everything is okay by executing this command:

```
$ java -version
java version "1.1.7"
```

Of course, the displayed version should correspond to the version you downloaded.

Compiling and Running a Program

Using your favorite text editor (emacs is a good option if you don't have a favorite editor yet), type the following program and save it in a file named `Example1.java`. This program will display a simple message to the screen.

```
public class Example1 {

    public static void

    main(String args[])
    {
        System.out.println("Hello World!");
    }

}
```

Now, compile it by typing at the command prompt

```
$ javac Example1.java
$
```

If you haven't made any typing mistakes, the compiler creates an `Example1.class` file that contains the Java bytecodes for your program. To execute it, you just need to invoke the JVM, like this:

```
$ java Example1
Hello World!
$
```

Now, we use the verbose option (`-v`) of the JVM to see how it dynamically loads the classes at runtime. Type at the command prompt

```
$ java -v Example1
[Loaded java/lang/Thread.class from /usr/java/bin/../lib/classes.zip]
[Loaded java/lang/Object.class from /usr/java/bin/../lib/classes.zip]
[Loaded java/lang/Class.class from /usr/java/bin/../lib/classes.zip]
.... (lines omitted for brevity)
[Loaded java/io/BufferedWriter.class from /usr/java/bin/../lib/classes.zip]
[Loaded java/lang/Compiler.class from /usr/java/bin/../lib/classes.zip]
[Loaded ./Example1.class]
Hello World!
```

Everything you see scrolling up in the window where you typed the command is the list of Java runtime classes that the JVM needed to load in order to run your program. You'll notice that the last class to be loaded was `Example1.class`, just before displaying the "Hello World!" message.

We make a small change in `Example1.java` to see a more interesting example of dynamic loading in action. Modify `Example1.java` by adding a new line after the one that prints the greeting. After the modification, the program should look like this:

```
public class Example1 {

    public static void
    main(String args[])
    {
        System.out.println("Hello World!");
        System.out.println(2000.0);
    }

}
```

Make sure you did not place the number between quotes.

Now, compile it and execute it again with the `-v` option:

```
$ java -v Example1
[Loaded java/lang/Thread.class from /usr/java/bin/../lib/classes.zip]
[Loaded java/lang/Object.class from /usr/java/bin/../lib/classes.zip]
[Loaded java/lang/Class.class from /usr/java/bin/../lib/classes.zip]
.... (lines omitted for brevity)
[Loaded java/io/BufferedWriter.class from /usr/java/bin/../lib/classes.zip]
[Loaded java/lang/Compiler.class from /usr/java/bin/../lib/classes.zip]
[Loaded ./Example1.class]
Hello World!
[Loaded java/lang/FloatingDecimal.class from /usr/java/bin/../lib/classes.zip]
[Loaded java/lang/Double.class from /usr/java/bin/../lib/classes.zip]
2000.0
```

Just after loading `Example1.class` and printing the greeting message, the JVM loaded and linked two more classes it needed before it could continue with the execution of your program. Now that you have created a quick example program, let's move on to more advanced programming with Java.

Programming in Java

Although Java is an object-oriented programming language, you can also use it to write programs the same way you would if you used a language such as C. This type of programming is definitely not the best way to use it, but right now, it will help us introduce other language features without having to worry about object-oriented programming issues. On the other hand, we won't be able to explain the meaning of certain keywords until we have explained classes and instances, so in the meantime, don't worry if we use a keyword without explaining why it has to be there. You'll still be able to understand what the program does.

Data Types

Java has just a few built-in data types: `byte`, `short`, `int`, `long`, `char`, `float`, `double`, and `boolean`. All except `boolean` are numeric data types. The numeric types `float` and `double` are used to represent IEEE single-precision and double-precision floating-point numbers. The `double` type is twice the size of the `float` type and has a larger range and greater accuracy. All the remaining numeric types are used to store integer numbers.

Table 25.1 lists all the integer data types with their main distinguishing features.

TABLE 25.1 Java Built-In Data Types

Type	*Size*	*Range*
`byte`	8 bits	–128 to 127
`short`	16 bits	–32,768 to 32,767
`int`	32 bits	–2,147,483,648 to 2,147,483,647
`long`	64 bits	–9,223,372,036,854,775,808 to 9,223,372,036,854,775,807
`char`	16 bits	0 to 65,535

As you can see in the table, all the integer types except `char` are signed. This is because the `char` data type is used to store Unicode character codes, which are always positive numbers. Supporting Unicode is also the reason for using 16 bits to represent one character; it must be able to encode all the characters for each language on our planet plus other codes used for special purposes. There are 47,402 different codes in the Unicode 2.1 standard.

Note

Please note that in Java, a string is not an array of `char`s. A Java string is implemented as an object. It is a special object because the compiler knows about it. This lets us use string constants in our source code, for which the compiler automatically generates the code needed to create a string object.

The architecture of the JVM forces all scalar variables to be either 32 or 64 bits long, so don't expect to save memory by declaring a scalar variable as a `byte`, `short`, `char`, or `boolean`: They are all stored as 32-bit variables in which the high order bits are ignored. On the other hand, an array of `bytes`, `shorts`, or `chars` will use just the bits it needs to store each element. Arrays of `booleans` require one byte for each element.

Besides the built-in types, in Java you can also declare variables that contain a reference—the Java substitute for a pointer—to either an object or an array.

Constants

Constant integer values can be written in decimal, octal, or hexadecimal. As in C and C++, octal constants are indicated by a leading `0` and hexadecimal constants by a leading `0x` or `0X`.

Integer constants are assumed to be of type `int` unless their last character is an `L`, which indicates a constant of type `long`.

Character constants can be written by placing the desired character or an accepted escape sequence between single quotes, as in `'A'` and `'\n'`.

Floating-point constants are assumed to be of type `double` unless their last character is an `f`, which indicates a constant of type `float`.

There are two `boolean` constants: `true` and `false`.

There is just one reference constant: `null`.

You can also write a constant that represents a reference to a string object by placing the desired sequence of characters between double quotes.

Operators

As shown in Table 25.2, the operators used for Java are similar to those used for C.

TABLE 25.2 Java Operators

Operator	*Arguments*	*Result*
`<`, `<=`, `>`, and `>=`	Numbers	Boolean
`==` and `!=`	Any type	Boolean
Unary `+` and `-`	Number	Number
`*`, `/`, and `%`	Numbers	Number
Binary `+` and `-`	Numbers	Number

continues

TABLE 25.2 continued

Operator	*Arguments*	*Result*
++ (prefix and postfix)	Number	Number
— (prefix and postfix)	Number	Number
>> and << (signed shifts)	Integers	Integer
>>> (unsigned shift left)	Integers	Integer
~ (bitwise complement)	Integers	Integer
&, ¦, and ^ (bitwise)	Integers	Integer
! (logical complement)	Boolean	Boolean
&, ¦, and ^ (logical)	Boolean	Boolean
&& (conditional AND)	Boolean	Boolean
¦¦ (conditional OR)	Boolean	Boolean
?: (conditional)	Boolean ? any : any	Any
+ (String concatenation)	String + any	String
`instanceof`	`obj-ref`	
`instanceof`	Class	Boolean

Control Structures

Control structures in Java are also similar to those you use when programming in C or C++. Control structures are the conditional, switching, and looping features of the language.

The `Example2` program in Listing 25.1 shows all of them. It isn't a really useful program, but at least it is simple to understand.

LISTING 25.1 `Example2`

```
public class Example2 {

    public static void printMultiplesOfTwo(int limit) {
        System.out.println("Multiples of Two:");
        int i = 0;
        while (i < limit)
        {
            System.out.println(i);
            i += 2;
```

```
        }
    }

    public static void printMultiplesOfThree(int limit) {
        System.out.println("Multiples of 3:");
        int i = 0;
        do {
            switch (i % 3) {
                case 0:
                    System.out.println(i);
                    break;

                default:
                    break;
            }
            i++;
        } while (i < limit);
    }

    public static void printPrimes(int limit) {
        System.out.println("Primes:");
    FindNextPrime:
        for (int i = 2; i < limit; i++) {
            for (int j = 2; j <= (int) Math.sqrt(i); j++) {
                if ((i / j) * j == i)
                    continue FindNextPrime;
            }
            System.out.println(i);
        }
    }

    public static void main(String args[]) {
        printMultiplesOfTwo(10);
        printMultiplesOfThree(20);
        printPrimes(30);
    }
}
```

If, for now, you ignore the `public`, `class`, and `static` keywords and you don't worry about why you have to write `Math.sqrt` to obtain the square root of a number, or `System.out.println` to display anything, then the rest of the program should be pretty easy to understand.

It is interesting to note that, as in C++, local variables can be introduced anywhere in a method, including in the initialization of a `for` loop.

If you examine the `printPrimes()` method, you notice how we used a label and a `continue` statement to break out of an inner loop and go on to next iteration of the outer loop. To do this in C or C++, you need to use a `goto` statement. Java does not have a `goto` statement, but it supports an optional label in its `continue` and `break` statements. Labels in Java can only be placed right before a looping construct.

Warning

The source code for a Java class must be stored in a file whose name is the name of the class with a `.java` extension.

Method Overloading

If you look closely at `Example1` and `Example2`, you see that we have used the `System.out.println` method with three different types of arguments: `string`, `int`, and `double`.

Actually, we used three different methods that share the same name. This is called *method overloading*.

You can write, in a single Java class, as many methods as you want with the same name as long as they all have different signatures. The signature of a method consists of the number and types of its arguments.

In other words, as long as they have a different number of arguments, or the arguments are of different types, two methods can share the same name.

This way, we avoid having to name one method `printDouble` and another `printString`.

Arrays and Memory Management

Java can have arrays of one or more dimensions. But unlike in C or C++, Java arrays are always dynamically allocated. Declaring a variable to be an array type means that the variable can contain a reference to an array. Likewise, the size of the array is a property of the array itself and not of the variable used to reference it.

In the `Example3` program in Listing 25.2, you can see how to declare an array variable, create an array and keep a reference to it in the variable (by using `new`), access the elements of the array, pass an array as an argument to a method, and find out the number of elements in an array (by using `.length`).

LISTING 25.2 Example3

```
public class Example3 {

    public static void print(int a[]) {
        for (int i = 0; i < a.length; i++)
            System.out.println(a[i]);
    }

    public static void main(String args[]) {
        int numbers[];
        numbers = new int[10];
        for (int i = 0; i < 10; i++)
            numbers[i] = i * 2;
        print(numbers);
    }

}
```

As in C and C++, for an array of size `n`, valid array indexes are numbered from 0 to `n`–1. Unlike in C and C++, each time you allocate memory for an array, all its contents are initialized to zero. (For an array of `booleans`, this means initialized to `false`, and for an array of objects, it means initialized to `null`.)

In each of the sample programs, you might have noticed that method `main` always has an parameter that is an array of strings. This parameter allows you to access the arguments with which your program was invoked. Unlike C or C++, `args[0]` is not the name of your program; it is the first argument. If you run the program with no arguments, then `args.length == 0`.

The program `Example4` in Listing 25.3 allocates an array with 1,024 integers of 32 bits each (4 bytes), so the array uses 4KB of memory. But it does this inside a loop that is executed a million times, so it allocates (and initializes to zero) 4,000,000KB of RAM.

For each 1,000 arrays, it allocates and displays the number of arrays it has already allocated, so you can see it is still working.

LISTING 25.3 Example4

```
public class Example4 {

    public static void main(String args[]) {
        int a[];
        for (int i = 1; i <= 1000000; i++) {
            a = new int[1024];
            if ((i % 1000) == 0)
                System.out.println(i);
        }
    }

}
```

Go ahead: Compile it and run it. Contrary to what you might expect, it won't crash, and it will not run out of memory. Why?

Each time we allocate a new array, we keep a reference to it in variable a, and the reference to the array we allocated in the previous iteration is lost. We cannot access it anymore: It becomes garbage. Java's memory management features a garbage collector, which finds all the memory we allocated but for which we don't have a reference anymore. This memory is unreachable; therefore, it is freed.

If you run `Example4` with the `-verbosegc` option, you'll be able to see the garbage collector in action:

```
$ java -verbosegc Example4
1000
2000
3000
<GC: managing allocation failure. need 4104 bytes, type=1, action=1>
<GC: freeing class java.lang.Compiler>
<GC: unloaded and freed 1 class>
<GC: freed 497 objects, 709720 bytes in 9 ms, 84% free (712352/838856)>
  <GC: init&scan: 2 ms, scan handles: 5 ms, sweep: 2 ms, compact: 0 ms>
<GC: managing allocation failure. need 4104 bytes, type=1, action=1>
<GC: freed 171 objects, 701784 bytes in 8 ms, 84% free (712352/838856)>
  <GC: init&scan: 1 ms, scan handles: 5 ms, sweep: 2 ms, compact: 0 ms>
[.... rest of listing omitted for brevity ]
```

Note

The exact messages might be different if you are running a different version of the JDK, but the concept remains the same.

It is interesting to note that the garbage collector first started by releasing the memory used by the `java.lang.Compiler` class, which was only needed shortly during the program initialization. Then, it later released 497 unreferenced objects, which accounted for 709,720 bytes of memory.

We can also see that it never used more than 838,856 of memory (slightly more than 800KB) and that garbage collection pauses took about 1/100 of a second (10ms).

Furthermore, it shows us that it is using 4,104 bytes for each array instance it allocates. That is 4KB (4,096) + 8 bytes. What are the 8 extra bytes for? Well, 4 of them are used to store the length of the array (so we can do `a.length` in our program), and the other 4 bytes are used for memory management. This 8 extra bytes are not part of the JVM specification. Another JVM implementation might do things differently.

Exception Handling

A fact of life for every programmer is that errors happen. Sometimes they might be due to a bug in your software, but in many cases, they can come from unexpected events such as a filesystem running out of disk space or a network problem.

The robustness of any program can be measured in terms of how well it handles these unexpected situations. By definition, however, you can't predict when an unexpected situation will occur or what will be its nature. This makes the task of writing robust software seem almost impossible. Fortunately, exception handling provides a simple and reliable solution to this complex problem.

To see how exception handling is used, we first need a program in which we can be sure that an exception is thrown at runtime. The easiest way to accomplish this is by intentionally placing a bug in our program.

The program `Example5` in Listing 25.4 has an intentional bug in it.

LISTING 25.4 `Example5`

```
public class Example5 {

    public static void printStrings(String str[]) {
        for (int i = 0; i <= str.length; i++)
            System.out.println(str[i]);
    }

    public static void main(String args[]) {
        System.out.println("The arguments are:");
        printStrings(args);
        System.out.println("That's all folks!");
    }

}
```

The bug is in the `printStrings()` method. The loop to print each element in the `String` array does one iteration too many and tries to access a string beyond the end of the array. This is what happens when you run the program:

```
$ java Example5 one two three
The arguments are:
one
two
three
java.lang.ArrayIndexOutOfBoundsException: 3
    at Example5.printStrings(Example5.java:5)
    at Example5.main(Example5.java:10)
```

You'll notice that the execution of the program was terminated unexpectedly, and it never got to write the last message (`"That's all folks!"`). The JVM didn't just terminate the execution of the program; it also printed a detailed stack trace explaining what kind of error happened and what the program was doing at that point in its execution.

This is the information displayed on the execution stack trace that was displayed when the error occurred:

- There was an attempt to access an array beyond its bounds.
- The illegal index value was `3`.
- This error happened while executing the `printStrings()` method of class `Example5`. In the source code, this corresponds to line 5 of the file `Example5.java`.
- The `printStrings()` method was called from the `main()` method in class `Example5`. In the source code, this corresponds to line 10 of the file `Example5.java`.

Not bad if you consider that this error message came from running compiled code without a debugger. From a user's point of view, the reaction might be, "So what? The program crashed anyway, didn't it?"

That's where exception handling comes into action. Listing 25.5 is a more robust version of `Example5`; the exception-handling code ensures that the program will continue working even if something unexpected happens while executing the `printStrings()` method.

LISTING 25.5 `Example5`

```
public class Example5 {

    public static void printStrings(String str[]) {
        for (int i = 0; i <= str.length; i++)
            System.out.println(str[i]);
    }

    public static void main(String args[]) {
        System.out.println("The arguments are:");
        try {
            printStrings(args);
        } catch (Exception e) {
            System.out.println("There was an unexpected error.");
        }
        System.out.println("That's all folks!");
    }

}
```

This is what happens when you run the program:

```
java Example5 one two three
The arguments are:
one
two
three
There was an unexpected error.
That's all folks!
```

This time, the program prints a warning about the unexpected error and continues with its execution as if nothing had happened.

The exception was handled through the use of the `try-catch` construct. You put the code for which you want to do exception handling in a block between the `try` and `catch` keywords. The `catch` keyword is followed by a single parameter declaration defining the kind of exceptions to be handled by the code in the statement block placed immediately after it.

There can be many `catch` clauses associated with a single `try` block. If there's an error while executing anything between `try` and `catch`, then the flow of execution jumps directly to the block of code of the first `catch` block that matches the type of the exception being thrown.

Objects and Inheritance

Now it's time to move on to the basics of object-oriented programming in Java. As Java is fundamentally based on object-oriented programming, these topics are important if you want to be able to accomplish many tasks in the language.

Objects

We now look at how to do object-oriented programming with Java. As I said before, don't worry; it's simpler than what you might have been led to believe.

Imagine that you want to write a computer game, some kind of strategy game played on a map. You need to store the location of each piece on the map, probably as a coordinate pair (x,y). If you were writing your computer game in C, you would define a data structure to represent a location on the map and some functions to help you manipulate it so that its internal representation is hidden from the rest of the program. Well, when you are working with Java, you do exactly the same thing.

Let's start by looking at the representation. In C, you would probably use a struct named `Point` to store the x and y coordinates. The Java equivalent of a C struct is called a *class*.

Here is the Java source code for our `Point` internal representation:

```
public class Point {

    public double x;

    public double y;

}
```

Remember that you must save it in a file named `Point.java`.

Now, let's look at the program in Listing 25.6, which uses the `Point` class we just defined.

LISTING 25.6 Example6

```
public class Example6 {

    public static void printPoint(Point p) {
        System.out.println("(" + p.x + ", " + p.y + ")");
    }

    public static void main(String args[]) {
        Point a;
        a = new Point();
        a.x = 3.4;
        a.y = 5.6;
        printPoint(a);
        Point b = new Point();
        b.x = a.x + 2.1;
        b.y = -5.6;
        printPoint(b);
        a = b;
        printPoint(a);
        b.x = 0;
        printPoint(a);
    }

}
```

Compile and run this program:

```
$ javac Example6.java Point.java
$ java Example6
(3.4, 5.6)
(5.5, -5.6)
(5.5, -5.6)
(0.0, -5.6)
```

Just like array variables, object variables in Java do not contain the object itself. They just hold a reference to it. When you declare a variable of type `Point`, what you get is a variable that can refer to an object of type `Point`. The `new` operator is used to create a new instance of an object and return a reference to it, which can be stored in a variable of the appropriate type.

Once a variable holds a reference to an object, you can use the variable to manipulate the object. We declared both `x` and `y` to be public members of class `Point`, which means that we can directly access them to get or set their value by using the `.` (dot) operator, just like in a C struct.

Remember that in Java, a variable contains a reference to an object, not the object itself; these variables are really equivalent to what in C would be a pointer to a struct. When you pass them as an argument, you are really passing a reference to the object. And when you assign one `Point` variable to another, as we did in the program with `a = b`, we get two variables that refer to the same object. As the example shows, when we use one of the variables to modify the object, the same change can be observed from the other variable.

When we copied the reference from variable `b` to variable `a`, not only did we make both variables refer to the same object, but also we lost the only reference to the object that was being referenced by `a`. That object became garbage, which is reclaimed automatically; we don't need to worry about it.

You can also create an array of `Point`. Just as we did for an array of `int`, you must allocate the memory for it dynamically. But be careful, each element of the array you allocated does not contain a `Point` but a reference to a `Point`. You still need to allocate one `Point` for each element in the array. If you fail to do this, the array only contains `null` references! Here is how it should be done:

```
Point pts[] = new Point[10];
for (int k = 0; k < pts.length; k++)
    pts[k] = new Point();
```

In `Example6`, we defined a `printPoint()` method. But it would be better to define this method in the same file where we defined our `Point` data structure. Any routine that interacts with the internal structure of a `Point` should also be defined there.

Here is a new definition of `Point`, which includes a method to print a representation of the point:

```
public class Point {

    public double x;

    public double y;

    public void print() {
```

```
        System.out.println("(" + x + ", " + y + ")");
    }

}
```

Listing 25.7 contains a new version of Example6, updated to use the new print method of class Point.

LISTING 25.7 Example6

```
public class Example6 {

    public static void main(String args[]) {
        Point a;
        a = new Point();
        a.x = 3.4;
        a.y = 5.6;
        a.print();
        Point b = new Point();
        b.x = a.x + 2.1;
        b.y = -5.6;
        b.print();
        a = b;
        a.print();
        b.x = 0;
        a.print();
    }

}
```

Running this program produces the same results as before.

Looking at the definition of the print() method in class Point, you can see that we referred to x and y without using a variable name and a dot before them. This is because they automatically refer to the x and y members of the object on which the print method was invoked. When you do a.print(), x and y refer to the values stored in the Point instance to which variable a holds a reference; if you do a b.print(), then x and y refer to the values in the object referenced by b.

You can define many methods in a class definition. Here is a new version of Point in which we have a method to calculate the distance from the current point to another point:

```
public class Point {

    public double x;

    public double y;

    public void print() {
```

```
        System.out.println("(" + x + ", " + y + ")");
    }

    public double distanceTo(Point other) {
        double dx = x - other.x;
        double dy = y - other.y;
        return Math.sqrt(dx * dx + dy * dy);
    }

}
```

`Example7` in Listing 25.8 shows how this can be used in a program.

LISTING 25.8 `Example7`

```
public class Example7 {

    public static void main(String args[]) {
        Point a = new Point();
        a.x = 2.3;
        a.y = 4.5;
        Point b = new Point();
        b.x = -5.2;
        b.y = 1.1;
        System.out.println(a.distanceTo(b));
    }

}
```

Here is what you get when you run `Example7`:

```
$ java Example7
8.234682750416072
```

Defining a Constructor

Allocating a `Point` object and then assigning values for each of its members is a little cumbersome. Wouldn't it be better to do both things at once? Actually, there is a way to do exactly that: by defining a constructor in class `Point`.

Here is what class `Point` looks like after we define a constructor:

```
public class Point {

    public double x;

    public double y;

    public void print() {
        System.out.println("(" + x + ", " + y + ")");
```

```
    }

    public double distanceTo(Point other) {
        double dx = x - other.x;
        double dy = y - other.y;
        return Math.sqrt(dx * dx + dy * dy);
    }

    public Point(double nx, double ny) {
        x = nx;
        y = ny;
    }

}
```

As you can see, a constructor is defined like a method, but its name must be same as the class name, and it doesn't return any value (not even void).

In Listing 25.9, we have `Example7`, now using the constructor we just defined for class `Point`.

LISTING 25.9 `Example7`

```
public class Example7 {

    public static void main(String args[]) {
        Point a = new Point(2.3, 4.5);
        Point b = new Point(-5.2, 1.1);
        System.out.println(a.distanceTo(b));
    }

}
```

Compared to the previous implementation, this looks much better, doesn't it? The program itself no longer has to take care of so many details of initializing the `Point`; these are all left to its constructor.

A class must always have a constructor. If you don't define one, then the compiler automatically generates one for you. The constructor generated by the compiler is always a constructor with no arguments, which is what allowed us to write `new Point()` in the previous examples. Now that we have defined our own constructor, the compiler won't generate the argumentless constructor anymore. Now it causes an error to write `new Point()` to create a new `Point` instance. If you want to have a constructor with arguments and still be able to use a constructor without arguments, then you have to add it yourself. You can define it like this:

```
public Point() {
}
```

You can have in a class as many constructors as you want. The only rule is that the signature—the number and type of its arguments—must be different from those of the other constructors.

Although objects by themselves are already a powerful concept in a programming language, another way to add power to the language is to implement object inheritance, which allows you to relate two different but similar objects to each other.

Inheritance

Let's suppose you also need to define a data structure to manipulate the concept of a geographical location. A geographical location is defined by a coordinate pair (x,y) and a name. You could copy the source for the `Point` class and paste it in a new file named `Location.java` and then make the changes you need. But there is a better way: Use inheritance.

When a class B inherits from a class A, it automatically has the same members as class A. This includes both data and method members. Class B, besides inheriting all the members from class A, can also define its own new members or provide alternate method definitions to replace those it inherited from A.

Inheritance Example

Here is an example of how we can define a geographical location inheriting from class `Point`:

```
public class Location extends Point {

    public String name;

    public void print() {
        System.out.println(name + ": (" + x + ", " + y + ")");
    }

    public Location(String nn, double nx, double ny) {
        super(nx, ny);
        name = nn;
    }

}
```

We used the `extends` keyword to indicate that `Location` inherits from `Point`. Inheritance can be interpreted as an is-a relationship. In other words, we can say that a `Location` is a special kind of `Point`. Sometimes, we say that `Point` is a superclass of `Location` and that `Location` is a subclass of `Point`. We can also say that `Point` is the parent class and `Location` is the child class.

We defined a new `print()` method for class `Location`. This new definition overrides the one inherited from `Point`. On the other hand, we didn't define a new `distanceTo()` method, so the one we inherited from `Point` is the one that is also used for `Location`.

`Location` has its own constructor (constructors are never inherited), which calls `Point`'s two-argument constructor using the notation `super(x, y)`, before using its `String` argument to initialize the name of the location. A constructor in a child class must always call a constructor in its parent class, and it must always be the first thing to be executed in the child's constructor. If you don't explicitly call the constructor of the parent class, then the compiler automatically generates an invocation of the parent's class constructor with no arguments.

Using the Inherited Class

`Example8` in Listing 25.10 shows how you might use class `Location`.

LISTING 25.10 `Example8`

```
public class Example8 {

    public static void main(String args[]) {
        Location a = new Location("New York", 10.2, 20.3);
        Location b = new Location("San Francisco", -7, -4.5);
        a.print();
        b.print();
        System.out.println(a.distanceTo(b));

        Point pts[] = new Point[3];
        pts[0] = new Point(3, 4);
        pts[1] = a;
        pts[2] = b;
        for (int i = 0; i < pts.length; i++)
            pts[i].print();
    }

}
```

It first creates two `Location` instances, prints them, and prints the distance between them. Next, it creates an array of `Points`, creates a `Point` object, and keeps a reference to it in the first element of the array, and—this is where it starts to get really interesting—stores, in the second and third elements of the array, references to the two location objects it had created previously.

At first sight, this might seem strange, maybe even like a mistake, but if you think about it, you realize it's completely normal. After all, a `Location` is a `Point`. Note that the inverse isn't always true: A `Point` is not necessarily a `Location`. Creating an array of

Locations and then trying to store a reference to a generic Point as one of its elements will give you a compile-time error.

It's even more amazing that when we ask each of the objects referenced in the array to print itself, each one of them automatically invokes the correct version of the print() method for itself. When you run the program, this is what you get:

```
$ java Example8
New York: (10.2, 20.3)
San Francisco: (-7.0, -4.5)
30.180788591420207
(3.0, 4.0)
New York: (10.2, 20.3)
San Francisco: (-7.0, -4.5)
```

Inheritance is one of the most useful features of object-oriented programming. It allows us to create generic routines where we can traverse a data structure asking each of its elements to do something—such as printing itself—without having to know all the kinds of objects that could be stored in the data structure. If in the future we decide to add another kind of object, we just need to provide it with its own print method, and we don't have to modify a single line of the generic routine for it to work with the new objects.

Static Variables

Maybe you also want your application to know how many Point objects have been created. The best way to do this is to keep a counter in the class itself, which is incremented by one each time a new Point instance is created.

Listing 25.11 is Point.java, modified to keep track of the number of Points created so far.

LISTING 25.11 Point Class, with Revisions

```
public class Point {

    public static int count;

    public double x;

    public double y;

    public void print() {
        System.out.println("(" + x + ", " + y + ")");
    }

    public double distanceTo(Point other) {
        double dx = x - other.x;
```

continues

LISTING 25.11 Continued

```
        double dy = y - other.y;
        return Math.sqrt(dx * dx + dy * dy);
    }

    public Point(double nx, double ny) {
        count++;
        x = nx;
        y = ny;
    }

    public Point() {
        count++;
    }
}
```

You'll notice that we have added a variable named `count` and that we declared that variable as `static`. What does static mean? Here, it says that there should be only one `count` variable shared by all instances of class `Point`. If we didn't use the `static` keyword, then each `Point` would have its own copy of the `count` variable, which would make it useless for our purposes.

To complement that, each of the constructors was modified to increment the `count` variable by one each time a `Point` object is created.

In Listing 25.12, `Example9` shows that a static variable can be accessed by prefixing the variable name with the class name and the dot operator. In other words, you don't need an instance in order to access a static variable. Sometimes static variables are called class variables, and non-static variables are referred to as instance variables.

LISTING 25.12 `Example9`

```
public class Example9 {

    public static void main(String args[]) {
        new Point();
        new Point();
        new Location("Mexico", 10, 20);
        System.out.println(Point.count);
    }
}
```

Not only variables can be declared static; a method can also be static. A static method can be invoked by following the class name with a dot and the name of the method.

When you invoke the JVM, it expects as an argument the name of a class. That class should have a static method called `main`, which should be public and expect an array of strings as its unique argument.

When we used `Math.sqrt()`, we were invoking a static method of class `Math`. The meaning of `System.out.println()` is to access a static variable (named `out`) of the `System` class, which contains a reference to a `PrintStream` object on which we invoke its `println()`method.

Interfaces

If you analyze inheritance closely, you'll find out that it combines two different features as if they were a single feature. One of them is the capability to describe a class of objects in generic terms: All `Points` or any of the classes that inherit from it can be printed by invoking their `print` method. The other feature is that it allows you to reutilize an implementation (as `Location` reutilizes the `distanceTo()` method implemented in class `Point`).

A few years ago, the use of inheritance for code reuse was thought to be one of the best features of object-oriented programming, but now many believe it is more of a liability than an asset because it can make programs harder to understand and maintain.

On the other hand, the use of inheritance to specify an interface as an abstract list of methods that can be applied to any object which implements (inherits) that interface is widely regarded as one of the cornerstones of modern object-oriented programming.

In Java, you can define an *interface*, which is like a kind of class for which you only define the available methods, their arguments, and return values but never write an implementation.

A class can implement as many interfaces as it wants to (or needs to). To implement the interface, it only has to declare its intention to do so (using the `implements` keyword) and provide an implementation for each of the methods defined in the interface.

As an example, we write a simple command interpreter that can dynamically load new commands at runtime.

The main feature of a command is that it can be executed. We represent this concept with the `Executable` interface:

```
public interface Executable {

    void execute();

}
```

The `Executable` interface specifies that for an object to be executable, its class must implement an `execute()` method with no arguments and that returns `void`. This code is placed by itself in a file `Executable.java`.

Here is `Exe1.java`, a simple implementation of `Executable`:

```
public class Exe1 implements Executable {

    public void execute() {
        System.out.println("I am Exe1!");
    }

}
```

To add a little variety to our command interpreter, here is `Exe2.java`, another implementation of `Executable`:

```
public class Exe2 implements Executable {

    public void execute() {
        System.out.println("Exe2:");
        for (int i = 0; i < 3; i++)
            System.out.println(i);
    }

}
```

Listing 25.13 contains the source for `Example10.java`, our dynamically extensible command interpreter.

LISTING 25.13 `Example10`

```
import java.io.*;

public class Example10 {

    public static void main(String args[]) throws IOException {
        BufferedReader reader =
            new BufferedReader(new InputStreamReader(System.in));
    MainLoop:
        while (true) {
            System.out.print(">+++:> ");
            String command = reader.readLine();
            if (command == null)
                break MainLoop;
            command = command.trim();
            if (command.equalsIgnoreCase("end"))
                break MainLoop;
            try {
                Executable executable =
```

```
                (Executable) Class.forName(command).newInstance();
            executable.execute();
        } catch (Exception e) {
            System.out.println("Command failed: " + e);
        }
    }
    System.out.println("Bye!");
  }
}
```

There are many new concepts in this example, so let's look at it line-by-line. The following line tells the compiler that we intend to use one or more classes in the `java.io` package:

```
import java.io.*;
```

Packages are a mechanism to avoid name clashes when using classes from two or more suppliers in a single program. Two different classes can have the same name only if they are in separate packages.

By default, the compiler only looks for classes in the current directory and in the `java.lang` package. If you need to use a class from another package, then you must either write the full class name (something like `java.io.BufferedReader`) or use an `import` statement to tell the compiler about the other packages being used by this class.

The next code declares that our main method can throw an `IOException`:

```
public class Example10 {

    public static void main(String args[]) throws IOException {
```

Some of the objects that we use to read the commands from the standard input have methods that can throw this exception. The Java compiler will refuse to compile our main method unless we use a `try-catch` to catch the exception or we declare that it can throw that exception. To keep the program simple, we chose not to worry about I/O exceptions.

`BufferedReader` is a class that, among other things, lets us read lines one-by-one from an `InputStreamReader`:

```
        BufferedReader reader =
            new BufferedReader(new InputStreamReader(System.in));
```

We can create an instance of `BufferedReader` by using its constructor with an `InputStreamReader` as its only argument.

We don't have an `InputStreamReader`, but we can create one by using its constructor with an `InputStream` as its only argument and `System.in` as a reference to an object of type `InputStream`.

We want to keep on reading commands until we reach the end of thefile or we receive an `end` command:

```
MainLoop:
    while (true) {
```

We display a prompt so the user knows we are waiting for a command (I call this the dead fish prompt):

```
        System.out.print(">+++:> ");
```

The `readLine()` method of class `BufferedReader` returns the next input line as a string, without the trailing new line. If it reaches the end of the file without reading any character, it returns `null`:

```
        String command = reader.readLine();
```

We reached the end of file; we can exit our interpreter loop:

```
        if (command == null)
            break MainLoop;
```

The `trim()` method of class `String` returns the current string without any leading or trailing blanks. Java strings are not modifiable; once created, they remain the same forever. Methods such as `trim()` create a new `String` object:

```
        command = command.trim();
```

The user wants to exit the interpreter; let's do what he wants:

```
        if (command.equalsIgnoreCase("end"))
            break MainLoop;
```

The class named `Class` lets us manipulate Java classes like standard objects. It has a static method `forName()`, which, given a string with the full name of a class, returns a reference to the `Class` object that is the memory representation for that class. (Watch out: It doesn't return an instance of the class you named; it returns an instance of `Class` with all the information about the class you named.) Then, you can use that `Class` object to create an instance of the class you named:

```
        try {
            Executable executable =
                (Executable) Class.forName(command).newInstance();
            executable.execute();
        } catch (Exception e) {
            System.out.println("Command failed: " + e);
        }
```

If you're slightly confused, don't worry. The only thing you need to understand is that `Class.forName("AnyClass").newInstance()` creates an instance of class `AnyClass`. With `Class.forName("Point").newInstance()`, you create a new instance of class `Point`.

Why use something so complex when it's so easy to just say `new Point()`? What happens is that when we use the `new` operator, we have to know at compile time for which class we want to create an instance. With this other method, we can create an object from any class specified by the user at runtime. That is exactly what we want to do in our extensible command interpreter.

We take the command the user typed as the name of a class. We create an instance for that class. We assume it implements the `Executable` interface (by casting the object returned from `newInstance()` into an `Executable`). Finally, we tell the executable to execute itself.

All of this code is inside a `try-catch` block so that our interpreter won't fail if the user types a command that is not a class, if the command is a class that does not implement `Executable`, or if executing the `Executable` throws an exception.

After exiting the loop, let the user know that the program is exiting:

```
        }
        System.out.println("Bye!");
    }

}
```

Here is what happens after we compile these classes and run the program:

```
$ java Example10
>+++:> Exe1
I am Exe1!
>+++:> Exe2
Exe2:
0
1
2
>+++:> Point
Command failed: java.lang.ClassCastException
>+++:> Exe3
Command failed: java.lang.ClassNotFoundException: Exe3
>+++:>
```

It "understood" the first two commands by dynamically loading `Exe1` and `Exe2`. The error message when you try to execute `Point` indicates that `Point` does not implement the `Executable` interface and therefore cannot be cast to an `Executable`.

The last command shows what happens when you try to load a non-existent class.

Now, let's try something interesting: Without exiting the interpreter, open another window to type in and compile `Exe3.java`:

```
public class Exe3 implements Executable {

    public void execute() {
        System.out.println("This is the new executable: Exe3");
    }

}
```

Return to the window where you left the interpreter running, and try again:

```
>+++:> Exe3
This is the new executable: Exe3
>+++:>
```

This time, it worked! You have just executed code from a component that was written and compiled while the interpreter was already running. You did not need to make any changes to the interpreter. You did not need to stop and restart the interpreter.

You should compare this to other component architectures in which you might even need to reboot the operating system after installing a new component.

Before exiting the interpreter, let's try a creating a component with an intentional bug, just to see what happens.

Here is `BugExe.java`:

```
public class BugExe implements Executable {

    public void execute() {
        int a[] = null;
        System.out.println(a.length);
    }

}
```

After compiling it, let's see what happens when you try to execute it:

```
>+++:> BugExe
Command failed: java.lang.NullPointerException:
>+++:> end
Bye!
```

It fails, but our interpreter keeps on running without a problem.

You have a dynamically extensible interpreter that can be modified at runtime without compromising its reliability, in less than 30 lines of code. Isn't Java powerful?

Threads

Java's thread support makes it easy to write portable multithreaded code. Multiple threads allow multiple sections of your program to run simultaneously—or at least appear to do so. Listing 25.14 contains a simple example that creates and runs four threads simultaneously.

LISTING 25.14 Example11

```
public class Example11 implements Runnable {

    int delay;

    public void run() {
        while (true) {
            System.out.print(delay);
            try {
                Thread.sleep(delay * 1000);
            } catch (InterruptedException e) {
                e.printStackTrace();
            }
        }
    }

    public Example11(int d) {
        delay = d;
    }

    public static void main(String args[]) {
        new Thread(new Example11(1)).start();
        new Thread(new Example11(2)).start();
        new Thread(new Example11(3)).start();
        new Thread(new Example11(4)).start();
    }
}
```

When you run this program, one thread displays a `1` every second, another thread displays a `2` every two seconds, the third thread displays a `3` every three seconds, and the last thread displays a `4` every four seconds. The output looks like this:

```
123412131214123112413121124311213124112311241312112431121312411
```

The four threads are in an endless loop, so if you don't kill the process, they will run forever. (A more realistic forecast is that they will run until you turn off your computer.)

Let's look at the source code line-by-line. `Runnable` is an interface that only defines one method: `run()`. This method does not have any arguments:

```
public class Example11 implements Runnable {
```

This instance variable is used to store the number of seconds the current thread should sleep after displaying this number:

```
int delay;
```

This is an implementation of the method `run()`, which the `Runnable` interface requires. It basically sits in an endless loop, printing the delay assigned to this instance and then sleeping for that number of seconds:

```
public void run() {
    while (true) {
        System.out.print(delay);
        try {
            Thread.sleep(delay * 1000);
        } catch (InterruptedException e) {
            e.printStackTrace();
        }
    }
}
```

Thread.sleep()

`Thread.sleep()` is a static method of class `Thread` that puts the current thread to sleep for the specified number of milliseconds. It can throw an `InterruptedException`, so we place it inside a `try-catch` block. Note that here we don't have the option to declare that method `run()` throws an `InterruptedException`: The definition for `run()` in the `Runnable` interface doesn't declare that it throws any exception, so it is forbidden to write an implementation that does throw one.

We don't ever expect to receive an `InterruptedException` in this program, but if we ever do, it never hurts to have the exception print a stack trace (exactly like the one the JVM prints when the execution of our program is interrupted due to an unexpected exception).

The constructor allows us to specify the desired delay for this instance:

```
public Example11(int d) {
    delay = d;
}
```

The `main` method creates four threads. One way to create a thread is by calling the `Thread` constructor, which expects a single parameter of type `Runnable`. When the `start()` method is invoked on the newly created `Thread` object, it uses the thread it is managing to execute the `run()` method of the `Runnable` object that was used to create it:

```
public static void main(String args[]) {
    new Thread(new Example11(1)).start();
    new Thread(new Example11(2)).start();
```

```
        new Thread(new Example11(3)).start();
        new Thread(new Example11(4)).start();
    }

}
```

In all the previous examples, exiting the `main()` method immediately terminated the execution of the JVM. But this won't happen in this program because the other four threads are still running. Actually, the JVM dies automatically when the last of the user threads finishes executing. In all the previous examples, the only user thread was the one used to execute the `main()` method.

AWT

Until now, all the examples we have seen have only used the standard input and the standard output to interact with the user. Our last example shows how easy it is to write GUI-based applications in Java.

The standard Java runtime libraries include a package called `java.awt`, which includes all the standard components of a modern GUI-based interface. These components include such things as windows, buttons, and menus.

Our sample program opens a window with a white background and draws a red square inside it. You can move the window, resize it, minimize it, and maximize it, just like any other window. You can move the red square by clicking and dragging inside the window.

Listing 25.15 is the complete source code for our GUI example.

LISTING 25.15 Example12

```
import java.awt.*;
import java.awt.event.*;

public class Example12 extends Frame {

    int x = 100;

    int y = 100;

    void moveSquare(int mx, int my) {
        x = mx;
        y = my;
        repaint();
    }

    public void paint(Graphics g) {
        g.setColor(Color.red);
        g.fillRect(x, y, 50, 50);
```

continues

LISTING 25.15 continued

```
    }

    public Example12() {
        setSize(new Dimension(400, 300));
        setVisible(true);
        addMouseListener(new MouseAdapter() {
            public void mousePressed(MouseEvent event) {
                moveSquare(event.getX(), event.getY());
            }
        });
        addMouseMotionListener(new MouseMotionAdapter() {
            public void mouseDragged(MouseEvent event) {
                moveSquare(event.getX(), event.getY());
            }
        });
    }

    public static void main(String args[]) {
        new Example12().addWindowListener(new WindowAdapter() {
            public void windowClosing(WindowEvent event) {
                System.exit(0);
            }
        });
    }
}
```

Let's look at it line-by-line. The first two lines tell the compiler to look in the `java.awt` and `java.awt.event` packages for the classes we'll be using in this program:

```
import java.awt.*;
import java.awt.event.*;

public class Example12 extends Frame {
```

Frame

`Example12` inherits from `Frame`. A `Frame` is a rectangular container that can have any kind of GUI components inside it. It typically has border decorations that the users use to move and resize the frame. Maybe you already guessed it: A frame is what any user would simply call a window.

All the normal window behavior such as being able to be moved or resized is already programmed into the `Frame` component, and by inheriting from it, you automatically inherit its behavior. You don't need to do anything else about it.

Next, we declare two integer variables used to hold the x,y coordinates for the red square:

```
int x = 100;

int y = 100;
```

Something we haven't seen in the previous examples: You can declare an initial value for any instance variable; upon creating a new instance, the variables are automatically initialized to their declared initial values.

The `moveSquare` method is used to update the position of the red square on the screen:

```
void moveSquare(int mx, int my) {
    x = mx;
    y = my;
    repaint();
}
```

It simply updates the values of the red square's coordinates and requests for the window to be repainted.

The `paint` Method

The window system can, at any time, send a request to a window to repaint its contents. This might happen because the window was resized or another window that was in front of it has moved, and it is necessary to repaint what was underneath it. Even the program itself can request that the window be repainted, maybe to update its contents with new data that should be displayed:

```
public void paint(Graphics g) {
    g.setColor(Color.red);
    g.fillRect(x, y, 50, 50);
}
```

Each time a frame needs to be repainted, its `paint` method is invoked to do the actual redrawing. By default, this method does nothing; classes that inherit from `Frame` are supposed to override it with their own `paint` method.

The `paint()` method has only one parameter of type `Graphics`. It is a handle to the graphics context that can be used to draw inside the window.

Our `paint` method just selects red as its current color and uses it to draw a square at the coordinates indicated by the x,y instance variables. The area to be repainted is always filled with a white background before calling the `paint()` method, so we don't have to worry about erasing the previous contents.

In the constructor, we define the initial size for the window and make it visible:

```
public Example12() {
    setSize(new Dimension(400, 300));
    setVisible(true);
```

If we forget this last step, nothing will appear onscreen.

Listeners

In Java, for each kind of event that can be received by a GUI component, you can register a list of listeners that want to be informed whenever one of these events is received. A listener is an instance that belongs to a class that implements a specific listener interface:

```
        addMouseListener(new MouseAdapter() {
            public void mousePressed(MouseEvent event) {
                moveSquare(event.getX(), event.getY());
            }
        });
        addMouseMotionListener(new MouseMotionAdapter() {
            public void mouseDragged(MouseEvent event) {
                moveSquare(event.getX(), event.getY());
            }
        });
    }
```

The `addMouseListener()` method is used to register objects that are interested in mouse pressed, mouse released, and mouse clicked events.

The `addMouseMotionListener()` method is used to register objects that are interested in mouse move and mouse drag events.

Listeners tend to be simple objects, so they are typically implemented inline using a Java feature known as an *anonymous inner class*.

Inner Classes

An inner class is a class that is completely defined inside another class. An anonymous inner class is an inner class that doesn't have a name; the complete definition for the class is used as an argument for the `new()` operator.

The only requirement for an anonymous inner class is that it must specify either what interface it implements or from which class it inherits.

Our first anonymous inner class inherits from the `MouseAdapter` class, which is an empty implementation of the `MouseListener` interface. It is an empty implementation because it provides, for each of the methods in the `MouseListener` interface, an implementation that does nothing. Adapter classes are used when you need to implement an interface but you aren't interested in providing an implementation for each one of its methods.

The `MouseListener` interface specifies a `mousePressed()`, a `mouseReleased()`, and a `mouseClicked()` method. The `MouseAdapter` class implements the `MouseListener` interface by providing for each of this methods a "do nothing" implementation. By inheriting from `MouseAdapter`, we can easily implement `MouseListener` and only implement the method we are interested in—which in this case is `mousePressed()`.

When you press the mouse button inside the window, all the mouse listeners registered with it are notified by calling their `mousePressed` method with a `MouseEvent` argument. From the `MouseEvent` argument, we can extract the mouse's x,y coordinates relative to the window's origin at the time the mouse button was pressed.

An interesting feature of inner classes is that when an instance is created, it is automatically linked to the instance of the containing class where it was created, and it can access all of the methods and instance variables of its outer class. This means that from any method in the inner class, we can get or set the value of the x and y instance variables or call an outer class method that will be executed in the context of the outer class.

Specifically, we use this feature of inner classes to update the square's position and repaint the window whenever the mouse button is pressed inside the window.

The inner class we defined as a `MouseMotionListener` does exactly the same thing whenever the mouse is dragged inside the window.

Our `main()` method creates an instance of `Example12` and registers with it a listener to terminate execution whenever it receives a window close event:

```
    public static void main(String args[]) {
        new Example12().addWindowListener(new WindowAdapter() {
            public void windowClosing(WindowEvent event) {
                System.exit(0);
            }
        });
    }

}
```

As in the threads example, the JVM stays alive even after our main method finishes. This happens because the `java.awt.Frame` implementation starts new threads to handle the window events.

Summary

What we saw in this chapter is just the tip of the iceberg.

We didn't look at how Java manages files, the standard data structures it supports such as vectors and hashtables, low-level networking support using sockets, high-level networking using RMI (Remote Method Invocation), database access with JDBC, or file compression. And all these features are included in the standard JDK 1.1 runtime library.

There are also many standard libraries, extensions, and specifications: Java 2D, Java 3D, Java Media Framework, Java Sound API, Java Advanced Imaging API, Servlets, Java Server Pages, Java Beans, Enterprise Java Beans, and many more.

CHAPTER 26

`tcl` and `tk` Programming

by Steve Wells

In This Chapter

The `tcl` (pronounced "tickle") scripting language and the `tk` toolkit are programming environments for creating graphical user interfaces for the X Window system. `tcl` and `tk` are easy to learn and use, and with them, you can construct user interfaces much faster than with traditional X Window programming methods.

`tcl/tk` was written by John K. Ousterhout while he was a professor of electrical engineering and computer science at the University of California, Berkeley. It was originally designed to provide a reusable command language for interactive tools, but it has expanded far beyond that and is used in a wide range of software products, such as client/server and database support.

The true power of `tcl/tk` is that complex graphical applications can be written almost entirely in the `tcl` scripting language, thus hiding many of the complexities of interface programming encountered in writing interfaces using the C language. This means you could write a graphical Internet browser such as Netscape entirely in `tcl/tk`.

The official `tcl/tk` Web site is located at `http://www.scriptics.com/`.

According to its Web site, Scriptics Corporation is the `tcl` platform company. Formed by John Ousterhout, Scriptics is focused on bringing the `tcl` scripting language into the corporate mainstream. Scriptics will provide development tools, technology extensions, and commercial support services for `tcl` while continuing to develop the open source `tcl` and `tk` packages.

The site also has links for downloading and installing the latest versions of `tcl/tk`.

`tcl` binaries `tcl`, `tclsh`, `wish`, and `tclhelp` are installed by Debian's rpm in `/usr/bin`. Voluminous help on both `tcl` and `tk` is available by running the `tclhelp` command. There are also `man` pages for `tclsh` and `wish`.

The programs discussed in this chapter are compatible with most versions of `tcl` and `tk` and should work fine for the current version.

tcl Basics

`tcl` is an interpreted language similar to Perl or the UNIX shell, which means `tcl` commands are first read and then evaluated. `tk` is a windowing toolkit that uses the `tcl` syntax for creating graphical user interface (GUI) components, such as buttons, scrollbars, dialogs, and windows.

To run `tcl`, the `tcl` shell (`tclsh`) or the windowing shell (`wish`) is required. Both `tclsh` and `wish` are similar to standard UNIX shells such as `sh` or `csh`; they allow commands to be executed interactively or read in from a file. In practice, these shells are seldom used interactively because their interactive capabilities are quite limited.

The main difference between tclsh and wish is that tclsh understands only tcl commands, and wish understands both tcl and tk commands.

Interactive Use of tcl

This section briefly covers the interactive use of the tcl shells to illustrate one of its hazards.

To start using tcl interactively, type **tclsh** (or wish, which works only in a graphical environment) at the UNIX shell's prompt. The following prompt should appear:

```
%
```

In this chapter, interactive commands start with the percent character (%). At the prompt, type

```
% echo "hello world"
```

The words hello world should appear, followed by a new prompt. Now try

```
% puts "hello world"
```

The same output should appear, but there is a big difference between the two. The first command ran the echo binary to echo the string "hello world", whereas the second command uses the puts (put string) tcl command. The echo version of "hello world" works only when tclsh is run interactively, which is one of the hazards of using tclsh and wish interactively. For example, if you put the command

```
echo "hello world"
```

into the file helloworld.tcl and then source that file from tclsh, as in

```
% source helloworld.tcl
```

you get the following error:

```
invalid command name "echo"
```

This executes the command with its arguments in a UNIX shell. This is only one example of things that work differently in the interactive mode of the tcl shells.

Noninteractive Use of tcl

Interactive mode has severe limitations because you need to enter each command individually and execute it. The real power of tcl is derived from the use of noninteractive scripts. Commonly, tclsh and wish are used noninteractively, which means they are invoked on scripts from the UNIX prompt ($), such as

```
$ tclsh myprog.tcl
$ wish myprog.tcl
```

or are called from within a script that has as its first line something like the following:

```
#!/usr/bin/tclsh
```

Usually, this first line must be changed for each installation of the script, because `wish` or `tclsh` will be in different places. To avoid the need to edit the script for each installation, the `man` page for `tclsh` recommends that the following three lines be used as the first three lines of all `tcl/tk` scripts:

```
#!/bin/sh
# the next line restarts using tclsh \
exec wish "$0" "$@"
```

This means users need to have only `tclsh` in their path to use the script. Individual results with this approach could vary, depending on the version of `sh` on the system.

The real advantage of noninteractive use of `tcl` is the same as for noninteractive use of the UNIX shell. Noninteractive use allows many commands to be grouped together and executed by simply typing the name of the script and allows faster development and debugging of large programs. Use the interactive portion of the language to test commands before committing them to your noninteractive scripts. Next, we will discuss the syntax of the language.

The `tcl` Language

This section contains an introduction to the `tcl` language syntax and its use in scripts. The code in the following section can be run interactively or from a script. The spacing of the output will vary slightly in interactive mode. It is likely you will find it easier to edit and run scripts.

Command Structure

The basic structure of a `tcl` command is

```
commandname arguments
```

where *`commandname`* is the command that `tcl` is to execute, and *`arguments`* is the optional arguments to give to that command. The entire line (*`commandname`* and *`arguments`*) is called the command. Commands are separated by newlines (`\n`) or by a semicolon (`;`). If only one command is given on a line, the semicolon is not required. As an illustration, the two commands can be written one per line:

```
set foo 0
set bar 1
```

or on the same line:

```
set foo 0; set bar 1;
```

Sometimes you need to use the value of one expression in another. To do that, you use brackets:

```
puts [expr 1000 / 4];
```

This prints the number 250. These brackets can be nested as necessary.

Comments

Other than commands, the only other lines in a tcl script are comments. As in UNIX shells and Perl, a comment line is a line that begins with a pound symbol (#):

```
# this is a comment
```

but unlike in a shell, the following is not a comment:

```
set foo 0 # initialize foo
```

This will result in an error, because the tcl parser thinks a command is terminated either by a newline or a semicolon. To include comments on the same line as a command, the command needs to be terminated by a semicolon:

```
set foo 0;# initialize foo
```

It is probably a good idea to terminate all commands with a semicolon, although it is not required.

Data Types

tcl doesn't support variable types, such as int, float, double, or char. This means a variable can be set to a number, a character, or a string at different times in the same program. tcl inherently understands when you are using a variable as a number or a string and appropriately performs the actions needed with it; therefore, the programmer does not need to explicitly set them.

Internally, however, tcl treats all variables as strings. When a variable needs to be manipulated, tcl allows numbers (real and integer) to be given in all the forms that are understood by ANSI C. The following are examples of valid numeric values for variables:

Value	*Data Type*
74	Integer
0112	Octal, starts with a 0
0x4a	Hexadecimal, starts with 0x
74.	Real
74.0	Real
7.4e1	Real
7.4e+1	Real

Other values are treated as strings and will generate errors if used in mathematical expressions.

Variables

`tcl` defines two types of variables, *scalars* and *arrays*. To create a scalar variable and assign it a value, use the `set` command. For example:

```
set banana 1;
```

creates the variable `banana` and gives it a value of `1`. To set the value of `banana` to something different, simply use `set` again:

```
set banana "Fresh from Brazil";
```

Now the variable `banana` has the value `"Fresh from Brazil"`. The double quotes tell `tcl` that all the characters including the spaces make up the value of the variable. (Quoting and substitution are covered later in this chapter in the section "Quoting and Substitution.")

To print the value of `banana`, use the `puts` command:

```
puts $banana;
```

This prints the value of the variable `banana` to the standard output (sometimes referred to as `STDOUT`). Putting `$` before the name of the variable tells `tcl` to access the value assigned to that variable. This convention, known as variable substitution, is similar to conventions used in UNIX shells.

> **Note**
>
> When should you use the dollar sign? Use the dollar sign when looking at or using the contents of the variable. Do not use the dollar sign when setting or changing the variable.

Creating a One-Dimensional Array

To create a one-dimensional array, enter the following:

```
set fruit(0) banana;
set fruit(1) orange;
```

This creates the array `fruit` and assigns the values `banana` and `orange` to the first and second elements, `0` and `1`.

Note

Remember: Computers start counting with the number zero (0), not one (1).

The assignments to array indexes need not be in order. The commands

```
set fruit(100) peach;
set fruit(2) kiwi;
set fruit(87) pear;
```

create only three items in the array `fruit`. Arrays in `tcl` are like associative arrays, which associate a "key" with a value. Arrays in `tcl` associate a given string with another string. This makes it possible to have array indexes that are not numbers. The command

```
set fruit(banana) 100
```

sets the value of item `banana` in the array `fruit` to `100`. The assigned values need not be numeric:

```
set food(koala) eucalyptus;
set food(chipmunk) acorn;
```

To access the value stored in a one-dimensional array variable, use the `$` convention:

```
puts $food(koala);
```

This prints the value stored in the array `food` at index `koala`. The array index can also be a variable:

```
set animal chipmunk;
puts $food($animal);
```

These commands output `acorn`, given the previous assignments.

Multidimensional arrays are a simple extension of one-dimensional arrays and are set as follows:

```
set myarray(1,1) 0;
```

This sets the value of the item at `1,1` in the array `myarray` to `0`. By separating the indexes by commas, you can make arrays of three, four, or more dimensions:

```
set array(1,1,1,1,1,1) "foo";
```

array and parray

In addition to setting array values, `tcl` provides the `array` command for getting information about arrays and the `parray` command for printing information about arrays. First, take a look at the `parray` command. Given the declarations

```
set food(koala) eucalyptus;
set food(chipmunk) acorn;
set food(panda) bamboo;
```

the command

```
parray food
```

produces the following output:

```
food(chipmunk) = acorn
food(koala)    = eucalyptus
food(panda)    = bamboo
```

Now look at the `array` command and its arguments, which are used to get information about an array and its elements. The basic syntax for an `array` command is as follows:

```
array option arrayname
```

The supported options are discussed later in this section.

One of the most frequently used pieces of information about an array is its size. Given the declarations

```
set fruit(0) banana;
set fruit(1) peach;
set fruit(2) pear;
set fruit(3) apple;
```

the command

```
array size fruit;
```

returns `4`. This number is often useful in loops because it returns the number of values set within the array, and a loop usually needs to run through each element.

Because arrays can have nonsequential or nonnumeric indexes, the `array` command provides an option for getting elements from an array. Assuming that the `food` array has been defined as presented earlier, the first thing you need to do to start getting elements is to use `startsearch` through the array. This is accomplished by first getting a search ID for the array:

```
set food_sid [array startsearch food];
```

The command

```
array startsearch food
```

returns a string, which is the name of the search (see the section "Quoting and Substitution," later in this chapter). You will need this for future reference, so set its value to that of a variable—in this case, `food_sid`.

To get the first element (and every subsequent element) of the `food` array, use

```
array nextelement food $food_sid;
```

When the array search is done, terminate the search for the array by using

```
array donesearch food $food_sid;
```

One other option to the `array` command that is frequently in use while iterating through an array is the `anymore` option. It returns true (a value of `1`) if there are any more items in the search. For example:

```
array anymore food $food_sid;
```

returns `1` the first two times it is used with the `food` array declared earlier.

unset

To dispose of a variable (scalar or array), use the `unset` command:

```
unset banana;
```

This unsets the variable `banana`. If you use `unset $banana` (assuming that `banana` was set to the value shown earlier) instead of just `banana`, you get an error:

```
can't unset "0": no such variable
```

This occurs because when `$` precedes a variable's name, the value of the variable is substituted before the command is executed.

Manipulating String Values

You might need to manipulate a string if you need to remove, modify, or add data to a file or database or you need to display information to the screen. The simplest form of string manipulation is the `append` command, which concatenates multiple strings and variables together. As an illustration, the following commands

```
set str1 "Begin";
append str1 " a String";
set str2 " even more text";
append str1 " with some text" " and add" $str2 " to it.";
puts $str1;
```

give this output:

```
Begin a String with some text and add even more text to it.
```

You can achieve the same results by using the following commands:

```
set str1 "Begin";
set str1 "$str1 a String";
set str2 " even more text";
set str1 "$str1 with some text and add$str2 to it.";
```

but this will be slower than using `append`, because `append` does not do character copying as `set` does.

For more advanced string manipulation, `tcl` provides the `string` command, which understands a whole host of options. The basic syntax of the `string` command is

```
string option string1 string2
```

where *`string1`* and *`string2`* can be either literal strings (`"this is a string"`) or variables, and *`option`* is one of the following:

Option	*Action*
`compare`	Returns `-1`, `0`, or `1`, depending on whether *`string1`* is lexographically less than, equal to, or greater than *`string2`* (similar to the C library function `strcmp`)
`first`	Returns the index of the first occurrence of *`string1`* in *`string2`*, or `-1` if *`string1`* does not occur in *`string2`*
`last`	Returns the index of the last occurrence of *`string1`* in *`string2`*, or `-1` if *`string1`* does not occur in *`string2`*

The following options to the `string` command interpret *`string2`* as a list of characters to trim from *`string1`*:

Option	*Action*
`trim`	Removes any leading and trailing characters present in *`string2`* from *`string1`*
`trimleft`	Removes any leading characters present in *`string2`* from *`string1`*
`trimright`	Removes any trailing characters present in *`string2`* from *`string1`*

The following options to the `string` command take only *`string1`* as an argument:

Option	*Action*
`length`	Returns the number of characters in *`string1`*
`tolower`	Returns a new string with all the characters in *`string1`* converted to lowercase
`toupper`	Returns a new string with all the characters in *`string1`* converted to uppercase

Now look at a few examples. First, create a string and get its length:

```
set str " Here Is A Test String ";
string length $str;
```

This gives a length of `23` (the `length` option counts whitespace characters). Now get the location of the first and last occurrences of the string `"st"` in `$str`:

```
string first "st" $str;
string last "st" $str
```

This gives a value of `13` for the first occurrence of `"st"` (corresponding to the occurrence in `Test`) and a value of `13` for the last occurrence of `"st"` (`Test` again). What about the "st" in String? Well, most of the string comparison functions are case- and whitespace-sensitive, so temporarily convert $str to lowercase and try again:

```
string last "st" [string tolower $str];
```

This gives a value of 16, which corresponds to the "st" in String. Finally, strip off the leading and trailing spaces and get a length for the string:

```
string length [string trim $str " "];
```

The value 21 is returned, which means the first and last spaces were stripped off.

Manipulating Numeric Values

If you ever have any sort of mathematical fuction or data manipulation to perform within your program, you may need to manipulate a numeric value. tcl provides two commands for manipulating numeric variables and constants: incr and expr.

The incr command gives tcl an equivalent to the C language operators +=, -=, ++, and --. The basic syntax is

```
incr variable integer
```

where *variable* must be an integer. The incr command adds the given *integer* to the *variable*; thus, decrementing is handled by giving negative integers. Let's demonstrate its usage. First, create a variable and do an incr on it:

```
set a 81;
incr a;
puts $a;
```

$a has a value of 82. By default, incr is the same as ++; if it is not given an integer argument, it adds one to the named variable. Now decrement $a by 3:

```
incr a -3
puts $a
```

Note that $a has a value of 79. One last point is that the integer can be the value of a variable:

```
set a 6;
set b 9;
incr a $b;
puts $a;
```

$a has a value of 15.

For more complex mathematical operations, tcl provides the expr command, which works with all standard ANSI C operators. Operator precedence is mostly the same as in ANSI C.

When any mathematical operations are required, they must be preceded by the `expr` command. For example, the commands

```
set a 20;
set b 4;
set c $a/$b;
puts $c;
```

result in the output

```
20/4
```

rather than `5`, the desired result. To get the right answer, use the `expr` command:

```
set c [expr $a / $b];
```

Other Numerical Operators

In addition to the standard operators `+`, `-`, `*`, and `/`, the `expr` command can be given several options that enable it to perform mathematical operations. The basic syntax is

```
expr function number
```

Some of the functions `expr` understands, along with the values they return, are shown in the following table

Function	*Value*
`abs(x)`	Absolute value of x
`round(x)`	The integer value resulting from rounding x
`cos(x)`	Cosine of x (x in radians)
`cosh(x)`	Hyperbolic cosine of x
`acos(x)`	Arccosine of x (0 to pi)
`sin(x)`	Sine of x (x in radians)
`sinh(x)`	Hyperbolic sine of x
`asin(x)`	Arcsine of x (-pi/2 to pi/2)
`tan(x)`	Tangent of x (x in radians)
`tanh(x)`	Hyperbolic tangent of x
`atan(x)`	Arctangent of x (-pi/2 to pi/2)
`exp(x)`	e raised to the power of x
`log(x)`	Natural log of x
`log10(x)`	Log base 10 of x
`sqrt(x)`	The square root of x

The following math function takes two number arguments:

`pow(x,y)`	x raised to the power of y

This is used as follows:

```
set a 2;
set b [expr pow($a,3)];
puts $b;
```

The output will be `8.0`, the value of 2 raised to the third power.

Quoting and Substitution

Quoting and substitution are both used heavily in relation to variables. You saw the most basic version of quoting (using double quotes to make strings) and substitution earlier in this chapter. `tcl` supports one more type of quoting, brace quoting, and one more type of substitution, command substitution.

To review, the most common use of double quotes is to create strings with embedded whitespace:

```
set kiwi "Fresh from New Zealand";
```

Double quotes can also be used to make multiline strings:

```
set kiwi "Fresh from
New Zealand 3 for a dollar";
```

In addition to making multiline strings, the standard ANSI C language escape sequences can be used in `tcl` strings:

```
set kiwi "Fresh from New Zealand\n\t3 for a dollar."
```

This outputs the following:

```
Fresh from New Zealand
3 for a dollar.
```

Variable and Command Substitution

The two types of substitution can also be applied within double-quoted strings. The first type of substitution, variable substitution, is explained in the "Variables" section earlier in this chapter. In a double-quoted string, you can access the value of a variable by preceding the variable's name with `$`. Thus, the following commands

```
set fruit kiwi;
set place "New Zealand";
set how_many 3;
puts "$fruit, fresh from $place, $how_many for a dollar";
```

output this:

```
kiwi, fresh from New Zealand, 3 for a dollar
```

The other type of substitution is command substitution. A command substitution block begins with a left bracket (`[`) and ends with a right bracket (`]`). For example:

```
set len_in 2;     puts "$len_in inches is [expr $len_in*2.54] cm";
```

outputs

```
2 inches is 5.08 cm
```

The `5.08` is the result of the command

```
expr $len_in*2.54
```

Because this command is in brackets, the value it returns is substituted. In this case, the `tcl` command `expr` is used, but any `tcl` command can be placed between brackets. Command substitution can be used in most commands and is not limited to double-quoted commands. For example, the commands

```
set len_in 2;
set len_cm [expr $len_in*2.54];
puts "$len_in inches is $len_cm cm";
```

produce the same output as

```
set len_in 2;     puts "$len_in inches is [expr $len_in*2.54] cm";
```

Brace Quoting

The other type of quoting available in `tcl` isbrace quoting, which is similar to using single quotes in UNIX shells. Brace quoting creates a string with the given characters, no substitution (command or variable) takes place, and the C language escape sequences are not interpreted. For example, the command

```
puts "This\nis a\nmulti-line\nstring"
```

produces the following output:

```
This
is a
multi-line
string
```

The command

```
puts {This\nis a\nmulti-line\nstring}
```

produces the following output:

```
This\nis a\nmulti-line\nstring
```

To get tabs, newlines, and other special characters in a brace-quoted string, they must be entered physically:

```
puts {This
is a
multi-line
string}
```

This produces the desired output. The real use for brace-quoted strings comes when certain characters with special meanings need to be given as values for variables. For example, the commands

```
set price 1.00;
puts "Pears, $$price per pound";
```

give this output:

```
Pears, $1.00 per pound
```

Because the `$$price` has the potential to be confusing, it would be better if the variable `price` had the value `$1.00`. You could use brace quoting to achieve the following:

```
set price {$1.00};
puts "Pears, $price per pound";
```

Brace quoting is also used to defer evaluation in control structures and procedure definitions. In such cases, the values of variables are substituted after the entire block is read.

Flow Control—if and switch

Flow control is the process of using comparison operators to make decisions and "control the flow" of the programs execution. `tcl` provides several commands for flow control and supports all the standard ANSI C comparison operators for both string and numeric data.

This section starts with the `if/elseif/else` commands. The simplest `if` statement is one like the following:

```
if {$x < 0} {
   set x 10;
}
```

Warning

`tcl` is very picky about braces and spaces. The beginning brace of an `if`, `elseif`, or `else` statement must be on the same line as the `if`, `elseif`, or `else`. The outside of braces must always border on a space. An `else` or `elseif` statement must always be on the same line as the closing brace of the previous `if` or `elseif`.

This example has only one line in the body of the `if` clause, but any number of lines and subblocks can be added. If additional tests need to be performed, each test is given in parentheses as follows:

```
if { ($x == "SJ") || ($x == "LA") } {
   puts "You Live in California!";
}
```

Tests can be nested as in the following example:

```
if { ( ($arch == "ppc") || ($arch == "intel") ) && ($os != "Linux") } {
   puts "Get Linux!";
}
```

Adding an `else` clause to an `if` statement is done like this:

```
if {$x <= 0} {
   set x 10;
} else {
   set x 0;
}
```

You can also add as many `elseif` statements as desired:

```
if {$x == 0} {
   set x 10;
} elseif {$x == 10} {
   incr x -1;
} elseif {$x == 100} {
   set x 50;
} else {
   set x 0;
}
```

In many cases, adding extra `elseif` statements becomes cumbersome and difficult to understand. To provide a more compact way of expressing the same logic, `tcl` implements the `switch` command. `switch` works by associating a value (string or number) with a block. The preceding `if` statement, when written as a `switch` statement, becomes

```
switch $x {
   0 {set x 10;}
   10 {incr x -1;}
   100 {set x 50;}
}
```

By default, only the block corresponding to the matched value is executed, but a `switch` statement can implement "fallthrough" if the block is designated as a single minus sign (`-`). *Fallthrough* simply means that if a statement fails, then execution falls through to the next statement. The `switch` statement

```
switch $x {
   0 -
   10 -
   100 {incr x -1}
}
```

is equivalent to the following `if` statement:

```
if { ($x == 0) || ($x == 10) || ($x == 100) } {
   incr x -1;
}
```

Loops

`tcl` provides three loop commands:

- `for`
- `foreach`
- `while`

`tcl` also provides two loop control commands:

- `break`
- `continue`

`while`

The `while` loop executes its body while its test condition is true. The structure can be thought of as

`while {`*`condition`*`} {`*`block`*`}`

The following is a simple `while` loop that counts to 10:

```
set x 0;
while {$x < 10} {
   incr x;
   puts $x;
}
```

`foreach`

The `foreach` loop iterates over a set of arguments and executes its body each time. The `foreach` loop has the following structure:

`foreach `*`variable`*` {`*`items`*`} {`*`block`*`}`

`variable` is the name of the variable to which each item in the set *`items`* is assigned in turn. Here is an example:

```
foreach element {o c n p li} {
   switch $element {
      o -
      n {puts gas;}
      c -
      p -
      li {puts solid;}
   }
}
```

In thiscase, the list of items to check is specified, but a variable can be used also:

```
set elements "o c n p li";
foreach element $elements {
   switch $element {
      o -
      n {puts gas;}
      c -
      p -
      li {puts solid;}
   }
}
```

If a variable instead of a list of items is given, braces should not be used, because the braces would be treated as if used for quoting.

for

The `for` loop allows the most control while looping. It can be broken down as

```
for {initialization} {condition} {increment} {body}
```

A simple `for` loop example that counts to 10 is

```
for {set i 0} {$i <= 10} {incr i} { puts $i; }
```

You have seen simple initialization statements, but the initialization and increment parts of the `for` loop can be as complicated as required.

Loop Control Commands: break and continue

Now for a look at the loop control commands, `break` and `continue`. The `break` commandbreaks out of loop and executes the next line of code after the loop's block; the `continue` command skips to the next iteration of the loop.

The `continue` command is handy for reading in initialization files where comment lines need to be allowed. If the following statement is included in a loop that reads in a file, all lines that start with a pound sign (#) will be skipped:

```
if { [regexp {^#} [string trim $line] ]} {continue;}
```

File I/O and File Info

`tcl` provides a simple and effective method for file input and output similar to the methods in the C standard I/O library. The first step in file I/O is to open a file and get a file handle or file ID. As an example, the command

```
set f [ open /etc/passwd r];
```

opens the file `/etc/passwd` with mode `r` and returns a file handle assigned to the variable `f`. `tcl` supports the following file open modes:

File Attribute	*Action*
`r`	Open for reading only; the file must exist.
`r+`	Open for reading and writing; the file must exist.
`w`	Open for writing. The file will be created if it does not exist; otherwise, it is truncated.
`w+`	Same as `w`, except the file is opened for reading also.
`a`	Open the file for appending text; the file will be created if it does not exist.
`a+`	Same as `a`, except the file is opened for reading also.

The `open` command can also be overloaded to run subprocesses with more control than the `exec` command provides. To open a process instead of a file, replace the filename with a brace-quoted string beginning with a pipe character (`¦`) and containing the command to run. For example, the following command opens a `ps` for reading:

```
set f [ open {¦ ps } r ];
```

For processes opened in this manner, the `tcl` command`pid` returns the process ID of the file handle associated with a process. For the preceding example:

```
pid $f
```

returns the `pid` associated with `$f`, the file handle for the `ps` command that was opened.

If a file (or process) is opened in a mode that supports reading, you can read from the file by using the `gets` command. To process all the lines of a file, the following `while` command is often used:

```
while { [ gets $f line ] >= 0 }
```

This works because the `gets` command returns `-1` when `EOF` is reached. In this case, the `gets` command reads in a line from the file handle `$f` and assigns the value to the variable `line`. In the body of the loop, `$line` can be accessed and manipulated.

If a file is opened for writing, the `puts` command can be used to write output to the file. If the file handle `$f` corresponds to a file opened for writing, the command

```
puts $f "This is a line of text";
```

writes the string `"This is a line of text"` to the open file.

The only other file I/O command is the `close` command, which takes as its argument a file handle. To close the file you opened earlier, you simply use

```
close $f;
```

It is probably a good idea to close any file handles that are open at the end of a program. Also, if the same file handle variable is to be reused several times in a program, it is a good idea to close it before the next `open`.

The `file` command

In addition to reading and writing from files, it is sometimes necessary to obtain information about files. `tcl` provides the `file` command to accomplish this. The `file` command's syntax is

```
file option filename
```

where *`filename`* is the name of the file to run the tests on and *`option`* is one of the following options, which return true (`1`) or false (`0`) information about files:

Command	*Value*
`executable`	True if the file is executable by the current user
`exists`	True if the file exists
`isdirectory`	True if the file is a directory
`isfile`	True if the file is a regular file
`owned`	True if the current user owns the file
`readable`	True if the file is readable by the current user
`writable`	True if the file is writable by the current user

The following options return additional information about a file:

Command	*Value*
`atime`	Returns the time the file was last accessed in seconds since January 1, 1970
`mtime`	Returns the time the file was last modified in seconds since January 1, 1970
`size`	Returns the size of the file in bytes
`readlink`	Returns the value of a symbolic link if the given file is a symbolic link
`type`	Returns a string giving the type of the file

Procedures

Procedures are the `tcl` equivalent of functions in the C language. To create a procedure, the `proc` command is used, which has the following syntax:

```
proc procedure_name {arguments} {body}
```

The number of arguments is variable, and an empty argument list is specified by `{}`. *`body`* can contain any valid `tcl` statement and can be as long as required.

A simple procedure that takes no arguments is

```
proc test_proc {} { puts "procedure test"; }
```

To invoke this procedure, simply give its name

```
test_proc;
```

to get the output

```
procedure test
```

A more realistic example is a file output procedure, which takes in a filename as an argument

```
proc cat {filename} {
   set f [open $filename r];
   while { [ gets $f line ] >= 0 } {
      puts $line;
   }
   close $f;
}
```

Warning

The beginning brace of a procedure must be on the same line as the `proc` keyword. The outside of braces must always border on a space.

To invoke this procedure with `/etc/passwd` as its argument, use the following:

```
cat /etc/passwd
```

This prints the contents of `/etc/passwd`.

Three important commands for use in procedures are `return`, `global`, and `catch`. The `global` command is used to give a procedure access to global variables, and the `return` command is used to return a value from a procedure. The `catch` command is useful for detecting errors and returning a failure value.

You can rewrite the `cat` procedure to be a little more robust by doing the following:

```
proc cat {filename} {
   set ret_code 0;
   catch {
      set f [open $filename r];
      while { [ gets $f line ] >= 0 } {
         puts $line;
      }
      close $f;
      set ret_code 1;
   }
return $ret_code;
}
```

This code demonstrates the use of both catch and return. If any parts of the procedure fail, it returns 0 (false); but if the catch is successful, it returns 1 (true). This information will be useful if catch is called with a process to execute as its argument.

You have learned to set and alter variables, change and find the status of files, and change and find the various comparison operators at your disposal. Now that we have covered the command syntax of tcl, we will overview the tk section. tk allows you to create the graphical elements of the language.

The tk Toolkit

The tk toolkit enables X Window GUIs to be written, using the tcl scripting language. The tk toolkit adds to the tcl language by enabling the creation of GUI components called *widgets*. This section looks briefly at the available tk widgets and shows how to create them.

Introduction to Widgets

A widget is a GUI component such as a button or a menu. The basic method for creating a widget is

```
widget_type path option
```

where *widget_type* is one of the widget types given in the following list, *path* is a window pathname (usually starting with a dot, which is the name of the root window), and *option* is any option the widget understands.

The tk toolkit defines the following widget types:

Widget	*Meaning*
canvas	Allows drawing objects
entry	Allows the input of a single line of text
frame	Used to contain other widgets
listbox	Displays a set of strings and allows choosing one or more of them
menu	Displays a menu bar and menu items
text	Displays multiple lines of text
label	Displays a single line of static text
button	Displays a clickable button
checkbutton	Displays a checkable box
radiobutton	Displays several mutually exclusive checkable boxes
scale	Similar to a slider that sets a value

To create and manipulate widgets, the windowing shell, wish, must be used. To invoke wish interactively, type **wish** at the UNIX prompt. The following wish prompt appears:

```
%
```

Along with this, an empty window pops up on the screen. This window is the wish root window (called .) and all the widgets that are created will appear with it.

Creating Widgets

This section shows how to create a widget and manipulate it. First, create a button:

```
button .button;
```

What did that do?

Well, the widget type is specified as button, so tk created a button. The path is .button, so tk created the button in the root window (. is the root tk window) and named it button.

So where is the button, anyway?

The button isn't displayed right now; tk simply created it. To display the button, you need to tell tk how to display the widget. For this, use the pack command and give it the path to the widget you want to display:

```
pack .button;
```

The button is showing, but it's blank. Now the widget's options come into play.

Widget Options

All tk widgets use standard options that control appearance and function. Most widgets understand the following options:

Widget Attribute	*Meaning*
-background *color*, -bg *color*	The background color of the widget. Valid values are of the form #RRGGBB, #RRRGGGBBB, or one of the names defined in /usr/lib/X11/rgb.txt.
-foreground *color*, -fg *color*	The foreground color of the widget. Valid values are of the form #RRGGBB, #RRRGGGBBB, or one of the names defined in /usr/lib/X11/rgb.txt.
-height *pixels*	The widget's height in pixels.
-width *pixels*	The widget's width in pixels.
-borderwidth *pixels*, db *pixels*	The width of the widget's border in pixels.
-padx *pixels*	Extra space required by the widget in the x direction.

continues

Widget Attribute	Meaning
-pady *pixels*	Extra space required by the widget in the y direction.
-relief *type*	The 3D effect of the widget, where *type* is one of these strings: flat, raised, groove, ridge, sunken.
-text *string*	The string to display in the widget.
-font *font*	The font to be used for the text displayed in a widget; valid font definitions are given by the command xlsfonts.
-command *command*	The tcl command to execute when the widget is used; usually, this is the name of a procedure or an exec statement.

In addition to these options, the pack command understands the following options of its own:

Widget Attribute	Meaning
-side *type*	Controls the order in which widgets are placed. Valid types are left, right, top, or bottom. For example, left indicates that new widgets should be placed to the left of existing widgets.
-fill *type*	Controls whether widgets are stretched to fill up open space in the window. Valid values are none, x, y, or both. For example, both indicates that widgets should fill all open space.
-expand *value*	Controls whether widgets expand if the window's size increases. *value* is either 0 or 1, with 1 indicating true.

After progressing through the various widgets and the various attributes that work with them, we will now go over an example of their use.

A tcl/tk Widget Programming Example

Now that you know about the options for widgets and for pack, you can start using them. One of the interesting features of widgets is their reliefs, the widgets' 3D look. To get an idea of how each relief looks, make some labels, using the following:

```
foreach i {raised sunken flat groove ridge} {
   label .$i -relief $i -text $i;
   pack .$i
}
```

This example iterates through the set of relief types, creating one `label` for each type, along with setting each label's `text` to be the `relief` type.

The labels are not all the same size. In addition, the labels are stacked one on top of the other. This is an example of the `pack` command's default behavior; it determines the size of each widget automatically and then places each widget below the preceding widget that was placed.

Now make all the labels the same size and pack them next to each other, instead of one on top of the other. There are two ways to do this. The first is to rewrite the loop:

```
foreach i {raised sunken flat groove ridge} {
   label .$i -relief $i -text $i -height 10 -width 10;
   pack .$i -side left
}
```

The second way is to reconfigure the labels by using the `configure` option, which has the following syntax:

```
widget configure option
```

In this case, you could use the following loop (after the labels are created):

```
foreach i {raised sunken flat groove ridge} {
   .$i configure -height 10 -width 10;
   pack .$i -side left;
}
```

So why use `configure`?

If `wish` is run interactively and one version of the loop is given, modifying it and running it again produces the following error:

```
window name "raised" already exists in parent
```

This is how `wish` tells the programmer that the program has attempted to re-create an existing widget (this time, with the label raised). So you need to use `configure`; in fact, `configure` is required any time an existing widget needs to be changed.

In this case, the only way to use the new version of the loop is to destroy the existing labels, using the `destroy` command:

```
foreach i {raised sunken flat groove ridge} { destroy .$i }
```

We need to make two fixes. First, it is difficult to tell the labels apart. Second, most of the window is blank.

Distinguishing Labels Using `borderwidths`

You can make the labels easier to distinguish by padding them when they are packed and by increasing their `borderwidths`. To make the labels take up all the available space, give `pack` the `fill` option for both `x` and `y` and set the `expand` option to true:

```
foreach i {raised sunken flat groove ridge} {
   label .$i -relief $i -text $i;
   .$i configure -height 5 -width 5 -borderwidth 5;
   pack .$i -side left -padx 5 -pady 5 -fill both -expand 1;
}
```

Note

To see the effect of the `fill` and `expand` options, you need to resize the window and watch the labels expand and contract to fit the window.

This example can be easily changed to use any of the widget types by replacing `label` with a different type ofwidget. Let's look at another example by interfacing `xsetroot` to our GUI front-end.

A `tcl/tk` Interface to `xsetroot`

This section introduces some of the other capabilities of the `tk` toolkit by applying them to the development of a GUI front-end for the X Window program `xsetroot`.

Most X Window users will be familiar with the X Window program `xsetroot` that can be used to set the background color of the `root` window, under X11. The actual command is

```
xsetroot -solid color
```

where *`color`* can be given in the form `#RRGGBB`. The front-end will allow for colors to be previewed and then applied.

Warning

On systems with eight-bit (256-color) or less color resolutions, many colors will cause an error to the effect of `xsetroot: unable to allocate color for #590000`. This is not a problem with your program, but instead is a property of your video. Doing `xsetroot` to that color from the command line produces the same result. On limited color monitors, always test your program with each slider either all the way up or all the way down.

The first thing you need is a variable that holds the color. Then you need to create two basic frames, one for the main area of the application and another in which to put messages. You also need a third frame for the controls.

Frames

Frames are handy because they can be used to pack items of a particular type or function together. Also, they are useful in partitioning a window into sections that don't change.

Create the frames and the color globally:

```
set color "#000000";
frame .main_frame;
frame .message_frame;
frame .control_frame;
```

Now pack the frames:

```
pack .control_frame -in .main_frame -expand 1 -fill both;
pack .main_frame -anchor c -expand 1;
pack .message_frame -anchor s -padx 2 -pady 2 \
-fill x -expand 1;
```

Creating a Label

You also need to create a label to handle messages. Let's do this as a procedure, so it will be easy to modify and execute:

```
proc make_message_label {} {
   label .message_label -relief sunken;
   pack .message_label -anchor c \
   -in .message_frame -padx 2 \
   -pady 2 -fill both -expand 1;
}
```

Pack the message label into the `.message_frame` so it is at the bottom of the window at all times.

Now create the scales. You need three scales—one each for red, blue, and green—with each one going from 0 to 255. You also need to pack the scales and their corresponding labels in their own frames:

```
proc make_scales {} {
   frame .scale_frame;
   foreach i {red green blue} {
      frame .scale_frame_$i -bg $i;
      label .label_$i -text $i -bg $i \
      -fg white;
      scale .scale_$i -from 0 -to 255 \
      -command setColor;
      pack .label_$i .scale_$i \
      -in .scale_frame_$i;
      pack .scale_frame_$i -in .scale_frame \
      -side left -padx 2 -pady 2;
   }
   pack .scale_frame -in .control_frame \
   -side left -expand 1;
}
```

This procedure is a good example of using frames. In all, this example creates four frames, one for each slider and label pair and overall frame. Adding the labels and sliders to their own frames simplifies the overall layout strategy.

Another example in this procedure is the use of the `-command` option for a widget. Each time the scales change, the command specified by the `-command` option is executed. In this case, the `setColor` command, which sets the global variable `color`, is executed:

```
proc setColor {value} {
   global color;
   foreach i {red green blue} {
      set $i [format %02x [.scale_$i get]];
   }
   set color "#$red$green$blue";
   .preview_label configure -bg $color;
   .message_label configure -text "$color";
}
```

Previewing the Color Change

You can preview the color change by setting the background color of the widget, `.preview_label`. To create `.preview label`, use the following procedure:

```
proc make_preview {} {
   global color;

   frame .preview_frame;
   label .preview_label -bg $color \
   -height 5 -width 5;
   pack .preview_label -in .preview_frame \
   -padx 2 -pady 2 -fill both \
   -anchor c -expand 1;
   pack .preview_frame -in .control_frame \
   -side bottom -fill both -expand 1 \
   -padx 2 -pady 2;
}
```

Now you need to add a few buttons—one to apply the changes and a couple to quit the program. Use the following procedure:

```
proc make_buttons {} {
   frame .button_frame;
   button .apply -text "apply" \
   -command setRootColor;
   button .quit -text "quit" -command exit;
   pack .apply .quit -in .button_frame \
   -fill both -expand 1 -padx 2 \
   -pady 2 -side left;
   pack .button_frame -in .main_frame \
   -fill both;
}
```

You also need the following procedure, which sets the `root` color:

```
proc setRootColor {} {
   global color;

   catch {
      exec xsetroot -solid $color;
   } msg;

   if {$msg != {}} {
      set msg "An ($msg) error occurred";
   } else {
      set msg "$color";
   }

   .message_label configure -text $msg;
}
```

Now that you are done with the procedures, invoke them:

```
make_message_label;
make_scales;
make_preview;
make_buttons;
```

You are now ready to test your little `tcl` application.

Listing 26.1 contains the complete source code of the `tksetroot` application.

LISTING 26.1 `tksetroot`

```
set color "#000000";
frame .main_frame;
frame .message_frame;
frame .control_frame;

pack .control_frame -in .main_frame -expand 1 -fill both;
pack .main_frame -anchor c -expand 1;
pack .message_frame -anchor s -padx 2 -pady 2 \
-fill x -expand 1;

proc make_message_label {} {
   label .message_label -relief sunken;
   pack .message_label -anchor c -in .message_frame \
   -padx 2 -pady 2 -fill both -expand 1;
}

proc make_scales {} {
   frame .scale_frame;
   foreach i {red green blue} {
      frame .scale_frame_$i -bg $i;
      label .label_$i -text $i -bg $i -fg white;
      scale .scale_$i -from 0 -to 255 \
      -command setColor;
```

continues

LISTING 26.1 continued

```
      pack .label_$i .scale_$i -in .scale_frame_$i;
      pack .scale_frame_$i -in .scale_frame -side left \
      -padx 2 -pady 2;
   }
   pack .scale_frame -in .control_frame -side left -expand 1;
}

proc setColor {value} {
   global color;
   foreach i {red green blue} {
      set $i [format %02x [.scale_$i get]];
   }
   set color "#$red$green$blue";
   .preview_label configure -bg $color;
   .message_label configure -text "$color";
}

proc make_preview {} {
   global color;

   frame .preview_frame;
   label .preview_label -bg $color \
   -height 5 -width 5;
   pack .preview_label -in .preview_frame \
   -padx 2 -pady 2 -fill both -anchor c \
   -expand 1;
   pack .preview_frame -in .control_frame \
   -side top -fill both -expand 1 \
   -padx 2 -pady 2;
}

proc make_buttons {} {
   frame .button_frame;
   button .apply -text "apply" -command setRootColor;
   button .quit -text "quit" -command exit;
   pack .apply .quit -in .button_frame -fill both \
   -expand 1 -padx 2 -pady 2 -side left;
   pack .button_frame -in .main_frame -fill both;
}

proc setRootColor {} {
   global color;

   catch {
      exec xsetroot -solid $color;
   } msg;

   if {$msg != {}} {
      set msg "An ($msg) error occurred";
   } else {
      set msg "$color";
   }
```

```
    .message_label configure -text $msg;
}

make_message_label;
make_scales;
make_preview;
make_buttons;
```

Summary

This chapter has been an introduction to programming in `tcl/tk`. The examples demonstrated the power of `tcl/tk`, which lies in its capability of making user interfaces within a short amount of time and with little code. Although this chapter covered many of the features of `tcl/tk`, many more were not discussed. I hope that with this chapter as a stepping stone, you will enjoy many years of developing `tcl/tk` applications.

CHAPTER 27

Programming in Python

by Steve Wells

In This Chapter

Python is a public domain, object-oriented, dynamic language. Developed in 1990 by Guido van Rossum and named after the Monty Python troop, Python has become popular as both a scripting language and a rapid-development tool. Python is truly freeware because there are no rules about copying the software or distributing any applications developed with it. When you obtain a copy of Python, you get all the source code, a debugger, a code profiler, and a set of interfaces for most GUIs in use today. Python runs on practically any operating system platform, including Linux.

Python, which has quickly become one of the most popular languages in use, is often referred to as a bridging language between compiled languages such as C and scripting languages such as Perl and `tcl/tk`. What makes Python so popular? The language lends itself to scripting, but several aspects of Python make it much more than a simple scripting tool. For example, Python is extensible, allowing the language to adapt and expand to meet your requirements. Python code is simple to read and maintain. Python is also object-oriented, although you do not need to use object-oriented features as part of your developments. Sounds powerful, doesn't it? Yet Python is remarkably easy to use, with no type declarations to worry about and no compile-link cycles to go through. Throughout this chapter you will be shown the building blocks of the Python language, on which you could build a solid foundation of the fundamentals of programming with this extremely powerful language.

Note

The Python Software Activity (PSA) group was formed to provide a development center for Python. A Web site devoted to Python can be found at `http://www.python.org`. This Web site contains voluminous Python documentation, and should be consulted whenever this chapter recommends looking at Python documentation.

To support the Python language, the Usenet newsgroup `comp.lang.python` sees lots of traffic. Distributions of Python are available from many Web and FTP sites, and Debian offers Python as part of its CD-ROM bundle.

Getting Ready to Run Python

If you want to play with Python as we go through the programming language in more detail, you need to install the Python programming tools on your Linux system if they aren't installed already. You also need to set up your environment so that it knows about Python and the directories to search for Python files.

Installing Python

The easiest place to find the code is through the Python FTP site, `ftp://ftp.python.org/pub/python/src`. You can use anonymous FTP to obtain the source code.

Python source files are usually supplied as C source code, which you need to compile and link using any C compiler on your system. The FTP site also contains precompiled binaries for many target hardware and operating system combinations, making compilation unnecessary. Make sure you download the binary that's appropriate for your machine.

Note

To make obtaining the proper binaries or source code even simpler, the Python Web site has been updated to allow you to choose the proper platform and operating system. The appropriate binaries are then transferred for you. Even if you have the binaries, you might want to obtain the source code. This is especially true if you plan to add any C extensions to Python. Any time Python is extended, the entire binary has to be recompiled and relinked, so the source code is necessary.

At the time of this writing, the 1.5.2 release of Python was available on the FTP and Web sites. Versions of Python for several UNIX versions, Linux, Windows, and Macintosh are all available.

If you download just the source code, Python is usually supplied as a gzipped file that requires `gunzip` to unpack. The packed file usually shows the version number as part of the name, such as `python1.3`, which means version 1.3 of the system. One or more `README` files are usually included with the Python distribution, often containing the compilation process and hints for your operating system. To begin the installation process, use the command

```
tar -zxvf python1.X.tgz
```

This will unpack the gzipped file as well as untar it (you must substitute your filename for `python1.X.tar.gz` in the command, of course).

The Python files are then untarred in the current directory. The next step is to run the auto-configuration routine by issuing the command

```
./configure
```

and then start the compilation of the executables with the command

```
make
```

This command compiles and links the Python files. You can also run a self-test program to ensure everything is completed properly and all files are accounted for by issuing the command

```
make test
```

Finally, you can complete the installation process by copying the compiled executables and all support files to the proper Linux directories with the command

```
make install
```

Following that, Python is ready to roll. Of course, all these steps are unnecessary if you use the precompiled deb version of Python.

> **Note**
>
> The Python FAQ is posted at regular intervals to the Usenet `comp.lang.python` newsgroup and is available through several FTP and Web sites, including `http://www.python.org`. The FAQ contains up-to-date information about the language and its versions, as well as hints on building the Python executables on many platforms.

Setting Python Environment Variables

You will most likely need to set up several shell environment variables to allow Python to work properly. This is so the Python command can be executed. The Python path for library locations and so on needs to be set. This process doesn't take very long, and you don't need to be a Linux guru. Python needs two environment variables, called `PATH` and `PYTHONPATH`. The `PATH` variable already exists for you, set when you log in to a shell. If you use Debian's package, you don't have to modify the PATH variable at all because the Python executable will be placed in `/usr/bin`, which is in your path by default.

A quick way of making sure Python is installed in your path is to execute the `python` command

```
python
```

and watch the output. If you get an error message, the `PATH` environment variable might not be properly set. If Python launches properly, you will see three right-angle brackets. This means the executable is in your search path. You can exit Python by pressing Ctrl+D. You can confirm your current path with the command

```
echo $PATH
```

which displays your default search path like this:

```
/bin:/usr/bin:$HOME/bin:.
```

Your path might be different from this. The only important thing is that /usr/bin is in your path.

If the Python executables are in the /usr/bin directory, this path finds them without a problem. If your path does not have the Python executable location in it, you need to modify the startup file for your shell (.cshrc, .login, .profile, or .kshrc, depending on the shell). Simply add the executable location to the existing PATH setting, using colons to separate entries. If you don't have a PATH statement in your startup files, add one, using the existing default path $PATH as one of the directory names.

The PYTHONPATH environment variable needs to be set for each user who will use Python. This path is used to locate files during runtime, and because many of the files are not kept in the default path, you need to set this variable in your startup files in most cases. The PYTHONPATH variable is usually set to include the current directory, the library location for the Python files (set during installation and usually /usr/lib), and any other directories Python needs, such as tcl/tk directories.

Finally, you can create an initialization file for Python to read when it launches (like the shell startup files). The name of the file is given in an environment variable called PYTHONSTARTUP and should be set to the absolute pathname of the startup file. The startup file can contain any valid Python commands you want running.

If you are using tcl/tk to integrate GUIs with Python, you also need to make sure environment variables such as TK_LIBRARY and TCL_LIBRARY are set. Python uses these variables to find the tcl/tk files it needs.

Now that we have set up Python, let's see how to use it.

Python Command-Line Interpreter

The Python executable can be used as both a line-by-line and a command-line interpreter (just as the Linux shells can be). To use the command-line interpreter, you need to start the Python program, called python (note lowercase). When you do, you'll see a line of three right angle brackets that represent the Python prompt:

```
$ python
>>>
```

You can exit the python program by pressing Ctrl+D.

Typing any valid Python command at the prompt results in carrying out the action (if one exists):

```
>>> print "Hello World!"
Hello World!
```

As you can see, the print command acts like the UNIX echo statement. Double quotation marks help prevent interpretation of the string and should be used with all print statements. You also can use single quotation marks to enclose a string, but do not use the single back quotes. By default, the `print` statement sends output to the standard output (usually the screen).

Command-Line Interpreter as Calculator

You can use the command-line interpreter as a calculator. If you use variables, they are set automatically to the proper type and can be used later in the program. To generate output from Python, don't use an assignment operator:

```
>>> a = 2
>>> b = 5
>>> a * b
10
>>> bigvar = 37465
>>> smallvar = a / 2
>>> bigvar / smallvar
37465
>>>
```

In the preceding example, the variables are set by using the equal sign. Spaces on either side of the equal sign are ignored, so you can adopt whichever style you want. The statements

```
A = 2
A=2
```

are identical. Case is important in Python, as it is in most UNIX-based languages, so the variables `A` and `a` are different. You can use long variable names to help differentiate variables and their purposes, with mixed case if you want. To display the current value of a variable, you can type its name at the prompt, and an assigned value is shown. If the variable has no value set, an error message is displayed.

Standard mathematical order of precedence applies, so the statement

```
>>> 4 + 8 / 2
```

results in 8 (4 + 4) and not 6 (4 + 8 divided by 2). Division and multiplication are carried out before addition and subtraction. For a complete reference on the mathematical order of precedence within `http://www.python.org/doc/ref/summary.html`

You can assign numeric and string values to variables and print them both at the same time, like this:

```
>>> a = "Python"
>>> b = "1"
>>> c = "statements"
>>> print b, a, c
1 Python statements
```

You can also set multiple values at once, like this:

```
>>> a = b = c = 19
```

This example sets all three variables to 19. You could, of course, set them separately, but setting multiple values often saves time during coding.

Note

In Python, the type of a variable is set by the operations performed on it. In any mathematical operation, if any of the variables are floating point, all are converted to floating point automatically.

If you are typing a compound expression, such as an `if` or `for` loop, the command-line interpreter switches the prompt to a set of three dots, allowing you to complete the expression:

```
>>> if b < 10:
...
```

After the three dots, you can complete the compound expression.

To start Python executing a file, you supply the name as an argument. If the program needs any arguments, you can specify them on the command line, too. For example, the command

```
python big_prog 12 24 36
```

starts the Python executable running the program `big_prog`, using the three arguments following the program name in the program. You'll see how these arguments are read later in this chapter.

Python supports unlimited precision numbers. By default, numbers are tracked only to a considerable number of significant digits, but appending an `L` to the number switches to unlimited precision mode, as the following example shows:

```
>>> 123456789 * 123456789
Traceback (innermost last):
  File "<interactive input>", line 0, in ?
OverflowError: integer multiplication
>>> 123456789L * 123456789L
15241578750190521L
>>>
```

The first multiplication here overflows the allowed number of digits and generates an error message. By appending the `L` to the end of the numbers (with no spaces between the number and the `L`), you can impose unlimited precision.

Because you have been introduced to the basics of programming, you will be introduced to some conventions used within Python.

Python Programs

A Python *program* is a straightforward ASCII file that you can create with any text editor. You can also use any word processor, if it can save files in ASCII format. By convention, Python filenames end in the extension `.py` (such as `primes.py` and `sort.py`). This filetype convention is not strictly necessary because Python can open any type of file and execute it, but it does help identify the files quickly to other users or programmers.

Each Python script file is called a *module*. A module is the largest program unit in Python and can be thought of as the main or master file. A module can import other modules. Lines of a Python module can contain comments, statements, and objects.

As with any programming language, Python has a number of statements. The majority of Python statements will be familiar to programmers, such as `if` and `for` loops and the equal sign for assignments. Python does add a few statements for functions and object-oriented tasks, but they are not difficult to learn (especially if you have programmed in other languages). If you do not feel comfortable with these more advanced statements, you have the option to code without them. After all, not all programs are suited to object-oriented approaches.

Python objects are handled by statements and define the types of data being handled. If you have done any object-oriented programming before, you will be familiar with Python's use of objects. For non–object-oriented programmers, objects define simple things such as the type of variable (`string`, `integer`, and so on), as well as other entities such as modules and filenames.

If you have never seen a Python module before, you might be surprised to see how simple it is. Python is similar to the UNIX languages `awk` and Perl in that you don't have to define variable types before assigning them. When you assign a value to a variable, the variable is dynamically created, removing the need for declaration and typing statements at the top of the module and making Python an ideal language for rapid programming. It also makes Python programs much shorter and easier to read. Python's excellent object implementation makes it an ideal candidate for substantial software development.

The first line in a Python program usually looks like this:

```
#!/usr/bin/python
```

which tells the shell to use the `python` executable to run the script. If you aren't sure where the Python executable is located on your system, try using the `whereis` command. The full path might be different on your system, depending on where you installed your

Python files. Following this line can come any number of valid Python commands. Python ignores whitespace, so you can use blank lines to separate sections of the program, making your code more readable.

Python comment lines start with a # sign. You can embed as many comments as you want in your code because the Python interpreter ignores any line with a pound sign at the beginning. You can also place a comment anywhere on a line, with everything after the comment symbol ignored by Python, as you can see in this example:

```
Var1 = 6    # sets Var1
```


At the top of most Python programs, you might see `import` statements. The `import` statement is used to read in another module (similar to an `include` in C). The most-used module for Python code is called `sys`. The `sys` module contains a set of system-level components. If you don't use any of these components in your code, you don't need to have the following statement at the top of your program, but it also doesn't cause any harm:

```
import sys
```

Command-Line Arguments and Environment Variables

Command-line arguments are accessed in Python through the `sys` module's `argv` list. The number of arguments, including the program name as one of those arguments (comparable to `argc` in C or C++), is available as `len(sys.argv)`. `sys.argv[0]` is the program name, whereas `sys.argv[1]` to `sys.argv[len(sys.argv)-1]` are the rest of the arguments. To shed more light on the subject, let's look at the following code, which is saved as `test.py`:

```
#!/usr/bin/python

import sys
print "Args are:", sys.argv
print "Counting program name,",
print "number of args is", len(sys.argv)
print "Program name is", sys.argv[0]
print "Final arg is", sys.argv[len(sys.argv)-1]
```

You can run this code by using the following command from the command line (after `chmod a+x test.py`):

```
$ ./test.py one two three
```

The output is as follows:

```
Args are: ['./test.py', 'one', 'two', 'three']
Counting program name, number of args is 4
Program name is ./test.py
Final arg is three
```

Environment variables are accessed in Python through the `os` module's `environ` dictionary. Because it's a dictionary, lookups are done with the `os.environ[VARNAME]` syntax, with the environment variable's name in quotes. That syntax throws a `KeyError` exception if `VARNAME` isn't in the environment. Unfortunately, an uncaught `KeyError` exception will clumsily terminate the program. To prevent the program from terminating, you use the `try,except,else` syntax to handle any `KeyError` exception. Note the following code:

```
#!/usr/bin/python
import os

def printenv(s):
   try:
      x = os.environ[s]
   except KeyError:
      print "No such environment var:", s
   else:
      print "Env var", s, "has value:", x


printenv("SHELL")
printenv("OSTYPE")
printenv("JUNK")
```

Try this code on your system. You'll almost certainly have environment variables `SHELL` and `OSTYPE`, and probably will not have `JUNK`. Based on those assumptions, you can expect the following output:

```
Env var SHELL has value: /bin/bash
Env var OSTYPE has value: Linux
No such environment var: JUNK
```

You can add, change, and delete environment variables in `os.environ` with standard dictionary manipulation, as shown here:

```
os.environ["JUNK"] = "added"
printenv("JUNK")
os.environ["JUNK"] = "changed"
printenv("JUNK")
del os.environ["JUNK"]
printenv("JUNK")
```

The preceding code adds environment variable `JUNK`, changes its value, and then deletes it, calling the `printenv()` function defined previously. The output is predictable:

```
Env var JUNK has value: added
Env var JUNK has value: changed
No such environment var: JUNK
```

This feature is useful because any such environment changes are available in subprocesses started with the `os.system()`, `os.popen()`, `os.fork()`, and `os.execv()`.

In the next section we will discuss some important control statements that Python has in common with many other languages.

Control Statements

Like many programming languages, Python has the usual assortment of control statements. The most commonly used statements are the `if` conditional test and the `for` and `while` loops. If you have programmed any other language before, or if you are familiar with shell scripts, you'll find little new about these statements. If you are new to programming, you will probably find the use of these statements a little confusing at first (that's not Python's fault; all languages are like this), but a little practice quickly makes their usage clear.

The `if` Statement

The Python `if` statement syntax uses the condition to be tested on the `if` line, followed by any statements to be executed if the test is true. An `else` can be used to execute statements if the test is negative. The syntax for the Python `if` statement looks like this:

```
if condition:
   statements
else:
   statements
```

The `else` section and its subsequent statements are optional. Notice the use of colons at the end of the `if` and `else` lines, indicating to Python that the section continues on the next line. This `if` statement doesn't have a termination statement, such as an `endif` or `fi`, which many other languages have.

Note

Python decides where the blocks of code to be executed start and end by the statement's indents (when executing a script) or blank lines (when running interactively). This way of working is different from most programming languages that use braces or some special statement or symbol to terminate each block. The number of spaces or tabs you use to indent statements in a block doesn't matter, as long as you are consistent.

The following is a simple `if` statement:

```
#!/usr/bin/python
if var1 < 10:
  var2 = 0
  print "the value is less than ten"
```

```
else:
  var2 = 1
  print "the value is ten or more"
```

The condition allows all the usual mathematical comparisons (==, !=, >, >=, <, <=). Note that you can't use the single equal sign in the `if` statement for a condition test. The single equal sign is used for assignment, not comparison. The double equal sign is used for "exactly equal to."

As with the C programming language, the Python `if` statement doesn't test for actual values but determines a simple true or false. If the condition is true, it has a return code of non-zero, whereas a false has a return code of zero. The value of the return code dictates whether the statements below the `if` or the `else` are executed. You can show this with a simple Python program:

```
X = 4
Y = 5
A = X > Y
print A
```

The zero result shows that the test of `X` being greater than `Y` is false, assigning the return value of zero to the variable `A`.

Python also allows the `elif` (`else if`) structure in the `if` statement. You can be have several cascaded `elifs`, which might be necessary for multiple branching tests because Python does not offer a `switch` or `case` statement. The following is an example of using `elif`:

```
#!/usr/bin/python
if var2 >= 10:
  print "The value is greater than or equal to ten"
elif var2 <= 5:
  print "The value is less than or equal to five"
else:
  print "The value is between five and ten"
```

Python allows a virtually unlimited number of nests, which is `if` statements within `if` statements, although your code will start to bog down after too many nests. If you need to nest more than three or four levels deep, you should probably try to find a better way to code the section.

When any section of the `if` statement has been completed as the result of a condition's being true or false, the Python interpreter jumps to the end of the `if` statement. As a result, the second part of a nested `if` might never be executed. For example, in the following program, when the first test proves true, the first `print` is executed:

```
#!/usr/bin/python
x = 6
if x > 5:
   print "X is greater than 5"
elif x > 2:
```

```
    print "X is greater than 2"
else:
    print "X is less than 2"
```

Even though the second test (where the `elif` is) is also true, it does not get executed because the Python interpreter jumps to the statements after the end of the `else` section.

The `if` statement can contain Booleans, as you might expect; however, you should write out Booleans in Python instead of using symbols, as in C and shell scripts. The Boolean statements are `and`, `or`, and `not`. The following are all legal statements in Python:

```
if a < 5 and b > 6:
if a < b or c > d:
if not a < b:
if a < b or ( a > 5 and b < 10):
```


The use of `not` negates the test, so the third example shown here is the same as testing `a >= b`. The last example uses parentheses to add another layer of testing, at which Python excels. As long as you use the conditions and Booleans properly, you can construct very long, complex statements in Python that would be almost impossible to construct in a few lines with other programming languages.

If you are reading Python programs written by others, you will often see the `if` condition and statement compressed onto a single line, like this:

```
if x < 5: print "X is less than five"
```

This approach is perfectly legal. Another common sight in code is comparisons run together, like this:

```
if 3 < X < 5: print "X is four"
```

This line is the same as writing the following:

```
if x > 3 and x < 5: print "X is four"
```

The `while` Loop

The Python `while` loop continues to loop as long as some condition is true. The general syntax for the `while` loop is as follows:

```
while condition:
    statements
```

As you can guess by now, the block of statements to be executed when the condition is true is indicated by indenting. The following simple `while` loop shows its use:

```
a = 0
while a < 10:
    print "a is currently set at ", a
    a = a + 1
print "all done!"
```

The last print statement is executed after the while loop condition tests false, or even if the while loop is not executed at all. This statement is executed because it is not indented to match the rest of the statements in the while block.

Note

You can use C-like formatting operations in print functions to produce the results you want, like this:

```
>>> print "The result of %d times %d is %d. %s!" % (2, 3, 2*3, "Excellent")
The result of 2 times 3 is 6. Excellent!
```

The condition is always tested and assigned a return code, and the while loop executes as long as the return code is non-zero. You could use this fact to abort the loop when a value hits zero, like this:

```
a = 10
while a:
  print "a is currently set at ", a
  a = a - 1
print "all done!"
```

This example starts counting with a set to 10, and because 10 is non-zero, the while loop is true. When the decrement results in a value of zero for a, the while loop stops. This type of syntax might look confusing but is quite common.

Python allows you to use a break statement to exit from a while statement at any time. Whenever a break is encountered, the interpreter immediately assumes the while condition is false and carries on execution after the last line of the while block. Consider the following program:

```
a = 10
while a:
  print "a is currently set at ", a
  a = a - 1
  if a == 4:
     break
print "all done!"
```

Here, the countdown proceeds as you would expect until the value of a is set to 4, at which point the if condition is true and the break executed. The "all done!" message is printed right after the break is reached because it is the first statement after the while block. Usually, a break is used in an if block as a way of escaping the while loop if certain conditions are met. By using the break, you can save a lot of coding in the while condition.

The for Loop

The `for` loop is used to iterate through a list or a string. The statements subservient to the `for` statement must not alter the list or string in any way. The syntax for the `for` loop under Python is as follows:

```
for var in list or string:
  statements
```

As with the `if` statement, Python knows where the body of the `for` loop is by the indentation. The colon at the end of the `for` statement also indicates a continuation to the interpreter. The `var` in the preceding syntax assumes individual values in the list or string.

The following simple `for` loop iterates the string:

```
for ltr in "Hello World":
  print ltr,
```

The preceding code prints each letter of the string, followed by a space:

```
H e l l o   W o r l d
```

Note

A comma on the end of a `print` statement eliminates the newline from the output, instead inserting a single space.

The "Lists and the `range()` Function" section examines `for` loops in greater detail.

Lists and the range() Function

A *list* is any sequence of zero or more items. You can specify a list in Python by using brackets. A simple list using numbers looks like this:

```
A = [1, 2, 3, 4, 5]
```

This list, called `A`, has five elements. You can recall the entire list by using the variable name, as this code example shows:

```
A = [1, 2, 3, 4, 5]
print A
```

The preceding code simply prints the list in brackets, as shown in the output:

```
[1, 2, 3, 4, 5]
```

To recall any single element from the list, you can use the variable name and the subscript of the element number in brackets, as shown here. Remember that Python is a zero-origin subscripting language, meaning the counting of elements starts at zero.

```
A = [1, 2, 3, 4, 5]
print A[2]
print A[0]
```

The preceding code prints `3` (`A[2]`) and then `1` (`A[0]`). If you try to access an element that doesn't exist, you usually get an error message from the interpreter.

> **Note**
>
> Even though Python performs some bounds checking for elements in a list, you should not expect Python to ensure that your code uses list elements correctly. For example, although Python rejects a reference to `A[10]` if the list `A` has only five elements, Python does allow a reference to the same list using `A[-4]`. We won't discuss the uses of negative list elements here, but you should be careful when using list elements in your code to prevent errors within your program.

Creating Lists with Strings

You can create lists with strings just as easily, separating each string with a comma and using quotation marks to surround each string:

```
A = ["Python", " powerful", "is", "language", "a"]
print A[0], A[2], A[4], A[1], A[3]
```

The preceding code prints list `A`'s elements in the order invoked in the `print` statement, outputting the sentence `"Python is a powerful language"`. You can mix lists between strings and numeric values just as easily. If you define each element properly, Python lets you manipulate them however you like:

```
Z = [ 5, "good", "is", 6, "This", 2]
print Z[4], Z[2], Z[1]
print Z[0] + Z[3] / Z[5]
```

Once again, the elements are printed according to the `print` statement, yielding this output:

```
This is good
8
```

Note that the order of precedence in the last statement results in the value 8, not 5.5.

To find the number of elements in a list, you can use Python's built- in `len()` function as follows:

```
a = [1,3,5,7]
print len(a)
```

The preceding code yields `4`, the number of elements in the list.

You can also add and delete members from a list. Remember in this discussion that element numbers start at zero. The following insertion and deletion examples assume the following list string:

```
a = ["zero","one","two","three","four"]
```

To delete `a[2]` (`"two"`), you do the following:

```
a[2:3] = []
```

The `"two"` is now missing from the list. To reinsert it, you do the following:

```
a[2:2] = ["two"]
```

A good way to remember where the preceding syntax chooses to insert is to remember you're adding back a new element 2, thus pushing the present element 2 out to element 3.

The following is an example of a multiple deletion (delete elements 2 and 3):

```
a[2:4] = []
```

You can create a multiple insertion by placing multiple elements on the right side of the equal sign. Consider this code, which reinserts elements 2 and 3 deleted previously:

```
a[2:2] = ["two", "three"]
```

The `for` loop is ideal for stepping through a list. In the following code, a list is displayed one element at a time:

```
A = [1, 2, 3, 4, 5, 6, 7, 8, 9, 10]
for x in A:
   print x
```

The preceding code creates a new variable `x` that holds the value of the indexes in `A`, one after another. You can do exactly the same with string lists, as the following example shows:

```
A = ["a", "b", "c", "d", "e", "f", "g"]
print A
for x in A:
   print x
```

The preceding code prints list A and then steps through the list, assigning each element to x and printing x, as shown in the following output:

```
['a', 'b', 'c', 'd', 'e', 'f', 'g']
a
b
c
d
e
f
g
```

To print all the elements one after another on a single line, with a single space between them, instead of in a column, you need to place a comma after the print statement at the end of the for statement. Note that the following print statement ends with a comma:

```
A = ["a", "b", "c", "d", "e", "f", "g"]
for x in A:
   print x,
```

Here's the output:

```
a b c d e f g
```

Testing for Inclusion

You can test for the inclusion of a particular value as an element, which yields a return code of zero (false) or non-zero (true). For example, look at the following code:

```
A = [1, 2, 3, 4, 5]
print "This should be 1:", 3 in A
print "But this should be 0:", 8 in A
```

The tests performed cause a search of all the elements to check for a match, and the proper return code is then displayed. This approach could be handy for some if or for loops when you need to make sure particular elements exist before continuing processing.

You can change individual elements in a list by using the element subscript, as the following example shows:

```
A = [1, 2, 3, 4, 5]
print A
A[3] = 7
print A
```

The preceding code changes A[3] from 4 to 7, as shown by the following output:

```
[1, 2, 3, 4, 5]
[1, 2, 3, 7, 5]
```

Lists Spanning a Contiguous Range

To create lists spanning a contiguous range, you can use the `range()` command, which comes in a one-argument and two-argument syntax, as shown here:

```
#This is the one argument syntax:
mylist = range(4)
print "range(4) is:", mylist

#This is the two argument syntax:
mylist = range(5,10)
print "range(5,10) is:", mylist
```

The rather surprising results are as follows:

```
range(4) is: [0, 1, 2, 3]
range(5,10) is: [5, 6, 7, 8, 9]
```

This might not be what is expected because you stated `range 4`, but instead of getting `1,2,3,4` you received `0,1,2,3`.

In the one-argument `range()` call, the argument represents the number of elements in the zero-based list. In the two-argument `range()`, the first argument is the first element in the list, and the last number is one greater than the last element.

You can use `range()` anywhere you can place a list. You can assign it to variables or use it as part of a command structure.

Upper and lower limits may be positive or negative, as in these examples:

```
print "range(-10, -5) is: ", range(-10, -5)
print "range(-5, 5) is: ", range(-5, 5)
print "range(-5, -10) is: ", range(-5, -10)
```

The preceding code's output is as follows:

```
range(-10, -5) is:  [-10, -9, -8, -7, -6]
range(-5, 5) is:  [-5, -4, -3, -2, -1, 0, 1, 2, 3, 4]
range(-5, -10) is:  []
```

Notice the last range in the preceding code. It's perfectly legal to specify a lower limit higher than the upper limit (although doing so is a little silly). The result is a list with no elements.

Understanding Tuples

Now we're ready for the slightly more complicated issue of *tuples*. A tuple is a Python data structure that works like a list but is more efficiently stored and managed. A tuple's elements cannot be moved around and extracted with the same ease as a list's elements.

The difference between lists and tuples, at least as far as Python's interpreter is concerned, is that a list is a variable-sized array of elements that might need to grow in size. A tuple has a fixed size and doesn't change, and hence is more efficiently stored and managed by the interpreter. A tuple's element values can't be changed without redefining the entire tuple, but a list's elements can be easily changed. This leads to the use of tuples for defining invariant constants in Python, much as the `#define` statement does in C. Tuples are also returned by many Python functions.

To define a tuple, you set it up much the same way as a list, but with parentheses instead of brackets. Python isn't all that fussy about the parentheses as long as there is no ambiguity. Still, it is advisable to always use parentheses when you're defining a tuple because they help make clear in your mind that you are working with a tuple. The following are some examples of defining tuples and displaying their values at the command-line interpreter:

```
a = (1,2,3,4)
print "This is a numerical tuple:", a
a = ("This", "is", "a", "tuple", "of", "strings")
print a
```

Here, variable `a` is set to a numerical tuple and then a string tuple, as shown by the following output:

```
This is a numerical tuple: (1, 2, 3, 4)
('This', 'is', 'a', 'tuple', 'of', 'strings')
```

Why bother with tuples? They are useful when you want to use either the full tuple value or specific elements from a tuple as a complete set of information. Each element in a tuple can be assigned to a specific variable, as long as the number of variables matches the number of elements in the tuple. The following code assigns the elements of a tuple to variables `w`, `x`, `y`, and `z`; changes the value of `y`; and then creates a new tuple from `x` and `y`:

```
w, x, y, z = (1, 2, 3, 4)
y = 7
mytuple = (x, y)
print mytuple
```

The preceding code assigns element 0 (`1`) to variable `w`, element 1 (`2`) to `x`, and so on. It then changes `y` to 7, producing the following output:

```
(2, 7)
```

To convert between lists and tuples, you need to do a little coding that assembles each structure from the other. Often, an easier way is simply to redefine the variable as either a list or a tuple instead of performing a conversion in your program code.

Now we will discuss dictionaries and their capabilities within Python.

Dictionaries

Python is a high-level language and, as such, has some special data types designed to take advantage of some aspect of the language's features. One of these special data types is the *dictionary*. Dictionaries are associative arrays. In plainer English, this statement means data is referred to by a key, similar to a variable. Perl programmers will recognize Python dictionaries as being similar to Perl hashes. To Python, a dictionary is a simple hash table that can grow at any time.

Creating a One-Element Dictionary

To create a one-element dictionary, you can specify both a key and the value to which that key refers. These *key-value* pairs (in Python-speak) are enclosed in braces, with the key and value separated by a colon. Python allows you to use almost any kind of data as a key or a value. Any number of key-value pairs can appear in a dictionary. An example of setting up a dictionary is a good place to start. The following code creates a dictionary called a that uses the key "python" to refer to a value "language" (two strings for key and value in this case):

```
a = {"python": "language"}
```

Brackets are used to refer to the value, either in whole or in part. Using the preceding definition, you can recall the whole value with this command-line sequence:

```
a = {"python": "language"}
print a["python"]        #prints the word "language"
```

As you can see, referring to the element "python" in the dictionary, a brings up the value assigned to "python", which is "language". Note, however, that only the key (not the value) can be used inside the brackets. The following code fails:

```
a = {"python": "language"}
print a["language"]        #Aborts with a KeyError"
```

So far, this example is rather unexciting, and it is hard to see why you would want to use dictionaries. The advantage of using dictionaries comes when you start using multiple values. The following is an example of a dictionary set up to hold computer languages and their categories:

```
a = {"C": "Compiler", "C++": "Compiler", "Python": "Interpreter"}
b = "Python"
print b, "is a", a[b]
```

Here, a[b] produces the word "Interpreter", as shown in the following output:

```
Python is a Interpreter
```

Note that when you're defining multiple key-value pairs, you separate them in the braces by using commas. Note also that values can be duplicates (both C and C++ are `"Compilers"` according to the preceding code), but the keys must never duplicate.

Trying to access a non-existent key in a dictionary produces an error. Thus, the following program aborts with a `KeyError` exception:

```
a = {"python": "language"}
Print a["perl"]
```

You can handle this situation gracefully by using the following `try,except,else` syntax:

```
def printelement(dict,key):
   try:
      x = dict[key]
   except KeyError:
      print "No key", key, "in dictionary."
   else:
      print "Key", key, "has value:", x + "."


a = {"python": "language"}
printelement(a, "perl")
printelement(a, "python")
```

Here, the `KeyError` exception is handled and processing continues. The output looks like this:

```
No key perl in dictionary.
Key python has value: language.
```

You also can add, change, and delete dictionary elements, as follows:

```
a = {"SIZE": "BIG", "WEIGHT": "HEAVY"}
a["STATUS"] = "added"
printelement(a, "STATUS")
a["STATUS"] = "changed"
printelement(a, "STATUS")
del a["STATUS"]
printelement(a, "STATUS")
```

Given the previous definition of the function `printelement()`, the output of the preceding code is exactly as expected:

```
Key STATUS has value: added.
Key STATUS has value: changed.
No key STATUS in dictionary.
```

Dictionaries bestow immense power because their values can be class instances (discussed later this chapter). When used this way, dictionaries can eliminate huge sections of `if,elif,else` code, and they are excellent for lookups.

In the next section we will explore the `print` statement and how to use it effectively.

Console I/O

As mentioned previously, console output in Python is created with the `print` statement. Each `print` statement prints a newline (linefeed) after the desired output, unless the `print` statement ends with a comma (`,`), in which case the output ends with a single space, as demonstrated in the following code:

```
print "This is a complete line."
print "This is the first half of a line, and",
print "this is the second and final half."
```

In the preceding code, the second line does not linefeed but instead appends a single space. The first and third lines linefeed to produce the following output:

```
This is a complete line.
This is the first half of a line, and this is the second and final half.
```


If you don't want the space inserted by the ending comma, you can use the plus sign to concatenate strings (but not numbers):

```
a="Python"
b="is"
c="great"
print a+b+c
```

The preceding code concatenates three string variables without spaces, producing the following output:

```
Pythonisgreat
```

Note that numbers cannot be concatenated without first converting them to strings. String conversions are covered later in this chapter.

You can use C-like formatting operations in `print` functions to produce the results you want, like this:

```
print "The result of %d times %d is %d. %s!" % (2, 3, 2*3, "Excellent")
```

The arguments inside the parentheses are assigned the substitution strings inside the format string, as shown in the following output:

```
The result of 2 times 3 is 6. Excellent!
```

You can create console input by using the `raw_input()` function. This function takes a single string argument, which is used as a prompt, and accepts a single line of keyboard input. It does not read individual keystrokes but rather accepts the entire line when the Enter key is pressed. Consider this example:

```
x = raw_input("Please type your name==>")
print x
```

The preceding code prints whatever you type at the prompt. Note that the input is always interpreted as a string; the `eval()` function must be used to acquire numbers. In contrast, the following code prints double the number you type:

```
x = raw_input("Please type number to be doubled==>")
x = 2 * eval(x)
print x
```

Typing a non-number causes an error, so a real program would check to see that the variable contains a number before invoking the `eval()` function.

With the inclusion of the `readline` module, `raw_input()` becomes much more powerful, including line editing and history. To demonstrate its power, run the following program:

```
import readline
x = "Anything but q to ensure first iteration"
while(x != "q"):
   x = raw_input("Please type your name==>")
   print x
```

The preceding code repeatedly asks for your name (until you type a single lowercase **q** at the prompt) and prints whatever is typed at the prompt. The addition of the `import readline` statement enables command-line editing and history, which can be explored using the keyboard's arrow keys. This capability is enabled even inside GUI Telnet sessions.

File I/O

A major portion of programming involves reading and writing files. Python has a rich variety of file functions. The following sections discuss the basic file I/O functions: `open()`, `close()`, `read()`, `readline()`, `readlines()`, and `write()`.

File Output

You can create file output by using the `write()` function on a file that has been opened for output with the `open()` function. The command to open file `test.tst` for output is as follows:

```
outfile = open("test.tst", "w")
```

The first argument is the name of the file to open, and the second is the mode in which it is open. Frequently used modes are `"r"` for read, `"w"` for write (delete any existing file), and `"a"` for append (write to the end of any existing file).

Note

An optional third argument, the buffer size, can be used with `open()`. In its absence, file I/O operations buffer according to the system default. A test conducted on an unloaded Celeron 333 with a 7200 RPM 14.4GB disk wrote a 4.5MB file in 12 seconds using the two-argument version. A buffer size of a million did not appreciably decrease that time, leading to the conclusion that the two-argument form is sufficient for most work.

The `open()` statement can fail because the filename is a directory, the disk is full, the user lacks the proper permissions in the directory, or for other reasons. The `open()` for read fails if the file does not exist. When an `open()` fails, the program is terminated with an error message. If you want to gracefully handle such failures, you can use the `try,except,else` syntax for `IOError` exceptions, as shown here:

```
try:
   outfile = open("test.tst", "w")
except IOError:
   print "Failed to open test.tst for write."
else:
   #place  file writes and close statement in this block
```

The preceding code does all file writes and closes the file if the `open` succeeds, but prints an error message and then skips file writes and closes if the `open` fails. This syntax also works on files open for read. If this syntax becomes obfuscated because of excessive nesting of multiple files, each `open`'s `except IOError` block can set a variable to be evaluated by subsequent code.

For simplicity's sake, the remainder of this chapter's sample code does not include error-handling code. However, real programs should handle their own file errors.

When the file is opened, it is written with the `write()` function:

```
outfile.write("Hello World\n")
```

When the preceding code is run, assuming `outfile` has been successfully opened for write, a single line containing the text `Hello World` is written to the file. Only strings can be written to the file. Numbers must be converted using the `str()` or `repr()` function.

As soon as all data has been written to the file, the file should be closed with the `close()` function. Although the file will be closed on normal termination of the Python program, it remains subject to change and/or corruption while open. The following is a short program to create a four-line file called `test.tst`:

```
outfile = open("test.tst", "w")
for x in ["Spring", "Summer", "Fall", "Winter"]:
   outfile.write(x + "\n")
outfile.close()
```

The preceding code opens file `test.tst`, iterates through the seasons printing one per line, and then closes the file. You should save the resulting file because it will serve as the input file in file input examples that follow.

File Input

You create file input by using the `read()`, `readline()`, and `readlines()` functions, operating on a file that has been opened for input with the `open()` function. One occasion to use file input is when you have an address book with the person's information all on one line. You usually don't need all the names at once, so you can use the readline function to extract one line (one person's record.) The command to open a file for input is as follows:

```
outfile = open("test.tst", "r")
```

The first argument is the name of the file to be opened, and the second is a string containing a lowercase `r`, which stands for "read."

Function `readline()` is used to read a single line from a file. It returns a single line, complete with newline. If the line is blank, it returns only the newline. At end-of-file, it returns the null string (`""`). After you test for EOF, you can remove the newline from string `x` by using the following syntax:

```
x = x[:-1]
```

The following is the Python code necessary to read file `test.tst`, surround each line with angle brackets, and print it:

```
infile = open("test.tst", "r")
x = infile.readline()
while x != "":
   x = x[:-1]
   print "<" + x + ">"
   x = infile.readline()
infile.close()
```

The preceding code uses a priming read and a loop-bottom read to simulate a test-at-bottom loop, thereby avoiding `if` statements inside the loop and (technically non-structured) `break` statements.

When the file size is known to be consistently tiny in comparision to system memory, the file can be read straight into a list using the `readlines()` function:

```
infile = open("test.tst", "r")
xl = infile.readlines()          #note readlines is plural
infile.close()
for x in xl:
   x = x[:-1]
   print "<" + x + ">"
```

The preceding syntax closes the file faster, eliminates the priming and bottom reads, and is much more readable. However, the results become undefined (and likely unpleasant) if memory is ever insufficient to hold list `xl`.

The function of choice for non line-oriented input is `read()`. Assuming an open file called `infile`, here is the syntax:

```
x = read(numbytes)
```

Function `read()` is used for fast file input, reading fixed-length sequential record files, file copy operations, translations, and the like. The following code copies file `test.tst` to file `test2.tst`:

```
infile = open("test.tst", "r")
outfile = open("test2.tst", "w")
x = infile.read(10)
while x != "":
   outfile.write(x)
   x = infile.read(10)
outfile.close()
infile.close()
```

The preceding code reads `test.tst`, 10 bytes at a time, into variable `x` and then writes variable `x` to file `test2.tst`. After running this code, you can verify its success by running this command at the command line:

```
$ diff test.tst test2.tst
```

If the files are identical, the command produces no output. If they are different, or if either file doesn't exist, a message prints. Note that the byte argument of `10` would result in snail-like performance in a real program. For general file input, you should use a large number such as `5000` as the byte argument. For fixed-length record operations, you can use the record length or a multiple of the record length.

Warning

Make sure `fname` is opened for read and not for write, or you will overwrite the file described on the command line.

File I/O Example

The following is a Python program to convert text file `test.tst` to a numbered listing in HTML-formatted file `o.html`:

```
#!/usr/bin/python

fname = "test.tst"
ouf = open("o.html", "w")
ouf.write("<html><body><P><H1>\n")
ouf.write(fname + " Listing</H1><PRE>\n")

inf=open(fname, "r")
line = inf.readline()
n=10001
while line != "":
   line = line[0:-1]
   ouf.write(str(n) + "     " + line + "\n")
   n = n + 1
   line = inf.readline()
inf.close()

ouf.write("</PRE></body></html>\n");
ouf.close()
```

Assigning `sys.argv[1]` to `fname` makes it a general program.

If you change all the `ouf.write()` statements to `print` statements, this code becomes a handy CGI script (once again, be careful of security).

Functions and Modules

Like many high-level languages, Python uses functions to break large programs into smaller functional blocks. The use of functions also leads directly to code reuse, allowing you to write functions for specific tasks that can be incorporated with little or no change into any future programs you write. Functions and modules may seem similar, which they are, but there is one major difference: Functions are written into a program while modules are files that are imported. Defining a function is straightforward. The following is an example of a simple function with a single input:

```
def simplefunction(name):
   print name
```

The keyword `def` identifies the code as a function to Python, followed by the name of the function and the variable names to be assigned to any incoming data (in this case, a single object), followed by a colon signifying that the following indented text is part of the function. Indenting indicates the body of the function.

When called, the function executes, using whatever data object is passed, as the following command-line interpreter output shows:

```
def simplefunction(name):
   print name

simplefunction("Python")
```

In the preceding code, the call to `simplefunction()` leads to the execution of function `simplefunction()`, using argument `"Python"`, to print the word `"Python"` to the screen.

You can use local variables in a function, as you can in most other languages. A local variable is valid only inside the function and has no meaning when tried outside that function. For example, the following function computes the average of any numbers passed to it:

```
def average(array):
  numvars = 0
  total = 0
  for a in array:
    numvars = numvars + 1
    total = total + a
  print "There are ", numvars, " numbers"
  print "The total is ", total
  print "The average is ", total/numvars
```

The variables `numvars` and `total` are valid only inside the function `average`. If a global variable conflicts with a local variable, the local variable takes precedence inside the function. When this function is called with a list containing 1 through 5 inclusive, the following output is generated:

```
There are 5 numbers
The total is 15
The average is 3
```

Warning

Any variable used outside all functions is global, and is accessible inside all functions. Because global variables represent a modularity breach, it is best, in all but the simplest programs, to place all top-level procedural code inside a function (typically called `main()`). Thus, the only code existing outside all functions would be the path to `python`, the `import` statements (covered later in this chapter), and a single call to function `main()`. If the imported modules do not declare global variables, such a construction prevents accidental creation of global variables in your program.

If you want to pass a result back to the calling function (which often is the case), you use the `return` statement. The following modification of the `average` function returns a numeric average value because of the `return` statement:

```
def average(array):
  numvars = 0
  total = 0
  for a in array:
    numvars = numvars + 1
    total = total + a
  return total/numvars
```

Modules

Modules, as we mentioned at the beginning of this chapter, are files or scripts of Python code, with filenames usually ending with `.py`. Again, modules are designed to allow code reuse, so you can write self-contained modules that can be dropped into future applications. You can write modules with any ASCII editor and call them from another module by using the `import` statement. The main module in Python is called `main`.

To see how modules work, put the `average` function demonstrated in the preceding section into a module called `average.py`. Save it to disk, and place it in either the current directory (which must also contain the main module) or the search path of the Python interpreter, defined by the environment variable `PYTHONPATH`. To use the `average.py` file in either the command-line interpreter or another module, embed the line as shown in this short program:

```
import average

a = [1,2,3,4,5]
average.average(a)
```

The preceding code imports module `average` and calls the `average` function inside the module `average`. The module name need not be identical to the function name.

To call a specific function inside a module, you can use the module name and the function name separated by a period. For example, if you have a file called `mymath.py` that includes functions called `average()`, `mean()`, and `deviation()`, you can call each from another module (after the `import` statement) as `mymath.average()`, `mymath.mean()`, and `mymath.deviation()`. By doing so, you can prevent conflicts with function names that are identical in different modules.

Now we will discuss strings and regular expressions, which have been a fundamental part of all programs since the first programming language.

Strings and Regular Expressions

To a great extent, the productivity of a computer language depends on how easily the programmer can modify and parse strings. It is precisely these qualities that have contributed to the recent popularity of both Python and Perl.

Strings

Strings are an integral part of being able to write effective programs, from reader input to value holders. Every language uses strings to some extent, and their effective use is important to writing worthwhile programs. Python has a rich variety of string- handling features. Features such as appending with the plus sign, string slicing, and conversion functions `str()` and `num()` are built into the language. If they aren't enough, Python's `string` module offers most of the C language's `string.h` functionality.

Appending with the + Sign

The plus sign allows concatenation of strings, as shown in the following source code:

```
fname = "resolv.conf"
dname = "/etc"
fullpath = dname + "/" + fname
print fullpath
```

The preceding code concatenates the directory, a slash, and the filename, resulting in the following output:

```
/etc/resolv.conf
```

String Slices

String slices are Python's ultra-flexible, built-in method of extracting substrings from larger strings. They can slice off the beginning or the end of a string or slice out the middle, relative to either the beginning or end. When you're using string slices, remember the first character is element 0. Perhaps the simplest string slice is grabbing a single character (this could also be considered subscripting), as shown here:

```
a="ABCDEFGHIJKLMNOPQRSTUVWXYZ"
print a[2]
```

The preceding prints element 2, the third character, `C`. Next, consider the following code, which prints the first five characters of the string:

```
a="ABCDEFGHIJKLMNOPQRSTUVWXYZ"
print a[0:5]
```

The preceding prints `"ABCDE"`. Often you might want to remove a certain number of characters from the end of a string. Most often you do so to remove a newline from the end of the string. Using a zero before the colon and a negative number after trims off characters from the last part of the string back:

```
a="ABCDEFGHIJKLMNOPQRSTUVWXYZ"
print a[0:-1]
```

The preceding code trims the `Z` off the end of the string. Often you need just a portion from the middle of the string, as shown here:

```
a="ABCDEFGHIJKLMNOPQRSTUVWXYZ"
print a[2:5]
```

The preceding code prints elements 2, 3, and 4—the string `"CDE"`. The best way to remember this is that the number of elements in the slice is the difference between the second and first numbers—unless, of course, the second number goes past the end of the string, in which case the effect is simply to trim off the characters before the element corresponding to the first number. Consider this example:

```
a="ABCDEFGHIJKLMNOPQRSTUVWXYZ"
print a[2:1000]
```

The preceding prints `"CDEFGHIJKLMNOPQRSTUVWXYZ"`. It strips elements 0 and 1, printing element 2 as the first character.

To print the last three characters of the string, you can combine a huge second number with a negative first number like this:

```
a="ABCDEFGHIJKLMNOPQRSTUVWXYZ"
print a[-3:1000]
```

The preceding code prints the last three characters, `"XYZ"`. If you find providing an arbitrarily large number unappealing, you can use the `len()` function to get the exact string length and accomplish the same thing, as illustrated in the following example:

```
a="ABCDEFGHIJKLMNOPQRSTUVWXYZ"
print a[-3:len(a)]
```

Once again, the output is `"XYZ"`. Occasionally, you might want to extract a substring from "almost" the end. In that case, both numbers are negative. For instance, to get the fourth-to-last, third-to-last, and second-to-last characters of the string, you use the following:

```
a="ABCDEFGHIJKLMNOPQRSTUVWXYZ"
print a[-4:-1]
```

The preceding code prints `"WXY"`. Remember that the number of characters returned is the difference between the numbers, assuming the original string contains enough characters.

String slicing is a versatile tool built in to the Python language. We can think of more uses for string slicing, but the preceding discussion gives you a strong foundation.

Converting with `str()`, `repr()`, and `eval()`

Python is more strongly typed than some languages (Perl, for instance), so strings and numbers can't be mixed without conversion. The `str()` and `repr()` functions convert a number to a string, whereas the `eval()` function converts a string to a number. The difference between `str()` and `repr()` is that `repr()` attempts to return a string that can be converted back to a number by `eval()`, whereas `str()` attempts to return a printable string. In practice, both `str()` and `repr()` usually do an excellent job of returning a string convertible back to a number. Consider this example:

```
pi_string = "3.14159"
r = 2.0
area = eval(pi_string) * r * r
print "Area = " + repr(area)
print "Area = " + str(area)
print "Area =",
print 3.14159 * 2 * 2
```

The preceding code prints the area of a radius 2 circle three times. The first two times it converts a string representation of pi to a number before doing the calculation; the third time it calculates from numeric constants. The first and second times differ only in that the first uses `repr()`, whereas the second uses `str()`. All three produce the identical results shown here:

```
Area = 12.56636
Area = 12.56636
Area = 12.56636
```

Rearranging a String

You also can use string slicing and appending to rearrange strings. Consider the following function to convert a date represented as MM/DD/YYYY to YYYYMMDD:

```
def yyyymmdd:
   return(d[-4:1000] + d[0:2] +d[3:5])

print yyyymmdd("07/04/1999")
print yyyymmdd("12/25/1999")
print yyyymmdd("01/01/2000")
```

Function `yyyymmdd` returns the last four characters, then the first two, and then the fourth and fifth (elements 3 and 4) to produce this output:

```
19990704
19991225
20000101
```

This simplistic function assumes an exact format for the input date. Later in this chapter, we'll build a "smarter" converter using string and number conversions and regular expressions.

The string Module

Occasionally, the previously described string capabilities aren't enough. Python's string module is used for those cases. Some functions included in the string module are explained in this section.

atof(), atoi(), and atol() arc sophisticated alternatives for the capabilities yielded by eval() because they are capable of working with number systems other than decimal.

Various case conversions return copies of their arguments rather than change the string in-place. capitalize() capitalizes the first character of a string, and capwords() capitalizes the first letter of each word (but has the side effect of removing redundant whitespace and leading and trailing whitespace). upper() completely capitalizes its argument. lower() converts every letter to lowercase. swapcase() converts all lowercase to uppercase, and vice versa.

Functions lstrip(), rstrip(), and strip() return copies of their arguments with whitespace stripped from the left, the right, and both, respectively.

split(s[, sep[, maxsplit]]) returns a list of substrings from string s. The default for sep is whitespace runs (in other words, it splits the string into space-delimited words). Used with a sep argument, this function becomes a powerful aid in parsing delimited data files. maxsplit defaults to 0, but if positive, it declares the maximum number of split, with any remainder becoming the last entry in the list. The following can split a quote- and comma-delimited record into fields. Note the actual parsing is accomplished in two lines:

```
import string
s="\"Smith\",\"John\",\"developer\""

s = s[1:-1]                 #strip first and last quote
z = string.split(s,'","')  #split by ","

for x in z:                 #print fields
   print x
```

Join(list[, sep]) is the inverse of split(). It joins the list into a single string, with each separated by sep if it's used. If sep is not used, sep defaults to a single space. Thus, string.join(string.split(s)) removes extra whitespace from string s, whereas string.join(string.split(s),"") removes all whitespace, and string.join(string.split(s),"¦") pipe-character–delimits the former whitespace-delimited words.

find() and rfind() are used to find substrings from the left and right, respectively. Function count() counts the number of non-overlapping substring occurrences in the string.

zfill(s, width) left-fills a string with zeros.

The `string` module contains several more functions. They can be found in the module documentation. To use the `string` module, remember these two requirements:

1. The `import string` command must appear at the program's top.
2. Each function must be preceded by the word `"string"` and a dot.

Regular Expressions

Regular expressions enable you to complete parsing tasks in a few lines of code instead of the 20 to 100 lines required in the C language. Regular expressions are flexible, wildcard-enabled strings used to match, pick apart, and translate other strings.

Regular Expressions: Python and Perl

The Perl language's success can be attributed partially to its inclusion of regular expressions. Python also supports regular expressions with the new, Perl-compatible `re` module, as well as the obsolete `regex` module (don't use this module). The syntax for invoking regular expressions and retrieving groups between the two languages is as different as can be. But the regular expressions themselves are identical. So, if you can construct a Perl regular expression, you can do the same in Python. The following is a Perl example to find the seven characters before the word `"Linux"` in a string:

```
#!/usr/bin/perl

my($a) = "I like Debian Linux for development.";
$a =~ m/(.{7})Linux /;
my($b) = $1;    #group 1
print "<$b>\n";
```

And here's the same code written in Python:

```
#!/usr/bin/python
import re

a = "I like Debian Linux for development."
m = re.search("(.{6})Linux", a)
b = m.group(1)
print "<" + b + ">"
```

Each prints the string `"<Debian >"`. The syntax is completely different, but the regular expression—in this case `"(.{6})Linux"`—remains the same.

The preceding code uses the `re` module's `search` function. The `re` module also contains a `match` function, which is not covered in this chapter.

Note the `import re` line. It must be included in every module using the `re` module's regular expressions.

Simple Matches

The simplest use of a regular expression is to determine whether a string conforms to the specified regular expression. Perhaps the simplest is searching the string for the existence of a substring, as shown here:

```
a = "I like Debian Linux for development."
m = re.search("Linux", a)
if m -- Nonc:
   print "Not found"
else:
   print "Found"
```

Function `re.search()` returns a match object. The match object, which is assigned to variable `m` in the preceding code, contains all information concerning the application of the regular expression against the string. If nothing in the string matches the regular expression, `re.search()` returns the special value `None`.

You can use several wildcards. The following are the most important ones:

`.`	Any character
`^`	Beginning of the string
`$`	End of the string
`\s`	Whitespace character
`\S`	Non-whitespace character
`\d`	Digit character
`\D`	Non-digit character

You also can use several repetition specifiers. You can place them after a character or wildcard to indicate repetition of the character or wildcard. The following are the most important ones:

`*`	Zero or more repetitions
`+`	One or more repetitions
`?`	One or zero repetitions
`{n}`	Exactly *n* repetitions
`{n,}`	At least *n* repetitions
`{n,m}`	At least *n* but not more than *m* repetitions

Several flags can be used to modify the behavior of the regular expression search. These flags are numeric constants used as an optional third argument to the `re.search()` function. You can `OR` these flags using the pipe symbol to accomplish multiple modifications. By far, the most common flag is `re.IGNORECASE`, which ignores case during searches. You can find several others in Python's documentation.

Let's look at a comparison of a search with and without `re.IGNORECASE`:

```
m = re.search("Linux", a, re.IGNORECASE)
m = re.search("Linux", a)
```

The first search finds `"Linux"`, `"LINUX"`, `"linux"`, `"lInUx"`, and any other combination of upper- and lowercase spelling of *Linux*. The second search finds only the exact string `"Linux"`.

A Demonstration of Wildcards and Repetitions

To demonstrate wildcards and repetitions, let's look at this overly simple regular expression to identify whether a date exists in a line:

```
a = "Valentines is 2/14/2000. Don\'t forget!"
m = re.search("\D\d{1,2}/\d{1,2}/\d{2,4}\D", a)
if m == None:
   print "No date in string."
else:
   print "String contains date."
```

The preceding code checks for the existence, anywhere in the string, of a non-digit followed by one or two digits; followed by a slash; followed by one or two digits; followed by another slash; followed by two, three, or four digits; followed by a non-digit.

> **Note**
>
> You also can use an alternative syntax that precompiles the regular expression for faster use in tight loops. In our experiments, it improved regular expression performance roughly 15 percent. However, it is not covered in this chapter. If you need better regular expression performance in loops, look up `re.compile()` in your Python documentation.

Simple Parsing with Groups

Classifying strings is nice, but the real power comes from the ability to parse strings. Perhaps the simplest example is changing a file extension. Consider this example:

```
src = "myfile.conf"
m = re.search("(\S+)\.conf", src)
dst = m.group(1) + ".bak"
print dst
```

The preceding code searches the source string for a group of one or more non-whitespace characters, followed by `".conf"`, and creates a match object that is assigned to variable `m`. The group, which is specified by the parentheses around the `\S+`, is available as `m.group(1)`, to which is appended `".bak"` to complete the destination name.

An Example of Parsing Dates

Now consider this example to parse dates. Note that this example is not complete enough for use in applications:

```
a = "11/21/1999"
m = re.search("^([01]?\d)[/-]([0123]?\d)[/-](\d{2,4})$", a)
print m.groups()
month = m.group(1)
day = m.group(2)
year = m.group(3)
print year, month, day
```

Carefully consider the `search` statement in the preceding code sample. It looks for a string consisting of a date as a one- or two-digit number, with the tens' place being 0 or 1 if existing; followed by either a slash or hyphen; followed by another one- or two-digit number (this one with the tens' place being 0, 1, 2, or 3). This second one- or two-digit number is followed by another slash or hyphen, followed by any number of two to four digits. Note that this is about as much validation as can be done without integer arithmetic.

Each number in the regular expression is surrounded by parentheses so that each is accessible as a group in the match object. The groups are then evaluated and assigned to month, day, and year. The sample code prints the following:

```
1999 11 21
```

Another way to accomplish the same objective is to use the `groups()` function to return a tuple that can then be assigned the groups, as shown here:

```
a = "11/21/1999"
m = re.search("^([01]?\d)[/-]([0123]?\d)[/-](\d{2,4})", a)
month,day,year = m.groups()
print year, month, day
```

Note that the assignment of `m.groups()` to three variables works only if the number of variables equals the number of elements in the tuple returned by `m.group`. You know in advance how many elements you will have by the number of parentheses pairs inserted in the regular expression. You can also access the number of elements in the tuple by using the `len()` function.

Regular Expression Example

The following complete program takes a file called `test.tst`, searches it for lines containing text inside square brackets, and returns that text minus any left or right space:

```
#!/usr/bin/python
import re

infile = open("test.tst", "r")
x = infile.readline()
```

```
while x != "":
   x = x[:-1]
   m = re.search("\[\s*(.*)\s*\]", x)
   if m:
      print m.group(1)
   x = infile.readline()
infile.close()
```

The preceding code reads every line of file `test.tst`, checks it for text between brackets, and if such text exists, prints it. Because many types of configuration files use brackets for headers, this example can be molded into useful code.

Strings and Regular Expressions Example

Listing 27.1 illustrates many features of strings and regular expressions. It repeatedly queries the user to type dates, and then evaluates, checks, and prints those dates until the user types a single lowercase '**q**'.

LISTING 27.1 Sample Date Program

```
#!/usr/bin/python

##############################################################################
# Sample Only. Do not use in production.
##############################################################################

import re            #regular expressions
import string        #string manipulation
import readline      #command line editing

def std(s):
   m=re.search("^([01]?\d)[/-]([0123]?\d)[/-](\d{2,4})",s)
   if m:
      mm =   eval(m.group(1))
      dd =   eval(m.group(2))
      yyyy = eval(m.group(3))
      if yyyy < 40:
         yyyy = yyyy + 2000
      elif yyyy < 100:
         yyyy = yyyy + 1900
      rv = (yyyy,mm,dd)
   else:
      rv = None
   return(rv)

def mdy(t):
   if t:
      mstring = string.zfill(t[1],2)
      dstring = string.zfill(t[2],2)
      return(mstring + "/" + dstring + "/" + str(t[0]))
```

continues

LISTING 27.1 continued

```
   else:
      return("bad date")

def ymd(t):
   if t:
      mstring = string.zfill(t[1],2)
      dstring = string.zfill(t[2],2)
      ystring = string.zfill(t[0],4)
      return(ystring +  mstring  + dstring)
   else:
      return("bad date")

def printdates(s):
   print std(s);
   print mdy(std(s))
   print ymd(std(s))

def main():
   x = raw_input("Please type a date, q to quit==>")
   while(x != "q"):
      printdates(x)
      print
      x = raw_input("Please type a date, q to quit==>")

main()
```

In this listing, function `std()` creates a standard `ymd` tuple from its string argument, returning `None` if the string is not a date. Function `mdy()` formats a standard `ymd` tuple as a `mm/dd/yyyy` string, and function `ymd()` formats a standard `ymd` tuple as a `yyyymmdd` string. Both `mdy()` and `ymd()` return the string `"bad date"` if passed `None`.

In the next section we discuss classes, which are a building block in object-oriented programming technique.

Classes

Because Python is an object-oriented language, it has features such as classes. If you are not familiar with object-oriented programming (OOP), this discussion might seem confusing. In fact, you can skip the use of classes without reducing the utility of Python for simple and moderate programs. However, classes do add OOP capabilities to Python that, when properly used, extend the language considerably.

Class Definition and Instantiation

Python treats classes much as C++ does. To define a class, you use a modification of the function syntax, defining the class that holds the functions, as shown here:

```
class myclass:
   def printout(self, string):
      print string
```

Here, the first line defines a class called `myclass`. The `myclass` class contains a single function, called `printout`. In OOP terms, `myclass` is the *class*, and `printout` is the *method*.

To use the class, you create an *instance* of the class. Another word often used for a class instance is the word *object*. The process of creating this instance is called *instantiation*. The following code creates an instance of the `myclass` class, assigning that instance to variable `my` and operating that instance:

```
my = myclass()
my.printout("This is a string")
```

The first line creates the object (instance). The second line invokes the `my` object's `printout()` method, as defined in the class. This code prints out the phrase `"This is a string"`.

You might wonder why the function definition has two arguments, `self` and `string`. The variable `string` is whatever is being passed in to the function. The `self` keyword is required for classes because, when an instance's method is called, the instance passes itself as the first argument. The use of the word `self` takes care of this method pass. If you were calling a function that had no input, you would have only the single `self` name in the function definition (the word `self` is used by convention, but it could be anything), as in this example:

```
class yourclass:
def printit(self):
   print "This is a function string!"
```

Tip

A good way to describe the relationship between a class and an instance of that class (an object) is that the class is a blueprint. Instances are built from that blueprint like a housing developer builds houses from a blueprint. The houses are the thing of value, but they're defined by the blueprint. In the same way that same-designed houses have different colors and swimming pools, objects from the same class can have different properties.

Encapsulation and Private Identifiers

The more modular the design of a system, the easier it is to build and troubleshoot the system, and the less likely it is to contain design flaws. Consider a home audio system. Almost any pair of speakers will connect to almost any receiver via speaker wires. Almost any CD player will connect to almost any receiver via patch cords. Likewise, tapedecks and equalizers. A car is another example. The only knowledge the driver requires is the operation of the gas pedal, brake, and steering wheel.

Imagine driving a car with driver-controlled spark timing, driver control of each of the four brake calipers, and driver control of each wheel's angle. How many crashes would result? Imagine an audio receiver requiring tapedeck inputs and outputs for head angle, bias, and tape speed. How many people could make good recordings on such a system?

The same principle applies to computer programs. Programs are separated into parts. The less each part needs to know about other parts, the more modular the program, and the more reliably the program works.

This is what's so exciting about object-oriented programming. Instead of simply dividing a program into tasks (functions), the OOP programmer divides the program into distinct parts, called classes, each with its own tasks, behaviors, properties, and most important, *public methods*.

A public method is a function contained by the class that is publicized to other classes and the program in general. Public methods are the equivalent of the patch cord jacks on the back of a CD player. Every CD player has them, and everyone knows it.

Class Description of a Person

Consider the following simple class describing a person:

```
class person:
   def getFirstname(self):
      return(self.__fname)
   def getLastname(self):
      return(self.__lname)
   def putFirstname(self, s):
      self.__fname = s
   def putLastname(self, s):
      self.__lname = s
   __fname = ""
   __lname = ""
```

The rest of the program knows instances of the `person` class by four public functions: `getFirstname()`, `getLastname()`, `putFirstname()`, and `putLastname()`. The rest of the program need know nothing else about the `person` class.

Note

Python defines any function or variable inside a class as private if the name of that function or variable begins with at least two underscores and ends with no more than one underscore. Private variables are inaccessible to code outside the class definition.

Python provides a "back door" way of accessing private variables outside the class definition. This chapter does not discuss that method because doing so would defeat the purpose of object-oriented programming and defeat your program's modularity.

To the programmer using instances of the `person` class, it is of absolutely no interest that the person's name happens to be kept in private class variables `__fname` and `__lname`. In fact, those two variables cannot be accessed outside of class code. Consider this attempt to access `__fname` directly:

```
p = person()
print p.__fname
```

The preceding code errors out with an attribute error. Because `__fname` is private, it can't be accessed as `p.__fname`. It cannot be seen or changed anywhere outside the class definition. `__fname` and `__lname` are the equivalents of a tapedeck's bias circuit or a car's timing. They're internally necessary to the class, but the other code operating class instances needn't, and definitely shouldn't, know about them. Thus, `__fname` and `__lname` are said to be encapsulated. The process of encapsulating all variables and methods except those intended to be accessed is called *encapsulation*. Good encapsulation requires each class to offer the minimum public functions necessary for other program parts to operate that class' objects. Such a "thin interface" makes an OOP program ultra modular, reliable, easy to modify, and easy to troubleshoot. And yes, it makes the program's classes reusable.

The `person` class previously defined provides for any necessary access to `__fname` via the `getFirstname()` and `putFirstname()` methods, in the same way a car provides any necessary access to the brake calipers via the brake pedal. The working of the `person` class is fairly obvious. A call to `putFirstname()` changes `__fname`, and a call to `getFirstname()` retrieves `__fname`. The same is true for methods and variables for the last name.

Now you can add the following code to exercise the person class code:

```
p = person()
print "*", p.getFirstname(), p.getLastname(), "*"
p.putFirstname("John")
p.putLastname("Smith")
print "*", p.getFirstname(), p.getLastname(), "*"
```

The preceding code instantiates a person object called p, prints the (presently empty) first and last names, sets the first and last names, and then prints them again. The output looks like this:

```
*  *
* John Smith *
```

Class Constructor

Now we're ready to add a class constructor. Class constructors are always called `__init__()`. There can be only one defined class constructor. In this case, we've made our class constructor so the person's name is defined on instantiation:

```
class person:
   def __init__(self, lname, fname):
      self.__lname = lname
      self.__fname = fname
   def getFirstname(self):
      return(self.__fname)
   def getLastname(self):
      return(self.__lname)
   def putFirstname(self, s):
      self.__fname = s
   def putLastname(self, s):
      self.__lname = s
   __fname = ""
   __lname = ""

p = person("Jones", "Paul")
print "*", p.getFirstname(), p.getLastname(), "*"
```

In the preceding code, the person's name is set upon instantiation by the `__init__()` method, so the `print` statement prints the correct name:

```
* Paul Jones *
```

Modularity has been the basis of cost-effective, reliable, easy-to-repair systems since the dawn of the industrial revolution. Object-oriented programming's potential for encapsulation enables those advantages in software. Tight encapsulation makes programs scalable, meaning they can grow without reaching a point where the interaction combinations grow geometrically and prevent further growth. The road to tight encapsulation is deciding what each class represents and creating a very few public functions to allow other software entities to control its behavior and query it for information.

Note

Inheritance is an advanced OOP topic, of concern primarily to those doing serious development. If you're doing small- to moderate-sized projects, you can safely choose to skip the "Inheritance" section.

Inheritance

Object orientation allows construction of programs in parts rather than tasks. Often these parts represent tangible objects or business entities. At such times, it's handy to classify these objects or entities the way we do in English. Consider the following:

```
Animal
  |--Bird
  |    |--Duck
  |    |--Robin
  |    `--Owl
  `--Fish
       |--Trout
       `--Catfish
```

You can think of the relationships of this hierarchy as an "is a" relationship. In other words, a bird *is a(n)* animal with wings. A robin *is a* bird. The robin "inherits" traits from birds (wings) and traits from animals (movement).

Here's another example:

```
Person
  '--Employee
```

An employee *is a* person.

Now let's look at some code:

```
class person:
   def __init__(self, lname, fname):
      self.__lname = lname
      self.__fname = fname
   def getFirstname(self):
      return(self.__fname)
   def getLastname(self):
      return(self.__lname)
   def putFirstname(self, s):
      self.__fname = s
   def putLastname(self, s):
      self.__lname = s
   __fname = ""
   __lname = ""

p = person("Jones", "Paul")
print "*", p.getFirstname(), p.getLastname(), "*"
```

In the physical world, an employee is a person (who works for the employer). Here, we've created a class called employee, which *inherits* traits from class person. employee is said to be a *subclass* of person, and person is said to be the *superclass*, and an *ancestor*, of employee. The act of creating a new class that inherits from another class is sometimes called *subclassing* or *deriving*.

The employee class has not only the getNumber() and putNumber() methods, but also the getFirstname(), getLastname(), putFirstname(), and putLastname() methods it inherits from person. Thus, assuming the preceding coding of person and employee, the code

```
e = employee()
e.putFirstname("Maria")
e.putLastname("Garcia")
e.putNumber("1234")
print "Employee", e.getFirstname(), e.getLastname(),
print "has employee #", e.getNumber()
```

prints this output:

```
Employee Maria Garcia has employee # 1234
```

Notice the benefits we've obtained. Creating the new class was trivial because we merely added the trait (employee number) that makes a person an employee. And if the person class is changed later, those changes will "filter down" to the employee class.

Inheritance can greatly simplify the creation and maintenance of large programs. Consider using inheritance in large programs when you observe program entities having an "is a" relationship.

Next we will discuss other Python capabilities, including a quick walkthrough of some of the more used modules.

Additional Python Capabilities

Python ships with several modules giving it additional capabilities. You enable a module by placing an import statement for the module at the top of the program.

The sys module enables access to command-line arguments via sys.argv. The sys module also provides exit() to exit the program and several other useful functions.

The os module enables execution of shell commands via the exec() and system() functions. It provides for directory navigation and manipulation, environment variable access and manipulation, file descriptor I/O, file manipulation, pathname manipulation, and date and time functions.

The os.path module, which is enabled by importing the os module, contains various file information such as file time, and whether it's a directory, file, link, and so on. Functions from the os.path module must be prefaced with os.path, not just os.

The glob module is used for filename expansion. Programs scanning multiple files or walking directory trees use this type of expansion.

The following short program uses the sys, os, os.path (imported automatically with os), and glob modules to walk a directory tree and print the files:

```
#!/usr/bin/python
import sys
import os
import glob

def do1dir(s):
   s = s + "/*"
   files = glob.glob(s)
   for x in files:
      if os.path.isfile(x):
         print x
      elif os.path.isdir(x):
         do1dir(x)

if len(sys.argv[1]) > 2:  # prevent /,. or ..
   do1dir(sys.argv[1])
else:
   print "Cannot do:", sys.argv[1], "-- too short."
```

The math module provides trig functions, logarithmic functions, square root functions, functions for raising to powers, and other math functions expected from a full-featured language. The cmath (complex math) module provides most of those same functions for complex numbers.

If you need a nice GUI front-end to your Python program, import the Tkinter module, which provides a nice interface to the tk widgets of the tcl programming language. Documentation on the Tkinter module is available at http://www.python.org/topics/tkinter/doc.html.

Python's built-in functions are sufficient for CGI (Web programming). However, various included modules greatly simplify complex CGI tasks. When you're considering what language to use for Web programming, investigate Python's cgi module to make forms handling easier, the urllib module for opening Web resources, and urlparse for splitting and building URLs.

If you want to go deeper, you can investigate the xmllib, htmllib, ftplib, poplib, SocketServer, socket, thread, threading, Queue, zlib, and gzip modules.

Summary

In this chapter, you examined the primary programming features of the Python language. For more information about Python's more advanced features, look for programming guidelines in the Python distributions at `http://www.python.org` or in a dedicated Python book.

Python is easy to learn, making it a great first language. Yet its power, features, add-ons, and object orientation make Python ideal for large-scale application development. Add the spectacular programmer productivity gained through Python's concise command set, and it's clear why Python is increasingly the language of choice for challenging software projects.

CHAPTER

Programming with Scheme and Expect

by Steve Wells

In This Chapter

Scheme is used as any other scripting language in that you can create common gateway interface (CGI) scripts and System Administration scripts, such as warning devices. You can even send email with it. Scheme allows you to manipulate files and is very easy to learn compared to its parent language, Lisp. Guy Lewis Steele and Gerald Jay Sussman created Scheme as a dialect of Lisp in 1975. It is simpler than Lisp in that it is easier to learn, but it is still powerful in its ability to process. The name Scheme has an interesting heritage as well. The FAQ (`http://www.cs.cmu.edu/Groups/AI/html/faqs/lang/scheme/`) states

> According to Steele and Gabriel's "The Evolution of Lisp" paper, Scheme was originally called Schemer, in the tradition of the AI languages Planner and Conniver. But the ITS operating system had a six-character limitation of filenames, so the names were shortened to `PLNR`, `CNVR`, and `SCHEME`. Eventually, the truncated name Scheme stuck.

There are hundreds of variations of Scheme. A few of the more popular distributions include

Chez (`http://www.scheme.com/`)

Elk (`http://www-rn.informatik.uni-bremen.de/software/elk/`)

Gambit (`http://www.iro.umontreal.ca/~gambit/`)

Guile (`http://www.gnu.ai.mit.edu/software/guile/guile.html`)

Kali (`http://www.neci.nj.nec.com/PLS/Kali.html`)

Kawa (`http://www.gnu.org/software/kawa/`)

LispMe (`http://www.geocities.com/SiliconValley/Lab/9981/`)

PcScheme (`ftp://swiss-ftp.ai.mit.edu:/archive/pc-scheme/`)

PocketScheme (`http://www.angrygraycat.com/scheme/pscheme.htm`)

MzScheme, MrEd, DrScheme, and DrScheme Jr.
(`http://www.cs.rice.edu/CS/PLT/packages/`)

RScheme (`http://www.rscheme.org/`)

Scsh (`http://www-swiss.ai.mit.edu/scsh/`)

Scheme48 (`http://www.neci.nj.nec.com/homepages/kelsey/`)

Scm (`http://www-swiss.ai.mit.edu/~jaffer/SCM.html`)

Siod (`http://people.delphi.com/gjc/siod.html`)

Stk (`http://kaolin.unice.fr/STk/`)

Larceny (`http://www.ccs.neu.edu/home/will/Larceny/index.html`)

We are going to focus on the MzScheme implementation, but you should be aware that they are all similar in style, although the underlying implementations are quite diverse. The MzScheme development, for example, provides added benefits such as threads for Linux, Solaris, and Windows, among other added benefits. It was created by Mathew Flatt and was originally based on LibScheme. It has developed considerably since then and provides a basis for the MrEd, DrScheme, and DrScheme Jr. programs.

We will start by ensuring that Scheme is on your machine and, if it's not, walk through the process of installing it. This will provide you with the ability to upgrade your version as well. From there, we will cover how to run Scheme within the command line provided by the language. This will allow you to test small parts of a program that you may be developing without having to run it as a script. Building on this, the next step is to create a standalone script entirely using Scheme. Finishing touches such as command-line arguments that affect the way Scheme works, file input and output, as well as the data types that are available to Scheme programmers wrap up our discussion.

Installing MzScheme

The easiest method for installing MzScheme is to download the binary distribution from Rice University. If you want to dig into the source, it is also available from the same FTP site as the binary distributions.

You can download MzScheme for Linux from `http://www.cs.rice.edu/cs/PLT/packages/download/mzscheme/`. The name of the file is `mzscheme.i386-linux.tar.gz`. After you download the file, I recommend placing it in your `/usr/local` directory before unpacking it:

```
mv mzscheme.i386-linux.tar.gz /usr/local
```

Then, unpack the file using the command

```
tar zxvf mzscheme.i386-linux.tar.gz
```

This creates the directory `PLT` and places all the files and programs you need within it. Next, you need to set up the scripting files for installation. It is recommended that you use the install program that comes with the binary distribution. To do this, issue the following command:

```
cd plt; ./install
```

Partway through the installation, you should answer `y` to the following:

```
Create ".zo" files now (y/n)? [y]
```

If you decide to use DrScheme at a later date, it starts up much faster after creating the `.zo` files.

At this point, you have MzScheme installed and ready to go. Two more things will make your work easier when dealing with Scheme at this stage: First, you should create a link from your `/usr/local/bin/` directory to the `mzscheme` startup script located in the `./bin` subdirectory. This enables you to start `mzscheme` from anywhere on your computer, assuming that your path is set up to read from the /usr/local/bin directory (which is the default).

The command to make the link is

```
ln -s /usr/local/plt/bin/mzscheme /usr/local/bin/mzscheme
```

Now, you should be able to type mzscheme from anywhere to start the interactive Scheme programming environment, but you will have a hard time running scripts.

The problem is that your link from /usr/local/bin/mzscheme to /usr/local/plt/bin/mzscheme is actually a pointer to another script. This script allows you run your Scheme program from multiple operating systems, assuming you are running something like NFS to give you access to the files. In most instances, this is not the case. To make things a bit easier, we copy the real binary, which is located in a hidden directory at /usr/local/plt/.bin/i386-linux/mzscheme, and place it in our /usr/local/bin directory as scheme:

```
cp /usr/local/plt/.bin/i386-linux/mzscheme /usr/local/bin/scheme
```

With this command, we cut out an extra line from every script that we plan to build.

If all has gone well, you have successfully installed MzScheme. To test it, type

```
scheme -v
```

The version should appear and welcome you to the program.

If you run into any problems, go through the steps again and carefully follow the directions. If you have issues beyond that, then review the README file that comes with MzScheme to track down the problem. Otherwise, we will start running Scheme from its own user interface.

Running Scheme

Scheme has its own user interface that allows you to type commands directly into it. To activate this interface, you simply type the command

```
scheme
```

This displays the same message you viewed when you looked over the version information by using the -v argument. The next line shows a prompt preceded by a greater than symbol (>). We are about to enter our first command into Scheme, so it is only fitting that it displays the words "Hello World" on the terminal.

First, a word of caution is due. Perl is another scripting language; the name is an acronym for Practical Extraction and Reporting Language. Larry Wall, the author of Perl, claims that it actually stands for Pathologically Eclectic Rubbish Lister. Upon mentioning this to a friend of mine, he was quick to respond with

> If Perl is the Pathologically Eclectic Rubbish Lister, then Lisp is the Language Involving Several Parentheses, making Scheme the Simplified Code Having Even More Encapsulation.

As we begin this first "Hello World" program, you will see exactly what he means by this.

Enter the following code exactly as it appears into the MzScheme program:

```
(begin
    (display "Hello World")
    (newline))
```

As you can see, every command in Scheme is surrounded by parentheses. The `display` command in this case defaults to `STDOUT`, which in most cases is your console. The program displays the "Hello World" and then enters a newline so that "Hello World" is on a line by itself before completing.

You want to use the interface in this way as you learn more about Scheme because it is easy to test new programming paradigms or algorithms you would like to implement. Eventually, however, you want standalone scripting capabilities so you can create a file with your commands and simply execute that. The command line is powerful, but for any project in which you wouldn't want to type the commands each time you run them, it is simply not feasible.

Scripting Scheme

There are several methods available to run your Scheme programs from the command line. First, you need to know how to exit the command interface. The command to exit is `exit`, but of course, it must be surrounded by parentheses to work:

```
(exit)
```

Next, you need to enter the program into a file. Because this is the first time we are running Scheme from a file, we once again use the "Hello World" example. Choose your favorite editor to create a file with the following code in it:

```
(begin
    (display "Hello World")
    (newline)
)
```

Save your file as `hello.scm` and then make it executable:

```
chmod +x hello.scm
```

The program does not run because we haven't told it how it is to be executed. The documentation that comes with MzScheme explains that you need to enter the first line of every script you create with the following code:

```
":"; exec mzscheme -r $0 "$@"
```

This works, but we should have something easier to remember.

If you are used to other scripting languages, such as Python, you recall that to run them, you enter the first line of your scripts like so:

```
#!/usr/local/bin/python
```

So what makes Scheme so much more difficult? Actually, it's not.

The MzScheme program has the file attribute `-r` that tells it to run as a script as opposed to the command interface. You can just run your script from the shell using

```
mzscheme -r hello.scm
```

If you want to run it as a standalone program, you might try entering the first line as

```
#!/usr/local/bin/mzscheme -r
```

Although you would be close to having something that worked, it simply won't do. The reason is that `/usr/local/bin/mzscheme` is a link to `/usr/local/plt/bin/mzscheme`, and `/usr/local/plt/bin/mzscheme` is a shell script as opposed to the real file, which is located at `/usr/local/plt/.bin/i386-linux/mzscheme`.

Confused? Recall earlier that we copied the real MzScheme to `/usr/local/bin/scheme`. This allows us to run our Scheme scripts in the same method as our other scripting languages by causing the first line in our script to read

```
#!/usr/local/bin/scheme -r
```

MzScheme uses the other script to figure out which platform you are running on so it can direct you to the correct binary version, which explains why they set up their files this way. In our case, we are using Linux and no other operating systems within our environment, so we do not need this capability.

Edit your `hello.scm` file once again and change the first line to read

```
#!/usr/local/bin/scheme -r
```

Now, run the program from the command line using

```
./hello.scm
```

You see the output on its own line:

```
Hello World
```

Using Command-Line Arguments

Several command-line arguments come with MzScheme. If you want to read through them all using your man pages, you can move the man pages that come with the program to a place where your other man pages are located, change your `/etc/man.conf` file to read them where they are, or read them directly.

To read them directly, enter the command

```
man /usr/local/plt/man/man1/mzscheme.1
```

Each of your man pages that come with MzScheme is located in the `/usr/local/plt/man/man1/` directory and can be viewed from there.

Many programs use the `-e` command-line switch to invoke some short scripts as an argument. MzScheme is no exception. If you want to invoke your "Hello World" program without having to create a new file or enter the command interface, you can use this switch in this way:

```
scheme -e '(begin(display "hello world")(newline)(exit))'
```

The `-l` switch allows you to locate and execute a library file before loading your script or starting the command interface. This means that if you want to include some subroutines within your current program, you may do so from the command line using this switch. To run this from your script, simply have the first line in your script read

```
#!/usr/local/bin/scheme -r -l library.scm
```

This assumes of course that `library.scm` is the library file you need to have executed before your script runs.

By now, you already know the `-r` switch sets up the environment for script access. It invokes the use of command-line arguments, among other things. Each time you invoke a Scheme script, be sure to use the `-r` switch. It is easier to remember its longer name, `--script`, which does the same thing as `-r`. Use whichever form you are most comfortable with.

You can customize your version of MzScheme using a file in your home directory. The filename is `~/.mkschemerc`, which follows a UNIX pattern of personal customizing files in that it is located in your home directory, it starts with a period, and it ends in `rc`. This file is executed before anything else runs, so if you have some commands you want to have run before anything else, this is the place to keep them.

If you want to run a script that doesn't use your custom file, then you need to use the command-line switch `-q`. It tells the compiler not to load your personal `~/.mkschemerc` file. The long version of the switch is `--no-init-file`.

Now that you know how to customize your scripts, let's cover the data files you can use to do it effectively.

Available Data Types

Scheme has a vast quantity of data types. As with virtually every other language, it builds on simple data types to provide more complex types that are linked in some way. We will start with Boolean types and build up to Scheme's equivalent of an array, vectors.

Boolean

Boolean data types are the simplest in that they are either true or false. In Scheme, they are invoked by using

```
(boolean? #t)
```

This returns `true` because it is a Boolean value. If the Boolean type is checked using

```
(boolean? #f)
```

it also returns true because `#f` is in reference to the word `false`. If I use a command such as

```
(boolean? "hello world")
```

it returns `false` because "hello world" is certainly not a Boolean value, in that Boolean values are either `#t` for `true` or `#f` for `false`.

Numbers

If you want to know whether a value is a number as opposed to a letter (if you were checking for a phone number or zip code for instance), simply use the `number` command:

```
(number? 100)
```

This command returns `true` because 100 is indeed a number, but numbers in Scheme do not stop there. In fact, they can get quite complex:

```
(complex? 7+8i)
```

You can guess this allows you to check for complex numbers. If you want to check for real numbers, rationals, or integers, use one of these commands:

```
(real? 1.999e10)
(rational? 99.005)
(integer? 12)
```

Each of these returns a `true` value.

Let's say we were looking for the cheapest price of two items and needed to compare them. Comparing two numbers using Scheme is simple. The syntax is to put the comparison operator at the beginning of the command and the numbers to compare after that. Here are some examples:

`(= 100 100)`	Returns `true` as 100 does equal 100
`(<= 100 80)`	Returns `false` as 100 is not less than or equal to 80
`(= i 3)`	Returns an error
`(>= 14 12)`	Returns `true` as 14 is greater than 12

Enter some of the comparison operators to get a feel for them. Use the command interface by entering `scheme` at the prompt and enter the examples as you see them here at the > prompt.

Scheme provides special properties to check numbers of different base types other than 10. To do this, you simply add a code to the beginning of the number. Here's a list of codes you can use:

`#b`	Binary (base 2)
`#o`	Octal (base 8)
`#x`	Hexadecimal (base 16)
`#d`	Decimal (base 10) default

When you compare the binary number 1011 to the integer 11, they turn out to be equal:

`(= 11 #b1011)`	Returns `true`

The same method is applied to adding, subtracting, multiplying, and dividing numbers. Use the action you want to take first and then proceed with the number to be acted on after:

`(+ 1 2)`	Returns `3`
`(- 5 3)`	Returns `2`
`(* 3 2)`	Returns `6`
`(/ 6 3)`	Returns `2`

You can use these special types in such operations as adding the binary number 1011:

`(+ #b1011 4)`	Returns `15` (11 + 4)

To achieve negative numbers, use the syntax

`(- 4)`	Returns `-4`

If the division symbol is used with only one argument, it is translated into its reciprocal:

`(/ 4)`	Returns `1/4`

Although most scripting languages use a more intuitive sense of writing formulas, it doesn't take long to get used to Scheme's technique. Every command is encapsulated by parentheses, so you avoid problems of precedence.

Characters

Characters in Scheme are always prefixed with `#\`. Special characters usually have a full word describing the key:

```
#\newline
#\tab
#\space
```

To check whether something is a character data type, use the `char` command:

`(char? #\c)`	Returns `true`

This checks whether the character `c` is in fact a character. It is, so the expression evaluates to `true`. It also evaluates to `true` if you use the command

`(char? #\1)`	Returns `true`

The number `1` is being used as a character as opposed to an integer or some other data type. The prefix `#\` designates it as a character. It returns `false`, however, if the number is used as a number:

`(char? 1)`	Returns `false`

In this case, we are using the number `1` as an integer as opposed to a character.

Character Equality

You can check character equality using a similar technique as you do for number equality. Characters are ordered by their listing in the ASCII table. Those characters associated with larger numbers in the table are considered larger. The commands are

`(char=? #\a #\a)`	Returns `true`
`(char>=? #\a #\b)`	Returns `false`
`(char<? #\a #\b)`	Returns `true`

Character Conversion

Character conversion allows you to change the case of a character. Enter the commands:

`(char-downcase #\A)`	Returns `#\a`
`(char-upcase #\a)`	Returns `#\A`

These commands change the case of the characters. To test them on your command interface, enter the following script:

```
(begin
  (display (char-downcase #\A))
  (newline))
```

The lowercase letter a is printed to the screen on its own line. If you simply enter

```
(char-downcase #\A)
```

the return value #\a is returned. This occurs because the display function cleans up the return value before sending output to the STDOUT port.

Symbols

Symbols help to identify variables. For instance, if I enter on the command interface

```
"Debian"
```

The return value is

```
"Debian"
```

The reason this happens is that the command interface analyzes the return value and outputs that. In this case, it includes the quotes. If I didn't want to include the quotes, I could use the quote command:

```
(quote debian)
```

which instead returns

```
debian
```

As you can guess, this command is used quite often. A popular shortcut simply uses the ' character. Enter the command

```
'debian
```

Observe that it sends back the same return value as the previous command.

To check whether something is a symbol, the command is symbol. Here are examples:

`(symbol? 'debian)`	Returns true
`(symbol? (quote debian))`	Returns true
`(symbol? 1)`	Returns false

Symbols are case insensitive when searching for equality. The command to check whether two symbols are the same is eqv:

`(eqv? 'Debian 'debian)`	Returns true
`(eqv? 'Linux 'lInUx)`	Returns true
`(eqv? 'Debian 'Linux)`	Returns false

Variables

Scheme variables are scoped either lexically or globally. Lexically means that the variable exists only within its own subroutine or function, whereas you can use globally scoped variables throughout the script. Where you define and set your variables identifies under what conditions the variable is scoped.

Globally Scoped Variables

Globally scoped variables use the `define` command to initialize themselves:

```
(define pi 3.141559265359)
```

This defines the variable `pi` and set its value at `3.14`....

To call it, I simply need to enter it at the prompt without the surrounding parentheses. Its return value is the value associated with it.

To define a variable as global, you must declare it outside of any subroutine or function. Where you declare your variables in Scheme is very important.

Lexically Scoped Variables

Lexically scoped variables are variables declared within a specific function or subroutine. Here is an experiment to help you better understand the difference.

First, create a global variable `x` and set it to `12` using the command

```
(define x 12)
```

You might want to enter `x` at the command interpreter to verify that `x` is equal to `12`.

Next, we need to identify a function. We call our function `third`, and any number passed to it has as its return value the number divided by three. To accomplish this, enter the command

```
(define third (lambda(x) (/ x 3)))
```

Observe that we use the same variable name. In this case, it is lexically scoped because it was declared within the scope of `third`. To test it, we enter some commands:

`(third 12)`	Returns `4`
`(third 15)`	Returns `5`
`(third 21)`	Returns `7`

It should be obvious at this stage that `x` is set and changed each time that `third` is called, but the changes are taking place internally within `third` and are not affecting the global variable `x`. To prove this, type

`x`	Returns `12`

The return value indicates that the global variable has maintained its value through the process. To prove it now, you could type

```
(third x)                    Returns 4
```

This occurs because the global variable x's value has never changed from 12.

set

To change the value of a variable, use the set! command:

```
(set! x 15)
```

This command changes the value of the global variable x to 15. To test that it worked, enter x and it returns its new value.

If you want to set a variable within a scope, you need to place the set command within the same scope. Going back to the third example, we could write it as

```
(define third (lambda(x)
                 (set! x (+ x 2))
                  (/x3)))
```

This adds 2 to the lexical variable x before dividing by 3. It has no effect on the global variable of the same name because the placement of the set command is within the scope of the lexical variable.

let

Lambda allows you to grab arguments and pass them through your subroutine as local variables, and let initializes local variables in the same manner as define initializes global variables. Let's try another example:

```
(let ((x 1)
      (y 2)
      (z 3))
     (list x y z))
```

The output from this code segment should print (1 2 3), which indicates that within the let statement, x, y, and z were initialized to 1, 2, and 3. If you call a global variable within let, that value is accessed until the local variable has been determined:

```
(define x 12)
(let ((x 1)
      (y x)
      (z 3))
     (list x y z))
```

The output might seem unexpected until you understand the scope of the situation. It outputs (1 12 3) because the x has not been initialized until the last parenthesis after (z 3). let still grabs the global value and sets y to that, which in this case is 12.

let*

Referring to the previous example, Scheme allows you to override this instance using the `let*` command. This command initializes each variable as soon as it is set, allowing you to use other variables in the process:

```
(define x 12)
(let* ((x 1)
       (y (+ 1 x))
       (z 3))
       (list x y z))
```

This code segment outputs `(1 2 3)` because the `let*` command initializes each portion as it is seen by the compiler. In this case, we add 1 to `x` and set that value to `y`. Because `x` was initialized as `1` locally rather than `12` globally, the result is the number `2` as opposed to `13`.

Strings

A string is merely an ordered group of characters. In other words, a sequence of characters makes up a string. In an earlier example, we found that if we enter

```
"Debian"
```

the return value is `"Debian"` as well. In this case, `"Debian"` is a string because it is an ordered sequence of characters. We can duplicate this using the `string` command and listing each letter:

```
(string #\D #\e #\b #\i #\a #\n)
```

This has the same return value as the quoted string.

string-ref

We can reference and set parts of a string by knowing the number of the character placement. Scheme provides the command `string-ref` for referencing a specific character within a string, and `string-set!` replaces a character with a new character.

Let's look an example. First, we need to up set a variable that we can manipulate:

```
(define distribution "Debian")
```

This sets the global variable `distribution` to hold the value of `"Debian"` and gives us something to work with. As with most languages (such as Python, Perl, C, C++, `tcl`), references start at the number `0` and increase from there, so to reference the first character of the string, use the command

```
(string-ref distribution 0)
```

This returns the letter `D` because the first character in the string is the letter `D`. If we reference `4`, it picks up the fifth character because counting the characters starts at zero.

string-set!

If instead we want to change a character in the string, we can access it using the `string-set!` command. If, for instance, we decide to make the first `D` lowercase, we use the command

```
(string-set! distribution 0 #\d)
```

Although the command does not return anything, it changes the value of the variable. If you now enter the variable name

```
distribution
```

you find that it has changed the first letter to lowercase. If you want to change the fifth character, you can access it using the number `4`, and so forth.

string-append

Yet another useful command is the `string-append` command. As you might guess, it writes its output to the end of the string. If you want to append `rocks!` to the end of your `distribution` string, you can use the command

```
(define distribution
    (string-append distribution " rocks!"))
```

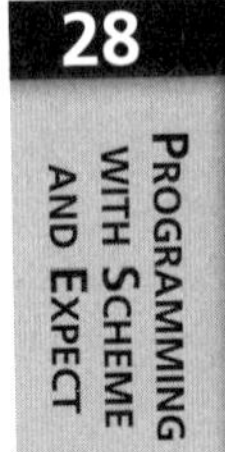

In this case, the return value of the `string-append` command is the `distribution` value (`debian`) with the string, `rocks!` appended to the end. This causes the global variable `distribution` to be reset to the new string:

```
debian rocks!
```

You can test this, of course, by simply entering `distribution` from the command interface to display the return value.

make-string

The `make-string` command allows you to define the size of the string before it has been set. For instance, if I want to define a string that is five characters long, I can use the command

```
(define a-5-character-string (make-string 5))
```

Although no value has been set on the string, it takes up five characters that can be manipulated using the `string-ref` and `string-set!` commands. It can be appended and manipulated just as any other string.

string?

To check whether something is a string, you can use the `string?` command. It works like the `number?` command you learned earlier in that it returns `true (#\t)` or `false (#\f)` when dealing with a possible string:

`(string? #\S)`	Returns `false`
`(string? 'hello)`	Returns `false`
`(string? "hello")`	Returns `true`
`(string? distribution)`	Returns `true`
`(string? (quote hello))`	Returns `false`

Commands ending with a question mark are useful in identifying a variable type. This can prove useful with conditional operators such as `if` or `case` statements, which we cover in the next section.

Vectors

Although a string can consist only of characters, a vector can be numbers, letters, binary characters, other strings, or vectors themselves—virtually anything. A vector is a list of items that seem similar to strings in its command set. To start, we create a list of numbers 0 to 5 and manipulate it. To create your list, enter the command

```
(define vec (vector 0 1 2 3 4 5))
```

Upon entering the variable `vec`, you find a return value of

```
#(0 1 2 3 4 5)
```

Vectors are always displayed this way with a space between each of the values.

vector-ref

To access an individual component of the vector, use the `vector-ref` command in the same manner as you did when accessing individual components of a string:

```
(vector-ref vec 3)
```

This command returns the fourth number in the list, which in this case is `3`.

vector-set!

If you want to set an individual component of a vector, use the command `vector-set!`. It works in the same manner as the `string-set!` command. To change the fourth number in the list (`3`) to the number `9`, for instance, you use the command

```
(vector-set! vec 3 9)
```

Now, enter the `vec` variable on a line by itself, and you see that the result has changed to

```
#(0 1 2 9 4 5)
```

This indicates that the fourth number has been changed.

Now that you know the various data types and how to set them, we will cover the techniques that use them.

Implementing Conditional Statements

Conditional statements help to organize control throughout the program. They are the brains behind the manipulation of data, and they control the flow of information through the system. They start with the if - else statement, which is the most common conditional, and end with the when statement, which is similar to the if statement in programming languages such as Perl, Python, or C/C++. Conditional statements do not allow for an else clause.

if Statement

The if statement is the most basic statement available to any programmer and, as such, it is probably the most useful as well. To implement the if statement in Scheme, you give it a conditional; if the conditional returns true, then some other process can take place. If it returns false, either that process is skipped or some other function occurs instead.

Here's an example of the if statement checking whether 100 – 50 is indeed 50. If it is, then Scheme returns the value excellent. Otherwise, it returns nothing:

```
(if (=(-100 50) 50)
    'excellent)
```

The optional else statement allows you to return something only if the if statement returns false. It is invoked as follows:

```
(if (=(-100 50) 40)
    'excellent
    'oops)
```

It returns oops because 100 – 50 is not 40.

unless Statement

The opposite of the if statement is the unless statement. This allows you to perform a series of actions based on the fact that a condition is false instead of true. It is invoked using a similar method as the if statement:

```
(unless (= 100 50)
        (display "100 is not equal to 50")(newline)
        (display "There's not much we can do about it")(newline))
```

This code segment displays

```
100 is not equal to 50
There's not much we can do about it
```

The unless statement executes its commands unless the expression returns true. In this case, it is false. Observe that the unless statement doesn't include an else expression, so you can place a number of commands within it—as opposed to the one command in the `if` statement.

when Statement

The `when` statement works identically to the `unless` statement but only executes its routines if the condition is true.

Now that you understand the conditionals that make up Scheme, the next step is to look into the manipulation of files.

File Input and Output

Files are designated as either input files or output files in Scheme. An output file allows you to write to the file, and an input file is read from. The `read` command reads in from a file, whereas the `display` and `write` commands are used to write out to a file. In this section, we will cover both reading from and writing to a file.

Reading from a File

To read from a file, you need to open it as an input file and read in either a line or a character. Subsequent calls to `read` invoke the next line or character until the end-of-file (`eof`) character has been read. This example assumes that a file called `test.dat` contains the text `"This is a test"`:

```
(define a (open-input-file "test.dat"))
  (read-char a) - returns the character 'T'
  (define b(read a))
(close-input-port a)
```

The first line opens the file for reading and sets the filehandle to `a`. The next line returns the letter `T` from the first word `This`. The next line reads in the rest of the line and therefore contains `his is a test`. The last line closes the file.

Creating a File

Creating a file is similar to reading one. First, you open an output stream, and then you use either `write` or `display` to write to it:

```
(define a (open-output-file "test.txt"))
  (display "Debian" a)
  (write-char #\space a)
  (display "Rocks!" a)
(close-output-port a)
```

The first line opens the file and creates the filehandle `a`. The line is the `display` command you've seen earlier, but the filehandle is appended as a second argument, in order to have the display write to the filehandle instead of the console. The next line enters a space using the write-char command. Finally, the display command is used once again, and the file is closed.

Echo Example

This program works in exactly the same way as the UNIX echo command, in that it displays what is placed in it as arguments. Name the program echo.scm, make it executable, and then call it like so:

```
./echo.scm This is what is displayed back to the screen.
```

Unlike the UNIX echo command, it deletes extra spaces:

```
#!/usr/local/bin/scheme -r
(let args((x 0))
    (unless (>= x (vector-length argv))
    (display (vector-ref argv x))
    (write-char #\space)
    (args (+ x 1))))
```

First, we set up the function called args and initialize the variable x to zero. The next step is to check whether we are at the end of the command-line arguments and display the next one if we are not. A space is inserted between each one, and then the call is done recursively to get at the next argument.

Expect

Expect was written in 1990 by Don Libes as the answer to a lot of nagging problems facing script hackers. Libes wrote this amazing scripting language soon after he discovered tcl, and it is inherently integrated into tcl. tcl, or Tool Command Language, is a well-developed scripting language in its own right. Expect extends tcl, allowing you to automate interactive programs.

Libes nearly named his language SEX for "Super Exec" or "Send-Expect," a day before he submitted his paper to the 1990 Winter USENIX Conference in Washington, D.C. Libes works for the government and ended up presenting it at the USENIX conference as Expect. Once you learn to use Expect, you will wonder how you ever got along without it.

Before we get started, we need to clarify a couple things: Expect is an extension of the tcl scripting language, and as such, it uses the same syntax in dealing with variables, arguments, procedures, libraries, and virtually everything else surrounding tcl.

Because this book has a complete chapter on tcl, Chapter 26, "tcl and tk Programming," there is little need to rehash the syntax here as well. So we only cover a few commands and then walk through a script that allows you to download the latest Netscape Communicator with a single command.

Installing Expect

Debian Linux comes with Expect, so you already have a copy of it built into your system. If you want to upgrade it because your version might not be the latest version out there, then read on; otherwise, you can skip this section and start using Expect.

It should be noted that you need `tcl` already installed on your computer to use Expect. Refer to Chapter 26 for information about how to install it on your system.

You need access to the `tcl` source to build Expect, and the configuration script assumes that it is located under your current directory. If it is not, you might need to make a symbolic link to the source before Expect can find it.

The latest version of Expect is always located at `http://expect.nist.gov/expect.tar.gz`. Once you have it downloaded, unpack it using the command

```
tar zxvf expect.tar.gz
```

This creates a directory with the name `expect-VERSION`, where *`VERSION`* is the latest version number of the program. You need to change your current directory to that one in order to proceed.

Once you have your current directory set up in the Expect section, it is a simple matter to compile. Run the `./configure` program, which generates a makefile:

```
./configure
```

Next, you need to run the `make` command to compile the program and use the `tcl` code as well. It might take a while to run, so you can grab a cup of java and a good book while you wait:

```
make
```

Once the program has compiled, the next step is to install it. The command to install Expect is

```
make install
```

If you are not already familiar with compiling and installing programs on your Linux system, you will find that most programs install this way.

Once it is installed, you should type

```
rehash
```

This causes the shell to rebuild your path and ensures that you are able to run Expect without having to log out and back in. It's a good idea to use this command whenever you add a new program or link from any of your `bin` directories.

At this point, you should verify that everything went smoothly by entering the command

```
expect -v
```

If all went well, you see the Expect version on the screen. If there was a problem, you might want to go through the steps again or read the `INSTALL` file that comes with Expect for possible solutions.

Command-Line Switches

Many command-line switches come with Expect. If you are interested in improving your skills, you are urged to read the man page that comes with Expect to learn the details of each switch.

The `-f` switch tells Expect to read commands from a file. I tend to use this notation when building scripts because it is the same command you use when running your script from the command line.

Diagnostic output can be enabled with the `-d` option. If you are having trouble with your script, I recommend the `-D` option. This is the interactive debugger, which helps in diagnosing problem areas.

If you installed Expect in the last section, then you recall that version information can be retrieved using the `-v` switch. After displaying this information, Expect immediately exits, allowing you to continue.

send

Expect allows you to automate interactive processes. You can automate virtually any program on your machine that normally requires you to be present. For instance, if I want to know the server load on another machine on the network, I can Telnet to that machine and look at the file contents of `/proc/loadavg`.

Expect has the ability to quickly automate that task. Because it uses `tcl` as its base, it is equally easy to send you an email or beep your console when the server load rises above a certain number. It can log that information as well.

Understandably, it is possible to write a server on the other machine to serve up the load averages and then have a client on your current computer poll the server, looking at the load every few minutes. With Expect, I can get the information with only eight lines of code.

First, let's run Expect in its interactive mode. To access this, enter the command

```
expect
```

You see a blinking cursor next to the Expect prompt, and you can enter commands. Enter the command

```
send "Hello World\n"
```

Here, you have an entire "Hello World" program in only 20 characters.

The `\n` stands for newline. A newline moves to the next line when the screen displays it. It is quite common to develop programs using the newline character, but Expect makes you look at programming from another point of view.

Expect programs act as if you, the user, were typing commands. Outputting a newline uses the key `\n`, but inputting uses the key `\r`. There are debates about why this is, but suffice to say that when sending information to another program, use the `\r`, and when sending information to the screen, use the `\n` notation—and you will be fine.

In this case, it worked properly because the "Hello World" string is being sent back to the screen.

It's not very useful to enter your programs on the Expect prompt each time you want to run something, so let's create a simple script to start.

First, you need to exit the Expect prompt. The command to exit is

```
exit
```

This brings you back to the prompt.

Next, you need to use your favorite editor (we recommend vi or emacs, both of which have chapters in this book) and create a new file called `hello`. Then, add the following lines to it:

```
#!/usr/bin/expect -f

send "Hello World\n"
```

Now, make sure that the script is executable before continuing, using the command

```
chmod +x hello
```

and then running your "Hello World" program using the command

```
./hello
```

`send` is used to send information to another program in most cases. In this case, we used it in its default mode, which sends to the terminal you are running the command from (`STDOUT`).

expect

The expect command works in the opposite way from how send works. expect waits for the other program to send information back to you before it processes the next command.

To see an example of this command, we need to edit the hello file you created with the send command. It should now read

```
#!/usr/bin/expect -f

send "Hello World\n"
send "What's the best OS in the world? "
expect "linux"
send "Exactly!"
```

What is happening when you run this program is that Expect is waiting for you to type the word linux. Until you do, the program waits. This is useful when performing networking or program interaction on heavily used servers because the timing might be different under different traffic levels or server loads. You can enter anything you want, and Expect waits patiently—for about 10 seconds. After that, it feels you are never going to interact with it so it continues.

If you want to change the amount of time it takes to time out, you reset the timeout variable. If, for instance, you want your program to time out after only five seconds, simply add the following line as the second line in the file:

```
set timeout 5
```

Run your program again without entering anything.

If you do not want the program to time out, then change the timeout variable again, but this time, make it -1:

```
set timeout -1
```

This causes the timeout to wait forever.

spawn

spawn is the command used to start a new process. It runs as if you are running a program from the shell. If I want to run a Telnet session to log in to expect.nist.gov using Expect, I need to spawn off the session with

```
spawn telnet expect.nist.gov
```

In the next section, we look at a full example of the spawn command.

interact

`interact` allows you to stop the script temporarily and read from the keyboard as well as send its output to the screen. It is useful for speeding up processes that you might use a great deal.

For example, suppose you tend to do a lot of anonymous FTP. You can create an Expect script that easily automates the process of logging in. Anonymous FTP requires the user-name `anonymous` and your email address as the password.

To FTP to the Netscape `anonymous` FTP site, you can create the following file:

```
#!/usr/bin/expect -f

spawn ftp.netscape.com

expect "Name"
send "anonymous\r"

expect "Password"
send "username@mysite.com"

interact
```

Of course, you should change `username@mysite.com` to your email address. Now, you can log in to Netscape's FTP site without having to type anything but the name of your script.

Sample Script—Netscape Download

Right now, you have gained enough experience to tackle some otherwise daunting tasks. What does it normally take to create a program that, given the version number of the Netscape Communicator you want, retrieves it for you?

We go through it line-by-line and then write the whole program (more than 20 lines of it) that does just that. I should warn you that there is no error checking built in, and organizing this code into something more efficient is left as an exercise for the reader.

The first line sets up our script and consists of the line

```
#!/usr/bin/expect -f
```

The second line spawns off an FTP process and hands the argument `ftp20.netscape.net` to it just as if you had typed it from the prompt:

```
spawn ftp ftp.netscape.com
```

The next line sets the timeout for one hour in seconds (60[ts]60). If your download takes longer than an hour, you might want to increase this or change it to `-1` to remove the timeout feature:

```
set timeout 3600
```

After that, we need to get the version from the command line. The version is simply a number such as 2.0, 3.2, or, at the time of this writing, 4.7. This number comes from the command line, and we load it into the variable `version` using the `tcl` command

```
set version [lindex $argv 0]
```

When you download Communicator, the version information is placed within the filename, but the `.` has been removed. This means that we need another variable that holds the file version and has the period removed. To accomplish this, we use regular expressions that are built into `tcl` and the command

```
regsub -all \\. $version {} fv
```

The rest of the file consists of Expect-specific commands.

At this point, we have attached ourselves to the remote server. The next step is to log in. First, we need to `expect Name` and `send anonymous`:

```
expect "Name"
send "anonymous\r"
```

This takes care of the login name. The next prompt is for a password, which is your email address. Be sure to change it in your script from the one I have here:

```
expect "Password:"
send "username@mysite.com\r"
```

Now, we need to wait again for the prompt. The prompt will state `ftp>` and, after each command, we need to wait for it. The directory we need to move to is quite long, so I split it into two commands so you can read it. In your own program, however, you might not want to do this because it is less efficient:

```
expect "ftp>"
send "cd /pub/communicator/$version/english/unix\r"
```

The `$version` in this line is the variable we collected from the command line argument. Expect substitutes the value for the version symbol before it sends it to the server.

The next step is to move into the directory where the file is located, using the commands

```
expect "ftp>"
send "cd supported/linux20_libc5/complete_install\r"
```

Next, we make sure we are downloading in binary format and get the latest Communicator. Within the filename itself, we add the `fileversion` variable to be sure it downloads the correct one:

```
expect "ftp>"
send "bin\r"
expect "ftp>"
send "get communicator-v$fv-export.x86-unknown\ linux2.0.tar.gz\r"
```

After the download is complete, we exit the FTP program and come to the last line of the Expect program as well:

```
expect "ftp>"
send "exit\r"
```

To use this program to download Communicator 4.7, I save the file as `getnetscape` and call it like so:

```
./getnetscape 4.7
```

In a few moments (or hours, depending on your connection rate), Netscape Communicator 4.7 is sitting in the same directory.

Here is the complete listing:

```
#!/usr/bin/expect -f
spawn ftp ftp.netscape.net
set timeout 3600
set version [lindex $argv 0]
regsub -all \\. $version {} fileversion
expect "Name"
send "anonymous\r"
expect "Password:"
send "username@mysite.com"
expect "ftp>"
send "cd /pub/communicator/$version/english/unix\r"
expect "ftp>"
send "cd /supported/linux20_libc5/complete_install\r"
expect "ftp>"
send "bin\r"
expect "ftp>"
send "get communicator-v$fv-export.x86-unknown-linux2.0.tar.gz\r";
expect "ftp>"
send "exit\r"
```

Start combining your knowledge of `tcl` and Expect, and you can see that complex tasks suddenly become a breeze. You can have a program check each week whether a new version of Communicator has been released and have it automatically download and install it if it has. Anything that you find yourself doing each day can suddenly be automated very quickly.

Summary

We have covered the basics of Scheme. For more information concerning Scheme, review the Scheme Web site at `http://www.scheme.org/` or consult a book dedicated entirely to the language. The MzScheme Web site has an extensive range of documentation as well when dealing with MzScheme specifically (`http://www.cs.rice.edu/CS/PLT/packages/mzscheme/`).

Scheme has matured a great deal since its creation in 1975. It is no wonder that there are so many variations of it and that it has been ported to so many platforms with its useful range of features. It currently runs on computers as small as a palmtop as well as those as large as a Cray, and the development continues today.

Expect is a powerful language and can wipe away those persistent boring jobs that you have always taken for granted. While reading the FAQ on Expect, I came across this email:

> Then, I found out about Expect. I automated everything! My boss didn't like hearing that I was working on something else in order to get out of work, and I got tired of explaining it to him.
>
> Although I accomplished all the aspects of my duties, I was infamous for being the laziest person at work, and it showed. (I made my job SO easy.) I got a new boss after a while, and he hated me from the start and fired me soon after. Oh well, I guess my mentality didn't click with theirs.

I'm not suggesting that anyone automate himself out of a job as this guy did, but I do hope you look into what Expect can offer in making your job easier.

Linux Applications

PART V

IN THIS PART

CHAPTER 29

Tying Them All Together in Projects: make and autoconf

by Matthew Hunter

IN THIS CHAPTER

The make utility is a traditional UNIX development tool. It was designed as an aid to the compilation process, saving some effort by analyzing the source and object files already in existence and compiling only the ones that actually needed to be updated. On early systems, this could save quite a lot of time if you changed only a single file. On more modern systems, projects normally compile quickly enough for this not to be as much of an issue (though large projects may still take hours or days!), but make remains a development staple due to the convenience of storing all the commands needed for compilation in a central location.

The version of make included with Debian Linux (and most other Linux distributions) is GNU make. Other UNIX systems often ship with their own versions of the make utility that behave in similar but not identical fashions.

To use make, you need to create a Makefile describing the dependency information and the commands needed to build the project. Normally, these will be calls to the compiler to compile your source code, but in fact, any command will do; Makefiles often have groups of commands defined to perform helpful tasks, such as running a test suite or producing automated documentation, that don't have anything to do with compilation.

make is useful for more than just programming. Any sort of project where a number of files need to be run through a processor of some kind in order to produce the final result can be made easier to manage with make. For example, many people using HTML preprocessors to maintain a large set of HTML pages can use make to manage that project just as they would a programming project. C programmers need to use a compiler, a linker, and possibly an assembler to process their files and generate a final executable.

Without a doubt, make is one of the most flexible project management tools around. Getting to know make is an investment in time that will certainly pay off.

Making Things with make

make relies on the presence of a file (called a Makefile) to describe the dependency tree of the project. The Makefile contains an entry for each file to be created as part of the project build process (called *target files*), and each entry specifies the files it is dependent on. When executed, make will check the last-modified date for each of the files. If the last-modified date for the target file is older than the last-modified date for one of its dependencies, the target file is rebuilt. The commands to rebuild each target file are usually specified (but can rely on default values).

Thus, when the user runs make, the Makefile is parsed into a dependency tree. The tree is then analyzed to determine which files need to be rebuilt and in what order. The commands to accomplish this are then executed, stopping if an error is encountered.

make Targets

The concept of a target in make refers to the end product of a series of steps. Each target is associated with a list of dependencies, which must be up to date before the target can be made. Your primary target is usually the application executable file, and its dependencies are the source files used to create it, along with any other files (often intermediate object files) it may depend on.

A Makefile can, and usually does, specify multiple targets. Typically, the primary target is the first target in the Makefile and will be built by default if make is called with no arguments:

```
# make
```

You can specify a target by giving the desired target on the command line:

```
# make mytarget
```

Typically, a Makefile will include a primary target as the default (which compiles the entire project), along with several virtual targets that perform installation, cleanup, or similar common tasks. More on the concept of virtual targets will be discussed later.

Other Command-Line Options for make

There are a few options that you might find useful in your daily interactions with make. These options are used to modify make's behavior in some certain conditions or adjust its interaction with you and are summarized below.

- keep-going

When this option is given, make will continue processing even if a target in the Makefile cannot be made. This can occur because of an error in the build process or because one or more dependency of the target does not have a defined rule for making the target. (More on rules later.) You may want to use this option if you are building a large number of files and would like to continue building the ones that can be successfully dealt with.

--ignore-errors

When this option is given, make will continue processing even after a command returns an error. A command returning an error is somewhat less serious than a target, which cannot be made, because the error is not necessarily fatal (that is, a compiler warning). This can also be specified on a permanent basis in the Makefile itself; commands prefaced by the - character (a single dash) will have any errors ignored.

-q --question

The option requests that `make` check the status of the dependencies without actually doing anything. The exit status of `make` itself indicates whether the specified targets are up to date. This is primarily useful in scripts.

-j [*n*] --jobs[=*n*]

This option indicates how many *threads* `make` should use when building. Using multiple threads is a good way to get more effective use of systems with a fast CPU and lots of memory and is particularly effective on SMP systems. When this option is given, `make` will try to process *n* different rules at once (or less, if using more would result in race conditions). If you do not specify *n*, `make` will use as many threads as it can; this is generally not very efficient and can produce massive load on large projects.

-l [*n*] --load-average=[*n*]

This option is closely linked with the `-j` option. It uses the system load average to limit the number of running jobs, rather than requiring an absolute number. It is typically used in conjunction with `-j` (meaning to start as many parallel threads as possible). When this option is given, `make` checks the load average before starting any new thread and starts the new thread only if the system load is below *n*.

-t --touch

Instead of remaking targets, `touch` them. This is most useful if your system clock has been reset or you are using files from an archive generated from a system with an unusual system time. `touch` is a common utility that updates the last modified date of a file to the present time, without making any changes.

-n --dry-run

This option is intended for testing. It displays all the commands that would be executed based on the current state, but does not actually do anything. It's also useful when installing software from a source using the `make install` arrangement, because it enables you to see what the installation will do before actually doing it.

You should examine the `make` documentation for a full list of options.

The Makefile Format

Listing 29.1 shows a simple Makefile for a C programming project. There are three files: `main`, `main.c`, and `main.h`. They should be immediately familiar to anyone used to C; `main` is the program binary, and `main.c` and `main.h` contain the source code for the project. The Makefile also contains a call to gcc (the standard Linux C compiler), which will produce the application executable from the source files.

LISTING 29.1 A Very Simple Makefile

```
main: main.c main.h
	gcc -o main main.c
```

The line beginning with gcc is indented with a single tab character; in fact, it must have at least one tab character there. The reason for this is primarily for compatibility with older versions of make; those versions used the tab as a separator for performance reasons. Modern versions have no need of the minor performance benefit but preserve the custom for compatibility, and because it isn't anything more than mildly inconvenient. Make sure your text editor is configured to save real tab characters and not to simulate them with spaces.

When this Makefile is processed, make will check the modification times for all three files. If main.c or main.h (or both) has been modified more recently than main, the command specified in the file will be run; in this case, that is the call to the gcc compiler. If the two source files have not been modified since the main file was created, nothing will be done.

This simple example gets right to the heart of make. It checks the dependencies of a file, and uses these to determine whether and how a file should be built. Every other feature and function that exists in make has been added in an attempt to make this process easier. If you understand this, the rest is window dressing—albeit occasionally for very large and complex windows.

Naming Conventions for Makefiles

The make utility generally searches for a Makefile in the current directory (normally the top level of the project's directory tree). Also typically, it looks for a Makefile under a number of different names. GNU make looks for Makefiles in the following order: GNUMakefile, makefile, Makefile. It will use the first Makefile it finds. The first is used only to allow coexistence with other make utilities.

Because the make utility exists in many different versions, sometimes projects written on one system have a Makefile that uses features that are not available or function differently on another. This will obviously prevent the Makefile from operating as intended, even if the project itself works just fine on both systems otherwise. If a project was developed under a non-GNU make or is used

continues

regularly with a non-GNU make, you may find a number of different Makefiles in the project directory.

The make utility processes only one of the Makefiles, not all of them. If you are having problems with make, you should ensure that you are using the correct Makefile for your version of make.

After looking at the previous example, however, you may be wondering, "Why not just type that command?" After all, it's not terribly long or complex. True enough, make itself wasn't intended to be used with projects of such trivial size, although it handles them perfectly well. In order to understand the usefulness of make, examine Listing 29.2.

LISTING 29.2 A Slightly More Complex Makefile

```
main: main.c main.h graphics.o
        gcc -o main main.c

graphics.o: graphics.c graphics.h
        gcc -c -o graphics.o graphics.c
```

In this example, we add a new set of source files (`graphics.c` and `graphics.h`), along with the file they produce as output (`graphics.o`). The `.o` file is called an *object file* and is a sort of intermediate step between a set of source files and a complete application. The old source files and target file remain the same.

In this case, the additional files represent a program module. The code in those files doesn't depend on anything in `main.c` or `main.h`, but the code in `main.c` does depend on the functions provided in `graphics.c` and `graphics.h`. The `main.c` or `main.h` file will likely have an `#include` directive referencing `graphics.h`, so that the compiler knows it can expect to be linked with the functions in that file.

When this Makefile is processed, the same basic procedure is followed. In this case, however, there are two target files: `main` and `graphics.o`. Because `main` comes first in the file, and we are invoking `make` with no arguments, `main` is the default target. Processing begins with building the dependency tree for `main`, which consists of the two source files and the `graphics.o` object file. Obviously, if the two source files have been modified, `make` will have to rebuild `main`.

Here, we start to see the first real, although admittedly minor, benefit from the use of `make`. If the `graphics.c` and `graphics.h` files have not been changed since they were last compiled into the `graphics.o` object file, they do not need to be recompiled; `main` can be rebuilt from its source files and linked with the unchanged `graphics.o` file. If the graphics.c and graphics.h source files have in fact changed, make will automatically rebuild graphics.o before rebuilding main.

Although you could still do the same task manually, make is already starting to save us some work. This will become even more important when you are working with extremely large projects (which may take hours to fully compile) or with other programmers on the same project. Either case involves a lot of extra work that can be avoided by using make.

The Evolving Makefile

Now that you understand the basics, let's move on to some of the more advanced features of make. Whenever possible, we will continue to use simple examples to demonstrate each feature; this should not deter you from building on the examples here to suit a more complex project.

Variables with make

Listing 29.3 shows another example of a Makefile, this one demonstrating the use of variables within the Makefile itself.

LISTING 29.3 A Makefile with Environment Variables

```
# This Makefile includes some variables

CC    = gcc
FLAGS = --debug
main: main.c main.h graphics.o
        $(CC) $(FLAGS) main main.c graphics.o

graphics.o: graphics.c graphics.h
        $(CC) $(FLAGS) -c -o graphics.o graphics.c
```

The Makefile in Listing 29.3 shows the basic use of variables in a Makefile. In the example, the compiler command and the flags passed to the compiler are defined as variables and are referenced in the build rules instead of being entered directly. This has the advantage of allowing the compiler and compiler flags used to build the entire project modifiable from a single, central location. When doing debugging for the project, a user might want to build with one set of options and use another set for producing distributable binaries. To do this, the user needs to change the options in only one location, no matter how many different source files he has.

This same feature also sees use on multiplatform projects, where the compiler may be different across two platforms. Whoever is compiling the project simply fills in the appropriate compiler for his or her current platform.

Exporting Variables

If you want to access the variables defined within the Makefile from within a program called by the Makefile, you need to include this line:

```
EXPORT_ALL_VARIABLES:
```

in the Makefile. This line tells `make` that any variables defined in the Makefile should be inserted into the environment of the subprocesses `make` uses to execute the actual build commands. Most of the time this isn't needed, but it does show up in some odd situations, particularly when using recursive Makefiles.

All the variables given previously are defined as *recursively expanding variables*. Variables of this type are defined in memory with references to other functions and variables, rather than expanding their values immediately. This results in a (minor) penalty in CPU time, but allows some additional flexibility. `make` also supports a different type of variable, called *simply expanded* variables. This type of variable has its value set only once, with other variables and functions expanded and executed only once when the Makefile is read.

Separating the Source and Object Directories

For some projects, it is useful to be able to separate the source and build directories. This results in one directory (or directory tree) with source files and another for the intermediate object files and the final binary. This capability is useful primarily with very large or cross-platform projects being developed on a single (probably network-based) filesystem. In the former case it simply provides more organization, and in the latter case it is necessary due to differences between the object formats of most platforms.

Certain types of nonprogramming projects may also benefit from this separation. For those using an HTML preprocessor, for example, putting the processed HTML files in a separate directory from their source files simplifies updating the Web server immensely since you can simply upload all files from a single directory.

There are two ways to separate the source and destination directories. The first is somewhat less flexible but simpler to understand. The latter makes use of `GNU make`'s `VPATH` feature, which is easy to use but slower. Listing 29.4 is an example of the former.

LISTING 29.4 Separate Source and Object Directories

```
DESTDIR = objs

$(DESTDIR)/main.o: main.c

main: main.o
```

When VPATH is specified, make will search the paths specified in the VPATH variable for any dependencies not found in the current directory. This can simplify dependency specification, because you do not have to specify the full path to every file, but you pay the price in the extra time it takes for make to search the additional locations.

Automatic Variables

make defines a number of automatic variables for use in the commands being executed to rebuild a target. Those variables are vital for defining pattern rules (see the next section, "Using Pattern and Implicit Rules") and can come in handy elsewhere. The automatic variables provided by make are

`$e:`

This variable holds the filename of the target.

`$%:`

This variable holds the member name, when the target is a member of an archive. See the make documentation for information on supported archive types, because this does not mean traditional zip or tar archives.

`$<:`

The variable holds the name of the first dependency; if the target is getting its commands from an implicit rule, this will be based on the first dependency added by the implicit rule.

`$?:`

This holds the names of the dependencies that are newer than the target, space-separated.

`$^:`

This variable expands to a list of the unique dependencies of this target, again space-separated.

`$+:`

This variable is the same as `$^`, only nonunique.

`$*:`

This variable matches the stem that caused an implicit or pattern rule to match. The exact details depend on the pattern rule that caused the match. For most pattern rules, based on the file suffix, this will simply be the filename without the suffix.

Using Pattern and Implicit Rules

A pattern rule, in the make context, is a generic procedure for building a specific type of file when a procedure for that exact file has not been expressly defined. This serves mainly to save typing the same procedure for many different source files of the same type. By defining a rule for a certain type of file (for example, a file containing C source code), you can type a procedure for generating the next step (an object file) from that C file. Then repeat the process for translating an object file into an executable. When you have defined all the necessary rules, you can simply input the various stages as targets.

Pattern rules are so named because they are defined according to filename and extension patterns. Rules are applied when a file is listed that matches one of the pattern rules.

For large projects, using pattern rules reduces the amount of time you spend updating your Makefile tremendously. For small projects, it generally won't matter one way or the other.

Listing 29.5 shows a Makefile using pattern rules. Note that the target `main` depends on `main.c`, but no actions are specified for making that file. `make` will examine the pattern rules and apply the rule defined earlier. Pattern rules must match on both the left and right sides (that is, both the target and the dependencies must match the pattern) in order to be applied.

LISTING 29.5 A Makefile Using Pattern Rules

```
%: %.c
	@gcc $<

main: main.c
```

GNU `make` also has a collection of *implicit rules,* which operate in an almost identical fashion to the rules just described. However, implicit rules are predefined by the `make` utility itself. Rules for many common languages exist, particularly C and C++. Although using implicit rules can be convenient, they are more difficult for someone else to read and understand, so it is usually best to explicitly define the pattern rules in use. Listing 29.6 demonstrates a Makefile that uses implicit rules.

LISTING 29.6 A Makefile Using `make`'s Implicit Rules

```
main: main.c
```

Pattern rules can be chained; that is, if you have a `.y` file (input to the `yacc` parser generator), you can define a rule for `make` that will call `yacc` to create a `.c` file, and then apply the rule for `.c` files to produce an `.o` file. In fact, `make`'s implicit rules do just that.

`make` has implicit rules for compiling and linking C, C++, Pascal, FORTRAN/Ratfor, modula-2, assembler, `yacc` parsers, Lex for C and Ratfor, TeX, lint libraries from C, `yacc`, or Lex programs, info and Texinfo files, and the RCS and SCCS version control systems. Most of these rules make use of environment variables that can be defined by the user to modify the commands used. For example, the command used to make an `.o` file from a `.c` file by the implicit rule is

```
$(CC) -c $(CPPFLAGS) $(CFLAGS)
```

The words beginning with a dollar sign are Makefile variables. Simply set those variables to the value you desire:

```
CC = gcc
CFLAGS = -O3
```

These commands, when inserted into a Makefile using the implicit rules for C, tell `make` to use the C compiler `gcc` with the option `-O3` (for optimization, level 3).

Using Phony Targets

`make` can be used for more than just compiling a project. Many basic maintenance tasks, such as cleaning up temporary build files or installation procedures, can be added to the Makefile and performed easily through the use of phony targets. The targets are "phony" because they typically do not refer to any actual file that should be created in the build process. Instead, they are symbolic names intended to be invoked from the command line. In this way, they function somewhat like a shell script, but with the added advantage of having dependency information available.

Phony targets are invoked as you would any other specific target, by invoking `make` with the name of the target as an argument.

One of the common uses for phony targets is as an aid to installation, with the target usually named simply install. Thus, the user compiles the program, then types make install to install it. Other common uses include cleaning old files out of the project directory tree (typically the backup files left by editors and the intermediate object files left by compilers). Listing 29.8 shows a simple Makefile with phony install and clean rules.

LISTING 29.8 A Simple Makefile with Phony Rules

```
main: main.c main.h
    @gcc -o main main.c

install: main
    @/usr/bin/install main /usr/local/bin

clean:
    @-rm -rf *.o *~

.PHONY: install clean
```

This Makefile makes the `main` program from two source files when run with no arguments. When run with `install` as the target, it checks to see whether the `main` target is up to date (and update it if not), and then installs the resulting binary when `main` is up to date. The `clean` target simply deletes any files in the current directory ending with `.o` (object files) or the ~ character (typically backup files left by editors).

The final target in the Makefile, `.PHONY`, specifies that the targets it depends on (in this case, `install` and `clean`) are phony targets. This specification is not strictly necessary but, if not included, `make` will become confused if it finds a filename matching that of onc of thc fakc targcts.

There are several other new features used in this Makefile. The `@` character prefacing each command indicates that the command should not be printed before executing it. This is not a big deal, but it cuts down on screen clutter if you already know what's going to happen. The `-` (single-dash) character included before the `rm` command indicates that the Makefile should ignore any errors returned by the command. `rm` returns an error if it doesn't find anything to delete, but that doesn't have any bearing on success or failure of cleaning the project directory, so we tell `make` to ignore failure results from `rm`.

The `install` program referenced in the `install` target is a common program on UNIX systems. It functions similarly to the `cp` (copy) command, with some slightly different options for modifying ownership and protection of the installed file. See the man and info pages for more information.

Sometimes, you might want to build a list or manipulate variables for your specific project. `make` has some internal functions that can help with that.

Using `make`'s Internal Functions

`make` has a number of internal functions that can be used to manipulate the contents of variables, including automatic variables. Most of the time, you won't need `make`'s internal functions, but they are nice to have when a situation arises where you do need them. These functions typically may be useful to automatically generate lists of filenames, generate lists of files you think are dependencies, and the like. In general, they can help to make your Makefiles more dynamic. `make` also includes basic support for conditionals, although those are not covered in this chapter. Function calls are made as follows:

```
$(function argument1,argument2,...)
```

As you can see, calls to internal functions look like and function similarly to calls referencing a variable. The documentation has detailed information on the `make` internal functions, including several not described here.

Functions for Manipulating Filenames

`$(suffix files)`

This function takes a space-separated list of filenames and returns the suffix portion of each filename.

`$(basename files)`

This function takes a space-separated list of filenames and returns the base portion of each filename (that is, all the filename except the suffix).

`$(addsuffix suffix, files)`

This function adds the provided suffix to each component of the space-separated filename list in the second argument.

`$(addprefix prefix, files)`

This function adds the specified prefix to each of the space-separated filenames in the second argument.

`$(wildcard pattern)`

This function returns a space-separated list of all files matching the provided pattern.

`$(dir files)`

The `dir` function extracts the directory portion of each file in the space-separated list of filenames.

`$(notdir files)`

The `notdir` function extracts only the filename (excluding the directory name) for the space-separated filenames in the argument.

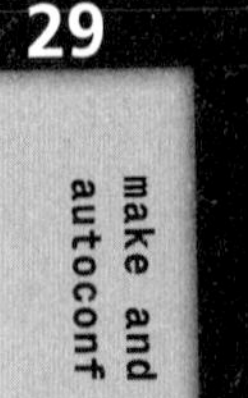

Functions for Manipulating Strings

`$(sort words)`

This function sorts the list of space-separated words in the argument.

`$(strip string)`

The `strip` function removes whitespace from the beginning and end of the argument and converts each occurrence of whitespace within the argument to a single space.

`$(findstring search, text)`

This function searches the second argument for the string provided in the first, returning the value of the first argument if it is found or nothing if not.

`$(subst find, replace, text)`

The `subst` function replaces each occurrence of `find` in text with `replace`.

Functions are one way that you can make your Makefiles more dynamic; `make` can find out things about its environment and task on-the-fly when you use them. Another method is to generate dependencies automatically.

Generating Dependencies Automatically

Obviously, updating all the dependencies for a large project can get very tedious. Because each object file depends on its source file(s) plus each header file it includes, you will be forced to update your Makefile essentially every time you add or remove an `#include` directive, create a new source file, and so on. Even if you ignore the files that aren't likely to change (primarily the system `include` files), you still end up with quite a lot of work.

Luckily, many modern compilers allow you to generate dependencies automatically in a format that `make` can understand. The traditional way of using this feature was to include a special target called `depend` and have the commands for that target generate a file of dependencies (usually `Makefile.depend`). This dependency file would be included from the `main` Makefile and contain lists of all the compiler-generated dependencies. Listing 29.8 is an example of such a situation.

LISTING 29.8 A Makefile Using Automatically Generated Dependencies

```
include Makefile.depend

depend:
    gcc -M main.c >Makefile.depend
```

The `-M` command-line option tells most compilers to generate `make`-style dependency information. The `gcc` compiler also accepts `-MM`, which asks for dependency information with any system header files excluded.

Going one step beyond this, however, you can use `make` to track and update the dependencies when needed. Although this is a bit tricky to set up, it can pay off in the long term, because you need to set it up only once. You create a small, simple Makefile corresponding to each source file.

Although most of the focus of this chapter has been on C programming, you can also use `make` with a variety of other languages and tasks as well.

Using make with Other Projects

make can be used with any programming language that requires or permits compilation. Although make was designed for C development, which can have very complex dependency trees, other languages can often make just as much use of it.

Using make with C and C++

make was designed for use with C, but the only place this shows clearly is in the default build rules in GNU make. Those default rules describe how make should rebuild files of a certain type (based on the file extension). make will know that to rebuild an .o file, you call the default C compiler on the appropriate .c file, and so on. This can save you some typing in the Makefile but generally isn't used extensively.

Using make with Web Sites

HTML preprocessors are designed to take input in some form of marked up HTML source and output normal HTML. They can make maintaining a large Web site with many common elements much easier. Because these preprocessors have essentially the same problems as C compilers (namely, a lot of files that need to be recompiled only if they change), they are equally well suited for use with make.

Using make with Java

Java includes its own basic dependency management system. Because the Java language specifies very precisely where each source file must be located and how it must be named, Java compilers can develop the dependency information from the source file passed on the command line and check the modification dates of the other source files as well. This renders make somewhat less useful.

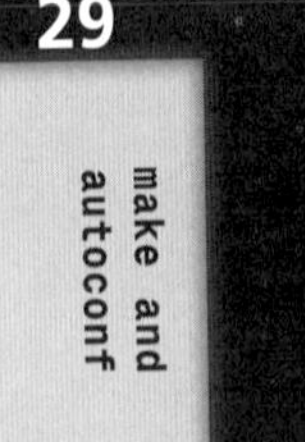

Luckily, the Java compiler cannot do everything make can do. This allows make to preserve some usefulness. Java developers can use make to generate distribution-ready packages (that is, jar files with documentation and the like included). These can even be arranged to automatically recompile first if needed. For those projects that don't really have a central class on which everything else depends (such as many API libraries), make provides better dependency processing than the Java compiler.

Listing 29.10 shows an example Makefile for a Java project. The pattern rule at the top of the file tells make how to build a Java class from a Java source file. There are two ways to handle the remaining dependencies.

If you want to use the Java automatic dependency tracking system, you can list only the main classes (that is, the classes with a main() method to start execution). The Java compiler will check all the class files referenced from the class file you provide and recompile those that need it. This is generally sufficient, but in certain situations it will miss some files that need to be recompiled. If you experience unusual problems, check to make sure all your classes are up to date.

The alternative is to try to specify the dependencies completely in the Makefile and let make worry about what should be recompiled. This is a lot more work than most people are willing to put up with, especially since the javac compiler does not support generating dependencies automatically. Luckily, the Jikes compiler (available from IBM's alphaWorks, http://www.research.ibm.com/jikes/) does allow just that.

Finally, some people just pass all their Java classes to the compiler at once and go for coffee. You don't need make for that.

LISTING 29.10 A Makefile for Use with a Java Project

```
%.class: %.java
    @javac $<

packagename: package/directory/MyClass.class
```

More Documentation for make

make is officially a GNU project and is documented in the GNU info format. You can access the GNU documentation using the info browser, if it is installed, by typing

```
# info make
```

The info documentation is very complete and documents everything a new or experienced user might want to know about make. It also includes several sample Makefiles, which are well worth perusing for ideas on how to create your own.

Man pages for make also exist but are derived from the info page and generally contain less information and sometimes out-of-date information.

Using autoconf

autoconf is a GNU tool designed to help configure source code to compile properly on a system it was not necessarily developed on. For instance, if you write a program on a FreeBSD machine, you'd also like it to be able to be compiled and run on a Linux box. It obviously isn't much of a chore for the developers of a package to ensure it will compile on all their systems without problems, because the number of systems is limited and can be configured identically in most cases. However, with the growing popularity of source-based distributions, along with the much more diverse nature of open-source development, the need arose for projects to compile on widely diverse platforms.

autoconf was developed to meet that need. Developers use autoconf to create shell scripts that handle software configuration automatically on each system. The user simply runs the generated script:

```
# /configure
```

The configure script then tests for all the features the package needs, one by one. In most cases, this is done automatically; for unusual configurations, the user may need to specify desired options or the locations of required packages. If all the required features are detected successfully, a set of configuration files is created. The project itself will use the contents of those configuration files to adjust its behavior, depending on the available features.

Before autoconf, developers needing features of this type had to write their own detection routines and rely on the user to modify the appropriate files manually. This was annoying for the developer and difficult or impossible for the user (who was increasingly likely to be an administrator, who doesn't have time to sweat over installing each new software package, or an end user, who simply doesn't have the knowledge). autoconf enables a collaborative effort in detecting certain features, thus eliminating a large part of the problem.

It should be noted that autoconf is licensed under the GPL but has a specific exception for the files it generates. Thus, you do *not* need to distribute under the GPL if you are using only include files generated by autoconf (that is, using autoconf as intended and distributing the generated configure scripts). If you are using the actual source code to autoconf itself, you need to abide by the GPL as usual. Check the documentation if you are unsure.

autoconf requires the GNU m4 macro package. Other m4 packages have historically had bugs that affect autoconf. This is probably installed on your Linux system already.

This chapter does not cover autoconf in any depth. It is intended to provide a brief introduction to help you decide whether you should use it. Check the man and info pages for more detail, particularly if you intend to make use of autoconf.

Summary

This chapter describes the GNU make project management tool. make is a widely used development tool for many different types of projects; it can be used with any system that has a number of changeable input files that need to be reprocessed after each change but can be left alone otherwise. The `make` environment is a rich one, supporting variables and a large set of internal functions for use in manipulating dependencies and filenames. Finally, a brief introduction to `autoconf`, a tool for configuring source code to compile on varying platforms, is provided.

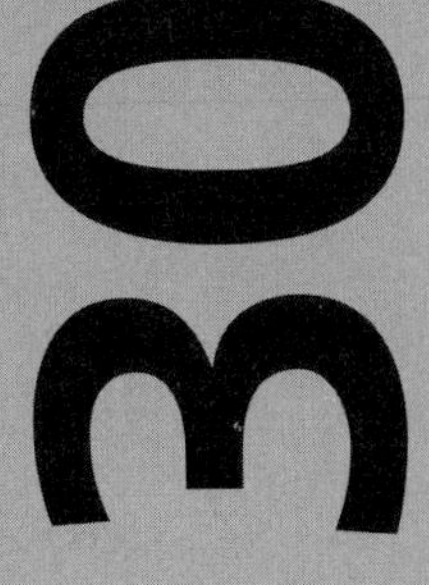

CHAPTER

Distributed Project Management

by Steve Wells

In This Chapter

Distributed project management is a complex issue. It starts debates among very intelligent people as to which methodology is the correct implementation. However, over the years several methods and programs have risen to the top as a being noteworthy. There is little need to pay for a project management solution today, because these products have proven themselves time and again—using literally thousands of programmers and yielding some of the profound software in use today.

Starting with programs that enable programmers and documentation experts to work together concurrently on a large project, we will work our way through techniques to handle bugs and finish up with the ability to use several machines at once to compile your programs.

CVS

When it comes to version control software for freeware programs, no other software is as popular as Concurrent Versions Systems (CVS). In 1986, Dick Grune created CVS; in April 1998, it went through a major overhaul by Brian Berliner, who is the current author. Revision Control Systems (RCS) makes up the base of CVS. RCS was created at Purdue University by Walter Tichy and was used to manage text-based documents, including programs, as multiple authors revised them.

CVS is a management tool that allows authors over a wide area network the ability to add, modify, and delete parts of a program or documentation. It enables each of these authors to work together to create a final product by managing who has done what, when, and where. For instance, if you and a friend were working on a paper you had written, you could use CVS to track any changes your friend made and merge them with your changes. Each of you keeps updating the paper until you have a final product.

One advantage of CVS over other version control software is that it uses a hierarchy of directories instead of a single directory or file. This allows much larger developments and libraries. It manages concurrent editing of the files under its control as well as releases. Using CVS, it is possible to fix a bug in an already released product and maintain an order to the version numbers. Its greatest strength is in allowing multiple users to get along well when dealing with large software projects without having to lock them out when making a change.

Netscape has used CVS for years in its development of Netscape Communicator. When Netscape changed its business model to allow for open source, it implemented CVS on a grand scale. Today, hundreds of programmers around the world work together on the core parts of Netscape Communicator. They have a Sun Ultra Enterprise 450 with four 250MHz processors, a full 2GB of RAM, and an 80GB hard drive to run all their CVS traffic. To warrant having such a huge machine, they obviously value CVS very highly.

Open-BSD, ECGS development (a GNU C/C++ compiler), and Bentley Systems are three other major users of CVS. It has a long history and has been tested and implemented in extreme environments. Obviously, you will not need to have such a large machine or use it with so many clients to make use of CVS. However, you could use it if you were implementing your own GNU software and wanted to allow others to work on it with you, or you knew someone else who was running it and wanted to test or help out with that person's program. Many sites distribute the latest version of their software using CVS, and you will need a basic understanding of it to use that software.

We will start by talking about installing CVS and setting up new accounts and then go over some features offered by CVS over other systems, such as its remote access capabilities.

Installation

Installing CVS may be easier than you think. It comes standard as part of the Debian distribution, so you should already have it installed on your machine. If you want to see whether you already have CVS on your system, enter this command:

```
cvs -v
```

This shows you the version number if it is installed but will not run the program. If you see something similar to "file not found," it has not yet been installed; if a newer version has been released and you would like to upgrade, please continue. Otherwise, feel free to skip to the next section.

CVS is installed in the same manner as most every other GNU product. The installation steps start with downloading the software in compressed form, unpacking it, compiling it, and installing it.

CVS can be obtained via anonymous FTP from

```
ftp prep.ai.mit.edu
```

First, log in as `anonymous` and then enter your email address as the password. When you have logged in, the next step is to find the software.

It is archived in the `/pub/gnu/cvs` directory, so you need to change your current directory to that directory with this command:

```
cd /pub/gnu/cvs
```

At this point, you need to list the files in that directory and make a judgment call as to which is the most current released version of the software. At the time of this writing, the latest version is version 1.10 and is labeled as `cvs-1.10.tar.gz`. If you see a later version (larger number) within this directory, you are urged to download that one, because it means a new version was created after this writing. To download the program, type

```
get cvs-1.10.tar.gz
```

Be sure to replace `1.10` with the most current version you can find. After you have downloaded the file, type

```
quit
```

to leave FTP and return to your local machine's prompt.

The next step is to unpack the file. The `tar` command has the capability of unzipping files that have been compressed using the gzip program by using the `z` option, so you can use one command to unpack the whole file:

```
tar zxvf cvs-1.10.tar.gz
```

where `1.10` is your version number, of course. This command creates a directory with the same name as the file and places all the source code, documentation, and test suites with it. You will change your current directory to this new one in order to continue:

```
cd cvs-1.10
```

Configuration

After you have changed to the new directory, the next step is to configure the software. This is a script that reads information about your current operating system, placement of shared libraries, and other things you need when compiling. To configure the CVS software, you simply type

```
./configure
```

A series of text lines will scroll by, explaining what it is doing. It is not meant to be read by a human in this manner, but can be outputted to file if something goes wrong, so do not try to keep up with reading it. When the `configure` script has finished, it creates a Makefile. The Makefile is used when compiling, so you'll use that next. To compile your CVS program, type

```
make
```

`make` uses the Makefile that was created by the `configure` script and compiles the program. When it is done, you have two options: Either test it and install it or take your chances and simply install it.

To test it before installing your program, enter this command:

```
make check
```

Then get a good book and a hot cup of java because it takes a couple of minutes to run. When it's done, you will be able to see whether any errors have occurred in the build process. If they have, you need to read the `INSTALL` file, which explains possible problems and how to fix them. To do this, enter

```
less INSTALL
```

If, on the other hand, all went well, install the files. This creates the man pages, installs the executables, and sets up any libraries that are needed. To install CVS at this stage, enter

```
make install
```

Now the program is installed, but you may not be able to use it yet. You need to either log out and log back in or simply type

```
rehash
```

This builds a list of the files you have access to from your prompt environment variable and enables you to start using CVS. If at any time during the installation you run into trouble or find an error, please read through the documentation within that file. Some especially useful commands are

```
less INSTALL
less README
less NEWS
less BUGS
```

These should help you locate the source of your trouble and provide possible solutions. In almost every case, though, everything goes fine and you are ready to start using CVS.

Starting a Project

I run a small freeware program that enables you to search for the most inexpensive book price on the Internet, given an ISBN number. Throughout the remainder of the text, I show you how I went about setting up and developing this program with other programmers. This will provide a real-world example and help to show you some of the pitfalls that may be incurred and how to avoid them.

If you would like to download the program and try to re-create the CVS features discussed here, it can be found at

```
http://www.price-hunter.net/
```

The name of the project is `bookprice`, and I have created a directory under the same name and put it in my home directory. With your own projects, you should choose a relevant name and do the same thing.

The next step is to inform CVS of the `root` directory for my projects. This is where CVS will store the project information, including modifications and version numbers. CVS recognizes this directory by searching your environment variables for the `CVSROOT` variable. Now create the following environment variable based on your shell. Notice that we have not created the directory yet. CVS will create it for us when we tell it to initialize later.

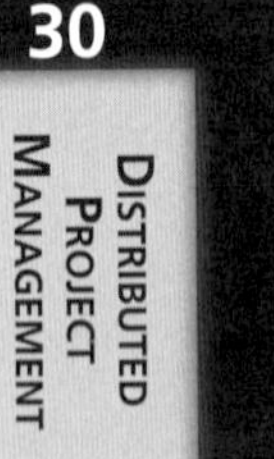

If you are using the `csh` or `tcsh` shell, use this command:

```
setenv CVSROOT ~/cvsroot
```

If you are using the `bash` or `ksh` shell, use the following command:

```
CVSROOT=~/cvsroot
export CVSROOT
```

Be sure that ~ is the full path to your home directory. CVS complains that it cannot use relative paths when you run it otherwise.

Setting Environment Variables

It is a good idea at this stage to set these environment variables each time you log in. The easiest technique for implementing this is to edit your login script. To do this, place the command you used to set your environment variable in your login script. Your login script is dependent on the shell you use.

If you are using the `csh` or `tcsh` shell, edit the following file:

```
~/.login
```

If you are using the `bash` or `ksh` shell, edit this file:

```
~/.profile
```

This assures that each time you log in to your system, the CVS `root` is always located by setting the environment variable at the onset.

At this stage, CVS needs to initialize itself using the new directory. To do this, enter the following command:

```
cvs init
```

If you now look in your home directory, you will see the new directory that CVS created as well as the files within it.

Importing Current Files

The next step is to import all your current files from your project into CVS. This enables you to retrieve them from CVS when you want to edit them and keep everything current with other developers. To start my `bookprice` project, I will ensure that my current directory is the topmost directory of the source tree and enter

```
cvs import -m "Book Price" bookprice steve start
```

The `import` command first requires that that you attach a message to the action using the `-m "`*`MESSAGE`*`"` attribute. If you leave this out, it will open an editor and ask for a message there. In this case, the message is simply a title to the project; because there is little need to get multiple lines involved, we are using the `-m` argument instead.

The next attribute is the repository or main directory for the source tree. After running this command, the `bookprice` directory is created under the `$CVSROOT` directory.

Following that is the vendor tag, `steve`. It does not have any real impact with this program, but because it is required, I decided to place my name there as the main author.

The last component is the release tag. Whenever I start a new project, I use the `start` attribute. These last two arguments are used for tracking purposes, and `start` helps identify the start of the project.

Finally, you should test the CVS tree, and to do that you need to move your project directory to a backup area and then try to retrieve the files:

```
cd ..
mv bookprice bookprice.bak
```

After this is complete, the next step is checking out the source tree from the CVS program:

```
cvs checkout bookprice
```

It then builds the directory tree. Now you can check for any differences between the CVS tree and the backup you just created:

```
diff -r bookprice.bak bookprice
```

The only difference that shows up on my setup is that the CVS directory is located in the `bookprice` directory and not the backup. This is a directory that CVS has created to keep track of the files, so there are no problems.

At this stage, it is recommended that you remove your original sources or move them to places where they won't be tampered with. They make good backups, but if you were to make your changes there instead of using a CVS copy at this stage, you could overwrite a large part of your data.

Modifying a Project

To make changes to your current project, you need to open the latest copy of it from CVS. Then make your changes, test it, and commit those changes back into the original. CVS will merge them back in with the original, including any changes that others have made. If there are conflicts, you will be warned of them at this time.

In this case, I would add some names of people who informed me of new sites to add to the `bookprice` program. These names are placed in the `README` file, so I first check out the `bookprice` directory from CVS:

```
cvs checkout bookprice
cd bookprice
```

Then I edit the README file within that directory and commit those changes back to CVS:

```
cvs commit -m "Added Additional Informers" README
```

As before, the commit command needs to have a message explaining what you are doing in order to continue. If you do not supply a message on the command line, it will open an editor and have you supply it there. The last argument of the commit command is the file you have edited. After you make any changes to a file within a distribution, be sure to use the commit command to update it after you have tested it and are sure it works properly.

Dealing with Multiple Developers

In most cases, you keep checking out and committing revisions as you always have, but there are a few commands that you should know in order to work well with others. In the following section, I cover changes I made to my bookprice project while another developer, Brian, was also making changes. In almost every case, you never have developers working on the same file, at the same section of the file, and at the same time—but in this one instance we did.

Books.com had changed its layout, and the bookprice program would not read in the correct price because of the new design. Both Brian and I noticed it at about the same time, and here is what happened.

First, I downloaded the bookprice program from CVS into a new directory:

```
cvs checkout bookprice
```

Remote Login

Brian did the same thing not long after on his own server, but his CVSROOT environment variable is set up to remotely log in to my machine. His CVSROOT environment variable is very different from mine because it contains

```
CVSROOT=:pserver:brian@price-hunter.net:/home/steve/cvsroot
```

This tells the CVS client to connect to price-hunter.net with the username brian. Brian must have an account on my machine, of course, for it to work. He then connects to the same cvsroot directory that I created earlier and uses the pserver authentication method to connect.

A bit of explanation is due here concerning how to set up the CVS pserver method so that outside developers can connect. You need to log in as root to make these changes, and I did that first. To set up the pserver, I edited my /etc/inetd.conf file and added this line:

```
cvspserver stream tcp nowait nobody /usr/bin/cvs cvs -allow-root=/home/steve/
➥cvsroot pserver
```

This needs to be on a single line in order to work.

Next, I needed to link that server to a port, and the default port for CVS is 2401. To be sure that clients could connect properly, I felt it best to leave it at that port, although I do have the option to change it if needed. To tie the server to the port, I edited the `/etc/services` file and added this line:

```
cvspserver 2401/tcp  # CVS Pserver
```

Restarting the Daemon

After making these changes, the `inetd` daemon needs to be restarted. First, you find the process identification number (PID) of the `inetd` program. This is located by listing all the processes that are currently running and searching that list for the program. To accomplish this I used the following command:

```
ps ax ¦ grep inetd
```

This command returns the PID in the first column and the name of the program in the last column. In some cases, it will return two entries because your command itself is a process. The PID in this case is 253, so to restart the `inetd` program I used this command:

```
kill -HUP inetd
```

The `inetd` program now reads in the changes from the configuration files and makes sure that CVS is running as a server on port 2401.

Issuing the Command

Brian issued this command:

```
cvs login
```

and was prompted to enter his password. After this was done, he had access to all the commands that come with CVS just as if he were doing everything locally. This means that when Brian entered

```
cvs checkout bookprice
```

his CVS client connected to the `price-hunter.net` server and downloaded the latest version of the `bookprice` program from the CVS server located there. This is exactly the same command I entered locally.

Each of us tested the program and found the problem with books.com. Now we needed to make the necessary changes to the file and upload it back to the server.

Brian located the `Books.pm` file and quickly discovered that books.com had changed its page. He used a regular expression to fix the page and, rather than read in one line at a time, he gathered the whole page in as one file as the previous library had before locating the price.

His code consisted of removing five lines and adding only three new ones. It was clean and yielded a lot of room for error if books.com made any other changes to its page in the future. Brian quickly committed it back to the CVS server using this command:

```
cvs commit -m "Page Change - Slurp Whole File " lib/Books.pm
```

He then went back to playing Quake.

I, on the other hand, was struggling with the parsing routines and reading in one line at a time. I first built up an array of each line and traversed through it. The keywords I was looking for were on a line by themselves, and the price was on a line after that. I was reading in each line, looking for the keywords, and grabbing and parsing the next line. Obviously, it took me longer using this method, and when I was finally done I went back to commit my changes:

```
cvs commit -m "Page Change - Price on own line" lib/Books.pm
```

To my surprise, I received this message:

```
cvs commit: Up-to-date check failed for 'lib/Books.pm'
cvs [commit aborted]: correct above errors first!
```

At this point, I had to assume that someone else had worked on the file in the meantime, so I issued the `update` command to see what had happened. This command merged the two changes and displayed what had changed:

```
cvs update lib/Books.pm
```

CVS returned the following:

```
RCS File: /home/steve/cvsroot/bookprice/lib/Books.pm,v
retrieving revision 1.4
retrieving revision 1.5
Merging differences between 1.4 and 1.5 into Books.pm
cvs update: conflicts found in Books.pm
C Books.pm
```

It told me that the revisions that Brian made were now merged with the revisions I created. I needed to resolve the conflicts before I could update the CVS tree with my changes.

Editing the `Books.pm` File

Next, I edited the `Books.pm` file to see what changes Brian had made. Near the end of the file I saw that CVS had inserted some lines into my code:

```
<<<<<<< Books.pm
   my (@lines) = get($url);
   my $count=0;
   foreach (@lines) {
            $count++;
           next unless /Our Price/;
           last;
```

```
    }
    $lines[$count] =~ /\$(\d+\.\d\d)/;
=======
    my ($content) = get($url);
    $content =~ s/\n//g;
    $content =~ /Our Price.*?\$(\d+\.\d\d)/;
>>>>>>> 1.5
```

Now I knew exactly what had happened. Someone changed the file at the same time that I had and used a different technique as well. It was up to me to decide to either go with Brian's code or incorporate my own. Weighing the decision carefully, I opted to go with Brian's code. It was usable under a more diverse set of circumstances and easier to maintain. If I had found that I could use both techniques to gain a greater advantage, I could certainly have implemented that as well.

To resolve this conflict, I removed the markers <<<<<<<, =======, >>>>>>>, and the lines I had created, and then committed it back to CVS:

```
cvs commit -m "Nice Job Brian!" Books.pm
```

At this point, you should also know the `status` command. This gives you information about any file in the distribution. The command is executed like so:

```
cvs status Books.pm
```

where `Books.pm` is the file whose status you want to check.

Using the `status` command on the `Books.pm` file in this distribution yields

```
===================================================================
File: Books.pm          Status: Up-to-date

    Working revision:  1.6    Wed Jun 30 20:34:51 1999
Repository revision:  1.6 /home/steve/cvsroot/bookprice/lib/Books.pm,v
Sticky Tag:    (none)
Sticky Date:     (none)
Sticky Options:   (none)
```

This displays the filename, the status when it was last updated, and the version number, as well as where the file is held within CVS. It is useful in deciding whether you should download a new version or not.

If you are in need of even more detail, use the `log` command. This command shows all the revisions, the date, the author, and any messages that were added after a revision.

For instance, if I enter

```
cvs log lib/Books.pm
```

I will see each change that was made, as well as the revision numbers. The first output is the total number of revisions, any symbolic names, and the location of the CVS `root`. The next output is a series of revisions that looks something like this:

```
----------------------------
revision 1.6
date:1999/06/30 20:25:13; author: steve; state: Exp; lines: +3 -1
Nice Job Brian
----------------------------
revision 1.5
date: 1999/06/30 20:17:12; author: brian; state: Exp lines: +4 -4
Page Change Price on own Line
```

As you can see, CVS is a powerful program when used with multiple users, and its remote capabilities make it especially important in the role of open source projects. After you have the program created and released, the next step is to gather bugs from your users to fix any problems that will occur in every large project.

Fixing Bugs in Released Versions

Here's the scenario: You have finally released version 1.0 of your software project as a stable, capable system and are starting work on the next version. Soon, you start receiving reports that there is a bug in the released software that needs to be fixed. Normally, you could just make sure that it is fixed in the next version and, when it is updated there, it will be fixed. This may be how some large companies work, but it is not recommended with good software. Linux released version 2.0, and before 2.2 was ever released as a stable version, it had over 35 patches applied to it. All good software should be dynamic in how it meets the needs of its users.

With CVS, fixing bugs in stable versions is just one of its many features. You can create as many different released versions as you want by *branching*. The best way to think of branching is to visualize a tree. You start off with the trunk of the tree, which is where your program starts, with a single version evolving upward. After a while, you need to release a stable version. This is called a *branch*. It spawns outward in a new direction, eventually tapering off.

Another branch has sprung up, though, that holds your development work—the work you do to cause the software to evolve with even more features. As time rolls on, you will find problems that need to be fixed within your released branch, without having to start over with the development version. You can have as many of these branches as you need, and you may call them whatever you want.

Releasing a Stable Version

The first step is to release a version of your software. This means creating a new branch that you tag as different from the standard development branch. Referring back to the `bookprice` program, after Brian made the change to the `Books.pm` file, it was ready to be released to the public. The command I used to create a new branch of the software was

```
cvs tag release-1-0
```

It then returned

```
cvs tag: Tagging .
T ARTISTIC.license
T CHANGES
T CONFIG
...
T test.pl
cvs tag: Tagging lib
```

Now when a user (let's call her Hope for this example) wants to download the released version, she enters this command:

```
cvs checkout -r release-1-0 bookprice
```

It works the same way as the normal `cvs checkout` command, but the `-r` attribute allows it to grab from a different branch of the software tree, as in `release-1-0`.

After working for several weeks on new features, Hope then comes back to inform the developers that several of the book sites are no longer working and need to be updated. Our development has only just begun. It has taken us several weeks ahead, and it may not come out as a released version for a couple of months. In the meantime, the released software is becoming a less useful tool, so it needs to be updated without having to release partial changes.

Someone (let's call him Matt) steps forward and volunteers to fix the engines on the released version. The first command he enters is

```
cvs rtag -b -r release-1-0 release-1-0-patches bookprice
```

With this, Matt creates a branch off the released version 1.0 and calls it `release-1-0-patches`. After issuing this command, CVS returns with

```
cvs rtag: tagging bookprice
```

Next, Matt downloads a working copy of the official first release to make the appropriate changes:

```
cvs checkout -r release-1-0-patches bookprice
```

When it has downloaded all the files, he can address the problems that Hope uncovered. When he is done testing those changes, he commits them back to CVS for inclusion within the new branch:

```
cvs commit -m "Fixed RegExp" lib/Amazon.pm
cvs commit -m "Replaced Return Value" lib/Spree.pm
cvs commit -m "Changed GET to POST" lib/Books.pm
```

Merging Changes to the Released Version

After all the changes are made and committed, Matt decides to merge the changes back into the released version. To achieve this, he must first release the old version and then merge the changes. To release the version, he issues this command:

```
cd ..
cvs release -d bookprice
```

After it's released, he needs to use the `-j` option of the `checkout` attribute to merge the two:

```
cvs checkout -j release-1-0-patches bookprice
```

After he enters this command, CVS then returns

```
cvs checkout: Updating project
```

along with a list of each file and a short status of the file that explains whether it was merged or not. If there are conflicts, those problems need to be worked out before the command will be successfully implemented, as we did in the "Editing the `Books.pm` File" section.

At this stage, the only thing left is to commit the merged patch:

```
cvs commit -m "Merged Patches"
```

This incorporates the changes that Matt made with the current development of the software so we are sure that each of the engines works as well.

Adding and Removing Files

When you add a new library or some documentation to the distribution, you need to be sure to add that new file to CVS. For instance, the last book site that I added to the `bookprice` distribution was `www.vcss.com`, which specializes in computer books. I created a new library file, which I named `VCSS.pm`, and added it to the CVS tree:

```
cvs add VCSS.pm
```

Then I committed that file:

```
cvs commit VCSS.pm
```

On another occasion, I had built a library file for the site `www.clbooks.com`. Everything was working great until John asked me to add `www.fatbrain.com`, which I later discovered was the new name that `clbooks` had chosen. It was the same company. There was no reason to keep the `clbooks.pm` library file now, because it would simply return the same results as `fatbrain.com`. So I removed it from the distribution:

```
cvs remove clbooks.pm
```

I was sure to commit that change as well:

```
cvs commit clbooks.pm
```

It may seem a little odd at first to commit a file that you do not want anymore, but without it the main distribution set is not updated.

Summary of CVS

There are several ways to handle version control and to be sure that multiple developers do not trip over each other while working on the same project. CVS allows you to lock files in the same manner as RCS or other types of software. Personally, I would rather developers had the opportunity to create without inhibition. If a developer plans on changing a file, for instance, and does not get around it for a couple days, no other developer could get access to the file in the meantime. CVS has the right approach because it allows everyone the freedom to work on any file he or she chooses and warns of problems that may pop up only if a developer took a lot longer than another developer to get the file patched.

I hope that you can see the results that CVS can bring to your software management and that it allows you to have your software grow with the help of many hands. It is easy to set up, and the basics are quick to learn. I suppose that is why it is the most widely used version control system for freeware projects in use today.

Version control software is useful in developing programs and adding new functionality, but one of the toughest components of writing software is fixing the software as it is released. Open-source advocates like to point out that with so many people providing immediate feedback on the software as it is released, bugs seem to float to the surface sooner and are taken care of more quickly. Programs such as Bugzilla, the Debian Bug Tracking System software, and Jitterbug all help to provide an organized way to track bug reports and get them to the appropriate people for squashing.

Bugzilla

Bugzilla is the name of the bug-reporting software developed for Mozilla. Mozilla, you might recall, is the mascot for Netscape. In fact, if you run Netscape on your Linux machine and type `about:mozilla` in the location bar, the icon in the top corner of your browser will change to Mozilla taking over the world by fire.

Bugzilla was created as a method of tracking and accepting bugs that were found by alpha users of Mozilla (Netscape). It was originally written in `tcl` (pronounced “tickle”) but has since been ported to Perl and uses MySQL as its database. The entire system is run over CGI and your Web browser, allowing anyone to send you bug reports by simply logging in and filling out a form.

Installation

Installation of Bugzilla is not trivial. It is recommended that you read the `INSTALL` file that comes with the distribution as you go through this section for other clues if you run into trouble. It is a powerful program and, as such, installation requires many steps. In most cases, this chapter will be all you need, but if you have changed your system settings for one reason or another, you will need to be aware of those subtle alterations that Bugzilla requires to work and ways around them.

First, download the source for Bugzilla from

```
http://www.mozilla.org/bugs/source.html
```

Next, you need to be running MySQL to use Bugzilla. Rather than go through how to install each item used by Bugzilla, I will direct you to the various sites, downloads, and installation files. These files are more current in case things change a bit. If you have already installed a certain package, then you should simply skip that part of the install.

MySQL can be located at

```
MAINPAGE: http://www.mysql.com/
DOWNLOAD: http://www.mysql.com/download.html
DOCUMENTATION: http://www.mysql.com/doc.html
```

I highly recommend downloading the binary versions of MySQL as opposed to the source code. I have never been very successful installing or compiling the source distribution on a standard Debian distribution. This may change in future distributions and it might work for you, but the binary distribution has proven trivial to install over the source.

After you have installed the MySQL server, be sure to have it start up as part of your boot sequence. It is a fearsome thing to rely on your database only to have to remember the start sequence for MySQL when your machine crashes.

The next step is to install Perl. This is much easier than it sounds. Every Linux distribution installs Perl as a standard component. So you already have it, but you may want to check the version number to be sure that it is at least version 5.004 or better. This can easily be accomplished by entering

```
perl -v
```

This version of Debian has 5.005, so you do not have to do anything; but if you want to upgrade when a new release comes out, you may find the following useful:

```
HOMEPAGE: http://www.perl.com/
DOWNLOAD: http://language.perl.com/info/software.html
DOCUMENTATION: http://language.perl.com/info/documentation.html
```

Though Perl has become a *huge* program with lots of extra features, it has one of the best install scripts of any program I have installed. It is exhaustively automated and searches your system to optimize itself when building. It is also a bit humorous as it gives back technical information.

Installing Perl Modules

The next step is to install some Perl modules. I'm going to make this much easier to do than the documentation that comes with Bugzilla—so pay careful attention.

One of the greatest Perl packages to come preinstalled with the distribution in my opinion is the `CPAN` module. To use it, enter this command:

```
perl -MCPAN -e shell
```

This command tells Perl to load the `CPAN` module (`-M`) and then execute the `shell` subroutine of that module. It will walk you though a quick installation, and you will find that installing Perl packages is a breeze.

After installing `CPAN`, enter the following commands to have Perl itself download, unpack, compile, test, and install each one for you:

```
install DBI
install DBD::MySQL
install TimeDate
install GD
install Chart::Base
```

You do not need to install `Data::Dumper`, because it comes as a standard part of the Perl distribution. The `DBI` module is a terrific program for connecting to almost any database type. The `DBD::MySQL` is specific to MySQL with its commands and works closely with `DBI` for its back-end. The `TimeDate` module is used to manipulate time and date routines, and the `GD` library is used for manipulating graphics through Perl. The `Chart::Base` is used to build specific types of charts and graphs.

It is assumed that you are running Apache, but you can run any type of Web server to make this program work. You should set up your Web server in such a way as to allow `.cgi` files to run from any directory when you use Bugzilla.

In Apache, this is invoked by adding the following line to your `srm.conf` file:

```
AddHandler cgi-script .cgi
```

Adding a Line to Your `access.conf` File

You will also want to add a line to your `access.conf` file:

```
Options Execcgi
```

Make sure that the directory that you un-`tar` the Bugzilla files into is writable by a Web user. Apache uses the username `nobody`, and in most cases this works fine. To accomplish this, you either need to make the directory writable by the general population:

```
chmod -R o+w Bugzilla-X.X
```

where `X.X` is your version number, or you could change the ownership of the files to `nobody` (you need to be `root` to do this):

```
chown -R nobody:nobody Bugzilla-X.X
```

Either one of these works fine, but the second option will make things harder for users on your machine to edit the files without going through the Web. Please do not look at this as a security measure, though, because if your users can execute `.cgi` files that run as `nobody`, they have access to everything anyway.

After you have your Web server set up and ready to execute `.cgi` files, the next step is to update the dates on the `comments`, `nomail`, and `mail` files that are located in the base directory. To do this, enter these commands:

```
touch comments
touch nomail
touch mail
```

Each of the `cgi` scripts is set up to access Perl from `/usr/bonsaitools/bin`. The easiest way to fix this is to create the directories and then a symbolic link to Perl. Your only other option is to change the first line of every file ending in `.cgi` to read the location of Perl correctly. To make the link, enter these commands:

```
mkdir /usr/bonsaitools
mkdir /usr/bonsaitools/bin
ln -s /usr/bin/perl /usr/bonsaitools/bin/perl
```

Setting Up the MySQL Database

The next step is to set up the MySQL database. You need to create the username `bugs`. This username cannot have any password associated with it. You may have to read the documentation on getting the permissions set up for MySQL or just open up everything if you are feeling secure.

Next, create a `bugs` database by entering

```
mysql
```

After which you should see

```
mysql>
```

Enter the following command:

```
create database bugs;
quit
```

This creates a new database called `bugs`. Honestly, it just creates a directory name in a special place on the MySQL directory tree, but this is the correct way to do it.

The INSTALL file that comes with Bugzilla now directs you to install each of the eight shell scripts to initialize each of the sites:

```
./makeactivitytable.sh
./makebugtable.sh
./makecctable.sh
./makecomponenttable.sh
./makelogincoookiestable.sh
./makeproducttable.sh
./makeprofilestable.sh
./makeversionstable.sh
./makegroupstable.sh
```

You may need to edit the global.pl file if your MySQL program is located on another machine or you need to set up passwords and the like. The database connection occurs where it states

```
$::db = Mysql->Connect("
```

To set yourself up as the administrator, you need to first create a Bugzilla account. Open the index.html file within your browser. Be sure to use a full URL to access the page so that the server executes the .cgi files on subsequent requests for cgi pages.

After you have opened that page, click on the link part far down on the page that states

```
Open a new Bugzilla Account
```

The next page will direct you to enter your email address and click on Submit Query. This program sends your password by email. Your login name from here on is your email address.

The final step is to add yourself to every group through the mysql interface. From the prompt, enter this command:

```
mysql
```

and wait for the prompt

```
mysql>
```

At this point, enter the following line of SQL code:

```
update profiles set groupset=0x7fffffffffffffff
    where login_name = 'YOUR_EMAIL';
```

where *YOUR_EMAIL* is your email address.

You have now installed Bugzilla, and you can edit and find its features from your new Web site.

Using Bugzilla

It is a good idea to put the bug report URL into your documentation. You will want your users to enter bug reports through this system, and they need some way to find it. Anyone can log in and send in a report.

Because each part of the system is forms based, it is designed to be easy to understand. To get started in setting up the parameters for your project, you simply access the Query Page, which is the first page you will see after logging into the system. A link was created for you because of the permissions you set up earlier. You click on that link, which states

```
edit parameters
```

Bugzilla provides an excellent interface for searching and has an excellent help system. Each area is clickable and brings you to the help screen for that command. It describes the options and features that each one supports. Those knowledgeable in regular expressions can implement them as part of the searching routines as well as supporting case-sensitive and case-insensitive searches. Sorting algorithms are in place, enabling sorts by importance, Big Number, and assignee. You can even search for only those bugs submitted within a certain number of days.

The reports are then summarized and compiled, giving you access to a wealth of information, but the most useful feature is that your developers now have a technique to track their bug fixes, and your users can log in to see how things are coming along. Bugs can be annoying, but at least with Bugzilla they annoy you into getting them cleaned up.

Bugzilla is a great program if all your users and developers have access to the Web. In almost every case this holds true, but what if it doesn't?

Bugzilla is used to track bugs for Netscape Navigator, whereas the Debian Bug Tracking System has different needs and requires another tracking system. When creating your programs, please decide how you expect bugs to be reported and use the type that is appropriate to your needs. We will cover the Debian approach next.

The Debian Bug Tracking System

Ian Jackson first introduced the Debian Bug Tracking System in 1994. It has features unlike most tracking systems: Its core does not require CGI access to work and is based entirely on email. It works in the same manner as a listserv; you can send commands to the tracking system and it responds in like manner. Web-based access does play a role because it is used to view reports, although it is possible to obtain reports through email as well.

This system boasts of handling more than 16,000 reports. It is copyrighted using the GNU Public License and is available for download for your own projects. These sets of scripts can be downloaded from

```
http://www.chiark.greenend.org.uk/~ian/debbugs/
```

Installing the Bug Tracking System

Take your time when installing the system because it is not a trivial process and the documentation is sparse. Rather than go over the entire process here, I urge you to go through the `README` file that comes with the build files for more complete coverage if you have specific needs during installation.

The first step is to unpack the distribution into its own directory. I recommend using your `/tmp` directory in this case because it can be found on every machine and you don't need to have these files hanging around when you are done. Move the file you downloaded in the previous section to the temporary directory and unpack it:

```
mv debbugs.tar.gz /tmp
cd /tmp
tar zxvf debbugs.tar.gz
```

This creates a new subdirectory and places all the build files into it. You then need to change your current directory to this new one before continuing:

```
cd /tmp/debbugs-1.0
```

If you have a later release, be sure that your version number corresponds to it when changing directories.

The next step in installing the Debian Bug Tracking System is to build the configuration files. Creating the subdirectory `config/local` and then copying the template files into it accomplishes this:

```
mkdir config/local
cp config/template/* config/local
```

When you have copied the template files, you simply edit the configuration files to hold your own values. Contrary to my previous statement, this is anything but simple, because there is no documentation outlining the process. Read through the configuration file carefully and change the various variable values to match your system settings. After it is built, you will see the impact of those decisions and you can make changes later and rebuild if needed. Just be sure that, at this stage, you leave the brackets in place as you make your changes.

Here is a quick example that illustrates using the `config/local/config.m4` file.

If your email address is `wall@nut.com`, the line that reads

```
m4_define([[DBC_MAINTACCOUNT_ADDR]],  [[smith@example.com]])
```

should read

```
m4_define([[DBC_MAINTACCOUNT_ADDR]], [[wall@nut.com]])
```

Be sure that the brackets are in place and make your changes over the exact areas that are outlined in the example.

Email Configurations

The last step before running the build script is to be sure that the email addresses you set up in the configuration files are set up on your system and work properly. In many cases, this will mean editing your alias file and being sure that an email name points to the correct alias.

For instance, if I need to have all mail that goes to

```
bugs@price-hunter.net
```

actually end up in my mailbox at

```
steve@price-hunter.net
```

I add the following line to my `/etc/alias` file:

```
bugs: steve
```

To instate the change, use this command:

```
newaliases
```

Now all mail that is sent to `bugs@price-hunter.net` ends up at `steve@price-hunter.net`.

Building the Program

After you have your new accounts and aliases set up to correctly handle email, you are finally ready to build the program. To do this, use the build script that comes with it and enter this command:

```
./build
```

This script is located in the `root` portion of the distribution and uses your configuration changes to compile and set up the program. If there is an error during the build process, look in the file `config/trace` for help. You may need to change your configuration files and recheck your email addresses before trying again.

After the build script has successfully completed, it is time to install the program. To do this, use the install script that comes with the distribution and enter this command:

```
./install
```

If everything worked properly, you can test the bug tracking system by sending it some mail messages. It is also recommended that you run `scripts/processall` as well as `scripts/update-html`.

When you feel secure that everything is working properly, add the lines from `misc/crontab.out` to your cronfile. If you do not already have a cronfile, it can be created as follows:

```
mkdir /home/root/crontab
cd /home/root/crontab
```

Now copy the `misc/crontab.out` file to the new directory and rename it `cronfile`. Add it to the `crontab` using this command:

```
crontab /home/root/crontab/cronfile
```

You can double-check the results by entering the following command:

```
crontab -l
```

Now that the program is built, the next step is to start using it to report bugs.

Reporting Bugs

Reporting a bug is as easy as sending an email. It depends on how you set up your configuration files and email addresses, but your users send in bugs by simply sending an email to the appropriate address.

For instance, on the `price-hunter.net` domain, I created the `submit@bugs.price-hunter.net` email address. If you were submitting a bug, you would send mail to this address. It is important to explain to each of your users the method in which you want your bugs displayed. They need to understand what information you need included within a bug report in order to deal with it effectively.

Be sure that the subject is very descriptive, because it is the basis for looking through the bug reports. It can save a lot of time for the administrator as well as future lookups.

In most cases, your testers/users need to enter, at a minimum, the following:

Program Name:

Version:

Description of Problem:

You may also choose to have them add optional fields, such as

Transcript:	What did you enter and what was output?
Suggestion:	What needs to be fixed? Do you have a patch?
System Information:	What versions of contributing software or hardware are affected?

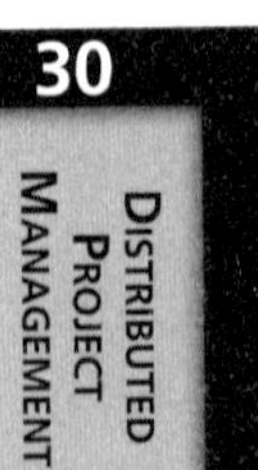

In some cases, you may want to create a Web page that the user fills in to be sure that each of the fields is entered correctly. Using the Debian Bug Tracking System, you have this page send an email to the system with the information to do the tracking. In many cases, you may want to have your program send an email to the Debian Bug Tracking System when a problem occurs. This is what happens with later versions of Netscape when it crashes. It sends a bug report back with system information to help track down the problem.

Next, the bug is assigned a code. This is used to track it, and the sender of the bug is informed that the bug was submitted successfully. It is then forwarded to the developer list. If a package name was included in the pseudo-headers (see next section) and a maintainer has been assigned to that package, that individual gets a personal copy of the bug.

The subject line from this point changes to include

```
Bug#XX
```

where *XX* is the number assigned to that particular bug. The mail headers are also altered to allow replies to go back to the sender, as well as a special Debian Bug Tracking System email address.

Implementing Pseudo-Headers

Pseudo-headers are actually commands that are read by the tracking system and processed by it. There are several different commands, but the most common are

```
Package:
Version:
Severity:
```

Those who are familiar with mail headers will realize that pseudo-headers are very similar. They are located at the top of the body or message of your email and are invoked by using the command name followed by a colon.

Here's an example:

```
To: submit@price-hunter.net
From: tester@someplace.org
Subject: Error Accessing Amazon.com

Package: Amazon.pm
Version: 0.9
Severity: grave
```

Amazon always returns `$ERROR` when I run it from the command line.

The Debian Bug Tracking System reads in the Subject line and uses that as its initial title for the bug. Then it grabs the pseudo-headers Package, Version, and Severity and archives those as well. Package, in this case, is the name of the library file that is affected;

Version is the `bookprice` program version that is awry, and Severity identifies how critical this bug is to the program.

Severity should be explained in a little more detail as well. It consists of five possible inputs (in order of severity):

```
critical
grave
important
normal
wishlist
```

If the Severity header is not in place, it defaults to normal.

Receiving a Bug

What do you do if you receive a bug? First, you should fix the bug. You have the address of the person who submitted it, so if you have further questions he can be asked over email.

After you have nailed it down and fixed the bug, notification of the fix is sent to the developers list as well as the individual who reported the bug.

All this is done over email; the developer replies to the email. The reply-to fields have been altered so that the email will go to the appropriate places.

There is one change that triggers that the bug is fixed: Append `-done` to the email when replying. If my email came from

```
123@price-hunter.net
```

I would reply to

```
123-done@price-hunter.net
```

This is retrieved from the tracking system and notes that the bug has been fixed. In some cases, you may want to announce the fix to the mailing list as well, and you can carbon copy the list.

Another command within the email address that is much like `-done` is `-quiet`. This assures that when you simply want to record something within the tracking system, it is not forwarded on to the developer list as well.

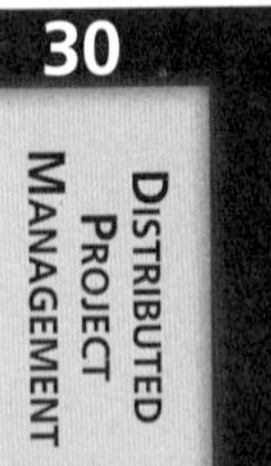

Wrapping Up the Debian Bug Tracking System

The Debian Bug Tracking System is well suited to a core group of developers. Each of these maintainers is then able to dish out bugs to specific developers who actually make the changes and move the results back up the line to completion. If there are too many developers on the discussion list, it can become troublesome trying to wade through the vast quantities of email to find your specific instance, so a hierarchical approach seems appropriate.

Of all the bug tracking systems tested in this chapter, only the Debian Bug Tracking System doesn't require a Web server to function. This means that developers who do not have graphical user interfaces can still be involved in the testing and implementation of bug fixes. It is also very current because it comes into your email when a bug arrives. You do not have to keep checking back on a Web page to see your results, which enables you to make timely responses to important questions.

The Web-based interface that does come with the tracking system allows you to search and view archived bug fixes. These reports can also be generated by email if that is more desirable. The greatest strength of the Debian Bug Tracking System is certainly its versatility.

Yet another approach is to have core developers who hand off component tasks to other developers in their group. Jitterbug works this way as well and allows both the Web-based and the email approaches.

As you can see, the Debian Bug Tracking System has many key elements that give it advantages over other tracking systems. The next system is called Jitterbug, which holds to yet another philosophy when concerning bug tracking, which we will cover next.

Jitterbug

Jitterbug is a Web-based bug tracker. Andrew Tridgell created it as the bug tracker in the development of Samba (`http://samba.anu.edu.au`). Samba is an amazing program that enables Linux machines to act like NT machines on a Windows network and is definitely worth looking into.

A Web-based system has the ability to accept bug reports and display results directly from a URL. These have the advantage of monitoring reporting systems in a GUI environment as well as provide a more user-friendly environment for reporting bugs. All of this comes with the real-time efficiency of the Internet.

Jitterbug uses separate files, as opposed to a database such as Bugzilla. This means that if your applications are growing quickly and have a lot of individual files, you may want to invest in a searching program, such as Glimpse. Glimpse can be easily integrated into Jitterbug and polls through the files creating an index file for searching.

Jitterbug defaults to a regular expression syntax when searching its records if you are not using Glimpse or some other search system. This enables you to complete very complex searches that may otherwise be impossible.

Jitterbug is used in several very large software distribution organizations, such as

Gnome:	`http://www.gnome.org/`
The Gimp:	`http://www.gimp.org/`

Gnu Cash:	`http://www.gnucash.org/`
Window Maker:	`http://www.windowmaker.org/`

Download Jitterbug from

`ftp://jitterbug.samba.org/pub/jitterbug/`

The main Web site for Jitterbug is located at

`http://samba.anu.edu.au/jitterbug/`

Installing Jitterbug

The first installation of Jitterbug requires patience and an understanding of what is trying to be accomplished. Read this section before attempting to install Jitterbug.

After you have downloaded the Jitterbug software distribution set, the first step is to unpack it in its own directory:

```
mv jitterbug-X.X.X.tar.gz /tmp
cd /tmp
tar zxvf jitterbug-X.X.X.tar.gz
```

where *`X.X.X`* is the version number of the release you want to install. This creates a subdirectory that you should change your current directory to in order to install Jitterbug:

```
cd jitterbug-X.X.X
```

The *`X.X.X`* is the version number of Jitterbug.

There are several techniques that you could use to install Jitterbug. I'm going with the easiest technique to avoid potential pitfalls, but after you understand what is trying to be accomplished, you are free to test your own methods.

First, log in as the superuser `root` and create a new account for Jitterbug. I created an account called `jitterbug`:

```
adduser jitterbug
passwd jitterbug
```

This prompts you to change the password and allows you to set up a new account. You are welcome to add any groups that you like or touch up the password file if you think there is a need.

The next step is to enter the source directory and enter the following:

```
./configure
```

`configure` reads your specific setup and creates a Makefile based on what it saw. This Makefile is then used to actually compile the program, which is what you do next by entering this command:

```
make
```

This starts your compiler and fills in attributes that were uncovered in the `./configure` script using the Makefile. The next step is to create a directory for the data files. In this case, I use the following command:

```
mkdir ~/jitterbug/tracking/
```

Now copy the default configuration files to your new directory:

```
cp -R /tmp/jitterbug-X.X.X/configs/* ~/jitterbug/tracking
```

Editing Your Web Server Configuration Files

You need to be sure that a user logs in when accessing the private part of the Jitterbug server. The easiest way to do this is to update your HTTPD server configurations. Edit your `access.conf` file and add these lines:

```
# Jitterbug Authentication
<Location /cgi-bin/jitterbug.private>
AuthType Basic
AuthName Jitterbug
AuthUserFile /home/jitterbug/apache.auth
<Limit GET POST>
  require user jitterbug
</Limit>
</Location>
```

This uses the `apache.auth` file (we are about to create it) to authenticate a user trying to access `/cgi-bin/jitterbug.private`. The user can access it only if he or she successfully logs in as `jitterbug`.

Creating the Password File

Next, you create the password file for authenticating users to the private directory. In this case, I'm going to try to keep all the Jitterbug files together within the account that I create. To do this, I need to use the `htpasswd` command. This program does not come precompiled as part of Apache (although the man pages are put into place), so if you have not used it in the past you need to compile it. Log in or use `su` to change to `root` and enter this command:

```
locate htpasswd.c
```

Then go to the directory it is located in and enter

```
make htpasswd
```

After it has compiled, there will be an executable called `htpasswd` in the directory. Copy it to your `/usr/local/bin` directory and you can start using it:

```
cp htpasswd /usr/local/bin
```

If you used su to change to root, exit and enter this command:

```
rehash
```

Otherwise, just log in as jitterbug again to continue.

Now we need to create the password file. The command for doing this is

```
htpasswd -c apache.auth jitterbug
```

The -c option tells Apache to create a new password file. If you want to add other users to an existing file, drop the -c option. This command creates the apache.auth file and immediately asks for a password to the jitterbug username.

Initializing Jitterbug

The next step is to initialize your Jitterbug program. Start by copying the config files that came with your Jitterbug distribution to the tracking directory you created earlier:

```
cp -R /tmp/jitterbug-X.X.X/config/* /home/jitterbug/tracking
```

Copy the binary to the /cgi-bin portion of your server. It can be found in the sources directory where you compiled it using make. Next, make a copy of the Jitterbug program within the same directory to use as your private version—in this case, jitterbug.private.

The permissions for these files may seem a bit tricky until you know what is going on. You want the file to be executable by the group nobody, which is what your Web server runs all CGIs as. Yet, you want to be secure enough that no one can abuse the Jitterbug program and have it write to other directories that it should not have access to. This dilemma is overcome by having the program run as root. As root, it is allowed to run the chroot command, which locks it into a specified directory, denying access to other directories on the system.

To accomplish this, you first change the owners of the file. The owner should be root and the group should be nobody:

```
chown root:nobody jitterbug
chown root:nobody jitterbug.private
```

Now change the rights to the files, causing the programs to run as root but be executed as nobody:

```
chmod 04710 jitterbug
chmod 04710 jitterbug.private
```

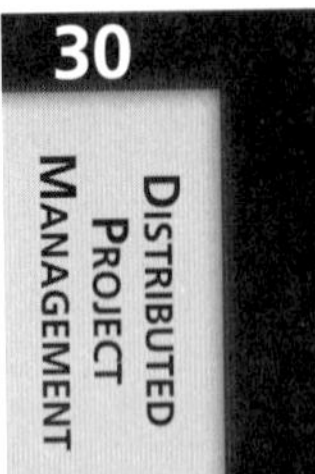

You should realize that if you do not follow these processes exactly, you could compromise your system, giving everyone in the group nobody access to run programs as user root. The end result should read

```
# ls -al
-rws--x--   1 root nobody  183963 Jul   7 21:11 jitterbug
-rws--x--   1 root nobody  183963 Jul 7 21:12 jitterbug.private
```

The numbers may change, but the rights and ownership information should be the same.

The main configuration files for Jitterbug are located in the same spot as almost every configuration file on your system. You first need to create a directory in your `/etc` directory called `jitterbug`:

```
mkdir /etc/jitterbug
```

Then add the following simple configuration file to that directory by creating a file called `jitterbug` and filling it with

```
from address = bugs@DOMAIN
chroot directory = /home/jitterbug/tracking
base directory = /
guest gid = 65534
guest uid = 65534
uid = XXXX
gid = XXXX
```

Note the following:

- The `from address` should be the email address that you want to have bugs sent to.
- The next-to-last line, `uid = XXXX`, is the user ID of `root`. On almost every UNIX machine, the value is `0`, so you probably should enter that.
- The last line, `gid = XXXX`, is the group ID of `nobody`; to find the number, enter

  ```
  grep nobody /etc/group
  ```

After you have created the configuration file, make a link to it using the `jitterbug.private` filename:

```
ln -s jitterbug jitterbug.private
```

At this point, you should be able to access the Jitterbug program from your Web site. It will be located in your `cgi-bin` directory, and if you log in as a guest, call it using

```
http://YOUR_DOMAIN/cgi-bin/jitterbug
```

Otherwise, you can log in with some rights using this command:

```
http://YOUR_DOMAIN/cgi-bin/jitterbug.private
```

In both cases, *`YOUR_DOMAIN`* needs to be changed to the domain name of the server you are running Jitterbug on.

After you have installed and set up Jitterbug, let's go over how to make use of it to track bugs.

Using Jitterbug

Jitterbug is very easy to use if you understand the concepts. The Guest account does not require a login, so it is given only the capability of submitting new bugs, searching using regular expressions with case-sensitive options, or browsing the current categories. The best way to use Jitterbug is to play with it a bit. Try adding a new bug.

You will see that the default files are in serious need of your help to become useful. Each of them is located in the `/home/jitterbug/tracking` directory, and you are urged to edit those files. Each has a description of what you should add.

Each user can set preferences according to his or her own style. These pages are configurable according to color, personal information, and even backgrounds. These personalization techniques are just another part of this unique bug tracking system.

Upon entering Jitterbug as a registered user, you have access to create a username. After a username has been generated, you can access as that user and then edit your personal preferences. When access has been granted, you have all the benefits of a guest user as well as extras, such as being able to create new users or directories.

As you move through the pages, you will notice that security is actually handled by the Web server instead of the program. When the Web server contacts the program, it sends the username as an environment variable to it so you have simulated logging in. The fact that the `chroot` command is used makes this a very secure and yet easily adaptable program to use.

Both bug tracking software and version control systems enable you to save time and effort in getting your software done. This last product makes the compiling and building much faster by allowing you to take your large project and distribute the build over several machines.

Doozer

One of the problems with today's very large programs is that they take so long to compile. If you have ever downloaded and compiled Netscape, you know what a hassle it can be to tie up a machine for several hours while it compiles. A good friend of mine, Matt Messier, works for a large software firm, and it can take him more than 12 hours to compile an entire build.

Graydon Hoare had to tie up his machine compiling Berlin. Berlin is very much like Xfree86—it is yet another windowing system. It is based on several open standards, and its creators hope to someday overtake the GUI market. It was introduced by Matt Messier and Jim Fetters in 1996 and has since become a huge project. Graydon has done a remarkable amount of work lately in helping to achieve Berlin's lofty goals.

Because its size has grown so dramatically over the last few years, it takes a long time to compile. This was the motivation behind Graydon's success in building small wrapper scripts to GNU make. Graydon had the distinct advantage that GNU make would run in parallel on a single machine, so he created two Perl scripts that provide access to other machines via client/server methodology.

By using several different Perl modules, he was able to put together a client for his distributed program in only 70 lines of code, if you strip away the comments. His server came up at even less than half that. Graydon has achieved something of note here; he is using protocols and standards already implemented. He was able to make use of preexisting programs to achieve something greater than the sum of its parts. He has a distributed building environment.

This Perl script works by starting a server on the first machine to coordinate the clients. It uses `GET` and `PUT` methods in much the same way as a Web server, except it checks out parts from the host and checks in compiled code. The default method of transfer is to use the `ssh` protocol, which is a secure shell. It is a good idea if you are not sure of your network security, because UNIX passwords are sent in plain text. Of course, it is configurable as well.

Note that the server runs on port 9000; if that is a problem, you may consider changing it to another open port. If you change it, be sure to update the clients as well.

Another important note is that this script makes assumptions as to how the computers are connected to the network. If you run into any problems with your setup, you might try reading the documentation at

`http://www.interlog.com/~gray/doozer.html`

The other approach is that if you have ever built client/server programs in Perl, the source code to this program is very simple and may provide some handy documentation.

You should download `doozer.pl` and `doozmaster.pl` from the previous site before continuing.

To run Doozer, you first need to start the server. To do this, enter

```
doozmaster.pl HOST1 HOST2 HOST3 ...
```

This tells the server that the following hosts are available for compiling. The next step is to alter the Makefile that you are using to compile your programs. Change the line that sets the variable for your c++ compiler to read

```
$(CC) = doozer.pl g++
```

This assures that `doozer.pl` will be run instead of your g++ alone. The next step is to be sure that when you run `make`, you use the `-j` extension. The `-j` attribute tells `make` to run in parallel (jobs), and if you do not provide an attribute it will run an unlimited number of them. It is normally useful if you have more than one processor on a machine. This program exploits that issue and runs the Makefile across many machines.

If you do run into problems, such as not having the proper Perl modules to run your client or server, it is suggested that you use the `CPAN` module to install them. For instance, if you get an error back stating that `String::ShellQuote` was not located as a valid module, use the following command to install or upgrade it:

```
perl -MCPAN -e shell
```

At the prompt

```
cpan>
```

enter the command

```
install String::ShellQuote
```

It is much easier than downloading, unpacking, and installing. Now it comes as part of the Perl distribution.

Wrapping Up Doozer

It is remarkable what you can accomplish in a few simple methods, and this program is a testament to the power of using other resources to get there. The method is simple and the implementation is small, yet the result is a very powerful feature that makes you wonder why you didn't think of it first.

However, there is little need to use something like Doozer when it comes to compiling small programs. If you don't have access to many machines on your LAN, it might not prove itself—but it is interesting to those of us who do.

Summary

As you can see, there are numerous programs for providing distributed project management software for a fraction of the cost you might incur if you were to buy these types of programs. Some of them, such as CVS, have been tested by literally thousands of programmers over many years—something you cannot expect from other programs. Depending on your needs when it comes to bug tracking software, the three covered in this chapter have diverse sets of rules, giving you several options to choose from.

Linux itself was built using distributed project management software as it was built over the years. Linus, the inventor of Linux, claims to have built only about 50% of the kernel, with so many others working on it today. Over the years, it is no wonder that these techniques have been hewn into the programs you see today.

Appendixes

Part VI

In This Part

APPENDIX

Installing Debian Linux

by Matthew Hunter

In This Appendix

finished 001001
040202 (not always carefully)

Installing an operating system can be a daunting task the first time and is not trivial even to the expert. Installing Linux is no different in that respect. However, most computers come with Microsoft Windows installed, which means installing Linux may well be your first experience with installing an OS. The important thing is not to panic; if you follow the steps outlined here carefully, you should not have any trouble.

The Debian CD-ROM contains a set of detailed installation instructions in at least one of the subdirectories under this directory:

`/cdrom/debian/dists/slink/main/disks-i386/`

Start at the `install.html` file (you can read this file in any Web browser), and it will cover many of the installation procedures in detail. You should read this whole section, along with the documentation on the CD-ROM, before beginning the installation procedure; this will give you a better idea of what is happening, in case something goes wrong.

You should pay close attention to the hardware compatibility section of the Debian documentation in the `install.html` directory. That section is not covered here at all, and the hardware requirements for installation are different than the generic hardware requirements for running Linux.

The online address to get the install information is
`http://www.debian.org/releases/slink/`.

It should be noted that Debian Linux is distributed without any warranty, and that installing Linux can be dangerous to your existing operating system and data. If you follow the procedures correctly and know what you are doing, it's no more dangerous than installing any other operating system or repartitioning your hard drive.

The following components will be addressed in this Appendix: preparing your computer for a Linux installation, disk partitioning, booting Linux, and installing the system, among others.

Preparing Your Computer for Linux

You need to make some changes to your computer system before starting to install Linux in order to preserve your present setup. The exact details vary depending on your system. Most people have a single hard drive with some version of Microsoft Windows installed on that drive, taking up the entire drive. Unfortunately, Linux will not be able to coexist with Windows in a setup such as that; you need to repartition the hard drive to make room for Linux.

Understanding Disk Partitioning

You are already familiar with the idea of a hard drive, which stores the information you keep on your computer in a permanently accessible manner. Modern computers typically have a lot of disk space (more than enough to support Windows and Linux together, in fact). However, that space is often configured as a single *partition*—that is, a single piece of contiguous space. In order to have space for its own use, Linux needs its own partition on the drive. To give it that space, you probably have to repartition your drive.

What Is a Partition, Exactly? And What Is a Filesystem?

Think of a hard drive in terms of a very large field, with room for several different sports played at once. The entire field represents the available space on your hard drive, but as just an empty field, it's not very useful.

A partition could be represented in that analogy as the painted lines for a particular sport. The playing field is a section of the empty space with defined boundaries that confine each "game," and they should have no effect on anything outside those boundaries.

In addition, there are painted markings within each playing field. The paint gives you a point of reference, so that you have an idea of where you are in the field in relation to the markings.

The painted markings represent the filesystem, which is essentially a way of finding data that you have left ìon the fieldî when you want it again. Different filesystems, of course, have different rules, and hence different markings. If you try to use the rules for one game/filesystem to find something relative to another game/filesystem's markings, you won't have much luck.

Debian Linux needs about 40MB of disk space as an absolute minimum. It can make use of a lot more, and of course, you want space for your data. There are two things to look for within Windows; double-click on My Computer and look for the hard drive icon (those are the rectangular, mostly solid ones). Typically, you have just one partition shown there, labeled C:. If you have more than one hard drive icon present (be careful not to confuse this with the floppy disk drive—typically labeled A:, but similar in appearance—or the CD-ROM drives, which are represented by a shiny circle), you should already have more than one partition available and may be able to avoid repartitioning.

Partitioning the Disk

Repartitioning in itself is not particularly difficult. Most of the time, however, you want to keep the data already on the Windows partition. That can complicate the process considerably. There are several ways to repartition without losing the data. No matter which one you choose, you have to accept some risk of losing your data, so you should ensure that everything important is safely backed up before beginning, regardless of the method you choose.

Note

If you do not care about Windows, and do not care about your data on the Windows partition, you can simply begin the install process. You still need to make some partitioning changes, but these can be performed within the install process. If you decide to do this, you will not be able to recover your Windows data!

Implementing Partitioning

First, you can back the data up, using a backup program, and then restore the backup after performing the repartition. This can be tricky, because you will not have a working OS to use to restore the backup! However, most backup programs have some provision for this. Using this method ensures that you still have a valid copy of your data afterward, but you may have to manually install Windows if your backup program needs that.

Second, you can back up your data manually (just by copying it to another computer), repartition the drive, reinstall Windows and your applications, and then copy the data back. This approach is often the easiest if you are comfortable installing Windows from scratch and you don't mind setting up Windows again.

Finally, you can use a program intended to resize the partition dynamically, without damaging your data. This is the most convenient option, but also the most dangerous. If it works, your Windows partition will become smaller, allowing the Linux install process to put a new partition into the remaining space. The data on the Windows partition is (in theory) not altered or lost. However, if an error occurs, you can lose all your data. You should be sure to back up all your important data before trying this.

There are several commercial utilities for Windows that enable you to resize partitions in this manner. If you have one, you should probably use it, especially if you are already familiar with its use. If not, there is a free utility available from most Debian FTP sites called `FIPS`, by Arno Schaefer, which will attempt the same task. `FIPS` is not included on this Debian CD-ROM. You should read the `FIPS` documentation and the installation documentation carefully before deciding to use it, because you can still lose your data if you make a mistake.

`FIPS` can be downloaded from `ftp://ftp.debian.org/tools/fips20.zip`.

Most versions of Windows and MS-DOS include versions of `fdisk`, a DOS utility for partitioning your hard drive. This utility is designed to handle only MS-DOS partitions and will cause problems if you try to use it with the Linux partitions. However, you can use it to create space for a Linux installation by deleting your Windows partition and creating it with a new, smaller size. Using `fdisk` this way will almost certainly cause you to lose some or all of your data on the Windows partition; you will very likely need to reinstall Windows from scratch. Using `fdisk` should be the option of last resort.

Another great tool that facilitates the partitioning of your hard drive is Partition Majic. This utility takes the headache out of a sometimes complex task.

Using MS-DOS/Windows `fdisk`

There are detailed instructions for using MS-DOS/Windows `fdisk` to make room for Linux later in this appendix. This sidebar briefly explains how the DOS version of `fdisk` works and what to expect when using it. You will not actually need this information, but it may be useful as background.

MS-DOS first included the `fdisk` tool in order to provide a way to create and manipulate partitions. It handles that task properly, but in a way that is oriented toward people using only MS-DOS. Thus, it enables you to perform basic partitioning operations, but makes the assumption you will be using those partitions only with MS-DOS and does not deal properly with other operating systems.

Making any changes with MS-DOS `fdisk` results in your losing the data from the partitions you made changes to.

If you do not want to risk altering your Windows installation, you can buy a second hard drive and install Linux on that drive. This will not require you to alter your Windows installation and should be completely safe, but it obviously involves additional expense, and you need to be comfortable installing the new hard drive in your computer (or ask someone who is to do it for you).

Another possibility, though requiring a great deal more research, is to perform a UMS-DOS installation. UMS-DOS is a UNIX-style filesystem that overlays the Windows/MS-DOS filesystem, enabling you to install Linux onto your existing Windows or MS-DOS partition while leaving all the Windows data intact (assuming there is enough free space, of course).

If this seems like a lot of work even before Linux is installed—well, you're right. Normally, the manufacturer preinstalls the operating system for you, on an entirely unused hard drive, and thus does not care about overwriting old data or arranging for multiple partitions.

Using FIPS

FIPS is an MS-DOS program designed to help you repartition your hard drive without losing data. It is not perfect, so you should still make a backup before using it, but it is quite a bit better than doing things the hard way and losing your data for certain. Unfortunately, FIPS has not been included directly on this Debian CD-ROM, although references to its location can be found.

You need a defragmentation utility in addition to FIPS. The defragmentation utility included with MS-DOS (called, unsurprisingly, DEFRAG) works fine for this.

An important requirement of this process is having sufficient free space. Before resizing with FIPS, or even performing the defragmentation step, you must ensure you have sufficient free space on the original partition to hold the entire new partition you want to add. FIPS checks the actual free space, so you shouldn't be able to lose data this way; but if you aren't paying attention, your new partition could be smaller than you had hoped for.

You should run a filesystem verification utility (such as MS-DOS's `scandisk` or `chkdsk`) both before and after using FIPS, in case of subtle errors. Such utilities ensure that the filesystem itself is valid and consistent, and may be able to repair some errors.

Understanding the Boot Process

Most modern computers use a simple procedure to boot an operating system. Their BIOS (software code usually packaged with the motherboard) contains very basic drivers for accessing disks, configuring some of the hardware, and so on. When the computer is turned on, the BIOS contains code that looks in various places on your computer for an operating system. Depending on the exact settings, it looks on floppy disks or CD-ROMs, and then on hard drives and possibly other devices. The first operating system it finds will be loaded.

In modern operating systems, this first operating system is actually a boot loader, which knows a bit more about the system and where to find the operating system. The Windows 95/98 boot loader is almost invisible; it just boots Windows immediately. Linux normally uses a more advanced boot loader called LILO, which can be told about several different operating systems to load. When installing Linux, you typically install LILO as the first boot loader the system finds, and configure LILO to enable you to boot Linux, your Windows system, and any other operating system you may be using.

Unfortunately, if you are using Windows NT and want to continue using it, the situation is a little more complex. Windows NT includes a more advanced boot loader of its own, which must be used to load NT. This boot loader typically includes NT, and may include a Windows 95 installation as well. Some versions of this boot loader can also be told to

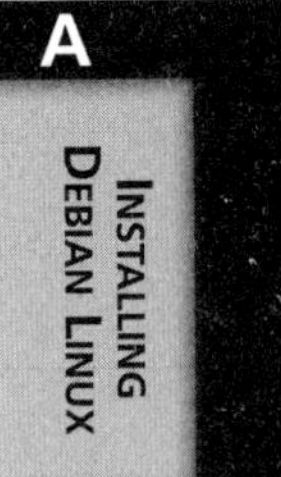

boot Linux, but the task is very difficult. Please see the sidebar for more information on using NT and Linux on the same computer.

You may have purchased a commercial application designed to help manage booting different operating systems (System Commander is a popular option for Windows systems). If you want to use that program or a similar one with Linux, you should consult the documentation of that program specifically.

If for some reason you do not want to boot Linux directly from your hard drive, you can easily boot Linux using a floppy disk or even via a command from within Windows.

Using Windows NT and Linux

If you want to use Linux and NT on the same system, be prepared for a bit of trouble; NT does not like to coexist with other operating systems. Read the Linux+NT Mini-HOWTO (available from the Linux Documentation Project at `http://metalab.unc.edu/LDP/`), and follow the directions there. Using NT and Linux on the same system is not recommended, if you can reasonably avoid it, but should work if you are careful.

Linux can coexist with just about any other operating system, although some of them are more complicated to set up than others. Once you know how to make Linux coexist with your other operating system, all that's needed is to partition the hard disk and start the install.

Disk Partitioning

This section describes the basic layout of the Linux system on the disk, including suggestions on how to configure the partition layout.

Partitions Needed for Linux

Unlike Windows, Linux systems often make use of more than one partition. Although defining more than one partition for Linux is not strictly necessary, there are a number of good reasons for doing so. At minimum, you should have two Linux partitions: one for your Linux system, and one for use as a swap partition.

The swap partition is used as a kind of extra memory. When you do not have enough memory for all the applications you are running, some of the less-used memory can be written to disk and then later read back if needed. Although you can use a file for a similar purpose, performance is better when using a partition. Opinions vary on the proper size for a swap partition, but a good rule of thumb is to use a swap partition equal in size to the amount of RAM in your computer.

After your swap partition, the remaining partitions will be used for your Linux system. The available space can be used in a single, large partition, or in a number of smaller partitions. For normal use, there is little difference between using a single system partition and using several, but using separate partitions is a big help in some unusual situations. If you are new to Linux and want to keep things simple, you can use a single partition for your filesystem and a swap partition.

Linux typically uses a single hierarchical filesystem, containing directories and files. Each directory can hold a number of additional files and directories. A partition will be added to your filesystem so that it takes the place of an empty directory (the process is called *mounting*). The directory hierarchy is basically the same across all Linux systems. Each directory generally contains a certain type of file. The following are the system directories commonly used as separate partitions:

- `/` (30MB) This is the `root` directory, automatically mounted at boot time, which contains the other system directories. This must have its own partition. Any elements of the directory structure that do not have their own partition are counted against the space allocated by the `root` partition.
- `/usr` (400MB) This contains standard applications and similar system resources. The size of this partition should be decided by how many programs you want to install. It is generally a good idea to give plenty of space for future expansion.
- `/usr/local` This contains the same sort of thing as `/usr`, only it's designated for the local system specifically. Historically, in a networked environment, where `/usr` may be mounted over a network, `/usr/local` is on a local hard drive and contains supplementary programs not available from the network. On standalone systems, `/usr/local` is used for programs installed by the user (that is, that are not part of the standard distribution). This makes it easier to keep track of what you installed and what your distribution installed.
- `/home` This holds the home directories of the users (except `root`). This is where most of your personal data will be placed. The size depends on how many users you want, and how much space each one will need. Generally this is a good place to put all the unused space you have left.
- `/var` (40MB) This directory contains variable files, often including logs, email queues, and so on.

Sizing the Partitions

The size of partitions depends a great deal on how many partitions you intend to use, and how much space you have available. The directory list in the previous section shows minimum sizes for each directory. You should make sure the partition you intend to use for that directory is at or above the minimum size. The minimum size of the `root` partition (`/`)

consists of the minimum requirement listed, plus the requirements for any of the directories that are not given a separate partition.

As a practical matter, you need a minimum of 40MB of space, at least 600MB for a reasonable installation, and 1.5GB for a complete installation—not counting personal data files, of course.

Changing Your Partition Layout

The preceding section should have given you an idea of what is necessary to make room for your Linux system. This section explains how to make the actual changes to your partition layout, *assuming you have already backed up your data and will be able to restore it*. Because backup and restore methods differ widely, they cannot be described in detail here.

When your system backup has been completed, type the command `fdisk` at a DOS prompt or DOS window. This brings up the `fdisk` program.

```
C:> fdisk
```

You will see a list of options. The first option you want is number 4, Display partition information. This lists the primary partitions on that hard drive and asks whether you want to see extended partition information (which it calls Logical DOS drives) if there are any extended partitions. Before responding to the prompt, you should examine the drive information provided closely.

Each partition has a size displayed in megabytes (look under the column labeled Megabytes). The total space on the disk is displayed below the individual partitions. Subtract the space occupied by all the partitions from the total space to find the space free; if the free space is at least 200MB, you might be able to fit a Linux installation into it by simply adding a partition. If you have other hard drives, do the same for them (press Esc to return to the previous menu, `5` to change to the other hard drive, and then `4` again).

If you don't have at least 200MB of disk space allocated to any partition, or a partition you can throw away with at least that much space, you have to make some room the hard way by deleting or moving files.

Making the Partitions

You should follow these steps only if you do not have a free partition, or enough free space to make a free partition, for Linux. Following these steps will cause you to *delete* one of your partitions—possibly your Windows system partition. This will result in your Windows system *not working* until you have created a new partition for it and reinstalled Windows. *You will lose anything you had on the partition.* Your computer may not boot Windows or DOS properly until you have properly reinstalled the system software:

1. Determine where to add the space. If you have more than one Windows/MS-DOS partition, consider moving all your data to your system partition and using the (now empty) partition for Linux. If you can do this, skip ahead to the section "Booting Linux," later in this chapter. If not, choose which partition will be shrunk and go to step 2.
2. Back up any data on the partition you chose. Take note of how much space your Windows partition is currently occupying, and how much of that is actually used. Make sure you know how to restore your data, *and* how to restore Windows if you want to continue using it. Make sure you have a set of floppies or a CD-ROM to restore Windows from. Make sure you have the drivers you need to access your Windows restoration disks. Make sure you have a simple DOS boot disk to install the drivers on. If you are not comfortable doing this, find someone who is and ask them to help.
3. If you have a partition-shrinking commercial program, such as Partition Majic, or intend to use the `FIPS` utility, use it, then begin the installation procedure by proceeding to the "Booting Linux" section later in this chapter. Otherwise, if you are going to use `fdisk`, continue.
4. Come back to `fdisk` and select number 3, Delete Partition. You will be presented with a menu asking which kind of partition to delete. The odds are that you are deleting a primary partition, but select the type of partition you chose earlier.
5. You will be presented with a menu showing each partition. Select the one you chose earlier. *This partition will be deleted! Make sure your data is backed up!*
6. Create a new primary partition for Windows/MS-DOS by typing `1`, and then `1` again. You will be asked to specify the size of the new partition, which is whatever you determined the size your Windows partition should be. This is presumably smaller than it was before, in order to give you more space to use for Linux, but also at least large enough to put all your Windows software back on. You should make sure the new partition is the first primary partition, and you should set it to be the active partition. You don't need to actually create a new partition for Linux here—just make sure there is space available.
7. Reinstall Windows/MS-DOS, or restore your prior installation from your backups. (You did keep backups, right?). This step is obviously important if you want to keep using Windows; get it right before going any further with Linux. If everything goes well, you'll be back to installing Linux soon enough, and if not, you don't want to complicate the situation!

If something goes wrong and you cannot get Windows to work again, try asking someone who has Linux and Windows working together. If such a person isn't available, the best thing to do is to reinstall Windows and look for some documentation about your problem. The Linux Documentation Project (`http://metalab.unc.edu/LDP/`) is a good place to look.

Understanding Primary and Extended Partitions

The partition format used by most Intel-architecture personal computers understands two types of partitions, *primary* and *extended*. Each hard drive can have up to four primary partitions. This wasn't enough, so later designs added the concept of an extended partition. The extended partition occupies one of the four primary partition spaces and can contain a number of additional partitions, up to the maximum size allocated to the extended partition.

Typically, your base partitions (MS-DOS or Windows partitions, Linux `root` partition) are primary partitions, and less important partitions are placed within the extended partition space. Some systems have trouble booting from extended partitions, so you should ensure your `root` filesystem is on a primary partition. The other partitions, if any, can go elsewhere.

After going through these steps, you should have free space or a predefined free partition available for Linux, along with a working Windows system.

The installation process will walk you through defining the partitions. You need to go through these steps even if you have used the MS-DOS/Windows `fdisk` utility to create the partitions, because those utilities assume the partitions are for DOS or Windows systems.

Booting Linux

Linux typically uses the `LILO` boot loader to boot up. However, `LILO` is a Linux utility; it won't operate under Windows. To boot Linux the first time, you need to use a different method. The most common method is a boot disk, traditionally a floppy, but newer computers can often use the Linux CD-ROM as a boot disk as well.

Before deciding on a boot method, you should adjust your Windows partitions as described in the earlier sections. When you have free space on your hard drive (not allocated to a partition) for your Linux partitions, you can begin the boot process.

It's easiest to just boot from the CD-ROM, if your computer supports that. This usually involves making a change in the BIOS, however. Somewhere in your computer BIOS there should be options for boot devices. You need to set the first boot device to the CD-ROM drive. If you don't know what the BIOS is, it's probably best not to try to boot from the CD-ROM. After the changes are made to the BIOS, you just put the CD-ROM in the drive and turn the computer on. If your computer supports booting from a CD-ROM, you see the first Linux boot screen after a moment. If your computer boots normally instead, you need to make a boot floppy disk.

Making a boot floppy disk consists of choosing a floppy image, which is a file on the Debian CD-ROM containing the exact data that should appear on the floppy disk, and writing that image to an actual floppy disk. The Debian CD-ROM contains several boot images. Most of the time, you can use the basic boot disk image, but some computers require special options to boot properly (laptops are notorious for this). For those systems, you need to choose one of the alternate images. However, it won't do any harm to try the standard image first.

You can make a boot disk from either Linux or Windows, but obviously doing so from Windows will be easiest the first time. The Windows utility for making a boot disk is called `rawrite.exe` and is included on the Debian CD-ROM (which you should be able to read easily from Windows). Running this program (from a DOS window or double-clicking the file) produces a prompt for the disk image filename. Type the name of the file you want to use, including the drive letter and directory if the file is not in the current directory, and make sure you have a formatted floppy disk in the floppy disk drive. Your system will spend a minute or so writing to the floppy disk, and then you should be done.

Making a Boot Floppy

Creating a boot floppy disk from a Linux system is a little more complicated. You can make use of the `dd` utility (a standard part of most distributions) to write the disk image to one of your own floppy disks:

```
# dd if=resc1440.bin of=/dev/fd0
```

If the floppy disks do not work, you can try using `loadlin`. `loadlin` is a program that will boot Linux from a DOS partition. There are two `loadlin` batch files on the CD-ROM that you can try. To use them, boot your computer to a DOS prompt with a CD-ROM drive that works in DOS. Then try running either `D:\dists\slink\main\disks-i386\2.1.8-1999-02-22\install.bat` or `D:\install\boot.bat`. Either one of these should work.

If you have tried all the floppy disk images on the CD-ROM or `loadlin`, and none of them have brought you to the basic installation screen, go to the "Troubleshooting" section, later in this chapter.

Installing Without a CD-ROM Drive OR If Linux Can't Find Your CD-ROM Drive

It is possible, though potentially difficult, to install Linux using only a boot floppy disk and some kind of network connection. This is not the recommended option, especially if a modem is your only network access, but it will work if you are patient.

The Debian install procedure makes use of the Debian package manager for the majority of the installation. That package manager is capable of acquiring the packages it needs for the installation from a number of different sources, including HTTP (the protocol used for Web pages), FTP, NFS, and directly from a CD-ROM image (that is, from the CD-ROM itself or from the CD-ROM files copied to a hard drive).

If you already have a network and want to install Debian Linux on a computer without a CD-ROM drive, your best option will be to make the CD available on the network and install from there. Barring that, if your network has access to the Internet, you can install from one of the main Debian sites—though this will probably be slow.

Choosing a Floppy Disk Image

Disk images are contained in the `debian/dists/slink/main/disks-i386/` directory—possibly in one of several subdirectories, depending on the kernel version. Start with the basic boot image `resc1440.bin`. You can make the boot disk with the `rawrite2.exe` file, also found on the Debian CD-ROM. Just run the `rawrite2.exe` program, and you will be prompted for the filename of the image to write to your floppy disk drive.

The `resc1200.bin` image is for 5 1/4-inch double sided double density disks. The `resc1440` images with `tecra` and `safe` appended to the filenames are specially prepared versions that may work on systems that cause the other disks to fail (including one version that has both of the changes).

The files beginning with `base12` and `base14` are disk images for a very basic floppy disk distribution of Debian (for 1.2MB, 5 1/4-inch disks and 1.44MB, 3 1/2-inch disks, respectively). The images titled `lowmem.bin` and `lowmemrd.bin` are designed for low memory systems. The `root.bin` image contains a `root` filesystem sufficient for very basic operation and system repair, but it is not bootable. The images beginning with `drv` contain additional drivers, which will be necessary to use certain installation methods (ethernet drivers and so on).

Boot Options

After you have successfully booted to the installation screen, you have a number of options. Normally, you will want to use the default, which boots the Linux kernel on that disk in installation mode. Assuming the kernel boots correctly and detects the necessary hardware properly, you then start the installation procedure. If there is a problem at this stage, see the "Troubleshooting" section later in this chapter for help. You may be able to cause the kernel to detect your hardware by feeding special options at boot time. It is worth noting, however, that this kernel is intended only for the installation procedure; as long as it detects everything you need for installation, it will be fine.

Installing the System

Debian uses a two-boot sequence to install. First, you boot from the CD-ROM or a boot disk, and then you use that to install and configure a kernel and the very basic elements of the system. Then, you boot a second time (this time, using the kernel you installed on your hard drive) and configure or install additional applications. This section will walk you through both boot processes.

This is convenient for installation because you can find out whether the kernel works immediately, before installing and configuring the rest of the system, but unfortunately it makes things difficult if the kernel in fact does not work; you don't have the tools readily to correct the problem. If you had to boot from one of the `safe` or `tecra` disks, you should expect to have a bit of trouble with the standard kernel and the second boot. If the standard boot disk worked for you, so should the standard kernel.

If the second boot (from the kernel installed on your hard drive) fails, go to the "Troubleshooting" section, where the recovery method is described.

The First Boot

If your first boot manages to load the kernel, you will see a scrolling text display. This is just the kernel initializing itself and the devices it knows about. You don't need to worry about it unless it stops in the middle. However, if you have problems, watching the display carefully can sometimes point you to the cause of the problem. The text is typically stored for reference after boot to the file `/var/log/kern.log`.

After the kernel boots successfully, the installation script begins. You will be prompted to indicate whether you are using a color or monochrome screen; this is your sign that you have booted the kernel successfully and are ready to begin the install. Pick whichever option is appropriate, and then select next. You will see a brief text describing the floppy disk you booted from; read it if you like, and then press Enter to continue. You are then at the first substantial step in the installation.

The Debian install process is broken into a series of steps. You can skip some steps or perform them in a different order, but it is recommended to simply go through the steps one-by-one in order. None of these settings are permanent; you can always go back and change them. The main thing is to get the installation complete and working at this stage.

Configuring the Keyboard

Just pick your keyboard layout from the list. You probably have a qwerty/us keyboard.

Partitioning Your Hard Drive

After configuring your keyboard, you will be asked to partition your hard drive. This time, you use a Linux utility to do so (which is much friendlier than MS-DOS `fdisk`). You should be careful not to mess with the partition you are using for Windows (because doing so will ruin all the hard work you have gone through earlier to keep Windows working). If you already have a partition you want to use with Linux, you will use this utility only to change the type of those partitions to appropriate Linux values.

The Debian partition utility (`cfdisk`) presents a listing of defined partitions across the screen (with an entry for free space not allocated to a partition, if any), and presents a list of operations at the bottom of the screen. Moving the cursor keys up and down selects the partition to operate on. Moving left and right selects the operation to perform from the bottom. There are some options you should be aware of: Write writes your changes to the disk. Quit exits without saving the changes you've made; this is a good emergency out, if you have modified or deleted your Windows partition by mistake.

You will want to create a Linux swap partition and one or more filesystem partitions. Linux uses an entire partition for swap as opposed to the way Windows does it, which is by using a single large file. To create these partitions, select the new operator at the bottom, if you have free space available, and create the partitions you want. If you set up the partitions you wanted previously with MS-DOS `fdisk`, all you have to do here is change the type.

Linux uses two different partition types: filesystem and swap. Partitions you create with this utility are assumed to be Linux filesystem partitions, but you can define them to be any other type you like, and you need to do this if you want to use a swap partition. Simply select the partition you want to use for swap, and select the type operation at the bottom. You will see a menu of partition types; enter the one you want and press Enter. Standard Linux filesystems are type 82, and standard Linux swap partitions are type 83.

When you have arranged your partition scheme to your satisfaction, select Write, type `yes`, and then select Quit. You will then be back in the install process. The next step is to initialize and activate a swap partition, assuming you defined one; if not, select Do without a swap partition. Pick the appropriate option and continue.

Initializing Your Swap Partition

You will be asked to select the swap partition to initialize and be presented with a menu of available swap partitions. You should see only one entry in the menu (unless you defined multiple swap partitions, which is usually not necessary). Select it and continue.

You will be asked whether the partition should be scanned for bad blocks. Say yes.

You will be asked if you are sure. Double-check to make sure you are operating on the right partition. Your Windows partition is usually `/dev/hda1` in the Linux notation, so make sure you aren't about to use that for swap! Luckily, the installation program shows partitions of only the type Linux swap, so this isn't a risk unless you mislabeled something when partitioning earlier.

Initializing and Mounting the Linux Partitions

You need to initialize and mount your other partitions here before beginning to install the system. This is similar to the process for installing a swap partition a moment ago. Select initialize, pick the Linux partition from the menu, say yes to the two questions (don't wipe your Windows partition here!), and then go on to the next partition, until you have initialized all the partitions that appear on the initialization menu. The menu displays partitions with only the Linux filesystem type, so you can safely initialize them all (unless you mislabeled one of your other partitions earlier). Start with the partition you intend to use for the `root` partition.

When you have finished initializing the `root` partition, you will be asked whether you want to mount it as `root`. Say yes. You will then be returned to the previous screen, with the choice of initializing and mounting more partitions, or beginning to install the base system. When all the Linux partitions have been initialized, you should mount each one and continue with the install only when all Linux partitions are initialized and mounted.

Installing the Operating System and Modules

You will be asked to select the medium you are using to install. Choose the medium and provide any more precise specification asked for. For CD-ROM installation, you are asked for the location of the CD-ROM; most systems have the CD-ROM as one of the options 2–5, with the most common being option 4. There's no harm in trying each one if the one you think is right doesn't work. If you are using an unusual medium, such as a network install or installing from an MS-DOS partition, select that option from this menu.

You will be asked to provide a path to the Debian archive on the installation medium. Usually the default will work, but for FTP sites or using an MS-DOS partition, you may need to specify the path in more detail. If you get it wrong, the installation program won't be able to find the data it needs and will complain; just try again.

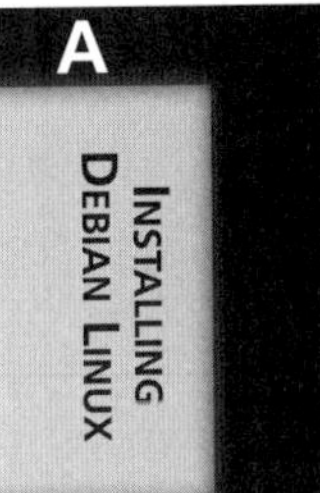

After the installation script has found the files you need, you will be asked to choose the path to locate the kernel images you used to boot. Normally, you can simply pick from the listed archive directory. The installation script will then install the floppy disk images to your system as the default kernel.

Configuring the Drivers and Modules

You will be presented with a list of module categories. These correspond very closely to the kernel modules that Debian includes on its driver's floppy disk. Go through and select the ones you want (don't forget that you can scroll down the screen to see more). You will, at the very least, want to examine the options in `fs` (this enables Linux to read and write other filesystem types, including MS-DOS/Windows partitions), `misc` (miscellaneous drivers, particularly mice, serial ports, and ISDN), and `net` (various hardware network interfaces).

When you are done, select Exit, and you will be brought to the network configuration section.

Configuring the Network

This section is very simple. If you have a network, input the options you want (ask your network administrator for the options if you are on a network you do not control).

If you are not on a network, you still need to go through this step, but you will be asked only to choose a name for your system (you can skip the other questions).

The primary purpose of this network configuration is to enable access to network-located Debian archives for network installations. You will be able to change the configuration later.

Installing the Base System

You will be asked a similar set of questions about where to find the base system archive. Generally, the same answers you gave before will work, although the less common installation procedures might expect the locations to differ.

Configuring the Base System

You will be asked a number of questions about your basic system and environment. None of them are difficult.

The first question concerns the time zone you are located in. You can pick the three-letter abbreviation from the left or press the right cursor key to select a time zone by name.

You will next be asked to choose between GMT and local time being stored in the system hardware clock. If you want to keep running Windows and don't want it to get confused, choose local time. If you are running Linux only, or don't care if Windows is confused, you can pick GMT. It won't make a big difference to Linux either way.

The next step will be configuring the boot process. You can make Linux bootable from the hard drive (which is normally what you want), or make a boot floppy disk (which requires you to use a boot floppy disk whenever you want to boot Linux), or just reboot (which is probably not what you want yet).

You will be asked which partition to install `LILO` on; as long as the partition is not your MS-DOS/Windows partition, it doesn't matter which you use. You will be asked whether you want to install `LILO` in your master boot record. Typically, the answer is yes, though if you are using NT or already have a boot manager, you may prefer not to. You will be asked whether Debian should be the default OS to boot; this is a matter of personal preference.

When you have completed this process, you will be asked to make a boot floppy disk just in case. This is a good idea if you aren't sure whether the installed kernel will work (for example, if you had trouble getting Linux to boot with the boot disk images), but it is not strictly necessary in most cases. Just put the floppy disk in the drive and let the installation script write the boot image. Use a different floppy disk than the one you used to get this far, in case you need this one again.

Finally, reboot the system. You may need to remove the Debian CD-ROM temporarily if you were able to boot directly from that, so that the system can boot from the hard disk instead of the CD-ROM. Booting from the CD-ROM would just start the install all over again.

The Second Boot

If everything goes as planned, your system will now boot into the next phase of the installation process. If it does not, go to the "Troubleshooting" section later in this chapter. After the computer boots, you will have to do some configuration before you can actually use the computer. You will be prompted for the needed configurations with plenty of information about the options.

Choosing a `root` Password

You will be asked to choose a `root` password. Read the explanatory text presented.

Adding a User

You should probably take the opportunity to create a normal user for yourself when asked. If you don't, do so yourself as soon as possible; doing most things as `root` is a security problem. You should use the `root` account only to perform system maintenance.

Shadow Passwords

Yes, you almost certainly want shadow passwords. This option creates a file called `/etc/shadow` which holds all the password information. This file can only be read or written to by `root` and adds an extra level of security.

PCMCIA

PCMCIA is a laptop expansion standard. Most desktop systems don't need PCMCIA support, but the installation procedure installs it anyway so laptops can get through the install. Unless you have a laptop, you can let the kernel remove the PCMCIA packages.

After you finish with these configuration options, you will be taken to `dselect` to finish the installation. `dselect` is a Debian package management system that you use to install or remove programs.

Using `dselect` to Install Applications

As mentioned previously, Debian Linux uses a package manager. There are several front-ends to that package manager; the standard front-end for this version of Debian is `dselect`. The installation procedure makes use of `dselect` to install the vast majority of the distribution.

Selecting an Access Method

The `dselect` menu shows a list of steps to install packages. The first thing you want to do is select an access method, so just press Return. You are probably installing from a single CD-ROM, so select that option unless you know better.

The next step requires you to know the layout of your selected installation medium. For the single CD-ROM, it is the following path: `debian/dists/slink`. For other installation methods, it may vary, but should at least resemble this one. You will be asked to enter a source for the `contrib` packages. These are not on the single CD-ROM, so you enter `none`. You can configure `dselect` to access them later, via the Internet, if you want. The same applies to the non-free, non-U.S., and local packages.

You will then be returned to the main menu with the next option (update list of available packages) selected.

Updating the List of Available Packages

Select this option by pressing Enter, and everything should work. If not, return to specifying an access method and try again.

If this step requires you to access a network, it may be slow.

Selecting Packages to Install

The next option enables you to select the packages you want to install. There are a number of recommended packages, which will be automatically installed, and a number of additional packages, which can be installed if desired but are not required. Pay attention to the help screens; this is your first exposure to the `dselect` front-end, which you will usually use to update the packages installed on your system.

The `dselect` application knows enough about the various packages to alert you when installing one package also requires you to install another. Just scroll down the list and use the plus key (+) to select the packages you want. You can't install all the packages you see in `dselect` because some packages conflict with others. You don't have to install any extra packages if you feel this is too complicated a task right now, but it's a good idea to at least take a look at the descriptions of the packages there. When you are finished selecting packages, press Enter. You will be presented with conflict and dependency resolution screens if there are problems; normally, you should be able to press Enter and accept the default solution.

Installing Selected Packages

This option will read the packages you have selected from the CD-ROM, over the network, or wherever you have defined as the source of the packages. Each package will then be installed on your system. If everything is configured properly, you should be able to select this option, and then lean back and watch the show for a while.

Configuring Installed Packages

Some of the basic system packages require you to configure them before they can be useful. This step enables you to perform that configuration. Just answer the questions as they appear.

Configuring `gpm`

The `gpm` package is a mouse server for console (that is, text mode) operation, enabling simple copying and pasting. The configuration is a little tricky. There is a default configuration command line provided, which is suitable for a common type of mouse on the first serial port. If your mouse does not match that type, is not on that serial port, or is a ps/2 mouse, you will want to make changes.

You will be asked if you want to use the mouse-test program. You probably do; just say yes. You will be asked to perform a series of tasks with your mouse, allowing the program to watch the possible mouse connections and detect which one you are using. As you perform each task in sequence, the program will narrow down the possibilities, until you are left with only one (you hope). You shouldn't use any programs that access the mouse while configuring this (normally, that isn't an option at this stage anyway), and it may be a good idea to disconnect or just turn off your modem.

After running through all the tests, the program will ask you to enter the location and protocol your mouse uses. It will display a line listing what it thinks the correct values are, but will not set the defaults to conform to those values! Look at the recommended values and enter them when asked. Write them down on a sheet of paper as well, because you will need them again later to configure X (see Chapter 3, "The X Window System Environment," for more information).

At this point, you can start celebrating because Linux has been installed successfully. Something most users will want to do is allow `lilo` to boot to another operating system besides Linux.

Booting Multiple Operating Systems

Linux typically uses the `LILO` boot loader. As mentioned previously, this loader is capable of booting multiple versions of the Linux kernel, as well as non-Linux operating systems, and enables you to choose between the configured operating systems at boot time. It performs this function by presenting a prompt, at which you can type a label to determine which operating system to boot and in the case of Linux, any additional options you want passed to the kernel.

The available operating systems are configured (by default) in the file `/etc/lilo.conf`. This will be set up for Linux, and possibly for Windows, in the default configuration. This basic file is shown in Listing A.1.

LISTING A.1 The `/etc/lilo.conf` File, Configured to Boot Windows and Linux

```
boot=/dev/hda
install=/boot/boot.b
map=/boot/map
prompt
vga=normal
delay=20

image=/vmlinuz-2.2.9
        root=/dev/hda3
        label=linux
        read-only

image=/vmlinuz.old

        label=old
        read-only

other=/dev/hda1
        label=win
```

The `boot` option at the beginning indicates where you want the code that does the actual loading to be installed; normally, this is configured according to your answer to a question during one of the earlier installation steps. You should not have to change it, unless you want to change where the system finds the default boot procedure.

The `install` and `map` options indicate the location of certain files on the Linux filesystem. Again, you shouldn't need to change these.

The `prompt` option specifies that you want to be prompted at boot time to select an OS. If you omit the option, `LILO` automatically boots the default kernel. You will almost always want to be prompted.

The `vga` line specifies some video options; it can be left as is for now. You may want to change it later.

The delay option specifies a delay, in seconds, to wait for a response to the prompt before booting the default OS. This can be as long or short as you like, within reason. This option is used only if you have the prompt option turned off, however. If you want a delay with the prompt option turned on, you need to use the timeout option.

The remaining sections (lines beginning with `image` and `other`) specify booting methods. Each `image` section specifies a kernel image, the `root` filesystem to use when booting that image, a label for that option, and `read-only`,which indicates the filesystem should be read-only to begin with (allowing it to be checked for errors) and then remounted to allow writing later on.

The `other` line specifies a partition to boot from and is used to boot other operating systems. MS-DOS, Windows 95/98, and BIOS all boot fine in this manner. Windows NT is known to be somewhat picky about its operation, however. Other operating systems may or may not work, but probably will.

The Linux Drive and Partition Naming System

Linux includes a `/dev/` directory, which contains a number of virtual files representing the devices available to the system.

Thus, you have files representing available hard drives, available partitions on each drive, and so on. The files that concern IDE hard drives present in the system are `/dev/hda`, `/dev/hdb`, `/dev/hdc`, and `/dev/hdd`. They are, in sequence, the drive on the first channel of the primary controller, the drive on the second channel of the primary controller, the first channel of the secondary controller, and the second channel of the secondary controller. Partitions are referred to by number, as in `/dev/hda1` for the first partition on the first channel of the primary controller. SCSI uses `/dev/sda` through `/dev/sdg` in a similar manner.

After making any changes you like, you should run `lilo` as the `root` user to make those changes permanent.

If you are wondering why the example includes two Linux kernel images, the answer is simple: Sometimes, the new kernel you are saving will not work properly. Anything from simply typing the wrong filename by mistake, to a bug in the kernel, or just a kernel compiled with the wrong options for your machine, may cause the new kernel to fail. When this happens, all you need to do is reboot the system and choose the other kernel image, which is usually a "known-good" kernel that you know works.

If you don't do this, it will be easy to end up with a nonbootable system if you make a mistake when building or installing your kernel. If you won't be doing any of that, you don't have to worry about it. If you do intend to compile your own kernels and run into a problem that prevents you from booting, you can usually use a boot disk to get access to your system (enough to fix the system, anyway). But using `LILO` with at least two kernel images is easier.

If you have access to only one computer regularly, it's a good idea to keep a boot disk handy as well. It's no fun to get locked out of your computer by a simple mistake. If you have other computers available, you can always use them to make a boot disk, which reduces the annoyance factor considerably. The next section provides some help for common problems.

Troubleshooting

There are a number of places where your Linux installation can run into problems. The tips in the following sections should cover most of the common situations. The newsgroup `comp.os.linux.setup` is an excellent resource for getting help with installation problems. Use one of the Usenet search engines to search for questions similar to yours. There are a number of mailing lists dealing with Linux; of particular use is the Linux Laptop mailing list, because laptops can present problems that are difficult to solve. The most useful of these methods are the debian-user mailing list and #debian on the `irc.debian.org` IRC server network. The Debian home page (`www.debian.org`) has information about both of these.

Most common systems should work with Linux. It may take a bit of work to find the proper kernel options if you have a system with unusual or proprietary hardware since all of your hardware may not be supported, but it should at least boot successfully. If it doesn't, ask; it's likely that someone else has had similar problems and may know the right options to use. It can be more work than you expect, but is usually possible.

If you are trying to use Linux with an Alpha, PowerPC (usually an Apple Macintosh), StrongARM, Amiga, or other uncommon hardware, you need to make sure you have the right version of Linux for your platform. The CD-ROM included with this book is for

Intel-architecture systems (386 and up). Most of the information in the book should be transferable to a different architecture, but the CD-ROM will not be.

Why Can't I Boot from My Linux Partition?

In order to boot properly, your computer must first find the boot loader. This is typically `LILO` on a Linux system, but may be something else if you are using NT or if you have purchased a commercial boot loader. `LILO` presents a boot prompt and (depending on the configuration) should enable you to choose which operating system and kernel to boot from. After you have selected the OS to load, `LILO` will attempt to load the kernel for that operating system and transfer control to the new kernel.

There are several potential problems with this process. The following sections present some questions you should ask yourself when something goes wrong.

Did You Rerun LILO After Making Configuration Changes?

`LILO`'s configuration file (`/etc/lilo.conf`) is not read at boot time. Instead, within Linux, you must run the `lilo` program, which reads the configuration file and writes the changes to the appropriate places on your hard drive.

Is the System Finding LILO?

It is possible to install `LILO` to a place where the system can't find it, or where the system will find another boot loader first. If your `LILO` is configured in such a way, read the `LILO` documentation to determine where it should be. The default Debian configuration of `LILO` should work fine; if your system cannot find `LILO`, either you have changed the default location `LILO` is installing to, or something has overwritten the `LILO` information. Remember: `lilo` must be run as `root`.

If your system can't find `LILO`, the first thing to try is simply running it again. Microsoft operating systems are notorious for overwriting the boot sectors whenever they are installed or upgraded, which will destroy the `LILO` installation. If this is your problem, boot from a boot disk and rerun `LILO`.

My Windows Partition Is Very Large, but LILO Won't Boot My Kernel.

Due to a peculiarity of the PC BIOS, `LILO` cannot always access all your hard drive space. Instead, it can access the space below a certain (somewhat arcane) size limit, imposed by the design of the BIOS itself. This doesn't affect Linux (or Windows, for that matter), because those operating systems can talk directly to the hard drive controller, but `LILO` must go through the BIOS in order to load the operating system kernel. Thus, `LILO` must abide by the limitations of the BIOS.

The only real solution is to put your Linux `root` partition as early as possible on the hard drive. Windows will still insist on its own partition being first, but you can make the Windows system partition relatively small and then add the Linux `root` partition immediately afterward, followed by another Windows partition if desired. Another common possibility is to define a separate partition only to hold the kernel images, which can be much smaller than the entire `root` partition.

If Your Second Boot Fails...

The Debian install is a two-boot process—first from the CD-ROM or a boot disk, and then from the installed kernel. If the second boot, from the installed kernel, fails, you can still recover from this.

Boot again from the boot disk (the same one that worked before), but instead of bypassing the boot options screen, type the following(replace `/dev/hda1` with your Linux `root` partition):

```
boot: rescue root=/dev/hda1
```

This should continue the install procedure, using the kernel from the boot disk. You then have to compile and install your own kernel to make one that boots properly. To do this, you need to download the kernel source and install `gcc`, the standard C compiler for Linux systems. Until you have built and installed a working kernel, you need to boot from the boot disk with the options given previously.

If you are having problems with a laptop, read the kernel documentation for the APM options; many boot problems with laptops can be resolved there.

Boot Disk Problems

The most common problem to have with boot disks is simply having a bad disk. You can try writing the disk image again, or try another disk. The disks should be 1.44MB (two holes), and preferably formatted before writing the disk image. Make sure the write-protect tab is down, so that it covers the hole in the disk, before writing the disk image.

If you have managed to rule out bad floppy disks, try using some of the alternate boot disks (those labeled `safe` and `tecra`). Make sure you are using the appropriate size (1440 or 14, not 1200 or 12, assuming 3 1/2-inch disks). Make sure your `dd` command is correct. Test your disks on other computers to try to eliminate your computer as the source of the problem. The following `dd` command writes the `resc1440.bin` file to the first floppy disk drive:

```
# dd if=resc1440.bin of=/dev/fd0
```

Another possibility is simply needing to pass parameters to the kernel in order for it to recognize your hardware properly. The initial boot is performed by the BIOS, which should be aware of your boot hardware; but after this, more information must be loaded from the floppy disk by the kernel itself. If the kernel can't find your floppy disk, this will be difficult. Similarly, if your kernel can't find your keyboard or hard drive, installation is difficult or impossible. Examine the help screens available by pressing F4 and F5 from the boot prompt in order to see the various options you can try.

Booting the Kernel with Options

If your boot disk isn't working, or it is not finding all the hardware you need to install, you may be able to help by providing options to the kernel indicating what to look for and where. These should be specified at the first boot prompt you see after booting from a boot disk. The exact options available are specified in the kernel documentation and summarized in the help screens available at that stage by pressing the function keys.

In some cases, you need to pass these options to the kernel every time you boot, not just when you are using the boot disk. If this is the case, you can specify them through the `LILO` prompt just as you did with the boot disk, or by adding them to `LILO` using the `append` option:

```
append = ìoptionî
```

You should make a practice of testing the options by hand first, just in case.

Getting Packages When Other Methods Fail

If you can't get Linux to see your CD-ROM, read the sidebar earlier in the chapter titled "Installing Without a CD-ROM Drive Or If Linux Can't Find Your CD-ROM Drive." If you cannot use either of the options described there, you can try to do things manually. This usually means making the CD-ROM files available on your Windows or DOS partition, and then loading them from Linux. You need to get enough of Linux installed to access that partition, which may be tricky, but should be possible. After that, you can tell the installation procedure where to find the packages and proceed normally.

Online Resources

There are a number of online resources devoted to installing Linux. This section provides pointers to several of them. However, your most important reference will be the documentation on the CD-ROM that you have available, because it describes the exact version of Linux you will attempt to install. Many of the other documents available online provide detailed instructions for overcoming specific problems with your Linux installation, or for installing Linux in one particular way. These often contain valuable hints, but should not be relied upon to be completely accurate or complete with a version or distribution of Linux they are not written for. They should be read with an eye toward combining their

advice with the normal install procedures, rather than relied upon as an alternate installation procedure entirely.

The following resources are all available from the Linux Documentation Project at `http://metalab.unc.edu/LDP/`.

- The Boot Disk HOWTO
- The Boot Prompt HOWTO
- The CD-ROM HOWTO (not necessary for most modern systems)
- The Linux Install Guide

Summary

This appendix described the installation procedure for Debian Linux, along with the necessary procedures for reallocating space from existing Windows partitions. Basic information regarding partitions, filesystems, and system booting was provided in order to help deal with potential problems. Pointers to information about some of the less common, but occasionally necessary, installation procedures were included.

APPENDIX

Online References

by Mario Camou

In This Appendix

This Appendix presents some references you may use to get more information on the topics covered in most chapters of this book. Most references are to Web sites, although there are some useful newsgroups and email lists as well.

Web Sites

These are some Web sites that contain useful information on the topics covered in this book. For each chapter, a list of links relevant to the information presented is given for you. You may still be able to find other information on these topics elsewhere; a search engine such as `http://www.google.com/` may prove useful if you need to do some online research into Linux topics.

Chapter 1—Introduction to Debian Linux

`http://www.debian.org/` The Debian home site

Chapter 3—The X Window System Environment

`http://www.x.org/`	The X Consortium
`http://www.xfree86.org/`	The XFree86 site
`http://www.mesa3d.org/`	The Mesa home page
`http://www.linux3d.org/`	The Linux 3D home page
`http://www.fvwm.org/`	The FVWM home page
`http://www.kiss.uni-lj.si/~k4fr0235/icewm/`	The IceWM home page
`http://www.windowmaker.org/`	The WindowMaker home page
`http://people.delphi.com/crc3419/WMUserGuide/index.htm`	The WindowMaker User's Guide
`http://www.kde.org/`	The KDE Web site
`http://www.enlightenment.org`	The Enlightenment home page
`http://www.gnome.org/`	The GNOME Web site
`http://www.dejanews.com/`	DejaNews

Chapter 4—User Applications

`http://www.netscape.com`	Netscape home page
`http://www.gnome.org`	The GNOME project home page
`http://www.stardivision.com/`	StarDivision, the creators of StarOffice
`http://www.applix.com`	ApplixWare home page
`http://linux.corel.com`	Corel's Linux page, home of WordPerfect for Linux
`http://www.gimp.org`	The GIMP

Chapter 8—Conventional Means, Extraordinary Ends: Powerful Scripting Tools

`http://www.ns.utk.edu/tech/bash/bashref_toc.html`	Bash Reference
`http://www.perl.com/`	The source for Perl
`http://language.perl.com/`	Perl language page
`http://www.perl.org/`	The Perl Institute
`http://www.cpan.org/`	The Comprehensive Perl Archive Network

Chapter 9—Regular Expressions

`http://www.perl.com/`	Perl home page

Chapter 11—Administration Essentials

`http://metalab.unc.edu/LDP/`	The Linux Documentation Project
`http://www.linux.org`	The Linux home page
`http://www.astart.com/LPRng.html`	LPR: the Next Generation home page

Chapter 14—Disaster Recovery

`http://linas.org/linux/Software-RAID/Software-RAID.html`	Software RAID HOWTO

Chapter 15—Advanced System Administration

`http://slashdot.org`	Slashdot
`http://linuxtoday.com`	Linux Today
`http://www.linuxgazette.com`	Linux Gazette
`http://freshmeat.net`	Freshmeat
`http://www.debian.org`	Debian Home Page
`http://www.debian.org/Lists-Archives`	Debian List Archives Page
`http://metalab.unc n.edu/LDP`	Linux Documentation Project

Chapter 16—TCP/IP Networking Essentials

`http://sunsite.auc.dk/RFC/`	Internet RFCs

Chapter 17—Information Servers

`http://www.sendmail.org/`	Sendmail home page
`http://www.apache.org/`	Apache home page
`www.isc.org/view.cgi?/products/BIND/index.phtml`	BIND home page
`www.isc.org/view.cgi?/products/INN/index.phtml`	INN home page

Chapter 18—Interacting with Microsoft Networks Using Samba

`http://www.samba.org`	The Samba home page
`http://lists.samba.org/`	Samba mailing lists

Chapter 19—Tools for Advanced Network Administration

`http://www.suse.de/~kukuk/linux/nis.html`	Linux NIS home page

Chapter 20—Conceptual Overview of Security Issues

http://www.ciac.llnl.com/	Computer Incident Advisory Capability archive
http://www.cs.purdue.edu/coast/coast.html	Computer Operations, Audit, and Security Technology site
http://www.digicrime.org/	Full-service criminal computer hacking organization
http://www.cert.org/	Computer Emergency Response Team
ftp:///info.cert.org/	Archived past CERT advisories

Chapter 23—Encryption

http://www.openmarket.com/techinfo/applied.htm	Applied Cryptography
http://www.ssh.fi/	Secure SHell home page
http://www.ssh.fi/tech/crypto/	Cryptography A–Z
http://www.wassenaar.org/	The Wassenaar Arrangement
http://www.nai.com/	Network Associates, the current owner of PGP
http://www.pgp.com/	Commercial version of PGP
http://web.mit.edu/network/pgp.html	Noncommercial U.S. version of PGP
http://www.pgpi.com/	Noncommercial non-U.S. version of PGP
http://www.pgp.net/	Information on PGP key-servers

Chapter 25—Java Programming

http://java.sun.com	The official Java Web site at Sun Microsystems
http://www.blackdown.org	Home of the Linux port of Sun's JDK
http://www.javaworld.com	An online Java magazine

`http://www.gamelan.com`	A directory of Java resources
`http://www.transvirtual.com`	Kaffe: an independent implementation of Java (there is even an open-source version of Kaffe)
`ftp://gonzalez.cyberus.ca/pub/Linux/java`	TYA: a JIT compiler for the Blackdown/Linux port of the JDK (Intel)
`http://developer.javasoft.com`	Sun's Java Developer Connection

Newsgroups

Newsgroups are a convenient way of discussing different topics. If you don't have a news server available, you may visit `Deja.com` at `http://www.deja.com`.

Chapter 8—Conventional Means, Extraordinary Ends: Powerful Scripting Tools

`comp.lang.perl.announce`	Announcements relating to Perl
`comp.lang.perl.misc`	General Perl discussion

Chapter 16—TCP/IP Networking Essentials

`comp.protocols.tcp-ip`	General discussion of TCP/IP
`comp.linux.networking`	Discussion of networking in Linux

Chapter 18—Interacting with Microsoft Networks Using Samba

`comp.protocols.smb`	Discussion on the SMB protocol
`linux.samba`	General discussion on Samba

Chapter 19—Tools for Advanced Network Administration

`comp.protocols.nfs`	General discussion of NFS
`comp.linux.networking`	Discussion of networking in Linux

Chapter 20—Conceptual Overview of Security Issues

`comp.security.unix`	UNIX security
`comp.security.announce`	Computer security announcements, including new CERT advisories
`comp.security.misc`	Miscellaneous computer and network security

Chapter 23—Encryption

`sci.crypt`	Discussions about cryptography research and application
`alt.security.pgp`	Discussions on PGP
`comp.security.pgp.announce`	Announcements of new PGP versions, tools, FAQs, and so on
`comp.security.pgp.discuss`	General discussion on PGP
`comp.security.pgp.resources`	Pointers to PGP resources
`comp.security.pgp.tech`	Technical details about PGP

Chapter 25—Java Programming

`comp.lang.java.*`	Everything about Java

Email Lists

The original way of communicating over a network was email. There are still many useful email lists.

Chapter 1—Introduction to Debian Linux

`debian-user` This list if for discussion with users of Debian. You can use it to ask a question and get answers when you have a problem. To subscribe, email `debian-user-request@lists.debian.org` with `subscribe` in the message subject.

Chapter 18—Interacting with Microsoft Networks Using Samba

`samba` General discussion on Samba. To subscribe, send email to `listproc@samba.org` with `subscribe samba` *`Your Full Name`* in the message body.

`samba-announce` Samba announcements. To subscribe, send email to `listproc@samba.org` with `subscribe samba-announce` *`Your Full Name`* in the message body.

Chapter 20—Conceptual Overview of Security Issues

`CERT-advisory` New CERT advisories. To subscribe, email `cert-advisory-request@cert.org` with `subscribe` in the message body.

`Best of Security` Nondiscussion list for remailing items from other security lists. To subscribe, send email to `best-of-security-request@suburbia.net` with `subscribe best-of-security` in the message body.

Chapter 23—Encryption

`pgp-users@joshua.riverton.net` Discussion list for users of PGP. To subscribe, send email to `pgp-users subscribe@joshua.riverton.net` with `subscribe` in the message subject and body.

Chapter 25—Java Programming

`java-linux@blackdown.org` Discussion about Java on Linux. To subscribe, send email to `java-linux-request@blackdown.org` with `subscribe` in the subject.

APPENDIX

DFSG-Compliant Licenses

by Mario Camou

In This Appendix

This appendix presents the three most commonly used open-source licenses. All are compliant with the Debian Free Software Guidelines, which can be found at `http://www.debian.org/social_contract`.

For more details on the history, purpose, and applicability of each of these licenses, see Chapter 1, "Introduction to Debian Linux," and the `http://www.gnu.org/` and `http://www.opensource.org` Web sites.

The GNU General Public License (GPL)

GNU GENERAL PUBLIC LICENSE

Version 2, June 1991

Copyright © 1989, 1991 Free Software Foundation, Inc.

59 Temple Place, Suite 330, Boston, MA 02111-1307 USA

Everyone is permitted to copy and distribute verbatim copies of this license document, but changing it is not allowed.

Preamble

The licenses for most software are designed to take away your freedom to share and change it. By contrast, the GNU General Public License is intended to guarantee your freedom to share and change free software—to make sure the software is free for all its users. This General Public License applies to most of the Free Software Foundation's software and to any other program whose authors commit to using it. (Some other Free Software Foundation software is covered by the GNU Library General Public License instead.) You can apply it to your programs, too.

When we speak of free software, we are referring to freedom, not price. Our General Public Licenses are designed to make sure that you have the freedom to distribute copies of free software (and charge for this service if you wish), that you receive source code or can get it if you want it, that you can change the software or use pieces of it in new free programs; and that you know you can do these things.

To protect your rights, we need to make restrictions that forbid anyone to deny you these rights or to ask you to surrender the rights. These restrictions translate to certain responsibilities for you if you distribute copies of the software, or if you modify it.

For example, if you distribute copies of such a program, whether gratis or for a fee, you must give the recipients all the rights that you have. You must make sure that they, too, receive or can get the source code. And you must show them these terms so they know their rights.

We protect your rights with two steps: (1) copyright the software, and (2) offer you this license which gives you legal permission to copy, distribute and/or modify the software.

Also, for each author's protection and ours, we want to make certain that everyone understands that there is no warranty for this free software. If the software is modified by someone else and passed on, we want its recipients to know that what they have is not the original, so that any problems introduced by others will not reflect on the original authors' reputations.

Finally, any free program is threatened constantly by software patents. We wish to avoid the danger that redistributors of a free program will individually obtain patent licenses, in effect making the program proprietary. To prevent this, we have made it clear that any patent must be licensed for everyone's free use or not licensed at all.

The precise terms and conditions for copying, distribution and modification follow.

GNU GENERAL PUBLIC LICENSE TERMS AND CONDITIONS FOR COPYING, DISTRIBUTION AND MODIFICATION

0. This License applies to any program or other work which contains a notice placed by the copyright holder saying it may be distributed under the terms of this General Public License. The "Program", below, refers to any such program or work, and a "work based on the Program" means either the Program or any derivative work under copyright law: that is to say, a work containing the Program or a portion of it, either verbatim or with modifications and/or translated into another language. (Hereinafter, translation is included without limitation in the term "modification".) Each licensee is addressed as "you".

   Activities other than copying, distribution and modification are not covered by this License; they are outside its scope. The act of running the Program is not restricted, and the output from the Program is covered only if its contents constitute a work based on the Program (independent of having been made by running the Program). Whether that is true depends on what the Program does.

1. You may copy and distribute verbatim copies of the Program's source code as you receive it, in any medium, provided that you conspicuously and appropriately publish on each copy an appropriate copyright notice and disclaimer of warranty; keep intact all the notices that refer to this License and to the absence of any warranty; and give any other recipients of the Program a copy of this License along with the Program.

   You may charge a fee for the physical act of transferring a copy, and you may at your option offer warranty protection in exchange for a fee.

2. You may modify your copy or copies of the Program or any portion of it, thus forming a work based on the Program, and copy and distribute such modifications or work under the terms of Section 1 above, provided that you also meet all of these conditions:

a. You must cause the modified files to carry prominent notices stating that you changed the files and the date of any change.

b. You must cause any work that you distribute or publish, that in whole or in part contains or is derived from the Program or any part thereof, to be licensed as a whole at no charge to all third parties under the terms of this License.

c. If the modified program normally reads commands interactively when run, you must cause it, when started running for such interactive use in the most ordinary way, to print or display an announcement including an appropriate copyright notice and a notice that there is no warranty (or else, saying that you provide a warranty) and that users may redistribute the program under these conditions, and telling the user how to view a copy of this License. (Exception: if the Program itself is interactive but does not normally print such an announcement, your work based on the Program is not required to print an announcement.)

These requirements apply to the modified work as a whole. If identifiable sections of that work are not derived from the Program, and can be reasonably considered independent and separate works in themselves, then this License, and its terms, do not apply to those sections when you distribute them as separate works. But when you distribute the same sections as part of a whole which is a work based on the Program, the distribution of the whole must be on the terms of this License, whose permissions for other licensees extend to the entire whole, and thus to each and every part regardless of who wrote it.

Thus, it is not the intent of this section to claim rights or contest your rights to work written entirely by you; rather, the intent is to exercise the right to control the distribution of derivative or collective works based on the Program.

In addition, mere aggregation of another work not based on the Program with the Program (or with a work based on the Program) on a volume of a storage or distribution medium does not bring the other work under the scope of this License.

3. You may copy and distribute the Program (or a work based on it, under Section 2) in object code or executable form under the terms of Sections 1 and 2 above provided that you also do one of the following:

   a. Accompany it with the complete corresponding machine-readable source code, which must be distributed under the terms of Sections 1 and 2 above on a medium customarily used for software interchange; or,

b. Accompany it with a written offer, valid for at least three years, to give any third party, for a charge no more than your cost of physically performing source distribution, a complete machine-readable copy of the corresponding source code, to be distributed under the terms of Sections 1 and 2 above on a medium customarily used for software interchange; or,

c. Accompany it with the information you received as to the offer to distribute corresponding source code. (This alternative is allowed only for noncommercial distribution and only if you received the program in object code or executable form with such an offer, in accord with Subsection b above.)

The source code for a work means the preferred form of the work for making modifications to it. For an executable work, complete source code means all the source code for all modules it contains, plus any associated interface definition files, plus the scripts used to control compilation and installation of the executable. However, as a special exception, the source code distributed need not include anything that is normally distributed (in either source or binary form) with the major components (compiler, kernel, and so on) of the operating system on which the executable runs, unless that component itself accompanies the executable.

If distribution of executable or object code is made by offering access to copy from a designated place, then offering equivalent access to copy the source code from the same place counts as distribution of the source code, even though third parties are not compelled to copy the source along with the object code.

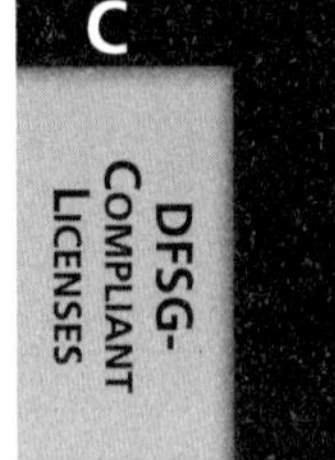

4. You may not copy, modify, sublicense, or distribute the Program except as expressly provided under this License. Any attempt otherwise to copy, modify, sublicense or distribute the Program is void, and will automatically terminate your rights under this License. However, parties who have received copies, or rights, from you under this License will not have their licenses terminated so long as such parties remain in full compliance.

5. You are not required to accept this License, since you have not signed it. However, nothing else grants you permission to modify or distribute the Program or its derivative works. These actions are prohibited by law if you do not accept this License. Therefore, by modifying or distributing the Program (or any work based on the Program), you indicate your acceptance of this License to do so, and all its terms and conditions for copying, distributing or modifying the Program or works based on it.

6. Each time you redistribute the Program (or any work based on the Program), the recipient automatically receives a license from the original licensor to copy, distribute or modify the Program subject to these terms and conditions. You may not impose any further restrictions on the recipients' exercise of the rights granted herein. You are not responsible for enforcing compliance by third parties to this License.

7. If, as a consequence of a court judgment or allegation of patent infringement or for any other reason (not limited to patent issues), conditions are imposed on you (whether by court order, agreement or otherwise) that contradict the conditions of this License, they do not excuse you from the conditions of this License. If you cannot distribute so as to satisfy simultaneously your obligations under this License and any other pertinent obligations, then as a consequence you may not distribute the Program at all. For example, if a patent license would not permit royalty-free redistribution of the Program by all those who receive copies directly or indirectly through you, then the only way you could satisfy both it and this License would be to refrain entirely from distribution of the Program.

   If any portion of this section is held invalid or unenforceable under any particular circumstance, the balance of the section is intended to apply and the section as a whole is intended to apply in other circumstances.

   It is not the purpose of this section to induce you to infringe any patents or other property right claims or to contest validity of any such claims; this section has the sole purpose of protecting the integrity of the free software distribution system, which is implemented by public license practices. Many people have made generous contributions to the wide range of software distributed through that system in reliance on consistent application of that system; it is up to the author/donor to decide if he or she is willing to distribute software through any other system and a licensee cannot impose that choice.

   This section is intended to make thoroughly clear what is believed to be a consequence of the rest of this License.

8. If the distribution and/or use of the Program is restricted in certain countries either by patents or by copyrighted interfaces, the original copyright holder who places the Program under this License may add an explicit geographical distribution limitation excluding those countries, so that distribution is permitted only in or among countries not thus excluded. In such case, this License incorporates the limitation as if written in the body of this License.

9. The Free Software Foundation may publish revised and/or new versions of the General Public License from time to time. Such new versions will be similar in spirit to the present version, but may differ in detail to address new problems or concerns.

   Each version is given a distinguishing version number. If the Program specifies a version number of this License which applies to it and "any later version", you have the option of following the terms and conditions either of that version or of any later version published by the Free Software Foundation. If the Program does not specify a version number of this License, you may choose any version ever published by the Free Software Foundation.

10. If you wish to incorporate parts of the Program into other free programs whose distribution conditions are different, write to the author to ask for permission. For software which is copyrighted by the Free Software Foundation, write to the Free Software Foundation; we sometimes make exceptions for this. Our decision will be guided by the two goals of preserving the free status of all derivatives of our free software and of promoting the sharing and reuse of software generally.

NO WARRANTY

11. BECAUSE THE PROGRAM IS LICENSED FREE OF CHARGE, THERE IS NO WARRANTY FOR THE PROGRAM, TO THE EXTENT PERMITTED BY APPLICABLE LAW. EXCEPT WHEN OTHERWISE STATED IN WRITING THE COPYRIGHT HOLDERS AND/OR OTHER PARTIES PROVIDE THE PROGRAM "AS IS" WITHOUT WARRANTY OF ANY KIND, EITHER EXPRESSED OR IMPLIED, INCLUDING, BUT NOT LIMITED TO, THE IMPLIED WARRANTIES OF MERCHANTABILITY AND FITNESS FOR A PARTICULAR PURPOSE. THE ENTIRE RISK AS TO THE QUALITY AND PERFORMANCE OF THE PROGRAM IS WITH YOU. SHOULD THE PROGRAM PROVE DEFECTIVE, YOU ASSUME THE COST OF ALL NECESSARY SERVICING, REPAIR OR CORRECTION.
12. IN NO EVENT UNLESS REQUIRED BY APPLICABLE LAW OR AGREED TO IN WRITING WILL ANY COPYRIGHT HOLDER, OR ANY OTHER PARTY WHO MAY MODIFY AND/OR REDISTRIBUTE THE PROGRAM AS PERMITTED ABOVE, BE LIABLE TO YOU FOR DAMAGES, INCLUDING ANY GENERAL, SPECIAL, INCIDENTAL OR CONSEQUENTIAL DAMAGES ARISING OUT OF THE USE OR INABILITY TO USE THE PROGRAM (INCLUDING BUT NOT LIMITED TO LOSS OF DATA OR DATA BEING RENDERED INACCURATE OR LOSSES SUSTAINED BY YOU OR THIRD PARTIES OR A FAILURE OF THE PROGRAM TO OPERATE WITH ANY OTHER PROGRAMS), EVEN IF SUCH HOLDER OR OTHER PARTY HAS BEEN ADVISED OF THE POSSIBILITY OF SUCH DAMAGES.

END OF TERMS AND CONDITIONS

How to Apply These Terms to Your New Programs

If you develop a new program, and you want it to be of the greatest possible use to the public, the best way to achieve this is to make it free software which everyone can redistribute and change under these terms.

To do so, attach the following notices to the program. It is safest to attach them to the start of each source file to most effectively convey the exclusion of warranty; and each file should have at least the "copyright" line and a pointer to where the full notice is found.

<one line to give the program's name and a brief idea of what it does.>
Copyright <year> <name of author>

This program is free software; you can redistribute it and/or modify it under the terms of the GNU General Public License as published by the Free Software Foundation; either version 2 of the License, or (at your option) any later version.

This program is distributed in the hope that it will be useful, but WITHOUT ANY WARRANTY; without even the implied warranty of MERCHANTABILITY or FITNESS FOR A PARTICULAR PURPOSE. See the GNU General Public License for more details.

You should have received a copy of the GNU General Public License along with this program; if not, write to the Free Software Foundation, Inc., 59 Temple Place, Suite 330, Boston, MA 02111-1307 USA

Also add information on how to contact you by electronic and paper mail.

If the program is interactive, make it output a short notice like this when it starts in an interactive mode:

Gnomovision version 69, Copyright 19yy name of author Gnomovision comes with ABSOLUTELY NO WARRANTY; for details type 'show w'. This is free software, and you are welcome to redistribute it under certain conditions; type 'show c' for details.

The hypothetical commands 'show w' and 'show c' should show the appropriate parts of the General Public License. Of course, the commands you use may be called something other than 'show w' and 'show c'; they could even be mouse-clicks or menu items—whatever suits your program.

You should also get your employer (if you work as a programmer) or your school, if any, to sign a "copyright disclaimer" for the program, if necessary. Here is a sample; alter the names:

Yoyodyne, Inc., hereby disclaims all copyright interest in the program `Gnomovision' (which makes passes at compilers) written by James Hacker.

<signature of Ty Coon>, 1 April 1989 Ty Coon, President of Vice

This General Public License does not permit incorporating your program into proprietary programs. If your program is a subroutine library, you may consider it more useful to permit linking proprietary applications with the library. If this is what you want to do, use the GNU Lesser General Public License instead of this License.

The GNU Lesser General Public License (LGPL)

GNU LESSER GENERAL PUBLIC LICENSE

Version 2.1, February 1999

[This is the first released version of the Lesser GPL. It also counts as the successor of the GNU Library Public License, version 2, hence the version number 2.1.]

Preamble

The licenses for most software are designed to take away your freedom to share and change it. By contrast, the GNU General Public Licenses are intended to guarantee your freedom to share and change free software—to make sure the software is free for all its users.

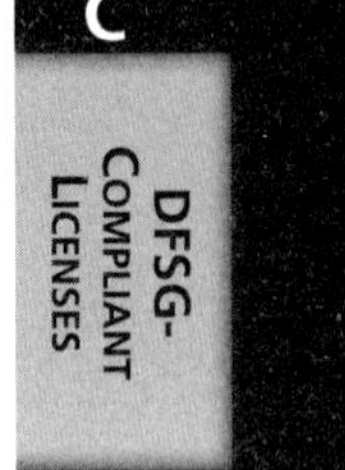

This license, the Lesser General Public License, applies to some specially designated software packages—typically libraries—of the Free Software Foundation and other authors who decide to use it. You can use it too, but we suggest you first think carefully about whether this license or the ordinary General Public License is the better strategy to use in any particular case, based on the explanations below.

When we speak of free software, we are referring to freedom of use, not price. Our General Public Licenses are designed to make sure that you have the freedom to distribute copies of free software (and charge for this service if you wish); that you receive source code or can get it if you want it; that you can change the software and use pieces of it in new free programs; and that you are informed that you can do these things.

To protect your rights, we need to make restrictions that forbid distributors to deny you these rights or to ask you to surrender these rights. These restrictions translate to certain responsibilities for you if you distribute copies of the library or if you modify it.

For example, if you distribute copies of the library, whether gratis or for a fee, you must give the recipients all the rights that we gave you. You must make sure that they, too, receive or can get the source code. If you link other code with the library, you must provide complete object files to the recipients, so that they can relink them with the library after making changes to the library and recompiling it. And you must show them these terms so they know their rights.

We protect your rights with a two-step method: (1) we copyright the library, and (2) we offer you this license, which gives you legal permission to copy, distribute and/or modify the library.

To protect each distributor, we want to make it very clear that there is no warranty for the free library. Also, if the library is modified by someone else and passed on, the recipients should know that what they have is not the original version, so that the original author's reputation will not be affected by problems that might be introduced by others.

Finally, software patents pose a constant threat to the existence of any free program. We wish to make sure that a company cannot effectively restrict the users of a free program by obtaining a restrictive license from a patent holder. Therefore, we insist that any patent license obtained for a version of the library must be consistent with the full freedom of use specified in this license.

Most GNU software, including some libraries, is covered by the ordinary GNU General Public License. This license, the GNU Lesser General Public License, applies to certain designated libraries, and is quite different from the ordinary General Public License. We use this license for certain libraries in order to permit linking those libraries into non-free programs.

When a program is linked with a library, whether statically or using a shared library, the combination of the two is legally speaking a combined work, a derivative of the original library. The ordinary General Public License therefore permits such linking only if the entire combination fits its criteria of freedom. The Lesser General Public License permits more lax criteria for linking other code with the library.

We call this license the "Lesser" General Public License because it does Less to protect the user's freedom than the ordinary General Public License. It also provides other free software developers Less of an advantage over competing non-free programs. These disadvantages are the reason we use the ordinary General Public License for many libraries. However, the Lesser license provides advantages in certain special circumstances.

For example, on rare occasions, there may be a special need to encourage the widest possible use of a certain library, so that it becomes a de-facto standard. To achieve this, non-free programs must be allowed to use the library. A more frequent case is that a free library does the same job as widely used non-free libraries. In this case, there is little to gain by limiting the free library to free software only, so we use the Lesser General Public License.

In other cases, permission to use a particular library in non-free programs enables a greater number of people to use a large body of free software. For example, permission to use the GNU C Library in non-free programs enables many more people to use the whole GNU operating system, as well as its variant, the GNU/Linux operating system.

Although the Lesser General Public License is Less protective of the users' freedom, it does ensure that the user of a program that is linked with the Library has the freedom and the wherewithal to run that program using a modified version of the Library.

The precise terms and conditions for copying, distribution and modification follow. Pay close attention to the difference between a "work based on the library" and a "work that uses the library". The former contains code derived from the library, whereas the latter must be combined with the library in order to run.

GNU LESSER GENERAL PUBLIC LICENSE TERMS AND CONDITIONS FOR COPYING, DISTRIBUTION AND MODIFICATION

0. This License Agreement applies to any software library or other program which contains a notice placed by the copyright holder or other authorized party saying it may be distributed under the terms of this Lesser General Public License (also called "this License"). Each licensee is addressed as "you".

   A "library" means a collection of software functions and/or data prepared so as to be conveniently linked with application programs (which use some of those functions and data) to form executables.

   The "Library", below, refers to any such software library or work which has been distributed under these terms. A "work based on the Library" means either the Library or any derivative work under copyright law: that is to say, a work containing the Library or a portion of it, either verbatim or with modifications and/or translated straightforwardly into another language. (Hereinafter, translation is included without limitation in the term "modification".)

   "Source code" for a work means the preferred form of the work for making modifications to it. For a library, complete source code means all the source code for all modules it contains, plus any associated interface definition files, plus the scripts used to control compilation and installation of the library.

   Activities other than copying, distribution and modification are not covered by this License; they are outside its scope. The act of running a program using the Library is not restricted, and output from such a program is covered only if its contents constitute a work based on the Library (independent of the use of the Library in a tool for writing it). Whether that is true depends on what the Library does and what the program that uses the Library does.

1. You may copy and distribute verbatim copies of the Library's complete source code as you receive it, in any medium, provided that you conspicuously and appropriately publish on each copy an appropriate copyright notice and disclaimer of warranty; keep intact all the notices that refer to this License and to the absence of any warranty; and distribute a copy of this License along with the Library.

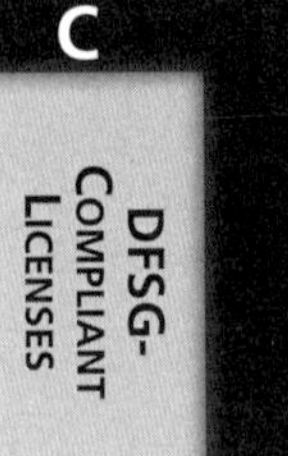

You may charge a fee for the physical act of transferring a copy, and you may at your option offer warranty protection in exchange for a fee.

2. You may modify your copy or copies of the Library or any portion of it, thus forming a work based on the Library, and copy and distribute such modifications or work under the terms of Section 1 above, provided that you also meet all of these conditions:

    a. The modified work must itself be a software library.

    b. You must cause the files modified to carry prominent notices stating that you changed the files and the date of any change.

    c. You must cause the whole of the work to be licensed at no charge to all third parties under the terms of this License.

    d. If a facility in the modified Library refers to a function or a table of data to be supplied by an application program that uses the facility, other than as an argument passed when the facility is invoked, then you must make a good faith effort to ensure that, in the event an application does not supply such function or table, the facility still operates, and performs whatever part of its purpose remains meaningful.

    (For example, a function in a library to compute square roots has a purpose that is entirely well-defined independent of the application. Therefore, Subsection 2d requires that any application-supplied function or table used by this function must be optional: if the application does not supply it, the square root function must still compute square roots.)

    These requirements apply to the modified work as a whole. If identifiable sections of that work are not derived from the Library, and can be reasonably considered independent and separate works in themselves, then this License, and its terms, do not apply to those sections when you distribute them as separate works. But when you distribute the same sections as part of a whole which is a work based on the Library, the distribution of the whole must be on the terms of this License, whose permissions for other licensees extend to the entire whole, and thus to each and every part regardless of who wrote it.

    Thus, it is not the intent of this section to claim rights or contest your rights to work written entirely by you; rather, the intent is to exercise the right to control the distribution of derivative or collective works based on the Library.

    In addition, mere aggregation of another work not based on the Library with the Library (or with a work based on the Library) on a volume of a storage or distribution medium does not bring the other work under the scope of this License.

3. You may opt to apply the terms of the ordinary GNU General Public License instead of this License to a given copy of the Library. To do this, you must alter all the notices that refer to this License, so that they refer to the ordinary GNU General Public License, version 2, instead of to this License. (If a newer version than version 2 of the ordinary GNU General Public License has appeared, then you can specify that version instead if you wish.) Do not make any other change in these notices.

   Once this change is made in a given copy, it is irreversible for that copy, so the ordinary GNU General Public License applies to all subsequent copies and derivative works made from that copy.

   This option is useful when you wish to copy part of the code of the Library into a program that is not a library.

4. You may copy and distribute the Library (or a portion or derivative of it, under Section 2) in object code or executable form under the terms of Sections 1 and 2 above provided that you accompany it with the complete corresponding machine-readable source code, which must be distributed under the terms of Sections 1 and 2 above on a medium customarily used for software interchange.

   If distribution of object code is made by offering access to copy from a designated place, then offering equivalent access to copy the source code from the same place satisfies the requirement to distribute the source code, even though third parties are not compelled to copy the source along with the object code.

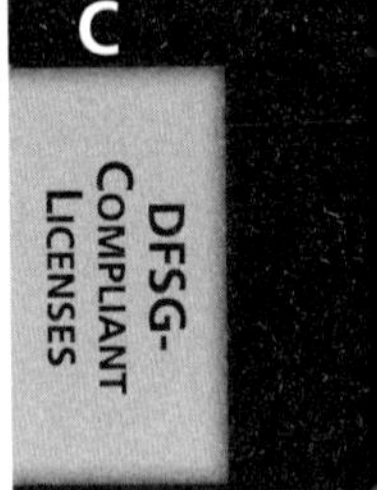

5. A program that contains no derivative of any portion of the Library, but is designed to work with the Library by being compiled or linked with it, is called a "work that uses the Library". Such a work, in isolation, is not a derivative work of the Library, and therefore falls outside the scope of this License.

   However, linking a "work that uses the Library" with the Library creates an executable that is a derivative of the Library (because it contains portions of the Library), rather than a "work that uses the library". The executable is therefore covered by this License. Section 6 states terms for distribution of such executables.

   When a "work that uses the Library" uses material from a header file that is part of the Library, the object code for the work may be a derivative work of the Library even though the source code is not. Whether this is true is especially significant if the work can be linked without the Library, or if the work is itself a library. The threshold for this to be true is not precisely defined by law.

   If such an object file uses only numerical parameters, data structure layouts and accessors, and small macros and small inline functions (ten lines or less in length), then the use of the object file is unrestricted, regardless of whether it is legally a derivative work. (Executables containing this object code plus portions of the Library will still fall under Section 6.)

Otherwise, if the work is a derivative of the Library, you may distribute the object code for the work under the terms of Section 6. Any executables containing that work also fall under Section 6, whether or not they are linked directly with the Library itself.

6. As an exception to the Sections above, you may also combine or link a "work that uses the Library" with the Library to produce a work containing portions of the Library, and distribute that work under terms of your choice, provided that the terms permit modification of the work for the customer's own use and reverse engineering for debugging such modifications.

   You must give prominent notice with each copy of the work that the Library is used in it and that the Library and its use are covered by this License. You must supply a copy of this License. If the work during execution displays copyright notices, you must include the copyright notice for the Library among them, as well as a reference directing the user to the copy of this License. Also, you must do one of these things:

   a. Accompany the work with the complete corresponding machine-readable source code for the Library including whatever changes were used in the work (which must be distributed under Sections 1 and 2 above); and, if the work is an executable linked with the Library, with the complete machine-readable "work that uses the Library", as object code and/or source code, so that the user can modify the Library and then relink to produce a modified executable containing the modified Library. (It is understood that the user who changes the contents of definitions files in the Library will not necessarily be able to recompile the application to use the modified definitions.)

   b. Use a suitable shared library mechanism for linking with the Library. A suitable mechanism is one that (1) uses at run time a copy of the library already present on the user's computer system, rather than copying library functions into the executable, and (2) will operate properly with a modified version of the library, if the user installs one, as long as the modified version is interface-compatible with the version that the work was made with.

   c. Accompany the work with a written offer, valid for at least three years, to give the same user the materials specified in Subsection 6a, above, for a charge no more than the cost of performing this distribution.

   d. If distribution of the work is made by offering access to copy from a designated place, offer equivalent access to copy the above specified materials from the same place.

   e. Verify that the user has already received a copy of these materials or that you have already sent this user a copy.

For an executable, the required form of the "work that uses the Library" must include any data and utility programs needed for reproducing the executable from it. However, as a special exception, the materials to be distributed need not include anything that is normally distributed (in either source or binary form) with the major components (compiler, kernel, and so on) of the operating system on which the executable runs, unless that component itself accompanies the executable.

It may happen that this requirement contradicts the license restrictions of other proprietary libraries that do not normally accompany the operating system. Such a contradiction means you cannot use both them and the Library together in an executable that you distribute.

7. You may place library facilities that are a work based on the Library side-by-side in a single library together with other library facilities not covered by this License, and distribute such a combined library, provided that the separate distribution of the work based on the Library and of the other library facilities is otherwise permitted, and provided that you do these two things:
    a. Accompany the combined library with a copy of the same work based on the Library, uncombined with any other library facilities. This must be distributed under the terms of the Sections above.
    b. Give prominent notice with the combined library of the fact that part of it is a work based on the Library, and explaining where to find the accompanying uncombined form of the same work.

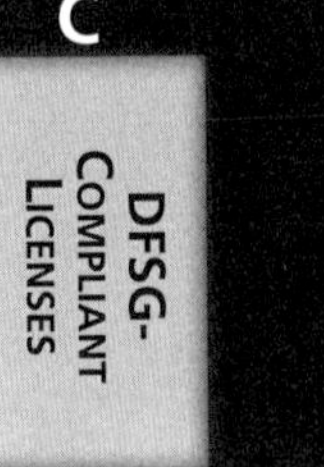

8. You may not copy, modify, sublicense, link with, or distribute the Library except as expressly provided under this License. Any attempt otherwise to copy, modify, sublicense, link with, or distribute the Library is void, and will automatically terminate your rights under this License. However, parties who have received copies, or rights, from you under this License will not have their licenses terminated so long as such parties remain in full compliance.
9. You are not required to accept this License, since you have not signed it. However, nothing else grants you permission to modify or distribute the Library or its derivative works. These actions are prohibited by law if you do not accept this License. Therefore, by modifying or distributing the Library (or any work based on the Library), you indicate your acceptance of this License to do so, and all its terms and conditions for copying, distributing or modifying the Library or works based on it.
10. Each time you redistribute the Library (or any work based on the Library), the recipient automatically receives a license from the original licensor to copy, distribute, link with or modify the Library subject to these terms and conditions. You may not impose any further restrictions on the recipients' exercise of the rights granted herein. You are not responsible for enforcing compliance by third parties with this License.

11. If, as a consequence of a court judgment or allegation of patent infringement or for any other reason (not limited to patent issues), conditions are imposed on you (whether by court order, agreement or otherwise) that contradict the conditions of this License, they do not excuse you from the conditions of this License. If you cannot distribute so as to satisfy simultaneously your obligations under this License and any other pertinent obligations, then as a consequence you may not distribute the Library at all. For example, if a patent license would not permit royalty-free redistribution of the Library by all those who receive copies directly or indirectly through you, then the only way you could satisfy both it and this License would be to refrain entirely from distribution of the Library.

    If any portion of this section is held invalid or unenforceable under any particular circumstance, the balance of the section is intended to apply, and the section as a whole is intended to apply in other circumstances.

    It is not the purpose of this section to induce you to infringe any patents or other property right claims or to contest validity of any such claims; this section has the sole purpose of protecting the integrity of the free software distribution system which is implemented by public license practices. Many people have made generous contributions to the wide range of software distributed through that system in reliance on consistent application of that system; it is up to the author/donor to decide if he or she is willing to distribute software through any other system and a licensee cannot impose that choice.

    This section is intended to make thoroughly clear what is believed to be a consequence of the rest of this License.

12. If the distribution and/or use of the Library is restricted in certain countries either by patents or by copyrighted interfaces, the original copyright holder who places the Library under this License may add an explicit geographical distribution limitation excluding those countries, so that distribution is permitted only in or among countries not thus excluded. In such case, this License incorporates the limitation as if written in the body of this License.

13. The Free Software Foundation may publish revised and/or new versions of the Lesser General Public License from time to time. Such new versions will be similar in spirit to the present version, but may differ in detail to address new problems or concerns.

    Each version is given a distinguishing version number. If the Library specifies a version number of this License which applies to it and "any later version", you have the option of following the terms and conditions either of that version or of any later version published by the Free Software Foundation. If the Library does not specify a license version number, you may choose any version ever published by the Free Software Foundation.

14. If you wish to incorporate parts of the Library into other free programs whose distribution conditions are incompatible with these, write to the author to ask for permission. For software which is copyrighted by the Free Software Foundation, write to the Free Software Foundation; we sometimes make exceptions for this. Our decision will be guided by the two goals of preserving the free status of all derivatives of our free software and of promoting the sharing and reuse of software generally.

NO WARRANTY

15. BECAUSE THE LIBRARY IS LICENSED FREE OF CHARGE, THERE IS NO WARRANTY FOR THE LIBRARY, TO THE EXTENT PERMITTED BY APPLICABLE LAW. EXCEPT WHEN OTHERWISE STATED IN WRITING THE COPYRIGHT HOLDERS AND/OR OTHER PARTIES PROVIDE THE LIBRARY "AS IS" WITHOUT WARRANTY OF ANY KIND, EITHER EXPRESSED OR IMPLIED, INCLUDING, BUT NOT LIMITED TO, THE IMPLIED WARRANTIES OF MERCHANTABILITY AND FITNESS FOR A PARTICULAR PURPOSE. THE ENTIRE RISK AS TO THE QUALITY AND PERFORMANCE OF THE LIBRARY IS WITH YOU. SHOULD THE LIBRARY PROVE DEFECTIVE, YOU ASSUME THE COST OF ALL NECESSARY SERVICING, REPAIR OR CORRECTION.

16. IN NO EVENT UNLESS REQUIRED BY APPLICABLE LAW OR AGREED TO IN WRITING WILL ANY COPYRIGHT HOLDER, OR ANY OTHER PARTY WHO MAY MODIFY AND/OR REDISTRIBUTE THE LIBRARY AS PERMITTED ABOVE, BE LIABLE TO YOU FOR DAMAGES, INCLUDING ANY GENERAL, SPECIAL, INCIDENTAL OR CONSEQUENTIAL DAMAGES ARISING OUT OF THE USE OR INABILITY TO USE THE LIBRARY (INCLUDING BUT NOT LIMITED TO LOSS OF DATA OR DATA BEING RENDERED INACCURATE OR LOSSES SUSTAINED BY YOU OR THIRD PARTIES OR A FAILURE OF THE LIBRARY TO OPERATE WITH ANY OTHER SOFTWARE), EVEN IF SUCH HOLDER OR OTHER PARTY HAS BEEN ADVISED OF THE POSSIBILITY OF SUCH DAMAGES.

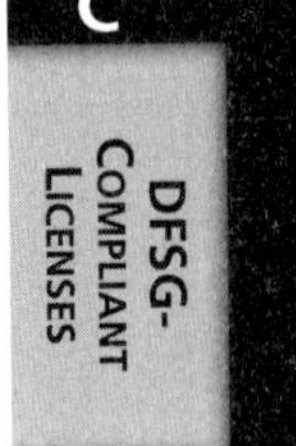

END OF TERMS AND CONDITIONS

How to Apply These Terms to Your New Libraries

If you develop a new library, and you want it to be of the greatest possible use to the public, we recommend making it free software that everyone can redistribute and change. You can do so by permitting redistribution under these terms (or, alternatively, under the terms of the ordinary General Public License).

To apply these terms, attach the following notices to the library. It is safest to attach them to the start of each source file to most effectively convey the exclusion of warranty; and each file should have at least the "copyright" line and a pointer to where the full notice is found.

<one line to give the library's name and a brief idea of what it does.>
Copyright <year> <name of author>

This library is free software; you can redistribute it and/or modify it under the terms of the GNU Lesser General Public License as published by the Free Software Foundation; either version 2 of the License, or (at your option) any later version.

This library is distributed in the hope that it will be useful, but WITHOUT ANY WARRANTY; without even the implied warranty of MERCHANTABILITY or FITNESS FOR A PARTICULAR PURPOSE. See the GNU Lesser General Public License for more details.

You should have received a copy of the GNU Lesser General Public License along with this library; if not, write to the Free Software Foundation, Inc., 59 Temple Place, Suite 330, Boston, MA 02111-1307 USA

Also add information on how to contact you by electronic and paper mail.

You should also get your employer (if you work as a programmer) or your school, if any, to sign a "copyright disclaimer" for the library, if necessary. Here is a sample; alter the names:

Yoyodyne, Inc., hereby disclaims all copyright interest in the library 'Frob' (a library for tweaking knobs) written by James Random Hacker.

<signature of Ty Coon>, 1 April 1990 Ty Coon, President of Vice

That's all there is to it!

The BSD License

Copyright © 1998, Regents of the University of California. All rights reserved.

Redistribution and use in source and binary forms, with or without modification, are permitted provided that the following conditions are met:

- Redistributions of source code must retain the above copyright notice, this list of conditions and the following disclaimer.
- Redistributions in binary form must reproduce the above copyright notice, this list of conditions and the following disclaimer in the documentation and/or other materials provided with the distribution.
- All advertising materials mentioning features or use of this software must display the following acknowledgement:

    This product includes software developed by the University of California, Berkeley and its contributors.

- Neither name of the University nor the names of its contributors may be used to endorse or promote products derived from this software without specific prior written permission.

THIS SOFTWARE IS PROVIDED BY THE REGENTS AND CONTRIBUTORS "AS IS" AND ANY EXPRESS OR IMPLIED WARRANTIES, INCLUDING, BUT NOT LIMITED TO, THE IMPLIED WARRANTIES OF MERCHANTABILITY AND FITNESS FOR A PARTICULAR PURPOSE ARE DISCLAIMED. IN NO EVENT SHALL THE REGENTS OR CONTRIBUTORS BE LIABLE FOR ANY DIRECT, INDIRECT, INCIDENTAL, SPECIAL, EXEMPLARY, OR CONSEQUENTIAL DAMAGES (INCLUDING, BUT NOT LIMITED TO, PROCUREMENT OF SUBSTITUTE GOODS OR SERVICES; LOSS OF USE, DATA, OR PROFITS; OR BUSINESS INTERRUPTION) HOWEVER CAUSED AND ON ANY THEORY OF LIABILITY, WHETHER IN CONTRACT, STRICT LIABILITY, OR TORT (INCLUDING NEGLIGENCE OR OTHERWISE) ARISING IN ANY WAY OUT OF THE USE OF THIS SOFTWARE, EVEN IF ADVISED OF THE POSSIBILITY OF SUCH DAMAGE.

Open-Source Licenses

by Aaron Von Cowenberghe

What Exactly Is Open-Source Software?

What is open-source software? Believe it or not, there are a few very distinct camps that take very well-rationalized stances on this issue. Some of these groups engage in bloody flamefests with one another over the slightest difference.

However, notwithstanding all this internal bickering, the open software community has agreed on a few basic tenets that make up *open source*. The community allows the term *open source* to be applied only to any software that is free, redistributable, and modifiable, and which comes with fully disclosed source code.

To a lawyer, this may appear to be a foggy definition for such a huge, unregulated community of volunteers. Over the years, this vague popular definition has led to the creation of a gamut of software licenses, all of them different in subtle yet significant ways.

A few years ago, the term *open source* had not even been coined yet. To refer to this idea that developers had in common, the term *free software* was being used. However, this term was greatly misleading, because other software that could be called free was widely available on the Internet—consider shareware sites such as `www.download.com`.

It was decided that in order to secure the movement's integrity, a new term was needed to describe it. There was no way anybody could keep businesses from calling closed-source (or proprietary) applications *free*. Free software, much of which was proprietary despite being provided at no cost, was already too widely spread to try to regulate.

SPI Versus OSI—The Open-Source Trademark

In response to this dilemma, Eric S. Raymond coined the term *open source* and registered the domain `www.opensource.org`, where he posted his Open Source Definition. This was the first major attempt at a unified description of this movement to the world.

When Debian anticipated the misuse of this term, Software in the Public Interest (SPI), Debian's legal group, put in an application to trademark it. The person who originally made this move left Debian (and SPI) abruptly, leaving SPI with questions as to what should be done with the trademark if it were obtained.

After much deliberation, management of the trademark (should it eventually be obtained) was ceded to Eric S. Raymond (henceforth referred to as ESR), because he seemed to represent the interests of the community. In addition, because he had coined the term in the first place, it seemed the most reasonable thing to do to give him control of its trademark.

During this time, Raymond began an organization that is known today as OSI, the Open Source Initiative. This is an organization of individuals that's very similar to SPI in its mission, which is to guard and direct the interests of the open-source community at large. Both OSI and SPI act as police, their sole purpose being to see the open-source movement proceed into the next century with its rights intact, unfettered by external commercial interests that might seek to exploit the work of others.

However, two groups with such different backgrounds are bound to disagree on at least a few basic points. Both groups' attempts at describing the whole will of a community so large have predictably alienated some of its members. More notably, SPI and OSI disagree on some substantial points.

Not only do they disagree doctrinally on some (usually minor) issues, OSI and SPI each consider themselves to have more legal right to the final say in any dispute. OSI makes this claim on the notion that Raymond coined the term *open source,* SPI on the circumstances that give them most immediate claim to the trademark.

Realistically, both SPI and OSI are working to the same common goal: the furtherance of open source to the point where the majority of software is not only free, but open. In order to see progress in this area, a clear message must be sent to the world outlining exactly what open source *is,* and this concept must be guarded faithfully. Both of these groups have altruistically stepped up to this challenge, and both have the same goal. However, each sees mistakes the other has made and is reluctant to let control slip from its grasp, for fear that the goal will be undermined.

The only reason any of this has been a problem stems from commercial interest in open-source software. No business can comprehend a pool of individuals working for free to produce a superior product—much less one where the number of available developers is directly correlated to the size of the Internet. Many corporations would like to tap into this market and exploit the good will of these visionary individuals.

Usually, this is done by sly wording in software licenses. A company may, for example, open source to a product, but by shrewd licensing claim all ownership of any changes made to the source. Any such licensing identifies the software as definitely not open source; instead of nurturing the community (which is the spirit of the open-source movement), it blatantly takes advantage of developers.

The DFSG and the OSD

In a community that incurs zero costs and brings in zero income, this kind of weakness is unavoidable. In addition, with all the new open-source licenses being written and published by rich corporations (mostly to attract attention), it's difficult to tell which projects are legitimate and which aren't. The language used in some of these is so obfuscating as to demand the presence of a lawyer for accurate interpretation.

This is where SPI and OSI come in. These two have come to be known as the guardians of open-source standards, applauding those licensing schemes that uphold them and disowning those that are lined with traps.

Both SPI and OSI have very basic sets of criteria for deciding whether a license is open source, and both are written in plain English. So, if you use a software package that's under a license condoned by either one of these groups, you can be certain of what you're getting. Just read OSI's Open Source Definition (OSD) and SPI's Debian Free Software Guidelines (DFSG) below.

When looking over the OSD and the DFSG, take note of the fact that they are identical except for a few specific points (which are outlined in the OSD).

The Open-Source Definition

The text of the Open Source Definition is taken directly from the Open Source Web site at `http://www.opensource.org/osd.html`.

Open source doesn't just mean access to the source code. The distribution terms of open-source software must comply with the following criteria:

1. Free Redistribution

   The license may not restrict any party from selling or giving away the software as a component of an aggregate software distribution containing programs from several different sources. The license may not require a royalty or other fee for such sale.

2. Source Code

   The program must include source code, and must allow distribution in source code as well as compiled form. Where some form of a product is not distributed with source code, there must be a well-publicized means of obtaining the source code for no more than a reasonable reproduction cost—preferably, downloading via the Internet without charge. The source code must be the preferred form in which a programmer would modify the program. Deliberately obfuscated source code is not allowed. Intermediate forms such as the output of a preprocessor or translator are not allowed.

3. Derived Works

   The license must allow modifications and derived works, and must allow them to be distributed under the same terms as the license of the original software.

4. Integrity of The Author's Source Code.

   The license may restrict source-code from being distributed in modified form only if the license allows the distribution of "patch files" with the source code for the purpose of modifying the program at build time. The license must explicitly permit distribution of software built from modified source code. The license may require derived works to carry a different name or version number from the original software.

5. No Discrimination Against Persons or Groups.

   The license must not discriminate against any person or group of persons.

6. No Discrimination Against Fields of Endeavor.

   The license must not restrict anyone from making use of the program in a specific field of endeavor. For example, it may not restrict the program from being used in a business, or from being used for genetic research.

7. Distribution of License.

   The rights attached to the program must apply to all to whom the program is redistributed without the need for execution of an additional license by those parties.

8. License Must Not Be Specific to a Product.

   The rights attached to the program must not depend on the program's being part of a particular software distribution. If the program is extracted from that distribution and used or distributed within the terms of the program's license, all parties to whom the program is redistributed should have the same rights as those that are granted in conjunction with the original software distribution.

9. License Must Not Contaminate Other Software.

   The license must not place restrictions on other software that is distributed along with the licensed software. For example, the license must not insist that all other programs distributed on the same medium must be open-source software.

Conformance

(This section is not part of the Open Source Definition.)

We think the Open Source Definition captures what the great majority of the software community originally meant, and still mean, by the term "Open Source." However, the term has become widely used and its meaning has lost some precision. The OSI Certified mark is OSI's way of certifying that the license under which the software is distributed conforms to the OSD; the generic term "Open Source" cannot provide that assurance, but we still encourage use of the term "Open Source" to mean conformance to the OSD. For information about the OSI Certified mark, and for a list of licenses that OSI has approved as conforming to the OSD, see this page.

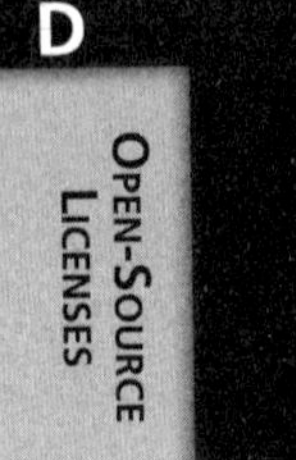

Change history:

1.0—Identical to DFSG, except for addition of MPL and QPL to clause 10.

1.1—Added LGPL to clause 10.

1.2—Added public-domain to clause 10.

1.3—Retitled clause 10 and split off the license list, adding material on procedures.

1.4—Now explicit about source code requirement for PD software.

1.5—Allow "reasonable reproduction cost" to meet GPL terms.

1.6—Edited section 10; this material has moved.

1.7—Section 10 replaced with new "Conformance" section.

Bruce Perens wrote the first draft of this document as "The Debian Free Software Guidelines," and refined it using the comments of the Debian developers in a month-long e-mail conference in June, 1997. He removed the Debian-specific references from the document to create the "Open Source Definition."

The Debian Social Contract (DFSG Included)

The text of the Debian Social Contract and Debian Free Software Guidelines is taken directly from the Debian Web site at `http://www.debian.org/social_contract`.

"Social Contract" with the Free Software Community

1. Debian Will Remain 100% Free Software

   We promise to keep the Debian GNU/Linux Distribution entirely free software. As there are many definitions of free software, we include the guidelines we use to determine if software is "free" below. We will support our users who develop and run non-free software on Debian, but we will never make the system depend on an item of non-free software.

2. We Will Give Back to the Free Software Community

   When we write new components of the Debian system, we will license them as free software. We will make the best system we can, so that free software will be widely distributed and used. We will feed back bug-fixes, improvements, user requests, etc. to the "*upstream*" authors of software included in our system.

3. We Won't Hide Problems

   We will keep our entire bug-report database open for public view at all times. Reports that users file online will immediately become visible to others.

4. Our Priorities Are Our Users and Free Software

   We will be guided by the needs of our users and the free-software community. We will place their interests first in our priorities. We will support the needs of our users for operation in many different kinds of computing environment. We won't object to commercial software that is intended to run on Debian systems, and we'll allow others to create value-added distributions containing both Debian and commercial software, without any fee from us. To support these goals, we will provide an integrated system of high-quality, 100% free software, with no legal restrictions that would prevent these kinds of use.

5. Programs That Don't Meet Our Free-Software Standards

   We acknowledge that some of our users require the use of programs that don't conform to the Debian Free Software Guidelines. We have created "contrib" and "non-free" areas in our FTP archive for this software. The software in these directories is not part of the Debian system, although it has been configured for use with Debian. We encourage CD manufacturers to read the licenses of software packages in these directories and determine if they can distribute that software on their CDs. Thus, although non-free software isn't a part of Debian, we support its use, and we provide infrastructure (such as our bug-tracking system and mailing lists) for non-free software packages.

The Debian Free Software Guidelines

1. Free Redistribution

   The license of a Debian component may not restrict any party from selling or giving away the software as a component of an aggregate software distribution containing programs from several different sources. The license may not require a royalty or other fee for such sale.

2. Source Code

   The program must include source code, and must allow distribution in source code as well as compiled form.

3. Derived Works

   The license must allow modifications and derived works, and must allow them to be distributed under the same terms as the license of the original software.

4. Integrity of The Author's Source Code

   The license may restrict source-code from being distributed in modified form-_only_if the license allows the distribution of "patch files" with the source code for the purpose of modifying the program at build time. The license must explicitly permit distribution of software built from modified source code. The license may require derived works to carry a different name or version number from the original software. (*This is a compromise. The Debian group encourages all authors to not restrict any files, source or binary, from being modified.*)

5. No Discrimination Against Persons or Groups

   The license must not discriminate against any person or group of persons.

6. No Discrimination Against Fields of Endeavor

   The license must not restrict anyone from making use of the program in a specific field of endeavor. For example, it may not restrict the program from being used in a business, or from being used for genetic research.

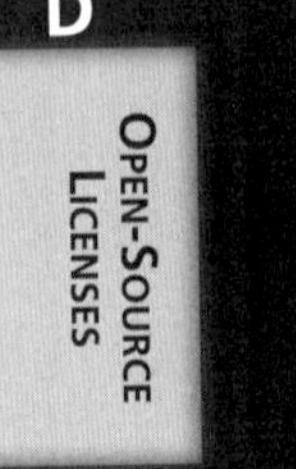

7. Distribution of License

   The rights attached to the program must apply to all to whom the program is redistributed without the need for execution of an additional license by those parties.

8. License Must Not Be Specific to Debian

   The rights attached to the program must not depend on the program's being part of a Debian system. If the program is extracted from Debian and used or distributed without Debian but otherwise within the terms of the program's license, all parties to whom the program is redistributed should have the same rights as those that are granted in conjunction with the Debian system.

9. License Must Not Contaminate Other Software

   The license must not place restrictions on other software that is distributed along with the licensed software. For example, the license must not insist that all other programs distributed on the same medium must be free software.

10. Example Licenses

    The "GPL", "BSD", and "Artistic" licenses are examples of licenses that we consider *"free."*

Bruce Perens wrote the first draft of this document and refined it using the comments of the Debian developers during a month-long e-mail conference in June 1997. He later removed the Debian-specific references from the Debian Free Software Guidelines to create "The Open Source Definition."

Other organizations may derive from and build on this document. Please give credit to the Debian project if you do.

Important Issues: Interpreting Software Licenses

Both the DFSG and the OSD lay out exactly what important pieces of information you should look for when evaluating a software license. Examining these terms could save you a great deal of time in the future:

1. Does the license allow redistribution?
2. Is use of the software restricted in any way?
3. Are you granted full source code?
4. Are you allowed to make and distribute modifications?
5. Does the license affect any other part of your system?
6. Is the integrity of the project retained? If not, it is not being paranoid to expect to see the project hijacked in the future.

Please keep in mind that not every license is listed here. Such a document would be well over a hundred pages long. Notable licenses that have been accepted by the community for ages are printed in their entirety and discussed in the following sections. Afterward, a few examples of more questionable commercial open-source licenses are presented briefly, along with the issues each presents.

The three licenses that are reviewed here are those that have gained the official sanction of Debian.

GNU GPL

The GNU General Public License (GPL) is by far the most widely recognized open-source license. After Richard Stallman played one of the greatest parts in beginning the open-source movement, he recognized how easily exploitable open-source code is. If not every situation is considered in the development of an open-source license agreement, business can often hijack projects covered by it. With this in mind, a lawyer friend of Stallman's was given the task of coming up with a license that would protect the integrity of open source but still grant the community as many rights as possible. The GPL was the result.

The GPL was the pioneer of a new concept, which came to be known as *copyleft*. When a piece of code is under GPL, all future revisions must be GPL. This limits somebody's right to step in, make a few modifications to a program, and sell it as his or her own.

There are a few long-standing problems with GPL. First and foremost, you cannot link any non-redistributable work to a GPL library. For example, if *X* were GPL, nobody could sell a program for *X* without fully disclosing and granting all rights to its source. This definitely would make *X* an unusable environment for commercial software development. Because of this trait, it has been criticized for being "insidious." That is, the GPL is fairly exclusive to itself and attempts to extinguish any other type of licensing from any system where most software is covered by it. In other words, the GNU GPL tries to weaken commercial software's rights to exist on a GNU-based system (which Linux is).

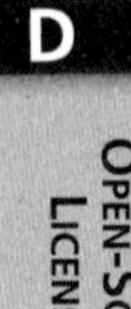

However, these provisions were made with good intention, knowing that GPL wouldn't be fully suited to every piece of software. All in all, anything released under GPL is completely open and will remain open for up to three years (read the GPL for further details). This is the essence of both the OSD and the DFSG; for being a pioneer, GPL is owed a great debt of gratitude.

GNU LGPL

The GNU Lesser GPL (LPGL), known previously as the Library GPL, although aiming to retain the integrity of free software projects like the GPL, is different in a few subtle ways.

The major difference lies in GPL's banishment of proprietary software products. Specifically, a library under LGPL can be linked into any type of software, as long as the library's code remains free and unfettered.

This allows proprietary software to operate in a free environment but still does not allow the free environment to be hijacked.

BSD

The BSD license is fairly short and to the point. Its wording is a bit more intuitive than that of the GPLs and the artistic license (see next section). No restrictions at all are placed on the code's redistribution, modification, and so forth.

As opposed to the GPL, the BSD license specifically allows what I have previously called hijacking. GPL supporters call this a weakness of BSD and a strength of GPL; many on the other side of the fence declare the exact opposite.

Artistic

The artistic license gives everybody a great deal of freedom in dealing with a piece of software and its source. Like the GPL and LGPL, it expressly demands that source be made available (but only if binaries you're distributing are built from source with modifications) and allows modification.

However, the artistic license is much friendlier to the commercial world than are GPL and friends (which tend to pollute one another, as described earlier). Any code under the artistic license can be used in a commercial project.

If a library under artistic is linked into a commercial product, that product can be distributed with the library and sold, as long as the distributor of said project doesn't claim the library as his or her own work. In other words, if you're going to be selling a program that needs to link against an artistic library, you can distribute both and charge for your product, as long as you give credit to the original author of your artistic support library.

Proprietary changes to artistic codebases are explicitly allowed by the license. However, if you choose to not release code to your changes, you can't distribute binaries with them—they must be used only within your organization. This is a move to protect artistic projects from being hijacked; if this clause didn't exist, any corporation could capitalize on the effort that went into an open-source project.

Finally, the artistic license explicitly discusses program output. In many scenarios, program output is deemed a *derived work*; under this license, ownership of any program output is explicitly given to the person who generated it.

Full Text

The artistic license is taken directly from
`http://language.perl.com/misc/Artistic.html`.

Preamble

The intent of this document is to state the conditions under which a Package may be copied, such that the Copyright Holder maintains some semblance of artistic control over the development of the package, while giving the users of the package the right to use and distribute the Package in a more-or-less customary fashion, plus the right to make reasonable modifications.

Definitions

"Package" refers to the collection of files distributed by the Copyright Holder, and derivatives of that collection of files created through textual modification.

"Standard Version" refers to such a Package if it has not been modified, or has been modified in accordance with the wishes of the Copyright Holder as specified below.

"Copyright Holder" is whoever is named in the copyright or copyrights for the package.

"You" is you, if you're thinking about copying or distributing this Package.

"Reasonable copying fee" is whatever you can justify on the basis of media cost, duplication charges, time of people involved, and so on. (You will not be required to justify it to the Copyright Holder, but only to the computing community at large as a market that must bear the fee.)

"Freely Available" means that no fee is charged for the item itself, though there may be fees involved in handling the item. It also means that recipients of the item may redistribute it under the same conditions they received it.

1. You may make and give away verbatim copies of the source form of the Standard Version of this Package without restriction, provided that you duplicate all of the original copyright notices and associated disclaimers.
2. You may apply bug fixes, portability fixes and other modifications derived from the Public Domain or from the Copyright Holder. A Package modified in such a way shall still be considered the Standard Version.
3. You may otherwise modify your copy of this Package in any way, provided that you insert a prominent notice in each changed file stating how and when you changed that file, and provided that you do at least ONE of the following:
    a. place your modifications in the Public Domain or otherwise make them Freely Available, such as by posting said modifications to Usenet or an equivalent medium, or placing the modifications on a major archive site such

as uunet.uu.net, or by allowing the Copyright Holder to include your modifications in the Standard Version of the Package.

b. use the modified Package only within your corporation or organization.

c. rename any non-standard executables so the names do not conflict with standard executables, which must also be provided, and provide a separate manual page for each non-standard executable that clearly documents how it differs from the Standard Version.

d. make other distribution arrangements with the Copyright Holder.

4. You may distribute the programs of this Package in object code or executable form, provided that you do at least ONE of the following:

   a. distribute a Standard Version of the executables and library files, together with instructions (in the manual page or equivalent) on where to get the Standard Version.

   b. accompany the distribution with the machine-readable source of the Package with your modifications.

   c. give non-standard executables non-standard names, and clearly document the differences in manual pages (or equivalent), together with instructions on where to get the Standard Version.

   d. make other distribution arrangements with the Copyright Holder.

5. You may charge a reasonable copying fee for any distribution of this Package. You may charge any fee you choose for support of this Package. You may not charge a fee for this Package itself. However, you may distribute this Package in aggregate with other (possibly commercial) programs as part of a larger (possibly commercial) software distribution provided that you do not advertise this Package as a product of your own. You may embed this Package's interpreter within an executable of yours (by linking); this shall be construed as a mere form of aggregation, provided that the complete Standard Version of the interpreter is so embedded.

6. The scripts and library files supplied as input to or produced as output from the programs of this Package do not automatically fall under the copyright of this Package, but belong to whomever generated them, and may be sold commercially, and may be aggregated with this Package. If such scripts or library files are aggregated with this Package via the so-called "undump" or "unexec" methods of producing a binary executable image, then distribution of such an image shall neither be construed as a distribution of this Package nor shall it fall under the restrictions of Paragraphs 3 and 4, provided that you do not represent such an executable image as a Standard Version of this Package.

7. C subroutines (or comparably compiled subroutines in other languages) supplied by you and linked into this Package in order to emulate subroutines and variables of the language defined by this Package shall not be considered part of this Package, but are the equivalent of input as in Paragraph 6, provided these subroutines do not change the language in any way that would cause it to fail the regression tests for the language.
8. Aggregation of this Package with a commercial distribution is always permitted provided that the use of this Package is embedded; that is, when no overt attempt is made to make this Package's interfaces visible to the end user of the commercial distribution. Such use shall not be construed as a distribution of this Package.
9. The name of the Copyright Holder may not be used to endorse or promote products derived from this software without specific prior written permission.
10. THIS PACKAGE IS PROVIDED "AS IS" AND WITHOUT ANY EXPRESS OR IMPLIED WARRANTIES, INCLUDING, WITHOUT LIMITATION, THE IMPLIED WARRANTIES OF MERCHANTIBILITY AND FITNESS FOR A PARTICULAR PURPOSE.

The End

An Explosion of Commercial Open-Source Licenses

More than ever, it's important for the goals of the open-source community to be clearly defined. Many companies are jumping on the bandwagon to get a piece of the press generated by this movement, often without heed to the dilution of the community's goals.

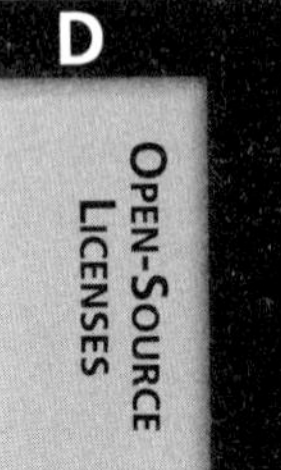

Several large corporations, such as Netscape (the NPL and MPL) and Apple (the APSL), have drafted their own licenses and jumped on the opportunity to call their products open source. However, history dictates that the motives of these organizations are usually not in sync with those of the community; sometimes the two are quite opposed. This is the time when it's important that OSI and SPI work with these commercial interests to make both worlds come together with the same interests.

Many say that this cannot be accomplished. However, some dare to nurture hope. Stallman and his camp, in particular, suggest that we do not want the involvement of commerce in this dimension at all, but others hold that it's vital to our survival.

A list of some of the more notable corporate open-source licenses is presented next, with the qualms each has created within the open-source community.

Apple's APSL

Apple recently began releasing code to old versions of its software. However, all developers must register centrally (with Apple) to gain access to any code. In addition, any modifications made to the code cannot be redistributed until they are registered with Apple, which gains complete rights over them. In a word, this makes Apple look guilty of exploiting the good will of the open source community for its own gain.

Troll Tech's QPL

Recently, Linux's graphical desktop has been divided two ways, between the K Desktop Environment (KDE) and the GNU Network Object Model (GNOME). KDE was originally based on a non-commercial[nd]use widget kit known as Qt. Because KDE's base libraries were so restricted in their use, interest dwindled a little and shifted to GNOME. Everything under GNOME is 100% free.

In the midst of this debacle, some held that Troll Tech would wait for KDE to mature and then quickly rescind the free part of Qt's license. For them, this would mean conquering a new desktop market for their product overnight. Troll Tech responded with the release of Qt 2.0, which is licensed under a completely open-source license, known as the QPL.

This is definitely a great victory for KDE, which at this point is not only more user friendly than GNOME, but further along in development. There is one problem with this scenario, however: QPL isn't compatible with GPL. At this point, many of the KDE components cannot be run legally with the new Qt.

For this reason, Debian does not distribute KDE or any portion thereof. However, it would have no qualms with including Qt.

Other Open Software Licenses

Some other licenses modeled after the Open Source licenses include

Netscape's MPL (Mozilla Public License):

`http://www.mozilla.org/NPL/MPL-1.0.html`

> **Note**
>
> Many other groups and companies have adopted the MPL as a model for their own licenses.

The X Consortium License:

http://www.opensource.org/licenses/mit-license.html

References and Additional Reading

More detailed descriptions of these licenses as well as other information on Open Source issues can be obtained from the following Web sites:

- http://www.opensource.org
- http://www.opensource.org/osd.html
- http://www.debian.org/intro/free
- http://www.spi-inc.org
- http://www.spi-inc.org/projects/opensource

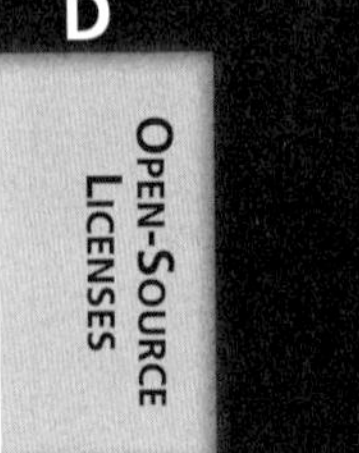

Kernel Configuration Options

In This Appendix

If we described every one of the more than 400 kernel options, it would take you weeks to read this appendix. Instead, we cover the more widely useful options with respect to their application.

The size of this section might seem a little daunting, but after you've been over it, there is no way you can possibly take a wrong turn in rolling your own task-specific kernel. However, more information is always available in the `Documentation/` subdirectory of your Linux sources.

The most important command in any of the configuration mechanisms is `help`. Some options are so simple that you don't need any more information than the page or so of help text. If you're still unsure about anything, take the approach suggested by these friendly help texts.

Code Maturity Level Options

Although a "stable" kernel release such as the 2.2 series is considered to be ready for prime time, the kernel still offers some features that are deemed experimental. These features might support new technology for which the standard is not yet resolved or simply add new techniques that were considered essential enough but not stable at the time of the release.

All these features are clearly marked as experimental, so Linux users are not saddled with them without knowing what they are doing. People are invited to try these new features, report on their results, and file proper bug reports, but we are asked not to flood the mailing lists and newsgroups with complaints.

Alpha-release drivers should not be considered something only for the brave or the foolish. In some cases, "experimental" code might be essential to your purpose—such as the Amiga filesystem support or enhanced support for certain PCI subsystems—and it is the real-world testing of these features that is worth most to the developers. The main caveat here is only that, if your kernel fails to load or crashes midstream, you should suspect the experimental modules first and remove all experimental modules before you suspect you have found a bug among the stable modules.

Processor Type and Features

The processor type might be the first kernel option you change: Most distributions are preset for the safest setting, the old Intel 386 computer.

When selecting the processor type, keep in mind that compiling for an advanced CPU might mean your kernel will not boot or will fail on an older machine. This is also true for excluding the floating-point co-processor emulation: A 386-SX might not run if the emulator is missing. Table E.1 shows the recommended mapping of processor types to processor options.

Table E.1 CPU Kernel Options

Kernel Option	*Recommended CPU*
386	AMD/Cyrix/Intel 386DX/DXL/SL/SLC/SX, Cyrix/TI 486DLC/DLC2, and UMC 486SX-S. Only "386" kernels will run on an i386 machine.
486	AMD/Cyrix/IBM/Intel DX4 or 486DX/DX2/SL/SX/SX2, AMD/Cyrix 5x86, NexGen Nx586, and UMC U5D or U5S.
586	Generic Pentium, possibly lacking the timestamp counter register.
Pentium	Intel Pentium/Pentium MMX, AMD K5, K6, and K63D.
Pentium Pro	Cyrix/IBM/National Semiconductor 6x86MX, MII, and Intel Pentium II/ Pentium Pro.

SMP and MTRR

For Pentium II and Pentium Pro machines, Linux includes optional support for the Memory Type Range Register (MTRR); where supported by the hardware and software, this option can double the performance of video transfers. To use MTRR, you need an X-Server that is aware of the interface through either `ioctl()` calls or through the `/proc/mtrr` pseudofile. You can query your MTRR system by `cat /proc/mtrr`, and code for manipulating the interface is provided in `linux/Documentation/mtrr.txt`. You can also correct an initialization bug on some Symmetric Multi-Processor machines by including MTRR support.

The last processor feature option enables support for Symmetric Multi-Processors (SMP); with the 2.2 kernels, SMP support for up to 16 processors on Intel x86 machines is now a standard feature and is not experimental, although SMP support for other architectures is still considered experimental. For many enterprise applications, SMP support is a primary reason for upgrading to Linux 2.2.

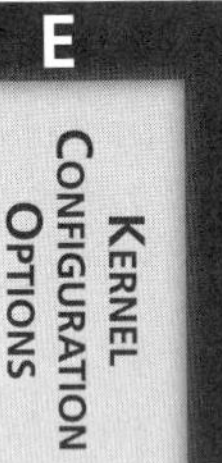

Tip

If you require SMP support, you also need to include the Realtime Clock option under Character Devices.

Note

Support for up to 64 processors is expected soon and may be in general release by the time this book is published.

On machines with only one CPU, selecting SMP support can degrade performance, and it might not run on some hardware; unselecting this option for machines that do have more than one CPU causes Linux to only use the primary processor. To use SMP, you also need to include the Realtime Clock option, and you might need to set your BIOS options for UnixWare. For more information on SMP support, look up the SMP-FAQ at `http://www.irisa.fr/prive/mentre/smp-faq/`.

Loadable Module Support

It is hard to imagine circumstances where you would not want to include module support and enable the kernel module loader. For most situations, module support allows the kernel to support many devices and filesystems without incurring the overhead of including this support at all times; in some situations, incompatible devices can share ports through loading and unloading of modules, for example, when using a single parallel port for both a printer and for a parallel-port SCSI drive.

Note

Actually, there are a few situations where you'd want a staticly linked kernel. One example is a floppy-only firewall. In this situation, there's minimal hardware (floppy and two ethernet cards—no monitor and so forth) and little in terms of other software support except for firewall extensions.

Keeping the module version information is also a fairly rare situation. Without version details, the kernel uses the `modprobe` utility to determine whether modules are compatible with the current kernel (and fails to compile if the modules utility package is missing or out of date), whereas a kernel with the version symbols enabled can load binary modules from third-party sources but might run into trouble when modules are of the same kernel version but belong to a different build.

Modules are usually loaded by `init` scripts or other shell scripts that explicitly call the `insmod` and `rmmod` utilities to load and unload modules as needed. The 2.2 kernel now includes support for automagically loading modules as needed: When the kernel detects a missing module, it uses the program specified in `/proc/sys/kernel/modprobe` (usually `/sbin/modprobe`) to load the module. To clear unused modules, you need to call `rmmod-a` yourself or schedule it periodically through the `root crontab` entry:

```
0-59/5 * * * * /sbin/rmmod -a
```

General Setup

General options includes enabling networking, PCI hardware, microchannel and parallel ports, and advanced power management and support for `ELF`, `aout`, and other binary executables. For most new Linux systems, the important details here are the `parport` and `PCI` options. Advanced administrators will likely want to pay close attention to the `PCI` options and to the new `sysctl` interface.

Networking Support

Unless you have a good technical reason (that is, you know what you are doing), you need to include networking support; many applications require this module even on non-networked machines and do not run if this option is not included. For the 2.2 kernel, you must also ensure your `net-tools` package understands the new `/proc/dev/net`. `net-tools` 1.50 is also required to accommodate the IPv6 protocol.

BSD Accounting

BSD accounting is of most interest to ISPs and other organizations that need to trace and track the use of their systems for billing or other accounting purposes. Adding BSD accounting creates a special file to log and measure each process, allowing compatible software to gather detailed usage information.

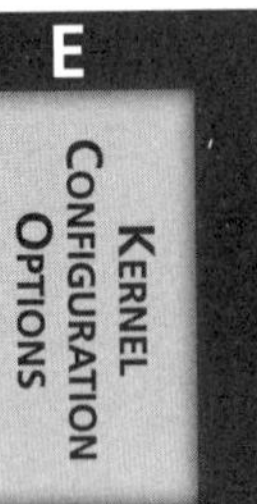

SysV IPC (DOSEMU)

Interprocess communications (IPC) is a protocol for synchronizing and exchanging data between separate programs; if you plan to run the DOSEMU MS-DOS Emulator, you need to include IPC. However, now that `kmod` has replaced `kerneld`, there is no longer any need to include IPC in the main kernel. The 2.2 kernel now offers IPC as a loadable module, and removing `kerneld` support from the IPC module has reduced its size by 40 percent.

`sysctl` Support

Adding `sysctl` provides a means for controlling the running kernel either through system calls or, if the `/proc` filesystem is enabled, by writing to pseudofiles in the `/proc/sys` directory. This directory is partitioned into several areas governing different aspects of the kernel:

`dev/`	Device-specific information (`dev/cdrom/info`)
`fs/`	Control of specific filesystems—for example, setting the number of filehandles and inodes, quota tuning, and configuring the support for arbitrary binaries (see the section "Support for Misc Binaries," later in this appendix)
`kernel/`	Kernel status and tuning
`net/`	Networking parameters
`sunrpc/`	SUN Remote Procedure Call (RPC)
`vm/`	Virtual memory and buffer and cache management

These services are both powerful and dangerous; know what you are getting into before you fiddle with these files! Kernel parameters include the interpretation of Ctrl+Alt+Del, the time delay for a reboot after a kernel panic, your system host and domain name, and a number of architecture-dependent features for the Sparc and Mac platforms. The `sunrpc` directory includes debug flags for kernel hacking of remote procedure calls.

Virtual memory tuning allows for tweaking the machine for disk activity. For example, if you set the system's tolerance for dirty memory pages to a higher value, the kernel will have less disk activity (which saves power and improves speed), although it increases the risk of thrashing, should real memory become scarce. For example, on a very large-memory machine, the default behavior of the caching algorithm could be modified with

```
echo "80 500 64 64 80 6000 6000 1884 2" >/proc/sys/vm/bdflush
```

This restricts flushing the dirty buffers until memory is 80 percent full (plus some other changes; see `linux/Documentation/sysctl/vm.txt`). For a single-purpose machine that has to run many processes, you can modify other options to have the buffer cache claim a major chunk of the total memory and to then restrict pruning this cache until nearly all of this memory is consumed:

```
echo "60 80 80" >/proc/sys/vm/buffermem
```

Keep in mind these changes might improve file or process performance for one purpose but upset this machine terribly for many other purposes: Be certain you know what you are doing before you install any optimization.

Other tunable `vm` parameters include setting the number of pages that can be read in one transaction or removing the page table caching for single CPU machines with limited memory (such as embedded systems and older machines).

The most common use of the `sysctrl` files is in the filesystem (`fs`) directory. This holds a collection of diagnostic pseudofiles for reading the number of file handles, inodes, superblock, and quota entries with corresponding files for setting maximum values for these items. For example, systems that require many open files (such as very busy Web servers) might see a flurry of filehandle messages in the logs; the current number of files can be queried by `cat file-nr` and a new limit set by echoing a higher number to the `sysctrl file-max`.

Detailed information on using and interpreting all these features appears in `linux/Documentation/sysctl/`.

Support for Misc Binaries

Long before other operating systems provided for running Java applications from the command line, the support for misc binaries was added to the Linux kernel. Later, this feature was generalized to all binary and interpreter types: Using the `sysctl` pseudofiles, Linux integrates Java, MS-DOS programs, Windows programs, tk/tcl, Perl, or any other strange executable as seamlessly as an `ELF` binary or a shell script.

To use the misc binaries support, you need to register the "magic cookie" of the file type and the corresponding interpreter through the `sysctl` pseudofiles in `/proc/sys/fs/binfmt_misc`. You can derive the magic cookie from the first few bytes of the file or from the filename (such as `.com` or `.exe`) and register it by echoing a string to `/proc/sys/fs/binfmt_misc/register`, where the format of the string specifies

```
:name:type:offset:magic:mask:interpreter:
```

`name` is an arbitrary identifier for this executable type. *`type`* specifies `'M'` or `'E'` for whether the cookie is by mask or extension. *`offset`* is the count in bytes from the front of the file; if omitted, a default is `0`.

magic is the sequence of bytes to match; hex codes may be specified as `\x0A` or `\xFF`. (Be careful to escape the slash character if you set the `binfmt` through a shell statement.) For 'E'xtension matching, the magic pattern is the filename extension, that is, the string that follows the last dot.

mask is also optional and if included must be the same length as the magic sequence. The bits in the mask are applied against the file contents before comparison to the magic cookie sequence.

interpreter is the program that is used to run the executable.

To use misc binary support, you can create a script in `/etc/rc.d/init.d` to echo the control strings to the `binfmt_miscfile` or add these statements to your `rc.local` script. For example, to emulate the original Java support, you might add the following line to the end of `/etc/rc.d/rc.local`:

```
echo ':Java:M::\xca\xfe\xba\xbe::/usr/local/jdk/bin/javawrapper:' >  \
/proc/sys/fs/binfmt_misc/register
```

This creates a new `/proc/sys/fs/binfmt_misc/Java` entry in the `sysctl` directories and lets you run a Java application by simply using the full filename. You can add support for running applets through `appletviewer` with

```
echo ':Applet:E::html::/usr/local/jdk/bin/appletviewer:'  > \
/proc/sys/fs/binfmt_misc/register
```

Note that for this to work, we need to create a special wrapper script to run the Java interpreter; Brian Lantz provides a sample script in `linux/Documentation/java.txt`. Once it is installed and the `binfmt_misc` is registered, you can run Java applications and applets from the command line; use `chmod +x` to set the `.class` or `.html` file as executable and then simply call it from the command line:

```
./HelloWorld.class
```

You can also use

```
./HelloApplet.html
```

To run Windows applications via the WINE emulator, you could add the following line

```
echo ':DOSWin:M::MZ::/usr/local/bin/wine:' >
 /proc/sys/fs/binfmt_misc/register
```

You can read the status of a `binfmt_misc` file by using `cat` on the filename, for example `cat /proc/sys/fs/binfmt_misc/Java` might produce

```
enabled
interpreter /usr/local/jdk/bin/javawrapper
offset 0
magic cafebabe
```

Caution

When configuring binfmt_misc support, the register control string cannot exceed 255 characters. The magic cookie must be within the first 128 bytes of the file; *offset + size(magic)* must be less than 128. The interpreter string cannot exceed 127 characters.

For more information on binfmt_misc and on creating the magic cookie patterns, see Richard Günther's binfmt_misc home page, http://www.anatom.uni-tuebingen.de/~richi/linux/binfmt_misc.html.

Parallel Ports (Parports)

One major change between the 2.0 and 2.2 kernels is the introduction of parports, an abstract representation of the parallel ports that separates architecture-dependent code from the parallel interface and allows sharing the same physical parallel port between many devices—for example, to use the same port for both a printer and a zip drive or Qcam video camera.

Parallel ports are often dangerous beasts to probe, especially when many on-board ports are fixed at IRQ numbers that can conflict with sound and network cards. It is best to avoid probing and to specify the port addresses and IRQ settings of the parallel port hardware either by appending the parameters to the boot command or by loading the parport as a module and specifying the parameters on the insmod command line. By default, the parport module does not probe for IRQs and initializes all parallel ports in polling mode.

The new parport modules also split parallel port control into two modules, the basic parport to manage port sharing and an architecture-dependent layer, for example, the parport_pc module. Either can be compiled into the kernel or built as a module and loaded as needed, but in both cases, you probably need to add port configuration details in the boot or the insmod command line. For example, to load parport and the parport_pc as modules, you might use the following command lines:

```
# insmod parport.o
# insmod parport_pc.o io=0x3bc,0x378,0x278 irq=none,7,auto
```

This installs three parallel ports where the first is in polling mode, the second is on IRQ7, and the third probes for the current values.

Once the modules are installed, the parport_probe module can be inserted to query IEEE1284-compliant devices. This outputs a status report to the system messages and to

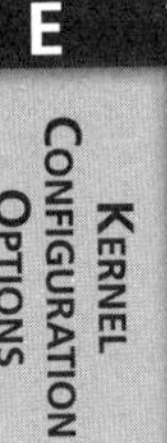

`/proc/parport/x/autoprobe`. Other files in `/proc/parport/x` include the devices file where parport will record the attached devices and flag those currently using the port, and the `irq` file. You can use `irq` to query the IRQ number of the port and also to set this value by echoing either the number or "none" to that file.

To use the parports, you can give modules that require the parallel port options to direct the module to a particular port:

```
# insmod lp.o parport=0,2
```

This installs the printer module only on ports 0 and 2 rather than the default action of installing the module on all available ports. You can also do this by adding `"lp=parport0 lp=parport2"` to the boot prompt or in `/etc/lilo.conf`.

A common use of parport modules is to share a parallel port between several devices by dynamically inserting device support and then removing that device before inserting the module for an alternate device. For example, you can share the printer port with a parallel-port camera, a zip drive, or PLIP (parallel port based network connection) by scripting the use of these facilities to first remove the other module before installing itself.

Note

In most instances, many modules can be assigned to a parport simultaneously without needing to first remove the prior module. When conflicts occur, however, modules can be removed and inserted as needed.

APM Support

Advanced power management does not power-down hard drives or trigger "green" monitors to go into Sleep mode: The Linux APM system is almost exclusively restricted to battery-powered computers such as laptops. Although APM is a good idea in principle, there are many different interpretations of the standard among laptop manufacturers and, as a result, APM support is a prime suspect when debugging laptop kernel problems. When in doubt, turn off all APM options and only enable each as you verify that it is either useful or benign.

Watchdog Support

Detailed support for hardware-based watchdog systems is set further down, but the General options also allow for a software-based watchdog. Using this option, the kernel monitors and periodically updates `/dev/watchdog` and forces a reboot if the updates fail to occur. This can be useful for small ISPs and other applications where the machine might be unattended and must be rebooted if any sort of crash occurs. Because this support is embedded in the kernel, it has a slightly better chance of being able to do its job even if all other processes have been halted or are being blocked. If you are using the software watchdog, you might also want to append `panic60` as a boot argument (in `/etc/lilo.conf`).

Alan Cox has included information on watchdog hardware manufacturers and the source for creating a software watchdog update program; these appear in `Documentation/watchdog.txt`.

Plug and Play Support

The Plug and Play support section contains options to enable kernel support of generic Plug and Play devices and to enable probing of devices attached to the parallel ports for mapping parallel port peripherals to the parports. In general, probing parallel ports for IRQ numbers can cause problems, and a better option is to explicitly specify your parport options through the append line in `/etc/lilo.conf`.

Block Devices

The Block Devices dialog contains options for disks from ancient MFM and RLL IDE drives through modern IDE/ATAPI devices to parallel-port IDE and ATAPI and RAID systems.

Floppy Disk Driver

Because of its use for other devices (such as tape backup units) and its ability to run multiple disk controllers, the floppy disk driver is worth some attention. You can also configure this driver through boot commands using the following options:

`floppy=daring` for well-behaved (usually all modern Pentium systems) controllers. This option allows for optimizations that can speed up floppy access but might fail on incompatible systems.

`floppy=one_fdc` tells the driver that only one controller is available; this is the default setting for the FDC driver.

`floppy=two_fdc` or `floppy=<address>,two_fdc` tells the driver to use two controllers with the second located at the specified address. The default address is 0x370 or is taken from CMOS memory if the `cmos` option is selected.

`floppy=thinkpad` alerts the driver to the inverted convention for the disk change line used in some ThinkPad laptops.

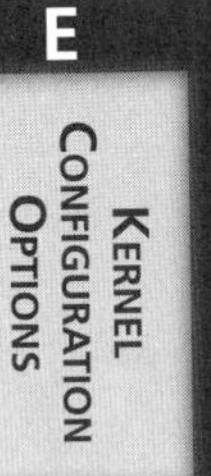

`floppy=omnibook` or `floppy=nodma` prevents using DMA for data transfers. You need this option if you get frequent "Unable to allocate DMA memory" messages or if you are using an HP Omnibook. DMA is also not available on 386 computers or if your FDC does not have a FIFO buffer (8272A and 82072). When using `nodma`, you should also set the FIFO threshold to `10` or lower to limit the number of data transfer interrupts.

`floppy=yesdma` can be used to force DMA mode. When using a FIFO-enabled controller, the driver falls back to `nodma` mode if it cannot find the contiguous memory it needs; the `yesdma` option prevents this. This option is the default setting.

`floppy=nofifo` is required if you receive "Bus master arbitration" errors from the ethernet card (or any other devices) while using your floppy controller. The default is the `fifo` option.

`floppy=<threshold>,fifo_depth` sets the FIFO depth for DMA mode. A higher setting tolerates more latency but triggers more interrupts and imposes more load on the system; a lower setting generates fewer interrupts but requires a faster processor.

Tip

If the floppy driver is compiled as a module, you can experiment with the `floppy=<threshold>,fifo_depth` driver option to find the optimum settings. To do this, you need the `floppycontrol` utility with the `--messages` flag to log controller diagnostics. After inserting the `floppy.o` module and running `floppycontrol --messages`, access the floppy disk; a rush of "Over/Underrun - retrying" messages will indicate your FIFO threshold is too low. You can then find an optimum value by unloading the module and trying again with higher values until these messages are infrequent.

`floppy=<drive>,<type>,cmos` sets the CMOS type of the specified drive to the given type and is a required option on systems with more than two floppy drives. Codes for the CMOS types appear in `drivers/block/README.fd`.

`floppy=L40SX` prevents printing messages when unexpected interrupts are received and is required on IBM L40SX laptops to escape a conflict between the video and floppy disk controllers.

`floppy=broken_dcl` avoids using the disk change line and assumes the disk may have been changed whenever the device is re-opened. In most situations, this symptom can be traced to other physical causes such as loose or broken cables and mistaken jumper settings but can be a real issue on older floppy drives and some laptop computers.

`floppy=<nr>,irq` and `floppy=<nr>,dma` sets the IRQ and DMA for the given device. The defaults are 6 and 2, respectively.

`floppy=slow` is required on some PS/2 machines that have a dramatically slower step rate.

The full list of FDC module options appears in `drivers/block/README.fd`, and you can download the `fdutils` package, a set of floppy driver utility programs, including an enhanced `mtools` kit, from `ftp://metalab.unc.edu/pub/Linux/system/Misc/`.

Tip

Floppy driver options are specified using the `floppy=` syntax, but unlike some kernel drivers, the device expects only one such declaration. For example, to set both `daring` and `two_fdc`, both options should be included, separated by a space, in one command:

```
insmod floppy 'floppy="daring two_fdc"'
```

You can pass options to the Linux floppy disk driver using the usual `/etc/lilo.conf` append line on the boot prompt or using `/sbin/insmod` when compiled as a module and also through using the older environment variable syntax.

Enhanced IDE Support

Linux supports up to eight IDE drives; you can set many options for tuning the runtime performance of the IDE drives using the `hdparm` utility. With Linux 2.1/2.2, support was also been for IDE ATAPI floppy drives, tape drives, and CD-ROM drives with autodetection for interfaces, IRQs, and disk geometries. The new driver also adds support for PIO modes on OPTi chipsets, SCSI host adapter emulation and PCI Busmaster DMA, as well as experimental support for many PCI chipsets.

The driver also detects buggy PCI IDE systems such as the prefect feature of the RZ1000 or "IRQ unmasking" on the CMD640. Full details of the IDE driver and supported systems appear in `linux/Documentation/ide.txt`.

Although the driver automatically probes for disk drives, geometries, and IRQs, you can specify these interfaces using kernel command-line options—such as to set the IO port addresses and the IRQ for controller three:

```
ide3=0x168,0x36e,10
```

If the IRQ number is omitted, the driver probes for it. Any number of interfaces can also share an IRQ, although this degrades performance; the driver detects and accounts for this situation, but your controller cards may suffer damage in the process (theoretically).

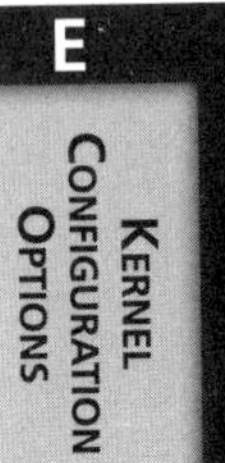

You can also specify disk geometry on the command line as three numbers for sectors, cylinders, and head, as in `hdc=768,16,32`, and if your CD-ROM is not being detected, you can give the kernel an extra nudge by using the `hdd=cdrom` option.

IDE interfaces on sound cards require initialization before you can use them; the program to initialize the driver is most often among the software that comes with the card and is usually part of the MS-DOS driver. The only alternative for using these devices is to boot your computer under MS-DOS to allow the drivers to initialize the device and then use `loadin` to switch to Linux.

Older hard drives might not be compatible with the newer IDE driver and, in this situation, you can include both interfaces in the kernel. The older driver commands the primary IDE interface while still allowing newer hardware to be used on the other interfaces.

Caution

When passing IDE driver options to loadable modules using `/sbin/insmod`, substitute `;` for any commas in the command line:

```
insmod ide.o options="ide0=serialize ide2=0x1e8;0x3ee;11"
```

Loopback Disk Devices

Loopback disks are somewhat cool: Loopback allows you to treat a normal file as a separate filesystem, for example, to mount and test a CD-ROM or floppy disk image before committing the image to the physical disk. Loopback also allows you to use cryptographic methods to secure a filesystem. Before using the loopback disk devices, you need to ensure your `util-linux` package is up to date with the requirements of `linux/Documentation/Changes`.

Network Block Devices

Using network block devices allows the client to transparently use a remote block device over TCP/IP. This is very different from NFS or Coda. For example, a thin client could use an NBD disk for any filesystem type, including as a swap disk.

Multiple Devices and Software-RAID

For people needing reliable and reasonably efficient redundant filesystems on a tight budget, Linux now includes a Software-RAID package, which can bind several disks as one RAID unit; you can use MD support to append, stripe, or mirror partitions together to form one logical partition.

More information on Software-RAID appears on the Software-RAID HOWTO at `ftp://metalab.unc.edu/pub/Linux/docs/HOWTO/mini`.

Paride and Parports

For the parallel IDE support (PARIDE), you can safely combine both parports and paride devices on the same physical parallel port. However, if parports are included as a loadable module, the paride driver must also be included as a module. Also, if paride is included directly into the kernel, individual protocols for disks, tapes, and CD drives can still be included as modules and loaded dynamically as needed.

Networking Options

UNIX is a networking operating system, and Linux follows in this tradition. In the UNIX world, computers are not thought of as isolated personal possessions but as nodes, as mere portals, points of entry into the whole network. Building a workstation without network services is not unlike building an office with no windows or doors: Yes, it is very secure, but….

For most single networked or SOHO workstations, networking options are only a matter of choosing TCP/IP network support and perhaps including IPX support to co-exist with Windows machines or to run the DOSEMU MS-DOS emulator. Some might add the Coda or NFS network file systems to share their local disk resources or configure Linux as a firewall and dial-up gateway for a home office or small enterprise. Small Novell shops might also use this section to use the Linux IPX support en route to using Linux as a high-powered NetWare fileserver.

For the enterprise network administrator, however, this dialog box is a playground of protocols and options, system diagnostics, and controls to position Linux as the glue holding the enterprise together. You can optimize Linux for routing or forwarding between interfaces and set it as a secure WAN router for a virtual private network over the Internet. Linux speaks IPX and AppleTalk, Acorn Econet, and Ipv6. It can log attacks, perform multicast (MBONE) routing, encapsulate IP over IP, do IP masquerading (to allow machines inside the firewall access to services without using a proxy server), provide ARP services over huge networks, and boot a diskless client. It's pretty darn amazing, and it keeps getting better.

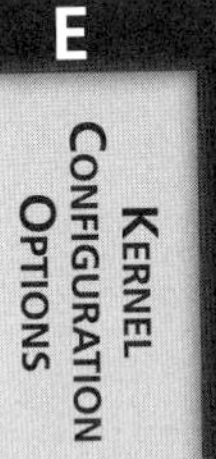

Kernel Netlink Socket

Netlink is a communication channel between kernel services and user programs through a special character device in the `/dev` directory. This interface can be used by the

Routing Messages package to log network behavior or by the IP Firewall Netlink device to log information about possible attacks. Netlink is also required when using the `arpd` daemon to map IP numbers to local network hardware addresses outside of kernel space or when using `ethertap` (user programs using raw ethernet frames).

Network Firewall

The head of network services for Bell Global Solutions once confirmed my suspicion: The only firewall that is impervious is the one implemented with scissors. That said, we all do what we can to be as secure as we need to be. It is all a matter of cost and necessity and of being realistic and practical. If you need to use almost-scissors, Linux will take you there, too, but for the more modest requirements of the masses, the stock kernel firewall provides decent protection for a minimal fuss.

The network firewall is packet-based protection that you can configure to accept or deny incoming or outbound packets based on the port, the protocol, and the originating and the destination network IP addresses. Proxy-based firewalls can expand this protection and use knowledge about the protocols to provide additional security, but this most often requires modified software and is a great deal more work to install. Even if you plan to use a proxy-based system, these systems most often also require including the packet-based firewall. For most situations of a gateway firewall for a small- or medium-size enterprise or a home office, packet-based protection is simple and easy to install and offers pretty good security.

Setting Up a TCP/IP Firewall

To set up a TCP/IP firewall, you need to include the Network Firewall option and IP:firewalling. Many installations also include the IP:masquerading option to allow inside machines access to services outside the firewall; using IP:masq, the remote computer perceives these connections as originating from the firewall machine and thereby removes the need to register IP addresses for all local network hosts who require these outside connections.

For example, our office LAN includes a workstation that needs HTTP and ICQ access. Using IP:masquerading, this workstation can run Netscape or ICQ without any proxy and can connect directly to the Web site or Mirabilis servers; because their packets appear to come from the firewall, remote ICQ users are not able to call in directly. You can add an extra level of security to this scheme by enabling the IP:Transparent Proxy support; transparent proxy silently redirects traffic from local machines to a predesignated proxy server address.

Warning

Network firewall support is not compatible with the fast-switching ultra-fast network option.

Basic IP:masquerading only redirects UDP and TCP traffic; this prevents some Windows applications such as ping and `tracert`, which depend on ICMP packets. You can enable support for these applications through the IP:ICMP masquerading option.

Inside hosts are also unable to receive connections unless you enable port forwarding using the Special Modules options. Through the external port administration utilities `ipautofw` and `ipportfw`, the Linux firewall can provide a gateway for outside machines to reach services on inside machines by forwarding packets for predefined ports. As a sample application of port forwarding, if the gateway machine is not using X11, port 6001 can be forwarded to another machine, which will then be able to run remote X11 applications. Port forwarding support is considered experimental.

Optimize as Router

In the current Linux kernel, the optimize as router switch only prevents some checksum operations on incoming packets that are not required when using the machine exclusively as a router. In the future, this option might contain other router-only optimizations.

IP Tunneling

IP tunneling is a technique for connecting two LANs across another network while staying under the same network address. A sample application might be to allow machines at a trade show to use services only available inside the corporate firewall or to give a roaming user in a hotel room full access to her office files. The basic support for IP tunneling wraps plain IPv4 inside IPv4; the GRE tunnel support is more useful if you are connecting through Cisco routers and is able to also encode IPv6 inside IPv4.

You can also use GRE/IP to create what appears to be a normal ethernet network, but that can be distributed all over the Internet. This would allow, for example, all branch offices of a global enterprise to use the same LAN IP numbers and to appear to be within the overall firewall. This feature requires the GRE tunneling option with the GRE broadcast and the IP:multicast option.

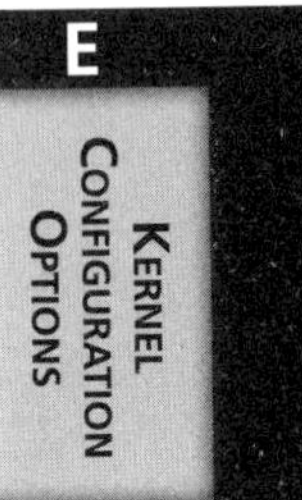

Webmasters and IP Aliasing

The Webmasters and IP aliasing option is of most interest to Webmasters who need "multi-homing," that is, to provide different documents or services to outside hosts according to the IP address they've called. IP aliasing allows for creating virtual domains attached to distinct IP addresses registered to `ifconfig` as `eth0:1`, `eth0:2`, and so on. Newer editions of Apache are able to provide much the same service from using only the hostnames, which removes some of the need for this feature, but there are other applications, such as the RealMedia PNM server, where the support for the virtual interface must be provided at the kernel level. More information on configuring virtual hosts and IP aliasing appears in `Documentation/networking/alias.txt`.

Another option valuable to Webmasters is the TCP SYN-cookie trap; SYN cookies are an easy but effective means to mount a denial-of-service attack on a public site and, although enabling this protection might not accurately report the source of the attack, it ensures that legitimate users can get access to your machine. To use the SYN-cookie option, you also need to enable the `/proc` filesystem and the `sysctl` feature and enable the support in your boot scripts with

```
echo 1 >/proc/sys/net/ipv4/tcp_syncookies
```

Tuning Linux and Apache for Performance

Although most Web sites perform quite adequately for their traffic loads, there is always a need for more speed. Before delving into kernel tuning, Webmasters seeking high performance should first look at their CGI and data servers as possible bottlenecks, and Apache Webmasters should check into the Apache performance-tuning FAQ at `http://www.apache.org/docs/misc/perf-tuning.html`.

Although any detailed tuning of the kernel is extremely dependent on the specific release, you can still do a few things at the kernel level to fit your machine to Apache. The first and most obvious change is to simply add more RAM or to redefine the behavior of the virtual memory manager to limit swapping and avoid expensive disk activity. Other areas to investigate include increasing the number of tasks and file descriptors by writing new values to the `/proc/sys` files `file-max` and `inode-max` and by editing the value of `NR_TASKS` in `include/linux/tasks.h`. Bill Hawes also posted a patch to the `linux-kernel` mailing list (1998-09-22) that improves forking speed by using dynamic `fd` arrays.

Other alternatives include switching Web server software; Apache is not the only Web server in the world (only half of them!), and its process forking method is not exactly the most efficient Web server for Linux. The current 1.3 Apache is designed more for robustness and portability than for raw performance.

Although the Apache model of pre-forking child processes is good enough for most applications, a better approach is to capitalize on the Linux kernel threads (pthreads) and avoid the forking overhead. An intelligent use of thread-pools might produce orders of magnitude performance gains. Although the core of the 1.3 Apache Server is already multithread-aware, and there are projects afoot to adapt Apache to a multithread model for version 2, the excellent and also open-source Roxen server can offer this performance today (see `http://www.roxen.com/`).

IPX and AppleTalk Support

IPX adds support for Novell NetWare services and enables your Linux machine to communicate with NetWare file and print servers through the `ncpfs` client program available at `ftp://metalab.unc.edu/pub/Linux/system/filesystems/`. IPX also allows DOSEMU programs to access the network. AppleTalk support provides a similar facility for communicating with Apple services using the `netatalk` program (see `http://threepio.hitchcock.org/cgi-bin/faq/netatalk/faq.pl`). Linux also supports the AppleTalk and LocalTalk Mac protocols. According to the recent kernel help files, the GNU boycott of Apple is now over and even politically correct people can now set this option.

Linux can be configured as a fully functional NetWare server and now even provides experimental support for the SPX protocol. For more information on IPX services, see the IPX HOWTO, which can be found at the Linux Documentation Project Web site `http://linuxdoc.org/HOWTO/IPX-HOWTO.html`. Installing Linux as a Grand Unifying Force is probably content enough for its own book, but general information on configuring Linux to glue together a heterogeneous network of Novell, Macintosh, and TCP/IP workstations appears at `http://www.eats.com/linux_mac_win.html`.

Enterprise Networks and X.25 Support

Enterprise administrators will be most interested in the Linux support for the X.25 protocol, a means for putting many virtual circuits through one high-speed line. This support is presently marked experimental and does not yet include support for dedicated X.25 network cards. Linux does provide X.25 services over ordinary modems and ethernet networks using the 802.2 LLC or LAPB protocol.

The WAN option is also of interest to enterprise admins who are looking for an inexpensive alternative to a dedicated WAN router. Using commercially available WAN interface cards and the `wan-tools` package from `ftp://ftp.sangoma.com`, a low-cost Linux machine makes a perfectly serviceable router. In addition, you can also still use the Linux router for other purposes, such as providing a firewall, a Web server, or anonymous FTP.

For the serious enterprise, the FreeS/WAN project in Toronto now offers a free encryption layer for the Linux WAN, using 1,024-bit keys and 168-bit Triple-DES technology, and incorporates the Internet Protocol Security (IPSEC). FreeS/WAN also uses encryption technology from outside the U.S. to avoid export restrictions (3DES).

Related to X.25 and WAN, Linux also provides support for frame relay; see the DLCI options under Network Devices.

Forwarding on High-Speed Interfaces and Slow CPUs

One very popular use of Linux is to breathe new life into aging hardware. This can, however, lead to some networking problems, as even a 120MHz machine can be overrun by a 10MB/sec ethernet connection. If you experience trouble with network overruns, you can use these options to modify the network support to accommodate the slower machines.

QoS and/or Fair Queuing

Packet schedules need to decide the order for sending out waiting network packets, and although the default algorithm is suitable for most purposes, special situations where certain packets must be given priority require alternative approaches. The QoS option offers several alternative packet scheduling algorithms.

SCSI Support

SCSI drives tend to be more expensive than IDE but give much higher performance and are the method of choice for large enterprise servers. Linux SCSI support is also required for certain parallel-port disk devices such as the 100MB Omega zip drive. Linux also supports SCSI CD-writers, scanners, and synthesizers via the SCSI Generic option and provides options for logging errors and activity on these devices.

To use the SCSI support, you need to know your hardware; the Low-Level Drivers dialog presents a long list of supported adapters with some options for setting device parameters.

Network Device Support

If you have a network card installed, you need to specify the network hardware. For those who have a network card but are certain they do not know what it is—if it is a cheap one, it is more than likely an NE2000 compatible.

You also need to enable network device support even if you only connect to networks via SLIP, PPP, or PLIP. If your machine will be used to dial an ISP to connect to the Internet, it needs this module.

Dummy Network Device

The dummy device is just that: It simply holds a place for a device and discards any traffic sent to it. This is most often used for machines that connect via SLIP or PPP to make these interfaces appear to be active even while offline. For example, if you are using a demand-dialing program such as `diald`, the dummy device enables network programs to function, but the packets sent there are re-routed to the Internet after the dialer has established the connection.

EQL

The EQL option is rarely used but extremely useful: In these days of wave modems and cheap xDSL lines, we often forget that many locations do not have the luxury of cheap high-speed dial-up lines. Using EQL, Linux can bind together several modems as the same IP interface and effectively multiply the bandwidth. For example, a rural school could install a Linux gateway server with demand dialing sensitive to the bandwidth requirements. When one phone line became saturated (rural lines are often 31.2Kbps), a second line could be opened to the same ISP and then a third and so on, giving the school symmetric ISDN-like bandwidth for the cost of a few extra phone lines. EQL does require support at both ends of the connection; it works well with the Livingstone Portmaster 2e, which is fortunately a popular choice among smaller ISPs.

PLIP, PPP, and SLIP Dial-Up Networking Support

PLIP provides a means to network two Linux machines over a null printer (Turbo Laplink) cable to give four or eight parallel data channels and is often used as a means to NFS-install to a laptop where there is no CD-ROM. Wiring for this cable is described in `Documentation/networking/PLIP.txt`, and the connection can be up to 15m long. Russell Nelson has also created MS-DOS drivers for PLIP to enable networking of DOS-based machines such as that old PS/1 space heater I keep in the workshop.

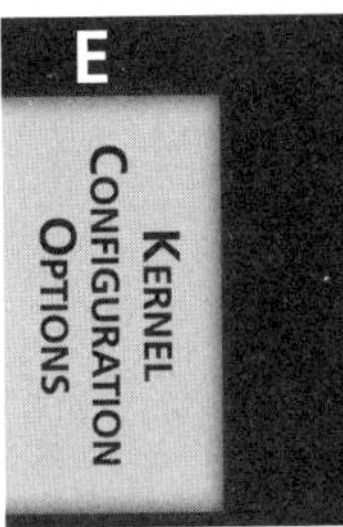

Linux 2.2 requires an update for the pppd tools or a patch applied to the pppd-2.2.0f package, as outlined in Documentation/networking/ppp.txt. The usual symptom of this problem is pppd crashing from a fatal error after using an ioctl operation.

SLIP is the ancestor to PPP, and although 99.9 percent of all ISPs only offer PPP connections, SLIP still has some viable uses. SLIP is an essential ingredient as an intermediary device in the diald demand dialer or to gain a network connection over a Telnet session (using SliRP).

Amateur Radio and Wireless Support

Another low-cost solution to nearly impossible remote access requirements is the amateur radio support; by encoding packets over shortwave radio, Linux systems have been used to provide as much as 64Kbps of bandwidth to very remote regions. For example, see the Wireless Papers at http://www.ictp.trieste.it/~radionet/papers or in the Linux-without-borders archive at http://www.tux.org/, or visit the Packet Radio home page at http://www.tapr.org/tapr/html/pkthome.html.

A related feature of interest in campus or development projects is the support for wireless LAN and the AT&T WaveLAN and DEC RoamAbout DS (see Documentation/networking/wavelan.txt). There is also support for the MosquitoNet StarMode Radio IP systems used by many laptop owners (see http://mosquitonet.stanford.edu/).

IrDA Subsystem and Infrared Port Device Drivers

InfraRed Data Association protocols provide wireless infrared communications between laptops and PDAs at speeds up to 4Mbps. Using the Linux driver, supported devices are transparent to the networking system. For more information on this support and on the utility programs for IrDA, see the IR-HowTo at http://linuxdoc.org/HOWTO/IR-HOWTO.html, or from the Linux IrDA home page at http://www.cs.uit.no/linux-irda/.

ISDN Subsystem

Using the ISDN subsystem requires the isdn4k-utils utility programs from ftp://ftp.franken.de/pub/isdn4linux/. When the module is loaded, isdn.o can support up to 64 channels (more can be added by changing the `isdn.h` file directly) where each channel is given read/write access to the D-Channel-messages and `ioctl` functions, with non-synchronized read/write to B-Channel and 128 tty devices. Modem emulation provides a standard AT-style command set that is compatible with most dial-up tools such as minicom, PPP, and `mgetty`.

The second step in configuring for ISDN is to select your specific ISDN modem card; some ISDN cards require initialization before the vendor-independent setup, and details about this appear in the appropriate `README` file under `linux/Documentation/isdn`.

Older CD-ROM Drivers (Not SCSI or IDE)

Old CD-ROM drivers include the early SoundBlaster Matsushita and Panasonic style CD-ROMs, which were included as part of 16-bit sound cards. If you have a clone card with a socket for a CD-ROM drive, and if it is older than 1994, it is likely to be one of these interfaces, but if it is newer, it could still be an IDE-type CD-ROM.

Character Devices

Character devices communicate with the kernel via a stream of characters. These include terminals, serial ports, printers, and also some special purpose devices such as the CMOS memory and the watchdog. For most desktop installations, this section is simply a matter of adding or removing printer support. On the other hand, some applications, especially in data acquisition projects, find this section very interesting.

Terminals and Consoles

Most applications configure the kernel for at least one console; there are some embedded applications where this code is not needed, but for most people, having multiple virtual consoles mapped to the Alt+F*n* keys is very useful.

Another somewhat useful feature is the ability to have console messages sent to a terminal attached to a serial device. You can use this feature to keep a printed log of system messages or have an emergency terminal port available on an otherwise console-less embedded application. Keep in mind that even if you do select this option, the serial console is not enabled by default if you have a VGA card installed, and it must be explicitly enabled using the `console=ttyN` kernel boot option.

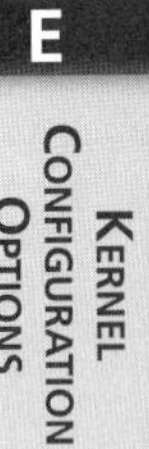

Serial Ports

In addition to plain old serial ports, Linux also permits IRQ sharing (where supported by your hardware) and systems with more than four serial ports. Many data-acquisition systems and smaller ISPs also use multiport serial boards, which can be included with these options.

Unix98 PTY

Linux 2.2 now supports the Unix98 standard for the `/dev/pts` ports; this option requires `glib`-2.1 and also requires the `/dev/pts` filesystem but is highly recommended. Although it will take some time to shift habits to the new naming convention, Linux has a clear resolve to move towards this system and obsolesce the old `/dev/tty` conventions. Under the new rules, pseudo-terminals are created on-the-fly under `/dev/pts/N`; the old convention of `/dev/ttyp2` will become `/dev/pts/2` under the Unix98 system.

Parallel Printer

You need the parallel printer option if you plan to add a parallel-port printer, but keep in mind this module supports the printer, not the port; you also need to install and configure the parallel port (parport) module. Also, by default, the `lp.o` module installs itself on all available parports unless specified in the boot command line, in the `/etc/lilo.conf` append line, or on the `/sbin/insmod` command line.

Mice

The mice section is for machines with bus mice and PS/2-style mouse connectors as found in some laptop computers. Note that although some laptops do support PS/2-style mice (such as the ThinkPad 560), the internal pointer might still be a plain COM1-based serial mouse.

Watchdog, NVRAM, and RTC Devices

The watchdog timer enables a character device (`mknod c/dev/watchdog c 10 130`), which can be used to reboot a locked machine. This feature is most often used with a watchdog daemon, which writes to this device within the time limit. Linux includes support for a software watchdog and also for watchdog boards, which are not only more reliable, but also can monitor the temperature inside your machine and force a shutdown/reboot when it moves out of the allowed range.

The `/dev/nvram` option enables a new character device (`mknod c/dev/nvram 10 144`) for read/write access to the 50-byte CMOS memory.

All computers have a real-time clock; Linux lets you use it. This option supports a new character device (`mknod c /dev/rtc 10135`) to generate reliable signals from 2Hz to 8KHz. You can also program the clock as a 24-hour alarm that raises IRQ8 when the alarm goes off. The `rtc` module is controlled by synchronized `ioctl` calls and is most often used for high-frequency data acquisition where you don't want to burn up CPU cycles polling through the time-of-day calls. Sample code for using the `rtc` module appears in `Documentation/rtc.txt`.

DoubleTalk Speech Synthesizer

No surprises here—but users of speech synthesizers might also be interested in Blinux (distribution for the blind) and Emacspeak. Linux stands alone as the one OS that can grant blind users total access to all the functions of their computers and full access to all services on the Internet.

Video for Linux

Video4linux grew out of a plethora of different interfaces and now provides a common programming API to audio/video capture or overlay cards, radio tuning sources, teletext, and other TV-related VBI data. V4l support is needed if you plan to use any of the current TV/FM cards and can be used for videoconferencing cameras such as the Connectix Qcam. To use these services, you also need v4l-aware applications; a few applications are currently archived at `ftp://ftp.uk.linux.org/pub/linux/video4linux` and a few more, including capture and webcam applications, are listed at the Room Three Web site at `http://roadrunner.swansea.linux.org.uk/v4l.shtml`.

Joystick Support

Although Linux supports many more joystick devices in the 2.2 kernel, still many more are coming. These include digital, serial, and USB controllers—and developers also hope to include support for force-feedback joysticks. A list of supported devices and applications that are compatible with the 2.2 kernel appears at `http://atrey.karlin.mff.cuni.cz/~vojtech/joystick/`.

Ftape, the Floppy Tape Device Driver

The ftape section is for tape drives that are connected to your existing floppy drive controller or that include their own high-performance FDC.

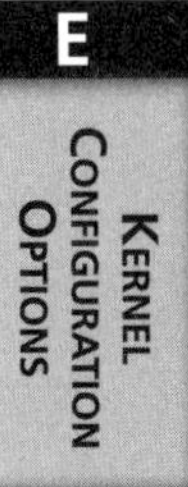

Filesystems

Linux is the only operating system that offers a common ground for heterogeneous computer networks. During your first installation, one of your first experiences was to select from a long list of supported filesystems for your Linux partition, and this tradition continues with the kernel filesystem and network filesystem support. When all of this is combined with the ability to launch arbitrary executables transparently through an emu lator (see the General Options), the degree of inter-OS integration in Linux becomes very clear.

The Filesystems dialog itself has few surprises; if you have any need to use floppy disks, CD-ROMs, zip drives, or hard drive partitions in any of the supported filesystems, you can include it as part of the core kernel or built as a module. The only exceptions to this are the `/proc` and `/dev/pts` filesystems, which are highly recommended unless the kernel is being built for a specialized embedded application; without these features, many standard utilities do not work.

MS-DOS and VFAT (Windows) Filesystems

The MS-DOS and VFAT filesystems are worth some special consideration if only because they are so ubiquitous. The current kernel support for the MS-DOS/VFAT disks used by DOS, Windows, Windows 95, and Windows NT only reads and writes to uncompressed disks and cannot be used on disks or partitions that have been DoubleSpaced. To access DoubleSpaced drives, you need to use the DOSEMU emulator or try the `dmsdosfs` tools at `ftp://metalab.unc.edu/pub/Linux/system/filesystems/dosfs`.

MS-DOS support in the kernel is not needed if you only plan to access MS-DOS disks through the `mtools` programs (`mdir`, `mcopy`, and so on). MS-DOS support is only needed if you plan to run Linux on a second partition or hard drive and need access to files on the MS-DOS side or if you want to mount a zip drive or other shared media to move files between Linux and MS-DOS. VFAT adds additional support for long filenames; VFAT also provides several options for the DOS code page and National Language Support and for the default behavior in coping with the DOS 11-character filename limit. Details of these translation options appear in `Documentation/filesystems/vfat.txt`.

ISO 9660, UDF, and DVD Support

UDF is the new standard for CD-ROM disks and is intended to someday replace the ISO 9660 standard. At this point in time, UDF support means Digital Video Disk (DVD) support. Although the kernel does support the conventional ISO 9660 format CD-ROMs and also supports the Microsoft Joliet extensions for Unicode file systems, it does not yet offer UDF. A driver for DVD and other UDF peripherals is available through the TryLinux UDF project (see `http://www.trylinux.com/projects/udf/`).

Network File Systems

Network file systems are only of interest to people with multiple machines that must share disk resources. Although there are obvious applications in a large network, even a small office or home office setting might want to distribute its resources. For example, our office uses an old salvage 486/33 machine as a multiuser X-terminal for the smoking lounge. This machine runs Linux 2.2.7 from a 60MB hard drive; 60MB is enough to get the system up and running, and from there, NFS is used to supply software directories and user disk resources from upstairs in the lab.

Tip

Using NFS or Coda, you can mount a common `/home` partition on all your workstations; no matter which workstation is used when a user logs in, he is working from the same home directory. With a little extra work (although POP3 and IMAP servers make this obsolete), you can even coordinate access to his own mail queue. Using Coda, Net workspaces can be extended to home-office teleworkers and laptop roamers; the physical computer is no longer their "personal workspace." A desktop is only another portal into their working environment, and any desktop will do.

As with the filesystems and partitions support, Linux provides a common glue for almost any heterogeneous network. Network file systems are no exception. The 2.2 kernel can create a hub where old and new UNIX protocol filesystems, Windows 95/NT, OS/2, and Novell can all be bound together in one workstation or server.

CODA Distributed File System

Coda is a new kid on the block: a distributed filesystem somewhat like NFS, only more flexible, more secure, and more efficient. Coda includes authentication and encryption features, disk replication, caching, and support for discontinuous connections such as laptops and teleworkers. Current Linux kernel support allows you to use Coda client programs; the latest Coda server software only runs in user space (which might be a good thing anyway). Client programs and other information about this filesystem are available from the Coda home page at `http://www.coda.cs.cmu.edu`; the Venus client support is also described in great detail in `Documentation/filesystems/coda.txt`.

NFS

The old workhorse of distributed filesystems, NFS takes a lot of criticism, but it is still the standard. Coda will probably take over more and more from NFS as time goes on, but for most purposes, NFS is all we have. NFS also requires running `portmap` with the `nfsd` and `mountd` daemons, and if you are configuring a kernel for a diskless workstation, NFS cannot be loaded as a module (obviously) and you need the IP:KernelLevel Autoconfiguration and NFS Root Partition options.

For NFS servers, you have the option of running the `nfsd` daemon or enabling the kernel-level NFS server. The latter choice has the advantage of being much faster (because it is in kernel space) but is still somewhat experimental.

SMB (Windows Shares) and NPC

If your LAN includes Windows for Workgroups, Windows 95/97, OS/2 LanManager, or NT machines that use TCP/IP, the SMB option will enable mounting shared directories from those machines. Note that SMB support is for the client side; you export directories to Windows machines through the Samba daemon.

NPC (NetWare Core Protocol) provides similar facilities for the NetWare (IPX) based file sharing used by Novell networks. As with the SMB support, this is for mounting remote NCP drives on this machine; you do not need this option to be an NPC server.

Partition Types

Linux is unique as the only OS to offer filesystem compatibility right down to the partition formats. The partition types section adds support for BSD, SunOS, Solaris, and Macintosh partitions and allows you to directly read and write disks in those proprietary formats, such as if you have a partitioned hard disk for a multi-boot machine (MacOS versus Linux or BSD versus Linux) or if you need to exchange optical disks or zip drives with one or more of the other systems.

Native Language Support

The native language support section is a bit of a misnomer: Although these options do support different cultural languages, they only support the reading and display of these character sets on Microsoft filesystems.

The first section lists Microsoft CodePages and is only an issue if your system needs to read filenames from an MS-DOS or Windows filesystem. Note that CodePage support applies to filenames only and not to the contents of the file. Similarly, to display characters from Microsoft VFAT or Joliet CD-ROM filesystems, you also need to include at least one of the NLS options. You can select any number of languages for both systems, and any of these can be built as a module to be loaded only when needed.

Console Drivers

The first two options under console drivers are very straightforward. The first enables support for the standard VGA graphics card (text mode), and the second adds support for the `vga=` option in `/etc/lilo.conf` to set the VGA text console during the boot sequence.

The remaining options are more obscure. Option 3 adds support for using old monochrome display adaptors such as a "second head." Your system could run with X on the VGA monitor while also displaying a text console on the alternate adaptor. The MDA option is only for this configuration and is not for systems that are using the MDA as the primary display.

Frame Buffer Support

Historically, Linux had no need for a graphical console, at least not until the Motorola 68k port, where there was no concept of a text console. With the 2.1 kernels, all ports have the same console code with a hardware-specific frame buffer supporting a graphical console device (`fbcon`).

Frame buffers become an alternate means to control the graphic system via a dedicated device (`/dev/fb0`) and are mostly an issue when compiling a kernel to run on platforms other than the Intel x86 or when using a Matrox Millennium or similar PC graphics card. To use frame buffers, your X-server must be aware of the feature; although you can include frame buffer support on an Intel platform (see `Documentation/fb/vesafb.txt`), be aware that some software that talks directly to the hardware but that is unaware of this method might cause a system crash. For more information, look up the frame buffer HOWTO at `http://www.tahallah.demon.co.uk/programming/prog.html` or read `Documentation/fb/framebuffer.txt`.

Note

Intel Binaries for the Xfree-3.3.3 with Framebuffer support are available through `http://www.in-berlin.de/User/kraxel/fb.html`.

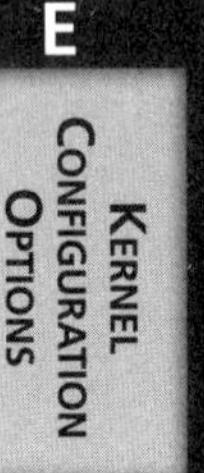

Sound

The Linux sound driver is derived from the OSS/Free driver by Hannu Savolainen; the current kernel driver is the result of work funded by Red Hat, and this should be taken into consideration when reporting problems. For very new or obscure sound card support, you might need to obtain the commercial edition of the OSS drivers (see `http://www.opensound.com/`).

The first option in the sound configuration section is a master switch for enabling sound support. If this option is switched off in a kernel previously configured for sound, all options are preserved in the `.config` file, but the sound module is not included in the resulting kernel; this is sometimes useful when experimenting with sound system options or when you suspect an IRQ conflict between the sound system and some other device such as a printer port (IRQ7) or a network card (IRQ10).

Most of this section is what you might expect: You need the IRQ numbers, DMA channels, and port addresses of your audio hardware, and when you're in doubt, the help option will offer some advice on the compatibility of various options. A few items provoke misunderstandings, such as enabling MIDI support versus enabling MIDI emulation in a SoundBlaster card, but all of these issues are explained in the help pages.

Linux includes support for a wide array of cards from the legacy AdLib cards to the latest high-performance wavetable systems. With the 2.2 kernel, OSS/Free also provides a software wavetable engine to bring realistic MIDI patches to even old 8-bit sound cards. This wavetable support allows for samples between 8KHz and 44KHz and up to 32 simultaneous voices; obviously, the sampling rate and the number of voices your system can handle depend on your RAM and CPU speed, but we find 22KHz in eight voices runs quite comfortably on a 486/33.

The most frequent causes of mishaps in configuring sound cards are due to IRQ or DMA and port conflicts from configuring a clone card as a SoundBlaster compatible (most clones that claim this mean SBPro compatible but can also run in MSS mode) or due to Plug and Play problems. Detailed information on compatibility issues and tips on troubleshooting sound support appear in `Documentation/sound/README.OSS`.

Plug and Play Sound Cards

Most modern Plug and Play sound cards have very little trouble with Linux, but in some situations, you might need to experiment with using `pnpdump` and `isapnp` to generate and then load acceptable settings into the card before you can use the sound system. In this situation, the sound card must be compiled as a module to allow using `isapnp` to set the device before the module is loaded.

To configure PnP devices, you first need to obtain the possible settings using the `pnpdump` utility:

```
pnpdump > /etc/isapnp.conf
```

This creates a long text file of configuration options for all Plug and Play devices on your system. You then must edit this file to uncomment the settings that will work with your configuration:

```
vi /etc/isapnp.conf
```

If you have a Windows partition or access to a Windows machine where you can test the card, you can obtain the correct (or likely) settings by using the Control Panel, System, Devices reports. Once you have set this configuration file to be compatible with your system, you can then add the lines to your boot scripts to first load the configuration and then to load the driver:

```
isapnp -c /etc/isapnp.conf
insmod sound.o
```

In rare circumstances, this technique does not work because the card needs to be initialized by Windows before it can accept any service requests. The only way around this, outside of lobbying the manufacturer to be more friendly, is to boot your system under Windows and then use the DOS-based `loadlin.exe` boot loader to switch to Linux.

Additional Low-Level Drivers

Although in its own section of the kernel configuration, the additional low-level drivers panel is an extension of the sound configuration and offers support for subsystems of the main sound driver. Such options include support for SoundBlaster AWE, Gallant, and Audio Excel DSP.

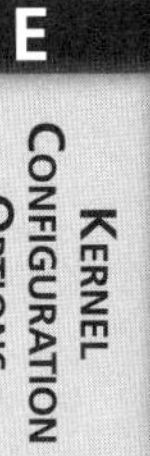

Kernel Hacking

In the 2.2 kernel, kernel hacking contains only one option, the flag to enable the SysRQ interrupt keys. SysRQ support adds several useful commands for recovering from a hung system through binding several critical operations to Ctrl+Alt+SysRq keys. For example, when using a development kernel or experimenting with kernel options, if the console or X-server becomes locked out because some renegade process is blocking all I/O, you might try to Telnet to the machine in hopes of opening a superuser shell to kill that process or reboot the machine, but if that fails (that is, you cannot start a login shell), you can use SysRQ commands to sync and unmount the filesystems and to force a reboot.

> **Caution**
>
> Workstations and production machines should not leave SysRQ enabled, and you might want to also disable the Ctrl+Alt+Backspace command to exit X-Windows. This prevents novice (or knowledgeable) users from bringing down the machine without authorization. In `/etc/inittab`, you can also customize the handling of the Ctrl+Alt+Del reboot interrupt, such as to give the machine a longer grace period or to disable the command entirely.

Table E.2 describes the SysRQ commands.

Table E.2 SysRQ Commands

Option	*Description*
`r`	Turns off keyboard raw mode and sets it to `XLATE`; this is useful when the console or the X-server is hung.
`k`	Kills all programs on the current virtual console, such as to shut down a locked X-server.
`b`	Immediately reboots the system without syncing or unmounting all filesystems; this command can corrupt your filesystem if you have not already synced and unmounted your disks.
`o`	Shuts off system power via APM (if configured and supported).
`s`	Attempts to sync all mounted filesystems to minimize the filesystem corruption that can occur from an ungraceful shutdown.
`u`	Attempts to remount all mounted filesystems read-only, much like the `shutdown` command. This allows your system to read the binaries required for an orderly shutdown.

Option	Description
p	Dumps the current registers and flags to your console (that is, generates a kernel panic).
t	Dumps a list of current tasks and their information to your console to give you the diagnostic details for isolating the cause of the hang.
m	Dumps current memory info to your console.
0–9	Sets the console log level that filters kernel messages. For example, a level of zero filters out everything except panics and oops messages.
e, i	Sends TeRM or KiLL signals to all processes except `init`, effectively throwing you into single-user mode.
l	Sends SIGKILL to all processes, including `init`, which effectively halts your system.

Load/Save Configuration

The load and save options are a convenience for those who need to maintain several alternate configurations, such as if one machine is used to compile kernels for several different machines or if the machine needs alternate kernels for different purposes. As you would expect, this option pops up a dialog asking for the filename and then saves the `.config` file to the named location.

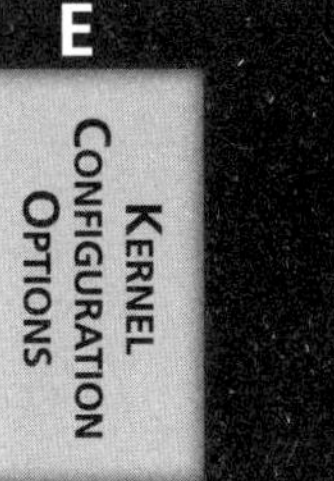

INDEX

SYMBOLS

A

F

G

N

O

Q -R

T

U

W

X

Y

Z

License Agreement

By opening this package, you are agreeing to be bound by the following agreement:

The CD-ROM contains Debian's GNU/Linux Release 2.1 binary distribution. Most of the programs included with this product are governed by the GNU General Public License, which allows redistribution. All packages in this release are covered under Debian's Free Software Guidelines, which allows redistribution in part or in whole. See the license information for each product for more information.